W9-AHL-969

PRENTICE HALL SERIES IN ACCOUNTING

FINANCIAL ACCOUNTING

CANADIAN THIRD EDITION

WALTER T. HARRISON, JR.

Baylor University

CHARLES T. HORNGREN

Stanford University

W. MORLEY LEMON

University of Waterloo

PRENTICE HALL CANADA INC., SCARBOROUGH, ONTARIO

Canadian Cataloguing in Publication Data

Harrison, Walter T.
          Financial accounting

Canadian 3rd ed.
First and second authors in reverse order on 2nd ed.
Also issued as part of: Harrison, Walter T.   Accounting.
Canadian 3rd ed.
ISBN 0-13-325770-3

1. Accounting.   I. Horngren, Charles T., 1926–   .
II. Lemon, W. Morley, 1939–   .   III. Title.

HF5635.H37 1996   657'.044   C95-931614-0

 © 1996, 1993, 1991 Prentice-Hall Canada Inc., Scarborough, Ontario
A Viacom Company

ALL RIGHTS RESERVED

No part of this book may be reproduced in any form without permission in writing from the publisher.

Prentice-Hall, Inc., Englewood Cliffs, New Jersey
Prentice-Hall International (UK) Limited, London
Prentice-Hall of Australia, Pty. Limited, Sydney
Prentice-Hall Hispanoamericana, S.A., Mexico City
Prentice-Hall of India Private Limited, New Delhi
Prentice-Hall of Japan, Inc., Tokyo
Simon & Schuster Asia Private Limited, Singapore
Editora Prentice-Hall do Brasil, Ltda., Rio de Janeiro

ISBN 0-13-325770-3

Acquisitions Editor: Patrick Ferrier
Developmental Editor: Dawn du Quesnay
Production Editor: Valerie Adams
Production Coordinator: Deborah Starks
Permissions/Photo Research: Marijke Leupen
Cover Design: Olena Serbyn
Cover Image: Image Bank/John W. Barragan
Page Layout: Debbie Fleming

      4 5   CC   00 99 98

Printed and bound in the U.S.A.

Original U.S. edition published by Prentice-Hall, Inc.
Englewood Cliffs, New Jersey. Copyright 1995, 1992, 1989 Prentice-Hall, Inc.

We welcome readers' comments, which can be sent by e-mail to
          phcinfo_pubcanada@prenhall.com

Brief Contents

Contents

4   Completing the Accounting Cycle   163

5   Merchandising and the Accounting Cycle   213

6   Accounting Information Systems   279

Preface

Financial Accounting, third Canadian edition, provides full introductory coverage of financial accounting.

Financial Accounting is in the mainstream for courses in introductory accounting. This book focuses on the most widely used accounting theory and practice.

Mission of the Book

Our mission is to present the fundamentals of financial accounting by challenging students to think and to make decisions. We emphasize the importance of connecting accounting to the business world and provide the student with the best support available for studying and learning accounting.

All the features of *Financial Accounting* have been extensively tested in the market. Professor focus groups, student focus groups, reviewer conferences, dozens of reviewers, solutions checkers, and two development editors have critiqued all aspects of this book.

Helping Students Become Decision Makers

Beginning with page 1 we create a business context for the student. The real-world environment promotes student interest. We integrate actual companies and their data into the text narrative and assignment materials. Familiar companies enliven the material and illustrate the role of accounting in business. Sometimes, however, "live" data drawn from real companies are too advanced for introductory students. In those situations, we illustrate the accounting with realistic examples to build a framework that invites students to participate in the learning process.

In this edition, we start the development of decision-making skills even before the first chapter—in a section called *Accounting's Role in Business*. Students are challenged to develop their own plan for running a business. By piecing together a business plan, students start to see how accounting serves an organization. Students are thus motivated to integrate the details into a broad view of accounting.

Each chapter opens with the actual business situation and often provides a quotation by a company manager, investor, or owner that gives insight into the chapter topic. Each chapter-opening story is illustrated with a photograph that draws students into the story. Students then revisit this story throughout the chapter, connecting accounting to a real business decision.

New or Expanded Features of the Third Edition

The third edition presents a number of new features:

- *Stop & Think* "speedbumps" ask students to do just that—stop and think about an application of accounting or an extension of the basic material—at various points in each chapter. These are not "boxes," which typically fall outside the running text and can be bypassed. They are part of the text, complete with answers to show students "how to do it," and they are identified by the icon you see here in the margin.

- A new category of exhibits called *Concept Highlights* contains tabular or visual summaries. The Concept Highlights give students another way to review the material. Exhibit 1-6 (page 18) and Exhibit 2-6 (page 62) are examples of Concept Highlights.

- There are many *new exhibits* in this edition. Most exhibits now use diagrams to illustrate concepts and relationships, helping students visualize accounting concepts and principles. Examples include Exhibit 1-1 (page 3) and Exhibit 2-3 (page 58).

- Our *Putting Skills to Work* features illustrate how particular businesses or individuals use accounting. An example is Chapter 4's feature "Ratios: Should a Bank Grant a Loan?" on p. 179.

- *Student annotations* in the margins provide a self-check or offer additional material of interest. Three types of student annotations are included. *Key Points* highlight concepts or topics that often cause students to stumble. *Short Exercises*—complete with solutions—give students immediate practice in applying new material. *Real-World Examples* illustrate the use of accounting in actual business situations.

- Each of the four Parts of *Financial Accounting* ends with a *Video Case* based on a real company. An accompanying CBC video clip is available. Each Video Case includes *Case Questions* that require critical-thinking skills and a basic understanding of the concepts and principles covered in the text.

- Each chapter has one or more new *Challenge Exercises* and two *Challenge Problems*, which go beyond the ordinary coverage to develop students' critical-thinking skills and offer instructors more variety in assignment material.

- Chapters 2 through 5 include a *Serial Exercise*. A single running example builds in complexity as it illustrates the accounting cycle.

- All-new *Financial Statement Problems* are based on the financial statements of Mark's Work Wearhouse Ltd.'s annual report, which appears in Appendix A.

- *Group Projects* are recommended to begin the course and are at the end of each of the four Parts of the book, within the Comprehensive Problems. These Group Projects challenge students to develop a plan for managing a business. The intent is for students to participate in the learning process by creating a familiar context. As students move through the course, they incorporate new material to refine the plan.

- *Decision-oriented assignment materials* have been expanded in this edition.

  1. Basic exercises and problems include ratios for decision making in the context of actual business practice. For example, the classified balance sheet is accompanied by the current ratio and the debt ratio. With inventories we introduce inventory turnover and gross profit percentage.

  2. Decision Problems ask students to make decisions that go beyond mere number crunching, such as determining the price to pay to acquire an existing business or whether a company is poised for a business expansion.

  3. We want students to step back and ponder the use of accounting information for decision making. To reach this target, selected problems now include this new requirement: "How will what you learned in this problem help you manage a business (or evaluate an investment)?"

- Assignment material has been updated. This includes the *Mid-Chapter Summary Problems for Your Review, Summary Problems for Your Review, Self-Study Questions* (with Answers), *Questions, Exercises, Challenge Exercises, Problems* (sets A and B and Challenge Problems), and *Extending Your Knowledge*. Many exercises and problems can be worked with a computer. Those that are coordinated with the Lotus Templates (provided in the Study Guide) have a spreadsheet icon.

- Each chapter *Summary* is now organized by Chapter Objective.

Chapter-by-Chapter revisions include the following:

- A new appendix to Chapter 1 discusses the accounting profession.

- Chapter 3 has a new appendix on alternate accounting treatment for prepaid expenses and unearned revenues. This material promotes the development of critical-thinking skills and illustrates that accounting is not so "cut and dried."

- In Chapter 4, reversing entries have been moved to an appendix.

- Chapter 5 uses a modern perpetual inventory system to illustrate accounting for inventory. More intuitive to students, the perpetual system helps them learn income measurement and the matching principle. At the same time, Chapter 5

maintains the strengths of the periodic inventory system—such as the computation of cost or goods sold—and offers a chapter supplement on the periodic system.

- Chapter 6 expands the coverage of computer information systems. Also, throughout the book we discuss computer applications in context to reinforce the fact that accountants use the computer as a tool.

- Chapter 7 has a new section on ethical decision making in accounting.

- Chapter 9 shows how to convert a LIFO company's income to the FIFO basis. This material is especially helpful for investment analysis and for credit decisions when companies are using different methods and the analyst must make a comparison. New sections of the chapter briefly discuss LIFO's potential use for manipulating income.

- To make room for more decision-relevant material, Chapter 12 (The Foundation for Generally Accepted Accounting Principles) and 13 (Accounting for Partnerships) have been streamlined, and stock subscriptions have been deleted from Chapter 14.

- Chapter 16's appendix now includes future value as we introduce the present-value techniques used to value bonds and amortize bond premium or to discount by the effective-interest method. This section of the appendix can be bypassed if instructors so desire.

- Chapter 18 now focuses on the indirect method of preparing the statement of changes in financial position.

Recommendations to Accounting Education _____

The recommendations of writings of and the reports of committees of academics and accounting practitioners about the need to change accounting eduction have inspired us in several ways.

- *Critical-Thinking Skills*—Each chapter includes Stop & Think "speedbumps" and new Challenge Exercises and Problems and places more emphasis on the Decision Problems, which require critical thinking.

- *User Perspective*—Most introductory students are not accounting majors. We motivate discussions on the basis of the experience of people who use accounting information.

- *Decision Making*—Chapter-opening stories, summaries of the material covered, and the assignment materials focus on decision making.

- *Group Learning Activities*—We propose a Group Project in *Accounting's Role in Business*, which precedes Chapter 1. In addition, each of the four Parts of the text includes a Group Project that asks students to devise their own business plan for financing, promoting, and operating a business.

- *Business Context for Accounting*—Students need a context for learning new material, and we have created Group Projects, chapter-opening stories, real-company examples, Putting Skills to Work, and margin annotations. All of these serve to build a picture of the real business world for students. These features are especially helpful to students who have little or no previous experience in business.

- *Ethical Issues in Business*—Chapter 7 includes a new section on ethical decision making. Also, each chapter includes an *Ethical Issue* among the assignment materials.

- *International Accounting*—Chapter 9 (Merchandise Inventory) and Chapter 10 (Capital Assets, Intangibles, and Related Expenses) include new discussions of international accounting for these assets. The second half of Chapter 17 also discusses accounting for international operations.

- *Communication Skills*—Each chapter includes assignment materials that require students to write business memoranda to explain the rationale for business decisions. Selected problems require students to explain how those problems will help them to, among other things, manage a business or evaluate an investment. The Group Projects can be presented orally in class.

Supplements

Supplements for the Instructor

Instructor's Manual and Video Guide   The *Instructor's Manual and Video Guide* contains the following elements for each chapter of the text: Chapter Overview, Chapter Outline, Assignment Grid, Suggested Readings, Ten-Minute Quiz, Answer Key to the Ten-Minute Quiz, and Supplement Grid. Video Write-Ups for each part-ending video case are also included.

Solutions Manual   The *Solutions Manual* contains answers to all questions, exercises, and problems in the text. The pages have been designed so that they can also be used as transparency masters.

Transparencies of Solutions   Every page from the *Solutions Manual* has been recreated as an acetate for use on the overhead projector.

Test Item File   Completely new for this edition of the text, a two-volume *Test Item File* contains a total of over 2,800 test items. Each chapter consists of over a hundred questions: true/false, multiple choice, exercises/problems, critical thinking/essay. Each chapter has been content-reviewed for clarity and solution-checked for accuracy. Available for Chapters 1–19 and Chapters 20–27.

PH Professor   The *Classroom Presentation Package* on PowerPoint 3.0 can be used to present chapter material using graphics and innovative ways of explaining concepts from the text. Other publishers provide this type of software but call it electronic transparencies. This item has been fully Canadianized.

Computerized Test Item File   A *Computerized Test Item File*, PH Custom Test, is available. It uses a state-of-the-art software program which provides fast, simple, and error-free test generation.

Entire tests can be previewed on-screen before printing. Tests can be saved to one of three word processing file formats: WordPerfect, Microsoft Word, or ASCII. PH Custom Test can print multiple variations of the same test, scrambling the order of questions and multiple-choice answers. A comprehensive, fully indexed desktop reference guide is included. This item has been fully Canadianized.

 ### *CBC/PH Video Library for Accounting*

Video is the most dynamic of all the supplements you can use to enhance your class. The quality of the video material and how well it relates to your course can make all the difference. For these reasons, Prentice Hall and CBC are working together to bring you the best video ancillaries available in the college market.

Through its program *Venture*, CBC offers a resource for feature and documentary-style videos related to text concepts and applications. The programs have extremely high production quality and present substantial content. Prentice Hall, its authors, and its editors provide the benefit of having selected videos on topics that will work well with this course and give the instructor teaching notes on how to use them in the classroom.

The CBC/PH Video Library offers video material for selected topics in the text. A video guide section in the Instructor's Manual is provided to integrate the videos into your lecture.

Supplements for Students

Study Guide and Lotus Templates Each *Study Guide* chapter contains the following parts: Chapter Overview, Chapter Review, and Test Yourself (with Matching, Multiple-Choice, and Completion Exercises and Critical-Thinking and Demonstration Problems). *Lotus Templates* can be used to solve selected exercises and problems in the text. Students are not required to know Lotus programming techniques. Instead, the templates are designed to focus on the accounting concepts presented in each template. Complexity of concepts increases as students gain knowledge.

Working Papers *Working Papers* is a set of tear-out forms that students can use to solve all exercises and problems in the text. Because T-accounts, general journals, cash receipts journals, purchase journals, and so on are already set up, students can focus on accounting concepts by filling in the necessary calculations to solve their assignments.

The forms are numbered in the same way as the textbook exercises and problems are arranged in the same order.

Practice Sets The *Runners Corporation Practice Set* is a computerized merchandising corporation practice set for a complete, one-year accounting cycle. It includes narrative of transactions.

A-1 Photography, Sole Proprietorship Practice Set is an unincorporated sole proprietorship practice set in business paper format. It is available only in a manual format.

PH Re-enforcer An interactive *Tutorial* consists of multiple-choice questions, problems, and case problems for each chapter of the text. This item has been fully Canadianized.

The Financial Post Supplements for Financial and Management Accounting The *Financial Post* and Prentice Hall are sponsoring *Contemporary Views*, a program designed to enhance student access to current information of relevance to the classroom. Through this program, the core subject matter provided in the text is supplemented by a collection of time-sensitive articles from a distinguished newspaper, *The Financial Post*. These articles demonstrate the connection between what is learned in the classroom and what is happening in the world around us.

Prentice Hall and *The Financial Post* are proud to co-sponsor *Contemporary Views*. We hope it will make the reading of both textbooks and newspapers a dynamic learning process.

The Financial Post

Software Supplements

PH Re-enforcer An interactive *Tutorial* consists of multiple-choice questions, problems, and case problems for each chapter of the text. This item has been fully Canadianized.

PH Professor The *Classroom Presentation Package* on PowerPoint 3.0 can be used to present chapter material using graphics and innovative ways of explaining concepts from the text. Other publishers provide this type of software but call it electronic transparencies. This item has been fully Canadianized.

Computerized Test Item File A *Computerized Test Item File*, PH Custom Test, is available. It uses a state-of-the-art software program which provides fast, simple, and error-free test generation.

Entire tests can be previewed on-screen before printing. Tests can be saved to one of three word processing file formats: WordPerfect, Microsoft Word, or ASCII. PH Custom Test can print multiple variations of the same test, scrambling the order of questions and multiple-choice answers. A comprehensive, fully indexed desktop reference guide is included. This item has been fully Canadianized.

Lotus Templates As mentioned earlier, *Lotus Templates* for selected exercises and problems are included in the Study Guide.

Practice Set The *Runners Corporation Practice Set* is a computerized merchandising corporation practice set for a complete, one-year accounting cycle. It includes narrative of transactions. This item has been fully Canadianized.

Testimonials

As a technical reviewer, I checked for accuracy in calculations, entries, statements, illustrations and formats for all text material.

As a solutions reviewer, I rigorously verified the accuracy of approximately 15 exercises and problems for each chapter as suggested by the publisher. As well, I independently verified other exercises and problems for accuracy.

In both cases suggestions for improvement and corrections were forwarded to the publisher for consultation with the author.

David C. Ferries

As solutions author, I solved each exercise and problem included in the text. Where clarification appeared desirable, I consulted with text co-author W. Morley Lemon. My final draft was subsequently reviewed by M.J. Pothier, and any remaining discrepancies were then resolved.

Donna P. Grace

On this third edition I had the dual role of supplements coordinator, and that of solutions reviewer.

As supplements coordinator, I assessed the suitability of the content and the format of all supplements and provided suggestions for improvement or changes. These suggestions were given from the professor's and student's points of view. In this regard, I included my experiences in using the second edition of this text in my accounting class at Seneca College. We also were conscious of the reading level used in the supplements, and strove to maintain consistency in terminology across all the supplements which will be especially helpful for ESL students.

As solutions reviewer, I reviewed the solutions to new problems added to this edition which were prepared by the authors. Whenever a discrepancy or error was discovered, I reworked the solution, made the appropriate corrections, and forwarded them to the authors for consultation.

Anne K. Chun

Acknowledgements to the Canadian Third Edition

I would like to thank Chuck Horngren and Tom Harrison for their encouragement and support.

Particular thanks are due to the following people for reviewing the manuscript, helping with supplements, writing new problems, and offering many useful suggestions: Wilson Balachandra, University of Waterloo; Anne Chun, Seneca College; Graham Clow, C.A.; David Crossley, Mohawk College; Johan de Rooy, University of British Columbia; Michael Douglas, Humber College; Gordon Farrell, B.C.I.T.; David Ferries, Algonquin College; Erik Genzer, Sheridan College; Donna Grace, Sheridan College; Jennifer McMillan, University of Waterloo; John Morelli, Seneca College; Abbe Nielsen, Langara College; Robert Nichols, B.C.I.T.; Melanie Russell, Price Waterhouse; Karin Vickars, Capilano College; Joel Ward, Sheridan College; Mandy White; and H. Barrie Yackness, B.C.I.T.

We are also grateful to the scores of instructors across the country who took the time to respond to a survey conducted while this edition was being planned. The thoughts and opinions of these respondents were a valuable guide as we mapped out a strategy for improving the text and its ancillaries.

Thanks are extended to Mark's Work Wearhouse Ltd. for permission to use the annual report. Thanks are also due to John Labatt Limited and National Trust for permission to use as exhibits a bond and a stock certificate, respectively issued by their companies.

Publications from the Canadian Institute of Chartered Accountants, the Butterworths series on Financial Statement Presentation prepared by the partners of Price Waterhouse and edited by Christina Drummond, *The Financial Post, The Globe and Mail*, and financial statements issued by a larger number of Canadian companies have been very helpful in the writing of this book.

I would like especially to acknowledge the people of Prentice Hall, especially the editorial work of and the support of Patrick Ferrier over the past months as this edition took shape. I would also like to acknowledge the editorial support of Dawn du Quesnay and Valerie Adams.

Finally, I would like to dedicate this book to William and Kelly-Anne, and I would like to thank them and my wife, Sandra, for their support.

W. Morley Lemon
Waterloo, Ontario
1996

Accounting's Role in Business

The Primary Mission of Business

Every organization has a primary mission. Hospitals provide health care. Law firms advise clients on legal matters. Automobile manufacturers produce cars. Auto dealers sell cars.

Consider a Ford automobile dealership, Pearson Ford Ltd. Most car dealerships are complex organizations that bring together the activities of a diverse group of people. The owners operate the business to earn a profit. They probably have to borrow money from the bank and other creditors. The Pearson dealership purchases automobiles from Ford Canada and sell the cars to customers such as you. Along the way, the business hires employees, buys and uses supplies, and pays bills for its building, insurance, and electric power. The following diagram shows these relationships, with the business at the center interacting with various parties.

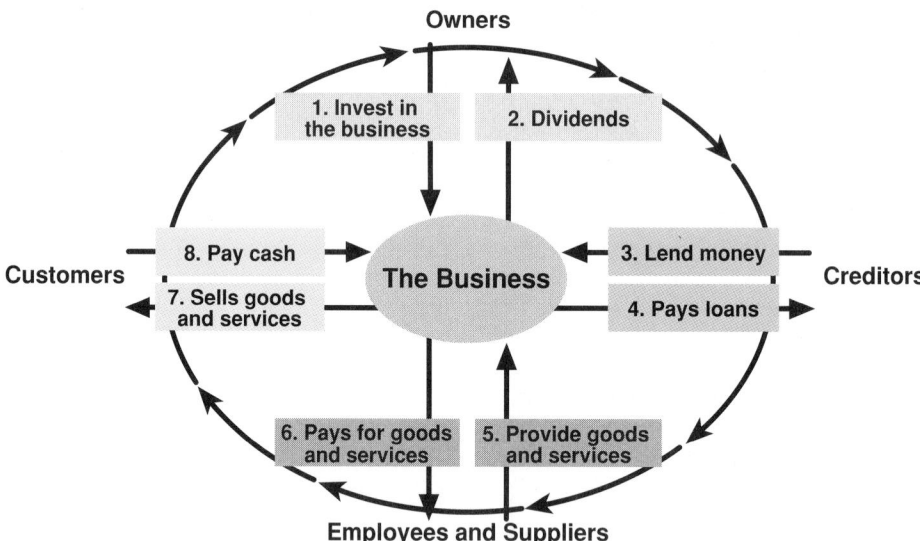

The primary mission of the Ford dealership is to sell cars to customers. For Ford Canada, headquartered in Oakville, Ontario, the mission is to manufacture the cars. But let's return to Pearson Ford. It must buy the cars that the public wants. It must hire productive employees and pay its bills to stay in business.

A dealership needs support services to accomplish its primary mission. For example, Pearson needs employees—salespersons, mechanics, and accountants. The dealership's personnel officer hires these employees. Someone else or some group must manage the overall business. We call this support function *administration* or *management*. The managers need information to make wise business decisions. Accountants produce much of this information. If the dealership borrows money (and most do), the lenders demand reports on how well the business is doing. Accountants supply much of this information, too. Virtually all businesses have an accounting function. Depending on the size and complexity of the organization, it may need additional support services. For now, however, let's focus on a business that has the functions we have mentioned.

Primary Mission of the Business—to Provide a Product or a Service

Functions directly related to the primary mission:	Support functions:
• Production (or purchasing)	• Personnel
• Sales	• Administration
	• Accounting

Accounting as a Business Function

Accounting is a support function in business. Unlike the sale of automobiles, which brings in money to the dealership, accounting by itself generates no cash. To earn its way, accounting must provide more benefit for the organization than the cost of operating the accounting department. What benefits does an accounting department bring to a car dealership? Simply, better decisions. For example, the owner must decide how many salespersons to hire and how to pay them: straight salary, commission, or salary plus commission. Accounting information aids these and many other decisions. Operating without an accounting department would be like driving blind from Vancouver to a remote village.

Business activity is complex. Suppose that Ford sales have been down for the past five years. Pearson is considering adding a Nissan dealership. If you were Pearson, how would you decide whether to invest? You probably would seek the advice of other people in the organization. The salespersons have valuable opinions about their ability to sell Nissans. The mechanics can predict the training they will need in order to work on foreign cars. The general manager may be reluctant to make so drastic a change. The accountant can answer the question, "How much will this changeover cost us?"

There is abundant evidence that groups can make better decisions than an individual can. "Two heads are better than one." That is why most business activity occurs in groups. In fact, more people fail in business because they cannot get along with others than because they are incompetent.

Innovations in Accounting Education

Over the past several years, academics working with practitioners in Canada and the United States have suggested innovations in the way accounting is taught at the university and college level. The authors believe that some key changes can enrich the teaching—and the learning—of accounting. This book incorporates several innovations that are a direct result of the work of these academics and practitioners.

Accounting in Context

The key innovation of this book is that accounting is presented in its business context. Throughout, we set the context before we launch into how to do accounting procedures. We want you t know *why* the accounting is done. In this way you will learn the subject better.

Accounting and Decision Making

Another innovation is that we present accounting as a tool for *decision making*. Every chapter has exercises and problems that ask you to make decision. You will learn how accounting generates information for decision making. You will also learn to use the information to make business decisions. We ask questions that lead you to think about what you will do with accounting information. As you progress through the book—specifically, as you finish each exercise and each problem in the assignment material—we encourage you to answer these questions:

1. What did you learn from working this exercise or problem?

2. How will what you learned help you manage a business?

To illustrate what we mean, consider Exercise 1-7. That exercise asks you to account for the transactions of Lisa Chen who is starting a design business. The exercise determines the amount of cash, supplies, and so ton that Chen's business has at the end of the first month. For this exercise, let's address our two key questions.

1. What did you learn from working this exercise or problem? Possible answers (there can be many):
   a. A business should account for its affairs separately from those of its owners.
   b. A business begins by raising money from its owners.
   c. To know where it stands, the business must account for its buying and selling transactions.
   d. Each business transaction, such as the purchase of land, has at least two effects.

2. How will what you learned help you manage a business?
   a. By keeping my personal affairs separate from those of my business, I am better able to evaluate the business. If I mix my personal finances with those of my business, I will not be able to tell how well the business is doing.
   b. If I go into business, I will probably have to invest some of my own money. Therefore, I should save. I will probably have to borrow, so I will need a good credit record.
   c. Accounting is necessary if I want to know how my business is doing.
   d. It makes sense that buying and selling have two effects on an organization because it takes two parties—a buyer and a seller—to complete a business transaction, such as the purchase of land.

To Instructors—A Group Project

To emphasize that accounting is best learned in the context of business decision making, the authors recommend that you begin the course with the following group activity (or some similar project). Divide the class into groups of four or five students. Allow 15 to 30 minutes for each group to list the decisions they must make to plan, promote, and present a **rock concert**. Each group's goal is to earn a profit. Instruct them to be as specific and as detailed as they can in describing the decisions for this business endeavor. At the end of the allotted time, have them report their business plan to the class. Your class can engage in this project at any time. It works particularly well as a structure builder at the beginning of the course. At the end of the term, you can revisit the exercise to summarize what the students have learned.[1] There are several benefits from beginning the study of accounting with the students' own business plan:

1. Starting a business is a stimulating endeavor that should capture student interest.

2. This strategy provides a context for illustrating the relevance of accounting.

3. The broad exercise helps students to think critically—beyond the details of accounting.

4. Student goals form the structure of learning.

5. The project develops group skills and communication skills—both oral and written.

6. Students become active participants in the learning process. The project is student-centered and learning-centered rather than instructor-centered and teaching-centered.

7. The exercise is decision-oriented.

We hope students will understand why accountants rise to leadership positions in their organizations in greater numbers than businesspersons trained in any other field.

The possibilities for implementation are virtually endless. Instructors may wish to have students refine their business plans as they cover new material in each chapter. The book includes a Comprehensive Problem at the end of each Part (after Chapters 6, 12, 17, and 19) to challenge students to incorporate and synthesize the material they learned in the preceding chapters. Students can write short memoranda or formal reports, as desired. Either individuals or groups can make class presentations. The authors encourage instructors to relay to us your experiences with this project. If you prefer to use e-mail, you can contact us at the following addresses:

Charles T. Horngren
fhorgren@GSB-lira.stanford.edu

Walter T. Harrison, Jr.
tom_harrison@baylor.edu

W. Morley Lemon
mlemon@uwaterloo.ca

---

[1]The authors thank J. R. Dietrich for suggesting this Group Project.

For our wives,
Nancy, Joan, and Sandra

CHAPTER 1
Accounting and Its Environment

"For two years running, we've achieved bottomline targets that were forecast in our Strategic Plan." (Mark Blumes, President of Mark's Work Wearhouse in "The President's Message" in the 1994 Mark's Work Wearhouse Annual Report.)

Mark's Work Wearhouse is a Canadian company whose head office is in Calgary, Alberta. The company sold $158,000,000 of workwear, casual wear, western wear, and other like clothing and footwear through 91 company stores and 43 franchise stores located from St. John's, Newfoundland, to Victoria, B.C. Part of the 1994 annual report referred to above is reproduced in Appendix A; you will be answering questions based on that annual report as you work your way through this text.

What role does accounting play in this real situation? Firstly, Mark Blumes and the men and women who run Mark's needed accounting information to prepare the forecast that was the basis of their Strategic Plan. Then, they needed accounting information to tell them how well they had done in meeting the forecast. For example, one of their goals for the year ended January 29, 1994, was to increase sales over 1993 sales of $133 million. The actual increase was almost $25 million to $158 million. A second goal was to earn a profit of $1,500,000; the actual profit fell somewhat short of that goal but was close at $1,266,000.

As you read Chapter 1 and the rest of the book, always remember that the accounting process is extensively concerned with recording and reporting the results of past transactions to assist users of the information in making decisions about *future* courses of action. Accounting is the language that records what happens between businesses or individuals and the environment with which they interact.

This chapter will introduce a number of terms that are part of the accounting vocabulary. Mark Blumes had to *finance* Mark's Work Wearhouse when the business was first founded. This chapter covers owner investments to start a business.

Source: Mark's Work Wearhouse Annual Report, January 29, 1994.

CHAPTER OBJECTIVES

After studying this chapter, you should be able to

1 Develop an accounting vocabulary for decision-making

2 Apply accounting concepts and principles to analyze business transactions

3 Use the accounting equation to describe an organization's financial position

4 Use the accounting equation to analyze business transactions

5 Prepare the financial statements

6 Evaluate the performance of a business

How did the management of Mark's Work Wearhouse and the users of Mark's financial statements know the total sales or *revenue* the company earned? The accounting records provided that information. Without records, the management of Mark's would have had to guess. *Revenue* is an accounting term that people use in everyday conversation. This chapter explains the concept of revenue more precisely.

Finally, Mark's earned a profit of $1,266,000 during 1994. What are *earnings*? In common usage, we might say Mark's "made" $1,266,000. This means that for the year ended January 29, 1994, Mark's Work Wearhouse earned a profit of $1,266,000 after all expenses were subtracted. *Earnings* and profit are accounting terms that mean the same thing. *Expenses* is another key accounting term. This chapter covers all those terms and introduces the financial statements that businesses use to report their financial affairs.

You may already know many accounting terms and relationships, because accounting affects people's behavior in many ways. This first accounting course will sharpen your focus by explaining how accounting works. As you progress through this course, you will see how accounting helps people like Mark Blumes—and you—achieve business goals.

What Is Accounting?

OBJECTIVE 1

Develop an accounting vocabulary for decision-making

Accounting is the system that measures business activities, processes that information into reports, and communicates the results to decision-makers. For this reason it is called "the language of business." The better you understand the language, the better you can manage the financial aspects of living. A recent survey indicates that business managers believe it is more important for college students to learn accounting than any other business subject. Personal financial planning, education expenses, loans, car payments, income taxes, and investments are based on the *information system* that we call accounting. A key product of an accounting information system, financial statements allow people to make informed business decisions. **Financial statements** are the documents that report on an individual's or an organization's business in monetary amounts.

Is my business making a profit? Should I hire assistants? Am I earning enough money to pay my rent? Intelligent answers to business questions like these are based on accounting information.

Please don't mistake bookkeeping for accounting. *Bookkeeping* is a procedural element of accounting, just as arithmetic is a procedural element of mathematics. Increasingly, people are using computers to do detailed bookkeeping—in households, businesses, and organizations of all types. Exhibit 1-1 illustrates the role of accounting in business. The process starts and ends with people making decisions.

EXHIBIT 1-1   *The Accounting System: the Flow of Information*

Users of Accounting Information: The Decision-Makers

Decision-makers need information to make decisions. The more important the decision, the greater the need for accurate information. Virtually all businesses and most individuals keep accounting records to aid decision-making. Most of the material in this book describes business situations, but the principles of accounting apply to the financial affairs of other organizations and individuals as well. The following sections discuss the range of people and groups who use accounting information.

Individuals   People such as you use accounting information in day-to-day affairs to manage bank accounts, to evaluate job prospects, to make investments, and decide whether to rent or buy a house.

Businesses   Managers of businesses, like Mark Blumes, use accounting information to set goals for their organizations, evaluate their progress toward those goals, and take corrective action if necessary. Decisions based on accounting information may include which building to purchase, how much merchandise inventory to keep on hand, and how much cash to borrow. Mark Blumes needed to know how much his company could spend on advertising.

Investors and Creditors   Investors provide the money a business needs to begin operations. To decide whether to help start up a new venture, potential investors evaluate what return they can reasonably expect on their investment. This means analyzing the financial statements of the new business. Those people who do invest monitor the progress of the business by analyzing the company's financial statements. They also keep up with developments in the business press, for example, *The Financial Post*, *The Financial Times of Canada*, and *Report on Business* published by *The Globe and Mail*. Before making a loan, banks determine the borrower's ability to meet scheduled payments. This evaluation includes a projection of future operations, which is based on accounting information.

Government Regulatory Agencies   Most organizations face government regulation. For example, the provincial securities commissions in British Columbia, Alberta, Saskatchewan, Manitoba, Ontario, and Quebec see that businesses, which sell their shares or borrow money from the public, disclose certain financial information to the investing public. The securities commissions, like many government agencies, base their regulatory activity in part on the accounting information they receive from the firms.

Taxing Authorities   Local, provincial, and federal governments levy taxes on individuals and businesses. The amount of the tax is figured using accounting information. Businesses determine their goods and services tax and sales tax based on their accounting records that show how much they have sold. Individuals and businesses compute their income tax based on how much money their records show they have earned.

Nonprofit Organizations   Nonprofit organizations such as churches, hospitals, government agencies, and colleges, which operate for purposes other than to earn a profit, use accounting information in much the same way that profit-oriented businesses do. Both profit organizations and nonprofit organizations deal with budgets, payrolls, rent payments, and the like—all from the accounting system.

Other Users   Employees and labor unions may make wage demands based on the accounting information that shows their employer's reported income. Consumer groups and the general public are also interested in the amount of income that businesses earn. For example, during times of fuel shortages, consumer groups have charged that oil companies have earned "obscene profits." And newspapers may report "improved profit pictures" of major companies as the nation emerges from an economic recession. Such news, based on accounting information, is related to our standard of living.

Users of accounting information are a diverse population, but they may be categorized as external users or internal users. This distinction allows us to classify accounting into fields—financial accounting and management accounting.

Financial accounting provides information to people outside the firm. Creditors and shareholders, for example, are not part of the day-to-day management of the company. Likewise, government agencies, such as Revenue Canada, and the general public are external users of a firm's accounting information. Chapters 2 through 19 of this book deal primarily with financial accounting.

Management accounting generates confidential information for internal decision-makers, such as top executives, department heads, college deans, and hospital administrators. Later courses cover management accounting.

The Development of Accounting

Accounting has a long history. Some scholars claim that writing arose in order to record accounting information. Account records date back to the ancient civilizations of China, Babylonia, Greece, and Egypt. The rulers of these civilizations used accounting to keep track of the cost of labor and materials used in building structures like the great pyramids. The need for accounting has existed as long as there has been business activity.

Accounting developed further as a result of the information needs of merchants in the city-states of Italy during the 1400s. In that busy commercial climate, the monk Luca Pacioli, a mathematician and friend of Leonardo da Vinci, published the first known description of double-entry bookkeeping in 1494.

In the nineteenth century, the growth of corporations spurred the development of accounting. The corporation owners—the shareholders—were no longer necessarily the managers of their business. Managers had to create accounting systems to report to the owners how well their businesses were doing. Because managers want their performance to look good, society needs a way to ensure that business information is reliable.

In Canada, the *Accounting Standards Board (AcSB)* of the Canadian Institute of Chartered Accountants (CICA) determines how accounting is practiced. The AcSB is made up of Chartered Accountants (CAs) from public accounting, industry, government, and academe, plus individuals nominated by the Canadian Council of Financial Analysts, the Financial Executives Insitute of Canada, the Canadian Academic Accounting Association, the Certified General Accountants Association of Canada, and the Society of Management Accountants of Canada. As you will learn in Chapter 12, the federal and provincial legislatures through the various companies acts and the various provincial securities commissions have given the standards or *generally accepted accounting principles (GAAP)* promulgated by the AcSB their legal status.

Computers have revolutionized accounting in the late twentieth century. Tasks that are time-consuming when done by hand are handled quickly and easily by computer. In addition to helping with accounting itself, microcomputers—personal computers, such as Apples, IBMs, and Compaqs—assist with many financial applications of accounting information and in business correspondence. Also, thanks to telecommunications, microcomputers can tap into the information stored in larger computers across the globe. As we progress through the study of accounting, we will consider computer applications that fit the topics under discussion.

Like other segments of society, accounting must be practiced in an ethical manner. We look next at the ethical dimension of accounting.

Ethical Considerations in Accounting and Business _____

Ethical considerations pervade all areas of accounting and business. Consider a situation that challenges the ethical conduct of the accountant.

A company is being sued by a competitor over an alleged patent infringement by the company. Loss of the lawsuit will impose significant financial hardship on the company, jeopardize the company's relationships with its customers and creditors, and likely cause the price of the company's stock to fall. Should the company disclose this sensitive information in its financial statements? Generally accepted accounting principles require the company to describe the lawsuit in its financial statements and the company's auditor to indicate if he or she thinks the company's disclosure is inadequate.

In 1992, 80 of the 300 companies surveyed in the CICA's 1993 edition of *Financial Reporting in Canada, Twentieth Edition,* reported information about lawsuits or possible judgments against the company in the notes to their financial statements.[1]

By what criteria do accountants address questions that challenge their ethical conduct? The three accounting bodies described above all have rules of conduct that govern their members' professional behavior. Many companies have codes of conduct that bind their management and employees to high levels of ethical conduct.

The Professional Accounting Bodies and Their Standards of Professional Conduct

CAs, CGAs, and CMAs are all governed by rules of conduct promulgated by their respective organizations. Many of the rules apply whether the members are public accountants working in public practice or private accountants working in industry or goverment, while other rules are applicable only to those members in public practice.

The rules of conduct serve both the members of the body promulgating them and the public. The rules serve members by setting standards that they must meet, and providing a benchmark against which they will be measured by their peers. The public is served because the rules of conduct provide it with a list of the standards to which the members of the body adhere. This helps it determine its expectations of members' behavior. However, the rules of conduct should be considered

---

[1] *Financial Reporting in Canada,* Twentieth Edition, Toronto: Canadian Institute of Chartered Accountants, 1993, p. 23.

a minimum standard of performance; ideally, the members should continually strive to exceed them.

There are certain rules that are fundamental to the practice of accounting and common to the rules of conduct of all three bodies. They concern the confidentiality of information the accountant is privy to, maintenance of the reputation of the profession, integrity and due care, competence, refusal to be associated with false and misleading information, and compliance by the accountant with professional standards such as the accounting standards found in the *CICA Handbook*.

There are other rules that are fundamental to the practice of public accounting. They deal with the public accountant's need for independence, and with the rules governing advertising and solicitation and the conduct of practice.

Codes of Business Conduct of Companies

Many companies have codes of conduct that apply to their employees in their dealings with each other and with the companies' suppliers and customers. Some of these companies mention their code in the report of management section of the annual report. For example, the Schneider Corporation 1994 annual report stated:

> The Corporation communicates throughout the organization the responsibility for employees to maintain high ethical standards in their conduct of the Corporation's affairs. This responsibility is characterized in the Code of Conduct, signed by each management employee, which provides for compliance with laws of each jurisdiction in which the Corporation operates and for observance of rules of ethical business conduct.

The company indicates to its employees how management expects employees to behave.

Types of Business Organizations

A business takes one of three forms of organization, and in some cases the accounting procedures depend on the organizational form. Therefore, you should understand the differences between a proprietorship, a partnership, and a corporation.

Proprietorships   A **proprietorship** has a single owner, called the proprietor, who is usually also the manager. Proprietorships tend to be small retail establishments and individual professional businesses, such as those of physicians, lawyers, and accountants. From the accounting viewpoint, each proprietorship is distinct from its proprietor. Thus the accounting records of the proprietorship do *not* include records of the proprietor's personal accounting records.

Partnerships   A **partnership** joins two or more individuals together as co-owners. Each owner is a partner. Many retail establishments, as well as some professional organizations of physicians, lawyers, and accountants, are partnerships. Most partnerships are small and medium-sized, but some are quite large; there are public accounting firms in Canada with more than 500 partners and law firms with more than 100 partners. Accounting treats the partnership as a separate organization, distinct from the personal affairs of each partner.

Corporations   A **corporation** is a business owned by **shareholders**, people who own stock in or shares of ownership in the business. The corporation is the dominant form of business organization in Canada. Although proprietorships and partnerships are more numerous, corporations enact more business and are generally larger in terms of total assets, income, and number of employees. Most well-known companies, such as Bombardier Inc., McCain Foods Ltd., and NOVA Corp. of Alberta, are corporations. In Canada, generally corporations must have *Ltd.* or

Limited, Inc. or *Incorporated,* or *Corp.* or *Corporation* in their legal name to indicate that they are incorporated. Some corporations bear the name "Company," such as Hudsons Bay Co. This title does not clearly identify the organization as a corporation because a proprietorship or partnership can also bear the name "Company." Corporations need not be large; a proprietorship or partnership with only a few assets and employees could be organized as a corporation. This book concentrates on corporations.

A business becomes a corporation when the federal or provincial government approves its articles of incorporation. From a legal perspective, a corporation is a distinct entity. The corporation operates as an artificial person that exists apart from its owners and that conducts business in its own name. The corporation has many of the rights that a person has. For example, a corporation may buy, own, and sell property. Assets and liabilities in the business belong to the corporation. The corporation may enter into contracts and sue and be sued. Unlike proprietors and partners, a shareholder has no personal obligation for corporation liabilities. The most that a shareholder can lose on an investment in a corporation's stock is the cost of the investment. But proprietors and partners are personally liable for the debts of their businesses.

The ownership interest of a corporation is divided into shares of stock. A person becomes an owner or shareholder by purchasing a share or shares of stock of the corporation.

Companies such as BCE, Inc. (the parent company of Bell Canada), the Bank of Montreal, and Canadian Pacific Limited have millions of shares of stock outstanding and tens of thousands of shareholders. An investor with no personal relationship either to the corporation or to any other shareholder can become an owner by buying 30, 100, 5,000, or any number of shares of its stock. For many corporations, the investor can sell the stock whenever he or she wishes. It is usually harder to sell out of a proprietorship or a partnership.

The ultimate control of the corporation rests with the shareholders, who receive one vote for each share of stock they own. The shareholders elect the members of the **board of directors**, which sets policy for the corporation and appoints the officers. The board elects a *chairperson,* who usually is the most powerful person in the corporation. The board also designates the president, who is the chief operating officer in charge of managing day-to-day operations. Most corporations also have vice-presidents in charge of sales, manufacturing, accounting and finance, and other key areas.

Exhibit 1-2 shows how the three types of business organizations compare.

EXHIBIT 1-2 *Comparison of a Proprietorship, a Partnership, and a Corporation*

Concept Highlight

	Proprietorship	Partnership	Corporation
1. Owner(s)	Proprietor—one owner	Partners—two or more owners	Shareholders—generally many owners
2. Life of entity	Limited by owner's choice or death	Limited by owners' choices or death	Indefinite
3. Personal liability of owner(s) for business debts	Proprietor is personally liable	Partners are personally liable	Shareholders are not personally liable
4. Accounting status	Accounting entity is separate from proprietor	Accounting entity is separate from partners	Accounting entity is separate from shareholders

OBJECTIVE 2

Apply accounting concepts and principles to analyze business transactions

Accounting Concepts and Principles

Accounting practices follow certain guidelines. The rules that govern how accountants measure, process, and communicate financial information fall under the heading GAAP, which stands for **generally accepted accounting principles**.

The term *accounting principles* is broader than you might at first think. Generally accepted accounting principles include not only principles but also concepts and methods that identify the proper way to produce accounting information. GAAP comprises all conventions, rules, and procedures that constitute accepted accounting practice at any given point in time. Generally accepted accounting principles are very much like the law—rules for conducting behavior in a way acceptable to the majority of people.

GAAP in Canada rests on Section 1000, "Financial Statement Concepts," of the *CICA Handbook. The primary objective of financial reporting is to provide information useful for making investment and lending decisions and for assessing management's stewardship.* To be useful, information must be understandable, relevant, reliable, and comparable. Accountants strive to meet these goals in the information they produce. This course will expose you to the generally accepted methods of accounting. We discuss GAAP fully in Chapter 12. First, however, you need to understand several basic concepts.

The Entity Concept

The most basic concept in accounting is that of the **entity**. An accounting entity is an organization or a section of an organization that stands apart from other organizations and individuals as a separate economic unit. From an accounting perspective, sharp boundaries are drawn around each entity so as not to confuse its affairs with those of other entities.

Consider Mazzio, a pizzeria owner whose bank account shows a $20,000 balance at the end of the year. Only half of that amount—$10,000—grew from the business's operations. The other $10,000 arose from a gift from his sister. If Mazzio follows the entity concept, he will keep separate the money generated by the business—one economic unit—from the money generated by the gift from his family—a second economic unit. This separation makes it possible to view the business's operating result clearly.

Suppose Mazzio disregards the entity concept and treats the full $20,000 amount as income from the pizzeria's operations. He will be misled into believing that the business has produced more cash than it has. Any steps needed to make the business more successful may not be taken.

Consider Bombardier Inc., a company with sales of almost $4.5 billion. It is made up of a transportation segment, an aerospace segment, a motorized consumer products segment, and a financial and real estate services segment. Each of these segments in turn is made up of groups which in turn are made up of units. If sales in the seadoo/skidoo unit were dropping drastically, Bombardier would do well to identify the reason. But if sales figures from all units, groups, and segments were analyzed as a single amount, then management would not even know that the company was not selling enough sea-doo/skidoos. Thus the entity concept also applies to the parts of a large organization—in fact to any entity that needs to be evaluated separately.

In summary, the transactions of different entities making up the whole organization should not be accounted for together. Each entity should be accounted for separately.

The Reliability (or Objectivity) Principle

Accounting records and statements are based on the most reliable data available so that they will be as accurate and useful as possible. This guideline is the *reliability principle,* also called the *objectivity principle*. Reliable data are verifiable. They may be confirmed by any independent observer. Ideally, accounting records are based on information that flows from activities that are documented by objective evidence.

Without the reliability principle, accounting records would be based on whims and opinions and would be subject to dispute.

Suppose you want to open a stereo shop, and in order to have a place for operations, you transfer a small building to the business. You believe the building is worth $55,000. To confirm its value, you hire two real-estate professionals, who appraise the building at $47,000. Is $55,000 or $47,000 the more reliable estimate of the building's value? The real-estate appraisal of $47,000 is, because it is supported by independent, objective observation. The business should record the building at a cost of $47,000, the cost of acquiring the building.

The Cost Principle

The *cost principle* states that assets and services that are acquired should be recorded at their actual cost (also called historical cost). Even though the purchaser may believe the price paid is a bargain, the item is recorded at the price paid in the transaction and not at the "expected" cost. Suppose your stereo shop purchases some stereo equipment from a supplier who is going out of business. Assume you get a good deal on this purchase and pay only $2,000 for merchandise that would have cost you $3,000 elsewhere. The cost principle requires you to record this merchandise at its actual cost of $2,000, not the $3,000 that you believe the equipment to be worth.

The cost principle also holds that the accounting records should maintain the historical cost of an asset for as long as the business holds the asset. Why? Because cost is a reliable measure. Suppose your store holds the stereo equipment for six months. During that time, stereo prices increase, and the equipment can be sold for $3,500. Should its accounting value—the figure "on the books"—be the actual cost of $2,000 or the current market value of $3,500? According to the cost principle, the accounting value of the equipment remains at actual cost, $2,000.

The Going-Concern Concept

Another reason for measuring assets at historical cost is the *going-concern concept*, which holds that the entity will remain in operation for the forseeable future. Most assets—that is, the firm's resources, such as supplies, land, buildings, and equipment—are acquired for use rather than to sell. Under the going-concern concept, accountants assume the business will remain in operation long enough to use existing assets for their intended purpose. The market value of an asset—the price for which the asset can be sold—may change many times during the asset's life. Therefore, an asset's current market value may not be relevant for decision-making. Moreover, historical cost is a more reliable accounting measure for assets than is market value.

To understand the going-concern concept, consider the alternative, which is to *go out of business*. A store that is holding a Going Out of Business Sale is trying to sell all its assets. In that case, the relevant measure of the assets is their current market value. However, going out of business is the exception rather than the rule, and for this reason accounting records list assets at their historical cost.

The Stable-Monetary-Unit Concept

We think of a loaf of bread and a month's apartment rent in terms of their dollar value. In Canada, accountants record transactions in dollars because the dollar is the medium of exchange. French accountants record transactions in terms of the franc, and in Japan transactions are recorded in yen.

Unlike the value of a liter, a kilometer or a tonne, the value of a dollar or a British pound changes over time. A rise in prices is called *inflation*. During inflation a dollar will purchase less milk, less toothpaste, and less of other goods. When prices are relatively stable—when there is little inflation—a dollar's purchasing power is also stable.

Accountants assume that the dollar's purchasing power is relatively stable. The *stable-monetary-unit concept* is the basis for ignoring the effect of inflation in the accounting records. It allows accountants to add and subtract dollar amounts as though each dollar has the same purchasing power as any other dollar at any other time. In certain countries in South America, where inflation rates are high, accountants make adjustments to report monetary amounts in units of current buying power—a very different concept.

The Accounting Equation

OBJECTIVE 3

Use the accounting equation to describe an organization's financial position

Financial statements tell us how a business is performing and where it stands. They are the final product of the accounting process. But how do we arrive at the items and amounts that make up the financial statements?

The most basic tool of the accountant is the **accounting equation**. This equation presents the resources of the business and the claims to those resources. **Assets** are the economic resources of a business that are expected to be of benefit in the future. Cash, office supplies, merchandise, furniture, land, and buildings are examples. Claims to those assets come from two sources.

Liabilities are "outsider claims," which are economic obligations—debts— payable to outsiders. These outside parties are called *creditors*. For example, a creditor who has loaned money to a business has a claim—a legal right—to a part of the assets until the business pays the debt. "Insider claims" are called **owner's equity** or **capital**. These are the claims held by the owners of the business. An owner has a claim to the entity's assets because he or she has invested in the business. Owner's equity is measured by subtracting liabilities from assets.

The accounting equation in Exhibit 1-3 shows the relationship among assets, liabilities, and owner's equity. Assets appear on the left-hand side of the equation. The legal and economic claims against the assets—the liabilities and owner's equity—appear on the right-hand side of the equation. The two sides must be equal:

EXHIBIT 1-3   *The Accounting Equation*

*Economic
Resources   Claims to Economic Resources*

ASSETS = LIABILITIES + OWNER'S EQUITY

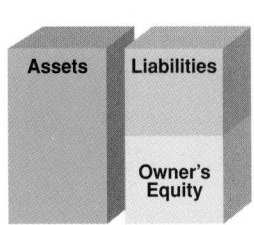

Let us take a closer look at the elements that make up the accounting equation. Suppose you run a business that supplies meat to Harvey's and other restaurants. Some customers may pay you in cash when you deliver the meat. Cash is an asset. Other customers may buy on credit and promise to pay you within a certain time after delivery. This promise is also an asset because it is an economic resource that will benefit you in the future when you receive cash from the customer. To you (the meat supplier) this promise is called an **account receivable**. If the promise that entitles you to receive cash in the future is formally written out, it is called a **note receivable**. All receivables are assets.

Harvey's promise to pay you in the future for the meat it purchases on credit creates a debt for the restaurant. This liability is an **account payable** of Harvey's, which means the debt is not formally out. Instead it is backed up by the reputation and credit standing of Harvey's. A written promise of future payment is called a **note payable**. All payables are liabilities.

Owner's equity is the amount of the assets that remains after the liabilities are subtracted. For this reason, owner's equity is often referred to as *net assets*. We often write the accounting equation to show that the owner's claim to business assets is a residual:

ASSETS – LIABILITIES = OWNER'S EQUITY

Owner's Equity

The owner's equity of a corporation—called shareholders' equity—is divided into two main categories: capital stock and retained earnings. For a corporation the accounting equation can be written as

ASSETS = LIABILITIES   +   SHAREHOLDERS' EQUITY

ASSETS = LIABILITIES   + CAPITAL STOCK + RETAINED EARNINGS

Capital stock is the amount invested in the corporation by its owners. The basic component of capital stock is **common stock** which the corporation issues to its shareholders as evidence of their ownership.

Retained earnings is the amount earned by income-producing activities and kept for use in the business. Two types of transactions that affect retained earnings are revenues and expenses. **Revenues** are increases in retained earnings from delivering goods or services to customers. For example, a laundry's receipt of cash from a customer for cleaning of a coat brings in revenue and increases the laundry's retained earnings. **Expenses** are the decreases in retained earnings that result from operations. For example, the wages that the laundry pays its employees is an expense and decreases retained earnings. Expenses are the cost of doing business and are the opposite of revenues. Expenses include office rent, salaries for employees, newspaper advertisements, and utility payments for light, electricity, gas, and so forth.

Businesses strive for profitability. When total revenues exceed total expenses, the result of operations is **net income, net earnings** or **net profit**. When expenses exceed revenues, the result is a **net loss**.

If the business is successful in earning a net income, it may pay dividends, the third type of transaction that affects retained earnings. Dividends are distributions to shareholders of assets (usually cash) generated by net income. Dividends are not expenses because the decision of whether or not to distribute them is made after expenses and revenues are recorded. First the business measures its net income or net loss. Then a corporation may (or may not) pay dividends. Exhibit 1-4 shows the relationships among retained earnings, revenues, expenses, net income or net loss, and dividends.

The owner's equity of proprietorships and of partnerships is different. These types of business make no distinction between capital stock and retained earnings. Instead, the equity of each owner is accounted for under the single heading of Capital—for example, Martel, Capital, for a proprietorship. The partnership of Chen and Paquette has a separate record of capital for each partner: Chen, Capital, and Paquette, Capital.

EXHIBIT 1-4   *Components of Retained Earnings*

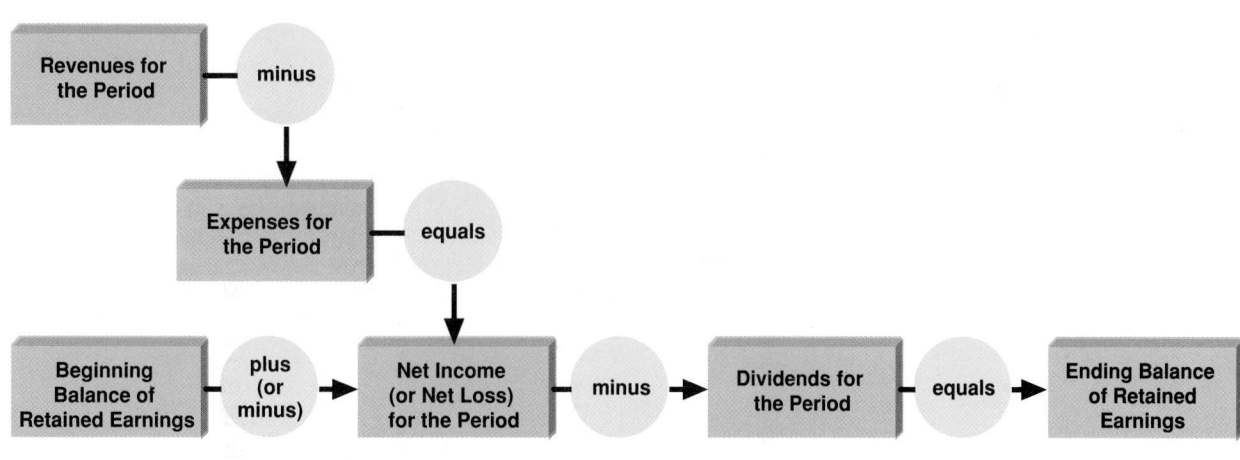

Accounting for Business Transactions

In accounting terms, a **transaction** is any event that *both* affects the financial position of the business entity *and* can be reliably recorded. Many events may affect a company, including (1) elections, (2) economic booms and recessions, (3) purchases and sales of merchandise inventory, (4) payment of rent, (5) collection of cash from customers, and so on. But, an accountant records only events with effects that can be measured reliably as transactions.

Which of the above five events would the accountant record? The answer is events (3), (4), and (5) because their dollar amounts can be measured reliably. Dollar effects that elections and economic trends have on a particular entity cannot be measured reliably. Therefore, an accountant would not record a key election or a trend even though it may affect the business more than events (3), (4), and (5).

To illustrate accounting for business transactions, let's assume that Gary and Monica Lyon open a travel agency that they incorporate as Air & Sea Travel, Inc. We now consider 11 events and analyze each in terms of its effect on the accounting equation of Air & Sea Travel, Inc. Transaction analysis is the essence of accounting.

OBJECTIVE 4

Use the accounting equation to analyze business situations

Transaction 1   The Lyons invest $50,000 of their money to begin the business. Specifically, they deposit $50,000 in a bank account entitled Air & Sea Travel, Inc. As evidence of the corporation, Air & Sea Travel issues common stock to Gary and Monica Lyon. The stock is printed on certificates and issued by the corporation. It provides tangible evidence that the Lyons have an ownership interest in the corporation. The effect of this transaction on the accounting equation of the business entity is

	Assets	=	Liabilities +	Shareholders' Equity	Type of Shareholders' Equity Transaction
	Cash			Common Stock	
(1)	+50,000			+50,000	Owner investment

The amount on the left side of the equation must equal the amount on the right side for every transaction. The first transaction increases both the assets (in this case, Cash) and the owners' equity of the business (Common Stock). The transaction involves no liabilities of the business because it creates no obligation for Air & Sea Travel to pay an outside party. To the right of the transaction we write "Owner investment" to keep track of the reason for the effect on shareholders' equity. This transaction is identical to an investment in a proprietorship except that the Lyons are investing in a corporation. Most businesses start with an investment by an owner, *not* with borrowed money. Why not? Because a lender usually requires the owners to have some of their own money in the business.

Transaction 2   Air & Sea Travel purchases land for a future office location, paying cash of $40,000. The effect of this transaction on the accounting equation is

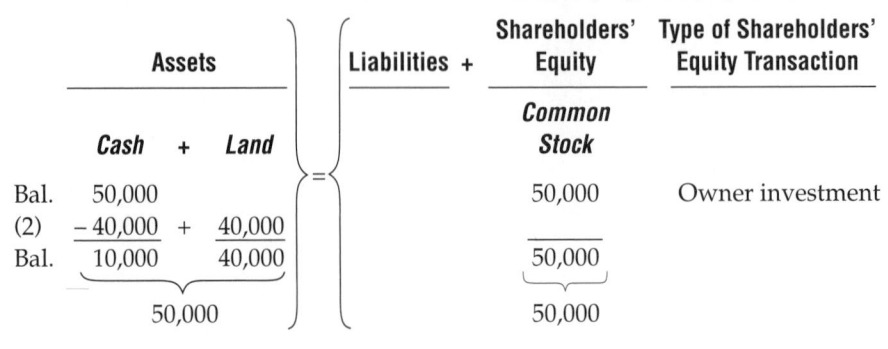

	Assets			Liabilities +	Shareholders' Equity	Type of Shareholders' Equity Transaction
	Cash	+	Land		Common Stock	
Bal.	50,000				50,000	Owner investment
(2)	−40,000	+	40,000			
Bal.	10,000		40,000		50,000	
		50,000			50,000	

The cash purchase of land increases one asset, Land, and decreases another asset, Cash, by the same amount. After the transaction is completed, Air & Sea Travel, Inc., has cash of $10,000, land of $40,000, no liabilities, and shareholders' equity of $50,000. Note that the sums of the balances (which we abbreviate Bal.) on both sides of the equation are equal. This equality must always exist.

STOP & THINK

The Lyons' realtor assures them that the land is worth $75,000. Could they ethically record the land at $75,000?

Answer: Regardless of the owners' belief about the true value of the land, it is recorded at $40,000 because of the *cost principle* and the *reliability principle.* Actual cost is a reliable measure of an asset.

Transaction 3   The business buys stationery and other office supplies, agreeing to pay $500 within 30 days. This transaction increases both the assets and the liabilities of the business. Its effect on the accounting equation is

	\multicolumn{5}{c}{**Assets**}		**Liabilities +**	**Shareholders' Equity**
	Cash	**+**	**Office Supplies**	**+**	**Land**	**=**	**Accounts Payable +**	**Common Stock**
Bal.	10,000				40,000			50,000
(3)			+500				+500	
Bal.	10,000		500		40,000		500	50,000
	\multicolumn{5}{c}{50,500}		\multicolumn{2}{c}{50,500}

The asset affected is Office Supplies, and the liability is called an account payable. The term *payable* signifies a liability. Because Air & Sea Travel, Inc., is obligated to pay $500 in the future but signs no formal promissory note, we record the liability as an Account Payable, not as a Note Payable. We say that purchases supported by the general credit standing of the buyer are made on an *open account.*

Transaction 4   Air & Sea Travel, Inc., earns service revenue by providing travel arrangement services for customers. Assume the business earns $5,500 and collects this amount in cash. The effect on the accounting equation is an increase in the asset Cash and an increase in Retained Earnings, as follows:

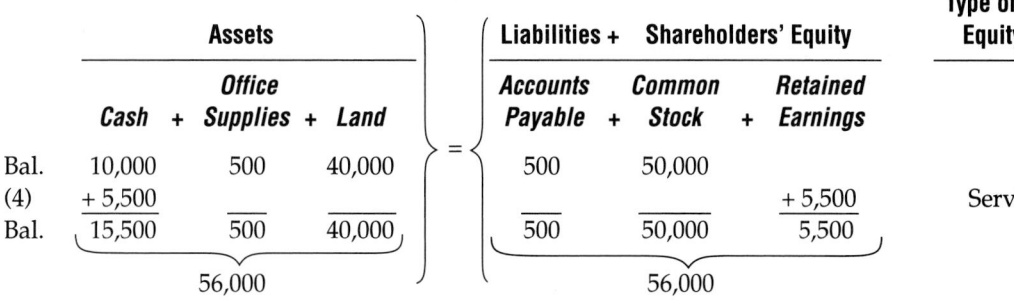

	\multicolumn{3}{c}{**Assets**}		\multicolumn{3}{c}{**Liabilities + Shareholders' Equity**}	**Type of Shareholders' Equity Transaction**
	Cash +	**Office Supplies +**	**Land**	**=**	**Accounts Payable +**	**Common Stock +**	**Retained Earnings**	
Bal.	10,000	500	40,000		500	50,000		
(4)	+ 5,500						+ 5,500	Service revenue
Bal.	15,500	500	40,000		500	50,000	5,500	
	\multicolumn{3}{c}{56,000}		\multicolumn{3}{c}{56,000}	

This revenue transaction caused the business to grow, as shown by the increase in total assets and in total liabilities plus shareholders' equity. A company that sells goods to customers is a merchandising business. Its revenue is called *sales revenue*. In contrast, Air & Sea Travel, Inc., performs services for clients; their revenue is called *service revenue*.

Transaction 5   Air & Sea Travel performs services for customers who do not pay immediately. In return for the services, Air & Sea receives the customers' promise to pay the $3,000 amount within one month. This promise is an asset to Air & Sea Travel, an account receivable because the business expects to collect the cash in the future. In accounting, we say that Air & Sea performed this service *on account*. When the business performs service for a client or a customer, the business earns revenue regardless of whether it receives cash immediately or expects to collect cash later. This $3,000 of service revenue is as real to the business as the $5,500 of revenue that was collected immediately in the preceding transaction. Air & Sea Travel records an increase in the asset Accounts Receivable and an increase in Service Revenue, which increases Retained Earnings as follows:

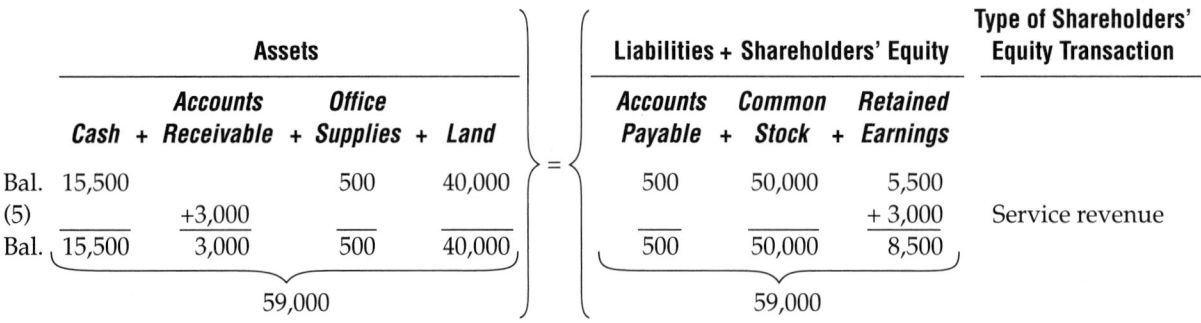

		Assets					Liabilities +	Shareholders' Equity		Type of Shareholders' Equity Transaction
	Cash +	Accounts Receivable +	Office Supplies +	Land	=		Accounts Payable +	Common Stock +	Retained Earnings	
Bal.	15,500		500	40,000			500	50,000	5,500	
(5)		+3,000							+ 3,000	Service revenue
Bal.	15,500	3,000	500	40,000			500	50,000	8,500	
		59,000						59,000		

Again, this revenue transaction caused the business to grow.

Transaction 6   During the month, Air & Sea Travel, Inc., pays $2,700 in cash expenses: office rent, $1,100; employee salary $1,200 (for a part-time assistant); and total utilities, $400. The effect on the accounting equation is

		Assets					Liabilities +	Shareholders' Equity		Type of Shareholders' Equity Transaction
	Cash +	Accounts Receivable +	Office Supplies +	Land	=		Accounts Payable +	Common Stock +	Retained Earnings	
Bal.	15,500	3,000	500	40,000			500	50,000	8,500	
(6)	−2,700								−1,100	Rent expense
									−1,200	Salary expense
									− 400	Utility expense
Bal.	12,800	3,000	500	40,000			500	50,000	5,800	
		56,300						56,300		

Because expenses have the opposite effect of revenues, they cause the business to shrink, as shown by the smaller amounts of total assets and total liabilities and shareholders' equity.

Each expense should be recorded in a separate transaction. Here, for simplicity, they are recorded together. Note that even though the figure $2,700 does not appear on the right-hand side of the equation, the three individual expenses add up to $2,700 total. As a result, the "balance" of the equation holds, as we know it must.

Transaction 7 Air & Sea Travel pays $400 to the store from which it purchased $500 worth of office supplies in Transaction 3. In accounting, we say that the business pays $400 *on account*. The effect on the accounting equation is a decrease in the asset Cash and a decrease in the liability Accounts Payable as follows:

	Assets				=	Liabilities + Shareholders' Equity		
	Cash +	Accounts Receivable +	Office Supplies +	Land		Accounts Payable +	Common Stock +	Retained Earnings
Bal.	12,800	3,000	500	40,000		500	50,000	5,800
(7)	– 400					– 400		
Bal.	12,400	3,000	500	40,000		100	50,000	5,800

55,900 = 55,900

The payment of cash on account has no effect on the asset Office Supplies because the payment does not increase or decrease the supplies available to the business.

Transaction 8 The Lyons remodel their home at a cost of $30,000, paying cash from personal funds. This event is *not* a transaction of Air & Sea Travel, Inc. It has no effect on Air & Sea's business affairs and therefore is not recorded by the business. It is a transaction of the *personal* entity the Lyon family, not the business entity Air & Sea Travel. We are focusing now solely on the *business* entity, and this event does not affect it. This transaction illustrates the application of the *entity concept*.

Transaction 9 In Transaction 5, Air & Sea Travel, Inc., performed services for customers on account. The business now collects $1,000 from a customer. We say that it collects the cash *on account*. It will record an increase in the asset Cash. Should it also record an increase in service revenue? No, because Air & Sea already recorded the revenue when it performed the service in Transaction 5. The phrase "collect cash on account" means to record an increase in Cash and a decrease in the asset Accounts Receivable. The effect on the accounting equation is

	Assets				=	Liabilities + Shareholders' Equity		
	Cash +	Accounts Receivable +	Office Supplies +	Land		Accounts Payable +	Common Stock +	Retained Earnings
Bal.	12,400	3,000	500	40,000		100	50,000	5,800
(9)	+ 1,000	– 1,000						
Bal.	13,400	2,000	500	40,000		100	50,000	5,800

55,900 = 55,900

Total assets are unchanged from the preceding transaction's total. Why? Because Air & Sea Travel merely exchanged one asset for another. Also, shareholders' equity is unchanged.

Transaction 10 An individual approaches the Lyons about selling a parcel of land owned by the Air & Sea Travel entity. They and the other person agree to a sale price of $22,000, which is equal to the business's cost of the land. Air & Sea sells the land and receives $22,000 cash, and the effect on the accounting equation is

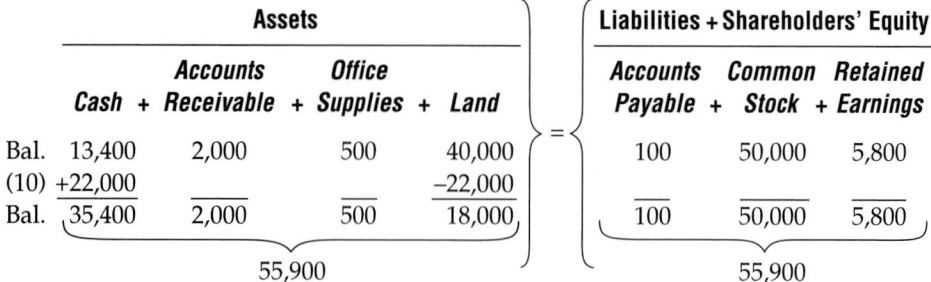

	Assets					Liabilities + Shareholders' Equity		
	Cash +	Accounts Receivable +	Office Supplies +	Land	=	Accounts Payable +	Common Stock +	Retained Earnings
Bal.	13,400	2,000	500	40,000		100	50,000	5,800
(10)	+22,000			−22,000				
Bal.	35,400	2,000	500	18,000		100	50,000	5,800
			55,900				55,900	

Transaction 11   The corporation declares a dividend and pays Gary and Monica Lyon $2,100 cash for their personal use. The effect on the accounting equation is

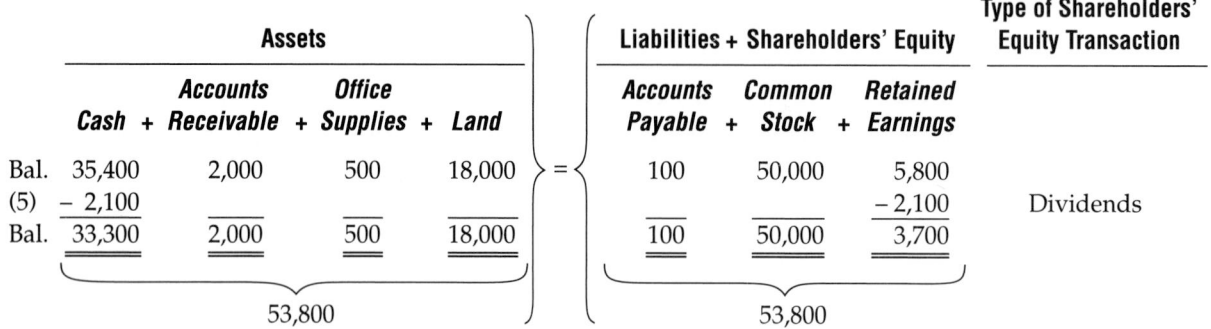

	Assets					Liabilities + Shareholders' Equity			Type of Shareholders' Equity Transaction
	Cash +	Accounts Receivable +	Office Supplies +	Land	=	Accounts Payable +	Common Stock +	Retained Earnings	
Bal.	35,400	2,000	500	18,000		100	50,000	5,800	
(5)	− 2,100							− 2,100	Dividends
Bal.	33,300	2,000	500	18,000		100	50,000	3,700	
			53,800				53,800		

The dividend decreases the asset Cash and also the shareholders' equity of the business.

Does the dividend decrease the business entity's holdings? The answer is yes, because the cash paid to the shareholders is no longer available for Air & Sea Travel business use. The dividend does *not* represent a business expense, however, because the cash is paid to the owners for their personal use. We record this decrease in shareholders' equity as Dividends.

Evaluating Business Transactions

Concept Highlight

Exhibit 1-5 summarizes the 11 preceding transactions. Panel A of the exhibit lists the details of the transactions, and Panel B presents the analysis. As you study the exhibit, note that every transaction maintains the equality

ASSETS = LIABILITIES + SHAREHOLDERS' EQUITY

STOP & THINK

Why do Gary and Monica Lyon, or anyone else, go into business? If you could identify only one reason, what would it be? How will accounting serve to meet this need?

Answer: The Lyons went into business to earn a profit—and thereby to make a living. They hope Air & Sea Travel's accounting revenues exceed its expenses to provide an excess—a net income. They hope to receive cash dividends from the business to pay their personal bills. Accounting tells the Lyons how much income the business has earned and how much cash and other assets the business has. The owners also need to know how much in liabilities the business owes. The financial statements help answer these questions.

EXHIBIT 1-5   *Analysis of Air & Sea Travel, Inc.*

Panel A: Details of Transactions

(1) The owners invested $50,000 cash in the business.
(2) Paid $40,000 cash for land.
(3) Bought $500 of office supplies on account payable.
(4) Received $5,500 cash from customers for service revenue earned.
(5) Performed services for customers on account, $3,000.
(6) Paid cash expenses: rent, $1,100; employee salary, $1,200; utilities, $400.
(7) Paid $400 on the account payable created in Transaction 3.
(8) Owners paid personal funds to remodel home. This is *not* a business transaction.
(9) Received $1,000 on the account receivable created in Transaction 5.
(10) Sold land for cash equal to its cost of $22,000.
(11) Declared and paid a dividend of $2,100 to the shareholders.

Panel B: Analysis of Transactions

	Cash	+	Accounts Receivable	+	Office Supplies	+	Land	=	Accounts Payable	+	Common Stock	+	Retained Earnings	Type of Shareholders' Equity Transaction
(1)	+50,000										+50,000			Owner investment
Bal.	50,000										50,000			
(2)	−40,000						+40,000							
Bal.	10,000						40,000				50,000			
(3)					500				+ 500					
Bal.	10,000				500		40,000		500		50,000			
(4)	+ 5,500												+ 5,500	Service revenue
Bal.	15,500				500		40,000		500		50,000		5,500	
(5)			+3,000										+ 3,000	Service revenue
Bal.	15,500		3,000		500		40,000		500		50,000		8,500	
(6)	− 2,700												− 1,100	Rent expense
													− 1,200	Salary expense
													− 400	Utilities expense
Bal.	12,800		3,000		500		40,000		500		50,000		5,800	
(7)	− 400								− 400					
Bal.	12,400		3,000		500		40,000		100		50,000		5,800	
(8)	Not a transaction of the business													
(9)	+ 1,000		−1,000											
Bal.	13,400		2,000		500		40,000		100		50,000		5,800	
(10)	+22,000						−22,000							
Bal.	35,400		2,000		500		18,000		100		50,000		5,800	
(11)	− 2,100												− 2,100	Dividends
Bal.	33,300		2,000		500		18,000		100		50,000		3,700	

53,800 = 53,800

Summary of Business Activities

Exhibit 1-6 summarizes (in clockwise fashion) the business activities that we have accounted for in this chapter. For a new entity such as Air & Sea Travel, Inc., the process begins when the owners supply financial resources to start the business. The entity may also borrow from creditors. These are the two ways of *financing* a business with money received from owners and with money lent by creditors.

Most businesses *invest* in long-term assets, such as the land that Air & Sea Travel purchased. There are other transactions between the business and its employees and suppliers—salary paid to employees (an expense) and the purchase of office supplies (an asset)—for the services and goods provided.

The *operations* of a business center on the sale of services and goods to customers and the collection of cash—items 7 and 8 in Exhibit 1-6. After a period the business pays off its loans, and, if it is profitable, distributes cash to its owners (dividends, for a corporation).

OBJECTIVE 5

Prepare the financial statements

Financial Statements

Once the analysis of the transactions is complete, what is the next step in the accounting process? How does a business present the results of the analysis? We now look at the *financial statements*, which are the formal reports of financial information about the entity. The primary financial statements are the (1) income statement, (2) statement of retained earnings, (3) balance sheet, and (4) statement of changes in financial position.

The **income statement** presents a summary of the *revenues* and *expenses* of an entity for a specific period of time, such as a month or a year. The income statement, also called the **statement of earnings** or **statement of operations**, is like a video of the entity's operations during the period. The income statement holds perhaps the most

Concept Highlight

EXHIBIT 1-6   *Business Activities*

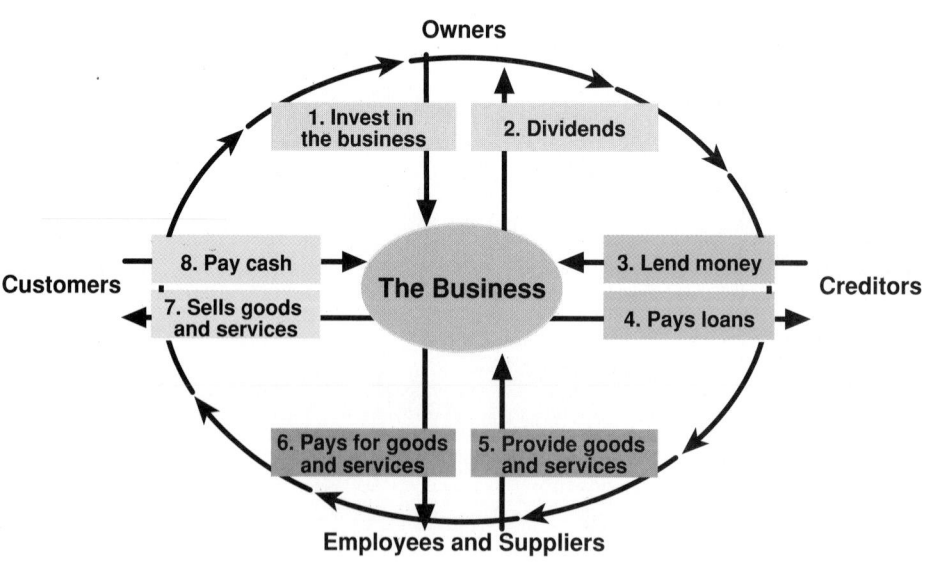

important single piece of information about a business—its *net income,* revenues minus expenses. If expenses exceed revenues, a net loss results for the period.

The **statement of retained earnings** presents a summary of the changes that occurred in the *retained earnings* of the entity during a specific time period, such as a month or a year. An increase in retained earnings arises from net income earned during the period. A decrease results from dividends to the owner and from a net loss for the period. Net income or net loss comes directly from the income statement. Dividends are capital transactions between the business and its owners, so they do not affect the income statement.

The **balance sheet** lists all the *assets, liabilities,* and *shareholders' equity* of an entity as of a specific date, usually the end of a month or a year. The balance sheet is like a snapshot of the entity. For this reason, it is also called the **statement of financial position**.

The **statement of changes in financial position** reports the amount of cash coming in—*cash receipts*—and the amount of cash going out—*cash payments* or *disbursements*—during a period. Business activities result in a net cash inflow (receipts greater than payments) or a net cash outflow (payments greater than receipts). The statement of changes in financial position shows the net increase or decrease in cash during the period and the cash balance at the end of the period. We will cover the statement of changes in financial position in greater depth in Chapter 18.

Computers and software programs for use in accounting have had a significant impact on the preparation of the financial statements. Financial statements can be produced instantaneously after the data from the financial records are entered into the computer. Of course, any errors that exist in the financial records will be passed on to the financial statements. For this reason, the person responsible for analyzing the accounting data is critical to the accuracy of the financial statements.

Each financial statement has a heading, which gives the name of the business (in our discussion Air & Sea Travel, Inc.), the name of the particular statement, and the date or period covered by the statement. A balance sheet taken at the end of year 19X4 would be dated December 31, 19X4. A balance sheet prepared at the end of March 19X7 is dated March 31, 19X7.

An income statement or a statement of retained earnings covering an annual period ending in December 19X5 is dated "For the year ended December 31, 19X5." A monthly income statement or statement of retained earnings for September 19X9 has in its heading "For the month ended September 30, 19X9" or simply "For the month of September 19X9." Income is meaningless unless identified with a particular time period.

Relationships among the Financial Statements _____

Exhibit 1-7 illustrates all four statements. Their data come from the transaction analysis in Exhibit 1-5. We are assuming the transactions occurred during the month of April 19X1. Study the exhibit carefully, because it shows the relationships among the four financial statements.

Observe the following in Exhibit 1-7:

1. The *income statement* for the month ended April 30, 19X1

    a. Reports all *revenues* and all *expenses* during the period. Revenues and expenses are reported only on the income statement.

    b. Reports *net income* of the period if total revenues exceed total expenses, as in the case of Air & Sea Travel's operations for April. If total expenses exceed total revenues, *a net loss* is reported instead. Normally, Air & Sea Travel would record income tax expense as a deduction from income; income tax has been ignored for purposes of this example.

2. The *statement of retained earnings* for the month ended April 30, 19X1

    a. Opens with the retained earnings balance at the beginning of the period.

    b. Adds *net income* (or subtracts *net loss*, as the case may be). Net income (or net loss) comes directly from the income statement, which includes the effect of all the revenues and all the expenses for the period (see arrow 1 in Exhibit 1-7).

    c. Subtracts *dividends*.

    d. Ends with the retained earnings balance at the end of the period.

3. The balance sheet at April 30, 19X1, the end of the period.

    a. Reports all *assets*, all *liabilities*, and *shareholders'* equity of the business at the end of the period. No other statement reports assets and liabilities.

    b. Reports that total assets equal the sum of total liabilities plus total shareholders' equity. This balancing feature gives the balance sheet its name. It is based on the accounting equation.

    c. Reports the ending retained earnings, taken directly from the statement of retained earnings (see arrow 2).

4. The *statement of changes in financial position* for the month ended April 30, 19X1

    a. Reports cash flows from three types of business activities (*operating, investing,* and *financing* activities) during the month. Each category results in net cash inflow or a net cash outflow for the period.

    b. Reports a net increase in cash during the month and ends with the cash balance at April 30, 19X1. This is the amount of cash to report on the balance sheet (see arrow 3).

STOP & THINK

How well did Air & Sea Travel perform during April?

Answer: Rather well. Business net income was $5,800—very good in relation to service revenue of $8,500. Gary and Monica Lyon were able to receive cash dividends of $2,100 for personal use. The business ended April with cash of $33,300. The total assets of $53,800 far exceed the total liabilities of $100. The shareholders' equity of $53,700 provides a good cushion against which the business can borrow. The business's financial position at April 30, 19X1, is strong. What identifies a strong financial position? Plenty of cash and assets far in excess of liabilities—hence a large amount of shareholders' equity. Lenders like to see these features before making a loan: "Those most able to borrow money need it the least."

Now read the chapter appendix to become familiar with accounting organizations and the structure of the profession.

EXHIBIT 1-7 *Financial Statements of Air & Sea Travel, Inc.*

Air & Sea Travel, Inc.
Income Statement
Month Ended April 30, 19X1

Revenue:		
Service revenue		$8,500
Expenses:		
Salary expense	$1,200	
Rent expense	1,100	
Utilities expense	400	
Total expenses		2,700
Net income		$5,800

Air & Sea Travel, Inc.
Statement of Retained Earnings
Month Ended April 30, 19X1

Retained Earnings, April 1, 19X1	$ 0
Add: Net income for the month	5,800
	5,800
Less: Dividends	2,100
Retained earnings, April 30, 19X1	$3,700

Air & Sea Travel, Inc.
Balance Sheet
April 30, 19X1

Assets		**Liabilities**	
Cash	$33,300	Accounts payable	$ 100
Accounts receivable	2,000		
Office supplies	500	**Shareholders' Equity**	
Land	18,000	Common Stock	50,000
		Retained earnings	3,700
		Total shareholders'	53,700
		Total liabilities and	
Total assets	$53,800	shareholders' equity	$53,800

Air & Sea Travel, Inc.
Statement of Changes in Financial Position*
Month Ended April 30, 19X1

Cash flows from operating activities:		
Receipts		
Collections from customers ($5,500 + $1,000)		$ 6,500
Payments:		
To suppliers ($1,100 + $400 + $400)	$(1,900)	
To employees	(1,200)	(3,100)
Net cash inflow from operating activities		3,400
Cash flows from financing activities:		
Investment by owners	$50,000	
Withdrawal by owner	(2,100)	
Net cash inflow from financing activities		47,900
Cash flows from investing activities:		
Acquisition of land	$(40,000)	
Sale of land	22,000	
Net cash outflow from investing activities		(18,000)
Net increase in cash		$33,300
Cash balance, April 1, 19X1		0
Cash balance, April 30, 19X1		$33,300

* The statement of changes in financial position is included here merely for completeness. Chapter 18 will explain how to prepare this statement.

Summary Problem for Your Review

Jill Smith opens an apartment-locator business in Regina. She names the corporation Fast Apartment Locators, Inc. During the first month of operations, July 19X1, the business engages in the following transactions:

a. Smith invests $35,000 of personal funds to acquire the common stock of the corporation.

b. She purchases on account office supplies costing $350.

c. Fast Apartment Locators pays cash of $30,000 to acquire a lot. She intends to use the land as a future building site for her business office.

d. The company locates apartments for clients and receives cash of $1,900.

e. The company pays $100 on the account payable she created in Transaction (b).

f. Jill Smith pays $2,000 of personal funds for a vacation for her family.

g. The company pays cash expenses for office rent, $400, and utilities, $100.

h. The business sells office supplies to another business for its cost of $150.

i. The company declares and pays a cash dividend of $1,200.

Required

1. Analyze the preceding transactions in terms of their effects on the accounting equation of Fast Apartment Locators, Inc. Use Exhibit 1-5 as a guide but show balances only after the last transaction.

2. Prepare the income statement, statement of retained earnings and balance sheet of the business after recording the transactions. Use Exhibit 1-7 as a guide.

SOLUTION TO REVIEW PROBLEM

1.   **Panel A: Details of Transactions**

a. Smith invested $35,000 cash to aquire the common stock of the corporation.

b. Purchased $350 in office supplies on account.

c. Paid $30,000 to acquire land as a future building site.

d. Earned service revenue and received cash of $1,900.

e. Paid $100 on account.

f. Paid for a personal vacation, which is not a business transaction.

g. Paid cash expenses for rent, $400, and utilities, $100.

h. Sold office supplies for cost of $150.

i. Paid dividends of $1,200.

Panel B: Analysis of Transactions

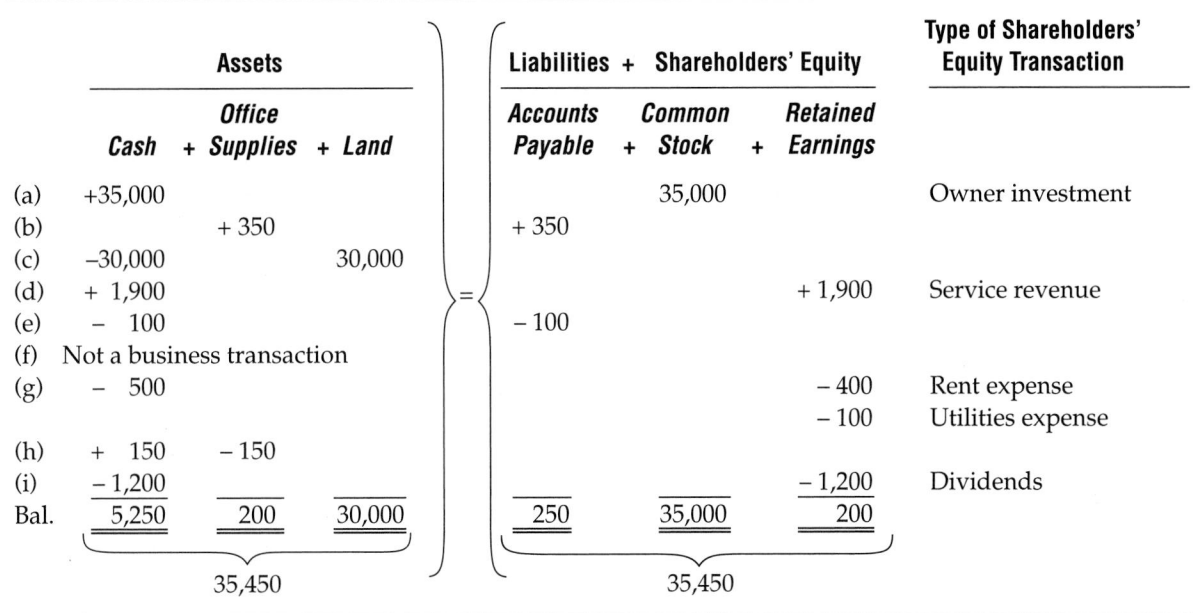

	Assets				Liabilities +	Shareholders' Equity		Type of Shareholders' Equity Transaction
	Cash	+	Office Supplies	+ Land	Accounts Payable	Common Stock +	Retained Earnings	
(a)	+35,000					35,000		Owner investment
(b)			+ 350		+ 350			
(c)	−30,000			30,000				
(d)	+ 1,900						+ 1,900	Service revenue
(e)	− 100				− 100			
(f)	Not a business transaction							
(g)	− 500						− 400	Rent expense
							− 100	Utilities expense
(h)	+ 150		− 150					
(i)	− 1,200						− 1,200	Dividends
Bal.	5,250		200	30,000	250	35,000	200	

35,450 = 35,450

2. *Financial Statements of Fast Apartment Locators, Inc.*

Fast Apartment Locators, Inc.
Income Statement
for the month ended July 31, 19X1

Revenues		
Service revenue		$1,900
Expenses		
Rent expense	$400	
Utilities expense	100	
Total expenses		500
Net Income		$ 1,400

Fast Apartment Locators, Inc.
Statement of Retained Earnings
for the month ended July 31, 19X1

Retained Earnings, May 1, 19X1	$ 0
Add:	
Net income for the month	1,400
	1,400
Less: Dividends	1,200
Retained earnings, May 31, 19X1	$ 200

Fast Apartment Locators, Inc.
Balance Sheet
July 31, 19X1

Assets		Liabilities	
Cash	$5,250	Accounts payable	$ 250
Office Supplies	200		
Land	30,000	**Shareholders' Equity**	
		Common Stock	35,000
		Retained earnings	200
		Total shareholders' equity	$35,200
		Total liabilities and	
Total assets	$35,450	shareholders' equity	$35,450

Summary _____

1. *Develop an accounting vocabulary for decision-making.* Accounting is a system for measuring, processing, and communicating financial information. As the "language of business," accounting helps a wide range of decision-makers. Accounting dates back to ancient civilizations, but its importance to society has been greatest since the Industrial Revolution.

2. *Apply accounting concepts and principles to analyze business transactions.* The three basic forms of business organization are the proprietorship, the partnership, and the corporation. Whatever form, accountants use the entity concept to keep the business's records separate from the personal records of the people who run it. Accountants at all levels must be ethical to serve their intended purpose. *Generally accepted accounting principles (GAAP)* guide accountants in their work. Among these guidelines are the *entity concept*, the *reliability principle*, the *cost principle*, the *going-concern concept*, and the *stable-monetary-unit concept*.

3. *Use the accounting equation to describe an organization's financial position.* In its most common form, the accounting equation is

ASSETS = LIABILITIES + OWNERS' EQUITY

4. *Use the accounting equation to analyze business transactions.* Transactions affect a business's assets, liabilities, and owner's equity. The owner's equity of a corporation is called *shareholders' equity*. Therefore, transactions are analyzed in terms of their effect on the accounting equation.

5. *Prepare the financial statements.* The *financial statements* communicate information for decision-making by the entity's managers, owners, and creditors and by government agencies. The *income statement* presents a video of the entity's operations in terms of revenues earned and expenses incurred during a specific period. Total revenues minus total expenses equal net income. Net income or net loss answers the question, How much income did the entity earn, or, How much loss did it incur during the period? The *statement of retained earnings* reports the changes in retained earnings during the period. The *balance sheet* provides a photograph of the entity's financial standing in terms of its assets, liabilities, and shareholders' equity at a specific time. It answers the question, What is the entity's financial position? The *statement of changes in financial position* reports the cash coming in and the cash going out during the period. It answers, Where did cash come from, and, Where did it go?

6. *Evaluate the performance of a business.* High net income indicates success in business; net loss indicates a bad year.

Self-Study Questions

Test your understanding of the chapter by marking the correct answer for each of the following questions:

1. The organization that formulates generally accepted accounting principles is *(p. 4)*
   a. Ontario Securities Commission
   b. Public Accountants Council of Canada
   c. Canadian Institute of Chartered Accountants (CICA)
   d. Revenue Canada

2. Which of the following forms of business organization is an "artificial person" and must obtain legal approval from the federal government or a province to conduct business? *(p. 7)*
   a. Law firm   c. Partnership
   b. Proprietorship   d. Corporation

3. You have purchased some unclaimed freight for $10,000 and can sell it imme-
   diately for $15,000. What accounting concept or principle governs the amount
   at which to record the goods you purchased? *(p. 9)*
   a. Entity concept
   b. Reliability principle
   c. Cost principle
   d. Going-concern concept

4. The economic resources of a business are called *(p. 10)*
   a. Assets   c. Owner's equity
   b. Liabilities   d. Receivables

5. A business has assets of $140,000 and liabilities of $60,000. How much is its
   owner's equity? *(p. 10)*
   a. $0   c. $140,000
   b. $80,000   d. $200,000

6. The purchase of office supplies on account will *(p. 13)*
   a. Increase an asset and increase a liability
   b. Increase an asset and increase owner's equity
   c. Increase one asset and decrease another asset
   d. Increase an asset and decrease a liability

7. The performance of service for a customer or client and immediate receipt of cash
   will *(p. 14)*
   a. Increase one asset and decrease another asset
   b. Increase an asset and increase owner's equity
   c. Decrease an asset and decrease a liability
   d. Increase an asset and increase a liability

8. The payment of an account payable will *(p. 15)*
   a. Increase one asset and decrease another asset
   b. Decrease an asset and decrease owner's equity
   c. Decrease an asset and decrease a liability
   d. Increase an asset and increase a liability

9. The report of assets, liabilities, and shareholders' equity is called the *(p. 18)*
   a. Financial statement   c. Income statement
   b. Balance sheet   d. Statement of owner's equity

10. The financial statements that are dated for a time period (rather than a specific
    time) are the *(p. 18)*
    a. Balance sheet and income statement
    b. Balance sheet and statement of owner's equity
    c. Income statement, statement of owner's equity, and statement of changes
       in financial position
    d. All financial statements are dated for a time period.

Answers to the Self-Study Questions follow the Accounting Vocabulary.

Accounting Vocabulary

Accounting, like many other subjects, has a special vocabulary. It is important that
you understand the following terms. They are explained in the chapter and also in
the glossary at the end of the book.

accounting *(p. 2)*
accounting equation *(p. 10)*
accounts payable *(p. 10)*
accounts receivable *(p. 10)*
assets *(p. 10)*
auditing *(p. 50)*
balance sheet *(p. 18)*
board of directors *(p. 7)*
capital *(p. 10)*

common stock *(p. 11)*
corporation *(p. 6)*
entity *(p. 8)*
expenses *(p. 11)*
financial accounting *(p. 4)*
financial statements *(p. 2)*
generally accepted accounting principles (GAAP) *(p. 8)*
income statement *(p. 18)*
liabilities *(p. 10)*
management accounting *(p. 4)*
net earnings *(p. 11)*
net income *(p. 11)*
net loss *(p. 11)*
net profit *(p. 11)*
note payable *(p. 10)*
note receivable *(p. 10)*
owner's equity *(p. 10)*
partnership *(p. 6)*
proprietorship *(p. 6)*
retained earnings *(p. 11)*
revenues *(p. 11)*
shareholders *(p. 6)*
statement of changes in financial position *(p. 18)*
statement of earnings *(p. 18)*
statement of financial position *(p. 18)*
statement of operations *(p. 18)*
statement of retained earnings *(p. 18)*
transaction *(p. 12)*

Answers to Self-Study Questions

1.	c	3.	c	5.	b	7.	b	9.	b
2.	d	4.	a	6.	a	8.	c	10.	c

ASSIGNMENT MATERIAL _____

Questions

1. Distinguish between accounting and bookkeeping.
2. Identify five users of accounting information and explain how they use it.
3. Name two important reasons for the development of accounting thought.
4. Name three professional titles of accountants. Also give their abbreviations.
5. What organization formulates generally accepted accounting principles? Is this organization a government agency?
6. Name the four principal types of services provided by public accounting firms.
7. Identify the owner(s) of a proprietorship, a partnership, and a corporation.
8. Why do ethical standards exist in accounting? Which organizations direct their standards more toward independent auditors? Which organizations direct their standards more toward management accountants?
9. Why is the entity concept so important to accounting?
10. Give four examples of accounting entities.
11. Briefly describe the reliability principle.
12. What role does the cost principle play in accounting?
13. If *assets = liabilities + owner's equity*, then how can liabilities be expressed?
14. Explain the difference between an account receivable and an account payable.
15. Identify the items that make up the balance of retained earnings.
16. What role do transactions play in accounting?

17. Give a more descriptive title for the balance sheet.
18. What feature of the balance sheet gives this financial statement its name?
19. Give another title of the income statement.
20. Which financial statement is like a snapshot of the entity at a specific time? Which financial statement is like a video of the entity's operation during a period of time?
21. What information does the statement of retained earnings report?
22. What piece of information flows from the income statement to the statement of retained earnings? What information flows from the statement of retained earnings to the balance sheet? What balance sheet item is explained by the statement of changes in financial position?

Exercises

Exercise 1-1 *Explaining the income statement and the balance sheet* *(Obj. 1)*

Felix and Charlotte Jiminez want to open a Mexican restaurant in Calgary. In need of cash, they ask the Bank of Montreal for a loan. The bank's procedures require borrowers to submit financial statements to show likely results of operations for the first year and likely financial position at the end of the first year. With little knowledge of accounting, Felix and Charlotte don't know how to proceed. Explain to them the information provided by the statement of operations (the income statement) and the statement of financial position (the balance sheet). Indicate why a lender would require this information.

Exercise 1-2 *Business transactions* *(Obj. 2)*

For each of the following items, give an example of a business transaction that has the described effect on the accounting equation:

a. Increase an asset and increase a liability.
b. Increase one asset and decrease another asset.
c. Decrease an asset and decrease owner's equity.
d. Decrease an asset and decrease a liability.
e. Increase an asset and increase owner's equity.

Exercise 1-3 *Transaction analysis* *(Obj. 2)*

Kreitze Contractors Inc., a corporation owned by Darren Kreitze, the major shareholder, experienced the following events. State whether each event (1) increased, (2) decreased, or (3) had no effect on the total assets of the business. Identify any specific asset affected.

a. Borrowed money from the bank.
b. Cash purchase of land for a future building site.
c. Kreitze increased his cash investment in the business.
d. Paid cash on accounts payable.
e. Purchased machinery and equipment for a manufacturing plant; signed a promissory note in payment.
f. Performed service for a customer on account.
g. Kreitze received a cash dividend.
h. Received cash from a customer on account receivable.
i. Kreitze used personal funds to purchase a swimming pool for his home.
j. Sold land for a price equal to the cost of the land; received cash.

Exercise 1-4 *Accounting equation* *(Obj. 3)*

Compute the missing amount in the accounting equation of each of the following three entities:

	Assets	Liabilities	Owner's Equity
Entity A	$?	$41,800	$84,400
Entity B	95,900	?	34,000
Entity C	81,700	29,800	?

Exercise 1-5   *Accounting equation*   **(Obj. 4, 5)**

Oriole Travel Agency balance sheet data, at May 31, 19X2, and June 30, 19X2, follow:

	May 31, 19X2	June 30, 19X2
Total assets	$150,000	$195,000
Total liabilities	109,000	131,000

Required

Below are three assumptions about investments by and dividends to the owner of the business during June. For each assumption, compute the amount of net income or net loss of the business during June 19X2.

a. The owner invested $20,000 in the business and made no withdrawals.

b. The owners made no additional investments in the business but received dividends of $16,000.

c. The owners invested $39,000 in the business and received dividends of $6,000.

Exercise 1-6   *Transaction analysis*   **(Obj. 4)**

Indicate the effects of the following business transactions on the accounting equation. Transaction *a* is answered as a guide.

a. Received cash of $20,000 from the owners, who were investing in the business.
   Answer: Increase asset (Cash)
   Increase shareholders' equity (Common Stock)

b. Paid $300 cash to purchase office supplies.

c. Performed engineering services for a client and received cash of $780.

d. Paid monthly office rent of $500.

e. Performed engineering service for a client on account, $2,000.

f. Purchased on account office furniture at a cost of $500.

g. Received cash on account, $900.

h. Paid cash on account, $250.

i. Sold land for $12,000, which was our cost of the land.

Exercise 1-7   *Transaction analysis, accounting equation*   **(Obj. 2, 4)**

Allison LaChappelle D.V.M. opens an animal hospital to specialize in small animals. During her first month of operation, January, her hospital, entitled Allison LaChappelle, Inc., experienced the following events:

Jan.   6   LaChappelle invested $120,000 in the hospital by opening a bank account in the name of Allison LaChappelle, Inc.

9   LaChappelle paid cash for land costing $90,000. She plans to build a clinic on the land.

12   She purchased medical supplies for $2,000 on account.

15   On January 15, LaChappelle officially opened for business.

15–31   During the rest of the month she treated patients and earned service revenue of $8,000, receiving cash.

15–31 She paid cash expenses: employee salaries, $1,400; office rent, $1,000; utilities, $300.

28 She sold supplies to another animal hospital for a cost of $500.

31 She paid $1,500 on account.

Required

Analyze the effects of these events on the accounting equation of the animal hospital of Allison LaChappelle, Inc. Use a format similar to that of Exhibit 1-5 in the chapter with headings for Cash; Medical Supplies; Land; Accounts Payable; Common Stock; and Retained Earnings.

Exercise 1-8   *Business organization, transactions, and net income*   **(Obj. 2, 3, 4)**

The analysis of the transactions that Krannig Leasing Corporation engaged in during its first month of operations follows. The company buys equipment that it leases out to earn revenue. The owners of the business made only one investment to start the business and received no dividends from Krannig Leasing.

	Cash	+	Accounts Receivable	+	Lease Equipment	=	Accounts Payable	+	Common Stock	+	Retained Earnings
a.	+50,000								+50,000		
b.					+100,000		+100,000				
c.	+ 750										+ 750
d.	+ 150		−150								
e.	− 1,000										−1,000
f.	+ 3,600										+3,600
g.			+500								+ 500
h.	− 10,000						− 10,000				

Required

1. Describe each transaction.

2. If these transactions fully describe the operations of Krannig Leasing during the month, what was the amount of net income or net loss?

Exercise 1-9   *Business organization, balance sheet*   **(Obj. 2, 5)**

Presented below are the balances of the assets and liabilities of Long-Gone Delivery Service Ltd., as of September 30, 19X2. Also included are the revenue and expense figures of the business for September.

Delivery service revenue.........	$4,100	Delivery equipment..........	$15,500
Accounts receivable	1,900	Supplies	600
Accounts payable	1,750	Note payable.....................	6,000
Common Stock	?	Rent expense	500
Salary expense	2,000	Cash....................................	750

Required

1. What type of business organization is Long-Gone Delivery Service? How can you tell?

2. Prepare the balance sheet of Long-Gone Delivery Service as of September 30, 19X2.

Exercise 1-10   *Income statement*   **(Obj. 2, 5)**

Presented below are the balances of the assets, liabilities, shareholders' equity, revenues and expenses of Toshi Consultants Inc. at December 31, 19X3, the end of its first year of business.

Note payable	$ 30,000	Office furniture	$ 45,000
Utilities expense....................	6,800	Rent expense.......................	24,000
Accounts payable..................	3,300	Cash	3,600
Retained earnings	17,100	Office supplies....................	4,800

Service revenue	151,200	Salary expense	49,000
Accounts receivable	9,000	Salaries payable	2,000
Supplies expense	4,000	Property tax expense	1,200
Equipment	10,000	Dividends	?
Common stock	10,000		

Required

1. Prepare the income statement of Toshi Consultants Inc. for the year ended December 31, 19X3.
2. What was the amount of the dividends during the year?

Challenge Exercises

Exercise 1-11   *Transaction analysis, effects on financial statements*   **(Obj. 4)**

Opportunity Associates Inc. conducts summer camps for children with disabilities. Because of the nature of its business, Opportunity experiences many unusual transactions. Evaluate each of the following transactions in terms of its effect on Opportunity Associates' income statement and balance sheet.

a. A camper suffered an injury that was not covered by insurance. Opportunity paid $320 for the child's medical care. How does this transaction affect the income statement and the balance sheet?

b. Opportunity sold land adjacent to the camp for $190,000, receiving cash of $50,000 and a note receivable for $140,000. When purchased five years earlier, the land cost Opportunity $120,000. How should Opportunity account for the sale of the land?

c. Some campers cannot pay their fees, so Opportunity solicits donations for camp scholarships. Because Opportunity Associates is organized to earn a profit, donation receipts are treated as revenue. How should Opportunity account for a donation receipt of a small building valued at $45,000?

d. One camper's mother is a physician. Opportunity allows this child to attend camp in return for the mother's serving part-time in the camp infirmary for the two-week term. The standard fee for a camp term is $600. The physician's salary for this part-time work would be $600. How should Opportunity account for this arrangement?

e. Camp counselors build playground equipment during their off-duty hours. If Opportunity had purchased this equipment, it would have cost $2,000. But counselors are paid only their room, board, and transportation to and from camp. Should this equipment be included in Opportunity's financial statements? If so, where, and at what dollar amount?

Exercise 1-12   *Using the financial statements*   **(Obj. 5)**

Compute the missing amounts for each of the following companies.

	Green Ltd.	White Ltd.	Black Ltd.
Beginning:			
Assets	$ 50,000	$ 90,000	$110,000
Liabilities	20,000	60,000	50,000
Ending:			
Assets	$ 70,000	$?	$160,000
Liabilities	35,000	80,000	70,000
Owner's Equity:			
Investments by owners	$ 0	$ 10,000	$?
Dividends	40,000	70,000	100,000
Income Statement:			
Revenues	$210,000	$400,000	$430,000
Expenses	?	300,000	320,000

Problems   *(Group A)*

Problem 1-1A   *Analyzing a loan request*   *(Obj. 1, 3)*

As an analyst for the Bank of Nova Scotia, it is your job to write recommendations to the bank's loan committee. Sigma Enterprises has submitted these summary data to support the company's request for a $100,000 loan:

Income Statement Data	19X5	19X4	19X3
Total revenues	$850,000	$770,000	$720,000
Total expenses	640,000	570,000	540,000
Net income	$210,000	$200,000	$180,000

Selected Statement of Retained Earnings	19X5	19X4	19X3
Dividends	$160,000	$140,000	$120,000

Balance Sheet Data	19X5	19X4	19X3
Total assets	$740,000	$670,000	$590,000
Total liabilities	$240,000	$220,000	$200,000
Total shareholders' equity	500,000	450,000	390,000
Total liabilities and shareholders' equity	$740,000	$670,000	$590,000

Required

Analyze these financial statement data to decide whether the bank should lend $100,000 to Sigma Enterprises. Write a one-paragraph recommendation to the loan committee.

Problem 1-2A   *Entity concept, transaction analysis, accounting equation*   *(Obj. 2, 4)*

Kathy Wood was an architect with a large firm, a partnership, for ten years after graduating from university. Recently she resigned her position to open her own architecture office, which she operates as a corporation. The name of the new entity is Kathy Wood, Design Inc.

Wood recorded the following events during the organizing phase of her new business and its first month of operations. Some of the events were personal and did not affect the practice of architecture. Others were business transactions and should be accounted for by the business.

July 1   Wood sold 4,000 shares of National Trust stock, which she had owned for several years, receiving $80,000 cash from her stockbroker.

2   Wood deposited the $80,000 cash from sale of the National Trust stock in her personal bank account.

3   Wood received $150,000 cash from her former partners in the architecture firm from which she resigned.

5   The business issued common stock to Wood for $120,000 cash.

6   A representative of a large real estate company telephoned Wood and told her of the company's intention to transfer its design business to the new entity of Kathy Wood, Design Inc.

7   Wood paid $550 cash for letterhead stationery for her new office.

9   Wood purchased office furniture for the office, on account, $11,500.

23   Wood finished design work on behalf of a client and submitted her bill for design services, $3,000. She expected to collect from this client within one month.

30   Wood paid office rent $1,900.

31   The business declared and paid a cash dividend of $500.

Required

1. Classify each of the preceding events as one of the following:
   a. A business transaction to be accounted for by the business of Kathy Wood, Design Inc.
   b. A business-related event but not a transaction to be accounted for by the business of Kathy Wood, Design Inc.
   c. A personal transaction not to be accounted for by the business of Kathy Wood, Design Inc.

2. Analyze the effects of the above events on the accounting equation of the business of Kathy Wood, Design Inc. Use a format similar to Exhibit 1-5.

Problem 1-3A   *Balance Sheet*   **(Obj. 2, 5)**

The bookkeeper of Murtz Auction Corp. prepared the balance sheet of the company while the accountant was ill. The balance sheet contains numerous errors. In particular, the bookkeeper knew that the balance sheet should balance, so he plugged in the shareholders' equity amount needed to achieve this balance. The shareholders' equity amount, however, is not correct. All other amounts are accurate.

Murtz Auction Corp.
Balance Sheet
Month Ended July 31, 19X7

Assets		Liabilities	
Cash..	$ 3,000	Accounts receivable.................	$ 3,000
Office supplies..........................	1,000	Service revenue	59,000
Land	44,000	Property tax expense	800
Advertising expense................	2,500	Accounts payable....................	9,000
Office furniture.........................	10,000		
Note payable.............................	16,000	**Shareholders' Equity**	
Rent expense.............................	4,000	Shareholders' equity...............	8,700
Total assets................................	$80,500	Total liabilities	$80,500

Required

1. Prepare the correct balance sheet, and date it correctly. Compute total assets, total liabilities, and shareholders' equity.

2. Identify the accounts listed above that should *not* be presented on the balance sheet and state why you excluded them from the correct balance sheet you prepared for Requirement 1.

Problem 1-4A   *Balance sheet, entity concept*   **(Obj. 2, 3, 5)**

Charlotte Braun is a realtor. She buys and sells properties on her own, and she also earns commission as a real estate agent for buyers and sellers. She organized her business as a corporation on November 24, 19X4, by investing $90,000 to acquire the business's common stock. Consider the following facts as of November 30, 19X4:

a. Braun owed $85,000 on a note payable for some undeveloped land that had been acquired by the business for a total price of $140,000.

b. Braun's business had spent $20,000 for a Re/Max Ltd. real estate franchise, which entitled her to represent herself as a Re/Max agent. Re/Max is a national affiliation of independent real estate agents. This franchise is a business asset.

c. Braun owed $120,000 on a personal mortgage on her personal residence, which she acquired in 19X1 for a total price of $170,000.

d. Braun had $10,000 in her personal bank account and $12,000 in her business bank account.

e. Braun owed $1,800 on a personal charge account with Eaton's.

f. Braun acquired business furniture for $17,000 on November 25. Of this amount, her business owed $6,000 on open account at November 30.

g. Office supplies on hand at the real estate office totaled $1,000.

Required

1. Prepare the balance sheet of the real estate business of Charlotte Braun, Realtor, Inc., at November 30, 19X4.

2. Identify the personal items given in the preceding facts that would not be reported on the balance sheet of the business.

Problem 1-5A   *Business transactions and analysis*   *(Obj. 4)*

Campanelli Corp. was recently formed. The balance of each item in the company's accounting equation is shown below for June 10 and for each of the nine following business days.

	Cash	Accounts Receivable	Supplies	Land	Accounts Payable	Shareholders' Equity
June 10	$ 8,000	$ 4,000	$1,000	$ 8,000	$4,000	$17,000
11	13,000	4,000	1,000	8,000	4,000	22,000
12	6,000	4,000	1,000	15,000	4,000	22,000
15	6,000	4,000	3,000	15,000	6,000	22,000
16	5,000	4,000	3,000	15,000	5,000	22,000
17	7,000	2,000	3,000	15,000	5,000	22,000
18	16,000	2,000	3,000	15,000	5,000	31,000
19	13,000	2,000	3,000	15,000	2,000	31,000
22	11,000	2,000	5,000	15,000	2,000	31,000
23	5,000	2,000	5,000	15,000	2,000	25,000

Required

Assuming that a single transaction took place on each day, describe briefly the transaction that was most likely to have occurred, beginning with June 11. Indicate which accounts were affected and by what amount. No revenue or expense transactions occurred on these dates.

Problem 1-6A   *Income statement, statement of retained earnings, balance sheet*   *(Obj. 5)*

Presented below are the amounts of (a) the assets and liabilities of Petoski Hardware Corporation as of December 31 and (b) the revenues and expenses of the company for the year ended on that date. The items are listed in alphabetical order.

Accounts payable	$ 19,000	Land	$ 58,000
Accounts receivable	12,000	Note payable	85,000
Advertising expense	13,000	Property tax expense	4,000
Building	170,000	Rent expense	23,000
Cash	10,000	Salary expense	63,000
Common stock	100,000	Salary payable	1,000
Furniture	20,000	Sales revenue	200,000
Interest expense	9,000	Supplies	3,000

The beginning amount of retained earnings was $50,000, and during the year dividends were $70,000.

Required

1. Prepare the entity's income statement for the year ended December 31 of the current year.
2. Prepare the statement of retained earnings of the company for the year ended December 31.
3. Prepare the balance sheet of the company at December 31.

Problem 1-7A   *Transaction analysis, accounting equation, financial statements*   **(Obj. 4, 5)**

Lisa Chen operates and is the major shareholder of an interior design studio called Chen Interiors, Inc. The following amounts summarize the financial position of the business on August 31, 19X2:

Assets				=	Liabilities +	Shareholders' Equity	
	Accounts				Accounts	Common	Retained
Cash +	Receivable +	Supplies +	Land	=	Payable +	Stock +	Earnings
Bal. 1,250	1,500		12,000		8,000	4,000	2,750

During September 19X2 the following events occurred:

a. Chen inherited $20,000 and deposited the cash in the business bank account. The business issued common stock to Chen.
b. Performed services for a client and received cash of $700.
c. Paid off the beginning balance of accounts payable.
d. Purchased supplies on account, $1,000.
e. Collected cash from a customer on account, $1,000.
f. Received cash of $1,000 and issued common stock to Chen.
g. Consulted on the interior design of a major office building and billed the client for services rendered, $2,400.
h. Recorded the following business expenses for the month:
   (1) Paid office rent—$900.
   (2) Paid advertising—$100.
i. Sold supplies to another business for $150 cash, which was the cost of the supplies.
j. Declared and paid a cash dividend of $1,800.

Required

1. Analyze the effects of the above transactions on the accounting equation of Chen Interiors, Inc. Adapt the format of Exhibit 1-5.
2. Prepare the income statement of Chen Interiors, Inc., for the month ended September 30, 19X2. List expenses in decreasing order by amount.
3. Prepare the entity's statement of retained earnings for the month ended September 30, 19X2.
4. Prepare the balance sheet of Chen Interiors, Inc., at September 30, 19X2.
5. What did you learn from working this problem?
6. How will what you learned help you manage a business?

Problem 1-8A *Accounting concepts/principles, transaction analysis, accounting equation* *(Obj. 2, 4)*

J. Mommesso has been operating a TV Repair business as a sole proprietorship for 4 years and had the following business assets and liabilities (at their historical costs) as of April 30, 19X1:

Cash	$ 4,000
Accounts receivable........................	3,000
Shop supplies	1,000
Shop equipment.............................	14,000
Accounts payable...........................	5,000

The following transactions took place during the month of May, 19X1:

May 1 J. Mommesso incorporated the business under the name "JM TV Repairs Co." This was done by transferring the assets (with the exception of the "Cash") and liabilities of the sole proprietorship over to the new company and issuing 5,000 shares in the corporation to Mommesso. The equipment had been purchased 4 years ago and Mommesso knew it would cost $12,000 to replace it today, but today's appraised value of the equipment was only $9,000. One of the Accounts Payable (Richards—$4,000) had been outstanding for 4 years and also had $800 of interest owing on it.

  3 Mommesso adjusted a TV for S. Smyle. Mommesso would normally have charged about $120 for the work, but had agreed to do it for $100 cash in order to promote more business from the client.

  5 The company was unable to pay one of the creditors (Richards) and, therefore, Mommesso agreed to give 2,000 shares of JM TV Repairs Co. in settlement of the debt. Mommesso noted that the debt was 4 years old and therefore the $4,000 plus the $800 interest was the equivalent of $5,500 in today's dollars.

  10 Mommesso signed a lease to rent additional shop space for the company at a cost of $900 per month. JM TV Repairs Co. will occupy the premises effective June 1, 19X1.

  12 The company gave 500 shares to a marketing company for promotions for the new company. Mommesso noted that the promotions would have cost only $1,000 if he had paid cash, because a personal friend owned the marketing company, but were actually worth at least $2,000.

  18 Finding the business low on cash, Mommesso went to the bank and borrowed $10,000 on a personal loan and transferred the money to the company in exchange for 5,000 more shares.

  22 The company did repairs to the equipment of NBB News for $5,000. They gave JM TV Repairs Co. equipment that had originally cost them $8,000 and agreed to pay $1,000 in 30 days. Mommesso estimated the equipment to be worth $5,800.

  25 Mommesso accepted $1,000 from a customer for $1,500 of repair work. Mommesso agreed to consider that as payment in full as the client had painted Mommesso's house this month.

  28 JM TV Repairs declared and distributed dividends of $3,000. Mommesso used $1,000 of his dividends to repay part of the loan taken out on May 18.

  31 Mommesso decided the equipment received on May 22 should be reduced to $2,500 as an independent appraisal shows that is what it would be sold for if JM TV Repairs Co. were to go out of business today.

Required

1. Identify any accounting "concept or principle" that would be applicable to each of the transactions and discuss the effects it would have on the books of JM TV Repairs Co.

2. Analyze the effects of the above transactions on the accounting equation of JM TV Repairs Co.

Problem 1-9A   *Accounting concepts/principles, transaction analysis, accounting equation, financial statements, evaluation* **(Obj. 2, 4, 5)**

The PAC Company Ltd. was incorporated on August 1, 19X1, by Jane Paully with an investment of $10,000. It has been operating for two years, during which time Paully has made additional investments but has been unable to pay any dividends. The company prepares marketing plans for clients and has seen business grow from a small, one-person business using rented equipment and having only two customers, to one with the following as of July 31, 19X3:

Cash	$ 1,000
Accounts receivable	9,000
Office supplies	5,000
Office furniture	34,000
Computer equipment	23,000
Accounts payable	11,000
Common stock	25,000

The following transactions took place during the month of August, 19X3:

Aug. 1   Paully borrowed $15,000 from her family and invested $6,000 in the business, receiving 2,000 shares. The other $9,000 was intended for Paully's living expenses.

1   Paid $3,000 to Offices R Us for the month's rent on the office space.

4   Signed a lease for the rental of additional office space at a cost of $2,000 per month. The lease is effective September 1st and Paully was required to pay the first month's rent in advance.

6   Developed a marketing plan for a client and received $800 with $400 payments to be made to Paully on the 15th of the month for the next three months.

10   Paid $100 to a courier service which had delivered the job of August 6th to her client.

12   Paully signed an agreement to provide marketing plans to a client for $12,000 to be paid upon completion of the work.

14   Purchased $2,000 of supplies that will be required for the new client. She paid $500 and promised to pay the balance by the end of the month.

15   Received $400 as the monthly payment from the client of August 6th.

18   Purchased computer equipment for $4,000 by paying $1,000 down with the balance due in 60 days.

20   Completed a marketing plan for ABC Rentals, the owner of her apartment building. They paid her $200 and waived next month's rent ($800) on the apartment.

23   Completed a marketing plan for a client who promised to pay $6,000 by the end of the month.

29   Paid the balance owing for the supplies purchased on August 14th.

30   Due to a shortage of funds in the company's account, Paully wrote a personal cheque to pay for the utilities of the office ($600) and her apartment ($200).

31   Paully calculated that she had used $1,800 of office supplies for the jobs completed in August.

Required

1. What are the total profits earned by the business over the period of August 1, 19X1 to July 31, 19X3?

2. Analyze the effects of the transactions on the accounting equation of PAC Company. Be sure to include the amounts from the prior periods.

3. Prepare the income statement for PAC Company for the month ended August 31, 19X3.

4. Prepare the statement of retained earnings for PAC Company for the month ended August 31, 19X3.

5. Prepare the balance sheet for PAC Company, at August 31, 19X3.

6. Paully has expressed concern that although the business seems to be profitable and growing, she constantly seems to be putting additional money into it and has been unable to take any salary for the work she has put into it. Prepare a reply to her concerns.

(Group B)

Problem 1-1B   *Analyzing a loan request*   **(Obj. 1, 3)**

As an analyst for The Royal Bank, it is your job to write recommendations to the bank's loan committee. Lomoni Ltd. has submitted these summary data to support its request for a $200,000 loan:

Income Statement Data:	19X8	19X7	19X6
Total revenues............................	$890,000	$840,000	$820,000
Total expenses............................	640,000	580,000	540,000
Net income	$250,000	$260,000	$280,000

Selected Statement of Retained Earnings Data:	19X8	19X7	19X6
Dividends....................................	$290,000	$280,000	$270,000

Balance Sheet Data:	19X8	19X7	19X6
Total assets	$730,000	$700,000	$660,000
Total liabilities.............................	$390,000	$320,000	$260,000
Total shareholders' equity..........	340,000	380,000	400,000
Total liabilities and shareholders' equity..................	$730,000	$700,000	$660,000

Required

Should the bank lend $200,000 to Lomoni Ltd.? Write a one-paragraph recommendation to the loan committee.

Problem 1-2B   *Entity concept, transaction analysis, accounting equation*   *(Obj. 2, 4)*

Melvin Kahn was a computer consultant with a large firm, a partnership, for five years after graduating from university. Recently he resigned his position to open his own consultancy practice, which he operates as a corporation. The name of the new entity is Melvin Kahn Systems Inc.

Kahn recorded the following events during the organizing phase of his new business and its first month of operations. Some of the events were personal and did not affect his consultancy practice. Others were business transactions and should be accounted for by the business.

May	4	Kahn received $50,000 cash from his former partners in the computer consulting firm from which he resigned.
	5	The business issued common stock to Khan for $50 cash.
	6	Kahn paid $300 cash for letterhead stationery for his new office.
	7	Kahn purchased office furniture for his office. He agreed to pay the account payable, $6,000, within six months.
	10	Kahn sold 800 shares of Dofasco stock, which he and his wife had owned for several years, receiving $16,000 cash from his stockbroker.
	11	Kahn deposited the $16,000 cash from sale of the Dofasco stock in his personal bank account.
	12	A representative of a large company telephoned Kahn and told him of the company's intention to transfer its consulting business to the new entity of Melvin Kahn Systems Inc.
	29	Kahn finished a systems design on behalf of a client and submitted his bill for services, $3,000. Kahn expected to collect from this client within two weeks.
	30	Kahn paid office rent expense, $1,000.
	31	The business declared and paid a cash dividend of $500.

Required

1. Classify each of the preceding events as one of the following:
   a. A business transaction to be accounted for by the business of Melvin Kahn Systems Inc.
   b. A business-related event but not a transaction to be accounted for by the business of Melvin Kahn Systems Inc.
   c. A personal transaction not to be accounted for by the business of Melvin Kahn Systems Inc.
2. Analyze the effects of the above events on the accounting equation of the business of Melvin Kahn Systems Inc. Use a format similar to Exhibit 1-5.

Problem 1-3B   *Balance sheet*   *(Obj. 2, 5)*

The bookkeeper of Stojko Travel Agency, Inc., prepared the balance sheet of the company while the accountant was ill. The balance sheet contains numerous errors. In particular, the bookkeeper knew that the balance sheet should balance, so she plugged in the shareholders' equity amount needed to achieve this balance. The shareholders' equity amount, however, is not correct. All other amounts are accurate.

Stojko Travel Agency, Inc.
Balance Sheet
Month ended October 31, 19X7

Assets		Liabilities	
Cash.....................................	$3,400	Notes receivable	$14,000
Advertising expense	300	Interest expense.......................	2,000
Land	40,500	Office supplies.........................	800
Salary expense	3,300	Accounts receivable................	2,600
Office furniture.....................	6,700	Note payable............................	30,000
Accounts payable................	3,000		
Utilities expense	2,100	**Shareholders' Equity**	
		Shareholders' equity...............	9,900
Total assets	$59,300	Total liabilities	$59,300

Required

1. Prepare the correct balance sheet, and date it correctly. Compute total assets, total liabilities, and shareholders' equity.

2. Identify the accounts listed above that should not be presented on the balance sheet and state why you excluded them from the correct balance sheet you prepared for Requirement 1.

Problem 1-4B *Balance sheet, entity concept* **(Obj. 2, 3, 5)**

James Renfro is a realtor. He buys and sells properties on his own, and he also earns commission as a real estate agent for buyers and sellers. He organized his business as a corporation on March 10, 19X2, by investing $60,000 to acquire the business's common stock. Consider the following facts as of March 31, 19X2:

a. Renfro had $5,000 in his personal bank account and $9,000 in his business bank account.

b. Office supplies on hand at the real estate office totaled $1,000.

c. Renfro's business had spent $15,000 for a Realty World Canada franchise, which entitled him to represent himself as a Realty World Canada real estate agent. This franchise is a business asset.

d. Renfro owed $33,000 on a note payable for some undeveloped land that had been acquired by his business for a total price of $70,000.

e. Renfro owed $65,000 on a personal mortgage on his personal residence, which he acquired in 19X1 for a total price of $90,000.

f. Renfro owed $950 on a personal charge account with The Bay.

g. He had acquired business furniture for $12,000 on March 26. Of this amount, Renfro's business owed $6,000 on open account at March 31.

Required

1. Prepare the balance sheet of the real estate business of James Renfro, Realtor, Inc., at March 31, 19X2.

2. Identify the personal items given in the preceding facts that would not be reported on the balance sheet of the business.

Problem 1-5B *Business transactions and analysis* **(Obj. 4)**

Clay Desta Oil Company was recently formed. The balance of each item in the company's accounting equation follows for August 4 and for each of the nine business days given:

	Cash	Accounts Receivable	Supplies	Land	Accounts Payable	Shareholders' Equity
Aug. 4	$3,000	$7,000	$ 800	$11,000	$3,800	$18,000
9	4,000	6,000	800	11,000	3,800	18,000
14	2,000	6,000	800	11,000	1,800	18,000
17	2,000	6,000	1,100	11,000	2,100	18,000
19	3,000	6,000	1,100	11,000	2,100	19,000
20	1,900	6,000	1,100	11,000	1,000	19,000
22	7,900	6,000	1,100	5,000	1,000	19,000
25	7,900	6,200	900	5,000	1,000	19,000
26	7,700	6,200	1,100	5,000	1,000	19,000
28	2,600	6,200	1,100	10,100	1,000	19,000

Required

Assuming that a single transaction took place on each day, describe briefly the transaction that was most likely to have occurred beginning with August 9. Indicate which accounts were affected and by what amount. No revenues or expense transactions occurred on these dates.

Problem 1-6B   *Income statement, statement of retained earnings, balance sheet*   **(Obj. 5)**

Presented below are the amounts of (a) the assets and liabilities of Seguin Delivery Service, Inc., as of December 31 and (b) the revenues and expenses of the company for the year ended on that date. The items are listed in alphabetical order.

Accounts payable	$12,000	Land	$ 8,000
Accounts receivable	6,000	Note payable	31,000
Building	26,000	Property tax expense	2,000
Cash	4,000	Rent expense	14,000
Common stock	10,000	Salary expense	38,000
Equipment	21,000	Service revenue	120,000
Interest expense	4,000	Supplies	17,000
Interest payable	1,000	Utilities expense	3,000

The beginning amount of retained earnings was $11,000, and during the year dividends were $42,000.

Required

1. Prepare the income statement of Seguin Delivery Service, Inc., for the year ended December 31 of the current year.

2. Prepare the statement of retained earnings of the company for the year ended December 31.

3. Prepare the balance sheet of the company at December 31.

Problem 1-7B   *Transaction analysis, accounting equation, financial statements*   **(Obj. 4, 5)**

K.T. Singh operates and is the major shareholder of an interior design studio called Singh Designers, Inc. The following amounts summarize the financial position of the business on April 30, 19X5:

	Assets				=	Liabilities	+	Shareholders' Equity	
Cash +	Accounts Receivable +	Supplies +	Land	=	Accounts Payable +	Common Stock +	Retained Earnings
Bal. 1,720	2,240		24,100		5,400	10,000	12,660

During May 19X5 the following events occurred:

a. Singh received $12,000 as a gift and deposited the cash in the business bank account. The business issued common stock to Singh.

b. Paid off the beginning balance of accounts payable.

c. Performed services for a client and received cash of $1,100.

d. Collected cash from a customer on account, $750.

e. Purchased supplies on account, $720.

f. Consulted on the interior design of a major office building and billed the client for services rendered, $5,000.

g. Received cash of $1,700 and issued common stock to Singh.

h. Recorded the following business expenses for the month:

(1) Paid office rent—$1,200.

(2) Paid advertising—$660.

i. Sold supplies to another interior designer for $80 cash, which was the cost of the supplies.

j. Declared and paid a cash dividend of $2,400.

Required

1. Analyze the effects of the above transactions on the accounting equation of Singh Designers, Inc. Adapt the format of Exhibit 1-5.

2. Prepare the income statement of Singh Designers, Inc., for the month ended May 31, 19X5. List expenses in decreasing order by amount.

3. Prepare the statement of retained earnings of Singh Designers, Inc., for the month ended May 31, 19X5.

4. Prepare the balance sheet of Singh Designers, Inc., at May 31.

5. What did you learn from working this problem?

6. How will what you learned help you manage a business?

Problem 1-8B   *Accounting concepts/principles, transaction analysis, accounting equation*
(Obj. 2, 4)

J. Simmons has been operating a Video Repair business as a sole proprietorship for 4 years and had the following business assets and liabilities (at their historical costs) as of May 31 19X1:

Cash	$ 6,000
Accounts receivable	5,000
Shop supplies	2,000
Shop equipment	15,000
Accounts payable	7,000

The following transactions took place during the month of June, 19X1:

June 1 J. Simmons incorporated the business under the name "JS Video Repairs Co.". This was done by transferring the assets (with the exception of the "Cash") and liabilities of the sole proprietorship over to the new company and issuing 5,000 shares in the corporation to Simmons. The equipment had been purchased 4 years ago and Simmons knew it would cost $13,000 to replace it today, but today's appraised value of the equipment was only $10,000. One of the Accounts Payable (Johnson—$5,000) had been outstanding for 4 years and also had $1,000 of interest owing on it.

3   Simmons adjusted a TV for S. Royce. Simmons would normally have charged about $200 for the work, but had agreed to do it for $150 cash in order to promote more business from the client.

5   The company was unable to pay one of the creditors (Johnson) and, therefore, Simmons agreed to give 2,000 shares of JS Video Repairs Co. in settlement of the debt. Simmons noted that the debt was 4 years old and therefore the $5,000 plus the $1,000 interest was the equivalent of $7,500 in today's dollars.

10   Simmons signed a lease to rent additional shop space for the company at a cost of $800 per month. JS Video Repairs Co. will occupy the premises effective July 1, 19X1.

12   The company gave 500 shares to a marketing company for promotions for the new company. Simmons noted that the promotions would have cost only $1,500 if he had paid cash, because a personal friend owned the marketing company, but were actually worth at least $3,000.

18   Finding the business low on cash, Simmons went to the bank and borrowed $12,000 on a personal loan and transferred the money to the company in exchange for 5,000 more shares.

22   The company did repairs to the equipment of CCM News for $7,000. They gave JS Video Repairs Co. equipment that had originally cost them $9,000 and agreed to pay $2,000 in 30 days. Simmons estimated the equipment to be worth $6,800.

25   Simmons accepted $2,000 from a customer for $3,000 of repair work. Simmons agreed to consider that as payment in full as the client had painted Simmons' house this month.

28   JS Video Repairs declared and distributed dividends of $4,000. Simmons used $2,000 of his dividends to repay part of the loan taken out on June 18.

31   Simmons decided the equipment received on June 22 should be reduced to $3,000 as an independent appraisal shows that is what it would be sold for if JS Video Repairs Co. were to go out of business today.

Required

1. Identify any accounting "concept or principle" that would be applicable to each of the transactions and discuss the effects it would have on the books of JS Video Repairs Co.

2. Analyze the effects of the above transactions on the accounting equation of JS Video Repairs Co.

Problem 1-9B   *Accounting concepts/principles, transaction analysis, accounting equation, financial statements, evaluation* **(Obj. 2, 4, 5)**

The ACE Company Ltd. was incorporated on January 1, 19X1 by Sally Reilly with an investment of $10,000. It has been operating for two years during which time Reilly has made additional investments but has been unable to pay any dividends. The company prepares marketing plans for clients and has seen business grow from a small one-person business using rented equipment and having only two customers to one with the following as of December 31, 19X2:

Cash	$ 2,000
Accounts receivable	8,000
Office supplies	6,000
Office furniture	34,000
Computer equipment	24,000
Accounts payable	13,000
Common stock	28,000

The following transactions took place during the month of January, 19X3:

Jan. 1 Reilly borrowed $12,000 from her family and invested $5,000 in the business, receiving 2,000 shares. The other $7,000 was intended for Reilly's living expenses.

1 Paid $2,000 to Offices R Us for the month's rent on the office space.

4 Signed a lease for the rental of additional office space at a cost of $1,800 per month. The lease is effective September 1st and Reilly was required to pay the first month's rent in advance.

6 Developed a marketing plan for a client and received $900 with $500 payments to be made to Reilly on the 15th of the month for the next three months.

10 Paid $50 to a courier service which had delivered the job of January 6 to her client.

12 Reilly signed an agreement to provide marketing plans to a client for $10,000 to be paid upon completion of the work.

14 Purchased $2,500 of supplies that will be required for the new client. She paid $1,000 and promised to pay the balance by the end of the month.

15 Received $500 as the monthly payment from the client of January 6.

18 Purchased computer equipment for $5,000 by paying $1,500 down with the balance due in 60 days.

20 Completed a marketing plan for ABC Rentals, the owner of her apartment building. They paid her $300 and waived next month's rent ($900) on the apartment.

23 Completed a marketing plan for a client who promised to pay $4,000 by the end of the month.

29 Paid the balance owing for the supplies purchased on January 14.

30 Due to a shortage of funds in the company's account, Reilly wrote a personal cheque to pay for the utilities of the office ($500) and her apartment ($100).

31 Reilly calculated that she had used $1,200 of office supplies for the jobs completed in January.

Required

1. What are the total profits earned by the business over the period of January 1, 19X1, to December 31, 19X2?

2. Analyze the effects of the transactions on the accounting equation of ACE Company. Be sure to include the amounts from the prior periods.

3. Prepare the income statement for ACE Company for the month ended January 31, 19X3.

4. Prepare the statement of retained earnings for ACE Company for the month ended January 31, 19X3.

5. Prepare the balance sheet for ACE Company, at January 31, 19X3.

6. Reilly has expressed concern that although the business seems to be profitable and growing, she constantly seems to be putting additional money into it and has been unable to take any salary for the work she has put into it. Prepare a reply to her concerns.

Challenge Problems

Problem 1-1C *Understanding the going-concern concept* **(Obj. 2)**

The going-concern concept is becoming an increasing source of concern for users of financial statements. There are instances of companies filing for bankruptcy several months after issuing their annual audited financial statements. The question is: why didn't the financial statements predict the problem?

A friend has just arrived on your doorstep; you realize she is very angry. After calming her down, you ask what the problem is. She tells you that she had inherited $5,000 from an uncle and invested the money in the common stock of Always Good Yogurt Corp. She had carefully examined Always Good Yogurt's financial statements for the year ended six months previously and concluded that the company was financially sound. This morning, she had read in the local paper that the company had gone bankrupt and her investment was worthless. She asks you why the financial statements valued the assets at values that are in excess of those the Trustee in Bankruptcy expects to realize from liquidating the assets. Why have the assets suddenly lost so much of the value they had six months ago?

Required

Explain to your friend why assets are valued on a going-concern basis in the financial statements and why they are usually worth less when the company goes out of business. Use inventory and accounts receivable as examples.

Problem 1-2C   *Accounting for business transactions*   *(Obj. 4)*

You and three friends have decided to go into the lawn care business for the summer to earn money to pay for your schooling in the fall. Your first step was to sign up customers to satisfy yourselves that the business had the potential to be profitable. Next, you planned to go to the bank to borrow money to buy the equipment you would need.

After considerable effort, the group obtained contracts for 200 lawns for the summer. One of your partners wants to prepare a balance sheet showing the value of the contracts as an asset. She is sure that you will have no trouble with borrowing the necessary funds from the bank on the basis of the proposed balance sheet.

Required

Explain to your friend why the commitments cannot be recognized as assets. What suggestions do you have that might assist your group in borrowing the necessary funds?

Extending Your Knowledge

Decision Problems

1.   Using financial statements to evaluate a request for a loan (Obj. 1, 2, 6)

Two businesses, Bouchard Drugs Ltd. and Leslie Falco Home Decorators Inc., have sought business loans from you. To decide whether to make the loans, you have requested their balance sheets.

Bouchard Drugs Ltd.
Balance Sheet
August 31, 19X4

Assets		Liabilities	
Cash	$ 9,000	Accounts payable	$ 12,000
Accounts receivable	14,000	Note payable	18,000
Merchandise inventory	85,000	Total liabilities	30,000
Store supplies	500		
Furniture and fixtures	9,000	**Shareholders' Equity**	
Building	82,000	Shareholders' equity	183,500
Land	14,000	Total liabilities and	
Total assets	$213,500	shareholders' equity	$213,500

Leslie Falco Home Decorators Inc.
Balance Sheet
August 31, 19X4

Assets		Liabilities	
Cash	$10,000	Accounts payable	$ 3,000
Accounts receivable	4,000	Note payable	18,000
Office supplies	2,000	Total liabilities	21,000
Office furniture	5,000		
Land	20,000	**Shareholders' Equity**	
		Shareholders' equity	20,000
		Total liabilities and	
Total assets	$41,000	shareholders' equity	$41,000

Required

1. Based solely on these balance sheets, which entity would you be more comfortable loaning money to? Explain fully, citing specific items and amounts from the balance sheets.

2. In addition to the balance sheet data, what other financial statement information would you require? Be specific.

2. *Using accounting information (Obj. 1, 2, 3, 4, 5)*

A friend learns that you are taking an accounting course. Knowing that you do not plan a career in accounting, the friend asks why you are "wasting your time." Explain to the friend:

1. Why you are taking the course.

2. How accounting information is used or will be used:
   a. In your personal life.
   b. In the business life of your friend, who plans to be a farmer.
   c. In the business life of another friend, who plans a career in sales.

Ethical Issue

The board of directors of Abrahamson Corporation is meeting to discuss the past year's results before releasing financial statements to the public. The discussion includes this exchange:

Mark Abrahamson, company president: "Well, this has not been a good year! Revenue is down and expenses are up—way up. If we don't do some fancy stepping, we'll report a loss for the third year in a row. I can temporarily transfer some land that I own into the company's name, and that will beef up our balance sheet. Gwen, can you shave $500,000 from expenses? Then we can probably get the bank loan that we need."

Gwen Netherton, company chief accountant: "Mark, you are asking too much. Generally accepted accounting principles are designed to keep this sort of thing from happening."

Required

1. What is the fundamental ethical issue in this situation?
2. Discuss how the company president's proposals violate generally accepted accounting principles. Identify the specific concept or principle involved.

Financial Statement Problems

1. Identifying items from a company's financial statements (Obj. 4)

This and similar problems in later chapters focus on the financial statements of a real company—Mark's Work Wearhouse Ltd., a chain of company-owned and franchise stores across Canada that sells workwear, casual wear, western wear, and other like clothing and footwear. As you study each problem, you will gradually build the confidence that you can understand and use actual financial statements.

Refer to the Mark's Work Wearhouse Ltd. financial statements in Appendix A.

Required

1. How much cash did Mark's Work Wearhouse have at January 29, 1994?
2. What were total assets at January 29, 1994? At January 30, 1993?
3. Write the company's accounting equation at January 29, 1994, by filling in the dollar amounts:

ASSETS = LIABILITIES + SHAREHOLDERS' EQUITY

4. Identify sales for the year ended January 29, 1994.
5. How much net income (net earnings) or net loss did Mark's Work Wearhouse experience for the year ended January 29, 1994? Was 1994 a good year or bad year compared to 1993?
6. Why did Mark's Work Wearhouse year end on January 29, 1994, but on January 30, 1993, and January 25, 1992? Is it usual for an organization to have their year end on the same date every year or on different dates?

2. Identifying items from an actual company's financial statements (Obj. 4)

Obtain the annual report of an actual company of your choosing. Annual reports are available in various forms including the original document in hard copy, microfiche, and computerized data bases.

Answer the following questions about the company. Concentrate on the current year in the annual report you select, except as directed for particular questions.

1. How much in cash (which may include cash equivalents) did the company have at the end of the current year? At the end of the preceding year? Did cash increase or decrease during the current year? By how much?
2. What were the total assets at the end of the current year? At the end of the preceding year?
3. Write the company's accounting equation at the end of the current year by filling in the dollar amounts:

Assets = Liabilities + Owner's or Shareholders' Equity

4. Identify net sales revenue for the current year. The company may label this as *Sales, Net Sales, Revenue,* or another title. How much was the corresponding revenue for the preceding year?

5. How much net income or net loss did the company experience for the current year? For the preceding year? Evaluate the current year's operations in comparison with the preceeding year.

Appendix

The Accounting Profession: Career Opportunities

This appendix discusses the accounting profession in a sequence that does not interrupt the flow of the text material. It discusses the work of accountants and the organizations that influence the accounting profession. Study it either before you cover the main text material or after.

The Work of Accountants

Positions in the field of accounting may be divided into several areas. Two general classifications are *public accounting* and *private accounting*.

In Canada, most accountants, both public and private, belong to one of three accounting bodies, which set the standards for admission of and deal with matters like the rules of professional conduct followed by their members: The Canadian Institute of Chartered Accountants (CICA), whose members are called *Chartered Accountants (CA)*; the Certified General Accountants Association of Canada (CGAAC), whose members are called *Certified General Accountants (CGA)*; and the Society of Management Accountants of Canada (SMAC), whose members are called *Certified Management Accountants (CMA)*. The role and activities of each of these bodies are discussed below.

Private accountants work for a single business, such as a local department store, the Swiss Chalet restaurant chain, or ATCO Ltd. Charitable organizations, educational institutions, and government agencies also employ private accountants. The chief accounting officer usually has the title of controller, treasurer, or chief financial officer. Whatever the title, this person usually carries the status of vice-president.

Public accountants are those who serve the general public and collect professional fees for their work, much as doctors and lawyers do. Their work includes auditing, income tax planning and preparation of returns, management consulting, and various accounting services. These specialized accounting services are discussed in the next section. Public accountants represent about a quarter of all professional accountants.

Some public accountants pool their talents and work together within a single firm. Public accounting firms are called CA firms, CGA firms, or CMA firms, depending on the accounting body from which the partners of the firm come. Public accounting firms vary greatly in size. Some are small businesses, and others are medium-sized partnerships. The largest firms are worldwide partnerships with over 2,000 partners. The six largest accounting firms in the world are often called the Big Six. They represent the first five and seventh largest CA firms in Canada and are, in alphabetical order:

Arthur Andersen	Ernst & Young
Coopers & Lybrand	KPMG Peat Marwick Thorne
Deloitte & Touche (Samson Belair/	Price Waterhouse
Deloitte & Touche in Quebec)	

Although these firms employ less than 20 percent of the more than 50,000 CAs in Canada, they audit almost 80 percent of the 1,000 largest corporations in Canada. The top partners in large accounting firms earn about the same amount as the top managers of other large businesses.

Exhibit 1A-1 shows the accounting positions within public accounting firms and other organizations. Of special interest in the exhibit is the upward movement of accounting personnel, as the arrows show. In particular, note how accountants may move from positions in public accounting firms to similar or higher positions in industry and government. This is a frequently traveled career path. Because accounting deals with all facets of an organization—such as purchasing, manufacturing, marketing, and distribution—it provides an excellent basis for gaining broad business experience.

Accounting Organizations and Designations

The position of accounting in today's business world has created the need for control over the professional, educational, and ethical standards of accountants. Through statutes passed by provincial legislatures, the three accounting organizations in Canada have received the authority to set educational requirements and professional standards for their members and to discipline members who fail to adhere to their codes of conduct. The acts make them self-regulating bodies, just as provincial associations of doctors and lawyers are.

The *Canadian Institute of Chartered Accountants (CICA)*, whose members are chartered accountants or CAs, is the senior accounting organization in Canada. Experience and education requirements for becoming a CA vary among the provinces. Generally, the educational requirement includes a university degree. All provinces, however, require that an individual, to qualify as a CA, pass a national four-day uniform final examination administered by the CICA. The province grants the right to use the professional designation CA.

CAs in Canada generally must earn their practical experience by working for a public accounting firm; subsequently, about half the CAs in Canada leave public

EXHIBIT 1A-1 *Accounting Positions within Organizations*

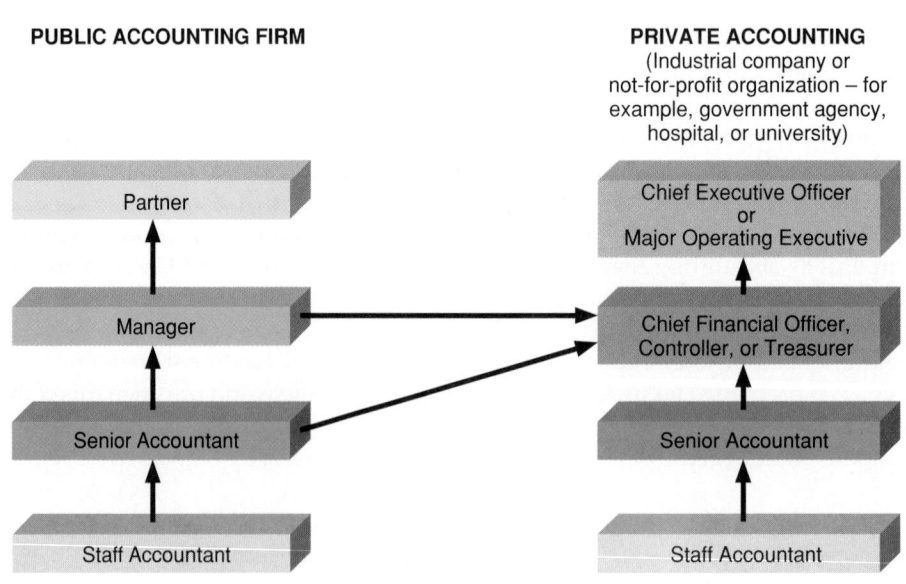

practice for jobs in industry, government, or education. A small number of CAs meet their experience requirements working for the federal or provincial governments. CAs in public accounting have the right to perform audits and issue opinions on the audited financial statements in all provinces in Canada.

CAs belong to a provincial institute (*Ordre* in Quebec) and through that body to the CICA. The provincial institutes have the responsibility for developing and enforcing the code of professional conduct which guides the actions of the CAs in that province.

The CICA, through the Accounting Standards Board and the Auditing Standards Board respectively, promulgates accounting standards or GAAP (discussed in Chapter 12) and auditing standards (Generally Accepted Auditing Standards or GAAS). These standards are enunciated in the *CICA Handbook*. Specific standards are italicized and called *Recommendations*. Accounting Recommendations are the standards or regulations that govern the preparation of financial statements in Canada. The Accounting Standards Board and the Auditing Standards Board publish Accounting Guidelines and Auditing Guidelines respectively; these do not have the force of Recommendations, but simply provide guidance on specific issues.

The Emerging Issues Committee, another committee of the CICA, publishes Abstracts of Issues Discussed which rank below Accounting Guidelines in terms of authority.

A fourth body, the Public Sector Accounting and Auditing Board (PSAAB), issues standards pertaining to public sector accounting and auditing. The CICA supports and publishes research relating primarily to financial reporting and auditing, and publishes a monthly professional journal *CA Magazine*.

The *Certified General Accountants Association of Canada (CGAAC)* is also regulated by provincial law. The experience and education requirements for becoming a CGA vary from province to province, but in all provinces the individual must either pass national examinations administered by the CGAAC in the various subject areas, or gain exemption by taking specified university courses. Certain subjects may only be passed by taking a national examination.

CGAs may gain their practical experience through work in public accounting, industry, or government. They are employed in public practice, industry, and government. Some provinces license CGAs in public practice, which gives them the right to conduct audits and issue opinions on financial statements, while some other provinces do not require a license for them to perform audits.

The association supports research in various areas pertaining to accounting through the Canadian CGA Research Foundation. CGAAC publishes a professional journal entitled *CGA Magazine*.

The *Society of Management Accountants of Canada (SMAC)* administers the Certified Management Accountant program which leads to the Certified Management Accountant (CMA) designation. The use of this designation is similarly controlled by provincial law. Students generally must have a university degree. The SMAC administers an admission or entrance examination which students must pass before embarking on a two-year professional program and completing two years of required work experience. After completing the professional program and the work experience, they write a final examination in order to obtain the CMA designation. The SMAC also administers the professional program and the final examination. CMAs earn their practical experience in industry or government, and are generally employed in industry or government although some CMAs are in public accounting. The Society promulgates standards relating to management accounting through the SMAC. The SMAC conducts and publishes research relating primarily to management accounting, and publishes a professional journal entitled *Cost and Management*.

The *Financial Executives Institute (FEI)* is an organization composed of senior financial executives from many of the larger corporations in Canada, who meet on a regular basis with a view to sharing information on how they can better manage their organizations. Most of these executives have one of the three designations just discussed. It supports and publishes research relating to management accounting, and also publishes a journal, the *Financial Executive*.

The *Institute of Internal Auditors (IIA)* is a world-wide organization of internal auditors. It administers the examinations leading to and grants the Certified Internal Auditor (CIA) designation. Internal auditors are employees of an organization whose job is to review the operations, including financial operations, of the organization with a view to making it more economical, efficient, and effective. Many Canadian internal auditors are members of Canadian chapters of the IIA. It supports and publishes research and conducts courses related in internal auditing. The IIA journal is *The Internal Auditor*.

The *Canadian Academic Accounting Association (CAAA)* directs its attention toward the academic and research aspects of accounting. A high percentage of its members are professors. The CAAA publishes a journal devoted to research in accounting and auditing, *Contemporary Accounting Research*.

Revenue Canada (RC) enforces the tax laws and collects the revenue needed to finance federal the government.

Specialized Accounting Services

As accounting affects so many people in so many different fields, public accounting and private accounting include specialized services.

Public Accounting

Auditing is one of the accounting profession's most significant services to the public. An audit is the independent examination that ensures the reliability of the reports that management prepares and submits to investors, creditors, and others outside the business. In carrying out an audit, public accountants from outside a business examine the business's financial statements. If the public accountants believe that these documents are a fair presentation of the business's operations, they offer a professional opinion stating that the firm's financial statements are in accordance with generally accepted accounting principles, which is the standard. Why is the audit so important? Creditors considering loans want assurance that the facts and figures the borrower submits are reliable. Shareholders, who have invested in the business, need to know that the financial picture management shows them is complete. Government agencies need information from businesses.

Tax accounting has two aims: complying with the tax laws and minimizing taxes to be paid. Because combined federal and provincial income tax rates range as high as 54 percent for individuals and 46 percent for corporations, reducing income tax is an important management consideration. Tax work by accountants consists of preparing tax returns and planning business transactions to minimize taxes. In addition, since the imposition of the Goods and Services Tax, public accountants have been involved in advising their clients how to properly collect and account for it. Public accountants advise individuals on what types of investments to make, and on how to structure their transactions.

Management consulting is the catchall term that describes the wide scope of advice public accountants provide to help managers run a business. As they conduct audits, public accountants look deep into a business's operations. With the insight they gain, they often make suggestions for improvements in the business's management structure and accounting systems. Management consulting is the fastest-growing service provided by accountants.

Accounting services is also a catchall term used to describe the wide range of services related to accounting provided by public accountants. These services include bookkeeping, write-up work, and preparation of financial statements on a monthly or annual basis. Some small companies have all their accounting done by a public accounting firm.

Private Accounting

Cost accounting analyzes a business's costs to help managers control expenses. Good cost accounting records guide managers in pricing their products to achieve greater profits. Also, cost accounting information shows management when a product is not profitable and should be dropped.

Budgeting sets sales and profit goals, and develops detailed plans—called budgets—for achieving those goals. Some of the most successful companies in Canada have been pioneers in the field of budgeting, for example, London Life Insurance Co., and J.M. Schneider Inc., the meat packing company.

Information systems design identifies the organization's information needs, both internal and external. Using flow charts and manuals, designers develop and implement the system to meet those needs.

Internal auditing is performed by a business's own accountants. Many large organizations, Ontario Hydro, Hudson's Bay Co., and the Toronto-Dominion Bank among them, maintain a staff of internal auditors. These accountants evaluate the firm's own accounting and management systems to improve operating efficiency, and to ensure that employees follow management's policies.

Exhibit 1A-2 summarizes these accounting specializations.

EXHIBIT 1A-2   *Specialization in Public and Private Accounting*

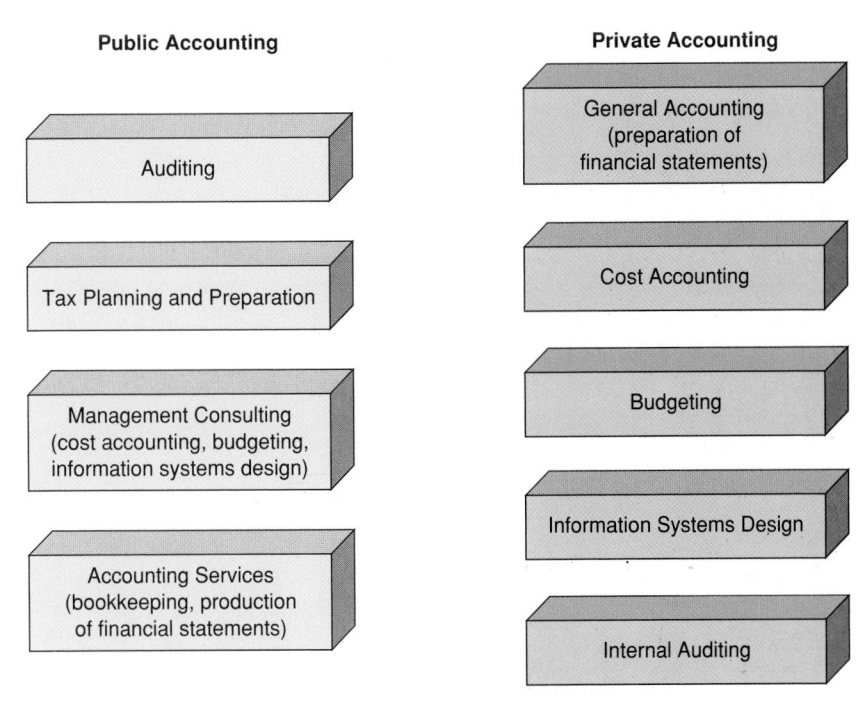

CHAPTER 2
Recording Business Transactions

"I had to create financial statements to generate more business. I hired an accountant to organize and present the information. This helped me run the business better. My accountant calls accounting the 'thermometer of business'—it tells you not just hot or cold, but *how* hot or *how* cold."

Renato Antonio Nahas graduated with a degree in engineering from the university in São Paulo, Brazil. After graduation, Nahas took a job with his brother Raul's building renovation firm. Within a couple of years, he had learned the business of cleaning and polishing the concrete exteriors of buildings and had made enough contacts in Rio de Janeiro to launch his own renovation company there. He called the company Compacta—Central de restauracao e revestimentos Ltda. Early on, the business had only a few clients. Expenses consisted of Nahas's salary, the salary of a small construction crew, and supplies. For several months Nahas kept his accounting records in a notebook.

At the end of the first year, Nahas tallied his revenue: 50 million cruzeiros (approximately $80,000). To expand the business, he needed to convince the owners of larger buildings, such as the Copacabana Palace Hotel, to hire him. The larger the deal, the more Nahas had to prove the strength of Compacta. Nahas was forced to consider the financial statements that customers required before they would accept his bid. He had to hire an accountant (a *contador*, in Portuguese) to prepare the statements to show how well Compacta had performed and where it stood financially.

CHAPTER OBJECTIVES

After studying this chapter, you should be able to

1 Define and use key accounting terms: *account*, *ledger*, *debit*, and *credit*

2 Apply the rules of debit and credit

3 Record transactions in the journal

4 Post from the journal to the ledger

5 Prepare a trial balance

6 Set up a chart of accounts of a business

7 Analyze transactions without a journal

Renato Nahas sounds a lot like Mark Blumes, the entrepreneur in the beginning of Chapter 1. Both appear headed for success. It takes several qualities to succeed in business: a product or service that customers demand, the ability to deliver the product or service at a competitive price, and the perseverance to keep working when it would be easier to quit.

At some point most businesses must keep score to measure the results of operations, cash flows, and financial position. Renato Nahas has an immediate need for accounting information. His potential clients require financial statements to learn how stable his business is. The statements include income information by which to predict Compacta's likely income over the next year or two, what resources the business has to work with (assets), and how much it already owes (liabilities). Overall, the clients want to predict the likelihood that Compacta can handle their renovation projects, and accounting information helps make the prediction.

Chapter 1 introduced accounting by analyzing the effects of transactions on the accounting equation. That approach emphasizes analysis, but it becomes unwieldy if many transactions occur. In practice, accountants do most of their work by computer. This chapter focuses on processing accounting information as it is done in practice. The illustrations show what is going on behind the scenes to help a business like Compacta operate more efficiently.

OBJECTIVE 1

Define and use key accounting terms: *account*, *ledger*, *debit*, and *credit*

The Account

The basic summary device of accounting is the **account**. This is the detailed record of the changes that have occurred in a particular asset, liability, or item of shareholders' equity during a period of time. For convenient access to the information, accounts are grouped together in a record called the **ledger**. In the phrases "keeping the books" and "auditing the books," *books* refers to the ledger. Today the ledger usually takes the form of a computer listing.

Accounts are grouped in three broad categories, according to the accounting equation:

ASSETS = LIABILITIES + SHAREHOLDERS' EQUITY

Assets

Assets are the economic resources that benefit the business and will continue to do so in the future. Most firms use the following asset accounts.

Cash   The Cash account shows the cash effects of a business's transactions. Cash means money and any medium of exchange that a bank accepts at face value, such as bank account balances, paper currency, coins, certificates of deposit, and cheques. Most business failures result from a shortage of cash.

Accounts Receivable   A business may sell its goods or services in exchange for an oral or implied promise of future cash receipt. Such sales are made on credit ("on account"). The Accounts Receivable account contains these amounts. Most sales in Canada and in other developed countries are made on account receivable.

Notes Receivable   A business may sell its goods or services in exchange for a promissory note, which is a written pledge that the customer will pay the business a fixed amount of money by a certain date. The Notes Receivable account is a record of the promissory notes that the business expects to collect in cash. Renato Nahas may demand a note receivable when Compacta completes a job because a note receivable offers more security for collection than a mere account receivable does.

Prepaid Expenses   A business often pays certain expenses in advance. A prepaid expense is an asset because the business avoids having to pay cash in the future for the specified expense. The ledger holds a separate asset account for each prepaid expense. Prepaid Rent, Prepaid Insurance, and Office Supplies are accounted for as prepaid expenses.

Land   The Land account is a record of the cost of land a business owns and uses in its operations. Land held for sale is accounted for separately—in an investment account.

Building   The cost of a business's buildings—office, warehouse, garage, and the like—appear in the Building account. Buildings held for sale are separate assets accounted for as investments.

Equipment, Furniture, and Fixtures   A business has a separate asset account for each type of equipment—Office Equipment and Store Equipment, for example. The Furniture and Fixtures account shows the cost of this asset, which is similar to equipment.

Other asset categories and accounts will be discussed as needed. For example, many businesses have an Investments account for their investments in the stocks and bonds of other companies.

Liabilities

Recall that a *liability* is a debt. A business generally has fewer liability accounts than asset accounts because a business's liabilities can be summarized under relatively few categories.

Accounts Payable   This account is the opposite of the Accounts Receivable account. The oral or implied promise to pay off debts arising from credit purchases appears in the Accounts Payable account. Such purchases are said to be made on account.

Notes Payable   The Notes Payable account is the opposite of the Notes Receivable account. Notes Payable has the amounts that the business must pay because it signed a promissory note to borrow money to purchase goods or services.

Accrued Liabilities   Liability categories and accounts are added as needed. Goods and Services Taxes Payable, Income Taxes Payable, Interest Payable, and Salary Payable are liability accounts used by most companies.

Shareholders' Equity

The owners' claims to the assets of the business are called *shareholders' equity*. In a proprietorship or a partnership, owner's equity is often split into separate accounts for the owner's capital balance and the owner's withdrawals.

Common Stock   The *Common Stock* account represents the owners' investment in the corporation. A person invests in a corporation by purchasing common stock. The corporation issues a stock certificate imprinted with the name of the shareholder as proof of ownership.

Short Exercise:
Name two things that (1) increase shareholders' equity; (2) decrease shareholders' equity.
A: (1) Investments by owner and net income (revenue greater than expenses). (2) Dividends and net loss (expenses greater than revenue).

Retained Earnings   A business must earn a profit to remain in operation. The *Retained Earnings* account shows the cumulative net income earned by the corporation over its lifetime, minus cumulative net losses and dividends. We will be using this account more in the chapters to follow and include it here merely for completeness.

Dividends   The owners of a corporation demand cash from their business. After profitable operations, the board of directors may (or may not) declare a dividend to be paid in cash at a later date. Dividends are not required but are optional and depend upon the action of the board of directors. The corporation keeps a separate account titled *Dividends*, which indicates a decrease in Retained Earnings.

Revenues   The increase in shareholders' equity from delivering goods or services to customers or clients is called *revenue*. The ledger contains as many revenue accounts as needed. Renato Nahas's renovation business would have a Service Revenue account for amounts earned by providing cleaning services for clients. If a business loans money to an outsider, it will need an Interest Revenue account for the interest earned on the loan. If the business rents a building to a tenant, it will need a Rent Revenue account.

Expenses   The cost of operating a business is called *expense*. Expenses have the opposite effect of revenues, so they decrease shareholders' equity. A business needs a separate account for each type of expense, such as Salary Expense, Rent Expense, Advertising Expense, and Utilities Expense. Businesses strive to minimize their expenses to maximize net income.

Exhibit 2-1 shows how asset, liability, and shareholders' equity accounts can be grouped into the ledger.

Double-Entry Bookkeeping

Accounting is based on a *double-entry system*, which means that we record the *dual effects* of a business transaction. *Each transaction affects at least two accounts*. For example, Gary and Monica Lyon's $50,000 cash investment in their travel agency increased both the Cash account and the Common Stock account of the business. It

EXHIBIT 2-1   *The Ledger (Asset, Liability, and Shareholders' Equity Accounts)*

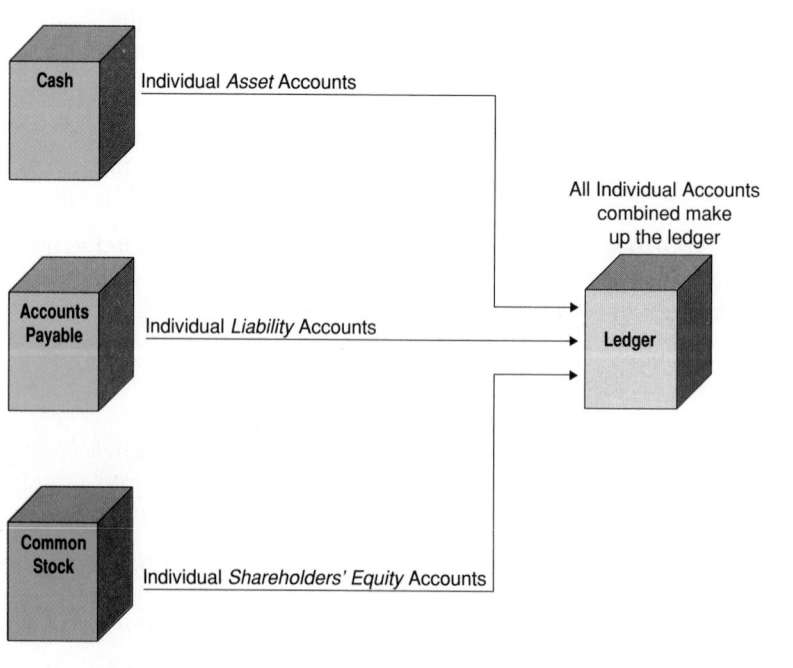

would be incomplete to record only the increase in the entity's cash without recording the increase in its shareholders' equity.

Consider a *cash purchase of supplies*. What are the dual effects of this transaction? The purchase (1) decreases cash and (2) increases supplies. A *purchase of supplies on credit* (1) increases supplies and (2) increases accounts payable. A *cash payment on account* (1) decreases cash and (2) decreases accounts payable. All transactions have at least two effects on the entity.

The T-Account

Key Point:
A T-account is a quick way to show the effect of transactions on a particular account—a useful shortcut in accounting.

How do we record transactions? The account format used for most illustrations in this book is called the *T-account*. It takes the form of the capital letter "T." The vertical line in the letter divides the account into its left and right sides. The account title rests on the horizontal line. For example, the Cash account of a business appears in the following T-account format:

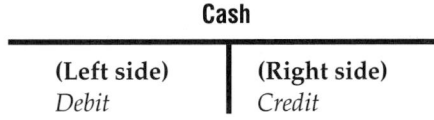

Cash

(Left side)	(Right side)
Debit	*Credit*

The left side of the account is called the **debit** side, and the right side is called the **credit** side. Often beginners in the study of accounting are confused by the words *debit* and *credit*. To become comfortable using them, simply remember this:

> debit = left side
> credit = right side

Even though *left side* and *right side* may be more convenient, *debit* and *credit* are too deeply entrenched in accounting to avoid using.[1]

OBJECTIVE 2

Apply the rules of debit and credit

Increases and Decreases in the Accounts

Key Point:
The accounting equation must balance after every transaction. But verifying that total assets = total liabilities + shareholders' equity is no longer necessary after every transaction. The equation will balance as long as the debits in each transaction equal the credits in the transaction.

The type of an account determines how increases and decreases in it are recorded. For any given account, all increases are recorded on one side, and all decreases are recorded on the other side. Increases in *assets* are recorded in the left (debit) side of the account. Decreases in assets are recorded in the right (credit) side of the account. Conversely, increases in *liabilities* and *shareholders' equity* are recorded by credits. Decreases in liabilities and shareholders' equity are recorded by debits. These are the rules of debit and credit.

In everyday conversation, we may praise someone by saying, "She deserves credit for her good work." In your study of accounting forget this general usage. Remember only that *debit means left side* and *credit means right side*. Whether an account is increased or decreased by a debit or credit depends on the type of account (see Exhibit 2-2).

This pattern of recording debits is based on the accounting equation:

ASSETS = LIABILITIES + SHAREHOLDERS' EQUITY

Assets are on the opposite side from liabilities and shareholders' equity. Therefore, increases and decreases in assets are recorded in the opposite manner from liabilities and shareholders' equity. And liabilities and shareholders' equity which are on the same side of the equal sign are treated in the same way. Exhibit 2-2 shows the relationship between the accounting equation and the rules of debit and credit.

---

[1] The words *debit* and *credit* have a Latin origin (*debitum* and *creditum*). Pacioli, the Italian monk who wrote about accounting in the fifteenth century, used these terms.

EXHIBIT 2-2   *The Accounting Equation and the Rules of Debit and Credit (The Effects of Debits and Credits on Assets, Liabilities, and Shareholders' Equity)*

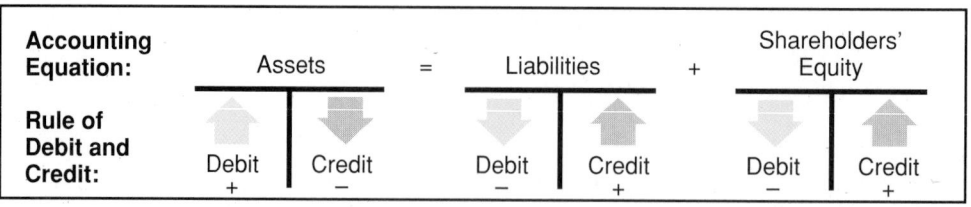

To illustrate the ideas diagrammed in Exhibit 2-2, reconsider the first transaction from Chapter 1. Gary and Monica Lyon invested $50,000 in cash to begin the travel agency. What accounts of Air & Sea Travel are affected? By what amounts? On what side (debit or credit)? The answer is that Assets and Common Stock would increase by $50,000, as the following T-accounts show:

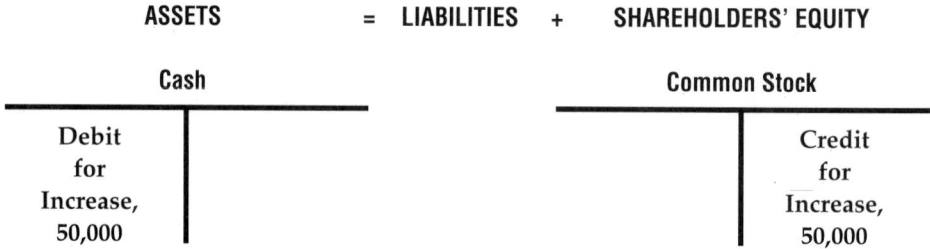

Notice that Assets = Liabilities + Shareholders' Equity *and* that total debit amounts = total credit amounts. Exhibit 2-3 illustrates the accounting equation and Air & Sea Travel's first three transactions.

The amount remaining in an account is called its *balance*. This initial transaction gives Cash a $50,000 debit balance, and Common Stock a $50,000 credit balance.

EXHIBIT 2-3   *The Accounting Equation and the First Three Transactions of Air & Sea Travel, Inc.*

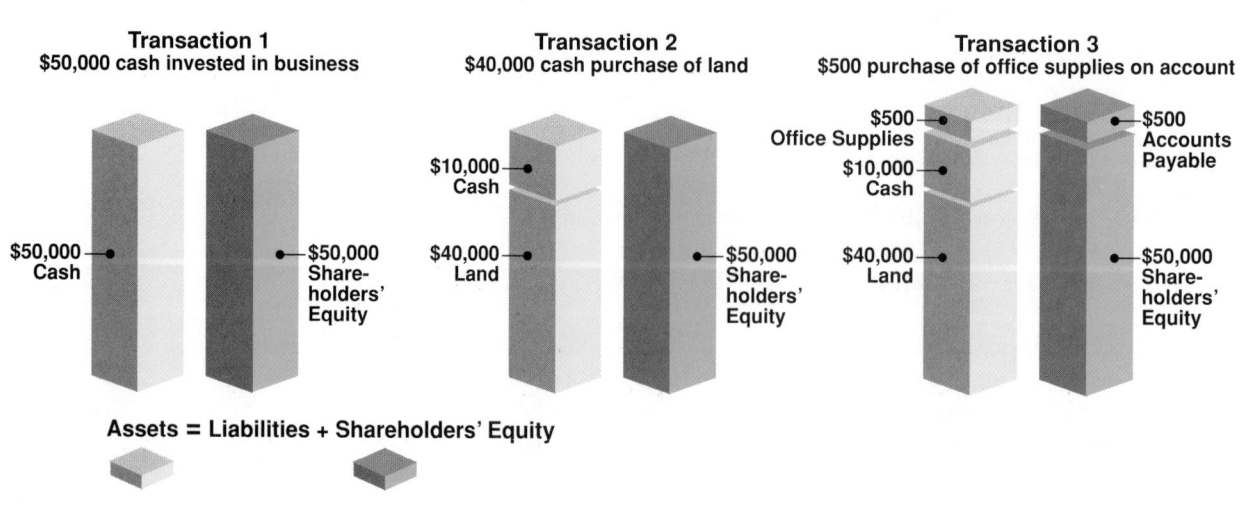

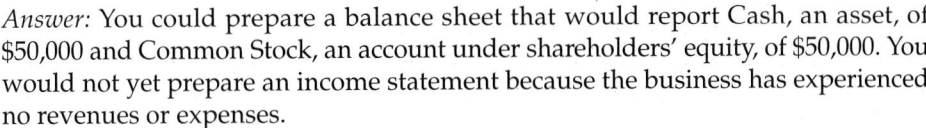

Can you prepare a balance sheet and an income statement for Air & Sea Travel at this point? What would the business's financial statements report?

Answer: You could prepare a balance sheet that would report Cash, an asset, of $50,000 and Common Stock, an account under shareholders' equity, of $50,000. You would not yet prepare an income statement because the business has experienced no revenues or expenses.

The second transaction is a $40,000 cash purchase of land. This transaction affects two assets: Cash and Land. It decreases (credits) Cash and increases (debits) Land, as shown in the T-accounts:

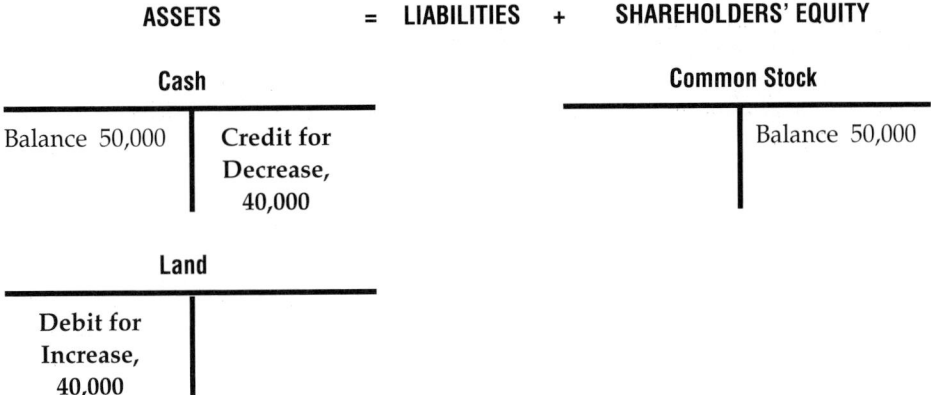

After this transaction, Cash has a $10,000 debit balance ($50,000 debit balance—$40,000 credit amount), Land has a debit balance of $40,000, and Common Stock has a $50,000 credit balance as shown in Exhibit 2-3.

Transaction 3 is a $500 purchase of office supplies on account. This transaction increases the asset Office Supplies and the liability Accounts Payable, as shown in the following accounts and Exhibit 2-3:

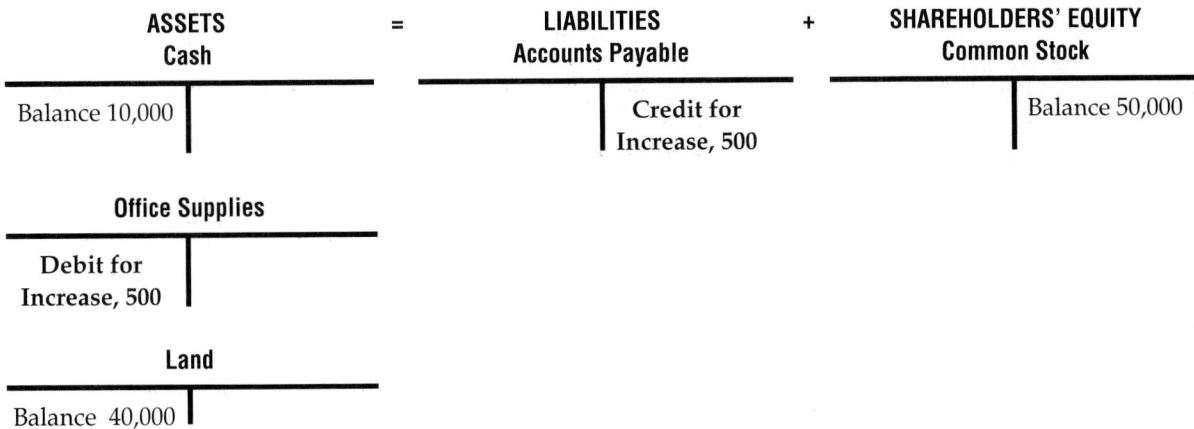

We can create accounts as needed. The process of writing a new T-account in preparation for recording a transaction is called *opening the account*. For Transaction 1, we opened the Cash account and the Common Stock account. For Transaction 2, we opened the Land account, and for Transaction 3, Office Supplies and Accounts Payable.

We could record all transactions directly in the accounts as we have shown for the first three transactions. However, that way of accounting is not practical because it does not leave a clear record of each transaction. Suppose you need to know what accounts were affected by a particular transaction. Looking at each account in the ledger does not answer this question because double-entry accounting always affects at least two accounts. Therefore, you may have to search through all the accounts to find both sides of a particular transaction. To save time, accountants keep a record of each transaction in a journal and then transfer this information into the accounts.

Recording Transactions in Journals

OBJECTIVE 3
Record transactions in the journal

In practice, accountants record transactions first in a **journal**, which is a chronological record of the entity's transactions. In this section, we describe the recording process and illustrate how to use the journal and the ledger.

The journalizing process follows these five steps:

Short Exercise:
Prepare the journal entry to record a $1,600 payment on account. (1) Identify the accounts. (2) Are they increased or decreased? (3) Debit or credit? (4) Enter transaction, debit first.
A: (1) Cash and Accounts Payable. (2) Both are decreased. (3) Debit Accounts Payable; reductions in liabilities are debits. Credit Cash; reductions in assets are credits. (4)

Accounts Payable....1,600

Cash 1,600

1. Identify the transactions from source documents, such as bank deposit slips, sales receipts, and cheque stubs.
2. Specify each account affected by the transaction and classify it by type (asset, liability, or shareholders' equity).
3. Determine whether each account is increased or decreased by the transaction.
4. Using the rules of debit and credit, determine whether to debit or credit the account to record its increase or decrease.
5. Enter the transaction in the journal, including a brief explanation for the journal entry. The debit side of the entry is entered first and the credit side next.

We have discussed steps 1, 2, 3, and 4. Step 5, "Enter the transaction in the journal," means to record the transaction in the journal. This step is also called "making the journal entry," or "journalizing the transaction." These five steps are completed in a computerized accounting system as well as in a manual system. In step 5, however, the journal entry is generally entered into the computer by account number, and the account name is then listed automatically. Most computer programs replace the explanation in the journal entry with some other means of tracing the entry back to its source documents.

Let us apply the five steps to journalize the first transaction of Air & Sea Travel, Inc.—receiving cash of $50,000 and issuing common stock.

Key Point:
In a journal entry, such as Exhibit 2-4, the account debited is always written first (not indented). The account credited is indented on the line below, and the explanation is not indented on the next line. Journal entries should always be recorded in this format.

Step 1.   The source documents are Air & Sea Travel's bank deposit slip and the stock certificate the business issued to Gary and Monica Lyon.

Step 2.   *Cash and Common Stock* are the accounts affected by the transaction. Cash is an asset account, and Common Stock is a shareholders' equity account.

Step 3.   Both accounts increase by $50,000. Therefore, Cash is the asset account that is increased, and Common Stock is the shareholders' equity account that is increased.

Step 4.   Debit Cash to record an increase in this asset account. Credit Common Stock to record an increase in this shareholders' equity account.

Step 5.   The journal entry is

Date	Accounts and Explanation	Debit	Credit
Apr. 2[a]	Cash[b]	50,000[d]	
	Common Stock[c]		50,000[e]
	Initial investment by owner.[f]		

The journal entry includes (a) the date of the transaction, (b) the title of the account debited (placed flush left), (c) the title of the account credited (indented slightly), the dollar amounts of the (d) debit (left) and (e) credit (right)—dollar signs are omitted in the money columns—and (f) a short explanation of the transaction.

A helpful hint: To get off to the right start when analyzing a transaction, first pinpoint its effects (if any) on cash. Did cash increase or decrease? Then find its effect on other accounts. Typically, it is much easier to identify the cash effect of a transaction on cash than to identify the effect on other accounts.

The journal offers information that the ledger accounts do not provide. Each journal entry shows the complete effect of a business transaction. Let us examine Air & Sea Travel's initial receipt of cash. The Cash account shows a single figure, the $50,000 debit. We know that every transaction has a credit, so in what account will we find the corresponding $50,000 credit? In this simple illustration, we know that the Common Stock account holds this figure. But imagine the difficulties you would face trying to link debits and credits for hundreds of daily transactions—without a separate record of each transaction. The journal solves this problem and presents the full story for each transaction. Exhibit 2-4 shows how a journal page might look after the first transaction is recorded. (It is customary to leave a space between each journal entry.)

In these introductory discussions we temporarily ignore the date of each transaction in order to focus on the accounts and their dollar amounts.

Regardless of the accounting system in use, an accountant must analyze every business transaction in the manner we are presenting in these opening chapters. Once the transaction has been analyzed, a computerized accounting package performs the same actions as accountants do in a manual system. For example, when a sales clerk runs your MasterCard through the credit card reader, the underlying accounting system records the store's sales revenue and receivable from MasterCard. The computer automatically records the transaction as a journal entry, but an accountant had to program the computer to do so. A computer's ability to perform routine tasks and mathematical operations fast and without error frees accountants for decision making.

Transferring Information (Posting) from the Journal to the Ledger

Posting means transferring the amounts from the journal to the appropriate accounts in the ledger. Debits in the journal are posted as debits in the ledger, and credits in the journal as credits in the ledger. The initial investment transaction of Air & Sea Travel is posted to the ledger as shown in Exhibit 2-5. Computers perform this tedious task quickly and without error.

Flow of Accounting Data

Exhibit 2-6 summarizes the flow of accounting data from the business transaction to the ledger. We continue the example of Air and Sea Travel, Inc., and account for six of the early transactions. Transactions that affect cash are the easiest to analyze. Therefore, when a transaction affects cash, we account for the cash effect first.

EXHIBIT 2-4   *The Journal*

	Journal			Page 6
Date	**Accounts and Explanation**		**Debit**	**Credit**
Apr. 2	Cash		50,000	
	Common stock			50,000
	Issued common stock to owners.			

EXHIBIT 2-5   *Journal Entry and Posting to the Ledger*

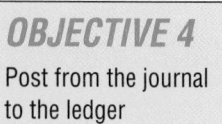

OBJECTIVE 4

Post from the journal to the ledger

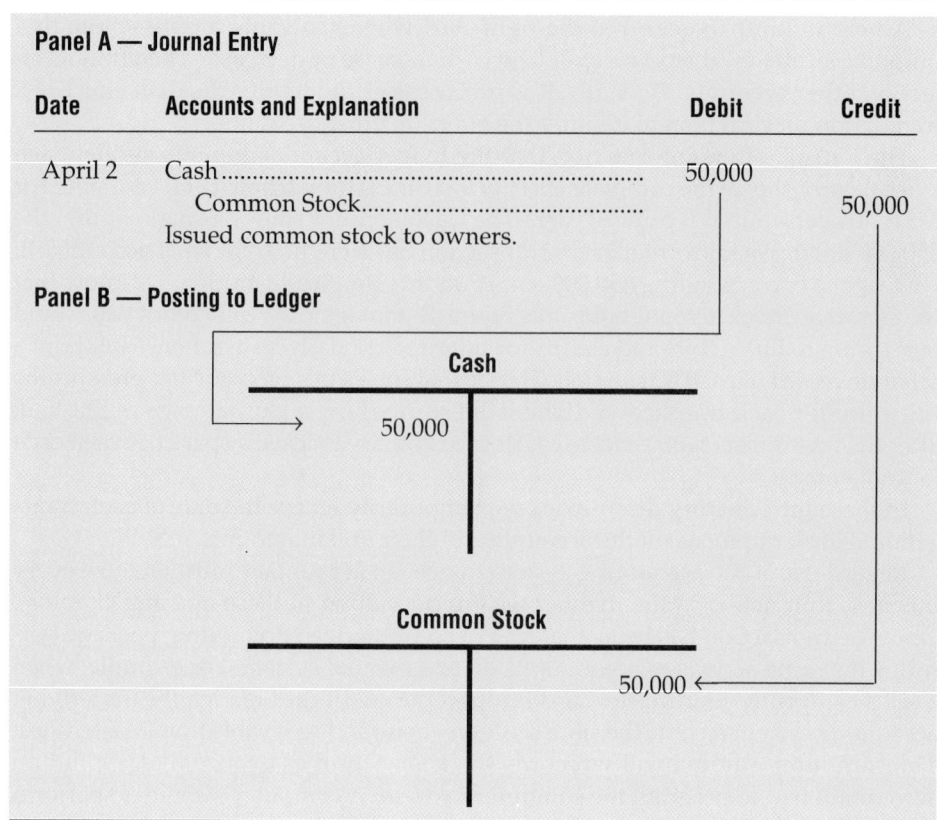

Panel A — Journal Entry

Date	Accounts and Explanation	Debit	Credit
April 2	Cash..	50,000	
	Common Stock......................................		50,000
	Issued common stock to owners.		

Panel B — Posting to Ledger

Cash

50,000

Common Stock

50,000

EXHIBIT 2-6   *Flow of Accounting Data*

Transaction Occurs	Source Documents Prepared	Transaction Analysis Takes Place	Transaction Entered in Journal	Amounts Posted to Ledger

Concept Highlight

Transaction Analysis, Journalizing, and Posting

We will now indicate the journal entries required to show the above Air & Sea transactions during April 19X1.

1.   *Transaction:*   The Lyons invested $50,000 to begin their travel agency.

      Analysis: The Lyons' investment in the business increased its asset cash; to record this increase, debit Cash. The investment also increased the shareholders' equity of the entity; to record this increase, credit Common Stock.

Journal   Cash 50,000
Entry: Common Stock   50,000
            Issued common stock to owners.

Ledger
Accounts:

Cash	Common Stock
(1) 50,000	(1) 50,000

2. *Transaction:* The business paid $40,000 cash for land as a future office location.

    Analysis: The purchase decreased cash; therefore, credit Cash.

            The purchase increased the entity's asset land; to record this increase, debit Land.

    Journal   Land 40,000
    Entry: Cash   40,000
               Paid cash for land.

    Ledger
    Accounts:

Cash		Land
(1) 50,000	(2) 40,000	(2) 40,000

STOP & THINK

Suppose you are a lender and Gary and Monica Lyon ask you to make a $10,000 business loan to Air & Sea Travel, Inc. After the initial investment of $50,000, how would you evaluate Air & Sea Travel as a credit risk? Would your evaluation differ if the Lyons had invested only $5,000 of their money and Air & Sea Travel owed $25,000 to another bank?

Answer: You would probably view the loan request favorably. The Lyons have invested $50,000 of their own money in the business. The travel agency has no debts, so it should be able to repay you. However, if the owners had invested only $5,000 in the business and it had liabilities of $25,000, Air & Sea Travel would be a less attractive credit risk.

3. *Transaction:* The business purchased $500 office supplies on account payable.

    Analysis: The credit purchase of office supplies increased this asset; to record this increase, debit Office Supplies. The purchase also increased the liability accounts payable; to record this increase, credit Accounts Payable.

    Journal   Office Supplies 500
    Entry: Accounts Payable   500
               Purchased office supplies on account.

    Ledger
    Accounts

Office Supplies	Accounts Payable
(3) 500	(3) 500

4.   *Transaction:*   The business paid $400 on the account payable created in Transaction 3.

      Analysis: The payment decreased the asset cash; therefore, credit Cash. The payment also decreased the liability, accounts payable; to record this decrease, debit Accounts Payable.

      Journal Entry:

      Accounts Payable   400
           Cash   400
      Paid cash on account.

      Ledger Accounts:

Cash				Accounts Payable			
(1)	50,000	(2)	40,000	(4)	400	(3)	500
		(4)	400				

5.   *Transaction:*   The Lyons remodeled their personal residence. This is not a business transaction of the travel business, so no journal entry is made.

6.   *Transaction:*   Air & Sea Travel, Inc. paid the Lyons a cash dividend of $2,100.

      Analysis: The dividends decreased the entity's cash; therefore, credit Cash. The transaction also decreased the shareholders' equity of the entity and must be recorded by a debit to a shareholders' equity account. Decreases in the shareholders' equity of a corporation that result from distributions to owners are debited to a separate corporation equity account entitled Dividends. Therefore, debit Dividends.

      Journal Entry:

      Dividends   2,100
           Cash   2,100
      Paid dividends.

      Ledger Accounts:

Cash				Dividends			
(1)	50,000	(2)	40,000	(6)	2,100		
		(4)	400				
		(6)	2,100				

Each journal entry posted to the ledger is keyed by date or by transaction number. In this way any transaction can be traced from the journal to the ledger, and, if need be, back to the journal. This linking allows you to locate efficiently any information needed.

Accounts after Posting

We next illustrate how the accounts look when the amounts of the preceding transactions have been posted. The accounts are grouped under the accounting equation's headings.

Each account has a balance, denoted as Bal. This amount is the difference between the account's total debits and its total credits. For example, the balance in the Cash account is the difference between the debits, $50,000 and the credits, $42,500 (i.e., $40,000 + $400 + $2,100). Thus the balance figure is $7,500. The balance amounts are not journal entries posted to the accounts, so we set an account balance apart by horizontal lines.

If the sum of an account's debits is greater than the sum of its credits, that account has a debit balance, as the Cash account does here. If the sum of its credits is greater, that account has a credit balance, as Accounts Payable does.

Assets   **=**   **Liabilities**   **+**   **Shareholders' Equity**

Cash				Accounts Payable				Common Stock	
(1)	50,000	(2)	40,000	(4)	400	(3)	500	(1)	50,000
		(4)	400			Bal.	100	Bal.	50,000
		(6)	2,100						
Bal.	7,500								

Office Supplies			Dividends		
(3)	500		(6)	2,100	
Bal.	500		Bal.	2,100	

Land		
(2)	40,000	
Bal.	40,000	

Trial Balance

A **trial balance** is a list of all accounts with their balances—assets first, followed by liabilities and then shareholders' equity. It provides a check on accuracy by showing whether the total debits equal the total credits. A trial balance may be taken at any time the postings are up to date, but the most common time is at the end of a period. Exhibit 2-7 is the trial balance of the general ledger of Air & Sea Travel, Inc. after the first six transactions have been journalized and posted.

Correcting Trial Balance Errors   The title *trial balance* is well chosen. The list is prepared to *test* the accounts' balances by showing whether the total debits and total credits are equal. If they are not equal, then accounting errors exist. Most computerized accounting systems prohibit the recording of unbalanced journal entries. Because the journal amounts are posted precisely as they have been journalized, trial balances will always balance. Hence computers minimize accounting errors. But they cannot *eliminate* errors, because human operators might input the amounts incorrectly.

Many out-of-balance conditions can be detected by computing the difference between total debits and total credits on the trial balance. Then perform one or more of the following:

> *Short Exercise:*
> Assume that Dividends, $2,100, is erroneously listed in the credit column on the trial balance in Exhibit 2-7. (1) Recompute the trial balance totals. (2) To find the mistake, calculate the difference between the column totals. (3) Then divide the difference by two.
> ***A:*** (1) Debit = $48,000; Credit = $52,200.
> (2) $52,200 − $48,000 = $4,200.
> (3) $4,200 ÷ 2 = $2,100.
>
> If you find that amount somewhere on the trial balance, you may have entered it in the wrong column. This is one easy way to find an error if your trial balance does not balance.

EXHIBIT 2-7   *Trial Balance*

> **OBJECTIVE 5**
> Prepare a trial balance

Air & Sea Travel, Inc.
Trial Balance
April 30, 19X1

Account Titles	Balance	
	Debit	Credit
Cash...	$ 7,500	
Office supplies...	500	
Land..	40,000	
Accounts payable..		$ 100
Common stock...		50,000
Dividends...	2,100	
Total...	$50,100	$50,100

1. Search the trial balance for a missing account. Trace each account and its balance from the ledger to the trial balance.
2. Search the journal for the amount of difference. For example, suppose the total credits on Air & Sea Travel's trial balance equal $50,100 and total debits are $49,900. A $200 transaction may have been recorded incorrectly in the journal or posted incorrectly to the ledger. Search the journal for a $200 transaction.
3. Divide the difference between total debits and total credits by two. A debit treated as a credit, or vice versa, doubles the amount of error. Suppose Air & Sea Travel debited $300 to Cash instead of crediting the Cash account, or assume the accountant posted a $300 credit as a debit. Total debits contain the $300, and total credits omit the $300. The out-of-balance amount is $600, and dividing by two identifies the $300 of the transaction. Then search the journal for a $300 transaction and trace to the account affected.
4. Divide the out-of-balance amount by nine. If the result is evenly divisible by nine, the error may be a *slide* (example: writing $61 as $610) or a transposition (example: treating $61 as $16). Suppose Air & Sea Travel listed the $2,100 Dividends balance as $21,000 on the trial balance—a slide-type error. Total debits would differ from total credits by $18,900 (i.e., $21,000 − $2,100 = $18,900). Dividing $18,900 by 9 yields $2,100, the correct amount of the dividends. Trace this amount through the ledger until you reach the Dividends account with a balance of $2,100. Computer-based systems avoid such errors.

Do not confuse the trial balance with the balance sheet. Accountants prepare a trial balance for their internal records. The company reports its financial position—both inside and outside the business—on the balance sheet, a formal financial statement. And remember that the financial statements are the focal point of the accounting process; the trial balance is merely a step in the preparation of the financial statements.

Mid Chapter Summary Problem for Your Review

On August 1, 19X5, Liz Shea opens Shea's Research Service, Inc. During the entity's first ten days of operations, the business completes the following transactions:

a. To begin operations, Shea deposits $50,000 of personal funds in a bank account entitled Shea's Research Service, Inc., and the business issues common stock to her.
b. Shea pays $40,000 cash for a small house to be used as an office.
c. Shea purchases office supplies for $500 on account.
d. Shea pays cash of $6,000 for office furniture.
e. Shea pays $150 on the account payable she created in Transaction (c).
f. The corporation pays a dividend of $1,000 to Shea.

Required

1. Prepare the journal entries to record these transactions. Key the journal entries by letter.
2. Post the entries to the ledger.
3. Prepare the trial balance of Shea's Research Service, Inc. at August 10, 19X5.

SOLUTION TO REVIEW PROBLEM

Requirement 1

Accounts and Explanation	Debit	Credit
a. Cash	50,000	
Common stock		50,000
Initial investment by owner.		
b. Building	40,000	
Cash		40,000
Purchased building for an office.		
c. Office Supplies	500	
Accounts Payable		500
Purchased office supplies on account.		
d. Office Furniture	6,000	
Cash		6,000
Purchased office furniture.		
e. Accounts Payable	150	
Cash		150
Paid cash on account.		
f. Dividends	1,000	
Cash		1,000
Paid dividends.		

Requirement 2

ASSETS

Cash

(a)	50,000	(b)	40,000
		(d)	6,000
		(e)	150
		(f)	1,000
Bal.	2,850		

Office Supplies

(c)	500	
Bal.	500	

Office Furniture

(d)	6,000	
Bal.	6,000	

Building

(b)	40,000	
Bal.	40,000	

LIABILITIES

Accounts Payable

(e)	150	(c)	500
		Bal.	350

SHAREHOLDERS' EQUITY

Common Stock

	(a)	50,000
	Bal.	50,000

Dividends

(f)	1,000	
Bal.	1,000	

Requirement 3

Shea's Research Service, Inc.
Trial Balance
August 10, 19X5

	Balance	
Account Titles	**Debit**	**Credit**
Cash	$ 2,850	
Office supplies	500	
Office furniture	6,000	
Building	40,000	
Accounts payable		$ 350
Common stock		50,000
Dividends	1,000	
Total	$50,350	$50,350

Details of Journals and Ledgers

To focus on the main points of journalizing and posting, we purposely omitted certain essential data. In practice, the journal and the ledger provide additional details that create a "trail" through the accounting records for future reference. For example, a supplier may bill us twice for the same item we purchased on account. To prove we paid the bill, we would search the accounts payable records and work backward to the journal entry that recorded our payment. To see how this works, let's take a closer look at the journal and the ledger.

Journal   Exhibit 2-8, Panel B presents a widely used journal format. The journal page number appears in the upper-right corner. As the column headings indicate, the *journal* displays the following information:

1. The *date*, which indicates when the transaction occurred. The year appears only when the journal is started or when the year has changed. For our purposes, the year appears with an X in the third, or decade's position. Thus 19X1 is followed by 19X2, and so on. The date of the transaction is recorded for every transaction.
2. The *account title* and explanation of the transaction, as in Exhibit 2-4.
3. The *posting reference*, abbreviated Post. Ref. How this column helps the accountant becomes clear when we discuss the details of posting.
4. The *debit* column, which shows the amount debited.
5. The *credit* column, which shows the amount credited.

Ledger   Exhibit 2-8, Panel C presents the *ledger* in T-account format. Each account has its own record in the illustrative ledger. Our example shows Air & Sea Travel's Cash account. This account maintains the basic format of the T-account but offers more information—for example, the account number at the upper-right corner. Each account has its own identification number.

The column headings identify the ledger account's features:

1. The date.
2. The item column. This space is used for any special notation.
3. The journal reference column, abbreviated Jrnl. Ref. The importance of this column becomes clear when we discuss the mechanics of posting.

EXHIBIT 2-8 *Details of Journalizing and Posting*

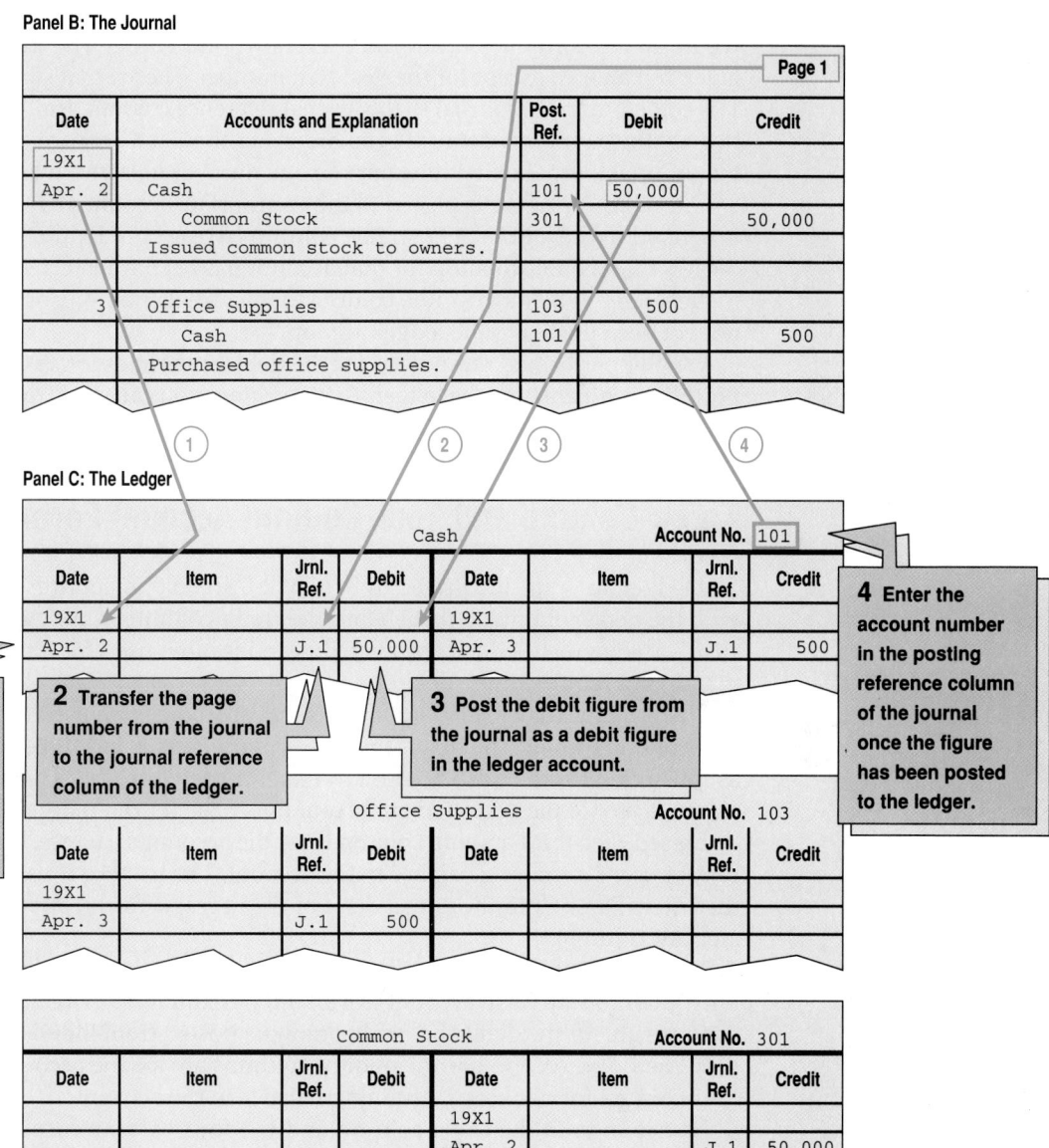

Panel A: Two of Air & Sea's Transactions

Date	Transaction
Apr. 2, 19X1	Gary and Monica Lyon invested $50,000 in travel
	agency, which issued common stock to the owners.
3	Paid $500 cash for office supplies.

Panel B: The Journal

Page 1

Date	Accounts and Explanation	Post. Ref.	Debit	Credit
19X1				
Apr. 2	Cash	101	50,000	
	Common Stock	301		50,000
	Issued common stock to owners.			
3	Office Supplies	103	500	
	Cash	101		500
	Purchased office supplies.			

① ② ③ ④

Panel C: The Ledger

Cash   Account No. 101

Date	Item	Jrnl. Ref.	Debit	Date	Item	Jrnl. Ref.	Credit
19X1				19X1			
Apr. 2		J.1	50,000	Apr. 3		J.1	500

1 Transfer the date of the transaction from the journal to the ledger.

2 Transfer the page number from the journal to the journal reference column of the ledger.

3 Post the debit figure from the journal as a debit figure in the ledger account.

4 Enter the account number in the posting reference column of the journal once the figure has been posted to the ledger.

Office Supplies   Account No. 103

Date	Item	Jrnl. Ref.	Debit	Date	Item	Jrnl. Ref.	Credit
19X1							
Apr. 3		J.1	500				

Common Stock   Account No. 301

Date	Item	Jrnl. Ref.	Debit	Date	Item	Jrnl. Ref.	Credit
				19X1			
				Apr. 2		J.1	50,000

4. The debit column, with the amount debited.

5. The credit column, with the amount credited.

Posting

We know that posting means transferring information from the journal to the ledger accounts. But how do we handle the additional details that appear in the journal and the ledger formats that we have just seen? Exhibit 2-8 illustrates the steps in full detail. Panel A lists the first two transactions of Air & Sea Travel, Inc.; Panel B presents the journal; and Panel C shows the ledger.

Because the flow of accounting data moves from the journal to the ledger, you would first record the journal entry, as shown in Panel B. The transaction data are given in Panel A, except for the Post Ref. number. The journal's page number, Page 1, is copied from the journal to the journal reference column, Jrnl. Ref., of the ledger. Why bother with this detail? If you are using the Cash account and need to locate the original journal entry, the journal page number tells you where to look.

Once a dollar figure is posted to the appropriate account, that account's number is entered in the journal's Post. Ref. column (Arrow 4 of Exhibit 2.8). This step indicates that the information for that account has been transferred from the journal to the ledger. A blank Post Ref. column for a journal entry means that the entry has not yet been posted to the ledger account.

Having performed these steps for the debit amount of $50,000, you would then post the credit entry to the ledger. After posting, you can draw up the trial balance, as we discussed earlier.

Three-Column and Four-Column Account Format

The ledger accounts illustrated in Exhibit 2-8 are in two-column T-account format, with the debit column on the left and the credit column on the right. The T-account clearly distinguishes debits from credits and is often used for illustrative purposes that do not require much detail.

There are two other standard formats that are more often used in practice than the two-column format. The first is the three-column which has three amount columns, as illustrated for the Cash account in Panel A of Exhibit 2-9. The first two amount columns are for the debit and credit amounts posted from individual entries as just discussed. The third amount column is for the account's balance. This three-column format keeps a running balance in the account. The balance is usually indicated by the letters Dr or Cr (indicating a debit or credit respectively) appearing in the third amount column.

The other standard format, the four-column format, has four amount columns, as illustrated for the Cash account in Panel B of Exhibit 2-9. The first pair of amount columns are for the debit and credit amounts posted from individual entries as just discussed. The second pair of amount columns are for the account's balance. This four-column format keeps a running balance in the account.

Notice in both the three-column and the four-column formats, illustrated in Exhibit 2-9, Cash has a debit balance of $50,000 after the first transaction is posted and a debit balance of $49,500 after the second transaction.

Chart of Accounts

OBJECTIVE 6

Set up a chart of accounts of a business

As you know, the ledger contains the business's accounts grouped under these headings:

1. Balance Sheet Accounts: Assets, Liabilities, and Shareholders' Equity
2. Income Statement Accounts: Revenues and Expenses.

EXHIBIT 2-9   *Account in Three-Column and Four-Column Format*

Panel A   Account in Three-Column Format

Account   Cash   Account No. 101

Date	Item	Jrnl. Ref.	Debit	Credit	Balance
19X1 Apr 2		J.1	50,000		50,000 Dr.
3		J.1		500	49,500 Dr.

Panel B   Account in Four-Column Format

Account   Cash   Account No. 101

Date	Item	Jrnl. Ref.	Debit	Credit	Balance Debit	Credit
19X1 Apr 2		J.1	50,000		50,000	
3		J.1		500	49,500	

To keep track of their accounts, organizations have a **chart of accounts**, which lists all the accounts and their account numbers. These account numbers are used as posting references, as illustrated by Arrow 4 in Exhibit 2-8. It is easier to input the account number, 101, in the posting reference column of the journal than to input the account title, Cash. Also, this numbering system makes it easy to locate individual accounts in the ledger.

Accounts are identified by account numbers with two or more digits. Assets are often numbered beginning with 1, liabilities with 2, shareholders' equity with 3, revenues with 4, and expenses with 5. The second, third, and higher digits in an account number indicate the position of the individual account within the category. For example, Cash might be account number 1001, which is the first asset account. Accounts receivable may be account number 1101, the second asset account. Accounts payable may be number 2001, the first liability account. All accounts are numbered by this system.

Organizations with many accounts use lengthy account numbers; some may have more than 25 digits. The account number can provide much useful information. For example, the account number might indicate the type of account (for example, Petty Cash) and the location of the account within the organization (for example, the Yorkton branch). The chart of accounts of Brown, Gunz, and Scace (in Exhibit 2-10) uses a three-digit account number. The assignment material reflects the variety found in practice.

The chart of accounts for Air & Sea Travel, Inc., appears in Exhibit 2-11. Notice the gap in account numbers between 111 and 141. The Lyons realize that at some later date the business may need to add another category of receivables—for example, Notes Receivable, numbered 121.

The chapter appendix gives two expanded charts of accounts that you will find helpful as you work through this course. The first chart lists the typical accounts of a large service corporation, such as Air & Sea Travel, after a period of growth. The second chart is for a merchandising corporation, one that sells a product rather than a service. Study the service corporation chart of accounts now, and refer to the second chart of accounts as needed later.

EXHIBIT 2-10   *Partial Chart of Accounts: Law Practice of Brown, Gunz, and Scace*

Account Number	Account Name
110	Petty Cash
120	Accounts Receivable
130	Office Supplies
160	Office Furniture
170	Computers
220	Accounts Payable
225	Notes Payable
230	Employee Withholdings
300	Partners' Capital
400	Fee Revenue
500	Rent Expense
510	Wages Expense
540	Supplies Expense

EXHIBIT 2-11   *Chart of Accounts—Air & Sea Travel, Inc.*

Balance Sheet Accounts:

Assets	Liabilities	Shareholders' Equity
101 Cash	201 Accounts Payable	301 Common Stock
111 Accounts Receivable	231 Notes Payable	311 Dividends
141 Office Supplies		
151 Office Furniture		**Income Statement Accounts (part of Shareholders' Equity)**
191 Land		

Revenues	Expenses
401 Service Revenue	501 Rent Exp.
	502 Salary Exp.
	503 Utilities Exp.

Normal Balance of an Account

Key Point:
The normal balance of an account is the side on which increases are recorded.

An account's *normal balance* is on the side of the account—debit or credit—where *increases* are recorded. That is, the normal balance is on the side that is positive. For example, Cash and other assets usually have a debit balance (the debit side is positive and the credit side negative), so the normal balance of assets is on the debit side, and assets are called *debit-balance accounts*. Conversely, liabilities and shareholders' equity usually have a credit balance, so their normal balances are on the credit side, and they are called *credit-balance accounts*. Exhibit 2-12 illustrates the normal balances of assets, liabilities, and shareholders' equity.

An account that normally has a debit balance may occasionally have a credit balance which indicates a negative amount of the item. For example, Cash will have a temporary credit balance if the entity overdraws its bank account. Similarly, the liability Accounts Payable—normally a credit balance account—will have a debit balance if the entity overpays its account. In other instances, the shift of a balance amount away from its normal column indicates an accounting error. For example, a credit balance in Office Supplies, Office Furniture, or Buildings indicates an error because negative amounts of these assets cannot exist.

EXHIBIT 2-12 *Normal Balances of Balance Sheet Accounts*

Assets	=	Liabilities	+	Shareholders' Equity
Normal Bal. Debit		Normal Bal. Credit		Normal Bal. Credit

Short Exercise:

Compute the missing amounts:

(1) Common Stock

	Bal. ?
22,000	56,000
	15,000
	Bal. 73,000

(2) Cash

Bal. 10,000	
20,000	13,000
Bal. ?	

(3) Accounts Payable

?	Bal. 12,800
	45,600
	Bal. 23,500

A: (1) $24,000; (2) $17,000; (3) $34,900

As we have explained, shareholders' equity usually contains several accounts. In total, these accounts show a normal credit balance for the shareholders' equity of the business. Each shareholders' equity account has a normal credit balance if it represents an *increase* in shareholders' equity (for example, the Common Stock account in Exhibit 2-14). However, if the individual shareholders' equity account represents a decrease in shareholders' equity, the account will have a normal debit balance (for example, the Dividends account in Exhibit 2-14).

Additional Shareholders' Equity Accounts: Revenues and Expenses

The shareholders' equity category includes two income statement accounts: Revenues and Expenses. As we have discussed, *revenues* are increases in shareholders' equity that result from delivering goods or services to customers. *Expenses* are decreases in shareholders' equity due to the cost of operating the business. Therefore, the accounting equation may be expanded as shown in Exhibit 2-13. Revenues and expenses appear in parentheses because their impact on the accounting equation arises from their effect on shareholders' equity. If revenues exceed expenses, the net effect—revenues minus expenses—equals net income, which increases shareholders' equity. If expenses are greater, the net effect is a net loss, which decreases shareholders' equity.

Key Point:

Because dividends reduce shareholders' equity, the Dividends account is sometimes referred to as a contra equity account, meaning that it has the opposite balance of shareholders' equity.

EXHIBIT 2-13 *Expansion of the Accounting Equation*

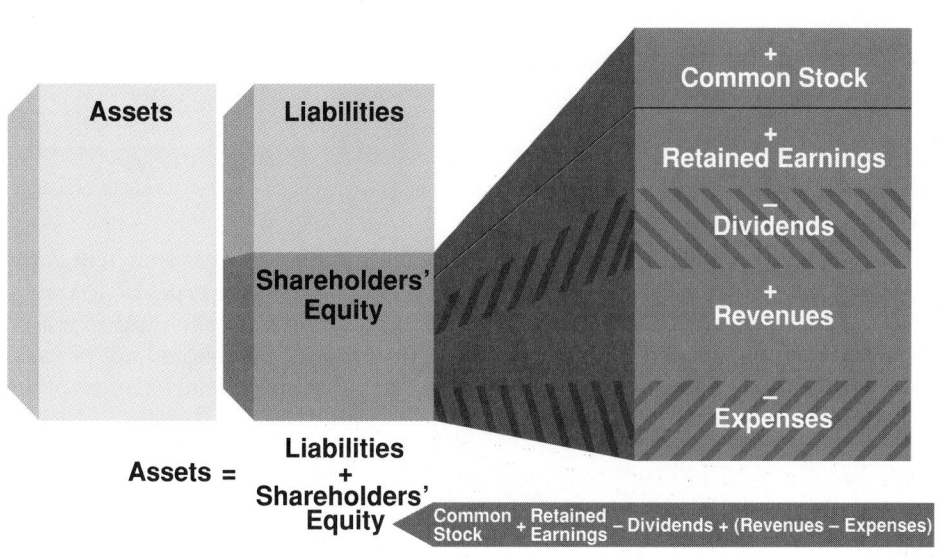

EXHIBIT 2-14   *Rules of Debit and Credit and Normal Balances of Accounts*

Panel A: Rules of Debit and Credit

Assets		=	Liabilities		+	Common Stock	
Debit for Increase	Credit for Decrease		Debit for Decrease	Credit for Increase		Debit for Decrease	Credit for Increase

						Retained Earnings	
						Debit for Decrease	Credit for Increase

						Dividends	
						Debit for Increase	Credit for Decrease

						Revenues	
						Debit for Decrease	Credit for Increase

						Expenses	
						Debit for Increase	Credit for Decrease

Panel B: Normal Balances

Assets	Debit	
Liabilities		Credit
Shareholders' equity—overall		Credit
Common stock		Credit
Retained earnings		Credit
Dividends	Debit	
Revenue		Credit
Expenses	Debit	

We can now express the rules of debit and credit in final form as shown in Panel A of Exhibit 2-14. Panel B shows the *normal* balances of the five types of accounts: *Assets*; *Liabilities*; and *Shareholders' Equity* and its subparts, *Revenue* and *Expenses*. All of accounting is based on these five types of accounts. You should not proceed until you have learned the rules of debit and credit and the normal balances of the five types of accounts.

Expanded Problem Including Revenues and Expenses

Let's account for the revenues and expenses of the systems design engineering practice of Sally Gunz and her business SG Systems Corp., for the month of July

19X1. We follow the same steps illustrated earlier: analyze the transaction, journalize, post to the ledger, and prepare the trial balance. Revenue accounts and expense accounts work just like asset, liability, and shareholders' equity accounts.

Transaction Analysis, Journalizing, and Posting

1. *Transaction:*   Sally Gunz invested $10,000 cash in a business bank account to open her systems design engineering practice. The business issues common stock to Gunz.

   Analysis: The asset cash is increased; therefore debit Cash. The shareholders' equity of the business increased; therefore, credit Common Stock.

   Journal Entry:

   Cash 10,000
        Common Stock   10,000
   Issued common stock to the owner.

   Ledger Accounts:

Cash		**Common Stock**	
(1) 10,000			(1) 10,000

2. *Transaction:*   Gunz performed systems design services for a client and received $3,000.

   Analysis: The asset cash is increased; therefore, debit Cash. The revenue service revenue is increased; credit Service Revenue.

   Journal Entry:

   Cash 3,000
        Service Revenue   3,000
   Performed service and received cash.

   Ledger Accounts:

Cash		**Service Revenue**	
(1) 10,000			(2) 3,000
(2) 3,000			

3. *Transaction:*   Gunz performed services for a local veterinarian and billed the client for $500 on account receivable. This means the veterinarian owes the business $500 even though the veterinarian signed no formal promissory note.

   Analysis: The asset accounts receivable is increased; therefore, debit Accounts Receivable. Service revenue is increased; credit Service Revenue.

   Journal Entry:

   Accounts Receivable 500
        Service Revenue   500
   Performed service on account.

   Ledger Accounts:

Accounts Receivable		**Service Revenue**	
(3) 500			(2) 3,000
			(3) 500

4.   *Transaction*:   Gunz performed systems design services of $700 for a doctor, who paid $300 cash immediately. Gunz billed the remaining $400 to the doctor on account receivable.

    Analysis: The assets cash and accounts receivable are increased; therefore, debit both of these asset accounts. Service revenue is increased; credit Service Revenue for the sum of the two debit amounts.

    Journal
    Entry:

Cash	300	
Accounts Receivable	400	
Service Revenue		700

Performed service for cash and on account.

    Note: Because this transaction affects more than two accounts at the same time, the entry is called a *compound entry*. No matter how many accounts a compound entry affects—there may be any number—total debits must equal total credits.

    Ledger
    Accounts:

Cash		**Accounts Receivable**	
(1)	10,000	(3)	500
(2)	3,000	(4)	400
(4)	300		

Service Revenue	
(2)	3,000
(3)	500
(4)	700

5.   *Transaction*:   The business paid the following cash expenses: office rent, $900; employee salary, $1,500; and utilities, $500.

    Analysis: The asset cash is decreased; therefore, credit Cash for each of the three expense amounts. The following expenses are increased: Rent Expense, Salary Expense, and Utilities Expense. Each should be debited.

    Journal
    Entry:

Rent Expense	900	
Salary Expense	1,500	
Utilities Expense	500	
Cash		2,900

Issued three cheques to pay cash expenses.

    Ledger
    Accounts:

Cash				**Rent Expense**	
(1)	10,000	(5)	2,900	(5)	900
(2)	3,000				
(4)	300				

Salary Expense		**Utilities Expense**	
(5)	1,500	(5)	500

6. *Transaction*: The business received a telephone bill for $120 and will pay this expense next week.

   Analysis: Utilities expense is increased; therefore, debit this expense. The liability accounts payable is increased; credit this account.

   Journal Entry:
   Utilities Expense 120
       Accounts Payable   120
   Received utility bill.

   Ledger Accounts:

Accounts Payable		Utilities Expense	
(6)	120	(5)	500
		(6)	120

7. *Transaction*: Gunz collected $200 cash from the client established in Transaction 3.

   Analysis: The asset cash is increased; therefore, debit Cash. The asset accounts receivable is decreased; therefore, credit Accounts Receivable.

   Journal Entry:
   Cash 200
       Accounts Receivable   200
   Received cash on account.

   Note: This transaction has no effect on revenue; the related revenue is accounted for in Transaction 3.

   Ledger Accounts:

Cash				Accounts Receivable			
(1)	10,000	(5)	2,900	(3)	500	(7)	200
(2)	3,000			(4)	400		
(4)	300						
(7)	200						

8. *Transaction*: The business paid the telephone bill that was received and recorded in Transaction 6.

   Analysis: The asset cash is decreased; credit Cash. The liability accounts payable is decreased; therefore, debit Accounts Payable.

   Journal Entry:
   Accounts Payable 120
       Cash   120
   Paid cash on account.

   Note: This transaction has no effect on expense because the related expense was recorded in Transaction 6.

   Ledger Accounts:

Cash				Accounts Payable			
(1)	10,000	(5)	2,900	(8)	120	(6)	120
(2)	3,000	(8)	120				
(4)	300						
(7)	200						

Key Point:
Recording an expense does not necessarily involve a credit to cash. In Transaction 6 the expense is recorded now, but the cash will be paid later. Likewise, a debit to cash does not always reflect revenue. Transaction 7 records cash collected on a receivable (the revenue was recorded in Transaction 3).

9.   *Transaction*:   SG Systems Corp. paid a dividend of $1,100.

   Analysis: The asset cash decreased; credit Cash. The dividend decreased shareholders' equity; therefore, debit Dividends.

   Journal Entry:

   Dividends 1,100
        Cash 1,100
   Withdrew for personal use.

   Ledger Accounts:

Cash					Dividends	
(1)	10,000	(5)	2,900		**(9)**	**1,100**
(2)	3,000	(8)	120			
(4)	300	**(9)**	**1,100**			
(7)	200					

Ledger Accounts After Posting

ASSETS

Cash			
(1) 10,000	(5) 2,900		
(2) 3,000			
(4) 300			
(7) 200	(8) 120		
	(9) 1,100		
Bal. 9,380			

Accounts Receivable			
(3) 500	(7) 200		
(4) 400			
Bal. 700			

LIABILITIES

Accounts Payable			
(8) 120	(6) 120		
	Bal. 0		

SHAREHOLDERS' EQUITY

Common Stock	
	(1) 10,000
	Bal. 10,000

Dividends	
(9) 1,100	
Bal. 1,100	

REVENUE

Service Revenue	
	(2) 3,000
	(3) 500
	(4) 700
	Bal. 4,200

EXPENSES

Rent Expense	
(5) 900	
Bal. 900	

Salary Expense	
(5) 1,500	
Bal. 1,500	

Utilities Expense	
(5) 500	
(6) 120	
Bal. 620	

Discussion Q:
Which side of the trial balance is affected by a debit to accounts payable? **A:** The credit side. (Students will want to say debit.)
Illustration:

Accounts Payable
| | Bal. | 6,000 |

A debit to accounts payable reduces the *credit* balance of Accounts Payable.

Accounts Payable
	Bal.	6,000
1,000		
	Bal.	5,000

Trial Balance

	SG Systems, Corp. Trial Balance July 31, 19X1		
		Balance	
Account Title		**Debit**	**Credit**
Cash		$ 9,380	
Accounts receivable		700	
Accounts payable			$ 0
Common stock			10,000
Dividends		1,100	
Service revenue			4,200
Rent expense		900	
Salary expense		1,500	
Utilities expense		620	
Total		$14,200	$14,200

Review the chapter-opening story and concentrate on Renato Nahas's need for financial statement information. How will the procedures you have applied in this chapter help Compacta convince potential customers that the business is stable?

Answer: The end product of the accounting process is a set of financial statements. Compacta's accounting records will generate the income statement and balance sheet that customers require of contractors before accepting a bid.

Use of Accounting Information for Quick Decision Making

OBJECTIVE 7
Analyze transactions without a journal

What dominates the accountant's analysis of transactions: the accounting equation, the journal, or the ledger? The accounting equation is most fundamental. And, the ledger is more useful than the journal in providing an overall model of the organization. The ledger includes all the accounts, which represent all the entity's assets, liabilities, shareholders' equity, revenues, and expenses. The journal is merely a record of transactions.

Businesspeople must often make quick decisions without the benefit of a complete accounting system. For example, Normal Erickson, a hair stylist in Brandon, Manitoba, may be renegotiating the rental of his shop. He may not have the time for a thorough recording of the effects of all the transactions. One who knows accounting can skip the journal and go directly to the ledger, compressing transaction analysis, journalizing, and posting into one step. This type of analysis saves time that may make the difference between a good business decision and a lost opportunity.

Erickson may be comparing the expense of renting the shop for $800 per month with the $75,000 cost of buying his own building. In the heat of negotiation, he doesn't have time to journalize and post all the likely transactions and prepare a trial balance. But if he knows some accounting, he can make this quick comparison:

Rent the Shop		Buy the Building	
Cash	**Rent Expense**	**Cash**	**Building**
| 800	800 |	| 75,000	75,000 |

Immediately Erickson can see that buying the building will require more cash. But he can also see that he will obtain the building as an asset. This may motivate him to borrow cash and buy the building.

Companies do not actually keep their records in this short-cut fashion. But a decision-maker who needs information immediately need not perform all the accounting steps to analyze the effect of a set of transactions on the company's financial statements.

Summary Problem for Your Review

The trial balance of Tomassini Computer Service Center Inc. on March 1, 19X2, lists the entity's assets, liabilities, and shareholders' equity on that date.

	Balance	
Account Titles	Debit	Credit
Cash	$26,000	
Accounts receivable	4,500	
Accounts payable		$ 2,000
Common stock		10,000
Retained earnings		18,500
Total	$30,500	$30,500

During March the business engaged in the following transactions:

a. Borrowed $45,000 from the bank. Tomassini signed a note payable in the name of the business.

b. Paid cash of $40,000 to a real estate company to acquire land.

c. Performed service for a customer and received cash of $5,000.

d. Purchased supplies on credit, $300.

e. Performed customer service and earned revenue on account, $2,600.

f. Paid $1,200 on account.

g. Paid the following cash expenses: salaries, $3,000; rent, $1,500; and interest, $400.

h. Received $3,100 on account.

i. Received a $200 utility bill that will be paid next week.

j. Paid dividend of $1,800.

Required

1. Open the following accounts, with the balances indicated, in the ledger of Tomassini Computer Service Center Inc. Use the T-account format.
   Assets: Cash, $26,000; Accounts Receivable, $4,500; Supplies, no balance; Land, no balance
   Liabilities: Accounts Payable, $2,000; Note Payable, no balance
   Shareholders' Equity: Common Stock, $10,000; Retained Earnings, $18,500.
   Revenues: Service Revenue, no balance
   Expenses: (none have balances) Salary Expense, Rent Expense, Utilities Expense, Interest Expense

2. Journalize the preceding transactions. Key journal entries by transaction letter.

3. Post to the ledger.

4. Prepare the trial balance of Tomassini Computer Service Centre Inc. at March 31, 19X2.

5. Compute the net income or net loss of the entity during the month of March. List expenses in order from the largest to the smallest.

SOLUTION TO REVIEW PROBLEM

Requirement 1

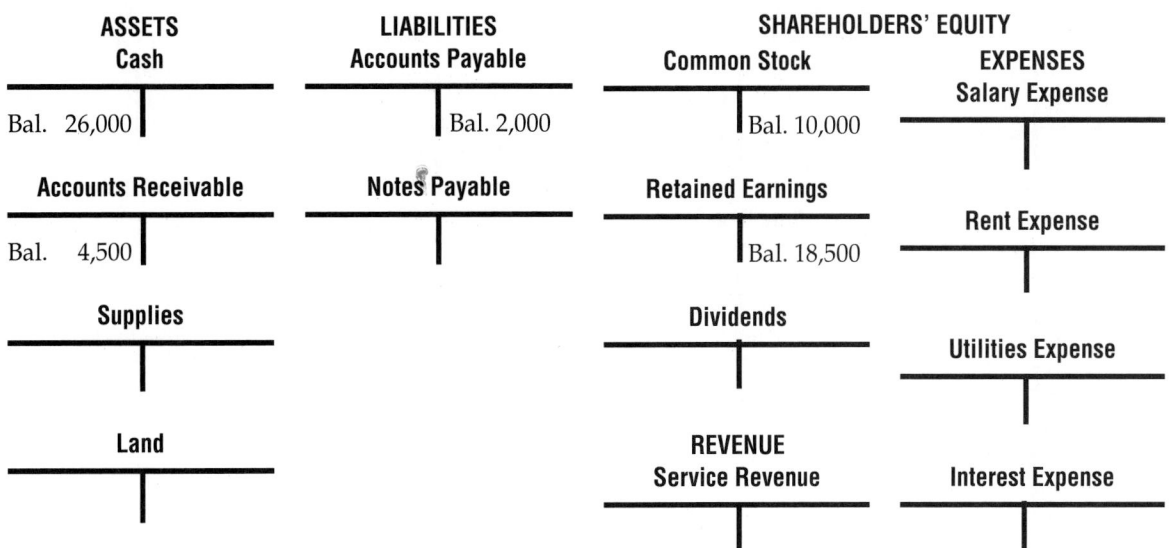

Requirement 2

	Accounts and Explanation	Debit	Credit
a.	Cash..	45,000	
	Note Payable		45,000
	Borrowed cash on note payable.		
b.	Land..	40,000	
	Cash		40,000
	Purchased land for cash.		
c.	Cash..	5,000	
	Service Revenue		5,000
	Performed service and received cash.		
d.	Supplies...	300	
	Accounts Payable.......................................		300
	Purchased supplies on account.		
e.	Accounts Receivable	2,600	
	Service Revenue		2,600
	Performed service on account.		
f.	Accounts Payable	1,200	
	Cash		1,200
	Paid on account.		
g.	Salary Expense...	3,000	
	Rent Expense...	1,500	
	Interest Expense	400	
	Cash		4,900
	Issued three cheques to pay cash expenses.		
h.	Cash..	3,100	
	Accounts Receivable..................................		3,100
	Received on account.		
i.	Utilities Expense	200	
	Accounts Payable.......................................		200
	Received utility bill.		
j.	Dividends	1,800	
	Cash		1,800
	Dividends paid to shareholder or owner.		

Requirement 3

ASSETS				
Cash				
Bal.	26,000	(b)	40,000	
(a)	45,000	(f)	1,200	
(c)	5,000	(g)	4,900	
(h)	3,100	(j)	1,800	
Bal.	31,200			

Accounts Receivable

Bal.	4,500	(h)	3,100
(e)	2,600		
Bal.	4,000		

Supplies

(d)	300	
Bal.	300	

Land

(b)	40,000	
Bal.	40,000	

LIABILITIES

Accounts Payable

(h)	1,200	Bal.	2,000
		(d)	300
		(i)	200
		Bal.	1,300

Note Payable

		(a)	45,000
		Bal.	45,000

SHAREHOLDERS' EQUITY

Common Stock

	Bal.	10,000

Retained Earnings

	Bal.	18,500

Dividends

(j)	1,800	
Bal.	1,800	

REVENUE

Service Revenue

		(c)	5,000
		(e)	2,600
		Bal.	7,600

EXPENSES

Salary Expense

(g)	3,000	
Bal.	3,000	

Rent Expense

(g)	1,500	
Bal.	1,500	

Utilities Expense

(i)	200	
Bal.	200	

Interest Expense

(g)	400	
Bal.	400	

Requirement 4

Tomassini Computer Service Centre Inc.
Trial Balance
March 31, 19X2

	Balance	
Account Title	**Debit**	**Credit**
Cash	$31,200	
Accounts Receivable	4,000	
Supplies	300	
Land	40,000	
Accounts Payable		$ 1,300
Note Payable		45,000
Common Stock		10,000
Retained Earnings		18,500
Dividends	1,800	
Service Revenue		7,600
Salary Expense	3,000	
Rent Expense	1,500	
Interest Expense	400	
Utilities Expense	200	
Total	$82,400	$82,400

Requirement 5

Tomassini Computer Service Centre Inc.
Income Statement
For the Month Ended March 31, 19X2

	Balance	
Account Title	**Debit**	**Credit**
Revenues		
Service Revenue		$7,600

Expenses		
Salary Expense	$3,000	
Rent Expense	1,500	
Interest Expense	400	
Utilities Expense	200	
Total expenses		5,100
Net income		$2,500

Summary

1. **Define key accounting terms: account, ledger, debit, and credit.** The *account* can be viewed in the form of the letter "T." The left side of each T-account is its *debit* side. The right side is its *credit* side. The *ledger*, which contains a record for each account, groups and numbers accounts by category in the following order: assets, liabilities, and shareholders' equity (and its subparts, revenues and expenses).

2. **Apply the rules of debit and credit.** *Assets* and *expenses* are increased by debits and decreased by credits. *Liabilities, shareholders' equity,* and *revenues* are increased by credits and decreased by debits. The side—debit or credit—of the account in which increases are recorded is that account's normal balance. Thus the normal balance of assets and expenses is a debit, and the normal balance of liabilities, shareholders' equity, and revenues is a credit. The Dividends account, which decreases shareholders' equity, normally has a debit balance. *Revenues,* which are increases in shareholders' equity, have a normal credit balance. *Expenses,* which are decreases in shareholders' equity, have a normal debit balance.

3. **Record transactions in the journal.** The accountant begins the recording process by entering the transaction's information in the *journal,* a chronological list of all the business's transactions.

4. **Post from the journal to the ledger.** The information is then posted—transferred—to the *ledger* accounts. Posting references are used to trace amounts back and forth between the journal and the ledger. Businesses list their account titles and numbers in a chart of accounts.

5. **Prepare a trial balance.** The *trial balance* is a summary of all the account balances in the ledger. When *double-entry accounting* has been done correctly, the total debits and the total credits in the trial balance are equal.

6. **Set up a chart of accounts for a business.** The first step in accounting is to set up the chart of accounts.

7. **Analyze transactions without a journal.** Decision makers must often make decisions without a complete accounting system. They can analyze the transactions without a journal.

We can now trace the flow of accounting information through these steps:

Business Transaction → Source Documents → Journal Entry →
Posting to Ledger → Trial Balance

Self-Study Questions

Test your understanding of the chapter by marking the correct answer for each of the following questions:

1. An account has two sides called the *(p. 57)*
   a. Debit and credit
   b. Asset and liability
   c. Revenue and expense
   d. Journal and ledger

2. Increases in liabilities are recorded by *(p. 57)*
   a. Debits
   b. Credits

3. Why do accountants record transactions in the journal? *(p. 60)*
   a. To ensure that all transactions are posted to the ledger
   b. To ensure that total debits equal total credits
   c. To have a chronological record of all transactions
   d. To help prepare the financial statements
4. Posting is the process of transferring information from the *(p. 61)*
   a. Journal to the trial balance   c. Ledger to the financial statements
   b. Ledger to the trial balance   d. Journal to the ledger
5. The purchase of land for cash is recorded by a *(p. 63)*
   a. Debit to Cash and a credit to Land
   b. Debit to Cash and a debit to Land
   c. Debit to Land and a credit to Cash
   d. Credit to Cash and a credit to Land
6. The purpose of the trial balance is to *(p. 65)*
   a. List all accounts with their balances
   b. Ensure that all transactions have been recorded
   c. Speed the collection of cash receipts from customers
   d. Increase assets and shareholders' equity
7. What is the normal balance of the Accounts Receivable, Office Supplies, and Rent Expense accounts? *(p. 72)*
   a. Debit   b. Credit
8. A business has Cash of $3,000, Notes Payable of $2,500, Accounts Payable of $4,300, Service Revenue of $7,000 and Rent Expense of $1,800. Based on these data, how much are its total liabilities? *(p. 73)*
   a. $5,500   c. $9,800
   b. $6,800   d. $13,800
9. The earning of revenue on account is recorded by a *(pp. 75–78)*
   a. Debit to Cash and a credit to Revenue
   b. Debit to Accounts Receivable and a credit to Revenue
   c. Debit to Accounts Payable and a credit to Revenue
   d. Debit to Revenue and a credit to Accounts Receivable
10. The account credited for a receipt of cash on account is *(p. 77)*
    a. Cash   c. Service Revenue
    b. Accounts Payable   d. Accounts Receivable

Answers to the Self-Study Questions follow the Accounting Vocabulary.

Accounting Vocabulary

Account *(p. 54)*
Chart of accounts *(p. 71)*
Credit *(p. 57)*
Debit *(p. 57)*
Journal *(p. 60)*
Ledger *(p. 64)*
Posting *(p. 61)*
Trial balance *(p. 65)*

Answers to Self-Study Questions

1. a	3. c	5. c	7. a		9. b
2. b	4. d	6. a	8. b ($6,800 = $2,500 + $4,300)		10. d

ASSIGNMENT MATERIAL _____

Questions

1. Name the basic summary device of accounting. What letter of the alphabet does it resemble? Name its two sides.

2. Is the following statement true or false? Debit means decrease and credit means increase. Explain your answer.

3. Write two sentences that use the term *debit* differently.

4. What are the three *basic* types of accounts? Name two additional types of accounts. To which one of the three basic types are these two additional types of accounts most closely related?

5. Suppose you are the accountant for Smith Courier Service Ltd. Keeping in mind double-entry bookkeeping, identify the *dual effects* of Mary Smith's investment of $10,000 cash in her business and the issuance of common stock to Smith.

6. Briefly describe the flow of accounting information.

7. To what does the *normal balance* of an account refer?

8. Complete the table by indicating the normal balance of the five types of accounts.

Account Type	Normal Balance
Assets	_____
Liabilities	_____
Shareholders' equity	_____
Revenues	_____
Expenses	_____

9. What does posting accomplish? Why is it important? Does it come before or after journalizing?

10. Label each of the following transactions as increasing shareholders' equity (+), decreasing shareholders' equity (–), or as having no effect on shareholders' equity (0). Write the appropriate symbol in the space provided.

___ Investment by owner   ___ Cash payment on account
___ Revenue transaction   ___ Dividends
___ Purchase of supplies   ___ Borrowing money on a note
     on credit   payable
___ Expense transaction   ___ Sale of services on account

11. What four steps does posting include? Which step is the fundamental purpose of posting?

12. Rearrange the following accounts in their logical sequence in the ledger:

Notes Payable   Cash
Accounts Receivable   Common Stock
Sales Revenue   Salary Expense

13. What is the meaning of the statement, Accounts Payable has a credit balance of $1,700?

14. Jack Brown Campus Cleaners Ltd. launders the shirts of customer Bobby Baylor, who has a charge account at the cleaners. When Bobby picks up his clothes and is short on cash, he charges it. Later, when he receives his monthly statement from the cleaners, Bobby writes a cheque on Dear Old Dad's bank account and mails the cheque to Jack Brown. Identify the two business transactions described here. Which transaction increases the business's shareholders' equity? Which transaction increases Jack Brown's cash?

15. Explain the difference between the ledger and the chart of accounts.

16. Why do accountants prepare a trial balance?

17. What is a compound journal entry?

18. The accountant for Bower Construction Corp. mistakenly recorded a $500 purchase of supplies on account as a $5,000 purchase. He debited Supplies and credited Accounts Payable for $5,000. Does this error cause the trial balance to be out of balance? Explain your answer.

19. What is the effect on total assets of collecting cash on account from customers?

20. What is the advantage of analyzing and recording transactions without the use of a journal? Describe how this "journal-less" analysis works.

21. Briefly summarize the similarities and differences between manual and computer-based accounting systems in terms of journalizing, posting, and the preparation of a trial balance.

Exercises

Exercise 2-1   Using accounting vocabulary   *(Obj. 1)*

Your employer, Metric Devices, Inc., has just hired an office manager who does not understand accounting. Metric's trial balance lists Cash of $43,900. Write a short memo to the office manager, explaining the accounting process that produced this listing on the trial balance. Mention *debits, credits, journals, ledgers, posting,* and so on.

Exercise 2-2   Analyzing and journalizing transactions   *(Obj. 2, 3)*

Analyze the following transactions in the manner shown for the December 1 transaction. Also, record each transaction in the journal.

Dec. 1 Paid monthly utilities expense of $1,200. (Analysis: The expense, utilities expense, is increased; therefore, debit Utilities Expense. The asset, cash, is decreased; therefore credit Cash.)

1	Utilities Expense	1,200
	Cash	1,200

    4 Borrowed $12,000 cash, signing a note payable.
    8 Performed service on account for a customer, $1,600.
   12 Purchased office furniture on account, $810.
   19 Sold for $74,000 land that had cost this same amount.
   24 Purchased building for $140,000; signed a note payable.
   27 Paid the liability created on December 12.

Exercise 2-3   Applying the rules of debit and credit   *(Obj. 2)*

Refer to Exercise 2-2.

Required

1. Open the following T-accounts with their December balances: Cash, debit balance $6,000; Land, debit balance $74,000; Common Stock, credit balance $80,000.

2. Record the transactions of Exercise 2-2 directly in the T-accounts affected. Enter the dates in the T-accounts.

3. Compute the December 31 balance in each account, and prove that total debits equal total credits.

Exercise 2-4   Journalizing transactions   *(Obj. 3)*

Chin Consulting Service, Inc. engaged in the following transactions during March 19X3, its first month of operations:

Mar. 1 Rudy Chin invested $65,000 of cash to start the business. The corporation issued common stock to Chin.
    2 Purchased supplies of $200 on account.
    4 Paid $40,000 cash for building to use as a future office.
    6 Performed service for customers and received cash, $2,000.
    9 Paid $100 on accounts payable.

   17   Performed service for customers on account, $1,600.
   23   Received $1,200 cash from a customer on account.
   31   Paid the following expenses: salary, $1,200; rent, $500.

Required

Record the preceding transactions in the journal of Chin Consulting Service, Inc. Key transactions by date and include an explanation for each entry, as illustrated in the chapter. Use the following accounts: Cash; Accounts Receivable; Office Supplies; Building; Accounts Payable; Common Stock; Service Revenue; Salary Expense; Rent Expense.

Exercise 2-5   *Posting to the ledger and preparing a trial balance*   **(Obj. 4, 5)**

Refer to Exercise 2-4.

Required

1. After journalizing the transactions of Exercise 2-4, post the entries to the ledger, using T-account format. Key transactions by date. Date the ending balance of each account Mar. 31.
2. Prepare the trial balance of Chin Consulting Service, Inc. at March 31, 19X3.

Exercise 2-6   *Describing transactions and posting*   **(Obj. 3, 4)**

The journal of Benesh Company Ltd. follows:

Journal   **Page 5**

Date	Accounts and Explanation	Post Ref.	Debit	Credit
Aug. 2	Cash...		6,000	
	Common Stock.................................			6,000
5	Cash...		15,000	
	Note Payable.................................			15,000
9	Supplies..		270	
	Accounts Payable...........................			270
11	Accounts Receivable.............................		2,630	
	Sales Revenue...............................			2,630
14	Rent Expense......................................		4,200	
	Cash...			4,200
22	Cash...		1,400	
	Accounts Receivable.......................			1,400
25	Advertising Expense.............................		350	
	Cash...			350
27	Accounts Payable.................................		270	
	Cash...			270
31	Utilities Expense..................................		220	
	Accounts Payable...........................			220

Required

1. Describe each transaction.
2. Post the transactions to the ledger using the following account numbers: Cash, 110; Accounts Receivable, 120; Supplies, 130; Accounts Payable, 210; Note Payable, 230; Common Stock, 310; Sales Revenue, 410; Rent Expense, 510; Advertising Expense,

520; Utilities Expense, 530. Use dates, journal references and posting references as illustrated in Exhibit 2-8. You may write the account numbers as posting references directly in your book unless directed otherwise by your instructor.

3. Compute the balance in each account after posting. Prepare Benesh Company Ltd.'s trial balance at August 31, 19X6.

Exercise 2-7   *Journalizing transactions   (Obj. 3)*

The first five transactions of Klassen Security Corp. have been posted to the company's accounts as follows:

Cash				Supplies		Equipment	
(1)	60,000	(3)	42,000	(2)	400	(5)	6,000
(4)	7,000	(5)	6,000				

Land		Accounts Payable		Note Payable	
(3)	42,000	(2)	400	(4)	7,000

Common Stock	
(1)	60,000

Required

Prepare the journal entries that served as the sources for the five transactions. Include an explanation for each entry as illustrated in the chapter.

Exercise 2-8   *Preparing a trial balance   (Obj. 5)*

Prepare the trial balance of Klassen Security, Corp. at April 30, 19X4, using the account data from Exercise 2-7.

Exercise 2-9   *Preparing a trial balance   (Obj. 5)*

The accounts of Japra Realty Ltd. are listed below with their normal balances at October 31, 19X4. The accounts are listed in no particular order.

Account	Balance
Common stock	$48,800
Advertising expense	650
Accounts payable	4,300
Sales commission revenue	22,000
Land	29,000
Note payable	25,000
Cash	5,000
Salary expense	6,000
Building	45,000
Rent expense	2,000
Dividends	6,000
Utilities expense	400
Accounts receivable	5,500
Supplies expense	300
Supplies	250

Required

Prepare the company's trial balance at October 31, 19X4, listing accounts in proper sequence, as illustrated in the chapter. Supplies comes before Building and Land. List the expense with the largest balance first, the expense with the next largest balance second, and so on.

Exercise 2-10   *Correcting errors in a trial balance*   **(Obj. 5)**

The trial balance of Thai Enterprises, Inc. at February 28, 19X9, does not balance.

Cash	$ 4,200	
Accounts receivable	2,000	
Supplies	600	
Land	46,000	
Account payable		$ 3,000
Common stock		41,600
Service revenue		9,700
Salary expense	1,700	
Rent expense	800	
Utilities expense	300	
Total	$55,600	$54,300

Investigation of the accounting records reveals that the bookkeeper

a. Recorded a $400 cash revenue transaction by debiting Accounts Receivable. The credit entry was correct.

b. Posted a $1,000 credit to Accounts Payable as $100.

c. Did not record utilities expense or the related account payable in the amount of $200.

d. Understated Common Stock by $400.

Required

Prepare the correct trial balance at February 28, complete with a heading. Journal entries are not required.

Exercise 2-11   *Recording transactions without a journal*   **(Obj. 7)**

Open the following T-accounts: Cash; Accounts Receivable; Office Supplies; Office Furniture; Accounts Payable; Common Stock; Dividends; Service Revenue; Salary Expense; Rent Expense.

Record the following transactions directly in the T-accounts without using a journal. Use the letters to identify the transactions.

a. Dolores Trevino opened a pension consulting firm by investing $7,200 cash and office furniture valued at $5,400. The business was incorporated and issued common stock to Trevino.

b. Paid monthly rent of $1,500.

c. Purchased office supplies on account, $800.

d. Paid employee salary, $800.

e. Paid $400 of the account payable credited in c.

f. Performed consulting service on account, $1,700.

g. Paid dividends of $200.

Exercise 2-12   *Preparing a trial balance*   **(Obj. 5)**

After recording the transactions in Exercise 2-11, prepare the trial balance of Trevino Pension Consulting Ltd., at May 31, 19X7.

Serial Exercise

Exercise 2-13 begins an accounting cycle that is completed in Chapter 5.

Exercise 2-13   *Recording transactions and preparing a trial balance*   **(Obj. 2, 3, 4, 5)**

Emily Schneider, Architect, Inc., completed these transactions during the first half of December:

Dec.   2 Received $12,000 cash from Emily Schneider. Issued common stock to Schneider.
      2 Paid monthly office rent, $500.
      3 Paid cash for a Macintosh computer, $3,000. The computer is expected to remain in service for five years.
      4 Purchased office furniture on account, $3,600. The furniture should last for five years.
      5 Purchased supplies on account, $300.
      9 Performed design services for a client and received cash for the full amount of $800.
     12 Paid utility expenses, $200.
     18 Performed design services for a client on account, $1,700.

Required

1. Open T-accounts in the ledger: Cash; Accounts Receivable; Supplies; Equipment; Furniture; Accounts Payable; Common Stock; Dividends; Service Revenue; Rent Expense; Utilities Expense; and Salary Expense.

2. Journalize the transactions. Explanations are not required.

3. Post to the T-accounts. Key all items by date, and denote an account balance as *Bal*. Formal posting references are not required.

4. Prepare a trial balance at December 18. In the serial Exercise of Chapter 3, we will add transactions for the remainder of December and will require a trial balance at December 31.

Challenge Exercise

Exercise 2-14   *Identifying the accounts of a new business*   **(Obj. 6)**

Jack Grimestad asks your advice in setting up the accounting records for his new business. He plans to organize as a corporation. The business will be a photography studio and will operate in a rented building. Grimestad will need office equipment, cameras, tripods, lights, backdrops, and so on. The business will borrow money to buy the needed equipment. Grimestad will purchase on account photographic supplies, such as film, paper, and developing solution, and office supplies. Each asset needs its own expense account, some of which have not yet been discussed. For example, equipment wears out (depreciates) and thus needs a depreciation account. As supplies are used up, the business must record a supplies expense.

Grimestad owns the land on which the studio building stands. He will contribute the land to the business, which will then pay the property tax on the land. A gas station located on a corner of the property will start paying its monthly rent to the photography studio. The studio will need an office manager to arrange appointments, keep the books, design advertisements, and pay the rent and the insurance in advance and the utility bills as they come due. Grimestad anticipates paying this person a weekly salary of $300.

He will want to know which aspects of the business are the most, and the least, profitable, so he will account for each category of service revenue separately: portraits, school pictures, and weddings. He will let his better customers open accounts with the business and expects to collect cash over a three-month period. The studio will carry an inventory of picture frames for sale to customers—a separate category of revenue.

Required

List all the accounts the studio will need, starting with assets and ending with expenses. Indicate which accounts will be reported on the balance sheet and which will be on the income statement.

Exercise 2-15   *Computing financial statement amounts without a journal*   (Obj. 7)

The owner of McBee Technical Services, Inc., is an engineer with little understanding of accounting. He needs to compute the following summary information from the accounting records:

a. Net income for the month of March.
b. Total cash paid during March.
c. Cash collections from customers during March.
d. Cash paid on a note payable during March.

The quickest way to compute these amounts is to analyze the following accounts:

	Balance		Additional Information for the Month of March
Account	Feb. 28	Mar. 31	
1. Retained Earnings.............	$ 9,200	$10,100	Dividends, $3,800
2. Cash	4,600	3,400	Cash receipts, $61,200
3. Accounts Receivable........	24,300	26,700	Sales on account, $53,500
4. Note Payable	13,900	17,400	New borrowing, $6,300

The net income for March can be computed as follows:

Retained Earnings

March Dividends	3,800	Feb. 28 Bal.	9,200
		March Net Income	x = $4,700
		March 31 Bal.	10,100

Use a similar approach to compute the other three items.

Exercise 2-16   *Analyzing accounting errors*   (Obj. 2, 3, 4, 5)

Klutz Accountant has trouble keeping his debits and credits equal. During a recent month he made the following errors:

a. In journalizing a cash sale, Klutz debited Cash for $900 but accidentally credited Accounts Receivable.
b. Klutz posted a $700 utility expense as $70. The credit posting to Cash was correct.
c. In preparing the trial balance, Klutz omitted a $20,000 note payable.
d. Klutz recorded a $120 purchase of supplies on account by debiting Supplies and crediting Accounts Payable for $210.
e. In recording a $400 payment on account, Klutz debited Supplies and credited Accounts Payable.

Required

1. For each of these errors, state whether the total debits equal total credits on the trial balance.
2. Identify any accounts with misstated balances, and indicate the amount and direction of the error (account balance too high or too low).

Problems   *(Group A)*

Problem 2-1A   *Analyzing a trial balance*   *(Obj. 1)*

The owner of Electrix Corp. is selling the business. She offers the following trial balance to prospective buyers:

Electrix Corp. Trial Balance December 31, 19XX		
Cash	$ 7,000	
Accounts receivable	11,000	
Prepaid expenses	4,000	
Land	31,000	
Accounts payable		$ 31,000
Note payable		20,000
Common stock		33,000
Dividends	21,000	
Sales revenue		47,000
Rent expense	14,000	
Advertising expense	3,000	
Wage expense	33,000	
Supplies expense	7,000	
Total	$131,000	$131,000

Your best friend is considering buying Electrix Corp. She seeks your advice in interpreting this information. Specifically, she asks whether this trial balance is the same as a balance sheet and an income statement. She also wonders whether Electrix is a sound company. She thinks it must be because the accounts are in balance.

Required

Write a short note to answer your friend's questions. To aid her decision, state how she can use the information on the trial balance to compute Electrix's net income or net loss for the current period. State the amount of net income or net loss in your note.

Problem 2-2A   *Analyzing and journalizing transactions*   *(Obj. 2, 3)*

High View Theater Corp. owns movie theaters in the shopping centers of a major metropolitan area. The business engaged in the following business transactions:

Feb.   1   Received cash of $60,000 and issued common stock to the investor.
        2   Paid $40,000 cash to purchase land for a theater site.
        5   Borrowed $220,000 from the bank to finance the construction of the new theater. The company signed a note payable to the bank.
        7   Received $20,000 cash from ticket sales and deposited this amount in the bank. (Label the revenue as Sales Revenue.)
       10   Purchased supplies on account, $1,700.

15   Paid theater employee salaries, $2,800, and rent on a theater building, $1,800.

15   Paid property tax expense on theater building, $1,200.

16   Paid $800 on account.

17   Declared and paid a cash dividend of $3,000.

High View uses the following accounts: Cash; Supplies; Land; Accounts Payable; Notes Payable; Common Stock; Dividends; Sales Revenue; Salary Expense; Rent Expense; Property Tax Expense.

Required

1. Prepare an analysis of each business transaction of High View Theater Company, as shown for the February 1 transaction:

   Feb. 1   The asset Cash is increased. Increases in assets are recorded by debits; therefore, debit Cash. The shareholders' equity of the entity is increased. Increases in shareholders' equity are recorded by credits; therefore, credit Common Stock.

2. Journalize each transaction. Explanations are not required.

Problem 2-3A   *Journalizing transactions, posting to T-accounts, and preparing a trial balance*   **(Obj. 2, 3, 4, 5)**

Oliver Goldsmith opened a renovation business on September 3 of the current year. During the first month of operations, he completed the following transactions:

Sept. 3   Goldsmith transferred $25,000 cash from his personal bank account to a business account entitled Oliver's Renovations Ltd. The corporation issued common stock to Goldsmith.

4   Purchased supplies, $200, and furniture, $1,800, on account.

6   Performed design services for a client and received $1,000 cash.

7   Paid $15,000 cash to acquire land for a future office site.

10   Designed a bathroom for a client, billed the client, and received her promise to pay the $600 within one week.

14   Paid for the furniture purchased September 4 on account.

15   Paid assistant's salary, $600.

16   Paid the telephone bill, $120.

17   Received partial payment from client on account, $500.

20   Prepared a recreation room design for a client on account, $800.

24   Paid the water and electricity bills, $110.

28   Received $1,500 cash for helping a client sell a cottage.

30   Paid assistant's salary, $600.

30   Paid rent expense, $500.

30   Declared and paid dividends of $2,400.

Required

Open the following T-accounts: Cash; Accounts Receivable; Supplies; Furniture; Land; Accounts Payable; Common Stock; Dividends; Service Revenue; Salary Expense; Rent Expense; Utilities Expense.

1. Record each transaction in the journal, using the account titles given. Key each transaction by date. Explanations are not required.

2. Post the transactions to the ledger, using transaction dates as posting references in the ledger. Label the balance of each account Bal., as shown in the chapter.

3. Prepare the trial balance of Oliver's Renovations Ltd. at September 30 of the current year.

4. How will what you have learned in this problem help you manage a business?

Problem 2-4A *Journalizing transactions, posting to ledger accounts, and preparing a trial balance* **(Obj. 2, 3, 4, 5)**

The trial balance of Elizabeth Vanza Design Inc. is dated February 14, 19X3.

Elizabeth Vanza Design Inc.
Trial Balance
February 14, 19X3

Account Number	Account	Debit	Credit
11	Cash..	$ 2,000	
12	Accounts receivable	8,000	
13	Supplies..	800	
14	Land...	18,600	
21	Accounts payable		$ 3,000
31	Common stock		10,000
32	Retained earnings..............................		15,000
33	Dividends	1,200	
41	Service revenue................................		7,200
51	Salary expense.................................	3,600	
52	Rent expense	800	
53	Utilities expense...............................	200	
	Total..	$35,200	$35,200

During the remainder of February, Vanza Design completed the following transactions:

Feb.	15	Vanza collected $2,000 cash from a client on account.
	16	Performed design services for a client on account, $900.
	18	Paid utilities, $300.
	20	Paid on account, $1,000.
	21	Purchased supplies on account, $100.
	21	Declared and paid dividends of $1,200.
	21	Paid for a swimming pool for private residence, using personal funds, $13,000.
	22	Received cash of $2,100 for consulting work just completed.
	28	Paid rent, $800.
	28	Paid employees' salaries, $1,600.

Required

1. Record the transactions that occurred during February 15 through 28 in page 3 of the journal. Include an explanation for each entry.

2. Open the ledger accounts listed in the trial balance, together with their balances at February 14. Use the three column account format illustrated in the chapter. Enter Bal. (for previous balance) in the Item column, and place a check mark (✓) in the journal reference column for the February 14 balance in each account

   Post the transactions to the ledger, using dates, account numbers, journal references and posting references.

3. Prepare the trial balance of Elizabeth Vanza Design Inc. at February 28, 19X3.

Problem 2-5A *Correcting errors in a trial balance* **(Obj. 2, 5)**

The following trial balance does not balance:

Zweig Counseling Services Inc.
Trial Balance
June 30, 19X2

Cash	$ 2,000	
Accounts receivable	10,000	
Supplies	900	
Office furniture	3,600	
Land	25,000	
Accounts payable		$ 4,000
Note payable		14,000
Common stock		18,600
Dividends	2,000	
Counseling service revenue		6,500
Salary expense	1,600	
Rent expense	1,000	
Advertising expense	500	
Utilities expense	300	
Property tax expense	100	
Total	$47,000	$43,100

The following errors were detected:

a. The cash balance is overstated by $300.

b. A property tax payment of $500 was omitted from the trial balance.

c. Land should be listed in the amount of $23,000.

d. A $200 purchase of supplies on account was neither journalized nor posted.

e. A $2,800 credit to Counselling Service Revenue was not posted.

f. Rent Expense of $200 was posted as a credit rather than a debit.

g. The balance of Advertising Expense is $600, but it was listed as $500 on the trial balance.

h. A $300 debit to Accounts Receivable was posted as $30.

i. The balance of Utilities Expense is overstated by $70.

j. A $900 debit to the Dividends account was posted as a debit to Common Stock.

Required

Prepare the correct trial balance at June 30. Journal entries are not required.

Problem 2-6A *Recording transactions directly in the ledger; preparing a trial balance*
(Obj. 2, 5, 7)

Diana Flori obtained articles of incorporation from the province of British Columbia and started a telecommunications consulting business called Flori Tele-Consulting Service Inc. During the first month of operations, the business completed the following selected transactions:

a. Flori began the business with an investment of $7,000 cash and a building valued at $60,000. The corporation issued common stock to Flori.

b. Borrowed $30,000 from the bank; signed a note payable.

c. Purchased office supplies on account, $1,300.

d. Paid $18,000 for office furniture.

e. Paid employee salary, $2,200.

f. Performed consulting service on account for client, $2,100.

g. Paid $800 of the account payable created in Transaction *c.*

h. Received a $600 bill for advertising expense that will be paid in the near future.

i. Performed consulting service for customers and received cash, $1,600.

j. Received cash on account, $1,200.

k. Paid the following cash expenses:

(1) Rent for automobile, $700.

(2) Utilities, $400.

l. Declared and paid dividends of $3,500.

Required

1. Open the following T-accounts: Cash; Accounts Receivable; Office Supplies; Office Furniture; Building; Accounts Payable; Note Payable; Common Stock, Dividends; Service Revenue; Salary Expense; Advertising Expense; Rent Expense; Utilities Expense.

2. Record each transaction directly in the T-accounts without using a journal. Use the letters to identify the transactions.

3. Prepare the trial balance of Flori Tele-Consulting Service Inc. at June 30, 19X3.

Problem 2-7A   *Apply the rules of debit and credit and record transactions in the journal (Obj. 2, 3)*

J. Hook operated a fishing charter business, Hookem Charters, Inc., with the following transactions for the month of September:

Sept. 1   J. Hook sold his personal automobile for $15,000. He then invested $14,000 cash and his 10-meter power boat in the charter business and was issued common stock. The boat had originally cost him $40,000, but had a fair market value of $25,000 today.

3   Purchased a new boat by paying $7,000 cash and promising to pay another $14,000 in one week. He felt that this was an excellent bargain as the boat had a list price of $30,000 and he knew it was worth at least $25,000.

4   Paid moorage fees of $1,200 for the month. These fees covered three moorage slips—two for the charter boats and one for Hook's personal live-onboard houseboat.

5   Hired a deckhand at a rate of $400 per week.

9   Took clients out on a charter for $1,000. They paid $600 and promised to pay the balance in 30 days.

10   Paid $1,000 of the amount owing on the boat (Sept. 3) and signed a promissory note for the balance as he was unable to pay the full amount today.

15   Purchased equipment from a supplier. The equipment normally would have cost $4,000 but Hook obtained it for only $3,000 as he took the supplier and her employees out on a day charter.

20   Received $300 from the clients of September 9th as payment on the charter.

26   Paid the deckhand for three weeks' work.

29   Received $2,000 from a client for the charter of the two boats for two days. The client was the owner of a service station and also provided Hook with $600 of gas for the boats as well as $1,400 of repair parts that can be used on the boats.

30   Used $200 of repair parts on each of the three boats.

Required:

Journalize each of the transactions.

Problem 2-8A   *Apply the rules of debit and credit, record transactions, post to the general ledger   (Obj. 2, 3, 4)*

Westco Moving and Storage Inc., owned by W. Westco, had the following account balances, in random order, on December 15, 19X1 (all accounts have their "normal" balances):

Moving fees earned.............	$ 87,200	Cash......................................	$ 1,500
Accounts receivable............	5,800	Storage fees earned	19,300
Rent expense........................	5,700	Notes receivable	15,000
Prepaid rent.........................	500	Utilities expense	800
Common stock......................	35,800	Office supplies	3,200
Office supplies expense......	700	Account payable..................	7,000
Mortgage payable	13,000	Retained earnings................	15,100
Salaries expense...................	63,700	Office equipment.................	4,100
Insurance expense...............	2,100	Moving equipment	49,600
Storage equipment..............	27,800	Income taxes payable..........	4,000

The following events also took place during the final days of the year:

Dec. 16   Realized that an error had been made in posting an entry to "Moving Fees Earned" account. The entry was correctly journalized but $1,200 was accidentally posted as $2,100 in the account. Note—no journal entry is required, but the account balance must be corrected.

   17   Moved a customer's goods to our warehouse for storage. The moving fees were $1,000 and storage fees are $500 per month, payable in 30 days.

   18   Collected a $5,000 note owed to Westco by D. Dalms and collected interest of $600.

   21   Purchased storage equipment for $6,000. Westco paid $1,200, provided moving services for $500 and promised to pay the balance in 60 days.

   22   Signed a lease to rent additional storage facilities in 19X2 for $700 per month and paid the first month's rent.

   23   Collected $1,000 from J. Jones; $750 of this was for moving goods on December 15th (recorded at that time) and the balance was for storage fees for the period of December 16th to 23rd.

   24   Westco paid $1,000 owing on the mortgage. They also issued 1,000 shares of common stock to the mortgage company in settlement of another $5,000 that was due today.

   27   Declared and distributed a dividend of $2,000.

   29   Provided moving services to L. Loma, a lawyer, for $800. Loma paid Westco $500 and provided legal work for the balance.

   31   W. Westco sold 1,000 shares he held in Westco Moving and Storage Inc. to V. Baffle for $4,000.

Required:

1. Journalize the appropriate events for the last part of December.
2. Set up a three-column general ledger account for the "Cash" account (only) and post the appropriate transactions to it.

Problem 2-1B   *Analyzing a trial balance*   *(Obj. 1)*

The owners of McBee Service Company Ltd. are selling the business. They offer the following trial balance to prospective buyers.

McBee Service Company Ltd. Trial Balance December 31, 19XX		
Cash	$ 12,000	
Accounts receivable	27,000	
Prepaid expenses	4,000	
Land	81,000	
Accounts payable		$ 35,000
Note payable		32,000
Common stock		30,000
Dividends	18,000	
Sales revenue		104,000
Rent expense	26,000	
Advertising expense	3,000	
Wage expense	23,000	
Supplies expense	7,000	
Totals	$201,000	$201,000

Your best friend is considering buying McBee Service Company Ltd. He seeks your advice in interpreting this information. Specifically, he asks whether this trial balance is the same as a balance sheet and an income statement. He also wonders whether McBee is a sound company. After all, the accounts are in balance.

Required

Write a short note to answer your friend's questions. To aid his decision, state how he can use the information on the trial balance to compute McBee's net income or state the net loss for the current period. State the amount of net income or net loss in your note.

Problem 2-2B   *Analyzing and journalizing transactions*   *(Obj. 2, 3)*

Lee Quinius practices civil engineering under the business title Lee Quinius, Ltd. During April his engineering practice engaged in the following transactions:

Apr. 1   Quinius deposited $50,000 cash in the business bank account. The business issued common stock to Quinius.
   5   Paid monthly rent on drafting equipment, $700.
   9   Paid $42,000 cash to purchase land for an office site.
  10   Purchased supplies on account, $1,200.
  19   Paid $1,000 on account.
  22   Borrowed $20,000 from the bank for business use. Quinius signed a note payable to the bank in the name of the business.
  30   Revenues earned during the month included $6,000 cash and $5,000 on account.
  30   Paid employee salaries ($2,400), office rent ($1,500), and utilities ($400).
  30   Declared and paid a cash dividend of $4,000.

Quinius's business uses the following accounts: Cash; Accounts Receivable; Supplies; Land; Accounts Payable; Notes Payable; Common Stock; Dividends; Service Revenue; Salary Expense; Rent Expense; Utilities Expense.

Required

1. Prepare an analysis of each business transaction of Lee Quinius, Ltd., as shown for the April 1 transaction:

   Apr. 1   The asset Cash is increased. Increases in assets are recorded by debits; therefore, debit Cash. The shareholders' equity is increased. Increases in shareholders' equity are recorded by credits; therefore, credit Common Stock.

2. Prepare the journal entry for each transaction. Explanations are not required.

Problem 2-3B   *Journalizing transactions, posting to T-accounts, and preparing a trial balance   (Obj. 2, 3, 4, 5)*

Marie Haley opened a translation business on January 2 of the current year. During the first month of operations the business completed the following transactions:

Jan. 2   Haley deposited $30,000 cash in a business bank account entitled Marie Haley, Translation Inc. The corporation issued common stock to Haley.
      3   Purchased supplies, $500, and furniture, $2,600, on account.
      4   Performed translation services for a client and received cash, $300.
      7   Paid cash to acquire land for a future office site, $22,000.
     11   Translated a brochure for a client, billed the client, and received his promise to pay the $800 within one week.
     15   Paid secretary salary, $650.
     16   Paid for the furniture purchased January 3 on account.
     17   Paid the telephone bill, $110.
     18   Received partial payment from client on account, $400.
     19   Translated legal documents for a client on account, $1,600.
     22   Paid the water and electricity bills, $130.
     29   Received $1,800 cash for helping a client in an overseas business transaction.
     31   Paid secretary salary, $650.
     31   Paid rent expense, $700.
     31   Declared and paid dividends of $400.

Required

Open the following T-accounts: Cash; Accounts Receivable; Supplies; Furniture; Land; Accounts Payable; Common Stock; Dividends; Service Revenue; Salary Expense; Rent Expense; Utilities Expense.

1. Record each transaction in the journal, using the account titles given. Key each transaction by date. Explanations are not required.
2. Post the transactions to the ledger, using transaction dates in the ledger. Label the balance of each account *Bal.* as shown in the chapter.
3. Prepare the trial balance of Marie Haley, Translation Inc. at January 31 of the current year.
4. How will what you have learned in this problem help you manage a business?

Problem 2-4B   *Journalizing transactions, posting to ledger accounts, and preparing a trial balance   (Obj. 2, 3, 4, 5)*

The trial balance of the desktop publishing business of William Pittenger at November 15, 19X3, is shown on the next page.

William Pittenger Publishing Inc.
Trial Balance
November 15, 19X3

Account Number	Account	Debit	Credit
11	Cash	$ 3,000	
12	Accounts receivable...........................	8,000	
13	Supplies....................................	600	
14	Land.......................................	35,000	
21	Accounts payable............................		$ 4,400
31	Common stock		18,000
32	Retained earnings		22,000
33	Dividends..................................	2,100	
41	Service revenue		7,100
51	Salary expense..............................	1,800	
52	Rent expense...............................	700	
53	Utilities expense............................	300	
	Total	$51,500	$51,500

During the remainder of November, the business completed the following transactions:

Nov. 16   Collected $4,000 cash from a client on account.
  17   Performed publishing services for a client on account, $1,700.
  19   Paid utilities, $100.
  21   Paid on account, $2,600.
  22   Purchased supplies on account, $200.
  23   Declared and paid dividends of $2,000.
  23   Used personal funds to pay for the renovation of private residence, $55,000.
  24   Received $1,900 cash for design work just completed.
  30   Paid rent, $700.
  30   Paid employees' salaries, $1,800.

Required

1. Record the transactions that occurred during November 16 through 30 in *Page 6* of the journal. Include an explanation for each entry.

2. Post the transactions to the ledger, using dates, account numbers, journal references and posting references. Open the ledger accounts listed in the trial balance together with their balances at November 15. Use the three-column account format illustrated in the chapter. Enter *Bal.* (for previous balance) in the Item column, and place a check mark (✓) in the journal reference column for the November 15 balance of each account.

3. Prepare the trial balance of William Pittenger Publishing Inc. at November 30, 19X3.

Problem 2-5B   *Correcting errors in a trial balance*   *(Obj. 2, 5)*

The trial balance for Woodway Copy Center Ltd., shown on the following page, does not balance. The following errors were detected:

a. The cash balance is overstated by $400.

b. Office maintenance expense of $200 is omitted from the trial balance.

c. Rent expense of $200 was posted as a credit rather than a debit.

d. The balance of Advertising Expense is $300, but it is listed as $400 on the trial balance.

e. A $600 debit to Accounts Receivable was posted as $60.

f. The balance of Utilities Expense is understated by $60.

g. A $1,300 debit to the Dividends account was posted as a debit to Common Stock.

h. A $100 purchase of supplies on account was neither journalized nor posted.

i. A $5,600 credit to Service Revenue was not posted.

j. Office furniture should be listed in the amount of $1,300.

Woodway Copy Center Ltd.		
Trial Balance		
October 31, 19X1		
Cash	$ 3,800	
Accounts receivable	2,000	
Supplies	500	
Office furniture	2,300	
Land	46,000	
Accounts payable		$ 2,000
Note payable		18,300
Common stock		29,500
Dividends	3,700	
Service revenue		4,900
Salary expense	1,000	
Rent expense	600	
Advertising expense	400	
Utilities expense	200	
Property tax expense	100	
Total	$60,600	$54,700

Required

Prepare the correct trial balance at October 31. Journal entries are not required.

Problem 2-6B   *Recording transactions directly in the ledger; preparing a trial balance*
(Obj. 2, 5, 7)

Ken Mazanec obtained articles of incorporation from the province of New Brunswick and started a cable television service called Clearview Cable Corp. During the first month of operations, the business completed the following selected transactions:

a. Mazanec began the business with an investment of $15,000 cash and a building valued at $50,000. The corporation issued common stock to Mazanec.

b. Borrowed $25,000 from the bank; signed a note payable.

c. Paid $32,000 for transmitting equipment.

d. Purchased office supplies on account, $400.

e. Paid employee salary, $1,300.

f. Received $500 for service performed for customers.

g. Sold cable service to customers on account, $2,300.

h. Paid $100 of the account payable created in Transaction (d).

i. Received a $600 bill for utility expense that will be paid in the near future.

j. Received cash on account, $1,100.

k. Paid the following cash expenses:
   (1) Rent on land, $1,000.
   (2) Advertising, $800.
l. Declared and paid dividends of $600.

Required

1. Open the following T-accounts: Cash; Accounts Receivable; Office Supplies; Transmitting Equipment; Building; Accounts Payable; Note Payable; Common Stock; Dividends; Service Revenue; Salary Expense; Rent Expense; Advertising Expense; Utilities Expense.
2. Record the following transactions directly in the T-accounts without using a journal. Use the letters to identify the transactions.
3. Prepare the trial balance of Clearview Cable Corp. at January 31, 19X7.

Problem 2-7B   *Apply the rules of debit and credit, record transactions in the journal*
                (Obj. 2, 3)

J. Lander operated a fishing charter business, U-Landem Charters, Inc., with the following transactions for the month of August:

Aug. 1   J. Lander sold his personal automobile for $16,000. He then invested $15,000 cash and his 10-meter power boat in the charter business. The boat had originally cost him $50,000, but had a fair market value of $30,000 today.

3   Purchased a new boat by paying $8,000 cash and promising to pay another $15,000 in one week. He felt that this was an excellent bargain as the boat had a list price of $28,000 and he knew it was worth at least $26,000.

4   Paid moorage fees of $1,500 for the month. These fees covered three moorage slips—two for the charter boats and one for Hook's personal live-onboard houseboat.

5   Hired a deckhand at a rate of $500 per week.

9   Took clients out on a charter for $1,200. They paid $800 and promised to pay the balance in 30 days.

10   Paid $2,000 of the amount owing on the boat (Aug. 3) and signed a promissory note for the balance as he was unable to pay the full amount today.

15   Purchased equipment from a supplier. The equipment normally would have cost $5,000 but Lander obtained it for only $4,000 as he took the supplier and her employees out on a day charter.

20   Received $200 from the clients of August 9th as payment on the charter.

26   Paid the deckhand for three weeks' work.

29   Received $2,500 from a client for the charter of the two boats for two days. The client was the owner of a service station and also provided Lander with $500 of gas for the boats as well as $2,000 of repair parts that can be used on the boats.

30   Used $300 of repair parts on each of the three boats.

Required:

Journalize each of the transactions.

Problem 2-8B   *Apply the rules of debit and credit, record transactions, post to the general ledger, prepare a trial balance*   **(Obj. 2, 3, 4, 5)**

Eastco Moving and Storage Inc., owned by E. Eastco, had the following account balances, in random order, on December 15, 19X1 (all accounts have their "normal" balances):

Moving fees earned..............	$84,400	Cash..	$ 1,900
Accounts receivable............	4,400	Storage fees earned	20,100
Rent expense.........................	5,900	Notes receivable	13,000
Prepaid rent..........................	600	Utilities expense	500
Common stock......................	37,000	Office supplies	2,900
Office supplies expense......	1,400	Account payable..................	6,000
Mortgage payable	15,000	Retained earnings................	9,900
Salaries expense...................	61,500	Office equipment.................	5,100
Insurance expense...............	3,400	Moving equipment	48,400
Storage equipment..............	28,900	Income taxes payable..........	4,600

The following events also took place during the final days of the year:

Dec. 16   Realized that an error had been made in posting an entry to "Moving Fees Earned" account. The entry was correctly journalized but $2,100 was accidentally posted as $1,200 in the account. Note: no journal entry is required, but the account balance must be corrected.

17   Moved a customer's goods to our warehouse for storage. The moving fees were $1,200 and storage fees are $400 per month, payable in 60 days.

18   Collected a $6,000 note owed to Eastco by A. Adams and collected interest of $900.

21   Purchased storage equipment for $7,000. Eastco paid $1,500, provided moving services for $800 and promised to pay the balance in 60 days.

22   Signed a lease to rent additional storage facilities in 19X2 for $800 per month and paid the first month's rent.

23   Collected $1,200 from L. Smith; $800 of this was for moving goods on December 15th (recorded at that time) and the balance was for storage fees for the period of December 16th to 23rd.

24   Eastco paid $2,000 owing on the mortgage. They also issued 1,000 shares of common stock to the mortgage company in settlement of another $6,000 that was due today.

27   Declared and distributed a dividend of $3,000.

29   Provided moving services to R. Roma, a lawyer, for $1,000. Roma paid Eastco $600 and provided legal work for the balance.

31   E. Eastco sold 1,000 shares he held in Eastco Moving and Storage Inc. to V. Baffle for $4,000.

Required:

1. Journalize the appropriate events for the last part of December.
2. Set up a three-column general ledger account for the "Cash" account (only) and post the appropriate transactions to it.

Challenge Problems

Problem 2-1C   *Understanding the rules of debit and credit*   **(Obj. 2)**

Some individuals, for whatever reason, do not pay income tax or pay less than they should. Often their business transactions are cash transactions so there is no paper trail to prove how much or how little they actually earned. Revenue Canada, however, has a way of dealing with these individuals; they use a model (based on the accounting equation), to calculate how much the individual must have earned.

Revenue Canada is about to audit Dawn Jolliffe for the period January 1, 19X1, to December 31, 19X1. Dawn buys and sells used cars for cash; the purchaser is responsible for having the car certified so it can be licensed and insured. Dawn has $2,000 cash, and no other assets at January 1, 19X1.

Required

1. Use the accounting equation to explain how the Revenue Canada model will be used to audit Dawn.
2. What do you think are the accounting concepts underlying the model?

Problem 2-2C   *Using a formal accounting system.* *(Obj. 3, 4, 6)*

Over the years you have become friendly with a farmer who raises crops, which she sells, and has small herds of beef cattle and sheep. She maintains her basic herds and markets the calves and lambs each fall. Her accounting system is quite simple; all her transactions are in cash. She pays tax each year on her income which she estimates. She indicated to you once that she must be doing it right because Revenue Canada audited her recently and assessed no additional tax.

You are taking your first accounting course and are quite impressed with the information one can gain from a formal accounting system.

Required

Explain to your friend why it would be to her advantage to have a more formal accounting system with accounts, ledgers, and journals.

Extending Your Knowledge

Decision Problems

1. Recording transactions directly in the ledger, preparing a trial balance, and measuring net income or loss   (Obj. 2, 5, 7)

You have been requested by a friend named Lyn Miske to give advice on the effects that certain business transactions will have on the entity she plans to start. Time is short, so you will not be able to do all the detailed procedures of journalizing and posting. Instead, you must analyze the transactions without the use of a journal. Miske will continue in the business only if she can expect to earn monthly net income of $3,500. The following transactions have occurred:

a. Miske deposited $5,000 cash in a business bank account and the corporation issued common stock to Miske.
b. Borrowed $4,000 cash from the bank and signed a note payable due within one year.

c. Paid $300 cash for supplies.

d. Purchased advertising in the local newspaper for cash, $800.

e. Purchased office furniture on account, $2,500.

f. Paid the following cash expenses for one month: secretary salary, $1,400; office rent, $400; utilities, $300; interest, $50.

g. Earned revenue on account $5,300.

h. Earned revenue and received $2,500 cash.

i. Collected cash from customers on account, $1,200.

j. Paid on account, $1,000.

k. Declared and paid dividends of $900.

Required

1. Open the following T-accounts: Cash; Accounts Receivable; Supplies; Furniture; Accounts Payable; Notes Payable; Common Stock; Dividends; Service Revenue; Salary Expense; Advertising Expense; Rent Expense; Utilities Expense; Interest Expense.

2. Record the transactions directly in the accounts without using a journal. Key each transaction by letter.

3. Prepare a trial balance at the current date. List expenses with the largest amount first, the next largest second, and so on. The business name will be Miske Apartment Locators Inc.

4. Compute the amount of net income or net loss for this first month of operations. Would you recommend Miske continue in business?

2. Using the accounting equation   (Obj. 2)

Although all the following questions deal with the accounting equation, they are not related:

1. Explain the advantages of double-entry bookkeeping over single-entry bookkeeping to a friend who is opening a used-book store.

2. When you deposit money in your bank account, the bank credits your account. Is the bank misusing the word *credit* in this context? Why does the bank use the term *credit* to refer to your deposit, and not *debit*?

3. Your friend asks, "When revenues increase assets and expenses decrease assets, why are revenues credits and expenses debits and not the other way around?" Explain to your friend why revenues are credits and expenses are debits.

Ethical Issue

Community Charities, a charitable organization in Winnipeg, Manitoba, has a standing agreement with National Trust. The agreement allows Community Charities to overdraw its cash balance at the bank when donations are running low. In the past, Community Charities managed funds wisely and rarely used this privilege. Greg Osborn has recently become the president of Community Charities. To expand operations, Osborn is acquiring office equipment and spending large amounts for fundraising. During his presidency, Community Charities has maintained a negative bank balance of approximately $1,000.

Required

What is the ethical issue in this situation? State why you approve or disapprove of Osborn's management of Community Charities funds.

Financial Statement Problems

1. *Journalizing transactions*   (Obj. 2, 3)

This problem helps to develop skill in recording by using an actual company's account titles. Refer to the Mark's Work Wearhouse Ltd. financial statements in Appendix A. Assume Mark's completed the following selected transactions during January, 1994:

Jan.   5   Earned sales revenues on account, $1,500,000.
       9   Borrowed $5,000,000 by signing a note payable (long-term debt).
      12   Purchased equipment on account, $9,000,000.
      17   Paid $1,200,000, which represents payment of $1,000,000 on long-term debt plus interest expense of $200,000.
      19   Earned sales revenues and immediately received cash of $500,000.
      22   Collected the cash on account that was earned on January 5.
      24   Paid operating lease rental of $1,300,000, for three months in advance.
      29   Received a home-office electricity bill for $10,000, which will be paid in February. (This is a back line-occupancy expense.)
      29   Paid half the account payable created on January 12.

Required

Journalize these transactions using the following account titles taken from the financial statements of Mark's Work Wearhouse: Accounts Receivable; Cash; Inventories; Prepaid Expenses; Fixed Assets; Accounts Payable; Long-Term Debt; Sales; Cost of Sales, Back Line Expenses–Occupancy; Interest. Explanations are not required.

2. *Journalizing transactions*   (Obj. 2, 3)

Obtain the annual report of an actual company of your choosing. Assume the company completed the following selected transactions during May of the current year:

May   3   Borrowed $350,000 by signing a short-term note payable (may be called short-term debt or other account title).
      5   Paid rent for six months in advance, $4,600.
      9   Earned revenue on account, $74,000.
     12   Purchased equipment on account, $33,000.
     17   Paid a telephone bill, $300 (this is a Selling Expense).
     19   Paid $90,000 of the money borrowed on May 3.
     26   Collected one half of the cash on account from May 9.
     30   Paid the account payable from May 12.

Required

1. Journalize these transactions using the company's actual account titles taken from its annual report. Explanations are not required.

2. Open a ledger account for each account that you used in journalizing the transactions. (For clarity, insert no actual balances in the accounts.) Post the transaction amounts to the accounts. Take the balance of each account.

3. Prepare a trial balance.

Appendix

Typical Charts of Accounts for Different Types of Businesses

SERVICE CORPORATION

ASSETS

Cash
Accounts Receivable
Allowance for Uncollectible
    Accounts
Notes Receivable, Short-
    Term
Interest Receivable
Supplies
Prepaid Rent
Prepaid Insurance
Notes Receivable, Long-
    Term
Land
Furniture
Accumulated
    Depreciation—Furniture
Equipment
Accumulated
    Depreciation—
    Equipment
Building
Accumulated
    Depreciation—Building

LIABILITIES

Accounts Payable
Notes Payable, Short-Term
Salary Payable
Wage Payable
Goods and Services Tax
    Payable
Employee Income Tax
    Payable
Unemployment Insurance
    Payable
Canada Pension Plan
    Payable
Employee Benefits Payable
Interest Payable
Unearned Service Revenue
Notes Payable, Long-Term

SHAREHOLDERS' EQUITY

Common Stock
Retained Earnings
Dividends

Revenues and Gains

Service Revenue
Interest Revenue
Gain on Sale of Land
    (Furniture, Equipment,
    or Building)

Expenses and Losses

Salary Expense
Payroll Benefits Expense
Insurance Expense for
    Employees
Rent Expense
Insurance Expense
Supplies Expense
Uncollectible Account
    Expense
Depreciation Expense—
    Furniture
Depreciation Expense—
    Equipment
Depreciation Expense—
    Building
Property Tax Expense
Interest Expense
Miscellaneous Expense
Loss on Sale (or Exchange)
    of Land (Furniture,
    Equipment, or
    Buildings)

SERVICE PARTNERSHIP

Same as Service Corporation, except for Owners' Equity:

OWNERS' EQUITY

Partner 1, Capital
Partner 2, Capital
Partner *N*, Capital
Partner 1, Drawing
Partner 2, Drawing
Partner *N*, Drawing

MERCHANDISING CORPORATION

ASSETS

Cash
Short-Term Investments
    (Trading Securities)
Accounts Receivable
Allowance for Uncollectible
    Accounts
Notes Receivable, Short-
    Term
Interest Receivable
Inventory
Supplies
Prepaid Rent
Prepaid Insurance
Notes Receivable, Long-
    Term
Investments in Subsidiaries
Investments in Stock
    (Available-for-Sale
    Securities)
Investments in Bonds
    (Held-to-Maturity
    Securities)
Other Receivables, Long-
    Term
Land
Land Improvements
Furniture and Fixtures
Accumulated
    Depreciation—Furniture
    and Fixtures
Equipment
Accumulated
    Depreciation—
    Equipment
Buildings
Accumulated
    Depreciation—Buildings
Organization Cost
Franchises
Patents
Leaseholds
Goodwill

LIABILITIES

Accounts Payable
Notes Payable, Short-Term
Current Portion of Bonds
    Payable
Salary Payable
Wage Payable
Goods and Services Tax
    Payable
Employee Income Tax
    Payable
Unemployment Insurance
    Payable
Canada Pension Plan
    Payable
Employee Benefits Payable
Interest Payable
Income Tax Payable
Unearned Service Revenue
Notes Payable, Long-Term
Bonds Payable
Lease Liability

SHAREHOLDERS' EQUITY

Common Stock
Retained Earnings
Dividends

Revenues and Gains

Sales Revenue
Interest Revenue
Dividend Revenue
Equity-Method Investment
    Revenue
Unrealized Holding Gain
    on Trading Investments
Gain on Sale of
    Investments
Gain on Sale of Land
    (Furniture and Fixtures,
    Equipment, or Building)
Discontinued Operations—
    Gain
Extraordinary Gains

Expenses and Losses

Cost of Goods Sold
Salary Expense
Wage Expense
Commission Expense
Payroll Benefits Expense
Insurance Expense for
    Employees
Rent Expense
Insurance Expense
Supplies Expense
Uncollectible Account
    Expense
Depreciation Expense—
    Land Improvements
Depreciation Expense—
    Furniture and Fixtures
Depreciation Expense—
    Equipment
Depreciation Expense—
    Building
Organization Expense
Amortization Expense—
    Franchises
Amortization Expense—
    Leaseholds
Amortization Expense—
    Goodwill
Income Tax Expense
Unrealized Holding Loss
    on Trading Investments
Loss on Sale of Investments
Loss on Sale (or Exchange)
    of Land (Furniture and
    Fixtures, Equipment, or
    Buildings)
Discontinued Operations—
    Loss
Extraordinary Losses

MANUFACTURING CORPORATION

Same as Merchandising Corporation, except for Assets:

ASSETS

Inventories:
    Materials Inventory
    Work in Progress
        Inventory
    Finished Goods
        Inventory
Factory Wages
Factory Overhead

CHAPTER 3
Measuring Business Income: The Adjusting Process

"We are very satisfied with Harris's leadership at Air Canada," says Captain Gary Dean, former national chairman of [Canadian Air Line Pilots' Association's] Air Canada executive unit. Cheryl Kryzaniwsky, president of the union representing Air Canada's airport and ground workers states: "Even though I don't always agree with everything [Harris] does, at least he has a plan."

The early 1990s were not good years for airlines all around the world. Between 1990 and 1992, airlines all over the world combined to lose US$15.7 billion. Air Canada lost $74 million in fiscal 1990, $218 million in fiscal 1991, $454 million in 1992, and $326 million in 1993.

In February, 1992, Hollis Harris was appointed the new Chief Executive Officer (CEO) of Air Canada with the mandate to make the airline profitable. He recognized that the only way to make the airline profitable was to cut expenses. He did this by cutting wages, from his own salary through pilots, cabin crew, ground crew and managers, reservations, and clerical staff. In 1992, he sold some older planes and reduced commitments for new planes. In addition, he entered into service contracts with other airlines, bought a part-interest in Continental Airlines in the U.S. and expanded Air Canada's overseas routes. All of these measures allowed Harris to cut $155 million from expenses in 1992 and $187 million in 1993. It is expected that Air Canada will break even in 1994 and earn a profit in 1995.

Source: Adapted from Cecil Foster, "Tough Guys Don't Cuss," *Canadian Business*, February, 1995, pp. 23–28.

CHAPTER OBJECTIVES

After studying this chapter, you should be able to

1 Distinguish accrual-basis accounting from cash-basis accounting

2 Apply the revenue and matching principles

3 Make adjusting entries at the end of the accounting period

4 Prepare an adjusted trial balance

5 Prepare the financial statements from the adjusted trial balance

A1 Account for a prepaid expense recorded initially as an expense

A2 Account for an unearned (deferred) revenue recorded initially as a revenue

Short Exercise:

All parts of the financial statements are important in describing the financial condition of a business. Which statement would be most helpful to Air Canada's management in evaluating the company's performance for the past year? **A:** The income statement, because it reports how profitable the company has been for that period.

This story shows how accounting income affects people's behavior—from airline executives to retail stores to investors across the country. Air Canada moved from a situation where losses were increasing every year to break-even to potential profit.

When Air Canada is able to control its costs and increase its revenues, its reported income figures make Air Canada a more attractive investment. In addition, Air Canada is able to expand its services and compete more successfully with other world carriers. On the other hand, when Air Canada loses money, investors sell its stock and it has to pay higher interest rates to borrow money. As can be seen from the vignette you just read, Hollis Harris was able to "turn Air Canada around" and put it on the path to profitability. It was accounting information, in the main, that allowed Harris to make the decisions that effected the change.

The primary goal of business is to earn a profit. Virtually all companies want to earn increasing amounts of profit each year, but, as the Air Canada story indicates, that is not always possible.

Air & Sea Travel, Inc., the travel agency we discussed in the earlier chapters, earns business income by providing travel services for clients. Whether the entity is Air & Sea Travel, or Air Canada, the profit motive increases the owner's drive to carry on the business. As you read this chapter, consider how important accounting income is to a business and how the pursuit of income effects people's behavior.

At the end of each accounting period, the entity prepares its financial statements. The period may be a month, three months, six months, or a full year. Air Canada is typical. The company reports on a quarterly basis—at the end of every three months, with audited financial statements at the end of the year.

Whatever the length of the period, the end accounting product is the financial statements. And the most important single amount in these statements is the net income or net loss—the profit or loss—for the period. Net income captures much information: total revenues minus total expenses for the period. In essence, net income—or net loss—measures the ability of the business to generate revenues from its outputs (products or services) that exceed the costs of its inputs (merchandise, employee labor, supplies, utilities, and so on). A business that consistently earns net income adds value to its owners, its employees, its customers, and society. The business is able to pay its debts. Net income captures these important aspects of a business.

An important step in financial statement preparation is the trial balance. The account balances in the trial balance include the effects of the transactions that occurred during the period—cash collections, purchases of assets, payments of bills, sales of assets and so on. To measure its income, however, a business must do some additional accounting at the end of the period to bring the records up to date before preparing the financial statements. This process is called *adjusting the books* and it consists of making special entries called *adjusting entries*. This chapter focuses primarily on these adjusting entries to help you better understand the nature of business income.

The accounting profession has concepts and principles to guide the measurement of business income. Chief among these are the concepts of accrual accounting, the accounting period, the revenue principle and the matching principle. In this chapter, we apply these (and other) concepts and principles to measure the income and prepare the financial statements of Air & Sea Travel for the month of April.

Accrual-Basis Accounting versus Cash-Basis Accounting

> **OBJECTIVE 1**
> Distinguish accrual-basis accounting from cash-basis accounting

There are two widely used bases of accounting: the accrual basis and cash basis. In **accrual-basis accounting**, an accountant recognizes the impact of a business event as it occurs. When the business performs a service, makes a sale, or incurs an expense, the accountant enters the transaction into the books, whether or not cash has been received or paid. In **cash-basis accounting**, however, the accountant does not record a transaction until cash is received or paid. Cash receipts are treated as revenues and cash payments are handled as expenses.

Suppose a client paid the Four Seasons Hotel in Toronto $15,000 on October 1, 1995, for a six-month stay in a suite to begin October 1, 1995. Exhibit 3-1 shows how hotel revenues would be recorded by the two methods of accounting over the six-month period October 1, 1995, through March 31, 1996. In actuality, the Four Seasons Hotels and Resorts, which operates nearly 40 luxury properties worldwide and serves 3.1 million guests a year, uses accrual-basis accounting to match the expenses and related revenues in a given fiscal period.

GAAP requires that a business use the accrual basis. This means that the accountant records revenues as they are *earned* and expenses as they are *incurred*— not necessarily when cash changes hands.

Using accrual-basis accounting, Air Canada records revenue when it provides transportation services to a client, not when it collects the cash later. Air & Sea Travel records revenue when the business performs services for a client on account. The travel agency has earned the revenue at that time because its efforts have generated an account receivable, a legal claim against the client for whom it did the work. In contrast, if Air & Sea Travel used cash-basis accounting, it would not record revenue at the time the business performed the service. It would wait until it received cash.

EXHIBIT 3-1   *Accrual-Basis Accounting versus Cash-Basis Accounting*

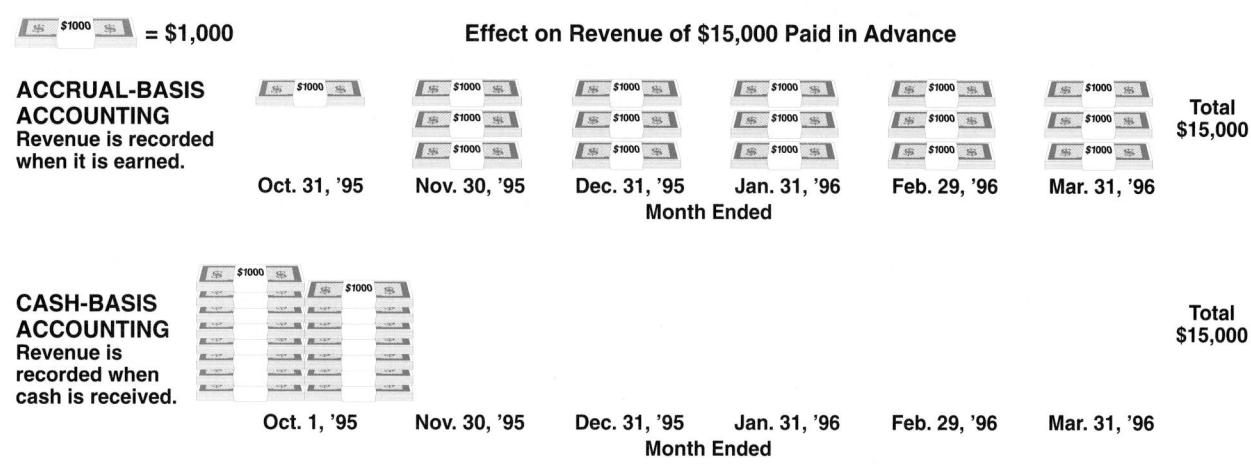

Why does GAAP require that businesses use the accrual basis? What advantage does accrual-basis accounting offer? Suppose Air & Sea Travel's accounting period ends after it has earned some revenue, but before it has collected the money. If it used the cash-basis method, its financial statements would not include this revenue or the related account receivable. As a result, the financial statements would be misleading. Revenue and the asset Accounts Receivable would be understated so the business would look less successful than it actually is. If Air & Sea Travel needs a bank loan to expand, the understated revenue and asset figures might hurt its chances.

Using accrual-basis accounting, Air & Sea Travel treats expenses in a like manner. For instance, salary expense includes amounts paid to employees plus any amount owed to employees but not yet paid. Air & Sea Travel's use of the employee's service, not the payment of cash to the employee, brings about the expense.

Under cash-basis accounting, a business records salary expense only when it actually pays the employee. Suppose Air & Sea owed a travel agent a salary, and the financial statements were drawn up before the business paid. Expenses and liabilities would be understated, so Air & Sea would look more successful than it really is. This incomplete information would give potential creditors an inaccurate accounting.

As these examples show, accrual-basis accounting provides more complete information than does cash-basis accounting. This difference is important because the more complete the data, the better equipped decision-makers are to reach accurate conclusions about the firm's financial health and future prospects. Three concepts used in accrual accounting are the accounting period, the revenue principle, and the matching principle.

The Accounting Period

The only way to know for certain how successfully a business has operated is to close its doors, sell all its assets, pay the liabilities, and return any leftover cash to the owner. This process, called *liquidation*, is the same as going out of business. Obviously, it is not practical for accountants to measure business income in this manner. Instead, businesses need periodic reports on their progress. Accountants slice time into small segments and prepare financial statements for specific periods. Until a business sells all its assets for cash and pays all its liabilities, the amounts reported in its financial statements must be regarded as estimates.

The most basic accounting period is one year, and virtually all businesses prepare annual financial statements. For about 60 percent of companies in a recent Canadian survey, the annual accounting period or *fiscal year* runs the calendar year from January 1 through December 31. The other companies in the survey use a fiscal year ending on some date other than December 31. The year-end date is usually the low point in business activity for the year. Depending on the type of business, the fiscal year may end on April 30, July 31 or some other date. Retailers are a notable example. Traditionally, they have used a fiscal year ending on January 31, because the low point in their business activity has followed the after-Christmas sales during January; Mark's Work Wearhouse and Hudson's Bay Co. are two examples. Eight percent of the companies in the survey mentioned above have a 52–53-week year like Mark's Work Wearhouse.

Managers and investors cannot wait until the end of the year to gauge a company's progress. Companies prepare financial statements for *interim* periods, which are less than a year. Publicly owned companies must issue quarterly financial statements. Managers want financial information more often so monthly financial statements are common. A series of monthly statements can be combined for quarterly and semiannual periods. Most of the discussions in this book are based on an annual accounting period. However, the procedures and statements can also be applied to interim periods as well.

Revenue Principle

The **revenue principle** tells accountants (1) *when* to record revenue, and (2) the *amount* of revenue to record. When we speak of "recording" something in accounting, the act of recording (or recognizing) the item naturally leads to posting to the ledger accounts and preparing the trial balance and the financial statements. Although the financial statements are the end product of accounting and what accountants are most concerned about, our discussions often focus on recording the entry in the journal because that is where the accounting process starts.

The general principle guiding *when* to record revenue is that revenue should be recorded as it has been earned—but not before. In most cases, revenue is earned when the business has delivered a completed good or service to the customer. The business has done everything required by the agreement, including transferring the item to the customer. Exhibit 3-2 shows two situations that provide guidance on when to record revenue. The first situation illustrates when *not* to record revenue. Situation 2 illustrates when revenue should be recorded. If the client pays for Air & Sea Travel's service immediately, the business will debit Cash. If the service is performed on account, Air & Sea will debit Accounts Receivable. In either case, the travel agency should record revenue by crediting the Service Revenue account.

The general principle guiding the *amount* of revenue to record is record revenue equal to the cash value of the goods or the service transferred to the customer. Suppose that in order to obtain a new client, the Lyons perform travel service for the price of $500. Ordinarily, they would have charged $600 for this service. How much revenue should the business record? The answer is $500 because that was the cash value of the transaction. Air and Sea Travel will not receive the full value of $600, so that is not the amount of revenue to record. The business will receive only $500 cash, and that pinpoints the amount of revenue earned.

Short Exercise:
A client pays Air & Sea $900 on March 15 for service to be performed April 1 to June 30. Has Air & Sea earned revenue on March 15? *A:* No. Air & Sea has received the cash but will not perform the service until later. Under the accrual method, Air & Sea will record Unearned Service Revenue on March 15. It is a liability because Air & Sea has an obligation to perform a service in the future.

OBJECTIVE 2
Apply the revenue and matching principles

Matching Principle

The **matching principle** is the basis for recording expenses. Recall that expenses, such as rent, utilities, and advertising, are the costs of operating a business. Expenses are the costs of assets and services that are used up in the earning of revenue. The matching principle directs accountants (1) to identify all expenses incurred during the accounting period, (2) to measure the expenses, and (3) to match them against

EXHIBIT 3-2 *Recording Revenue*

| No transaction has occurred. | The client has taken a trip arranged by Air & Sea Travel, Inc. |
| **Situation 1 — Do Not Record Revenue** | **Situation 2 — Record Revenue** |

EXHIBIT 3-3   *The Matching Principle*

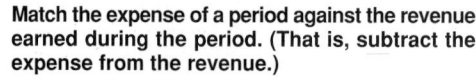

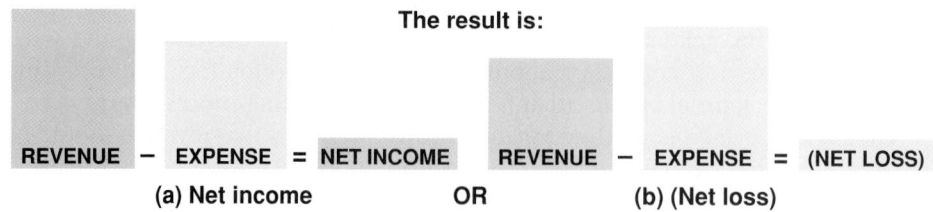

the revenues earned during that same span of time. To match expenses against revenues means to subtract the expenses from the revenues in order to compute net income or net loss. Exhibit 3-3 illustrates the matching principle.

Short Exercise:

Air & Sea Travel, Inc., pays $4,500 on July 31 for office rent for the next three months. Has Air & Sea incurred an expense on July 31? ***A:*** No. Air & Sea has paid cash, but the rent will not expire for three months. Under the accrual method, Air & Sea will record Prepaid Rent on July 31. It is an asset because Air & Sea has paid in advance for the use of an office in the future.

There is a natural link between revenues and some types of expenses. Accountants follow the matching principle by first identifying the revenues of a period and the expenses that can be linked to particular revenues. For example, a business that pays sales commissions to its sales persons will have commission expense if the employees make sales. If they make no sales, the business has no commission expense. *Cost of goods sold* is another example. When merchandise is sold, there must be a cost—the cost incurred by the seller—assigned to the goods sold. If there are no sales, there can be no cost of goods sold.

Other expenses are not so easy to link with particular sales. Monthly rent expense occurs, for example, regardless of the revenues earned during the period. The matching principle directs accountants to identify these types of expenses with a particular time period, such as a month or a year. If Air & Sea Travel employs a secretary at a monthly salary of $1,900, the business will record salary expense of $1,900 each month. Because financial statements appear at definite intervals, there must be some cutoff date for the necessary information. Most entities engage in so many transactions that some are bound to spill over into more than a single accounting period. Air & Sea Travel prepares a monthly statement for the business at April 30. How does it account for a transaction that begins in April but ends in May? How does it bring the accounts up to date for preparing the financial statements? To answer these questions, accountants use the time-period concept.

Time-Period Concept

Managers, investors and creditors make decisions daily and need periodic readings on the business's progress. To meet this need for information, accountants prepare financial statements at regular intervals. Virtually all companies report net income for an annual period and their assets, liabilities, and shareholders' equity at the end of the year. As suggested earlier, most companies also prepare monthly and quarterly financial statements.

The **time-period concept** ensures that accounting information is reported at regular intervals. It interacts with the revenue principle and matching principle to underlie the use of accruals. To measure income accurately, companies update the revenue and expense accounts immediately prior to the end of the period. For example, Finning Ltd., who sells Caterpillar earthmoving equipment, has a December 31 year end. When December 31 falls during a pay period (say, December 31, 1996, is on a Tuesday, and Finning pays its employees weekly on Friday), the company must record the employee compensation owed to the workers for unpaid services performed up to and including December 31. Assume weekly salary and wages expense for Finning is $2,300,000; the entry would be ($\frac{2}{5} \times$ $2,300,000 = $920,000):

1996
Dec. 31 Salary and Wages Expense   920,000
        Salary and Wages Payable.....................   920,000

This entry serves two purposes. It assigns the expense to the proper period. Without the accrual entry at December 31, total expenses for 1996 would be understated, and as a result, net income would be overstated. Incorrectly, the expense would fall in 1997 when Finning makes the next payroll disbursement. The accrual entry also records the liability for reporting on the balance sheet at December 31, 1996. Without the accrual entry, total liabilities would be understated.

At the end of the accounting period, companies also accrue revenues that have been earned but not collected. The remainder of the chapter discusses how to make the necessary adjustments to the accounts.

Adjustments to the Accounts _____

> **OBJECTIVE 3**
> Make adjusting entries at the end of the accounting period

At the end of the period, the accountant prepares the financial statements. This end-of-the-period process begins with the trial balance that lists the accounts and their balances after the period's transactions have been recorded in the journal and posted to the accounts in the ledger. Exhibit 3-4 is the trial balance of Air & Sea Travel, Inc. at April 30, 19X1.

This *unadjusted trial balance* includes some new accounts that will be explained here. It lists most, but not all, of the revenue accounts and the expenses of the travel agency for the month of April. These trial balance amounts are incomplete because they omit certain revenue and expense transactions that affect more than one accounting period. That is why it is called an *unadjusted* trial balance. In most cases, however, we refer to it simply as the trial balance, without the label "unadjusted."

Under the cash basis of accounting, there would be no need for adjustments to the accounts because all April cash transactions would have been recorded. The accrual basis requires adjusting entries at the end of the period in order to produce correct balances for the financial statements. To see why, consider the Supplies account in Exhibit 3-4.

Air & Sea Travel uses supplies in providing travel services for clients during the month. This use reduces the quantity of supplies on hand and thus constitutes an

EXHIBIT 3-4 *Unadjusted Trial Balance*

Air & Sea Travel, Inc.		
Unadjusted Trial Balance		
April 30, 19X1		
Cash..	$24,800	
Accounts receivable......................................	2,250	
Supplies	700	
Prepaid rent..	3,000	
Furniture..	16,500	
Accounts payable..		$13,100
Unearned service revenue		450
Common stock...		20,000
Retained earnings		11,250
Dividends...	3,200	
Service revenue		7,000
Salary expense	950	
Utilities expense	400	
Total...	$51,800	$51,800

expense, just like salary expense or rent expense. Gary and Monica Lyon do not bother to record this expense daily, and it is not worth their while to record supplies expense more than once a month. It is time-consuming to make hourly, daily, or even weekly journal entries to record the expense incurred by the use of supplies. So how does the business account for supplies expense?

By the end of the month, the Supplies balance is not correct. The balance represents the amount of supplies on hand at the start of the month plus any supplies purchased during the month. This balance fails to take into account the supplies used (supplies expense) during the accounting period. It is necessary, then, to subtract the month's expenses from the amount of supplies listed on the trial balance. The resulting new adjusted balance measures the cost of supplies that are still on hand at April 30. This is the correct amount of supplies to report on the balance sheet. Adjusting entries in this way brings the accounts up to date.

Adjusting entries assign revenues to the period in which they are earned and expenses to the period in which they are incurred. They are needed (1) to measure properly the period's income, and (2) to bring related asset and liability accounts to correct balances for the financial statements. For example, an adjusting entry is needed to transfer the amount of supplies used during the period from the asset account Supplies to the expense account Supplies Expense. The adjusting entry updates both the Supplies asset account and the Supplies Expense account. This achieves accurate measures of assets and expenses. Adjusting entries, which are the key to accrual-basis accounting, are made before preparing the financial statements. The end-of-period process of updating the accounts is called *adjusting the accounts, making the adjusting entries,* or *adjusting the books.*

A large company would use accounting software to print out a trial balance. At Canadian Occidental Petroleum Ltd., a multidivisional company that locates, produces, and transports oil and natural gas, each division has its own accounting software that prints a monthly trial balance. The accountants then analyze the amounts on the trial balance, testing them for reasonableness and tracing the balances back to the ledger. If necessary, the accountants might go back to the supporting documents that generated the transactions. This analysis results in the adjusting entries. Posting the adjusting entries updates the ledger accounts. The trial balance has now become the adjusted trial balance. At Canadian Occidental, the adjusted trial balances from all divisions are consolidated. Adjusting entries can be further divided into five categories:

1. Prepaid expenses
2. Depreciation of capital assets
3. Accrued expenses
4. Accrued revenues
5. Unearned revenues

Prepaid Expenses

Key Point:
Prepaid expenses are assets, not expenses.

Prepaid expenses is a category of miscellaneous assets that typically expire or are used up in the near future. Prepaid rent, prepaid insurance, and supplies are examples of prepaid expenses. They are called prepaid expenses because they are expenses that are paid in advance. Salary expense and utilities expense, among others, are *not* prepaid expenses because they are not paid in advance. All companies, large and small, must make adjustments regarding prepaid expenses. For example, Swiss Chalet must contend with such prepayments as rents, packaging supplies, and insurance.

Prepaid Rent   Landlords usually require tenants to pay rent in advance. This prepayment creates an asset for the renter, because that person has purchased the future benefit of using the rented item. Suppose Air & Sea Travel prepays three months' rent on April 1, 19X1, after negotiating a lease for the business office. If the lease specifies monthly rental amounts of $1,000 each, the entry to record the payment for three months is a debit to the asset account, Prepaid Rent, as follows:

Apr. 1   Prepaid Rent ($1,000 × 3)   3,000
         Cash   3,000
        Paid three months' rent in advance.

After posting, Prepaid Rent appears as follows:

Prepaid Rent	
Apr. 1 3,000	

The trial balance at April 30, 19X1 lists Prepaid Rent as an asset with a debit balance of $3,000. Throughout April, the Prepaid Rent account maintains this beginning balance, as shown in Exhibit 3-4.

At April 30, Prepaid Rent should be adjusted to remove from its balance the amount of the asset that has expired, which is one month's worth of the prepayment. By definition, the amount of an asset that has expired is *expense*. This adjusting entry transfers one third, or $1,000 ($3,000 × ⅓), of the debit balance from Prepaid Rent to Rent Expense. The debit side of the entry records an increase in Rent Expense and the credit records a decrease in the asset Prepaid Rent.

Apr. 30 Rent Expense ($3,000 × ⅓)   1,000
         Prepaid Rent   1,000
        To record rent expense.

After posting, Prepaid Rent and Rent Expense appear as follows:

Prepaid Rent				**Rent Expense**	
Apr. 1 3,000	Apr. 30 1,000	⟷	Apr. 30 1,000	
Bal. 2,000			Bal. 1,000	

Correct asset amount, $2,000	→	Total accounted for, $3,000	←	Correct expense amount, $1,000

The full $3,000 has been accounted for: two-thirds measures the asset, and one-third measures the expense. Recording this expense illustrates the matching principle. The same analysis applies to a prepayment of three months' insurance premiums. The only difference is in the account titles, which would be Prepaid Insurance and Insurance Expense instead of Prepaid Rent and Rent Expense. In a computerized system, the adjusting entry crediting the prepaid account and debiting the expense account could be established to recur automatically in each subsequent accounting period until the prepaid account has a zero balance.

The chapter appendix shows an alternate treatment of prepaid expenses. The end result on the financial statements is the same as that for the method given here.

Supplies

Supplies are accounted for the same way as prepaid expenses. On April 2, Air & Sea Travel paid cash of $700 for office supplies.

Apr. 2   Supplies   700
         Cash   700
        Paid cash for supplies.

Assume that the business purchased no additional supplies during April. The April 30 trial balance, therefore, lists Supplies with a $700 debit balance (Exhibit 3-4).

During April, Air Sea & Travel used supplies in performing services for clients. The cost of the supplies used is the measure of *supplies expense* for the month. To measure the business's supplies expense during April, the Lyons count the supplies on hand at the end of the month. This is the amount of the asset still available to the

Short Exercise:

At the beginning of the month, supplies were $5,000. During the month, $7,800 of supplies were purchased. At month's end, it was determined that $3,600 of supplies were still on hand. What are the adjusting entry and the ending balance in the Supplies account?

A:

Supplies Expense 9,200
   Supplies   9,200

Ending balance = $5,000 + $7,800 − $9,200 = $3,600

business. Assume the count indicates that supplies costing $400 remain. Subtracting the entity's $400 of supplies on hand at the end of April from the cost of supplies available during April ($700) measures supplies expense during the month ($300).

Cost of asset available during the period		Cost of asset on hand at the end of the period		Cost of asset used (expense) during the period
$700	−	$400	=	$300

The April 30 adjusting entry to update the Supplies account and to record the supplies expense for the month debits the expense and credits the asset:

Apr. 30 Supplies Expense ($700 – $400) 300
          Supplies..   300
         To record supplies expense.

After posting, the Supplies and Supplies Expense accounts appear as follows:

Supplies				Supplies Expense	
Apr. 2	700	Apr. 30	300	Apr. 30	300
Bal.	400			Bal.	300

Correct asset amount, $400 → Total accounted for, $700 ← Correct expense amount, $300

The Supplies account enters the month of May with a $400 balance, and the adjustment process is repeated each month.

Depreciation of Capital Assets

The logic of the accrual basis is best illustrated by how businesses account for capital assets. **Capital assets** are long-lived assets, such as land, buildings, furniture, machinery and equipment. As one accountant said, "All assets but land are on a march to the junkyard." That is, all capital assets but land decline in usefulness as they age. This decline is an *expense* to the business. Accountants systematically spread the cost of each capital asset, except land, over the years of its useful life. This process of allocating cost to expense is called **depreciation** or **amortization**.

Similarity to Prepaid Expenses   The concept underlying accounting for plant assets and depreciation expense is the same as for prepaid expenses. In a sense, plant assets are large prepaid expenses that expire over a number of periods. For both prepaid expenses and plant assets, the business purchases an asset that wears out or is used up. As the asset is used, more and more of its cost is transferred from the asset account to the expense account. The major difference between prepaid expenses and plant assets is the length of time it takes for the asset to lose its usefulness. Prepaid expenses usually expire within a year, whereas most plant assets remain useful for a number of years.

Consider Air & Sea Travel's operations. Suppose on April 3, the business purchased furniture on account for $16,500.

Apr. 3 Furniture 16,500
          Accounts Payable.......................................   16,500
         Purchased office furniture on account.

After posting, the Furniture account appears as follows:

Furniture	
Apr. 3	16,500

In accrual-basis accounting, an asset is recorded when the furniture is acquired. Then, a portion of the asset's cost is transferred from the asset account to Depreciation Expense each period that the asset is used. This method matches the asset's expense to the revenue of the period, which is an application of the matching principle. In many computerized systems, the adjusting entry for depreciation is programmed to occur automatically each month for the duration of the asset's life.

Gary and Monica Lyon believes the furniture will remain useful for five years and be virtually worthless at the end of its life. One way to compute the amount of depreciation for each year is to divide the cost of the asset ($16,500 in our example) by its useful life (5 years). This procedure—called the straight-line method—gives annual depreciation of $3,300 ($16,500/5 years = $3,300 per year). Depreciation for the month of April is $275 ($3,300/12 months = $275 per month). Chapter 10 covers depreciation in more detail.

The Accumulated Depreciation Account   Depreciation expense for April is recorded by the following entry:

Apr. 30 Depreciation Expense 275
          Accumulated Depreciation—Furniture.........   275
          To record depreciation expense on furniture.

> **Key Point:**
> Use a separate Depreciation Expense account and Accumulated Depreciation account for each type of asset (Depreciation Expense— Furniture, Depreciation Expense—Buildings, and so on). You must know the amount of depreciation recorded for each asset.

Accumulated Depreciation is credited instead of Furniture, because the original cost of the capital asset is an objective measurement, and that figure remains in the original asset account as long as the business uses the asset. Accountants may refer to that account if they need to know how much the asset costs. This information is useful in a decision about whether to replace the furniture and the amount to pay. The amount of depreciation, however, is an *estimate*. Accountants use the **Accumulated Depreciation** account to show the cumulative sum of all depreciation expense from the date of acquiring the asset. Therefore, the balance in this account increases over the life of the asset.

Accumulated Depreciation is a *contra asset* account, which means an asset account with a normal credit balance. A *contra account* has two distinguishing characteristics: (1) it always has a companion account, and (2) its normal balance is opposite that of the companion account. In this case, Accumulated Depreciation accompanies Furniture. It appears in the ledger directly after Furniture. Furniture has a debit balance, and therefore Accumulated Depreciation, a contra asset, has a credit balance. All contra asset accounts have credit balances.

A business carries an accumulated depreciation or amortization account for each depreciable asset. If a business has a building and a machine, for example, it will carry the accounts Accumulated Depreciation—Building, and Accumulated Depreciation—Machine.

After the depreciation entry has been posted, the Furniture, Accumulated Depreciation, and Depreciation Expense accounts of Air & Sea Travel, Inc. are

> **Short Exercise:**
> (1) What is the book value of Air & Sea Travel's furniture at the end of May? (2) Is that what the furniture could be sold for then? (3) What is the asset's book value at the end of its life? **A:** (1) $16,500 − $275 − $275 = $15,950. (2) Not necessarily. *Book value* represents the part of the asset's *cost* that has not yet been depreciated. (3) $0.

Furniture		Accumulated Depreciation—Furniture			Depreciation Expense—Furniture		
Apr. 3 16,500			Apr. 30	275	Apr. 30	275	
Bal. 16,500			Bal.	275	Bal.	275	

Book Value   The balance sheet shows the relationship between Furniture and Accumulated Depreciation. The balance of Accumulated Depreciation is subtracted from the balance of Furniture. This net amount of a capital asset (cost minus accumulated depreciation) is called its **book value**, or *net book value*, as shown below for Furniture:

Capital Assets

Furniture...	$16,500
Less: Accumulated Depreciation..	275
Book Value..	$16,225

Because Accumulated Depreciation is reported with its companion account to determine the asset's book value, Accumulated Depreciation is called a *valuation account*.

Suppose the travel agency owns a building that cost $48,000, on which annual depreciation is $2,400. The amount of depreciation for one month would be $200 (i.e., $2,400/12), and the following entry records depreciation for April.

Apr. 30	Depreciation Expense—Building	200	
	Accumulated Depreciation—Building		200
	To record depreciation on building.		

The balance sheet at April 30 would report Air & Sea Travel's capital assets as shown in Exhibit 3-5.

EXHIBIT 3-5   *Capital Assets on the Balance Sheet of Air & Sea Travel, Inc. (April 30)*

Capital Assets

Furniture..	$16,500	
Less: Accumulated Depreciation	275	$16,225
Building	48,000	
Less: Accumulated Depreciation	200	47,800
Book Value of Capital Assets....................................		$64,025

Exhibit 3-6 shows how Inco—producers of nickel, copper, alloys, and other primary metal products—displayed Property, Plant, and Equipment in its annual report. Inco has mines and mining plants located around the world; they are displayed in line 1 of Exhibit 3-6. Lines 2, 3, 5, and 6 list the costs of processing facilities and other buildings used for offices, production, and research as well as air conditioners, computers, plumbing, and so on, in those facilities and buildings. In addition, trucks and automobiles and other such vehicles would be included.

EXHIBIT 3-6   *Inco's Reporting of Property, Plant, and Equipment (Amounts in Thousands)*

Mines and mining plants	$2,089,476
Processing facilities	2,242,168
Other	413,508
Primary metals facilities	4,745,152
Alloys and engineered products	591,584
Other facilities	95,792
Total property, plant, and equipment at cost	5,432,528
Accumulated depreciation	2,233,479
Accumulated depletion	691,550
	2,925,029
Property, plant, and equipment, net	$2,507,499

Now, however, let's return to Air & Sea Travel's situation.

Accrued Expenses

Businesses often incur expenses before they pay cash. Payment is not due until later. Consider an employee's salary. The employer's salary expense and salary payable grow as the employee works, so the liability is said to *accrue*. Another example is interest expense on a note payable. Interest accrues as the clock ticks. The term **accrued expense** refers to an expense that the business has incurred but has not yet paid.

It is time-consuming to make hourly, daily, or even weekly journal entries to accrue expenses. Consequently, the accountant waits until the end of the period. Then an adjusting entry brings each expense (and related liability) up to date just before the financial statements are prepared.

Salary Expense Most companies pay their employees at set times. Suppose Air & Sea Travel pays its employee a monthly salary of $1,900, half on the 15th and half on the last day of the month. Here is a calendar for April that has paydays circled:

APRIL

S	M	T	W	T	F	S
					1	2
3	4	5	6	7	8	9
10	11	12	13	14	(15)	16
17	18	19	20	21	22	23
24	25	26	27	28	29	(30)

Assume that if either payday falls on a weekend, Air & Sea Travel pays the employee on the following Monday. During April, the agency paid its employee's first half-month salary of $950 on Friday, April 15, and recorded the following entry:

Apr. 15	Salary Expense	950	
	Cash		950
	To pay salary.		

After posting, the Salary Expense account is

Salary Expense

Apr. 15	950	

The trial balance at April 30 (Exhibit 3-4) includes Salary Expense, with its debit balance of $950. Because April 30, the second payday of the month, falls on a Saturday, the second half-month amount of $950 will be paid on Monday, May 2. Without an adjusting entry, this second $950 amount is not included in the April 30 trial balance amount for Salary Expense. Therefore, at April 30, the business adjusts for additional *salary expense* and *salary payable* of $950 by recording an increase in each of these accounts as follows:

Apr. 30	Salary Expense	950	
	Salary Payable		950
	To accrue salary expense.		

After posting, the Salary Expense and Salary Payable accounts appear as follows:

Salary Expense

Apr.15	950	
Apr. 30	**950**	
Bal.	1,900	

Salary Payable

		Apr. 30	950
		Bal.	950

Short Exercise:

What is the adjusting entry for this situation? Weekly salaries for a five-day week total $3,500, payable on Friday. April 30 falls on a Tuesday.

A: $3,500 × 2/5 = $1,400. The adjusting entry is:

Salary Expense 1,400
    Salary Payable 1,400

The accounts at April 30 now contain the complete salary information for the month. The expense account has a full month's salary, and the liability account shows the portion that the business still owes.

Air & Sea Travel, Inc. will record the payment of this liability on May 2 by debiting Salary Payable and crediting Cash for $950. This payment entry does not affect April or May expenses because the April expense was recorded on April 15 and April 30. May expense will be recorded in a like manner. All accrued expenses are recorded with similar entries—a debit to the appropriate expense account and a credit to the related liability account.

Many computerized systems contain a payroll module, or functional unit. The adjusting entry for accrued salaries is automatically journalized and posted at the end of each accounting period.

Accrued Revenues

Businesses often earn revenue before they receive the cash because collection occurs later. A revenue that has been earned but not yet received in cash is called an **accrued revenue**. Assume Air & Sea Travel is hired on April 15 by Guerrero Tours Co. Ltd. to perform services on a monthly basis. Under this agreement, Guerrero will pay Air & Sea Travel $500 monthly, with the first payment on May 15. During April, Air & Sea Travel will earn half a month's fee, $250. On April 30, Air & Sea Travel's accountant makes the following adjusting entry to record an increase in Accounts Receivable and Service Revenue:

Apr. 30	Accounts Receivable ($500 × ½)	250	
	Service Revenue		250
	To accrue service revenue.		

Short Exercise:

Suppose Air & Sea Travel held a note receivable from a client. At the end of April, there is $125 of interest due. Prepare the adjusting entry:

A: Interest
Receivable...........125
Interest Revenue 125

Recall that Accounts Receivable has an unadjusted balance of $2,250 and the Service Revenue unadjusted balance is $7,000 (Exhibit 3-4). Posting this adjustment has the following effects on these two accounts:

Accounts Receivable				Service Revenue	
	2,250				7,000
Apr. 30	250			**Apr. 30**	250
Bal.	2,500			Bal.	7,250

This adjusting entry illustrates accrual accounting and the revenue principle in action. Without the adjustment, the travel agency's financial statements would be misleading—they would understate Accounts Receivable and Service Revenue by $250 each. All accrued revenues are accounted for similarly—by debiting a receivable and crediting a revenue.

Unearned Revenues

Key Point:
An unearned revenue is a liability, not a revenue.

Some businesses collect cash from customers in advance of doing work for the customer. This creates a liability called **unearned revenue**, which is an obligation arising from receiving cash in advance of providing a product or service. Only when the job is completed will the business have earned the revenue. Suppose Baldwin Investments Ltd. engages Air Sea & Travel's services, agreeing to pay the travel agency $450 monthly, beginning immediately. If Baldwin makes the first payment on April 20, Air & Sea Travel records this increase in the business's liabilities as follows:

Apr. 20	Cash	450	
	Unearned Service Revenue		450
	Received revenue in advance.		

After posting, the liability account appears as follows:

Unearned Service Revenue

| | Apr. 20 | 450 |

Short Exercise:
In which, if any, of the five categories of adjusting entries would the following transactions fall? (1) Paid one year's insurance in advance. (2) Recorded part of a building's cost as an expense for the current period. (3) Recorded revenue from renting a building before receiving cash. (4) Paid a bill for maintenance of company automobiles.

A: (1) Prepaid expense. (2) Depreciation. (3) Accrued revenue. (4) No adjusting entry necessary.

Unearned Service Revenue is a liability because it represents Air & Sea Travel's obligation to perform service for the client. The April 30 unadjusted trial balance (Exhibit 3-4) lists this account with a $450 credit balance prior to the adjusting entries. During the last 10 days of the month—April 21 through April 30—the travel agency will have *earned* one third (10 days divided by April's total 30 days) of the $450, or $150. Therefore, the accountant makes the following adjustment to decrease the liability, Unearned Service Revenue, and to record an increase in Service Revenue:

Apr. 30	Unearned Service Revenue ($450 × ⅓).................	150	
	Service Revenue...		150
	To record service revenue that has been earned.		

This adjusting entry shifts $150 of the total amount from the liability account to the revenue account. After posting, the balance of Service Revenue is increased by $150 and the balance of Unearned Service Revenue has been reduced to $300.

Unearned Service Revenue

Apr. 30	150	Apr. 20	450
		Bal.	300

Service Revenue

			7,000
		Apr. 30	250
		Apr. 30	150
		Bal.	7,400

Correct liability amount, $300 → Total accounted for, $450 ← Correct revenue amount, $150

Short Exercise:
What is the result on the financial statements of omitting this adjusting entry?

A: Liabilities are overstated by $150; revenues, net income, and shareholders' equity are understated by $150.

All types of revenues that are collected in advance are accounted for similarly.
An unearned revenue to one company can be a prepaid expense to the company that made the payment. For example, suppose that two months in advance Xerox

STOP & THINK

Consider the tuition you pay. Assume that one semester's tuition costs $500 and that you make a single payment at the start of the term. Can you make the journal entries to record the tuition transaction on your own books and on the books of your college or university?

Answer:

	Your Entries		
Start of semester:	Prepaid Tuition	500	
	Cash.......................		500
	Paid semester tuition.		
End of semester:	Tuition Expense	500	
	Prepaid Tuition		500
	To record tuition expense.		

	Your College's Entries		
	Cash	500	
	Unearned Tuition......		500
	Received revenue in advance.		
	Unearned tuition:		
	Unearned Tuition...........	500	
	Tuition Revenue........		500
	To record unearned tuition revenue that has been earned.		

EXHIBIT 3-7   *Prepaid- and Accrual-Type Adjustments*

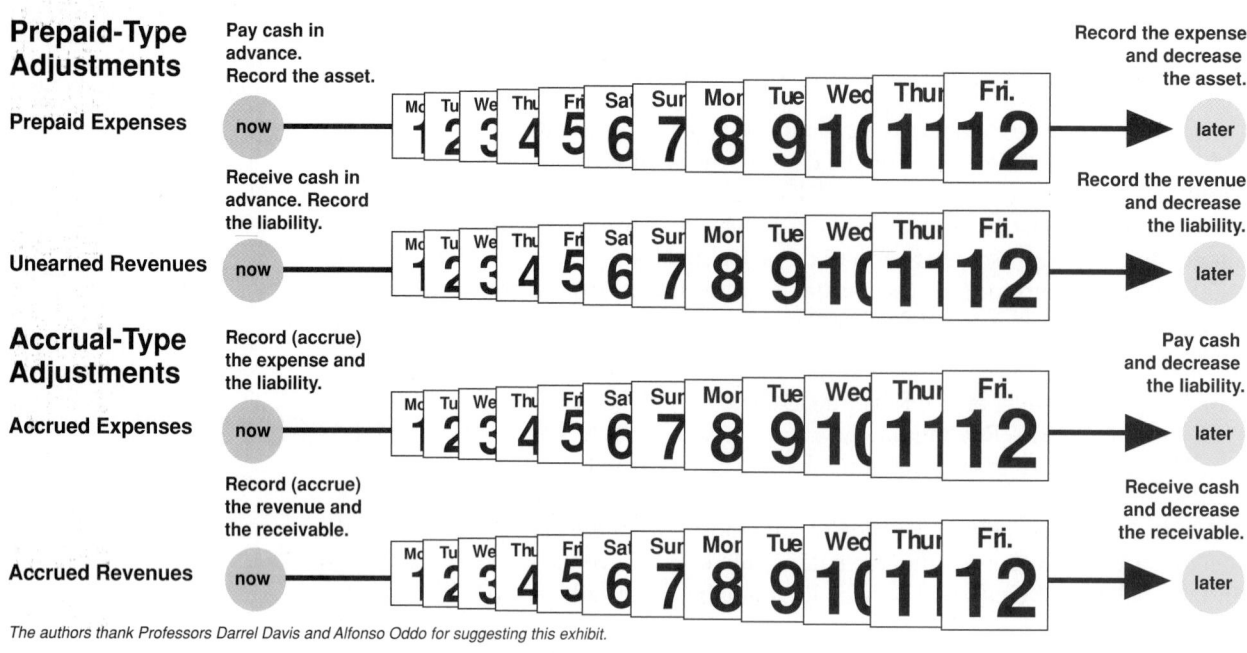

The authors thank Professors Darrel Davis and Alfonso Oddo for suggesting this exhibit.

Corporation paid American Airlines $1,800 for the airfare of Xerox executives. To Xerox the payment is Prepaid Travel Expense. To American Airlines, the receipt of cash creates Unearned Service Revenue. After the executives take the trip, American Airlines records the revenue.

The chapter appendix shows an alternate treatment of unearned revenues. Exhibit 3-7 diagrams the timing of prepaid-type and accrual-type adjusting entries.

Summary of the Adjusting Process

One purpose of the adjusting process is to measure business income, so each adjusting entry affects at least one income statement account—a revenue or an expense. The other purpose of the adjusting process is to update the balance sheet accounts. Therefore, the other side of the entry—a debit or a credit—affects an asset or a liability. No adjusting entry debits or credits Cash because the cash transactions are recorded at other times. The end-of-period adjustment process is reserved for the noncash transactions that are required by accrual-basis accounting. Exhibit 3-8 summarizes the adjusting entries.

EXHIBIT 3-8   *Summary of Adjusting Entries*

Type of Account Debited	Category of Adjusting Entries	Type of Account Credited
Expense	Prepaid expense	Asset
Expense	Depreciation/Amortization	Contra asset
Expense	Accrued expense	Liability
Asset	Accrued revenue	Revenue
Liability	Unearned revenue	Revenue

Adapted from Beverly Terry.

Concept Highlight

Overview of the Adjusting Entries ———————————

Exhibit 3-9 summarizes the adjusting entries of Air & Sea Travel, Inc. at April 30. Panel A of the exhibit briefly describes the data for each adjustment, Panel B gives the adjusting entries, and Panel C shows the accounts after they have been posted. The adjustments are keyed by letter.

Adjusted Trial Balance ———————————————

OBJECTIVE 4
Prepare an adjusted trial balance

This chapter began with the trial balance before any adjusting entries—the unadjusted trial balance (Exhibit 3-4). After the adjustments are journalized and posted, the accounts appear as shown in Exhibit 3-9, Panel C. A useful step in preparing the financial statements is to list the accounts, along with their adjusted balances, on an **adjusted trial balance**. This document has the advantage of listing all the accounts and their adjusted balances in a single place. Exhibit 3-10 shows the preparation of the adjusted trial balance.

The format of Exhibit 3-10 is called a *work sheet*. We will consider the work sheet further in Chapter 4. For now, simply note how clearly this format presents the data. The information in the Account Title column and in the Trial Balance columns is drawn directly from the trial balance. The two Adjustments columns list the debit and credit adjustments directly across from the appropriate account title. Each adjusting debit is identified by a letter in parentheses that refers to the adjusting entry.

EXHIBIT 3-9   *Journalizing and Posting the Adjusting Entries*

Panel A: Information for Adjustments at April 30, 19X1

a. Accrued service revenue, $250.
b. Supplies on hand, $400.
c. Prepaid rent expired, $1,000.
d. Depreciation on furniture, $275.
e. Accrued salary expense, $950.
f. Amount of unearned service revenue that has been earned, $150.

Panel B: Adjusting Entries

a. Accounts Receivable	250	
Service Revenue		250
To accrue service revenue.		
b. Supplies Expense	300	
Supplies		300
To record supplies used.		
c. Rent Expense	1,000	
Prepaid Rent		1,000
To record rent expense.		
d. Depreciation Expense—Furniture	275	
Accumulated Depreciation—Furniture		275
To record depreciation on furniture.		
e. Salary Expense	950	
Salary Payable		950
To accrue salary expense.		
f. Unearned Service Revenue	150	
Service Revenue		150
To record unearned revenue that has been earned.		*(cont'd…)*

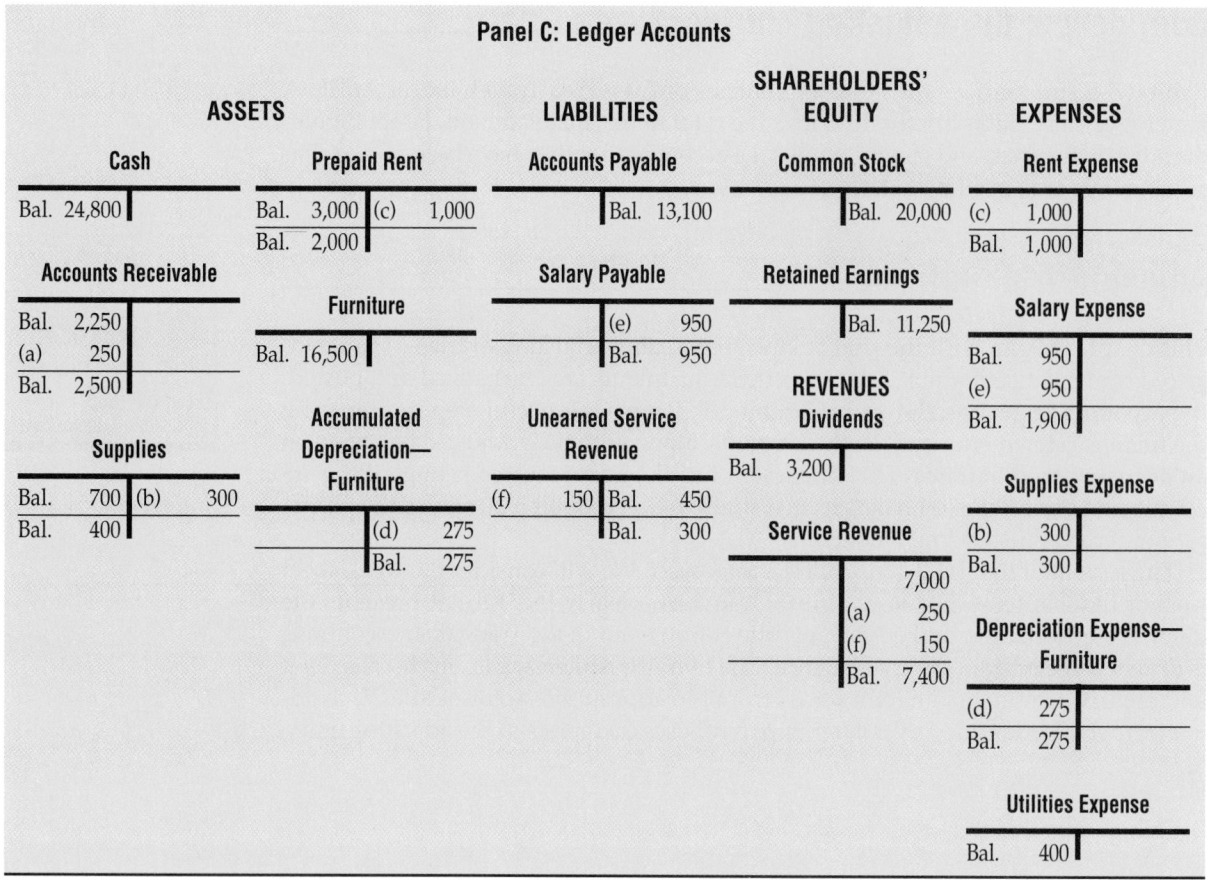

Panel C: Ledger Accounts

Key Point:

The differences between the amounts in the trial balance and in the adjusted trial balance of Exhibit 3-10 result from the adjusting entries. If the adjusting entries were not given, you could obtain them by computing the differences between the adjusted and unadjusted amounts.

For example, the debit labeled (a) on the work sheet refers to the debit adjusting entry of $250 to Accounts Receivable in Panel B of Exhibit 3-9. Likewise for credit adjusting entries, the corresponding credit, labeled (a), refers to the $250 credit to Service Revenue.

The Adjusted Trial Balance columns give the adjusted account balances. Each amount on the adjusted trial balance of Exhibit 3-10 is computed by combining the amounts from the unadjusted trial balance plus or minus the adjustments. For example, Accounts Receivable starts with a debit balance of $2,250. Adding the $250 debit amount from adjusting entry (a) gives Accounts Receivable an adjusted balance of $2,500. Supplies begins with a debit balance of $700. After the $300 credit adjustment, its adjusted balance is $400. More than one entry may affect a single account, as is the case for Service Revenue. If an account is unaffected by the adjustments, it will show the same amount on both the adjusted and unadjusted trial balances. This is true for Cash, Furniture, Accounts Payable, and the Dividends accounts.

OBJECTIVE 5

Prepare the financial statements from the adjusted trial balance

Preparing the Financial Statements from the Adjusted Trial Balance

The April financial statements of Air & Sea Travel, Inc., can be prepared from the adjusted trial balance. Exhibit 3-11 shows how the accounts are distributed from the adjusted trial balance to these three financial statements. The income statement (Exhibit 3-12) comes from the revenue and expense accounts. The statement of retained earnings (Exhibit 3-13) shows the reasons for the change in retained earnings during the period. The balance sheet (Exhibit 3-14) reports the assets, liabilities, and shareholders' equity.

EXHIBIT 3-10   *Preparation of Adjusted Trial Balance*

Air & Sea Travel, Inc.
Preparation of Adjusted Trial Balance
April 30, 19X1

Account Title	Trial Balance Debit	Trial Balance Credit	Adjustments Debit		Adjustments Credit		Adjusted Trial Balance Debit	Adjusted Trial Balance Credit
Cash	24,800						24,800	
Accounts receivable	2,250		(a)	250			2,500	
Supplies	700				(b)	300	400	
Prepaid rent	3,000				(c)	1,000	2,000	
Furniture	16,500						16,500	
Accumulated depreciation					(d)	275		275
Accounts payable		13,100						13,100
Salary payable					(e)	950		950
Unearned service revenue		450	(f)	150				300
Common stock		20,000						20,000
Retained earnings		11,250						11,250
Dividends	3,200						3,200	
Service revenue		7,000			(a)	250		7,400
					(f)	150		
Rent expense			(c)	1,000			1,000	
Salary expense	950		(e)	950			1,900	
Supplies expense			(b)	300			300	
Depreciation expense			(d)	275			275	
Utilities expense	400						400	
	51,800	51,800		2,925		2,925	53,275	53,275

EXHIBIT 3-11   *Preparing the Financial Statements of Air & Sea Travel, Inc., from the Adjusted Trial Balance*

Account Title	Adjusted Trial Balance Debit	Adjusted Trial Balance Credit	
Cash	24,800		
Accounts receivable	2,500		
Supplies	400		
Prepaid rent	2,000		
Furniture	16,500		Balance Sheet (Exhibit 3-14)
Accumulated depreciation		275	
Accounts payable		13,100	
Salary payable		950	
Unearned service revenue		300	
Common stock		20,000	
Retained earnings		11,250	Statement of Retained Earnings (Exhibit 3-13)
Dividends	3,200		
Service revenue		7,400	
Rent expense	1,000		
Salary expense	1,900		Income Statement (Exhibit 3-12)
Supplies expense	300		
Depreciation expense	275		
Utilities expense	400		
	53,275	53,275	

EXHIBIT 3-12   Income Statement

Air & Sea Travel, Inc. Income Statement for the month ended April 30, 19X1		
Revenue		
Service revenue		$7,400
Expenses		
Salary expense	$1,900	
Rent expense	1,000	
Utilities expense	400	
Supplies expense	300	
Depreciation expense	275	
Total expenses		3,875
Net income		$3,525

EXHIBIT 3-13   Statement of Retained Earnings

①

Air & Sea Travel, Inc. Statement of Retained Earnings for the month ended April 30, 19X1	
Retained earnings, April 1, 19X1	$11,250
Add: Net income	3,525
	14,775
Less: Dividends	3,200
Retained earnings, April 30, 19X1	$11,575

EXHIBIT 3-14   Balance Sheet

②

Air & Sea Travel, Inc. Balance Sheet April 30, 19X1				
Assets			**Liabilities**	
Cash		$24,800	Accounts payable	$13,100
Accounts receivable		2,500	Salary payable	950
Supplies		400	Unearned service	
Prepaid rent		2,000	revenue	300
Furniture	$16,500		Total liabilities	14,350
Less: Accumulated				
depreciation	275	16,225	**Shareholders' Equity**	
			Common stock	20,000
			Retained earnings	11,575
			Total shareholders' equity	31,575
			Total liabilities and	
Total assets		$45,925	shareholders' equity	45,925

Financial Statements

The financial statements are best prepared in the order shown: the income statement first, followed by the statement of retained earnings and then, the balance sheet. The essential features of all financial statements are (1) the name of the entity, (2) the title of the statement, (3) the date or the period covered by the statement and (4) the body of the statement.

It is customary to list expenses in descending order by amount, as shown in Exhibit 3-12. However, Miscellaneous Expense, a *catch-all* account for expenses that do not fit another category, is usually reported last regardless of its amount.

Relationships among the Three Financial Statements

The arrows in Exhibits 3-12, 3-13, and 3-14 illustrate the relationship among the income statement, the statement of shareholders' equity, and the balance sheet. Consider why the income statement is prepared first and the balance sheet last.

1. The income statement reports net income or net loss, figured by subtracting expenses from revenues. Because revenues and expenses are shareholders' equity accounts, their net figure is then transferred to the statement of retained earnings. Note that net income in Exhibit 3-12, $3,525, increases retained earnings in Exhibit 3-13. A net loss would decrease retained earnings.

2. Retained earnings is a balance sheet account, so the ending balance in the statement of retained earnings is transferred to the balance sheet. This amount is the final balancing element of the balance sheet. To solidify your understanding of this relationship, trace the $11,575 figure from Exhibit 3-13 to Exhibit 3-14.

You may be wondering why the total assets on the balance sheet ($45,925 in Exhibit 3-14) do not equal the total debits on the adjusted trial balance ($53,275 in Exhibit 3-11). Likewise, the total liabilities and shareholders' equity do not equal

STOP & THINK

Examine Air & Sea Travel's adjusted trial balance in Exhibit 3-10. If the accountant forgot to record the $950 accrual of salary expense at April 30, what net income would the travel agency have reported for April? What total assets, total liabilities, and total shareholders' equity would the balance sheet have reported at April 30?

Answer: Omission of the salary accrual would produce these effects:

1. Net income would have been reported on the income statement (Exhibit 3-12) as $4,475 (i.e., $3,525 + $950).
2. Total assets would have been unaffected by the error—$45,925, as reported on the balance sheet (Exhibit 3-14).
3. Total liabilities would have been reported as $13,400 (i.e., $14,350 – $950) on the balance sheet (Exhibit 3-14).
4. Shareholders' equity (Common Stock plus Retained Earnings) would have been reported at $32,525 (i.e., $31,575 + $950) on the balance sheet (Exhibit 3-14).

This specific example addresses an accounting-error question. But the analysis needed to compute these amounts is important to marketing, finance, statistics, and management personnel in business—because everyone is affected by the amount of the net income that a business reports.

the total credits on the adjusted trial balance. The reason for these differences is that Accumulated Depreciation and Dividends are *subtracted* from their related accounts on the balance sheet, but *added* in their respective columns on the adjusted trial balance.

Summary Problem for Your Review

The trial balance of O'Malley's Service Corp. pertains to December 31, 19X3, which is the end of its year-long accounting period.

O'Malley's Service Corp.
Trial Balance
December 31, 19X3

Cash	$ 198,000	
Accounts receivable	370,000	
Supplies	6,000	
Furniture and fixtures	100,000	
Accumulated depreciation—furniture and fixtures		$ 40,000
Building	250,000	
Accumulated depreciation—building		130,000
Accounts payable		380,000
Salary payable		
Unearned service revenue		45,000
Common stock		100,000
Retained earnings		193,000
Dividends	65,000	
Service revenue		286,000
Salary expense	172,000	
Supplies expense		
Depreciation expense—furniture and fixtures		
Depreciation expense—building		
Miscellaneous expense	13,000	
Total	$1,174,000	$1,174,000

Data needed for the adjusting entries include:

a. Supplies on hand at year's end, $2,000.

b. Depreciation on furniture and fixtures, $20,000.

c. Depreciation on building, $10,000.

d. Salaries owed but not yet paid, $5,000.

e. Accrued service revenue, $12,000.

f. Of the $45,000 balance of unearned service revenue, $32,000 was earned during the year.

Required

1. Open the ledger accounts with their unadjusted balances using T-account format. Show dollar amounts in thousands, as shown for Accounts Receivable.

Accounts Receivable

370

2. Journalize O'Malley's Service Corp.'s adjusting entries at December 31, 19X3. Key entries by letter as in Exhibit 3-9.

3. Post the adjusting entries.

4. Write the trial balance on a work sheet, enter the adjusting entries, and prepare an adjusted trial balance, as shown in Exhibit 3-10.

5. Prepare the income statement, the statement of retained earnings, and the balance sheet. Draw the arrows linking these three statements.

SOLUTION TO REVIEW PROBLEM

Requirements 1 and 3

ASSETS

Cash

Bal.	198		

Accounts Receivable

Bal.	370		
(e)	12		
Bal.	382		

Supplies

Bal.	6	(a)	4
Bal.	2		

Furniture and Fixtures

Bal.	100		

Accumulated Depreciation— Furniture and Fixtures

		Bal.	40
		(b)	20
		Bal.	60

Building

Bal.	250		

Accumulated Depreciation— Building

		Bal.	130
		(c)	10
		Bal.	140

LIABILITIES

Accounts Payable

		Bal.	380

Salary Payable

		(d)	5
		Bal.	5

Unearned Service Revenue

(f)	32	Bal.	45
		Bal.	13

SHAREHOLDERS' EQUITY

Common Stock

		Bal.	100

Retained Earnings

		Bal.	193

Dividends

Bal.	65		

REVENUE

Service Revenue

		Bal.	286
		(e)	12
		(f)	32
		Bal.	330

EXPENSES

Salary Expense

Bal.	172		
(d)	5		
Bal.	177		

Supplies Expense

(a)	4		
Bal.	4		

Depreciation Expense— Furniture and Fixtures

(b)	20		
Bal.	20		

Depreciation Expense— Building

(c)	10		
Bal.	10		

Miscellaneous Expense

Bal.	13		

Requirement 2

	19X1				
a.	Dec. 31	Supplies Expense ($6,000 – $2,000)	4,000	
		Supplies..		4,000
		To record supplies used.		
b.	31	Depreciation Expense—Furniture and Fixtures......	20,000	
		Accumulated Depreciation—Furniture and Fixtures...		20,000
		To record depreciation expense on furniture and fixtures.		
c.	31	Depreciation Expense—Building..............................	10,000	
		Accumulated Depreciation—Building................		10,000
		To record depreciation expense on building.		
d.	31	Salary Expense..	5,000	
		Salary Payable...		5,000
		To accrue salary expense.		

e.	31	Accounts Receivable	12,000
		Service Revenue..		12,000
		To accrue service revenue.	
f.	31	Unearned Service Revenue	32,000
		Service Revenue..		32,000
		To record unearned service revenue that has been earned.	

Requirement 4

O'Malley's Service Corp.
Preparation of Adjusted Trial Balance
December 31, 19X3
(amounts in thousands)

Account Title	Trial Balance		Adjustments				Adjusted Trial Balance	
	Debit	Credit	Debit		Credit		Debit	Credit
Cash	198						198	
Accounts receivable	370		(e)	12			382	
Supplies	6				(a)	4	2	
Furniture and fixtures	100						100	
Accumulated depreciation —furniture and fixtures		40			(b)	20		60
Building	250						250	
Accumulated depreciation —building		130			(c)	10		140
Accounts payable		380						380
Salary payable					(d)	5		5
Unearned service revenue		45	(f)	32				13
Common stock		100						100
Retained earnings		193						193
Dividends	65						65	
Service revenue		286			(e)	12		330
					(f)	32		
Salary expense	172		(d)	5			177	
Supplies expense			(a)	4			4	
Depreciation expense —furniture and fixtures			(b)	20			20	
Depreciation expense —building			(c)	10			10	
Miscellaneous expense	13						13	
	1,174	1,174		83		83	1,221	1,221

Requirement 5

O'Malley's Service Corp.
Income Statement
for the year ended December 31, 19X3
(amounts in thousands)

Revenues		
Service revenue..		$330
Expenses		
Salary expense	$177	
Depreciation expense—furniture and fixtures	20	
Depreciation expense—building	10	
Supplies expense...	4	
Miscellaneous expense	13	
Total expenses..		224
Net income		$106

O'Malley's Service Corp.
Statement of Retained Earnings
for the year ended December 31, 19X3
(amounts in thousands)

Retained earnings, January 1, 19X3	$193
Add: Net income	106
	299
Less: Dividends...	65
Retained Earnings, December 31, 19X3...	$234

①

O'Malley's Service Corp.
Balance Sheet
December 31, 19X3
(amounts in thousands)

Assets			**Liabilities**	
Cash..		$198	Accounts payable.........................	$380
Accounts receivable		382	Salary payable	5
Supplies		2	Unearned service revenue	13
Furniture and fixtures	$100		Total liabilities	398
Less: Accumulated				
depreciation..............	60	40	**Shareholders' Equity**	
Building	$250		Common stock	100
Less: Accumulated			Retained earnings........................	234
depreciation..............	140	110	Total shareholders' equity	334
			Total liabilities and	
Total assets		$732	shareholders' equity	$732

②

Summary

1. Distinguish accrual-basis accounting from cash-basis accounting. In *accrual-basis accounting*, business events are recorded as they affect the entity. In *cash-basis accounting*, only those events that affect cash are recorded. The cash basis omits important events such as purchases and sales of assets on account. It also distorts the financial statements by labeling as expenses those cash payments that have long-term effects, such as the purchases of buildings and equipment. Some small organizations use cash-basis accounting, but the generally accepted method is the accrual basis.

2. Apply the revenue and matching principles. Businesses divide time into definite periods—such as a month, a quarter, and a year—to report the entity's financial statements. The year is the basic *accounting period*, but companies prepare financial statements as often as they need the information. Accountants have developed the *revenue principle* to determine when to record revenue and the amount of revenue to record. The *matching principle* guides the accounting for expenses.

3. Make adjusting entries at the end of the accounting period. *Adjusting entries* are a result of the accrual basis of accounting. These entries, made at the end of the period, update the accounts for preparation of the financial statements. One of the most important pieces of business information is net income or net loss, and the adjusting entries help to measure the *net income* of the period. Adjusting entries can be divided into five categories: *prepaid expenses, depreciation, accrued expenses, accrued revenues,* and *unearned revenues.*

4. Prepare an adjusted trial balance. To prepare the *adjusted trial balance*, enter the adjusting entries next to the *unadjusted trial balance* and compute each account's balance.

5. Prepare the financial statements from the adjusted trial balance. The adjusted trial balance can be used to prepare the financial statements. The three financial statements are related as follows: Income, shown on the *income statement*, increases the retained earnings, which also appears on the *statement of retained earnings*. The ending balance of shareholders' equity combines common stock and retained earnings and appears on the *balance sheet*.

Self-Study Questions

Test your understanding of the chapter by marking the correct answer for each of the following questions:

1. Accrual-basis accounting *(pp. 111–112)*
   a. Results in higher income than cash-basis accounting
   b. Leads to the reporting of more complete information than does cash-basis accounting
   c. Is not acceptable under GAAP
   d. Omits adjusting entries at the end of the period

2. Under the revenue principle, revenue is recorded *(pp. 113)*
   a. At the earliest acceptable time
   b. At the latest acceptable time
   c. After it has been earned, but not before
   d. At the end of the accounting period

3. The matching principle provides guidance in accounting for *(p. 113–114)*
   a. Expenses   c. Assets
   b. Shareholders' equity   d. Liabilities

4. Adjusting entries *(pp. 115–116)*
   a. Assign revenues to the period in which they are earned
   b. Help to properly measure the period's net income or net loss
   c. Bring asset and liability accounts to correct balances
   d. All of the above

5. A building-cleaning firm began November with supplies of $160. During the month, the firm purchased supplies of $290. At November 30, supplies on hand total $210. Supplies expense for the period is *(pp. 117–118)*
   a. $210   c. $290
   b. $240   d. $450

6. A building that cost $120,000 has accumulated depreciation of $50,000. The book value of the building is *(p. 119)*
   a. $50,000   c. $120,000
   b. $70,000   d. $170,000

7. The adjusting entry to accrue salary expense *(p. 122)*
   a. Debits Salary Expense and credits Cash
   b. Debits Salary Payable and credits Salary Expense
   c. Debits Salary Payable and credits Cash
   d. Debits Salary Expense and credits Salary Payable

8. A business received cash of $3,000 in advance for service that will be provided later. The cash receipt entry debited Cash and credited Unearned Revenue for $3,000. At the end of the period, $1,100 is still unearned. The adjusting entry for this situation will *(pp. 122–123)*
   a. Debit Unearned Revenue and credit Revenue for $1,900
   b. Debit Unearned Revenue and credit Revenue for $1,100
   c. Debit Revenue and credit Unearned Revenue for $1,900
   d. Debit Revenue and credit Unearned Revenue for $1,100

9. The links between the financial statements are *(p. 128)*
   a. Net income from the income statement to the statement of retained earnings
   b. Ending retained earnings from the statement of retained earnings to the balance sheet
   c. Both of the above
   d. None of the above

10. Accumulated Depreciation is reported on the *(p. 128)*
    a. Balance sheet   c. Statement of retained earnings
    b. Income statement   d. Both a and b

Answers to the Self-Study Questions follow the Accounting Vocabulary.

Accounting Vocabulary

Accrual-basis accounting *(p. 111)*
Accrued expenses *(p. 121)*
Accrued revenue *(p. 122)*
Accumulated depreciation *(p. 119)*
Adjusted trial balance *(p. 125)*
Adjusting entry *(p. 116)*
Amortization *(p. 118)*
Book value of a capital asset *(p. 119)*
Capital asset *(p. 118)*
Cash-basis accounting *(p. 111)*
Depreciation *(p. 118)*
Matching principle *(p. 113)*
Prepaid expenses *(p. 116)*
Revenue principle *(p. 113)*
Time-period concept *(p. 114)*
Unearned revenue *(p. 122)*

Answers to Self-Study Questions

1. b   4. d   7. d   9. c
2. c   5. b ($160 + $290 – $210 = $240)   8. a ($3,000 received – $1,100   10. a
3. a   6. b ($120,000 – $50,000 = $70,000)   unearned = $1,900 earned)

ASSIGNMENT MATERIAL _____

Questions

1. Distinguish accrual-basis accounting from cash-basis.
2. How long is the basic accounting period? What is a fiscal year? What is an interim period?
3. What two questions does the revenue principle help answer?
4. Briefly explain the matching principle.
5. What is the purpose of making adjusting entries?
6. Why are adjusting entries made at the end of the accounting period, not during the period?
7. Name five categories of adjusting entries and give an example of each.
8. Do all adjusting entries affect the net income or net loss of the period? Include the definition of an adjusting entry.
9. Why does the balance of Supplies need to be adjusted at the end of the period?
10. Manning Supply Company Ltd. pays $1,800 for an insurance policy that covers three years. At the end of the first year, the balance of its Prepaid Insurance account contains two elements. What are the two elements, and what is the correct amount of each?
11. The title Prepaid Expense suggests that this type of account is an expense. If so, explain why. If it is not, what type of account is it?
12. What is a contra account? Identify the contra account introduced in this chapter, along with the account's normal balance.
13. The manager of a Quickie-Pickie convenience store presents his entity's balance sheet to a banker to obtain a loan. The balance sheet reports that the entity's capital assets have a book value of $135,000 and accumulated depreciation of $65,000. What does *book value* of a capital asset mean? What was the cost of the capital assets?
14. Give the entry to record accrued interest revenue of $800.
15. Why is an unearned revenue a liability? Give an example.
16. Identify the types of accounts (assets, liabilities, and so on) debited and credited for the five types of adjusting entries.
17. What purposes does the adjusted trial balance serve?
18. Explain the relationship among the income statement, the statement of retained earnings, and the balance sheet.
19. Bellevue Corp. failed to record the following adjusting entries at December 31, the end of its fiscal year: (a) accrued expenses, $500; (b) accrued revenues, $850; and (c) depreciation, $1,000. Did these omissions cause net income for the year to be understated or overstated and by what overall amount?

Exercises

Exercise 3-1   *Cash-basis versus accrual-basis accounting*   **(Obj. 1)**

Oak Lodge Ltd. had the following selected transactions during August:

Aug.	1	Prepaid cash for rent for three months, $3,000.
	5	Paid electricity expenses, $700.
	9	Received cash for the day's room rentals, $1,400.
	31	Purchased six television sets, $3,000.
	31	Served a banquet, receiving a note receivable, $1,200.
	31	Made an adjusting entry for rent (from Aug. 1).
	31	Accrued salary expense, $900.

Show how each transaction would be handled using the cash basis and the accrual basis of accounting. Under each column give the amount of revenue or expense for August. Journal entries are not required. Use the following format for your answer, and show your computations:

Oak Lodge Ltd.—Amount of Revenue or Expense for August

Date	Cash-Basis	Accrual-Basis

Exercise 3-2   *Applying accounting concepts and principles*   *(Obj. 2)*

Identify the accounting concept or principle that gives the most direction on how to account for each of the following situations:

a. A customer states her intention to switch travel agencies. Should the new travel agency record revenue based on this intention?

b. The owner of a business desires monthly financial statements to measure the progress of the entity on an ongoing basis.

c. Expenses of the period total $6,100. This amount should be subtracted from revenue to compute the period's income.

d. Expenses of $2,600 must be accrued at the end of the period to measure income properly.

Exercise 3-3   *Applying accounting concepts*   *(Obj. 2)*

Write a short paragraph to explain in your own words the concept of depreciation as it is used in accounting.

Exercise 3-4   *Allocating prepaid expense to the asset and expense*   *(Obj. 2, 3)*

Compute the amounts indicated by question marks for each of the following Prepaid Insurance situations. For situations 2, 3, and 4, journalize the missing entry. Consider each situation separately.

	Situation			
	1	2	3	4
Beginning Prepaid Insurance	$ 300	$500	$ 600	$ 900
Payments for Prepaid Insurance during the year	1,100	?	?	1,100
Total amount to account for	?	?	1,300	2,000
Ending Prepaid Insurance	200	600	500	?
Insurance Expense	$?	$400	$ 800	$1,400

Exercise 3-5   *Journalizing adjusting entries*   *(Obj. 3)*

Journalize the entries for the following adjustments at December 31, the end of the accounting period:

a. Prepaid insurance expired, $600.

b. Interest revenue accrued, $4,100.

c. Unearned service revenue earned, $800.

d. Depreciation, $6,200.

e. Employee salaries owed for two days of a five-day workweek; weekly payroll, $9,000.

Exercise 3-6   *Analyzing the effects of adjustments on net income   (Obj. 3)*

Suppose the adjustments required in Exercise 3-5 were not made. Compute the overall overstatement or understatement of net income as a result of the omission of these adjustments.

Exercise 3-7   *Journalizing adjusting entries   (Obj. 3)*

Journalize the adjusting entry needed at December 31 for each of the following independent situations.

a. The business owes interest expense of $1,400 that it will pay early in the next period.

b. Interest revenue of $900 has been earned but not yet received. The business holds a $20,000 note receivable.

c. On July 1, when we collected $6,000 rent in advance, we debited Cash and credited Unearned Rent Revenue. The tenant was paying for two years' rent.

d. Salary expense is $1,000 per day—Monday through Friday—and the business pays employees each Friday. This year December 31 falls on a Thursday.

e. The unadjusted balance of the Supplies account is $3,100. The total cost of supplies on hand is $1,200.

f. Equipment was purchased last year at a cost of $10,000. The equipment's useful life is four years. Record the year's depreciation.

g. On September 1, when we prepaid $1,800 for a one-year insurance policy, we debited Prepaid Insurance and credited Cash.

Exercise 3-8   *Recording adjustments in T-accounts   (Obj. 3)*

The accounting records of Lucca Galvez, Artist Supplies Inc. include the following unadjusted balances at May 31: Accounts Receivable, $1,200; Supplies, $600; Salary Payable, $0; Unearned Service Revenue, $400; Service Revenue, $4,700; Salary Expense, $1,200; and Supplies Expense, $0.

Galvez's accountant develops the following data for the May 31 adjusting entries:

a. Supplies on hand, $400.

b. Salary owed to employee, $400.

c. Service revenue accrued, $350.

d. Unearned service revenue that has been earned, $250.

Open the foregoing T-accounts and record the adjustments directly in the accounts, keying each adjustment amount by letter. Show each account's adjusted balance. Journal entries are not required.

Exercise 3-9   *Adjusting the accounts   (Obj. 3, 4)*

Preparation of the Ship-n-Go Service, Inc., adjusted trial balance is incomplete. Enter the adjustment amounts directly in the adjustment columns of the questions. Service Revenue is the only account affected by more than one adjustment.

Ship-n-Go Service, Inc.
Preparation of Adjusted Trial Balance
October 31, 19X2

Account Title	Trial Balance		Adjustments		Adjusted Trial Balance	
	Debit	Credit	Debit	Credit	Debit	Credit
Cash	3,000				3,000	
Accounts receivable	6,500				7,400	
Supplies	1,040				800	
Office furniture	29,300				29,300	
Accumulated depreciation		11,060				11,420
Salary payable						600
Unearned revenue		900				690
Common stock		10,000				10,000
Retained earnings		16,340				16,340
Dividends	6,200				6,200	
Service revenue		11,830				12,940
Salary expense	2,690				3,290	
Rent expense	1,400				1,400	
Depreciation expense					360	
Supplies expense					240	
	50,130	50,130			51,990	51,990

Exercise 3-10 *Journalizing adjustments* **(Obj. 3, 4)**

Make journal entries for the adjustments that would complete the preparation of the adjusted trial balance in Exercise 3-9. Include explanations.

Exercise 3-11 *Preparing the financial statements* **(Obj. 5)**

Refer to the adjusted trial balance in Exercise 3-9. Prepare Ship-n-Go Service, Inc.'s income statement and statement of retained earnings for the three months ended October 31, 19X2, and its balance sheet on that date. Draw the arrows linking the three statements.

Exercise 3-12 *Preparing the financial statements* **(Obj. 5)**

The accountant for Judy Wong, P. Eng., Inc., has posted adjusting entries (a) through (e) to the accounts at September 30, 19X2. Selected balance sheet accounts and all the revenues and expenses of the entity follow in T-account form:

Accounts Receivable			Supplies			Accumulated Depreciation —Furniture		
23,000			4,000	(a)	2,000			5,000
(e)	4,500					(b)		4,000

Accumulated Depreciation —Building			Salaries Payable			Service Revenue		
		33,000	(d)		1,500			135,000
	(c)	5,000				(e)		4,500

Salary Expense		Supplies Expense		Depreciation Expense— Furniture		Depreciation Expense— Building	
28,000		(a)	2,000	(b)	4,000	(c)	5,000
(d)	1,500						

Required

Prepare the income statement of Judy Wong, P. Eng., Inc. for the year ended September 30, 19X2. List expenses in order from the largest to the smallest.

Exercise 3-13   *Computing financial statement amounts   (Obj. 5)*

The adjusted trial balances of KPMG Corporation at December 31, 19X6, and December 31, 19X5, include these amounts:

	19X6	19X5
Supplies	$ 1,100	$ 1,500
Salary payable	3,400	3,700
Unearned service revenue	14,200	16,300

Analysis of the Cash account at December 31, 19X6, reveals these cash disbursements and cash receipts for 19X6.

Cash disbursements for supplies	$ 9,100
Cash disbursements for salaries	81,600
Cash receipts for service revenue	731,200

Compute the amount of supplies expense, salary expense, and service revenue to report on the 19X6 income statement.

Serial Exercise

Exercise 3-14 continues the Emily Schneider, Architect, Inc., situation begun in Exercise 2-13 of Chapter 2.

Exercise 3-14   *Adjusting the accounts, preparing an adjusted trial balance, and preparing the financial statements   (Obj. 3, 4, 5)*

Refer to Exercise 2-13 of Chapter 2. Start from the trial balance and the posted T-accounts that Emily Schneider, Architect, Inc., prepared for her architectural practice at December 18. Later in December, the business completed these transactions:

Dec. 21   Received $900 in advance for architectural work to be performed evenly
         over the next 30 days.

   21   Hired a secretary to be paid $1,500 on the 21st day of each month.
   26   Paid for the supplies purchased on December 5.
   28   Collected $600 from the consulting client on December 18.
   30   Declared and paid dividends of $1,600.

Required

1. Open these T-accounts: Accumulated Depreciation—Equipment; Accumulated Depreciation—Furniture; Salary Payable; Unearned Service Revenue; Retained Earnings; Depreciation Expense—Equipment; Depreciation Expense—Furniture; Supplies Expense.

2. Journalize the transactions of December 21 through 30.

3. Post to the T-accounts, keying all items by date.

4. Prepare a trial balance at December 31. Also set up columns for the adjustments and for the adjusted trial balance, as illustrated in Exhibit 3-10.

5. At December 31, Schneider gathers the following information for the adjusting entries:
   a. Accrued service revenue, $400.
   b. Earned a portion of the service revenue collected in advance on December 21.
   c. Supplies on hand, $100.
   d. Depreciation expense—equipment, $50; furniture, $60.
   e. Accrued expense for secretary salary.

   Make these adjustments directly in the adjustments columns, and complete the adjusted trial balance at December 31.

6. Journalize and post the adjusting entries. Denote each adjusting amount as *Adj.* and an account balance as *Bal.*

7. Prepare the income statement and statement of retained earnings of Emily Schneider, Architect, Inc., for the month ended December 31, and prepare the balance sheet at that date.

Challenge Exercise

Exercise 3-15   *Computing the amount of revenue*   *(Obj. 3)*

Lei Ma Enterprises Ltd. aids Singaporean students upon their arrival in Canada. Paid by the Singaporean government, Lei Ma collects some service revenue in advance. In other cases Lei Ma Enterprises receives cash after performing relocation services. At the end of August—a particularly busy period—Lei Ma's books show the following:

	July 31	August 31
Accounts receivable	$1,900	$2,200
Unearned service revenue.....................	1,200	300

During August Lei Ma Enterprises Ltd. received cash of $6,100 from the Singaporean government. How much service revenue did the business earn during August? Show your work.

Exercise 3-16   *Computing cash amounts*   *(Obj. 3)*

For the situation of Exercise 3-15, take the service revenue of Lei Ma Enterprises Ltd. as $5,700 during August. How much cash did the business collect from the Singaporean government that month? Show your work.

Problems   *(Group A)*

Problem 3-1A   *Cash basis versus accrual basis* **(Obj. 1, 2)**

Samaritan Counseling Service Inc. had the following selected transactions during October:

Oct.	1	Prepaid insurance for October through December, $450.
	4	Purchased office equipment for cash, $800.
	5	Performed counseling services and received cash, $700.
	8	Paid advertising expense, $300.
	11	Performed counseling service on account, $1,200.
	19	Purchased office furniture on account, $150.
	24	Collected $400 on account for the October 11 service.
	31	Paid account payable from October 19.
	31	Paid salary expense, $900.
	31	Recorded adjusting entry for October insurance expense (see Oct. 1).
	31	Debited unearned revenue and credited revenue to adjust the accounts, $600.

Required

1. Show how each transaction would be handled using the cash basis and the accrual basis. Under each column give the amount of revenue or expense for October. Journal entries are not required. Use the following format for your answer, and show your computations:

Samaritan Counseling Service, Inc.—Amount of Revenue or Expense for October

Date	Cash Basis	Accrual Basis

2. Compute October net income or net loss under each method.

3. Indicate which measure of net income or net loss is preferable. Give your reason.

Problem 3-2A   *Applying accounting principles*   **(Obj. 2, 3)**

As the controller of Binswanger Auto Glass Company Ltd., you have hired a new bookkeeper, whom you must train. He objects to making an adjusting entry for accrued salaries at the end of the period. He reasons, "We will pay the salaries soon. Why not wait until payment to record the expense? In the end, the result will be the same." Write a reply to explain to the bookkeeper why the adjusting entry for accrued salary expense is needed.

Problem 3-3A   *Journalizing adjusting entries*   **(Obj. 3)**

Journalize the adjusting entry needed on December 31, end of the current accounting period, for each of the following independent cases affecting Randolph Engineering Consulting Corp.:

a. Each Friday Randolph pays its employees for the current week's work. The amount of the payroll is $3,500 for a five-day work week. The current accounting period ends on Thursday.

b. Randolph has received notes receivable from some clients for professional services. During the current year, Randolph has earned accrued interest revenue of $9,575, which will be received next year.

c. The beginning balance of Engineering Supplies was $3,800. During the year the entity purchased supplies costing $12,530, and at December 31 the inventory of supplies on hand is $2,970.

d. Randolph is conducting tests of the strength of the steel to be used in a large building, and the client paid Randolph $36,000 at the start of the project. Randolph recorded this amount as Unearned Engineering Revenue. The tests will take several months to complete. Randolph executives estimate that the company has earned three-fourths of the total fee during the current year.

e. Depreciation for the current year includes: Office Furniture, $5,500; Engineering Equipment, $6,360; and Building, $3,790. Make a compound entry.

f. Details of Prepaid Insurance are shown in the account:

Prepaid Insurance

Jan. 1 Bal. 1,200	
Apr. 30 1,800	
Oct. 31 1,800	

Randolph pays semiannual insurance premiums (the payment for insurance coverage is called a *premium*) on April 30 and October 31. At December 31, part of the last payment is still in force.

Problem 3-4A   *Analyzing and journalizing adjustments*   *(Obj. 3)*

Ahmed Rashad Ltd. unadjusted and adjusted trial balances at December 31, 19X7, are shown in the following.

Ahmed Rashad Ltd.
Adjusted Trial Balance
December 31, 19X7

Account Title	Trial Balance Debit	Trial Balance Credit	Adjusted Trial Balance Debit	Adjusted Trial Balance Credit
Cash	4,120		4,120	
Accounts receivable	11,260		14,090	
Supplies	1,090		780	
Prepaid insurance	2,600		1,330	
Office furniture	21,630		21,630	
Accumulated depreciation		8,220		10,500
Accounts payable		6,310		6,310
Salary payable				960
Interest payable				480
Note payable		12,000		12,000
Unearned commission revenue		1,840		1,160
Common stock		10,000		10,000
Retained earnings		3,510		3,510
Dividends	29,370		29,370	
Commission revenue		72,890		76,400
Depreciation expense			2,280	
Supplies expense			310	
Utilities expense	4,960		4,960	
Salary expense	26,660		27,620	
Rent expense	12,200		12,200	
Interest expense	880		1,360	
Insurance expense			1,270	
	114,770	114,770	121,320	121,320

Required

Journalize the adjusting entries that account for the differences between the two trial balances.

Problem 3-5A   *Journalizing and posting adjustments to T-accounts; preparing the adjusted trial balance and the financial statements*   *(Obj. 3, 4)*

The trial balance of Pettit Realty Inc. at August 31 of the current year and the data needed for the month-end adjustments follow:

Pettit Realty, Inc.		
Trial Balance		
August 31, 19XX		
Cash	$ 3,100	
Accounts receivable......................................	23,780	
Prepaid rent	2,420	
Supplies..	1,180	
Furniture	19,740	
Accumulated depreciation		$ 3,630
Accounts payable..		3,310
Salary payable		
Unearned commission revenue		2,790
Common stock...		15,000
Retained earnings		24,510
Dividends..	4,800	
Commission revenue.....................................		11,700
Salary expense..	3,800	
Rent expense...		
Utilities expense	550	
Depreciation expense		
Advertising expense......................................	1,570	
Supplies expense...		
Total..	$60,940	$60,940

Adjustment data:

a. Unearned commission revenue still unearned at August 31, $1,670.

b. Prepaid rent still in force at August 31, $620.

c. Supplies used during the month, $700.

d. Depreciation for the month, $400.

e. Accrued advertising expense at August 31, $610. (Credit Accounts Payable.)

f. Accrued salary expense at August 31, $550.

Required

1. Open T-accounts for the accounts listed in the trial balance, inserting their August 31 unadjusted balances.

2. Journalize the adjusting entries on August 31, and post them to the T-accounts. Key the journal entries and posted amounts by letter.

3. Prepare the adjusted trial balance.

Problem 3-6A   *Preparing the financial statements from an adjusted trial balance*
(Obj. 3, 4, 5)

The adjusted trial balance of Blitz Delivery Services at the end of the year or December 31, 19X8 follows:

Blitz Delivery Services, Inc.
Adjusted Trial Balance
December 31, 19X8

Cash	$ 2,340	
Accounts receivable	41,490	
Prepaid rent	1,350	
Supplies	970	
Equipment	75,690	
Accumulated depreciation—equipment		$ 22,240
Office furniture	24,100	
Accumulated depreciation—office furniture		18,670
Accounts payable		13,600
Unearned service revenue		4,520
Interest payable		2,130
Salary payable		930
Note payable		45,000
Common stock		12,000
Retained earnings		20,380
Dividends	48,000	
Service revenue		195,790
Depreciation expense—equipment	11,300	
Depreciation expense—office furniture	2,410	
Salary expense	102,800	
Rent expense	12,000	
Interest expense	4,200	
Utilities expense	3,770	
Insurance expense	3,150	
Supplies expense	1,690	
Total	$335,260	$335,260

Required

Prepare Blitz's 19X8 income statement, statement of retained earnings, and balance sheet. List expenses in decreasing order on the income statement and show total liabilities on the balance sheet. Draw the arrows linking the three financial statements. How will what you have learned in this problem help you manage a business?

Problem 3-7A   *Preparing an adjusted trial balance and the financial statements*   *(Obj. 3, 4, 5)*

Consider the unadjusted trial balance of Lori Morgan System Design, Inc., at October 31, 19X2 and the related month-end adjustment data.

Lori Morgan System Design, Inc.
Trial Balance
October 31, 19X2

Cash	$16,300
Accounts receivable	8,000
Prepaid rent	4,000
Supplies	600

Furniture	15,000	
Accumulated depreciation		$ 3,000
Accounts payable..		2,800
Salary payable		
Common stock..		15,000
Retained earnings		21,000
Dividends...	3,600	
Consulting service revenue		7,400
Salary expense...	1,400	
Rent Expense		
Utilities expense...	300	
Depreciation expense		
Supplies expense...		
Total...	$49,200	$49,200

Adjustment data:

a. Accrued consulting service revenue at October 31, $2,000.

b. Prepaid rent expired during the month. The unadjusted prepaid balance of $4,000 relates to the period October 1, 19X2, through January 19X3.

c. Supplies on hand at October 31, $200.

d. Depreciation on furniture for the month. The furniture's expected useful life is five years.

e. Accrued salary expense at October 31 for one day only. The five-day weekly payroll is $2,000.

Required

1. Write the trial balance on a work sheet, using as an example Exhibit 3-10, and prepare the adjusted trial balance of Lori Morgan System Design, Inc., at October 31, 19X2. Key each adjusting entry by letter.

2. Prepare the income statement, the statement of retained earnings, and the balance sheet. Draw the arrows linking the three financial statements.

Problem 3-8A   *Apply the revenue and matching principles, make adjusting entries, account for prepaid expenses recorded initially as an expense, account for unearned revenue recorded initially as a revenue   (Obj. 2, 3, A1, A2)*

The Cyborg Company, a consulting business, had the following information available at the close of their first year of business:

1. Insurance payments during the year were debited to "Prepaid Insurance" and an examination of the policies showed the following:
   - Policy # 1: a two-year policy purchased on March 31st at a cost of $2,400; it was recorded as a debit to "Prepaid Insurance."
   - Policy # 2: a one-year policy purchased on July 2nd at a cost of $1,000; it was recorded as a debit to "Insurance Expense."

2. On January 1st the company purchased $500 of supplies which was debited to "Supplies." Throughout the year the company purchased additional supplies totaling $1,200 which was debited to "Supplies Expense." An inventory count on December 31st showed that there was $800 of supplies on hand.

3. Equipment was purchased on July 2nd for $25,000. The equipment was expected to be used for 5 years and then discarded.

4. The thirty employees each earn an average of $200 per day for a five-day week and are paid each Friday. December 31st fell on a Wednesday this year.

5. An examination of the contracts signed with clients showed the following:
   - Customer #1 signed a contract on September 1st and paid $6,000 to Cyborg. The contract was for them to receive $600 of consulting work each month for ten months commencing October 1st.
   - Customer #2 signed a contract on October 30th to receive $1,000 of consulting work each month commencing November 1st, with payments to be made on the 15th of the month following the service provision.

   All money received to date on the two contracts was credited to "Consulting Fees Earned."

6. Cyborg Company had recorded and posted the following transaction of August 10th:

DR.	Repair Equipment	$5,000	
CR.	Cash		$5,000

   On December 31st the company realized that the transaction was actually for $500 (not $5,000) and was for repair supplies (not equipment). The supplies had all been used during the year.

Required

1. Record any adjusting or correcting entries that would be required on December 31st (the year-end).

2. Give the journal entry required to record the payment of wages on January 2nd of the following year (all employees are paid for January 1st).

3. What would be the *total effects* of the adjusting entries (parts 1 to 6) on each of the three financial statements?

Problem 3-9A   *Apply the revenue and matching principles, make adjusting entries, account for prepaid expenses recorded initially as an expense, prepare an adjusted trial balance, prepare an income statement*   **(Obj. 2, 3, 4, 5, A1)**

J. Joseph owns and operates a skydiving business called J. Joseph Skydiving Inc. On December 31, 19X1, the business had the following account balances (in alphabetical order):

Accounts payable	$ 3,000
Accounts receivable	2,800
Accumulated amortization—building	2,000
Accumulated amortization—equipment	4,800
Cash	1,200
Building	40,000
Equipment rental revenues	7,200
Common stock	26,000
Dividends	11,000
Plane rental expense	6,600
Prepaid consulting	2,000
Salaries expense	16,800
Skydiving equipment	9,600
Skydiving fees earned	52,000
Supplies	700
Supplies expense	3,400
Utilities expense	900

The following information was available on December 31, 19X1:

- A physical count showed there were $1,200 worth of supplies on hand on December 31st.
- The buildings had an expected useful life of 10 years with no expected salvage value.

- The skydiving equipment was expected to be used for 4 years with no expected salvage value.
- On November 1, Joseph hired a consultant to prepare a business plan and agreed to pay her $500 per month. Joseph paid her four months in advance.
- On December 15th, Joseph rented a plane for $2,000 to fly to San Francisco for a holiday. This was recorded as Plane Rental Expense.
- Joseph's assistant, who earns $200 per day has worked the last six days of the year and will be paid on January 4, 19X2.
- On December 30th, Joseph provided skydiving lessons to a customer for $200 to be paid in 30 days.

Required

1. Journalize the adjustments required on December 31, 19X1, the end of the year.
2. Prepare, with accounts in the correct sequence, an adjusted trial balance on December 31, 19X1.
3. Prepare an income statement for the year ended December 31, 19X1.
4. How old was the Building on December 31, 19X1? The skydiving equipment?

(Group B)

Problem 3-1B   *Cash-basis versus accrual-basis accounting   (Obj. 1, 2)*

Selective Placement Services, Inc., experienced the following selected transactions during January:

Jan. 1   Prepaid insurance for January through March, $600.
       4   Purchased office equipment for cash, $1,400.
       5   Received cash for services performed, $900.
       8   Paid gas bill, $400.
      12   Performed services on account, $1,500.
      14   Purchased office equipment on account, $300.
      28   Collected $500 on account from January 12.
      31   Paid salary expense, $1,100.
      31   Paid account payable from January 14.
      31   Recorded adjusting entry for January insurance expense (see Jan. 1)
      31   Debited unearned revenue and credited revenue in an adjusting entry, $700.

Required

1. Show how each transaction would be handled using the cash basis and the accrual basis. Under each column give the amount of revenue or expense for January. Journal entries are not required. Use the following format for your answer, and show your computations:

Selective Placement Services, Inc.—Amount of Revenue or Expense for January

Date	Cash Basis	Accrual Basis

2. Compute January net income or net loss under each method.
3. Indicate which measure of net income or net loss is preferable. Give your reason.

Problem 3-2B   *Applying accounting principles   (Obj. 1, 2)*

Write a short memo to a new bookkeeper to explain the differences between the cash basis of accounting and the accrual basis. Mention the roles of the revenue principle and the matching principle in accrual-basis accounting.

Problem 3-3B   *Journalizing adjusting entries*   *(Obj. 3)*

Journalize the adjusting entry needed on December 31, end of the current accounting period, for each of the following independent cases affecting Petrov Construction Contractors, Inc.:

a. Details of Prepaid Rent are shown in the account:

Prepaid Rent

Jan. 1 Bal.	600
Mar. 31	1,200
Sept. 30	1,200

Petrov pays semiannual payments on March 31 and September 30. At December 31, part of the last payment is still in force.

b. Petrov pays its employees each Friday. The amount of the weekly payroll is $2,000 for a five-day workweek, and the daily salary amounts are equal. The current accounting period ends on Monday.

c. Petrov has loaned money, receiving notes receivable. During the current year the entity has earned accrued interest revenue of $737 that it will receive next year.

d. The beginning balance of Supplies was $2,680. During the year the entity purchased supplies costing $6,180, and at December 31 the inventory of supplies on hand is $2,150.

e. Petrov is servicing the air-conditioning system in a large building, and the owner of the building paid Petrov $12,900 as the annual service fee. Petrov recorded this amount as Unearned Service Revenue. Efrim Zweig, the general manager, estimates that the company has earned one fourth of the total fee during the current year.

f. Depreciation for the current year includes: Office Furniture, $850; Equipment, $3,850; and Trucks, $10,320. Make a compound entry.

Problem 3-4B   *Analyzing and journalizing adjustments*   *(Obj. 3)*

Patricia Woo Court Reporting Corp. unadjusted and adjusted trial balances at November 30, 19X1 are as follows:

Patricia Woo Court Reporting Corp.
Adjusted Trial Balance
November 30, 19X1

Account Title	Trial Balance Debit	Trial Balance Credit	Adjusted Trial Balance Debit	Adjusted Trial Balance Credit
Cash	8,180		8,180	
Accounts receivable	6,360		6,540	
Interest receivable			300	
Note receivable	4,100		4,100	
Supplies	980		290	
Prepaid rent	2,480		720	
Building	66,450		66,450	
Accumulated depreciation		16,010		17,110
Accounts payable		6,920		6,920
Wages payable				320
Unearned service revenue		670		110
Common stock		18,000		18,000
Retained earnings		42,790		42,790

Dividends	3,600		3,600	
Service revenue		9,940		10,680
Interest revenue				300
Wage expense	1,600		1,920	
Rent expense			1,760	
Depreciation expense			1,100	
Insurance expense	370		370	
Supplies expense			690	
Utilities expense	190		210	
	94,310	94,330	96,230	96,230

Required

Journalize the adjusting entries that account for the differences between the two trial balances.

Problem 3-5B   *Journalizing and posting adjustments to T-accounts; preparing the adjusted trial balance   (Obj. 3, 4)*

The trial balance of Insurers Corp. of Saskatchewan at October 31, 19X2 and the data needed for the month-end adjustments are as follows:

Adjustment data:

a. Prepaid rent still in force at October 31, $700.

b. Supplies used during the month, $640.

c. Depreciation for the month, $900.

d. Accrued advertising expense at October 31, $320. (Credit Accounts Payable.)

e. Accrued salary expense at October 31, $180.

f. Unearned commission revenue still unearned at October 31, $2,000.

Insurers Corp. of Saskatchewan
Trial Balance
October 31, 19X2

Cash	$ 1,280	
Accounts receivable	14,750	
Prepaid rent	3,100	
Supplies	780	
Furniture	22,370	
Accumulated depreciation		$11,640
Accounts payable		1,940
Salary payable		
Unearned commission revenue		2,290
Common stock		5,000
Retained earnings		19,140
Dividends	2,900	
Commission revenue		8,400
Salary expense	2,160	
Rent expense		
Utilities expense	340	
Depreciation expense		
Advertising expense	730	
Supplies expense		
Total	$48,410	$48,410

Required

1. Open T-accounts for the accounts listed in the trial balance, inserting their October 31 unadjusted balances.

2. Journalize the adjusting entries and post them to the T-accounts. Key the journal entries and the posted amounts by letter.

3. Prepare the adjusted trial balance.

Problem 3-6B   *Preparing the financial statements from an adjusted trial balance*   **(Obj. 5)**

The adjusted trial balance of Halifax Travel Corp. at December 31, 19X6 follows:

Halifax Travel Corp. Adjusted Trial Balance December 31, 19X6		
Rent expense	$ 1,320	
Accounts receivable	8,920	
Supplies	2,300	
Prepaid rent	1,600	
Office equipment	20,180	
Accumulated depreciation —office equipment		$ 4,350
Office furniture	17,710	
Accumulated depreciation —office furniture		4,870
Accounts payable		3,640
Property tax payable		1,100
Interest payable		830
Unearned service revenue		620
Note payable		25,500
Common stock		5,000
Retained earnings		1,090
Dividends	44,000	
Service revenue		127,910
Depreciation expense—office equipment	6,680	
Depreciation expense—office furniture	2,370	
Salary expense	39,900	
Rent expense	17,400	
Interest expense	3,100	
Utilities expense	2,670	
Insurance expense	3,810	
Supplies expense	2,950	
Total	$174,910	$174,910

Required

Prepare Halifax Travel's 19X6 income statement, statement of retained earnings, and balance sheet. List expenses in decreasing order on the income statement and show total liabilities on the balance sheet. Draw the arrows linking the three financial statements. How will what you have learned in this problem help you manage a business?

Problem 3-7B   *Preparing an adjusted trial balance and the financial statements*   **(Obj. 3, 4, 5)**

The unadjusted trial balance of Tran TeleLogistics Ltd., at July 31, 19X2 and the related month-end adjustment data are as follows:

Tran TeleLogistics Ltd.
Trial Balance
July 31, 19X2

Cash	$14,600	
Accounts receivable	11,600	
Prepaid rent	3,600	
Supplies	800	
Furniture	16,800	
Accumulated depreciation		$ 3,500
Accounts payable		3,450
Salary payable		
Common stock		25,000
Retained earnings		13,650
Dividends	4,000	
Consulting revenue		8,750
Salary expense	2,400	
Rent expense		
Utilities expense	550	
Depreciation expense		
Supplies expense		
Total	$54,350	$54,350

Adjustment data:

a. Accrued consulting revenue at July 31, $900.

b. Prepaid rent expired during the month. The unadjusted prepaid balance of $3,600 relates to the period July through October.

c. Supplies on hand at July 31, $400.

d. Depreciation on furniture for the month. The estimated useful life of the furniture is four years.

e. Accrued salary expense at July 31 for one day only. The five-day weekly payroll is $1,000.

Required

1. Using Exhibit 3-10 as an example, write the trial balance on a work sheet and prepare the adjusted trial balance of Tran TeleLogistics Ltd., at July 31, 19X2. Key each adjusting entry by letter.

2. Prepare the income statement, the statement of retained earnings, and the balance sheet. Draw the arrows linking the three financial statements.

Problem 3-8B   *Apply the revenue and matching principles, make adjusting entries, account for prepaid expenses recorded initially as an expense, account for unearned revenue recorded initially as a revenue   (Obj. 2, 3, A1, A2)*

The Robotic Company, a consulting business, had the following information available at the close of their first year of business:

1. Insurance payments during the year were debited to "Prepaid Insurance" and an examination of the policies showed the following:
   - Policy # 1: a three-year policy purchased on July 1st at a cost of $3,000; it was recorded as a debit to "Prepaid Insurance."
   - Policy # 2: a one-year policy purchased on March 31st at a cost of $1,200; it was recorded as a debit to "Insurance Expense."

2. On January 1st the company purchased $800 of supplies which was debited to "Supplies." Throughout the year the company purchased additional supplies

totaling $1,400 which was debited to "Supplies Expense." An inventory count on December 31st showed that there was $1,000 of supplies on hand.

3. Equipment was purchased on July 2nd for $33,000. The equipment was expected to be used for 6 years and then discarded.

4. The twenty employees each earn an average of $150 per day for a five-day week and are paid each Friday. December 31st fell on a Wednesday this year.

5. An examination of the contracts signed with clients showed the following:
   - Customer #1 signed a contract on October 1st and paid $5,000 to Robotic. The contract was for them to receive $500 of consulting work each month for ten months commencing November 1st.
   - Customer #2 signed a contract on September 30th to receive $800 of consulting work each month commencing October 1st, with payments to be made on the 15th of the month following the service provision.

   All money received to date on the two contracts was credited to "Consulting Fees Earned."

6. Robotic Company had recorded and posted the following transaction of August 10th:

DR.	Repair Equipment	$6,000
CR.	Cash	$6,000

   On December 31st the company realized that the transaction was actually for $600 (not $6,000) and was for repair supplies (not equipment). The supplies had all been used during the year.

Required

1. Record any adjusting or correcting entries that would be required on December 31st (the year-end).

2. Give the journal entry required to record the payment of wages on January 2nd of the following year (all employees are paid for January 1st).

3. What would be the *total effects* of the adjusting entries (parts 1 to 6) on each of the three financial statements?

Problem 3-9B   *Apply the revenues and matching principles, make adjusting entries, account for prepaid expenses recorded initially as an expense, prepare an adjusted trial balance, prepare an income statement **(Obj. 2, 3, 4, 5, A1)***

J. Sharkley owns and operates a scuba-diving business as a corporation called J. Sharkley Scuba Diving Inc. On December 31, 19X1, the business had the following account balances (in alphabetical order):

Accounts payable	$ 4,000
Accounts receivable	3,800
Accumulated amortization—building	8,000
Accumulated amortization—equipment	4,500
Cash	2,000
Boat rental expense	8,600
Building	40,000
Equipment rental revenues	9,200
J. Sharkley, common stock	32,000
J. Sharkley, dividends	15,000
Prepaid consulting	2,500
Salaries expense	18,300
Scuba diving equipment	12,000
Scuba diving fees earned	50,000
Supplies	900
Supplies expense	3,900
Utilities expense	700

The following information was available on December 31, 19X1:

- A physical count showed there were $1,000 worth of supplies on hand on December 31st.

- The buildings had an expected useful life of 10 years with no expected salvage value.

- The scuba-diving equipment was expected to be used for 4 years with no expected salvage value.

- On October 1, Sharkley hired a consultant to prepare a business plan and agreed to pay her $500 per month. Sharkley paid her five months in advance.

- On December 15th, Sharkley rented a boat for $3,000 to go to San Francisco for a holiday. This was recorded as Boat Rental Expense.

- Joseph's assistant, who earns $200 per day, has worked the last five days of the year and will be paid on January 5, 19X2.

- On December 30th, Sharkley provided scuba-diving lessons to a customer for $400 to be paid in 30 days.

Required

1. Journalize the adjustments required on December 31, 19X1.
2. Prepare, with accounts in the correct sequence, an adjusted trial balance on December 31, 19X1.
3. Prepare an income statement for the year ended December 31, 19X1.
4. How old was the Building on December 31, 19X1? The scuba-diving equipment?

Challenge Problems

Problem 3-1C   *Understanding accrual-basis accounting*   *(Obj. 1, 2, 3)*

The basic accounting period is one year and all organizations report on an annual basis. It is common for large companies to report on an annual basis and some even report monthly. Interim reporting has a cost, however.

You are working part-time as an accounting clerk for Delray Corp. The company was private and prepared only annual financial statements for its shareholders. Delray has gone public and now must report quarterly. Mary Miller, your supervisor in the accounting department, is concerned about all the additional work that will be required to produce the quarterly statements.

Required

What does Mary mean when she talks about "additional work"?

Problem 3-2C   *Application of the matching principle*   *(Obj. 2)*

The matching principle is well-established as a basis for recording expenses.

Required

1. New accountants sometimes state the principle as matching revenues against expenses. Explain to a new accountant why matching revenues against expenses is incorrect.
2. It has been suggested that not-for-profit organizations, such as churches and hospitals, should flip their income statements and show revenues as a deduction from expenses. Why do you think that the suggestion has been made?

Extending Your Knowledge

Decision Problems

1. Valuing a business on the basis of its net income   (Obj. 4, 5)

Pat Simunic has owned and operated Simunic Biomedical Systems, Ltd., a management consulting firm for physicians, since its beginning 10 years ago. From all appearances the business has prospered. Simunic lives in the fast lane—flashy car, home located in an expensive suburb, frequent trips abroad, and other signs of wealth. In the past few years, you have become friends with her and her husband through weekly rounds of golf at the country club. Recently, she mentioned that she has lost her zest for the business and would consider selling it for the right price. She claims that her clientele is firmly established, and that the business "runs on its own." According to Simunic, the consulting procedures are fairly simple, and anyone could perform the work.

Assume you are interested in buying this business. You obtain its most recent monthly trial balance, which follows. Assume that revenues and expenses vary little from month to month and April is a typical month.

Your investigation reveals that the trial balance does not include the effects of monthly revenues of $1,100 and expenses totaling $2,100. If you were to buy Simunic Biomedical Systems, Ltd., you would hire a manager so you could devote your time to other duties. Assume that this person would require a monthly salary of $2,000.

Simunic Biomedical Systems, Ltd. **Trial Balance** **April 30, 19XX**		
Cash	$ 9,700	
Accounts receivable	4,900	
Prepaid expenses	2,600	
Capital assets	241,300	
Accumulated depreciation		$189,600
Land	158,000	
Accounts payable		13,800
Salary payable		
Unearned consulting revenue		56,700
Common stock		50,000
Retained earnings		107,400
Dividends	9,000	
Consulting revenue		12,300
Salary expense	3,400	
Rent expense		
Utilities expense	900	
Depreciation expense		
Supplies expense		
Total	$429,800	$429,800

Required

1. Is this an unadjusted or adjusted trial balance? How can you tell?

2. Assume that the most you would pay for the business is 30 times the monthly net income you could expect to earn from it. Compute this possible price.

3. Simunic states that the least she will take for the business is its shareholders' equity on April 30. Compute this amount.

4. Under these conditions, how much should you offer Simunic? Give your reasons.

2. Understanding the concepts underlying the accrual basis of accounting (Obj. 1, 2)

The following independent questions relate to the accrual basis of accounting:

1. It has been said that the only time a company's financial position is known for certain is when the company is wound up and its only asset is cash. Why is this statement true?

2. A friend suggests that the purpose of adjusting entries is to correct errors in the accounts. Is your friend's statement true? What is the purpose of adjusting entries if the statement is wrong?

3. The text suggested that furniture (and each other capital asset that is depreciated) is a form of prepaid expense. Do you agree? Why do you think some accountants view capital assets this way?

Ethical Issue

The net income of Adkin's Ltd., a department store, decreased sharply during 1996. Matthew Adkin, owner of the store, anticipates the need for a bank loan in 1997. Late in 1996 he instructed the accountant to record a $2,600 sale of furniture to the Adkin family, even though the goods will not be shipped from the manufacturer until January 1997. Adkin also told the accountant not to make the following December 31, 1996 adjusting entries:

Salaries owed to employees	$1,800
Prepaid insurance that has expired	530

Required

1. Compute the overall effect of these transactions on the store's reported income for 1996.

2. Why did Adkin take this action? Is this action ethical? Give your reason, identifying the parties helped and the parties harmed by Adkin's action.

3. As a personal friend, what advice would you give the accountant?

Financial Statement Problems

1. Journalizing and posting transactions, and tracing account balances to the financial statements   (Obj. 3, 4, 5)

Mark's Work Wearhouse Ltd.—like all other businesses—makes adjusting entries prior to year end in order to measure assets, liabilities, revenues, and expenses properly. Examine Mark's Work Wearhouse's balance sheet and pay particular attention to Prepaid Expenses and Deposits and Accounts Payable and Accrued Liabilities (which includes Salary Payable, Interest Payable, and Advance Payments from Customers—another name for unearned revenue). Assume the following balances at January 30, 1993, the beginning of the current year: Salary Payable, $268 thousand; Interest Payable, $81 thousand.

Required

1. Open T-accounts for: Prepaid Expenses and Deposits; Salary Payable; Interest Payable; and Advance Payments from Customers. Insert Mark's Work Wearhouse's balances (in thousands) at January 30, 1993. (Examples: Prepaid Expenses and Deposits $1,106; Interest Payable $81; Advance Payments from Customers $250.)

2. Journalize the following for the current year, ended January 29, 1994. Key entries by letter. Explanations are not required.

   Cash transactions (amounts in thousands):

   a. Paid prepaid expenses, $87.

   b. Paid the January 30, 1993, salary payable.

   c. Paid the January 30, 1993, interest payable.

   d. Received $76 cash for customers' advance payments on orders.

   Adjustments at January 29, 1994 (amounts in thousands):

   e. Prepaid expenses expired, $145. (Debit Back Line Expense.)

   f. Salary Payable, $301. (Debit Personnel Expense.)

   g. Accrued interest payable, $72.

   h. Earned sales revenue for which cash has been received from customers in advance, $250.

3. After these entries are posted, show that the balance in the Prepaid Expenses and Deposits account agrees with the corresponding amount reported in the January 29, 1994, balance sheet.

2. Adjusting the accounts of an actual company   (Obj. 2)

Obtain the annual report of an actual company of your choosing. Assume the company accountants *failed* to make four adjustments at the end of the current year. For illustrative purposes, we shall assume that the amounts reported for the related assets and liabilities are *incorrect*.

Adjustments omitted:

a. Depreciation of equipment, $800,000.

b. Salaries owed to employees but not yet paid, $230,000.

c. Prepaid rent used up during the year, $100,000.

d. Accrued sales (or service) revenue, $140,000.

Required

1. Compute the correct amounts for the following balance sheet items:
   a. Book value of capital assets
   b. Total liabilities
   c. Prepaid expenses
   d. Accounts receivable

2. Compute the amount of net income or net loss that the company would have reported if the accountants had recorded these transactions properly. Ignore income tax.

Appendix

Alternate Treatment of Accounting for Prepaid Expenses and Unearned Revenues

Chapters 1 through 3 illustrate the most popular way to account for prepaid expenses and unearned revenues. This appendix illustrates an alternate—equally appropriate—approach to handling prepaid expenses and unearned revenues.

OBJECTIVE A1

Account for a prepaid expense recorded initially as an expense

Short Exercise:
How does a business record
(1) the prepayment of
monthly rent in an expense
account; (2) utilities expense;
(3) the prepayment of three
months' rent?

A:

(1) Rent Expense   XX
    Cash   XX

(2) Utilities Expense   XX
    Cash   XX

(3) Rent Expense   XX
    Cash   XX

It is easier to record the
payment as an expense than
as an asset, like most
payments.

Prepaid Expenses

Prepaid expenses are advance payments of expenses. Prepaid Insurance, Prepaid Rent, Prepaid Advertising, and Prepaid Legal Cost are prepaid expenses. Supplies that will be used up in the current period or within one year are also accounted for as prepaid expenses.

When a business prepays an expense—rent, for example—it can debit an *asset* account (Prepaid Rent) as follows:

Aug. 1	Prepaid Rent	XXX
	Cash..	XXX

Alternatively, it can debit an *expense* account in the entry to record this cash payment:

	Rent Expense	XXX
	Cash..	XXX

Regardless of the account debited, the business must adjust the accounts at the end of the period. Making the adjustment allows the business to report the correct amount of expense for the period and the correct amount of asset at the period's end.

Prepaid Expense Recorded Initially as an Expense

Prepaying an expense creates an asset, as recorded in this chapter. However, the asset may be so short-lived that it will expire in the current accounting period—within one year or less. Thus the accountant may decide to debit the prepayment to an expense account at the time of payment. A $6,000 cash payment for rent (one year, in advance) on August 1 may be debited to Rent Expense:

19X6		
Aug. 1	Rent Expense	6,000
	Cash..	6,000

At December 31 only five months' prepayment has expired, leaving seven months' rent still prepaid. In this case, the accountant must transfer 7/12 of the original prepayment of $6,000, or $3,500, to Prepaid Rent. The adjusting entry decreases the balance of Rent Expense to 5/12 of the original $6,000, or $2,500. The December 31 adjusting entry is

Adjusting Entries

19X6		
Dec. 31	Prepaid Rent ($6,000 × 7/12)	3,500
	Rent Expense...............................	3,500

After posting, the two accounts appear as follows:

Prepaid Rent			Rent Expense		
19X6			19X6		19X6
Dec. 31 Adj. 3,500			Aug. 1 CP 6,000		Dec. 31 Adj. 3,500
Dec. 31 Bal. 3,500			Dec. 31 Bal. 2,500		

CP = Cash payment entry   Adj. = Adjusting entry

The balance sheet for 19X6 reports Prepaid Rent of $3,500, and the income statement for 19X6 reports Rent Expense of $2,500. Whether the business initially debits the prepayment to an asset account or to an expense account, the financial statements report the same amounts for prepaid rent and rent expense.

Unearned (Deferred) Revenues

Unearned (deferred) revenues arise when a business collects cash in advance of earning the revenue. The recognition of revenue is *deferred* until later when it is earned. Unearned revenues are liabilities because the business that receives cash owes the other party goods or services to be delivered later.

Unearned (Deferred) Revenue Recorded Initially as a Revenue

Receipt of cash in advance of earning the revenue creates a liability, as recorded in this chapter. Another way to account for the initial transaction is to credit a *revenue* account when the cash is received. If the business has earned all the revenue within the period during which it received the cash, no adjusting entry is necessary. However, if the business earns only a part of the revenue at the end of the period, it must make adjusting entries.

Suppose on October 1, 19X2, a law firm records the receipt of cash for a nine-month advance fee of $7,200 as revenue. The cash receipt entry is

19X6			
Oct. 1	Cash...	7,200	
	Legal Revenue............................		7,200

At December 31 the attorney has earned only 3/9 of the $7,200, or $2,400. Accordingly, the firm makes an adjusting entry to transfer the unearned portion (6/9 of $7,200, or $4,800) from the revenue account to a liability account.

Adjusting Entries

19X2			
Dec. 31	Legal Revenue ($7,200 × 6/9).........	4,800	
	Unearned Legal Revenue..........		4,800

The adjusting entry leaves the earned portion (3/9, or $2,400) of the original amount in the revenue account. After posting, the total amount ($7,200) is properly divided between the liability account (4,800) and the revenue account ($2,400), as follows:

Unearned Legal Revenue			Legal Revenue			
	19X2		19X6		19X6	
	Dec. 31 Adj. 4,800		Dec. 31 Adj. 4,800		Oct. 1 CR. 7,200	
	Dec. 31 Bal. 4,800				Dec. 31 Bal. 2,400	

CR = Cash receipt entry   Adj. = Adjusting entry

The lawyer's 19X2 income statement reports legal revenue of $2,400, and the balance sheet at December 31, 19X2, reports as a liability the unearned legal revenue of $4,800. Whether the business initially credits a liability account or a revenue account, the financial statements report the same amounts for unearned legal revenue and legal revenue.

OBJECTIVE A2

Account for an unearned (deferred) revenue recorded initially as a revenue

Short Exercise:

The required adjusting entry depends on the way the transaction was originally recorded. (1) If the receipt of cash is recorded as a liability before it is earned, what adjusting is required? (2) If the receipt of cash is originally recorded as revenue, what adjusting entry is required?

A:

(1) Unearned Rev. XX
        Revenue XX

(2) Revenue XX
        Unearned Rev. ... XX

These entries are not interchangeable.

Short Exercise:

Co. X receives $3,000 for magazine subscriptions in advance and records it as a liability. (1) If $1,600 is unearned at the end of the year, what is the adjusting entry? (2) If the subscriptions were originally recorded as revenue, what is the adjusting entry?

A:

(1) Unearned Rev. 1,400
         Revenue   1,400

(2) Revenue 1,600
         Unearned Rev. 1,600

Only $1,400 of the $3,000 had been earned. The revenue account needs a $1,400 balance. That account must be reduced (debited) by $1,600.

Appendix Exercises

Exercise 3A-1   *Recording supplies transactions two ways*   *(Obj. A1)*

At the beginning of the year, supplies of $1,690 were on hand. During the year, the business paid $3,400 cash for supplies. At the end of the year, the count of supplies indicates the ending balance is $1,360.

Required

1. Assume that the business records supplies by initially debiting an *asset* account. Therefore, place the beginning balance in the Supplies T-account, and record the above entries directly in the accounts without using a journal.
2. Assume that the business records supplies by initially debiting an *expense* account. Therefore, place the beginning balance in the Supplies Expense T-account, and record the above entries directly in the accounts without using a journal.
3. Compare the ending account balances under both approaches. Are they the same? Explain.

Exercise 3A-2   *Recording unearned revenues two ways*   *(Obj. A2)*

At the beginning of the year, the company owed customers $6,750 for unearned service revenue collected in advance. During the year, the business received advance cash receipts of $10,000. At year end, the unearned revenue liability is $3,700.

Required

1. Assume that the company records unearned revenues by initially crediting a *liability* account. Open T-accounts for Unearned Service Revenue and Service Revenue, and place the beginning balance in Unearned Service Revenue. Journalize the cash collection and adjusting entries, and post their dollar amounts. As references in the T-accounts, denote a balance by *Bal.*, a cash receipt by *CR*, and an adjustment by *Adj.*
2. Assume that the company records unearned revenues by initially crediting a *revenue* account. Open T-accounts for Unearned Service Revenue and Service Revenue, and place the beginning balance in Service Revenue. Journalize the cash collection and adjusting entries, and post their dollar amounts. As references in the T-accounts, denote a balance by *Bal.*, a cash receipt by *CR*, and an adjustment by *Adj.*
3. Compare the ending balances in the two accounts. Explain why they are the same or different.

Appendix Problem

Problem 3A-1 *Recording prepaid rent and rent revenue collected in advance two ways*   *(Obj. A1, A2)*

Diebolt Sales and Service Inc. completed the following transactions during 19X4:

Aug. 31   Paid $6,000 store rent covering the six-month period ending February 28, 19X5.

Dec. 1   Collected $3,200 cash in advance from customers. The service revenue will be earned $800 monthly over the period ending March 31, 19X5.

Required

1. Journalize these entries by debiting an asset account for Prepaid Rent and by crediting a liability account for Unearned Service Revenue. Explanations are unnecessary.

2. Journalize the related adjustments at December 31, 19X4.

3. Post the entries to the ledger accounts, and show their balances at December 31, 19X4. Posting references are unnecessary.

4. Repeat Requirements 1 through 3. This time debit Rent Expense for the rent payment and credit Service Revenue for the collection of revenue in advance.

5. Compare the account balances in Requirements 3 and 4. They should be equal.

CHAPTER 4
Completing the Accounting Cycle

"People often ask, what's the value of closing the books faster? Clearly, the value of information today is greater than the value of that same information tomorrow. The fast close provides time for more important functions, such as planning and analysis, and reduces overtime, thereby improving morale. It is a distinct competitive advantage," says Kenneth Johnson, Corporate Vice President and Controller of Motorola Inc.

Motorola Inc., best known for its semiconductors, cellular telephones, pagers, and other electronic products, was awarded the first Malcolm Baldrige National Quality Award for superior management of its quality control processes, or total quality management (TQM). The U.S. Department of Commerce grants this award every year to companies that do exemplary work in each of three categories. Motorola won the Malcolm Baldrige Award in the manufacturing category.

To compete in a swiftly changing economy, companies must get financial data to decision-makers fast and at low cost. Motorola accomplishes this goal by rapidly *closing its accounts*, or *closing its books*— the process of preparing the accounts at the end of each period for recording the transactions of the next period. The company amasses detailed financial information in a computerized system that allows its finance division to analyze the information continuously. Motorola can close its accounts in just two days and is working toward the goal of closing its books on a continuous basis. Compared with that of other companies that take two to four weeks to assemble the same type of information, Motorola's statement-preparation process is lightning-fast. This means that Motorola's managers can have up-to-date financial information virtually all the time.

Source: Adapted from Sandy Denarski, "Benchmarking the Best-Summary of Results," *Financial Management News*, April 1993, p. 4

CHAPTER OBJECTIVES
After studying this chapter, you should be able to

1 Prepare an accounting work sheet

2 Use the work sheet to complete the accounting cycle

3 Close the revenue, expense, and dividends accounts

4 Correct typical accounting errors

5 Classify assets and liabilities as current or long-term

6 Use the current and debt ratios to evaluate a business

In Chapter 3 we prepared the financial statements from an adjusted trial balance. That approach works well for quick decision making, but organizations of all sizes take the accounting process a step further. Whether it's Motorola or Air & Sea Travel, the closing process follows the basic pattern outlined in this chapter. It marks the end of the *accounting cycle* for a given period.

Often included in the accounting process is a document known as the accountant's *work sheet*. There are many different types of work sheets in business—as many as there are needs for summary information. Businesspersons who can visualize a useful summary of relevant information—a work sheet—are valuable because work sheets aid decision making.

Overview of the Accounting Cycle

Key Point:

The accounting cycle is repeated each accounting period. The goal of the cycle is the financial statements.

The **accounting cycle** is the process by which companies produce their financial statements for a specific period of time. For a new business, the cycle begins with setting up (opening) the ledger accounts. Gary and Monica Lyon started Air & Sea Travel, Inc. on April 1, 19X1, so the first step in the cycle was to open the accounts. After a business has operated for one period, however, the account balances carry over from period to period. Therefore, the accounting cycle usually starts with the account balances at the beginning of the period, as shown in Exhibit 4-1. The exhibit highlights the new steps that we will be discussing in this chapter.

The accounting cycle is divided into work that is performed during the period — journalizing transactions and posting to the ledger—and work performed at the end of the period to prepare the financial statements. The end-of-period work also readies the accounts for the next period. The greater number of individual steps at the end of the period may seem to suggest that most of the work is done at the end. But, the recording and posting during the period take far more time than the end-of-period work, as is reflected in the organization of this book. We cover the end-of-period accounting in a couple of chapters. The remainder of the book deals with the information needed for decisions on an ongoing basis.

Companies prepare financial statements on a monthly or a quarterly basis, and steps 1 to 6a in Exhibit 4-1 are adequate for statement preparation. Steps 6b through 7 can be performed monthly or quarterly but are necessary only at year's end.

Accounting Work Sheet

Accountants often use a **work sheet**, a multi-columned document that is designed to help move data from the trial balance to the financial statements. The work sheet provides an orderly way to summarize and arrange the data for the financial statements. Listing all the accounts and their unadjusted balances helps identify the accounts that need adjustment. Although it is not essential, the work sheet is helpful

Concept Highlight

EXHIBIT 4-1 *The Accounting Cycle*

PANEL A

During the Period	End of the Period

1. Start with the account balances in the ledger at the beginning of the period.
2. Analyze and journalize transactions as they occur.
3. Post journal entries to the ledger accounts.
	4. Compute the unadjusted balance in each account at the end of the period.
	5. **(Optional) Enter the trial balance on the work sheet, and complete the work sheet.**
	6. Using the adjusted trial balance or the full work sheet as a guide,
	   a. Prepare the financial statements.
	   b. Journalize and post the adjusting entries.
	   c. **Journalize and post the closing entries.**
	7. **Prepare the postclosing, or afterclosing, trial balance. This trial balance becomes step 1 for the next period.**

PANEL B

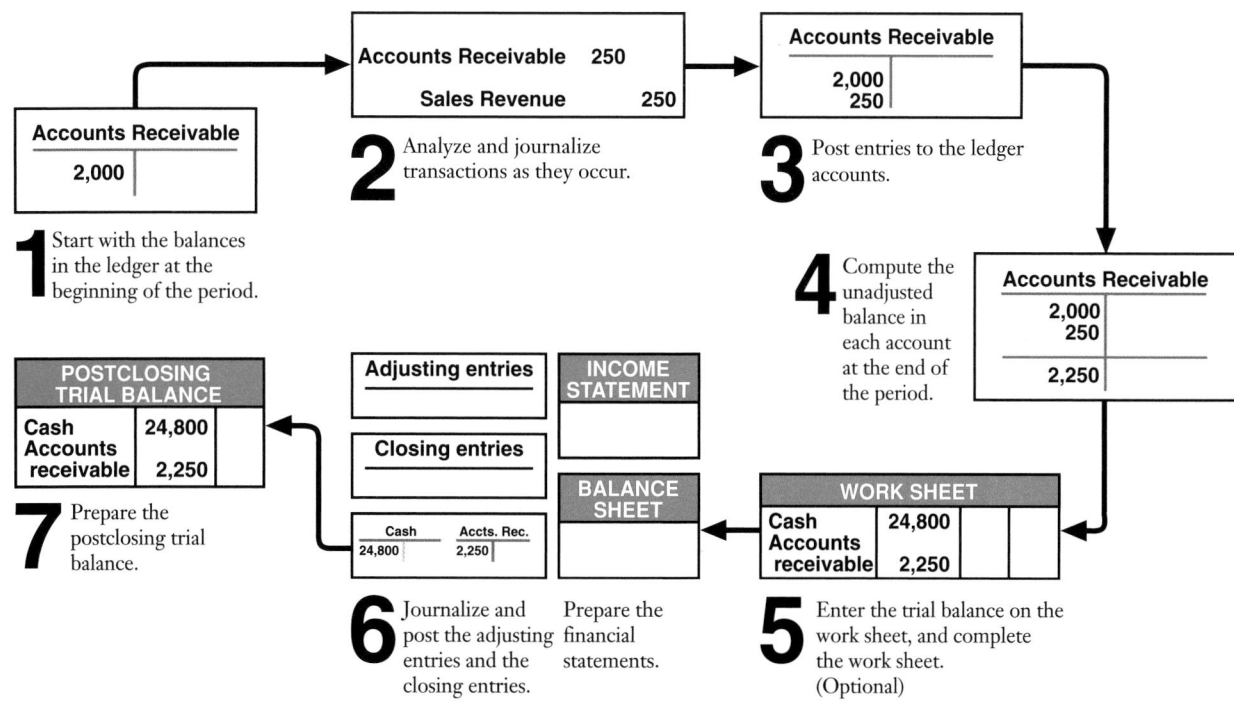

because it brings together in one place the effects of all the transactions of a particular period. The work sheet aids the closing process by listing the adjusted balances of all the accounts. It can also reveal errors.

The work sheet is not part of the ledger or the journal, nor is it a financial statement. Therefore, it is not part of the formal accounting system. Instead, it is a summary device that exists for the accountant's convenience.

Exhibits 4-2 through 4-6 illustrate the development of a typical work sheet for Air & Sea Travel, Inc. The heading at the top names the business, identifies the document, and states the accounting period. A step-by-step description of its preparation follows.

Steps introduced in Chapter 3 to prepare the adjusted trial balance:

1. Print the account titles and their unadjusted ending balances in the Trial Balance columns of the work sheet and total the amounts.

2. Enter the adjustments in the Adjustments columns and total the amounts.

EXHIBIT 4-2 *Trial Balance*

Air & Sea Travel, Inc.
Accounting Work Sheet
For the Month Ended April 30, 19X1

Account Title	Column (1) Trial Balance Dr.	Cr.	Column (2) Adjustments Dr.	Cr.	Column (3) (1) + (2) Adjusted Trial Balance Dr.	Cr.	Column (4) Income Statement Dr.	Cr.	Column (5) Balance Sheet Dr.	Cr.
Cash	24,800									
Accounts receivable	2,250									
Supplies	700									
Prepaid rent	3,000									
Furniture	16,500									
Accumulated depreciation										
Accounts payable		13,100								
Salary payable										
Unearned service revenue		450								
Common stock		20,000								
Retained earnings		11,250								
Dividends	3,200									
Service revenue		7,000								
Rent expense										
Salary expense	950									
Supplies expense										
Depreciation expense										
Utilities expense	400									
	51,800	51,800								

Net income

Write account
titles.

Step 1

Enter
unadjusted
ending balances
in Column (1).

Step 2

3. Compute each account's adjusted balance by combining the trial balance and adjustment figures. Enter the adjusted amounts in the Adjusted Trial Balance columns.

New steps introduced in this chapter:

4. Extend the asset, liability, and shareholder's equity amounts from the Adjusted Trial Balance to the Balance Sheet columns. Extend the revenue and expense amounts to the Income Statement columns. Total the statement columns.

5. Compute net income or net loss as the difference between total revenues and total expenses on the income statement. Enter net income or net loss as a balancing amount on the income statement and the balance sheet, and compute the adjusted column totals.

1. Print the account titles and their unadjusted ending balances in the Trial Balance columns of the work sheet and total the amounts. Total debits must equal total credits as shown in Exhibit 4-2. The account titles and balances come directly from the ledger accounts before the adjusting entries are prepared. Accounts are grouped on the work sheet by category and are usually listed in the order they appear in the ledger. By contrast, their order on the financial statements follows a different pattern. For example, the expenses on the work sheet in Exhibit 4-2 indicate no particular order. But on the income statement, expenses are ordered by amount with the largest first (see Exhibit 4-7).

Accounts may have zero balances (for example, Depreciation Expense). All accounts are listed on the trial balance because they appear in the ledger. Electronically prepared work sheets list all the accounts, not just those with a balance.

2. Enter the adjusting entries in the Adjustments columns and total the amounts. Exhibit 4-3 includes the April adjusting entries. These are the same adjustments that were illustrated in Chapter 3 to prepare the adjusted trial balance.

How can we identify the accounts that need to be adjusted? By scanning the trial balance. Cash needs no adjustment because all cash transactions are recorded as they occur during the period. Consequently, Cash's balance is up to date.

Accounts Receivable is listed next. Has Air & Sea Travel earned revenue that it has not yet recorded? Yes. At April 30, the business has earned $250, which must be accrued because the cash will be received during May. Air & Sea Travel's accountant debits Accounts Receivable and credits Service Revenue on the work sheet in Exhibit 4-3. A letter is used to link the debit and the credit of each adjusting entry. By moving down the trial balance, the accountant identifies the remaining accounts that need adjustment. Supplies is next. The business has used supplies during April, so it debits Supplies Expense and credits Supplies. The other adjustments are analyzed and entered on the work sheet.

The process of identifying accounts that need to be adjusted is aided by listing the accounts in their proper sequence. However, suppose one or more accounts is omitted from the trial balance. It can always be written below the first column totals, $51,800. Assume that Supplies Expense was accidentally omitted and thus did not appear on the trial balance. When the accountant identifies the need to update the Supplies account, he or she knows that the debit in the adjusting entry is to Supplies Expense. In this case, the accountant can write Supplies Expense on the line beneath the amount totals and enter the debit adjustment, $300, on the Supplies Expense line. Keep in mind that the work sheet is not the finished version of the financial statements, so the order of the accounts on the work sheet is not critical. Supplies Expense can be listed in its proper sequence on the income statement. After the adjustments are entered on the work sheet, the amount columns are totaled.

Key Point:
Remember how posting references help track data from the journal to the ledger. These identifiers are equally important for organizing the adjusting entries on the work sheet.

3. Compute each account's adjusted balance by combining the trial balance and adjustment figures. Enter the adjusted amounts in the Adjusted Trial Balance columns. Exhibit 4-4 shows the work sheet with the adjusted trial balance added. This step is performed as illustrated in Chapter 3. For example, the Cash balance is up to date, so it receives no adjustment. Accounts Receivable's adjusted balance of $2,500 is computed by adding the trial balance amount of $2,250 to the $250 debit adjustment. Supplies' adjusted balance of $400 is determined by subtracting the $300 credit adjustment from the unadjusted debit balance of $700. An account may receive more than one adjustment, as does Service Revenue. The column totals should maintain the equality of debit and credits.

4. Extend (that is, transfer) the asset, liability and shareholder's equity amounts from the Adjusted Trial Balance to the Balance Sheet columns. Extend the revenue and expense amounts to the Income Statement columns. Total the statement columns. Every account is either a balance sheet account or an income statement account. The asset, liability, and shareholder's equity accounts go to the balance sheet, and the revenues and expenses go to the income statement. Debits on the adjusted trial balance remain debits in the statement columns, and likewise for credits. Each account's adjusted balance should appear in only one statement column, as shown in Exhibit 4-5.

The income statement indicates total expenses in the debit column ($3,875) and total revenues ($7,400) in the credit column. The balance sheet shows total debits of $49,400 and total credits of $45,875. At this stage, the column totals should not necessarily be equal.

STOP & THINK

Study Exhibit 4-5. How much was Air & Sea Travel's net income or net loss during April? How can you compute net income or net loss from the work sheet?

Answer: Net Income for April was $3,525: total revenues of $7,400 minus total expenses of $3,875—all from the income statement columns of the work sheet.

5. Compute net income or net loss as the difference between total revenues and total expenses on the income statement. Enter net income or net loss as a balancing amount on the income statement and on the balance sheet and compute the adjusted column totals. Exhibit 4-6 presents the completed work sheet, which shows net income of $3,525, computed as follows:

Key Point:
Net income is the difference between the debit and credit Income Statement columns

Revenue (total credits on the income statement)	$7,400
Expenses (total debits on the income statement)	3,875
Net income..	$3,525

Net income of $3,525 is entered in the debit column of the income statement, to balance with the credit column of the income statement, which totals at $7,400. The net income amount is then extended to the credit column of the balance sheet because an excess of revenues over expenses increases retained earnings, and increases in retained earnings are recorded by a credit. In the closing process, net income will find its way into the Retained Earnings account, as we shall soon see.

If expenses exceed revenue, the result is a net loss. In that event, *Net loss* is printed on the work sheet. The loss amount should be entered in the credit column of the income statement and in the debit column of the balance sheet, because an excess of expenses over revenue decreases retained earnings, and decreases in retained earnings are recorded by a debit. After completion, total debits equal total credits in the Income Statement columns. The balance sheet columns are totaled at $49,400.

Mid-Chapter Summary Problem for Your Review

The trial balance of O'Malley's Service Corp. at December 31, 19X1, the end of its fiscal year, is presented below:

	O'Malley's Service Corp. Trial Balance December 31, 19X1	
Cash	$ 198,000	
Accounts receivable.................................	370,000	
Supplies..	6,000	
Furniture and fixtures	100,000	
Accumulated depreciation —furniture and fixtures		$ 40,000
Building..	250,000	
Accumulated depreciation—building......		130,000
Accounts payable.....................................		380,000
Salary payable		
Unearned service revenue		45,000
Common stock		100,000
Retained earnings		193,000
Dividends..	65,000	
Service revenues......................................		286,000
Salary expense..	172,000	
Supplies expense......................................		
Depreciation expense —furniture and fixtures		
Depreciation expense—building.............		
Miscellaneous expense............................	13,000	
Total...	$1,174,000	$1,174,000

Data needed for the adjusting entries include:

a. Supplies on hand at year end, $2,000

b. Depreciation on furniture and fixtures, $20,000

c. Depreciation on building, $10,000

d. Salaries owed but not yet paid, $5,000

e. Accrued service revenue, $12,000

f. Of the $45,000 balance of Unearned Service Revenue, $32,000 was earned during 19X1.

Required

Prepare the work sheet of O'Malley's Service Corporation for the year ended December 31, 19X1. Key each adjusting entry by the letter corresponding to the data given.

SOLUTION TO REVIEW PROBLEM

O'Malley's Service Corp.
Work Sheet
for the year ended December 31, 19X1

Account Title	Trial Balance Debit	Trial Balance Credit	Adjustments Debit	Adjustments Credit	Adjusted Trial Balance Debit	Adjusted Trial Balance Credit	Income Statement Debit	Income Statement Credit	Balance Sheet Debit	Balance Sheet Credit
Cash	198,000				198,000				198,000	
Accounts receivable	370,000		(e) 12,000		382,000				382,000	
Supplies	6,000			(a) 4,000	2,000				2,000	
Furniture and fixtures	100,000				100,000				100,000	
Accumulated depreciation —furniture and fixtures		40,000		(b) 20,000		60,000				60,000
Building	250,000				250,000				250,000	
Accumulated depreciation —building		130,000		(c) 10,000		140,000				140,000
Accounts payable		380,000				380,000				380,000
Salary payable				(d) 5,000		5,000				5,000
Unearned service revenue		45,000	(f) 32,000			13,000				13,000
Common stock		100,000				100,000				100,000
Retained earnings		193,000				193,000				193,000
Dividends	65,000				65,000				65,000	
Service revenue		286,000		(e) 12,000 (f) 32,000		330,000		330,000		
Salary expense	172,000		(d) 5,000		177,000		177,000			
Supplies expense			(a) 4,000		4,000		4,000			
Depreciation expense —furniture and fixtures			(b) 20,000		20,000		20,000			
Depreciation expense—building			(c) 10,000		10,000		10,000			
Miscellaneous expense	13,000				13,000		13,000			
	1,174,000	1,174,000	83,000	83,000	1,221,000	1,221,000	224,000	330,000	997,000	891,000
Net income							106,000			106,000
							330,000	330,000	997,000	997,000

OBJECTIVE 2

Use the work sheet to complete the accounting cycle

Using the Work Sheet

The work sheet helps organize accounting data and compute the net income or net loss for the period. It also aids in preparing the financial statements, recording the adjusting entries, and closing the accounts.

Preparing the Financial Statements

Even though the work sheet shows the amount of net income or net loss for the period, it is still necessary to prepare the financial statements. The sorting of accounts to the balance sheet and income statement eases the preparation of the statements. The work sheet also provides the data for the statement of retained earnings. Exhibit 4-7 presents the April financial statements for Air & Sea Travel, Inc. (based on the data from the work sheet in Exhibit 4-6).

EXHIBIT 4-7 *April Financial Statements of Air & Sea Travel, Inc.*

Air & Sea Travel, Inc.
Income Statement
for the month ended April 30, 19X1

Revenues		
Service revenue		$7,400
Expenses		
Salary expense	$1,900	
Rent expense	1,000	
Utilities expense	400	
Supplies expense	300	
Depreciation expense	275	
Total expenses		3,875
Net income		$3,525

Air & Sea Travel, Inc.
Statement of Retained Earnings
for the month ended April 30, 19X1

Retained Earnings, April 1, 19X1	$11,250
Add: Net income	3,525
	14,775
Less: Dividends	3,200
Retained earnings, April 30, 19X1	$11,575

Air & Sea Travel, Inc.
Balance Sheet
April 30, 19X1

Assets			**Liabilities**		
Cash		$24,800	Accounts payable		$13,100
Accounts receivable		2,500	Salary payable		950
Supplies		400	Unearned service revenue		300
Prepaid rent		2,000	Total liabilities		14,350
Furniture	$16,500				
Less: Accumulated			**Shareholders' Equity**		
depreciation	275	16,225	Common stock		20,000
			Retained earnings		11,575
			Total shareholders' equity		31,575
			Total liabilities and		
Total assets		$45,925	shareholders' equity		$45,925

Recording the Adjusting Entries

The adjusting entries are a key element of accrual-basis accounting. The work sheet helps identify the accounts that need adjustments, which may be conveniently entered directly on the work sheet (Exhibits 4-2 through 4-6). But, actual adjustment of the accounts requires journal entries that are posted to the ledger accounts; see Panel A of Exhibit 4-8. Panel B of the exhibit shows the postings to the accounts, with "Adj." denoting an amount posted from an adjusting entry. Only the revenue and expense accounts are to focus on the closing process, which is discussed in the next section.

EXHIBIT 4-8   *Journalizing and Posting the Adjusting Entries*

Panel A: Journalizing Adjusting Entries   Page 4

Apr. 30	Accounts Receivable	250	
	Service Revenue		250
30	Supplies Expense...	300	
	Supplies		300
30	Rent Expense...	1,000	
	Prepaid Rent		1,000
30	Depreciation Expense	275	
	Accumulated Depreciation............................		275
30	Salary Expense..	950	
	Salary Payable...		950
30	Unearned Service Revenue...............................	150	
	Service Revenue		150

Short Exercise:

Where is each account extended—Income Statement, debit column; Income Statement, credit column; Balance Sheet, debit column; or Balance Sheet, credit column?

1. Cash. **A:** Balance Sheet, debit

2. Supplies. **A:** Balance Sheet, debit

3. Supplies Expense. **A:** Income Statement, debit

4. Unearned Revenue. **A:** Balance Sheet, credit

5. Service Revenue. **A:** Income Statement, credit

6. Common Stock. **A:** Balance Sheet, credit

Panel B: Posting the Adjustments to the Revenue and Expense Accounts

REVENUE

Service Revenue

	7,000
Adj. 250	
Adj. 150	
Bal. 7,400	

EXPENSES

Rent Expense

| Adj. 1,000 | |
| Bal. 1,000 | |

Salary Expense

950	
Adj. 950	
Bal. 1,900	

Depreciation Expense

| Adj. 275 | |
| Bal. 275 | |

Utilities Expense

| 400 | |
| Bal. 400 | |

Supplies Expense

| Adj. 300 | |
| Bal. 300 | |

Adj. = Amount posted from an adjusting entry
Bal. = Balance

The adjusting entries can be recorded in the journal as they are entered on the work sheet, but it is not necessary to journalize them at the same time. Most accountants prepare the financial statements immediately after completing the work sheet. They can wait to journalize and post the adjusting entries before they make the closing entries. Delaying the journalizing and posting of the adjusting entries illustrates another use of the work sheet. Many companies journalize and post the adjusting entries—as in Exhibit 4-8—only at the end of the year. The need for monthly and quarterly financial statements, however, requires a tool like the work sheet. The entity can use the work sheet to aid in preparing interim statements without entering the adjusting entries in the journal and posting them to the ledger.

OBJECTIVE 3

Close the revenue, expense, and dividend accounts

Closing the Accounts

The term **closing the accounts** refers to the step at the end of the period that prepares the accounts for recording the transactions of the next period. Closing the accounts consists of journalizing and posting the closing entries. Closing sets the balances of the revenue and expense accounts back to zero in order to measure the net income of the next period. Closing is a clerical procedure that requires only accounting procedures that we have already covered. Recall that the income statement reports only one period's income. For example, net income for Journey's End Corp., owner of Journey's End motels, for the year ended July 31, 1997, relates exclusively to the twelve months ended on that date. At July 31, 1997, Journey's End accountants close the company's revenues and expense accounts for that year. Because these accounts' balances relate to a particular accounting period and are therefore closed at the end of the period, the revenue and expense accounts are called **temporary (nominal) accounts**. The Dividends account—although not a revenue or an expense—is also a temporary account, because it measures dividends declared during a specific period. The closing process applies only to temporary accounts.

To better understand the closing process, contrast the nature of the temporary accounts with the nature of the **permanent (real) accounts**—the assets, liabilities, and shareholders' equity. The permanent accounts are *not* closed at the end of the period because their balances are not used to measure income. Consider Cash, Supplies, Accounts Receivable, Buildings, Accounts Payable, Notes Payable, Common Stock, and Retained Earnings. These accounts do not represent increases and decreases for a single period as do revenues and expenses, which relate only to one accounting period. Instead the permanent accounts represent assets, liabilities, and shareholders' equity that are on hand at a specific time. This is why their balances at the end of one accounting period carry over to become the beginning balances of the next period. For example, the Cash balance at December 31, 19X1 is also the beginning balance for 19X2.

Briefly, **closing entries** transfer the revenue, expense, and dividends balances from their respective accounts to the Retained Earnings account. As you know, revenues increase retained earnings, and expenses and dividends decrease it. It is when we post the closing entries that the Retained Earnings account absorbs the impact of the balances in the temporary accounts. As an intermediate step, however, the revenues and the expenses are transferred first to an account entitled **Income Summary**, which collects in one place the total debit for the sum of all expenses and the total credit for the sum of all revenues of the period. The Income Summary account is like a temporary "holding tank" used only in the closing process. Then the balance of Income Summary is transferred to Retained Earnings. The steps in closing the accounts of a corporation like Air & Sea Travel, Inc., are as follows:

① Debit each revenue account for the amount of its credit balance. Credit Income Summary for the sum of the revenues. This entry transfers the sum of the revenues to the credit side of the Income Summary.

② Credit each expense account for the amount of its debit balance. Debit Income Summary for the sum of the expenses. This entry transfers the sum of the expenses to the debit side of the Income Summary.

③ Debit Income Summary for the amount of its credit balance (revenues minus expenses) and credit the Retained Earnings account. If Income Summary has a debit balance, then credit Income Summary for this amount and debit Retained Earnings. This entry transfers the net income or loss from Income Summary to the Retained Earnings account.

④ Credit the Dividends account for the amount of its debit balance. Debit the Retained Earnings account. Dividends are not expenses and do not affect net income or net loss. This entry transfers the Dividends amount to the debit side of the Retained Earnings account.

To illustrate, suppose Air & Sea Travel closes the books at the end of April. Exhibit 4-9 presents the complete closing process for the business. Panel A gives the closing journal entries, and Panel B shows the accounts after the closing entries have been posted.

 Key Point:
There is no account for Net Income, which is the net result of all revenue and expense accounts. The Income Summary combines all revenue and expense amounts into one account.

EXHIBIT 4-9   *Journalizing and Posting the Closing Entries*

Panel A: Journalizing

Closing Entries   **Page 5**

① Apr. 30	Service Revenue	7,400	
	Income Summary............................		7,400
② 30	Income Summary	3,875	
	Rent Expense		1,000
	Salary Expense		1,900
	Supplies Expense		300
	Depreciation Expense......................		275
	Utilities Expense		400
③ 30	Income Summary ($7,400 – $3,875)	3,525	
	Retained Earnings...........................		3,525
④ 30	Retained Earnings	3,200	
	Dividends..		3,200

Panel B: Posting

Rent Expense

Adj.	1,000		
Bal.	1,000	Clo.	1,000

Salary Expense

	950		
Adj.	950		
Bal.	1,900	Clo.	1,900

Supplies Expense

Adj.	300		
Bal.	300	Clo.	300

Depreciation Expense

Adj.	275		
Bal.	275	Clo.	275

Utilities Expense

	400		
Bal.	400	Clo.	400

Income Summary

Clo.	3,875	Clo.	7,400
Clo.	3,525	Bal.	3,525

Service Revenue

			7,000
		Adj.	250
		Adj.	150
Clo.	7,400	Bal.	7,400

Dividends

Bal.	3,200	Clo.	3,200

Retained Earnings

Clo.	3,200		11,250
		Clo.	3,525
		Bal.	11,575

Adj. = Amount posted from an adjusting entry
Clo. = Amount posted from a closing entry
Bal. = Balance

Key Point: ☑
It is not necessary to make a separate closing entry for each expense. In one closing entry, record one debit to Income Summary and a separate credit to each expense account.

The amount in the debit side of each expense account is its adjusted balance. For example, Rent Expense has a $1,000 debit balance. Also note that Service Revenue has a credit balance of $7,400 before closing. These amounts come directly from the adjusted balances in Exhibit 4-8, Panel B.

Closing entry ①, denoted in the Service Revenue account *Clo.*, transfers Service Revenue's balance to the Income Summary account. This entry zeroes out Service Revenue for April and places the revenue on the credit side of Income Summary.

Closing entry ② zeroes out the expenses and moves their total ($3,875) to the debit side of Income Summary. At this point, Income Summary contains the impact of April's revenues and expenses; hence Income Summary's balance is the month's net income ($3,525). Closing entry ③ closes the Income Summary account by transferring net income to the credit side of Retained Earnings.[1] The last closing entry, ④, moves the dividends to the debit side of Retained Earnings, leaving a zero balance in the Dividends account.

After all the closing entries, the revenues, the expenses, and the Dividends account are set back to zero to make ready for the next period. The Retained Earnings account includes the full effects of the April revenues, expenses, and dividends. These amounts, combined with Retained Earning's beginning balance, give Retained Earnings an ending balance of $11,575. This balance agrees with the amount reported on the statement of retained earnings and on the balance sheet in Exhibit 4-7.

Closing a Net Loss   What would the closing entries be if Air & Sea Travel, Inc., had suffered a net *loss* during April? Suppose April expenses totaled $7,700 and all other factors were unchanged. Only closing entries ② and ③ would be altered. Closing entry ② would transfer expenses of $7,700 to Income Summary, as follows:

Income Summary

Clo.	7,700	Clo.	7,400
Bal.	300		

Closing entry ③ would then credit Income Summary to close its debit balance and to transfer the net loss to Capital:

③ Apr. 30   Retained Earnings... 300
                      Income Summary   300

After posting, these two accounts would appear as follows:

Income Summary						**Retained Earnings**		
Clo.	7,700	Clo.	7,400		Clo.	300		11,250
Bal.	300	Clo.	300					

Finally, the Dividends balance would be closed to Retained Earnings, as before.

As outlined, the closing process is fundamentally mechanical and is completely automated in a computerized system. Accounts are identified as either temporary or permanent. The temporary accounts are closed automatically by selecting that option from the software's menu. Posting also occurs automatically.

Postclosing Trial Balance

The accounting cycle ends with the **postclosing trial balance** (see Exhibit 4-10). The postclosing trial balance is the final check on the accuracy of journalizing and posting the adjusting and closing entries. Like the trial balance that begins the work sheet, the postclosing trial balance is a list of the ledger's accounts and balances. This step ensures that the ledger is in balance for the start of the next accounting period. The postclosing trial balance is dated as of the end of the period for which the statements have been prepared.

Short Exercise:

(1) Would the Income Summary have a debit or a credit balance if the company suffers a net loss? (2) In the event of a loss, how is Income Summary closed?

A: (1) Expenses would exceed revenues, and Income Summary would have a debit balance (2) Income Summary is credited, and Retained Earnings is debited.

Key Point:

The double line in an account means that the account has a zero balance; nothing more will be posted to it in the current period. The double line is drawn immediately after the closing entry is posted. In the general ledger, the account has a zero balance.

---

[1] The Income Summary account is a convenience for combining the effects of the revenues and expenses prior to transferring their income effect to Retained Earnings. It is not necessary to use the Income Summary account in the closing process. Another way of closing the revenues and expenses makes no use of this account. In this alternative procedure, the revenues and expenses are closed directly to Retained Earnings.

Short Exercise:

A company pays its employees $1,500 every Friday, the end of a 5-day work week. What journal entry is made each Friday?

Salary Expense   1,500
   Cash   1,500

If December 31 falls on a Tuesday, what would be the adjusting entry?

Salary Expense   600
   Salary Payable   600

What would be the reversing entry on January 1?

Salary Payable   600
   Salary Expense   600

What would be the entry to record the payroll the next Friday?

Salary Expense   1,500
   Cash   1,500

Short Exercise:

(1) John Doe recorded the collection of a $1,000 receivable as a debit to Cash and a credit to Service Revenue for $1,000. Prepare the correcting entry. (2) If Doe's net income before the correction was $26,000, how much is the corrected net income?

A:

(1) Service Rev.   1,000
   Accounts Rec.   1,000

(2) $25,000
   ($26,000 − $1,000)

EXHIBIT 4-10 *Postclosing Trial Balance*

Air & Sea Travel, Inc. Postclosing Trial Balance April 30, 19X1		
Cash	$24,800	
Accounts receivable..	2,500	
Supplies..	400	
Prepaid rent	2,000	
Furniture	16,500	
Accumulated depreciation		$ 275
Accounts payable..		13,100
Salary payable		950
Unearned service revenue...		300
Common stock		20,000
Retained earnings		11,575
Total	$46,200	$46,200

The postclosing trial balance resembles the balance sheet. It contains the ending balances of the permanent accounts—the balance sheet accounts: the assets, liabilities, and shareholders' equity. No temporary accounts—revenues, expenses, or withdrawal accounts—are included because their balances have been closed. The ledger is up to date and ready for the next period's transactions.

Correcting Journal Entries

In Chapter 2 we discussed errors that affect the trial balance: treating a debit as a credit and vice versa; transpositions; and slides. Here we show how to correct errors in journal entries.

When a journal entry contains an error, the entry can be deleted and corrected—if the error is caught immediately. A computerized accounting system makes easy work of retrieving an incorrect entry. When you delete the original entry, the posting is also cancelled. You can then record the correct entry, which is posted automatically.

If the error is detected after posting, the accountant makes a *correcting entry*. Suppose Air & Travel, Inc., paid $5,000 cash for furniture and erroneously debited Supplies as follows:

OBJECTIVE 4
Correct typical accounting errors

Incorrect Entry

May 13	Supplies	5,000	
	Cash		5,000
	Bought supplies.		

The debit to Supplies is incorrect, so it is necessary to make a correcting entry as follows:

Correcting Entry

May 15	Furniture...	5,000	
	Supplies		5,000
	To correct May 13 entry.		

The credit to Supplies in the second entry offsets the incorrect debit of the first entry. The debit to Furniture in the correcting entry places the furniture's cost in the correct account. Now both Supplies and Furniture are correct. Cash was unaffected by the error because Cash was credited correctly in the entry to purchase the furniture.

Classification of Assets and Liabilities _____

On the balance sheet, assets and liabilities are classified as either *current* or *long-term* to indicate their relative *liquidity*. **Liquidity** is a measure of how quickly an item can be converted to cash. Cash is the most liquid asset. Accounts receivable is a relatively liquid asset because the business expects to collect the amount in cash in the near future. Supplies are less liquid than accounts receivable, and furniture and buildings are even less so.

Users of financial statements are interested in liquidity because business difficulties often arise owing to a shortage of cash. How quickly can the business convert an asset to cash and pay a debt? How soon must a liability be paid? These are questions of liquidity. Balance sheets list assets and liabilities in the order of their relative liquidity.

OBJECTIVE 5
Classify assets and liabilities as current or long-term

Current Assets   **Current assets** are assets that are expected to be converted to cash, sold, or consumed during the next 12 months or within the business's normal operating cycle if longer than a year. The **operating cycle** is the time span during which (1) cash is used to acquire goods and services, and (2) those goods and services are sold to customers, who in turn pay for their purchases with cash. For most businesses, the operating cycle is a few months. A few types of business have operating cycles longer than a year. Cash, Accounts Receivable, Notes Receivable due within a year or less, and Prepaid Expenses are current assets. Merchandising entities such as Eaton's, The Bay, and Zellers have an additional current asset, Inventory. This account shows the cost of goods that are held for sale to customers.

Long-Term Assets   **Long-term assets** are all assets other than current assets. They are not held for sale, but rather they are used to operate the business. One category of long-term assets is capital assets or fixed assets. Land, Buildings, Furniture and Fixtures, and Equipment are capital assets. Of these, Air & Sea Travel has only Furniture. There are other categories of long-term assets such as Investments and other Assets (a catchall category for assets that are not classified more precisely).

Financial statement users such as creditors are interested in the due dates of an entity's liabilities. The sooner a liability must be paid, the more current it is. Liabilities that must be paid on the earliest future date create the greatest strain on cash. Therefore, the balance sheet lists liabilities in the order in which they are due. Knowing how many of a business's liabilities are current and how many are long-term helps creditors assess the likelihood of collecting from the entity. Balance sheets usually have at least two liability classifications, *current liabilities* and *long-term liabilities*.

Current Liabilities   **Current liabilities** are debts that are due to be paid within one year or one of the entity's operating cycles if the cycle is longer than a year. Accounts Payable, Notes Payable due within one year, Salaries Payable, Unearned Revenue, Goods and Services Tax Payable, and Interest Payable owed on notes payable are current liabilities.

Long-Term Liabilities   All liabilities that are not current are classified as **long-term liabilities**. Many notes payable are long-term. Other notes payable are paid in installments, with the first installment due within one year, the second installment due the second year, and so on. In this case, the first installment would be a current liability and the remainder long-term liabilities.

An Actual Classified Balance Sheet

Exhibit 4-11 is an actual classified balance sheet of John Labatt Limited. John Labatt labels its balance sheet as the Statement of Financial Position, a more descriptive title. The statement is labeled Consolidated because it reports the accounts of John Labatt and its component companies as well. Dollar amounts are reported in millions to avoid clutter. John Labatt's year end is April 30, 1994. It is customary to present

EXHIBIT 4-11   *Consolidated Statements of Financial Position*

John Labatt Limited
As at April 30, 1994 (millions)

	1994
Assets	
Current assets	
Cash and short-term investments	$ 368
Accounts receivable and advances	376
Inventories	193
Prepaid expenses	93
Discontinued operations	72
	1,102
Fixed assets	813
Other assets	539
Discontinued operations	82
	$2,536
Liabilities	
Current liabilities	
Bank advances and short-term notes	$ 100
Accounts payable and accrued charges	401
Deferred revenue	99
Taxes payable	52
Long-term debt due within one year	4
Discontinued operations	65
	721
Non-convertible long-term debt	610
Deferred income taxes	
Continuing operations	86
Discontinued operations	—
	1,417
Convertible debentures and shareholders' equity	
Convertible debentures	$ 91
Shareholders' equity	
Share capital	
Preferred shares	300
Common shares	363
Retained earnings	364
Cumulative translation adjustment	1
	1,028
	1,119
	$2,536

two or more years' statements together to let people compare one year with the other—1994 and 1993 in this case.

You should be familiar with all but a few of John Labatt's account titles. One title you might not be familiar with is *Discontinued Operations*; note that this account title appears as a current asset, a long-term asset, and as a current liability. Those balances are explained in the notes to the financial statements and relate to the disposal of the company's dairy business in Canada and the United States

John Labatt includes marketable or short-term securities together with cash on the balance sheet under the title "Cash and Short-term Investments." "Other Assets," a long-term asset, is made up mainly of securities and investments in other companies and goodwill (a term used to describe the excess of the cost of a purchased company over the market value of its net assets—you will study this term later in the text).

You should recognize John Labatt's current liabilities. Bank Advances and Short-term Notes are like Notes Payable. John Labatt collects revenue from customers in advance. This practice explains the account titled Deferred Revenue, which is another name for the Unearned Revenues account.

Notice that John Labatt has long-term debt titled Non-convertible Long-term Debt, which is included with long-term liabilities, and other long-term debt grouped with shareholders' equity titled Convertible Debentures. They are different in that the latter is convertible into common shares in the future at the option of the holder. Since management believes that such conversion is likely, the debt is grouped with shareholders' equity. (You will learn more about convertible debt later in the course.)

John Labatt reports a long-term liability for Deferred Income Taxes. These are corporate income taxes payable that the company may pay beyond one year in the future.

Formats of Balance Sheets

The balance sheet of John Labatt Limited shown in Exhibit 4-11 lists the assets at the top, with the liabilities and shareholders' equity below. This is the *report format*. The balance sheet of Air & Sea Travel, Inc., presented in Exhibit 4-7 lists the assets at the left, with the liabilities and the shareholders' equity at the right. That is the *account format*.

Either format is acceptable. A recent survey of 300 Canadian companies indicated that slightly over 82 percent used the report format and slightly over 14 percent used the account format.

STOP & THINK

IBM reported less shareholders' equity at December 31, 1992, than at December 31, 1991. Why might shareholders' equity have decreased?

Answer: The main reasons were that IBM suffered a net loss during 1992 and that the company paid dividends to its shareholders. You may be wondering why a company would pay dividends during a loss year. Suppose Air & Travel had a bad year and lost money. Gary and Monica Lyon would still need to pay household and other personal expenses. If the business had accumulated assets and retained earnings in previous years, the Lyons could draw on those resources in a lean year.

It is the same for a large corporation. Prior to 1992 IBM had built up lots of assets and retained earnings, which were available to absorb losses and pay dividends in a bad year. This is why investors and creditors feel comfortable investing in, and lending to, a business with a large amount of retained earnings. It has the shareholders' equity to survive hard times.

Use of Accounting Information in Decision-Making

The purpose of accounting is to provide information for decision-making. Chief users of accounting information include managers, investors, and creditors. A creditor considering lending money must predict whether the borrower can repay the loan. If the borrower already has lots of debt, the probability of repayment is lower than if the borrower has a small amount of liabilities. To assess financial position, decision-makers use ratios computed from various items drawn from a company's financial statements.

> **OBJECTIVE 6**
> Use the current and debt ratios to evaluate a business

Current Ratio

One of the most common ratios is the **current ratio**, which is the ratio of an entity's current assets to its current liabilities:

Short Exercise:

A company has current assets of $100, 000 and current liabilities of $50,000. How will the payment of a $10,000 account payable affect the current ratio? **A:** The payment of an account payable would cause both cash and accounts payable to decrease and thus would increase the current ratio from 2.00 to 2.25

$$\text{Current Ratio} \ = \ \frac{\text{Total current assets}}{\text{Total current liabilities}}$$

The current ratio measures the ability to pay current liabilities with current assets. A company prefers a high current ratio, which means the business has plenty of current assets to pay current liabilities. An increasing current ratio from period to period generally indicates improvement in financial position.

A rule of thumb: A strong current ratio would be in the range of 2.00; it would indicate that the company has approximately $2.00 in current assets for every $1.00 in current liabilities. A company with a current ratio of 2.00 would probably have little trouble paying its current liabilities. Most successful businesses operate with current ratios between 1.30 and 2.00. A current ratio of 1.0 is considered quite low. Lenders and investors would view a company with a current ratio of 1.50 to 2.00 as substantially less risky. Such a company could probably borrow money on better terms and also attract more investors.

Debt Ratio

Real-World Example:

John Labatt has a current ratio of 1.52 (1.52 = $1,102,000,000/$721,000). The ratio indicates that John Labatt is in a fairly strong liquidity position.

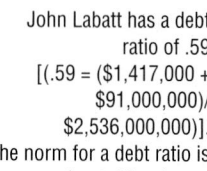

A second aid to decision-making is the **debt ratio**, which is the ratio of total liabilities to total assets:

$$\text{Debt ratio} \ = \ \frac{\text{Total liabilities}}{\text{Total assets}}$$

Real-World Example:

John Labatt has a debt ratio of .59 [(.59 = ($1,417,000 + $91,000,000)/ $2,536,000,000)]. The norm for a debt ratio is about .50 or lower.

The debt ratio indicates the proportion of a company's assets that are financed with debt. This ratio measures a business's ability to pay both current and long-term debts—total liabilities. A low debt ratio is safer than a high debt ratio. Why? Because a company with a small amount of liabilities has low required payments. Such a company is unlikely to get into financial difficulty. By contrast, a company with a high debt ratio may have trouble paying its liabilities, especially when sales are low and cash is scarce. When a company fails to pay its debts on a timely basis, the creditors take the business away from its owners.

The largest retail bankruptcy in history, Federated Department Stores (owned at one point by Campeau Corporation) was due largely to high debt during a retail-industry recession. Federated was unable to weather the downturn and had to declare bankruptcy.

In general, a *high* current ratio is preferred over a low current ratio. *Increases* in the current ratio indicate improving financial position. By contrast, a *low* debt ratio is preferred over a high debt ratio. Improvement is indicated by a *decrease* in the debt ratio.

Financial ratios are an important aid to decision-makers. However, it is unwise to place too much confidence in a single ratio or group of ratios. For example, a company may have a high current ratio, which indicates financial strength. It may also have a high debt ratio, which suggests weakness. Which ratio gives the more reliable signal about the company? Experienced managers, lenders and investors evaluate a company by examining a large number of ratios over several years to spot trends and turning points. These people also consider other facts, such as the company's cash position and its trend in net income. No single ratio gives the whole picture about a company.

As you progress through the study of accounting, we will introduce key ratios used for decision-making. Chapter 19 summarizes all the ratios discussed throughout this book. This chapter provides a good overview of ratios used in decision-making.

PUTTING SKILLS TO WORK

Ratios: Should a Bank Grant a Loan?

Suppose John Labatt, the company in Exhibit 4-11, needed a bank loan to purchase a new division. How would a bank evaluate the company's financial position to judge whether to grant the loan? The example above shows just two pieces of information a bank loan officer would consider.

Excerpts from John Labatt's balance sheet

• Total current assets: $1,102,000,000

• Total current liabilities: $721,000,000

• Total assets: $2,536,000,000

• Total liabilities and convertible debentures: $1,508,000,000

The Current Ratio

The bank might look at John Labatt's current ratio to determine the company's ability to pay current liabilities with current assets. The bank could use John Labatt's balance sheet to calculate a current ratio of 1.53 at April 30,1994:

$$\text{Current ratio} = \frac{\$1,102,000,000}{\$721,000,000} = 1.53$$

The value of this ratio indicates that John Labatt has a ratio that is in the mid-range of current ratios indicating that the company has sufficient current assets to pay off its current liabilities and still have funds to operate. One year earlier, John Labatt's ratio stood at 1.27 ($1,187,000,000/ $932,000,000 = 1.27) which is not as good.

The Debt Ratio

The bank would want more information than just the current ratio before making a decision about a loan. It could compute John Labatt's debt ratio to measure the company's ability to pay current and long-term debts. From the balance sheet, John Labatt's debt ratio is calculated to be 0.65 at April 30, 1994:

$$\text{Debt ratio} = \frac{\$1,508,000,000}{\$2,536,000,000} = 0.595$$

That figure is in line with other large companies and somehow higher than John Labatt's debt ratio of one year earlier, at April 30, 1993 ($1,814,000,000/$3,020,000,000 = 0.60).

The Final Decision

How would a decision-maker use John Labatt's ratios? John Labatt's current ratio would not worry the loan officer since it is within an acceptable range and did improve over the previous year. The decision-maker may suggest that while John Labatt's debt ratio is not a problem, it has deteriorated from 1993. In summary, John Labatt could probably arrange the loan at a favorable interest rate.

Summary Problem for Your Review

Refer to the data in the Mid-Chapter Summary Problem for Your Review, presented on pp. 167–168

Required

1. Journalize and post the adjusting entries. (Before posting to the accounts, enter into each account its balance as shown in the trial balance. For example, enter the $370,000 balance in the Accounts Receivable account before posting its adjusting entry.) Key adjusting entries by *letter*, as shown in the work sheet solution to the mid-chapter review problem. You can take the adjusting entries straight from the work sheet on p. 168.

2. Journalize and post the closing entries. (Each account should carry its balance as shown in the adjusted trial balance.) To distinguish closing entries from adjusting entries, key the closing entries by *number*. Draw the arrows to illustrate the flow of data, as shown in Exhibit 4-9, p. 172. Indicate the balance of the Retained Earnings account after the closing entries are posted.

3. Prepare the income statement for the year ended December 31, 19X1. List Miscellaneous Expense last among the expenses, a common practice.

4. Prepare the statement of retained earnings for the year ended December 31, 19X1. Draw the arrow that links the income statement to the statement of retained earnings.

5. Prepare the classified balance sheet at December 31, 19X1. Use the report form. All liabilities are current. Draw the arrow that links the statement of retained earnings to the balance sheet.

SOLUTION TO REVIEW PROBLEM

Requirement 1

a. Dec. 31		Supplies Expense		4,000	
		Supplies			4,000
b.	31	Depreciation Expense—Furniture and Fixtures		20,000	
		Accumulated Depreciation —Furniture and Fixtures			20,000
c.	31	Depreciation Expense—Building		10,000	
		Accumulated Depreciation—Building			10,000
d.	31	Salary Expense		5,000	
		Salary Payable			5,000
e.	31	Accounts Receivable		12,000	
		Service Revenue			12,000
f.	31	Unearned Service Revenue		32,000	
		Service Revenue			32,000

Accounts Receivable

370,000	
(e)　12,000	

Supplies

6,000	(a)　4,000

Accumulated Depreciation —Furniture and Fixtures

	40,000
	(b)　20,000

Accumulated Depreciation —Building

	130,000
	(c)　10,000

Salary Payable

	(d)　5,000

Unearned Service Revenue

(f)　32,000	45,000

Service Revenue

	286,000
	(e)　12,000
	(f)　32,000
	Bal. 330,000

Salary Expense

172,000	
(d)　5,000	
Bal. 177,000	

Supplies Expense

(a)　4,000	
Bal.　4,000	

Depreciation Expense —Furniture and Fixtures

(b)　20,000	
Bal.　20,000	

Depreciation Expense —Building

(c)　10,000	
Bal.　10,000	

Requirement 2

a. Dec. 31	Service Revenue...	330,000	
		Income Summary		330,000
b.	31	Income Summary	224,000	
		Salary Expense...		177,000
		Supplies Expense.....................................		4,000
		Depreciation Expense		
		—Furniture and Fixtures........................		20,000
		Depreciation Expense—Building...............		10,000
		Miscellaneous Expense.............................		13,000
c.	31	Income Summary ($330,000 – $224,000).........	106,000	
		Retained Earnings		106,000
d.	31	Retained Earnings	65,000	
		Dividends..		65,000

Salary Expense

	172,000			
(d)	5,000			
Bal.	177,000	(2)	177,000	

Supplies Expense

(a)	4,000			
Bal.	4,000	(2)	4,000	

Depreciation Expense
— Furniture and Fixtures

(b)	20,000			
Bal.	20,000	(2)	20,000	

Depreciation Expense
— Building

(c)	10,000			
Bal.	10,000	(2)	10,000	

Miscellaneous Expense

	13,000			
Bal.	13,000	(2)	13,000	

Income Summary

(2)	224,000	(1)	330,000	
(3)	106,000	Bal.	106,000	

Service Revenue

			286,000	
		(e)	12,000	
		(f)	32,000	
(1)	330,000	Bal.	330,000	

Dividends

Bal.	65,000	(4)	65,000	

Retained Earnings

(4)	65,000		193,000	
		(3)	106,000	
		Bal.	234,000	

Requirement 3

O'Malley's Service Corp.
Income Statement
for the year ended December 31, 19X1

Revenues		
Service revenue		$330,000
Expenses		
Salary expense	$177,000	
Depreciation expense—furniture and fixtures	20,000	
Depreciation expense—building	10,000	
Supplies expense	4,000	
Miscellaneous expense	13,000	
Total expenses		224,000
Net Income		$106,000

Requirement 4

O'Malley's Service Corp.
Statement of Retained Earnings
for the year ended December 31, 19X1

Retained earnings, January 1, 19X1	$193,000
Add: Net income	106,000
	299,000
Less: Dividends	65,000
Retained earnings, December 31, 19X1	$234,000

Requirement 5

O'Malley's Service Corp.
Balance Sheet
December 31, 19X1

Assets

Current assets		
Cash		$198,000
Accounts receivable		382,000
Supplies		2,000
Total current assets		582,000
Capital assets		
Furniture and fixtures	$100,000	
Less: Accumulated depreciation	60,000	40,000
Building	250,000	
Less: Accumulated depreciation	140,000	110,000
		150,000
Total assets		$732,000

Liabilities

Current liabilities		
Accounts payable		$380,000
Unearned service revenue		13,000
Salary payable		5,000
Total current liabilities		398,000

Shareholders' Equity

Common stock	100,000	
Retained earnings	234,000	334,000
Total liabilities and shareholders' equity		$732,000

Summary

1. *Prepare an accounting work sheet.* The *accounting cycle* is the process by which accountants produce the financial statements for a specific period of time. The cycle starts with the beginning account balances. During the period, the business journalizes transactions and posts them to the ledger accounts. At the end of the period, the trial balance is prepared, and the accounts are adjusted in order to measure the period's net income or net loss. Completion of the accounting cycle is aided by use of a *work sheet*. This multicolumned document summarizes the effects of all the activity of the period.

2. *Use the work sheet to complete the accounting cycle.* The work sheet is neither a journal nor a ledger but merely a convenient device for completing the accounting cycle. It has columns for the trial balance, the adjustments, the adjusted trial balance, the income statement, and the balance sheet. It aids the adjusting process, and it is the place where the period's net income or net loss is first computed. The work sheet also provides the data for the financial statements and the *closing entries*. It is not, however, a necessity. The accounting cycle can be completed from the less elaborate adjusted trial balance.

3. *Close the revenue, expense, and dividends accounts.* Revenues, expenses, and dividends represent increases and decreases in retained earnings for a specific period. At the end of the period, their balances are closed out to zero, and, for this reason, they are called *temporary accounts*. Assets, liabilities, and shareholders' equity are not closed because they are the *permanent accounts*. Their balances at the end of one period become the beginning balances of the next period. The final accuracy check of the period is the *postclosing trial balance*.

4. *Correct typical accounting errors.* Accountants correct errors by making correcting journal entries.

5. *Classify assets and liabilities as current or long-term.* The balance sheet reports *current* and *long-term assets* and *current* and *long-term liabilities*. It can be presented in *report format* or *account format*.

6. *Use the current and debt ratios to evaluate a business.* Two decision-making aids are the *current ratio*—total current assets divided by total current liabilities—and the *debt ratio*—total liabilities divided by total assets.

Self-Study Questions

Test your understanding of the chapter by marking the correct answer to each of the following questions:

1. The focal point of the accounting cycle is the *(p. 162)*
   a. Financial statements
   b. Trial balance
   c. Adjusted trial balance
   d. Work sheet

2. Arrange the following accounting cycle steps in their proper order *(p. 163)*
   a. Complete the work sheet
   b. Journalize and post adjusting entries
   c. Prepare the postclosing trial balance
   d. Journalize and post cash transactions
   e. Prepare the financial statements
   f. Journalize and post closing entries

3. The work sheet is a *(pp. 162–163)*
   a. Journal
   b. Ledger
   c. Financial statement
   d. Convenient device for completing the accounting cycle

4. The usefulness of the work sheet is *(pp. 162–163)*
   a. Identifying the accounts that need to be adjusted
   b. Summarizing the effects of all the transactions of the period
   c. Aiding the preparation of the financial statements
   d. All of the above

5. Which of the following accounts is not closed? *(pp. 170–171)*
   a. Supplies Expense   c. Interest Revenue
   b. Prepaid Insurance   d. Dividends

6. The closing entry for Salary Expense, with a balance of $322,000, is *(pp. 171–172)*

   a. Salary Expense... 322,000
        Income Summary   322,000

   b. Salary Expense... 322,000
        Salary Payable...   322,000

   c. Income Summary 322,000
        Salary Expense...   322,000

   d. Salary Payable... 322,000
        Salary Expense...   322,000

7. The purpose of the postclosing trial balance is to *(p. 173)*
   a. Provide the account balances for preparation of the balance sheet
   b. Ensure that the ledger is in balance for the start of the next period
   c. Aid the journalizing and posting of the closing entries
   d. Ensure that the ledger is in balance for completion of the work sheet

8. A payment on account was recorded by debiting Inventory and crediting Cash. This entry was posted. The correcting entry is *(p. 174)*
   a. Accounts Payable   X
        Inventory   X
   b. Inventory   X
        Accounts Payable   X
   c. Cash   X
        Accounts Payable   X
   d. Cash   X
        Inventory   X

9. The classification of assets and liabilities as current or long-term depends on *(p. 175)*
   a. Their order of listing in the general ledger
   b. Whether they appear on the balance sheet or the income statement
   c. The relative liquidity of the item
   d. The format of the balance sheet—account format or report format

10. In 19X4, Air & Sea Travel debited Depreciation Expense for the cost of a computer used in the business. For 19X4, this error *(p. 174)*.
   a. Overstated net income
   b. Understated net income
   c. Either a or b, depending on the circumstances
   d. Had no effect on net income

Answers to the Self-Study Questions follow the Accounting Vocabulary.

Accounting Vocabulary

Accounting cycle *(p. 164)*
Closing the accounts *(p. 170)*
Closing entries *(p. 171)*
Current assets *(p. 175)*
Current liabilities *(p. 175)*
Current ratio *(p. 177)*
Debt ratio *(p. 178)*
Income Summary *(p. 171)*
Liquidity *(p. 175)*
Long-term assets *(p. 175)*
Long-term liabilities *(p. 175)*

Nominal account *(p. 171)*
Operating cycle *(p. 175)*
Permanent account *(p. 171)*
Postclosing trial balance *(p. 173)*
Real account *(p. 171)*
Reversing entries *(p. 209)*
Temporary account *(p. 171)*
Work sheet *(p. 164)*

Answer to Self-Study Questions

1. a   3. d   5. b   7. b   9. c
2. d, a, e, b, f, c   4. d   6. c   8. a   10. b

ASSIGNMENT MATERIAL _____

Questions

1. Identify the steps in the accounting cycle, distinguishing those that occur during the period from those that are performed at the end.
2. Why is the work sheet a valuable accounting tool?
3. Name two advantages the work sheet has over the adjusted trial balance.
4. Why must the adjusting entries be journalized and posted if they have already been entered on the work sheet?
5. Why should the adjusting entries be journalized and posted before the closing entries are made?
6. Which types of accounts are closed?
7. What purpose is served by closing the accounts?
8. State how the work sheet helps with recording the closing entries.
9. Distinguish between permanent accounts and temporary accounts; indicate which type is closed at the end of the period. Give five examples of each type of account.
10. Is Income Summary a permanent account or a temporary account? When and how is it used?
11. Give the closing entries for the following accounts (balances in parentheses): Service Revenue ($4,700), Salary Expense ($1,100), Income Summary (credit balance of $2,000), Dividends ($2,300).
12. Why are assets classified as current or long-term? On what basis are they classified? Where do the classified amounts appear?
13. Indicate which of the following accounts are current assets and which are long-term assets: Prepaid Rent, Building, Furniture, Accounts Receivable, Merchandise Inventory, Cash, Note Receivable (due within one year), Note Receivable (due after one year).
14. In what order are assets and liabilities listed on the balance sheet?
15. Name an outside party that is interested in whether a liability is current or long-term. Why would this party be interested in this information?
16. A friend tells you that the difference between a current liability and a long-term liability is that they are payable to different types of creditors. Is your friend correct? Include in your answer the definitions of these two categories of liabilities.
17. Show how to compute the current ratio and the debt ratio. Indicate what ability each ratio measures, and state whether a high value or a low value is safer for each.

18. Capp Corp. purchased supplies of $120 on account. The accountant debited Supplies and credited Cash for $120. A week later, after this entry has been posted to the ledger, the accountant discovers the error. How should he correct the error?

Exercises

Exercise 4-1 *Preparing a work sheet* **(Obj. 1)**

The trial balance of Makovic Pest Control Service Ltd. follows.

Additional information at September 30, 19X6:

a. Accrued service revenue, $210.

b. Depreciation, $40.

c. Accrued salary expense, $500.

d. Prepaid rent expired, $600.

e. Supplies used, $1,650.

Makovic Pest Control Service Ltd.
Trial Balance
September 30, 19X6

Cash	$ 3,560	
Accounts receivable	3,440	
Prepaid rent	1,200	
Supplies	3,390	
Equipment	12,600	
Accumulated depreciation		$ 2,840
Accounts payable		1,600
Salary payable		
Common stock		5,000
Retained earnings		11,030
Dividends	3,000	
Service revenue		9,300
Depreciation expense		
Salary expense	1,800	
Rent expense		
Utilities expense	780	
Supplies expense		
Total	$29,770	$29,770

Required

Complete Makovic's work sheet for September 19X6.

Exercise 4-2 *Journalizing adjusting and closing entries* **(Obj. 2)**

Journalize the adjusting and closing entries in Exercise 4-1.

Exercise 4-3 *Posting adjusting and closing entries* **(Obj. 2)**

Set up T-accounts for those accounts affected by the adjusting and closing entries in Exercise 4-1. Post the adjusting and closing entries to the accounts, denoting adjustment amounts by *Adj.*, closing amounts by *Clo.*, and balances by *Bal*. Double underline the accounts with zero balances after you close them and show the ending balance in each account.

Exercise 4-4   *Preparing a postclosing trial balance*   **(Obj. 2)**

Prepare the postclosing trial balance in Exercise 4-1.

Exercise 4-5   *Identifying and journalizing closing entries*   **(Obj. 3)**

From the following selected accounts that Higginbotham Catering Service, Inc., reported in its June 30, 19X4 annual financial statements, prepare the entity's closing entries.

Retained earnings.................	$45,600	Interest expense.........................	$ 2,200
Service revenue......................	96,100	Accounts receivable.................	30,000
Unearned revenues	1,350	Salary payable	850
Salary expense........................	12,500	Depreciation expense	10,200
Accumulated depreciation ...	35,000	Rent expense............................	5,900
Supplies expense...................	1,700	Dividends.................................	40,000
Interest revenue	700	Supplies	1,400

Exercise 4-6   *Identifying and journalizing closing entries*   **(Obj. 4)**

The accountant for Loren Chin System Design, Inc., has posted adjusting entries (a) through (e) to the accounts at December 31, 19X2. All the revenue, expense, and shareholders' equity accounts of the entity are listed here in T-account form.

Accounts Receivable	**Supplies**	**Accumulated Depreciation —Furniture**	**Retained Earnings**
26,000 (a) 3,500	4,000 | (b) 2,000	5,000 (c) 1,100	276,000

Accumulated Depreciation —Building	**Salary Payable**	**Common Stock**
33,000 (d) 6,000	(e) 700	25,000

Dividends	**Service Revenue**	**Salary Expense**
52,400	102,000 (a) 3,500	26,000 (e) 700

Supplies Expense	**Depreciation Expense —Furniture**	**Depreciation Expense —Building**
(b) 2,000	(c) 1,100	(d) 6,000

Required

Journalize Loren Chin System Design's closing entries at December 31, 19X2.

Exercise 4-7   *Preparing a statement of retained earnings*   **(Obj. 3)**

From the following accounts of Overhead Door Corp., prepare the entity's statement of retained earnings for the year ended December 31, 19X5.

Retained Earnings				Dividends			
Dec. 31	42,000	Jan. 1	52,000	Mar. 31	9,000	Dec. 31	42,000
		Dec. 31	43,000	Jun. 30	7,000		
				Sept. 30	9,000		
				Dec. 31	17,000		

Income Summary			
Dec. 31	85,000	Dec. 31	128,000
31	43,000		

Exercise 4-8   *Identifying and recording adjusting and closing entries*   *(Obj. 2, 3)*

The trial balance and income statement amounts from the March work sheet of Sisam Management Corp. are presented below.

Account Title	Trial Balance		Income Statement	
Cash	$ 5,100			
Supplies	2,400			
Prepaid rent	1,100			
Office equipment	30,100			
Accumulated depreciation		$ 6,200		
Accounts payable		4,600		
Salary payable				
Unearned service revenue		4,400		
Common stock		7,500		
Retained earnings		10,300		
Dividends	1,000			
Service revenue		11,700		$16,000
Salary expense	3,000		$ 3,800	
Rent expense	1,200		1,400	
Depreciation expense			300	
Supplies expense			400	
Utilities expense	800		800	
	$44,700	$44,700	$ 6,700	$16,000
			9,300	
Net income			$16,000	$16,000

Required

Journalize the adjusting and closing entries of Sisam Management Corp. at March 31.

Exercise 4-9   *Preparing a classified balance sheet*   *(Obj. 5, 6)*

Refer to Exercise 4-8.

Required

1. After solving Exercise 4-8, use the data in that exercise to prepare Sisam Management Corp.'s classified balance sheet at March 31 of the current year. Use the report format.

2. Compute Sisam's current ratio and debt ratio at March 31. One year ago, the current ratio was 1.20 and the debt ratio was .30. Indicate whether Sisam's ability to pay its debts has improved or deteriorated during the current year.

Exercise 4-10 *Correcting accounting errors* *(Obj. 4)*

Prepare a correcting entry for each of the following accounting errors:

a. Debited Supplies and credited Accounts Payable for a $2,900 purchase of office equipment on account.

b. Adjusted prepaid rent by debiting Prepaid Rent and crediting Rent Expense for $900. This adjusting entry should have debited Rent Expense and credited Prepaid Rent for $900.

c. Debited Salary Expense and credited Cash to accrue salary expense of $900.

d. Recorded the earning of $3,200 service revenue collected in advance by debiting Accounts Receivable and crediting Service Revenue.

e. Accrued interest revenue of $800 by a debit to Accounts Receivable and a credit to Interest Revenue.

f. Recorded a $600 cash purchase of supplies by debiting Supplies and crediting Accounts Payable.

Serial Exercise

This exercise continues the Emily Schneider, Architect, Inc., situation begun in Exercise 2-13 of Chapter 2 and extended to Exercise 3-14 of Chapter 3.

Exercise 4-11 *Closing the books, preparing a classified balance sheet, and evaluating a business* *(Obj. 3, 5, 6)*

Refer to Exercise 3-14 of Chapter 3. Start from the posted T-accounts and the adjusted trial balance that Emily Schneider, Architect, Inc., prepared for her architectural practice at December 31.

Required

1. Journalize and post the closing entries at December 31. Denote each closing amount as *Clo.* and an account balance as *Bal.*

2. Prepare a classified balance sheet at December 31.

3. Compute the current ratio and the debt ratio of Schneider's architectural practice and evaluate these ratio values as indicative of a strong or weak financial position.

4. If your instructor assigns it, complete the accounting work sheet at December 31.

Challenge Exercise

Exercise 4-12 *Computing financial statement amounts* *(Obj. 2, 5)*

The unadjusted trial balance of ElsiMate Corp. follows:

Cash	$ 1,900	Unearned service revenue	$ 5,300
Accounts receivable	7,200	Note payable, long-term	6,000
Rent receivable		Common stock	10,000
Supplies	1,100	Retained earnings	50,100
Prepaid Insurance	2,200	Dividends	16,200
Furniture	8,400	Service revenue	93,600
		Rent revenue	1,900
Accumulated depreciation—		Salary expense	32,700
furniture	1,300	Depreciation expense—	
Building	57,800	furniture	
Accumulated depreciation—		Depreciation expense—building	
building	14,900	Supplies expense	

Land	51,200	Insurance expense	
Accounts payable	6,100	Interest expense	
Salary payable		Advertising expense	7,800
Interest payable		Property tax expense	
Property tax payable		Utilities expense	2,700

Adjusting data at the end of the year include:

a. Unearned service revenue that has been earned, $3,600.

b. Accrued rent revenue, $1,200.

c. Accrued property tax expense, $900.

d. Accrued service revenue, $1,700.

e. Supplies used in operations, $600.

f. Accrued salary expense, $1,400.

g. Insurance expense, $1,800.

h. Depreciation expense—furniture, $800; building, $2,100.

i. Accrued interest expense, $500.

Elsie Sharp, the owner, has received an offer to sell ElsiMate Corp. She needs to know the following information within one hour:

1. Net income for the year covered by these data.

2. Total assets.

3. Total liabilities.

4. Total shareholders' equity.

5. Proof that total assets = total liabilities + total shareholders' equity after all items are updated.

Required

Without opening any accounts, making any journal entries, or using a work sheet, provide Elsie Sharp with the requested information. Show all computations.

Problems   *(Group A)*

Problem 4-1A   *Preparing a work sheet*   *(Obj. 1)*

The trial balance of Krup Painting Contractors at July 31, 19X3 appears below.

Krup Painting Contractors, Inc. **Trial Balance** **July 31, 19X3**		
Cash...	$ 1,200	
Accounts receivable	37,820	
Supplies..	17,660	
Prepaid insurance..	2,300	
Equipment..	32,690	
Accumulated depreciation—equipment....		$ 26,240
Building	36,890	
Accumulated depreciation—building.......		10,500
Land..	28,300	
Accounts payable		22,690
Interest payable..		
Wage payable		
Unearned service revenue...........................		10,560
Note payable, long-term..............................		22,400
Common stock..		20,000
Retained earnings..		39,130
Dividends	4,200	
Service revenue..		14,190
Depreciation expense—equipment............		
Depreciation expense—building................		
Wage expense...	3,200	
Insurance expense		
Interest expense		
Utilities expense..	270	
Property tax expense...................................	840	
Advertising expense	340	
Supplies expense		
Total...	$165,710	$165,710

Additional data at July 31, 19X3:

a. Depreciation: equipment, $630; building, $370.

b. Accrued wage expense, $240.

c. Supplies on hand, $14,740.

d. Prepaid insurance expired during July, $500.

e. Accrued interest expense, $180.

f. Unearned service revenue earned during July, $4,970.

g. Accrued advertising expense, $100. (Credit Accounts Payable.)

h. Accrued service revenue, $1,100.

Required

Complete Krup's work sheet for July.

Problem 4-2A   *Preparing financial statements from an adjusted trial balance; journalizing adjusting and closing entries   (Obj. 2, 5, 6)*

The adjusted trial balance of Armoured Car Security Couriers Corp. at June 30, 19X1, the end of the company's fiscal year, follows:

Armoured Car Security Couriers Corp. Adjusted Trial Balance June 30, 19X1		
Cash	$ 19,350	
Accounts receivable	26,470	
Supplies	1,290	
Prepaid insurance	3,200	
Equipment	55,800	
Accumulated depreciation—equipment		$ 16,480
Building	144,900	
Accumulated depreciation—building		16,850
Accounts payable		38,400
Interest payable		1,490
Wage payable		770
Unearned service revenue		2,300
Note payable, long-term		97,000
Common stock		10,000
Retained earnings		58,390
Dividends	45,300	
Service revenue		109,860
Depreciation expense—equipment	7,300	
Depreciation expense—building	3,970	
Wage expense	18,800	
Insurance expense	3,100	
Interest expense	11,510	
Utilities expense	4,300	
Property tax expense	2,670	
Supplies expense	3,580	
Total	$351,540	$351,540

Additional data at June 30, 19X1:

a. Depreciation for the year: equipment, $7,300; building, $3,970.

b. Supplies used during the year, $3,580.

c. Prepaid insurance expired during the year, $3,100.

d. Accrued interest expense, $690.

e. Accrued service revenue, $940.

f. Unearned service revenue earned during the year, $7,790.

g. Accrued wage expense, $770.

Required

1. Journalize the adjusting and closing entries.

2. Prepare Armoured Car's income statement and statement of retained earnings for the year ended June 30, 19X1 and the classified balance sheet on that date. Use the account format for the balance sheet.

3. Compute Armoured Car's current ratio and debt ratio at June 30, 19X1. One year ago, the current ratio stood at 1.01, and the debt ratio was .71. Did Armoured Car's ability to pay debts improve or deteriorate during 19X1?

4. How will what you have learned in this problem help you manage a business?

Problem 4-3A   *Taking the accounting cycle through the closing entries*   **(Obj. 2, 3)**

The unadjusted T-accounts of Christine Ciancia Design, Inc., at December 31, 19X2, and the related year-end adjustment data follow:

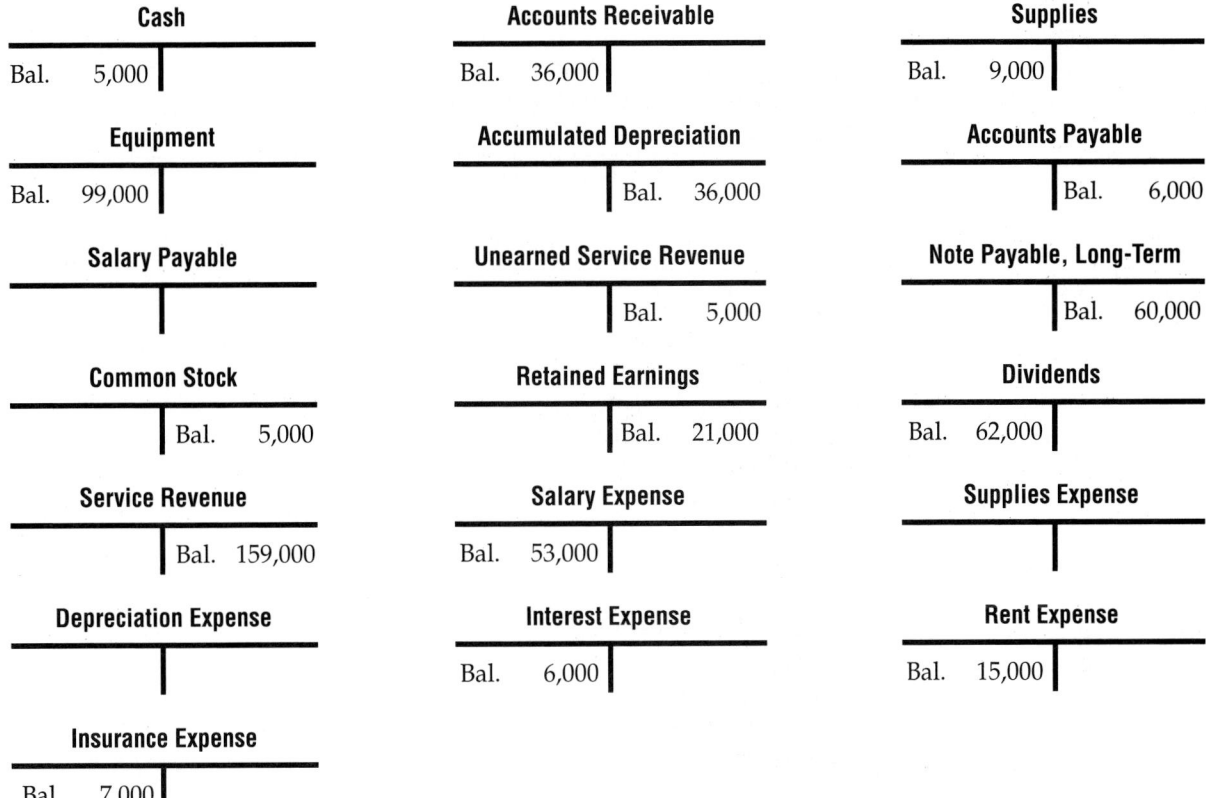

| **Cash** | | | |
| Bal. | 5,000 | | |

| **Accounts Receivable** | | | |
| Bal. | 36,000 | | |

| **Supplies** | | | |
| Bal. | 9,000 | | |

| **Equipment** | | | |
| Bal. | 99,000 | | |

| **Accumulated Depreciation** | | | |
| | | Bal. | 36,000 |

| **Accounts Payable** | | | |
| | | Bal. | 6,000 |

| **Salary Payable** | | | |

| **Unearned Service Revenue** | | | |
| | | Bal. | 5,000 |

| **Note Payable, Long-Term** | | | |
| | | Bal. | 60,000 |

| **Common Stock** | | | |
| | | Bal. | 5,000 |

| **Retained Earnings** | | | |
| | | Bal. | 21,000 |

| **Dividends** | | | |
| Bal. | 62,000 | | |

| **Service Revenue** | | | |
| | | Bal. | 159,000 |

| **Salary Expense** | | | |
| Bal. | 53,000 | | |

| **Supplies Expense** | | | |

| **Depreciation Expense** | | | |

| **Interest Expense** | | | |
| Bal. | 6,000 | | |

| **Rent Expense** | | | |
| Bal. | 15,000 | | |

| **Insurance Expense** | | | |
| Bal. | 7,000 | | |

Adjustment data at December 31, 19X2 include:

a. Unearned service revenue earned during the year, $5,000.

b. Supplies on hand, $1,000.

c. Depreciation for the year, $9,000.

d. Accrued salary expense, $1,000.

e. Accrued service revenue, $2,000.

Required

1. Write the trial balance on a work sheet, and complete the work sheet. Key each adjusting entry by the letter corresponding to the data given.

2. Prepare the income statement, the statement of retained earnings, and the classified balance sheet in account format.

3. Journalize the adjusting and closing entries.

Problem 4-4A   *Completing the accounting cycle*   **(Obj. 2, 3)**

This problem should be used only in conjunction with Problem 4-3A. It completes the accounting cycle by posting to T-accounts and preparing the postclosing trial balance.

Required

1. Using the Problem 4-3A data, post the adjusting and closing entries to the T-accounts, denoting adjusting amounts by *Adj.*, closing amounts by *Clo.*, and

account balances by *Bal.*, as shown in Exhibit 4-9. Double underline all accounts with a zero ending balance.

2. Prepare the postclosing trial balance.

Problem 4-5A   *Completing the accounting cycle*   *(Obj. 2, 3, 5)*

The trial balance of Leung Insurance Agency Ltd. at August 31, 19X9, and the data needed for the month-end adjustments follow.

Leung Insurance Agency Ltd.
Trial Balance
August 31, 19X9

Account Number	Account Title	Debit	Credit
11	Cash	$ 3,800	
12	Accounts receivable	15,560	
13	Prepaid rent	1,290	
14	Supplies	900	
15	Furniture	15,350	
16	Accumulated depreciation—furniture		$ 12,800
17	Building	89,900	
18	Accumulated depreciation—building		28,600
21	Accounts payable		4,240
22	Salary payable		
23	Unearned commission revenue		8,900
31	Common stock		50,000
32	Retained earnings		21,920
33	Dividends	4,800	
41	Commission revenue		7,300
51	Salary expense	1,100	
52	Rent expense		
53	Utilities expense	410	
54	Depreciation expense—furniture		
55	Depreciation expense—building		
56	Advertising expense	650	
57	Supplies expense		
	Total	$133,760	$133,760

Adjustment data:

a. Unearned commission revenue still unearned at August 31, $6,750.

b. Prepaid rent still in force at August 31, $1,050.

c. Supplies used during the month, $340.

d. Depreciation on furniture for the month, $370.

e. Depreciation on building for the month, $130.

f. Accrued salary expense at August 31, $460.

Required

1. Open the accounts listed in the trial balance, inserting their August 31 unadjusted balances. Also open the Income Summary account, number 34. Date the balances of the following accounts as of August 1: Prepaid Rent, Supplies, Furniture, Accumulated Depreciation—Furniture, Building, Accumulated Depreciation—Building, Unearned Commission Revenue, and Retained Earnings.

2. Write the trial balance on a work sheet and complete the work sheet of Leung Insurance Agency Ltd. for the month ended August 31, 19X9.

3. Prepare the income statement, the statement of retained earnings, and the classified balance sheet in report format.

4. Using the work sheet data, journalize and post the adjusting and closing entries. Use dates and posting references. Use page 7 as the number of the journal page.

5. Prepare a postclosing trial balance.

Problem 4-6A *Preparing a classified balance sheet in report format* **(Obj. 5, 6)**

The accounts of Zak Travel Agency Ltd. at December 31, 19X6 are listed in alphabetical order.

Accounts payable	$ 5,100	Interest receivable	$ 200
Accounts receivable	6,600	Note payable, long-term	27,800
Accumulated depreciation		Note receivable, long-term	4,000
—building	37,800	Other assets	3,600
Accumulated depreciation		Other current assets	1,700
—furniture	11,600	Other current liabilities	4,700
Advertising expense	2,200	Prepaid insurance	1,100
Building	104,400	Prepaid rent	6,600
Cash	6,500	Retained earnings,	
Commission revenue	93,500	December 31, 19X5	35,300
Common stock	15,000	Salary expense	24,600
Current portion of		Salary payable	3,900
note payable	2,200	Supplies	2,500
Current portion of		Supplies expense	5,700
note receivable	1,000	Unearned commission	
Depreciation expense	1,300	revenue	5,400
Dividends	47,400		
Furniture	22,700		
Insurance expense	800		
Interest payable	600		

Required

1. All adjustments have been journalized and posted, but the closing entries have not yet been made. Prepare the company's classified balance sheet in report format at December 31, 19X6. Use captions for total assets, total liabilities, and shareholders' equity.

2. Compute Zak's current ratio and debt ratio at December 31, 19X6. At December 31, 19X5, the current ratio was 1.52 and the debt ratio was .37. Did Zak's ability to pay debts improve or deteriorate during 19X6?

Problem 4-7A *Analyzing and journalizing corrections, adjustments, and closing entries* **(Obj. 3, 4)**

Accountants for Osaka Catering Service Inc., encountered the following situations while adjusting and closing the books at December 31. Consider each situation independently.

a. The $39,000 balance of Equipment was entered as $3,900 on the trial balance.
   (1) What is the name of this type of error?
   (2) Assume this is the only error in the trial balance. Which will be greater, the total debits or the total credits, and by how much?
   (3) How can this type of error be identified?

b. The company bookkeeper made the following entry to record a $600 credit purchase of office equipment:

Nov. 12   Office Supplies 600
            Accounts Payable 600

Prepare the correcting entry, dated December 31.

c. A $750 debit to Cash was posted as a credit.
   (1) At what stage of the accounting cycle will this error be detected?
   (2) Describe the technique for identifying the amount of the error.

d. The accountant failed to make the following adjusting entries at December 31:
   (1) Accrued property tax expense, $200.
   (2) Supplies expense, $1,090.
   (3) Accrued interest revenue on a note receivable, $650.
   (4) Depreciation of equipment, $4,000.
   (5) Earned service revenue that had been collected in advance, $5,100.
   Compute the overall net income effect of these omissions.

e. Record each of the adjusting entries identified in item d.

f. The revenue and expense accounts, after the adjusting entries had been posted, were Service Revenue, $56,800; Interest Revenue, $2,000; Salary Expense, $14,200; Rent Expense, $5,100; Depreciation Expense, $5,550; Supplies Expense, $1,530; and Property Tax Expense, $1,190. Two balances prior to closing were Retained Earnings, $58,600, and Dividends, $30,000. Journalize the closing entries.

Problem 4-8A   *Prepare a work sheet, journalize the adjustments, close the accounts*
                  (Obj. 1, 3)

RV Mobile Repairs Inc. performs overhauls and repairs to motor homes and trailers at the customer's location. The company had the following trial balance for the year ended March 31, 19X1:

Cash	$ 3,400	
Accounts receivable	11,200	
Repair supplies	8,900	
Prepaid insurance	3,900	
Repair equipment	70,000	
Accumulated depreciation—equipment		$ 28,000
Building	94,000	
Accumulated depreciation—building		18,800
Land	65,000	
Accounts payable		7,200
Unearned repair revenues		1,500
Income taxes payable		2,000
Notes payable (2 years)		8,000
Mortgage payable		70,000
Common stock		80,000
Retained earnings		15,700
Dividends	9,000	
Repair fees earned		64,300
Wages expense	21,400	
Utilities expense	1,100	
Travel expenses	7,600	
Totals	$295,500	$295,500

Additional information:

- On March 31st, a physical count of the repair supplies showed $1,300 worth were still on hand.
- An examination of the insurance policies showed $2,100 worth had expired in the year ended March 31, 19X1.
- An examination of the repair equipment and the building showed the following:

	Repair Equipment	*Building*
Estimated useful life	5 years	10 years
Estimated salvage value	$0	$0

- The company had performed $800 of services for a client who had paid $1,500 in advance.
- Accrued expenses included:
      interest on the mortgage, $600
      wages, $900
      income taxes, $200
- An examination of the accounting records showed that $1,800 of service performed on credit was incorrectly recorded as a cash transaction.

Required

1. Complete a work sheet for the year ended March 31, 19X1.
2. Journalize the adjusting and correcting entries required on March 31, 19X1.
3. Journalize the closing entries that would be required on March 31, 19X1.
4. Prepare a postclosing trial balance for March 31, 19X1.

Problem 4-9A   *Prepare a work sheet, close the accounts, classify the assets and liabilities, evaluate the current and debt ratios*   **(Obj. 1, 3, 4, 6)**

J. Rapids, the accountant, had prepared the work sheet shown on the next page on a computer spreadsheet but has lost much of the data. The only particular item the accountant can recall is that there was an adjustment made to correct an error made where $400 of supplies, purchased on credit, had been incorrectly recorded as $4,000 of equipment.

Required:

1. Complete the work sheet by filling in the missing data.
2. Journalize the closing entries that would be required on December 31, 19X1.
3. Prepare the company's classified balance sheet as of December 31, 19X1.
4. Compute Whitewater Trips Co.'s current ratio and debt ratio for December 31, 19X1. On December 31, 19X0 the current ratio was 2.14 and the debt ratio was .47. Comment on the changes in the ratios.

Account Title	Trial Balance Debit	Trial Balance Credit	Adjustments Debit	Adjustments Credit	Adjusted Trial Balance Debit	Adjusted Trial Balance Credit	Income Statement Debit	Income Statement Credit	Balance Sheet Debit	Balance Sheet Credit
Cash	1,000								1,000	
Accounts receivable	3,600				3,800					
Supplies	1,900			(b) 800						
Prepaid rent	2,000				1,600					
Equipment	27,500				23,500					
Accumulated depreciation—equipment		2,400								
Building	40,000				40,000					
Accumulated depreciation—building		4,000		(e) 2,000		3,600				
Land	30,000			(f) 600	30,000					
Accounts payable		5,000								
Wages payable		1,200								
Unearned revenues		3,500	(g) 500							
Mortgage payable		50,000								50,000
Common stock		30,000								30,000
Retained earnings		11,000								11,000
Dividends	6,000				6,000				6,000	
Rafting fees earned		33,300						34,000		
Wages expense	23,500				24,100					
Rent expense	4,400									
Utilities expense	500				500					
Totals	140,400	140,400								
Supplies expense			(b) 800				800			
Depreciation expense—equipment										
Depreciation expense—building			(d) 1,200				1,200			
Totals										

Problems   *(Group B)*

Problem 4-1B   *Preparing a work sheet*   **(Obj. 1)**

The trial balance of Wentworth Learning Center, Inc., at May 31, 19X2 follows:

Wentworth Learning Center, Inc. Trial Balance May 31, 19X2		
Cash	$ 3,670	
Notes receivable	10,340	
Interest receivable		
Supplies	560	
Prepaid insurance	1,790	
Furniture	27,410	
Accumulated depreciation—furniture		$ 1,480
Building	58,900	
Accumulated depreciation—building		34,560
Land	13,700	
Accounts payable		14,730
Interest payable		
Salary payable		
Unearned service revenue		8,800
Note payable, long-term		18,700
Common stock		14,000
Retained earnings		20,290
Dividends	3,800	
Service revenue		11,970
Interest revenue		
Depreciation expense—furniture		
Depreciation expense—building		
Salary expense	2,170	
Insurance expense		
Interest expense		
Utilities expense	490	
Property tax expense	640	
Advertising expense	1,060	
Supplies expense		
Total	$124,530	$124,530

Additional data at May 31, 19X2:

a. Depreciation: furniture, $480; building, $460.

b. Accrued salary expense, $600.

c. Supplies on hand, $410.

d. Prepaid insurance expired during May, $390.

e. Accrued interest expense, $220.

f. Unearned service revenue earned during May, $4,400.

g. Accrued advertising expense, $60. Credit Accounts Payable.

h. Accrued interest revenue, $170.

Required

Complete Wentworth's work sheet for May.

Problem 4-2B   *Preparing financial statements from an adjusted trial balance; journalizing adjusting and closing entries   **(Obj. 2, 5, 6)***

The adjusted trial balance of Scace Golf School Inc. at April 30, 19X2, the end of the company's fiscal year, follows:

	Scace Golf School Inc. **Adjusted Trial Balance** **April 30, 19X2**	
Cash	$ 1,370	
Accounts receivable	23,740	
Supplies	3,690	
Prepaid insurance	2,290	
Equipment	63,930	
Accumulated depreciation—equipment		$ 28,430
Building	74,330	
Accumulated depreciation—building		18,260
Accounts payable		19,550
Interest payable		2,280
Wage payable		830
Unearned service revenue		3,660
Note payable, long-term		69,900
Common stock		10,000
Retained earnings		34,200
Dividends	47,500	
Service revenue		98,550
Depreciation expense—equipment	6,900	
Depreciation expense—building	3,710	
Wage expense	29,800	
Insurance expense	5,370	
Interest expense	8,170	
Utilities expense	4,970	
Property tax expense	3,010	
Supplies expense	6,880	
Total	$285,660	$285,660

Additional data at April 30, 19X2:

a. Unearned service revenue earned during the year, $4,180.

b. Supplies used during the year, $5,880.

c. Prepaid insurance expired during the year, $5,370.

d. Accrued interest expense, $1,280.

e. Accrued service revenue, $2,200.

f. Depreciation for the year: equipment, $6,900; building, $3,710.

g. Accrued wage expense, $830.

Required

1. Journalize the adjusting and closing entries.

2. Prepare Scace's income statement and statement of retained earnings for the year ended April 30, 19X2 and the classified balance sheet on that date. Use the account format for the balance sheet.

3. Compute Scace's current ratio and debt ratio at April 30, 19X2. One year ago, the current ratio stood at 1.21, and the debt ratio was .82. Did Scace's ability to pay debts improve or deteriorate during 19X2?

Problem 4-3B   *Taking the accounting cycle through the closing entries*   *(Obj. 2, 3)*

The unadjusted T-accounts of Pierre Fortin Televideo Corp. at December 31, 19X2, and the related year-end adjustment data follow:

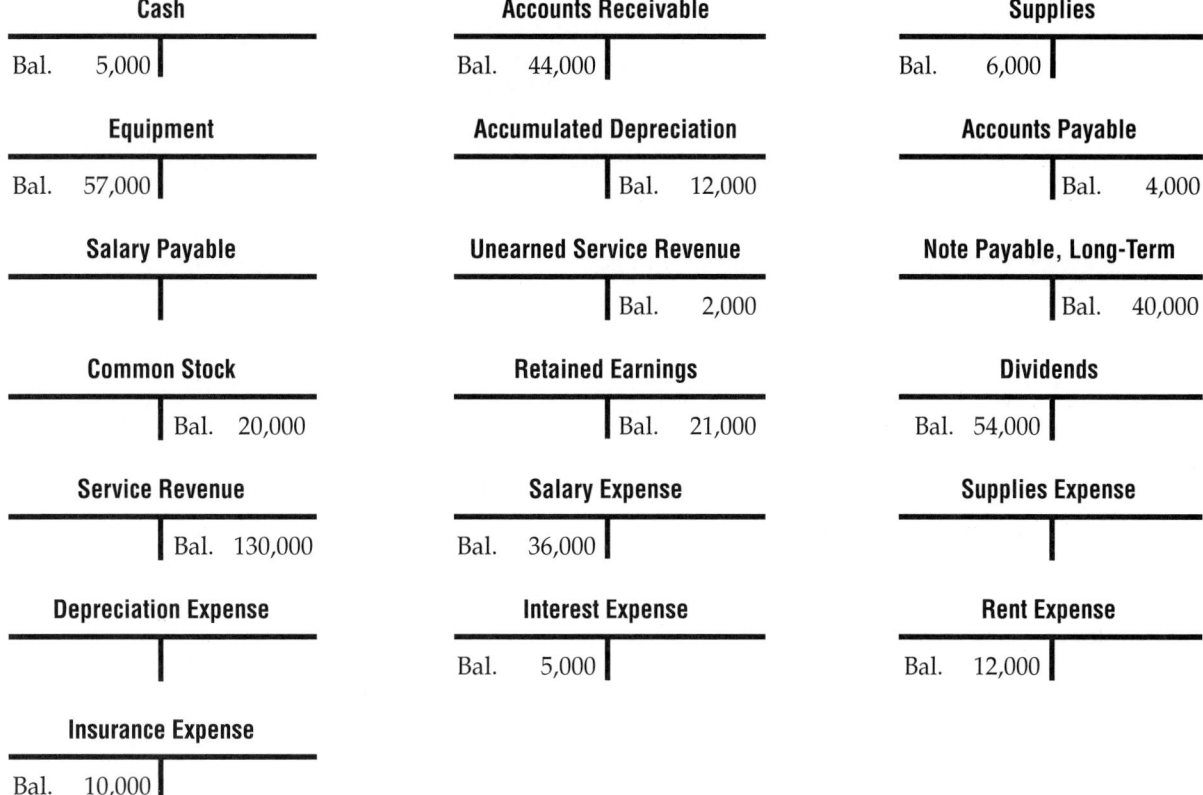

Cash		Accounts Receivable		Supplies	
Bal. 5,000		Bal. 44,000		Bal. 6,000	

Equipment		Accumulated Depreciation		Accounts Payable	
Bal. 57,000			Bal. 12,000		Bal. 4,000

Salary Payable		Unearned Service Revenue		Note Payable, Long-Term	
			Bal. 2,000		Bal. 40,000

Common Stock		Retained Earnings		Dividends	
	Bal. 20,000		Bal. 21,000	Bal. 54,000	

Service Revenue		Salary Expense		Supplies Expense	
	Bal. 130,000	Bal. 36,000			

Depreciation Expense		Interest Expense		Rent Expense	
		Bal. 5,000		Bal. 12,000	

Insurance Expense	
Bal. 10,000	

Adjustment data at December 31, 19X2 include:

a. Depreciation for the year, $5,000.
b. Supplies on hand, $2,000.
c. Accrued revenue, $4,000.
d. Unearned service revenue earned during the year, $2,000.
e. Accrued salary expense, $4,000.

Required

1. Write the trial balance on a work sheet and complete the work sheet. Key each adjusting entry by the letter corresponding to the data given.
2. Prepare the income statement, the statement of retained earnings, and the classified balance sheet in account format.
3. Journalize the adjusting and closing entries.

Problem 4-4B   *Completing the accounting cycle*   *(Obj. 2, 3)*

This problem should be used only in conjunction with Problem 4-3B. It completes the accounting cycle by posting to T-accounts and preparing the postclosing trial balance.

Required

1. Using the Problem 4-3B data, post the adjusting and closing entries to the T-accounts, denoting adjusting amounts by *Adj.*, closing amounts by *Clo.*, and account balances by *Bal.*, as shown in Exhibit 4-9. Double underline all accounts with a zero ending balance.
2. Prepare the postclosing trial balance.

Problem 4-5B   *Completing the accounting cycle*   *(Obj. 2, 3, 5)*

The trial balance of Garner Insurance Agency Ltd. at October 31, 19X0, and the data needed for the month-end adjustments are as follows:

Garner Insurance Agency Ltd.
Trial Balance
October 31, 19X0

Account Number	Account Title	Debit	Credit
11	Cash	$ 1,900	
12	Accounts receivable	15,310	
13	Prepaid rent	2,200	
14	Supplies	840	
15	Furniture	26,830	
16	Accumulated depreciation—furniture		$ 3,400
17	Building	68,300	
18	Accumulated depreciation—building		12,100
21	Accounts payable		7,290
22	Salary payable		
23	Unearned commission revenue		5,300
31	Common stock		25,000
32	Retained earnings		59,490
33	Dividends	3,900	
41	Commission revenue		9,560
51	Salary expense	1,840	
52	Rent expense		
53	Utilities expense	530	
54	Depreciation expense—furniture		
55	Depreciation expense—building		
56	Advertising expense	490	
57	Supplies expense		
	Total	$122,140	$122,140

Adjustment data:

a. Unearned commission revenue still unearned at October 31, $4,900.

b. Prepaid rent still in force at October 31, $2,000.

c. Supplies used during the month, $770.

d. Depreciation on furniture for the month, $250.

e. Depreciation on building for the month, $580.

f. Accrued salary expense at October 31, $310.

Required

1. Open the accounts listed in the trial balance, inserting their October 31 unadjusted balances. Also open the Income Summary account, number 34. Date the balances of the following accounts October 1: Prepaid Rent, Supplies, Building, Accumulated Depreciation—Building, Furniture, Accumulated Depreciation—Furniture, Unearned Commission Revenue, and Retained Earnings.

2. Write the trial balance on a work sheet and complete the work sheet of Garner Insurance Agency Inc. for the month ended October 31, 19X0.

3. Prepare the income statement, the statement of retained earnings, and the classified balance sheet in report format.

4. Using the work sheet data, journalize and post the adjusting and closing entries. Use dates and posting references. Use 12 as the number of the journal page.

5. Prepare a postclosing trial balance.

Problem 4-6B   *Preparing a classified balance sheet in report format*   **(Obj. 5, 6)**

The accounts of Pilote Environmental Corp., at March 31, 19X3, are listed in alphabetical order.

Accounts payable................	$14,700	Interest payable......................	$ 300
Accounts receivable............	11,500	Interest receivable..................	900
Accumulated depreciation		Note payable, long-term........	3,200
—building.......................	47,300	Note receivable, long-term....	6,900
Accumulated depreciation		Other assets	2,300
—furniture......................	7,700	Other current assets	900
Advertising expense...........	900	Other current liabilities.........	1,100
Building..............................	55,900	Prepaid insurance..................	600
Cash	3,400	Prepaid rent...........................	4,700
Common stock	12,000	Retained earnings,	
Current portion of		March 31, 19X2	30,800
note payable	800	Salary expense	17,800
Current portion of		Salary payable.......................	2,400
note receivable	3,100	Service revenue.....................	71,100
Depreciation expense.........	1,900	Supplies.................................	3,800
Dividends............................	31,200	Supplies expense	4,600
Furniture	43,200	Unearned service revenue....	2,800
Insurance expense	600		

Required

1. All adjustments have been journalized and posted, but the closing entries have not yet been made. Prepare the company's classified balance sheet in report format at March 31, 19X3. Use captions for total assets, total liabilities, and total liabilities and shareholders' equity.

2. Compute Pilote's current ratio and debt ratio at March 31, 19X3. At March 31, 19X2, the current ratio was 1.28, and debt ratio was .32. Did Pilote's ability to pay debts improve or deteriorate during 19X3?

Problem 4-7B   *Analyzing and journalizing corrections, adjustments, and closing entries*
   (Obj. 3, 4)

The auditors of Polanski Catering Service Ltd. encountered the following situations while adjusting and closing the books at February 28. Consider each situation independently.

a. The $1,620 balance of Utilities Expense was entered as $16,200 on the trial balance.

(1) What is the name of this type of error?
(2) Assume this is the only error in the trial balance. Which will be greater, the total debits or the total credits, and by how much?
(3) How can this type of error be identified?

b. The company bookkeeper made the following entry to record a $950 credit purchase of supplies:

Feb. 26	Equipment	950	
	Accounts Payable		950

Prepare the correcting entry, dated February 28.

c. A $690 credit to Accounts Receivable was posted as $960.
   (1) At what stage of the accounting cycle will this error be detected?
   (2) Describe the technique for identifying the amount of the error.

d. The accountant failed to make the following adjusting entries at February 28:
   (1) Accrued service revenue, $900.
   (2) Insurance expense, $360.
   (3) Accrued interest expense on a note payable, $520.
   (4) Depreciation of building, $3,700.
   (5) Earned service revenue that had been collected in advance, $2,700.
      Compute the overall net income effect of these omissions.

e. Record each of the adjusting entries identified in item d.

f. The revenue and expense accounts after the adjusting entries had been posted were Service Revenue, $97,330; Wage Expense, $29,340; Depreciation Expense, $6,180; Interest Expense, $4,590; Utilities Expense, $1,620; and Insurance Expense, $640. Two balances prior to closing were Retained Earnings, $75,150, and Dividends, $44,000. Journalize the closing entries.

Problem 4-8B   *Prepare a work sheet, journalize the adjustments, close the accounts*
                   (Obj. 1, 3)

Mobile Boat Repairs Inc. performs overhauls and repairs to motor homes and trailers at the customer's location. The company had the following trial balance for the year ended June 30, 19X1:

Cash	$ 2,300	
Accounts receivable	12,200	
Repair supplies	9,800	
Prepaid insurance	4,700	
Repair equipment	60,000	
Accumulated depreciation—equipment		$ 24,000
Building	88,000	
Accumulated depreciation—building		17,600
Land	55,000	
Accounts payable		6,500
Unearned repair revenues		2,000
Income taxes payable		1,000
Notes payable (2 years)		9,000
Mortgage payable		80,000
Common stock		50,000
Retained earnings		7,600
Dividends	7,000	
Repair fees earned		72,500
Wages expense	24,600	
Utilities expense	800	
Travel expenses	5,800	
Totals	$270,200	$270,200

Additional information:

• On June 30th, a physical count of the repair supplies showed supplies costing $2,200 were still on hand.

• An examination of the insurance policies showed policies costing $2,900 had expired in the year ended June 30, 19X1.

• An examination of the repair equipment and the building showed the following:

	Repair Equipment	Building
Estimated useful life	5 years	10 years
Estimated salvage value	$0	$0

• The company had performed $1,000 of services for a client who had paid $2,000 in advance.

- Accrued expenses included:
    - interest on the mortgage, $800
    - wages, $1,200
    - income taxes, $4,000
- An examination of the accounting records showed that $2,000 of service performed on credit was incorrectly recorded as a cash transaction.

Required

1. Complete a work sheet for the year ended June 30, 19X1.
2. Journalize the adjusting and correcting entries required on June 30, 19X1.
3. Journalize the closing entries that would be required on June 30, 19X1.
4. Prepare a postclosing trial balance for June 30, 19X1.

Problem 4-9B *Prepare a work sheet, close the accounts, classify the assets and liabilities, evaluate the current and debt ratios* **(Obj. 1, 3, 4, 6)**

J. Rapids, the accountant for Mountainhigh Trips Corp., had prepared the work sheet shown on the next page on a computer spreadsheet but has lost much of the data. The only particular item the accountant can recall is that there was an adjustment made to correct an error made where $300 of supplies, purchased on credit, had been incorrectly recorded as $3,000 of equipment.

Required

1. Complete the work sheet by filling in the missing data.
2. Journalize the closing entries that would be required on December 31, 19X1.
3. Prepare the company's classified balance sheet as of December 31, 19X1.
4. Compute Mountainhigh Trips' current ratio and debt ratio for December 31, 19X1. On December 31, 19X0 the current ratio was 2.25 and the debt ratio was .41. Comment on the changes in the ratios.

Challenge Problems

Problem 4-1C *Closing the revenue and expense accounts* **(Obj. 3)**

Small businesses used to use a simplified journal called a "synoptic" journal to account for their businesses. The synoptic journal usually had columns for cash, accounts receivable, other assets, accounts payable, revenues, expenses, and so on. It required double-entry bookkeeping and the columns were usually totaled every month.

The synoptic journal was much like the journals you learned about in Chapters 2, 3, and 4 with one major exception. The accounts in the synoptic journal were never closed; each year flowed into the next year. The column totals for revenues and expenses grew ever larger.

Required

1. Explain why the synoptic journal was used by small businesses. What was the advantage it provided?
2. What do you think was the principal disadvantage of the synoptic journal? Why is it a disadvantage?

Problem 4-2C *Understanding the current ratio* **(Obj. 6)**

It is July 15, 19X1. A friend, who works in the office of a local company that has four fast-food restaurants, has come to you with a question. He knows you are studying accounting and asks if you could help him sort something out. He acknowledges that although he has worked for the company for three years as a general clerk, he really does not understand the accounting work he is doing.

Account Title	Trial Balance Debit	Trial Balance Credit	Adjustments Debit	Adjustments Credit	Adjusted Trial Balance Debit	Adjusted Trial Balance Credit	Income Statement Debit	Income Statement Credit	Balance Sheet Debit	Balance Sheet Credit
Cash	2,000								2,000	
Accounts receivable	2,700				2,800					
Supplies	1,400			(b) 700						
Prepaid rent	1,600				1,400					
Equipment	26,000				23,000					
Accumulated depreciation—equipment		3,000								
Building	46,000				46,000					
Accumulated depreciation—building		4,600		(e) 2,300		4,500				
Land	24,000				24,000					
Accounts payable		6,000								
Wages payable		900	(g) 400	(f) 400						
Unearned revenues		2,700								
Mortgage payable		40,000								40,000
Common stock		35,000								35,000
Retained earnings		14,000								14,000
Dividends	8,000				8,000				8,000	
Rafting fees earned		35,100						35,600		
Wages expense	26,700				27,100					
Rent expense	2,200									
Utilities expense	700				700					
Totals	141,300	141,300								
Supplies expense			(b) 700				700			
Depreciation expense—equipment										
Depreciation expense—building			(d) 1,500				1,500			
Totals										

The company has a large bank loan and, as your friend understands it, the company has agreed with the bank to maintain a current ratio (he thinks that is what it is called) of 1.8 to 1 (1.8:1). The company's year end is June 30. The owner came to him on July 7, 19X1 and asked him to issue a batch of cheques to suppliers but to date them June 30. Your friend recognizes that the cheques will have an effect on the June 30, 19X1 financial statements but doesn't think the effect will be too serious.

Required

Explain to your friend what the effect of paying invoices after June 30 but dating the cheques prior to June 30 has on the current ratio. Provide an example to illustrate your explanation.

Extending Your Knowledge

Decision Problems

1. Completing the accounting cycle to develop the information for a bank loan   (Obj. 4, 6)

One year ago, your friend Sally Van Evra founded Van Evra Computing Service, Inc. The business has prospered. Van Evra, who remembers that you took an accounting course while in college, comes to you for advice. She wishes to know how much net income her business earned during the past year. She also wants to know what the entity's total assets, liabilities, and shareholders' equity are. Her accounting records consist of the T-accounts of her ledger, which were prepared by an accountant who moved to another city. The ledger at December 31 of the current year appears as follows:

Cash		Accounts Receivable		Prepaid Rent	
Dec. 31 5,830		Dec. 31 12,360		Jan. 2 2,800	

Supplies		Equipment		Accumulated Depreciation	
Jan. 2 2,600		Jan. 2 23,600			

Accounts Payable		Unearned Service Revenue		Salary Payable	
	Dec. 31 18,540		Dec. 31 4,130		

Common Stock		Retained Earnings		Dividends	
	Jan. 2 25,000			Dec. 31 43,420	

Service Revenue		Salary Expense		Depreciation Expense	
	Dec. 31 60,740	Dec. 31 17,000			

Rent Expense		Utilities Expense		Supplies Expense	
		Dec. 31 800			

Van Evra indicates that at the year's end customers owe her $1,600 accrued service revenue, which she expects to collect early next year. These revenues have not been recorded. During the year she collected $4,130 service revenue in advance from customers, but she earned only $600 of that amount. Rent expense for the year was $2,400, and she used up $2,100 in supplies. Van Evra estimates that depreciation on her equipment was $5,900 for the year. At December 31, she owes her employee $1,200 accrued salary.

At the conclusion of your meeting, Van Evra expresses concern that her dividends during the year might have exceeded her net income. To get a loan to expand the business, Van Evra must show the bank that her capital account has grown from its original $25,000 balance. Has it? You and Van Evra agree that you will meet again in one week. You perform the analysis and prepare the financial statements to answer her questions.

2. Finding an error in the work sheets   (Obj. 1, 4)

You are preparing the financial statements for the year ended October 31, 19X5, for Woodside Publishing Company Ltd., a weekly newspaper. You began with the trial balance of the ledger, which balanced, and then made the required adjusting entries. To save time, you omitted preparing an adjusted trial balance. After making the adjustments on the work sheet, you extended the balances from the trial balance, adjusted for the adjusting entries, and computed amounts for the income statement and balance sheet columns.

a. You added the debits and credits on the income statement and found that the credits exceeded the debits by $X. According to your finding, did Woodside Publishing have a profit or a loss?

b. You entered the balancing amount from the income statement columns in the balance sheet columns and found the total debits exceeded total credits in the balance sheet. The difference between the debits and credits is twice the amount ($2X) you calculated in question (a). What is the likely cause of the difference? What assumption have you made in your answer?

Ethical Issue

McBride Associates, Inc., a management consulting firm, is in its third year of operations. The company was initially financed by owner's equity as the three partners each invested $30,000. The first year's slim profits were expected because new businesses often start slowly. During the second year, McBride Associates landed a large contract with a paper mill, and referrals from that project brought in several other large jobs. To expand the business, McBride borrowed $100,000 from the Bank of British Columbia. As a condition for making this loan, the bank required McBride to maintain a current ratio of at least 1.50 and a debt ratio of no more than .50.

Business during the third year has been good, but slightly below the target for the year. Expansion costs have brought the current ratio down to 1.47 and the debt ratio up to .51 at December 15. Glenda McBride and her partners are considering the implication of reporting this current ratio to the Bank of British Columbia. One course of action that the partners are considering is to record in December of the third year some revenue on account that McBride Associates will earn in January of their fourth year of operations. The contract for this job has been signed, and McBride will perform the management consulting services for the client during January.

Required

1. Journalize the revenue transaction, and indicate how recording this revenue in December would affect the current ratio and the debt ratio.

2. State whether it is ethical to record the revenue transaction in December. Identify the accounting principle relevant to this situation.

3. Propose an ethical course of action for McBride Associates, Inc.

Financial Statement Problems

1. *Using an actual balance sheet (Obj. 6)*

This problem, based on Mark's Work Wearhouse balance sheet in Appendix A, will familiarize you with some of the assets and liabilities of this actual company. Answer these questions, using Mark's Work Wearhouse's balance sheet:

a. Which balance sheet format does Mark's use?

b. Name the company's largest current asset and largest current liability at January 29, 1994?

c. How much were total current assets and total current liabilities at January 30, 1993? Which had decreased by the greater percentage during the year ended January 29, 1994: total current assets or total current liabilities?

d. Compute Mark's current ratio at January 29, 1994 and January 30, 1993. Also compute the debt ratios at these dates. Did the ratio values improve or deteriorate during 1994?

e. What is the cost of the company's fixed assets at January 29, 1994? What is the book value of these assets? To answer this question, refer to the fixed assets note.

2. *Using an actual balance sheet (Obj. 6)*

Obtain the annual report of an actual company of your choosing. Answer these questions about the company:

a. Which balance sheet format does the company use?

b. Name the company's largest asset and largest liability at the end of the current year and at the end of the preceding year. Name the largest current asset and the largest current liability at the end of the current year and at the end of the preceding year.

c. Compute the company's current ratio at the end of the current year and the current ratio at the end of the preceding year. Also compute the debt ratio at the end of the current year and at the end of the preceding year. Did these ratio values improve or deteriorate during the current year? Does the income statement help to explain why the ratios improved or deteriorated? Give your reason.

Appendix

Reversing Entries

Reversing entries are special types of entries that ease the burden of accounting after adjusting and closing entries have been made at the end of a period. Reversing entries are used most often in conjunction with accrual-type adjustments such as an accrued salary expense and accrued service revenue. GAAP do not require reversing entries. They are used only for convenience and to save time.

Reversing Entries for Accrued Expense Accrued expenses accumulate with the passage of time and are paid at a later date. At the end of the period, the business makes an adjusting entry to record the expense that has accumulated up to that time.

To see how reversing entries work, return to the adjusting entries (Exhibit 4-8) that Air & Sea Travel, Inc., used to update its accounting records for the April financial statements. At April 30—before the adjusting entries—Salary Expense has a debit balance of $950 from salaries paid during April. At April 30, the business owes employees an additional $950 for service during the last part of the month. Assume for the purpose of this illustration that on May 5, the next payroll date, Air & Sea Travel will pay $950 of accrued salary plus $100 in salary that the employee has earned in the first few days of May. The next payroll payment will be $1,050 ($950 + $100). However, to present the correct financial picture, the $950 in salaries incurred in April must be included in the April statements, not in the May statements. Accordingly, Air & Sea Travel's accountant makes the following adjusting entry on April 30:

Adjusting Entries

April 30	Salary Expense	950	
	Salary Payable		950

After posting, the Salary Payable and Salary Expense accounts appear as follows:[2]

Salary Payable

	Apr. 30 Adj.[2] 950
	Apr. 30 Bal. 950

Salary Expense

Paid during April CP 950	
Apr. 30 Adj. 950	
Apr. 30 Bal. 1,900	

After the adjusting entry, the April income statement reports Salary Expense of $1,900, and the balance sheet at April 30 reports Salary Payable, a liability, of $950. The $1,900 debit balance of Salary Expense is eliminated by this closing entry at April 30, 19X1, as follows:

Closing Entries

April 30	Income Summary	1,900	
	Salary Expense		1,900

After posting, Salary Expense appears as follows:

Salary Expense

Paid during April CP 950	
Apr. 30 Adj. 950	
Apr. 30 Bal. 1,900	Apr. 30 Clo. 1,900

In the normal course of recording salary payments during the year, Air & Sea Travel's accountant makes the standard entry, as follows:

Salary Expense...	XXX	
Cash..		XXX

In our example, however, payday does not land on the day the accounting period ends, and Air & Sea Travel's accountant has made an adjusting entry to accrue salary payable of $950. On May 5, the next payday, assume the total payroll is $1,050. Air & Sea Travel credits Cash for $1,050, but what account—or accounts—should the accountant debit? The cash payment entry is

---

[2] Entry explanations used throughout this discussion are

Adj. = Adjusting entry	CP = Cash payment entry—includes a credit to Cash
Bal. = Balance	CR = Cash receipt entry—includes a debit to Cash
Clo. = Closing entry	Rev. = Reversing entry

May 5	Salary Payable	950	
	Salary Expense	100	
	Cash		1,050

This method of recording the cash payment is correct, but inefficient: the accountant must refer back to the adjusting entries of April 30. Otherwise, he does not know the amount of the required debit to Salary Payable (in this example, $950). Searching through the preceding period's adjusting entries takes time, and in business, time is money. To avoid having to separate the debit of a later cash payment entry into two accounts, accountants have devised a technique called reversing entries.

Making a Reversing Entry   A *reversing entry* switches the debit and the credit of a previous adjusting entry. A reversing entry, then, is the exact opposite of a prior adjusting entry. The reversing entry is dated the first day of the period following the adjusting entry.

To illustrate reversing entries let's return to Air & Sea Travel. Recall that on April 30, 19X1, the travel agency made the following adjusting entry to accrue Salary Payable:

Adjusting Entries

| Apr. 30 | Salary Expense .... | 950 | |
| | Salary Payable .... | | 950 |

The reversing entry simply reverses the position of the debit and the credit:

Reversing Entries

| May 1 | Salary Payable .... | 950 | |
| | Salary Expense .... | | 950 |

The reversing entry is dated the first day of the new period. It is the exact opposite of the April 30 adjusting entry. Ordinarily, the accountant who makes the adjusting entry also prepares the reversing entry at the same time. Air & Sea Travel post-dates—that is, assigns a later date to—the reversing entry to the first day of the next period, however, so that it affects only the new period. Note how the accounts appear after the accountant posts the reversing entry:

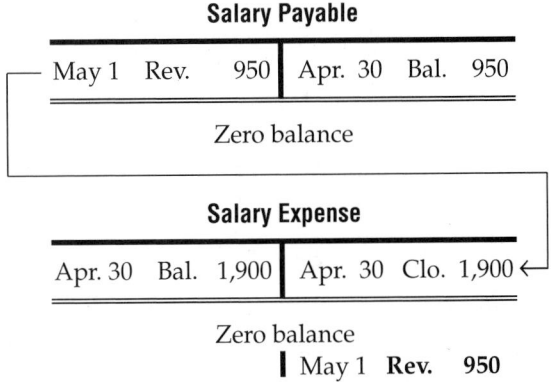

The arrow shows the transfer of the $950 credit balance from Salary Payable to Salary Expense. This credit balance in Salary Expense does not mean that the entity has negative salary expense, as might be suggested by a credit balance in an Expense account. Instead, the odd credit balance is merely a temporary result of the reversing entry. The credit balance is eliminated on May 5 when the $1,050 cash payment for salaries is debited to Salary Expense in the customary manner:

May 5   Salary Expense...   1,050
   Cash...   1,050

Then this cash payment entry is posted:

Salary Expense

May 5 CP	1,050	May 1 Rev.	950
May 5 Bal.	100		

Now Salary Expense has its correct debit balance of $100, which is the amount of salary expense incurred thus far in May. The $1,050 cash disbursement also pays the liability for Salary Payable. Thus the Salary Payable account has a zero balance, which is correct, as shown on the previous page.

The adjusting and reversing process is repeated period after period. Cash payments for salaries are debited to Salary Expense, and these amounts accumulate in that account. At the end of the period, the accountant makes an adjusting entry to accrue salary expense incurred but not yet paid. At the same time, the accountant also makes a reversing entry, which allows him or her to record all payroll entries in the customary manner by routinely debiting Salary Expense. Even in computerized systems, making reversing entries is more efficient than writing a program to locate the amount accrued from the preceding period and making the more complicated journal entry. Reversing entries may be made for all types of accrued expenses.

Appendix Problem

Problem 4A-1   *Using reversing entries*

Refer to the data in Problem 4-5A, page 194.

Required

1. Open accounts for Salary Payable and Salary Expense. Insert their unadjusted balances at August 31, 19X9.
2. Journalize adjusting entry *f* and the closing entry for Salary Expense at August 31. Post to the accounts.
3. On September 5, Leung Insurance Agency paid the next payroll amount of $580. Journalize this cash payment, and post to the accounts. Show the balance in each account.
4. Repeat Requirements 1 through 3 using a reversing entry. Compare the balances of Salary Payable and Salary Expense computed by using a reversing entry with those balances computed without using a reversing entry (as appear in your answer to Requirement 3).

CHAPTER 5
Merchandising and the Accounting Cycle

"It's a David and Goliath struggle to own the most exclusive niche in the sky—long-distance executive jets. But here's the kicker: Goliath hails from Canada."

Most Canadians have some vague notion of Bombardier as an ambitious Quebec company with a flair for inventing recreational vehicles and a knack for attracting government support. The fact is that Bombardier, with 37,000 employees manufacturing operations in eight countries and markets in more than 60, is an international powerhouse in transportation equipment. Revenues for the whole company for the year ended Jan. 31, 1995, increased to $5.9 billion.

Bombardier entered the aerospace industry in 1986 and presently is the sixth-largest civil aviation company in the world. Bombardier has received international notice for its accomplishments in the aerospace industry.

However, it has not been content to rest on its laurels. Its most recent venture has been the development of an ultralong-range corporate jet named the Bombardier Global Express. Such a jet will be able to fly eight passengers and a crew of four from Montreal to Tokyo in 13 hours without refueling. The market for such planes is estimated to be 350 to 800 planes, which will sell for $42 million, over the next 15 to 20 years. Bombardier's main competitor is a U.S. company, Gulfstream Aerospace Corp. of Savannah, Georgia.

Usually the Canadian company in such a struggle is described as David against the American Goliath. However, in this case, because of its "considerable manufacturing and technical capabilities" and its "financial acumen," Bombardier is Goliath and Gulfstream is David.

Source: Quoted from "Bombardier's Billion-Dollar Space Race," *Canadian Business*, June, 1994, pp. 91–101.

CHAPTER OBJECTIVES

After studying this chapter, you should be able to

1 Use sales, gross margin, and operating income to evaluate a company

2 Account for the purchase and sale of inventory

3 Compute cost of goods sold and gross margin

4 Adjust and close the accounts of a merchandising business

5 Prepare a merchandiser's financial statements

6 Use the gross margin percentage and inventory turnover ratio to evaluate a business

S1 Account for the purchase and sale of inventory

S2 Compute the cost of goods sold

S3 Adjust and close the accounts of a merchandising business

How do the operations of Bombardier differ from those of the businesses we have studied so far? In the first four chapters, Air & Sea Travel, Inc., provided an illustration of a business that earns revenue by selling its services. Service enterprises include Four Seasons Hotels, Canadian Airlines, physicians, lawyers, public accountants, the Edmonton Oilers hockey team, and the twelve-year-old who cuts lawns in your neighborhood. A *merchandising entity* earns its revenue by selling products, called *merchandise inventory* or, simply, *inventory*.

This chapter shows the central role of inventory in a business that sells merchandise. *Inventory* includes all goods that the company owns and expects to sell in the normal course of their operations. Some businesses, such as department stores, gas stations, and grocery stores, buy their inventory in finished form ready for sale to customers. Others, such as Sony, Hershey Foods, and the Goodyear Tire and Rubber Company, manufacture their own products. Both groups sell products rather than services.

We illustrate accounting for the purchase and sale of inventory plus how to adjust and close the books of a merchandiser. The chapter ends with two ratios that managers, investors, and creditors use to evaluate companies' operations.

OBJECTIVE 1

Use sales, gross margin, and operating income to evaluate a company

Merchandising Operations

Real-World Example:

Many businesses use the gross margin percentage (also known as the markup percentage) as a means of determining how well inventory is selling. If too much inventory is purchased and it must be marked down, the gross margin percentage will decline. By monitoring the gross margin percentage, problems can be corrected quickly.

Exhibit 5-1 shows the income statement of Sony Corporation for two recent years. Sony's income statement differs from those of the service business discussed in previous chapters. The highlighted items are unique to merchandising operations.

The amount that a business earns from selling merchandise inventory is called **sales revenue**, often abbreviated as **sales**. (Net sales equals sales revenue minus any deductions from sales.) The major revenue of a merchandising entity, sales revenue, represents the increase in retained earnings from delivering inventory to customers. The major expense of a merchandiser is *cost of goods sold*. The title of this expense is well chosen, because it represents the entity's cost of the goods (inventory) it has sold to customers. As long as inventory is held by a business, the inventory is an asset because the goods are an economic resource with future value to the company. When the inventory is sold, however, the inventory's cost becomes an expense to the seller because the goods are no longer available. When Sony sells its MiniDisc to an audio store, the product's cost is expensed as cost of goods sold on Sony's books.

The excess of sales revenue over cost of goods sold is called **gross margin** or **gross profit**. This important business statistic helps measure a business's success. A sufficiently high gross margin is vital to success. Sony's operations were not very successful during the year ended March 31, 1992, despite an increase in sales.

EXHIBIT 5-1   *A Real Company's Income Statement*

Short Exercise:
Calculate (1) Sony's gross margin percentage for 1992 and (2) Sony's COGS as a percentage of sales for 1992. (3) What do these percentages mean to Sony management? **A:** (1) ¥983,238/¥3,821,582 = 25.7%; (2) ¥2,838,344/ ¥3,821,582 = 74.3%; (3) Per dollar of sales, Sony spends (on average) ¥0.74 to acquire their products, and they earn (on average) ¥0.26 of gross margin per dollar of sales revenue.

Sony Corporation
Income Statement*
Years Ended March 31, 1992 and 1991

	In millions of yen (¥)	
	1992	1991
Net sales	¥3,821,582	¥3,616,517
Cost of sales [same as Cost of goods sold]	2,838,344	2,505,554
Gross margin	983,238	1,110,963
Selling, general & administrative expenses [salaries, rent, insurance, depreciation, advertising, delivery, utilities, supplies, and so on]	910,774	887,773
	72,464	223,190
[Other] operating revenue	93,814	74,259
Operating income	166,278	297,449
Other items summarized	(46,157)	(180,524)
Net income	¥ 120,121	¥ 116,925

*Rearranged for instructional purposes

The following example will clarify the nature of gross margin. Suppose Sony's cost to manufacture a compact disc player is $500 and Sony sells the product to stores in Canada for $700. Sony's gross margin per unit is $200 ($700 − $500). The gross margin reported on Sony's income statement, ¥983 billion, is the sum of the gross margins on all the products the company sold during its 1992 fiscal year.

The Operating Cycle for a Merchandising Business

A merchandising entity buys inventory, sells the inventory to its customers, and uses the cash to purchase more inventory to repeat the cycle. Exhibit 5-2 diagrams the operating cycle for *cash sales* and for *sales on account*. For a cash sale—Panel A—the cycle is from cash to inventory, which is purchased for resale and back to cash. For a sale on account—Panel B—the cycle is from cash to inventory to accounts receivable and back to cash. In all lines of business, managers strive to shorten the cycle in order to keep assets active. The faster the sale of inventory and the collection of cash, the higher the profits.

Inventory Systems

Two main types of inventory accounting systems exist: the periodic system and the perpetual system. The **periodic inventory system** is used by businesses that sell relatively inexpensive goods. A grocery store without an optical-scanning cash register does not keep a daily running record of every loaf of bread and package of bacon that it buys and sells. The cost of record keeping would be overwhelming. Instead, grocers would count their inventory periodically—at least once a year—to determine the quantities on hand. The inventory amounts are used to prepare the annual financial statements. Other businesses such as office supply outlets, restaurants, and variety stores also use the periodic inventory system. To them, detailed inventory records in the ledger are not necessary for controlling merchandise and managing day-to-day operations. In small businesses, the owner can visually inspect the goods on hand for control purposes. The end-of-chapter supplement covers the periodic inventory system. That system is rapidly decreasing in importance as computers have decreased in price but have greatly increased in processing power.

EXHIBIT 5-2   *Operating Cycle of a Merchandiser*

Panel A—Purchase and Cash Sale

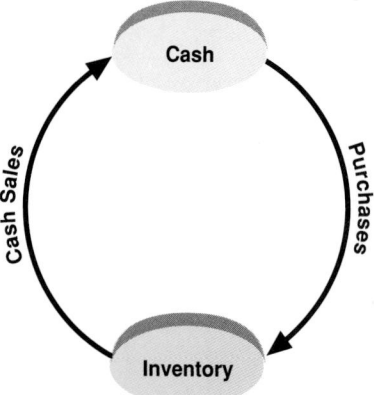

Panel B—Purchase and Sale on Account

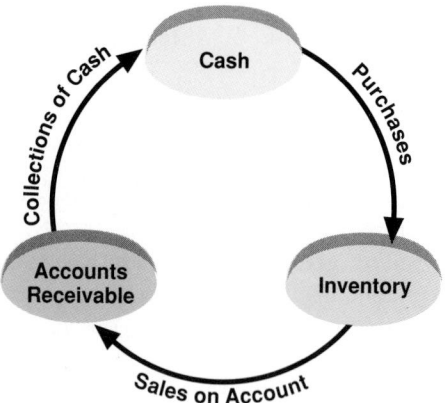

Under the **perpetual inventory system**, the business maintains a running record of inventory on hand. This system achieves control over expensive goods such as automobiles, jewelry, and furniture. The loss of one item would be significant, and this justifies the cost of a perpetual system. Inventory record keeping is a demanding accounting task, from the paperwork required in purchasing and selling inventory to the job of periodically counting it. Computers have dramatically reduced the time required to manage inventory and have greatly increased a company's ability to control its merchandise. But even under a perpetual system the business counts the inventory on hand annually. The physical count establishes the correct amount of ending inventory and serves as a check on the perpetual records.

The following chart compares the periodic and perpetual systems:

Periodic Inventory System
- Does not keep a running record of all goods bought and sold.
- Inventory counted at least once a year.
- Used for inexpensive goods.

Perpetual Inventory System
- Keeps a running record of all goods bought and sold.
- Inventory counted once a year.
- Used for all types of goods.

A computerized system enhances management control over inventory because the computer can keep accurate, up-to-the-minute records of the number of units purchased, the number of units sold, and the quantities on hand. For a purchase made on account, the goods received are entered in a computer as a debit to Inventory and a credit to Accounts Payable.

Computerized inventory systems are often integrated with accounts receivable and sales. For example, when a prospective customer's order is entered into the computer, the computer checks warehouse records to see if the requested units are in stock. If they are, details of the shipment are entered into the computer, which then multiplies the number of units shipped by the unit sale price. The computer then prints an invoice for the customer and calculates the debit to Accounts Receivable (for that customer), the credit to Sales Revenue, and the decrease in inventory units.

The computer can keep up-to-the-minute records, so managers can call up current inventory information at any time. For example, in a perpetual system the "cash register" at many retail and discount stores is a computer terminal that records the sale and also updates the inventory records. Bar codes, which are scanned by a laser, are an integral part of the perpetual inventory system. The combinations of lines of different widths and lengths represent the data used to keep track of each item.

When you ask if a certain item is in stock, the clerk usually consults a computer printout of the perpetual inventory records. Because most businesses today use them, we base our inventory discussions on modern perpetual systems.[1]

Purchase of Merchandise Inventory in the Perpetual System

The cycle of a merchandising entity begins with cash which is used to purchase inventory, as Exhibit 5-2 shows. For example, a stereo center records the purchase of cassette players, compact disc (CD) players, and other items of inventory acquired for resale by debiting the inventory account. Most businesses have good credit and can purchase inventory on account, so a $500 purchase on account is recorded as follows:

June 14	Inventory	500	
	Accounts payable		500
	Purchased inventory on account.		

> **OBJECTIVE 2**
> Account for the purchase and sale of inventory

The Purchase Invoice: A Basic Business Document

Business documents are the tangible evidence of transactions. As we trace the steps that Austin Sound Stereo Center, Inc., takes in ordering, receiving and paying for inventory, we point out the roles that documents play in carrying on business.

1. Suppose Austin Sound wants to stock JVC brand CD players, cassette decks, and speakers. Austin prepares a *purchase order* and mails it to JVC.

2. On receipt of the purchase order, JVC scans its warehouse for the inventory that Austin Sound ordered. JVC ships the equipment and mails the invoice to Austin on the same day. The *invoice* is the seller's request for payment from the purchaser. It is also called the *bill*.

3. Often the purchaser receives the invoice before the inventory arrives. Austin Sound does not pay immediately. Instead, Austin waits until the inventory arrives in order to ensure that it is the correct type, the quantity ordered, and in good condition. After the inventory is inspected and approved, Austin Sound pays JVC the invoice amount.

Exhibit 5-3 is an updated copy of an actual invoice from JVC Canada Inc. to Austin Sound Stereo Center Ltd. From Austin Sound's perspective, this document is a *purchase invoice* (it is being used to purchase goods), whereas to JVC it is a *sales invoice* (it is being used to sell goods).

Discounts from Purchase Prices

There are two major types of discounts from purchase prices: quantity discounts and cash discounts (called purchase discounts).

Quantity Discounts   A *quantity discount, which is a type of trade discount*, works this way. The larger the quantity purchased, the lower the price per item. For example, JVC may offer no trade discount for the purchase of only one or two CD players, and charge the *list* price—the full price—of $200 per unit. However, JVC may offer the following quantity discount terms in order to persuade customers to buy more CD players:

---

[1]For professors who prefer to concentrate on the periodic inventory system, comprehensive treatment of that system begins on p. 263. Follow Chapter Objectives S1 through S4 instead of 2 through 5.

EXHIBIT 5-3 *Business Invoice*

①	The seller.
②	The invoice date, needed for determining whether the purchaser gets a discount for prompt payment (see 5).
③	The purchaser. This inventory is invoiced (billed) and shipped to the same address.
④	Austin Sound's purchase order (P.O.) date.
⑤	Credit terms of the transaction: If it pays within 15 days of the invoice date, Austin Sound may deduct 3% of the total amount. Otherwise, the full amount—net—is due in 30 days.*
⑥	Austin ordered 6 CD players, 3 cassette decks, and 2 speakers.
⑦	JVC shipped 5 CD players, no cassette decks, and no speakers.
⑧	Total invoice amount.
⑨	Austin's payment date. How much did Austin pay? (See 10.)
⑩	Payment occurred 14 days after the invoice date—within the discount period—so Austin paid $685.79 ($707 – 3% discount).

*A full discussion of discounts appears in the next section.

Quantity	Quantity Discount	Net Price Per Unit
Buy minimum quantity, 3 CD players	5%	$190 [$200 – .05($200)]
Buy 4–9 CD players	10	$180 [$200 – .10($200)]
Buy more than 9 CD players	20	$160 [$200 – .20($200)]

Suppose Austin Sound purchases five CD players from this manufacturer. The cost of each CD player is, therefore, $180. Purchase of five units on account would be recorded by debiting Inventory and crediting Accounts Payable for the total price of $900 ($180 × 5).

There is no Quantity Discount account and no special accounting entry for a quantity discount. Instead, all accounting entries are based on the net price of a purchase after the quantity discount has been subtracted.

Purchase Discounts   Many businesses also offer purchase discounts to their customers. A *purchase discount* is a reward for prompt payment. If a quantity discount is also offered, the purchase discount is computed on the net purchase amount after the quantity discount has been subtracted, further reducing the cost of the inventory.

JVC's credit terms of 3% 15, NET 30 DAYS can also be expressed as 3/15 n/30. This means that Austin Sound Center may deduct 3 percent of the total amount due if Austin pays within 15 days of the invoice date. Otherwise, the full amount—net—is due in 30 days. Terms of simply n/30 indicate that no discount is offered, and that payment is due 30 days after the invoice date. Terms of *eom* mean that payment is due by the end of the current month. However, a purchase after the 25th of the current month on terms of *eom* can be paid at the end of the next month.

Short Exercise:

(1) What is meant by the terms 1/10 n/60? (2) By the terms 2/10 n/eom? (3) By the terms n/30? **A:** (1) 1% discount if paid within 10 days, or the full ("net") amount is due in 60 days. (2) 2% discount if paid within 10 days, or the full amount is due at the end of the month. (3) No discount allowed, and the full amount is due in 30 days.

Let us use the Exhibit 5-3 transaction to illustrate accounting for a purchase discount. Austin Sound records this purchase on account as follows:

May 25	Inventory..	707.00	
	Accounts Payable		707.00
	Purchased inventory on account.		

Austin paid within the discount period so its cash payment entry is

June 10	Accounts Payable...	707.00	
	Cash ($707.00 × .97)		685.79
	Inventory ($707.00 × .03)..................................		21.21
	Paid on account within discount period.		

Alternatively, if Austin Sound pays this invoice after the discount period, it must pay the full invoice amount. In this case, the payment entry is

June 29	Accounts Payable...	707.00	
	Cash		707.00
	Paid on account after discount period.		

Without the discount, Austin Sound's cost of the inventory is the full amount of $707, as shown in the following T-account:

Inventory	
May 27 707.00	

Purchase Returns and Allowances

Most businesses allow their customers to *return* merchandise that is defective, damaged in shipment, or otherwise unsuitable. Or if the buyer chooses to keep damaged goods, the seller may deduct an *allowance* from the amount the buyer owes. Because returns and allowances decrease the cost of inventory, returns and allowances are recorded by crediting the inventory account.

Suppose the $70 CD player purchased by Austin Sound (in Exhibit 5-3) was not the CD player ordered. Austin returns the merchandise to the seller and records the purchase return as follows:

June 3	Accounts Payable..	70.00	
	Inventory...		70.00
	Returned inventory to seller.		

Now assume that one of the JVC CD players is damaged in shipment to Austin Sound. The damage is minor, and Austin decides to keep the CD player in exchange for a $10 allowance from JVC. To record this purchase allowance, Austin Sound makes this entry:

June 4	Accounts Payable..	10.00	
	Inventory...		10.00
	Received a purchase allowance.		

The return and the allowance had two effects: (1) They decreased Austin Sound's liability, which is why we debit Accounts Payable. (2) They decreased the net cost of the inventory, which is why we credit Inventory.

Assume that Austin Sound has not paid its debt to JVC. After these return and allowance transactions are posted, Austin Sound's accounts will show these balances:

Short Exercise:

Austin Sound Center purchases $1,000 of merchandise on account, terms 2/10, n/30 on 9/15; $100 of merchandise is returned for credit on 9/20. Payment in full is made on 9/25. Journalize the transactions.

A:

9/15 Inventory	1,000	
Accts. Pay.		1,000
9/20 Accts. Pay.	100	
Inventory		100
9/25 Accts. Pay.		
($1,000 – $100)	900	
Inventory		
(2% × $900)		18
Cash		
($900 – $18)		882

No discount is given on the return.

Inventory					Accounts Payable			
May 27	707.00	June 3	70.00		June 3	70.00	May 27	707.00
		June 4	10.00		June 4	10.00		
Bal.	627.00						Bal.	627.00

Transportation Costs

The transportation cost of moving inventory from seller to buyer can be significant. The purchase agreement specifies FOB terms to indicate who pays the shipping charges. The term *FOB* stands for *free on board* and governs when the legal title—ownership—to the goods passes from seller to buyer. When FOB *shipping point* terms are in effect, title passes when the inventory leaves the seller's place of business—the shipping point. The buyer owns the goods while they are in transit, and therefore pays the transportation cost. Under FOB *destination* terms, title passes when the goods reach the destination, so the seller pays transportation cost. Exhibit 5-4 summarizes these terms.

EXHIBIT 5-4 *FOB Terms*

	FOB Shipping Point	FOB Destination
When does title pass to buyer?	Shipping point	Destination
Who pays transportation cost?	Buyer	Seller

FOB shipping point terms are the most common, so generally, the buyer bears the shipping cost. A freight cost that the buyer pays on an inventory purchase is called *freight in*. In accounting, the cost of an asset includes all costs incurred to bring the asset to its intended use. For inventory, cost includes the net cost after all discounts taken, plus any transportation charges paid. To record the payment for freight in, the buyer debits Inventory and credits Cash or Accounts Payable for the amount. Suppose Austin Sound receives a $60 shipping bill directly from the freight company. Austin's entry to record payment of the freight charge is:

June 1	Inventory	60	
	Cash		60
	Paid a freight bill.		

The freight charge increases the cost of the inventory as follows:

Inventory			
May 27	707.00	June 3	70.00
June 1	60.00	June 4	10.00
Bal.	687.00		

After the returns, allowances, and transportation costs are considered, this inventory has a cost of $687. Any discounts would be computed only on the account payable to the seller, not on the transportation costs, because the freight company offers no discount.

STOP & THINK

Refer to the Accounts Payable account on page 220 (Purchase Returns and Allowances). After all returns, allowances, and transportation charges, what amount of discount can Austin Sound take if it pays JVC on June 9 (within the discount period)? How much should Austin Sound pay JVC on June 9? What is Austin Sound's net cost of this inventory?

Answer:

$$3\% \text{ Discount} = \$18.81\ (\$707.00 - \$70.00 - \$10.00) \times 0.03$$
$$\text{Payment to JVC} = \$608.19 = \$627.00 - \$18.81$$
$$\text{Net cost of inventory} = \$668.19 = \$608.19 + \$60.00 \text{ transportation charge}$$

Under FOB shipping point terms, the seller sometimes prepays the transportation cost as a convenience, and lists this cost on the invoice. The buyer can debit Inventory for the combined cost of the inventory and the shipping cost because both costs apply to the merchandise. A $5,000 purchase of goods, coupled with a related freight charge of $400, would be recorded as follows:

March 12	Inventory	5,400	
	Accounts Payable		5,400
	Purchased inventory on account plus freight.		

If the buyer pays within the discount period, the discount will be computed on the $5,000 merchandise cost, not on the $5,400. No discount is offered on transportation cost.

Freight out is the cost of freight charges paid to ship goods sold to customers. It is paid by the seller, not by the purchaser. Freight out, which is also called *delivery expense*, is an operating expense for the seller. It is debited to an account such as Delivery Expense.

Alternative Procedures for Purchase Discounts, Returns and Allowances, and Transportation Costs

 Key Point:
A contra account always has a companion account with the opposite balance. Thus both Purchase Discounts and Purchase Returns and Allowances (credit balances) are reported with Inventory (debit balance) on the balance sheet.

Some businesses may want to keep a detailed record of purchase discounts, returns and allowances, and transportation costs. For example, Austin Sound may receive too many defective CD players from an off-brand manufacturer. In recording purchase returns, Austin could credit a special account, Purchase Returns and Allowances, that would serve as a running record of the defective merchandise. The Purchase Returns and Allowances account would carry a credit balance and be treated as a contra account to Inventory. Freight In would be debited for transportation costs. Then for reporting on the financial statements these accounts could be combined with the Inventory account as follows (amounts assumed):

Inventory..		$35,000
Less: Purchase discounts...............................	$700	
Purchase returns and allowances	800	1,500
Net purchases of inventory		33,500
Freight in		2,100
Total cost of inventory..................................		$35,600

Sale of Inventory and Cost of Goods Sold

The sale of inventory may be for cash or on account, as Exhibit 5-2 shows.

Cash Sale   Sales of retailers such as grocery stores, drug stores, gift shops, and restaurants are often for cash. A $120.00 cash sale is recorded by debiting Cash and crediting the revenue account, Sales Revenue, as follows:

Jan. 9	Cash..	120	
	Sales Revenue..		120
	Cash sale.		

To update the inventory records, the business also must decrease the Inventory balance. Suppose these goods cost the seller $70. An accompanying entry is needed to transfer the $70 cost of the goods—not their selling price of $120—from the Inventory account (an asset) to Cost of Goods Sold (an expense) as follows:

Jan. 9	Cost of Goods Sold..	70	
	Inventory..		70
	Recorded the cost of goods sold.		

Cost of goods sold (also called **cost of sales**) is the largest single expense of most businesses that sell merchandise, such as Bombardier and Austin Sound. It is the cost of the inventory that the business has sold to customers. The Cost of Goods Sold account keeps a current balance as transactions are journalized and posted.

After posting, the Cost of Goods Sold account holds the cost of the merchandise sold:

Inventory				Cost of Goods Sold		
Purchases 50,000 (amount assumed)	Jan. 9	70		Jan. 9	70	

The computer automatically records this entry when the cashier keys in the code number of the inventory that is sold. Optical scanners perform this task in most stores.

Sale on Account   Most sales by department stores, furniture stores, and other consumer goods stores are made on account using either the store's credit card or some other credit card such as Visa or MasterCard. To simplify the discussion, we will assume the seller records the receivable as a regular account receivable rather than a special receivable from the credit card company.

Most sales by wholesalers and manufacturers are also made on account or on credit. A $5,000 sale on account is recorded by a debit to Accounts Receivable and a credit to Sales Revenue, as follows:

Jan. 11	Accounts Receivable	5,000	
	Sales Revenue..		5,000
	Sale on account.		

The related cash receipt from the January 11 sale on account is journalized as follows:

Jan. 19	Cash	5,000	
	Accounts Receivable		5,000
	Collection on account.		

STOP & THINK

Why is there no January 19 entry to Sales Revenue, Cost of Goods Sold, or Inventory?

Answer: On January 19 the seller merely receives one asset—Cash—in place of another asset—Accounts Receivable. The sales revenue, the related cost of goods sold, and the decrease in inventory for the goods sold were recorded on January 11.

Sales Discounts and Sales Returns and Allowances

Just as purchase discounts and purchase returns and allowances decrease the cost of inventory purchases, **sales discounts** and **sales returns and allowances**, which are contra accounts to Sales Revenue, decrease the revenue earned on sales. Companies keep close watch on their customers' paying habits and on their own sales of defective and unsuitable merchandise. They maintain separate accounts for Sales Discounts and Sales Returns and Allowances. Let's examine a sequence of the sale transactions of JVC.

On July 7, JVC sells stereo components for $7,200 on credit terms of 2/10 n/30. JVC's entry to record this credit sale and the cost of goods sold follows:

July 7	Accounts Receivable	$7,200	
	Sales Revenue		$7,200
	Sale on account.		

July 7	Cost of Goods Sold	$4,700	
	Inventory		$4,700
	Recorded the cost of goods sold.		

Assume the buyer returns goods that cost $600. JVC's cost of this inventory was $400. JVC records the sales return and the related decrease in Accounts Receivable as follows:

July 12	Sales Returns and Allowances	600	
	Accounts Receivable		600
	Received returned goods.		

JVC would also update the inventory records to include the goods returned by the customer and to decrease cost of goods sold as follows:

July 12	Inventory	400	
	Cost of Goods Sold		400
	Returned goods to inventory.		

JVC grants a $100 sales allowance for damaged goods. JVC journalizes this transaction by debiting Sales Returns and Allowances and crediting Accounts Receivable as follows:

July 15	Sales Returns and Allowances	100	
	Accounts Receivable		100
	Granted a sales allowance for damaged goods.		

No inventory entry is needed for a sales allowance transaction because the seller receives no returned goods from the customer. Instead, JVC will receive less cash from the customer.

After the preceding entries are posted, Accounts Receivable has a $6,500 debit balance as follows:

Accounts Receivable

July 7	7,200	July 12	600
		15	100
Bal.	6,500		

On July 17, the last day of the discount period, JVC collects half ($3,250) of this receivable ($6,500 × ½ = $3,250). The cash receipt is $3,185 [$3,250 − (.02 × $3,250)], and the collection entry is

July 17	Cash	3,185	
	Sales Discounts (.02 × $3,250)	65	
	Accounts Receivable		3,250
	Cash collection with the discount period.		

Suppose JVC collects the remainder on July 28. That date is after the discount period, so there is no sales discount. To record this collection on account, JVC debits Cash and credits Accounts Receivable for the same amount, as follows:

July 28	Cash	3,250	
	Accounts Receivable		3,250
	Cash collection after the discount period.		

Net sales is computed by subtracting the contra accounts as follows:

>   **Sales Revenue (*credit* balance account)**
> − **Sales Discounts (*debit* balance account)**
> − **Sales Returns and Allowances (*debit* balance account)**
> ───
> = **Net sales (a *credit* subtotal, not a separate account)**

In Exhibit 5-1, Sony Corporation—like most other businesses—reports to the public only the net sales figure. But Sony managers use the return and allowance data to track customer satisfaction and product quality.

Cost of Goods Sold and Gross Margin

OBJECTIVE 3

Compute cost of goods sold and gross margin

The inventory accounting system illustrated thus far is designed to produce up-to-date records of inventory on hand. This system provides the data for many inventory decisions and for preparation of the financial statements. However, managers have other information needs that the perpetual inventory system does not meet. For example, the owners of Austin Sound Stereo Center, Inc., plan their operations a year in advance to prepare the budget—a summary of the business strategies—for the coming year. Another computation of cost of goods sold helps managers budget their purchases of inventory. Banks also need another computation of the cost of goods sold because they do not have access to the internal accounting records of their borrowers but must monitor their borrower's financial affairs. We now turn to the alternate computation of cost of goods sold.

Panel A of Exhibit 5-5 gives the computation of cost of goods sold, and Panel B diagrams it.

By studying Exhibit 5-5, you will see that the computation and the diagram tell the same story. That is, a company's goods available for sale during a period come from beginning inventory and the period's net purchases and freight costs. Either the merchandise is sold during the period or it remains on hand at the end. The merchandise that remains is an asset, Inventory. The cost of the inventory that has been sold is an expense, Cost of Goods Sold. Panel A summarizes the relationship between the expense, Cost of Goods Sold, and the related asset, Inventory, during a period of time. The computation of net purchases is also shown. Panel B reveals that the cost of goods available for sale must wind up either as expense for the period or as an asset.[2]

---

[2]This computation of cost of goods sold is based on the periodic inventory system described in the end-of-chapter supplement.

EXHIBIT 5-5   *Measurement of Cost of Goods Sold*

Panel A

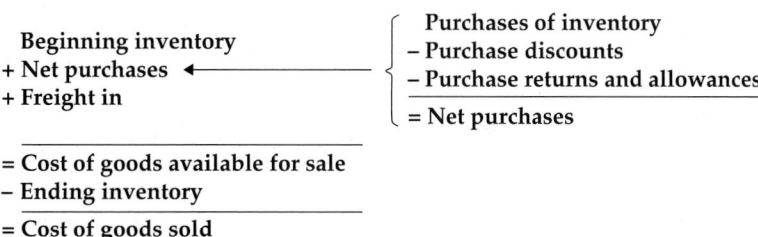

```
                                        ⎧  Purchases of inventory
  Beginning inventory                   ⎪  – Purchase discounts
+ Net purchases  ◄──────────────────────⎨  – Purchase returns and allowances
+ Freight in                            ⎪  ────────────────────────────────
                                        ⎩  = Net purchases
  ──────────────────────────
= Cost of goods available for sale
– Ending inventory
  ──────────────────────────
= Cost of goods sold
```

Panel B

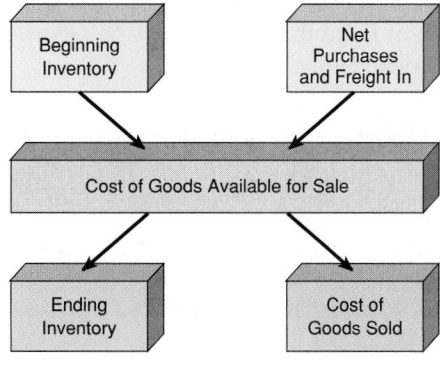

Exhibit 5-6 summarizes the first half of the chapter by showing Austin Sound's net sales revenue, cost of goods sold, and gross margin on the income statement. (All amounts are assumed.) *Gross margin equals net sales revenue minus cost of goods sold.*

Contra accounts—discounts, returns and allowances, and the like—are frequently netted against their related accounts parenthetically. Austin Sound could report:

Net sales revenue (net of sales discounts, $1,400,
    and returns and allowances, $2,000) $165,900

Goods and Services Tax

This topic is introduced here to make you aware of the goods and services tax because most goods and services sold today in Canada have the goods and services tax (GST)

EXHIBIT 5-6   *Partial Income Statement*

Austin Sound Stereo Center, Inc. Income Statement for the year ended December 31, 19X6		
Sales revenue		$169,300
Less: Sales discounts	$ 1,400	
Sales returns and allowances	2,000	3,400
Net sales revenue		$165,900
Cost of goods sold		90,800
Gross margin		$ 75,100

levied on them by the federal government at the time of sale. However, it was decided to omit consideration of the GST from the discussion and examples in the early chapters to avoid making the material overly complicated. The following discussion provides a brief introduction to the topic; GST is dealt with more fully in Chapter 11.

The manufacturer, wholesaler, and retailer pay the GST on the cost of their purchases, and then pass it on to the next link in the economic chain by collecting it on their respective sales. The consumer, the last link in the chain, pays the final tax. Each entity that collects the GST remits the tax collected to the Receiver General.

The GST is designed to be a consumption tax and, as was suggested above, the entity ultimately paying the tax is the final purchaser of the product or service. Earlier links in the chain (for example, the retailer) pay tax on their purchases, but are then allowed to deduct that tax from the tax they themselves collect on their sales. Therefore the GST paid on purchases does not really affect the cost of the purchase. For example, Austin Sound paid the GST of 7 percent, or $4.90 ($70 × .07), on the LA100 purchased on Exhibit 5-3. The entry to record the purchase of the single CD player would have been

May 27	Inventory	70.00	
	GST on purchases	4.90	
	Accounts payable		74.90
	Purchased JVC LA100 CD player on account.		

Assume Austin Sound sold the JVC LA100 CD player for $110.00 to a customer; the GST on the sale would be $7.70 ($110.00 × .07). The entry to record the sale would be

June 10	Cash	117.70	
	GST payable		7.70
	Net sales		110.00
	Sold turntable for cash.		

Subsequently, Austin Sound would have to remit the GST collected. The entry would be

July 31	GST payable..	7.70	
	GST on purchases		4.90
	Cash		2.80
	Payment of GST collected net of GST paid on purchases.		

Mid-Chapter Summary Problem for Your Review

Brun Sales Corp. engaged in the following transactions during June of the current year:

June	3	Purchased inventory on credit terms of 1/10 net eom (end of month), $1,610.
	9	Returned 40 percent of the inventory purchased on June 3. It was defective.
	9	Sold goods for cash, $920 (cost, $550).
	15	Purchased merchandise of $5,100, less a $100 quantity discount. Credit terms were 3/15 n/30.
	16	Paid a $260 freight bill on goods purchased.

18 Sold inventory on credit terms of 2/10 n/30, $2,000 (cost, $1,180).

22 Received damaged merchandise from the customer to whom the June 18 sale was made, $800 (cost, $480).

24 Borrowed money from the bank to take advantage of the discount offered on the June 15 purchase. Signed a note payable to the bank for the net amount.

24 Paid supplier for goods purchased on June 15, less all discounts.

28 Received cash in full settlement of the account from the customer who purchased inventory on June 18.

29 Paid the amount owed on account from the purchase of June 3.

30 Purchased inventory for cash, $900, less a quantity discount of $35.

Required

1. Journalize the above transactions. Explanations are not required.

2. Calculate the ending balances in the Inventory and Cost of Goods Sold accounts.

3. Assume the note payable signed on June 24 requires the payment of $95 interest expense. Was the decision wise or unwise to borrow funds to take advantage of the cash discount?

SOLUTION TO REVIEW PROBLEM

Requirement 1

June	3	Inventory	1,610	
		Accounts Payable		1,610
	9	Accounts Payable ($1,610 × .40)	644	
		Inventory		644
	9	Cash	920	
		Sales Revenue		920
	9	Cost of Goods Sold	550	
		Inventory		550
	15	Inventory ($5,100 – $100)	5,000	
		Accounts Payable		5,000
	16	Inventory	260	
		Cash		260
	18	Accounts Receivable	2,000	
		Sales Revenue		2,000
	18	Cost of Goods Sold	1,180	
		Inventory		1,180
	22	Sales Returns and Allowances	800	
		Accounts Receivable		800
	22	Inventory	480	
		Cost of Goods Sold		480
	24	Cash [$5,000 – .03($5,000)]	4,850	
		Note Payable		4,850
	24	Accounts Payable	5,000	
		Inventory ($5,000 × .03)		150
		Cash ($5,000 × .97)		4,850
	28	Cash [($2,000 – $800) × .98]	1,176	
		Sales Discounts [($2,000 – $800) × .02]	24	
		Accounts Receivable ($2,000 – $800)		1,200
	29	Accounts Payable ($1,610 – $644)	966	
		Cash		966
	30	Inventory ($900 – $35)	865	
		Cash		865

Requirement 2

Inventory: $1,610 + $5,000 − $644 − $550 + $260 − $1,180 + $480 − $150 + $865 = $5,691. Cost of goods sold: $550 + $1,180 − $480 = $1,250.

Requirement 3

The decision to borrow funds was wise, because the discount ($150) exceeded the interest paid on the amount borrowed ($95). Thus the entity was $55 better off as a result of its decision.

OBJECTIVE 4

Adjust and close the accounts of a merchandising business

The Adjusting and Closing Process for a Merchandising Business

A merchandising business adjusts and closes the accounts much as a service entity does. The steps of this end-of-period process are the same. If a work sheet is used, the trial balance is entered and the work sheet is completed to determine net income or net loss. The work sheet provides the data for journalizing the adjusting and closing entries and for preparing the financial statements.

Key Point:

As a result of this inventory adjustment, cost of goods sold is higher and gross margin is lower. The cost associated with buying these units is not accompanied by the revenue from a sale. Therefore gross margin shrinks by this amount (cost).

Adjusting Inventory Based on a Physical Count

In theory, the Inventory account stays current at all times. However, the actual amount of inventory on hand may differ from what the books show. Theft losses and damage can be significant. Also, accounting errors can cause Inventory's balance to need adjustment. For this reason virtually all businesses, such as the bookstore chain W.H. Smith, take a physical count of inventory at least once each year. The most common time for a business to count its inventory is at the end of the fiscal year, before the financial statements are prepared. The business then adjusts the Inventory account to the correct amount on the basis of the physical count.

Exhibit 5-7, Austin Sound's trial balance at December 31, 19X6, lists a $40,500 balance for inventory. With no shrinkage—due to theft or error—the business should have on hand inventory costing $40,500. But on December 31, when the Ernests, owners of Austin Sound, count the merchandise in the store, the total cost of the goods on hand comes to only $40,200. Austin Sound would record the inventory shrinkage with this adjusting entry:

Dec. 31	Cost of Goods Sold	300	
	Inventory ($40,500 − $40,200)		300

This entry brings Inventory and Cost of Goods Sold to their correct balances. Austin Sound's December 31, 19X6, adjustment data, including this inventory information (item (b)), are given at the bottom of Exhibit 5-7.

The physical count can indicate that more inventory is present than the books show. A search of the records may reveal that Austin Sound made a purchase it did not record. This could be entered the standard way: debit Inventory and credit Cash or Accounts Payable. If the excess inventory could not be accounted for, the business would adjust the accounts by debiting Inventory and crediting Cost of Goods Sold.

To illustrate a merchandiser's adjusting and closing process, let's use Austin Sound's December 31, 19X6, trial balance in Exhibit 5-7. All the new accounts—Inventory, Cost of Goods Sold, and the contra accounts—are highlighted for emphasis. The additional data item (b) gives the ending inventory figure $40,200.

EXHIBIT 5-7   *Trial Balance*

Austin Sound Stereo Center, Inc.
Trial Balance
December 31, 19X6

Cash	$ 2,850	
Accounts receivable	4,600	
Note receivable, current	8,000	
Interest receivable		
Inventory	**40,500**	
Supplies	650	
Prepaid insurance	1,200	
Furniture and fixtures	33,200	
Accumulated depreciation		$ 2,400
Accounts payable		47,000
Unearned sales revenue		2,000
Wages payable		
Interest payable		
Note payable, long-term		12,600
Common stock		10,000
Retained earnings		15,900
Dividends	54,100	
Sales revenue		**168,000**
Sales discounts	**1,400**	
Sales returns and allowances	**2,000**	
Interest revenue		600
Cost of goods sold	**90,500**	
Wage expense	9,800	
Rent expense	8,400	
Depreciation expense		
Insurance expense		
Supplies expense		
Interest expense	1,300	
Total	$258,500	$258,500

Additional data at December 31, 19X6:

a. Interest revenue earned but not yet collected, $400.

b. Inventory on hand, $40,200.

c. Supplies on hand, $100.

d. Prepaid insurance expired during the year, $1,000.

e. Depreciation, $600.

f. Unearned sales revenue earned during the year, $1,300.

g. Accrued wage expense, $400.

h. Accrued interest expense, $200.

Accounting Work Sheet of a Merchandising Business

The Exhibit 5-8 work sheet is similar to the work sheets we have seen so far, but a few differences appear. This work sheet does not include adjusted trial balance columns. In most accounting systems, a single operation combines trial balance amounts with the adjustments and extends the adjusted balances directly to the income statement and balance sheet columns. Therefore, to reduce clutter, the adjusted trial balance columns are omitted.

EXHIBIT 5-8   *Work Sheet*

Austin Sound Stereo Center, Inc.
Accounting Work Sheet
for the year ended December 31, 19X6

Account Title	Trial Balance Debit	Trial Balance Credit	Adjustments Debit	Adjustments Credit	Income Statement Debit	Income Statement Credit	Balance Sheet Debit	Balance Sheet Credit
Cash	2,850						2,850	
Accounts receivable	4,600						4,600	
Note receivable, current	8,000						8,000	
Interest receivable			(a) 400				400	
Inventory	**40,500**			(b) 300			**40,200**	
Supplies	650			(c) 550			100	
Prepaid insurance	1,200			(d)1,000			200	
Furniture and fixtures	33,200						33,200	
Accumulated depreciation		2,400		(e) 600				3,000
Accounts payable		47,000						47,000
Unearned sales revenue		2,000	(f) 1,300					700
Wages payable				(g) 400				400
Interest payable				(h) 200				200
Note payable, long-term		12,600						12,600
Common stock		10,000						10,000
Retained earnings		15,900						15,900
Dividends	54,100						54,100	
Sales revenue		168,000		(f) 1,300		169,300		
Sales discounts	1,400				1,400			
Sales returns and allowances	2,000				2,000			
Interest revenue		600		(a) 400		1,000		
Cost of goods sold	**90,500**		(b) 300		90,800			
Wage expense	**9,800**		(g) 400		10,200			
Rent expense	8,400				8,400			
Depreciation expense			(e) 600		600			
Insurance expense			(d)1,000		1,000			
Supplies expense			(c) 550		550			
Interest expense	1,300		(h) 200		1,500			
	258,500	258,500	4,750	4,750	116,450	170,300	143,650	89,800
Net income					53,850			53,850
					170,300	170,300	143,650	143,650

Account Title Columns   The trial balance lists a number of accounts without balances. Ordinarily, these accounts are affected by the adjusting process. Examples include Interest Receivable, Wages Payable, and Depreciation Expense. The accounts are listed in the order they appear in the ledger. If additional accounts are needed, they can be written in at the bottom of the work sheet above the net income amount.

Trial Balance Columns   Examine the Inventory account, $40,500 in the Trial Balance. This $40,500 is the ending balance before the physical count. Cost of Goods Sold's balance of $90,500 precedes any adjustment based on the physical count of goods on hand at December 31. We shall assume that any difference between the Inventory amount on the trial balance and the correct amount based on the physical count is unexplained and should be debited or credited directly to Cost of Goods Sold.

Adjustments Columns   The adjustments are similar to those discussed in Chapters 3 and 4. They may be entered in any order desired. The debit amount of each entry should equal the credit amount, and total debits should equal total credits.

Income Statement Columns   The income statement columns contain adjusted amounts for the revenues and expenses. Sales Revenue, for example, is $169,300, which includes the $1,300 adjustment.

The income statement column subtotals on the work sheet indicate whether the business earned net income or incurred a net loss. If total credits are greater, the result is net income, as shown in Exhibit 5-8. Inserting the net income amount in the debit column brings total debits into agreement with total credits. If total debits are greater, a net loss has occurred. Inserting a net loss amount in the credit column would equalize total debits and total credits. Net income or net loss is then extended to the opposite column of the balance sheet.

Balance Sheet Columns   The only new item on the balance sheet is Inventory. The balance listed is the ending amount of $40,200, which is determined by a physical count of inventory on hand at the end of the period.

Key Point:
If you were preparing a work sheet, you could omit the adjusted trial balance columns. Once you understand the mechanics of the work sheet, you can take a trial balance amount, add or subtract the adjustments, and extend the new amount to either the income statement or balance sheet columns.

Financial Statements of a Merchandising Business

OBJECTIVE 5
Prepare a merchandiser's financial statements

Exhibit 5-9 presents Austin Sound Stereo Center's financial statements. The *income statement* through gross margin repeats Exhibit 5-6. This information is followed by the **operating expenses**, which are those expenses other than cost of goods sold incurred in the entity's major line of business—merchandising. Austin Sound's operating expenses include wage expense, rent, insurance, depreciation of furniture and fixtures, and supplies expense.

Many companies report their operating expenses in two categories. *Selling expenses* are those expenses related to marketing the company's products—sales salaries; sales commissions; advertising; depreciation, rent, utilities and property taxes on store buildings; depreciation on store furniture; delivery expense, and so on. *General expenses* include office expenses, such as the salaries of the company president and office employees, depreciation, rent, utilities, property taxes on the home office building, and office supplies.

Gross margin minus operating expenses equals **income from operations**, or **operating income**. Many businesspeople view operating income as the most reliable indicator of a business's success because it measures the entity's major ongoing activities.

The last section of Austin Sound's income statement is **other revenue and expense**. This category reports revenues and expenses that are outside the main operations of the business. Examples include gains and losses on the sale of capital assets (not inventory) and gains and losses on lawsuits. Accountants have traditionally viewed Interest Revenue and Interest Expense as "other" items, because they arise from loaning money and borrowing money—financing activities that are outside the operating scope of selling merchandise or, for a service entity, rendering services.

The bottom line of the income statement is net income. We often hear the term *bottom line* used to refer to a final result. The term originated in the position of net income on the income statement.

A merchandiser's *statement of retained earnings* looks exactly like that of a service business. In fact, you cannot determine whether the entity is merchandising- or service-oriented from looking at the statement of retained earnings.

If the business is a merchandiser, the *balance sheet* shows inventory as a major asset. In contrast, service businesses usually have minor amounts of inventory.

Adjusting and Closing Entries for a Merchandising Business

Exhibit 5-10 presents Austin Sound's adjusting entries, which are similar to those you have seen previously, except for the inventory adjustment (entry (b)). The closing en-

EXHIBIT 5-9   Financial Statements of Austin Sound Stereo Center, Inc.

Austin Sound Stereo Center, Inc.
Income Statement
for the year ended December 31, 19X6

Sales revenue		$169,300	
Less: Sales discounts	$1,400		
Sales returns and allowances	2,000	3,400	
Net sales revenue			$165,900
Cost of goods sold			90,800
Gross margin			75,100
Operating expenses			
Wage expense		10,200	
Rent expense		8,400	
Insurance expense		1,000	
Depreciation expense		600	
Supplies expense		550	20,750
Income from operations			54,350
Other revenue and expense			
Interest revenue		1,000	
Interest expense		(1,500)	(500)
Net income			$ 53,850

Austin Sound Stereo Center, Inc.
Statement of Retained Earnings
for the year ended December 31, 19X6

Retained earnings, January 1, 19X6	$15,900
Add: Net income	53,850
	69,750
Less: Dividends	54,100
Retained earnings, December 31, 19X6	$15,650

Austin Sound Stereo Center, Inc.
Balance Sheet
December 31, 19X6

Assets			Liabilities		
Current			Current		
Cash		$ 2,850	Accounts payable		$47,000
Accounts receivable		4,600	Unearned sales revenue		700
Note receivable		8,000	Wages payable		400
Interest receivable		400	Interest payable		200
Inventory		40,200	Total current liabilities		48,300
Prepaid insurance		200	Long-term		
Supplies		100	Note payable		12,600
Total current assets		56,350	Total liabilities		60,900
Capital			**Shareholders' Equity**		
Furniture and fixtures	$33,200		Common stock		10,000
Less: Accumulated			Retained earnings		15,650
depreciation	3,000	30,200	Total shareholders' equity		25,650
Total assets		$86,550	Total liabilities and		
			shareholders' equity		$86,550

EXHIBIT 5-10 *Journalizing and Posting the Adjusting and Closing Entries*

		Journal		
		Adjusting Entries		
a. Dec. 31		Interest receivable...	400	
		Interest revenue...		400
b.	31	Cost of goods sold	300	
		Inventory..		300
c.	31	Supplies expense ($650 – $100)......................	550	
		Supplies..		550
d.	31	Insurance expense..	1,000	
		Prepaid insurance......................................		1,000
e.	31	Depreciation expense	600	
		Accumulated depreciation		600
f.	31	Unearned sales revenue.................................	1,300	
		Sales revenue..		1,300
g.	31	Wage expense	400	
		Wages payable...		400
h.	31	Interest expense...	200	
		Interest payable..		200
		Closing Entries		
Dec. 31		Sales revenue	169,300	
		Interest revenue	1,000	
		Income summary...		170,300
	31	Income summary...	116,450	
		Cost of goods sold......................................		90,800
		Sales discounts...		1,400
		Sales returns and allowances..................		2,000
		Wage expense..		10,200
		Rent expense		8,400
		Depreciation expense................................		600
		Insurance expense		1,000
		Supplies expense		550
		Interest expense		1,500
	31	Income summary ($170,300 – $116,450)	53,850	
		Retained earnings......................................		53,850
	31	Retained earnings...	54,100	
		Dividends		54,100

tries in the exhibit also follow the pattern exhibited in Chapter 4. The first closing entry debits the revenue accounts for their ending balances. The offsetting credit of $170,300 transfers their sum to Income Summary. This amount comes directly from the credit column of the income statement on the work sheet (Exhibit 5-8).

The second closing entry includes credits to Cost of Goods Sold and to the contra revenue accounts, Sales Discounts, Sales Returns and Allowances, which are new, and to the expense accounts. The offsetting $116,450 debit to Income Summary comes from the debit column of the income statement on the work sheet. The last two closing entries close net income from Income Summary, and also close Dividends, into the Retained Earnings account.

Study Exhibits 5-8, 5-9, and 5-10 carefully because they illustrate the entire end-of-period process that leads to the financial statements. As you progress through this book, you may want to refer to these exhibits to refresh your understanding of the adjusting and closing process for a merchandising business.

Income Statement Format

We have seen that the balance sheet appears in two formats: the account format and report format. There are also two basic formats for the income statement: *multiple step* and *single step*. A recent survey indicated the multiple-step format was used by almost two-thirds of the companies surveyed; the remainder used the single-step format.

Multiple-Step Income Statement

The **multiple-step income statement** format contains subtotals to highlight significant relationships. In addition to net income, it also presents gross margin and operating income, or income from operations. This format communicates a merchandiser's results of operations especially well, because gross margin and income from operations are two key measures of operating performance. Schneider Corporation (maker of Schneider's meat products) and John Labatt use the multiple-step format. The income statements presented thus far in this chapter have been multiple-step income statements. Austin Sound's multiple-step income statement for the year ended December 31, 19X6 appears in Exhibit 5-9.

Single-Step Income Statement

The **single-step income statement** format groups all revenues together, and then lists and deducts all expenses together without drawing any subtotals. IBM uses this format. The single-step format has the advantage of listing all revenues together and all expenses together, as shown in Exhibit 5-11. Thus it clearly distinguishes revenues from expenses. The income statements in Chapters 1 through 4 were single-step. This format works well for service entities because they have no gross margin to report.

Most published financial statements are highly condensed. Appendix A at the end of the book gives the income statement for Mark's Work Wearhouse Ltd. Of course, condensed statements can be supplemented with desired details.

EXHIBIT 5-11   *Single-Step Income Statement*

Austin Sound Stereo Center, Inc. Income Statement for the year ended December 31, 19X6	
Revenues	
Net sales (net of sales discounts, $1,400, and returns and allowances, $2,000)	$165,900
Interest revenue	1,000
Total revenues	166,900
Expenses	
Cost of goods sold	$ 90,800
Wage expense	10,200
Rent expense	8,400
Interest expense	1,500
Insurance expense	1,000
Depreciation expense	600
Supplies expense	550
Total expenses	113,050
Net income	$ 53,850

Use of Accounting Information in Decision-Making

OBJECTIVE 6
Use the gross margin percentage and the inventory turnover ratio for evaluating a business

Merchandise inventory is the most important asset to a merchandising business because it captures the essence of the entity. To manage the firm, owners and managers focus their energies on the best way to sell the inventory. They use several ratios to evaluate operations.

Gross Margin Percentage

A key decision tool for a merchandiser relates to gross margin, which is net sales minus cost of goods sold. Merchandisers strive to increase the **gross margin percentage**, which is computed as follows:

**For Austin Sound Stereo Center, Inc.
(Exhibit 5-9)**

$$\text{Gross margin percentage} = \frac{\text{Gross margin}}{\text{Net sales revenue}} = \frac{\$75,100}{\$165,900} = .453 = 45.3\%$$

EXHIBIT 5-12
Gross Margin on $1.00 of Sales for Two Merchandisers

The gross margin (or gross profit) percentage is one of the most carefully watched measures of profitability because it is fundamental to a merchandiser. For most firms, the gross margin percentage changes little from year to year, and a small downturn may signal an important drop in income. A 45-percent gross margin means that each dollar of sales generates 45 cents of gross profit. On average, the goods cost the seller 55 cents. A small increase in the gross margin percentage usually indicates an increase in profitability.

Austin Sound's gross margin percentage of 45.3 percent compares favorably with the industry average for electronic retailers, which is 34.9 percent. By contrast, the average gross margin percentage is 14.1 percent for automobile dealers, 22.8 percent for grocery stores, and 55.7 percent for restaurants. Exhibit 5-12 compares Austin Sound's gross margin to Wal-Mart.

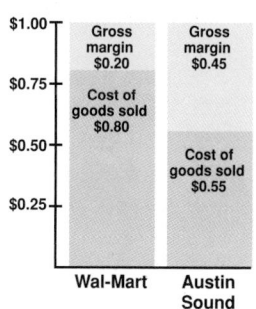

Inventory Turnover

Owners and managers strive to sell inventory as quickly as possible because it generates no profit until it is sold. The faster the sales occur, the higher the income. The slower the sales, the lower the income. Ideally, a business could operate with zero inventory. Most businesses, however, including retailers such as Austin Sound, must keep goods on hand for customers. Successful merchandisers purchase carefully to keep the goods moving through the business at a rapid pace. **Inventory turnover**, the ratio of cost of goods sold to average inventory, indicates how rapidly inventory is sold. Its computation follows:

Short Exercise:
Calculate inventory turnover given the following data:

Beg. inventory ....$ 2,350
End. inventory 1,980
Purchases....................14,550
Freight in 390

A: Cost of goods sold/Avg. inv. turn. = $15,310/ $2,165 = 7 times

**For Austin Sound Stereo Center, Inc.
(Exhibit 5-9)**

$$\text{Inventory turnover} = \frac{\text{Cost of goods sold}}{\text{Average inventory}} = \frac{\text{Cost of goods sold}}{(\text{Beginning inventory} + \text{ ending inventory})/2} = \frac{\$90,800}{(\$38,600 + \$40,200)/2}$$

$$= \text{ 2.3 times per year} \atop \text{(about every 159 days)}$$

EXHIBIT 5-13   *Rate of Inventory Turnover for Two Merchandisers*

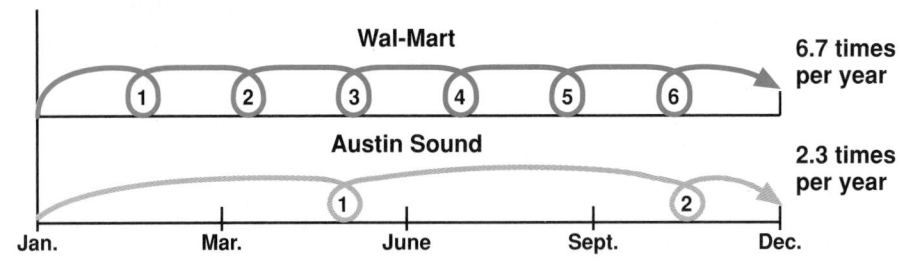

Inventory turnover is usually computed for an annual period, and the relevant cost-of-goods sold figure is the amount from the entire year. Average inventory is computed from the beginning and ending amounts. (Austin Sound's beginning would be taken from the business's balance sheet at the end of the preceding year.) The resulting inventory turnover statistic shows how many times the average level of inventory was sold during the year. A high rate of turnover is preferred over a low rate of turnover. An increase in turnover usually means higher profits.

Inventory turnover varies from industry to industry. Grocery stores, for example, turn their goods over faster than automobile dealers do. Drug stores have a higher turnover than furniture stores do. Retailers of electronic products, such as Austin Sound, have an average turnover of 3.6 times per year. Austin Sound's turnover rate of 2.3 times per year suggests that Austin Sound is not very successful. The lower one-fourth of electronics retailers average a turnover rate of 2.7, so Austin Sound's turnover rate of 2.2 looks rather bad. Exhibit 5-13 compares the inventory turnover rate of Austin Sound and Wal-Mart Stores, Inc.

Financial analysis is complex. Exhibits 5-12 and 5-13 tell an interesting story. Wal-Mart sells lots of inventory at a relatively low gross profit margin. Wal-Mart earns its profits by turning its inventory over rapidly. Austin Sound, a mom-and-pop business, prices inventory to earn a higher gross margin on each dollar of sales. But Austin Sound cannot sell its merchandise nearly as rapidly as Wal-Mart can. Gross margin percentage and rate of inventory turnover do not provide enough information to yield an overall conclusion about either firm, but the example shows how owners and managers may use accounting information to evaluate a company.

Summary Problem for Your Review

The accompanying trial balance and additional data are related to Jan King Distributing Company, Inc.

Jan King Distributing Company, Inc.
Trial Balance
December 31, 19X3

Cash	$ 5,670	
Accounts receivable	37,100	
Inventory	60,500	
Supplies	3,930	
Prepaid rent	6,000	
Furniture and fixtures	26,500	
Accumulated depreciation		$ 21,200
Accounts payable		46,340
Salary payable		

Interest payable..		
Unearned sales revenue..		3,500
Note payable, long-term...		35,000
Common stock		5,000
Retained earnings		18,680
Dividends...	48,000	
Sales revenue...		346,700
Sales discounts	10,300	
Sales returns and allowances	8,200	
Cost of goods sold	171,770	
Salary expense...	82,750	
Rent expense..	7,000	
Depreciation expense		
Utilities expense..	5,800	
Supplies expense...		
Interest expense...	2,900	
Total	$476,420	$476,420

Additional data at December 31, 19X3:

a. Supplies used during the year, $2,580.

b. Prepaid rent in force, $1,000.

c. Unearned sales revenue still not earned, $2,400. The company expects to earn this amount during the next few months.

d. Depreciation. The furniture and fixtures' estimated useful life is 10 years, and they are expected to be worthless when they are retired from service.

e. Accrued salaries, $1,300.

f. Accrued interest expense, $600.

g. Inventory on hand, $65,800.

Required

1. Enter the trial balance on a work sheet and complete the work sheet.

2. Journalize the adjusting and closing entries at December 31. Post to the Income Summary account as an accuracy check on the entries affecting that account. The credit balance closed out of Income Summary should equal net income computed on the work sheet.

3. Prepare the company's multiple-step income statement, statement of retained earnings, and balance sheet in account format.

4. Compute the inventory turnover for 19X3. Inventory at December 31, 19X2, was $60,500. Turnover for 19X2 was 2.1. Would you expect Jan King Distributing Company, Inc., to be more or less profitable in 19X3 than in 19X2? Give your reason.

Requirement 1

Jan King Distributing Company, Inc.
Work Sheet
for the year ended December 31, 19X3

Account Title	Trial Balance Debit	Trial Balance Credit	Adjustments Debit	Adjustments Credit	Income Statement Debit	Income Statement Credit	Balance Sheet Debit	Balance Sheet Credit
Cash	5,670						5,670	
Accounts receivable	37,100						37,100	
Inventory	60,500		(g)5,300				65,800	
Supplies	3,930			(a) 2,580			1,350	
Prepaid rent	6,000			(b) 5,000			1,000	
Furniture and fixtures	26,500						26,500	
Accumulated depreciation		21,200		(d)2,650				23,850
Accounts payable		46,340						46,340
Salary payable				(e) 1,300				1,300
Interest payable				(f) 600				600
Unearned sales revenue		3,500	(c)1,100					2,400
Note payable, long-term		35,000						35,000
Common stock		5,000						5,000
Retained earnings		18,680						18,680
Dividends	48,000						48,000	
Sales revenue		346,700		(c) 1,100		347,800		
Sales discounts	10,300				10,300			
Sales returns and allowances	8,200				8,200			
Cost of goods sold	171,770			(g) 5,300	166,470			
Salary expense	82,750		(e)1,300		84,050			
Rent expense	7,000		(b)5,000		12,000			
Depreciation expense			(d)2,650		2,650			
Utilities expense	5,800				5,800			
Supplies expense			(a)2,580		2,580			
Interest expense	2,900		(f) 600		3,500			
	476,420	476,420	18,530	18,530	295,550	347,800	185,420	133,170
Net income					52,250			52,250
					347,800	347,800	185,420	185,420

SOLUTION TO REVIEW PROBLEM

Requirement 2

Adjusting entries

19X3				
Dec. 31	Supplies expense		2,580	
	Supplies			2,580
31	Rent expense		5,000	
	Prepaid rent			5,000
31	Unearned sales revenue		1,100	
	Sales revenue			1,100
31	Depreciation expense ($26,500/10)		2,650	
	Accumulated depreciation			2,650
31	Salary expense		1,300	
	Salary payable			1,300
31	Interest expense		600	
	Interest payable			600
31	Inventory		5,300*	
	Cost of goods sold			5,300

*Excess of inventory on hand over the balance in the Inventory amount. This adjustment brings Inventory to its correct balance.

Closing entries

19X3

Dec. 31	Sales revenue		347,800	
	Income summary			347,800
31	Income summary		295,550	
	Cost of goods sold			166,470
	Sales discounts			10,300
	Sales returns and allowances			8,200
	Salary expense			84,050
	Rent expense			12,000
	Depreciation expense			2,650
	Utilities expense			5,800
	Supplies expense			2,580
	Interest expense			3,500
31	Income summary ($347,800 − $295,550)		52,250	
	Retained earnings			52,250
31	Retained earnings		48,000	
	Dividends			48,000

Income Summary

Clo.	295,550	Clo.	347,800
Clo.	52,250	Bal.	52,250

Requirement 3

Jan King Distributing Company, Inc.
Income Statement
for the year ended December 31, 19X3

Sales revenue		$347,800	
Less: Sales discounts	$10,300		
Sales returns and allowances	8,200	18,500	
Net sales revenue			$329,300
Cost of goods sold			166,470
Gross margin			162,830
Operating expenses			
Salary expense		84,050	
Rent expense		12,000	
Utilities expense		5,800	
Depreciation expense		2,650	
Supplies expense		2,580	107,080
Income from operations			55,750
Other expense			
Interest expense			3,500
Net income			$ 52,250

Jan King Distributing Company, Inc.
Statement of Retained Earnings
for the year ended December 31, 19X3

Retained earnings, December 31, 19X2	$18,680
Add: Net income	52,250
	70,930
Add: Dividends	48,000
Retained earnings, December 31, 19X3	$22,930

Jan King Distributing Company, Inc.
Balance Sheet
December 31, 19X3

Assets			Liabilities		
Current			Current		
Cash..............................	$ 5,670		Accounts payable................	$ 46,340	
Accounts receivable.....	37,100		Salary payable......................	1,300	
Inventory........................	65,800		Interest payable	600	
Supplies.........................	1,350		Unearned sales revenue	2,400	
Prepaid Rent	1,000		Total current liabilities........	50,640	
Total current assets....	110,920		Long-term		
Capital			Note payable........................	35,000	
Furniture and fixtures . $26,500			Total liabilities	85,640	
Less: Accumulated					
depreciation................ 23,850	2,650		**Shareholders' Equity**		
			Common stock	5,000	
			Retained earnings.....................	22,930	
			Total shareholders' equity	27,930	
			Total liabilities and		
Total assets..........................	$113,570		shareholders' equity	$113,570	

Requirement 4

$$\text{Inventory turnover} = \frac{\text{Cost of goods sold}}{\text{Average inventory}} = \frac{\$166,470}{(\$60,500 + \$65,800)/2} = 2.6$$

The increase in the rate of inventory turnover from 2.1 to 2.6 suggests higher profits in 19X3 than in 19X2.

Summary

1. Use sales, gross margin, and operating income to evaluate a company. The major revenue of a merchandising business is *sales revenue*, or *net sales*. The major expense is *cost of goods sold*. Net sales minus cost of goods sold is called *gross margin*, or *gross profit*. This amount measures the business's success or failure in selling its products at a higher price than it paid for them.

The *invoice* is the business document generated by a purchase or sale transaction. Most merchandising entities offer *discounts* to their customers and allow them to *return* unsuitable merchandise. They also grant *allowances* for damaged goods that the buyer chooses to keep. Discounts and Returns and Allowances are contra accounts to Sales Revenue.

2. Account for the purchase and sale of inventory. The merchandiser's major asset is *inventory*. In a merchandising entity the accounting cycle is from cash to inventory as the inventory is purchased for resale, and back to cash as the inventory is sold.

3. Compute cost of goods sold and gross margin. *Cost of goods sold*, or *cost of sales*, is the cost of the inventory that the business has sold. It is the largest single expense of most merchandising businesses. Gross margin equals net sales revenue minus cost of goods sold.

4. Adjust and close the accounts of a merchandising business. The end-of-period adjusting and closing process of a merchandising business is similar to that of a service business. In addition, a merchandiser adjusts inventory for theft losses, damage, and accounting errors.

5. Prepare a merchandiser's financial statements. The income statement may appear in the *single-step format* or the *multiple-step format*. A single-step income statement has only two sections—one for revenues and the other for expenses—and a single income amount for net income. A multiple-step income statement has subtotals for gross margin and income from operations. Both formats are widely used.

6. Use the gross margin percentage and the inventory turnover ratio to evaluate a business. Two key decision aids for a merchandiser are the *gross margin percentage* and the *rate of inventory turnover*. Increases in these measures usually signal an increase in profits.

Self-Study Questions

Test your understanding of the chapter by marking the correct answer for each of the following questions:

1. The major expense of a merchandising business is *(p. 214)*
   a. Cost of goods sold   c. Rent
   b. Depreciation   d. Interest

2. Sales total $440,000, cost of goods sold is $210,000, and operating expenses are $160,000. How much is gross margin? *(p. 214)*
   a. $440,000   c. $210,000
   b. $230,000   d. $70,000

3. A purchase discount results from *(p. 218)*
   a. Returning goods to the seller
   b. Receiving a purchase allowance from the seller
   c. Buying a large enough quantity of merchandise to get the discount
   d. Paying within the discount period

4. Which one of the following pairs includes items that are the most similar? *(pp. 223–224)*
   a. Purchase discounts and purchase returns
   b. Cost of goods sold and inventory
   c. Net sales and sales discounts
   d. Sales returns and sales allowances

5. Which of the following is *not* an account? *(p. 224)*
   a. Sales revenue   c. Inventory
   b. Net sales   d. Supplies expense

6. Cost of goods sold is computed by adding beginning inventory and net purchases and subtracting X. What is X? *(p. 224)*
   a. Net sales   c. Ending inventory
   b. Sales discounts   d. Net purchases

7. Which account causes the main difference between a merchandiser's adjusting and closing process and that of a service business? *(pp. 231–233)*
   a. Advertising expense   c. Cost of goods sold
   b. Interest revenue   d. Accounts receivable

8. The major item on a merchandiser's income statement that a service business does not have is *(p. 214)*
   a. Cost of goods sold   c. Salary expense
   b. Inventory   d. Total revenue

9. The closing entry for Sales Discounts is *(p. 233)*
   a. Sales Discounts   b. Sales Discounts   c. Income Summary
         Income Summary   Sales Revenue   Sales Discounts
   d. Not used: Sales Discounts is a permanent account, which is not closed.

10. Which income statement format reports income from operations? *(p. 234)*
    a. Account format   c. Single-step format
    b. Report format   d. Multiple-step format

Answers to the Self-Study Questions follow the Accounting Vocabulary.

Accounting Vocabulary

Cost of goods sold *(p. 222)*
Cost of sales *(p. 222)*
Gross margin *(p. 214)*
Gross margin percentage *(p. 234)*
Gross profit *(p. 214)*
Income from operations *(p. 231)*
Inventory turnover *(p. 235)*
Multiple-step income statement *(p. 233)*
Net purchases *(p. 263)*
Net sales *(p. 224)*
Operating expenses *(p. 231)*
Operating income *(p. 231)*
Other expense *(p. 231)*
Other revenue *(p. 231)*
Periodic inventory system *(p. 215)*
Perpetual inventory system *(p. 216)*
Sales *(p. 214)*
Sales discountsy *(p. 223)*
Sales returns and allowances *(p. 223)*
Sales revenue *(p. 214)*
Single-step income statement *(p. 234)*

Answers to Self-Study Questions

1. a
2. b ($440,000 – $210,000 = $230,000)
3. d

4. d   7. c   10. d
5. b   8. a
6. c   9. c

ASSIGNMENT MATERIAL _____

Questions

1. Gross margin is often mentioned in the business press as an important measure of success. What does gross margin measure, and why is this important?

2. Describe the operating cycle for (a) the purchase and cash sale of inventory, and (b) the purchase and sale of inventory on account.

3. Identify 10 items of information on an invoice.

4. Indicate which accounts are debited and credited for (a) a credit purchase of inventory and the subsequent cash payment, and (b) a credit sale of inventory and the subsequent cash collection. Assume no discounts, returns, allowances, or freight.

5. Inventory costing $1,000 is purchased and invoiced on July 28 under terms of 3/10 n/30. Compute the payment amount on August 6. How much would the payment be on August 8? What explains the difference? What is the latest acceptable payment date under the terms of sale?

6. Inventory listed at $35,000 is sold subject to a quantity discount of $3,000 and under payment terms of 2/15 n/45. What is the net sales revenue on this sale, if the customer pays within 15 days?

7. Name the new contra accounts introduced in this chapter.

8. Briefly discuss the similarity in computing supplies expense and computing cost of goods sold by the method shown on page 224.

9. Why is the title of Cost of Goods Sold especially descriptive? What type of account is Cost of Goods Sold?

10. Beginning inventory is $5,000, net purchases total $30,000, and freight in is $1,000. If ending inventory is $8,000, what is cost of goods sold?

11. You are evaluating two companies as possible investments. One entity sells its services and the other entity is a merchandiser. How can you identify the merchandiser by examining the two entities' balance sheets and income statements?

12. You are beginning the adjusting and closing process at the end of your company's fiscal year. Does the trial balance carry the final ending amount of inventory? Give your reason.

13. Give the adjusting entry for inventory if shrinkage is $9,100.

14. What is the identifying characteristic of the "other" category of revenues and expenses? Give an example of each.

15. Name and describe the two income statement formats and identify the type of business to which each format best applies.

16. List eight different operating expenses.

17. Which financial statement reports sales discounts and sales returns and allowances? Show how they are reported, using any reasonable amounts in your illustration.

18. Does a merchandiser prefer a high or low rate of inventory turnover? Give your reason.

19. In general, what does a decreasing gross margin percentage, coupled with an increasing rate of inventory turnover, suggest about a business's pricing strategy?

Exercises

Exercise 5-1   *Evaluating a real company's revenues, gross margin, operating income, and net income*   **(Obj. 1)**

IBM recently reported its operations on this income statement:

Consolidated Statement of Earnings International Business Machines Corporation and Subsidiary Companies (Dollars in millions)			
For the year ended December 31:	1992	1991	1990
Revenue:			
Sales..	**$33,755**	$37,093	$43,959
Software..	**11,103**	10,498	9,865
Maintenance..	**7,635**	7,414	7,198
Services...	**7,352**	5,582	4,124
Rentals and financing.................................	**4,678**	4,179	3,785
	64,523	64,766	68,931
Cost:			
Sales..	**19,698**	18,571	19,401
Software..	**3,924**	3,865	3,118
Maintenance..	**3,430**	3,379	3,302
Services...	**6,051**	4,531	3,315
Rentals and financing.................................	**1,966**	1,727	1,579
	35,069	32,073	30,715
Gross Profit	**29,454**	32,693	38,216

Operating Expenses:			
Selling, general and administrative..........	**19,526**	21,375	20,709
Research, development and engineering	**6,522**	6,644	6,554
Restructuring charges................................	**11,645**	3,735	—
	37,693	31,754	27,263
Operating Income	**(8,239)**	939	10,953
Other Income, principally interest	**573**	602	495
Interest Expense	**1,360**	1,423	1,324
Earnings before Income Taxes.................	**(9,026)**	118	10,124
Provision for Income Taxes......................	**(2,161)**	716	4,157
Net Earnings before Changes in			
Accounting Principles...........................	**(6,865)**	(598)	5,967
Effect of Changes in Accounting			
Principles...	**1,900**	(2,263)	—
Net Earnings...	**$(4,965)**	$(2,861)	$ 5,967

Required

1. Is IBM a merchandising entity, a service business, or both? How can you tell?

2. Compute IBM's gross margin on sales (not total revenues) for 1992, 1991, and 1990. Compare this trend with the company's trend of total gross margin.

3. Write a brief memo to investors advising them of IBM's two-year trend of sales, total revenues, gross margin, operating income, and net income. In which year did IBM experience the larger change from the preceding year, 1992 or 1991?

Exercise 5-2   *Journalizing purchase and sale transactions*   *(Obj. 2)*

Journalize, without explanations, the following transactions of Mariposa, Inc. during July:

July	3	Purchased $1,000 of inventory under terms of 2/10 n/eom (end of month) and FOB shipping point.
	7	Returned $300 of defective merchandise purchased on July 3.
	9	Paid freight bill of $110 on July 3 purchase.
	10	Sold inventory for $2,200, collecting cash of $400. Payment terms on the remainder were 2/15 n/30. The goods cost Mariposa $1,300.
	12	Paid amount owed on credit purchase of July 3, less the discount and the return.
	16	Granted a sales allowance of $800 on the July 10 sale.
	23	Received cash from July 10 customer in full settlement of her debt, less the allowance and the discount.

Exercise 5-3   *Journalizing transactions from a purchase invoice*   *(Obj. 2)*

As the proprietor of Kendrick Tire Corp., you receive the accompanying invoice from a supplier.

Required

1. Record the May 14 purchase on account.

2. The R39 truck tires were ordered by mistake and therefore were returned to ABC. Journalize the return on May 19.

3. Record the May 22 payment of the amount owed.

ABC TIRE WHOLESALE DISTRIBUTORS, INC.
2600 Victoria Avenue
Regina, Saskatchewan S4P 1B3

Invoice date: May 14, 19X3   **Payment terms:** 2/10 n/30

Sold to: Kendrick Tire Corp.
4219 Cumberland Avenue
Saskatoon, SK S7M 1X3

Quantity Ordered	Description	Quantity Shipped	Price	Amount
6	P135-X4 Radials.........	6	$37.14	$222.84
8	L912 Belted-bias........	8	41.32	330.56
14	R39 Truck tires.........	10	50.02	500.20
	Total..			$1,053.60

Due date: **Amount:**
May 24, 19X3 $1,032.53
May 25 through June 13, 19X3 $1,053.60

Paid:

Exercise 5-4   *Journalizing purchase transactions*   *(Obj. 2)*

On April 30, Corwin Jewelers Ltd. purchased inventory of $5,300 on account from La Roche Fine Gems Ltd., a wholesale jewelry supplier. Terms were 3/15 n/45. On receiving the goods Corwin checked the order and found $800 worth of items that were not ordered. Therefore, Corwin returned this amount of merchandise to the supplier on May 4.

To pay the remaining amount owed, Corwin had to borrow from the bank because of a temporary cash shortage. On May 14 Corwin signed a short-term note payable to the bank and immediately paid the borrowed funds to La Roche. On May 31 Corwin paid the bank the net amount of the invoice, which Corwin had borrowed, plus $30 interest.

Required

Record the indicated transactions in the journal of Corwin Jewelers. Explanations are not required.

Exercise 5-5   *Journalizing sale transactions*   *(Obj. 2)*

Refer to the business situation in Exercise 5-4. Journalize the transactions of La Roche Fine Gems Ltd. La Roche's gross margin is 40 percent. Explanations are not required.

Exercise 5-6   *Computing the elements of a merchandiser's income statement*   *(Obj. 3)*

Supply the missing income statement amounts in each of the following situations:

Sales	Sales Discounts	Net Sales	Beginning Inventory	Net Purchases	Ending Inventory	Cost of Goods Sold	Gross Margin
$94,300	(a)	$92,800	$32,500	$66,700	$39,400	(b)	$33,000
72,400	$2,100	(c)	27,450	43,000	(d)	$44,100	(e)
91,500	1,800	89,700	(f)	54,900	22,600	59,400	(g)
(h)	3,000	(i)	40,700	(j)	48,230	62,500	36,600

Exercise 5-7   *Computing cost of goods sold for an actual company*   **(Obj. 3)**

For the year ended December 31, 19X9, House of Fabrics Ltd., a retailer of home-related products, reported net sales of $338 million and cost of goods sold of $154 million. The company's balance sheet at December 31, 19X8 and 19X9 reported inventories of $133 million and $129 million, respectively. What were House of Fabrics' net purchases during 19X9?

Exercise 5-8   *Preparing a merchandiser's multiple-step income statement to evaluate the business*   **(Obj. 3, 5, 6)**

Selected accounts of Handy Dan Ltd., a Home Hardware franchise, are listed in alphabetical order.

Accounts receivable	$48,300		Purchase of inventory	$91,300
Accumulated depreciation	18,700		Purchase discounts	3,000
Cost of goods sold	?		Purchase returns	2,000
Freight in	2,200		Sales discounts	9,000
General expenses	23,800		Sales returns	4,600
Interest revenue	1,500		Sales revenue	201,000
Inventory, June 30	21,870		Selling expense	37,840
Inventory, May 31	19,450		Shareholders' equity	126,070
			Unearned sales revenue	6,500

Required

Prepare the business's multiple-step income statement for June of the current year. In a separate schedule, show the computation of cost of goods sold. Compute the rate of inventory turnover. Last year the turnover was 3.8 times. Does this two-year trend suggest improvement or deterioration in profitability?

Exercise 5-9   *Preparing a single-step income statement for a merchandising business*   **(Obj. 3, 5, 6)**

Prepare Handy Dan's single-step income statement for June, using the data from Exercise 5-8. In a separate schedule, show the computation of cost of goods sold. Compute the gross margin percentage, and compare it to last year's value of 58 percent for Handy Dan. Does this two-year trend suggest better or worse profitability during the current year?

Exercise 5-10   *Using work sheet data to prepare a merchandiser's income statement and evaluate the business*   **(Obj. 4, 6)**

The trial balance and adjustments columns of the work sheet of Midway Auto Supply Ltd. include the following accounts and balances at March 31, 19X2:

Account Title	Trial Balance Debit	Trial Balance Credit	Adjustments Debit	Adjustments Credit
Cash	$ 2,000			
Accounts receivable	8,500		(a) 2,100	
Inventory	36,070			(b) 1,170
Supplies	13,000			(c) 8,600
Store fixtures	22,500			
Accumulated depreciation		$ 11,250		(d) 2,250
Accounts payable		9,300		
Salary payable				(e) 1,200
Note payable, long-term		7,500		

Common stock...............................		20,000		
Retained earnings...........................		13,920		
Dividends.......................................	45,000			
Sales revenue		213,000		(a) 2,100
Sales discounts..............................	2,000			
Cost of goods sold.........................	111,600		(b) 1,170	
Selling expense	21,050		(c) 5,200	
			(e) 1,200	
General expense	10,500		(c) 3,400	
			(d) 2,250	
Interest expense.............................	2,750			
Total..	$274,970	$274,970	$15,320	$15,320

Ending inventory at March 31, 19X2 is $34,500.

Prepare the company's multiple-step income statement for the year ended March 31, 19X2. Compute the gross margin percentage and the inventory turnover for the year. Compare these figures with the gross margin percentage of 49 percent and the inventory turnover of 3.16 for 19X1. What does the two-year trend suggest about the company's sales-pricing strategy this year?

Exercise 5-11   *Use work sheet data to prepare the closing entries of a merchandising business*   *(Obj. 4)*

Use the data from Exercise 5-10 to journalize Midway Auto Supply Ltd.'s closing entries at March 31, 19X2.

Serial Exercise

This exercise completes the Emily Schneider situation begun in Exercise 2-13 of Chapter 2 and extended to Exercise 3-14 of Chapter 3 and Exercise 4-11 of Chapter 4.

Exercise 5-12   *Accounting for merchandising and service transactions*   *(Obj. 2, 4, 5)*

The architecture practice of Emily Schneider now includes a great deal of systems consulting business. In conjunction with the consulting, the business has begun selling design software. During January the business completed these transactions:

Jan. 2 Completed a consulting engagement and received cash of $5,800.
2 Prepaid three months' office rent, $1,500.
7 Purchased design software on account for merchandise inventory, $4,000.
16 Paid employee salary, $1,400.
18 Sold design software on account, $1,100 (cost $700).
19 Consulted with a client for a fee of $900 on account.
21 Paid on account, $2,000.
24 Paid utilities, $300.
28 Sold design software for cash, $600 (cost $400).
31 Recorded these adjusting entries:
Accrued salary expense, $1,400.
Accounted for expiration of prepaid rent.
Depreciation of office furniture, $200.

Required

1. Open the following T-accounts in the ledger: Cash, Accounts Receivable, Accounting Software Inventory, Prepaid Rent, Accumulated Depreciation—

Office Furniture, Accounts Payable, Salary Payable, Retained Earnings, Income Summary, Service Revenue, Sales Revenue, Cost of Goods Sold, Salary Expense, Rent Expense, Utilities Expense, and Depreciation Expense—Office Furniture.

2. Journalize and post the January transactions. Key all items by date. Compute each account balance, and denote the balance as *Bal.* Journalize and post the closing entries. Denote each closing amount as *Clo.* After posting, prove the equality of debits and credits in the ledger.

3. Prepare the January income statement of Emily Schneider, Architect. Use the single-step format.

Challenge Exercise

Exercise 5-13   *Evaluating a company's profitability*   *(Obj. 1, 6)*

Compensation Management Services, Inc. (CMSI), is a leading provider of products for workers' compensation insurance purposes. The company recently reported these figures.

Compensation Management Services, Inc., and Subsidiaries Consolidated Statements of Operations For the Years Ended July 31, 1995 and 1994		
	1995	1994
Sales	$106,115,984	$81,685,715
Cost of sales	76,424,328	60,981,847
Gross margin	29,691,656	20,703,868
Cost and expenses		
Selling, general and administrative	21,801,737	16,576,484
Depreciation and amortization	2,169,196	918,693
Restructuring charges	7,096,774	—
	31,067,707	17,495,177
Operating income (loss)	(1,376,051)	3,208,691
Other items (summarized)	(635,153)	(1,315,490)
Net income (loss)	$ (2,011,204)	$ 1,893,201

Required

Evaluate CMSI's operations during 1995 in comparison with 1994. Consider sales, gross margin, operating income, and net income. Track the gross margin percentage and inventory turnover in both years. CMSI's inventories at December 31, 1995, 1994, and 1993, were $7,755,322, $12,163,053, and $10,176,722, respectively. In the annual report CMSI's management describes the restructuring charges in 1995 as a one-time event. How does this additional information affect your evaluation?

Problems   (Group A)

Problem 5-1A   *Explaining the accounting for inventory by a retailer*   *(Obj. 1)*

Eaton's is one of the most famous retailers in the world. The women's sportswear department of Eaton's purchases clothing from many well-known manufacturers. Eaton's uses a sophisticated perpetual inventory system.

Required

You are the manager of an Eaton's store in Vancouver. Write a memo to a new employee in the women's sportswear department that explains how the company accounts for the purchase and sale of merchandise inventory.

Problem 5-2A   *Accounting for the purchase and sale of inventory*   *(Obj. 2)*

The following transactions occurred between Allcare Medical Supply Corp. and Ridgewood Nursing Homes Ltd. during February of the current year.

Feb.   6   Allcare Medical Supply sold $6,300 worth of merchandise to Ridgewood on terms of 2/10 n/30, FOB shipping point. Allcare prepaid freight charges of $500 and included this amount in the invoice total. (Allcare's entry to record the freight payment debits Accounts Receivable and credits Cash.) These goods cost Allcare $4,100.

       10   Ridgewood returned $900 of the merchandise purchased on February 6. Allcare issued a credit memo for this amount and returned the goods to inventory (cost, $590).

       15   Ridgewood paid $3,000 of the invoice amount owed to Allcare for the February 6 purchase. This payment included none of the freight charge.

       27   Ridgewood paid the remaining amount owed to Allcare for the February 6 purchase.

Required

Journalize these transactions, first on the books of Ridgewood Nursing Homes Ltd., and second on the books of Allcare Medical Supply.

Problem 5-3A   *Computing cost of goods sold and gross margin to evaluate the business*
                    (Obj. 3, 6)

Selected accounts from the accounting records of Miske Lock and Safe Company Ltd. had these balances at November 30, 19X1.

Accumulated depreciation—furniture and fixtures	$ 13,600
Note payable	14,000
Purchase discounts	600
Sales discounts	2,100
General expenses	19,300
Accounts receivable	7,200
Purchases of inventory	132,000
Selling expenses	8,800
Furniture and fixtures	37,200
Purchase returns and allowances	900
Salary payable	300
Retained earnings	52,800
Sales revenue	184,600
Sales returns and allowances	3,200
Inventory: November 30, 19X0	41,700
November 30, 19X1	41,500
Accounts payable	9,500
Cash	3,700
Freight in	1,600

Required

1. Show the computation of Miske's net sales, cost of goods sold, and gross margin for the year ended November 30, 19X1.

2. Lynn Miske, principal shareholder and manager of Miske Lock and Safe, strives to earn a gross margin percentage of 25 percent. Did she achieve this goal?

3. Did the rate of inventory turnover reach the industry average of 3.4?

4. How will what you have learned in this problem help you manage a business?

Problem 5-4A   *Preparing a merchandiser's financial statements*   **(Obj. 3, 5)**

Items from the accounts of Superior Milk Company Ltd. follow, listed in alphabetical order.

Accounts payable	$ 16,950	Note payable, long-term	45,000
Accounts receivable	43,700	Office equipment	$ 58,680
Accumulated depreciation		Purchases of inventory	364,000
—office equipment	22,450	Purchase discounts	1,990
Accumulated depreciation		Purchase returns	
—store equipment	16,000	and allowances	3,400
Cash	7,890	Retained earnings: April 30	24,620
Common stock	50,000	Salary payable	2,840
Cost of goods sold	?	Sales discounts	10,400
Dividends	9,000	Sales returns and allowances	18,030
General expenses	116,700	Sales revenue	731,000
Interest expense	5,400	Selling expenses	132,900
Interest payable	1,100	Store equipment	88,000
Inventory: April 30	69,350	Supplies	5,100
May 31	65,520	Unearned sales revenue	13,800

Required

1. Prepare the business's multiple-step income statement for May of the current year. In a separate schedule, show the computation of cost of goods sold.

2. Prepare the income statement in single-step format.

3. Prepare the balance sheet in report format at May 31 of the current year. Show your computation of the May 31 balance of Retained Earnings.

Problem 5-5A   *Using accounting work sheet data to prepare financial statements and evaluate the business*   **(Obj. 3, 5, 6)**

The trial balance and adjustments columns of the work sheet of Scarlatti Development Corp. include the following accounts and balances at November 30, 19X4:

Account Title	Trial Balance Debit	Trial Balance Credit	Adjustments Debit	Adjustments Credit
Cash	$ 4,000			
Accounts receivable	14,500		(a) 6,000	
Inventory	46,330		(b) 1,010	
Supplies	2,800			(c) 2,400
Furniture	39,600			
Accumulated depreciation		$ 4,900		(d) 2,450
Accounts payable		12,600		
Salary payable				(f) 1,000
Unearned sales revenue		13,570	(e) 6,700	
Note payable, long-term		15,000		
Common stock		20,000		
Retained earnings		40,310		
Dividends	42,000			
Sales revenue		164,000		(a) 6,000
				(e) 6,700

Sales returns	6,300			
Cost of goods sold	72,170			(b) 1,010
Selling expense	28,080		(f) 1,000	
General expense	13,100		(c) 2,400	
			(d) 2,450	
Interest expense	1,500			
Total	$270,380	$270,380	$19,560	$19,560

Required

1. Inventory on hand at November 30, 19X3, is $52,650. Without entering the preceding data on a formal work sheet, prepare the company's multiple-step income statement for the year ended November 30, 19X4, and its November 30, 19X4, balance sheet. Show your computation of the ending balance of Retained Earnings.

2. Compute the gross margin percentage and the rate of inventory turnover for 19X4. For 19X3, Scarlatti's gross margin percentage was 58 percent, and inventory turnover was 1.1. Does the two-year trend in these ratios suggest improvement or deterioration in profitability?

Problem 5-6A   *Preparing a merchandiser's work sheet*   **(Obj. 4)**

The trial balance of Chenot Apparel Inc. pertains to December 31 of the current year.

Chenot Apparel, Inc.
Trial Balance
December 31, 19XX

Cash	$ 1,270	
Accounts receivable	4,430	
Inventory	73,900	
Prepaid rent	4,400	
Store fixtures	22,100	
Accumulated depreciation		$ 8,380
Accounts payable		6,290
Salary payable		
Interest payable		
Note payable, long-term		18,000
Common stock		12,000
Retained earnings		43,920
Dividends	39,550	
Sales revenue		170,150
Cost of goods sold	67,870	
Salary expense	24,700	
Rent expense	7,700	
Advertising expense	4,510	
Utilities expense	3,880	
Depreciation expense		
Insurance expense	2,770	
Interest expense	1,660	
Total	$258,740	$258,740

Additional data at December 31, 19XX:

a. Rent expense for the year, $2,500.

b. Store fixtures have an estimated useful life of 10 years, and are expected to be worthless when they are retired from service.

c. Accrued salaries at December 31, $900.

d. Accrued interest expense at December 31, $360.

e. Inventory on hand at December 31, $73,200.

Required

Complete Chenot's work sheet for the year ended December 31 of the current year.

Problem 5-7A   *Journalizing the adjusting and closing entries of a merchandising business*   *(Obj. 4)*

Refer to the data in Problem 5-6A.

Required

1. Journalize the adjusting and closing entries.
2. Determine the December 31 balance of Retained Earnings.

Problem 5-8A   *Account for the purchase and sale of inventory, compute cost of goods sold and gross margin, use the gross margin percentage to evaluate a business (Obj. 2, 3, 6)*

A1 Computer Sales Co. uses the perpetual inventory method in tracking its inventory purchases and sales. All sales and purchases that result in a return, allowance, or discount are tracked in separate accounts in order to give management the proper information to control operations. The following information is available for the month of April, 19X1:

April 1   The balance of inventory on hand at the beginning of the month was $13,800.

      2   Purchased $5,000 of merchandise from Ronning Co., terms 2/10 n/30. The goods were expected to be resold for $11,000.

      4   Sold merchandise for $7,000 to Pecka Co., terms 2/10 n/60. The goods had a cost of $4,000 to A1 Computer.

      6   A1 Computer returned $2,000 of defective merchandise purchased from Ronning Co. on April 2.

      8   Sold merchandise for $8,000 cash; the goods had a cost of $6,000.

      9   Purchased $9,000 of merchandise from ABC Co., terms 2/10 n/30.

   10   A1 Computer paid the balance owing to Ronning Co.

   12   A1 Computer accepted the return of 1/2 of the merchandise sold on April 8 as it was not compatible with the customer's needs. The goods were returned to the shelf and a cash refund paid.

   16   A1 Computer took $1,000 of merchandise out of inventory to use in their own office.

   18   Paid the balance owing to ABC Co. from the purchase of April 9.

   20   Sold merchandise for $4,000 to Jones Tent Co., terms 2/10 n/60. The goods had cost $3,000.

   22   Jones Tent Co. complained about the quality of goods they received and A1 Computer agreed to give them a reduction of $500.

   25   Purchased $6,000 of merchandise for cash and paid $500 for freight.

   29   A1 Computer sold merchandise for $6,000 to USA Tomorrow Co., terms 2/10 n/30. The goods had cost $3,000. The terms of the sale where FOB shipping point, but, as a convenience, A1 Computer prepaid $400 of freight for USA Tomorrow Co.

   30   Collected the balance owing from Jones Tent Co.

Required

1. Record any journal entries required for the above transactions.
2. What would be the total cost of the inventory on April 30, 19X1?
3. Prepare a multi-step income statement, to the point of Gross Margin, for the month of April, 19X1.
4. The average gross margin percentage for the industry is 55%; how does A1 Computer compare to the industry?

Problem 5-9A   *Compute cost of goods sold and gross margin, adjust and close the accounts of a merchandising company, prepare a merchandiser's financial statements   (Obj. 3, 4, 5)*

The Beta Kite Sales Co. has the following account balances (in alphabetical order) as of July 31, 19X1:

Accounts payable	$ 2,900
Accounts receivable	3,100
Accumulated depreciation	8,600
Cash	1,000
Common stock	20,000
Cost of goods sold	47,300
Dividends	2,000
Equipment	21,500
Interest earned	800
Inventory	18,700
Operating expense control	36,200
Retained earnings	11,500
Supplies	3,800
Sales discounts	1,100
Sales returns and allowances	7,600
Sales revenues	96,500
Unearned sales revenue	2,000

Note: For simplicity, all operating expenses have been summarized in the account "Operating Expense Control."

The following information was also available on July 31st:

a. a physical count of items on hand on July 31st showed:
   - $400 of supplies were on hand
   - $16,900 of inventory was on hand

b. the equipment was expected to last 5 years and have no salvage value

c. sales of $500, to customers who had paid in advance, were completed

Required

1. Record all adjustments and closing entries that would be required on July 31st.
2. Prepare the financial statements of Beta Kite Sales for the year ended July 31, 19X1.

(Group B)

Problem 5-1B   *Explaining the operating cycle of a retailer   (Obj. 1)*

Claire Vision Inc. is a regional chain of optical shops in Manitoba. They specialize in offering a large selection of eyeglass frames, and they provide while-you-wait service. Claire Vision has launched a vigorous advertising campaign promoting its two-for-the-price-of-one frame sales.

Required

Claire Vision expects to grow rapidly and increase its level of inventory. As chief accountant of the company, you wish to install a perpetual inventory system. Write a memo to the company president to explain how the system would work.

Problem 5-2B   *Accounting for the purchase and sale of inventory   (Obj. 2)*

The following transactions occurred between MDS Health Group Ltd. and Victoria Sports Medicine Clinic during June of the current year.

June   8   MDS sold $4,900 worth of merchandise to Victoria Sports Medicine on terms of 2/10 n/30, FOB shipping point. MDS prepaid freight charges of $200 and included this amount in the invoice total. (MDS's entry to record the freight payment debits Accounts Receivable and credits Cash.) These goods cost MDS $2,100.

11   Victoria Sports Medicine returned $600 of the merchandise purchased on June 8. MDS issued a credit memo for this amount and returned the goods to inventory (cost $250).

17   Victoria Sports Medicine paid $2,000 of the invoice amount owed to MDS for the June 8 purchase. This payment included none of the freight charge.

26   Victoria Sports Medicine paid the remaining amount owed to MDS for the June 8 purchase.

Required

Journalize these transactions, first on the books of Victoria Sports Medicine, and second on the books of MDS.

Problem 5-3B   *Computing cost of goods sold and gross margin to evaluate the business (Obj. 3, 6)*

Selected accounts from the accounting records of Fundy Supply Company Ltd. at June 30, 19X9, were as follows:

Selling expenses	$ 29,800
Equipment	44,700
Purchase discounts	1,300
Accumulated depreciation—equipment	6,900
Note payable	30,000
Sales discounts	3,400
General expenses	16,300
Accounts receivable	22,600
Accounts payable	23,800
Cash	13,600
Purchases of inventory	98,100
Freight in	4,300
Sales revenue	173,100
Purchases returns and allowances	1,400
Salary payable	1,800
Retained earnings	36,000
Sales returns and allowances	12,100
Inventory: June 30, 19X8	33,800
June 30, 19X9	32,500

Required

1. Show the computation of Fundy Supply's net sales, cost of goods sold, and gross margin for the year ended June 30, 19X9.
2. John Wilfong, president of Fundy Supply, strives to earn a gross margin percentage of 40 percent. Did he achieve this goal?
3. Did the rate of inventory turnover reach the industry average of 2.8?
4. How will what you have learned in this problem help you manage a business?

Problem 5-4B   *Preparing a merchandiser's financial statements   (Obj. 3, 5)*

The accounts of Waslow Stereo Super Store Ltd. are listed in alphabetical order.

Accounts payable	$127,380	Note payable, long-term	$160,000
Accounts receivable	31,200	Office equipment	79,000
Accumulated depreciation		Purchases of inventory	373,100
—office equipment	9,500	Purchase discounts	4,670
Accumulated depreciation		Purchase returns and	
—store equipment	6,880	allowances	10,190
Cash	12,320	Retained earnings, June 30	53,720
Common stock	20,000	Salary payable	6,120
Cost of goods sold	?	Sales discounts	8,350
Dividends	11,000	Sales returns and	
General expenses	75,830	allowances	17,900
Interest expense	7,200	Sales revenue	531,580
Interest payable	3,000	Selling expenses	84,600
Inventory: June 30	190,060	Store equipment	47,500
July 31	187,390	Supplies	4,350
		Unearned sales revenue	9,370

Required

1. Prepare the entity's multiple-step income statement for July of the current year. In a separate schedule, show the computation of cost of goods sold.

2. Prepare the income statement in single-step format.

3. Prepare the balance sheet in report format at July 31 of the current year. Show your computation of the July 31 balance of Retained Earnings.

Problem 5-5B   *Using work sheet data to prepare financial statements and evaluate the business*   **(Obj. 3, 5, 6)**

The trial balance and adjustments columns of the work sheet of Carmen Candy Company Ltd. include the following accounts and balances at September 30, 19X5:

Account Title	Trial Balance Debit	Trial Balance Credit	Adjustments Debit	Adjustments Credit
Cash	$ 7,300			
Accounts receivable	4,360		(a) 1,800	
Inventory	29,630		(b) 2,100	
Supplies	10,700			(c) 7,640
Equipment	79,450			
Accumulated depreciation		$ 29,800		(d) 9,900
Accounts payable		13,800		
Salary payable				(f) 200
Unearned sales revenue		3,780	(e) 2,600	
Note payable, long-term		10,000		
Common stock		25,000		
Retained earnings		33,360		
Dividends	35,000			
Sales revenue		242,000		(a) 1,800
				(e) 2,600
Sales returns	3,100			
Cost of goods sold	125,600			(b) 2,100
Selling expense	40,600		(c) 7,640	
			(f) 200	
General expense	21,000		(d) 9,900	
Interest expense	1,000			
Total	$357,740	$357,740	$24,240	$24,240

Required

1. Inventory on hand at September 30, 19X4 was $32,580. Without entering the preceding data on a formal work sheet, prepare the company's multiple-step income statement for the year ended September 30, 19X5 and its September 30, 19X5 balance sheet. Show your computation of the ending balance of Retained earnings.

2. Compute the gross margin percentage and the inventory turnover for 19X5. For 19X4, Carmen's gross margin percentage was 57 percent and the rate of inventory turnover was 4.2. Does the two-year trend in these ratios suggest improvement or deterioration in profitability?

Problem 5-6B   *Preparing a merchandiser's work sheet*   **(Obj. 5)**

Li-Chong Paint Company Ltd.'s trial balance pertains to December 31 of the current year.

<table>
<tr><td colspan="3" align="center">**Li-Chong Paint Company Ltd.**
Trial Balance
December 31, 19XX</td></tr>
<tr><td>Cash ....</td><td>$ 2,910</td><td></td></tr>
<tr><td>Accounts receivable................................</td><td>6,560</td><td></td></tr>
<tr><td>Inventory...</td><td>101,760</td><td></td></tr>
<tr><td>Store supplies ....</td><td>1,990</td><td></td></tr>
<tr><td>Prepaid insurance ....</td><td>3,200</td><td></td></tr>
<tr><td>Store fixtures...</td><td>63,900</td><td></td></tr>
<tr><td>Accumulated depreciation ....</td><td></td><td>$ 37,640</td></tr>
<tr><td>Accounts payable....................................</td><td></td><td>29,770</td></tr>
<tr><td>Salary payable ....</td><td></td><td></td></tr>
<tr><td>Interest payable......................................</td><td></td><td></td></tr>
<tr><td>Note payable, long-term...........................</td><td></td><td>37,200</td></tr>
<tr><td>Common stock ....</td><td></td><td>10,000</td></tr>
<tr><td>Retained earnings ....</td><td></td><td>53,120</td></tr>
<tr><td>Dividends...</td><td>36,300</td><td></td></tr>
<tr><td>Sales revenue ....</td><td></td><td>286,370</td></tr>
<tr><td>Cost of goods sold..................................</td><td>161,090</td><td></td></tr>
<tr><td>Salary expense.......................................</td><td>46,580</td><td></td></tr>
<tr><td>Rent expense...</td><td>14,630</td><td></td></tr>
<tr><td>Utilities expense.....................................</td><td>6,780</td><td></td></tr>
<tr><td>Depreciation expense ....</td><td></td><td></td></tr>
<tr><td>Insurance expense..................................</td><td>5,300</td><td></td></tr>
<tr><td>Store supplies expense ....</td><td></td><td></td></tr>
<tr><td>Interest expense.....................................</td><td>3,100</td><td></td></tr>
<tr><td>Total..</td><td>$454,100</td><td>$454,100</td></tr>
</table>

Additional data at December 31, 19XX:

a. Insurance expense for the year, $790.

b. Store fixtures have an estimated useful life of 10 years, and are expected to be worthless when they are retired from service.

c. Accrued salaries at December 31, $1,260.

d. Accrued interest expense at December 31, $870.

e. Store supplies on hand at December 31, $760.

f. Inventory on hand at December 31, $99,650.

Required

Complete Li-Chong Paint Company's work sheet for the year ended December 31 of the current year.

Problem 5-7B   *Journalizing the adjusting and closing entries of a merchandising business*
                    (Obj. 4)

Refer to the data in Problem 5-6B.

Required

1. Journalize the adjusting and closing entries.
2. Determine the December 31 balance of Retained Earnings.

Problem 5-8B   *Account for the purchase and sale of inventory, compute cost of goods sold*
                    and gross margin, use the gross margin percentage to evaluate a business
                    (Obj. 2, 3, 6)

EZ Computer Sales Co. uses the perpetual inventory method in tracking its inventory purchases and sales. All sales and purchases that result in a return, allowance or discount are tracked in separate accounts in order to give management the proper information to control operations. The following information is available for the month of April, 19X1:

April 1   The balance of inventory on hand at the beginning of the month was $15,500.

       2   Purchased $4,000 or merchandise from Muzac Co., terms 2/10 n/30. The goods were expected to be resold for $9,000.

       4   Sold merchandise for $6,000 to Pills Co., terms 2/10 n/60. The goods had a cost of $3,000 to EZ Computer.

       6   EZ Computer returned $1,000 of defective merchandise purchased from Muzac Co. on April 2.

       8   Sold merchandise for $9,000 cash; the goods had a cost of $7,000.

       9   Purchased $8,000 of merchandise from XYZ Co., terms 2/10 n/30.

      10   EZ Computer paid the balance owing to Muzac Co.

      12   EZ Computer accepted the return of 1/2 of the merchandise sold on April 8 as it was not compatible with the customer's needs. The goods were returned to the shelf and a cash refund paid.

      16   EZ Computer took $1,200 of merchandise out of inventory to use in their own office.

      18   Paid the balance owing to XYZ Co. from the purchase of April 9.

      20   Sold merchandise for $5,000 to Randell Co., terms 2/10 n/60. The goods had cost $3,500.

      22   Randell Co. complained about the quality of goods they received and EZ Computer agreed to give them a reduction of $600.

      25   Purchased $7,000 of merchandise for cash and paid $400 for freight.

      29   EZ Computer sold merchandise for $5,000 to England Enterprises Co., terms 2/10 n/30. The goods had cost $3,000. The terms of the sale were FOB shipping point, but as a convenience, EZ Computer prepaid $300 of freight for England Enterprises Co.

      30   Collected the balance owing from Randell Co.

Required

1. Record any journal entries required for the above transactions.
2. What would be the total cost of the inventory on April 30, 19X1?

3. Prepare a multiple-step income statement, to the point of Gross Margin, for the month of April, 19X1.

4. The average gross margin percentage for the industry is 55%; how does EZ Computer compare to the industry?

Problem 5-9B   *Compute cost of goods sold and gross margin, adjust and close the accounts of a merchandising company, prepare a merchandiser's financial statements   (Obj. 3, 4, 5)*

The Delta Kite Sales Co. has the following account balances (in alphabetical order) as of July 31, 19X1:

Accounts payable	$ 5,800
Accounts receivable	6,200
Accumulated depreciation	17,200
Cash	2,000
Common stock	40,000
Cost of goods sold	94,600
Dividends	4,000
Equipment	43,000
Interest earned	1,600
Inventory	37,400
Operating expense control	72,400
Retained earnings	23,000
Supplies	7,600
Sales discounts	2,200
Sales returns and allowances	15,200
Sales revenues	193,000
Unearned sales revenue	4,000

Note: For simplicity, all operating expenses have been summarized in the account "Operating Expense Control."

The following information was also available for the year ended July 31, 19X1:

a. a physical count of items on hand on July 31st showed:
  • $80 of supplies were on hand
  • $33,800 of inventory was on hand

b. the equipment was expected to last 5 years and have no salvage value

c. sales of $1,000, to customers who had paid in advance, were completed

Required

1. Record all adjustments and closing entries that would be required on July 31st.

2. Prepare the financial statements of Delta Kite Sales for the year ended July 31, 19X1.

Challenge Problems

Problem 5-1C   *Understanding purchasing and gross margin   (Obj. 1, 2, 6)*

You have been recently hired as an accountant by AllSave Stores Ltd., a small chain of discount stores. One of your first activities is to review the accounting system for AllSave.

In your review, you discover that the company determines selling prices by adding a standard markup of 10 percent to the cost of all products. The company uses a perpetual inventory system. You also discover that your predecessor had set the accounting system up so that all purchase discounts and purchase returns and allowances were accumulated in an account that was treated as "other income" for financial statement purposes because he believed that they were financing items and not related to operations.

Marion Farouk, President of AllSave has an MBA and utilizes modern decision-making techniques in running AllSave. Two ratios she particularly favors are the gross margin percentage and inventory turnover ratio.

Required

1. What is a possible effect of the accounting system described on the pricing of products and thus operations of AllSave Stores?
2. What is the effect of the accounting system instituted by your predecessor on the two models Ms. Farouk favors?

Problem 5-2C   *Using an inventory system for control*   *(Obj. 1)*

Arthur Leung is concerned about theft by shoplifters in his chain of three electronics stores and has come to your public accounting firm for advice. Specifically, he has several questions he would like you to answer.

a. He wonders if there is any inventory system he can use that will allow him to keep track of products that leave his stores as legitimate purchases and merchandise that is stolen?

b. He realizes that carrying inventory is expensive and wants to know if you have any suggestions as to how he can keep close tabs on his inventory at the three stores so he can be sure that the stores don't run out of product.

c. The space in the stores is limited. Arthur also wants to install an inventory system that will tell him when a product is slow-moving or obsolete so he can clear it out and replace it with a potentially faster-moving product.

Required

Suggest an inventory system that Arthur might install that will provide him with answers to the three questions he has asked. Explain how the inventory system you have suggested will provide the specific information he has requested.

Extending Your Knowledge

Decision Problems

1. Using the financial statements to decide on a business expansion (Obj. 5, 6)

David and Steph Garner own Heights Pharmacy, Inc., which has prospered during its second year of operation. In deciding whether to open another pharmacy in the area, the Garners' accountant has prepared the current financial statements of the business.

Heights Pharmacy, Inc.
Income Statement
for the year ended December 31, 19X1

Sales revenue	$175,000
Interest revenue	24,600
Total revenue	199,600
Cost of goods sold	85,200
Gross margin	114,400

Operating expenses:

Salary expense	18,690	
Rent expense	12,000	
Interest expense	6,000	
Depreciation expense	4,900	
Utilities expense	2,330	
Supplies expense	1,400	
Total operating expense		45,320
Income from operations		69,080
Other expense:		
Sales discounts ($3,600) and returns ($7,100)		10,700
Net income		$58,380

Heights Pharmacy, Inc.
Statement of Retained Earnings
for the year ended December 31, 19X1

Retained earnings, January 1, 19X1	$35,000
Add:	
Net income	58,380
Retained earnings, December 31, 19X1	$93,380

Heights Pharmacy, Inc.
Balance Sheet
December 31, 19X1

Assets

Current	
Cash	$ 5,320
Accounts receivable	9,710
Inventory	30,100
Supplies	2,760
Store fixtures	63,000
Total current assets	110,890
Other	
Dividends	45,000
Total assets	$155,890

Liabilities

Current	
Accumulated depreciation—store fixtures	$ 6,300
Accounts payable	10,310
Salary payable	900
Total current liabilities	17,510
Other	
Note payable due in 90 days	40,000
Total liabilities	57,510

Shareholders' Equity

Common stock	5,000
Retained earnings	93,380
Total shareholders' equity	98,380
Total liabilities and shareholders' equity	$155,890

The Garners recently read in an industry trade journal that a successful pharmacy meets all of these criteria:

a. Gross margin of at least 50 percent.

b. Current ratio is at least 2.0.

c. Debt ratio is no higher than .50.

d. Inventory turnover is at least 4.0. Inventory at December 31, 19X0, was $19,200.

Basing their opinion on the entity's financial statement data, the Garners believe the business meets all four criteria. They plan to go ahead with the expansion plan, and ask your advice on preparing the pharmacy's financial statements in accordance with generally accepted accounting principles. They assure you that all amounts are correct.

Required

1. Prepare a correct multiple-step income statement, a statement of retained earnings, and a balance sheet in report format.

2. On the basis of the corrected financial statements, compute correct measures of the four criteria listed in the trade journal.

3. Assuming the criteria are valid, make a recommendation about whether to undertake the expansion at this time.

2. Understanding the operating cycle of a merchandiser   (Obj. 1, 3)

A. Gayle Yip-Chuck has come to you for advice. Earlier this year, she opened a record store in a plaza near the university she had attended. The store sells cassettes and compact discs for cash and on credit cards and, as a special feature, on credit to certain students. Many of the students at the university are co-op students who alternate school and work terms. Gayle allows co-op students to buy on credit while they are on a school term, with the understanding that they will pay their account shortly after starting a work term. Business has been very good. Gayle is sure it is because of her competitive prices and the unique credit terms she offers. Her problem is that she is short of cash, and her loan with the bank has grown significantly. The bank manager has indicated that he wishes to reduce Yip-Chuck's line of credit because he is worried that she will get into financial difficulties.

Required

1. Explain to Yip-Chuck why you think she is in this predicament.

2. Yip-Chuck has asked you to explain her problem to the bank manager and to assist in asking for more credit. What might you say to the bank manager to assist Yip-Chuck?

B. The employees of Klassen Ltd. made an error when they performed the periodic inventory count at year end, October 31, 19X2. Part of one warehouse was not counted and therefore was not included in inventory.

Required

1. Indicate the effect of the inventory error on cost of goods sold, gross margin, and net income for the year ended October 31, 19X2.

2. Will the error affect cost of goods sold, gross margin, and net income in 19X3? If so, what will the effect be?

Ethical Issue

Kingston & Barnes, a partnership, makes all sales of industrial conveyor belts under terms of FOB shipping point. The company usually receives orders for sales approximately one week before shipping inventory to customers. For orders received late in December, Lisa Kingston and Meg Barnes, the owners, decide when to ship the goods. If profits are already at an acceptable level, they delay shipment until January. If profits are lagging behind expectations, they ship the goods during December.

Required

1. Under Kingston & Barnes's FOB policy, when should the company record a sale?

2. Do you approve or disapprove of Kingston & Barnes's means of deciding when to ship goods to customers? If you approve, give your reason. If you disapprove, identify a better way to decide when to ship goods. (There is no accounting rule against the Kingston & Barnes practice.)

Financial Statement Problems

1. Closing entries for a merchandising corporation; evaluating ratio data (Obj. 5)

This problem uses both the income statement (statement of operations) and the balance sheet of Mark's Work Wearhouse Ltd. in Appendix A. It will aid your understanding of the closing process of a business with inventories.

1. Journalize Mark's closing entries for the year ended January 29, 1994. You will be unfamiliar with certain costs and expenses, but you should treat them all similarly.

2. What amount was closed to Retained Earnings?

3. Compute Mark's gross margin percentages and inventory turnover rates for the years ended January 29, 1994, and January 30, 1993. (In addition to the information in the Mark's report in Appendix A, you will also need the January 25, 1992 Inventories balance, which was $30,606,000.) Did these ratio values of Mark's improve or deteriorate during 1994? Summarize these results in a sentence.

2. Identifying items from an actual company's financial statements (Obj. 5)

Obtain the annual report of an actual incorporated company of your choosing. *Make sure that the company's balance sheet reports Inventories, Merchandise Inventories, or a similar asset category.* Answer these questions about the company:

1. What was the balance of total inventories reported on the balance sheet at the end of the current year? At the end of the preceding year? (If you selected a manufacturing company, you may observe more than one category of inventories. If so, name these categories and briefly explain what you think they mean.)

2. Give the company's journal entry to close Income Summary and Dividends.

3. Compute the company's gross margin percentage for the current year and for the preceding year. Did the gross margin percentage increase, decrease, or hold steady during the current year? Is this a favorable or an unfavorable signal about the company?

4. Compute the rate of inventory turnover for the current year. Would you expect your company's rate of inventory turnover to be higher or lower than that of a grocery chain such as Loblaws or IGA? Higher or lower than that of an aircraft manufacturer such as Boeing or Bombardier? State your reasoning.

Supplement

Accounting for Merchandise Inventory in a Periodic System

Purchase of Merchandise Inventory in the Periodic System

Some businesses find it uneconomical to invest in a computerized (perpetual inventory system that keeps up-to-the-minute records of merchandise on hand and cost of goods sold. For example, a Harvey's restaurant may experience such rapid inventory turnover that a perpetual inventory system costs more than it is worth. These types of businesses use a periodic system that relies on visual inspection for inventory control during the period. Accountants make entries to the Inventory account only in response to the physical count at the end of the period.

Purchases of Inventory

The periodic system uses the Inventory account. But purchases, purchase discounts, purchase returns and allowances, and transportation costs are recorded in separate accounts bearing these titles. Let's account for the purchase of the JVC goods in Exhibit 5S-1 by Austin Sound Stereo Center, Inc. The following entries record the purchase and payment on account within the discount period:

May 27	Purchases...	707.00	
	Accounts Payable..		707.00
	Purchased inventory on account.		
June 10	Accounts Payable.......................................	707.00	
	Cash ($707.00 × 0.97)		685.79
	Purchase Discounts ($707.00 × 0.03)...		21.21

Purchase Returns and Allowances

Suppose instead that prior to payment Austin Sound returned to JVC goods costing $70 and also received from JVC a purchase allowance of $10. Austin Sound would record these transactions as follows:

June 3	Accounts Payable...	70.00	
	Purchase Returns and Allowances...............		70.00
	Returned inventory to seller.		
June 4	Accounts Payable...	10.00	
	Purchase Returns and Allowances...............		10.00
	Received a purchase allowance.		

During the period, the business records the cost of all inventory bought in the Purchases account. The balance of Purchases is a *gross* amount because it does not include subtractions for purchase discounts, returns, or allowances. **Net purchases** is the remainder computed by subtracting the contra accounts from Purchases:

> **Purchase (*debit* balance account)**
> − **Purchase Discounts (*credit* balance account)**
> − **Purchase Returns and Allowances (*credit* balance account)**
> = **Net purchases (a *debit* subtotal, not a separate account)**

OBJECTIVE S1
Account for the purchase and sale of inventory

Key Point:
A contra account always has a companion account with the opposite balance. Thus both Purchase Discounts and Purchase Returns and Allowances (credit balances) are reported with Purchases (debit balance) on the income statement.

EXHIBIT 5-S1   *Business Invoice*

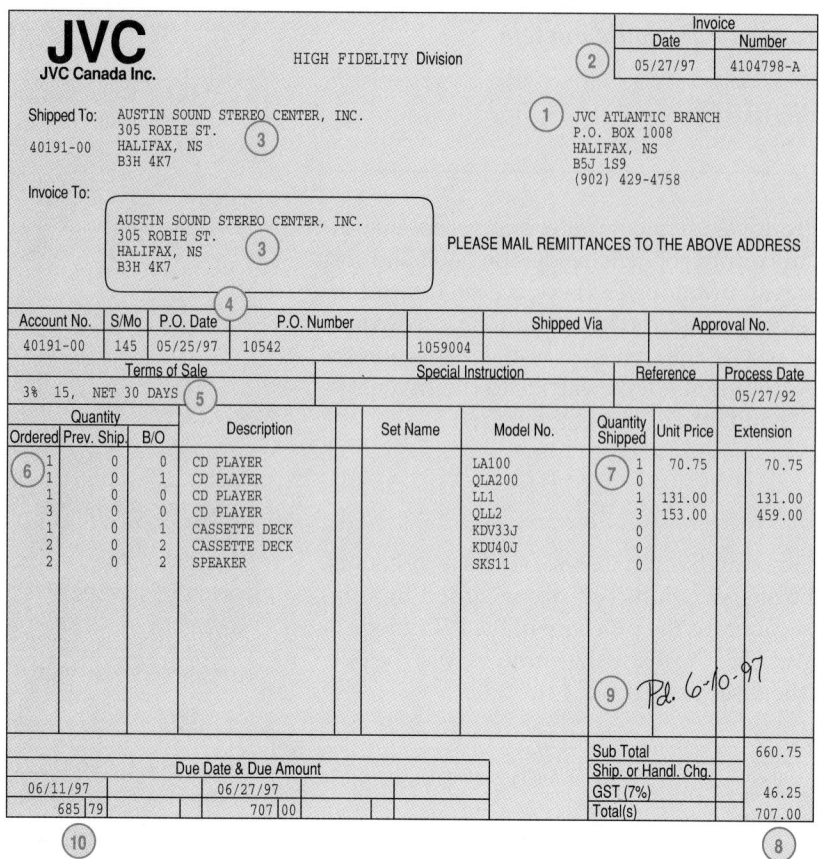

① The seller.

② The invoice date, needed for determining whether the purchaser gets a discount for prompt payment (see 5).

③ The purchaser. This inventory is invoiced (billed) and shipped to the same address.

④ Austin Sound's purchase order (P.O.) date.

⑤ Credit terms of the transaction: If it pays within 15 days of the invoice date, Austin Sound may deduct 3% of the total amount. Otherwise, the full amount—net—is due in 30 days.

⑥ Austin ordered 6 CD players, 3 cassette decks, and 2 speakers.

⑦ JVC shipped 5 CD players, no cassette decks, and no speakers.

⑧ Total invoice amount.

⑨ Austin's payment date. How much did Austin pay? (See 10.)

⑩ Payment occurred 14 days after the invoice date—within the discount period—so Austin paid $685.79 ($707 – 3% discount).

Transportation Costs

Under the periodic system, costs to transport purchased inventory from seller to buyer are debited to a separate account, as shown for payment of a $60 freight bill:

June 1	Freight In..	60.00	
	Cash		60.00
	Paid a freight bill.		

Sale of Inventory

Recording sales is streamlined in the periodic system. With no running record of inventory to maintain, we can record a $120 sale as follows:

June 1	Accounts Receivable..	120	
	Sales Revenue		120
	Sale on account.		

No accompanying entry to Inventory and Cost of Goods Sold is required. Also, sales discounts and sales returns and allowances are recorded as shown for the perpetual system on page 184, but with no entry to Inventory and Cost of Goods Sold.

OBJECTIVE S2

Compute the cost of goods sold

Cost of Goods Sold

Cost of goods sold (also called *cost of sales*) is the largest single expense of most businesses that sell merchandise, such as Electrohome and Austin Sound. It is the cost of the inventory that the business has sold to customers. In a periodic system, cost of goods sold must be computed as in Exhibit 5S-2 and is *not* a ledger account. It is the residual left when we subtract ending inventory from the cost of goods available for sale.

EXHIBIT 5-S2   *Measurement of Cost of Goods Sold*

Panel A

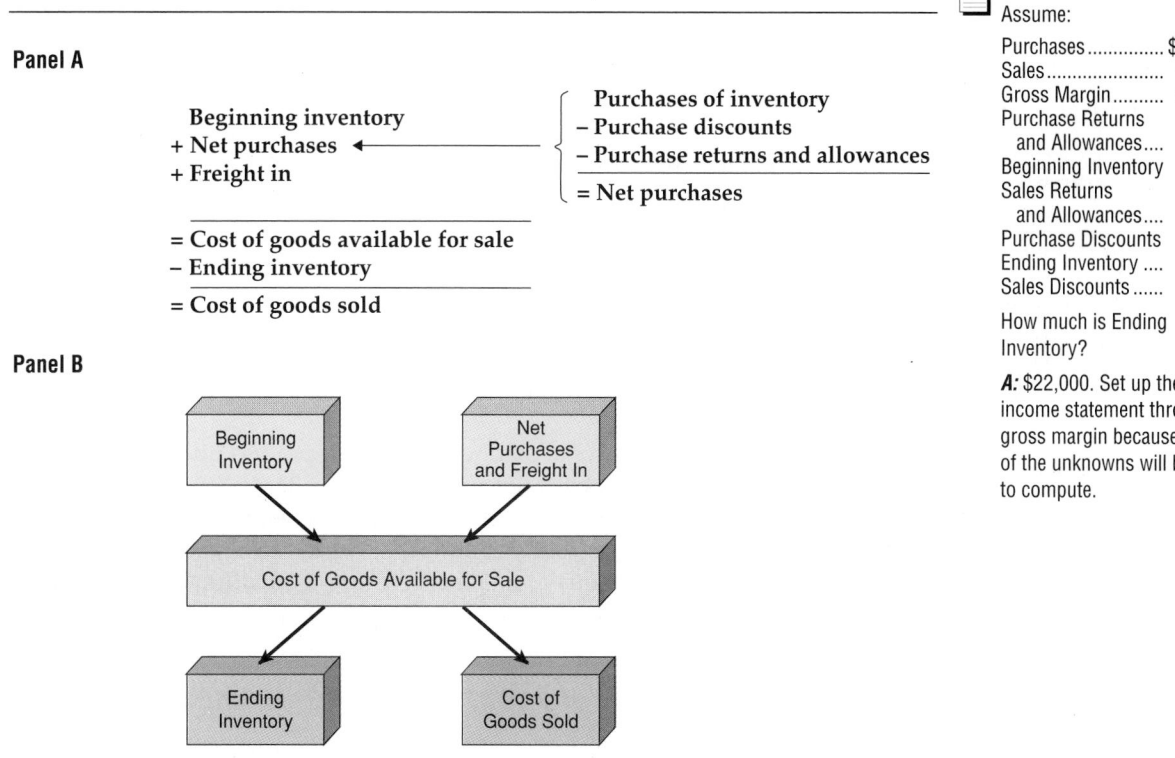

Beginning inventory
+ Net purchases ◄——————
+ Freight in

= Cost of goods available for sale
− Ending inventory

= Cost of goods sold

Purchases of inventory
− Purchase discounts
− Purchase returns and allowances

= Net purchases

Panel B

Short Exercise:

Assume:

Purchases	$265,000
Sales	463,000
Gross Margin	200,000
Purchase Returns and Allowances	2,600
Beginning Inventory	12,000
Sales Returns and Allowances	4,500
Purchase Discounts	2,400
Ending Inventory	?
Sales Discounts	8,500

How much is Ending Inventory?

A: $22,000. Set up the income statement through gross margin because many of the unknowns will be easier to compute.

Exhibit 5S-3 summarizes the first half of the chapter by showing Austin Sound's net sales revenue, cost of goods sold—including net purchases and freight in—and gross margin on the income statement for the periodic system. (All amounts are assumed.)

EXHIBIT 5S-3   *Partial Income Statement*

Austin Sound Stereo Center, Inc.
Income Statement
for the year ended December 31, 19X6

PANEL A—Detailed Gross Margin Section—Often Required by Management

Sales revenue			$169,300	
Less: Sales discounts		$ 1,400		
Sales returns and allowances		2,000	3,400	
Net sales				$165,900
Cost of goods sold:				
Beginning inventory			$ 38,600	
Purchases		$91,400		
Less: Purchase discounts	$3,000			
Purchase returns and allowances	1,200	4,200		
Net purchases			87,200	
Freight in			5,200	
Cost of goods available for sale			131,000	
Less: Ending inventory			40,200	
Cost of goods sold				90,800
Gross margin				$ 75,100

PANEL B—Summary Gross Margin Section—Most Common in Annual Reports to Outsiders

Net sales	$165,900
Cost of goods sold	90,800
Gross margin	$ 75,100

OBJECTIVE S3

Adjust and close
the accounts of
merchandising
business

The Adjusting and Closing Process
for a Merchandising Business

A merchandising business adjusts and closes the accounts much as a service entity does. The steps of this end-of-period process are the same: If a work sheet is used, the trial balance is entered and the work sheet completed to determine net income or net loss. The work sheet provides the data for journalizing the adjusting and closing entries and for preparing the financial statements.

The Inventory account affects the adjusting and closing entries of a merchandiser. At the end of the period, before any adjusting or closing entries, the Inventory account balance is still the cost of the inventory that was on hand at the beginning date. It is necessary to remove this beginning balance and replace it with the cost of the ending inventory. Various techniques might be used to bring the inventory records up to date.

To illustrate a merchandiser's adjusting and closing process under the periodic inventory system, let's use Austin Sound's December 31, 19X6, trial balance in Exhibit 5S-4. All the new accounts—Inventory, Freight In, and the contra accounts—are highlighted for emphasis. Inventory is the only account that is affected by the new closing procedures. The additional data item (h) gives the ending inventory figure $40,200.

Accounting Work Sheet of a Merchandising Business

The Exhibit 5S-5 work sheet is similar to the work sheets we have seen so far, but a few differences appear. This work sheet does not include adjusted trial balance columns. In most accounting systems, a single operation combines trial balance amounts with the adjustments and extends the adjusted balances directly to the income statement and balance sheet columns. Therefore, to reduce clutter, the adjusted trial balance columns are omitted.

Account Title Columns   The trial balance lists a number of accounts without balances. Ordinarily, these accounts are affected by the adjusting process. Examples include Interest Receivable, Interest Payable, and Depreciation Expense. The accounts are listed in the order they appear in the ledger. If additional accounts are needed, they can be written in at the bottom, above net income.

Trial Balance Columns   Examine the Inventory account, $38,600 in the trial balance. This $38,600 is the cost of the beginning inventory. The work sheet is designed to replace this outdated amount with the new ending balance, which in our example is $40,200 (additional data item (h) in Exhibit 5S-4). As we shall see, this task is accomplished later in the columns for the income statement and the balance sheet.

Adjustments Columns   The adjustments are similar to those discussed in Chapters 3 and 4. They may be entered in any order desired. The debit amount of each entry should equal the credit amount, and total debits should equal total credits.

Income Statement Columns   The income statement columns contain adjusted amounts for the revenues and the expenses. Sales Revenue, for example, is $169,300, which includes the $1,300 adjustment.

You may be wondering why the two inventory amounts appear in the income statement columns. The reason is that both beginning inventory and ending inventory enter the computation of cost of goods sold. *Placement of beginning inventory ($38,600) in the work sheet's income statement debit column has the effect of adding beginning inventory in computing cost of goods sold. Placing ending inventory ($40,200) in the credit column has the opposite effect.*

Purchases and Freight In appear in the debit column because they are added in computing cost of goods sold. Purchase Discounts and Purchase Returns and Allowances appear as credits because they are subtracted. All these items are used to compute cost of goods sold—$90,800 on the income statement in Exhibit 5S-6.

Key Point:

Recall that Purchases (not Inventory) was debited for merchandise purchased. In the periodic system, no entries are made to the Inventory account for purchases or sales. Beginning inventory remains on the books and on the trial balance until ending inventory replaces it at the end of the period.

Key Point:

If you were preparing a work sheet, you could omit the adjusted trial balance columns. Once you understand the mechanics of the work sheet, you can take a trial balance amount, add or subtract the adjustments, and extend the new amount to either the income statement or balance sheet columns.

EXHIBIT 5S-4   *Trial Balance*

Austin Sound Stereo Center, Inc.
Trial Balance
December 31, 19X6

Cash	$ 2,850	
Accounts receivable	4,600	
Note receivable, current	8,000	
Interest receivable		
Inventory	**38,600**	
Supplies	650	
Prepaid insurance	1,200	
Furniture and fixtures	33,200	
Accumulated depreciation		$ 2,400
Accounts payable		47,000
Unearned sales revenue		2,000
Wages payable		
Interest payable		
Note payable, long-term		12,600
Common stock		10,000
Retained earnings		15,900
Dividends	54,100	
Sales revenue		**168,000**
Sales discounts	**1,400**	
Sales returns and allowances	**2,000**	
Interest revenue		600
Purchases	**91,400**	
Purchase discounts		**3,000**
Purchase returns and allowances		**1,200**
Freight in	**5,200**	
Wage expense	9,800	
Rent expense	8,400	
Depreciation expense		
Insurance expense		
Supplies expense		
Interest expense	1,300	
Total	$262,700	$262,700

Additional data at December 31, 19X6:

a. Interest revenue earned but not yet collected, $400.

b. Supplies on hand, $100.

c. Prepaid insurance expired during the year, $1,000.

d. Depreciation, $600.

e. Unearned sales revenue earned during the year, $1,300.

f. Accrued wage expense, $400.

g. Accrued interest expense, $200.

h. Inventory on hand, $40,200.

The income statement column subtotals on the work sheet indicate whether the business earned net income or incurred a net loss. If total credits are greater, the result is net income, as shown in Exhibit 5S-5. If total debits are greater, a net loss has occurred.

EXHIBIT 5S-5   Accounting Work Sheet

Austin Sound Stereo Center, Inc.
Accounting Work Sheet
for the year ended December 31, 19X6

Account Title	Trial Balance Debit	Trial Balance Credit	Adjustments Debit	Adjustments Credit	Income Statement Debit	Income Statement Credit	Balance Sheet Debit	Balance Sheet Credit
Cash	2,850						2,850	
Accounts receivable	4,600						4,600	
Note receivable, current	8,000						8,000	
Interest receivable			(a) 400				400	
Inventory	38,600				38,600	40,200	40,200	
Supplies	650			(b) 550			100	
Prepaid insurance	1,200			(c) 1,000			200	
Furniture and fixtures	33,200						33,200	
Accumulated depreciation		2,400		(d) 600				3,000
Accounts payable		47,000						47,000
Unearned sales revenue		2,000	(e) 1,300					700
Wages payable				(f) 400				400
Interest payable				(g) 200				200
Note payable, long-term		12,600						12,600
Common stock		10,000						10,000
Retained earnings		15,900						15,900
Dividends	54,100						54,100	
Sales revenue		168,000		(e) 1,300		169,300		
Sales discounts	1,400				1,400			
Sales returns and allowances	2,000				2,000			
Interest revenue		600		(a) 400		1,000		
Purchases	91,400				91,400			
Purchase discounts		3,000				3,000		
Purchase returns and allowances		1,200				1,200		
Freight in	5,200				5,200			
Wage expense	9,800		(f) 400		10,200			
Rent expense	8,400				8,400			
Depreciation expense			(d) 600		600			
Insurance expense			(c) 1,000		1,000			
Supplies expense			(b) 550		550			
Interest expense	1,300		(g) 200		1,500			
	262,700	262,700	4,450	4,450	160,850	214,700	143,650	89,800
Net income					53,850			53,850
					214,700	214,700	143,650	143,650

Balance Sheet Columns   The only new item on the balance sheet is inventory. The balance listed is the ending amount of $40,200, which is determined by a physical count of inventory on hand at the end of the period.

Financial Statements of a Merchandising Business

OBJECTIVE S4

Prepare a merchandiser's financial statements

Exhibit 5S-6 presents Austin Sound's financial statements. The *income statement* through gross margin repeats Exhibit 5S-3. This information is followed by the *operating expenses,* expenses other than cost of goods sold that are incurred in the entity's major line of business—merchandising. Wage expense is Austin Sound's cost of

EXHIBIT 5S-6   *Financial Statements of Austin Sound Stereo Center, Inc.*

Austin Sound Stereo Center, Inc.
Income Statement
for the year ended December 31, 19X6

Sales revenue			$169,300
Less: Sales discounts		$ 1,400	
Sales returns and allowances		2,000	3,400
Net sales revenue			$165,900
Cost of goods sold			
Beginning inventory			$ 38,600
Purchases		$91,400	
Less: Purchase discounts	$ 3,000		
Purchase returns and allowances	1,200	$ 4,200	
Net purchases		87,200	
Freight in		5,200	
Cost of goods available for sale		131,000	
Less: Ending inventory		40,200	
Cost of goods sold			90,800
Gross margin			75,100
Operating expenses			
Wage expense		10,200	
Rent expense		8,400	
Insurance expense		1,000	
Depreciation expense		600	
Supplies expense		550	20,750
Income from operations			54,350
Other revenue and (expense)			
Interest revenue		1,000	
Interest expense		(1,500)	(500)
Net income			$ 53,850

Austin Sound Stereo Center, Inc.
Statement of Retained Earnings
for the year ended December 31, 19X6

Retained earnings, December 31, 19X5	$15,900
Add: Net income	53,850
	69,750
Less: Dividends	54,100
Retained earnings, December 31, 19X6	$15,650

Austin Sound Stereo Center, Inc.
Balance Sheet
December 31, 19X6

Assets			Liabilities		
Current			Current		
Cash		$ 2,850	Accounts payable		$47,000
Accounts receivable		4,600	Unearned sales revenue		700
Note receivable		8,000	Wages payable		400
Interest receivable		400	Interest payable		200
Inventory		40,200	Total current liabilities		48,300
Prepaid insurance		200	Long-term		
Supplies		100	Note payable		12,600
Total current assets		56,350	Total liabilities		60,900
Plant:			**Shareholders' Equity**		
Furniture and fixtures	$33,200		Retained earnings		15,650
Less: Accumulated			Common stock		10,000
depreciation	3,000	30,200	Total shareholders' equity		25,650
			Total liabilities and		
Total assets		$86,550	shareholders' equity		$86,550

employing workers. Rent is the cost of obtaining store space. Insurance helps to protect the inventory. Store furniture and fixtures wear out; the expense is depreciation. Supplies expense is the cost of stationery, mailing, and the like, used in operations.

Many companies report their operating expenses in two categories. *Selling expenses* are those expenses related to marketing the company's products—sales salaries; sales commissions; advertising; depreciation, rent, utilities, and property taxes on store buildings; depreciation on store furniture; delivery expense; and so on. *General expenses* include office expenses, such as the salaries of office employees; and depreciation, rent, utilities, and property taxes on the home office building.

Gross margin minus operating expenses and plus any other operating revenues equals *operating income*, or *income from operations*. As was true for Sony, many businesspeople view operating income as the most reliable indicator of a business's success because it measures the entity's major ongoing activities.

The last section of Austin Sound's income statement is *other revenue and expenses*, which is handled the same way in both inventory systems.

Adjusting and Closing Entries for a Merchandising Business

Exhibit 5S-7 presents Austin Sound's adjusting entries. The closing entries in the exhibit include two new effects. The first closing entry debits Inventory for the ending balance of $40,200 and also debits the revenue and expense accounts that have credit balances. For Austin Sound these accounts are Sales Revenue, Interest Revenue, Purchase Discounts, and Purchase Returns and Allowances. The offsetting credit of $214,700 transfers their sum to Income Summary. This amount comes from the credit column of the income statement on the work sheet (Exhibit 5S-5).

Key Point:

Closing entries for a merchandising company accomplish the same tasks as in Chapter 4 and also replace beginning inventory with the ending inventory balance. The debit and credit to Income Summary match the Income Statement column totals from the work sheet.

The second closing entry includes a credit to Inventory for its beginning balance and credits to the revenue and expense accounts with debit balances. These are Sales Discounts, Sales Returns and Allowances, Purchases, Freight In, and the expense accounts. The offsetting $160,850 debit to Income Summary comes from the debit column of the income statement on the work sheet. Some accountants prefer to include these Inventory entries among the adjustments.

The entries to the Inventory account deserve additional explanation. Recall that before the closing process Inventory still has the period's beginning balance. At the end of the period, this balance is one year old and must be replaced with the ending balance in order to prepare the financial statements at December 31, 19X6. The closing entries give Inventory its correct ending balance of $40,200, as shown here:

Inventory

Jan. 1 Bal.	38,600		Dec. 31 Clo.	38,600
Dec. 31 Clo.	40,200			
Dec. 31 Bal.	40,200			

The inventory amounts for these entries are taken directly from the income statement columns of the work sheet. The offsetting debits and credits to Income Summary in these entries also serve to record the dollar amount of cost of goods sold in the accounts. Income Summary contains the cost of goods sold amount after Purchases and its related contra accounts and Freight In are closed.[1]

---

[1]Some accountants make the inventory entries as adjustments rather than as part of the closing process. The adjusting-entry approach adds these adjustments (shifted out of the closing entries):

Adjusting Entries

Dec. 31	Income Summary	38,600	
	Inventory (beginning balance)		38,600
31	Inventory (ending balance)	40,200	
	Income Summary		40,200

When these entries are posted, the Inventory account will look exactly as shown above, except that the journal references will be "Adj." instead of "Clo." The financial statements are unaffected by the approach used for these inventory entries.

EXHIBIT 5S-7 *Adjusting and Closing Entries*

		Journal		
		Adjusting Entries		
a.	Dec. 31	Interest receivable...	400	
		Interest revenue..		400
b.	31	Supplies expense ($650 – $100).......................	550	
		Supplies..		550
c.	31	Insurance expense...	1,000	
		Prepaid insurance.......................................		1,000
d.	31	Depreciation expense	600	
		Accumulated depreciation..........................		600
e.	31	Unearned sales revenue..................................	1,300	
		Sales revenue..		1,300
f.	31	Wage expense	400	
		Wages payable...		400
g.	31	Interest expense..	200	
		Interest payable...		200
		Closing Entries		
	Dec. 31	Inventory (ending balance).........................	40,200	
		Sales revenue	169,300	
		Interest revenue	1,000	
		Purchase discounts...	3,000	
		Purchase returns and allowances..............	1,200	
		Income summary.....................................		214,700
	31	Income summary......................................	160,850	
		Inventory (beginning balance)		38,600
		Sales discounts...		1,400
		Sales returns and allowances.................		2,000
		Purchases..		91,400
		Freight in..		5,200
		Wage expense...		10,200
		Rent expense		8,400
		Depreciation expense..............................		600
		Insurance expense		1,000
		Supplies expense		550
		Interest expense		1,500
	31	Income summary ($214,700 – $160,850)	53,850	
		Retained earnings.....................................		53,850
	31	Retained earnings..	54,100	
		Dividends		54,100

Study Exhibits 5S-5, 5S-6, and 5S-7 carefully because they illustrate the entire end-of-period process that leads to the financial statements. As you progress through this book, you may want to refer to these exhibits to refresh your understanding of the adjusting and closing process for a merchandising business.

Net sales, cost of goods sold, operating income, and net income are unaffected by the choice of inventory system. You can prove this by comparing Austin Sound's financial statements given in Exhibit 5S-6 with the corresponding statements in Exhibit 5-9. The only differences appear in the cost-of-goods-sold section of the income statement, and those differences are unimportant. In fact, virtually all companies report cost of goods sold in streamlined fashion, as shown for Sony in Exhibit 5-1 and for Austin Sound in Exhibit 5-9.

Summary Problem for Your Review

The accompanying trial balance pertains to Jan King Distributing Company, Inc.

Jan King Distributing Company, Inc.
Trial Balance
December 31, 19X3

Cash	$ 5,670	
Accounts receivable	37,100	
Inventory	60,500	
Supplies	3,930	
Prepaid rent	6,000	
Furniture and fixtures	26,500	
Accumulated depreciation		$ 21,200
Accounts payable		46,340
Salary payable		
Interest payable		
Unearned sales revenue		3,500
Note payable, long-term		35,000
Common stock		5,000
Retained earnings		18,680
Dividends	48,000	
Sales revenue		346,700
Sales discounts	10,300	
Sales returns and allowances	8,200	
Purchases	175,900	
Purchase discounts		6,000
Purchase returns and allowances		7,430
Freight in	9,300	
Salary expense	82,750	
Rent expense	7,000	
Depreciation expense		
Utilities expense	5,800	
Supplies expense		
Interest expense	2,900	
Total	$489,850	$489,850

Additional data at December 31, 19X3:

a. Supplies used during the year, $2,580.

b. Prepaid rent in force, $1,000.

c. Unearned sales revenue still not earned, $2,400. The company expects to earn this amount during the next few months.

d. Depreciation. The furniture and fixtures' estimated useful life is 10 years, and they are expected to be worthless when they are retired from service.

e. Accrued salaries, $1,300.

f. Accrued interest expense, $600.

g. Inventory on hand, $65,800.

Required

1. Enter the trial balance on a work sheet and complete the work sheet.

2. Journalize the adjusting and closing entries at December 31. Post to the Income Summary account as an accuracy check on the entries affecting that account. The credit balance closed out of Income Summary should equal net income computed on the work sheet.

3. Prepare the company's multiple-step income statement, statement of retained earnings, and balance sheet in account format.

4. Compute the inventory turnover for 19X3. Turnover for 19X2 was 2.1. Would you expect Jan King Distributing Company to be more or less profitable in 19X3 than in 19X2? Give your reason.

SOLUTION TO REVIEW PROBLEM

Requirement 1

Jan King Distributing Company, Inc.
Work Sheet
for the year ended December 31, 19X3

Account Title	Trial Balance Debit	Trial Balance Credit	Adjustments Debit	Adjustments Credit	Income Statement Debit	Income Statement Credit	Balance Sheet Debit	Balance Sheet Credit
Cash	5,670						5,670	
Accounts receivable	37,100						37,100	
Inventory	60,500				60,500	65,800	65,800	
Supplies	3,930			(a) 2,580			1,350	
Prepaid rent	6,000			(b) 5,000			1,000	
Furniture and fixtures	26,500						26,500	
Accumulated depreciation		21,200		(d) 2,650				23,850
Accounts payable		46,340						46,340
Salary payable				(e) 1,300				1,300
Interest payable				(f) 600				600
Unearned sales revenue		3,500	(c) 1,100					2,400
Note payable, long-term		35,000						35,000
Common stock		5,000						5,000
Retained earnings		18,680						18,680
Dividends	48,000						48,000	
Sales revenue		346,700		(c) 1,100		347,800		
Sales discounts	10,300				10,300			
Sales returns and allowances	8,200				8,200			
Purchases	175,900				175,900			
Purchase discounts		6,000				6,000		
Purchase returns and allowances		7,430				7,430		
Freight in	9,300				9,300			
Salary expense	82,750		(e) 1,300		84,050			
Rent expense	7,000		(b) 5,000		12,000			
Depreciation expense			(d) 2,650		2,650			
Utilities expense	5,800				5,800			
Supplies expense			(a) 2,580		2,580			
Interest expense	2,900		(f) 600		3,500			
	489,850	489,850	13,230	13,230	374,780	427,030	185,420	133,170
					52,250			52,250
Net income					427,030	427,030	185,420	185,420

Requirement 2

Adjusting Entries

19X3

Dec. 31	Supplies expense	2,580	
	Supplies		2,580
31	Rent expense	5,000	
	Prepaid rent		5,000
31	Unearned sales revenue	1,100	
	Sales revenue		1,100
31	Depreciation expense ($26,500/10)	2,650	
	Accumulated depreciation		2,650
31	Salary expense	1,300	
	Salary payable		1,300
31	Interest expense	600	
	Interest payable		600

Closing Entries

19X3

Dec. 31	Inventory (ending balance)	65,800	
	Sales revenue	347,800	
	Purchase discounts	6,000	
	Purchase returns and allowances	7,430	
	Income summary		427,030
31	Income summary	374,780	
	Inventory (beginning balance)		60,500
	Sales discounts		10,300
	Sales returns and allowances		8,200
	Purchases		175,900
	Freight in		9,300
	Salary expense		84,050
	Rent expense		12,000
	Depreciation expense		2,650
	Utilities expense		5,800
	Supplies expense		2,580
	Interest expense		3,500
31	Income summary ($427,030 – $374,780)	52,250	
	Retained earnings		52,250
31	Retained earnings	48,000	
	Dividends		48,000

Income Summary

Clo.	374,780	Clo.	477,030
Clo.	52,250	Bal.	52,250

Requirement 3

Jan King Distributing Company, Inc.
Income Statement
for the year ended December 31, 19X3

Sales revenue...			$347,800
Less: Sales discounts..		$ 10,300	
Sales returns and allowances..................		8,200	18,500
Net sales revenue			$329,300
Cost of goods sold:			
Beginning inventory		60,500	
Purchases..		175,900	
Less: Purchase discounts...............................	$6,000		
Purchase returns and allowances...........	7,430	13,430	
Net purchases		162,470	
Freight in		9,300	
Cost of goods available for sale		232,270	
Less: Ending inventory...................................		65,800	
Cost of goods sold..			166,470
Gross margin			162,830
Operating expenses:			
Salary expense		84,050	
Rent expense..		12,000	
Utilities expense		5,800	
Depreciation expense......................................		2,650	
Supplies expense..		2,580	107,080
Income from operations			55,750
Other expense			
Interest expense..			3,500
Net income			$ 52,250

Jan King Distributing Company, Inc.
Statement of Retained Earnings
for the year ended December 31, 19X3

Retained earnings, December 31, 19X2	$18,680
Add: Net income	52,250
	70,930
Less: Dividends	48,000
Retained earnings, December 31, 19X3	$22,930

Jan King Distributing Company, Inc.
Balance Sheet
December 31, 19X3

Assets			**Liabilities**		
Current			Current		
Cash.............................		$ 5,670	Accounts payable................		$ 46,340
Accounts receivable.....		37,100	Salary payable......................		1,300
Inventory......................		65,800	Interest payable		600
Supplies........................		1,350	Unearned sales revenue		2,400
Prepaid rent		1,000	Total current liabilities........		50,640
Total current assets....		110,920	Long-term note payable		35,000
Plant			Total liabilities............................		85,640
Furniture and fixtures .	$26,500				
Less: Accumulated			**Shareholders' Equity**		
depreciation.....	23,850	2,650	Common stock		5,000
			Retained earnings.....................		22,930
			Total shareholders' equity.......		27,930
			Total liabilities and		
Total assets.........................		$113,570	shareholders' equity..............		$113,570

Requirement 4

$$\text{Inventory turnover} = \frac{\text{Cost of goods sold}}{\text{Average inventory}} = \frac{\$166,470}{(\$60,500 + \$65,800)/2} = 2.6$$

The increase in the rate of inventory turnover from 2.1 to 2.6 suggests higher profits in 19X3 than in 19X2.

Supplement Problems

Problem 5S-1   *Accounting for the purchase and sale of inventory*   *(Obj. S1)*

The following transactions occurred between Glendale Medical Supply Corp. and Halifax Rehab Clinic during February of the current year.

Feb. 6	Glendale Medical Supply sold $5,300 worth of merchandise to Halifax Rehab Clinic on terms of 2/10 n/30, FOB shipping point. Glendale prepaid freight charges of $300 and included this amount in the invoice total. (Glendale's entry to record the freight payment debits Accounts Receivable and credits Cash.)
10	Halifax Rehab Clinic returned $900 of the merchandise purchased on February 6. Glendale issued a credit memo for this amount.
15	Halifax Rehab Clinic paid $3,000 of the invoice amount owed to Glendale for the February 6 purchase. This payment included none of the freight charge.
27	Halifax Rehab Clinic paid the remaining amount owed to Glendale for the February 6 purchase.

Required

Journalize these transactions, first on the books of Halifax Rehab Clinic and second on the books of Glendale Medical Supply.

Problem 5S-2   *Preparing a merchandiser's accounting work sheet, financial statements, and adjusting and closing entries*   *(Obj. S2, S3, S4)*

The year-end trial balance of Bliss Sales Corp. (on p. 277) pertains to March 31 of the current year.

a. Accrued interest revenue, $1,030.
b. Insurance expense for the year, $3,000.
c. Furniture has an estimated useful life of 6 years. Its value is expected to be zero when it is retired from service.
d. Unearned sales revenue still unearned, $8,200.
e. Accrued salaries, $1,200.
f. Accrued sales commissions, $1,700.
g. Inventory on hand, $133,200.

Required

1. Enter the trial balance on an accounting work sheet, and complete the work sheet for the year ended March 31 of the current year.
2. Prepare the company's multiple-step income statement and statement of retained earnings for the year ended March 31 of the current year. Also prepare its balance sheet at that date. Long-term notes receivable should be reported on the balance sheet between current assets and plant assets in a separate section labeled Investments.

3. Journalize the adjusting and closing entries at March 31.
4. Post to the Retained Earnings account and to the Income Summary account as an accuracy check on the adjusting and closing process.

Bliss Sales Corp.
Trial Balance
March 31, 19XX

Cash	$ 7,880	
Notes receivable, current	12,400	
Interest receivable		
Inventory...	130,050	
Prepaid insurance	3,600	
Notes receivable, long-term	62,000	
Furniture	6,000	
Accumulated depreciation		$ 4,000
Accounts payable...		12,220
Sales commission payable		
Salary payable		
Unearned sales revenue...............................		9,610
Common stock		50,000
Retained earnings		122,780
Dividends..	66,040	
Sales revenue		440,000
Sales discounts	4,800	
Sales returns and allowances	11,300	
Interest revenue...		8,600
Purchases..	233,000	
Purchase discounts		3,100
Purchase returns and allowances		7,600
Freight in	10,000	
Sales commission expense............................	78,300	
Salary expense...	24,700	
Rent expense..	6,000	
Utilities expense	1,840	
Depreciation expense		
Insurance expense...		
Total...	$657,910	$657,910

CHAPTER 6
Accounting Information Systems

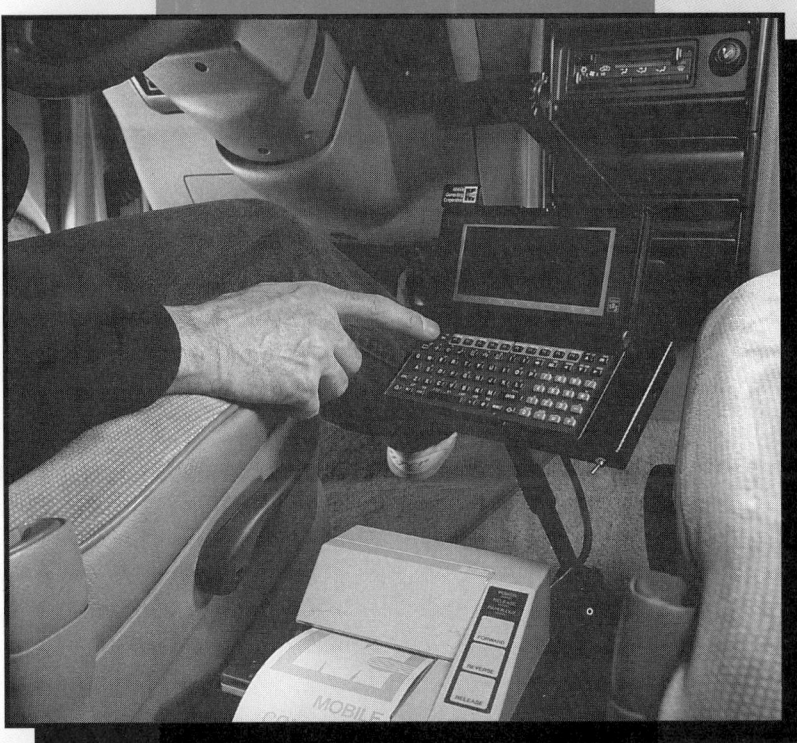

"[Mobile Computing Corp.'s] technology can monitor inventory levels, provide a repair history and help deal with problems over time [for customers of a home-heating company using its technology]," says Kim Killen, Marketing Manager, Mobile Computing Corp.

Mobile Computing Corp., a Toronto company, puts computers on board trucks so that companies such as waste-haulers and fuel-delivery companies can monitor such things as a customer's fuel oil inventory level and can provide on-the-spot invoicing—on their trucks. The company has developed software for field service technicians for home fuel trucks that can let a technician know when the customer was last visited and can suggest if routine servicing of the customer's furnace is needed. Work orders can be dispatched from a central dispatch office. The computer lets the central dispatch office know where the technicians are and promotes more efficient scheduling of the technicians.

In addition, the company does business with "Waste Management Industries, Browning Ferris, and Laidlaw, the largest waste haulers in North America and Europe." The on-board computers can, utilizing a radio-frequency device fixed to a garbage container, record the customer's name, and the weight of the garbage in the container.

The technology allows the companies using it to operate more efficiently and effectively. Information is provided to them quickly so they can best utilize their resources and better serve their customers. With respect to home-heating oil and gas firms such as Esso Home Comfort, Shell, Ultramar, and Superior Propane, Killen stated, "[The technology] helps [them] improve receivables, cash flow, and productivity for drivers and dispatching functions."

Source: Quoted from "Mobil Computing Corp. puts Data Processing on Wheels," *Challenges* (published by the Ontario Ministry of Economic Development and Trade), Fall, 1994, p. 23.

CHAPTER OBJECTIVES

After studying this chapter, you should be able to

1 Describe the features of an effective accounting information system

2 Understand how computerized and manual accounting systems are used

3 Understand how spreadsheets are used in accounting

4 Use the sales journal, the cash receipts journal, and the accounts receivable subsidiary ledger

5 Use the purchases journal, the cash disbursements journal, and the accounts payable subsidiary ledger

The systems installed by Mobile Computing Corp. are more than accounting systems. They are accounting *information systems*. An **accounting information system** is a combination of personnel, records and procedures that a business uses to meet its needs for financial data. A fuel delivery company would link the system provided by Mobile Computing Corp. with other systems such as *ACCPAC Plus Accounting*. The word *information* in the title indicates that the fuel delivery company can get more than routine financial statements from their system. Special management reports, such as sales by product and service and cash-flow projections, provide valuable information for their business decisions.

We have already been using an accounting information system in this text. That simple accounting system consists of two basic components:

- A general journal
- A general ledger

The journal and the ledger we have been using are the *general* journal and the *general* ledger. Every accounting system has these components, but this simple system can efficiently handle only a few transactions per period. Accounting systems cope with heavy transaction loads in two ways: computerization and specialization. We *computerize* to journalize, post, and prepare reports faster and more reliably. *Specialization* comes when we deal with similar transactions in groups to speed the process. We will explore special journals in the second half of this chapter.

Features of an Effective Accounting Information System

OBJECTIVE 1

Describe the features of an effective accounting information system

Several design features make accounting systems run efficiently. A good system—whether computerized or manual—includes four features: control, compatibility, flexibility, and a favorable cost/benefit relationship.

Control

Managers need *control* over operations. *Internal controls* are the methods and procedures used to safeguard assets, to prevent and detect error and fraud, to optimize the use of resources (that is, to ensure as far as practicable that reliable information is provided to determine business policies and to monitor the implementation of such policies), and to maintain reliable control systems (that is, to ensure that reliable and timely information is provided to management).

For example, in companies such as John Labatt, McCain Foods, and Kinko's, managers exert tight control over cash disbursements to avoid theft through unauthorized payments. Also, keeping accurate records of accounts receivable is the only way for VISA, MasterCard, Diners Club/en Route, and other credit-card companies to ensure that customers are billed and collections are received on time.

Compatibility

A *compatible* system is one that works smoothly with the business's operations, personnel, and organizational structure. An example is The Toronto Dominion Bank which is organized into a network of branch offices. The Toronto Dominion Bank's top managers want to know revenues in each region where the bank does business. They also want to analyze the bank's loans in different geographic regions. If revenues and loans in Alberta or Nova Scotia are lagging, the managers can concentrate their efforts in that region. They may relocate some branch offices, hire new personnel, or purchase a successful local bank to increase their revenues and net income. A compatible accounting *information* system conforms to the particular needs of the business.

Flexibility

Organizations evolve. They develop new products, sell off unprofitable operations and acquire new ones, and adjust employee pay scales. Changes in the business often call for changes in the accounting system. A well-designed system meets the *flexibility* guideline by accommodating changes without needing a complete overhaul. Consider Bombardier's acquisition of Canadair. Bombardier's accounting system had the flexibility to fold Canadair's financial statements into those of itself, the parent company.

Favorable Cost/Benefit Relationship

Achieving control, compatibility, and flexibility costs money. These costs reduce a company's net income, so managers often must settle for less than the perfect accounting information system. They strive for a system that offers maximum benefits at a minimum cost—that is, a favorable *cost/benefit relationship*. Most small companies, such as Westmount Drugs, use off-the-shelf computerized accounting packages, and the very smallest businesses might not computerize at all. But large companies, such as the brokerage firm Midland Walwyn, have specialized needs for information. For them, customized programming is a must because the benefits—in terms of information tailored to the company's needs—far outweigh the cost of the system. The result? Better decisions.

Components of a Computerized Accounting System

Three components form the heart of a computerized accounting system:

1. Hardware
2. Software
3. Company personnel

Each component is critical to the system's success.

Hardware is the electronic equipment that includes computers, disk drives, monitors, printers, and the network that connects them. Most modern accounting systems require a **network**, the system of electronic linkages that allows different computers to share the same information. In a networked system many computers can be connected to the main computer, or **server**, which stores the program and the data. With the right communications hardware and software, a Price Waterhouse auditor in London can access the data of a client located in Sydney, Australia. The result is a speedier audit for the client, often at lower cost than if the auditor had to perform all the work on site in Sydney.

Software is the set of programs that cause the computer to perform the work desired. Accounting software accepts, edits (alters), and stores transaction data and

Real-World Example:
Computers can make an information system less controllable because many employees have access to a terminal. At a Canadian Tire store, it would be risky for all employees to gain access to customer accounts. An unauthorized employee could change a customer's account or learn confidential information about the customer. Hence, access codes limit access to certain information. Source documents should support all sensitive changes to computer files.

generates the reports managers use to run the business. Many accounting software packages operate independently from the other computing activities of the system. For example, a company that is only partly computerized may use software programs to account for employee payrolls and sales and accounts receivable. The other parts of the accounting system may not be fully automated.

For large enterprises, such as TransCanada PipeLines and McCain Foods, the accounting software is integrated within the overall company *database*, or computerized storehouse of information. Many business databases, or *management information systems*, include both accounting and nonaccounting data. For example, in the U.S., in negotiating a union contract, the Union Pacific Railroad often needs to examine the relationship between the service time and salary levels of company employees. Union Pacific's database will provide the needed data and enable managers to negotiate effectively with their unions and to develop impact statements, which show the possible effects of union demands on the company. During Union Pacific negotiations, both parties carry laptop computers so that they can access the database and continue to analyze the effects of decisions under consideration.

Personnel are critical to the success of any endeavor because people operate the system. Modern accounting systems give nonaccounting personnel access to parts (but not all) of the system. For example, an Old Dutch Food Co. marketing manager (a nonaccountant) may use a microcomputer and regional sales data (accounting information) to identify the territory that needs a promotional campaign. Management of a computerized accounting system requires careful consideration of data security and screening of the people in the organization who will have access to the data. Security is usually achieved with *passwords*, codes that permit access to computerized records.

The Three Stages of Data Processing: A Comparison of Computerized and Manual Accounting Systems

OBJECTIVE 2

Understand how computerized and manual accounting systems are used

Computerized accounting systems have replaced manual systems in many organizations—even small businesses such as Westmount Pharmacy. As we discuss the three stages of data processing, observe the differences between a computerized system and a manual system. The relationship among the three stages of data processing is shown in Exhibit 6-1.

Inputs represents data from source documents, such as sales receipts and bank deposit slips, and electronically generated data from fax orders and other telecommunications. Inputs are usually grouped by type. For example, a firm would enter cash sale transactions separately from credit sales and purchase transactions.

Key Point:

The output (financial reports) can be only as reliable as the input. If the input is incorrect or incomplete, the output will be flawed.

Computerized accounting systems require that data inputs be arranged in specific formats. Transactions that are missing dates, account numbers, or other critical information are not accepted by the system. Transactions for which debits do not equal credits are also rejected.

In a manual system, *processing* includes journalizing transactions, posting to the accounts, and preparing the financial statements. A computerized system also processes but without the intermediate steps (journal, ledger, and trial balance).

EXHIBIT 6-1   *The Three Stages of Data Processing*

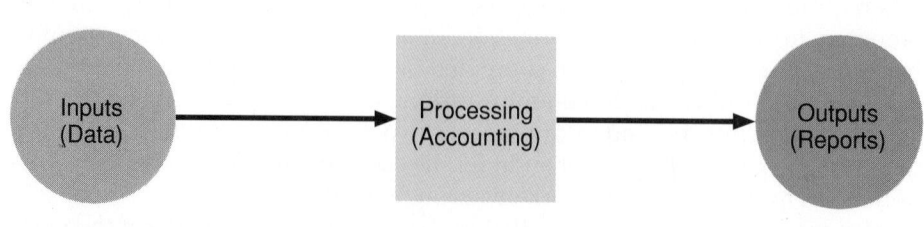

Inputs (Data) → Processing (Accounting) → Outputs (Reports)

Outputs are the reports used for decision making, including the financial statements (income statement, balance sheet, and so on). The fuel oil companies using the Mobile Computing Corp. software in the opening story are making better decisions—and prospering—because of the reports their accounting system produces. From the computer's point of view, a trial balance is also a report. But a manual system would treat the trial balance as a processing step leading to the statements. Exhibit 6-2 is an expanded diagram of the relationship between the components of a computerized accounting system and the three stages of data processing.

In a computerized accounting system, the software controls how the hardware operates. Input enters the system, subject to editing for the balancing of debits and credits, numerical limits, and so on. Accounting records, or files, are accessed by the computer and updated (posted). Reports are displayed on the screen and printed in response to operator command, which requires access to the computerized accounting records. All steps are under the control of the software and the operator (accountant).

Accounting Systems Designed: The Chart of Accounts

Design of the accounting system begins with the chart of accounts. In the accounting system of a company such as Southam Inc., account numbers take on added importance. It is efficient to represent a complex account title, such as Accumulated Depreciation—Photographic Equipment, with a concise account number (for example, 16570).

Recall the asset accounts generally begin with the digit 1, liabilities with the digit 2, owner equity accounts with the digit 3, revenues with 4, and expenses with 5. Exhibit 6-3 diagrams one structure for computerized accounts. Assets are divided into current assets, capital assets (property, plant, and equipment), and other assets. Among the current assets we illustrate only three general ledger accounts: Cash in Bank (Account No. 111), Accounts Receivable (No. 112), and Prepaid Insurance (No. 115). Accounts Receivable holds the total dollar amount receivable from all customers. To ensure collection and follow-up, companies also keep records

EXHIBIT 6-2   *Overview of a Computerized Accounting System*

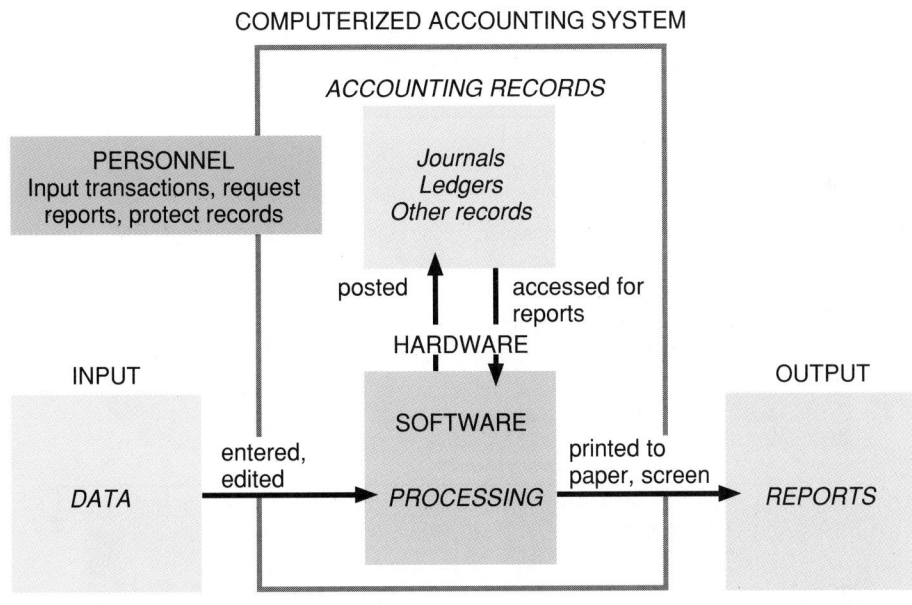

of the amount receivable from each customer. (We discuss the individual customer records in the second half of the chapter.)

The account numbers in Exhibit 6-3 get more detailed as you move from top to bottom. For example, Customer A's account number is 1120001, in which 112 represents Accounts Receivable and 0001 refers to Customer A.

The choice of number groups for account categories is not as critical in a manual system as it is in a computerized system, except for the ease of looking up accounts in the accounting records. Computerized accounting systems rely instead on number ranges to translate accounts and their balances into properly organized financial statements and other reports. For example, the accounts numbered 101–399 (assets, liabilities, and owner equity) are sorted to the balance sheet; the accounts numbered 401–599 (revenues and expenses) go to the income statement.

Key Point:
The general journal will have the fewest entries. Most transactions fall into one of these four categories: credit sales, cash receipts, credit purchases, or cash disbursements.

Classifying Transactions: Computerized and Manual Systems

Recording transactions in an actual accounting system requires an additional step that we have skipped thus far. A business of any size must *classify* transactions by type for efficient handling. In a manual system, credit sales, purchases on account, cash receipts, and cash payments are treated as four separate categories, with each type entered into its own special journal. For example, credit sales are recorded in a special journal called a sales journal. Cash receipts are entered into a cash receipts journal, and so on. Transactions that do not fit any of the special journals, such as the adjusting entries at the end of the period, are recorded in the general journal, which serves as the "journal of last resort."

Computerized systems also require you to preclassify transactions. Suppose you are accruing salary expense (debit Salary Expense; credit Salary Payable). In a manual system, you record the data in the general journal and post to the general ledger. But there is no "set of books" in a computerized system. To record this entry, you choose within the system software the appropriate processing environment from a menu. A **menu** is a list of options for choosing computer functions.

EXHIBIT 6-3 *Structure for Computerized Accounts*

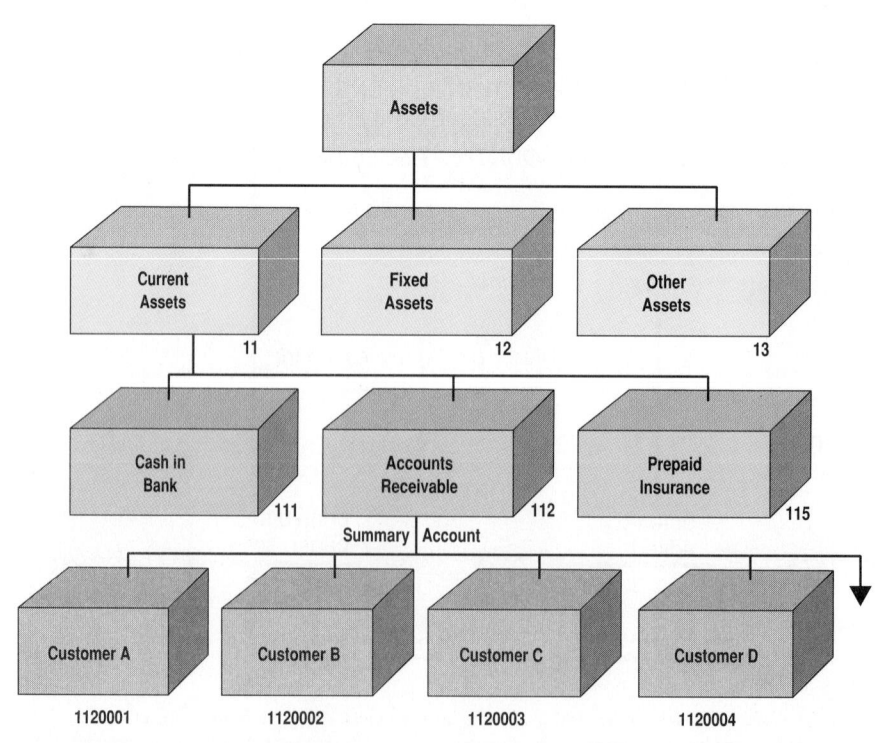

Menu-Driven Accounting Systems

Computerized systems are organized by function, or task. Access to functions is arranged in terms of menus. In such a *menu-driven* system, you first access the most general group of functions, called the *main menu*. You then choose from one or more submenus until you finally reach the function you want. Most computerized systems have similar functions, but their menu structures differ.

Exhibit 6-4 illustrates one type of menu structure. The row at the top of the exhibit shows the main menu. The computer operator (or accountant) had chosen the General option (short for General Ledger), as shown by the highlighting. This action opened a submenu of four items—Transactions, Posting, Account Maintenance, and Closing. The Transactions option was then chosen (highlighted).

Posting in a computerized system can be performed continuously as transactions are being recorded—**on-line processing**—or later for a group of similar transactions—**batch processing**. In either case posting is automatic. Batch processing of accounting data allows accountants to check the entries for accuracy before posting them. In effect, the transaction data are "parked" in the computer to await posting, which simply updates the account balances.

Accounting Reports

Outputs—accounting reports—are the final stage of data processing. In a computerized system the financial statements can be printed automatically. For example, the Reports option in the main menu gives the operator various report choices, which are expanded in the Reports submenu of Exhibit 6-5. In the exhibit the operator is working with the financial statements, specifically the balance sheet, as shown by the highlighting.

Summary of the Accounting Cycle: Computerized and Manual

Exhibit 6-6 summarizes the accounting cycle in a computerized system and in a manual system. As you study the exhibit, compare and contrast the two types of systems.

EXHIBIT 6-4   *Main Menu of a Computerized Accounting System*

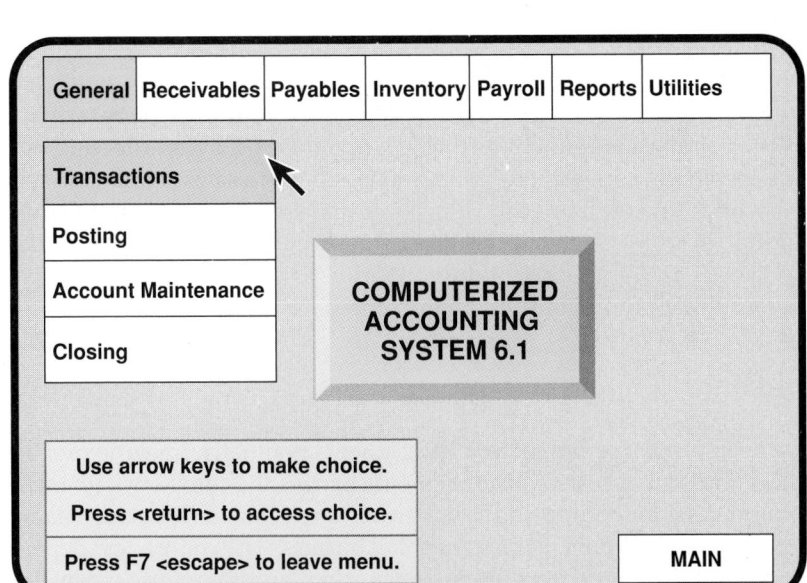

EXHIBIT 6-5   *Reports Menu of a Computerized Accounting System*

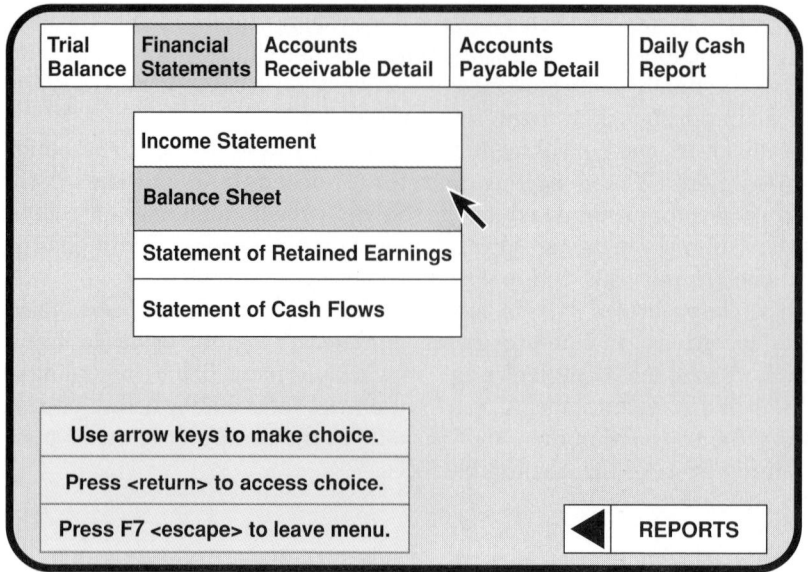

STOP & THINK

Why does every business need an accounting information system? Give several reasons.

Answer: Managers and owners of businesses must make decisions, and they need information to run the organization. The business's accounting system provides much of this information. Likewise, lenders and outside investors use accounting information in their lending and investment decisions. And most businesses are subject to some form of taxation. An accounting system provides tax information as well.

Integrated Accounting Software

Computerized accounting packages are organized by **modules**, separate but *integrated* units—compatible units that function together. Changes affecting one module will affect others. For example, entry and posting of a sales transaction will update two modules: Accounts Receivable/Sales and Inventory/Cost of Goods Sold. Accounting packages, such as ACCPAC Plus Accounting, Business Works, Peachtree, DacEasy, One-Write Plus, and RealWorld Accounting, come as a complete set of accounting modules to form an integrated system.

OBJECTIVE 3

Understand how spreadsheets are used in accounting

Spreadsheets

You may have been preparing homework assignments manually. Imagine preparing a work sheet for Bombardier. Each adjustment changes the company's financial statement totals. Consider computing Bombardier's revenue amounts by hand. The task would be overwhelming. For even a small business with only a few departments, the computations are tedious, time-consuming, and therefore expensive. Furthermore, errors are likely.

EXHIBIT 6-6   *Comparison of the Accounting Cycle in a Computerized and a Manual System*

Key Point:

A computerized system performs all the steps a manual system does, except for the work sheet. Even if you never keep a manual set of books, you still need to understand the entire accounting system.

Computerized System	Manual System
1. Start with the account balances in the ledger at the beginning of the period.	1. Same.
2. Analyze and classify business transactions by type. Access appropriate menus for data entry.	2. Analyze and journalize transactions as they occur.
3. Computer automatically posts transactions as a batch or when entered on-line.	3. Post journal entries to the ledger accounts.
4. The unadjusted balances are available immediately after each posting.	4. Compute the unadjusted balance in each account at the end of the period.
5. The trial balance, if needed, can be accessed as a report.	5. Enter the trial balance on the work sheet, and complete the work sheet.
6. Enter and post adjusting entries. Print the financial statements. Run automatic closing procedures after backing up the period's accounting records.	6. Prepare the financial statements. Journalize and post the adjusting entries. Journalize and post the closing entries.
7. The next period's opening balances are created automatically as a result of closing.	7. Prepare the postclosing trial balance. This trial balance becomes step 1 for the next period.

Spreadsheets are computer programs that link data by means of formulas and functions. These electronic work sheets are invented to automate budget updates. Spreadsheets are organized as a rectangular grid composed of hundreds or thousands of grid points called *cells*, each defined by a row number and a column number. A cell can contain words (called labels), numbers, or formulas (relationships among cells). The *cursor*, or electronic highlighter, indicates which cell is active, and it can be moved around the spreadsheet. When the cursor is placed over any cell, information can be entered there for processing.

Exhibit 6-7 shows a simple income statement on a spreadsheet screen. The words are entered in cells A1 through A4. The dollar amount of revenues was entered in cell B2 and expenses in cell B3. A formula was placed in B4 as follows: +B2–B3. This formula subtracts expenses from revenues to compute net income in cell B4. If revenues in cell B2 increase to $105,000, net income in B4 automatically increases to $45,000. No other cells will change.

Spreadsheets are ideally suited to preparing a budget, the financial goal of a business. Consider Canada's Procter & Gamble Inc., whose Health-Care Sector has an annual advertising budget of $30–$40 million. Procter & Gamble allocates $4–5 million for its Crest Complete toothbrush and $500,000 for a new stand-up tube for Crest toothpaste. Procter & Gamble's advertising expenses will increase in both cases. The company will also forecast an increase in sales revenue, cost of goods sold, and other expenses. A spreadsheet computes all these changes automatically in response to the advertising. The spreadsheet lets Procter & Gamble's managers track relative profitability of each product. Their budget can stay abreast of the latest developments. Armed with current data, the managers can make informed decisions. The result is higher profits.

We can add or delete whole rows and columns of data and move blocks of numbers and words on a spreadsheet. The power and versatility of spreadsheets are apparent when enormous amounts of data are entered on the spreadsheet with formula relationships. Change only one number, and save hours of manual recalculation. Exhibit 6-8 shows the basic arithmetic operations in some popular spreadsheet programs such as Lotus 1-2-3.

EXHIBIT 6-7   *A Spreadsheet Screen*

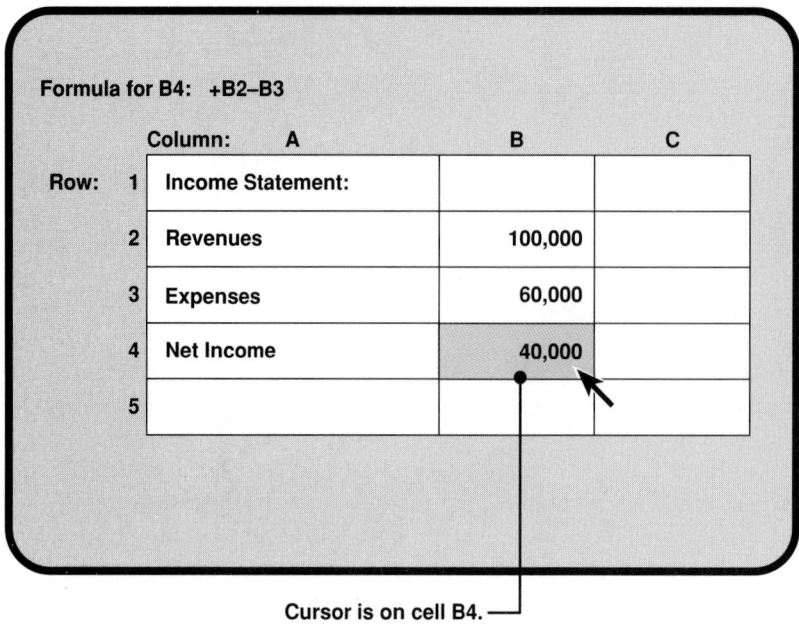

Formula for B4:   +B2–B3

Column:	A	B	C
Row: 1	Income Statement:		
2	Revenues	100,000	
3	Expenses	60,000	
4	Net Income	40,000	
5			

Cursor is on cell B4.

Computerized accounting packages often come with the ability to export data to spreadsheets. For example, the B.C. division of PetroCanada may export a list of accounts receivable (thousands of customers and their balances) as a spreadsheet to the home office in Calgary. The spreadsheet can sort the PetroCanada customers by name, size of balance, sales to the customer during the last quarter, and so on. Other software called **database programs** organize information so that it can be summarized in a variety of report forms. A database program can merge information from various sources to generate even more complex reports than spreadsheets can handle. Some of the common database programs are dBase, Access, and Paradox.

The purpose of an accounting system is to provide information for decision making. The financial statements and other reports are used by managers, creditors, and others who evaluate the business. Each entity designs its accounting system to meet its own needs for information while keeping the cost of the system within its budget. Exhibit 6-9 diagrams a typical accounting system for a merchandising business. The remainder of this chapter describes some of the more important aspects of the system described in Exhibit 6-9.

EXHIBIT 6-8   *Basic Arithmetic Operations in Spreadsheets*

Operation	Symbol
Addition	+
Subtraction	–
Multiplication	*
Division	/
Addition of a range of cells	@SUM (beginning cell..ending cell)
	or
	=SUM (beginning cell..ending cell)
Examples:	
Add the contents of cells A2 through A9	@SUM(A2..A9)
Divide the contents of cell C2 by the	
contents of cell D1	+C2/D1

EXHIBIT 6-9   *Overview of an Accounting Information System*

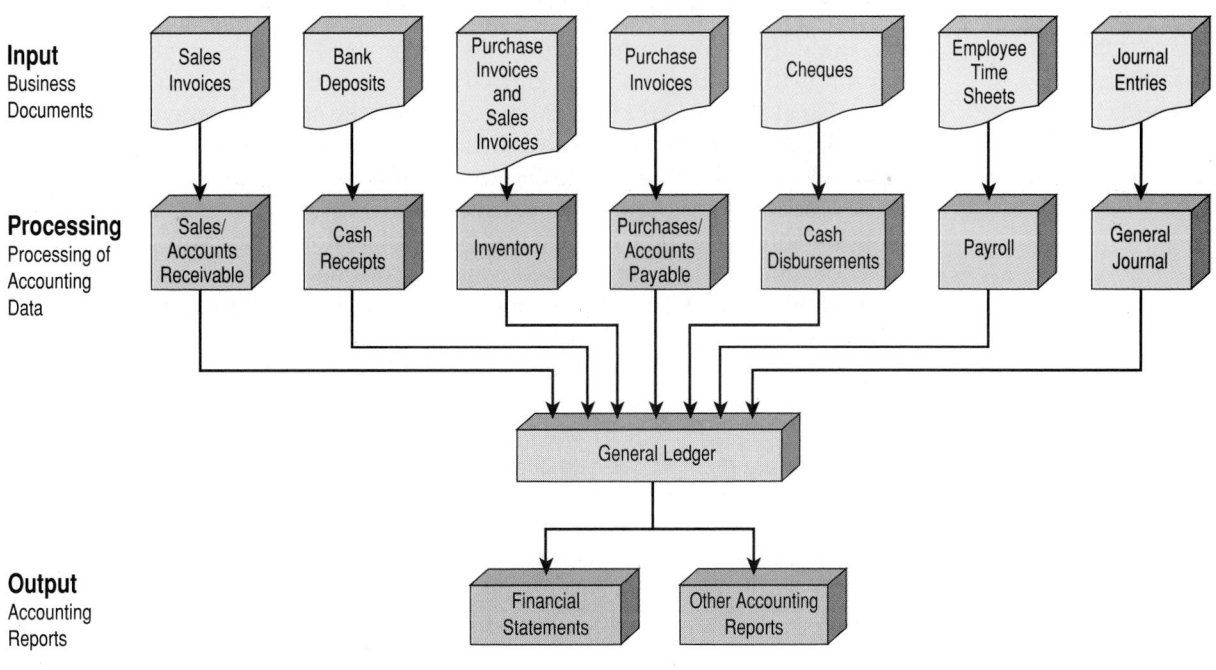

Special Accounting Journals

The journal entries illustrated so far in this book have been made in the general journal. The **general journal** is used to record all transactions that do not fit one of the special journals. In practice, it is inefficient to record all transactions in the general journal, so we use special journals. A **special journal** is an accounting journal designed to record one specific type of transaction, such as credit sales, which would be recorded in the special journal called the sales journal.

Both manual systems and computerized systems must specialize by organizing transaction entry by type. Special journals and accounting modules accomplish that task. In a computerized system, accountants do not enter transaction data in these journals. Instead, they input data through various modules, such as the Accounts Receivable module for credit sales. But the underlying accounting principles are the same in manual and computerized systems.

In all likelihood, you will be working with a computerized system. We would rather you *not* view the process as a black box. To help you understand the basic accounting, we take you through the steps in a manual system.

Most of a business's transactions fall into one of four categories, so accountants use special journals to record these transactions. This system reduces the time and cost otherwise spent journalizing, as we will see. The four categories of transactions, the related special journal and the posting abbreviations follow:

 Key Point:
Transactions are recorded in either the general journal or a special journal, but not in both.

Transaction	Special Journal	Posting Abbreviation
1. Sales on account	Sales journal	S
2. Cash receipt	Cash receipts journal	CR
3. Purchase on account	Purchases journal	P
4. Cash disbursement	Cash disbursements journal	CD

Adjusting and closing entries are entered in the general journal. Its posting abbreviation is J.

OBJECTIVE 4

Use the sales journal, the cash receipts journal, and the accounts receivable subsidiary ledger

Sales Journal

Most merchandisers sell at least some of their inventory on account. These *credit sales* are recorded in the **sales journal**. Credit sales of assets other than inventory—for example, buildings—occur infrequently and are recorded in the general journal.

Exhibit 6-10 illustrates a sales journal (Panel A) and the related posting to the ledgers (Panel B) of Austin Sound Stereo Center, the stereo shop we introduced in Chapter 5. Each entry in the Accounts Receivable/Sales Revenue column of the sales journal in Exhibit 6-10 is a debit (Dr.) to Accounts Receivable and a Credit (Cr.) to Sales Revenue, as the heading above this column indicates. For each transaction, the accountant enters the date, invoice number, and customer account, along with the transaction amount. This streamlined way of recording sales on account saves a vast amount of time that, in a manual system, would be spent entering account titles and dollar amounts in the general journal.

Key Point:
Only credit sales are recorded in the sales journal.

In recording credit sales in the previous chapter, we did not keep a record of the names of credit-sale customers. In practice the business must know the amount receivable from each customer. How else can the company keep track of who owes it money, when payment is due—and how much?

Consider the first transaction in Panel A. On November 2, Austin Sound sold stereo equipment on account to Claudette Trudeau for $935. The invoice number is 422. All this information appears on a single line in the sales journal. No explanation is necessary. The transaction's presence in the sales journal means that it is a credit sale, debited to Accounts Receivable—Claudette Trudeau and credited to Sales Revenue. To gain any additional information about the transaction, we would look up the actual invoice.

In a computerized system, accountants do not enter credit sales in a sales journal. The transaction data may be input through point-of-sales terminals, as in an Eaton's or Zellers store. When managers wish to review credit sales, they can print a report that resembles the sales journal. The report may show the date and amount of each transaction, the invoice number, and the customer name. The other special journals discussed in this chapter are likewise similar to the reports generated by a computerized system.

Recall from Chapter 5 that Austin Sound uses a *perpetual* inventory system. At the time of recording the sale, Austin Sound also records the cost of goods sold and the decrease in inventory. Many computerized accounting systems are programmed to read both the sales amount (from the bar code on the package of the item sold) and the cost of goods sold. A separate column of the sales journal holds the cost of goods sold and inventory amount—$505 for the sale to Claudette Trudeau. If Austin Sound used a *periodic* inventory system, it would not record cost of goods sold and the decrease in inventory at the time of sales. The sales journal would need only one column to debit Accounts Receivable and to credit Sales Revenue for the amount of the sale.

Posting to the General Ledger
The ledger we have used so far is the **general ledger**, which holds the accounts reported in the financial statements. We will soon introduce other ledgers.

Posting from the sales journal to the general ledger can be done *monthly*. In Exhibit 6-10 (Panel A), the total credit sales for November are $4,319. This column has two headings, Accounts Receivable and Sales Revenue. When the $4,319 is posted to these accounts in the general ledger, their account numbers are written beneath the total in the sales journal. In Panel B of Exhibit 6-10, the account number for Accounts Receivable is 112 and the account number for Sales Revenue is 410. These account numbers are entered beneath the credit sales total in the sales journal to signify that the $4,319 has been posted to the two accounts.

The debit to Cost of Goods Sold and the credit to Inventory for the monthly total of $1,814 can also be posted at the end of the month. After posting, these accounts' numbers are entered beneath the total to show that Cost of Goods Sold and Inventory have been updated.

EXHIBIT 6-10   *Sales Journal and Posting to Ledgers*

Panel A: Sales Journal

		Sales Journal			Page 3
Date	Invoice No.	Account Debited	Post. Ref		Accounts Receivable Dr. Sales Revenue Cr.
19X6					
Nov. 2	422	Claudette Trudeau	✔		935
13	423	Brent Harmon	✔		694
18	424	Susan Levy	✔		907
27	425	Clay Schmidt	✔		1,783
30		Total			4,319
					(112/410)

Individual acoounts receivable are posted daily.

Totals can be posted at the end of the month.

Panel B: Posting to Ledgers

Accounts Receivable Ledger

Claudette Trudeau

Date	Jrnl. Ref.	Debit	Credit	Balance
Nov. 2	S.3	935		935

Brent Harmon

Date	Jrnl. Ref.	Debit	Credit	Balance
Nov.13	S.3	694		694

Susan Levy

Date	Jrnl. Ref.	Debit	Credit	Balance
Nov.18	S.3	907		907

Clay Schmidt

Date	Jrnl. Ref.	Debit	Credit	Balance
Nov.27	S.3	1,783		1,783

General Ledger

Accounts Receivable   No. 112

Date	Jrnl. Ref.	Debit	Credit	Balance
Nov.30	S.3	3,319		4,319

Sales Revenue   No. 410

Date	Jrnl. Ref.	Debit	Credit	Balance
Nov.30	S.3		3,319	4,319

Posting to the Subsidiary Ledger   The $4,319 sum of the November debits to Accounts Receivable does not identify the amount receivable from any specific customer. Most businesses would find keeping a separate Accounts Receivable account in the general ledger for each customer to be unmanageable. A business may have tens of thousands of customers. Imagine how many pages thick the general ledger for Canadian Tire would be with their hundreds of thousands of customers.

Key Point:
In a manual system, the dates recorded in the subsidiary ledger and the general ledger must reflect the date of the transaction, not the date on which the transaction was posted. In a computerized system, the computer will automatically record the date entered by the computer operator.

To streamline operations, businesses instead place the accounts of their individual credit customers in a subsidiary ledger, called the Accounts Receivable ledger. A **subsidiary ledger** is a book or file of accounts that provides supporting details on individual balances, the total of which appears in a general ledger account. The customer accounts are arranged in alphabetical order.

Amounts in the sales journal are posted to the subsidiary ledger *daily* to keep a current record of the amount receivable from each customer. The amounts are debits. Daily posting allows the business to answer customer inquiries promptly. Suppose Claudette Trudeau telephones Austin Sound on November 11 to ask how much money she owes. The subsidiary ledger readily provides that information.

When each transaction amount is posted to the subsidiary ledger, a check mark or some other notation is written in the posting reference column of the sales journal.

Journal References in the Ledgers When amounts are posted to the ledgers, the journal page number is written in the account to identify the source of the data. All transaction data in Exhibit 6-10 originated on page 3 of the sales journal so all posting references in the ledger accounts are S.3. The "S." indicates sales journal.

Trace all the postings in Exhibit 6-10. The most effective way to learn about accounting systems and special journals is to study the flow of data. The arrows indicate the direction of the information. The arrows show the links between the individual customer accounts in the subsidiary ledger and the Accounts Receivable account. These links are summarized as follows:

Accounts Receivable debit balance $4,319

Customer Accounts Receivable

Customer	Balance
Claudette Trudeau	$ 935
Brent Harmon...	694
Susan Levy...	907
Clay Schmidt	1,783
Total accounts receivable	$4,319

Accounts Receivable in the general ledger is a **control account**, which is an account whose balance equals the sum of the balances of a group of related accounts in a subsidiary ledger. The individual customer accounts are subsidiary accounts. They are "controlled" by the Accounts Receivable account in the general ledger.

Additional data can be recorded in the sales journal. For example, a company may add a column to record sale terms, such as 2/10 n/30. The design of the journal depends on the manager's needs for information.

STOP & THINK

Suppose Austin Sound had 400 credit sales for the month. How many postings to the general ledger would be made from the sales journal? (Ignore Cost of Goods Sold and Inventory.) How many would there be if all sales transactions were routed through the general journal?

Answer: There are only two postings from the sales journal to the general ledger: one to Accounts Receivable and one to Sales Revenue. There would be 800 postings from the general journal: 400 to Accounts Receivable and 400 to Sales Revenue. This difference clearly shows the benefit of using a sales journal.

Cash Receipts Journal

Key Point:
Every entry in the cash receipts journal includes a debit to Cash. Cash sales are recorded here rather than in the sales journal.

Cash transactions are common in most businesses because cash receipts from customers are the lifeblood of business. To record repetitive cash receipt transactions, accountants use the **cash receipts journal**.

Panel A in Exhibit 6-11 illustrates the cash receipts journal. The related posting to ledgers is shown in Panel B. The exhibit illustrates November transactions for Austin Sound Stereo Center, Inc.

Every transaction recorded in this journal is a cash receipt, so the first column is for debits to the Cash account. The next column is for debits to Sales Discounts on collections from customers. In a typical merchandising business, the main sources of cash are collections on account and cash sales. Thus the cash receipts journal has credit columns for Accounts Receivable and Sales Revenue. The journal also has a credit column for Other Accounts, which lists sources of cash other than cash sales and collections on account. This Other Accounts column is also used to record the names of customers from whom cash is received on account.

In Exhibit 6-11, cash sales occurred on November 6, 19, and 28. Observe the debits to Cash and the credits to Sales Revenue ($517, $853, and $1,802). Each sale entry is accompanied by an entry that debits Cost of Goods Sold and credits Inventory for the cost of the merchandise sold. The column for this entry is at the far right side of the cash receipts journal. Some companies may record this entry separately.

On November 11, Austin Sound borrowed $1,000 from Fundy Bank. Cash is debited, and Note Payable to Fundy Bank is credited in the Other Accounts column because no specific credit column is set up to account for borrowings. For this transaction, it is necessary to write the account title, Note Payable to Fundy Bank, in the Other Accounts/Account Title column to record the source of cash.

On November 25, Austin Sound collected $762 of interest revenue. The account credited, Interest Revenue, must be written in the Other Accounts column. The November 11 and 25 transactions illustrate an important fact about business. Different entities have different types of transactions, and they design their special journals to meet their particular needs for information. In this case, the Other Accounts Credit column is the catch-all that is used to record all nonroutine cash receipt transactions.

On November 14, Austin Sound collected $900 from Claudette Trudeau. Referring back to Exhibit 6-10, we see that on November 2 Austin Sound sold merchandise for $935 to Ms. Trudeau. Assume that the terms of sale allowed a $35 discount for prompt payment and that she paid within the discount period. Austin's cash receipts is recorded by debiting Cash for $900 and Sales Discounts for $35 and by crediting Accounts Receivable for $935. The customer's name appears in the Other Accounts/Account Title column. This procedure enables the business to keep exact track of each customer's account in the subsidiary ledger.

On November 22, the business collected $300 on account from Brent Harmon, who was paying for part of the November 13 purchase. No discount applied to this collection.

Total debits should equal total credits in the cash receipts journal. This equality holds for each transaction and for the monthly totals. For example, the first transaction has a $517 debit and an equal credit. For the month, total debits ($6,134 + $35 = $6,169) equal total credits ($1,235 + $3,172 + $1,762 = $6,169).

Posting to the General Ledger   The column totals can be posted monthly. To indicate their posting, the account number is written below the column total in the cash receipts journal. Note the account number for Cash (101) below the column total $6,134, and trace the posting to Cash in the general ledger. Likewise, the Sales Discounts, Accounts Receivable, and Sales Revenue column totals also are posted to the general ledger.

The column total for *Other Accounts* is not posted. Instead, these credits are posted individually. In Exhibit 6-11, the November 11 transaction reads "Note Payable to Fundy Bank." This account's number (221) in the Post. Ref. column indicates that the transaction amount was posted individually. The check mark, instead of an account

EXHIBIT 6-11 *Cash Receipts Journal and Posting to Ledgers*

Panel A: Cash Receipts Journal

		Debits			Credits				Cost of Goods Sold Dr.
						Other Accounts			
Date	Cash	Sales Discounts	Accounts Receivable	Sales Revenue	Account Title	Post. Ref.	Amount		Inventory Cr.
19X6									
Nov. 6	517			517					290
11	1,000				Note payable to Fundy Bank	222	1,000		
14	900	35	935		Claudette Trudeau	✔			
19	853			853					426
22	300		300		Brent Harmon	✔			
25	762				Interest Revenue	460	762		
28	1,802			1,802					991
30	6,134	35	1,235	3,172	Totals		1,762		1,707
	(101)	(420)	(112)	(410)			(✔)		(511/131)

Cash Receipts Journal — Page 5

- Totals are posted at the end of the month.
- Individual accounts receivable are posted daily.
- Individual amounts are posted at the end of the month.
- Total is not posted.
- Totals can be posted at the end of the month.

Panel B: Posting to Ledgers

Accounts Receivable Ledger

Claudette Trudeau

Date	Jrnl. Ref.	Debit	Credit	Balance
Nov. 2	S.3	935		935
14	CR.5		935	-0-

Brent Harmon

Date	Jrnl. Ref.	Debit	Credit	Balance
Nov.13	S.3	694		694
22	CR.5		300	394

Susan Levy

Date	Jrnl. Ref.	Debit	Credit	Balance
Nov.18	S.3	907		907

Clay Schmidt

Date	Jrnl. Ref.	Debit	Credit	Balance
Nov.27	S.3	1,783		1,783

General Ledger

Cash — No. 101

Date	Jrnl. Ref.	Debit	Credit	Balance
Nov.30	CR.5	6,134		

Accounts Receivable — No. 112

Date	Jrnl. Ref.	Debit	Credit	Balance
Nov.30	S.3	3,319		3,319
30	CR.5		1,235	2,084

Inventory — No. 131

Date	Jrnl. Ref.	Debit	Credit	Balance
Nov.30	Bal.	3,885		3,885
30	S.3		1,814	2,071
30	CR.5		1,707	364

Note Payable to Fundy Bank — No. 222

Date	Jrnl. Ref.	Debit	Credit	Balance
Nov.11	CR.5		1,000	1,000

Sales Revenue — No. 410

Date	Jrnl. Ref.	Debit	Credit	Balance
Nov.30	S.3		3,319	3,319
30	CR.5		3,172	6,491

Sales Discounts — No. 420

Date	Jrnl. Ref.	Debit	Credit	Balance
Nov.30	CR.5	35		35

Interest Revenue — No. 460

Date	Jrnl. Ref.	Debit	Credit	Balance
Nov.25	CR.5		762	762

Cost of Goods Sold — No. 511

Date	Jrnl. Ref.	Debit	Credit	Balance
Nov.30	S.3	1,814		1,814
30	CR.5	1,707		3,521

number, below the column total indicates that the column total was not posted. The November 25 collection of interest revenue is also posted individually. These amounts can be posted to the general ledger at the end of the month. But, they should be dated in the ledger accounts based on their actual date in the journal so that it is easy to trace the amounts back to the journal.

Posting to the Subsidiary Ledger   Amounts from the cash receipts journal are posted to the subsidiary accounts receivable ledger daily to keep the individual balances up to date. The postings to the accounts receivable ledger are credits. Trace the $935 posting to Claudette Trudeau's account. It reduces the balance in her account to zero. The $300 receipt from Brent Harmon reduces his accounts receivable balance to $394.

After posting, the sum of the individual balances that remain in the accounts receivable ledger equals the general ledger balance in Accounts Receivable ($3,084). Austin Sound may prepare a November 30 list of account balances from the subsidiary ledger to follow up on slow-paying customers:

Customer Accounts Receivable

Customer	Balance
Brent Harmon	$ 394
Susan Levy	907
Clay Schmidt	1,783
Total accounts receivable	$3,084

Good accounts receivable records help a business manage its cash.

Purchases Journal

OBJECTIVE 5
Use the purchases journal, the cash disbursements journal, and the accounts payable subsidiary ledger

A merchandising business purchases inventory and supplies frequently. Such purchases are usually made on account. The **purchases journal** is designed to account for all purchases of inventory, supplies and other assets *on account*. It can also be used to record expenses incurred on account. Cash purchases are recorded in the cash disbursements journal.

Exhibit 6-12 illustrates Austin Sound's purchases journal (Panel A) and posting to ledgers (Panel B).[1] The purchases journal in Exhibit 6-12 has amount columns for credits to Accounts Payable and debits to Inventory, Supplies, and Other Accounts. A periodic inventory system would replace the Inventory column with a column entitled "Purchases." The Other Accounts columns accommodate purchases of assets other than inventory and supplies. Each business designs its purchases journal to meet its own needs for information and efficiency. Accounts Payable is credited for all transactions recorded in the purchases journal.

On November 2, Austin Sound Stereo Center purchased from JVC Canada Inc. stereo inventory costing $700. The creditor's name (JVC Canada Inc.) is entered in the Account Credited column. The purchase terms of 3/15 n/30 are also entered to help identify the due date and the discount available. Accounts Payable is credited and Inventory is debited for the transaction amount. On November 19, a credit purchase of supplies is entered as a debit to Supplies and a credit to Accounts Payable.

Note the November 9 purchase of fixtures from City Office Supply. The purchases journal contains no column for fixtures, so the Other Accounts debit column is used. Because this was a credit purchase, the accountant enters the creditor name (City Office Supply) in the Account Credited column and writes "Fixtures" in the Other Accounts/Account Title column.

The total credits in the journal ($2,876) are compared to the total debits ($1,706 + $103 + $1,067 = $2,876). This equality proves the accuracy of the entries in the purchases journal.

 Key Point:
Every transaction in the purchases journal will include a credit to Accounts Payable.

---

[1]This is the only special journal that we illustrate with the credit column placed to the left and the debit columns to the right. This arrangement of columns focuses on Accounts Payable, which is credited for each entry to this journal, and on the individual supplier to be paid.

EXHIBIT 6-12   Purchases Journal and Posting to Ledgers

Panel A: Purchases Journal

Purchases Journal									Page 8
				Credits	Debits				
							Other Accounts		
Date	Account Credited	Terms	Post. Ref.	Accounts Payable	Inventory	Supplies	Account Title	Post. Ref.	Amount
Nov. 2	JVC Canada Inc.	3/15 n/30	✔	700	700				
5	Electrohome Ltd.	n/30	✔	319	319				
9	City Office Supply Co.	2/10 n/30	✔	440			Fixtures	191	440
12	Audio Electronics Inc.	n/30	✔	236	236				
13	JVC Canada Inc.	3/15 n/30	✔	451	451				
19	City Office Supply Co.	2/10 n/30	✔	103		103			
23	O'Leary Furniture Corp.	n/60	✔	627			Furniture	181	627
30	Totals			2,876	1,706	103			1,067
				(210)	(131)	(161)			(✔)

Individual accounts payable are posted daily.

Totals are posted at the end of the month.

Total is not posted.

Individual amounts are posted at the end of the month.

Panel B: Posting to Ledgers

Accounts Payable Ledger

Audio Electronics Inc.

Date	Jrnl. Ref.	Debit	Credit	Balance
Nov. 12	P.8		236	236

City Office Supply Co.

Date	Jrnl. Ref.	Debit	Credit	Balance
Nov. 9	P.8		440	440
19	P.8		103	543

Electrohome Ltd.

Date	Jrnl. Ref.	Debit	Credit	Balance
Nov. 5	P.8		319	319

JVC Canada Inc.

Date	Jrnl. Ref.	Debit	Credit	Balance
Nov. 2	P.8		700	700
13	P.8		451	1,151

O'Leary Furniture Corp.

Date	Jrnl. Ref.	Debit	Credit	Balance
Nov. 23	P.8		627	627

General Ledger

Inventory   No. 131

Date	Jrnl. Ref.	Debit	Credit	Balance
Nov. 30	P.8	1,706		1,706

Supplies   No. 161

Date	Jrnl. Ref.	Debit	Credit	Balance
Nov. 30	P.8	103		103

Furniture   No. 181

Date	Jrnl. Ref.	Debit	Credit	Balance
Nov. 23	P.8	627		627

Fixtures   No. 191

Date	Jrnl. Ref.	Debit	Credit	Balance
Nov. 9	P.8	440		440

Accounts Payable   No. 210

Date	Jrnl. Ref.	Debit	Credit	Balance
Nov. 30	P.8		2,876	2,876

To pay debts efficiently, a company must know how much it owes particular creditors. The Accounts Payable account in the general ledger shows only a single total, however, and therefore does not indicate the amount owed to each creditor. Companies keep an accounts payable subsidiary ledger. The accounts payable ledger lists the creditors in alphabetical order, along with the amounts owed to them. Exhibit 6-12, Panel B shows Austin Sound's accounts payable subsidiary ledger, which includes accounts for Audio Electronics, City Office Supply, and others. After posting, the total of the individual balances in the subsidiary ledger equals the balance in the Accounts Payable control account in the general ledger. This system is much like the accounts receivable system discussed earlier in the chapter.

Posting from the Purchases Journal   Posting from the purchases journal is similar to posting from the sales journal and the cash receipts journal. Exhibit 6-12, Panel B, illustrates the posting process.

Individual accounts payable in the *accounts payable subsidiary ledger* are posted daily, and column totals and other amounts can be posted to the *general ledger* at the end of the month. In the ledger accounts, P.8 indicates the source of the posted amounts—that is, page 8 of the purchases journal.

Key Point:
The posting procedure is the same as for the other special journals: column totals can be posted to the general ledger at the end of the month; other accounts are posted individually to the general ledger; and individual accounts payable amounts are posted daily to the subsidiary.

STOP & THINK

Contrast the number of general ledger postings from the purchases journal in Exhibit 6-12 with the number that would be required if the general journal were used to record the same seven transactions.

Answer: Use of the purchases journal requires only five general ledger postings—$2,876 to Accounts Payable, $1,706 to Inventory, $103 to Supplies, $440 to Fixtures, and $627 to Furniture. Without the purchases journal, there would have been 14 postings, two for each of the seven transactions.

Cash Disbursements Journal

Businesses make most cash disbursements by cheque. All payments by cheque are recorded in the **cash disbursements journal**. Other titles of this special journal are the *cheque register* and the *cash payments journal*. Like the other special journals, it has multiple columns for recording cash payments that occur frequently.

Exhibit 6-13, Panel A, illustrates the cash disbursements journal, and Panel B shows the postings to the ledgers of Austin Sound. This cash disbursements journal has two debit columns—for Accounts Payable and Other Accounts—and two credit columns—for Cash and purchase discounts, which are credited to the Inventory account in a perpetual inventory system. This special journal also has columns for the date and cheque number of each cash payment.

Suppose a business makes numerous cash purchases of inventory. What additional column would its cash disbursements journal need to be most useful? A column for Inventory, which would appear under the Debits heading, would streamline the accounting.

All entries in the cash disbursements journal include a credit to Cash. Payments on account are debits to Accounts Payable. On November 15, Austin Sound paid JVC Canada on account, with credit terms of 3/15 n/30 (for details, see the first transaction in Exhibit 6-12). Therefore, Austin took the 3 percent discount and paid $679 ($700 less the $21 discount). The discount is credited to the Inventory account.

The Other Accounts column is used to record debits to accounts for which no special column exists. For example, on November 3, Austin Sound paid rent expense of $1,200, and on November 8, the business purchased supplies for $61.

As with all other journals, the total debits ($3,461 + $819 = $4,280) should equal the total credits ($21 + $4,259 = $4,280).

Posting from the Cash Disbursements Journal   Posting from the cash disbursements journal is similar to posting from the cash receipts journal. Individual creditor amounts are posted daily, and column totals and Other Accounts can be posted at the end of the month. Exhibit 6-13, Panel B, illustrates the posting process.

Real-World Example:
Businesses make most cash disbursements by cheque to control their cash. Imagine the confusion and the opportunity for theft if all employees could take cash from the register to pay for purchases.

Short Exercise:
(1) How many postings would be in the general ledger Cash account?
(2) How many postings would be in the Sales Revenue Account?
A: (1) Two—one from cash receipts and one from cash disbursements. (2) Two—one from the sales journal and one from cash receipts. (In addition, there may also be adjustments.)

EXHIBIT 6-13   *Cash Disbursements Journal and Posting to Ledgers*

Panel A: Cash Disbursements Journal

Cash Disbursements Journal							Page 6
Date	Ch. No.	Account Debited	Post. Ref.	Debits		Credits	
				Other Accounts	Accounts Payable	Inventory	Cash
Nov. 3	101	Rent Expense	541	1,200			1,200
8	102	Supplies	161	61			61
15	103	JVC Canada Inc.	✔		700	21	679
20	104	Electrohome Ltd.	✔		119		119
26	105	Inventory	131	2,200			2,200
30		Totals		3,461	819	21	4,259
				(✔)	(210)	(131)	(101)

Total is not posted.

Totals can be posted at the end of the month.

Individual accounts payable are posted daily.

Individual amounts can be posted at the end of the month.

Panel B: Posting to Ledgers

Accounts Payable Ledger

Audio Electronics Inc.

Date	Jrnl. Ref.	Debit	Credit	Balance
Nov.12	P.8		236	236

City Office Supply Co.

Date	Jrnl. Ref.	Debit	Credit	Balance
Nov. 9	P.8		440	440
19	P.8		103	543

Electrohome Ltd.

Date	Jrnl. Ref.	Debit	Credit	Balance
Nov. 5	P.8		319	319
20	CD.6	119		200

JVC Canada Inc.

Date	Jrnl. Ref.	Debit	Credit	Balance
Nov. 2	P.8		700	700
13	P.8		451	1,151
15	CD.6	700		451

O'Leary Furniture Co.

Date	Jrnl. Ref.	Debit	Credit	Balance
Nov.23	P.8		627	627

General Ledger

Cash   No. 101

Date	Jrnl. Ref.	Debit	Credit	Balance
Nov.30	CR.5	6,134		6,134
30	CD.6		4,259	1,875

Inventory   No. 131

Date	Jrnl. Ref.	Debit	Credit	Balance
Nov.30	P.8	1,706		1,706
26	CD.6	2,200		3,906
30	CD.6		21	3,885

Supplies   No. 161

Date	Jrnl. Ref.	Debit	Credit	Balance
Nov.30	P.8	103		103
8	CD.6	61		164

Accounts Payable   No. 210

Date	Jrnl. Ref.	Debit	Credit	Balance
Nov.30	P.8		2,876	2,876
30	CD.6	819		2,057

Rent Expense   No. 541

Date	Jrnl. Ref.	Debit	Credit	Balance
Nov. 3	CD.6	1,200		1,200

Observe the effect of posting to the Accounts Payable account in the general ledger. The first posted amount in the Accounts Payable account (credit $2,876) originated in the purchases journal, page 8 (P.8). The second posted amount (debit $819) came from the cash disbursements journal, page 6 (CD.6). The resulting credit balance in Accounts Payable is $2,057. Also, see the Cash account. After posting, its debit balance is $2,175.

Amounts in the Other Accounts column are posted individually (for example, Rent Expense—debit $1,200). When each Other Accounts amount is posted to the general ledger, the account number is written in the Post. Ref. column of the journal.

To review their accounts payable, companies list the individual creditor balances in the accounts payable subsidiary ledger:

Creditor Accounts Payable

Creditor	Balance
Audio Electronics	$ 236
City Office Supply	543
Electrohome Ltd.	200
JVC Canada Inc..	451
O'Leary Furniture	627
Total accounts payable..	$2,057

This total agrees with the Accounts Payable balance in Exhibit 6-13. Agreement of the two amounts indicates that the resulting account balances are correct.

Sales Tax

In Chapter 4, the federal Goods and Services Tax (GST) was discussed; recall that the GST is collected at each level of transaction right down to the consumer, the final level. The discussion that follows relates to consumption or sales taxes levied by all the provinces except Alberta. The Yukon and the Northwest Territories also do not have a sales tax. Sellers must add the tax to the sale amount, then pay the tax to the provincial government. In most jurisdictions, sales tax is levied only on final consumers, so retail businesses usually do not pay sales tax on the goods they purchase for resale. For example, Gunz Stereo Ltd. would not pay sales tax on a purchase of equipment from JVC Canada, a wholesaler. However, when retailers like Gunz Stereo make sales, they must collect sales tax from the consumer. In effect, retailers serve as collecting agents for the taxing authorities. The amount of tax depends on the total sales.

Retailers set up procedures to collect the sales tax, account for it and pay it on time. Invoices may be preprinted with a place for entering the sales tax amount, and the general ledger has an account entitled Sales Tax Payable. The sales journal may include a special column for sales tax, such as the one illustrated in Exhibit 6-14. The sales tax rate in the exhibit is 7 percent, the rate of sales tax in Saskatchewan and Manitoba.

Note that the amount debited to Accounts Receivable ($3,551.33) is the sum of the credits to Sales Tax Payable ($232.33) and Sales Revenue ($3,319.00). This is so because the customers' payments, the Accounts Receivable figures, are partly for the purchase of merchandise (Sales Revenue) and partly for tax created by the sale. Individual customer accounts are posted daily to the accounts receivable subsidiary ledger, and each column total is posted at the end of the month. The check marks in the Posting Reference column show that individual amounts have been posted to the customer accounts. The absence of account numbers under the column totals shows that the total amounts have not yet been posted.

Most companies that use cash registers have them programmed to calculate separate totals, as sales are being rung in, of taxable items and nontaxable items; the register then calculates the relevant taxes—sales tax, if applicable, and GST—and computes the total owing. Due to the fact that the provincial sales tax and the federal GST are not applicable to all items (for example, food and prescription medicines are excluded from both; reading material is excluded from most sales taxes but not from the GST), most businesses calculate sales tax and GST at the time of sale.

Short Exercise:
In which journal would you record each transaction?
(1) Owner withdraws cash
(2) Sale of unused business auto (3) Owners invest additional cash (4) Owner invests a personal computer (5) Purchase of supplies on credit (6) Accrue salary payable. ***A:*** (1) Cash disbursements (2) Cash receipts (3) Cash receipts (4) General (5) Purchases (6) General.

EXHIBIT 6-14   *Sales Journal Designed to Account for Sales Tax*

Sales Journal   Page 4

Date	Invoice No.	Account Debited	Post. Ref.	Accounts Receivable Dr.	Sales Tax Payable Cr.	Sales Revenue Cr.
19X6						
Nov. 2	422	Anne Fortin	✔	1,000.45	65.45	935.00
13	423	Brent Mooney	✔	742.58	48.58	694.00
18	424	Debby Levy	✔	970.49	63.49	907.00
27	425	Dan Girardi	✔	837.81	54.81	783.00
30		Totals		3,551.33	232.33	3,319.00

A business, whose sales are all taxable, may use a simplified approach to account for sales tax as follows. The business enters a single amount, which is the sum of sales revenue and sales tax, in the Sales Revenue account. This amount is what the customer pays the retailer. At the end of the period, the business computes the tax collected and transfers that amount from Sales Revenue to Sales Tax Payable through a general journal entry. This procedure eliminates the need for a special multicolumn journal.

Suppose a retailer's Sales Revenue account shows a $11,100 balance at the end of the period. This retailer chooses to enter the full amount of each sale—the actual sales revenue and the sales tax—as Sales Revenue. How does the retailer divide the total amount into its two parts?

To compute the actual sales revenue, the Sales Revenue balance is divided by 1 plus the tax rate. Assume that sales tax is 11 percent, the sales tax rate in New Brunswick. Thus the retailer divides $11,100 by 1.11 (1 + .11), which yields $10,000. Subtracting the actual sales revenue, the $10,000, from the $11,100 total yields $1,100, the sales tax. The retailer makes the following entry in the general journal:

General Journal   Page 9

Date	Accounts	Post. Ref.	Debit	Credit
July 31	Sales Revenue..	41	1100	
	Sales Tax Payable...............................	28		1100
	To transfer sales tax to the liability account.			

Sales tax and GST are more fully discussed in Chapter 11.

Balancing the Ledgers

At the end of the period, after all postings, equality should exist between

1. Total debits and total credits in the general ledger. These amounts are used to prepare the trial balance that has been used throughout Chapters 3 to 5.
2. The balance of the Accounts Receivable control account in the general ledger and the sum of individual customer accounts in the accounts receivable subsidiary ledger.
3. The balance of the Accounts Payable control account in the general ledger and the sum of individual creditor accounts in the accounts payable subsidiary ledger.

This process is called *balancing the ledgers* or proving the ledgers. It is an important control procedure because it helps assure the accuracy of the accounting records.

Documents as Journals in a Manual Accounting System ___

Many small businesses streamline their accounting systems to save money by using the actual business documents as the journals. For example, Austin Sound could let its sales invoices serve as its sales journal and keep all invoices for credit sales in a looseleaf binder. At the end of the period, the accountant simply totals the sales on account and posts that amount to Accounts Receivable and Sales Revenue. Also, the accountant can post directly from invoices to customer accounts in the accounts receivable ledger. This "journal-less" system reduces accounting cost, because the accountant does not have to write in journals the information already in the source documents.

Computers and Special Journals _____

The manual accounting system we discuss in this chapter should help you understand the importance of computers for companies with large numbers of customers and suppliers and a high volume of transactions. Imagine entering manually the few transactions in this chapter—multiplied by a thousand or even ten thousand.

Computerizing special journals requires no drastic change in the accounting system's design. Systems designers create a special screen for each accounting application (module)—credit sales, cash receipts, credit purchases, and cash payments. The special screen for credit sales would ask the person entering the data, for example, on a terminal or a cash register, to type in the following information: date, customer number, customer name, invoice number, and the dollar amount of the sale. These data can generate debits to the subsidiary accounts receivable, and files from which are generated monthly customer statements that show activity and ending balance. For purchases on account, additional computer files keep the subsidiary ledger information on individual vendors.

Summary Problem for Your Review

A company completed the following selected transactions during March:

Mar. 4 Received $500 from a cash sale to a customer (cost $319).
  6 Received $60 on account from Brady Lee. The full invoice amount was $65, but Lee paid within the discount period to gain the $5 discount.
  9 Received $1,080 on a note receivable from Beverly Mann. This amount includes the $1,000 note receivable plus $80 of interest revenue.
 15 Received $800 from a cash sale to a customer (cost $522).
 24 Borrowed $2,200 by signing a note payable to the Bank of the Rockies.
 27 Received $1,200 on account from Lance Au. Payment was received after the discount period lapsed.

The general ledger showed the following balances at February 28: Cash, $1,117; Accounts Receivable, $2,790; Note Receivable—Beverly Mann, $1,000. The accounts receivable subsidiary ledger at February 28 contained debit balances as follows: Lance Au, $1,840; Melinda Fultz, $885; Brady Lee, $65.

Required

1. Record the transactions in the cash receipts journal, page 7.

2. Compute column totals at March 31. Show that total debits equal total credits in the cash receipts journal.

3. Post to the general ledger and the accounts receivable subsidiary ledger. Use complete posting references, including the account numbers illustrated: Cash, 11; Accounts Receivable, 12; Note Receivable—Beverly Mann, 13; Note Payable—Bank of the Rockies, 22; Sales Revenue, 41; Sales Discounts, 42; Interest Revenue, 46, and Cost of Goods Sold, 51. Insert a check mark (✔) in the posting reference column for each February 28 account balance.

4. Show that the total of the balances in the subsidiary ledger equals the general ledger balance in Accounts Receivable.

SOLUTION TO REVIEW PROBLEM

Requirements 1 and 2

Cash Receipts Journal   Page 7

	Debits		**Credits**						
					Other Accounts				**Cost of Goods Sold Debit**
Date	**Cash**	**Sales Discounts**	**Accounts Receivable**	**Sales Revenue**	**Account Title**	**Post. Ref.**	**Amount**		
Mar. 4	500			500					319
6	60	5	65		Brady Lee	✔			
9	1,080				Note Receivable — Beverly Mann	13	1,000		
					Interest Revenue	46	80		
15	800			800					
24	2,200				Note Payable— Bank of the Rockies	22	2,200		522
27	1,200		1,200		Lance Au	✔			
31	5,840	5	1,265	1,300	Total		3,280		841
	(11)	(42)	(12)	(41)			(✔)		(51/14)

5,845   5,845

Requirement 3

Accounts Receivable Ledger
Lance Au

Date	Jrnl. Ref.	Debit	Credit	Balance
Feb. 28	✔			1,840
Mar. 27	CR. 7		1,200	640

Melinda Fultz

Date	Jrnl. Ref.	Debit	Credit	Balance
Feb. 28	✔			885

General Ledger
Cash   No. 11

Date	Jrnl. Ref.	Debit	Credit	Balance
Feb. 28	✔			1,117
Mar. 31	CR. 7	5,840		6,957

Accounts Receivable   No. 12

Date	Jrnl. Ref.	Debit	Credit	Balance
Feb. 28	✔			2,790
Mar. 31	CR. 7		1,265	1,525

Brady Lee

Date	Jrnl. Ref.	Debit	Credit	Balance
Feb. 28	✔			65
Mar. 6	CR. 7		65	—

Note Receivable—Beverly Mann   No. 13

Date	Jrnl. Ref.	Debit	Credit	Balance
Feb. 28	✔			1,000
Mar. 9	CR. 7		1,000	—

Inventory   No. 14

Date	Jrnl. Ref.	Debit	Credit	Balance
Mar. 31	✔			1,819
31	CR. 7		841	978

Note Payable—Bank of the Rockies   No. 22

Date	Jrnl. Ref.	Debit	Credit	Balance
Mar. 24	CR. 7		2,200	2,200

Sales Revenue   No. 41

Date	Jrnl. Ref.	Debit	Credit	Balance
Mar. 31	CR. 7		1,300	1,300

Sales Discount   No. 42

Date	Jrnl. Ref.	Debit	Credit	Balance
Mar. 31	CR. 7	5		5

Interest Revenue   No. 46

Date	Jrnl. Ref.	Debit	Credit	Balance
Mar. 9	CR. 7		80	80

Cost of Goods Sold   No. 51

Date	Jrnl. Ref.	Debit	Credit	Balance
Mar. 31	CR. 7	841		841

Requirement 4

Customer balances in the Accounts Receivable subsidiary ledger.

Lance Au	$ 640
Melinda Fultz	885
Total accounts receivable	$1,525

This total agrees with the balance in Accounts Receivable.

Summary _____

1. *Describe the features of an effective accounting information system.* An effective *accounting information system* should capture and summarize transactions quickly, accurately, and usefully. It should generate a variety of accounting reports, including financial statements and trial balances, that aid management in operating a business. The four major aspects of a good accounting system are (1) control over operations, (2) compatibility with the particular features of the business, (3) flexibility in response to changes in the business, (4) a favorable cost/benefit relationship such that benefits outweigh costs.

2. *Understand how computerized and manual accounting systems are used.* Computerized accounting systems process inputs faster than do manual systems and can generate more types of reports. The key components of a computerized accounting system are *hardware, software,* and company personnel. Account numbers play a bigger role in the operation of computerized systems than they do in manual systems, because computers classify accounts by account numbers. Both computerized and manual accounting systems require transactions to be classified by type.

Computerized systems are a *menu* structure to organize accounting functions. Posting, trial balances, financial statements, and closing procedures are carried out automatically in a computerized accounting system. Computerized accounting systems are integrated so that the different *modules* of the system are updated together.

3. *Understand how spreadsheets are used in accounting. Spreadsheets* are electronic work sheets whose grid points, or cells, are linked by means of formulas. The numerical relationships in the spreadsheet are maintained whenever changes are made to the spreadsheet. Spreadsheets are ideally suited to detailed computations as in budgeting.

4. *Use the sales journal, the cash receipts journal, and the accounts receivable subsidiary ledger.* Manual accounting systems use special journals to record transactions by category. Credit sales are recorded in a *sales journal,* and cash receipts in a *cash receipts journal.* Posting goes to the *general ledger* and to the accounts receivable *subsidiary ledger,* which lists each customer and the amount receivable from that customer. The accounts receivable subsidiary ledger is the main device for ensuring that the company collects from customers.

5. *Use the purchases journal, the cash disbursements journal, and the accounts payable subsidiary ledger.* Credit purchases in a manual system are recorded in a *purchases journal,* and cash payments in a *cash disbursements journal.* Posting from these journals is to the general ledger and to the accounts payable subsidiary ledger. The accounts payable subsidiary ledger helps the company stay current in payments to suppliers.

Self-Study Questions

Test your understanding of the chapter by marking the correct answer for each of the following questions:

1. Why does a jewelry store need an accounting system different from that which a physician uses? *(p. 280)*
   a. They have different kinds of employees.
   b. They have different kinds of journals and ledgers.
   c. They have different kinds of business transactions.
   d. They work different hours.
2. Which feature of an effective information system is most concerned with safeguarding assets? *(p. 280)*
   guarding assets? *(p. 280)*

   a. Control   c. Flexibility
   b. Compatibility   d. Favorable cost/benefit relationship

3. The account number 211031 most likely refers to *(p. 283)*
   a. Liabilities
   b. Current liabilities
   c. Accounts payable
   d. An individual vendor

4. If the amount of total revenues is in cell E7 of a spreadsheet and the amount for total expenses is in cell E20, then net income would be computed by the formula *(p. 287)*
   a. +E7 + E20
   b. +E7 – E20
   c. +E20 – E7
   d. None of the above formulas will work

5. Special journals help most by *(p. 289)*
   a. Limiting the number of transactions that have to be recorded
   b. Reducing the cost of operating the accounting system
   c. Improving accuracy in posting to subsidiary ledgers
   d. Easing the preparation of the financial statements

6. Galvan Company recorded 523 credit sale transactions in the sales journal. Ignoring Cost of Goods Sold and Inventory, how many postings would be required if these transactions were recorded in the general journal? *(pp. 290–291)*
   a. 523   c. 1,569
   b. 1,046   d. 2,092

7. Which two dollar-amount columns in the cash receipts journal will be used the most by a department store that makes half of its sales for cash and half on credit? *(pp. 293–295)*
   a. Cash Debit and Sales Discounts Debit
   b. Cash Debit and Accounts Receivable Credit
   c. Cash Debit and Other Accounts Credit
   d. Accounts Receivable Debit and Sales Revenue Credit

8. Entries in the purchases journal are posted to the *(pp. 295–297)*
   a. General ledger only
   b. General ledger and the accounts payable ledger
   c. General ledger and the accounts receivable ledger
   d. Accounts receivable ledger and the accounts payable ledger

9. Every entry in the cash disbursements journal includes a *(pp. 295–297)*
   a. Debit to Accounts Payable   c. Credit to Inventory
   b. Debit to an Other Account   d. Credit to Cash

10. Balancing the ledgers at the end of the period is most closely related to *(p. 300)*
    a. Control   c. Flexibility
    b. Compatibility   d. Favorable cost/benefit relationship

Answers to the Self-Study Questions follow the Accounting Vocabulary.

Accounting Vocabulary

Accounting information system *(p. 280)*
Batch processing *(p. 285)*
Cash disbursements journal *(p. 297)*
Cash receipts journal *(p. 293)*
Control account *(p. 292)*
Database programs *(p. 288)*
General journal *(p. 289)*
General ledger *(p. 290)*
Hardware *(p. 281)*

Menu *(p. 284)*
Module *(p. 286)*
Network *(p. 281)*
On-line processing *(p. 285)*
Purchases journal *(p. 295)*
Sales journal *(p. 290)*
Server *(p. 281)*
Software *(p. 281)*
Special journal *(p. 289)*
Spreadsheet *(p. 287)*
Subsidiary ledger *(p. 292)*

Answers to Self-Study Questions

1. c	6. c [523 × 3 (one debit, one credit, and	8. b
2. a	one to the accounts receivable ledger)	9. d
3. d	= 1,569]	10. a
4. b	7. b	
5. b		

ASSIGNMENT MATERIAL _____

Questions

1. Describe the four criteria of an effective accounting system.

2. Distinguish batch computer processing from on-line computer processing.

3. What accounting categories correspond to the account numbers 1, 2, 3, 4, and 5 in a typical computerized accounting system?

4. Why might the number 112 be assigned to Accounts Receivable and the number 1120708 to Carl Erickson, a customer?

5. Describe the function of menus in a computerized accounting system.

6. How do formulas in spreadsheets speed the process of budget preparation and revision?

7. Name four special journals used in accounting systems. For what type of transaction is each designed?

8. Describe the two advantages that special journals have over recording all transactions in the general journal.

9. What is a control account, and how is it related to a subsidiary ledger? Name two common control accounts.

10. Graff Company's sales journal has one amount column headed Accounts Receivable Dr. and Sales Revenue Cr. In this journal, 86 transactions are recorded. How many posting references appear in the journal? State what each posting reference represents.

11. The accountant for Bannister Company posted all amounts correctly from the cash receipts journal to the general ledger. However, she failed to post three credits to customer accounts in the accounts receivable subsidiary ledger. How would this error be detected?

12. At what two times is posting done from a special journal? What items are posted at each time?

13. Describe two ways to account for sales tax collected from customers.

14. What is the purpose of balancing the ledgers?

15. Posting from the journals of McKedrick Realty is complete. However, the total of the individual balances in the accounts payable subsidiary ledger does not equal the balance in the Accounts Payable control account in the general ledger. Does this necessarily indicate that the trial balance is out of balance? Give your reason.

16. Assume that posting is completed. The trial balance shows no errors, but the sum of the individual accounts payable does not equal the Accounts Payable control balance in the general ledger. What two errors could cause this problem?

Exercises

Exercise 6-1   *Assigning account numbers* **(Obj. 2)**

Assign account numbers (from the list that follows) to the accounts of LP Gas Corp. Identify the headings, which are *not* accounts and would not be assigned an account number.

Assets	Common Stock
Current Assets	Dividends
Property, Plant, and Equipment	Revenues
Accounts Payable	Selling Expenses

Numbers from which to choose:

1	14
2	21
3	31
4	32
5	33
11	121
12	131
13	411

Exercise 6-2   *Using a trial balance* **(Obj. 2)**

The following accounts in the computerized accounting system of FAX Supply Company Ltd. show some of the company's adjusted balances before closing:

Total assets	?
Current assets	5,600
Plant assets	13,400
Total liabilities	?
Current liabilities	1,100
Long-term liabilities	?
Common stock	1,000
Retained earnings	12,600
Dividends	7,000
Total revenues	18,000
Total expenses	11,000

Compute the missing amounts.

Exercise 6-3   *Using a spreadsheet to compute depreciation* **(Obj. 3)**

An asset listed on a spreadsheet has a cost of $60,000; this amount is located in cell E7. The number of years of the asset's useful life is found in cell E9. Write the spreadsheet formula to express annual depreciation expense for this asset.

Exercise 6-4   *Computing financial statement amounts with a spreadsheet* **(Obj. 3)**

Suppose the values of the following items are stored in the cells of a spreadsheet:

Item	Cell
Total assets	E7
Current assets	E8
Fixed assets	E9
Total liabilities	E10
Current liabilities	E11
Long-term liabilities	E12

Write the spreadsheet formula to calculate:

a. Current ratio
b. Total owner equity
c. Debt ratio

Exercise 6-5   *Using the sales and cash receipts journals* **(Obj. 4)**

The sales and cash receipts journals of CompuGraphics Corp. include the following entries:

Sales Journal

Date	Account Debited	Post. Ref.	Accounts Receivable Dr. Sales Revenue Cr.	Cost of Goods Sold Dr. Inventory Cr.
Oct. 7	C. Carlson	✔	930	550
10	T. Muecke	✔	3,100	1,970
10	E. Lovell	✔	690	410
12	B. Goebel	✔	5,470	3,340
31	Total		10,190	6,270

Cash Receipts Journal

	Debits			Credits				
					Other Accounts			
Date	Cash	Sales Discounts	Accounts Receivable	Sales Revenue	Account Title	Post. Ref.	Amount	Cost of Goods Sold Dr. Inventory Cr.
Oct. 16					C. Carlson	✔		
19					E. Lovell	✔		
24	300			300				190
30					T. Muecke	✔		

CompuGraphics makes all sales on credit terms of 2/10 n/30. Complete the cash receipts journal for those transactions indicated. Also, total the journal and show that total debits equal total credits. Each cash receipt was for the full amount of the receivable.

Exercise 6-6   *Classifying postings from the cash receipts journal* **(Obj. 4)**

The cash receipts journal of Schwarzkopf, Inc. follows:

Cash Receipts Journal   **Page 7**

Date	Cash	Sales Discounts	Accounts Receivable	Sales Revenue	Account Title	Post Ref.	Amount
		Debits			Credits		
					Other Accounts		
Dec. 2	794	16	810		Magna Corp.	(a)	
9	1,291		1,291		Kamm, Inc.	(b)	
14	3,904			3,904		(c)	
19	4,480				Note Receivable	(d)	4,000
					Interest Revenue	(e)	480
30	314	7	321		J. T. Franz	(f)	
31	4,235			4,235		(g)	
31	15,018	23	2,422	8,139	Totals		4,480
	(h)	(i)	(j)	(k)			(l)

Required

Identify each posting reference (a) through (l) as (1) a posting to the general ledger as a column total, (2) a posting to the general ledger as an individual amount, (3) a posting to a subsidiary ledger account, or (4) an amount not posted.

Exercise 6-7   *Identifying transactions from postings to the accounts receivable ledger* **(Obj. 4)**

An account in the accounts receivable ledger of Wu Computers Ltd. follows:

Lind Lumber Inc.

Date		Jrnl. Ref.	Dr.	Cr.	Balance
July 1	....				403 (Dr)
10	....	S.5	1,180		1,583 (Dr)
15	....	J.8		191	1,392 (Dr)
21	....	CR.9		703	689 (Dr)

Required

Describe the three posted transactions.

Exercise 6-8   *Recording purchase transactions in the general journal and purchases journal* **(Obj. 5)**

During April, Ippolito, Inc., completed the following credit purchase transactions:

April 4   Purchased inventory, $1,904, from McGraw Ltd. Ippolito uses a perpetual inventory system.
     7   Purchased supplies, $107, from Paine Corp.
    19   Purchased equipment, $1,903, from Liston-Fry Corp.
    27   Purchased inventory, $2,210, from Milan, Inc.

Record these transactions first in the general journal—with explanations—and then in the purchases journal. Omit credit terms and posting references. Which procedure for recording transactions is quicker?

Exercise 6-9   *Posting from the purchases journal; balancing the ledgers* **(Obj. 5)**

The purchases journal of Odegaard Company Ltd. follows:

Purchases Journal   **Page 7**

| Date | Account Credited | Terms | Post. Ref. | Account Payable Cr. | Purchases Dr. | Other Accounts Dr. | | | |
						Supplies Dr.	Acct. Title	Post. Ref.	Amt. Dr.
Sept. 2	Erb Corp.	n/30		1,300	1,300				
5	Ling Office Supply	n/30		175		175			
13	Erb Corp.	2/10 n/30		847	847				
26	Marks Equipment Company Ltd.	n/30		916			Equipment		916
30	Totals			3,238	2,147	175			916

Required

1. Open general ledger accounts for Supplies, Equipment, Accounts Payable and Inventory, Post to these accounts from the purchases journal. Use dates and posting references in the ledger accounts.

2. Open accounts in the accounts payable subsidiary ledger for Erb Corp., Ling Office Supply, and Marks Equipment Company Ltd. Post from the purchases journal. Use dates and journal references in the ledger accounts.

3. Balance the Accounts Payable control account in the general ledger with the total of the balances in the accounts payable subsidiary ledger.

Exercise 6-10   *Using the cash disbursements journal* **(Obj. 5)**

During April, Crest Products Ltd. had the following transactions:

July 3   Paid $892 on account to Hellenic Corp. net of an $8 discount.
6   Purchased inventory for cash, $1,267.
11   Paid $375 for supplies.
15   Purchased inventory on credit from Monroe Corporation, $774.
16   Paid $8,062 on account to LaGrange Associates; there was no discount.
21   Purchased furniture for cash, $960.
26   Paid $3,910 on account to Graff Software for an earlier purchase of inventory. The discount was $90.
31   Made a semiannual interest payment of $800 on a long-term note payable. The entire payment was for interest.

Required

1. Draw a cash disbursements journal similar to the one illustrated in this chapter. Omit the cheque number (Ch. No.) and posting reference (Post. Ref.) columns.

2. Record the transactions in the journal. Which transaction should not be recorded in the cash disbursements journal? In what journal does it belong?

3. Total the amount columns of the journal. Determine that the total debits equal the total credits.

Exercise 6-11   *Using business documents to record transactions* **(Obj. 5)**

The following documents describe two business transactions:

Invoice		
Date:	March 14, 19X0	
Sold to:	Tailwind Bicycle Shop Ltd.	
Sold by:	Schwinn Company	
Terms:	2/10 n/30	
Items Purchased	Bicycles	

Quantity	Price	Total
4	$95	$380
2	70	140
5	60	300
Total		$820

Debit Memo		
Date:	March 20, 19X0	
Issued to:	Schwinn Company	
Issued by:	Tailwind Bicycle Shop Ltd.	
Items Returneed	Bicycles	

Quantity	Price	Total
1	$95	$ 95
1	70	70
Total		$165

Reason: Wrong sizes

Use the general journal to record these transactions and Tailwind's cash payment on March 21. Record the transactions first on the books of Tailwind Bicycle Shop and, second, on the books of Schwinn Company, which makes and sells bicycles. Round to the nearest dollar. Explanations are not required. Using the perpetual system of inventory, set up your answer in the following format:

Date	Tailwind Journal Entries	Schwinn Journal Entries

Problems   *(Group A)*

Problem 6-1A   *Using a spreadsheet to prepare an income statement and evaluate operations* **(Obj. 3)**

The following spreadsheet shows the income statement of DeGraff Wholesale Grocery Ltd.

Row Number	Column A	Column B
5	Revenues:	
6	Service revenue ⟶	
7	Rent revenue ⟶	
8		————
9	Total revenue ⟶	
10		
11	Expenses:	
12	Salary expense ⟶	
13	Supplies expense ⟶	
14	Rent expense ⟶	
15	Depreciation expense ⟶	
16		————
17	Total expenses ⟶	
18		————
19	Net income ⟶	
20		════

Required

1. Write the word *number* in the cells (indicated by arrows) where numbers will be entered.

2. Write the appropriate formula in each cell that will need a formula. Symbols from which to choose are:

+	add
–	subtract
*	multiply
/	divide
@SUM	(beginning cell..ending cell)

3. Last year DeGraff Wholesale Grocery Co. used this spreadsheet to prepare the company's budgeted income statement—which shows the company's net income goal—for the current year. It is now one year later, and DeGraff has prepared its actual income statement for the year. State how the president of the company can use this income statement in decision making.

Problem 6-2A   *Using the sales, cash receipts and general journals*   *(Obj. 4)*

The general ledger of Robertson, Inc., includes the following accounts, among others:

Cash	11	Sales Revenue	41
Accounts Receivable	12	Sales Discounts	42
Inventory	13	Sales Returns and Allowances	43
Notes Receivable	15	Interest Revenue	47
Supplies	16	Cost of Goods Sold	51
Land	18		

All credit sales are on the company's standard terms of 2/10 n/30. Transactions in May that affected sales and cash receipts were as follows:

May 2 Sold inventory on credit to Dockery Co., $1,700. Robertson's cost of these goods was $1,200.

4 As an accommodation to a competitor, sold supplies at cost, $85, receiving cash.

7 Cash sales for the week totaled $1,890 (cost $1,640).

9 Sold merchandise on account to A. L. Prince Ltd., $7,320 (cost $5,110).

10 Sold land that cost $10,000 for cash of $10,000.

11 Sold goods on account to Sloan Electric, $5,104 (cost $3,520).

12 Received cash from Dockery Co. in full settlement of its account receivable from May 2.

14 Cash sales for the week were $2,106 (cost $1,530).

15 Sold inventory on credit to the partnership of Wilkie & Blinn, $3,650 (cost $2,260).

18 Received inventory sold on May 9 to A. L. Prince Ltd. for $600. The goods shipped were unsatisfactory. These goods cost Robertson $440.

20 Sold merchandise on account to Sloan Electric, $629 (cost $450).

21 Cash sales for the week were $990 (cost $690).

22 Received $4,000 cash from A. L. Prince Ltd. in partial settlement of their account receivable.

25 Received cash from Wilkie & Blinn for its account receivable from May 15.

25 Sold goods on account to Olsen, Inc., $1,520 (cost $1,050).

27 Collected $5,125 on a note receivable, of which $125 was interest.

28 Cash sales for the week totaled $3,774 (cost $2,460).

29 Sold inventory on account to R. O. Bankston Inc., $242 (cost $170).

May 30 Received goods sold on May 25 to Olsen, Inc., for $40. The inventory was damaged in shipment. The salvage value of the goods was $10.

      31 Received $2,720 cash on account from A. L. Prince Ltd.

Required

1. Robertson records sales returns and allowances in the general journal. Use the appropriate journal to record the above transactions in a sales journal (omit the Invoice No. column), a cash receipts journal, and a general journal.

2. Total each column of the cash receipts journal. Show that the total debits equal the total credits.

3. Show how postings would be made from the journals by writing the account numbers and check marks in the appropriate places in the journals.

Problem 6-3A   *Correcting errors in the cash receipts journal* **(Obj. 4)**

The cash receipts journal below contains five entries. All five entries are for legitimate cash receipt transactions, but the journal contains some errors in recording the transactions. In fact, only one entry is correct, and each of the other four entries contains one error.

Required

1. Identify the correct entry.
2. Identify the error in each of the other four entries.
3. Using the following format, prepare a corrected cash receipts journal.

Cash Receipts Journal   **Page 13**

| | Debits | | | Credits | | | | |
| | | | | | Other Accounts | | | |
Date	Cash	Sales Discounts	Accounts Receivable	Sales Revenue	Account Title	P.R.	Amount	Cost of Goods Sold Dr. Inventory Cr.
5/6		600		600				290
7	429	22			Marc Fortin	✔	451	
12	2,160				Note Receivable	13	2,000	
					Interest Revenue	45	160	
18				330				150
24	1,100		770					
	3,689	622	770	930	Totals		2,611	440
	(11)	(42)	(12)	(41)			(✔)	51/13

Total Dr. = $4,311   Total Cr. = $4,311

Cash Receipts Journal Page 13

	Debits		Credits					
					Other Accounts			
Date	Cash	Sales Discounts	Accounts Receivable	Sales Revenue	Account Title	P.R.	Amount	Cost of Goods Sold Dr. Inventory Cr.
5/6 7 12 18 24					Marc Fortin Note Receivable Interest Revenue	✔ 13 45		
	4,289	22	1,221	930	Totals		2,160	
	(11)	(42)	(12)	(41)			(✔)	

Total Dr. = $4,311   Total Cr. = $4,311

Problem 6-4A *Using the purchases, cash disbursements and general journals* **(Obj. 5)**

The general ledger of Klassen, Inc., includes the following accounts:

Cash	111	Furniture	187
Inventory	131	Accounts Payable	211
Prepaid Insurance	161	Rent Expense	564
Supplies	171	Utilities Expense	583

Transactions in August that affected purchases and cash disbursements were as follows:

Aug. 1 Purchased inventory on credit from Wood Corp., $3,900. Terms were 2/10 n/30.
  1 Paid monthly rent, debiting Rent Expense for $2,000.
  5 Purchased supplies on credit terms of 2/10 n/30 from Ross Supply, $450.
  8 Paid electricity bill, $588.
  9 Purchased furniture on account from A-1 Office Supply Ltd., $4,100. Payment terms were net 30.
  10 Returned the furniture to A-1 Office Supply. It was the wrong color.
  11 Paid Wood Corp. the amount owed on the purchase of August 1.
  12 Purchased inventory on account from Wynne, Inc., $4,400. Terms were 3/10 n/30.
  13 Purchased inventory for cash, $655.
  14 Paid a semiannual insurance premium, debiting Prepaid Insurance, $1,200.
  15 Paid our account payable to Ross Supply, from August 5.
  18 Paid gas and water bills, $196.
  21 Purchased inventory on credit terms of 1/10 n/45 from Software, Inc., $5,200.
  21 Paid account payable to Wynne, Inc., from August 12.
  22 Purchased supplies on account from Office Sales, Inc., $274. Terms were net 30.
  25 Returned $1,200 of the inventory purchased on August 21 to Software, Inc., issuing a debit memo for $1,200.
  31 Paid Software, Inc., the net amount owed from August 21, less the return, on August 25.

Required

1. Klassen, Inc. records purchase returns in the general journal. Use the appropriate journal to record the above transactions in a purchases journal, a cash disbursements journal (omit the Cheque No. column), and a general journal.

2. Total each column of the special journals. Show that the total debits equal the total credits in each special journal.

3. Show how postings would be made from the journals by writing the account numbers and check marks in the appropriate places in the journals.

Problem 6-5A   *Understand how manual accounting systems are used, use the cash disbursements journal* **(Obj. 2, 4)**

The Tullis Company had the following transactions for the month of April:

April 1   Sold $2,000 of merchandise to J. James, terms 2/10 n/30.

3   Purchased $9,000 of merchandise from MNO Suppliers, terms net 30.

5   Sold old equipment for $10,000; receiving $1,000 and a note for the balance.

6   Paid for the purchase of April 3 (MNO Suppliers), cheque #12.

7   Paid $7,000 wages to employee, cheque #13.

9   Paid dividends of $10,000, cheque #14.

11   Collected $980 from J. James (April 1) with the discount allowed and issued a credit memo for $500 of merchandise returned as defective.

13   Purchased equipment from MB Machinery, $15,000, terms 2/10 n/30.

14   Issued a debit memo to MB Machinery (April 13) for $1,000 of equipment returned as defective.

15   Sold $6,000 of merchandise to S. Smith, receiving $1,000 and a promise to pay the balance in 30 days. Inventory had a cost of $4,000.

16   Paid the account owing to MB Machinery (April 13, 14), cheque #15.

17   Purchased $25,000 of equipment from Johnson equipment, terms net 60.

19   Sold 2,000 common shares at $2 per share.

20   Sold used equipment for $19,000 to D. Dawson, terms net 60.

21   The major shareholder (R. Aphid) sold 2,000 of her shares for $5 per share.

22   Paid a $6,000 note due to the Commercial Bank, plus interest of $600, cheque # 16.

24   Sold $1,500 of merchandise for cash; inventory cost was $1,000.

25   Paid $1,000 to Revenue Canada for taxes owing from 19X0, cheque #17.

26   Returned $3,000 of the merchandise purchased from MNO Suppliers.

27   Received $2,000 from D. Dawson from the sale of equipment on April 20.

28   Purchased inventory for $4,000 from R. Angel Co., paying $1,000 down (cheque #18) and promising to pay the balance in 30 days.

30   Recorded the adjustments for the month of April.

Required

1. Indicate which journal would be used to record each of the transactions assuming Tullis Company uses:
   - a General Journal
   - a Sales Journal (as illustrated in the chapter)
   - a Cash Receipts Journal (as illustrated in the chapter)
   - a Purchases Journal (as illustrated in the chapter) and
   - a Cash Disbursements Journal as illustrated on the following page.

2. Record the appropriate transactions in the "Cash Disbursements Journal" as shown on the following page.

3. Show the appropriate posting references for the "Cash Disbursements Journal" assuming all postings have been made. Select your own three-digit account numbers.

Cash Disbursements Journal   **Page 11**

| Date | CH. # | Account Debited | P R | Debits | | Credits | |
				Other Accounts	Accounts Payable	Inventory	Cash

Problem 6-6A   *Understand how manual accounting systems are used, use the cash receipts journal   (Obj. 4)*

The Robotics Company had the following transactions for the month of June:

June 1   Sold $5,000 of merchandise to J. Jones, terms 2/10 n/30.

3   Purchased $8,000 of merchandise from ABC Suppliers, terms net 30.

5   Sold old equipment for $10,000, receiving $1,000 and a note for the balance. The equipment had cost Robotics $30,000 and had been depreciated by $20,000.

6   Sold $2,000 of merchandise for cash; inventory cost was $ 1,500.

7   Sold $7,000 of merchandise to A. Abbott, terms 2/10 n/30.

9   Paid wages of $1,500.

11   Collected $980 from J. Jones (June 1) with the discount allowed and issued a credit memo for $2,000 of merchandise returned as defective.

13   Received the balance owing from J. Jones (June 1 and 11).

14   Issued a credit memo to A. Abbott (June 7) for $1,000 of merchandise returned as defective.

15   Sold $6,000 of merchandise to S. Smith, receiving $1,000 and a promise to pay the balance in 30 days. Inventory had a cost of $4,000.

16   Received the balance owing from A. Abbott (June 7 and 14).

17   Purchased $25,000 of equipment from Johnson Equipment, terms net 60.

19   Sold 2,000 common shares at $2 per share.

20   Sold $1,500 of merchandise for cash; inventory cost was $1,000.

21   The major shareholder (R. Robot) sold 5,000 of her shares for $3 per share.

22   Borrowed $6,000 from the Royal Bank, signing a 60-day note.

24   Sold used equipment for $13,000 to D. Davidson, terms net 60.

June 25   Paid $1,000 to ABC Suppliers for the purchase of June 3.

25   Returned $3,000 of the merchandise purchased from ABC Suppliers.

27   Received $1,000 from D. Davidson from the sale of equipment on June 24.

28   Sold $2,000 of merchandise to A. Cobbett, terms 2/10 n/30.

30   Recorded the adjustments for the month of June.

Required

1. Indicate which journal would be used to record each of the transactions assuming Robotics Company uses:
   - a General Journal
   - a Sales Journal (as illustrated in the chapter)
   - a Cash Disbursements Journal (as illustrated in the chapter)
   - a Purchases Journal (as illustrated in the chapter) and
   - a Cash Receipts Journal as illustrated below.

2. Record the appropriate transactions in the "Cash Receipts Journal" as shown below. Robotics Company operates in a province with a 5% Sales Tax applied to all sales.

3. Show the appropriate posting references for the "Cash Receipts Journal" assuming all postings have been made. Select your own three-digit account numbers.

Cash Receipts Journal   **Page 1**

| | Debits | | Credits | | | | | |
| | | | | | Other Accounts | | | |
Date	Cash	Sales Discounts	Accounts Receivable	Sales Revenue	Account Title	Post. Ref.	Amount	Cost of Goods Sold Dr. Inventory Cr.

Problem 6-1B   *Using a spreadsheet to prepare a partial balance sheet and evaluate financial positions   (Obj. 3)*

The following spreadsheet shows the assets section of the Quartz Products Company balance sheet:

Row Number	Column A	Column B
5	Assets:	
6	Current asset:	
7	Cash ⟶	
8	Receivables	_____
9	Inventory ⟶	
10		_____
11	Total current assets	
12		
13	Equipment ⟶	
14	Accumulated depreciation ⟶	
15		_____
16	Equipment, net ⟶	
17		_____
18	Total assets ⟶	
19		════════

Required

1. Write the word *number* in the cells (indicated by arrows) where numbers will be entered.

2. Write the appropriate formula in each cell that will need a formula. Symbols from which to choose are:

+	add
−	subtract
*	multiply
/	divide
@SUM	(beginning cell..ending cell)

3. Last year Quartz Products Company used this spreadsheet to prepare the company's balance sheet for the current year. The budgeted balance sheet shows the company's goal for total current assets at the end of the year. It is now one year later, and Quartz Products Company has prepared its actual year-end balance sheet. State how the company president can use this balance sheet in decision making.

Problem 6-2B   *Using the sales, cash receipts, and general journals   (Obj. 4)*

The general ledger of Vasquez Supply Corp. includes the following accounts:

Cash	111	Sales Revenue	411
Accounts Receivable	112	Sales Discounts	412
Notes Receivable	115	Sales Returns and Allowances	413
Inventory	131	Interest Revenue	417
Equipment	141	Gain on Sale of Land	418
Land	142	Cost of Goods Sold	511

All credit sales are on the company's standard terms of 2/10 n/30. Transactions in February that affected sales and cash receipts were as follows:

Feb. 1   Sold inventory on credit to Ruth Lott, $300. Vasquez's cost of these goods was $214.

5   As an accommodation to another company, sold new equipment for its cost of $770, receiving cash in this amount.

6   Cash sales for the week totaled $2,107 (cost $1,362).

8   Sold merchandise on account to McNair Co., $2,830 (cost $1,789).

9   Sold land that cost $22,000 for cash of $40,000.

11   Sold goods on account to Nickerson Builders Inc., $6,099 (cost $3,853).

11   Received cash from Ruth Lott in full settlement of her account receivable from February 1.

13   Cash sales for the week were $1,995 (cost $1,286).

15   Sold inventory on credit to Montez and Montez, a partnership, $800 (cost $517).

18   Received inventory sold on February 8 to McNair Co. for $120. The goods we shipped were unsatisfactory. These goods cost Vasquez $73.

19   Sold merchandise on account to Nickerson Builders, $3,900 (cost $2,618).

20   Cash sales for the week were $2,330 (cost $1,574).

21   Received $1,200 cash from McNair Co. in partial settlement of its account receivable. There was no discount.

22   Received cash from Montez and Montez for its account receivable from February 15.

22   Sold goods on account to Diamond, Inc., $2,022 (cost $1,325).

25   Collected $4,200 on a note receivable, of which $200 was interest.

27   Cash sales for the week totaled $2,970 (cost $1,936).

27   Sold inventory on account to Littleton Corporation, $2,290 (cost $1,434).

28   Received goods sold on February 21 to Diamond, Inc. for $680. The goods were damaged in shipment. The salvage value of these goods was $96.

28   Received $1,510 cash on account from McNair Co. There was no discount.

Required

1. Use the appropriate journal to record the above transactions in a sales journal (omit the Invoice No. column), a cash receipts journal, and a general journal. Vasquez records sales returns and allowances in the general journal.

2. Total each column of the cash receipts journal. Determine that the total debits equal the total credits.

3. Show how postings would be made from the journals by writing the account numbers and check marks in the appropriate places in the journals.

Problem 6-3B   *Correcting errors in the cash receipts journal*   **(Obj. 4)**

The cash receipts journal below contains five entries. All five entries are for legitimate cash receipt transactions, but the journal contains some errors in recording the transactions. In fact, only one entry is correct, and each of the other four entries contains one error.

Required

1. Identify the correct entry.

2. Identify the error in each of the other four entries.

3. Using the following format, prepare a corrected cash receipts journal.

Cash Receipts Journal   Page 5

Date		Debits				Credits				
							Other Accounts			
										Cost of Goods
										Sold Dr.
		Sales	Accounts	Sales						Inventory Cr.
Date	Cash	Discounts	Receivable	Revenue	Account Title		P.R.	Amount	
7/5	711	34	745		Meg Davis		✔		
9			346	346	Carl Ryther		✔		
10	8,000			8,000	Land		19		
19	73								44
31	1,060			1,133					631
	9,844	34	1,091	9,479	Totals			0	675
	(11)	(42)	(12)	(41)				(✔)	51/13

Total Dr. = $9,878   Total Cr. = $10,570

Cash Receipts Journal   Page 5

Date		Debits				Credits				
							Other Accounts			
										Cost of Goods
										Sold Dr.
		Sales	Accounts	Sales						Inventory Cr.
Date	Cash	Discounts	Receivable	Revenue	Account Title		P.R.	Amount	
7/5					Meg Davis		✔		
9					Carl Ryther		✔		
10					Land		19		
19									
31									
	10,190	34	1,091	1,133	Totals			8,000	
	(11)	(42)	(12)	(41)				(✔)	51/13

Total Dr. = $10,224   Total Cr. = $10,224

Problem 6-4B   *Using the purchases, cash disbursements, and general journals*   **(Obj. 5)**

The general ledger of Greensboro Custom Frames includes the following accounts:

Cash	111	Equipment	189
Inventory	131	Accounts Payable	211
Prepaid Insurance	161	Rent Expense	562
Supplies	171	Utilities Expense	565

Transactions in March that affected purchases and cash disbursements were as follows:

Mar. 1   Paid monthly rent, debiting Rent Expense for $1,350.
3   Purchased inventory on credit from Broussard Ltd., $4,900. Terms were 2/15 n/45.
4   Purchased supplies on credit terms of 2/10 n/30 from Harmon Sales Ltd., $800.

Mar. 7   Paid gas and water bills, $406.

10   Purchased equipment on account from Lancer Corp., $1,050. Payment terms were 2/10 n/30.

11   Returned the equipment to Lancer Corp. It was defective.

12   Paid Broussard Ltd. the amount owed on the purchase of March 3.

12   Purchased inventory on account from Lancer Corp., $1,100. Terms were 2/10 n/30.

14   Purchased inventory for cash, $1,585.

15   Paid an insurance premium, debiting Prepaid Insurance, $2,416.

16   Paid our account payable to Harmon Sales Ltd. from March 4.

17   Paid electricity bill, $165.

20   Paid account payable to Lancer Corp., less the discount, from March 12.

21   Purchased supplies on account from Master Supply, $754. Terms were net 30.

22   Purchased inventory on credit terms of 1/10 n/30 from Linz Brothers, $3,400.

26   Returned part of inventory purchased for $500 on March 22, to Linz Brothers.

31   Paid Linz Brothers the net amount owed from March 22, less the return on March 26.

Required

1. Use the appropriate journal to record the above transactions in a purchases journal, a cash disbursements journal (omit the Cheque No. column), and a general journal. Greensboro records purchase returns in the general journal.

2. Total each column of the special journals. Show that the total debits equal the total credits in each special journal.

3. Show how postings would be made from the journals by writing the account numbers and check marks in the appropriate places in the journals.

Problem 6-5B   *Understand how manual accounting systems are used, use the cash disbursements journal*   **(Obj. 2, 4)**

The Venos Company had the following transactions for the month of April:

April 1   Sold $8,000 of merchandise to J. Thoms, terms 2/10 n/30.

3   Purchased $6,000 of merchandise from STU Suppliers, terms net 30.

5   Sold old equipment for $7,000; receiving $1,000 and a note for the balance.

6   Paid for the purchase of April 3 (STU Suppliers), cheque #12.

7   Paid $11,000 wages to employee, cheque #13.

9   Paid dividends of $15,000, cheque #14.

11   Collected $1,960 from J. Thoms (April 1) with the discount allowed and issued a credit memo for $1,000 of merchandise returned as defective.

13   Purchased equipment from DE Machinery, $10,000, terms 2/10 n/30.

14   Issued a debit memo to DE Machinery (April 13) for $2,000 of equipment returned as defective.

15   Sold $5,000 of merchandise to S. DePloy, receiving $2,000 and a promise to pay the balance in 30 days. Inventory had a cost of $3,000.

16   Paid the account owing to DE Machinery (April 13, 14), cheque #15.

17   Purchased $30,000 of equipment from Alfreds Equipment, terms net 60.

19   Sold 6,000 common shares at $2 per share.

20   Sold used equipment for $13,000 to S. Lawson, terms net 60.

21   The major shareholder (R. Balfry) sold 6,000 of cher shares for $5 per share.

22   Paid a $10,000 note due to the Commercial Bank, plus interest of $1,000, cheque #16.

April 24   Sold $3,500 of merchandise for cash; inventory cost was $2,000

25   Paid $1,500 to Revenue Canada for taxes owing from 19X0, cheque #17.

26   Returned $1,000 of the merchandise purchased from STU Suppliers.

27   Received $3,000 from S. Lawson from the sale of equipment on April 20.

28   Purchased inventory for $6,000 from R. Demon Co., paying $2,000 down (cheque #18) and promising to pay the balance in 30 days.

30   Recorded the adjustments for the month of April.

Required

1. Indicate which journal would be used to record each of the transactions assuming Venos Company uses:
   - a General Journal
   - a Sales Journal (as illustrated in the chapter)
   - a Cash Receipts Journal (as illustrated in the chapter)
   - a Purchases Journal (as illustrated in the chapter) and
   - a Cash Disbursements Journal as illustrated below.

2. Record the appropriate transactions in the "Cash Disbursements Journal" as shown below.

3. Show the appropriate posting references for the "Cash Disbursements Journal" assuming all postings have been made. Select your own three-digit account numbers.

Cash Disbursements Journal   Page 11

| | | | | Debits | | Credits | |
Date	CH. #	Account Debited	P R	Other Accounts	Accounts Payable	Inventory	Cash

Problem 6-6B   *Understand how manual accounting systems are used, use the cash receipts journal*   **(Obj. 2, 4)**

The Autotron Company had the following transactions for the month of June:

June   1   Sold $6,000 of merchandise to A. Allen, terms 2/10 n/30.

3   Purchased $9,000 of merchandise from XYZ Suppliers, terms net 30.

5   Sold old equipment for $9,000, receiving $1,000 and a note for the balance. The equipment had cost Autotron $20,000 and had been depreciated by $11,000.

June   6   Sold $3,000 of merchandise for cash, inventory cost was $2,000.

7   Sold $8,000 of merchandise to A. Collin, terms 2/10 n/30.

9   Paid wages of $2,500.

11   Collected $1,960 from A. Allen (June 1) with the discount allowed and issued a credit memo for $1,000 of merchandise returned as defective.

13   Received the balance owing from A. Allen (June 1 and 11).

14   Issued a credit memo to A. Collin (June 7) for $2,000 of merchandise returned as defective.

15   Sold $7,000 of merchandise to S. Davis, receiving $2,000 and a promise to pay the balance in 30 days. The inventory had cost $4,500.

16   Received the balance owing from A. Collin (June 7 and 14).

17   Purchased $20,000 of equipment from Nickells equipment, terms net 60.

19   Sold 4,000 common shares at $3 per share.

20   Sold $2,500 of merchandise for cash; inventory cost was $1,500.

21   The major shareholder (R. Falter) sold 6,000 of her shares for $3 per share.

22   Borrowed $9,000 from the Royal Bank, signing a 60-day note.

24   Sold used equipment for $12,000 to D. Gallanty, terms net 60.

25   Paid $3,000 to XYZ Suppliers for the purchase of June 3.

26   Returned $2,000 of the merchandise purchased from XYZ Suppliers.

27   Received $2,000 from D. Gallanty from the sale of equipment on June 24.

28   Sold $3,000 of merchandise to A. Melissa, terms 2/10 n/30.

30   Recorded the adjustments for the month of June.

Required

1. Indicate which journal would be used to record each of the transactions assuming Autotron Company uses:
   - a General Journal
   - a Sales Journal (as illustrated in the chapter)
   - a Cash Disbursements Journal (as illustrated in the chapter)
   - a Purchases Journal (as illustrated in the chapter) and
   - a Cash Receipts Journal as illustrated below.

2. Record the appropriate transactions in the "Cash Receipts Journal" as shown at the top of p. 324. Autotron Company operates in a province with a 5% Sales Tax applied to all sales.

3. Show the appropriate posting references for the "Cash Receipts Journal" assuming all postings have been made. Select your own three-digit account numbers.

Challenge Problems

Problem 6-1C   *Advantage of an effective accounting system*   *(Obj. 1)*

An accounting information system that provides timely, accurate information to management is an important asset of any organization. This is especially true as organizations become larger and move into different parts of the world. The integration of computers into many organization's information systems has enhanced their usefulness to the organization.

Required

Assume your older sister is a pharmacist. She regards an information system as simply an accounting system that keeps track of her revenues and expenses. Explain to her how an effective accounting information system can make her a more effective pharmacist.

Cash Receipts Journal

Date	Debits		Credits					Cost of Goods Sold Dr. Inventory Cr.
					Other Accounts			
	Cash	Sales Discounts	Accounts Receivable	Sales Revenue	Account Title	Post. Ref.	Amount	

Problem 6-2C   *Providing advice about a computerized accounting system*   *(Obj. 2)*

Information technology is a "buzz word" you hear more and more frequently. Everyone wants the latest technology. Your brother has asked you about installing this wonderful computer system in his car dealership and auto repair business. The salesperson has promised your brother that the system "will do everything you want and then some." Your brother has come to you for advice about acquiring this new computerized accounting information system. At present he uses a manual accounting system.

Required

Provide the advice your brother wants, focusing on the costs of the new computerized accounting information system; your brother has been told all the positive aspects of purchasing the system.

Extending Your Knowledge

Decision Problems

1. Reconstructing transactions from amounts posted to the accounts receivable ledger   (Obj. 4)

A fire destroyed some accounting records of Roemer Corp. The owner, Anne Roemer, asks for your help in reconstructing the records. *She needs to know the beginning and ending balances of Accounts Receivable and the credit sales and cash receipts on account from customers during March.* All Roemer Corp. sales are on credit, with payment terms of 2/10 n/30. All cash receipts on account reached Roemer within the 10-day discount period, except as noted. The only accounting record preserved from the fire is the accounts receivable subsidiary ledger, which follows:

Adam Cline

Date	Item	Jrnl. Ref.	Debit	Credit	Balance
Mar. 8		S6	2,378		2,378
16		S.6	903		3,281
18		CR.8		2,378	903
19		J.5		221	682
27		CR.8		682	-0-

Lou Gross

Date	Item	Jrnl. Ref.	Debit	Credit	Balance
Mar. 1	Balance				1,096
5		CR.8		1,096	-0-
11		S.6	396		396
21		CR.8		396	-0-
24		S.6	1,944		1,944

Norris Associates Ltd.

Date	Item	Jrnl. Ref.	Debit	Credit	Balance
Mar. 1	Balance				883
15		S.6	2,635		3,518
29		CR.8		883*	2,635

---

* Cash receipt did not occur within the discount period.

Suzuki, Inc.

Date	Item	Ref. Jrnl.	Debit	Credit	Balance
Mar. 1	Balance				440
3		CR.8		440	-0-
25		S.6	3,655		3,655
29		S.6	1,123		4,778

2. Understanding an accounting system   (Obj. 4, 5)

The external auditor must ensure that the amounts shown on the balance sheet for Accounts Receivable represent actual amounts that customers owe the company. Each customer account in the accounts receivable subsidiary ledger must represent an actual credit sale to the person indicated, and the customer's balance must not have been collected. This auditing concept is called *validity,* or *validating* the accounts receivable.

The auditor must also ensure that all amounts that the company owes are included in Accounts Payable and other liability accounts. For example, all credit purchases of inventory made by the company (and not yet paid) should be included in the balance of the Accounts Payable account. This auditing concept is called *completeness.*

Required

Suggest how an auditor might test a customer's account receivable balance for validity. Indicate how the auditor might test the balance of the Accounts Payable account for completeness.

Ethical Issue

On a recent trip to Poland, Randolph Buchholz, sales manager of Microelectronic Devices Inc., took his wife at company expense. Erika Schwartz, vice-president of sales and Buchholz's boss, thought his total travel and entertainment expenses of $10,000 seemed excessive. However, Schwartz approved the reimbursement because she owed Buchholz a favor. Schwartz, well aware that the company president routinely reviewed all expenses recorded in the cash disbursements journal, had the accountant record the expenses of Buchholz's wife in the general journal as follows:

Sales Promotion Expense...	3,500	
Cash		3,500

Required

1. Does recording the transaction in the general journal rather than in the cash disbursements journal affect the amounts of cash and total expenses reported in the financial statements?
2. Why did Ms. Schwartz want this transaction recorded in the general journal?
3. What is the ethical issue in this situation? What role does accounting play in the ethical issue?

Comprehensive Problems for Part One

1. Completing a Merchandiser's Accounting Cycle

The end-of-month trial balance of Regina Building Materials at January 31 of the current year follows:

Regina Building Materials Ltd.
Trial Balance
January 31, 19XX

Account Number	Account	Debit	Credit
		Balance	
11	Cash	$ 6,430	
12	Accounts receivable	19,090	
13	Inventory	65,400	
14	Supplies	2,700	
15	Building	188,170	
16	Accumulated depreciation—building		$ 36,000
17	Fixtures	45,600	
18	Accumulated depreciation—fixtures		5,800
21	Accounts payable		28,300
22	Salary payable		
23	Interest payable		
24	Unearned sales revenue		6,560
25	Note payable, long-term		87,000
31	Common stock		20,000
32	Retained earnings		124,980
33	Dividends	9,200	
41	Sales revenue		177,970
42	Sales discounts	7,300	
43	Sales returns and allowances	8,140	
51	Cost of goods sold	103,000	
54	Selling expense	21,520	
55	General expense	10,060	
56	Interest expense		
	Total	$486,610	$486,610

Additional data at January 31, 19XX:

a. Supplies consumed during the month, $1,500. One half is selling expense, and the other half is general expense.

b. Depreciation for the month: building, $4,000; fixtures, $4,800. One fourth of depreciation is selling expense, and three fourths is general expense.

c. Unearned sales revenue still unearned, $1,200.

d. Accrued salaries, a general expense, $1,150.

e. Accrued interest expense, $780.

f. Inventory on hand, $63,720.

Required

1. Using three-column accounts, open the accounts listed on the trial balance, inserting their unadjusted balances. Date the balances of the following accounts January 1: Supplies; Building; Accumulated Depreciation—Building; Fixtures; Accumulated Depreciation—Fixtures; Unearned Sales Revenue; and Retained Earnings. Date the balance of Dividends, January 31.

2. Enter the trial balance on an accounting work sheet, and complete the work sheet for the month ended January 31 of the current year. Regina groups all operating expenses under two accounts, Selling Expense and General Expense. Leave two blank lines under Selling Expense and three blank lines under General Expense.

3. Prepare the company's multiple-step income statement and statement of retained earnings for the month ended January 31 of the current year. Also prepare the balance sheet at that date in report form.

4. Journalize the adjusting and closing entries at January 31, using page 3 of the journal.

5. Post the adjusting and closing entries, using dates and posting references.

6. Compute Regina's current ratio and debt ratio at January 31, and compare these values with the industry averages of 1.9 for the current ratio and .57 for the debt ratio. Compute the gross margin percentage and the rate of inventory turnover for the month (the inventory balance at the end of December was $67,100) and compare these ratio values with the industry averages of .26 for the gross margin percentage and 1.0 for inventory turnover. Does Regina Building Materials Ltd. appear to be stronger or weaker than the average company in the building materials industry?

2. Completing the Accounting Cycle for a Merchandising Entity

Note: This problem can be solved with or without special journals. See Requirement 2.

Canmore Ltd. closes its books and prepares financial statements at the end of each month. The company completed the following transactions during August.

Aug. 1   Issued cheque no. 682 for August office rent $2,000. (Debit Rent Expense.)

2   Issued cheque no. 683 to pay salaries of $1,240, which includes salary payable of $930 from July 31. Canmore does not use reversing entries.

2   Issued invoice no. 503 for sale on account to R. T. Loeb, $600. Canmore's cost of this merchandise was $190.

3   Purchased inventory on credit terms of 1/15 n/60 from Grant Publishers Ltd., $1,400.

4   Received net amount of cash on account from Fullam Corp., $2,156, within the discount period.

4   Sold inventory for cash, $330 (cost, $104).

5   Received from Park-Hee, Inc., merchandise that had been sold earlier for $550 (cost, $174).

5   Issued cheque no. 684 to purchase supplies for cash, $780.

6   Collected interest revenue of $1,100.

7   Issued invoice no. 504 for sale on account to K. D. Skipper, $2,400 (cost, $759).

8   Issued cheque no. 685 to pay Federal Corp. $2,600 of the amount owed at July 31. This payment occurred after the end of the discount period.

11   Issued cheque no. 686 to pay Grant Publishers the net amount owed from August 3.

Aug. 12	Received cash from R. T. Loeb in full settlement of her account receivable from August 2.
16	Issued cheque no. 687 to pay salary expense of $1,240.
19	Purchased inventory for cash, $850, issuing cheque no. 688.
22	Purchased furniture on credit terms of 3/15 n/60 from Beaver Corporation, $510.
23	Sold inventory on account to Fullam Corp., issuing invoice no. 505 for $9,966 (cost, $3,152).
24	Received half the July 31 amount receivable from K. D. Skipper—after the end of the discount period.
25	Issued cheque no. 689 to pay utilities, $432.
26	Purchased supplies on credit terms of 2/10 n/30 from Federal Corp., $180.
30	Returned damaged inventory to company from whom Canmore made the cash purchase on August 19, receiving cash of $850.
30	Granted a sales allowance of $175 to K. D. Skipper.
31	Purchased inventory on credit terms of 1/10 n/30 from Suncrest Supply, $8,330.
31	Issued cheque no. 690 for dividends, $1,700.

Required

1. Open these accounts with their account numbers and July 31 balances in the various ledgers.

General Ledger:

101	Cash	$ 4,490
102	Accounts Receivable	22,560
104	Interest Receivable	
105	Inventory	41,800
109	Supplies	1,340
117	Prepaid Insurance	2,200
140	Note Receivable, Long-term	11,000
160	Furniture	37,270
161	Accumulated Depreciation	10,550
201	Accounts Payable	12,600
204	Salary Payable	930
207	Interest Payable	320
208	Unearned Sales Revenue	
220	Note Payable, Long-term	42,000
301	Common Stock	25,000
302	Retained Earnings	29,260
303	Dividends	
400	Income Summary	
401	Sales Revenue	
402	Sales Discounts	
403	Sales Returns and Allowances	
410	Interest Revenue	
501	Cost of Goods Sold	
510	Salary Expense	
513	Rent Expense	
514	Depreciation Expense	
516	Insurance Expense	
517	Utilities Expense	
519	Supplies Expense	
523	Interest Expense	

Accounts Receivable Subsidiary Ledger: Fullam Corp., $2,200; R. T. Loeb; Park-Hee, Inc., $11,590; K. D. Skipper, $8,770.

Accounts Payable Subsidiary Ledger: Beaver Corporation; Federal Corp., $12,600; Grant Publishers; Suncrest Supply.

2. Ask your professor for directions. Journalize the August transactions either in the general journal (page 9; explanations not required) or, as illustrated in Chapter 6, in a series of special journals: a sales journal (page 4), a cash receipts journal (page 11), a purchases journal (page 8), a cash disbursements journal (page 5), and a general journal (page 9). Canmore makes all credit sales on terms of 2/10 n/30 and uses a perpetual inventory system as illustrated in Chapter 5.

3. Post daily to the accounts receivable subsidiary ledger and the accounts payable subsidiary ledger. On August 31, post to the general ledger.

4. Prepare a trial balance in the Trial Balance columns of a work sheet, and use the following information to complete the work sheet for the month ended August 31.
   a. Accrued interest revenue, $100.
   b. Supplies on hand, $990.
   c. Prepaid insurance expired, $550.
   d. Depreciation expense, $230.
   e. Accrued salary expense, $1,030.
   f. Accrued interest expense, $320.
   g. Unearned sales revenue, $450.*
   h. Inventory on hand, $46,700.

5. Prepare Canmore's multiple-step income statement and statement of retained earnings for August. Prepare the balance sheet at August 31.

6. Journalize and post the adjusting and closing entries.

7. Prepare a postclosing trial balance at August 31. Also, balance the total of the customer accounts in the accounts receivable subsidiary ledger against the Accounts Receivable balance in the general ledger. Do the same for the accounts payable subsidiary ledger and Accounts Payable in the general ledger.

3. Group Project: Preparing a Business Plan for a Service Entity

List what you have learned thus far in the course. On the basis of what you have learned, refine your plan for promoting a rock concert to include everything you believe you must do to succeed in this business venture.

4. Preparing a Business Plan for a Merchandising Entity

As you work through Part 2 of this book (Chapters 7–12), you will be examining in detail the current assets, current liabilities, and plant assets of a business. Most of the organizations that form the context for business activity in the remainder of the book are merchandising entities. Therefore, in a group or individually—as directed by your instructor—develop a plan for beginning and operating an audio/video store or other type of business. Develop your plan in as much detail as you can. Remember that the business manager who attends to the most details delivers the best product at the lowest price for customers.

At the end of each Part (after Chapters 12, 17, and 19), we will revisit this plan. Each time we will ask you to refine your plan on the basis of what you learned in that Part. At the end of the course, you will have a good idea of how to plan and operate a business. That is what accounting is all about.

---

*On August 2, Canmore Ltd. sold inventory to R. T. Loeb and collected in full on August 12. Upon learning that the shipment to Loeb was incomplete, Canmore plans to ship the goods to her during September. At August 31, $450 of unearned sales revenue needs to be recorded. The cost of this merchandise is $142.

VIDEO CASE

CBC ❋

Earth Buddy:
The Role of Accounting in a New Business

Many young people dream of owning their own business. The four partners started their own business after graduating from university in 1993; the company they formed was Earth Buddies. The product they were producing and selling is a head-shaped object that spouts hair (grass) when watered. The concept is very simple: a nylon stocking or panty-hose leg is filled with sawdust and some grass seed; the head is then shaped and a face is painted on it; finally, the head is placed in a printed box and it is ready for shipping.

The company has been very succesful and has some large Canadian orders from KMart, Canadian Tire, and Zellers. Then they landed a possible order from KMart U.S. for 500,000 Earth Buddies that could provide the partners with a half-million dollars profit. But they must produce the 500,000 units quickly to get the order. The level of production must be increased substantially to 16,000 units a day. More production staff is needed.

The partners are good at marketing and production. They were able to get the large order and produce the needed Earth Buddies. But successful companies need more than than a product; they need more than marketing and production skills. They also need accounting skills.

Their accountant tells Anton, the president, that the partners regard the administration of the company as something they do in their spare time. He tells Anton and the other partners that the books are a mess. The partners have been too busy making money to keep track of it.

The partners think the company needs a large loan from the bank to finance the production of Earth Buddies for the KMart U.S. order. They go to their banker and are able to obtain a line-of-credit for the necessary funds. Then, when the books are straightened out, the partners discover that they have sufficent funds without the bank loan.

The order from KMart U.S. comes in; the partners will earn the $500,000 plus profit. They are a success; so much so that Anton is asked to address a class at Ryerson University in Toronto about entrepreneurship.

CASE QUESTIONS

1. What do you think the partners in Earth Buddies would need "accounting skills" to do based on the video?

2. Why do you think KMart U.S. might be interested in the partner's financial statements?

3. What are some potential problems that the books' being in a mess might cause?

4. What have you learned about accounting from this video case?

CHAPTER 7
Internal Control and Cash Transactions

"Fraud costs more than you think. Why is this important in business today? . . . The threat of fraud has never been greater, and the police and government have fewer and fewer resources to combat it. . . . No one is immune from fraud," say Tedd Avey and Hazel de Burgh (quoted from the *Financial Post* Conference "Combating Fraud," October 5, 1994).

"The main point to consider when developing strategies for overcoming . . . fraud is to look at the human element of fraud . . . [H]ire honest people . . . and . . . keep people honest [through psychological deterrents, physical deterrents, and improved detection controls]."

Jan Gibson was a cashier at an office of the brokerage firm Brown Monroe & Company Ltd. Her problems began when appendicitis forced her to miss work and office manager Bruce Ritchie received complaints from customers who had not received credit for their deposits. Ritchie uncovered an elaborate embezzlement scheme that Gibson had begun five years earlier.

The court found that Gibson had stolen a total of $610,934 in a "rob-Peter-to-pay-Paul scheme": She was transferring customer deposits into her personal account and concealing the missing amounts with deposits from other customers. In this way customer accounts always balanced as long as Gibson was present to respond to customer inquiries. She simply explained that the account was temporarily out-of-balance. But while she was recovering in the hospital, her replacement was unable to explain the irregularities to customers' accounts. When all the evidence came to light, it pointed in the direction of the missing employee, who was sentenced to jail. Ritchie then understood why Gibson had never taken a vacation.

CHAPTER OBJECTIVES

After studying this chapter, you should be able to

1 Define internal control

2 Identify the characteristics of an effective system of internal control

3 Prepare a bank reconciliation and related journal entries

4 Apply internal controls to cash receipts

5 Apply internal controls to cash disbursements

6 Account for petty cash transactions

7 Weigh ethical judgments in business

A1 Use the voucher system

What went wrong at the Brown Monroe office? Jan Gibson was able to control not only the cash received from customers, but also part of her company's accounting records. By manipulating the records she was able to hide her theft for several years. Evidently, no one checked her work on a regular basis. Several procedures that we discuss in this chapter will explain how this embezzlement could have been avoided. How could the embezzlement have been uncovered sooner? By the requirement that employees take vacations. This example illustrates a key feature of control systems in business: They cannot prevent all employee misbehavior, but they can help to detect misbehavior and thereby to limit its effects.

The need for laws requiring internal control has received increased attention since the 1970s. During that time some illegal payments, embezzlements, and other criminal business practices came to light. Concerned citizens wanted to know why the companies' internal controls had failed to alert management to these illegalities.

This chapter discusses *internal control*—the organizational plan and integrated framework that managers use to keep the business under control. The chapter applies these control techniques mainly to transactions of cash, the most liquid asset, and provides a framework for making ethical judgments in business. Later chapters discuss how managers control other assets.

Internal Control

OBJECTIVE 1

Define internal control

A key responsibility of the manager of a business is to keep its operations under control. The owners and the top managers set the entity's goals, the managers lead the way, and the employees carry out the plan. Good managers must decide where the organization is headed for the next several years. But unless they control operations today, they may not remain long enough to put lofty plans into effect. Managers are responsible for the control of their business. The *CICA Handbook* states that **internal control** consists of the policies and procedures established and maintained by management to assist in achieving its objective of ensuring the orderly and efficient conduct of a company's business. The *Handbook* indicates that management's internal control objectives are

1. Optimizing the use of resources.
2. Preventing and detecting error and fraud.
3. Safeguarding assets.
4. Maintaining reliable control systems.

Internal control is the organizational plan and all related measures adopted by an entity to meet management's objectives of discharging statutory responsibilities, profitability, prevention and detection of fraud and error, safeguarding of assets, reliability of accounting records, and the timely preparation of reliable financial information.

A company's internal control consists of two elements: (1) the control environment, which in essence consists of the actions, policies, and procedures that reflect the attitudes of top management and the owners of a company about control and its importance to the entity; and (2) the control systems, which can be divided into two components—the accounting system and the control procedures. The accounting system refers to the policies and procedures that pertain to the collection, recording, and processing of data and reporting information, while the control procedures pertain to enhancing the reliability of the data and information.

Internal control is a management priority, not merely a part of the accounting system. Thus it is not a responsibility only of accountants but of managers as well. A business's internal control system is only as effective as the quality of the people in the organization. For example, top managers who expect workers to behave ethically must themselves exhibit ethical behavior. Suppose that the cashier in our opening story had observed unethical behavior by her office manager. Such an act could motivate an employee to take a little money here, a little money there.

Internal controls are most effective when employees at all levels adopt the goals and objectives of the organization. Top managers are wise to communicate these goals to workers. Lee Iacocca, former president of Chrysler Corporation, instilled management's goals in Chrysler employees by getting out of the executive suite and spending time with assembly-line workers. (Japanese firms pioneered this style of participative management.) The result? Defects decreased dramatically, and Chrysler products became more competitive. Its sales of cars and trucks increased 14 percent in one year.

The only thing that is constant in business is that things are going to change. Companies take risks when they move into new industries.

An effective system of internal control is designed to manage change in the organization.

Exhibit 7-1 presents the management report from the 1994 John Labatt Ltd. annual report. John Labatt's top managers take responsibility for the financial statements and for the related system of internal control. The second paragraph indicates that the company's controls are "designed to provide reasonable assurance that the financial information is relevant, reliable, and accurate and that the Company's assets are appropriately accounted for and adequately safeguarded." The fifth paragraph describes the role of John Labatt's audit committee.[1] Another example of a management report is that of Mark's Work Wearhouse in Appendix A. Note that the management of Mark's states, "Management recognizes its responsibility for conducting the Company's affairs in compliance with established financial standards and applicable laws and maintains proper standards of conduct for its activities."

Let's examine in detail how companies accomplish the goals of an effective system of internal control.

Effective Internal Control

Whether the business is Brown Monroe, Air Canada, or a local department store, its system of internal controls, if effective, has the following noteworthy characteristics.

Competent, Reliable, and Ethical Personnel

Employees should be *competent*, *reliable*, and *ethical*. Paying top salaries to attract top-quality employees, training them to do their job well, and supervising their

> **OBJECTIVE 2**
>
> Identify the characteristics of an effective internal control

---

[1] An audit committee is a committee of the board of directors of a corporation. Incorporating acts such as the *Canada Business Corporations Act* require that a corporation has an audit committee, and that a majority of the members of the audit committee be independent of the company (that is, that they not be officers or employees of the company). In many companies, both the internal and external auditors report to the audit committee (see Exhibit 7–2).

EXHIBIT 7-1   *Excerpts from Management Statements of John Labatt Limited*

Management's Responsibility for Financial Statements

The accompanying consolidated financial statements of John Labatt Limited and all the information in this annual report are the responsibility of management.

The financial statements have been prepared by management in accordance with generally accepted accounting principles. When alternative accounting methods exist, management has chosen those it deems most appropriate in the circumstances. Financial statements are not precise since they include certain amounts based on estimates and judgment. Management has determined such amounts on a reasonable basis in order to ensure that the financial statements are presented fairly, in all material respects. Management has prepared the financial information presented elsewhere in the annual report and has ensured that it is consistent with that in the financial statements.

The Company maintains systems of internal accounting and administrative controls of high quality, consistent with reasonable cost. Such systems are designed to provide reasonable assurance that the financial information is relevant, reliable and accurate and that the Company's assets are appropriately accounted for and adequately safeguarded.

The Board of Directors is responsible for ensuring that management fulfills its responsibilities for financial reporting and is ultimately responsible for reviewing and approving the financial statements. The Board carries out this responsibility principally through its Audit Committee.

The Audit Committee is appointed by the Board, and is comprised of non-management directors. The Committee meets periodically with management as well as the independent external auditors to discuss internal controls over the financial reporting process, auditing matters and financial reporting issues, to satisfy itself that each party is properly discharging its responsibilities, and to review the annual report, the financial statements and the external auditors' report. The Committee reports its findings to the Board for consideration when the Board approves the financial statements for issuance to the Company's shareholders. The Committee also considers, for review by the Board and approval by the shareholders, the engagement or re-appointment of the external auditors.

On behalf of the shareholders, the financial statements have been audited by Ernst & Young, the external auditors, in accordance with generally accepted auditing standards. Ernst & Young has full and free access to the Audit Committee.

Toronto, Canada
June 23, 1994

Robert G. Vaux
Senior Vice-President,
Finance and Corporate Development

---

work all help to build a competent staff. A business adds flexibility to its staffing by rotating employees through various jobs. If one employee is sick or on vacation, a second employee is already trained to step in and do the job.

Rotating employees through various jobs also promotes reliability. Employees are less likely to handle their jobs improperly if they know that their misconduct may come to light when a second employee takes over the job. This same reasoning leads businesses to require that employees take an annual vacation. A second employee, stepping in to handle the position, may uncover any wrongdoing. Periodic reviews by other employees have a way of keeping workers honest and ethical.

Assignment of Responsibilities

In a business with effective internal control, no important duty is overlooked. Each employee is assigned certain responsibilities. A model of such *assignment of responsibilities* appears in the corporate organizational chart in Exhibit 7-2. Notice that the corporation has a vice-president of finance and accounting. Two other officers, the treasurer and the controller, report to the vice-president. The treasurer is responsible for cash management. The controller performs accounting duties.

Within this organization, the controller may be responsible for approving invoices for payment and the treasurer may actually sign the cheques. Working under the controller, one accountant may be responsible for property taxes, a second for income taxes, and a third for sales tax and the GST. In sum, all duties are clearly defined and assigned to individuals who bear responsibility for carrying them out.

EXHIBIT 7-2   *Organization Chart of a Corporation*

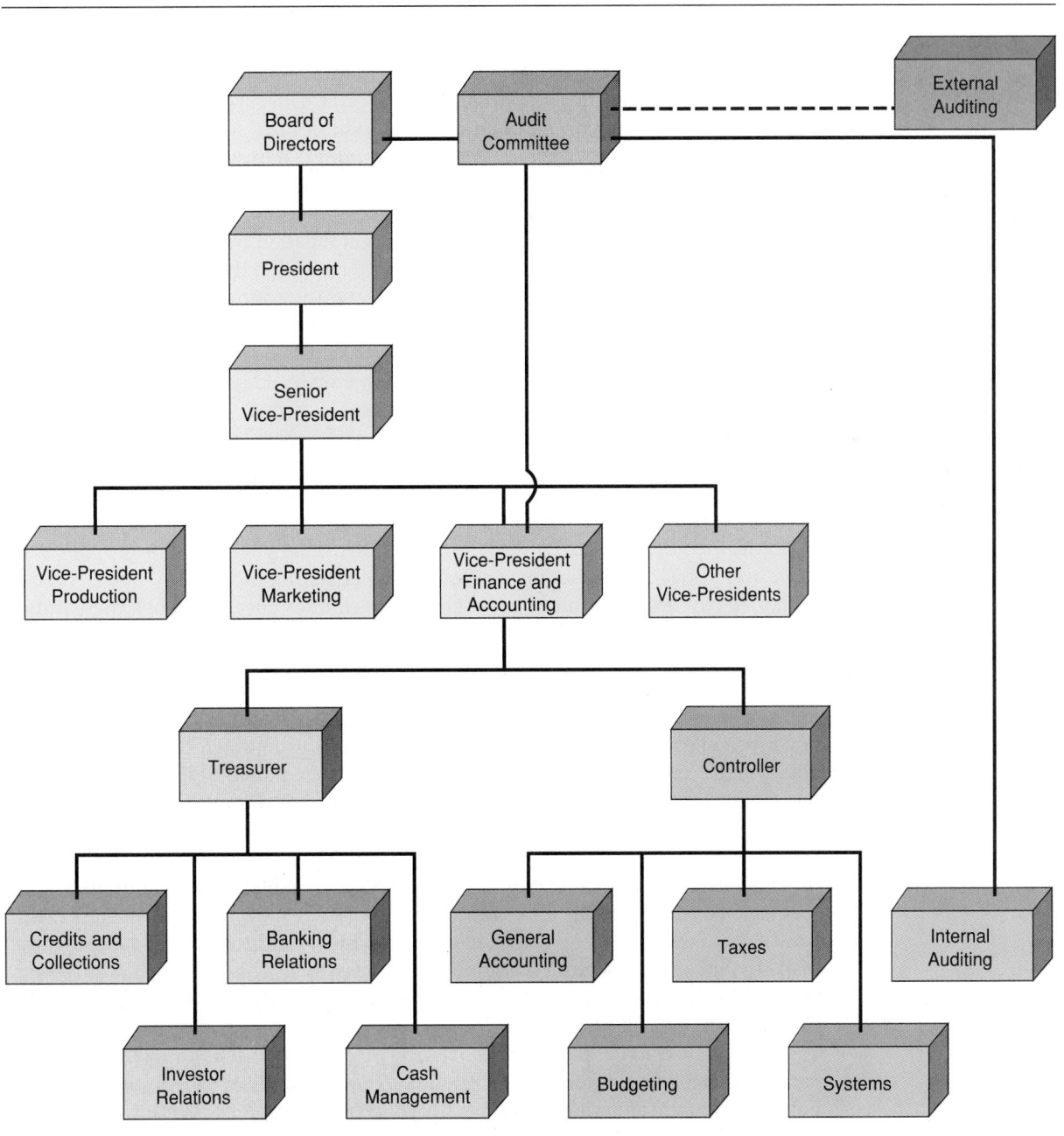

Proper Authorization

An organization generally has a written set of rules that outlines approved procedures. Any deviation from standard policy requires *proper authorization*. For example, managers or assistant managers of retail stores must approve customer cheques for amounts above the store's usual limit. Likewise, deans or department chairpersons of colleges and universities must give the authorization for a first- or second-year student to enroll in courses otherwise restricted to upper-year students.

Separation of Duties

Smart management divides the responsibilities for transactions between two or more people or departments. *Separation of duties* limits chances for fraud and promotes the accuracy of accounting records. This crucial and often neglected component of internal control may be subdivided into four parts.

Short Exercise:
What problems can result when a sales clerk can also grant credit approval and record the sales?
A: The clerk could grant credit approval to friends who do not meet the credit standards, steal merchandise and hide the theft in the accounting records, fail to do all three jobs well and make mistakes, or forget to perform a task when the sales floor is busy.

1. *Separation of operations from accounting.* The entire accounting function should be completely separate from operating departments such as manufacturing or sales so that reliable records may be kept. For example, product inspectors, not machine operators, should count units produced by a manufacturing process. Accountants, not salespersons, should keep inventory records. Observe the separation of accounting from production and marketing in Exhibit 7-2.

2. *Separation of the custody of assets from accounting.* Temptation and fraud are reduced if the accountant does not handle cash and the cashier does not have access to the accounting records. If one employee had both cash-handling and accounting duties, that person can steal cash and conceal the theft by making a bogus entry on the books. We see this component of internal control in the organization chart in Exhibit 7-2. The treasurer has custody of cash and the controller accounts for cash. Neither person has both responsibilities.

Warehouse employees with no accounting duties should control inventory. If they were allowed to account for the inventory, they could steal it and write it off as obsolete. In a computerized accounting system, a person with custody of assets should not have access to the computer programs. Similarly, the programmer should not have access to tempting assets like cash.

3. *Separation of the authorization of transactions from the custody of related assets.* If possible, persons who authorize transactions should not handle the related asset. For example, the same individual should not authorize the payment of a supplier's invoice and also sign the cheque to pay the invoice. With both duties, the person can authorize payments to him- or herself and then sign the cheques. When these duties are separated, only legitimate bills get paid.

For another example, an individual who handles cash receipts should not have the authority to write off accounts receivable. (Businesses that sell on credit declare certain of their accounts receivable as uncollectible, realizing that these receivables will never be collected. Chapter 8 looks at uncollectible accounts receivable in detail.) Suppose the company shown in Exhibit 7-2 employs V. Saucier. He works in Credits and Collections (under the treasurer), and handles cash receipts from customers.

Among the business's accounts receivable in the subsidiary ledger is Gina Kowalski's $500 balance. Saucier could label Kowalski's account as uncollectible, and the business might cease trying to collect from her. When Kowalski mails a $500 cheque to pay off her balance, Saucier forges the endorsement and pockets the money. Kowalski, of course, has no reason to notify anyone else at the business that she has mailed a cheque so that Saucier's crime goes undetected. This theft would have been avoided by denying Saucier either the access to cash receipts or the authority to declare accounts uncollectible.

4. *Separation of duties within the accounting function.* Independent performance of various phases of accounting helps minimize errors and the opportunities for fraud. For example, different accountants should be responsible for recording cash receipts and cash disbursements. The employees who process accounts payable and cheque requests should have nothing to do with the approval process.

Internal and External Audits

It is not economically feasible for auditors to examine all the transactions during a period, so they must rely to some degree on the accounting system to produce accurate records. To gauge the reliability of the company's accounting system, auditors evaluate its system of internal controls. Auditors also spot weaknesses in internal control and recommend corrections. Auditors offer *objectivity* in their reports, while managers, immersed in operations, may overlook their own weaknesses.

Audits are internal or external. Exhibit 7-2 shows *internal auditors* as employees of the business reporting directly to the audit committee. Some organizations have internal auditors report directly to a vice-president. Throughout the year, they audit various segments of the organization. *External auditors* are entirely independent of the business. Employed by a public accounting firm, they are hired by an entity as outsiders to audit the entity as a whole. The external auditors are and the internal auditors should be independent of the operations they examine.

An auditor may find that an employee has both cash-handling and cash-accounting duties, or may learn that a cash shortage has resulted from lax efforts to collect accounts receivable. In such cases, the auditor suggests improvements. Auditors' recommendations assist the business in running efficiently.

Documents and Records

Business *documents and records* vary considerably, from source documents such as sales invoices and purchase orders to special journals and subsidiary ledgers. Documents should be prenumbered. A gap in the numbered sequence calls attention to a missing document.

Prenumbering cash sales receipts discourages theft by the cashier because the copy retained by the cashier, which lists the amount of the sale, can be checked against the actual amount of cash received. If receipts are not prenumbered, the cashier can destroy the copy and pocket the cash sale amount. However, if receipts are prenumbered, the missing copy can easily be identified.

In a computerized system, a permanent record of the sale is stored electronically when the transaction is completed.

In a bowling alley, for example, a key document is the score sheet. The manager can check on cashiers by comparing the number of games scored with the amount of cash received. By multiplying the number of games by the price per game and comparing the result with each day's cash receipts, the manager can see whether all the bowling revenue is being collected by the business. If cash on hand is low, the cashier might be stealing.

Real-World Example:
In a retail business, if a clerk makes a mistake on the sales ticket, the ticket is not destroyed but is marked VOID. Most companies use prenumbered sales receipts, so a missing receipt would be noted.

Electronic and Other Controls

Businesses use electronic devices to meet their needs for control over assets and operations. For example, retailers such as The Bay and Eaton's control their inventories by attaching an *electronic sensor* to merchandise. The cashier removes the sensor when a sale is made. If a customer tries to remove from the store an item with the sensor attached, an alarm is activated. According to Checkpoint Systems, which manufactures electronic sensors, these devices reduce loss due to theft by as much as 50 percent.

Accounting systems are relying less and less on documents and more and more on digital storage devices. Computers produce accurate records and enhance operational efficiency, but that does not automatically safeguard assets or encourage employees to behave in accordance with company policies. What computers have done is shift the internal controls to the people who write the programs. Programmers carry out the plans of managers and accountants. All the controls that apply to accountants apply to computer programmers as well.

Businesses of all types keep cash and important business documents such as titles to property and contracts in *fireproof vaults*. They use burglar alarms to protect buildings and other property.

Retailers receive most of their cash from customers on the spot. To safeguard cash they use *point-of-sale terminals* that serve as a cash register and record each transaction as it is entered in the machine. Several times each day a supervisor removes the cash for deposit in the bank.

Employees who handle cash are in an especially tempting position. Many businesses purchase *fidelity bonds* on cashiers. The bond is an insurance policy that reimburses the company for any losses due to the employee's theft. Before issuing a fidelity bond, the insurance company investigates the employee's past to ensure a record of ethical conduct.

Within a single company, each department may take steps to maintain control over its assets and accounting records. Consider a large company like Northern Telecom Ltd., a manufacturer of a wide range of electronic equipment especially for the telecommunications industry. Computerized record keeping means that the raw data provided by one department leads to a whole array of *accurate* output—from journals to ledgers to cheques and so on—all consistent with the original information. Manually copying information, a time-consuming, error-prone process, is reduced or eliminated.

If Northern Telecom's system is well designed, each department can ensure that its transactions are processed correctly. The user department needs to maintain record counts or dollar control totals. For example, the accounts receivable department submits daily credit sales totals for processing by the computing department. The accounts receivable department expects a printout showing a total sales amount agreeing with the control total that was calculated *before* its documents went to the computer department. This amount is the control figure.

The accounts receivable department—and every other department—relies on the computing department to post correctly the thousands of customer accounts. To assure proper posting, customer account numbers may have been devised so that the last digit is a mathematical function of the previous digits, for example, 1,359, where $1 + 3 + 5 = 9$. Any miskeying of a customer account number would trigger an error message to the data entry clerk, and the computer would not accept that number.

STOP & THINK

Ralph works the late movie at Big-Hit Theater. Occasionally Ralph must sell tickets *and* take the tickets as customers enter the theater. Standard procedure requires that Ralph tear the tickets, give one half to the customer, and keep the other half. To control cash receipts, the theater manager compares each night's cash receipts with the number of ticket stubs on hand.

What is the internal control weakness in this situation? What might a dishonest employee do? What additional steps should the manager take to strengthen the control over cash receipts?

Answer: The internal control weakness is the lack of separation of duties. Ralph receives cash from customers and also controls the tickets. Good internal control would require that Ralph handle either cash or the tickets, but not both. If he were dishonest, he could issue no ticket and keep the customer's cash. To control that dishonest behavior, the manager could physically count the people watching a movie and compare that number with the number of ticket stubs retained. Or a dishonest employee could destroy some ticket stubs and keep the cash received from customers. To catch that dishonest behavior, the manager could account for all ticket stubs by serial number. Missing serial numbers would raise questions that would lead to investigations.

Limitations of Internal Control

Most internal control measures can be overcome. Systems designed to thwart an *individual* employee's fraud may be beaten by two or more employees working as a team—*colluding*—to defraud the firm. Consider the Big-Hit Theater again. Ralph and a fellow employee could could put together a scheme in which the ticket seller pockets the cash from ten customers and the ticket taker admits the customers without tickets. Who would catch them? The manager could take the additional control measure of counting the people in the theatre and matching that figure against the number of ticket stubs retained. But that would take time away from other duties. As you see, the stricter the internal control, the more expensive it becomes.

A system of internal control that is too complex may strangle people in red tape. Efficiency and control are hurt rather than helped. The more complicated the system, the more time and money it takes to maintain. Just how tight should internal control be? Managers must make sensible judgments. Investments in internal control must be judged in the light of costs and benefits.

The Bank Account as a Control Device

Keeping cash in a *bank account* is part of internal control because banks have established practices for safeguarding cash. Banks also provide depositors with detailed records of cash transactions. To take full advantage of these control features, the business should deposit all cash receipts in the bank account and make all cash payments through it (except petty cash disbursements, which we look at later). We now discuss banking records and documents.

For many businesses, cash is the most important asset. After all, cash is the most common means of exchange, and most transactions ultimately affect cash. But cash is the most tempting asset for theft. Consequently, internal controls for cash are more elaborate than for most other assets. We consider cash to be not just paper money and coins but also cheques, money orders, and money kept in bank accounts. Cash reported on a company's balance sheet may also include *cash equivalents*, liquid investments that can be converted to cash within a few months. Cash equivalents include bank certificates of deposits (CDs), money-market funds, and government treasury bills and notes. We treat cash equivalents as cash. Cash includes neither stamps, because they are supplies, nor IOUs payable to the business, because they are receivables.

The documents used to control a bank account include the signature card, the deposit ticket, the cheque, the bank statement, and the bank reconciliation.

Signature Card   Banks require each person authorized to transact business through an account in that bank to sign a *signature card*. The bank compares the signatures on documents against the signature card to protect the bank and the depositor against forgery.

Deposit Ticket   Banks supply standard forms as *deposit tickets* or *deposit slips*. The customer fills in the dollar amount and date of deposit. The customer retains either (1) a duplicate copy of the deposit ticket or slip, or (2) a deposit receipt, depending on the bank's practice, as proof of transaction.

Cheque   To draw money from an account, the depositor writes a **cheque**, which is a document that instructs the bank to pay the designated person or business the specified amount of money. There are three parties to a cheque: the *maker*, who signs the cheque; the *payee*, to whose order the cheque is drawn; and the *bank* on which the cheque is drawn.

Most cheques are serially numbered and preprinted with the name and address of the maker and the bank. The cheques have places for the date, the name of the payee, the signature of the maker, and the amount. The bank name and identification number and the depositor account number are usually imprinted in magnetic ink for machine processing.

EXHIBIT 7-3 *Cheque with Remittance Advice*

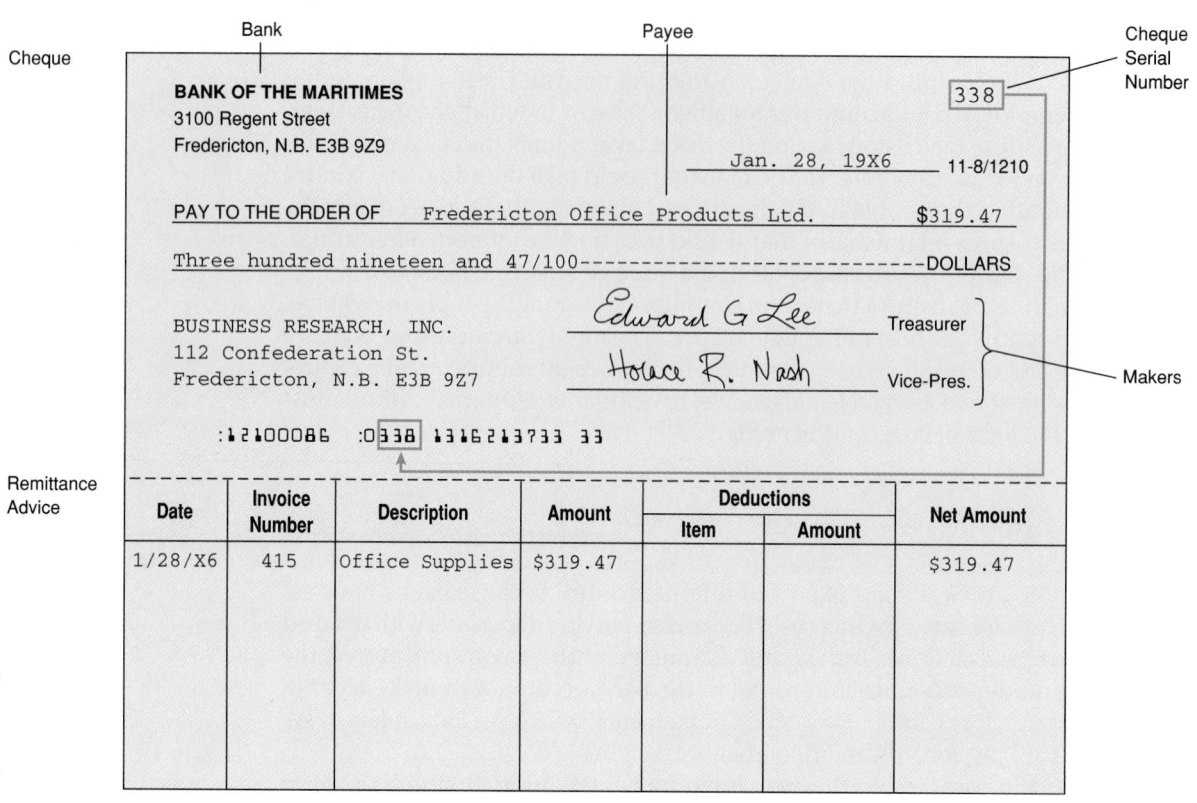

Exhibit 7-3 shows a cheque drawn on the bank account of Business Research, Inc. The cheque has two parts: the cheque itself and the remittance advice. The *remittance advice,* an optional attachment, tells the payee the reason for payment. The maker (Business Research) retains a duplicate copy of the cheque for its recording in the cheque register (cash disbursements journal). Note that internal controls at Business Research require two signatures on cheques.

Bank Statement   Most banks send monthly **bank statements** to their depositors. The statement shows the account's beginning and ending balance for the period and lists the month's transactions. Included with the statement are the maker's *cancelled cheques,* those cheques that have been paid by the bank on behalf of the depositor. The bank statement also lists any other deposits and changes in the account. Deposits appear in chronological order, and cheques in a logical order, along with the date each cheque cleared the bank.

Exhibit 7-4 is the bank statement of Business Research, Inc., for the month ended January 31, 19X6. At some banks, some depositors receive their statements on the first of the month, some on the second, and so on. This spacing eliminates the clerical burden of supplying all the statements at one time. Most businesses, like Business Research, receive their bank statement at the end of each calendar month.

Electronic funds transfer (EFT) is a system that relies on electronic impulses—not paper documents—to transfer cash. More and more businesses today rely on EFT for repetitive cash transactions. It is much cheaper for a company to pay employees by EFT (direct deposit) than by issuing hundreds of payroll cheques. Also, many people make mortgage, rent, and insurance payments by prior arrangement with their bank and never write cheques for those payments. The bank statement lists cash receipts by EFT among the deposits, and cash payments by EFT among the cheques and other bank charges. The bank statement may be the depositor's only notification of the transaction.

Exhibit 7-4 *Bank Statement*

SPECIAL ACCOUNT	**THE TORONTO-DOMINION BANK** KING SQUARE BRANCH FREDERICTON, NEW BRUNSWICK E3B 8Z1

```
                          1024/  0/  5
        BUSINESS RESEARCH INC.
        112 CONFEDERATION ST.
        FREDERICTON, NB

        E3B 9Z7
```

For Current Interest Rates:	Statement of Account		Statement From - To	
CALL TD GREEN INFOLINE 1-800-387-2092 QUEBEC 1-800-387-1500 TORONTO 982-7730	**Branch No.**	**Account No.**	JAN 1/x6 JAN 31/x6	
	1024	136213733	**Page 1 of 1**	

BEGINNING BALANCE	TOTAL DEPOSITS	TOTAL WITHDRAWALS	SERVICE CHARGE	ENDING BALANCE
6556.12	4352.64	4963.00	14.25	5931.51

```
                    CHEQUING ACCOUNT TRANSACTIONS

   DEPOSITS

   DEPOSIT                                          01-04    1000.00
   DEPOSIT                                          01-04     112.00
   DEPOSIT                                          01-08     194.60
   EFT    COLLECTION OF RENT                        01-17     904.03
   BANK COLLECTION                                  01-26    2114.00
   INTEREST                                         01-31      28.01


   CHARGES

   SERVICE CHARGE                                   01-31      14.25
```

CHEQUES			CHEQUES			BALANCE	
NUMBER	DATE	AMOUNT	NUMBER	DATE	AMOUNT	DATE	BALANCE
332	01-12	3000.00	334	01-10	100.00	12-31	6556.12
656	01-06	100.00	335	01-06	100.00	01-04	7616.12
333	01-12	150.00	336	01-31	1100.00	01-06	7416.12
						01-08	7610.72
						01-10	7510.72
						01-12	4360.72
						01-17	5264.75
						01-20	4903.75
						01-26	7017.75
						01-31	5931.51

OTHER CHARGES	DATE	AMOUNT
NSF	01-04	52.00
EFT INSURANCE	01-20	361.00

```
                        MONTHLY SUMMARY

   8 WITHDRAWALS        4360 MINIMUM BALANCE      6091.00 AVERAGE BALANCE
```

Bank Reconciliation   There are two records of the business's cash: its Cash account in its own general ledger, and the bank statement which tells the actual amount of cash the business has in the bank. The balance in the business's Cash account rarely equals the balance shown on the bank statement.

The books and the bank statement may show different amounts, but both are correct. The difference arises because of a time lag in recording certain transactions. When a firm writes a cheque, it immediately credits its Cash account. The bank, however, will not subtract the amount of the cheque until the cheque reaches it for payment. This may take days, even weeks, if the payee waits to cash the cheque. Likewise, the business debits Cash for all cash receipts, and it may take a day or so for the bank to add this amount to the business's bank balance.

Good internal control means knowing where a company's money comes from, how it is spent, and the current cash balance. How else can the accountant keep the accurate records that management needs to make informed decisions? The accountant must report the correct cash amount on the balance sheet. To ensure accuracy, the accountant explains the reasons for the difference between the firm's records and bank statement figures on a certain date. This process is called the **bank reconciliation**. Properly done, the bank reconciliation ensures that all cash transactions have been accounted for, and that bank and book records of cash are correct. Internal control is enhanced if an independent person reviews the reconciliation.

Common items that cause differences between the bank balance and the business are

1. Items recorded by the company but not yet recorded by the *bank*:
   a. **Deposits in transit** (outstanding deposits). The company has recorded these deposits, but the bank has not.
   b. **Outstanding cheques**. These cheques have been issued by the company and recorded on its books but have not yet been paid by its bank.

2. Items recorded by the bank but not yet recorded by the *company*:
   a. **Bank collections**. The bank sometimes collects money on behalf of depositors. Many businesses have their customers pay directly to the company bank account. This practice, called a lock-box system, reduces the possibility of theft and places the business's cash in circulation faster than if the cash had to be collected and deposited by company personnel. An example is a bank's collecting cash on a note receivable and interest revenue for the depositor. The bank may notify the depositor of these bank collections on the bank's statement.
   b. *Electronic funds transfers*. The bank may receive or pay cash on behalf of the depositor. The bank statement will list the EFT and may serve as notification for the depositor to record these transactions.
   c. *Service charge*. This amount is the bank's fee for processing the depositor's transactions. Banks commonly base service charge on the balance in the account. The depositor learns the amount of service charge from the bank statement.
   d. *Interest revenue on chequing account*. Banks often pay interest to depositors who keep a large enough balance of cash in the account. This is especially true of business chequing accounts. The bank notifies the depositor of this interest on the bank statement.
   e. **NSF (nonsufficient funds) cheques** received from customers. To understand how to handle NSF cheques, also called hot cheques, you first need to know the route a cheque takes. The maker writes the cheque, credits Cash to record the payment on the books and gives the cheque to the payee. On receiving the cheque, the payee debits Cash on his or her books and deposits the cheque in the bank. The payee's bank immediately adds the receipt amount to the payee's bank balance on the assumption that the cheque is good. The cheque is returned to the maker's bank, which then deducts the cheque amount from the maker's bank balance. If the maker's bank balance is insufficient to pay the cheque, the maker's bank refuses to pay the cheque, reverses this deduction and sends an NSF notice back to the payee's bank. The payee bank

Key Point:

Your chequing account is a liability on the bank's balance sheet. When the bank reduces your account for a service charge, the bank will debit your account. Banks may send a debit memo to inform you that the deduction has been made. They may send a credit memo to notify you when interest revenue has been added (credited) to your account.

subtracts the cheque amount from the payee's bank balance and notifies the payee of this action. This process may take from three to seven days. The company may learn of an NSF cheque through the bank statement, which lists the NSF cheque as a charge (subtraction), as shown near the bottom of Exhibit 7-4.

   f. *Cheques collected, deposited, and returned to the payee by the bank for reasons other than NSF.* Banks return cheques to the payee if (1) the maker's account has been closed, (2) the date is stale (the cheque has not been cashed within six month's of the cheque issue date), (3) the signature is not authorized, (4) the cheque has been altered, or (5) the cheque form is improper (for example, a counterfeit). Accounting for all returned cheques is the same as for NSF cheques.

   g. *The cost of printed cheques.* This charge against the company's bank account balance is handled like a service charge.

3. Errors by either the company or the bank. For example, a bank may improperly charge (decrease) the bank balance of Business Research, Inc., for a cheque drawn by another company, perhaps Business Research Associates. Or a company may miscompute its bank balance on its own books. Computational errors are becoming less frequent with the widespread use of computers. Nevertheless, all errors must be corrected, and the corrections will be a part of the bank reconciliation.

Steps in Preparing the Bank Reconciliation

OBJECTIVE 3
Prepare a bank reconciliation and related journal entries

The steps in preparing the bank reconciliation are

1. Start with two figures, the balance shown on the bank statement (*balance per bank*) and the balance in the company's Cash account (*balance per books*) as in Exhibit 7-5, Panel B. These two amounts will probably disagree because of the timing differences discussed earlier.

2. Add to, or subtract from, the *bank* balance those items that appear on the books but not on the bank statement.

   a. Add *deposits in transit* to the bank balance. Deposits in transit are identified by comparing the deposits listed on the bank statement to the company list of cash receipts. They show up as cash receipts on the books but not as deposits on the bank statement. As a control measure, the accountant should also ensure that deposits in transit from the preceding month appear on the current month's bank statement. If they do not, the deposits may be lost.

   b. Subtract *outstanding cheques* from the bank balance. Outstanding cheques are identified by comparing the canceled cheques returned with the bank statement to the company list of cheques in the cash disbursements journal. They show up as cash payments on the books but not as paid cheques on the bank statement. This comparison also verifies that all cheques paid by the bank were valid company cheques and correctly recorded by the bank and by the company. Outstanding cheques are usually the most numerous item on a bank reconciliation.

3. Add to, or subtract from, the *book* balance those items that appear on the bank statement but not on the company books.

   a. Add to the book balance (1) *bank collections*, (2) *EFT cash collections*, and (3) *interest revenue* earned on the money in the bank. These items are identified by comparing the deposits listed on the bank statement with the list of cash receipts. They show up as cash receipts on the bank statement but not on the books.

   b. Subtract from the book balance (1) *EFT cash payments*, (2) *service charges*, (3) *cost of printed cheques*, and (4) *other bank charges* (for example, charges for NSF or stale-date cheques). These items are identified by comparing the other charges listed on the bank statement to the cash disbursements recorded on the company books. They show up as subtractions on the bank statement but not as cash payments on the books.

Key Point:
Preparing the bank reconciliation does not change the Cash balance on the books; it just shows what the balance should be. An entry is needed for every reconciling item on the book side to bring the Cash account to its correct balance.

Key Point:
A journal entry is needed for each reconciling item on the book side. There are no entries for items on the bank side.

EXHIBIT 7-5 *Bank Reconciliation*

Panel A: Reconciling Items

1. Deposit in transit, $1,591.63.
2. Bank error; add $100 to bank balance.
3. Outstanding cheques: no. 337, $286.00; no. 338, $319.47; no. 339, $83.00; no. 340, $203.14; no. 341, $458.53.
4. EFT receipt of rent revenue, $904.03.

5. Bank collection, $2,114, including interest revenue of $214.
6. Interest earned on bank balance, $28.01.
7. Book error; add $360 to book balance.
8. Bank service charge, $14.25.
9. NSF cheque from L. Ross, $52.
10. EFT payment of insurance expense, $361.00.

Panel B: Bank Reconciliation

Business Research, Inc.
Bank Reconciliation
January 31, 19X6

Bank			Books		
Balance, January 31		$5,931.51	Balance, January 31		$3,294.21
Add:			Add:		
1. Deposit of Janaury 30 in transit		1,591.63	4. EFT receipt of rent revenue		904.03
2. Correction of bank error —Business Research Associates cheque erroneously charged against company account		100.00	5. Bank collection of note receivable, including interest revenue of $214		2,114.00
		$7,623.14	6. Interest revenue earned on bank balance		28.01
3. Less: outstanding cheques			7. Correction of book error—Overstated amount of cheque no. 333		360.00
No. 337	$286.00				6,700.25
338	319.47		Less:		
339	83.00		8. Service charge	$14.25	
340	203.14		9. NSF cheque	52.00	
341	458.53	(1,350.14)	10. EFT payment of insurance expense	361.00	427.25
Adjusted bank balance		$6,273.00	Adjusted book balance		$6,273.00

Key Point:

Each reconciling item is treated in the same way in every situation. Here is a summary:

Bank Balance—always
• *Add* deposits in transit
• *Subtract* outstanding cheques

Book Balance—always
• *Add* bank collection items, interest revenue, and EFT receipts
• *Subtract* service charges, NSF cheques, and EFT payments

Errors—adjust the side where the error was made

Entries—only for items on the book side

4. Compute the *adjusted bank balance* and *adjusted book balance*. The two adjusted balances should be equal.

5. Journalize each item in step 3, that is, each item listed on the book portion of the bank reconciliation. These items must be recorded on the company books because they affect cash.

6. Correct all book errors, and notify the bank of any errors it has made.

Recording Entries from the Reconciliation

The bank reconciliation does not directly affect the journals or ledgers. Like the work sheet, the reconciliation is an accountant's tool, separate from the company's books.

The bank reconciliation acts as a control device by signaling the company to record transactions listed as reconciling items in the Books section because the company has not yet done so. For example, the bank collected the note receivable on behalf of the company, but the company has not yet recorded this cash receipt. In fact, the company learned of the cash receipt only when it received the bank statement.

PUTTING SKILLS TO WORK

Bank Reconciliation Illustrated

The bank statement in Exhibit 7-4 indicates that the January 31 bank balance of Business Research, Inc., is $5,931.51. However, the company's Cash account has a balance of $3,294.21. In following the steps outlined in the text, the accountant finds these reconciling items:

1. The January 30 deposit of $1,591.63 does not appear on the bank statement.

2. The bank erroneously charged to the Business Research, Inc., account a $100 cheque—number 656—written by Business Research Associates.

3. Five company cheques issued late in January and recorded in the cash disbursements journal have not been paid by the bank:

Cheque	Date	Amount
337	Jan. 27	$286.00
338	28	319.47
339	28	83.00
340	29	203.14
341	30	458.53

4. By EFT the bank received $904.03 on behalf of Business Research, Inc. The bank statement serves as initial notification of this receipt of monthly rent revenue on unused office space.

5. The bank collected on behalf of the company a note receivable, $2,114 (including interest revenue of $214). This cash receipt has not been recorded by Business Research, Inc.

6. The bank statement shows interest revenue of $28.01 that the company has earned on its cash balance.

7. Cheque number 333 for $150 paid to Brown Company on account was recorded in the cash disbursements journal as a $510 amount, creating a $360 understatement of the Cash balance per books.

8. The bank services charge for the month was $14.25.

9. The bank statement shows an NSF cheque for $52, which was received from customer L. Ross. The bank charged no collection fee.

10. Business Research, Inc., pays insurance expense monthly by EFT. The company has not yet recorded this $361 payment.

Exhibit 7-5 is the bank reconciliation based on the above data. Panel A lists the reconciling items, which are keyed by number to the reconciliation in Panel B. After the reconciliation, the adjusted bank balance equals the adjusted book balance. This equality is an accuracy check.

Short Exercise:

The bank statement balance is $4,500 and shows a service charge of $15, interest earned of $5, and an NSF cheque for $300. Deposits in transit total $1,200; outstanding cheques are $575. The bookkeeper recorded as $152 a cheque of $125 in payment of an account payable. (1) What is the adjusted bank balance? (2) What was the book balance of cash before the reconciliation?

A: (1) $5,125 ($4,500 + $1,200 – $575); (2) $5,408 ($5,125 + $15 + $300 – $27– $5). The adjusted book and bank balances are the same. The answer can be determined by working backward from the adjusted balance.

STOP & THINK

Why does the company *not* need to record the reconciling items on the Bank side of the reconciliation?

Answer: Those items have already been recorded on the company books.

On the basis of the reconciliation in Exhibit 7-5, Business Research, Inc., makes these entries. They are dated January 31 to bring the Cash account to the correct balance on that date.

Jan.	31	Cash..	904.03	
		Rent revenue...		904.03
		Receipt of monthly rent.		
	31	Cash..	2,114.00	
		Notes receivable...		1,900.00
		Interest revenue		214.00
		Note receivable collected by bank.		
	31	Cash..	28.01	
		Interest revenue		28.01
		Interest earned on bank balance.		

Short Exercise:

Prepare the adjusting journal entry(ies) for the previous Short Exercise.

A:

Cash......................	27	
Acct. Payable		27
Misc. Exp	15	
Cash....................		15
Acct. Receivable.....	300	
Cash....................		300
Cash......................	5	
Interest Rev.........		5

31	Cash...	360.00	
	Accounts payable—Brown Co....................		360.00
	Correction of cheque no. 333.		
31	Miscellaneous expense	14.25	
	Cash...		14.25
	Bank service charges.		
31	Accounts receivable—L. Ross.......................	52.00	
	Cash...		52.00
	NSF cheque returned by bank.		
31	Insurance Expense...	361.00	
	Cash...		361.00
	Payment of monthly insurance.		

Note: Miscellaneous Expense is debited for the bank service charge because the service charge pertains to no particular expense category.

These entries bring the business's books up to date.

The entry for the NSF cheque needs explanation. Upon learning that L. Ross's $52 cheque was not good, Business Research credits Cash to bring the Cash account up to date. Since Business Research still has a receivable from Ross, it debits Accounts Receivable—L. Ross and pursues collection from him.

Mid-Chapter Summary Problem for Your Review

The cash account of Kao Corp. at February 28, 19X3 follows:

Cash

Feb.	1 Balance	3,995	Feb.	3	400
	6	800		12	3,100
	15	1,800		19	1,100
	23	1,100		25	500
	28	2,400		27	900
	28 Balance	4,095			

Kao Corp. receives this bank statement on February 28, 19X3 with the information shown below (as always, negative amounts appear in parentheses):

Bank Statement for February, 19X3

Beginning balance...		$3,995
Deposits:		
Feb. 7	$ 800	
15	1,800	
24	1,100	3,700
Cheques (total per day):		
Feb. 8	$ 400	
16	3,100	
23	1,100	(4,600)
Other items:		
Service charge		(10)

NSF cheque from M. E. Crown......................................	(700)
Bank collection of note receivable for the company..	1,000*
EFT monthly rent expense	(330)
Interest on account balance..	15
Ending balance...	$3,070

*Includes interest of $119.

Additional data: Kao Corp. deposits all cash receipts in the bank and makes all cash disbursements by cheque.

Required

1. Prepare the bank reconciliation of Kao Corp. at February 28, 19X3.
2. Record the entries based on the bank reconciliation.

SOLUTION TO REVIEW PROBLEM

Requirement 1

Kao Corp.
Bank Reconciliation
February 28, 19X3

Bank

Balance, February 28, 19X3		$3,070
Add: Deposit of February 28 in transit		2,400
		5,470
Less: Outstanding cheques issued on Feb. 25 ($500)		
and Feb. 27 ($900)...		(1,400)
Adjusted bank balance, February 28, 19X3		$4,070 ←

Books

Balance, February 28, 19X3		$4,095
Add: Bank collection of note receivable,		
including interest of $119		1,000
Add: Interest earned on bank balance		15
		5,110
Less: Service charge...	$ 10	
NSF cheque	700	
EFT—Rent expense...	330	(1,040)
Adjusted book balance, February 28, 19X3		$4,070 ←

Requirement 2

Feb.	28	Cash..	1,000	
		Note Receivable ($1,100 – $119)...................		881
		Interest Revenue		119
		Note receivable collected by bank.		
	28	Cash..	15	
		Interest Revenue		15
		Interest earned on bank balance.		
	28	Miscellaneous Expense.......................................	10	
		Cash...		10
		Bank service charge.		
	28	Accounts Receivable—M. E. Crown...............	700	
		Cash...		700
		NSF cheque returned by bank.		
	28	Rent Expense..	330	
		Cash...		330
		Monthly rent expense.		

Reporting of Cash

Cash is the first current asset listed on the balance sheet of most companies. Even small businesses have several bank accounts and one or more *petty cash* funds—small sums that are kept on hand for making small disbursements. But, companies usually combine all cash amounts into a single total for reporting on the balance sheet. They also include liquid assets such as time deposits and certificates of deposit. These are interest-bearing accounts that can be withdrawn with no penalty after a short period of time. Although they are slightly less liquid than cash, they are sufficiently similar to be reported along with cash. For example, the balance sheet of National Trustco. Inc., Canada's third largest trust company with branches from Vancouver to Quebec City, recently reported (in thousands of dollars):

Assets

Cash and short-term investments		$ 1,609,058
Securities		907,367
Loans		
Mortgages	11,422,656	
Other	2,477,811	13,900,467
		$16,416,892

Companies perform the bank reconciliation on the balance sheet date in order to be assured of reporting the correct amount of cash.

Internal Control over Cash Receipts

OBJECTIVE 4

Apply internal controls to cash receipts

Internal control over cash receipts ensures that all cash receipts are deposited in the bank and the company's accounting records are correct. Many businesses receive cash over the counter and through the mail. Each source of cash receipts calls for *security measures*. Exhibit 7-6 outlines the controls over cash receipts.

Real-World Example:
Stores often give customers a bonus if the clerk fails to give them a receipt.

Cash Receipts Over the Counter   The point-of-sale terminal (cash register) offers management control over cash received in a store. Consider a Canadian Tire store. First, the machine should be positioned so that customers can see the amounts the cashier enters into the computer. No person willingly pays more than the marked price for an item, so the customer helps prevent the sales clerk from overcharging and pocketing the excess over actual prices. Company policy should require issuance of a receipt to make sure each sale is recorded in the register.

Short Exercise:
The bookkeeper in your company has stolen cash received from customers. The bookkeeper prepared fake credit memos to indicate that the customers had returned merchandise. What internal control feature could have prevented this theft? *A:* The bookkeeper should not have had access to cash.

Second, the cash drawer opens only when the salesclerk enters an amount on the keys, and a roll of tape locked inside the machine records each amount. At the end of the day, a manager proves the cash by comparing the total amount in the cash drawer against the tape's total. This step helps prevent outright theft by the clerk. For security reasons, the clerk should not have access to the tape.

Third, pricing merchandise at "uneven" amounts—say, $3.95 instead of $4.00—means that the clerk generally must make change, which in turn means having to get into the cash drawer. This requires entering the amount of the sale on the keys and so onto the register tape.

At the end of the day, the cashier or other employee with cash-handling duties deposits the cash in the bank. The tape goes to the accounting department as the basis for an entry in the cash receipts journal. These security measures, coupled with periodic on-site inspection by a manager, discourage fraud.

EXHIBIT 7-6   *Internal Controls over Cash Receipts*

Element of Internal Control	Internal Controls over Cash Receipts
Competent, reliable, ethical personnel	Companies carefully screen employees for undesirable personality traits. They also spend large sums for training programs.
Assignment of responsibility	Specific employees are designated as cashiers, supervisors of cashiers, or accountants for cash receipts.
Proper authorization	Only designated employees, such as department managers, can grant exceptions for customers, approve cheque receipts above a certain amount, and allow customers to purchase on credit.
Separation of duties	Cashiers and mailroom employees who handle cash do not have access to the accounting records. Accountants who record cash receipts have no opportunity to handle cash.
Internal and external audits	Internal auditors examine company transactions for agreement with management policies. External auditors examine the internal controls over cash receipts to determine whether the accounting system produces accurate amounts for revenues, receivables, and other items related to cash receipts.
Documents and records	Customers receive receipts as transaction records. Bank statement lists cash receipts for reconciliation with company records (deposit tickets). Customers who pay by mail include a remittance advice showing the amount of cash the company received.
Electronic and other controls	Cash registers serve as transaction records. Cashiers are bonded. Cash is stored in vaults and banks. Each day's receipts are matched with customer remittance advices and with the day's deposit ticket with the bank. Employees are rotated among jobs and are required to take vacations.

Concept Highlight

Cash Receipts by Mail   All incoming mail should be opened by a mail-room employee. This person should compare the actual enclosed amount of cash or cheque with the attached remittance advice. If no advice was sent, the mail-room employee should prepare one and enter the amount of each receipt on a control tape. At the end of the day, this control tape is given to a responsible official, such as the controller, for verification. Cash receipts should be given to the cashier, who combines them with any cash received over the counter and prepares the bank deposit.

Having a mail-room employee be the first to handle postal cash receipts is just another application of a good internal control procedure—in this case, separation of duties. If the accountants opened postal cash receipts, they could easily hide a theft.

The mail-room employee forwards the remittance advices to the accounting department. They provide the data for entries in the cash receipts journal and postings to customers' accounts in the accounts receivable ledger. As a final step, the controller compares the three records of the day's cash receipts: (1) the control tape total from the mail room, (2) the bank deposit amount from the cashier, and (3) the debit to Cash from the accounting department.

Cash Short and Over   A difference often exists between actual cash receipts and the day's record of cash received. Usually the difference is small and results from honest errors. When the recorded cash balance exceeds cash on hand, we have a *cash short* situation. When the actual cash exceeds the recorded cash balance, we have a *cash over*. Suppose the tapes from a cash register of Zellers indicate sales revenue of $25,000, but the cash received is $24,980. To record the day's sales for that register, the store would make this entry:

Cash in Bank...	24,980	
Cash Short and Over	20	
Sales Revenue..		25,000

As the entry shows, Cash Short and Over is debited when sales revenue exceeds cash receipts. This account is credited when cash receipts exceed sales. A debit balance in cash short and over appears on the income statement as Miscellaneous Expense, a credit balance as Other Revenue.

This account's balance should be small. The debits and credits for cash shorts and overs collected over an accounting period tend to cancel each other out. A large balance signals the accountant to investigate. For example, too large a debit balance may mean an employee is stealing. Cash Short and Over, then, acts as an internal control device.

OBJECTIVE 5

Apply internal controls to cash disbursements

Internal Control over Cash Disbursements (Payments) ____

Cash disbursements are at least as important as cash receipts because how a business spends its money determines the source and amount of cash receipts.

Controls over Payment by Cheque

Payment by *cheque* is an important control over cash disbursements. First, the cheque acts as a source document. Second, to be valid the cheque must be signed by an authorized official, so that each payment by cheque draws the attention of management. Before signing the cheque, the manager should study the evidence supporting the payment.

To illustrate the internal control over cash disbursements, suppose the business is buying inventory for sale to customers. Let's examine the process leading up to the cash payment.

Controls Over Purchasing   The purchasing process—outlined in Exhibit 7-7—starts when the sales department identifies the need for merchandise and prepares a *purchase request* (or requisition). A separate purchasing department specializes in

EXHIBIT 7-7   *Purchasing Process*

Business Document	Prepared by	Sent to
Purchase request	Sales department	Purchasing department
Purchase order	Purchasing department	Outside company that sells the needed merchandise (supplier or vendor)
Invoice	Outside company that sells the needed merchandise (supplier or vendor)	Accounting department
Receiving report	Receiving department	Accounting department
Disbursement packet	Accounting department	Officer who signs the cheque

EXHIBIT 7-8 Disbursement Packet

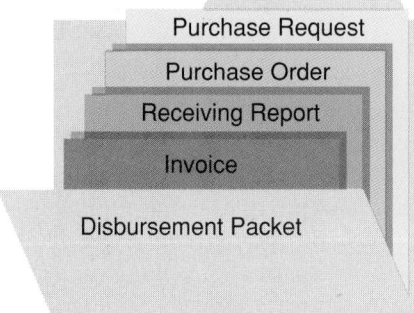

Purchase Request
Purchase Order
Receiving Report
Invoice
Disbursement Packet

locating the best buys and mails a *purchase order* to the supplier, the outside company that sells the needed goods. When the supplier ships the goods to the requesting business, the supplier also mails the *invoice*, or bill, which is a notification of the need to pay. As the goods arrive, the receiving department checks them for any damage and lists the merchandise received on a document called the *receiving report*. The accounting department attaches all the foregoing documents, checks them for accuracy and agreement, and forwards this disbursement packet to designated officers for approval and payment. The packet includes the invoice, receiving report, purchase order, and purchase request, as shown in Exhibit 7-8.

Controls Over Approval of Payments Before approving the disbursement, the controller and the treasurer should examine a sample of transactions to determine that the following control steps have been performed by the accounting department:

1. The invoice is compared with a copy of the purchase order and purchase request to ensure that the business pays cash only for the goods that it ordered.
2. The invoice is compared with the receiving report to ensure that cash is paid only for the goods that are actually received.
3. The mathematical accuracy of the invoice is proved.

Information technology is streamlining cash disbursement procedures in many businesses. Exhibit 7-9 summarizes the internal controls over cash disbursements. The use of **vouchers**, documents that authorize cash disbursements, improves the internal control over cash disbursements. (See the appendix at the end of this chapter for a discussion of the voucher system.) As further security and control over disbursements, many firms require two signatures on a cheque, as we saw in Exhibit 7-3. To avoid document alteration, some firms also use machines that indelibly stamp the amount on the cheque. After payment, the cheque signer can punch a

Short Exercise:
You manage a clothing store. The cheques are prepared by the bookkeeper and require two signatures—the bookkeeper's and yours. You are leaving on a two-week vacation. To minimize inconvenience, you have pre-signed 20 cheques so that only the bookkeeper must sign them in your absence. You have left strict instructions about allowable payments. What internal control feature is being violated? *A:* Never leave signed cheques. The bookkeeper can make unauthorized payments. Payments need your approval.

OBJECTIVE 6
Account for petty cash transactions

STOP & THINK

Talon Computer Concepts Ltd. processes payroll cheques for small businesses. Clients give their employees' time cards to Talon each week, and Talon programmers write computer programs to meet the clients' payrolls. Talon computer operators process and deliver the cheques to the clients for distribution to employees. Identify two employee functions of Talon's cash disbursements system that should be separated. Give your reason.

Answer: The programmers should not also be computer operators. Any person who performed both functions could write the program to process cheques to himself or herself or to a fictitious employee and then pocket the printed cheques.

EXHIBIT 7-9   *Internal Controls over Cash Disbursements*

Element of Internal Control	Internal Controls over Cash Disbursements
Competent, reliable, ethical personnel	Cash disbursements are entrusted to high-level employees, with larger amounts paid by the treasurer or assistant treasurer.
Assignment of responsibility	Specific employees approve purchase documents for payment. Executives examine approvals, then sign cheques.
Proper authorization	Large expenditures must be authorized by the company owner or board of directors to ensure agreement with organizational goals.
Separation of duties	Computer operators and other employees who handle cheques have no access to the accounting records. Accountants who record cash disbursements have no opportunity to handle cash.
Internal and external audits	Internal auditors examine company transactions for agreement with management policies. External auditors examine the internal controls over cash disbursements to determine whether the accounting system produces accurate amounts for expenses, assets, and other items related to cash disbursements.
Documents and records	Suppliers issue invoices that document the need to pay cash. Bank statements list cash payments (cheques and EFT disbursements) for reconciliation with company records. Cheques are prenumbered to account for payments in sequence.
Electronic and other controls	Blank cheques are stored in a vault and controlled by a responsible official with no accounting duties. Machines stamp the amount on a cheque in indelible ink. Paid invoices are punched to avoid duplicate payment.

Concept Highlight

hole through the disbursement packet. This hole denotes that the invoice has been paid and discourages a dishonest employee from running the documents through the system for a duplicate payment.

Petty Cash Disbursements

It would be uneconomical for a business to write a separate cheque for an executive's taxi fare, a box of pencils needed right away, or the delivery of a special message across town. Therefore, companies keep a small amount of cash on hand to pay for such minor amounts. This fund is called **petty cash**.

Even though the individual amounts paid through the petty cash fund may be small, such expenses occur so often that the total amount over an accounting period may grow quite large. Thus the business needs to set up these controls over petty cash: (1) designate an employee to administer the fund as its custodian, (2) keep a specific amount of cash on hand, (3) support all fund disbursements with a petty cash ticket, and (4) replenish the fund through normal cash disbursement procedures.

The petty cash fund is opened when a payment is approved for a predetermined amount and a cheque for this amount is issued to Petty Cash. Assume that on February 28 the business decides to establish a petty cash fund of $200. The custodian cashes the cheque and places the currency and coin in the fund, which may be a cash box, safe, or other device. The petty cash custodian is assigned the responsibility for controlling the fund. Starting the fund is recorded as follows:

Feb. 28   Petty Cash...   200
             Cash in Bank   200
        To open the petty cash fund.

For each petty cash disbursement, the custodian prepares a *petty cash ticket* like the one illustrated in Exhibit 7-10.

Observe the signatures (or initials, for the custodian) that identify the recipient of petty cash and the fund custodian. Requiring both signatures reduces unauthorized cash disbursements. The custodian keeps all the petty cash tickets in the fund. The sum of the cash plus the total of the ticket amounts should equal the opening balance at all times—in this case, $200. Maintaining the Petty Cash account keeps its prescribed $200 balance at all times. Maintaining the Petty Cash account at this balance, supported by the fund (cash plus tickets totaling the fund amount) is a characteristic of an **imprest system**. The control feature of an imprest system is that it clearly identifies the amount of money that the fund custodian is responsible for.

Disbursements reduce the amount of cash in the fund, so periodically the fund must be replenished. Suppose that on March 31st the fund has $118 in cash and $82 in tickets. A cheque for $82 is issued, made payable to Petty Cash. The fund custodian cashes this cheque for currency and coins, and puts the money in the fund to return its actual cash to $200. The petty cash tickets identify the accounts to be debited: Store Supplies for $23, Delivery Expense for $17 and Miscellaneous Selling Expense for $42. The entry to record replenishment of the fund is

Mar. 31   Store Supplies   23
            Delivery Expense   17
            Miscellaneous Selling Expense...........   42
              Cash in Bank...................................   82
            To replenish the petty cash fund.

If this cash payment exceeds the sum of the tickets—that is, if the fund comes up short, Cash Short and Over is debited for the missing amount. If the sum of the tickets exceeds the payment, Cash Short and Over is credited. Replenishing the fund does *not* affect the Petty Cash account. Petty Cash keeps its $200 balance at all times.

Whenever petty cash runs low, the fund is replenished. It *must* be replenished on the balance sheet date. Otherwise, the reported balance for Petty Cash will be overstated by the amount of the tickets in the fund. The income statement will understate the expenses listed on these tickets.

Petty Cash is debited only when starting the fund (see the February 28 entry) or changing its amount. In our illustration, suppose the business decides to raise the fund amount from $200 to $250 because of increased demand for petty cash. This step would require a $50 debit to Petty Cash.

> ☑ *Key Point:*
> No journal entries are made for petty cash disbursements until the fund is replenished. At that time, all petty cash payments will be recorded in a summary entry. This procedure avoids the need to journalize many payments for small amounts.

EXHIBIT 7-10   *Petty Cash Ticket*

```
                    PETTY CASH TICKET

Date    Mar. 25, 19X4                        No.  45

Amount    $23.00

For    Box of floppy diskettes

Debit    Office Supplies, Acct. No. 145

Received by   Lewis Wright      Fund Custodian   WAR
```

Ethics and Internal Controls

An article in *The Wall Street Journal* (August 2, 1993, page A1) quoted a young entrepreneur in Russia as saying that he was getting ahead in business by breaking laws. He stated that "Older people have an ethics problem. By that I mean they *have* ethics." Conversely, Roger Smith, former chairman of General Motors, said, "Ethical practice is, quite simply, good business." Which perspective is valid? The latter. There are at least two key differences between these competing perspectives. The young entrepreneur is operating in a country where legal, social, and ethical structures are in tremendous upheaval. In contrast, Smith's environment—Canada and the United States—is stable. Businesses in Russia are fledglings with little in the way of internal controls. Apparently, the young entrepreneur has not yet been caught. Smith has been in business long enough to see the danger in unethical behavior. Sooner or later unethical conduct comes to light, as was true in our chapter-opening story.

Corporate and Professional Codes of Ethics

Most large companies have a code of ethics designed to encourage employees to behave ethically and responsibly. A set of general guidelines may not be specific enough to identify misbehavior. A list of do's and don'ts can lead to the false view that anything is okay if it's not specifically forbidden. There is no easy answer. But most businesses are intolerant of unethical conduct by employees. One executive has stated, "I cannot describe all unethical behavior, but I know it when I see it."

Accountants have additional incentives to behave ethically. As professionals, they are expected to maintain higher standards than society in general. Why? The work of professionals such as accountants and physicians is difficult to judge. Their ability to attract business depends entirely on their reputation.

As you learned in Chapter 1, there are three bodies of professional accountants in Canada: the CAs; the CGAs; and the CMAs. Members of each of the bodies must adhere to the rules of professional conduct of their respective organizations.

These documents set minimum standards of conduct for members. Unacceptable actions can result in expulsion from the organization, which makes it difficult for the person to remain in the accounting profession.

Ethical Issues in Accounting

In many situations the ethical choice is easy. For example, stealing cash as in the chapter opener is illegal and unethical. The cashier's actions landed her in jail. In other cases, the choices are more difficult. But, in every instance, ethical judgments boil down to a personal decision. How should I behave in a given situation? Let's consider three ethical issues in accounting. The first two are easy to resolve. The third issue is more difficult.

Situation 1   Sonja Kleberg is preparing the income tax return of a client who has had a particularly good year—higher income than expected. On January 2, the client pays for newspaper advertising and asks Sonja to backdate the expense to the preceding year. The tax deduction would help the client more in the year just ended than in the current year. Backdating would decrease taxable income of the earlier year and save the client a few dollars in tax payments. After all, there is a difference of only two days between January 2 and December 31. This client is important to Kleberg. What should she do? She should refuse the request because the transaction took place in January of the new year. What internal control device could prove that Kleberg behaved unethically if she backdated the transaction in the accounting records? A Revenue Canada audit of the documents and records: The date of the cash payment could prove that the expense occurred in January rather than in December.

Situation 2   Jack Mellichamp's software company owes $40,000 to the Toronto-Dominion Bank. The loan agreement requires Mellichamp's company to maintain a current ratio (current assets divided by current liabilities) of 1.50 or higher. It is late in the year, and the bank will review Mellichamp's situation early next year. At present, the company's current ratio is 1.40. At this level, Mellichamp is in violation of his loan agreement. He can increase the current ratio to 1.53 by paying off some current liabilities right before year end. Is it ethical to do so? Yes, because the action is a real business transaction. But paying off the liabilities is only a delaying tactic. It will hold off the creditors for now, but time will tell whether the business can improve its underlying operations.

Situation 3   Emilia Gomez, an accountant for Hoover Electronics Ltd., discovers that her supervisor, Myles Packer, made several errors last year. Overall, the errors overstated net income by 20 percent. It is not clear whether the errors were deliberate or accidental. Gomez is deciding what to do. She knows that Packer evaluates her job performance, and lately her work has been marginal. What should Gomez do? The answer is uncertain.

Framework for Ethical Judgments

Situation 3 poses a difficult question because the best course of action is not clear. Some would consider this an ethical dilemma. Weighing tough ethical judgments carefully requires a decision framework. Consider these six steps as they apply to Emilia Gomez's situation.

1. *Determine the facts.* These are clear from the description of the situation.

2. *Identify the ethical issues.* The root word of *ethical* is ethics, which Webster's dictionary defines as "the discipline dealing with what is good and bad and with moral duty and obligation." Gomez's ethical dilemma is to decide what is the right thing to do with the information she has uncovered.

3. *Specify the alternatives.* Three reasonable alternatives include (a) reporting the errors to Packer, (b) reporting the errors to the owner of the company, and (c) correcting the errors while saying nothing.

4. *Identify the people involved.* Individuals who could be affected include Gomez, Packer, the owner of the company, Gomez's co-workers who observe her behavior, and outsiders who rely on Hoover's financial statements.

5. *Assess the possible consequences.* (a) If Gomez reported the errors to Packer, he might penalize her or reward her for careful work. Her reporting the errors would preserve her integrity and probably would lead to correction of the errors. But Hoover Electronics could suffer embarrassment in notifying users of the changes required to correct the financial statements. (b) If Gomez reported to the company owner—going over Packer's head—her integrity would be preserved. Her relationship with Packer would surely be strained, and it might be difficult for them to work together in the future. The owner might reward Gomez for careful work. But if the owner had colluded with Packer in deliberately overstating income, Gomez could be penalized. If the error was corrected and outsiders were notified, Hoover would be embarrassed. Other accountants who observed this situation would be affected by the outcome. (c) If Gomez quietly corrected the error, she would avoid a confrontation with Packer or the owner. They might or might not discover the error and its correction. If they discovered it, they might or might not notify outsiders. All might criticize Gomez for not bringing the error to their attention. Fellow accountants might or might not learn of the situation.

6. *Make the decision.* The best choice is unclear. Gomez must balance the likely effects on the various people against the dictates of her own conscience. Even though this framework does not provide an easy decision, it identifies the relevant factors. Reporting the error to Packer is preferable because he is Gomez's supervisor. Moreover, Gomez must protect her reputation and consider the interests of outsiders who may be relying on Hoover's financial statements.

Ethics and External Controls _____

There is another dimension to most ethical issues: external controls, which refer to the discipline on business conduct placed by outsiders who interact with the company. In situation 1, for example, Sonja Kleberg could give in to the client's request to backdate the advertising expense. But because this would be dishonest, it would be risky. To backdate the expense record would be illegal, however insignificant the amount of the transaction. These external controls arise from the business's interaction with the taxing authorities. A Revenue Canada audit of Kleberg's client could uncover her action.

In situation 2, the external controls arise from Jack Mellichamp's relationship with the bank that lent money to his software company. As long as the loan agreement is in effect, the company must maintain a current ratio of 1.50 or higher. Paying off current liabilities to improve the current ratio would be a short-term solution to Mellichamp's problem. Over the long run, his business must generate more current assets through operations. Almost certainly his business will need to borrow in the future and will probably face similar loan restrictions. Managers are wise to focus on long-term solutions to their problems if they hope to succeed in business.

The primary external control in situation 3 results from creditors and other outside users of Hoover Electronics' financial statements. If these people suffered a financial loss because they were deceived by Hoover's overstated income, they could file a lawsuit against Hoover. The legal system in Canada places the burden of proof on companies to show that their financial information is accurate. A lender or an investor who can demonstrate that a loss resulted from reliance on fraudulent information can recover damages against the company.

A shifting of income to one year usually causes a corresponding decrease in the income of a later year. Thus Hoover's reporting 20 percent too much income last year may cause the company to report 20 percent too little income the next year. The ethical implication is that companies that are caught manipulating their reported income lose their good reputations very quickly. This loss would make it difficult to attract investors and to borrow money on favorable terms. Honest errors can occur, and lenders and investors can be forgiving, but companies must work hard to keep their reputations clean. That is why they have codes of conduct and why, as Roger Smith put it, "Ethical practice is…good business."

Summary Problem for Your Review

Grudnitski Ltd. established a $300 petty cash fund. James C. Brown is the fund custodian. At the end of the first week, the petty cash fund contains the following:

1. Cash: $171
2. Petty cash tickets

No.	Amount	Issued to	Signed by	Account Debited
44	$14	B. Jarvis	B. Jarvis and JCB	Office Supplies
45	9	S. Bell	S. Bell	Miscellaneous Expense
47	43	R. Tate	R. Tate and JCB	—
48	33	G. Ghiz	G. Ghiz and JCB	Travel Expense

Required

1. Identify the four internal control weaknesses revealed in the given data.
2. Prepare the general journal entries to record
   a. Establishment of the petty cash fund.

   b. Replenishment of the fund. Assume petty cash ticket no. 47 was issued for
      the purchase of office supplies.
3. What is the balance in the Petty Cash account immediately before replenishment?
   Immediately after replenishment?

SOLUTION TO REVIEW PROBLEM

Requirement 1

The four internal control weaknesses are

a. Petty cash ticket no. 46 is missing. Coupled with weakness b, this omission raises
   questions about the administration of the petty cash fund and about how the
   petty cash funds were used.
b. The $171 cash balance means that $129 has been disbursed ($300 – $171 = $129).
   However, the total amount of the petty cash tickets is only $99 ($14 + $9 + $43 +
   $33). The fund, then, is $30 short of cash ($129 – $99 = $30). Was petty cash ticket
   no. 46 issued for $30? The data in the problem offer no hint that helps answer
   this question. In a real-world setting, management would investigate the problem.
c. The petty cash custodian (JCB) did not sign petty cash ticket no. 45. This omission
   may have been an oversight on his part. However, it raises the question of whether
   he authorized the disbursement. Both the fund custodian and recipient of cash
   should sign the ticket.
d. Petty cash ticket no. 47 does not indicate which account to debit. What did Tate
   do with the money, and what account should be debited? At worst, the funds
   have been stolen. At best, asking the custodian to reconstruct the transaction
   from memory is haphazard. With no better choice available, debit Miscellaneous
   Expense.

Requirement 2

Petty cash journal entries
a. Entry to establish the petty cash fund

Petty Cash	300	
Cash in Bank		300

b. Entry to replenish the fund

Office Supplies ($14 + $43)	57	
Miscellaneous Expense	9	
Travel Expense	33	
Cash Short and Over	30	
Cash in Bank		129

Requirement 3

The balance in Petty Cash is *always* its specified balance, in this case $300, as shown
by posting the above entries to the account.

Petty Cash

(a)   300

The entry to establish the fund (entry a) debits Petty Cash. The entry to replenish the
fund (entry b) neither debits nor credits Petty Cash.

Summary

1. *Define internal control.* Internal control objectives are to optimize the use of resources, prevent and detect error and fraud, safeguard assets, and maintain reliable control systems.

Internal control is the organizational plan and all related measures adopted by an entity to meet management's objectives of discharging statutory responsibilities, profitability, prevention and detection of fraud and error, safeguarding of assets, reliability of accounting records, and timely preparation of reliable financial information.

2. *Identify the characteristics of an effective system of internal control.* An effective internal control system includes these features: *reliable personnel, clear-cut assignment of responsibility, proper authorization,* and *separation of duties,* which is the primary element of internal control. Many businesses use security devices, audits, and specially designed documents and records in their internal control systems. Effective computerized internal control systems must meet the same basic standards that good manual systems do.

3. *Prepare a bank reconciliation and the related journal entries.* The *bank account* helps to control and safeguard cash. Businesses use the *bank statement* and the *bank reconciliation* to account for banking transactions.

4. *Apply internal controls to cash receipts.* Different methods are used to control cash receipts over the counter and cash receipts by mail.

5. *Apply internal controls to cash disbursements.* A key control over cash disbursements is payment by cheque.

6. *Account for petty cash transactions.* An *imprest system* is used to control petty cash disbursements.

7. *Weigh ethical judgments in business.* Ethical judgments can be aided by a process that identifies the ethical issues, specifies the alternative actions, identifies the people involved, and assesses the possible consequences.

Self-Study Questions

Test your understanding of the chapter by marking the correct answer for each of the following questions:

1. Which of the following is an objective of internal control? *(p. 334)*
   a. Safeguarding assets
   b. Maintaining reliable control systems
   c. Optimizing the use of resources
   d. Preventing and detecting fraud and error
   e. All the above are objectives of internal control.

2. Which of the characteristics of an effective system of internal control is violated by allowing the employee who handles inventory to also account for inventory? *(p. 338)*
   a. Competent and reliable personnel   c. Proper authorization
   b. Assignment of responsibilities   d. Separation of duties

3. What control function is performed by auditors? *(p. 339)*
   a. Objective opinion of the effectiveness of the internal control system
   b. Assurance that all transactions are accounted for correctly
   c. Communication of the results of the audit to regulatory agencies
   d. Guarantee that a proper separation of duties exists within the business

4. The bank account serves as a control device over *(pp. 341–345)*
   a. Cash receipts   c. Both of the above
   b. Cash disbursements   d. None of the above

5. Which of the following items appears on the bank side of a bank reconciliation? *(p. 345)*
   a. Book error   c. NSF cheque
   b. Outstanding cheque   d. Interest revenue earned on bank balance

6. Which of the following reconciling items requires a journal entry on the books of the company? *(pp. 346–347)*
    a. Book error
    b. Outstanding cheque
    c. NSF cheque
    d. Interest revenue earned on bank balance
    e. All of the above, except (b)
    f. None of the above

7. What is the major internal control measure over the cash receipts of a Zellers store? *(p. 350)*
    a. Reporting the day's cash receipts to the controller
    b. Preparing a petty cash ticket for all disbursements from the fund
    c. Pricing merchandise at uneven amounts, coupled with use of a cash register
    d. Channeling all cash receipts through the mail room, whose employees have no cash-accounting responsibilities

8. Before signing a cheque to pay for goods purchased, the company should determine that the *(p. 353)*
    a. Invoice is for the goods ordered
    b. Merchandise was received
    c. Amount of the bill is correct
    d. All of the above are correct

9. The internal control feature that is specific to petty cash is *(p. 354)*
    a. Separation of duties   c. Proper authorization
    b. Assignment of responsibility   d. The imprest system

10. Ethical judgments in accounting and business *(pp. 356–358)*
    a. Require employees to break laws to get ahead
    b. Force decisions about what is good and bad
    c. Always hurt someone
    d. Are affected by internal controls but not by external controls

Answers to the Self-Study Questions follow the Accounting Vocabulary.

Accounting Vocabulary

Bank collections *(p. 344)*
Bank reconciliation *(p. 344)*
Bank statement *(p. 342)*
Cheque *(p. 341)*
Deposits in transit *(p. 344)*
Electronic funds transfer (EFT) *(p. 342)*
Imprest system *(p. 355)*
Internal control *(p. 334)*
NSF (nonsufficient funds) cheques *(p. 344)*
Outstanding cheques *(p. 344)*
Petty cash *(p. 354*
Voucher *(p. 353)*

Answers to Self-Study Questions

1. e   3. a   5. b   7. c   9. d
2. d   4. c   6. e   8. d   10. b

ASSIGNMENT MATERIAL _____

Questions

1. Which of the features of effective internal control is the most fundamental? Why?

2. What is the role of the Audit Committee? Does the example of the report from management in the text support your answer? How?

3. Which company employees bear primary responsibility for a company's financial statements and for maintaining the company's system of internal control? How do these persons carry out this responsibility?

4. Identify features of an effective system of internal control.

5. Separation of duties may be divided into four parts. What are they?

6. How can internal control systems be circumvented?

7. Are internal control systems designed to be foolproof and perfect? What is a fundamental constraint in planning and maintaining systems?

8. Briefly state how each of the following serves as an internal control measure over cash: bank account, signature card, deposit ticket, and bank statement.

9. What is the remittance advice of a cheque? What use does it serve?

10. Each of the items in the following list must be accounted for in the bank reconciliation. Next to each item, enter the appropriate letter from the following possible treatments: (a) bank side of reconciliation—add the item; (b) bank side of reconciliation—subtract the item; (c) book side of reconciliation—add the item; and (d) book side of reconciliation—subtract the item.

    _____   Outstanding cheque
    _____   NSF cheque
    _____   Bank service charge
    _____   Cost of printed cheques
    _____   EFT receipt
    _____   Bank error that decreased bank balance
    _____   Deposit in transit
    _____   Bank collection
    _____   EFT payment
    _____   Customer's cheque returned because of unauthorized signature
    _____   Book error that increased balance of Cash account

11. What purpose does a bank reconciliation serve?

12. Suppose a company has six bank accounts, two petty cash funds, and three certificates of deposit that can be withdrawn on demand. How many cash amounts would this company likely report on its balance sheet?

13. What role does a cash register play in an internal control system?

14. Describe internal control procedures for cash received by mail.

15. What documents make up the disbursement packet? Describe three procedures that use the disbursement packet to ensure that each payment is appropriate.

16. What balance does the Petty Cash account have at all times? Does this balance always equal the amount of cash in the fund? When are the two amounts equal? When are they unequal?

17. Why should accountants adhere to a higher standard of ethical conduct than many other members of society do?

18. "Our managers know that they are expected to meet budgeted profit figures. We don't want excuses. We want results." Discuss the ethical implications of this policy.

19. Why should the same employee not write the computer programs for cash disbursements, sign cheques, and mail the cheques to payees?

Exercises

Exercise 7-1   *Identifying internal control strengths and weaknesses*   *(Obj. 2)*

The following situations suggest either a strength or weakness in internal control. Identify each as strength or weakness and give the reason for your answer.

a. Cash received by mail goes straight to the accountant, who debits Cash and credits Accounts Receivable from the customer.

b. The vice-president who signs cheques assumes the accounting department has matched the invoice with other supporting documents and therefore does not examine the disbursement packet.

c. Top managers delegate all internal control measures to the accounting department.

d. The accounting department orders merchandise and approves vouchers for payment.

e. The operator of the computer has no other accounting or cash-handling duties.

f. Cash received over the counter is controlled by the salesclerk, who rings up the sale and places the cash in the register. The salesclerk has access to the control tape stored in the register.

Exercise 7-2   *Identifying internal controls*   *(Obj. 2)*

Identify the missing internal control characteristic in the following situations:

a. In the course of auditing the records of a company, you find that the same employee orders merchandise and approves invoices for payment.

b. Business is slow at the White Water Park on Tuesday, Wednesday, and Thursday nights. To reduce expenses the owner decides not to use a ticket taker on those nights. The ticket seller (cashier) is told to keep the tickets as a record of the number sold.

c. The manager of a discount store wants to speed the flow of customers through check-out. She decides to reduce the time spent by cashiers making change, so she prices merchandise at round dollar amounts—such as $8.00 and $15.00—instead of the customary amounts—$7.95 and $14.95.

d. Grocery stores such as Save-on-Foods and Great Canadian Superstore purchase large quantities of their merchandise from a few suppliers. At another grocery store the manager decides to reduce paper work. He eliminates the requirement that a receiving department employee prepare a receiving report, which lists the quantities of items received from the supplier.

e. When business is brisk, Beckers and many other retail stores deposit cash in the bank several times during the day. The manager at another convenience store wants to reduce the time spent by employees delivering cash to the bank, so he starts a new policy. Cash will build up over Saturdays and Sundays, and the total two-day amount will be deposited on Sunday evening.

Exercise 7-3   *Classifying bank reconciliation items*   *(Obj. 3)*

The following seven items may appear on a bank reconciliation:

1. Book error: We debited Cash for $200. The correct debit was $2,000.
2. Outstanding cheques.
3. Bank error: the bank charged our account for a cheque written by another customer.
4. Service charge.
5. Deposits in transit.
6. NSF cheque.
7. Bank collection of a note receivable on our behalf.

Classify each item as (1) an addition to the bank balance, (2) a subtraction from the bank balance, (3) an addition to the book balance, or (4) a subtraction from the book balance.

Exercise 7-4 *Bank reconciliation* *(Obj. 3)*

Tracy Mann's chequebook lists the following:

Date	Cheque No.	Item	Cheque	Deposit	Balance
9/1					$ 525
4	622	Treats Gift Shop	$ 19		506
9		Dividends		$ 116	622
13	623	B.C. Telephone	43		579
14	624	Petro Canada	58		521
18	625	Cash	50		471
26	626	St. Alban's Anglican Church	25		446
28	627	Bent Tree Apartments	275		171
30		Paycheque		2,000	2,171

The September bank statement shows:

Balance		$525
Add: Deposits..		116
Deduct cheques: No.	Amount	
622	$19	
623	43	
624	68*	
625	50	(180)
Other charges		
Printed cheques	$ 8	
Service charge	12	(20)
Balance		$441

* This is the correct amount of cheque number 624.

Required

Prepare Tracy's bank reconciliation at September 30.

Exercise 7-5 *Bank reconciliation* *(Obj. 3)*

Pierre Vincelette operates four Petro Canada stations. He has just received the monthly bank statement at October 31 from the Bank of Nova Scotia, and the statement shows an ending balance of $3,840. Listed on the statement are an EFT rent collection of $400, a service charge of $12, two NSF cheques totaling $74, and a $9 charge for printed cheques. In reviewing his cash records, Vincelette identifies outstanding cheques totaling $467 and an October 31 deposit of $788 which does not appear on the bank statement. During October, he recorded a $290 cheque for the salary of a part-time employee by debiting Salary Expense and crediting Cash for $29. Vincelette's cash account shows an October 31 cash balance of $4,117. Prepare the bank reconciliation at October 31.

Exercise 7-6 *Journal entries from a bank reconciliation* *(Obj. 3)*

Using the data from Exercise 7-5, record the entries that Vincelette should make in the general journal on October 31. Include an explanation for each of the entries.

Exercise 7-7   *Internal controls and the bank reconciliation*   **(Obj. 2, 3)**

A jury convicted the treasurer of On-Time Taxi Company Ltd. for stealing cash from the company. Over a 10-year period the treasurer allegedly took almost $50,000 and attempted to cover the theft by manipulating the bank reconciliation.

Required

What is the most likely way that a person would manipulate a bank reconciliation to cover a theft? Be specific. What internal control arrangement could have avoided this theft?

Exercise 7-8   *Internal control over cash receipts*   **(Obj. 4)**

A cash register is located in each department of Woodwyn's Discount Store. The register shows the amount of each sale, the cash received from the customer, and any change returned to the customer. The machine also produces a customer receipt but keeps no record of transactions. At the end of the day, the clerk counts the cash in the register and gives it to the cashier for deposit in the company bank account.

Required

Write a memo to convince the store manager that there is an internal control weakness over cash receipts. Identify the weakness that gives an employee the best opportunity to steal cash, and state how to prevent such a theft.

Exercise 7-9   *Accounting for petty cash*   **(Obj. 5, 6)**

United Way of Regina, Saskatchewan, created a $300 imprest petty cash fund. During the first month of use, the fund custodian authorized and signed petty cash tickets as follows:

Ticket No.	Item	Account Debited	Amount
1	Delivery of pledge cards to donors	Delivery Expense	$22.19
2	Stamp purchase	Postage Expense	52.80
3	Newsletter	Supplies Expense	34.14
4	Key to closet	Miscellaneous Expense	.85
5	Waste basket	Miscellaneous Expense	3.78
6	Staples	Supplies Expense	85.37

Required

1. Make general journal entries for creation of the petty cash fund and its replenishment. Include explanations.
2. Immediately prior to replenishment, describe the items in the fund.
3. Immediately after replenishment, describe the items in the fund.

Exercise 7-10   *Petty cash voucher system*   **(Obj. 6, 7)**

Record the following selected transactions in general journal format (explanations are not required):

April 1   Established a petty cash fund with a $500 balance.
       2   Journalized the day's cash sales. Cash register tapes show a $2,869 total, but the cash in the register is only $2,863.
      10   The petty cash fund has $169 in cash and $271 in petty cash tickets issued to pay for Office Supplies ($61), Delivery Expense ($113) and Entertainment Expense ($97). Replenished the fund.

Challenge Exercises

Exercise 7-11   *Internal control over cash disbursements, ethical considerations*   *(Obj. 5, 7)*

Amy Fisk, the owner of Amy's Dress Shop, has delegated management of the business to Micah Floyd, a friend. Fisk drops by the business to meet customers and checks up on cash receipts, but Floyd buys the merchandise and handles cash disbursements. Business has been brisk lately, and cash receipts have kept pace with the apparent level of sales. However, for a year or so the amount of cash on hand has been too low. When asked about this, Floyd explains that designers are charging more for dresses than in the past. During the past year Floyd has taken two expensive vacations, and Fisk wonders how Floyd could afford these trips on his $35,000 annual salary and commissions.

Required

List at least three ways Floyd could be defrauding the business of cash. In each instance, also identify how Fisk can determine whether Floyd's actions are ethical. Limit your answers to the dress shop's cash disbursements. The business pays all suppliers by cheque (no EFTs).

Exercise 7-12   *Ethical conduct by government legislators*   *(Obj. 5, 7)*

Several years ago, the newspapers carried stories revealing that approximately 300 current and former members of the U.S. House of Representatives—on a regular basis—wrote a quarter-million dollars of cheques without having the cash in their accounts. Later investigations revealed that no public funds were involved. The House bank was a free-standing institution that recirculated House members' cash. In effect, the delinquent cheque writers were borrowing money from each other on an interest-free, no-service-charge basis. Nevertheless, the House closed its bank after the events became public.

Required

You have been given the assignment in a political science course to comment on the issue. Apply the six-step framework for analysis outlined in the chapter to decide whether a congressional representative would write NSF cheques on a regular basis through the House bank.

Problems   *(Group A)*

Problem 7-1A   *Identifying the characteristics of an effective internal control system*   *(Obj. 1)*

An employee of CanAir Aircraft Service Corp. recently stole thousands of dollars of the company's cash. The company has decided to install a new system of internal controls.

Required

As controller of CanAir Aircraft Service Corp., write a memo to the president explaining how a separation of duties helps to safeguard assets.

Problem 7-2A   *Identifying internal control weaknesses*   *(Obj. 2, 4, 5)*

Each of the following situations has an internal control weakness:

a. Luann Sorella employs three professional interior designers in her design studio. She is located in an area with a lot of new construction, and her business is booming. Ordinarily, Luann does all the purchasing of furniture, draperies, carpets, fabrics, sewing services, and other materials and labor needed to complete jobs. During the summer she takes a long vacation, and in her absence she allows each designer to purchase materials and labor. At her return, Sorella reviews operations and notes that expenses are much higher and net income much lower than in the past.

b. Discount stores such as Kmart and Zellers receive a large portion of their sales revenue in cash, with the remainder in credit card sales. To reduce expenses, a store manager ceases purchasing fidelity bonds on the cashiers.

c. The office supply company from which Champs Sporting Goods purchases cash receipt forms recently notified Champs that the last shipped receipts were not prenumbered. Stephanie Champion, the owner, replied that she did not use the receipt numbers, so the omission is not important.

d. Lancer Computer Programs Ltd. is a software company that specializes in computer programs with accounting applications. The company's most popular program prepares the general journal, cash receipts journal, voucher register, cheque register, accounts receivable subsidiary ledger and general ledger. In the company's early days, the owner and eight employees wrote the computer programs, lined up manufacturers to produce the diskettes, sold the products to stores such as Compu Centre and Office Depot and performed the general management and accounting of the company. As the company has grown, the number of employees has increased dramatically. Recently, the development of a new software program stopped while the programmers redesigned Lancer's accounting system. Lancer's own accountants could have performed this task.

e. Myra Jones, a widow with no known sources of outside income, has been a trusted employee of Stone Products Company Ltd. for 15 years. She performs all cash handling and accounting duties, including opening the mail, preparing the bank deposit, accounting for all aspects of cash and accounts receivable, and preparing the bank reconciliation. She has just purchased a new Cadillac and a new home in an expensive suburb. Lou Stone, the owner of the company, wonders how she can afford these luxuries on her salary.

Required

1. Identify the missing internal control characteristic in each situation.
2. Identify the business's possible problem.
3. Propose a solution to the problem.

Problem 7-3A   *Identifying internal control weakness*   *(Obj. 2)*

Algonquin Dental Supply Inc. makes all sales on credit. Cash receipts arrive by mail, usually within 30 days of the sale. Brad Mooney opens envelopes and separates the cheques from the accompanying remittance advices. Mooney forwards the cheques to another employee who makes the daily bank deposit but has no access to the accounting records. Mooney sends the remittance advices, which show the amount of cash received, to the accounting department for entry in the accounts. Mooney's only other duty is to grant sales allowances to customers. When he receives a customer cheque for less than the full amount of the invoice, he records the sales allowance and forwards the document to the accounting department.

Required

You are the outside auditor of Algonquin Dental Supply. Write a memo to the company president to identify the internal control weakness in this situation. State how to correct the weakness.

Problem 7-4A   *Bank reconciliation and related journal entries*   *(Obj. 3)*

The May 31 bank statement of Pressler Institute has just arrived from the Royal Bank. To prepare the Pressler bank reconciliation, you gather the following data:

a. The May 31 bank balance is $4,530.82.

b. The bank statement includes two charges for returned cheques from customers. One is an NSF cheque in the amount of $67.50 received from Harley Doherty, a customer, recorded on the books by a debit to Cash and deposited on May 19. The other is a $195.03 cheque received from Maria Gucci and deposited on May 21. It was returned by Ms. Gucci's bank with the imprint "Unauthorized Signature."

c. The following Pressler cheques are outstanding at May 31:

Cheque No.	Amount
616	$403.00
802	74.25
806	36.60
809	161.38
810	229.05
811	48.91

d. A few students pay monthly fees by EFT. The May bank statement lists a $200 deposit for student fees.

e. The bank statement includes two special deposits: $899.14, which is the amount of dividend revenue the bank collected from Canadian General Electric on behalf of Pressler; and $16.86, the interest revenue Pressler earned on its bank balance during May.

f. The bank statement lists a $6.25 subtraction for the bank service charge.

g. On May 31, the Pressler treasurer deposited $381.14, but this deposit does not appear on the bank statement.

h. The bank statement includes a $410.00 deduction for a cheque drawn by Marimont Freight, Inc. Pressler promptly notified the bank of its error.

i. Pressler's Cash account shows a balance of $3,521.55 on May 31.

Required

1. Prepare the bank reconciliation for Pressler Institute at May 31.

2. Record in general journal form the entries necessary to bring the book balance of Cash into agreement with the adjusted book balance on the reconciliation. Include an explanation for each entry.

Problem 7-5A   *Bank reconciliation and related journal entries*   *(Obj. 3)*

Selected columns of the cash receipts journal and cheque register of Lethbridge Resources Inc. at March 31, 19X5 appear as follows:

Cash Receipts Journal (Posting reference is CR)		Cheque Register (Posting reference is CD)	
Date	Cash Debit	Cheque No.	Cash Credit
Mar. 4	$2,716	1413	$ 1,465
9	544	1414	1,004
11	1,655	1415	450
14	896	1416	8
17	367	1417	775
25	890	1418	88
31	2,038	1419	4,126
Total	$9,106	1420	970
		1421	200
		1422	2,267
		Total	$11,353

Assume the Cash account of Lethbridge Resources shows the following information on March 31, 19X5:

Cash

Date	Item	Jrnl. Ref.	Debit	Credit	Balance
Mar. 1	Balance				15,188
31		CR. 10	9,106		24,294
31		CD. 16		11,353	12,941

Lethbridge Resources received the following bank statement on March 31, 19X5:

Bank Statement for March 19X5

Beginning Balance..		$15,188
Deposits and Other Credits		
Mar. 1..	$ 625 EFT	
5..	2,716	
10..	544	
11..	1,655	
15..	896	
18..	367	
25..	890	
31..	1,000 BC	8,693
Cheques and Other Debits		
Mar. 8..	441 NSF	
9..	1,465	
13..	1,004	
14..	450	
15..	8	
19..	340 EFT	
22..	775	
29..	88	
31..	4,216	
31..	25 SC	(8,812)
Ending Balance...		$15,069

Explanation: EFT = Electronic Funds Transfer; BC = Bank Collection; NSF = Nonsufficient Fund Cheque; SC = Service Charge

Additional data for the bank reconciliation include:

a. The EFT deposit was a receipt of monthly rent. The EFT debit was payment of monthly insurance.

b. The NSF cheque was received late in February from J. Schlegal.

c. The $1,000 bank collection of a note receivable on March 31 included $122 interest revenue.

d. The correct amount of cheque no. 1419, a payment on account, is $4,216. (The Lethbridge Resources accountant mistakenly recorded the cheque for $4,126.)

Required

1. Prepare the bank reconciliation of Lethbridge Resources at March 31, 19X5.
2. Record the entries based on the bank reconciliation. Include explanations.

Problem 7-6A   *Accounting for petty cash transactions*   *(Obj. 5, 6)*

Suppose that on April 1, Ontario Hydro opens a regional office in Orillia and creates a petty cash fund with an imprest balance of $400. During April, Eleanor McGillicuddy, the fund custodian, signs the following petty cash tickets:

Ticket Number	Item	Amount
101	Office supplies	$86.89
102	Cab fare for executive	25.00
103	Delivery of package across town	37.75
104	Dinner money for sales manager entertaining a customer	80.00
105	Postage for package received	10.00
106	Decorations for office party	19.22
107	Six boxes of floppy disks	44.37

On April 30, prior to replenishment, the fund contains these tickets plus $84.77. The accounts affected by petty cash disbursements are Office Supplies Expense, Travel Expense, Delivery Expense, Entertainment Expense, and Postage Expense.

Required

1. Explain the characteristics and internal control features of an imprest fund.

2. Make general journal entries to create the fund and to replenish it. Include explanations. Also, briefly describe what the custodian does on these dates.

3. Make the entry on May 1 to increase the fund balance to $500. Include an explanation and briefly describe what the custodian does.

Problem 7-7A   *Making an ethical judgment*   *(Obj. 7)*

The Canadian Imperial Bank of Commerce (CIBC) in Brandon, Manitoba, has a loan receivable from Magellan Manufacturing Corp. Magellan is six months late in making payments to the bank, and Sheila Boswell, a CIBC vice-president, is assisting Magellan to restructure its debt. With unlimited access to Magellan's records Boswell learns that the company is depending on landing a manufacturing contract from Loew's Brothers Ltd., another CIBC client. Boswell also serves as Loew's loan officer at the bank. In this capacity she is aware that Loew's is considering declaring bankruptcy. No one else outside Loew's Brothers knows this. Boswell has been a great help to Magellan Manufacturing, and Magellan's owner is counting on her expertise in loan workouts to carry the company through this difficult process. To help the bank collect on this large loan, Boswell has a strong motivation to help Magellan survive.

Required

Apply the ethical judgment framework outlined in the chapter to help Sheila Boswell plan her next action.

Problem 7-8A   *Apply internal controls to cash disbursements, account for petty cash transactions*   *(Obj. 5, 6)*

Wayburn Wholesale Greenhouses Inc. operates out of White Rock, B.C. (in the lower mainland), with a sales territory covering the lower mainland and Vancouver Island. Employees live on both the mainland and the island, but all report to work at the company's offices in White Rock.

The company has established a large petty cash fund to handle small cash payments and cash advances to their sales force to cover frequent ferry trips to and from the island on sales trips.

The controller, J. Roberts, has decided that two people (D. Davis and L. Connor) should be in charge of the fund as money is often needed when one person may be out for coffee or lunch. Roberts also feels this will increase internal control, as the work of one person will serve as a check on that of the other.

Regular small cash payments required are handled by either Davis or Connor, who make the payment and have the person receiving the money sign a sheet of paper listing the date and reason for the payment. Whenever a salesperson requires an advance for a trip to the island, he or she simply signs a receipt for the money received. The salespeople later submit receipts for the cost of the ferry ride to either Davis or Connor to offset the cash advance.

A summary of transactions for the month of March, 19X1, is as follows:

- Balance of the fund and the actual cash on hand plus outstanding advances on March 1, 19X1 was $1,000.

- Reports from the fund managers included:

D. Davis		L. Conner	
Receipts for supplies	$ 20	Receipts for postage	$ 30
Miscellaneous receipts	40	Receipts for deliveries	50
Total advances given	230	Total advances given	320
Receipts for ferry rides	160	Receipts for ferry rides	210
Outstanding advances	70	Outstanding advances	110

- On March 31st, the fund had cash on hand of $120.

Required

1. Prepare a journal entry on March 31st to replenish the fund and increase its balance to $1,200. The fund should be replenished for the amount of all expenses incurred to date so that the cash on hand plus the outstanding advances will be equal to the balance of the fund.

2. Comment on the internal control procedures of Wayburn Wholesale Greenhouses Inc., including suggested improvements.

Problem 7-9A   *Prepare a bank reconciliation and related journal entries*   **(Obj. 3)**

The Matlocks Security Corporation had a computer failure on February 1, which resulted in the loss of data, including the balance of their cash account and their bank reconciliation from January 31, 19X1. The accountant, R. Springe, has been able to obtain the following information from the records of the company and their bank:

- An examination showed that two cheques (#131 for $180 and #144 for $325) had not been cashed as of February 1st. Springe recalled that there was only one deposit in transit on the January 31st bank reconciliation, but was unable to recall the amount.

- The cash receipts and cash disbursements journal contained the following entries for February, 19X1:

Cash Receipts:	Cash Disbursements:	
Amounts	**Cheque #**	**Amount**
$ 485	157	$ 195
680	158	165
510	159	230
920	160	435
270	161	215
$2,865	162	370
	163	void
	164	110
	165	460
		$2,180

- Their bank provided the following statement as of February 28, 19X1:

Date	Cheques and Other Debits		Deposits and Other Credits		Balance
Feb. 1	#158	165.00		880.00	2,005.00
3	#144	325.00			1,680.00
5	#159	230.00			1,450.00
8				485.00	1,935.00
14	#157	195.00		550.00	2,290.00
17	EFT	210.00			2,080.00
19			EFT	160.00	2,240.00
21	#161	215.00		680.00	2,705.00
22	#162	730.00	EFT	410.00	2,385.00
24			EFT	175.00	2,560.00
26	NSF	195.00		510.00	2,875.00
27	SC	25.00			2,850.00
28	#165	460.00		920.00	3,310.00

- The deposit made on February 14th was for the collection of a note receivable ($500) plus interest.
- The electronic funds transfers (EFT's) had not been recorded by Matlocks yet as the bank statement was the first notification of them. They consisted of:
  - February 17th was for the monthly payment on an insurance policy for Matlocks Security Corporation.
  - February 19th and 24th were collections on accounts receivable.
  - February 22nd ($410) was in error—the transfer should have been to Matrocks Construction Corporation.
- The "NSF" cheque on February 26th was received from a customer as payment for security equipment purchased for $195 (cost to Matlocks was $120).
- Cheque #162 was correctly written for $730 for the purchase of office supplies, but incorrectly recorded by the cash disbursements clerk.

Required

1. Prepare a bank reconciliation as of February 28, 19X1 including the calculation of the book balance of February 28, 19X1.
2. Prepare all journal entries that would be required by the bank reconciliation.

(Group B)

Problem 7-1B *Identifying the characteristics of an effective internal control system* **(Obj. 1)**

Shah Real Estate Development Company Ltd. prospered during the lengthy economic expansion of the 1980s and early 1990s. Business was so good that the company bothered with few internal controls. The recent decline in the local real estate market, however, has caused Shah to experience a shortage of cash. Jai Shah, the company owner, is looking for ways to save money.

Required

As controller of the company, write a memorandum to convince Mr. Shah of the company's need for a system of internal control. Be specific in telling him how an internal control system could possibly lead to saving money. Include the definition of internal control, and briefly discuss each characteristic beginning with competent, reliable, and ethical personnel.

Problem 7-2B   *Identifying internal control weaknesses*   **(Obj. 2, 4, 5)**

Each of the following situations has an internal control weakness:

a. In evaluating the internal control over cash disbursements, an auditor learns that the purchasing agent is responsible for purchasing diamonds for use in the company's manufacturing process, approving the invoices for payment, and signing the cheques. No supervisor reviews the purchasing agent's work.

b. Eric Van Der Saar owns a firm that performs engineering services. His staff consists of twelve professional engineers, and he manages the office. Often his work requires him to travel to meet with clients. During the past six months, he has observed that when he returns from a business trip, the engineering jobs in the office have not progressed satisfactorily. He learns that when he is away several of his senior employees take over office management and neglect their engineering duties. One employee could manage the office.

c. Marta Sefcik has been an employee of Griffith's Shoe Store for many years. Because the business is relatively small, Marta performs all accounting duties, including opening the mail, preparing the bank deposit, and preparing the bank reconciliation.

d. Most large companies have internal audit staffs that continuously evaluate the business's internal control. Part of the auditor's job is to evaluate how efficiently the company is running. For example, is the company purchasing inventory from the least expensive wholesaler? After a particularly bad year, De Souza Design Co. Ltd. eliminates its internal audit department to reduce expenses.

e. Public accounting firms, law firms, and other professional organizations use paraprofessional employees to do some of their routine tasks. For example, an accounting paraprofessional might examine documents to assist a public accountant in conducting an audit. In the public accounting firm of Grosso Howe, Lou Grosso, the senior partner, turns over a significant portion of his high-level audit work to his paraprofessional staff.

Required

1. Identify the missing internal control characteristic in each situation.
2. Identify the business's possible problem.
3. Propose a solution to the problem.

Problem 7-3B   *Identifying internal control weakness*   **(Obj. 2)**

Rocky Mountain Supply Corp. makes all sales on credit. Cash receipts arrive by mail, usually within 30 days of the sale. Susan de Silva opens envelopes and separates the cheques from the accompanying remittance advices. De Silva forwards the cheques to another employee who makes the daily bank deposit but has no access to the accounting records. De Silva sends the remittance advices, which show the amount of cash received, to the accounting department for entry in the accounts. De Silva's only other duty is to grant sales allowances to customers. When she receives a customer cheque for less than the full amount of the invoice, she records the sales allowance and forwards the document to the accounting department.

Required

You are the outside auditor of Rocky Mountain Supply Corp. Write a memo to the company president to identify the internal control weakness in this situation. State how to correct the weakness.

Problem 7-4B   *Bank reconciliation and related journal entries*   **(Obj. 3)**

The August 31 bank statement of Master Security, Inc., has just arrived from The Bank of Montreal. To prepare the Master security bank reconciliation, you gather the following data:

a. Master Security's Cash account shows a balance of $6,866.14 on August 31.

b. The bank statement includes two charges for returned cheques from customers. One is a $395.00 cheque received from Shoreline Express and deposited on August 20, returned by Shoreline's bank with the imprint "Unauthorized Signature." The other is an NSF cheque in the amount of $146.67 received from Lipsey, Inc. This cheque had been deposited on August 17.

c. The following Master Security cheques are outstanding at August 31:

Cheque No.	Amount
237	$ 46.10
288	141.00
291	578.05
293	11.87
294	609.51
295	8.88
296	101.63

d. The bank statement includes a deposit of $1,191.17, collected by the bank on behalf of Master Security. Of the total, $1,011.81 is collection of a note receivable, and the remainder is interest revenue.

e. The bank statement shows that Master Security earned $38.19 in interest on its bank balance during August. This amount was added to Master Security's account by the bank.

f. The bank statement lists a $10.50 subtraction for the bank service charge.

g. On August 31, the Master Security treasurer deposited $316.15, but this deposit does not appear on the bank statement.

h. The bank statement includes a $300.00 deposit that Master Security did not make. The bank had erroneously credited the Master Security account for another bank customer's deposit.

i. The August 31 bank balance is $7,984.22.

j. Master Security pays rent ($750) and insurance ($290) each month by EFT.

Required

1. Prepare the bank reconciliation for Master Security, Inc., at August 31.

2. Record in general journal form the entries necessary to bring the book balance of Cash into agreement with the adjusted book balance on the reconciliation. Include an explanation for each entry.

Problem 7-5B   *Bank reconciliation and related journal entries*   **(Obj. 3)**

Assume selected columns of the cash receipts journal and the cheque register of a Hard Rock Café for April 30, 19X4, appear as follows:

Cash Receipts Journal (Posting reference is CR)		Cheque Register (Posting reference is CD)	
Date	Cash Debit	Cheque No.	Cash Credit
Apr. 2	$ 4,174	3113	$ 891
8	407	3114	147
10	559	3115	1,930
16	2,187	3116	664
22	1,854	3117	1,472
29	1,060	3118	1,000
30	337	3119	632
Total	$10,578	3120	1,675
		3121	100
		3122	2,413
		Total	$10,924

Assume the Cash account of the Hard Rock Café shows the following information at April 30, 19X4:

Cash

Date	Item	Jrnl. Ref.	Debit	Credit	Balance
Apr. 1	Balance				7,911
30		CR. 6	10,578		18,489
30		CD. 11		10,924	7,565

The Hard Rock Café received the following bank statement on April 30, 19X4:

Bank Statement for April 19X4

Beginning Balance..		$ 7,911
Deposits and Other Credits		
Apr. 1	$ 326 EFT	
4	4,174	
9	407	
12	559	
17	2,187	
22	1,368 BC	
23	1,854	10,875
Cheques and Other Debits		
Apr. 7	$ 891	
13	1,390	
14	903 US	
15	147	
18	664	
21	219 EFT	
26	1,472	
30	1,000	
30	20 SC	6,706
Ending Balance..		$12,080

Explanation: EFT = Electronic Funds Transfer; BC = Bank Collection; US = Unauthorized Signature; SC = Service Charge

Additional data for the bank reconciliation include:

a. The EFT deposit was a receipt of monthly rent. The EFT debit was a monthly insurance payment.

b. The unauthorized signature cheque was received from S.M. Holt.

c. The $1,368 bank collection of a note receivable on April 22 included $185 interest revenue.

d. The correct amount of cheque number 3115, a payment on account, is $1,390. (The Hard Rock Café accountant mistakenly recorded the cheque for $1,930.)

Required

1. Prepare the bank reconciliation of the Hard Rock Café at April 30, 19X4.

2. Record the entries based on the bank reconciliation. Include explanations.

Problem 7-6B   *Accounting for petty cash transactions   (Obj. 5, 6)*

Suppose that on June 1, Hitachi Electronics Inc. opens a district office in Gander, Newfoundland, and creates a petty cash fund with an imprest balance of $450. During June, Sharon Dietz, the fund custodian, signs the following petty cash tickets:

Ticket Number	Item	Amount
1	Postage for package received	$ 8.40
2	Decorations and refreshments for office party	13.19
3	Two boxes of floppy disks	20.82
4	Office Supplies	27.13
5	Dinner money for sales manager entertaining a customer	50.00
6	Plane ticket for executive business trip to St. John's	169.00
7	Delivery of package across town	6.30

On June 30, prior to replenishment, the fund contains these tickets plus $173.51. The accounts affected by petty cash disbursements are Office Supplies Expense, Travel Expense, Delivery Expense, Entertainment Expense, and Postage Expense.

Required

1. Explain the characteristics and the internal control features of an imprest fund.

2. Make the general journal entries to create the fund and to replenish it. Include explanations. Also, briefly describe what the custodian does on these dates.

3. Make the entry on July 1 to increase the fund balance to $550. Include an explanation and briefly describe what the custodian does.

Problem 7-7B   *Making an ethical judgment*   (Obj. 5, 7)

Zane O'Grady is a vice-president of the Bank of Nova Scotia in Burnaby, B.C. Active in community affairs, Zane serves on the board of directors of West Coast Publishing Company. West Coast is expanding rapidly and is considering relocating its plant. At a recent meeting, board members decided to try to buy 15 acres of land on the edge of town. The owner of the property is Amy Gao, a customer of the Bank of Nova Scotia. Gao is completing a bitter divorce. O'Grady knows that Gao is eager to sell her local property. In view of Gao's anguished condition, O'Grady believes she would accept almost any offer for the land. Realtors have appraised the property at $5 million.

Required

Apply the ethical judgment framework outlined in the chapter to help Zane O'Grady decide what his role should be in West Coast's attempt to buy the land from Amy Gao.

Problem 7-8B   *Apply internal controls to cash disbursements, account for petty cash transactions*   (Obj. 5, 6)

Farrell's Wholesale Greenhouses Inc. operates out of White Rock, B.C. (in the lower mainland), with a sales territory covering the lower mainland and Vancouver Island. Employees live on both the mainland and the island, but all report to work at the company's offices in White Rock.

The company has established a large petty cash fund to handle small cash payments and cash advances to their sales force to cover frequent ferry trips to and from the island on sales trips.

The controller, J. Briscall, has decided that two people (D. Sandy and L. Elifson) should be in charge of the fund as money is often needed when one person may be out for coffee or lunch. Briscall also feels this will increase internal control, as the work of one person will serve as a check on that of the other.

Regular small cash payments required are handled by either Sandy or Elifson, who make the payment and have the person receiving the money sign a sheet of paper listing the date and reason for the payment. Whenever a salesperson requires an advance for a trip to the island, they simply sign a receipt for the money received. The salespeople later submit receipts for the cost of the ferry ride to either Sandy or Elifson to offset the cash advance.

A summary of transactions for the month of March, 19X1, is as follows:

- Balance of the fund and the actual cash on hand plus outstanding advances on March 1, 19X1 was $1,200.
- Reports from the fund managers included:

D. Sandy		L. Elifson	
Receipts for supplies	$ 30	Receipts for postage	$ 20
Miscellaneous receipts	50	Receipts for deliveries	40
Total advances given	250	Total advances given	410
Receipts for ferry rides	170	Receipts for ferry rides	290
Outstanding advances	80	Outstanding advances	120

- On March 31st, the fund had cash on hand of $220.

Required

1. Prepare a journal entry on March 31st to replenish the fund and increase its balance to $1,400. The fund should be replenished for the amount of all expenses incurred to date so that the cash on hand plus the outstanding advances will be equal to the balance of the fund.

2. Comment on the internal control procedures of Farrell's Wholesale Greenhouses Inc., including suggested improvements.

Problem 7-9B   *Prepare a bank reconciliation and related journal entries* **(Obj. 3)**

The Highgates Security Corporation had a computer failure on April 1, which resulted in the loss of data including the balance of their cash account and their bank reconciliation from March 31, 19X1. The accountant, S. Ringles, has been able to obtain the following information from the records of the company and their bank:

- An examination showed that two cheques (#164 for $320 and #173 for $240) had not been cashed as of April 1st. Ringles recalled that there was only one deposit in transit on the March 31st bank reconciliation, but was unable to recall the amount.

- The cash receipts and cash disbursements journal contained the following entries for April, 19X1:

Cash Receipts:	Cash Disbursements:	
Amounts	Cheque #	Amount
$ 845	182	$ 245
410	183	340
380	184	195
860	185	465
320	186	180
$2,815	187	475
	188	void
	189	290
	190	480
		$2,670

- Their bank provided the following statement as of April 30, 19X1:

Date	Cheques and Other Debits		Deposits and Other Credits		Balance
April 1	#183	340.00		880.00	2,030.00
3	#173	240.00			1,790.00
5	#184	195.00			1,595.00
8				845.00	2,440.00
14	#182	245.00		440.00	2,635.00
17	EFT	320.00			2,315.00
19			EFT	420.00	2,735.00
21	#186	180.00		410.00	2,965.00
22	#187	745.00	EFT	190.00	2,410.00
24			EFT	145.00	2,555.00
26	NSF	570.00		380.00	2,365.00
27	SC	35.00			2,330.00
30	#190	480.00		860.00	2,710.00

- The deposit made on April 14th was for the collection of a note receivable ($400) plus interest.
- The electronic funds transfers (EFT's) had not been recorded by Highgates yet as the bank statement was the first notification of them. They consisted of:
  - April 17th was for the monthly payment on an insurance policy for Highgates Security Corporation.
  - April 19th and 24th were collections on accounts receivable.
  - April 22nd ($190) was in error—the transfer should have been to Highways Construction Corporation.
- The "NSF" cheque on April 26th was received from a customer as payment for security equipment purchased for $570 (cost to Highgates was $420).
- Cheque #187 was correctly written for $745 for the purchase of office supplies, but incorrectly recorded by the cash disbursements clerk.

Required

1. Prepare a bank reconciliation as of April 30, 19X1 including the calculation of the book balance of April 30, 19X1.
2. Prepare all journal entries that would be required by the bank reconciliation.

Challenge Problems

Problem 7-1C   *Management's role in internal control*   (Obj. 1)

Effective internal control must begin with management. The "tone at the top" is a necessary condition if an organization is to have an effective system of internal control. These statements are becoming a more important part of internal control literature and thought.

The chapter lists a number of characteristics that are important for an effective system of internal control. Many of these characteristics have been part of the internal control literature for years.

Required

Explain why you think a commitment to good internal control by top management is fundamental to an effective system of internal control.

Problem 7-2C   *Applying internal controls to cash transactions*   **(Obj. 4, 5)**

Many companies require some person other than the person preparing the bank reconciliation to review the reconciliation. Organizations routinely require cheques over a certain amount to be signed by two signing officers. The purchasing department orders goods but the receiving department receives the goods.

Required

All of the above illustrations have a common thread. What is that common thread and why is it important?

Extending Your Knowledge

Decision Problems

1. Using the bank reconciliation to detect a theft   *(Obj. 3)*

Erb Agricultural Equipment Company Ltd. has poor internal control over its cash transactions. Recently Grace Erb, the owner, has suspected the cashier of stealing. Details of the business's cash position at September 30 follow:

1. The Cash account shows a balance of $19,702. This amount includes a September 30 deposit of $3,794 that does not appear on the September 30 bank statement.

2. The September 30 bank statement shows a balance of $16,624. The bank statement lists a $200 credit for a bank collection, an $8 debit for the service charge and a $36 debit for an NSF cheque. The Erb Agricultural Equipment accountant has not recorded any of these items on the books.

3. At September 30 the following cheques are outstanding:

Cheque No.	Amount
154	$116
256	150
278	253
291	190
292	206
293	145

4. The cashier handles all incoming cash and makes bank deposits. He also reconciles the monthly bank statement. His September 30 reconciliation follows:

Balance per books, September 30		$19,702
Add: Outstanding cheques............................		560
Bank collection..		200
		20,462
Less: Deposits in transit	$3,794	
Service charge	8	
NSF cheque	36	3,838
Balance per bank, September 30		$16,624

Erb has requested that you determine whether the cashier has stolen cash from the business and, if so, how much. Erb also asks you to identify how the cashier has attempted to conceal the theft. To make this determination, you perform your own bank reconciliation using the format illustrated in the chapter. There are no bank or book errors. Erb also asks you to evaluate the internal controls and recommend any changes needed to improve them.

2. The role of internal control   (Obj. 2)

The following questions are unrelated except that they all pertain to internal control:

1. Separation of duties is an important consideration if a system of internal control is to be effective. Why is this so?
2. Cash may be a relatively small item on the financial statements. Nevertheless, internal control over cash is very important. Why do you think this is true?
3. Ling Ltd. requires that all documents supporting a cheque be canceled by the person who signs the cheque. Why do you think this practice is required? What might happen if it were not required?
4. Many managers think that safeguarding assets is the most important objective of internal control systems. Whereas auditors, on the other hand, emphasize reliable accounting data. Explain why auditors are more concerned about the quality of the accounting records.

Ethical Issue

Anne McMinn owns apartment buildings in British Columbia, Alberta, and Manitoba. Each property has a manager who collects rent, arranges for repairs, and runs advertisements in the local newspaper. The property managers transfer cash to McMinn monthly and prepare their own bank reconciliations.

The manager in Alberta has been stealing large sums of money. To cover the theft, he understates the amount of outstanding cheques on the monthly bank reconciliation. As a result, each monthly bank reconciliation appears to balance. However, the balance sheet reports more cash than McMinn actually has in the bank. In negotiating the sale of the Alberta property, McMinn is showing the balance sheet to prospective investors.

Required

1. Identify two parties other than McMinn who can be harmed by this theft. In what ways can they be harmed?
2. Discuss the role accounting plays in this situation.

Financial Statement Problems

1. Internal controls and cash   (Obj. 1)

Study the manangement report and the auditors' report on Mark's Work Wearhouse's financial statements, given in Appendix A. Answer the following questions about Mark's internal controls and cash position:

1. What is the name of Mark's Work Wearhouse's outside auditing firm? What office of this firm signed the auditor's report? How long after Mark's Work Wearhouse's year end did the auditors issue their opinion?
2. Who bears primary responsibility for the financial statements? How can you tell?
3. Does it appear that Mark's internal controls are adequate? How can you tell?
4. What standard of auditing did the outside auditors use in examining Mark's Work Wearhouse's financial statements? By what accounting standards were the statements evaluated?
5. By how much did Mark's Work Wearhouse's cash position change during 1994? The statement of changes in financial position (discussed in detail chapter 18) tells why this change occurred. Which type of activity—operating, financing, or investing—contributed most to this change?

2. *Audit opinion, management responsibility, internal controls, and cash (Obj. 1)*

Obtain the annual report of an actual company of your choosing. Study the auditor's report and the management statement of responsibility (if present) in conjunction with the financial statements. Answer these questions about the company:

1. What is the name of the company's outside auditing firm? What office of this firm signed the audit report? How long after the company's year end did the auditors issue their opinion?
2. Who bears primary responsibility for the financial statements? How can you tell?
3. Does it appear that the company's internal controls are adequate? Give your reason.
4. What standard of auditing did the outside auditors use in examining the company's financial statements? By what accounting standards were the statements evaluated?
5. By how much did the company's cash position (including cash equivalents) change during the current year? The statement of changes in financial position (discussed in Chapter 18) tells why this change occurred. Which type of activity—operating, financing, or investing—contributed most to this change?
6. Where is the balance of petty cash reported? Name the financial statement and the account, and identify the specific amount that includes petty cash.

Appendix

The Voucher System

The *voucher system* for recording cash payments improves a business's internal control over cash disbursements by formalizing the process of approving and recording invoices for payment. We will examine the voucher system as it is used by a merchandising business.

The voucher system uses (1) vouchers, (2) a voucher register, (3) an unpaid voucher file, (4) a cheque register, and (5) a paid voucher file. The merchandising business we discuss has separate departments for purchasing goods, receiving goods, disbursing cash, and accounting.

Vouchers   Recall that a *voucher* is a document authorizing a cash disbursement. The accounting department prepares vouchers. Exhibit 7A-1 illustrates the voucher of Bliss Wholesale Company Ltd. In addition to places for writing in the *payee, due date, terms, description,* and *invoice amount,* the voucher includes a section for designated officers to sign their approval for payment. The back of the voucher has places for recording the *account debited, date paid,* and *cheque number.* You should locate these nine items in Exhibit 7A-1.

Exhibit 7A-2 lists the various business documents used to ensure that the company receives the goods it ordered and pays only for the goods it has actually received.

Exhibit 7A-3 shows how a voucher added to the other documents can provide the evidence for a cash disbursement. The amounts on all these documents should agree.

The bundle of documents is called a *voucher packet.*

Voucher Register   After it is approved by the designated officers, the voucher goes to the accounting department where it is recorded in the **voucher register**. This journal is similar to the purchases journal (discussed in Chapter 6), but the voucher register is more comprehensive. In a voucher system, *all* expenditures are recorded first in the voucher register. This step is a fundamental control feature of

OBJECTIVE A1
Use the voucher system

Key Point:
In a voucher system, all expenditures must be approved before payment can be made. This approval takes the form of a voucher. The larger the business, the more likely it is to need strict control over disbursements. The voucher system helps supply this control.

EXHIBIT 7A-1 *Voucher*

Front of
Voucher

		Voucher No. 326
	BLISS WHOLESALE COMPANY LTD.	

Payee   John Forsyth Co.
Address   31 Young St.
            Kitchener, Ontario N2H 4Y7

Due Date   March 7
Terms   2/10 n/30

Date	Invoice No.	Description	Amount
Mar. 1	6380	144 men's shirts stock no. X14	$1,800

Approved *Jane Trent*   Approved *Bob Kraft*
          Controller   Treasurer

Back of
Voucher

Voucher No. 326
Payee John Forsyth Co.

Invoice Amount   1,800

Discount   36

Net Amount $1,764

Due Date   Mar. 7

Date Paid   Mar. 6

Cheque No.   694

Account Distribution

Account Debited	Acct. No.	Amount
Inventory	501	1,800
Store Supplies	145	
Salary Expense	538	
Advertising Expense	542	
Utilities Expense	548	
Delivery Expense	544	
Total		1,800

EXHIBIT 7A-2 *Purchasing Process*

Business Document	Prepared by	Sent to
Purchase request	Sales department	Purchasing department
Purchase order	Purchasing department	Outside company that sells the needed merchandise (supplier or vendor)
Invoice	Outside company that sells the needed merchandise (supplier or vendor)	Accounting department
Receiving report	Receiving department	Accounting department
Voucher	Accounting department	Officer who signs the cheque

EXHIBIT 7A-3   *Voucher Packet*

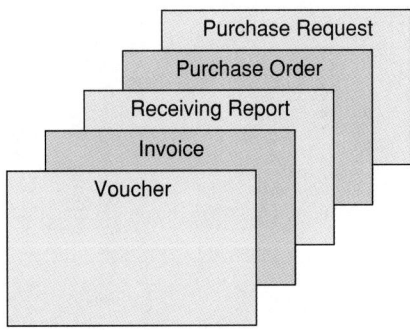

the voucher system because it centralizes the initial recording of all expenditures in this one journal. That is, all cash payments must be vouchered and approved prior to payment. For each transaction, the debit is to the account for which payment is being made, and the credit is to Vouchers Payable, the account that replaces Accounts Payable in many voucher systems. Exhibit 7A-4 illustrates the voucher register of Bliss Wholesale Company Ltd.

The voucher register has columns to record payment date and cheque number, which are entered when the voucher is paid. The absence of a payment date and cheque number means that the voucher is unpaid. In Exhibit 7A-4, for example, Bliss Wholesale has a $2,202 liability at March 31 for vouchers 330 ($369 payable to the *Daily Journal*), 348 ($1,638 payable to Carr Products), and 350 ($195 payable to Consumers Gas Company). If these were the company's only unpaid vouchers at March 31, the balance sheet would report:

Current liabilities
    Accounts payable* $2,202

*Usually reported as Accounts Payable, even by companies that use a voucher system.

Unpaid Voucher File   After recording a voucher in the voucher register, the accountant places the voucher packet in the unpaid voucher file, where it stays until the voucher is paid. The unpaid voucher file acts as the accounts payable subsidiary ledger because each voucher serves as an individual account payable. Thus no need exists for a separate accounts payable ledger.

The unpaid voucher file has 31 slots, one for each day of the month. Each voucher is filed according to its due date. For example, voucher no. 326 in Exhibit 7A-1 was due March 7, so it was filed in the slot marked 7.

Cheque Register   The *cheque register* is the journal in which all cheques issued in a voucher system are recorded. It replaces the cash disbursements journal. All entries in the cheque register debit Vouchers Payable and credit Cash (and Inventory, as appropriate). Exhibit 7A-5 shows a cheque register. Notice that all transactions include a credit to the Cash in Bank account.

On or before the due date, the accountant removes the voucher packet from the unpaid voucher file and sends it to the officers for signing. After the cheques are signed, the cheque number and payment date are entered on the back of the voucher, in the cheque register, and in the voucher register.

Paid Voucher File   After payment, the voucher packet is canceled to avoid paying the bill twice. Typically, a hole is punched through the voucher packet. It is then filed alphabetically by payee name. Most businesses also file a copy in numerical sequence by voucher number as a cross reference. With this dual filing system, a voucher can be located using either classification scheme.

EXHIBIT 7A-4   *Voucher Register*

Voucher Register

Page 16

Date	Voucher No.	Payee	Cheque No.	Date	Vouchers Payable	Inventory	Store Supplies	Salary Expense	Advertising Expense	Utilities Expense	Delivery Expense	Title	No.	Amount
			Payment		Credit	Debit						Other Accounts		
Mar. 1	326	John Forsyth Co.	694	3/6	1,800	1,800								
1	327	Howell Properties	693	3/2	1,500							Rent Expense	547	1,500
4	328	Bell Telephone	696	3/10	128					128				
5	329	Schick Supplies	697	3/11	85		85							
8	330	Daily Journal			369				369					
9	331	Ace Delivery Service	695	3/9	37						37			
26	348	Carr Products			1,638	1,638								
28	349	Petty Cash	717	3/31	82		23				17	Miscellaneous Selling Expense	563	42
29	350	Consumers Gas Co.			195					195				
30	351	Royal Bank	718	3/31	360							Interest Expense	546	360
31	352	Ralph Grant	719	3/31	864			864						
31		Totals			12,580	6,209	137	1,781	753	602	185			2,913
					(201)	(501)	(145)	(538)	(542)	(548)	(544)			(✓)

Account numbers in parentheses indicate the accounts to which these amounts have been posted.

EXHIBIT 7A-5 *Cheque Register*

				Debit		Credit
Date	Cheque No.	Payee	Voucher No.	Vouchers Payable	Inventory	Cash in Bank
Mar. 1	692	Trent Co.	322	600	18	582
2	693	Howell Properties	327	1,500		1,500
6	694	John Forsyth Co.	326	1,800	36	1,764
9	695	Ace Delivery Service	331	37		37
10	696	Bell Telephone	328	128		128
11	697	Schick Supplies	329	85		85
31	717	Petty Cash	349	82		82
31	718	Royal Bank	351	360		360
31	719	Ralph Grant	352	864		864
31	720	Krasner Supply Co.	336	92		92
31		Totals		11,406	317	11,089
				(201)	(105)	(103)

Cheque Register   Page 9

Account numbers in parentheses indicate the accounts to which these amounts have been posted.

In summary, the voucher system works as follows:

1. The accounting department prepares a *voucher* for each invoice to be paid.
2. Supporting documents (invoice, receiving report, purchase order, and purchase request) are compared in the accounting department for accuracy and attached to the voucher. These make up the *voucher packet*.
3. Designated officials examine the supporting documents and approve the voucher for payment.
4. The accounting department enters the voucher in the *voucher register*. The entry is a debit to the account of the item purchased (for example, Inventory) and a credit to Vouchers Payable. The voucher remains in the *unpaid voucher file* until payment.
5. Prior to the invoice due date, a cheque is issued to pay the voucher. The official reviews the supporting document and signs the cheque.
6. The accounting department enters the cheque in the *cheque register,* and updates the voucher and voucher register to record payment. All cheques are debits to Vouchers Payable and credits to Cash.
7. Paid vouchers are canceled and filed by payee name and by voucher number.

To gain a complete understanding of the voucher system, trace voucher no. 326 from Exhibit 7A-1 through the voucher register in Exhibit 7A-4 to the cheque register in Exhibit 7A-5. Also, trace the cheque register entries from Exhibit 7A-5 back to Exhibit 7A-4.

Appendix Problems

Problem 7A-1   *Voucher system entries*   *(Obj. A1)*

Assume that a CompuServ store in Fredericton, New Brunswick, uses a voucher system. Assume also that the store completed the following transactions during January:

Jan. 3   Issued voucher no. 135 payable to New Brunswick Telephone Co. for telephone service of $2,007.

5   Issued voucher no. 136 payable to IBM for the purchase of inventory costing $15,500, with payment terms of 3/10 n/30.

6   Issued voucher no. 137 payable to City Supply Company for inventory costing $350, with payment terms of 2/10 n/45.

7   Issued cheque no. 404 to pay voucher no. 136.

10   Issued cheque no. 405 to pay voucher no. 135.

14   Issued cheque no. 406 to pay voucher no. 137.

15   Issued voucher no. 138 payable to a Fredericton newspaper for advertising of $2,990.

17   Issued voucher no. 139 payable to replenish the petty cash fund. The payee is Petty Cash, and the petty cash tickets list Store Supplies ($16), Delivery Expense ($96), and Miscellaneous Expense ($64). Also issued cheque no. 407 to pay the voucher.

18   Issued voucher no. 140 payable to Apple Computer Company for inventory costing $27,600, with payment terms of 2/10 n/30.

24   Issued voucher no. 141 payable to city of Fredericton for property tax of $4,235.

27   Issued voucher no. 142 payable to the Royal Bank for payment of a note payable ($10,000) and interest expense ($1,200).

30   Issued cheque no. 408 to pay voucher no. 140.

31   Issued voucher no. 143 to pay salesperson salary of $2,309 to Lester Gibbs. Also issued cheque no. 409 to pay the voucher.

Required

1. Record CompuServ transactions in a voucher register and a cheque register like those illustrated in the appendix. Posting references are unnecessary.
2. Open the Vouchers Payable account and post amounts to that account.
3. Prepare the list of unpaid vouchers at January 31 and show that the total matches the balance of Vouchers Payable.

Problem 7A-2   *Voucher system entries*   *(Obj. A1)*

Assume that a Canadian Tire store in St. John's, Newfoundland, uses a voucher system. Assume also that the store completed the following transactions during July:

July 2   Issued voucher no. 614 payable to Black & Decker Canada for the purchase of inventory costing $23,000, with payment terms of 2/10 n/30.

3   Issued voucher no. 615 payable to Newfoundland Light & Power Co. for electricity usage of $2,189.

5   Issued cheque no. 344 to pay voucher no. 614.

6   Issued voucher no. 616 payable to Baylor Supply Corp. for inventory costing $850, with payment terms of 2/10 n/45.

7   Issued cheque no. 345 to pay voucher no. 615.

July 13 Issued voucher no. 617 payable to replenish the petty cash fund. The payee is Petty Cash, and the petty cash tickets list store supplies ($119), delivery expense ($48), and miscellaneous expense ($36). Also issued cheque no. 346 to pay the voucher.

14 Issued cheque no. 347 to pay voucher no. 616.

18 Issued voucher no. 618 payable to a St. John's newspaper for advertising, $2,800.

19 Issued voucher no. 619 payable to Michelin Tire Co. for inventory costing $65,800, with payment terms of 3/10 n/30.

28 Issued voucher no. 620 payable to city of St. John's for property tax of $9,165.

30 Issued cheque no. 348 to pay voucher no. 619.

31 Issued voucher no. 621 payable to Bank of Montreal for interest expense of $9,000.

31 Issued voucher no. 622 to pay executive salary of $4,644 to Sharon Kratzman. Also issued cheque no. 349 to pay the voucher.

Required

1. Record the Canadian Tire store's transactions in a voucher register and a cheque register like those illustrated in the appendix. Posting references are unnecessary.

2. Open the Vouchers Payable account with a zero beginning balance, and post amounts to that account.

3. Prepare the list of unpaid vouchers at July 31 and show that the total matches the balance of Vouchers Payable.

CHAPTER 8
Accounts and Notes Receivable

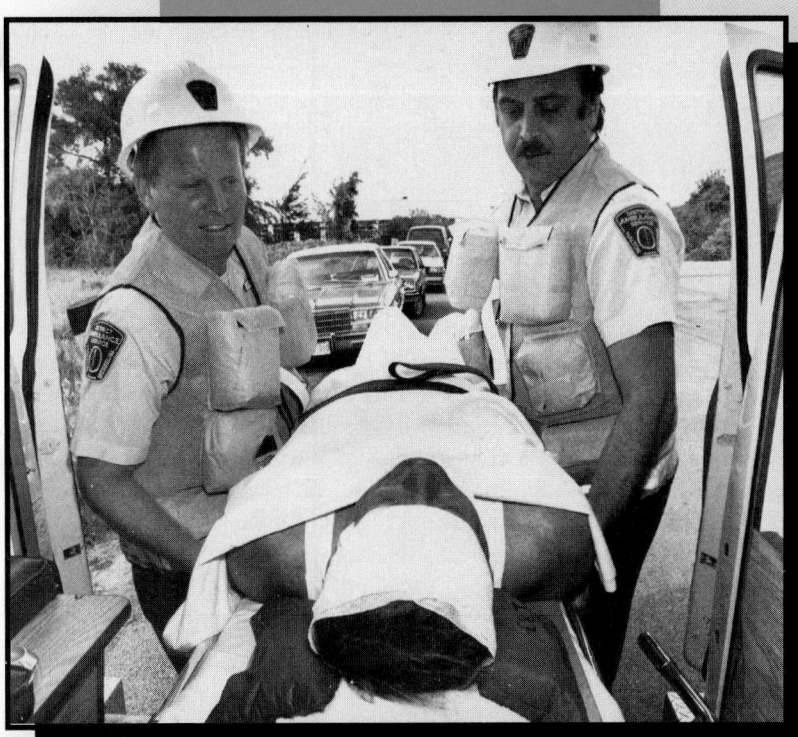

"Time is money. The longer a receivable goes unpaid, the more difficult and expensive it is to collect, and the less it is worth. Effective credit and collection policies and procedures improve net income by reducing write-offs of accounts receivable, increasing cash flow, and improving customer relations," says James R. Bohmann, Senior Vice-President of Corporate Development, Payco American Corporation (World's Largest Publicly Held Receivable Management Firm).

Rural Metro Corp. is a private ambulance company that provides services to a large number of communities. Some services are covered by the client's medical insurance but some are not. The company was growing rapidly but management found they were having to borrow more and more money and the company was incurring losses.

The company brought in a new chief executive. He reviewed operations and found that bad debt expense was running at almost 30 percent and that the cash shortage was caused by increasing accounts receivable.

The new chief executive realized the company was going to have to more aggressively try to collect its receivables if it was to survive. One of the steps he took was to speed up the billing process so invoices went out in 3 days rather than 21 as before. A second step was to increase the number of employees dealing with receivables. The company also installed software that assisted the collectors.

The result of these efforts was to reduce the bad debt rate to below 20 percent and to return the company to profitability.

Source: Adapted from Nina Munk, "Making the Customer Pay," *Forbes*, February 13, 1995, pp. 74–75.

xfprove 401-410

CHAPTER OBJECTIVES

After studying this chapter, you should be able to

1 Use the allowance method of accounting for uncollectibles

2 Estimate uncollectibles by the percentage of sales and the aging approaches

3 Use the direct write-off method of accounting for uncollectibles

4 Identify internal control weaknesses in accounts receivable

5 Account for notes receivable

6 Report receivables on the balance sheet

7 Use the acid-test ratio and days' sales in receivables to evaluate a company's position

---

Accounts receivable, like most other assets, can represent good news or bad news: Good news because receivables represent a claim to the customer's cash; bad news when the business fails to collect the cash. In the case of Rural Metro Corp., receivables got out of hand, and profits suffered. How could the company's revenue increase so much while net income turned into net losses? Because Rural Metro was not managing its receivables very well. Too much of Rural Metro's resources were tied up in accounts receivable—an asset that earns no income. Cash was not flowing into the business quickly enough. Rural Metro had to borrow money, and the related interest expense was draining profits.

This chapter discusses the role of the credit department in deciding to which customers the business will sell on account. It explains receivables, including how to account for them when they appear to be uncollectible, and internal control over receivables. It also covers notes receivable and introduces several measures that help a business manage customer accounts, including *days' sales in receivables*.

A receivable arises when a business (or person) sells goods or services to a second business (or person) on credit. A receivable is the seller's claim against the buyer for the amount of the transaction. Each credit transaction involves at least two parties—the **creditor**, who sells a service or merchandise and obtains a receivable, and the **debtor**, who makes the purchase and creates a payable. This chapter focuses on accounting for the creditor's receivables. We will discuss the accounts that generally appear on a creditor's balance sheet.

Different Types of Receivables

Receivables are monetary claims against businesses and individuals. They are acquired mainly by selling goods and services, and by lending money.

The two major types of receivables are accounts receivable and notes receivable. A business's *accounts receivable* are the amounts that its customers owe it. These accounts receivables are sometimes called *trade receivables*. They are *current assets*.

Accounts receivable should be distinguished from accruals, notes, and other assets not arising from everyday sales because accounts receivable pertain to sales or service revenue which represents the lifeblood of a business. Moreover, amounts included as accounts receivable should be collectible according to the business's normal sale terms, such as net 30, or 2/10 n/30.

Notes receivable are more formal than accounts receivable. The debtor in a note receivable arrangement promises in writing to pay the creditor a definite sum at a definite future date—the date of maturity. The terms of these notes usually extend for at least 60 days. A written document known as a *promissory note* serves as evidence of the receivable. A note may require the debtor to pledge *security* for the loan. This means that the borrower promises that the lender may claim certain assets if the borrower fails to pay the amount due at maturity.

Notes receivable due within one year, or operating cycle if longer, are *current as-sets*. Those notes due beyond one year are *long-term receivables*. Some notes receivable are collected in periodic installments. The portion due within one year is a current asset, with the remaining amount a long-term asset. The Toronto-Dominion Bank may hold a $6,000 note receivable from you, but only the $1,500 you owe on it this year is a current asset to the Toronto-Dominion Bank.

Other receivables is a miscellaneous category that includes loans to employees and branch companies. Usually these are long-term receivables, but they are current assets if receivable within one year or less. Long-term notes receivable, and other receivables are often reported on the balance sheet after current assets and before capital assets as shown in Exhibit 8-1.

Each type of receivable is a separate account in the general ledger, and may be supported by a subsidiary ledger if needed.

The Credit Department

A customer who uses a credit card to acquire goods or services is buying on account. This transaction creates a receivable for the seller. Most companies with a high proportion of sales on account (for example, Canadian Tire) have a separate credit department. This department evaluates customers who apply for credit cards by using standard formulas—which include the applicant's income and credit history, among other factors—for deciding which customers the store will sell to on account. After approving a customer, the credit department monitors customer payment records. Customers with a history of paying on time may receive higher credit limits. Those who fail to pay on time have their limits reduced or eliminated. The goal is to collect from customers quickly enough to keep cash circulating. The credit department also assists the accounting department in measuring collection losses on customers who do not pay.

EXHIBIT 8-1   *Balance Sheet*

Example Company Ltd.
Balance Sheet
Date

Assets			Liabilities		
Current			Current		
Cash		$X,XXX	Accounts payable		$X,XXX
Accounts receivable	**X,XXX**		Notes payable, short-term		X,XXX
Less: Allowance for			Accrued current liabilities		X,XXX
uncollectible accounts	**(XXX)**	**X,XXX**	Total current liabilities		X,XXX
Notes receivable, short-term		**X,XXX**			
Inventories		X,XXX	Long-term		
Prepaid expenses		X,XXX	Notes payable, long-term		X,XXX
Total		X,XXX	Total liabilities		$X,XXX
Investments and long-term receivables					
Investments in other companies		X,XXX			
Notes receivable, long-term		**X,XXX**	**Shareholders' Equity**		
Other receivables		**X,XXX**	Common stock		X,XXX
Total		X,XXX	Retained earnings		X,XXX
			Total shareholders' equity		X,XXX
Capital assets			Total liabilities and shareholder's		
Property, plant and equipment		X,XXX	equity		$X,XXX
Total assets		$X,XXX			

Key Point: ☑

Selling on credit enables a company to generate more sales revenue. But there is a cost associated with selling on credit; bad-debt expense arises as a result of not collecting from some customers.

Uncollectible Accounts (Bad Debts)

Selling on credit creates both a benefit and a cost. Customers unwilling or unable to pay cash immediately may make a purchase on credit. Revenue and profits rise as sales increase. The cost to the seller of extending credit arises when credit customers do not pay off their debts. Accountants label this cost uncollectible-account expense, doubtful-account expense, or **bad-debt expense**.

The extent of uncollectible-account expense varies from company to company. In some lines of business, a six-month-old receivable of $1 is worth only 67 cents. A five-year-old receivable of $1 is worth only 4 cents. Uncollectible-account expense depends on the credit risks that managers are willing to accept. At Albany Ladder, a $23 million construction-equipment and supply firm, 85 percent of company sales are on account. Albany's receivables grow in proportion to sales. Bad debts cost Albany Ladder about $100,000 a year, or about 1 to 1½ percent of total sales, a figure that has remained fairly constant as a result of careful credit screening and rigorous collection activity. It takes Albany Ladder an average of 70 days to collect its receivables.

Many small retail businesses accept a higher level of risk than large stores such as The Bay. Why? Small businesses often have personal ties to customers, which increases the likelihood that customers will pay their accounts.

Measuring Uncollectible Accounts

OBJECTIVE 1

Use the allowance method of accounting for uncollectibles

For a firm that sells on credit, uncollectible-account expense is as much a part of doing business as salary expense and depreciation expense. Uncollectible-Account Expense—an operating expense—must be measured, recorded, and reported. To do so, accountants use the allowance method or the direct write-off method (which will be covered on page 397).

Key Point: ☑

The amount of bad-debt expense depends on the volume of credit sales, the effectiveness of the credit department, and the diligence of the collection department.

Allowance Method   To present the most accurate financial statements possible, accountants in firms with large credit sales use the **allowance method** of measuring bad debts. This method records collection losses based on estimates instead of waiting to see which customers the business will not collect from.

Smart managers know that not every customer will pay in full. But at the time of sale, managers do not know which customers will not pay. If they did, they would not sell on credit to those customers.

Rather than try to guess which accounts will go bad, managers, based on collection experience, estimate the total bad-debt expense for the period. The business debits Uncollectible-Account Expense for the estimated amount, and credits **Allowance for Uncollectible Accounts** (or **Allowance for Doubtful Accounts**), a contra account related to Accounts Receivable. This account shows the amount of receivables that the business expects *not* to collect.

To match expense against revenue properly, the firm estimates the uncollectible account expense based on past collection experience, and records as an adjusting entry during the same period in which the sales are made. This expense entry has two effects: (1) *it decreases net income by debiting an expense account*, and (2) *it decreases net accounts receivable by crediting the allowance account*. Allowance for Uncollectible Accounts, the contra account, is subtracted from Accounts Receivable to measure *net* accounts receivable.

Assume the company's sales for 19X1 are $240,000, and that past collection experience suggests estimated bad debts of $3,100 for the year. The 19X1 journal entries follow, with accounts receivable from customers Rolf and Anderson separated for emphasis.

During the year:

19X1	Accounts Receivable—Rolf	1,300	
	Accounts Receivable—Anderson	1,700	
	Accounts Receivable—Various Customers	237,000	
	Sales Revenue		240,000
	To record credit sales.		

End-of-year adjusting entry:

19X1	Uncollectible-Account Expense	3,100	
	Allowance for Uncollectible Accounts....		3,100
	To record estimated bad-debt expense, based on past collection experience.		

The account balances at December 31, 19X1 appear as follows:

Accounts Receivable		Allowance for Uncollectible Accounts		Sales Revenue		Uncollectible Account Expense	
240,000			3,100		240,000	3,100	

Net accounts receivable
= $236,900

The entry to record uncollectible-account expense decreases net accounts receivable. The 19X1 financial statements will report:

Income Statement	19X1
Revenue	
Sales revenue..	$240,000
Expense	
Uncollectible account expense..	3,100

Balance Sheet	December 31,19X1
Current assets	
Accounts receivable	$240,000
Less: Allowance for uncollectible accounts.......................	3,100
Net accounts receivable...	$236,900

Writing Off Uncollectible Accounts

During 19X2, the company collects on most of the accounts receivable as follows:

19X2	Cash	235,000	
	Accounts Receivable—		
	Various Customers....................................		235,000
	To record collections on account		

However, the credit department determines that customers Rolf and Anderson cannot pay the amounts they owe. The accountant writes off their receivables with the following entry:

19X2	Allowance for Uncollectible Accounts.............	3,000	
	Accounts Receivable—Rolf		1,300
	Accounts Receivable—Anderson		1,700
	To write off uncollectible accounts.		

The write-off entry has no effect on net income because it includes no debit to an expense account. The entry also has no effect on net accounts receivable because both the Allowance account debited and the Accounts Receivable account credited are part of *net* accounts receivable. The account balances at December 31, 19X2 are as follows:

Short Exercise:

Given:

Accts. Rec.............	$90,000
– Allow. for Uncoll.	
Accts...............	– 3,500
= Net Accts. Rec.	
(Net Realizable	
Value)..............	$86,500

If a $700 Account Receivable for Kathy Brown is written off, the journal entry required and Net Accounts Receivable after the write-off are:

Allow. for Uncoll.

Accts.............	700
Accts. Rec.—	
K. Brown	700

Accts. Rec.

90,000	700
89,300	

Allow. for Uncoll. Accts.

700	3,500
	2,800

Net accts. rec. (NRV) is the same, $86,500:

Accts. Rec.............	$89,300
– Allow. for	
Uncoll. Accts.–2,800	
= Net Accts. Rec.	
(NRV)..............	$86,500

NRV (the net amount) does not change as a result of writing off a specific customer's account because the same amount is taken out of both Accts. Rec. and the contra account, Allow. for Uncoll. Accts.

Accounts Receivable		Allowance for Uncollectible Accounts	
240,000	235,000	3,000	3,100
	1,300		100
	1,700		
2,000			

The financial statements for 19X1 and 19X2 will report the following. In order to highlight the matching of expense and revenue, we are assuming no sales are made in 19X2.

Income Statement	19X1	19X2
Revenue		
Sales revenue	$240,000	$ 0
Expense		
Uncollectible account expense	3,100	0

The matching principle requires that uncollectible-account expense bear a reasonable relationship to sales revenue. This is why there is no expense for 19X2: There was no revenue that year.

Balance Sheet	December 31, 19X1	19X2
Current assets		
Accounts receivable..	$240,000	$2,000
Less: Allowance for uncollectible accounts	3,100	100
Net accounts receivable	$236,900	$1,900

After the accounting, the allowance for uncollectibles should hold the amount of the receivables the business expects *not* to collect ($100). Net accounts receivable is the amount the business *does* expect to collect ($1,900).

Bad Debt Write-Offs Rarely Equal Allowance for Uncollectibles

The allowance amount is based on estimates because it comes before the determination that any particular customer account receivable is uncollectible. Write-offs equal the allowance only if the estimate of bad debts is perfect—a rare occurrence. Usually the difference between write-offs and the allowance is small, as shown in the preceding example. If the allowance is too large for one period, the estimate of bad debts for the next period can be cut back. If the allowance is too low, an adjusting entry can increase it: Debit Uncollectible-Account Expense and credit Allowance for Uncollectible Accounts. This credit brings the Allowance account to a realistic balance. Estimating uncollectibles will be discussed shortly.

Recoveries of Uncollectible Accounts

When an account receivable is written off as uncollectible, the customer still has an obligation to pay. However, the likelihood of receiving cash is so low that the company ceases its collection effort and writes off the account. Some companies turn such accounts over to a lawyer for collection in the hope of recovering part of the receivable. To record a recovery, the accountant reverses the write-off and records the collection in the regular manner. The reversal of the write-off is needed to give the customer account receivable a debit balance.

Assume that the write-off of Rolf's account ($1,300) occurs in February 19X2. In August, Rolf pays the account in full. The journal entries for this situation follow:

Feb.	19X2	To write off Rolf's account as uncollectible (same entry as above):		
		Allowance for Uncollectible Accounts	1,300	
		Accounts Receivable—Rolf		1,300
Aug.	19X2	To reinstate Rolf's account:*		
		Accounts Receivable—Rolf	1,300	
		Allowance for Uncollectible Accounts ..		1,300
		To record collection from Rolf:		
		Cash	1,300	
		Accounts Receivable—Rolf		1,300

OBJECTIVE 2

Estimate uncollectibles by the percentage of sales and the aging approaches

* This entry places Rolf's account receivable back on the books. It also replaces the $1,300 removed from the Allowance when Rolf's account was written off in February.

Estimating Uncollectibles

The more accurate the estimate, the more reliable the information in the financial statements. How are bad debt estimates made? The most logical way to estimate bad debts is to look at the business's past records. Both the *percentage of sales* method and the *aging of accounts receivable* method use the company's collection experience.

Percentage-of-Sales   A popular way to estimate uncollectibles, **the percentage of sales approach** computes the expense as a percentage of net credit sales (or net sales). Uncollectible-account expense is recorded as an adjusting entry at the end of the period.

Basing its decision on figures from the previous four periods, a business estimates that bad debt expense will be 2.5 percent of credit sales. If credit sales for 19X3 total $500,000, the adjusting entry to record bad debt expense for the year is

> *Key Point:*
>
> The percentage of sales approach is often referred to as the income statement approach to estimating bad-debt expense because the entry is based on credit sales for the period (an income statement figure).

Adjusting Entries

Dec. 31	Uncollectible-Account Expense		
	($500,000 × .025)...	12,500	
	Allowance for Uncollectible Accounts......		12,500

Under the percentage of sales method, the amount of this entry ignores the prior balance in Allowance for Uncollectible Accounts.

A business may change the percentage rate from year to year, depending on its collection experience. Suppose collections of accounts receivable in 19X4 are greater, and write-offs are less, than expected. The credit balance in Allowance for uncollectible Accounts would be too large in relation to the debit balance of Accounts Receivable. How would the business change its bad debt percentage rate in this case? *Decreasing* the percentage rate would reduce the credit entry to the allowance account, and the allowance account balance would not grow too large.

New businesses, with no credit history on which to base their rates, may obtain estimated bad-debt percentages from industry trade journals, government publications, and other sources of collection data.

Aging of Accounts Receivable   The second popular method of estimating bad debts is called **aging of accounts receivable**. In this approach, individual accounts receivable are analyzed according to the length of time that they have been receivable from the customer. When performed manually, this method is time-consuming. Computers greatly ease the burden. Computerized accounting packages prepare a report for aging accounts receivable. The computer accesses files of customer data and sorts accounts by customer number and date of invoice. Schmidt Home Builders groups its accounts receivable into 30-day periods, as Exhibit 8-2 shows:

Schmidt bases the percentage figures on the company's collection experience.

EXHIBIT 8-2   *Aging the Accounts of Schmidt Home Builders*

	Age of Account				
Customer Name	1–30 Days	31–60 Days	61–90 Days	Over 90 Days	Total Balance
Oxwall Tools Corp.......	$20,000				$ 20,000
Calgary Pneumatic Parts Ltd.	10,000				10,000
Red Deer Pipe Corp. ...		$13,000	$10,000		23,000
Seal Coatings, Inc.........			3,000	$1,000	4,000
Other accounts*...........	39,000	12,000	2,000	2,000	55,000
Totals	$69,000	$25,000	$15,000	$3,000	$112,000
Estimated percentage uncollectible..............	.1%	1%	5%	90%	
Allowance for Uncollectible Accounts.....................	$69	$250	$750	$2,700	$3,769

* Each of the "Other accounts" would appear individually.

In the past, the business has collected all but .1 percent of accounts aged from 1 to 30 days, all but 1 percent of accounts aged 31 to 60 days, and so on.

The total amount receivable in each age group is multiplied by the appropriate percentage figure. For example, the $69,000 in accounts aged 1 to 30 days is multiplied by .1 percent (.001), which comes to $69.00. The total balance needed in the Allowance for Uncollectible Accounts—$3,769—is the sum of the amounts computed for the various groups ($69 + $250 + $750 + $2,700).

Suppose the Allowance account has a $2,100 *credit* balance from the previous period, that is, before any current-period adjustment:

Allowance for Uncollectible Accounts

	Unadjusted balance 2,100

Under the aging method, the adjusting entry is designed to adjust this account balance from $2,100 to $3,769, the needed amount determined by the aging schedule. To bring the Allowance balance up to date, Schmidt makes this entry:

Adjusting Entries

Dec. 31	Uncollectible-Account Expense	1,669	
	Allowance for Uncollectible Accounts ($3,769 – $2,100)		1,669

Under the aging method, the adjusting entry takes into account the prior balance in Allowance for Uncollectibles. Now the Allowance account has the correct balance:

Allowance for Uncollectible Accounts

	Unadjusted balance 2,100
	Adjustment amount 1,669
	Adjusted balance 3,769

It is possible for the allowance account to have a *debit* balance at year end prior to the adjusting entry. How can this occur? Bad debt write-offs during the year could have exceeded the allowance amount. Suppose the unadjusted Allowance for Uncollectible Accounts balance is a *debit* amount of $1,500:

Allowance for Uncollectible Accounts

Unadjusted balance	1,500		

In this situation, the adjusting entry is

Adjusting Entries

Dec. 31	Uncollectible-Account Expense........................	5,269	
	Allowance for Uncollectible Accounts		
	($3,769 + $1,500)...		5,269

After posting, the allowance account is up to date:

Allowance for Uncollectible Accounts

Unadjusted balance	1,500	Adjustment amount	5,269
		Adjusted balance	3,769

In the final analysis, the balance sheet reports the expected realizable value of the accounts receivable—$108,231—$112,000 balance of accounts receivable, minus the $3,769 balance in the allowance account (see the total balance in Exhibit 8-2).

In addition to supplying the information needed for accurate financial reporting, the aging method directs management's attention to the accounts that should be pursued for payment.

Using the Percentage of Sales and the Aging Methods Together   In practice, many companies use both the percentage of sales and the aging of accounts methods together (Exhibit 8-3). For interim statements (monthly or quarterly), companies use the percentage of sales method because it is easier to apply. At the end of the year, these companies use the aging method to ensure that Accounts Receivable is reported at expected realizable value—that is, the expected amount to be collected. The two methods work well together, because the percentage of sales approach focuses on measuring bad-debt expense on the income statement, whereas the aging approach is designed to measure net accounts receivable on the balance sheet.

Direct Write-Off Method   Under the **direct write-off method** of accounting for bad debts, the company waits until the credit department decides that a customer's account receivable is uncollectible. Then the accountant debits Uncollectible-Account Expense and credits the customer's account receivable to write off the account.

Assume it is 19X2 and most credit customers have paid for their 19X1 purchases. At this point, the credit department believes that two customers, Chou and Smith, will never pay. The department directs the accountant to write off Chou and Smith

OBJECTIVE 3

Use the direct write-off method of accounting for uncollectibles

Key Point:

This method is easier to use, but it fails to match expenses and revenues properly. It is acceptable only if bad debts are immaterial in amount.

EXHIBIT 8-3   *Two Methods of Estimating Uncollectibles*

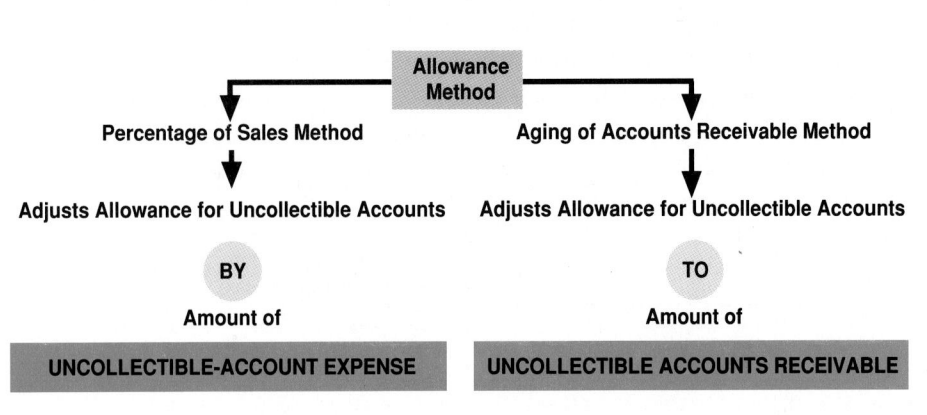

Concept Highlight

as bad debts using this entry:

19X2	Uncollectible-Account Expense..........................	2,000	
	Accounts Receivable—Chou..........................		800
	Accounts Receivable—Smith		1,200
	To write off uncollectible accounts and record bad-debt expense of $2,000.		

How does the direct write-off method affect the financial statement? The following are partial financial statements for 19X1 and 19X2, based on the assumption of $100,000 credit sales in 19X1 and $0 in 19X2:

Income Statement	**19X1**	**19X2**
Revenue		
Sales revenue	$100,000	$ 0
Expense		
Uncollectible account expense	0	2,000

Balance Sheet	**December 31,**	
	19X1	**19X2**
Accounts receivable..	$100,000	$1,000

STOP & THINK

1. How accurately does the write-off method measure income?

Answer: Following generally accepted accounting principles means matching each period's expenses against its revenues. The direct write-off method fails this test: In our example, the full amount of sales revenue appears for 19X1, but the bad-debt expense incurred to generate this revenue appears in 19X2. Consequently, this method gives misleading income figures for both years. The $2,000 bad-debt expense should be matched against the $100,000 sales revenue for 19X1.

2. How accurately does the direct write-off method value accounts receivable?

Answer: The 19X1 balance sheet shows accounts receivable at the full $100,000 figure. But any businessperson knows that bad debts are unavoidable when selling on credit. There are always a few customers who will fail to pay the amount they owe. Is the $100,000 figure, then, the expected realizable value of the accounts? No, showing the full $100,000 in the balance sheet falsely implies that these accounts receivable are worth their full amount.

The direct write-off method is simple to use, and it causes no great error if collection losses are insignificant in amount. However, the resulting accounting records are not as accurate as they could be. The allowance method is a more accurate way to apply the accrual basis for measuring uncollectible-account expense.

Credit Balances in Accounts Receivable _____

Occasionally, customers overpay their accounts or return merchandise for which they have already paid. The result is a credit balance in the customer's accounts receivable. Assume the company's subsidiary ledger contains 213 accounts, with balances as shown:

210 accounts with *debit* balances totaling	$185,000
3 accounts with *credit* balances totaling...	2,800
Net total of all balances	$182,200

The company should *not* report the asset Accounts Receivable at the net amount— $182,200. Why not? The credit balance—$2,800—is a liability. Like any other liability, customer credit balances are debts of the business. A balance sheet that did not indicate to management or to other financial statement users that the company had this liability amount would be misleading if the $2,800 is significant in relation to net income or total current assets. Therefore, the company would report on its balance sheet:

Assets		Liabilities	
Current		Current	
Accounts receivable...	$185,000	Credit balances in	
		customer accounts......	$2,800

Credit Card Sales _____

Credit card sales are common in retailing. American Express, Diners Club en Route, VISA, and MasterCard are popular. The customer presents the credit card as payment for a purchase. The seller prepares a sales invoice in triplicate. The customer and the seller keep copies as receipts. The third copy goes to the credit card company, which then pays the seller the transaction amount and bills the customer.

Credit cards offer consumers the convenience of buying without having to pay the cash immediately. Consumers receive a monthly statement from the credit card company, detailing each credit card transaction. They can write a single cheque to cover the entire month's credit card purchases.

Retailers also benefit from credit card sales. They do not have to check a customer's credit rating. The company that issues the card has already done so. Retailers do not have to keep an accounts receivable subsidiary ledger account for each customer, and they do not have to collect cash from customers. The copy of the sales invoice that retailers send to the credit card company signals the card issuer to pursue payment. Further, retailers receive cash more quickly from the credit card companies than they would from the customers themselves.

Of course, these services to the seller do not come free. The seller receives less than 100 percent of the face value of the invoice. The credit card company takes a discount[1] on the sale to cover its services. Suppose a friend treats you and two others to lunch at Hy's Steak House (the seller) and pays the bill—$100—with a Diners Club en Route card. The seller's entry to record the $100 Diners Club en Route card sale, subject to a 2-percent discount is

Accounts Receivable—Diners Club en Route	98	
Credit-Card Discount Expense	2	
Sales Revenue...		100

On collection of the discounted value, the seller records

Cash...	98	
Accounts Receivable—Diners Club en Route		98

_____

[1] The rate varies among companies and over time.

OBJECTIVE 4

Identify internal control weaknesses in accounts receivable

Internal Control over Collections of Accounts Receivable ___

Businesses that sell on credit receive most of their cash receipts by mail. Internal control over collections on account is an important part of overall internal control. Chapter 7 detailed control procedures over cash receipts, but a critical element of internal control deserves emphasis here: the separation of cash-handling and cash-accounting duties. Consider the following case.

Butler Supply Ltd. is a small, family-owned business that takes pride in the loyalty of its workers. Most company employees have been with the Butlers for at least five years. The company makes 90 percent of its sales on account.

The office staff consists of a bookkeeper and a supervisor. The bookkeeper maintains the general ledger and the accounts receivable subsidiary ledger. He also makes the daily bank deposit. The supervisor prepares monthly financial statements and any special reports the Butlers require. She also takes sales orders from customers and serves as office manager.

Can you identify the internal control weakness? The bookkeeper has access to the general ledger, accounts receivable subsidiary ledger, and cash. The bookkeeper could take a customer cheque and write off the customer's account as uncollectible.[2] Unless the supervisor or some other manager reviews the bookkeeper's work regularly, the theft may go undetected. In small businesses like Butler Supply Ltd., such a review may not be performed routinely.

How can this control weakness be corrected? The supervisor could open incoming mail and make the daily bank deposit. The bookkeeper should not be allowed to handle cash. Only the remittance slips would be forwarded to the bookkeeper to indicate which customer accounts to credit. Removing cash-handling duties from the bookkeeper and keeping the accounts receivable subsidiary ledger away from the supervisor, separates duties and strengthens internal control. These actions would reduce an employee's opportunity to steal cash and then cover it up with a false credit to a customer account.

Using a bank lock box would achieve the same separation of duties. Customers would send their payments directly to Butler Supply's bank, which would record and deposit the cash into the company's account. The bank would then forward the remittance advice to Butler Supply's bookkeeper to credit the appropriate customer accounts.

Another step should be taken. The bookkeeper should total the amount posted as credits to customer accounts receivable each day. The owner should then compare this total with the day's bank deposit slip. Agreement of the two records gives some assurance that the customer accounts were posted correctly and helps avoid accounting errors. Also, the owner should prepare the bank reconciliation.

Mid-Chapter Summary Problem for Your Review

Wolfville Lumber Ltd. is a chain of hardware and building supply stores concentrated in the Maritimes. The company's year-end balance sheets for 19X3 reported:

Accounts Receivables..	$7,455,648
Allowance for doubtful accounts	(224,000)

---

[2] The bookkeeper would need to forge the endorsements of the cheques and deposit them in a bank account he controls. This is easier than you might think.

Required

1. How much of the December 31, 19X3, balance of accounts receivable did Wolfville expect to collect? Stated differently, what was the expected realizable value of these receivables?

2. Journalize, without explanations, 19X4 entries for Wolfville Lumber, assuming:
   a. Estimated Doubtful-Account Expense of $225,000, based on the percentage of sales method.
   b. Write-offs of accounts receivable totaling $290,000.
   c. December 31, 19X4, aging of receivables, which indicates that $180,000 of the total receivables of $7,980,346 is uncollectible.

3. Show how Wolfville Lumber's receivables and related allowance will appear on the December 31, 19X4, balance sheet.

4. What is the expected realizable value of receivables at December 31, 19X4? How much is doubtful-account expense for 19X4?

SOLUTION TO REVIEW PROBLEM

Requirements

1. Wolfville Lumber expected to collect $7,231,648 (i.e. $7,455,648 – $224,000).

2. a. Doubtful-Account Expense 225,000
      Allowance for Doubtful Accounts   225,000

   b. Allowance for Doubtful Accounts.................................... 290,000
      Accounts Receivable   290,000

Allowance for Doubtful Accounts

19X4 Write-offs	290,000	Dec. 31, 19X3	224,000
		19X4 Expense	225,000
		19X4 balance prior to Dec. 31, 19X4	159,000

   c. Doubtful-Account Expense ($180,000 – $159,000)........... 21,000
      Allowance for Doubtful Accounts   21,000

3. Accounts receivable.. $7,980,346
   Less: Allowance for doubtful accounts...........................   180,000

4. Wolfville Lumber, at December 31, 19X4,
   expected to collect ($7,980,346 – $180,000) $7,800,346

   Doubtful-account expense for 19X4
   ($225,000 + $21,000)   246,000

Notes Receivable

As we pointed out earlier in this chapter, notes receivable are more formal arrangements than accounts receivable. Often the debtor signs a promissory note, which serves as evidence of the debt. Let's define the special terms used to discuss notes receivable:

Promissory note. A written promise to pay a specified sum of money at a particular future date.

Maker of a note. The person or business that signs the note and promises to pay the amount required by the note agreement; the debtor.

Payee of the note. The person or business to whom the maker promises future payment; the creditor.

Short Exercise:

Calculate the maturity dates of these notes:

(1) A 90-day note dated January 4, 19X3. (2) A 150-day note dated September 30, 19X1. (3) A 45-day note dated May 15, 19X2. Begin counting on the day following the date of the note, so that the due date on a 90-day note is day number 90. *A:* (1) April 4, 19X3 (2) February 27, 19X2 (3) June 29, 19X2

Principal amount or **principal**. The amount loaned out by the payee and borrowed by the maker of the note.

Interest. The revenue to the payee for loaning out the principal and the expense to the maker for borrowing the principal.

Interest period. The period of time during which interest is to be computed. It extends from the original date of the note to the maturity date. Also called the *note period*, *note term*, or simply *time*.

Interest rate. The percentage rate that is multiplied by the principal amount to compute the amount of interest on the note.

Maturity date (also called *due date*). The date on which final payment of the note is due. Debts with a maturity date are permitted by law to be paid three days after their maturity or due date. These three days are called "days of grace."

Maturity value. The sum of principal and interest due at the maturity date of a note.

Exhibit 8-4 illustrates a promissory note. Study it carefully.

Identifying the Maturity Date of a Note

Key Point:

Here *rate* means interest and *time* means interest period.

Key Point:

Interest rates are usually stated as an annual rate. Therefore, the time in the formula should also be expressed in terms of a year.

Some notes specify the maturity date of a note, as shown in Exhibit 8-4. Other notes state the period of the note, in days or months. When the period is given in months, the note's maturity date falls on the same day of the month as the date the note was issued. For example, a 6-month note dated February 16 matures on August 16. With the days of grace taken into account, the note must be repaid by August 19.

When the period is given in days, the maturity date is determined by counting the days from date of issue. A 120-day note dated September 14, 19X2, matures on January 12, 19X3, as shown below:

Month		Number of Days	Cumulative Total
Sept.	19X2	16*	16
Oct.	19X2	31	47
Nov.	19X2	30	77
Dec.	19X2	31	108
Jan.	19X3	12	120

*30 – 14 = 16

The note would have to be repaid by January 15, 19X3.

EXHIBIT 8-4 *A Promissory Note*

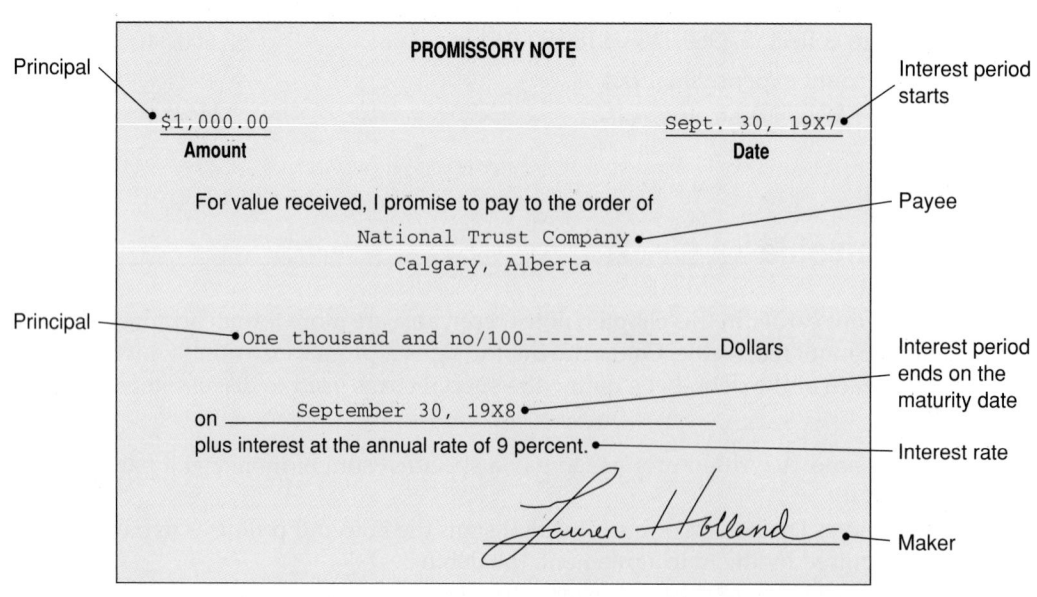

Computing Interest on a Note

The formula for computing interest is

Principal × Rate × Time = Amount of Interest

Using the data in Exhibit 8-4, National Trust Company computes its interest revenue for 1 year on its note receivable as:

Principal	Rate	Time	Interest
$1,000	× .09 ×	1 (yr.) =	$90

The *maturity value* of the note is $1,090 ($1,000 principal + $90 interest). Note that the time element is one (1) because interest is computed over a 1-year period.

When the interest period of a note is stated in months, we compute the interest based on the 12-month year. Interest on a $2,000 note at 15 percent for 3 months is computed as

Principal	Rate	Time	Interest
$2,000	× .15 ×	3/12 =	$75

When the interest period of a note is stated in days, we usually compute interest based on a 365-day year. The interest on a $5,000 note at 12 percent for 60 days is computed as

Principal	Rate	Time	Interest
$5,000	× .12 ×	60/365 =	$98.63

Short Exercise:

Practice calculating interest:

(1) $30,000, 12½%, 180-day note; (2) $8,500, 9%, 6-month note

A: (1) ($30,000 × .125 × 180/365 = $1,849.32
(2) ($8,500 × .09 × 6/12) = $383

Recording Notes Receivable

OBJECTIVE 5
Account for notes receivable

Consider the loan agreement shown in Exhibit 8-4. After Holland signs the note and presents it to the trust company, National Trust gives her $1,000 cash. At maturity date, Holland pays the trust company $1,090 ($1,000 principal + $90 interest). The trust company's entries are

Sept. 30, 19X7	Note Receivable—L. Holland..................	1,000	
	Cash..		1,000
	To record the loan.		
Sept. 30, 19X8	Cash...	1,090	
	Note Receivable—L. Holland............		1,000
	Interest Revenue ($1,000 × .09 × 1)....		90
	To record collection at maturity.		

Some companies sell merchandise in exchange for notes receivable. This arrangement occurs often when the payment term extends beyond the customary accounts receivable period, which generally ranges from 30 to 60 days.

Suppose that on October 20, 19X3, Canadian General Electric (CGE) sells equipment for $15,000 to Dorman Builders Inc. Dorman signs a 90-day promissory note at 10 percent interest. CGE's entries to record the sale and collection from Dorman are

Oct. 20, 19X3	Note Receivable		
	— Dorman Builders......................	15,000	
	Sales Revenue............................		15,000
	To record sale.		

Jan. 18, 19X4   Cash...   15,375
                    Note Receivable
                        —Dorman Builders.................   15,000
                    Interest Revenue
                        ($15,000 × .10 × 3/12).............   375
                To record collection at maturity.

A company may accept a note receivable from a trade customer who fails to pay an account receivable within the customary 30 to 60 days. The customer signs a promissory note—that is, becomes the maker of the note—and gives it to the creditor, who becomes the payee.

Suppose Maison Fortin Inc. sees that it will not be able to pay off its account payable to Hoffman Supply, which is due in 15 days. Hoffman may accept a one-year $2,400 note receivable, with 9 percent interest, from Maison Fortin October 1, 19X1. Hoffman's entry is

Oct. 1, 19X1   Note Receivable—Maison Fortin Inc.   2,400
                    Accounts Receivable—
                        Maison Fortin Inc.   2,400
                To receive a note on account from a customer.

Why does a company accept a note receivable instead of pressing its demand for payment of the account receivable? The company may pursue payment but learn that its customer does not have the money. A note receivable gives the company written evidence of the maker's debt, which may aid any legal action for collection. Also, the note receivable may carry a pledge by the maker that gives the payee certain assets if cash is not received by the due date. The company's reward for its patience in collecting is the interest revenue that it earns on the note receivable.

Accruing Interest Revenue

Notes receivable may be outstanding at the end of the accounting period. The interest revenue that was accrued on the note up to that point should be recorded as part of that period's earnings. Recall that interest revenue is earned over time, not just when cash is received.

Let's continue with the Hoffman Supply note receivable from Maison Fortin. Hoffman Supply's accounting period ends December 31. How much of the total interest revenue does Hoffman earn in 19X1? How much in 19X2?

Hoffman will earn three months' interest in 19X1—for October, November, and December. In 19X2, Hoffman will earn nine months' interest—for January through September. Therefore, at December 31, 19X1, Hoffman Supply will make the following adjusting entry to accrue interest revenue:

Oct. 31, 19X1   Interest Receivable ($2,400 × .09 × ³⁄₁₂).........   54
                    Interest Revenue   54
                To accrue interest revenue earned in
                19X1 but not yet received.

Then, on the maturity date Hoffman Supply may record collection of principal and interest as follows:

Short Exercise:

Calculate interest accrued at 12/31 on an 11%, $3,500, 90-day note receivable dated 10/15.

A: $3,500 × 0.11 × 77/365
    = $81 (rounded)

July 31, 19X2   Cash [$2,400 + ($2,400 × .09)]   2,616
                    Note Receivable   2,400
                    Interest Receivable
                        ($2,400 × .09 × ³⁄₁₂)..............................   54
                    Interest Revenue
                        ($2,400 × .09 × ⁹⁄₁₂)..............................   162
                To record collection of note receivable on
                which interest has been previously
                accrued.

The entries to accrue interest revenue earned in 19X1 and record collection in 19X2 assign the correct amount of interest to each year.

Discounting a Note Receivable

A payee of a note receivable may need the cash before the maturity date. When this occurs, the payee may sell the note. A note receivable is a *negotiable instrument*, which means it is readily transferable from one party to another, and may be sold. Selling a note is called **discounting a note receivable**. This practice is prevalent with long-term notes receivable secured by real estate as collateral. A bank that has lent money may discount the note receivable to another lender. The net result is that the banks and trust companies can quickly replenish their funds for lending. Moreover, more money is available for people to purchase homes and for businesses to invest in inventory and plant and equipment.

Computers can be used to discount notes. If the company deals with relatively few discounted notes, a spreadsheet may handle the accounting (if the accounting software package does not include a special function for discounting). Companies that discount notes on a regular basis would have a standard program to compute the proceeds.

The price the purchaser of a discounted note pays for the note receivable depends mainly on the interest rate the purchaser seeks to earn on its investment. In effect, the purchaser pays cash now—at a discounted price—to receive a larger amount at a later date. This is the concept of present value: Less money today grows to a larger sum in the future. More advanced accounting courses explore present-value concepts in more detail.

A payee may also discount a short-term note receivable, one with a maturity of one year or less. There are several ways to compute the price to be received. Fundamentally the price is determined by present-value concepts. But the transaction between the seller and the buyer of the note can take any form agreeable to the two parties. We illustrate one procedure used for discounting short-term notes receivable. To receive cash immediately, the seller is willing to accept a significantly discounted price. The purchaser of the note is interested mainly in the margin to be earned on the note—the difference between the purchase price and the amount to be collected at maturity.

Now we return to the preceding example with Canadian General Electric and Dorman on page 403. The maturity date of the Dorman note is January 18, 19X4. Let us assume CGE discounts the Dorman note at the National Bank on December 9, 19X3. The discount period—the number of days from the date of discounting to the date of maturity (the period the bank will hold the note)—is 40 days; 22 days in December and 18 days in January. Assume the bank applies a 12 percent interest rate in computing the discounted value of the note. The bank will want to use a discount rate that is higher than the interest rate on the note in order to increase its earnings. CGE may be willing to accept this higher rate in order to get cash quickly. The discounted value, called the *proceeds*, is the amount that CGE receives from the bank. The proceeds are computed as follows:

Key Point:
The discounting procedure follows five steps:
1. Compute the maturity value (principal + interest).
2. Compute the bank's discount period (length of note – days held prior to discounting).
3. Compute the bank's discount (maturity value × discount rate × discount period).
4. Compute the proceeds (maturity value – discount).
5. Prepare the general journal entry.

Cash (from Step 4) ...XXX
   Interest Revenue
   (or expense) XXX
   Note Receivable
   (principal) XXX

Principal amount	$15,000	
+ Interest ($15,000 × .10 × 90/365)	370	
= Maturity value...	$15,370	⎤ $168 ⎤ $168
− Discount ($15,370 × .12 × 40/365)....................	(202)	
= Proceeds	$15,168	

At maturity the bank collects $15,370 from the maker of the note, earning $202 of interest revenue.

Observe two points in the above computation: (1) the discount is computed on the *maturity value* of the note (principal plus interest) rather than on the original principal amount; and (2) the discount period extends *backward* from the maturity date (January 18, 19X4) to the date of discounting (December 9, 19X3). Follow Exhibit 8-5.

EXHIBIT 8-5 *The Timing of Discounting a Note Receivable*

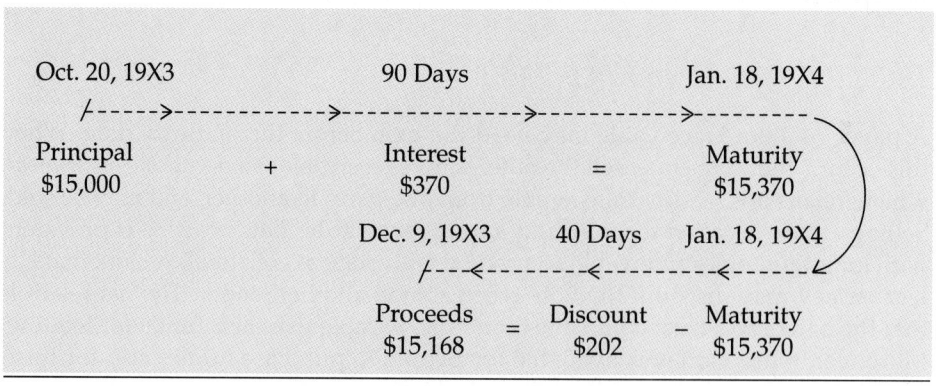

Canadian General Electric's entry to record discounting the note is

Dec. 9, 19X3	Cash	15,168	
	Note Receivable		
	— Dorman Builders...........................		15,000
	Interest Revenue		
	($15,168 – $15,000)		168
	To record discounting a note receivable.		

When the proceeds from discounting a note receivable are less than the principal amount of the note, the payee records a debit to Interest Expense for the amount of the difference. For example, CGE could discount the note receivable for cash proceeds of $14,980. The entry to record this transaction is

Short Exercise:

Dec. 9 19X3	Cash	14,980	
	Interest Expense..	20	
	Note Receivable—Dorman Builders....		15000

The term *discount* has been used here to distinguish the interest earned by the payee of the note from the interest to be earned by the purchaser of the note. Fundamentally, the discount is interest.

Contingent Liabilities on Discounted Notes Receivable

A **contingent liability** is a potential liability that will become an actual liability only if a potential event does occur.

Discounting a note receivable creates a contingent liability for the endorser. If the maker of the note (Dorman in our example) fails to pay the maturity value to the new payee (the bank), the original payee (Canadian General Electric, the note's endorser) legally must pay the bank the amount due.[3] Now we see why the liability is "potential." If Dorman pays the bank, CGE can forget the note. But if Dorman dishonors the note—fails to pay it—CGE has an actual liability.

This contingent liability exists from the time of endorsement to the maturity date of the note. In our example, the contingent liability exists from December 9, 19X3 when CGE endorsed the note to the January 18, 19X4 maturity date.

Contingent liabilities are not included with actual liabilities on the balance sheet. After all, they are not real debts. However, financial statement users should be alerted that the business has incurred *potential* debts. Most businesses report contingent liabilities in a footnote to the financial statements. Canadian General Electric's end-of-period financial statement might carry this note:

> As of December 31, 19X3, the Company is contingently liable on notes receivable discounted in the amount of $15,000.

Sidebar (left margin):

January 5, received a $5,000, 90-day, 10% note from Barney Fife. Sold the Fife note on January 25 by discounting it to a bank at 12%. Prepare the journal entry to record the discounted note on January 25. **A:**

1. Maturity value = $5,000 + ($5,000 × 10% × 90/365) = $5,123

2. Discount period = 90 – 20 = 70 days

3. Disct. = $5,123 × 12% × 70/365 = $118.

4. Proceeds = $5,123 – $118 = $5,005

5. Journal entry:
Cash 5,005
  Interest Revenue ...   5
  Note Receivable—
    ....Barney Fife 5,000

---

[3]The discounting agreement between the endorser and the purchaser may specify that the endorser has no liability if the note is dishonored at maturity.

Dishonored Notes Receivable

If the maker of a note does not pay a note receivable at maturity (plus the days of grace), the maker is said to **dishonor** or **default on** the note. Because the term of the note has expired, the note agreement is no longer in force, nor is it negotiable. However, the payee still has a claim against the maker of the note for payment, and usually transfers the claim from the note receivable account to Accounts Receivable. The payee records interest revenue earned on the note and debits Accounts Receivable for full maturity value of the note.

Suppose Rubinstein Jewelers Ltd. has a six-month, 10 percent note receivable for $1,200 from D. Hatachi. On the February 3 maturity date, Hatachi defaults. Rubinstein Jewelers would record the default as follows:

Feb. 3	Accounts Receivable—D. Hatachi		
	[$1,200 + ($1,200 × .10 × ⁶⁄₁₂)]	1,260	
	Note Receivable—D. Hatachi		1,200
	Interest Revenue ($1,200 × .10 × ⁶⁄₁₂)		60
	To record dishonor of note receivable.		

Rubinstein would pursue collection from Hatachi as a promissory note default. The company may treat accounts receivable such as this as a special category to highlight them for added collection efforts. If the account receivable later proves uncollectible, the account is written off against Allowance for Uncollectible Accounts in the manner previously discussed.

The maker may dishonor a note after it has been discounted by the original payee. For example, suppose Dorman Builders dishonors its note (maturity value, $15,370) to Canadian General Electric after CGE has discounted the note to the bank. On dishonor, the bank adds a *protest fee* to cover the cost of a statement about the facts of the dishonor and requests payment from CGE, which then becomes the holder of the dishonored note. Assume CGE pays the maturity value of the note, plus the $25 protest fee, to the bank. This payment creates an obligation for Dorman to CGE. CGE then presents the statement to Dorman and makes the following entry on the maturity date of the note:

Jan. 18, 19X4	Accounts Receivable—Dorman		
	Builders ($15,370 + $25)	15,395	
	Cash		15,395
	To record payment of dishonored note receivable that has been discounted, plus a protest fee.		

CGE's collection of cash or write-off of the uncollected account receivable would be recorded in the normal manner, depending on the ultimate outcome. If CGE charges Dorman additional interest, CGE's collection entry debits Cash and credits Accounts Receivable and Interest Revenue.

Reporting Receivables and Allowances: Actual Reports

OBJECTIVE 6
Report receivables on the balance sheet

Let us now look at how some companies report their receivables and allowances for uncollectibles in the financial statements. The terminology and setup vary, but you can understand these actual presentations based on what you have learned in this chapter.

Section 3020.01 in the *CICA Handbook* indicates that because "... it is ... assumed that adequate allowance for doubtful accounts has been made ... it is not considered necessary to refer to [the] allowance" in the financial statements. The 1993 edition of *Financial Reporting in Canada*, published by the CICA, indicates that 9 percent of the 300 companies surveyed made reference, on the balance sheet or in the notes, to the allowance in 1992.[4]

---

[4] *Financial Reporting in Canada 1993*, Twentieth edition (Toronto: CICA, 1993) p. 90.

One Canadian company that did provide information was Industra Service Corporation, an industrial plant engineering and environmental service company. In their 1993 annual report, they reported (amounts in millions):

	December	
	1993	**1992**
Current assets		
Accounts receivable (note 2)	18.3	14.9

Notes to the Consolidated Financial Statements
8. Accounts receivable
   Allowance for doubtful accounts was $.84 million
   (1992: $.16 million).

United Dominion Industries Limited, a Canadian manufacturing and engineering services company that is listed on the Toronto, Montreal, and New York stock exchanges, and that reports its financial statement in U.S. dollars, reports in its 1993 financial statement (U.S. dollars in thousands)

	December 31	
	1993	**1992**
Current assets		
Accounts and notes receivables, less allowance for doubtful accounts of $6,983 in 1993 and $9,693 in 1992	272,424	269,416

To figure the total accounts and notes receivables amount, add the allowance to the net receivables amount. For 1993, $272,424 + $6,983 = $279,407.

While some companies like Industra Service and United Dominion provide information about the allowance for doubtful accounts, as was suggested above, many companies in Canada such as Canadian General Electric tend to show only net accounts receivable. They do not show the allowance.

Intrawest Corporation, a Canadian company that operates Whistler/Blackcomb and Mount Tremblant ski resorts among its many activities, like many real estate companies, does not categorize its balance sheet. Assets include a single amount for receivables supplemented by a detailed note (amounts in thousands).

Amounts receivable (note 5)	$51,099

Note 5:	
Amounts receivable	
Receivable from sales of real estate	$22,395
Mortgages...	12,514
Loans and notes receivable..	3,706
Funded senior employee share purchase plan	2,125
Other accounts receivable..	10,359
	$51,099

Receivables are due as follows:

Year ending September 30, 1994	$44,750
1995...	933
1996...	111
1997...	52
1998...	1,526
Subsequent to 1998...	3,727
	$51,099

Tembec Inc., a forest products company, includes long-term receivables with other assets after fixed assets. The exact placement is less important than the fact that the long-term receivables are properly described and not included with current assets.

Nova Corporation of Alberta reported in its 1993 annual report in the notes to the financial statements:

> The Corporation sells trade receivables to certain financial institutions ... Recourse to [that is, the liability of] the Corporation is limited to a maximum of 10% of the amount outstanding at any point in time.

In other words, as the seller, Nova is contingently liable if the receivables sold are not paid to the financial institution when due but to a limit of 10 percent of the total outstanding.

Use of Accounting Information in Decision-Making

The balance sheet lists assets in the order of relative liquidity. Cash, of course, comes first because it is the medium of exchange, and can be used to purchase any item or pay any bill. Current receivables are less liquid than cash because receivables must be collected. Merchandise inventory is less liquid than receivables because the goods must first be sold; selling the goods creates a receivable that can be collected. Exhibit 8-1 provides an example of a balance sheet showing these accounts.

Acid-Test (or Quick) Ratio

In making decisions, owners and managers use some ratios based on the relative liquidity of assets. In Chapter 4, for example, we discussed the current ratio, which indicates the ability to pay current liabilities with current assets. A more stringent measure of the ability to pay current liabilities is the **acid-test** (or **quick**) ratio:

$$\text{Acid-test ratio} = \frac{\text{Cash + Short-term investments + Net current receivables}}{\text{Total current liabilities}}$$

The acid-test ratio assumes that all current liabilities are payable immediately, and that the debtor will convert the most liquid assets to cash. The three most liquid asset categories are cash, short-term investments, and current receivables. Short-term investments (covered in Chapter 17) are the second-most-liquid assets because they are readily convertible to cash at the will of the owner. All the owner must do to generate cash is sell these investments.

The higher the acid-test ratio, the better able the business is to pay its current liabilities. An acid-test ratio that increases over time usually indicates improving business operations.

Inventory, although included in the computation of the current ratio, is excluded from the acid-test ratio because it may not be easy to sell the goods. A company may have an acceptable current ratio and a poor acid-test ratio because of a large amount of inventory.

What is an acceptable acid-test ratio value? It depends on the industry. Automobile dealers can operate smoothly with an acid-test ratio of .20. Several things make this possible: Car dealers have almost no current receivables. They receive cash from customers, who borrow from banks and other lenders. Dealers carry large inventories, and the manufacturers—GM, Toyota, Mercedes-Benz, for example—allow dealers to pay the cost of automobiles as they are sold at retail prices. In summary, car dealers need little in the way of liquid assets. The average acid-test ratio for women's dress manufacturers is .90. Most department stores' ratio values cluster about .80, and travel agencies average 1.10. In general, an acid-test ratio of 1.00 is considered safe.

Short Exercise:

Compute the current and acid-test ratios for the following selected accounts and their balances at 12/31:

Equipment	$4,000
Supplies	500
Interest Payable	600
Accounts Receivable	2,600
Accounts Payable	3,400
Accum. Deprec.	1,200
Inventory	1,600
Cash	1,300

A: Current ratio = 1.5
($6,000*/$4,000†)
Acid-test ratio = 0.975
($3,900/$4,000)
($2,600 + $1,300 = $3,900)
* ($500 + $2,600 + $1,600 + $1,300 = $6,000)
† ($600 + $3,400 = $4,000)

OBJECTIVE 7

Use the acid-test ratio and days' sales in receivables to evaluate a company's position

Short Exercise:
Given:

Net Sales $48,000
Accts. Rec. (1/1) 10,000
Accts. Rec. (12/31) 14,000
What is the average collection period?
A: One day's sales = $132 ($48,000/365). Days' sales in average accounts receivable = 91 days ($12,000/$132)

Days' Sales in Receivables

After a business makes a credit sale, the next critical event in the business cycle is collection of the receivable. Several financial ratios center on receivables. **Days' sales in receivables**, also called the *collection period*, indicates how many days it takes to collect the average level of receivables. The shorter the collection period, the more quickly the organization can use cash for operations. The longer the collection period, the less cash is available to pay bills and expand. In the chapter-opening story, Rural Metro's days' sales in receivables increased, and this increase hurt the company. How could the collection period get so long? A company that doesn't collect its receivables cannot pay its bills. Companies like Rural Metro may write off lots of receivables as uncollectible. With tougher collection policies, the cash flow and profits improved.

Short Exercise:

Refer to the previous Short Exercise. If the company's credit sale terms were 3/10 n/45, how would you evaluate days' sales in receivables? *A:* Far too high; 91 days is nearly twice the allowable credit period of 45 days.

Days' sales in receivables can be computed in two steps, as follows:

$$1. \quad \text{One day's sales} = \frac{\text{Net sales}}{\text{365 days}}$$

$$2. \quad \begin{array}{c}\text{Days' sales in}\\ \text{average accounts}\\ \text{receivable}\end{array} = \frac{\text{Average net accounts receivable}}{\text{One day's sales}} = \frac{(\text{Beginning net receivables} + \text{Ending net receivables})/2}{\text{One day's sales}}$$

Real-World Example:
The average collection period for manufacturers of men's and boys' sport clothing was 47 days in 1993. The top 25% of those companies collected receivables every 26 days. Manufacturers of canned vegetables had an average collection period of 28 days; the top 25% had a 21-day collection period.

The length of the collection period depends on the credit terms of the company's sales. For example, sales on net 30 terms should be collected within approximately 30 days. When there is a discount, such as 2/10 net 30, the collection period may be shorter. Terms of net 45 or net 60 will result in longer collection periods. Companies watch their collection period closely. Whenever the collection period lengthens, the business must find other sources of financing, such as borrowing. During recessions, customers pay more slowly, and a longer collection period may be unavoidable.

This situation points to the challenge of financial analysis. Investors and creditors do not evaluate a company on the basis of one or two ratios. Instead they perform a thorough analysis of all the information available on a company. Then they stand back from the data and ask, "What is our overall impression about the strength of this business?"

STOP & THINK

Suppose you computed Klink Corp.'s acid-test ratio at two dates: In 1992 when the days' sales in receivables stood at 162 days, and in 1995, when the days' sales in receivables was 98 days. Considering only the receivables, which acid-test ratio would look better? Would this appearance be realistic?

Answer: Considering only the receivables, the 1992 acid-test ratio would be higher, and thus look better, because the receivables were much greater in 1992. The 1995 acid-test ratio would be lower, and thus look worse, because of the lower receivables. But appearances can be deceiving. The bloated receivables in 1992 indicated a problem, not a strength.

Computers and Accounts Receivable

Accounting for receivables for a company like McCain Foods Ltd. requires tens of thousands of postings to customer accounts each month for credit sales and cash collections. Manual accounting methods cannot keep up.

As Chapter 6 explained in more detail, Accounts Receivable can be set up on a computerized system. The order entry and logistics (shipping) systems interface with the billing system, which automatically creates the customers' invoices and debits their accounts in Accounts Receivable. The computer then creates a sales invoice. At the same time, the computer generates records that lead to the printout of sales for the period. The printout is checked and approved. Finally, computerized posting to the ledger and accounts receivable subledger occurs.

Summary Problem for Your Review

Suppose Petro-Canada engaged in the following transactions:

19X4

Apr. 1   Loaned $8,000 to Bland Ltd., a service station operator. Received a one-year, 10 percent note.

June 1   Discounted the Bland note at the bank at a discount rate of 12 percent.

Nov. 30   Loaned $6,000 to Houle, Inc., a regional distributor of Petro-Canada products, on a three-month, 11 percent note.

19X5

Feb. 28   Collected the Houle note at maturity.

Petro-Canada's accounting period ends on December 31.

Required

Explanations are not needed.

1. Record the 19X4 transactions on April 1, June 1, and November 30 on Petro-Canada's books.
2. Make any adjusting entries needed on December 31, 19X4.
3. Record the February 28, 19X5 collection of the Houle note.
4. Which transaction creates a contigent liability for Petro-Canada? When does the contingency begin? When does it end?
5. Write a footnote that Petro-Canada could use in its 19X4 financial statements to report the contingent liability.

SOLUTION TO REVIEW PROBLEM

Requirement 1

19X4				
Apr. 1	Note Receivable—Bland Ltd.	8,000		
	Cash			8,000
June 1	Cash..	7,920*		
	Interest Expense...	80		
	Note Receivable—Bland Ltd...............			8,000

*Computation of proceeds

Principal..	$8,000
+ Interest ($8,000 × .10 × ²⁄₁₂)	800
= Maturity value	8,800
− Discount ($8,800 × .12 × ¹⁰⁄₁₂).............	880
= Proceeds..	$7,920

Nov. 30	Note Receivable—Houle, Inc.	6,000		
	Cash			6,000

Requirement 2

Adjusting Entries

19X4

Dec. 31	Interest Receivable ($6,000 × .11 × ½)	55	
	Interest Revenue		55

Requirement 3

19X5

Feb. 28	Cash [$6,000 + ($6,000 × .11 × ³⁄₁₂)]........	6,165	
	Note Receivable—Houle, Inc.		6,000
	Interest Receivable		55
	Interest Revenue ($6,000 × .11 × ²⁄₁₂)		110

Requirement 4

Discounting the Bland note receivable creates a contingent liability for Petro-Canada. The contingency exists from the date of discounting the note receivable (June 1) to the maturity date of the note (April 1, 19X5).

Requirement 5

Note XX—Contingent liabilities: At December 31, 19X4, the Company is contingently liable on notes receivable discounted in the amount of $8,000.

Summary

1. **Use the allowance method of accounting for uncollectibles.** Credit sales create receivables. Accounts receivable are usually current assets, and notes receivable may be current or long-term. Uncollectible receivables are accounted for by the allowance method or the direct write-off method. The *allowance method* matches expenses to sales revenue and also results in a more realistic measure of net accounts receivable.

2. **Estimate uncollectibles by the percentage of sales and the aging approaches.** The *percentage of sales method* and the *aging of accounts receivable method* are the two main approaches to estimating bad debts under the allowance method.

3. **Use the direct write-off method of accounting for uncollectibles.** The *direct write-off method* is easy to apply, but it fails to match the uncollectible-account expense to the corresponding sales revenue. Also, Accounts Receivable are reported at their full amount, which misleadingly suggests that the company expects to collect all its accounts receivable.

In *credit-card sales,* the seller receives cash from the credit-card company (Diners Club en Route, for example), which bills the customer. For the convenience of receiving cash immediately, the seller pays a fee that is a percentage of the sale.

4. **Identify internal control weaknesses in accounts receivable.** Companies that sell on credit receive most customer collections in the mail. Good *internal control* over mailed-in cash receipts means separating cash-handling duties from cash-accounting duties.

5. **Account for notes receivable.** *Notes receivable* are formal credit agreements. Interest earned by the creditor is computed by multiplying the note's principal amount by the interest rate times the length of the interest period.

Because notes receivable are negotiable, they may be sold. Selling a note receivable—called *discounting a note*—creates a *contingent (possible) liability* for the note's payee.

6. **Report receivables on the balance sheet.** All accounts receivable, notes receivable, and allowance accounts appear in the balance sheet. However, companies use various formats and terms to report these assets.

7. *Use the acid-test ratio and days' sales in receivables to evaluate a company's position.* The *acid-test ratio* measures ability to pay current liabilities from the most liquid current assets. *Days' sales in receivables* indicates how long it takes to collect the average level of receivables.

Self-Study Questions

Test your understanding of the chapter by marking the correct answer for each of the following questions:

1. The party that holds a receivable is called the *(p. 390)*
   - a. Creditor
   - b. Debtor
   - c. Maker
   - d. Security holder

2. The function of the credit department is to *(p. 391)*
   - a. Collect accounts receivable from customers
   - b. Report bad credit risks to other companies
   - c. Evaluate customers who apply for credit
   - d. Write off uncollectible accounts receivable

3. Longview, Inc., made the following entry related to uncollectibles:

   Uncollectible-Account Expense................................. 1,900
       Allowance for Uncollectible Accounts..............   1,900

   The purpose of this entry is to *(pp. 392–393)*
   - a. Write off uncollectibles
   - b. Close the expense account
   - c. Age the accounts receivable
   - d. Record bad-debt expense

4. Longview, Inc., also made this entry:

   Allowance for Uncollectible Accounts...................... 2,110
       Accounts Receivable (detailed)..........................   2,110

   The purpose of this entry is to *(pp. 393–394)*
   - a. Write off uncollectibles
   - b. Close the expense account
   - c. Age the accounts receivable
   - d. Record bad debt expense

5. The credit balance in Allowance for Uncollectibles is $14,300 prior to the adjusting entries at the end of the period. The aging of the accounts indicates that an allowance of $78,900 is needed. The amount of expense to record is *(pp. 395–396)*
   - a. $14,300
   - b. $64,600
   - c. $78,900
   - d. $93,200

6. The most important internal control over cash receipts is *(p. 400)*
   - a. Assigning an honest employee the responsibility for handling cash
   - b. Separating the cash-handling and cash-accounting duties
   - c. Ensuring that cash is deposited in the bank daily
   - d. Centralizing the opening of incoming mail in a single location

7. A six-month, $30,000 note specifies interest of 9 percent. The full amount of interest on this note will be *(p. 403)*
   - a. $450
   - b. $900
   - c. $1,350
   - d. $2,700

8. The note in Self-Study Question 7 was issued on August 31, and the company's accounting year ends on December 31. The year-end balance sheet will report interest receivable of *(pp. 403–405)*
   - a. $450
   - b. $900
   - c. $1,350
   - d. $2,700

9. Discounting a note receivable is a way to *(p. 405)*
   - a. Collect on a note
   - b. Increase interest revenue
   - c. Both of the above
   - d. None of the above

10. Discounting a note receivable creates a (an) *(p. 406)*
    - a. Cash disbursement
    - b. Interest expense
    - c. Protest fee
    - d. Contingent liability

Answers to the Self-Study Questions follow the Accounting Vocabulary.

Accounting Vocabulary

Acid-test ratio *(p. 409)*
Aging of accounts receivable *(p. 395)*
Allowance for Doubtful Accounts *(p. 392)*
Allowance for Uncollectible Accounts *(p. 392)*
Allowance method *(p. 392)*
Bad-debt expense *(p. 392)*
Contingent liability *(p. 406)*
Creditor *(p. 390)*
Days' sales in receivables *(p. 410)*
Debtor *(p. 390)*
Direct write-off method *(p. 397)*
Discounting a note receivable *(p. 405)*
Default on a note *(p. 407)*
Dishonor of a note *(p. 402)*
Interest *(p. 401)*
Interest period *(p. 401)*
Interest rate *(p. 401)*
Maker of a note *(p. 401)*
Maturity date *(p. 401)*
Maturity value *(p. 401)*
Payee of a note *(p. 401)*
Percentage of sales approach *(p. 395)*
Principal amount *(p. 401)*
Promissory note *(p. 401)*
Quick ratio *(p. 409)*
Receivables *(p. 390)*

Answers to Self-Study Questions

1. a
2. c
3. d
4. a
5. b ($78,900 − $14,300 = $64,600)
6. b
7. c ($30,000 × .09 × ⁹⁄₁₂ = $1,350)
8. b ($30,000 × .09 × ⁶⁄₁₂ = $900)
9. a
10. d

ASSIGNMENT MATERIAL _____

Questions

1. Name the two parties to a receivable/payable transaction. Which party has the receivable? Which has the payable? The asset? The liability?

2. List three categories of receivables. State how each category is classified for reporting on the balance sheet.

3. Name the two methods of accounting for uncollectible receivables. Which method is easier to apply? Which method is consistent with generally accepted accounting principles?

4. Which of the two methods of accounting for uncollectible accounts, the allowance method on the direct write-off method, is preferable? Why?

5. Identify the accounts debited and credited to account for uncollectibles under (a) the allowance method, and (b) the direct write-off method.

6. What is another term for Allowance for Uncollectible Accounts? What are two other terms for Uncollectible-Account Expense?

7. Which entry decreases net income under the allowance method of accounting for uncollectibles: the entry to record uncollectible-account expense, or the entry to write off an uncollectible account receivable?

8. May a customer pay his or her account receivable after it has been written off? If not, why not? If so, what entries are made to account for reinstating the customer's account and for collecting cash from the customer?

9. Identify and briefly describe the two ways to estimate bad debt expense and uncollectible accounts.

10. Briefly describe how a company may use both the percentage-of-sales method and aging method to account for uncollectibles.

11. How does a credit balance arise in a customer's account receivable? How does the company report this credit balance on its balance sheet?

12. Many businesses receive most of their cash on credit sales through the mail. Suppose you own a business so large that you must hire employees to handle cash receipts and perform the related accounting duties. What internal control feature should you use to ensure that cash received from customers is not taken by a dishonest employee?

13. Use the terms *maker, payee, principal amount, maturity date, promissory note,* and *interest* in an appropriate sentence or two describing a note receivable.

14. Name three situations in which a company might receive a note receivable. For each situation, show the account debited and the account credited to record receipt of the note.

15. For each of the following notes receivable, compute the amount of interest revenue earned during 19X6:

	Principal	Interest Rate	Interest Period	Maturity Date
a. Note 1	$ 10,000	9%	60 days	11/30/19X6
b. 2	50,000	10%	3 months	9/30/19X6
c. 3	100,000	8%	1½ years	12/31/19X7
d. 4	15,000	12%	90 days	1/15/19X7

16. Suppose you hold a 180-day, $5,000 note receivable that specifies 10 percent interest. After 60 days you discount the note at 12 percent. How much cash do you receive?

17. How does a contingent liability differ from an ordinary liability? How does discounting a note receivable create a contingent liability? When does the contingency cease to exist?

18. When the maker of a note dishonors the note at maturity, what accounts does the payee debit and credit?

19. Why does the payee of a note receivable usually need to make adjusting entries for interest at the end of the accounting period?

20. Recall the real-world disclosures of receivables the chapter presents. Show three ways to report Accounts Receivable of $100,000 and Allowance for Uncollectible Accounts of $2,800 on the balance sheet or in the related notes.

21. Why is the acid-test ratio a more stringent measure of the ability to pay current liabilities than is the current ratio?

22. Which measure of days' sales in receivables is preferable, 30 or 40? Give your reason.

Exercises

Exercise 8-1   *Using the allowance method for bad debts* **(Obj. 1)**

On September 30, Rochford Nurseries Ltd. had a $28,000 debit balance in Accounts Receivable. During October, the company had sales of $137,000, which included $90,000 in credit sales. October collections were $91,000 and write-offs of uncollectible receivables totaled $1,070. Other data include:

a. September 30 credit balance in Allowance for Uncollectible Accounts, $2,100.

b. Uncollectible account expense, estimated as 2 percent of credit sales.

Required

1. Prepare journal entries to record sales, collections, uncollectible-account expense by the allowance method, and write-offs of uncollectibles during October.

2. Show the ending balances in Accounts Receivable, Allowance for Uncollectible Accounts, and *net* accounts receivable at October 31. Does Rochford expect to collect the net amount of the receivable?

Exercise 8-2   *Recording bad debts by the allowance method* **(Obj. 1)**

Prepare general journal entries to record the following transactions under the allowance method of accounting for uncollectibles:

Apr. 2   Sold merchandise for $3,900 on credit terms of 2/10 n/30 to Han Sales Company.

May 28   Received legal notification that Han Sales Company was bankrupt. Wrote off Han accounts receivable balance.

Aug. 11   Received $2,000 from Han Sales Company, together with a letter indicating that the company intended to pay its account within the next month.

     30   Received the remaining amount due from Han.

Exercise 8-3   *Using the aging approach to estimate bad debts* **(Obj. 1,2)**

At December 31, 19X7, the accounts receivable balance of Chung Ltd. is $269,000. The allowance for doubtful accounts has a $3,910 credit balance. Accountants for Chung prepare the following aging schedule for its accounts receivable:

Total Balance	Age of Accounts			
	1–30 Days	*31–60 Days*	*61–90 Days*	*Over 90 Days*
$269,000	$107,000	$78,000	$69,000	$15,000
Estimated percentage uncollectible	.3%	1.2%	6.0%	50%
	3,210	936	4140	750

Journalize the adjusting entry for doubtful accounts based on the aging schedule. Show the T-account for the allowance.

Exercise 8-4   *Using the direct write-off method for bad debts* **(Obj. 3)**

Refer to the situation of Exercise 8-1.

Required

1. Record uncollectible account expense for October by the direct write-off method.

2. What amount of net accounts receivable would Rochford Ltd. report on its October 31 balance sheet under the direct write-off method? Does Rochford expect to collect this much of the receivable? Give your reason.

Exercise 8-5   *Controlling cash receipts from customers **(Obj. 4)***

As a recent college graduate, you land your first job in the customer collections department of Rentz & Schwayze, a partnership. Lela Rentz, the president, has asked you to propose a system to ensure that cash received by mail from customers is properly handled. Draft a short memorandum identifying the essential element in your proposed plan, and state why this element is important. Refer to Chapter 7 if necessary.

Exercise 8-6   *Recording a note receivable and accruing interest revenue **(Obj. 5)***

Record the following transactions in the general journal.

Nov.   1   Loaned $45,000 cash to E. Tremblay on a one-year, 9 percent note.
Dec.   3   Sold goods to Lofland, Inc., receiving a 90-day, 12 percent note for $3,750.
    16   Received a $2,000, 6-month, 12 percent note on account from J. Barnecke.
    31   Accrued interest revenue on all notes receivable.

Exercise 8-7   *Recording a note receivable and accruing interest revenue **(Obj. 5)***

Record the following transactions in the general journal:

Apr.   1, 19X2   Loaned $8,000 to Linda Rutishauser on a 1-year, 9 percent note.
Dec. 31, 19X2   Accrued interest revenue on the Rutishauser note.
Dec. 31, 19X2   Closed the interest revenue account.
Apr.   1, 19X3   Received the maturity value of the note from Linda Rutishauser.

Exercise 8-8   *Accounting for a dishonored note receivable **(Obj. 5)***

Record the following transactions in the general journal, assuming the company uses the allowance method to account for uncollectibles:

May 18   Sold goods to Pavlor Computer Ltd., receiving a 120-day, 12 percent note for $2,900.
Sept. 15   The note is dishonored.
Nov. 30   After pursuing collection from Pavlor Computer, wrote off their account as uncollectible.

Exercise 8-9   *Recording notes receivable, discounting a note, and reporting the contingent liability in a footnote **(Obj. 5, 6)***

Prepare general journal entries to record the following transactions:

Aug. 14   Sold goods on account to Vaike Lewis, $3,900.
Dec.   2   Received a $3,900, 180-day, 10 percent note from Vaike Lewis in satisfaction of her past-due account receivable.
    30   Sold the Lewis note by discounting it to a bank at 15 percent. (Use a 365-day year, and round amounts to the nearest dollar.)

Write the footnote to disclose the contingent liability at December 31.

Exercise 8-10   *Recording bad debts by the allowance method **(Obj. 1, 2, 6)***

At December 31, 19X5, Geo. Knudsen Ltd. has an accounts receivable balance of $137,000. Sales revenue for 19X5 is $950,000, including credit sales of $600,000. For each of the following situations, prepare the year-end adjusting entry to record doubtful account expense. Show how the accounts receivable and the allowance for doubtful accounts are reported on the balance sheet.

a. Allowance for Doubtful Accounts has a credit balance before adjustment of $1,600. Geo. Knudsen Ltd. estimates that doubtful account expense for the year is ½ of 1 percent of credit sales.

b. Allowance for Doubtful Accounts has a debit balance before adjustment of $1,100. Geo. Knudsen Ltd. estimates that $4,600 of the accounts receivable will prove uncollectible.

Exercise 8-11   *Evaluating ratio data* *(Obj. 6)*

Sussman's Ltd., a department store, reported the following amounts in its 19X8 financial statements. The 19X7 figures are given for comparison.

		19X8		19X7
Current assets				
Cash..		$ 14,000		$ 9,000
Short-term investments..........		13,000		11,000
Accounts receivable	$ 80,000		$74,000	
Less: Allowance for				
uncollectibles	7,000	73,000	6,000	68,000
Inventory................................		192,000		189,000
Prepaid insurance...................		2,000		2,000
Total current assets.............		294,000		279,000
Total current liabilities.................		114,000		107,000
Net sales.....................................		813,000		762,000

Required

1. Determine whether the acid-test ratio improved or deteriorated from 19X7 to 19X8. How does Sussman's acid-test ratio compare with the industry average of .80?

2. Compare the days' sales in receivables measure for 19X8 with the company's credit terms of net 30.

Exercise 8-12   *Analyzing a real company's financial statements*   *(Obj. 6, 7)*

Wal-Mart Stores, Inc., is one of the largest retailers in North America. Recently, Wal-Mart reported these figures, in millions of dollars:

	19X2	19X1
Net sales	$43,887	$32,602
Receivables at end of year	419	305

The Wal-Mart financial statements include no uncollectible-account expense or allowance for uncollectibles.

Required

1. Compute Wal-Mart's average collection period on receivables during 19X2.

2. How can Wal-Mart have $419 million of receivables at January 31, 19X2, and no significant allowance for uncollectibles?

Challenge Exercise

Exercise 8-13   *Credit-card sales (Obj. 2)*

Village Oaks Men's Store Ltd. has sold on store credit and managed its own receivables. Average experience for the past three years has been:

	Cash	Credit	Total
Sales	$200,000	$150,000	$350,000
Cost of goods sold	120,000	90,000	210,000
Uncollectible-account expense	—	4,000	4,000
Other expenses	34,000	27,000	61,000

Lou Onassis, the owner, is considering whether to accept bank cards (VISA, MasterCard). Typically, the availability of bank cards increases sales by 10 percent. But VISA and MasterCard charge approximately 1 percent of sales. If Onassis switches to bank cards, he can save $2,000 on accounting and other expenses. He figures that cash customers will continue buying in the same volume regardless of the type of credit the store offers.

Required

Should Village Oaks Men's Store start selling on bank credit cards? Show the computations of net income under the present plan and under the bank credit-card plan.

Problems

(Group A)

Problem 8-1A   *Accounting for uncollectibles by the direct write-off and allowance methods (Obj. 1, 2, 3, 6)*

On February 28, Basu Fashions Ltd. had a $75,000 debit balance in Accounts Receivable. During March, the business had sales revenue of $509,000, which included $443,000 in credit sales. Other data for March include

a. Collections on account receivable, $451,600.

b. Write-offs of uncollectible receivables, $3,500.

Required

1. Record uncollectible account expense for March by the *direct write-off method*. Show all March activity in Accounts Receivable and Uncollectible-Account Expense.

2. Record uncollectible account expense and write-offs of customer accounts for March by the *allowance* method. Show all March activity in Accounts Receivable, Allowance for Uncollectible Accounts, and Uncollectible-Account Expense. The February 28 unadjusted balance in Allowance for Uncollectible Accounts was $800 (debit). Uncollectible-Account Expense was estimated at 2 percent of credit sales.

3. What amount of uncollectible account expense would Basu Fashions report on its March income statement under the two methods? Which amount better matches expense with revenue? Give your reason.

4. What amount of *net* accounts receivable would Basu Fashions report on its March 31 balance sheet under the two methods? Which amount is more realistic? Give your reason.

Problem 8-2A   *Uncollectibles, notes receivable, discounting notes, dishonored notes and accrued interest revenue* ***(Obj. 2, 5)***

Assume Snyder Ltd., producer of building products, completed the following selected transactions:

19X4

Dec. 1   Sold goods to Assaf Builders Ltd., receiving a $17,000, 3-month, 10 percent note.

     31   Made an adjusting entry to accrue interest on the Assaf Builders note.

     31   Made an adjusting entry to record doubtful-account expense based on an aging of accounts receivable. The aging analysis indicates that $355,800 of accounts receivable will not be collected. Prior to this adjustment, the credit balance in Allowance for Doubtful Accounts is $346,100.

19X5

Feb. 18   Received a 90-day, 10 percent, $5,000 note from Altex, Inc., on account. (February has 28 days this year.)

Mar. 1   Collected the maturity value of the Assaf Builders note.

       8   Discounted the Altex, Inc., note to the Royal Bank at 16 percent.

Apr. 21   Sold merchandise to K Chen Ltd., receiving a 60-day, 9 percent note for $4,000.

June 20   K Chen Ltd. dishonored its note at maturity and converted the maturity value of the note to an account receivable.

July 12   Loaned $60,000 cash to McNeice, Inc., receiving a 90-day, 13 percent note.

      13   Sold merchandise to Seigrist Contracting Ltd., receiving a 4-month, 12 percent, $2,500 note.

Aug.   2   Collected $4,059 on account from K Chen Ltd.

Sep. 13   Discounted the Seigrist Contracting note to the Royal Bank at 18 percent.

Oct. 10   Collected the maturity value of the McNeice, Inc., note.

Nov. 13   Seigrist Contracting dishonored its note at maturity; paid the Royal Bank the maturity value of the note plus a protest fee of $35, and debited an account receivable from Seigrist Contracting Ltd.

Dec. 31   Wrote off as uncollectible the account receivable from Seigrist Contracting.

Required

Record the transactions in the general journal. Explanations are not required.

Problem 8-3A   *Using the percent of sales and aging approaches for uncollectibles* ***(Obj. 2–6)***

Alomar Ltd. completed the following transactions during 19X1 and 19X2:

19X1

Dec. 31   Began using the allowance method to account for uncollectibles. Estimated that uncollectible account expense for the year was 1 percent on credit sales of $300,000 and recorded that amount as expense. The accounts receivable balance is $113,500.

      31   Made the appropriate closing entry.

19X2

Jan. 17   Sold inventory to LeVon Carter, $652, on credit terms of 2/10 n/30.

June 29   Wrote off Carter's account as uncollectible after repeated efforts to collect from her.

Aug.   6   Received $250 from LeVon Carter, along with a letter stating her intention to pay her debt in full within 30 days. Reinstated her account in full.

Sept.   4   Received the balance due from Carter.
Dec. 31   Made a compound entry to write off the following accounts as uncollectible: Kris Masse, $837; Bud Mandy, $348; and Diana Prince, $622.
        31   Estimated that uncollectible account expense for the year was ½ of 1 percent on credit sales of $420,000 and recorded that amount as expense.
        31   Made the appropriate closing entry.

Required

1. Open general ledger accounts for Allowance for Uncollectible Accounts and Uncollectible-Account Expense. Keep running balances.
2. Record the transactions in the general journal and post to the two ledger accounts.
3. The December 31, 19X2, balance of Accounts Receivable is $130,000. Show how Accounts Receivable would be reported at December 31, 19X1 and 19X2. Why do you think Alomar, Ltd., decreased its uncollectible accounts percentage from 1 percent to 1/2 percent of 1 percent in 19X2?
4. Assume that Alomar Ltd., begins aging accounts receivable on December 31, 19X2. The balance in Accounts Receivable is $130,000, the credit balance in Allowance for Uncollectible Accounts is $1,193, and the company estimates that $3,293 of its accounts receivable will prove uncollectible.
   a. Make the adjusting entry for uncollectibles.
   b. Show how Accounts Receivable will be reported on the December 31, 19X2, balance sheet. Compare net accounts receivable at December 31, 19X2, with the amount reported in Requirement 3 above. Why do you think the two sets of figures agree or disagree?

Problem 8-4A   *Using the percentage-of-sales and aging approaches for uncollectibles (Obj. 2, 6)*

The December 31, 19X6, balance sheet of Master Auto Glass Limited reports the following:

Accounts Receivable...	$256,000
Allowance for Doubtful Accounts (credit balance)	7,100

At the end of each quarter, Master estimates doubtful account expense to be 2 percent of credit sales. At the end of the year, the company ages its accounts receivable and adjusts the balance in Allowance for Doubtful Accounts to correspond to the aging schedule. During 19X7, Master completes the following selected transactions:

Jan. 31   Wrote off as uncollectible the $955 account receivable from Spinelli Inc. and the $3,287 account receivable from Delgado Corp.
Mar. 31   Recorded doubtful account expense based on credit sales of $130,000.
May   2   Received $1,000 from Delgado Corp. after prolonged negotiations with Delgado's lawyer. Master has no hope of collecting the remainder.
June 15   Wrote off as uncollectible the $1,120 account receivable from Lisa Brown.
June 30   Recorded doubtful account expense based on credit sales of $166,000.
July   14   Made a compound entry to write off the following uncollectible accounts: Caldwell Ltd., $766; Graphics, Inc., $2,413; and Ben McQueen, $134.
Sept. 30   Recorded doubtful account expense based on credit sales of $141,400.
Nov. 22   Wrote off the following accounts receivable as uncollectible: Monet, Inc., $1,345; Blocher Inc., $2,109; and Queen Street Plaza, $755.
Dec. 31   Recorded doubtful account expense based on the following summary of the aging of accounts receivable:

| | | Age of Accounts | | |
Total Balance	*1–30 Days*	*31–60 Days*	*61–90 Days*	*Over 90 Days*
$296,600	$161,500	$86,000	$34,000	$15,100
Estimated percentage uncollectible	.2%	.5%	4.0%	50.0%

Dec. 31   Made the closing entry for Doubtful-Account Expense for the entire year.

Required

1. Record the transactions in the general journal.
2. Open the Allowance for Doubtful Accounts and post entries affecting that account. Keep a running balance.
3. Most companies report two-year comparative financial statements. If Master's Accounts Receivable balance is $296,600 at December 31, 19X7, show how the company would report its accounts receivable in a comparative balance sheet for 19X7 and 19X6.

Problem 8-5A   *Controlling cash receipts from customers* **(Obj. 4)**

Rocky Mountain Sporting Goods Inc. distributes merchandise to sporting goods stores. All sales are on credit, so virtually all cash receipts arrive in the mail. Pelina Johnson, the company president, has just returned from a trade association meeting with new ideas for the business. Among other things, Johnson plans to institute stronger internal controls over cash receipts from customers.

Required

Outline a set of procedures to ensure that all cash receipts are deposited in the bank, and that the total amounts of each day's cash receipts are posted as credits to customer accounts receivable.

Problem 8-6A   *Accounting for notes receivable, including discounting notes and accruing interest revenue* **(Obj. 5)**

A company received the following notes during 19X3. Notes (a), (b), and (c) were discounted on the dates and at the rates indicated:

Note	Date	Principal Amount	Interest Rate	Term	Date Discounted	Discount Rate
(a)	July 12	$12,000	10%	3 months	Aug. 12	15%
(b)	Sept. 4	6,000	11%	90 days	Sept. 30	13%
(c)	Oct. 21	5,000	15%	60 days	Nov. 3	18%
(d)	Nov. 30	12,000	12%	6 months	—	—
(e)	Dec. 7	6,000	10%	30 days	—	—
(f)	Dec. 23	15,000	9%	1 year	—	—

Required

As necessary in Requirements 1 through 5, identify each note by letter, compute interest using a 365-day year for those notes with terms specified in days or years, round all interest amounts to the nearest dollar, and present entries in general journal form. Explanations are not required.

1. Determine the due date and maturity value of each note.
2. For each discounted note, determine the discount and proceeds from sale of the note.
3. Journalize the discounting of notes (a) and (b).
4. Journalize a single adjusting entry at December 31, 19X3, to record accrued interest revenue on notes (d), (e), and (f).
5. Journalize the collection of principal and interest on note (e).

Problem 8-7A   *Using ratio data to evaluate a company's position* **(Obj. 7)**

The comparative financial statements of Orvis Catalogue Merchants Ltd. for 19X4, 19X3, and 19X2 included the following selected data:

	Millions		
	19X4	19X3	19X2
Balance Sheet			
Current assets			
Cash	$ 27	$ 26	$ 22
Short-term investments	73	101	69
Receivables, net of allowance for doubtful accounts of $7, $6, and $4	136	154	127
Inventories	438	383	341
Prepaid expenses	42	31	25
Total current assets	716	695	584
Total current liabilities	440	446	388
Income Statement			
Sales revenue	$2,671	$2,505	$1,944
Cost of sales	1,380	1,360	963

Required

1. For 19X4 and 19X3 compute these ratios:
   a. Current ratio
   b. Acid-test ratio
   c. Inventory turnover
   d. Days' sales in average receivables
2. Explain for top management which ratio values showed improvement from 19X3 to 19X4, and which ratio values showed deterioration. Which item in the financial statements caused some ratio values to improve and others to deteriorate?

Problem 8-8A   *Use the direct write-off method and the allowance method of accounting for uncollectibles, estimate uncollectibles using the aging process, report receivables on the balance sheet* **(Obj. 3, 1, 2, 6)**

The Pacific Cleaners Company started business on January 1, 19X1. The company produced monthly financial statements and had total sales of $229,000 (of which $152,000 were on credit) during the first four months.

On April 30th, the Accounts Receivable account had a balance of $52,040 (no accounts have been written off to date) which was made up of the following accounts aged as to the date of the sale:

	Month of Sale:			
Customer:	January	February	March	April
Jones	$ 500	$ 350	$ 780	$ 470
Lawson	200	440	650	290
Shawney	1,560	1,250	3,440	1,890
Ullman	2,080	1,340	3,320	5,690
Other Accounts Receivable	3,800	6,240	8,500	9,250

The following transactions, with regard to the accounts receivable, took place in the month of May, 19X1:

May 12   Decided the account of Lawson was uncollectible and wrote it off.

15   Collected $1,630 from Jones for sales made in the first three months.

21   Decided the account of Shawney was uncollectible and wrote it off.

24   Collected $2,080 from Ullman for sales made in the month of January.

26   Received a cheque from Shawney for $4,140 plus four cheques, of $1,000 each, post-dated to the 26th day of June, July, August, and September.

31   Total sales in the month were $104,000; 80% of these were on credit and 70% of the credit sales were collected in the month.

Required

1. Journalize the transaction for the month of May, 19X1, assuming the company uses the direct write-off method of accounting for uncollectibles.

2. Pacific Cleaners Company has heard that other companies in the industry use the allowance method of accounting for uncollectibles with many of these estimating the uncollectibles through an aging of accounts receivable. Journalize the adjustments that would have to be made on April 30 (for the months of January through April) as well as the transactions of May, 19X1 and the month-end adjustment, assuming the following estimates of uncollectibles:

Age of Accounts Receivable:	Estimated percentage uncollectible:
from current month's sales	2%
from prior month's sales	4%
from two months' prior	8%
from three months' prior	25%
from four months' prior	40%

(Round your total estimate to the nearest whole dollar.)

3. For each of the alternative methods of accounting for the uncollectibles used in the above, show
   - the balance sheet presentation of the accounts receivable.
   - the overall effect of the credit sales and uncollectibles on the income statement for the month of May, 19X1.

4. Which method of accounting for uncollectibles would you recommend for Pacific Cleaners Company? Use the results from Requirement 3 to justify your answer.

Problem 8-9A   *Use the allowance method of accounting for uncollectibles, estimate uncollectibles by the percent of sales and the aging approaches, account for notes receivable   (Obj. 1, 2, 5)*

The Avengers Company uses the allowance method in accounting for uncollectible accounts with the estimate based on an aging of Accounts Receivable. They had the following account balances on June 30, 19X1:

Accounts Receivable	$237,500	
Allowance for Doubtful Accounts (credit balance)	43,900	(credit)

The following transactions took place during the month of July, 19X1:

July   1   A. Adams who owes $26,000 has come in to say that he is unable to pay on time and has given a 20-day, 10% note in settlement of the account.

5   The Avengers Company sold the Adams note by discounting it to the bank at 14%. (Use a 360-day year and round amounts to the nearest dollar.)

6   Decided the account receivable for R. Ransom ($7,500) was uncollectible and wrote it off.

9   Received notice that a customer (V. Vickers) has filed for bankruptcy. Vickers owes $14,000 to the Avengers Company.

11   Decided the account receivable for K. Korrect ($4,800) was uncollectible and wrote it off.

15   R. Ransom, whose account was written off on July 6th, has come in and paid $4,000 on his account and promises to pay the balance in 30 days.

18   Received a cheque from the courts in the amount of $8,400 as final settlement in regards to V. Vickers's bankruptcy (July 9th).

22   Received notice that A. Adams has dishonored the note received on July 1st. Avengers Company charges a $20 fee on dishonored notes in addition to the $30 fee charged by the bank.

25   Decided the account receivable for E. Effigy ($3,900) was uncollectible and wrote it off.

31   Sales for the month totaled $358,000 (of which 70% were on credit) and collections on account totaled $264,000.

31   The Avengers Company did an aging of Accounts Receivable which indicated that $51,600 is expected to be uncollectible. The company recorded the appropriate adjustment.

Required

1. Record the above transactions in a general journal.

2. What would be the adjusting entry required on July 31st if the company used the percent of sales method with an estimate of uncollectibles equal to 10% of credit sales?

3. Which of the two methods of estimating uncollectible accounts would normally be more accurate? Why?

(Group B)

Problem 8-1B   *Accounting for uncollectibles by the direct write-off and allowance methods* **(Obj. 1, 2, 3, 6)**

On May 31, L. Martel Inc. had a $219,000 debit balance in Accounts Receivable. During June, the company had sales revenue of $789,000, which included $640,000 in credit sales. Other data for June include:

a. Collections on account receivable, $599,400.
b. Write-offs of uncollectible receivables, $8,900.

Required

1. Record uncollectible account expense for June by the *direct write-off* method. Show all June activity in Accounts Receivable and Uncollectible-Account Expense.

2. Record uncollectible account expense and write-offs of customer accounts for June by the *allowance* method. Show all June activity in Accounts Receivable, Allowance for Uncollectible Accounts, and Uncollectible-Account Expense. The May 31 unadjusted balance in Allowance for Uncollectible Accounts was $2,800 (credit). Uncollectible-Account Expense was estimated at 2 percent of credit sales.

3. What amount of uncollectible account expense would L. Martel report on its June income statement under the two methods? Which amount better matches expense with revenue? Give your reason.

4. What amount of net accounts receivable would L. Martel Inc. report on its June 30 balance sheet under the two methods? Which amount is more realistic? Give your reason.

Problem 8-2B   *Uncollectibles, notes receivable, discounting notes, dishonored notes, and accrued interest revenue (Obj. 2, 5)*

Assume Schneider Corporation, manufacturer of meat products, completed the following selected transactions:

19X5

Nov. 1   Sold goods to Eckerd Grocery Co., receiving a $24,000, 3-month, 12 percent note.

Dec. 31   Made an adjusting entry to accrue interest on the Eckerd Grocery note.

      31   Made an adjusting entry to record doubtful account expense based on an aging of accounts receivable. The aging analysis indicates that $197,400 of accounts receivable will not be collected. Prior to this adjustment, the credit balance in Allowance for Doubtful Accounts is $189,900.

19X6

Feb. 1   Collected the maturity value of the Eckerd Grocery note.

      23   Received a 90-day, 15 percent, $4,000 note from Bliss, Inc., on account. (February has 28 days this year.)

Mar. 31   Discounted the Bliss, Inc., note to the Toronto-Dominion Bank at 20 percent.

Apr. 23   Sold merchandise to K Lynn Ltd., receiving a 60-day, 10 percent note for $9,000.

June 22   K Lynn Ltd. dishonored its note at maturity; converted the maturity value of the note to an account receivable.

July 15   Loaned $8,500 cash to McNeil, Inc., receiving a 30-day, 12 percent note.

      17   Sold merchandise to Grant Corp., receiving a 3-month, 10 percent, $8,000 note.

Aug. 5   Collected $6,100 on account from K Lynn Ltd.

      14   Collected the maturity value of the McNeil, Inc., note.

      17   Discounted the Grant Corp. note to the Toronto-Dominion Bank at 15 percent.

Oct. 17   Grant Corp. dishonored its note at maturity; paid the Toronto-Dominion Bank the maturity value of the note plus a protest fee of $50, and debited an account receivable from Grant Corp.

Dec. 15   Wrote off as uncollectible the account receivable from Grant Corp.

Required

Record the transactions in the general journal. Explanations are not required.

Problem 8-3B   *Using the percent of sales and aging approaches for uncollectibles (Obj. 2, 6)*

Jacina Ltd. completed the following selected transactions during 19X1 and 19X2:

19X1

Dec. 31   Estimated that uncollectible account expense for the year was 1 percent on credit sales of $450,000 and recorded that amount as expense. The accounts rerceivable balance is $142,000.

      31   Made the appropriate closing entry.

19X2

Feb. 4   Sold inventory to Gary Carter, $2,521, on credit terms of 2/10 n/30.

July 1   Wrote off Gary Carter's account as uncollectible after repeated efforts to collect from him.

Oct. 19   Received $521 from Gary Carter, along with a letter stating his intention to pay his debt in full within 30 days. Reinstated his account in full.

Nov. 15   Received the balance due from Gary Carter.

Dec. 31   Made a compound entry to write off the following accounts as uncollectible: Kris Moore, $899; Marie Mandue, $530; and Grant Frycer, $672.

      31   Estimated that uncollectible account expense for the year was ½ of 1 percent on credit sales of $540,000 and recorded the expense.

      31   Made the appropriate closing entry.

Required

1. Open general ledger accounts for Allowance for Uncollectible Accounts and Uncollectible-Account Expense. Keep running balances.

2. Record the transactions in the general journal and post to the two ledger accounts.

3. The December 31, 19X2 balance of Accounts Receivable is $169,300. Show how Accounts Receivable would be reported at December 31, 19X1 and 19X2. Why do you think Jacina Ltd. decreased its uncollectible accounts percentage from 1 percent to ½ of 1 percent in 19X2?

4. Assume that Jacina Ltd. begins aging its accounts receivable on December 31, 19X2. The balance in Accounts Receivable is $169,300; the credit balance in Allowance for Uncollectible Accounts is $2,399; and the company estimates that $5,099 of its accounts receivable will prove uncollectible.

   a. Make the adjusting entry for uncollectibles.

   b. Show how Accounts Receivable will be reported on the December 31, 19X2, balance sheet. Compare net accounts receivable at December 31, 19X2, with the amount reported in Requirement 3 above. Why do you think the two sets of figures agree or disagree?

Problem 8-4B *Using the percent of sales and aging approaches for uncollectibles* **(Obj. 2, 6)**

The December 31, 19X4, balance sheet of Ferrara Limited reports the following:

Accounts Receivable	$143,000
Allowance for Doubtful Accounts (credit balance)	3,200

At the end of each quarter, Ferrara estimates doubtful account expense to be 1½ percent of credit sales. At the end of the year, the company ages its accounts receivable and adjusts the balance in Allowance for Doubtful Accounts to correspond to the aging schedule. During 19X5, Ferrara completes the following selected transactions:

Jan. 16	Wrote off as uncollectible the $603 account receivable from Platt Ltd. and the $1,719 account receivable from Lum Corp.
Mar. 31	Recorded doubtful account expense based on credit sales of $100,000.
Apr. 15	Received $300 from Lum Corp. after prolonged negotiations with Lum's lawyer. Ferrara has no hope of collecting the remainder.
May 13	Wrote off as uncollectible the $2,980 account receivable from M. E. Cate.
June 30	Recorded doubtful account expense based on credit sales of $114,000.
Aug. 9	Made a compound entry to write off the following uncollectible accounts: Clifford, Inc., $235; Matz, Inc., $188; and Lew Norris, $706.
Sept. 30	Recorded doubtful-account expense based on credit sales of $130,000.
Oct. 18	Wrote off as uncollectible the $767 account receivable from Bliss, Inc., and the $430 account receivable from Micro Data Ltd.
Dec. 31	Recorded doubtful-account expense based on the following summary of the aging of accounts receivable.

Total Balance	Age of Accounts			
	1–30 Days	*31–60 Days*	*61–90 Days*	*Over 90 Days*
$129,400	$74,600	$31,100	$14,000	$9,700
Estimated percentage uncollectible	.1%	.4%	5.0%	30.0%

Dec. 31   Made the closing entry for Doubtful-Account Expense for the entire year.

Required

1. Record the transactions in the general journal.

2. Open the Allowance for Doubtful Accounts and post entries affecting that account. Keep a running balance.

3. Most companies report two-year comparative financial statements. If Ferrara's Accounts Receivable balance is $129,400 at December 31, 19X5, show how the company would report its accounts receivable on a comparative balance sheet for 19X5 and 19X4.

Problem 8-5B   *Controlling cash receipts from customers (Obj. 4)*

Medical Laboratory Service provides laboratory testing for samples that veterinarians send in. All work is performed on account, with regular monthly billing to participating veterinarians. Herb Winters, accountant for Medical Laboratory Service, receives and opens the mail. Company procedure requires him to separate customer cheques from the remittance slips, which list the amounts he posts as credits to customer accounts receivable. Winters deposits the cheques in the bank. He computes each day's total amount posted to customer accounts and agrees this total to the bank deposit slip. This is intended to ensure that all receipts are deposited in the bank.

Required

As the auditor of Medical Laboratory Service, write a memo to management to evaluate the company's internal controls over cash receipts from customers. If the system is effective, identify its strong features. If the system has flaws, propose a way to strengthen the controls.

Problem 8-6B   *Accounting for notes receivable, including discounting notes and accruing interest revenue (Obj. 5)*

A company received the following notes during 19X5. Notes (a), (b), and (c) were discounted on the dates and at the rates indicated.

Note	Date	Principal Amount	Interest Rate	Term	Date Discounted	Discount Rate
(a)	July 15	$ 8,000	8%	6 months	Oct. 15	12%
(b)	Aug. 19	12,000	12%	90 days	Aug. 30	15
(c)	Sept. 1	16,000	15%	120 days	Nov. 2	20
(d)	Oct. 30	7,000	12%	3 months	—	—
(e)	Nov. 19	15,000	10%	60 days	—	—
(f)	Dec. 1	11,000	9%	1 year	—	—

Required

As necessary in Requirements 1 through 5, identify each note by letter, compute interest using a 365-day year for those notes with terms specified in days or years, round all interest amounts to the nearest dollar, and present entries in general journal form. Explanations are not required.

1. Determine the due date and maturity value of each note.

2. For each discounted note, determine the discount and proceeds from sale of the note.

3. Journalize the discounting of notes (a) and (b).

4. Journalize a single adjusting entry at December 31, 19X5, to record accrued interest revenue on notes (d), (e), and (f).

5. Journalize the collection of principal and interest on note (d).

Problem 8-7B   *Using ratio data to evaluate a company's position* **(Obj. 7)**

The comparative financial statements of Timber Mills Corp. for 19X6, 19X5, and 19X4 included the following selected data:

	Millions		
	19X6	19X5	19X4
Balance Sheet..			
Current assets			
Cash	$ 59	$ 80	$ 60
Short-term investments..............................	131	174	122
Receivables, net of allowance for			
doubtful accounts of $6, $6, and $5......	237	265	218
Inventories	389	341	302
Prepaid expenses	61	27	46
Total current assets	877	887	748
Total current liabilities	483	528	413
Income statement			
Sales revenue..	$5,189	$4,995	$4,206
Cost of sales...	2,734	2,636	2,418

Required

1. For 19X6 and 19X5 compute these ratios:
   a. Current ratio   c. Inventory turnover
   b. Acid-test ratio   d. Days' sales in average receivables

2. Explain for top management which ratio values showed improvement from 19X5 to 19X6, and which ratio values showed deterioration. Which item in the financial statements caused some ratio values to improve and others to deteriorate?

Problem 8-8B   *Use the direct write-off method and the allowance method of accounting for uncollectibles, estimate uncollectibles using the aging process, report receivables on the balance sheet.* **(Obj. 3, 1, 2, 6)**

The Atlantic Cleaners Company started business on January 1, 19X1. The company produces monthly financial statements and had total sales of $229,000 (of which $152,000 were on credit) during the first four months.

On April 30th, the Accounts Receivable account had a balance of $55,080 (no accounts have been written off to date) which was made up of the following accounts aged as to the date of the sale:

Customer	Month of Sale:			
	January	February	March	April
Hughes..	$ 700	$ 400	$ 650	$ 540
Kinder	400	270	490	1,320
Roberts	1,920	1,300	2,730	2,140
Versall..	1,840	990	4,610	5,430
Other Accounts Receivable......	4,100	5,950	9,400	9,900

The following transactions, with regard to the accounts receivable, took place in the month of May, 19X1:

May 12   Decided the account of Kinder was uncollectible and wrote it off.

     15   Collected $1,750 from Hughes for sales made in the first three months.

     21   Decided the account of Roberts was uncollectible and wrote it off.

     24   Collected $1,840 from Versall for sales made in the month of January.

     26   Received a cheque from Roberts for $2,090 plus four cheques, of $1,500 each, post-dated to the 26th day of June, July, August, and September.

31   Total sales in the month were $140,000; 75% of these were on credit and 80% of the credit sales were collected in the month.

Required

1. Journalize the transaction for the month of May, 19X1, assuming the company uses the direct write-off method of accounting for uncollectibles.
2. Atlantic Cleaners Company has heard that other companies in the industry use the allowance method of accounting for uncollectibles with many of these estimating the uncollectibles through an aging of accounts receivable. Journalize the adjustments that would have to be made on April 30 (for the months of January through April) as well as the transactions of May, 19X1 and the month-end adjustment, assuming the following estimates of uncollectibles:

Age of Accounts Receivable	Estimated Percentage Uncollectible
from current month's sales	2%
from prior month's sales	4%
from two months prior	8%
from three months prior	25%
from four months prior	40%

(Round your total estimate to the nearest whole dollar.)

3. For each of the alternative methods of accounting for the uncollectibles used in the above, show
   - the balance sheet presentation of the accounts receivable.
   - the overall effect of the credit sales and uncollectibles on the income statement for the month of May, 19X1.
4. Which method of accounting for uncollectibles would you recommend for Atlantic Cleaners Company? Use the results from Requirement 3 to justify your answer.

Problem 8-9B   *Use the allowance method of accounting for uncollectibles, estimate uncollectibles by percent of sales and the aging approaches, account for notes receivable (Obj. 1, 2, 5)*

The Stevenson Company uses the allowance method in accounting for uncollectible accounts with the estimate based on an aging of Accounts Receivable. They had the following account balances on June 30, 19X1:

Accounts Receivable	$345,000	
Allowance for Doubtful Accounts (credit balance)	53,800	(credit)

The following transactions took place during the month of July, 19X1:

July   1   A. Downs, who owes $35,000, has come in to say that he is unable to pay on time and has given a 20-day, 12% note in settlement of the account.

   5   The Stevenson Company sold the Downs note by discounting it to the bank at 14%. (Use a 360-day year and round amounts to the nearest dollar.)

   6   Decided the account receivable for R. Reliant ($9,000) was uncollectible and wrote it off.

   9   Received notice that a customer (V. Beckers) has filed for bankruptcy. Beckers owes $18,000 to the Stevenson Company.

   11   Decided the account receivable for K. Kansick ($6,700) was uncollectible and wrote it off.

   15   R. Reliant, whose account was written off on July 6th, has come in and paid $3,000 on his account and promises to pay the balance in 30 days.

   18   Received a cheque from the courts in the amount of $10,500 as final settlement in regards to V. Beckers's bankruptcy (July 9th).

22   Received notice that A. Downs has dishonored the note received on July 1st. Stevenson Company charges a $30 fee on dishonored notes in addition to the $10 fee charged by the bank.

25   Decided the account receivable for E. Edison ($4,700) was uncollectible and wrote it off.

31   Sales for the month totaled $476,000 (of which 80% were on credit) and collections on account totaled $271,000.

31   The Stevenson Company did an aging of Accounts Receivable which indicated that $51,600 is expected to be uncollectible. The company recorded the appropriate adjustment.

Required

1. Record the above transactions in a general journal.

2. What would be the adjusting entry required on July 31st if the company used the percent of sales method with an estimate of uncollectibles equal to 10% of credit sales?

3. Which of the two methods of estimating uncollectible accounts would normally be more accurate? Why?

Challenge Problems

Problem 8-1C   *Understanding accounts receivable management   (Obj. 1, 2, 4)*

Confused Company Ltd. is a six-store chain of retain stores selling appliances and electronic equipment mainly on credit; the company has its own credit card and does not accept other cards. Confused had a tendency to institute policies that conflicted with each other. Management rarely became aware of these conflicts until they became serious.

Recently, the president, who has been reading all the latest management texts, has instituted a new bonus plan. All managers are to be paid bonuses based on the success of their department. For example, the sales manager's bonus is based on how much she can increase sales; the production manager's bonus is based on how efficiently he can produce the product; the credit manager's bonus is based on reducing the bad-debt expense.

Required

Describe the conflict that the bonus plan has created for the sales manager and the credit manager. How might the conflict be resolved?

Problem 8-2C   *Explaining days' sales in accounts   (Obj. 3)*

Days' sales in receivables is a good measure of a company's ability to collect the amounts owing to it. You have owned shares in Irwin Toy for some years and follow the company's progress by reading the annual report. You noticed the most recent report indicated that the days' sales in receivables had increased over the previous year, and are concerned.

Required

Suggest reasons that may have resulted in the increase in the number of days' sales in receivables.

Extending Your Knowledge

Decision Problems

1. Uncollectible accounts and evaluating a business   *(Obj. 1, 2, 3, 5, 6)*

PEI Hardware Mfg. Ltd. sells its products either for cash or on notes receivable that earn interest. The business uses the direct write-off method to account for bad debts. Ajit Singh, the owner, has prepared PEI Hardware's financial statements. The most recent comparative income statements, for 19X3 and 19X2, are as follows:

	19X3	19X2
Total revenue	$220,000	$195,000
Total expenses	157,000	143,000
Net income	$ 63,000	$ 52,000

Based on the increase in net income, Singh seeks to expand his operations. He asks you to invest $50,000 in the business. You and Singh have several meetings, at which you learn that notes receivable from customers were $200,000 at the end of 19X1, and $400,000 at the end of 19X2. Also, total revenues for 19X3 and 19X2 include interest at 15 percent on the year's beginning notes receivable balance. Total expenses include doubtful account expense of $2,000 each year, based on the direct write-off basis. Singh estimates that doubtful account expense would be 2 percent of sales revenue if the allowance method were used.

Required

1. Prepare for PEI Hardware Mfg. Ltd. a comparative single-step income statement that identifies sales revenue, interest revenue, doubtful-account expense, and other expenses, all computed in accordance with generally accepted accounting principles.
2. Is PEI Hardware's future as promising as Singh's income statement makes it appear? Give the reason for your answer.

2. Estimating the collectibility of accounts receivable   *(Obj. 1, 6, 7)*

Assume you work in the corporate loan department of the Bank of Nova Scotia. Maria Presti, owner of MP Manufacturing Inc., a manufacturer of wooden furniture, has come to you seeking a loan of $350,000 to buy new manufacturing equipment to expand her operations. She proposes to use her accounts receivable as collateral for the loan, and has provided you with the following information from her most recent audited financial statements:

	19X9	19X8	19X7
Sales	$1,475	$1,589	$1,502
Cost of goods sold	876	947	905
Gross profit	599	642	597
Other expenses	518	487	453
Net profit before taxes	$ 81	$ 155	$ 144

Accounts receivable......................................	458	387	374
Allowance for doubtful accounts	23	31	29

Required

1. What analysis would you perform on the information Presti has provided? Would you grant the loan based on this information? Give your reason.

2. What additional information would you request from Presti? Give your reason.

3. Assume Presti provided you with the information requested in Requirement 2. What would make you change the decision you made in Requirement 1?

Ethical Issue

Goodwill Finance Ltd. is in the consumer loan business. It borrows from banks, and loans out the money at higher interest rates. Goodwill's bank requires Goodwill to submit quarterly financial statements in order to keep its line of credit. Goodwill's main asset is Notes Receivable. Therefore, Uncollectible-Account Expense and Allowance for Uncollectible Accounts are important accounts.

Goodwill's owner, Jacob Featherstone, likes net income to increase in a smooth pattern rather than to increase in some periods and decrease in other periods. To report smoothly increasing net income, Featherstone underestimates Uncollectible-Account Expense in some periods. In other periods, Featherstone overestimates the expense. He reasons that the income overstatements roughly offset the income understatements over time.

Required

Is Goodwill's practice of smoothing income ethical? Give your reasons.

Financial Statement Problems

1. Accounts receivable and related uncollectibles   (Obj. 1)

Answer the following questions using the financial statements for Mark's Work Wearhouse in Appendix A.

1. Analyze the Accounts Receivable account at January 29, 1994. What is the total receivable? What are the two components of Accounts Receivable? What percentage of total accounts receivable is the allowance for doubtful accounts?

2. Mark's Work Wearhouse makes a determined effort to reduce the allowance for doubtful accounts as a percentage of sales and the number of days' sales in receivables.

   a. Did Mark's reduce the allowance for doubtful accounts as a percentage of sales from 1993 to 1994?

   b. Did Mark's reduce the number of days' sales in receivables from 1993 to 1994?

3. Mark's annual report reveals that the company is budgeting for sales of $169 million for fiscal 1995. What would accounts receivable have to be if the number of days' sales in receivables was to be reduced by 10 percent over 1994?

4. Why does a company such as Mark's want to reduce number of days' sales in receivables?

2.   Accounts receivable, uncollectibles, and notes receivable   (Obj. 1, 5)

Obtain the annual report of an actual company of your choosing.

Required

1. How much did customers owe the company at the end of the current year? Of this

amount how much did the company expect to collect? How much did the company expect *not* to collect?

2. Assume during the current year that the company recorded doubtful account expense equal to 1 percent of net sales. Starting with the beginning balance, analyze the Allowance for Doubtful Accounts to determine the amount of the receivable write-offs during the current year. If the company does not provide information on the allowance for doubtful accounts, assume it is 3 percent of accounts receivable.

3. If the company does not have notes receivable, you may skip this requirement. If notes receivable are present at the end of the current year, assume their interest rate is 9 percent. Also assume that no new notes receivable arose during the following year. Journalize these transactions that took place during the following year:
   a. Received cash for 75 percent of the interest revenue earned during the year.
   b. Accrued the remaining portion of the interest revenue earned during the year.
   c. At year end collected half the notes receivable.

4. Suppose the company discounted a $500,000 note receivable. Under what heading in the annual report would the company report the discounting of a note receivable? Show how the company would disclose this fact.

CHAPTER 9
Merchandise Inventory

It seems peculiar that three identical companies could have three very different net incomes or losses on the income statement and three different values for inventory on the balance sheet using accounting procedures that comply with generally accepted accounting principles.

The *CICA Handbook* states that "The method selected for determining cost [for inventory] should be one which results in the fairest matching of costs against revenues regardless of whether or not the method corresponds to the physical flow of goods." A second recommendation is that "The basis of valuation of inventories should be clearly stated in the financial statements."

The first statement is partly true in that all three methods are permitted, and as you will see as you read the chapter, they result in very different measurements of closing inventory and thus of net income. The second statement, while indicating that management has the latitude to select the method used, does require management to select that method that results in the most appropriate matching of costs against revenues. And perhaps more importantly, management is required to report the method chosen in the financial statements.

The importance of inventory is demonstrated by the fact that 269 or 90 percent of the companies included in *Financial Reporting in Canada*, 1993, Twentieth Edition[1] reported a figure for inventory. Forty-eight percent of those 269 companies used FIFO, 35 percent used average cost, 5 percent used the retail method while 4 percent used LIFO; the remaining 8 percent used a variety of other methods.

Merchandise inventory is very important to a merchandising entity such as Mark's Work Wearhouse.

---

[1]Source: *Financial Reporting in Canada*, 1993, Twentieth Edition, Toronto: Canada Institute of Chartered Accountants, 1993, p. 92.

CHAPTER OBJECTIVES

After studying this chapter, you should be able to

1 Account for inventory by the periodic and perpetual systems

2 Apply four inventory costing methods: specific unit costs, weighted-average cost, FIFO, and LIFO

3 Describe the income effects of the inventory costing methods

4 Prepare a perpetual inventory record

5 Apply to inventory the lower-of-cost-or-market rule

6 Compute the effects of inventory errors on cost of goods sold and on net income

7 Estimate inventory by the gross margin method

Real-World Example:
Typically, a business's year end coincides with the time of year when inventory is lowest, so that counting the inventory ("taking inventory") will be as simple as possible. Many retailers, such as Mark's Work Wearhouse, have a January 31 year end.

Merchandise inventory is the lifeblood of a merchandising entity—the entity's major current asset. What is the entity's major expense? It is *cost of goods sold or cost of sales*. For example, Wal-Mart Stores, Inc., reported cost of goods sold at U.S. $44.2 billion and operating, selling, and administrative expenses at U.S. $8.3 billion. For Wal-Mart and many other companies, cost of goods sold is greater than all other expenses combined.

If the business buys inventory that is in demand, it will be able to sell the goods at a profit. But there is much more to merchandising than buying and selling.

Accounting plays an important role in merchandising. The most obvious role is the record-keeping to stay abreast of quantities on hand in order to meet customer demand. Beyond that, there are several different methods of accounting for the cost of inventories. The chapter-opening discussion refers to the FIFO and LIFO inventory methods, which you will learn about shortly. *FIFO* stands for "first-in, first-out." *LIFO* stands for "last-in, first-out." These methods have some peculiar characteristics that managers, investors, and creditors need to understand. For example, FIFO and LIFO result in different amounts of reported income. In short, accounting for inventory goes far beyond record-keeping.

This chapter continues where Chapter 5 left off. We begin by reviewing the basic concept of accounting for inventories. Then we go into different inventory systems (perpetual and periodic), the different inventory methods (FIFO, LIFO, and average), and several additional topics.

The Basic Concept of Inventory Accounting

The basic concept of accounting for inventory is simple. The Brick buys three chairs for $300 each, marks them up $200, and sells two chairs for the retail price of $500 each. The Brick's balance sheet and income statement report the following:

Balance Sheet (partial):
Current assets:

Cash	$XXX
Short-term investments	XXX
Accounts receivable	XXX
Inventory	**300**
Prepaid expenses	XXX

Income Statement (partial):

Sales revenue	$1,000
Cost of goods sold	**600**
Gross margin	$ 400

In practice, the process is not so simple. Complexity arises from several sources. The following sections describe alternative techniques for measuring inventories and how they differ.

Periodic and Perpetual Inventory Systems _____

Different businesses have different inventory information needs. We now look at the two main inventory systems that we introduced in Chapter 5.

Perpetual Inventory System

In the **perpetual inventory system**, the business keeps a continuous record for each inventory item. The records thus show the inventory on hand at all times. Perpetual records are useful in preparing monthly, quarterly, or other interim financial statements. The business can determine the cost of ending inventory, and the cost of goods sold directly from the accounts without having to count the merchandise.

The perpetual system offers a higher degree of control because information is always up to date. In the past, businesses used the perpetual system for high-unit-cost inventories such as gemstones and automobiles. Recently, however, most businesses have switched to perpetual systems as accounting software has come down in price.

Computer systems have revolutionized accounting for inventory. Computerized perpetual systems can provide up-to-the-minute inventory data useful for managing the business. They help cut accounting cost by processing large numbers of transactions without computational error. Computer systems also enhance internal control. They increase efficiency because managers always know the quantity and cost of inventory on hand. Managers can make better decisions about quantities to buy, prices to pay for the inventory, prices to charge customers, and sale terms to offer. Knowing the quantity on hand helps to safeguard the inventory.

Perpetual inventory records can be a computer printout like the CompuSave Ltd. record shown in Exhibit 9-1. The quantities of goods on hand are updated on a daily basis. Some companies, such as CompuSave, keep their perpetual records in terms of quantities only. We shall soon see how these data can be used to determine the cost of ending inventory and the cost of goods sold. Perpetual inventory records provide information for the following decisions:

1. When a customer asks how soon they can get two RK42 computers for their office, the salesperson can answer the question after referring to the perpetual inventory record. CompuSave, like most other large retailers, keeps its goods in storerooms or warehouses. Employees cannot visually scan the merchandise on hand to answer every customer inquiry. On November 6, the salesperson would reply that the company's stock is low, and the customer may have to wait a few days. On November 27, the salesperson could offer immediate delivery.

OBJECTIVE 1

Account for inventory by the periodic and perpetual systems

 Key Point:
Remember the derivation of the balance of every account, including Inventory:

Beg. Bal.
+ Increases (purchases)
− Decreases (COGS)
= End. Bal.

The balance of the Inventory account under the perpetual system should give the cost of inventory on hand at any time.

EXHIBIT 9-1   *Perpetual Inventory Record—Quantities Only, CompuSave Ltd.*

Item: Computer Model RK42			
	Received	**Sold**	**Balance**
Date	**Qty.**	**Qty.**	**Qty.**
Nov. 1			10
5		6	4
7	10		14
12		9	5
26	7		12
30		8	4
✓	17	23	4

2. The perpetual records alert the business to reorder when inventory becomes low. On November 5, the company would be wise to purchase inventory. Sales might be lost if the business could not promise immediate delivery.

3. At November 30, the company prepares monthly financial statements. The perpetual inventory records show the company's ending inventory of RK-42 computers at 4 units. No physical count is necessary at this time. However, a physical inventory is needed once a year to verify the accuracy of the records.

Computer inventory systems vary considerably. At the extreme are complex systems used by huge retailers such as Sears, Eaton's, and The Bay. Purchases of inventory are recorded in perpetual records stored in a central computer. The inventory tags are coded electronically for updating the perpetual records when a sale is recorded on the cash register. Have you noticed a salesclerk passing the inventory ticket over a particular area of the checkout counter? A sensing device in the counter reads the stock number, quantity, cost, and sale price of the item sold. In other systems, the salesclerk passes an electronic device over the inventory tag. The computer records the sale and updates the inventory records. In effect, a journal entry is recorded for each sale, a procedure that is not economical without a computer.

Small companies also use minicomputers and microcomputers to keep perpetual inventory records. These systems may be similar to the systems used by large companies. In less-sophisticated operations, companies may have salesclerks write inventory stock numbers on sales slips. The stock number identifies the particular item of inventory, such as men's shirts or children's shoes. The business may accumulate all sales slips for the week. If the company has its own computer system, an employee may type the sales information into the computer and store the perpetual records on a magnetic disk. To learn the quantity, cost, or other characteristic of a particular item of inventory, a manager can view the inventory record on the computer monitor. For broader-based decisions affecting the entire inventory, managers use printouts of all items in stock. Many small businesses hire outside computer service centers to do much of the accounting for inventory. Regardless of the arrangement, managers get periodic printouts showing inventory data needed for managing the business. Manual reporting of this information is more time-consuming and expensive.

Perpetual inventory systems are becoming so sophisticated that, for example, Frito-Lay's Decision Support System can tell the company president (and other managers) the weekly sales of Ruffles Light potato chips by each route salesperson. In one case, Frito-Lay identified a drop in sales of tortilla chips by a particular chain of stores. Within two weeks, the company revised its marketing strategy and turned sales up again. Without the perpetual system, this process would have taken three months.

Entries under the Perpetual System   In the perpetual system, the business records purchases of inventory by debiting the Inventory account. When the business makes a sale, two entries are needed. The company records the sale in the usual manner—debits Cash or Accounts Receivable and credits Sales Revenue for the sale price of the goods. The company also debits Cost of Goods Sold and credits Inventory for cost. The debit to Inventory (for purchases) and the credit to Inventory (for sales) serve to keep an up-to-date record of inventory on hand.

The Inventory account and the Cost of Goods Sold account carry a current balance during the period. Exhibit 9-2 illustrates the accounting for inventory transactions in a perpetual system (and in a periodic system as well). Panel A gives the journal entries, and Panel B presents the income statement and balance sheet effects. All amounts are assumed.

Periodic Inventory System

In the **periodic inventory system**, the business does not keep a continuous record of the inventory on hand. Instead, at the end of the period, the business makes a physical count of the on-hand inventory and applies the appropriate unit costs to determine the cost of ending inventory. The business makes the standard end-of-period inventory entries, as discussed in Chapter 5 and shown in the example that follows. This system is also called the *physical system* because it relies on the actual physical count of inventory. The periodic system is used to account for inventory items that have a low unit cost. Low-cost items may not be valuable enough to warrant the cost of keeping a running record of the inventory on hand. To use the periodic system effectively, the owner must be able to control inventory by visual inspection. For example, when a customer inquires about quantities on hand, the owner or manager can eyeball the goods in the store.

Entries under the Periodic System   In the periodic system, the business records purchases of inventory in the Purchases account (an expense account). The Inventory account continues to carry the beginning balance left over from the end of the preceding period. At the end of the period, however, the Inventory account must be updated for the financial statements. A journal entry removes the beginning balance, crediting Inventory and debiting Income Summary. A second journal entry sets up the ending balance, based on the physical count. The debit is to Inventory, and the credit to Income Summary. These entries can be made either in the closing process or as an adjustment.

EXHIBIT 9-2   *Recording and Reporting Inventory Transactions of CompuSave Ltd.—Perpetual and Periodic Systems (amounts assumed)*

Perpetual System

Panel A—Recording in the Journal
1. Credit purchases of $560,000:

Inventory	560,000	
Accounts Payable		560,000

2. Credit sales of $900,000 (cost $540,000):

Accounts Receivable	900,000	
Sales Revenue		900,000
Cost of Goods Sold	540,000	
Inventory		540,000

3. End-of-period entries:
No entries required. Both Inventory and Cost of Goods Sold are up to date.

Periodic System

Panel A—Recording in the Journal
1. Credit purchases of $560,000:

Purchases	560,000	
Accounts Payable		560,000

2. Credit sales of $900,000 (cost $540,000):

Accounts Receivable	900,000	
Sales Revenue		900,000

End-of-period entries to update Inventory:

Income Summary	100,000	
Inventory (beginning balance)		100,000
Inventory (ending balance)	120,000	
Income Summary		120,000

Panel B—Reporting in the Financial Statements

Income Statement (partial):

Sales revenue	$900,000
Cost of goods sold	540,000
Gross margin	$360,000

Income Statement (partial):

Sales revenue		$900,000
Cost of goods sold:		
Beginning inventory	$100,000	
Purchases	560,000	
Ending inventory	(120,000)	
Cost of goods sold		540,000
Gross margin		$360,000

Ending Balance Sheet (partial):

Current assets:

Cash	$XXX,XXX
Short-term investments	XXX,XXX
Accounts receivable	XXX,XXX
Inventories	**120,000**
Prepaid expenses	XXX,XXX

Current Assets:

Cash	$XXX,XXX
Short-term investments	XXX,XXX
Accounts receivable	XXX,XXX
Inventories	**120,000**
Prepaid expenses	XXX,XXX

Exhibit 9-2 contrasts the perpetual and periodic inventory systems for one month's operations of CompuSave Ltd. Compare the entries under both inventory systems step by step. First study the perpetual system all the way through. On the income statement the perpetual system reports cost of goods sold on a single line. Then study the periodic sysytem, which reports a more detailed computation of cost of goods sold. Both inventory systems report the same amounts for inventory and cost of goods sold. (All amounts are assumed.)

Computing the Cost of Inventory

Under both accounting systems, a physical count establishes the cost of inventory on hand, or the *cost of ending inventory*. The *quantity* of inventory is multiplied by the *unit cost* of inventory to compute the cost of inventory on hand.

Quantity of Inventory on Hand × Unit Cost = Cost of Inventory on Hand

The CompuSave inventory record in Exhibit 9-1 follows the common practice of recording quantities only. The company can multiply the quantity of 8 RK42 computers on hand at November 30 by the unit cost of each computer to compute the value of the ending inventory for the balance sheet.

Determining the Quantity of Inventory   Most businesses—even those that use the perpetual system—physically count their inventory on the last day of the fiscal year. If you have worked at a grocery store, or some other type of retail business, you will recall the process of "taking inventory." Some entities shut the business down to get a good count of inventory on hand. Others count the goods on a weekend. Still others inventory the merchandise while business is being conducted.

Complications may arise in determining the inventory quantity. Suppose the business has purchased some goods that are in transit when the inventory is counted. Even though these items are not physically present, they should be included in the inventory count if title to the goods has passed to the purchaser. When title passes from seller to purchaser, the purchaser becomes the legal owner of the goods.

The FOB—free on board—terms of the transaction govern when title passes from the seller to the purchaser. **FOB shipping point** indicates that title passes when the goods leave the seller's place of business. **FOB destination** means that title passes when the goods arrive at the purchaser's location. Therefore, goods in transit that CompuSave has purchased FOB shipping point should be included in CompuSave's inventory. Goods in transit that are bought FOB destination should not be included.

Another complication in counting inventory arises from consigned goods. In a **consignment** arrangement, the owner of the inventory (the *consignor*) transfers the goods to another business (the *consignee*). For a fee, the consignee sells the inventory on the owner's behalf. The consignee does *not* take title to the consigned goods and, therefore, should not include them in its own inventory. Consignments are common in retailing. Suppose CompuSave is the consignee for a line of notebook computers in its store. Should CompuSave include this consigned merchandise in its inventory count? No, because CompuSave does not own the goods. Instead, the computer manufacturer—the consignor—includes the consigned goods in its inventory. A rule of thumb is to include in inventory only what the business owns.

Determining the Cost of Inventory   Inventories are normally accounted for at historical cost, as the *cost principle* requires. *Inventory cost* is the price the business pays to acquire the inventory—not the selling price of the goods. Suppose a business purchases inventory for $10 and offers it for sale at $15. The inventory cost is reported at $10, not at its selling price of $15. Inventory cost includes its invoice price, less any purchase discount, plus sales tax, tariffs, transportation charges, insurance while in transit, and all other costs incurred to make the goods ready for sale.

While the retailer paid GST on the purchase, the amount paid is recoverable as a deduction from the GST collected when the retailer sells the inventory. For example,

Key Point:

FOB shipping point means the goods are placed on board (on the carrier, such as UPS) and the buyer is responsible for paying the freight.

FOB destination means the freight is paid to the destination by the seller.

CompuSave would pay $63 GST ($900 × .07 percent, the GST rate) on a purchase of a $900 home computer from the manufacturer. When CompuSave sells the computer the following month for $1,400, they would charge the purchaser GST of $98 ($1,400 × .07). Later CompuSave would remit $35 ($98 − $63) to Revenue Canada in connection with the purchase and sale.

Inventory Costing Methods

Determining the unit cost of inventory is easy when the unit cost remains constant during the period. But, the unit cost often changes. For example, during times of inflation, prices rise. The software model that cost CompuSave $100 in January may cost $115 in June and $122 in October. Suppose CompuSave sells 15 of the software packages in November. How many of them cost $100, $115 and $122? To compute the cost of goods sold and ending inventory amounts, the accountant must have some means of assigning the business's cost to each item sold. The four costing methods that GAAP allows are

> **OBJECTIVE 2**
>
> Apply four inventory costing methods: specific unit cost, weighted average cost, FIFO, and LIFO

1. Specific unit cost
2. Average cost
3. First-in, first-out (FIFO) cost
4. Last-in, first-out (LIFO) cost

A company may use any of these methods. Many companies use several methods—different methods for different categories of inventory.

Specific Unit Cost

Some businesses deal in inventory items that may be identified individually, like automobiles, jewels, and real estate. These businesses usually cost their inventory at the specific unit cost of the particular unit. For instance, a Chevrolet dealer may have two vehicles in the showroom, a "stripped-down" model that cost $16,000 and a "loaded" model that cost $21,000. If the dealer sells the loaded model for $23,700, cost of goods sold is $21,000, the cost of the specific unit. The gross margin on this sale is $2,700 ($23,700 − $21,000). If the stripped-down auto is the only unit left in inventory at the end of the period, ending inventory is $16,000, the cost to the retailer of the specific unit on hand.

The **specific unit cost method** is also called the *specific identification* method. This method is not practical for inventory items that do not have unique characteristics, such as bushels of wheat, gallons of paint, or boxes of laundry detergent.

Weighted-Average Cost, FIFO Cost, and LIFO Cost

The weighted-average cost, FIFO (first-in, first-out), and LIFO (last-in, first-out) methods are fundamentally different from the specific unit cost method. These methods do not assign to inventory the specific cost of particular units. Instead, they assume different flows of costs into and out of inventory.

Weighted-Average Cost The **weighted-average cost method**, often called the *average cost method*, is based on the weighted-average cost of inventory during the period. This method weighs the cost per unit as the average unit cost during the period—that is, if the unit cost drops or rises during the period, the average of these costs is used. Weighted-average cost is determined as follows: Divide the cost of goods available for sale (beginning inventory plus purchases) by the number of units available. Compute the ending inventory and cost of goods sold by multiplying the number of units by the weighted-average cost per unit. If cost of goods available for sale is $90,000 and 60 units are available, the weighted-average cost is

$1,500 per unit ($90,000/60 = $1,500). Ending inventory of 20 units of the same item has an average cost $30,000 (20 × $1,500 = $30,000). Cost of goods sold (40 units) is $60,000 (40 × $1,500). Panel A of Exhibit 9-3 gives the data in more detail. Panel B shows the weighted-average cost computations.

First-in, First-out (FIFO) Cost   Under the **first-in, first-out (FIFO) method**, the company must keep a record of the cost of each inventory unit purchased. The unit costs used in computing the ending inventory may be different from the unit

EXHIBIT 9-3   *Inventory and Cost of Goods Sold under Weighted-Average, FIFO, and LIFO Inventory Costing Methods*

Panel A: Illustrative Data

Beginning inventory (10 units @ $1,000 per unit)		$ 10,000
Purchases		
No. 1 (25 units @ $1,400 per unit)..................................	$ 35,000	
No. 2 (25 units @ $1,800 per unit).................................	45,000	
Total		80,000
Cost of goods available for sale (60 units)...........................		$ 90,000
Ending inventory (20 units @ $? per unit)...........................		?
Cost of goods sold (40 units @ $? per unit)		$?

Panel B: Ending Inventory and Cost of Goods Sold

Weighted-Average Cost Method

Cost of goods available for sale—see Panel A		
(60 units @ average cost of $1,500* per unit)		$ 90,000
Ending inventory (20 units @ $1,500 per unit)...................................		30,000
Cost of goods sold (40 units @ $1,500 per unit)		$ 60,000

*Cost of goods available for sale...		$ 90,000
Number of units available for sale...		÷ 60
Average cost per unit		$ 1,500

FIFO Cost Method

Cost of goods available for sale (60 units—see Panel A)		$ 90,000
Ending inventory (cost of the *last* 20 units available)		
20 units @ $1,800 per unit (from purchase no. 2)		36,000
Cost of goods sold (cost of the *first* 40 units available)		
10 units @ $1,000 per unit (all of beginning inventory)	$ 10,000	
25 units @ $1,400 per unit (all of purchase no. 1)..........	35,000	
5 units @ $1,800 per unit (from purchase no. 2)..........	9,000	
Total		$ 54,000

LIFO Cost Method

Cost of goods available for sale (60 units—see Panel A)		$90,000
Ending inventory (cost of the *first* 20 units available)		
10 units @ $1,000 per unit (all of beginning inventory)	$ 10,000	
10 units @ $1,400 per unit (from purchase no. 1)	14,000	
Total		24,000
Cost of goods sold (cost of the last 40 units available)		
25 units @ $1,800 per unit (all of purchase no. 2)..........	$ 45,000	
15 units @ $1,400 per unit (from purchase no. 1)	21,000	
Total		$66,000

costs used in computing the cost of goods sold. Under FIFO, the first costs into inventory are the first costs out to cost of goods sold—hence the name *first-in, first-out*. Ending inventory is based on the costs of the most recent purchases. In our example, the FIFO cost of ending inventory is $36,000. Cost of goods sold is $54,000. Panel A of Exhibit 9-3 gives the data, and Panel B shows the FIFO computations.

Last-in, First-out (LIFO) Cost   The **last-in, first-out (LIFO) method** also depends on the costs of particular inventory purchases. LIFO is the opposite of FIFO. Under LIFO, the last costs into inventory are the first costs out to cost of goods sold. This leaves the oldest costs—those of beginning inventory and the earliest purchases of the period—in ending inventory. In our example, the LIFO cost of ending inventory is $24,000. Cost of goods sold is $66,000. Panel A of Exhibit 9-3 gives the data, and Panel B shows the LIFO computations.

Income Effects of FIFO, LIFO, and Average Cost

In our discussion and examples, the cost of inventory rose over the accounting period. When inventory unit costs change, the different costing methods produce different cost of goods sold and ending inventory figures, as Exhibit 9-3 shows. When inventory unit costs are increasing, FIFO ending inventory is *highest* because it is priced at the most recent costs, which are the highest. LIFO ending inventory is *lowest* because it is priced at the oldest costs, which are the lowest. When inventory unit costs are decreasing, FIFO ending inventory is lowest, and LIFO is highest.

Exhibit 9-4 summarizes the income effects of the three inventory methods using the data from Exhibit 9-3. Study the exhibit carefully, focusing on ending inventory, cost of goods sold, and gross margin.

> **OBJECTIVE 3**
> Describe the income effects of the inventory costing methods

> **Concept Highlight**

EXHIBIT 9-4   *Income Effects of FIFO, LIFO, and Weighted-Average Cost Inventory Methods*

	FIFO		LIFO		Weighted-Average	
Sales revenue (assumed)............................		$100,000		$100,000		$100,000
Cost of goods sold						
Goods available for sale (assumed)....	$90,000		$ 90,000		$ 90,000	
Ending inventory	36,000		24,000		30,000	
Cost of goods sold................................		54,000		66,000		60,000
Gross margin..		$ 46,000		$ 34,000		$ 40,000

Summary of Income Effects: When Inventory Costs Are Increasing

FIFO—Highest ending inventory	LIFO—Lowest ending inventory	Weighted-average—Results fall
Lowest cost of goods sold	Highest cost of goods sold	between the extremes of
Highest gross margin	Lowest gross margin	FIFO and LIFO

Summary of Income Effects: When Inventory Unit Costs Are Decreasing

FIFO—Lowest ending inventory	LIFO—Highest ending inventory	Weighted-average—Results fall
Highest cost of goods sold	Lowest cost of goods sold	between the extremes of
Lowest gross margin	Highest gross margin	FIFO and LIFO

Key Point: ✓

During a period of rising prices—

Advantages of FIFO:
1. Always reports current cost for ending inventory
2. Reports higher income

Advantages of LIFO:
1. Always matches ex-penses and revenues

Disadvantages of FIFO:
1. Violates the matching principle (FIFO matches some of the previous year's inventory cost against current revenue)
2. Does not adjust cost of goods sold for the effects of inflation

Disadvantages of LIFO:
1. Reports lower income
2. Reports understated ending inventory
3. Can be used to manipulate income

Generally Accepted Accounting Principles and Practical Considerations: A Comparison of the Inventory Methods

We may ask two questions to judge the inventory costing methods. (1) How well does each method match inventory expense—the cost of goods sold—to sales revenue on the income statement? (2) Which method reports the most up-to-date inventory amount on the balance sheet? The weighted-average cost method produces amounts between the extremes of LIFO and FIFO.

LIFO better matches the current value of cost of goods sold with current revenue by assigning to this expense the most recent inventory costs. By contrast, FIFO matches the oldest inventory costs against the period's revenue—a poor matching of current expense with current revenue.

FIFO reports the most current inventory costs on the balance sheet. LIFO can result in misleading inventory costs on the balance sheet because the oldest prices are left in ending inventory.

FIFO Produces So-Called Inventory Profits   FIFO is criticized because it overstates income by so-called inventory profit during periods of inflation. Briefly, **inventory profit** is the difference between gross margin figured on the FIFO basis and gross margin figured on the LIFO basis. Exhibit 9-4 illustrates inventory profit. The $12,000 difference between FIFO and LIFO gross margins ($46,000 – $34,000) results from the difference in cost of goods sold. This $12,000 amount is called *FIFO inventory profit, phantom profit,* or *illusory profit.* Why? Because to stay in business, the company must replace the inventory it has sold. The replacement cost of the merchandise is more closely approximated by the cost of goods sold under LIFO ($66,000), than by the FIFO amount ($54,000).

LIFO Allows Managers to Manipulate Reported Income—Up or Down
LIFO is criticized because it allows managers to manipulate net income. Assume inventory prices are rising rapidly, and a company wants to show less income for the year. Managers can buy a large amount of inventory near the end of the year. Under LIFO these high inventory costs immediately become expense—as cost of goods sold. As a result, the income statement reports a lower net income. Conversely, if the business is having a bad year, management may wish to increase reported income. To do so, managers can delay a large purchase of high-cost inventory until the next period. This inventory is not expensed as cost of goods sold in the current year. Thus management avoids decreasing the current year's reported income. In the process, management draws down inventory quantities.

International Perspective   Many companies manufacture their inventory in foreign countries to decrease transportation costs and to break down trade barriers. Companies that value inventory by the LIFO method in one country often must use another accounting method for their inventories in another country.

LIFO is very popular in the United States where its use is permitted for tax purposes. As you can see in Exhibit 9-4, in a period of rising prices (such as we have had since World War II), LIFO leads to the lowest income of the three methods and, in the United States, to the lowest taxes.

LIFO is not allowed for income tax purposes in Canada, Austria, or the United Kingdom, but a company can use it for accounting purposes. That is probably why in Canada, as the opening story pointed out, very few companies use LIFO (4 percent); here the largest percentage uses FIFO (48 percent), while the next largest number uses average cost (35 percent). In other countries, such as Australia and Sweden, LIFO is not permitted.

Which Method to Use?   A company may want to report higher income, and FIFO meets this need when prices are rising. When prices are falling, LIFO reports the higher income.

Which inventory method is best? There is no single answer to this question. Different companies have different motives for the inventory method they choose. Co-Steel Inc., a steel company, and Dover Industries Limited, a food products company, use average cost while Primex Forest Products Ltd., Emco Limited, and Nova Corporation of Alberta use FIFO. MDS Health Group Limited and Quebecor Inc., a publishing and printing company, use average cost and FIFO. Haley Industries Limited uses average cost for finished goods and work in process, specific cost for patterns, and FIFO for raw materials and supplies. Celanese Canada and Shell Canada are among the few companies that use LIFO. The companies disclose the method used under the heading "Significant Accounting Policies" or "Summary of Significant Accounting Policies" in the notes to the financial statements. Edmonton Telephones Corporation's specific disclosure is:

> **(c) Inventory:**
> Inventories are valued at the lower of cost and moving average cost and net realizable value. ...

Ivaco Inc.'s disclosure is

> **Inventories**
> Inventories are stated at the lower of cost (determined substantially on the first-in, first-out method) and net realizable value. ...

Mid-Chapter Summary Problem for Your Review

Suppose a Northern Telecom division that handles telephone components has these inventory records for January 19X6:

Date	Item	Quantity	Unit Cost	Sale Price
Jan. 1	Beginning inventory	100 units	$ 8	
6	Purchase	60 units	9	
13	Sale	70 units		$ 20
21	Purchase	150 units	9	
24	Sale	210 units		22
27	Purchase	90 units	10	
30	Sale	30 units		25

Company accounting records reveal that related operating expense for January was $1,900.

Required

1. Prepare the January income statement, showing amounts for FIFO, LIFO, and weighted-average cost. Label the bottom line "Operating Income." (Round figures to whole dollar amounts.)

2. Suppose you are the financial vice-president of Northern Telecom. Which inventory method would you use if your motive is to
   a. Minimize income taxes?
   b. Report the highest operating income?
   c. Report operating income between the extremes of FIFO and LIFO?
   d. Report inventory at the most current cost?
   e. Attain the best matching of current expense with current revenue?

   State the reason for each of your answers.

SOLUTION TO REVIEW PROBLEM

Requirement 1

Northern Telecom (Telephone Components Division)
Partial Income Statement
for the month ended January 31, 19X6

	FIFO		LIFO		Weighted-Average	
Sales revenue.............................		$6,770		$6,770		$6,770
Cost of goods sold						
Beginning inventory	$ 800		$ 800		$ 800	
Purchases.............................	2,790		2,790		2,790	
Cost of goods						
available for sale..............	3,590		3,590		3,590	
Ending inventory..................	900		720		808	
Cost of goods sold		2,690		2,870		2,782
Gross margin.............................		4,080		3,900		3,988
Operating expenses..................		1,900		1,900		1,900
Operating income......................		$2,180		$2,000		$2,088

Computations

Sales revenue	(70	× $20)	+ (210 × $22) + (30 × $25) = $6,770
Beginning inventory	100	× $8	= $800
Purchases	(60	× $9)	+ (150 × $9) + (90 × $10) = $2,790
Ending inventory: FIFO ..	90	× $10	= $900
LIFO ..	90*	× $8	= $720
Weighted-average	90	× $8.975**	= $808 (rounded from $807.75)

*Number of units in ending inventory = 100 + 60 – 70 + 150 – 210 + 90 – 30 = 90
**$3,590/400 units = $8.975 per unit
Number of units available = 100 + 60 + 150 + 90 = 400

Requirement 2

a. Use average cost to minimize income taxes. Operating income under LIFO is lowest when inventory unit costs are increasing, as they are in this case (from $8 to $10). Remember, LIFO cannot be used for income tax purposes in Canada. Average cost produces the next lowest income and, since it can be used for tax purposes, the lowest income taxes.

b. Use FIFO to report the highest operating income. Income under FIFO is highest when inventory unit costs are increasing, as in this situation.

c. Use weighted-average cost to report an operating income amount between the LIFO and FIFO extremes. This is true in this problem situation and in others whether inventory unit costs are increasing or decreasing.

d. Use FIFO to report inventory at the most current cost. The oldest inventory costs are expensed as cost of goods sold, leaving in ending inventory the most recent (most current) costs of the period.

e. Use LIFO to attain the best matching of current expense with current revenue. The most recent (most current) inventory costs are expensed as cost of goods sold.

Perpetual Inventory Records under FIFO, LIFO, and Weighted-Average Costing

Many companies keep their perpetual inventory records in quantities only, as illustrated in Exhibit 9-1. Other companies keep perpetual records in both quantities and dollar costs.

FIFO   CompuSave Ltd. uses the FIFO inventory method. Exhibit 9-5 shows CompuSave's perpetual inventory record for RK-42 Computers—in both quantities and dollar costs for the month of November.

To prepare financial statements at November 30, CompuSave can take the ending inventory cost ($3,280) straight to the balance sheet. Cost of goods sold for the November income statement is $18,560. Some companies combine elements of the perpetual and periodic inventory systems—the perpetual system for control and preparation of the financial statements, and the periodic system for analysis. Here is CompuSave's computation of cost of goods sold during November, with data taken from the perpetual record in Exhibit 9-5:

Cost of Goods Sold (RK-42 Computers)—November	
Beginning inventory	$8,000
+ Purchases	13,840
= Cost of goods available for sale	21,840
– Ending inventory	(3,280)
= Cost of goods sold	18,560

LIFO   Few companies keep perpetual inventory records at LIFO cost. The record-keeping is expensive, and LIFO liquidations can occur during the year. To avoid these problems, LIFO companies can keep perpetual inventory records in terms of quantities only, as illustrated in Exhibit 9-1. For financial statements, they can apply LIFO costs at the end of the period. Other companies maintain perpetual inventory records at FIFO cost and convert the FIFO amounts to LIFO costs for the financial statements. This topic is covered in intermediate accounting courses.

Weighted-Average Cost   Perpetual inventory records can be kept at weighted-average cost. Most companies that use this method compute the weighted-average

EXHIBIT 9-5   *Perpetual Inventory Record—FIFO Cost*

<table>
<tr><td colspan="10" align="center">CompuSave Ltd.</td></tr>
<tr><td colspan="10">Item: Computer Model RK42</td></tr>
<tr><td></td><td colspan="3" align="center">Received</td><td colspan="3" align="center">Sold</td><td colspan="3" align="center">Balance</td></tr>
<tr><td>Date</td><td>Qty.</td><td>Unit Cost</td><td>Total</td><td>Qty.</td><td>Unit Cost</td><td>Total</td><td>Qty.</td><td>Unit Cost</td><td>Total</td></tr>
<tr><td>Nov. 1</td><td></td><td></td><td></td><td></td><td></td><td></td><td>10</td><td>$800</td><td>$8,000</td></tr>
<tr><td>5</td><td></td><td></td><td></td><td>6</td><td>$800</td><td>$4,800</td><td>4</td><td>800</td><td>3,200</td></tr>
<tr><td>7</td><td>10</td><td>$810</td><td>$8,100</td><td></td><td></td><td></td><td>4</td><td>800</td><td>3,200</td></tr>
<tr><td></td><td></td><td></td><td></td><td></td><td></td><td></td><td>10</td><td>810</td><td>8,100</td></tr>
<tr><td>12</td><td></td><td></td><td></td><td>4</td><td>800</td><td>3,200</td><td></td><td></td><td></td></tr>
<tr><td></td><td></td><td></td><td></td><td>5</td><td>810</td><td>4,050</td><td>5</td><td>810</td><td>4,050</td></tr>
<tr><td>26</td><td>7</td><td>820</td><td>5,740</td><td></td><td></td><td></td><td>5</td><td>810</td><td>4,050</td></tr>
<tr><td></td><td></td><td></td><td></td><td></td><td></td><td></td><td>7</td><td>820</td><td>5,740</td></tr>
<tr><td>30</td><td></td><td></td><td></td><td>5</td><td>810</td><td>4,050</td><td></td><td></td><td></td></tr>
<tr><td></td><td></td><td></td><td></td><td>3</td><td>820</td><td>2,460</td><td>4</td><td>820</td><td>3,280</td></tr>
<tr><td>Total</td><td>17</td><td></td><td>$13,840</td><td>23</td><td></td><td>$18,560</td><td>4</td><td>820</td><td>$3,280</td></tr>
</table>

cost for the entire period. They apply this cost to both ending inventory and cost of goods sold. These procedures parallel those used in the periodic inventory system (Exhibit 9-3).

The use of computer software to account for inventory eases the computation of the average cost per at each time additional goods are purchased. The new average unit cost is then applied to each subsequent sale until more goods are purchased, at which time another new average cost is computed.

STOP & THINK

Examine Exhibit 9-5. What was CompuSave Ltd.'s weighted-average unit cost during November? How much were ending inventory and cost of goods sold at weighted-average unit cost?

Answer: Weighted-average unit cost $= \dfrac{\$8,000 + \$13,840}{10 \text{ units} + 17 \text{ units}} = \dfrac{\$21,840}{27 \text{ units}} = \$808.89$

Ending inventory	= 4 units × \$808.89	=	3,236
Cost of goods sold	= 23 units × \$808.89	=	18,604
Cost of goods available for sale		=	21,840

Key Point:

The accounting principles used by a company must be consistent from year to year to allow comparison of the financial results from one year to the next. If a company changes its inventory method, the change and its effect must be disclosed in the footnotes.

Consistency Principle

The **consistency principle** states that businesses should use the same accounting methods and procedures from period to period. Consistency makes it possible to compare a company's financial statements from one period to the next.

Suppose you are analyzing a company's net income pattern. The company has switched from LIFO to FIFO. Its net income has increased dramatically, but only as a result of the change in inventory method. If you did not know of the change, you might believe that the company's increased income arose from improved operations, which is not the case.

The consistency principle does not require that all companies within an industry use the same accounting method. Nor does it mean that a company may never change its own accounting method. However, a company making an accounting change must disclose the effect of the change on net income.

EXCERPT FROM NOTE 6 OF THE SUN COMPANY FINANCIAL STATEMENTS

... Sun changed its method of accounting for the cost of crude oil and refined product inventories at Sun from the FIFO method to the LIFO method. Sun believes that the use of the LIFO method better matches current costs with current revenues ... The change decreased the 19X1 net loss ... by \$3 million ...

Disclosure Principle

The **disclosure principle** holds that a company's financial statements should report enough information for outsiders to make knowledgeable decisions about the company. In short, the company should report *relevant*, *reliable*, and *comparable* information about its economic affairs. With respect to inventories, this means to disclose the method or methods in use. Without knowledge of the inventory method, a banker could gain an unrealistic impression of a company and make an unwise lending decision. For example, suppose the banker is comparing two companies—one that uses LIFO and the other, FIFO. The FIFO company reports higher net income, but only because it uses a particular inventory method. Without knowledge of the accounting methods the companies are using, the banker could loan money to the wrong business or could refuse a loan to a promising customer.

In conjunction with the consistency principle, the disclosure principle requires companies to report the net-income effect of a change in accounting method. For example, while considering an investment in Sun Company, Inc., you observe that Sun's net loss was less than expected. Would you be inclined to invest in the company? Perhaps. However, the foregoing note explains that Sun Company's change to the LIFO method reduced the net loss by $3 million. If the company had not changed inventory methods, the net loss would have been $3 million higher. This information casts a different light on Sun's operations and may influence your investment decision. This is the disclosure principle of action.

Materiality Concept

The **materiality concept** states that a company must perform strictly proper accounting *only* for items and transactions that are significant to the business's financial statements. Information is significant—what accountants call *material*—when its inclusion and correct presentation in the financial statements would cause a statement user to change a decision because of that information. Immaterial—nonsignificant—items justify less-than-perfect accounting. The inclusion and proper presentation of items aggregating to a less-than-material or *immaterial* amount would not affect a statement user's decision. The materiality concept frees accountants from having to compute and report every last item in strict accordance with GAAP. Thus the materiality concept reduces the cost of recording accounting information.

How does a business decide where to draw the line between the material and the immaterial? This decision rests to a great degree on how large the business is. Westcoast Energy, for example, has close to $650 million in assets. Management would likely treat as immaterial a $100 loss of inventory. A loss of this amount is immaterial to Westcoast Energy's total assets and net income, so company accountants may ignore the loss. Will this accounting treatment affect anyone's decision about Westcoast Energy? Probably not, so it doesn't matter whether the loss is reported separately.

Large companies may draw the materiality line at a figure as high as $10,000 and expense any smaller amount. Smaller firms may choose to expense only those items less than $50. Materiality varies from company to company. An amount that is material to your local service station may not be material to George Weston Limited.

Accounting Conservatism

Conservatism in accounting means to report items in the financial statements at amounts that lead to the gloomiest immediate financial results. Conservatism comes into play when there are alternative ways to account for an item. What advantage does conservatism give a business? Management often looks on the brighter side of operations, and may overstate a company's income and asset values. Many accountants regard conservatism as a counterbalance to management's optimistic tendencies. The goal is for financial statements to present realistic figures.

Conservatism appears in accounting guidelines like "anticipate no gains, but provide for all probable losses," and "if in doubt, record an asset at the lowest reasonable amount and a liability at the highest reasonable amount."

Accountants generally regard the historical cost of acquiring an asset to be its maximum value. Even if the current market value of the asset increases above its cost, businesses do not *write up* (that is, increase) the asset's accounting value. Assume that a company purchased land for $100,000, and its value increased to $300,000. Accounting conservatism dictates that the historical cost $100,000 be maintained as the accounting value of the land.

Conservatism also directs accountants to decrease the accounting value of an asset if it appears unrealistically high—even if no transaction occurs. Assume that a company paid $35,000 for inventory that has become obsolete, and its current value is only $12,000. Conservatism dictates that the inventory be *written down* (that is, decreased) to $12,000.

OBJECTIVE 5

Apply to inventory the lower-of-cost-or-market rule

Lower-of-Cost-or-Market Rule

The **lower-of-cost-or-market rule** (abbreviated as LCM) shows accounting conservatism in action. LCM requires that an asset be reported in the financial statements at whichever is lower—its historical cost or its market value. Applied to inventories, *market value* may mean *current replacement cost* (that is, how much the business would have to pay in the market on that day to purchase the amount of inventory that it has on hand), or it may mean *net realizable value* (that is, the gross amount the business could get if it sold the inventory less the costs of selling it). If the replacement cost or net realizable value of inventory falls below its historical cost, the business must write down the value of its goods because of the likelihood of incurring a loss on the inventory. This departure from historical cost accounting is required by GAAP. The business reports ending inventory at its LCM value on the balance sheet. All this can be done automatically by a computerized accounting system. How is the write-down accomplished?

Suppose a business paid $3,000 for inventory on September 26. By December 31, its value has fallen. The inventory can now be replaced for $2,200. Market value, defined in this instance as current replacement cost, is below cost, and the December 31 balance sheet reports this inventory at its LCM value of $2,200. Usually, the market value of inventory is higher than historical cost, so that inventory's accounting value is cost for most companies. Exhibit 9-6 presents the effects of LCM on the income statement and the balance sheet. The exhibit shows that the lower of (a) cost or (b) market value—replacement cost—is the relevant amount for valuing inventory on both the income statement and the balance sheet. Companies are not required to show both cost and market value amounts. However, they may report the higher amount in parentheses, as shown on the balance sheet in Exhibit 9-6.

LCM states that of the $3,000 cost of ending inventory in Exhibit 9-6, $800 is considered to have expired even though the inventory was not sold during the period.

EXHIBIT 9-6   *Lower-of-Cost-or-Market (LCM) Effects*

Income Statement

Sales revenue		$20,000
Cost of goods sold		
Beginning inventory (LCM = Cost)	**$ 2,800**	
Net purchases	11,000	
Cost of goods available for sale	13,800	
Ending inventory—		
Cost = $3,000		
Replacement cost (market value) = $2,200		
LCM = Market	**2,200**	
Cost of goods sold		11,600
Gross margin		$ 8,400

Balance Sheet

Current assets		
Cash	$ XXX	
Short-term investments	XXX	
Accounts reveivable	XXX	
Inventories, at market (which is lower		
than $3,000 cost)	2,200	
Prepaid investments	XXX	
Total current assets	$X,XXX	

Its replacement cost is only $2,200, and that amount is carried forward to the next period as the cost of beginning inventory. Suppose during the next period, the replacement cost of this inventory increases to $2,500. Accounting conservatism states that it would not be appropriate to write up the book value of inventory. The market value of inventory ($2,200 in this case) is used as its cost in future LCM determinations.

Examine the income statement effect of LCM in Exhibit 9-6. What expense absorbs the impact of the $800 inventory write down? Cost of goods sold is increased by $800 because ending inventory is $800 less at market ($2,200) than it would have been at cost ($3,000).

	Ending Inventory at	
	Cost	**LCM**
Cost of goods available for sale	$13,800	$13,800
Ending inventory		
Cost...	3,000	} $800 lower
Replacement cost (market value)		2,200 } at LCM
Cost of goods sold	$10,800	$11,600 } $800 higher at LCM

Exhibit 9-6 also reports the application of LCM for inventories in the body of the balance sheet. Companies often disclose LCM in notes to their financial statements, as shown below for Spar Aerospace Limited:

> FROM NOTE 1
> **(c) Inventories**
> Inventories of raw materials and finished goods are valued at the lower of cost ... and market value determined as the lesser of replacement cost or net realizable value.

Federal Pioneer Limited, a manufacturing company, states the following in the notes to the financial statements:

> FROM NOTE 2—SIGNIFICANT ACCOUNTING POLICIES
> **Inventories**
> Raw material inventories are valued at lower of cost and replacement cost while work in process and finished goods are valued at the lower of cost and net realizable value....

Effect of Inventory Errors

> **OBJECTIVE 6**
> Compute the effects of inventory errors on cost of goods sold and on net income

Businesses determine inventory amounts at the end of the period. In the process of counting the items, applying unit costs and computing amounts, errors may arise. As the period 1 segment of Exhibit 9-7 shows, an error in the ending inventory amount creates errors in the cost of goods sold and gross margin amounts. Compare period 1, when ending inventory is overstated, and cost of goods sold is understated, each by $5,000, with period 3, which is correct. Period 1 should look exactly like period 3.

Recall that one period's ending inventory is the next period's beginning inventory. Thus the error in ending inventory carries over into the next period. Note the highlighted amounts in Exhibit 9-7.

Because the same ending inventory figure that is *subtracted* in computing cost of goods sold in one period is *added* as beginning inventory to compute cost of goods sold in the next period, the error's effect cancels out at the end of the second period. The overstatement of cost of goods sold in period 2 counterbalances

EXHIBIT 9-7   *Effects of Inventory Errors*

	Period 1 Ending Inventory Overstated by $5,000		Period 2 Beginning Inventory Overstated by $5,000		Period 3 Correct	
Sales revenue		$100,000		$100,000		$100,000
Cost of goods sold						
Beginning inventory	$10,000		**$15,000**		$10,000	
Net purchases	50,000		50,000		50,000	
Cost of goods available for sale	60,000		65,000		60,000	
Ending inventory	**15,000**		10,000		10,000	
Cost of goods sold.........................		45,000		55,000		50,000
Gross margin...................................		$55,000		$45,000		$50,000
			$100,000			

The authors thank Carl High for this example.

PUTTING SKILLS TO WORK

Inventory and the Great Salad Oil Scandal

In 1963, a scandal rocked the business community and changed forever the way auditors verify inventory. The scandal involved salad oil, on which the financial empire of Anthony DeAngelis was built. As president of Allied Crude Vegetable Oil Refining Corp., DeAngelis was the top dealer in vegetable oils in the United States.

The Scam

The "Great Salad Oil Scandal" began when the price of vegetable oil fell dramatically. Unable to pay back creditors who demanded their money, DeAngelis's empire collapsed. Revealed in its wake was a sea of fraudulent inventory claims. The company had pumped water into its vegetable oil storage tanks. Oil floats on water, so inspectors who checked only some of the tanks and only from the top overestimated the quantity of inventory in each tank.

The scam took place on a "tank farm" in Bayonne, New Jersey, where DeAngelis supposedly stored about 770 million kilograms of oil worth about U.S.$150 million. No one believed it was necessary to check the accuracy of the inventory amounts, in part because American Express Warehousing leased the tanks. The American Express name was beyond reproach.

The Discovery

DeAngelis used the overstated inventory amounts as collateral for loans. When he could not pay the loans, creditors seized the vegetable oil. They then learned that only about 45 million kilograms of oil—not 770 million kilograms—existed. Some tanks were covered by solid matter, and others contained mixtures of oil, water, and sludge. Four tanks were empty, and eight were filled with sea water. There weren't enough tanks to hold all the oil DeAngelis claimed he owned, even if the tanks *had* been filled with salad oil! The empty or partly filled tanks spelled disaster for DeAngelis's creditors.

Postscript

Among the changes brought about by the Great Salad Oil Scandal was the requirement that independent auditors check the accuracy of the owner's claims. In this case, auditors would have had little trouble uncovering DeAngelis's scam.

the understatement in cost of goods sold in period 1. Thus the total gross margin amount for the two periods is the correct $100,000 figure, whether or not an error entered into the computation.

These effects are summarized in Exhibit 9-8. Inventory errors, however, cannot be ignored simply because they counterbalance. Suppose you are analyzing trends in the business's operations. Exhibit 9-7 shows a drop in gross margin from period 1 to period 2, followed by an increase in period 3. But that picture of operations is untrue because of the accounting error. The correct gross margin is $50,000 each period. Providing accurate information for decision-making requires all inventory errors be corrected.

EXHIBIT 9-8 *General Effects of Inventory Errors*

	Period 1		Period 2	
Inventory Error	**Cost of Goods Sold**	**Gross Margin and Net Income**	**Cost of Goods Sold**	**Gross Margin and Net Income**
Period 1 Ending inventory overstated	Understated	Overstated	Overstated	Understated
Period 1 Ending inventory understated	Overstated	Understated	Understated	Overstated

Estimating Inventory

Often a business must *estimate* the value of its inventory. Because of cost and inconvenience, few companies physically count and verify the accuracy of their inventories at the end of each month. Yet they may need monthly financial statements. A fire or a flood may destroy inventory, and to file an insurance claim, the business must estimate the value of its loss. In both cases, the business needs to know the value of ending inventory without being able to count it. A widely used method for estimating ending inventory is the *gross margin method*.

Gross Margin (Gross Profit) Method

The **gross margin method** (also known as the *gross profit method*) is a way of estimating inventory based on the familiar cost of goods sold model:

OBJECTIVE 7
Estimate inventory by the gross margin method

>   Beginning inventory
> + Net purchases*
> _____
> = Cost of goods available for sale
> − Ending inventory
> _____
> = Cost of goods sold

* Here "net purchases" includes freight in.

Rearranging *ending inventory* and *cost of goods sold*, the model becomes useful for estimating ending inventory as illustrated in Exhibit 9-9:

>   Beginning inventory
> + Net purchases
> _____
> = Cost of goods available for sale
> − Cost of goods sold
> _____
> = Ending inventory

Short Exercise:
Beginning inventory is $70,000, net purchases total $292,000, and net sales are $480,000. With a normal gross margin rate of 40%, how much is ending inventory?
A: $74,000 [$70,000 + $292,000 − (0.60 × $480,000)]

EXHIBIT 9-9 *Estimating Ending Inventory*

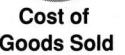

Step 1: Beginning Inventory + Net Purchases = Cost of Goods Available for Sale

Step 2: Cost of Goods Available for Sale − Cost of Goods Sold = Ending Inventory

EXHIBIT 9-10   *Gross Margin Method of Estimating Inventory (amounts assumed)*

Beginning inventory		$14,000
Net purchases		66,000
Cost of goods available for sale		80,000
Cost of goods sold		
Net sales revenue	$100,000	
Less estimated gross margin of 40%	40,000	
Estimated cost of goods sold		60,000
Estimated cost of *ending inventory*		$20,000

Suppose a fire destroys your business's inventory. To collect insurance, you must estimate the cost of the ending inventory. If the fire did not also destroy your accounting records, beginning inventory and net purchases amounts may be taken directly from the accounting records. The Sales Revenue, Sales Returns, and Sales Discounts accounts indicate net sales up to the date of the fire. Using the entity's normal *gross margin rate* (that is, gross margin divided by net sales revenue), you can estimate cost of goods sold. The last step is to subtract cost of goods sold from goods available to estimate ending inventory. Exhibit 9-10 illustrates the gross margin method.

Accountants, managers and auditors use the gross margin method to test the overall reasonableness of an ending inventory amount that has been determined by a physical count for all types of businesses. This method helps detect large errors.

Internal Control over Inventory

Internal control over inventory is important because inventory is the lifeblood of a merchandiser. Successful companies take great care to protect their inventory. Elements of good internal control over inventory include

1. Physically counting inventory at least once each year no matter which system is used.
2. Maintaining efficient purchasing, receiving, and shipping procedures.
3. Storing inventory to protect it against theft, damage, and decay.
4. Limiting access to inventory to personnel who do *not* have access to the accounting records.
5. Keeping perpetual inventory records for high-unit-cost merchandise.
6. Purchasing inventory in economical quantities.
7. Keeping enough inventory on hand to prevent shortages which lead to lost sales.
8. Not keeping too large an inventory stockpiled, thus avoiding the expense of tying up money in unneeded items.

The annual physical count of inventory (item 1) is necessary because the only way to be certain of the amount of inventory on hand is to count it. Errors arise in the best accounting systems, and the count is needed to establish the correct value of the inventory. When an error is detected, the records are brought into agreement with the physical count.

Keeping inventory handlers away from the accounting records (item 4) is an essential separation of duties, discussed in Chapter 7. An employee with access to inventory and the accounting records can steal the goods and make an entry to conceal the theft. For example, the employee could increase the amount of an inventory write-down to make it appear that goods decreased in value when in fact they were stolen.

Computerized inventory systems allow companies to minimize both the amount of inventory on hand and the chances of running out of stock (items 7 and 8). In an increasingly competitive business environment, companies cannot afford to have cash tied up in too much inventory.

Summary Problems for Your Review

Problem 1

Centronics Data Computer Ltd. reported a net loss for the year. In its financial statements, the company noted:

Balance Sheet
Current assets
Inventories (notes 1C and 2)..................................... $48,051,000

Note 1C: Inventories are stated at the lower of cost or market. Cost is determined on a first-in, first-out (FIFO) basis.

Note 2: Declining ... market conditions during [the] fiscal [year] adversely affected anticipated sales of the Company's older printer products; ... Accordingly, the statement of loss ... includes a [debit] of $9,600,000.

Required

1. At which amount did Centronics report its inventory, cost, or market value? How can you tell?
2. If the reported inventory of $48,051,000 represents market value, what was the cost of the inventory?

Problem 2

Beaver Building Supply Limited reported using the FIFO inventory method. Its inventory amount was $176 million.

Required

1. Suppose that during the period covered by this report, the company made an error that understated its inventory by $5 million. What effect would this error have on *cost of goods sold* and *gross margin* of the period? On *cost of goods sold* and *gross margin* of the following period? On *cost of goods sold* and *gross margin* of both periods combined?
2. When Beaver Building Supply reported the above amount for inventory, prices were rising. Would FIFO or LIFO have shown a higher gross margin? Why?

SOLUTIONS TO REVIEW PROBLEMS

Problem 1

1. Centronics reported its inventory at *market value*, as indicated by (a) their valuing inventories at LCM, and (b) the declining market conditions that caused the company to "include a [debit] of $9,600,000" in "the statement of loss." The company debited the $9,600,000 to a loss account or to cost of goods sold. The credit side of the entry was to Inventory—for a write-down to market value.

2. The cost of inventory before the write-down was $57,651,000 (i.e., $48,051,000 + $9,600,000). The $48,051,000 market value is what is left of the original cost. Thus the amount to be carried forward to future periods is $48,051,000.

Problem 2

1. Understating ending inventory by $5 million has the following effects on *cost of goods sold* and *gross margin*:

	Cost of Goods Sold	Gross Margin
Period during which error was made	OVERSTATED by $5 million	UNDERSTATED by $5 million
Following period	UNDERSTATED by $5 million	OVERSTATED by $5 million
Combined total	CORRECTLY STATED	CORRECTLY STATED

2. When prices are rising, FIFO results in higher gross margin than LIFO. FIFO matches against sales revenue the lower inventory costs of beginning inventory and purchases made during the early part of the period.

Summary

1. *Account for inventory by the perpetual and periodic systems.* Accounting for inventory plays an important part in merchandisers' accounting systems because selling inventory is the heart of their business. Inventory is generally the largest current asset on their balance sheet, and inventory expense—called cost of goods sold—is usually the largest expense on the income statements.

Merchandisers with high-price-tag items generally use the *perpetual inventory system*, which features a running inventory balance. In the past, most merchandisers handling low-price-tag items used the periodic system. Recent advances in information technology have led to replacement of periodic inventory systems with perpetual systems. A physical count of inventory is needed in both systems for control purposes.

2. *Apply four inventory costing methods: specific unit cost, weighted-average cost, FIFO, and LIFO.* Businesses multiply the quantity of inventory items by their unit cost to determine inventory cost. Inventory costing methods are *specific unit cost; weighted-average cost; first-in, first-out (FIFO) cost;* and *last-in, first-out (LIFO) cost.* Only businesses that sell unique items, such as automobiles and jewels, use the specific identification method. Most other companies use the other methods. FIFO reports ending inventory at the most current cost. LIFO reports costs of goods sold at the most current cost.

3. *Describe the income effects of the inventory costing methods.* When inventory costs increase, LIFO produces the highest cost of goods sold and the lowest income. FIFO results in the highest income. The weighted-average cost method avoids the extremes of FIFO and LIFO.

4. *Prepare a perpetual inventory record.* Some companies combine elements of the perpetual and periodic inventory systems at FIFO cost. Some companies keep perpetual inventory records at weighted-average cost, but few keep such records at LIFO cost.

5. *Apply to inventory the lower-of-cost-or-market rule.* The *consistency principle* demands that a business stick with rule inventory method it chooses. If a change in inventory method is warranted, the company must report the effect of the change on income. The *lower-of-cost-or-market rule*—an example of accounting *conservatism*—requires that businesses report inventory on the balance sheet at the lower of its cost or current replacement value.

6. Compute the effects of inventory errors on the cost of goods sold and on net income. Although inventory overstatements may be counterbalanced by inventory understatements in an adjacent period, effective decision making is aided by accurate inventory information.

7. Estimate inventory by the gross margin method. The *gross margin method* is a technique for estimating the cost of inventory. It comes in handy for preparing interim financial statements and for estimating the cost of inventory destroyed by fire or other casualties.

Self-Study Questions

Test your understanding of the chapter by marking the correct answer to each of the following questions:

1. Which of the following items is the greatest in dollar amount? *(p. 442)*
   a. Beginning inventory
   b. Purchases
   c. Cost of goods available for sale
   d. Ending inventory
   e. Cost of goods sold

2. Sound Warehouse counts 6,000 compact discs, including 1,000 CDs held on consignment, in its Halifax store. The business has purchased an additional 2,000 CDs on FOB destination terms. These goods are still in transit. Each CD costs $3.40. The cost of the inventory to report on the balance sheet is *(p. 440)*
   a. $17,000
   b. $20,400
   c. $23,800
   d. $27,200

3. The inventory costing method that best matches current expense with current revenues is *(p. 444)*
   a. Specific unit cost
   b. Weighted-average cost
   c. FIFO
   d. LIFO
   e. FIFO or LIFO, depending on whether inventory costs are increasing or decreasing

4. Why do companies prefer the LIFO inventory method during a period of rising prices? *(p. 444)*
   a. Higher reported income
   b. Lower reported income
   c. Lower cost of goods sold
   d. Higher ending inventory

5. The consistency principle has the most direct impact on *(p. 448)*
   a. Whether to include or exclude an item in inventory
   b. Whether to change from one inventory method or another
   c. Whether to write inventory down to a market value below cost
   d. Whether to use the periodic or the perpetual inventory system

6. Application of the lower-of-cost-or-market rule often results in *(pp. 450–451)*
   a. Higher ending inventory
   b. Lower ending inventory
   c. A counterbalancing error
   d. A change from one inventory method to another

7. An error understated ending inventory of 19X7. This error will *(pp. 451–453)*
   a. Overstate 19X7 cost of sales
   b. Understate 19X8 cost of sales
   c. Not affect owner equity at the end of 19X8
   d. All of the above

8. Beginning inventory was $35,000, purchases were $146,000, and sales totaled $240,000. With a normal gross margin rate of 35 percent, how much is ending inventory? *(pp. 453–454)*
   a. $25,000
   b. $35,000
   c. $97,000
   d. $181,000

9. The year-end entry to close beginning inventory in a perpetual inventory system is *(p. 441)*
   a. Income Summary XXX
      Inventory XXX

b. Inventory..   XXX

    Income Summary...   XXX

c. Either of the above, depending on whether inventory increased or decreased during the period

d. Not needed

10. Which of the following statements is true? *(p. 454)*

    a. Separation of duties is not an important element of internal control for inventories.

    b. The perpetual system is used primarily for low-unit-cost inventory.

    c. An annual physical count of inventory is needed regardless of the type of inventory system used.

    d. All the above are true.

Answers to the Self-Study Questions follow the Accounting Vocabulary.

Accounting Vocabulary

Conservatism *(p. 449)*
Consignment *(p. 440)*
Consistency principle *(p. 448)*
Disclosure principle *(p. 448)*
First-in, first-out (FIFO) method *(p. 442)*
FOB destination *(p. 440)*
FOB shipping point *(p. 440)*
Gross margin method *(p. 453)*
Inventory profit *(p. 444)*
Last-in, first-out (LIFO) method *(p. 443)*
Lower-of-cost-or-market (LCM) rule *(p. 450)*
Materiality concept *(p. 449)*
Periodic inventory system *(p. 438)*
Perpetual inventory system *(p. 437)*
Specific unit cost method *(p. 441)*
Weighted-average cost method *(p. 441)*

Answers to Self-Study Questions

1. c
2. a $(16,000 - 1,000) \times \$3.40 = \$17,000$
3. d
4. b
5. b
6. b
7. d
8. a $\$35,000 + \$146,000 = \$181,000$
   $\$240,000 - (.35 \times \$240,000) = \$156,000$
   $\$181,000 - \$156,000 = \$25,000$
9. d
10. c

ASSIGNMENT MATERIAL

Questions

1. Why is merchandise inventory so important to a retailer or wholesaler?

2. Suppose your company deals in expensive jewelry. Which inventory system should you use to achieve good internal control over the inventory? If your business is a hardware store that sells low-cost goods, which inventory system would you be likely to use? Why would you choose this system?

3. Identify the accounts debited and credited in the standard purchase and sale entries under (a) the perpetual inventory system, and (b) the periodic inventory system.

4. What is the role of the physical count of inventory in (a) the perpetual inventory system and (b) the periodic inventory system?

5. If beginning inventory is $10,000, purchases total $85,000, and ending inventory is $12,700, how much is cost of goods sold?

6. If beginning inventory is $32,000, purchases total $119,000, and cost of goods sold is $127,000, how much is ending inventory?

7. What role does the cost principle play in accounting for inventory?

8. What two items determine the cost of ending inventory?

9. Briefly describe the four generally accepted inventory cost methods. During a period of rising prices, which method produces the highest reported income? Which produces the lowest reported income?

10. Which inventory costing method produces the ending inventory valued at the most current cost? Which method produces the cost-of-goods-sold amount valued at the most current cost?

11. Why is LIFO the most popular method in the United States? Why is it so little used in Canada? Do these reasons accord with the notion that the inventory costing method should produce the most accurate data on the income statement?

12. Which inventory costing method produces the most accurate data on the balance sheet? Why?

13. What is inventory profit? Which method produces it?

14. How does the consistency principle affect accounting for inventory?

15. Briefly describe the influence that the concept of conservatism has on accounting for inventory.

16. Manley Ltd.'s inventory has a cost of $48,000 at the end of the year, and the current replacement cost of the inventory is $51,000. At which amount should the company report the inventory on its balance sheet? Suppose the current replacement cost of the inventory is $45,000 instead of $51,000. At which amount should Manley report the inventory? What rule governs your answers to these questions?

17. Gabriel Ltd. accidentally overstated its ending inventory by $10,000 at the end of period 1. Is gross margin of period 1 overstated or understated? Is gross margin of period 2 overstated, understated, or unaffected by the period 1 error? Is total gross margin for the two periods overstated, understated, or correct? Give the reason for your answers.

18. The market referred to in the lower-of-cost-or-market rule may have two meanings. Describe each of them.

19. Identify an important method of estimating inventory amounts. What familiar model underlies this estimation method?

20. A fire destroyed the inventory of Olivera Corp., but the accounting records were saved. The beginning inventory was $22,000, purchases for the period were $71,000, and sales were $140,000. Olivera's customary gross margin is 45 percent of sales. Use the gross margin method to estimate the cost of the inventory destroyed by the fire.

21. True or false? A company that sells inventory of low unit cost needs no internal controls over the goods. Any inventory loss would probably be small.

Exercises

Exercise 9-1 *Recording and reporting transactions under the perpetual and periodic inventory system* **(Obj. 1)**

Bar-Lev Enterprises Inc.'s accounting records yield the following data for 19X3:

Inventory, January 1	$98,000
Purchases of inventory (on account).......	1,613,000
Sales of inventory—1/2 on account;	
1/2 for cash (cost $1,539,000)	2,862,000
Inventory, December 31	?

Required

1. Journalize Bar-Lev's inventory transactions for the year—first under the perpetual system, then under the periodic system. Show all amounts in thousands.
2. Report ending inventory, sales, cost of goods sold, and gross margin on the appropriate financial statement (amounts in thousands). Show the computation of cost of goods sold in the periodic system.

Exercise 9-2 *Computing ending inventory by four method* **(Obj. 1)**

Bas Precision Instruments Ltd.'s inventory records for industrial switches indicate the following at October 31:

Oct.	1	Beginning inventory...................................	10 units @ $160
	8	Purchase...	4 units @ 160
	15	Purchase...	11 units @ 170
	26	Purchase...	5 units @ 176

Required

The physical count of inventory at October 31 indicates that eight units are on hand, and the company owns them. *Compute ending inventory and cost of goods sold using each of the following methods:*

1. Specific unit cost, assuming five $170 units and three $160 units are on hand
2. Weighted-average cost
3. First-in, first-out
4. Last-in, first-out

Exercise 9-3 *Recording inventory transactions* **(Obj. 2)**

Use the data in Exercise 9-2 to journalize, first for the perpetual inventory system, then for the periodic system:

1. Total October purchases in one summary entry. All purchases were on credit.
2. Total October sales in one summary entry. Assume the selling price was $300 per unit, and all sales were on credit.
3. October 31 entries for inventory. Bas Precision Instruments uses FIFO.

Exercise 9-4 *Converting LIFO financial statements to the FIFO basis* **(Obj. 3)**

Hennig Nursery Inc. reported:

Balance sheet	19X5	19X4
Inventories—note 4...	$ 67,800	$ 60,300

Income statement

Cost of goods sold..   399,600   381,400

Note 4: The company determines inventory cost by the last-in, first-out method. If the first-in, first-out method were used, ending inventories would be $6,100 higher at year end 19X5 and $3,500 higher at year end 19X4.

Required

Show the cost-of-goods-sold computations for 19X5 under LIFO and FIFO. Which method would result in higher reported income before taxes? Show the amount of the difference.

Exercise 9-5   *Note disclosure of a change in inventory method*   **(Obj. 3)**

A company has used the first-in, first-out inventory method for many years. At the start of the current year the company switched to the last-in, first-out method. This change decreased net income by $263,000. Write the note to disclose this accounting change in the company's financial statements.

Exercise 9-6   *Change from FIFO to LIFO*   **(Obj. 4)**

Walnut Lubricants Corp. is considering a change from the LIFO inventory method to the FIFO method. Managers are concerned about the effects of this change on reported pretax income. If the change is made, it will become effective on March 1. Inventory on hand at February 28 is $63,000. During March, Walnut managers expect sales of $250,000, net purchases between $159,000 and $182,000, and operating expenses of $83,000. Inventories at March 31 are budgeted as follows: FIFO, $85,000; LIFO, $78,000.

Required

Create a spreadsheet model to compute estimated net income for March under FIFO and LIFO. Format your answer as follows:

	A	B	C	D	E
1		**Walnut Lubricants**			
2		**Estimated Income under FIFO and LIFO**			
3		**March 19XX**			
4					
5		FIFO	LIFO	FIFO	LIFO
6					
7	Sales	$250,000	$250,000	$250,000	$250,000
8					
9	Cost of goods sold				
10	Beginning inventory	63,000	63,000	63,000	63,000
11	Net purchases	159,000	159,000	182,000	182,000
12					
13	Cost of goods available				
14	Ending inventory	85,000	78,000	85,000	78,000
15					
16	Cost of goods sold				
17					
18	Gross margin				
19	Operating expenses	83,000	83,000	83,000	83,000
20					
21	Net income before tax	$	$	$	$
22					

Exercise 9-7   *Computing the ending amount of a perpetual inventory*   **(Obj. 5)**

Music World Music Center Ltd. carries a large inventory of guitars, keyboards, and other musical instruments. Because each item is expensive, Music World uses a perpetual inventory system. Company records indicate the following for a particular line of Casio keyboards:

Date		Item	Quantity	Unit Cost
May	1	Balance	5	$90
	6	Sale	3	
	8	Purchase	11	95
	17	Sale	4	
	30	Sale	3	

Compute ending inventory and cost of goods sold for keyboards by the FIFO method. Also show the computation of cost of goods sold. Prepare a perpetual inventory card.

Exercise 9-8   *The effect of lower-of-cost-or-market on the income statement*   **(Obj. 5)**

From the following inventory records of Borg Corporation for 19X7, prepare the company's income statement through gross margin. Apply the lower-of-cost-or-market rule.

Beginning inventory (average cost)	300 @ $41.63	=	$ 12,489
(replacement cost)........	300 @ 41.91	=	12,573
Purchases during the year	2,600 @ 44.50	=	115,700
Ending inventory (average cost)	400 @ 45.07	=	18,028
(replacement cost)	400 @ 42.10	=	16,840
Sales during the year	2,500 @ 80.00*	=	200,000

*Selling price per unit.

Exercise 9-9   *Applying the lower-of-cost-or-market rule*   **(Obj. 5, 6)**

Imhoff Ltd.'s income statement for March reported the following data:

Income Statement

Sales revenue		$89,000
Cost of goods sold		
Beginning inventory...	$17,200	
Net purchases	51,700	
Cost of goods available for sale	68,900	
Ending inventory	23,800	
Cost of goods sold..		45,100
Gross margin...		$43,900

Before the financial statements were released, it was discovered that the current replacement cost of ending inventory was $20,400. Correct the above data to include the lower-of-cost-or-market value of ending inventory. Also, show how inventory would be reported on the balance sheet.

Exercise 9-10   *Correcting an inventory error*   **(Obj. 6)**

Rocky Mountain Auto Supply Ltd. reported the following comparative income statement for the years ended September 30, 19X8 and 19X7:

Rocky Mountain Auto Supply Ltd.
Income Statements
For the Year ended September 30,

	19X8		19X7	
Sales revenue		$137,300		$121,700
Cost of goods sold				
Beginning inventory	$14,000		$12,800	
Net purchases	72,000		66,000	
Cost of goods available	86,000		78,800	
Ending inventory	16,600		14,000	
Cost of goods sold.................		69,400		64,800
Gross margin.............................		67,900		56,900
Operating expenses		30,300		26,100
Net income before taxes............		$ 37,600		$ 30,800

During 19X8, accountants for the company discovered that ending 19X7 inventory was understated by $1,500. Prepare the corrected comparative income statement for the two-year period. What was the effect of the error on net income for the two years combined? Explain your answer.

Exercise 9-11   *Estimating inventory by the gross margin method*   **(Obj. 7)**

Jutzi Unpainted Furniture began April with inventory of $42,000. The business made net purchases of $37,600 and had net sales of $60,000 before a fire destroyed the company's inventory. For the past several years, Jutzi's gross margin on sales has been 42 percent. Estimate the cost of the inventory destroyed by the fire.

Challenge Exercises

Exercise 9-12   *Estimating inventory by the gross margin method*   **(Obj. 7)**

You are a claims investigator for All-Canada Insurance Co. You have been asked to investigate the loss claim filed by Jutzi Unpainted Furniture in Exercise 9-11. Your experience suggests to you that businesses such as Jutzi Unpainted Furniture have a markup of 50 percent or more.

Required

Why would Jutzi understate the gross margin? What might you do to verify the loss claim filed?

Exercise 9-13   *Inventory policy decisions*   **(Obj. 2, 3)**

For each of the following situations, identify the inventory method that you are using or would prefer to use, or, given the use of a particular method, state the strategy that you would follow to accomplish your goal.

a. Inventory costs are decreasing, and your company's board of directors wants to maximize income.

b. Inventory costs are increasing. Your company uses LIFO and is having an unexpectedly good year. It is near year end, and you need to keep net income from increasing too much.

c. Inventory costs have been stable for several years, and you expect costs to remain stable for the indefinite future. (Give your reason for your choice of method.)

d. Company management, like that of John Labatt Limited, prefers a middle-of-the-road inventory policy that avoids extremes.

e. Your inventory turns over very rapidly, and the company uses a perpetual inventory system. Inventory costs are increasing, and the company prefers to report high income.

f. Suppliers of your inventory are threatening a labor strike, and it may be difficult for your company to obtain inventory.

Problems (Group A)

Problem 9-1A   *Using the perpetual and periodic inventory systems*   *(Obj. 1)*

Elsinore Sporting Goods Ltd. began March with 50 units of inventory that cost $19 each. The sale price of each was $36. During March Elsinore completed these inventory transactions:

			Units	Unit Cost	Unit Sales Price
March	2	Purchase..	12	$ 20	$ 37
	8	Sale.......	27	19	36
	13	Sale.......	23	19	36
		....	1	20	37
	17	Purchase..	24	20	37
	22	Sale.......	31	20	37
	29	Purchase..	24	21	39

Required

1. The above data are taken from Elsinore's perpetual inventory records. Which cost method does Elsinore use?

2. Compute Elsinore's cost of goods sold for March under the
   a. Perpetual inventory system
   b. Periodic inventory system

3. Compute gross margin for March.

Problem 9-2A   *Computing inventory by three methods*   *(Obj. 2)*

Quality Vision Center Inc. began the year with 140 units of inventory that cost $79 each. During the year, Quality Vision made the following purchases:

Feb.	3	217 @ $81
Apr.	12	95 @ 82
Aug.	8	210 @ 84
Oct.	24	248 @ 87

The company uses the periodic inventory system, and the physical count at December 31 indicates that ending inventory consists of 229 units.

Required

Compute the ending inventory and cost of goods sold, amounts under (1) weighted-average cost, (2) FIFO cost, and (3) LIFO cost. Round weighted-average cost per unit to the nearest cent, and round all other amounts to the nearest dollar.

Problem 9-3A   *Computing inventory, cost of goods sold, and FIFO inventory profits*
(Obj. 2, 3)

Dave Delion Ltd. specializes in men's shirts. The store began operations on January 1, 19X1, with an inventory of 200 shirts that cost $13 each. During the year, the store purchased inventory as follows:

Purchase no. 1..	110 @ $14
Purchase no. 2..	80 @ 15
Purchase no. 3..	320 @ 15
Purchase no. 4..	100 @ 17

The ending inventory consists of 150 shirts.

Required

1. Complete the following tabulation, rounding average cost to the nearest cent and all other amounts to the nearest dollar:

	Ending Inventory	Cost of Goods Sold
a. Weighted-average cost........................	_____	_____
b. FIFO cost...	_____	_____
c. LIFO cost...	_____	_____

2. Compute the amount of inventory profit under FIFO.

3. Which method produces the most current ending-inventory cost? Which method produces the most current cost-of-goods-sold amount? Give the reason for your answers.

Problem 9-4A   *Preparing an income statement directly from the accounts*   **(Obj. 2, 3)**

The periodic inventory records of The Kitchen Cupboard Ltd. include the following accounts for one of its products at December 31 of the current year:

Inventory

Jan. 1	Balance	300 units @ $3.00 100 units @ 3.15 } 1,215	

Purchases

Feb. 6		800 units @ $3.15	2,520
May 19		600 units @ 3.35	2,010
Aug. 12		460 units @ 3.50	1,610
Oct. 4		800 units @ 3.70	2,960
Dec. 31	Balance		9,100

Sales Revenue

Mar. 12		500 units @ $4.10	2,050
June 9		1,100 units @ 4.20	4,620
Aug. 21		300 units @ 4.50	1,350
Nov. 2		600 units @ 4.50	2,700
Dec. 18		100 units @ 4.80	480
Dec. 31	Balance		11,200

Required

1. Compute the quantities of goods in (a) ending inventory, and (b) cost of goods sold during the year.

2. Prepare a partial income statement through gross margin under the weighted-average cost, FIFO cost, and LIFO cost methods. Round weighted-average cost to the nearest cent and all other amounts to the nearest dollar.

Problem 9-5A   *Converting a company's reported income from the LIFO basis to the FIFO basis   (Obj. 3)*

Shopper's Canada Corporation uses the LIFO method for inventories. In a recent annual report, Shopper's reported these amounts on the balance sheet (in thousands):

	End of Fiscal Year	
	19X6	**19X5**
Merchandise inventories..	$2,657	$2,613

A note to the financial statements indicated that if another method (assume FIFO) had been used, inventories would have been higher by $10 million at the end of fiscal year 19X6 and higher by $16 million at the end of 19X5. The income statement reported sales revenue of $14,740,000 and cost of goods sold of $9,786,000 for 19X6.

Required

1. Show the computation of Shopper's cost of goods sold and gross margin for fiscal year 19X6 by the LIFO method as actually reported.
2. Compute Shopper's cost of goods sold and gross margin for 19X6 by the FIFO method.
3. Which method produces the higher gross profit? Are inventory prices rising or falling between 19X5 and 19X6?

Problem 9-6A   *Using the perpetual inventory system; applying the lower-of-cost-or-market rule   (Obj. 4, 5)*

Northern Telecom Ltd. manufactures high-technology products used in communications and other industries. Assume the following data for Northern Telecom's product SR450:

		Purchased	**Sold**	**Balance**
Dec. 31,	19X1			110 @ $5 = $550
Feb. 10,	19X2	80 @ $6 = $480		
Apr.	7		160	
May 29		110 @ 7 = 770		
July 13			120	
Oct.	4	100 @ 9 = 900		
Nov. 22			80	

Required

1. Prepare a perpetual inventory record for product SR450, using the FIFO method.
2. Assume Northern Telecom sold the 160 units on April 7 on account for $13 each. Record the sale and related cost of goods sold in the general journal under the FIFO method.
3. Suppose the current replacement cost of the ending inventory of product SR450 is $305 at December 31, 19X2. Use the answer to requirement 1 to compute the lower-of-cost-or-market (LCM) value of the ending inventory.

Problem 9-7A   *Correcting inventory errors over a three-year period   (Obj. 6)*

The accounting records of the Harvey's restaurant chain show these data (in millions):

	19X3	19X2	19X1
Net sales revenue...................	$210	$165	$170
Cost of goods sold			
Beginning inventory..........	$ 15	$ 25	$ 40
Net purchases....................	135	100	90
Cost of goods available....	150	125	130
Less ending inventory......	30	15	25
Cost of goods sold	120	110	105
Gross margin	90	55	65
Operating expenses...............	74	38	46
Net income............................	$ 16	$ 17	$ 19

In early 19X4, a team of internal auditors discovered that the ending inventory of 19X1 had been understated by $8 million. Also, the ending inventory for 19X3 had been overstated by $5 million. The ending inventory at December 31, 19X2 was correct.

Required

1. Prepare corrected income statements for the three years.
2. State whether each year's net income as reported here and the related share-holders' equity amounts are understated or overstated. For each incorrect figure, indicate the amount of the understatement or overstatement.

Problem 9-8A *Estimating inventory by the gross margin method; preparing a multiple-step income statement **(Obj. 7)***

Assume Swiss Chalet estimates its inventory by the gross margin method when preparing monthly financial statements. For the past two years, gross margin has averaged 25 percent of net sales. Assume further that the company's inventory records for restaurants in Alberta reveal the following data:

Inventory, March 1	$ 392,000
Transactions during March	
Purchases..	6,585,000
Purchase discounts...	149,000
Purchase returns...	8,000
Sales...	8,657,000
Sales returns	17,000

Required

1. Estimate the March 31 inventory using the gross margin method.
2. Prepare the March income statement through gross margin for the Swiss Chalet restaurants in Alberta. Use the multiple-step format.

Problem 9-9A *Accounting for inventory by the periodic and perpetual systems, estimate inventory by the gross margin method **(Obj. 1, 7)***

The Raptors Company Inc. has a periodic inventory system and uses the gross margin method of estimating inventories for interim financial statements. The company had the following account balances for the fiscal year ended August 31, 19X5:

Merchandise inventory—Sept. 1, 19X4	$ 41,000
Purchases...	246,000
Purchases returns and allowances...	34,000
Transportation-in...	1,600
Sales..	374,000
Sales returns and allowances...	13,000

Required

1. Use the gross margin method to estimate the cost of the company's ending inventory, assuming the company has an average gross profit margin of 41 percent.

2. The company has done a physical count of the inventory on hand on August 31, 19X5. For convenience, this inventory was calculated based on the retail selling prices marked on the goods and amounted to $52,500. Use the information from part 1 to calculate the "cost" of the physical inventory count.

3. What is the company's estimated inventory shortage on a cost basis?

4. Give the summary journal entry(s) that would be appropriate if the company had used the perpetual inventory system, and the adjustment that would be required for the shortage.

5. Of what other use would this information be to the company?

Problem 9-10A   *Accounting for inventory by the perpetual system, applying the LIFO and FIFO costing methods, estimate inventory by the gross profit method* **(Obj. 1, 2, 7)**

The Coprice Company uses the perpetual inventory system for the purchase and sale of inventory and had the following information available from the accounts on October 31, 19X1:

Purchases/Sales		Number of Units	Cost/Selling Price per Unit
Oct. 1	Balance of inventory	2,600	$10
7	Purchased	4,000	$12
8	Sold	3,000	$17
12	Purchased	5,000	$11
16	Sold	6,000	$17
21	Purchased	3,000	$12
25	Purchased	7,000	$11
29	Sold	9,000	$17

Required

1. Calculate the cost of the ending inventory and the cost of goods sold in the month of October under each of the following inventory costing methods: (a) the LIFO method, (b) the FIFO method.

2. Prepare the journal entries required to record the transactions using the perpetual inventory system with FIFO costing.

3. An internal audit has discovered that two new employees—an accounting clerk and an employee from the purchasing department—have been stealing merchandise and covering up the shortage by changing the inventory records. For example, if 120 units were purchased at $10 per unit, they would record it as 100 units purchased at $12 per unit and then take the other 20 units.

   The internal auditors have examined accounting records prior to the employment of the two individuals and have noted that the company has an average gross profit margin of 45%. They estimate that 95% of the mis-costed units have been sold.

   Use the gross profit method to estimate the cost of the inventory shortage (under the FIFO costing method) and give the journal entry required to correct it.

4. What would be the effect on the net income for the year ending October 31, 19X1 if the inventory shortage had not been discovered? For the year ending October 31, 19X2?

(Group B)

Problem 9-1B   *Using the perpetual and periodic inventory systems*   *(Obj. 1)*

AAdvantage Luggage Company Ltd. began August 19X8 with 30 units of inventory that cost $40 each. The sale price of each was $70. During August AAdvantage completed these inventory transactions:

			Units	Unit Cost	Unit Sales Price
August	3	Sale	16	$40	$70
	8	Purchase	80	41	72
	11	Sale	14	40	70
			16	41	72
	19	Sale	9	41	72
	24	Sale	35	41	72
	30	Purchase	18	42	73
	31	Sale	6	41	72

Required

1. The above data are taken from AAdvantage's perpetual inventory records. Which cost method does AAdvantage use?

2. Compute AAdvantage's cost of goods sold for March under the
   a. Perpetual inventory system
   b. Periodic inventory system

3. Compute gross margin for August.

Problem 9-2B   *Computing inventory by three methods*   *(Obj. 2)*

Nemmer Electric Corp. began the year with 73 units of inventory that cost $26 each. During the year Nemmer made the following purchases:

Mar.	11	113 @ $27
May	2	81 @ 29
July	19	167 @ 32
Nov.	18	44 @ 35

   The company uses the periodic inventory system, and the physical count at December 31 indicates that ending inventory consists of 91 units.

Required

Compute the ending inventory and cost of goods sold amounts under (1) weighted-average cost, (2) FIFO cost, and (3) LIFO cost. Round weighted-average cost per unit to the nearest cent, and round all other amounts to the nearest dollar.

Problem 9-3B   *Computing inventory, cost of goods sold, and FIFO inventory profit*
   (Obj. 2,3)

Dorothy Thomson Beverage Distributors Ltd. specializes in soft drinks. The business began operations on January 1, 19X1, with an inventory of 500 cases of drinks that cost $2.01 per case. During the first month of operations, the store purchased inventory as follows:

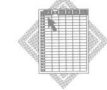

Purchase no. 1	60 @ $2.10
Purchase no. 2	120 @ 2.35
Purchase no. 3	600 @ 2.50
Purchase no. 4	40 @ 2.95

The ending inventory consists of 500 cases of drinks.

Required

1. Complete the following tabulation, rounding weighted-average cost to the nearest cent and all other amounts to the nearest dollar:

	Ending Inventory	Cost of Goods Sold
a. Weighted-average cost................................	_____	_____
b. FIFO cost..	_____	_____
c. LIFO cost..	_____	_____

2. Compute the amount of inventory profit under FIFO.

3. Which method produces the most current ending inventory cost? Which method produces the most current cost-of-goods-sold amount? Give the reason for your answers.

Problem 9-4B   *Preparing an income statement directly from the accounts*   **(Obj. 2, 3)**

The records of Dave Barr Golf Equipment Ltd. include the following accounts for one of its products at December 31 of the current year:

Inventory

Jan.	1	Balance	{700 units @ $7.00}	4,900	

Purchases

Jan.	6		300 units @ $7.05	2,115	
Mar.	19		1,100 units @ 7.35	8,085	
June	22		8,400 units @ 7.50	63,000	
Oct.	4		500 units @ 8.50	4,250	
Dec.	31	Balance		77,450	

Sales Revenue

			Feb.	5	1,000 units @ $12.00	12,000
			Apr.	10	700 units @ 12.10	8,470
			July	31	1,800 units @ 13.25	23,850
			Sept.	4	3,500 units @ 13.50	47,250
			Nov.	27	3,100 units @ 14.75	45,725
			Dec.	31	Balance	137,295

Required

1. Compute the quantities of goods in (a) ending inventory, and (b) cost of goods sold during the year.

2. Prepare a partial income statement through gross margin under the weighted-average cost, FIFO cost, and LIFO cost methods.

Problem 9-5B   *Converting an actual company's reported income from the LIFO basis to the FIFO basis*   **(Obj. 3)**

Colgate-Palmolive Canada uses the LIFO method for inventories. In a recent annual report, Colgate-Palmolive Canada reported these amounts on the balance sheet (in millions):

	December 31,	
	19X9	**19X8**
Inventories	$26	$28

A note to the financial statements indicated that if current cost (assume FIFO) had been used, inventories would have been higher by $1.2 million at the end of 19X9 and higher by $1.0 million at the end of 19X8. The income statement reported sales revenue of $244 million and cost of goods sold of $133 million for 19X9.

Required

1. Show the computation of Colgate-Palmolive Canada's cost of goods sold and gross margin for 19X9 by the LIFO method as actually reported.
2. Compute Colgate-Palmolive's cost of goods sold and gross margin for 19X9 by the FIFO method.
3. Which method makes the company look better in 19X9? Give your reason. What is the amount of inventory profit for 19X9?

Problem 9-6B   *Using the perpetual inventory system; applying the lower-of-cost-or-market rule*   *(Obj. 3, 6)*

Speedy is a popular brand of automobile mufflers. Assume the following data for a particular part at a Speedy Muffler shop:

		Purchased	**Sold**	**Balance**
Dec. 31,	19X3			120 @ $6 = $720
Mar. 15,	19X4	50 @ $7 = $350		
Apr. 10			80	
May 29		100 @ 8.50 = 850		
Aug. 3			130	
Nov. 16		70 @ 9 = 630		
Dec. 12			70	

Required

1. Prepare a perpetual inventory card for Speedy, using the FIFO method.
2. Assume Speedy sold the 130 units on August 3 on account for $22 each. Record the sale and related cost of goods sold in the general journal under the FIFO method.
3. Suppose the current replacement cost of the ending inventory of this Speedy shop is $750 at December 31, 19X4. Use the answer to requirement 1 to compute the lower-of-cost-or-market (LCM) value of the ending inventory.

Problem 9-7B   *Correcting inventory errors over a three-year period*   *(Obj. 6)*

The Scharr Custom Window Frames Corp. books show these data (in thousands):

	19X6		**19X5**		**19X4**	
Net sales revenue		$360		$285		$244
Cost of goods sold						
Beginning inventory	$ 65		$ 55		$ 70	
Net purchases	195		135		130	
Cost of goods available.........	260		190		200	
Less ending inventory	70		65		55	
Cost of goods sold.................		190		125		145

Gross margin..............................	170	160	99
Operating expenses....................	113	109	76
Net income	$ 57	$ 51	$ 23

In early 19X7, a team of internal auditors discovered that the ending inventory of 19X4 had been overstated by $12 thousand. Also, the ending inventory for 19X6 had been understated by $8 thousand. The ending inventory at December 31, 19X5 was correct.

Required

1. Prepare corrected income statements for the three years.
2. State whether each year's net income and owner's equity amounts are understated or overstated. For each incorrect figure, indicate the amount of the understatement or overstatement.

Problem 9-8B *Estimating inventory by the gross margin method; preparing a multiple-step income statement* **(Obj. 7)**

Assume Baldwin Piano Company Ltd. estimates its inventory by the gross margin method when preparing monthly financial statements. For the past two years, the gross margin has averaged 40 percent of net sales. Assume further that the company's inventory records for stores in British Columbia reveal the following data:

Inventory, July 1...	$ 267,000
Transactions during July	
Purchases...	3,789,000
Purchase discounts..	26,000
Purchase returns..	12,000
Sales...	6,430,000
Sales returns	25,000

Required

1. Estimate the July 31 inventory using the gross margin method.
2. Prepare the July income statement through gross margin for the Baldwin Piano stores in British Columbia. Use the multiple-step format.

Problem 9-9B *Accounting for inventory by the periodic and perpetual systems, estimate inventory by the gross margin method* **(Obj. 1, 7)**

The Dolphin Company Inc. has a periodic inventory system and uses the gross margin method of estimating inventories for interim financial statements. The company had the following account balances for the fiscal year ended August 31, 19X5:

Merchandise inventory—Sept. 1/X4.....................................	$ 38,000
Purchases..	327,000
Purchases returns and allowances......................................	47,000
Transportation-in...	2,400
Sales..	429,000
Sales returns and allowances...	18,000

Required

1. Use the gross margin method to estimate the cost of the company's ending inventory, assuming the company has an average gross profit margin of 45 percent.
2. The company has done a physical count of the inventory on hand on August 31, 19X5. For convenience, this inventory was calculated based on the

retail selling prices marked on the goods and amounted to $134,700. Use the information from part 1 to calculate the "cost" of the physical inventory count.

3. What is the company's estimated inventory shortage on a cost basis?

4. Give the summary journal entry(s) that would be appropriate if the company had used the perpetual inventory system, and the adjustment that would be required for the shortage.

5. Of what other use would this information be to the company?

Problem 9-10B *Accounting for inventory by the perpetual system, applying the LIFO and FIFO costing methods, estimate inventory by the gross profit method* **(Obj. 1, 2, 7)**

The Daltons Company uses the perpetual inventory system for the purchase and sale of inventory and had the following information available from the accounts on October 31, 19x1:

Purchases/Sales		Number of Units	Cost/Selling Price per Unit
Oct. 1	Balance of inventory	1,800	$12
7	Purchased	5,000	$11
8	Sold	4,000	$18
12	Purchased	3,500	$12
16	Sold	5,800	$18
21	Purchased	4,000	$13
25	Purchased	6,000	$14
29	Sold	8,000	$18

Required

1. Calculate the cost of the ending inventory and the cost of goods sold in the month of October under each of the following inventory costing methods: (a) the LIFO method, (b) the FIFO method.

2. Prepare the journal entries required to record the transactions using the perpetual inventory system with FIFO costing.

3. An internal audit has discovered that two new employees—an accounting clerk and an employee from the purchasing department—have been stealing merchandise and covering up the shortage by changing the inventory records. For example, if 130 units were purchased at $10 per unit, they would record it as 100 units purchased at $13 per unit and then take the other 30 units.

    The internal auditors have examined accounting records prior to the employment of the two individuals and have noted that the company has an average gross profit margin of 48%. They estimate that 90% of the mis-costed units have been sold.

    Use the gross profit method to estimate the cost of the inventory shortage (under the FIFO costing method) and give the journal entry required to correct it.

4. What would be the effect on the net income for the year ending October 31, 19X1 if the inventory shortage had not been discovered? For the year ending October 31, 19X2?

Challenge Problems

Problem 9-1C *Inventory measurement and income* **(Obj. 3)**

An anonymous source advised Revenue Canada that Mr. Joe Harrap, owner of Harrap's Grocery Store Ltd., has been filing fraudulent tax returns for the past several years. You, a tax auditor with Revenue Canada, are in the process of auditing

Harrap's Grocery Store Ltd. for the year ended December 31, 19X8. Harrap's tax returns for the past five years show a decreasing value for ending inventory from 19X3, when Mr. Harrap bought the business, to 19X7; the return for 19X8 shows the same sort of decrease. You have performed a quick survey of the large store and the attached warehouse and observed that both seemed very well stocked.

Required

Does the information set forth above suggest anything to you that might confirm the anonymous tip? What would you do to confirm or deny your suspicions?

Problem 9-2C   *Estimating inventory from incomplete records*   *(Obj. 7)*

It is Monday morning. You heard on the morning news that a client of your public accounting firm, Monarch Stereo Wholesalers Inc., had a fire overnight that destroyed Monarch's office and warehouse, and concluded that inventory records as well as inventory probably perished in the fire. Since you had been at Monarch on the previous Friday preparing the monthly income statement for the previous month which ended on Thursday, you realize you probably have the only current financial information available for Monarch Stereo.

Upon arrival at your firm's office, you meet your partner who confirms your suspicions. Monarch Stereo lost all their inventory and their records. She tells you that Monarch wants the firm to prepare information for a fire loss claim for Monarch's insurance company for the inventory.

You know the audit file for the fiscal year which ended three months earlier contains a complete section dealing with inventory and the four product lines Monarch Stereo carried including the most recent gross margin rate for each line. The file will show total inventory and how much inventory there was by product line at the year end. You also recall that the file contains an analysis of sales by product line for the past several years and that Monarch used a periodic inventory system.

Required

Explain how you would use the information available to you to calculate the fire loss by product line.

Extending Your Knowledge

Decision Problems

1. *Assessing the impact of a year-end purchase of inventory*   *(Obj. 2)*

Tailwind Cycling Center Ltd. is nearing the end of its first year of operations. The company made the following inventory purchases:

January	1,000	$100	$100,000
March	1,000	100	100,000
May	1,000	115	115,000
July	1,000	130	130,000
September	1,000	140	140,000
November	1,000	160	160,000
Totals	6,000		$745,000

Sales for the year will be 5,000 units for $1,200,000 revenue. Expenses other than cost of goods sold will be $200,000. The president of the company is undecided about whether to adopt FIFO or LIFO.

The company has storage capacity for 5,000 additional units of inventory. Inventory prices are expected to stay at $160 per unit for the next few months. The president is considering purchasing 4,000 additional units of inventory at $160 each before the end of the year. He wishes to know how the purchase would affect net income before taxes under both FIFO and LIFO.

Required

1. To help the company decide, prepare income statements under FIFO and under LIFO, both without and with the year-end purchase of 4,000 units of inventory at $160 per unit.

2. Compare net income before taxes under FIFO without and with the year-end purchase. Make the same comparison under LIFO. Under which method does the year-end purchase have the greater effect on net income before taxes?

3. Under which method can a year-end purchase be made in order to manipulate net income before taxes?

2. *Assessing the impact of the inventory costing method on the financial statements*   (Obj. 2, 3, 4)

The inventory costing method chosen by a company can affect the financial statements and thus the decisions of the users of those statements.

Required

1. A leading accounting researcher stated that one inventory costing method reports the most recent costs in the income statement, while another method reports the most recent costs in the balance sheet. In this person's opinion, this results in one or the other of the statements being "inaccurate" when prices are rising. What did the researcher mean?

2. Conservatism is an accepted accounting concept. Would you want management to be conservative in accounting for inventory if you were (a) a shareholder, and (b) a prospective shareholder? Give your reason.

3. Beechwood Ltd. follows conservative accounting and writes the value of its inventory of bicycles down to market, which has declined below cost. The following year, an unexpected cycling craze results in a demand for bicycles that far exceeds supply, and the market price increases well above the previous cost. What effect will conservatism have on the income of Beechwood over the two years?

Ethical Issue

During 19X6, Crocker-Hinds Company Inc. changed to the LIFO method of accounting for inventory. Suppose that during 19X7, Crocker-Hinds changes back to the FIFO method, and in the following year switches back to LIFO again.

Required

1. What would you think of a company's ethics if it changed accounting methods every year?

2. What accounting principle would changing methods every year violate?

3. Who can be harmed when a company changes its accounting methods too often? How?

Financial Statement Problems

1. Inventories   (Obj. 2, 3, 4)

The notes are an important part of a company's financial statements, giving valuable details that would clutter the tabular data presented in the statements. This problem will help you learn to use a company's inventory notes. Refer to the Mark's Work Wearhouse Ltd. statements and the related notes in Appendix A. Answer the following questions:

1. How much were Mark's Work Wearhouse's total inventories at January 29, 1994?
2. How does Mark's Work Wearhouse value its inventories? Which cost method does the company use?
3. Why do you think Mark's Work Wearhouse uses the inventory method that it does use?
4. By rearranging the cost-of-goods-sold formula, you can solve for net purchases, which are not disclosed in Mark's Work Wearhouse's statements. Show how to compute Mark's Work Wearhouse's net purchases for 1993 and 1994. Inventory on January 25, 1992, was $30,606,000.

2. Inventories   (Obj. 3, 4)

Obtain the annual report of an actual company *that includes inventories among its current assets.* Answer these questions about the company.

1. How much were the company's total inventories at the end of the current year? At the end of the preceding year?
2. How does the company value its inventories? Which cost method or methods does the company use?
3. Depending on the nature of the company's business, would you expect the company to use a periodic inventory system or a perpetual system? Give your reason.
4. By rearranging the cost-of-goods-sold formula, you can solve for net purchases, which are not disclosed. Show how to compute the company's net purchases during the current year. You should examine the company's note titled *Inventories, Merchandise inventories,* or by a similar term. If the company discloses several categories of inventories, including a title similar to Finished Goods, use the beginning and ending balances of Finished Goods for the computation of net purchases. If only one category of Inventories is disclosed, use these beginning and ending balances.

CHAPTER 10
Capital Assets, Intangibles, and Related Expenses

"Our resort development potential is virtually unlimited" says Joe S. Houssian, Chairman, President, and Chief Executive Officer of Intrawest Corporation. "The most talked about mountain resort development in the leisure world this past year is Tremblant, in the Laurentians of Quebec. This year's development activities at Tremblant represent the largest one-year program in the history of mountain development."

Intrawest Corporation is one of the leading companies in resort development in North America. The company's resorts include Blackcomb and Panorama in British Columbia and Tremblant in Quebec. It also has real estate developments in connection with those resorts and at other locations in Alberta, British Columbia, and Washington state.

Intrawest committed to spending $47 million to rejuvenate and expand the ski and resort facilities at Mont Tremblant. Expenditures on capital assets in 1993 were $18 million. The largest single component of the improvements was for snowmaking equipment. Mont Tremblant now has snowmaking capacity on 133 of its 175 hectares of skiable terrain. Intrawest expects a significant increase in skier visits and revenue as a result of these capital expenditures.

Source: *1993 Annual Report*, Intrawest Corporation, p. 43.

CHAPTER OBJECTIVES

After studying this chapter, you should be able to

1 Identify the elements of property, plant, and equipment's cost

2 Explain the concept of amortization (depreciation)

3 Account for depreciation by three methods

4 Identify the best depreciation method

for income tax purposes

5 Account for disposal of property, plant, and equipment

6 Account for wasting assets and amortization (depletion)

7 Account for intangible assets and amortization

What does it take for Intrawest to serve its more than a million skiers? Almost $150 million dollars invested in buildings, ski lifts and area improvements, and equipment. In Chapter 9 we looked at merchandise inventory. In this chapter we consider accounting for the long-term assets used in the operation of a business.

The revenue from Intrawest's ski and resort operations increased from $3 million in 1987 to almost $60 million in 1993, a twenty-fold increase. At the same time, it invested in capital assets to earn this revenue; capital assets increased from $45 million in 1987 to $137 million in 1993, an increase of just over 200 percent. The chapter-opening story indicates the sort of expenditure that was made.

The Intrawest annual report mentioned *capital expenditures*, a term used often in the business press. These are the costs of acquiring and adding to buildings, automobiles, and other long-lived assets. Capital expenditures are a major sign of growth in both business and nonprofit organizations such as churches, hospitals, and colleges and universities. Without capital expenditures, an organization falls behind its competitors. Intrawest and other leading companies work hard to keep that from happening.

Key Point:
Long-lived assets are often called long-term assets; property, plant, and equipment; or fixed assets.

Long-lived assets used in the operation of the business and not held for sale as investments are termed **capital assets**. They can be divided into property, plant, and equipment, wasting assets—for example, natural resources such as mining properties and oil and gas properties—and intangibles. *Property, plant*, and *equipment* and *wasting assets* are those long-lived assets that are tangible. Their physical form provides their usefulness. Of the capital assets, land is unique. Its cost is not amortized—expensed over time—because its usefulness does not decrease like that of other assets.

Key Point:
Land is not depreciated because it does not wear out as do buildings and equipment.

Intangible assets are useful not because of their physical characteristics, but because of the special rights they carry. Patents, copyrights, and trademarks are intangible assets. Accounting for intangibles is similar to accounting for property, plant, and equipment.

This area has its own terminology. The *CICA Handbook* uses the term **amortization** to describe the allocating of the *cost of a capital asset* over its useful life; companies in Canada more commonly use the terms shown in Exhibit 10-1 to describe amortization expenses with respect to the various capital assets listed.

The first half of the chapter discusses and illustrates how to identify the cost of property, plant, and equipment and how to expense its cost. The second half considers disposing of property, plant, and equipment and how to account for natural resources, intangible assets, and capital expenditures. Unless stated otherwise, we describe accounting in accordance with generally accepted accounting principles, as distinguished from reporting to Revenue Canada for income tax purposes.

EXHIBIT 10-1   *Terminology Used in Accounting for Capital Assets*

Asset Account on the Balance Sheet	Related Expense Account on the Income Statement
Land	None

Buildings, Machinery and Equipment,
    Furniture and Fixtures, and Land
    Improvements
	Depreciation

Wasting Assets (Natural Resources)	Depletion
Intangibles	Amortization

The Cost of Property, Plant, and Equipment

The cost principle directs a business to carry an asset on the balance sheet at the amount paid for it. The *cost of property, plant, and equipment* is the purchase price, taxes, purchase commissions, and all other amounts paid to acquire the asset and to ready it for its intended use. Because the types of cost differ for various categories of property, plant, and equipment, we discuss the major groups individually.

> **OBJECTIVE 1**
>
> Identify the elements of property, plant, and equipment's cost

Land

The cost of land includes its purchase price (cash plus any note payable given), brokerage commission, survey fees, legal fees, and any back property taxes that the purchaser pays. Land cost also includes any expenditures for grading and clearing the land, and for demolishing or removing any unwanted buildings.

The cost of land does *not* include the cost of fencing, paving, sprinkler systems, and lighting. These separate capital assets—called *land improvements*—are subject to amortization.

Suppose Intrawest signs a $300,000 note payable to purchase 100 hectares of land for subdivision into 5-hectare lots. The company also pays $10,000 in brokerage commission, $8,000 in transfer taxes, $5,000 for removal of an old building, a $1,000 survey fee, and $26,000 for the construction of fences, all in cash. What is the cost of this land?

Purchase price of land		$300,000
Add related costs:		
Brokerage commission	$10,000	
Transfer taxes	8,000	
Removal of building	5,000	
Survey fee	1,000	
Total incidental costs		24,000
Total cost of land		$324,000

Notice that all the costs except the cost of the fences is included in the cost of the land.

The entry to record purchase of the land is

Land	324,000	
Note Payable		300,000
Cash		24,000

Buildings

The cost of constructing a building includes architectural fees, building permits, contractors' charges, and payments for materials, labor, and overhead. The time between the first expenditure for a new building and its completion can be many months, even years, and the number of separate expenditures numerous. Computers keep track of these details efficiently and assist in monitoring costs as they accumulate.

When an existing building (new or old) is purchased, its cost includes the purchase price, brokerage commission, sales and other taxes, and cash or credit expenditures for repairing and renovating the building for its intended purpose.

Machinery and Equipment

Short Exercise:

Which of the following would you include in the cost of machinery: (1) installation charges; (2) testing of the machine; (3) repair to machinery due to installer's error; (4) first-year maintenance cost?

A: Include 1 and 2, not 3 or 4.

The cost of machinery and equipment includes its purchase price (less any discounts), transportation charges, insurance while in transit, sales and other taxes, purchase commission, installation costs, and any expenditures to test the asset before placing it in service.

Land Improvements

In the above example, the cost of the fences ($26,000) is not part of the cost of the land. Instead, the $26,000 would be recorded in a separate account entitled Land Improvements. This account includes cost for such other items as roads, driveways, parking lots and sprinkler systems. Although these assets are located on the land, they are subject to decay. Therefore their cost should be amortized. Also, the cost of a new building constructed on the land is a debit to the asset account Building.

Lump-Sum (or Basket) Purchases of Assets

Short Exercise:

How would a business divide a $120,000 lump-sum purchase price for land, building, and equipment with estimated market values of $40,000, $95,000, and $15,000, respectively?

A:

	Estimated Market Value	% of Total
Land	$ 40,000	26.7
Building	95,000	63.3
Equipment .	15,000	10
	$150,000	100

	Allocation of Purchase Price
Land	$ 32,000
Building	76,000
Equipment .	12,000
	$120,000

Businesses often purchase several assets (as a group or in a "basket") for a single amount. For example, a company may pay one price for land and an office building. The company must identify the cost of each asset. The total cost is divided between the assets according to their relative sales (or market) values. This allocation technique is called the *relative-sales-value method.*

Suppose Magna International Inc. purchases land and a building in Saint John for a Maritime plant. The building sits on 2 hectares of land and the combined purchase price of land and building is $280,000. An appraisal indicates that the land's market (sales) value is $30,000 and the building's market (sales) value is $270,000.

An accountant first figures the ratio of each asset's market price to the total market price. Total appraised value is $300,000. Thus land, valued at $30,000, is 10 percent of the total market value. Building's appraised value is 90 percent of the total.

Asset	Market (Sales) Value		Total Market Value		Percentage
Land	$ 30,000	÷	$300,000	=	10%
Building	270,000	÷	$300,000	=	90
Total	$ 300,000				100%

The percentage for each asset is multiplied by the total purchase price to give its cost in the purchase.

Asset	Total Purchase Price		Percentage		Allocated Cost
Land	$280,000	×	.10	=	$ 28,000
Building	$280,000	×	.90	=	252,000
Total			1.00		$ 280,000

Assuming Magna pays cash, the entry to record the purchase of the land and building is

Land	28,000	
Building...	252,000	
Cash		280,000

Amortization of Capital Assets

OBJECTIVE 2
Explain the concept of amortization (depreciation)

The process of allocating a capital asset's cost to expense is called *amortization* in Section 3060 of the *CICA Handbook*. The more common term used to describe the allocation of the cost when referring to capital assets such as property, plant, and equipment is *depreciation*, and that is the term we will use in this book. Depreciation is designed to match the expense of an asset against the revenue generated over that asset's life as the matching principle directs. Exhibit 10-2 shows this process for the purchase of a Boeing 737 jet by Canadian Airlines. The primary purpose of depreciation accounting is therefore to measure income. Of less importance is the need to account for the asset's decline in usefulness.

Suppose Mark's Work Wearhouse buys a computer to use in its accounting system. Mark's Work Wearhouse believes it will get four years of service from the computer which will then be worthless. Using straight-line depreciation (which we discuss later in this chapter), the business expenses one quarter of the asset's cost in each of its four years of use.

Let's contrast what depreciation accounting *is* with what it *is not*. (1) *Depreciation is not a process of valuation*. Businesses do not record depreciation based on appraisals of their capital assets made at the end of each period. Instead, businesses allocate the asset's cost to the periods of its useful life based on a specific depreciation method. (We discuss these methods in this chapter.) (2) *Depreciation does not mean that the business sets aside cash to replace assets as they become fully depreciated.* Establishing such a cash fund is a decision entirely separate from depreciation. *Accumulated depreciation* is that portion of the capital asset's cost that has already been recorded as an expense. Accumulated depreciation does not represent a growing amount of cash.

Determining the Useful Life of Property, Plant and Equipment

No asset (other than land) offers an unlimited useful life. For some property, plant, and equipment physical *wear and tear* from operations and the elements may be the important cause of depreciation. For example, physical deterioration takes its toll on the usefulness of Intrawest's Bombardier snow-grooming machines and the golf carts on its golf courses. The same is true of Mark's Work Wearhouse's store fixtures.

Assets such as computers, other electronic equipment, and airplanes may become *obsolete* before they physically deteriorate. An asset is obsolete when another asset can do the job better or more efficiently. Thus an asset's useful life may be much shorter than its physical life. Accountants usually depreciate computers over a

Key Point:
The total amount of depreciation recorded on an asset cannot exceed its depreciable cost. An asset can be used after it is fully depreciated.

EXHIBIT 10-2   *Depreciation and the Matching of Expense to Revenue*

Estimated useful life, 20 years

Annual revenue generated, $9 million

Annual depreciation expense, $1.6 million

Boeing 737 Cost, $32 million

short period of time—perhaps four years—even though they know the computers will remain in working condition much longer. Whether wear and tear or obsolescence causes depreciation, the asset's cost is depreciated over its expected useful life.

Measuring Depreciation

Key Point:
Three essential elements are used in determining depreciation expense: the asset's cost, estimated residual value, and estimated useful life.

To measure depreciation for a plant asset, we must know the asset's

1. Cost
2. Estimated useful life
3. Estimated residual value

We have already discussed cost, the purchase price of the asset.

Estimated useful life is the length of the service the business expects to get from the asset—an estimate of the asset's useful life. Useful life may be expressed in years, units of output, kilometers, or other measures. For example, the useful life of a building is stated in years. The useful life of a bookbinding machine may be stated as the number of books the machine is expected to bind—that is, its expected units of output. A reasonable measure of a delivery truck's useful life is the total number of kilometers the truck is expected to travel. Companies base such estimates on past experience and information from industry trade magazines and government publications.

Estimated residual value—also called *salvage value* or *scrap value*—is the expected cash value of the asset at the end of its *useful* life. For example, a business may believe that a machine's useful life will be seven years. After that time, the company expects to sell the machine as scrap metal. The amount the business believes it can get for the machine is the estimated residual value. In computations of depreciation, estimated residual value is *not* depreciated, because the business expects to receive this amount from disposing of the asset. The full cost of property, plant, and equipment is depreciated if the asset is expected to have no residual value. The asset's cost minus its estimated residual value is called the **depreciable cost**.

Of the factors entering the computation of depreciation, only one factor is known—cost. The other two factors—residual value and useful life—must be estimated. Depreciation, then, is an estimated amount.

OBJECTIVE 3

Account for depreciation by three methods

Depreciation Methods

Three methods for computing depreciation will be discussed in this text: straight-line, units-of-production, and declining-balance. These three methods allocate different amounts of depreciation expense to different periods. However, they all result in the same total amount of depreciation, the asset's depreciable cost over the life of the asset. Exhibit 10-3 presents the data used to illustrate depreciation computations by the three methods.

EXHIBIT 10-3   *Data for Depreciation Computations*

Data Item	Amount
Cost of truck...	$55,000
Estimated residual value	9,000
Depreciable cost	$46,000
Estimated useful life	
Years...	5 years
Units of production...	400,000 units (kilometers)

Straight-Line (SL) Method

In the **straight-line (SL) method**, an equal amount of depreciation expense is assigned to each year (or period) of asset use. Depreciable cost is divided by useful life in years to determine the annual depreciation expense. The equation for SL depreciation, applied to the truck data from Exhibit 10-3, is

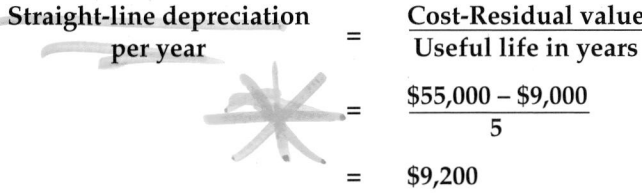

$$\text{Straight-line depreciation per year} = \frac{\text{Cost-Residual value}}{\text{Useful life in years}}$$

$$= \frac{\$55,000 - \$9,000}{5}$$

$$= \$9,200$$

The entry to record this depreciation is

Depreciation Expense	9,200	
Accumulated Depreciation		9,200

Assume that the truck was purchased on January 1, 19X1, and the business's fiscal year ends on December 31. A *straight-line depreciation schedule* is presented in Exhibit 10-4.

The final column of Exhibit 10-4 shows the asset's *book value*, which is its cost less accumulated depreciation. Book value is also called *carrying value.*

As an asset is used, accumulated depreciation increases and the book value decreases. (Compare the Accumulated Depreciation column and the Book Value column.) An asset's final book value is its *residual value* ($9,000 in Exhibit 10-3). At the end of its useful life, the asset is said to be fully depreciated.

Units-of-Production (UOP) Method

In the **units-of-production (UOP)** method, a fixed amount of depreciation is assigned to each unit of output produced by the capital asset. Depreciable cost is divided by useful life in units to determine this amount. This per-unit depreciation expense is multiplied by the number of units produced each period to compute depreciation for the period. The UOP depreciation equation for the truck data in Exhibit 10-3 is

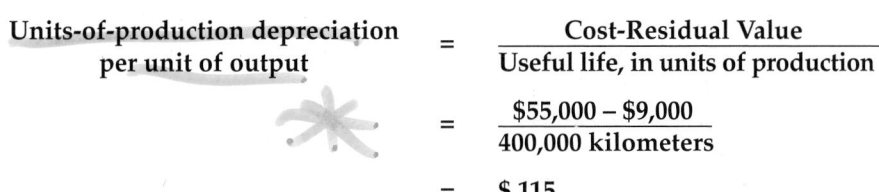

$$\text{Units-of-production depreciation per unit of output} = \frac{\text{Cost-Residual Value}}{\text{Useful life, in units of production}}$$

$$= \frac{\$55,000 - \$9,000}{400,000 \text{ kilometers}}$$

$$= \$.115$$

Short Exercise:

An asset with cost of $10,000, useful life of 5 years or 16,000 units, and residual value of $2,000 was purchased on 1/1. What was SL depreciation for the first year?

A: $1,600 ($10,000 − $2,000/5)

Short Exercise:

The asset in the preceding Short Exercise produced 3,000 units in the first year, 4,000 in the second, 4,500 in the third, 2,500 in the fourth, and 2,000 units in the last year. What was UOP depreciation for each year?

A: Depreciation per unit ($10,000 − $2,000)/ 16,000 = $0.50

Yr. 1:
$1,500 (3,000 × $0.50)

Yr. 2:
$2,000 (4,000 × $0.50)

Yr. 3:
$2,250 (4,500 × $0.50)

Yr. 4:
$1,250 (2,500 × $0.50)

Yr. 5:
$1,000 (2,000 × $0.50)

EXHIBIT 10-4 *Straight-Line Depreciation Schedule*

Date	Asset Cost	Depreciation Rate		Depreciable Cost		Depreciation Amount	Accumulated Depreciation	Asset Book Value
1-1-X1	$55,000							$55,000
12-31-X1		.20	×	$46,000	=	$9,200	$ 9,200	45,800
12-31-X2		.20	×	46,000	=	9,200	18,400	36,600
12-31-X3		.20	×	46,000	=	9,200	27,600	27,400
12-31-X4		.20	×	46,000	=	9,200	36,800	18,200
12-31-X5		.20	×	46,000	=	9,200	46,000	9,000

Assume the truck was driven 90,000 kilometers during the first year, 120,000 during the second, 100,000 during the third, 60,000 during the fourth, and 30,000 during the fifth. The UOP depreciation schedule for this asset is shown in Exhibit 10-5.

The amount of UOP depreciation per period varies with the number of units the asset produces. Note that the total number of units produced is 400,000—the measure of this asset's useful life. Therefore, UOP depreciation does not depend directly on time as the other methods do.

Declining-Balance (DB) Method

The **declining-balance method (DB)** is one of the accelerated-depreciation methods; the other is sum-of-years-digits, which is not widely used in Canada and so will not be discussed in this text. An **accelerated-depreciation method** writes off a relatively larger amount of the asset's cost nearer the start of its useful life than does straight-line. There are two methods in common use in Canada for computing DB depreciation; each is discussed in turn below.

Depreciation Based on Revenue Canada Rates　**Revenue Canada rates** are maximum depreciation rates for various capital assets that Revenue Canada will allow taxpayers (corporations and individuals) to use to compute deductions from income for income tax purposes. Depreciation allowed for income tax purposes is called **capital cost allowance**; and the rates allowed are called *capital cost allowance rates*.

Some typical Revenue Canada rates are

Automobiles	30%
Brick, concrete, or stone buildings	4
Computer software..	100
Office furniture and fixtures..	20
Video games, coin-operated	40

Thus, since the capital cost allowance rate allowed for automobiles is 30 percent, a company choosing to use the Revenue Canada rates would use a depreciation rate of 30 percent. Many companies, who use accelerated depreciation for accounting purposes, use the rates allowed by Revenue Canada for convenience. We now discuss the issue of depreciation and income taxes.

When a company uses the Revenue Canada rates, the annual depreciation is computed as follows:

First, the rate, which is obtained from Revenue Canada's *Income Tax Regulations*, is multiplied by the period's beginning asset book value (cost less accumulated depreciation).[1] The residual value of the asset is ignored in computing depreciation by the DB method except during the last year.

EXHIBIT 10-5　*Units-of-Production Depreciation Schedule*

		Depreciation for the Year				
Date	Asset Cost	Depreciation Per Unit	Number of Units	Depreciation Amount	Accumulated Depreciation	Asset Book Value
1-1-19X1	$55,000					$55,000
12-31-19X1		$.115 ×	90,000 =	$10,350	$10,350	44,650
12-31-19X2		.115 ×	120,000 =	13,800	24,150	30,850
12-31-19X3		.115 ×	100,000 =	11,500	35,650	19,350
12-31-19X4		.115 ×	60,000 =	6,900	42,550	12,450
12-31-19X5		.115 ×	30,000 =	3,450	46,000	9,000

[1] At the time of writing, Revenue Canada permits the taxpayer to use only 50 percent of the normal capital cost allowance in the first year and the full amount thereafter; for ease of computation in this chapter, we will claim full capital cost allowance every year it is claimed.

EXHIBIT 10-6 *Revenue Canada Rate Depreciation Schedule*

			Depreciation for the Year				
Date	Asset Cost	Depreciation Rate		Depreciable Cost		Depreciation Amount	Accumulated Depreciation	Asset Book Value
1-1-19X1	$55,000							$55,000
12-31-19X1		.30	×	$55,000	=	$16,500	$16,500	38,500
12-31-19X2		.30	×	38,500	=	11,550	28,050	26,950
12-31-19X3		.30	×	26,950	=	8,085	36,135	18,865
12-31-19X4		.30	×	18,865	=	5,660	41,795	13,205
12-31-19X5						4,205*	46,000	9,000

* Last-year depreciation is the amount needed to reduce asset book value to the residual value ($13,205 – $9,000 = $4,205).

Second, the final year's depreciation amount is used to reduce the asset's book value to its residual value. In Exhibit 10-6, the fifth and final year's depreciation is $4,205.

Double-Declining Balance (DDB)   This method involves computing annual depreciation by multiplying the asset's book value by a constant percentage, which is two times the straight-line depreciation rate. DDB rates are computed as follows:

First, the straight-line depreciation rate per year is computed. For example, a 5-year truck has a straight-line depreciation rate of $\frac{1}{5}$ or 20 percent. A 10-year asset has a straight-line rate of $\frac{1}{10}$ or 10 percent, and so on.

Second, the straight-line rate is multiplied by 2 to compute the DDB rate. The DDB rate for a 5-year asset is 40 percent (20% × 2 = 40%). For a 10-year asset the DDB rate is 20 percent (10% × 2 = 20%).

Third, the DDB rate is multiplied by the period's beginning asset book value (cost less accumulated depreciation). Residual value of the asset is ignored in computing depreciation by the DDB method, except during the last year.

The DDB rate for the truck in Exhibit 10-3 is

$$\text{DDB rate per year} = \left(\frac{1}{\text{Useful life in years}} \times 2\right) = \left(\frac{1}{5 \text{ years}} \times 2\right)$$

$$= (20\% \times 2) = 40\%$$

The DDB depreciation schedule for the asset is illustrated in Exhibit 10-7.

Fourth, the final year's depreciation amount is the amount needed to reduce the asset's book value to its residual value. In Exhibit 10-7, the fourth and second-last year's depreciation is $2,880 (the $11,880 book value less the $9,000 residual value). DDB can produce this result if the estimated residual value is much larger than 10 percent of the original cost.

Summary   The DB method differs from the other methods in two ways: (1) the asset's residual value is ignored initially (in the first year depreciation is calculated on the asset's full cost); (2) the final year's calculation is changed in order to bring the asset's book value to the residual value.

Most companies that use the DB method do not calculate depreciation on each capital asset separately, but rather they add the cost of each asset to a pool of similar assets and calculate depreciation on the undepreciated balance in the pool. This method is not as accurate as performing the individual calculations as illustrated in Exhibits 10-6 and 10-7, but it is much simpler and the degree of inaccuracy is small.

Short Exercise:
What is DDB depreciation of the asset in the Short Exercise at the top of page 483 for each year?
A:

Yr. 1:
$4,000 (10,000 × 40%)

Yr. 2:
$2,400 (6,000 × 40%)

Yr. 3:
$1,440 (3,600 × 40%)

Yr. 4:
$160 (2,160 – $2,000)*

* The asset is not depreciated below residual value.

 Key Point:
Rarely will the asset's book value equal its residual value in the final year. Depreciation expense in the final year is the amount that will reduce the asset's book value to the residual value.

EXHIBIT 10-7   *Double-Declining Balance Depreciation Schedule*

| | | | **Depreciation for the Year** | | | |
Date	Asset Cost	DDB Rate	Asset Book Value	Depreciation Amount	Accumulated Depreciation	Asset Book Value
1-1-19X1	$55,000					$55,000
12-31-19X1		.40	× $55,000 =	$22,000	$22,000	33,000
12-31-19X2		.40	× 33,000 =	13,200	35,200	19,800
12-31-19X3		.40	× 19,800 =	7,920	43,120	11,880
12-31-19X4				2,880*	46,000	9,000
12-31-19X5 **						

* Depreciation in year 19X4 is the amount needed to reduce asset book value to the residual value ($11,880 − $9,000 = $2,880).
**Because of the relatively high residual value, there would be no depreciation expense in the final year.

Comparison of the Depreciation Methods

Compare the three methods in terms of the yearly amount of depreciation:

| | | | **Amount of Depreciation per Year** | |
| | | | **Declining Balance** | |
Year	Straight-Line	Units-of-Production	Double-Declining-Balance	Revenue Canada Rates
1	$ 9,200	$10,350	$22,000	$16,500
2	9,200	13,800	13,200	11,550
3	9,200	11,500	7,920	8,085
4	9,200	6,900	2,880	5,660
5	9,200	3,450	—	4,205
Total	$46,000	$46,000	$46,000	$46,000

The yearly amount of depreciation varies by method, but the total $46,000 depreciable cost is expensed under all three methods.

Generally accepted accounting principles (GAAP) direct a business to match the expense of an asset to the revenue that the asset produces. For a capital asset that generates revenue fairly evenly over time, the straight-line method best meets the matching principle. During each period the asset is used, an equal amount of depreciation is recorded.

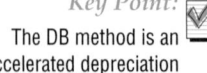

Key Point:
The DB method is an accelerated depreciation method. An accelerated method writes off more asset cost in the early years of an asset's life than in the later years. This method assumes that an asset is more useful (productive) in its early years and therefore should be depreciated more then.

The units-of-production method best fits those assets that wear out because of physical use, not obsolescence. Depreciation is recorded only when the asset is used, and the more units the asset generates in a given year, the greater the depreciation expense.

The declining balance or accelerated method applies best to those assets that generate greater revenue earlier in their useful lives. The greater expense recorded under the accelerated method in the early periods matches best against those periods' greater revenue.

Exhibit 10-8 graphs the relationship between annual depreciation amounts for straight-line, units-of-production, and the declining-balance methods. The graph of straight-line depreciation is flat because annual depreciation is the same amount in each period. Units-of-production depreciation follows no particular pattern because annual depreciation depends on the use of the asset. The greater the use, the greater is the amount of depreciation. Accelerated depreciation is greatest in the asset's first year and less in the later years.

EXHIBIT 10-8   *Depreciation Patterns Through Time*

Concept Highlight

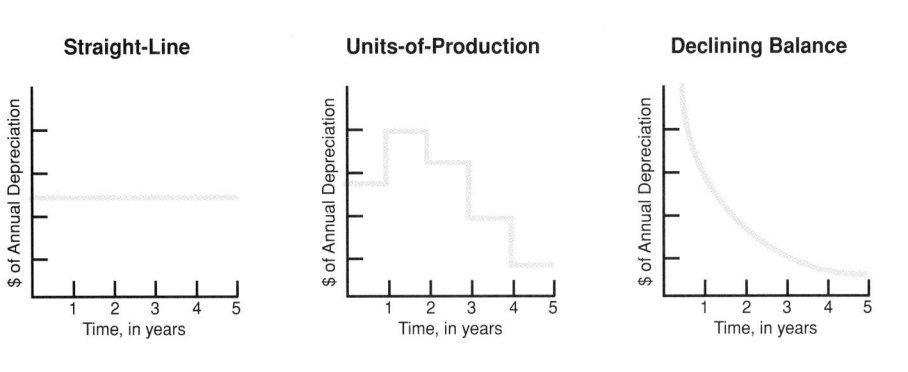

A recent survey indicated that over 87 percent of companies use the straight-line method, approximately 30 percent use an accelerated method, and approximately 23 percent use the units-of-production method. (Some companies use more than one method for different kinds of capital assets, so the total exceeds 100 percent.)[2] For example, John Labatt uses straight-line, while George Weston uses straight-line and units-of-production. Maclean Hunter uses straight-line for most fixed assets and declining-balance for some buildings, some equipment, and all vehicles.

Mid-Chapter Summary Problem for Your Review

Hubbard Corp. purchased office furniture on January 1, 19X5 for $44,000. The expected life of the furniture is 10 years and its residual value is $4,000. Under two depreciation methods, the annual depreciation expense and the balance of accumulated depreciation at the end of 19X5 and 19X6 are

	Method A		Method B	
Year	**Annual Depreciation Expense**	**Accumulated Depreciation**	**Annual Depreciation Expense**	**Accumulated Depreciation**
19X5	$4,000	$4,000	$8,800	$ 8,800
19X6	4,000	8,000	7,040	15,840

Required

1. Identify the depreciation method used in each instance, and show the equation and computation for each. (Round off to the nearest dollar.)
2. Assume continued use of the same method through the year 19X7. Determine the annual depreciation expense, accumulated depreciation, and book value of the equipment for 19X5 through 19X7 under each method.

[2] *Financial Reporting in Canada, 1993*, Twentieth Edition, Toronto: CICA, 1993, p. 154.

SOLUTION TO REVIEW PROBLEM

Requirement 1

Method A: Straight-line

Depreciable cost = $40,000 ($44,000 – $4,000)

Each year: $40,000/10 years = $4,000

Method B: Declining-balance (Revenue Canada rate)

Rate = 20%

19X5: .20 × $44,000 = $8,800

19X6: .20 × ($44,000 – $8,800) = $7,040

Requirement 2

	Method A Straight-Line			Method B Declining-Balance (Revenue Canada)		
Year	Annual Depreciation Expense	Accumulated Depreciation	Book Value	Annual Depreciation Expense	Accumulated Depreciation	Book Value
Start			$44,000			$44,000
19X5	$4,000	$ 4,000	40,000	$8,800	$ 8,800	35,200
19X6	4,000	8,000	36,000	7,040	15,840	28,160
19X7	4,000	12,000	32,000	5,632	21,472	22,528

Computations for 19X7

Straight-line:　　　　$40,000/10 years = $4,000

Declining-balance
(Revenue Canada):　　.20 × $28,160 = $5,632

Depreciation and Income Taxes

OBJECTIVE 4

Identify the best depreciation method for income tax purposes

The majority of companies use the straight-line method for reporting to their shareholders and creditors on their financial statements. But companies keep a separate set of records for calculating the capital cost allowance they claim on their tax return. The capital cost allowance rates published by Revenue Canada are maximums. A company may claim from zero to the maximum capital cost allowance allowed in a year. Most companies claim the maximum capital cost allowance using the Revenue Canada rates.

Suppose you are a business manager. Revenue Canada will allow you to use any one of the three methods we have discussed as long as the amount you are claiming does not exceed their maximum. Which method would you choose? You will probably choose Revenue Canada's capital cost allowance rate because it is the maximum allowed. It provides the largest deduction from income as quickly as possible, thus decreasing your immediate tax payments. The cash you save may be applied to best fit your business needs. This is the strategy most businesses follow.

To understand the relationships among cash flow (cash provided by operations), depreciation, and capital cost allowance and income tax, consider our earlier depreciation example. First-year depreciation is $9,200 under straight-line, while the maximum capital cost allowance allowed is $16,500. Assume the business has $400,000 in cash sales and $300,000 in operating expenses during the asset's first year, and the income tax rate is 25 percent. The cash flow analysis appears in Exhibit 10-9.

Exhibit 10-9 highlights several important business relationships. Compare the amount of cash provided by operations before income tax. Both columns show $100,000. If there were no income taxes, the total cash provided by operations would be the same regardless of the depreciation method used. Depreciation is a noncash expense and so does not affect cash from operations.

But, capital cost allowance is a tax-deductible expense. The higher the capital cost allowance, the lower the income before tax, and thus the lower the income tax payment. Therefore, using the maximum capital cost allowance available, the Revenue Canada rate helps conserve cash for use in the business. Exhibit 10-9 indicates that the business will have $1,825 more cash at the end of the first year if it uses RC depreciation instead of SL ($79,125 against $77,300). Suppose the company invests this money to earn a return of 10 percent during the second year. Then the company will be better off by $183 ($1,825 × 10% = $183). The cash advantage of using the RC method is the $183 of additional revenue.

Depreciation for Partial Years

Companies purchase capital assets as needed. They do not wait until the beginning of a year or a month. Therefore, companies must develop policies to compute *depreciation* for partial years. Suppose Nova Corporation of Alberta purchases a building as a maintenance shop on April 1 for $500,000. The building's estimated life

EXHIBIT 10-9 *Cash Flow Advantage of Declining-Balance (Revenue Canada—RC) Depreciation over Straight-Line (SL) Depreciation for Income Tax Purposes*

	Income Tax Rate 25 Percent	
	SL	RC
Revenues	$400,000	$400,000
Cash operating expense	300,000	300,000
Cash provided by operations before income tax	100,000	100,000
Capital cost allowance		
(Depreciation—a noncash expense)	9,200	16,500
Income before income tax	90,800	83,500
Income tax expense (25%)	22,700	20,875
Net income	$ 68,100	$ 62,625
Supplementary cash flow analysis		
Cash provided by operations		
before income tax	$100,000	$100,000
Income tax expense	22,700	20,875
Cash provided by operations	$ 77,300	$ 79,125
Extra cash available for investment		
if RC is used ($79,125 – $77,300)		$ 1,825
Assumed earnings rate		
on investment of extra cash		× .10
Cash advantage of using RC over SL		$ 183

Short Exercise:
Assume that the asset in the
Short Exercise on p. 485 was
acquired on 4/1. Compute SL
depreciation at 12/31 for the
life of the asset.

A: Yr. 1: $1,200 ($8,000/5
          = $1,600 × 9/12)
    Yr. 2–5: $1,600
    Yr. 6: $400 ($1,600
        × 3/12)

is 20 years and its estimated residual value is $80,000. Nova's fiscal year ends on December 31. Consider how the company computes depreciation for the year ended December 31.

Many companies compute partial-year depreciation by first computing a full year's depreciation. They then multiply this amount by the fraction of the year they held the asset. Assuming the straight-line method, the year's depreciation for the maintence shop is $15,750, computed as follows:

$$\frac{(\$500,000 - \$80,000)}{20} = \$21,000 \text{ per year} \times \frac{9}{12} = \$15,750$$

What if the company bought the asset on April 18? A widely used policy suggests businesses record no depreciation on assets purchased after the 15th of the month and record a full month's depreciation on an asset bought on or before the 15th. Thus the company would record no depreciation for April on an April 18 purchase. In this case, the year's depreciation would be $14,000 ($21,000 × 8/12).

How is partial-year depreciation computed under the other depreciation methods? Suppose this building is acquired on October 4, and the company uses the declining-balance (Revenue Canada) method. For brick buildings, the RC rate is 5 percent. The annual depreciation computations for 19X1, 19X2, and 19X3 are shown in Exhibit 10-10.

No special computation is needed for partial-year depreciation under the units-of-production method. Simply use the number of units produced, regardless of the time period the asset is held.

Most companies use computerized systems to account for fixed assets. They identify each asset with a unique identification number and indicate the asset's cost, estimated life, residual value, and depreciation method. The system will automatically calculate the depreciation expense for each period. Both Accumulated Depreciation and book value are automatically updated.

Change in the Useful Life of a Depreciable Asset _____

As previously discussed, a business must estimate the useful life of a capital asset to compute depreciation on that asset. This prediction is the most difficult part of accounting for depreciation. After the asset is put into use, the business is able to refine its estimate based on experience and new information. Such a change is called a change in accounting estimate. In an actual example, Electrohome Ltd. included the following note in a recent financial statement:

> **4. Changes in accounting estimates**
> ... The depreciation rate for broadcasting equipment was reviewed, and to represent more fairly the expected life of that equipment the rate was changed during the year from 25% to 20%. This change in accounting estimate has not been applied retroactively and has the effect of reducing depreciation expense for the current year by $108,000.

EXHIBIT 10-10   *Annual RC Depreciation for Partial Years*

Date	Asset Cost	Depreciation for the Year				Accumulated Depreciation	Asset Book Value Ending
		RC Rate	Asset Book Value— Beginning	Fraction of the Year	Depreciation Amount		
10-4-19X1	$500,000						$500,000
12-31-19X1		0.5 ×	$500,000 ×	3/12 =	$ 6,250	$ 6,250	493,750
12-31-19X2		.05 ×	493,750 ×	12/12 =	24,688	30,938	469,062
12-31-19X3		.05 ×	469,062 ×	12/12 =	23,453	54,391	445,609

Such accounting changes are common because no business has perfect foresight. Generally accepted accounting principles require the business to report the nature, reason, and effect of the change on net income, as the Electrohome example shows. To *record* a change in accounting estimate, the remaining book value of the asset is spread over its adjusted remaining useful life. The adjusted useful life may be longer or shorter than the original useful life. With computer-based systems, depreciation calculations resulting from revised useful lives or revised residual values are automatic and accurate.

Assume that a Big Rock Brewery Ltd. machine cost $40,000, and the company originally believed the asset had an 8-year useful life with no residual value. Using the straight-line method, the company would record $5,000 depreciation each year ($40,000/8 years = $5,000). Suppose Big Rock Brewery Ltd. used the asset for 2 years. Accumulated depreciation reached $10,000, leaving a book value of $30,000 ($40,000 – $10,000). From its experience with the asset during the first 2 years, management believes the asset will remain useful for an additional 10 years. The company would compute a revised annual depreciation amount and record it as follows:

Asset's Remaining Book Value	÷	(New) Estimated Useful Life Remaining	=	(New) Annual Depreciation Amount
$30,000	÷	10 years	=	$3,000

Yearly depreciation entry based on new estimated useful life is

Depreciation Expense—Machine	3,000	
Accumulated Depreciation—Machine		3,000

Short Exercise:

In 1974, ABC Ltd. purchased for $600,000 a building that had an estimated residual value of $100,000 and a life of 40 years. In 1994, a $200,000 addition to the building increased its residual value by $50,000. The accumulated depreciation on the building is $250,000. Calculate SL depreciation expense for 1994.

A: Calculate book value:
Cost (new) $800,000
Acc. Depr.   250,000
Revised book
  value $550,000
Revised SL depreciation
= $\frac{\$550,000 - \$150,000}{20}$
= $20,000

STOP & THINK

1. Suppose Hi Value Stores, Inc., was having a bad year—net income below expectations and lower than last year's income. For depreciation purposes Hi Value extended the estimated useful lives of its depreciable assets. How would this accounting change affect Hi Value's (a) depreciation expense? (b) net income? (c) owners' equity?

Answer: An accounting change that lengthens the estimated useful lives of depreciable assets (a) decreases depreciation expense and (b, c) increases net income and owners' equity.

2. Suppose that Hi Value's accounting change turned a loss year into a profitable year. Without the accounting change, the company would have reported a net loss for the year. But the accounting change enabled Hi Value to report net income. Under GAAP, Hi Value's annual report must disclose the accounting change and its effect on net income. Would investors evaluate Hi Value as better or worse in response to these disclosures?

Answer: Investors' reactions are not always predictable. There is evidence, however, that companies cannot fool investors. If investors have enough information—such as the knowledge of an accounting change disclosed in the annual report—they can process the information correctly. In this case, investment advisers would *probably* subtract from Hi Value's reported net income the amount caused by the accounting change. Investors could then use the remaining net *loss* figure to evaluate Hi Value's lack of progress during the year. Investors would probably view Hi Value worse for having made this accounting change.

Using Fully Depreciated Assets

A fully depreciated asset is one that has reached the end of its estimated useful life. No more depreciation is recorded for the asset. If the asset is no longer suitable for its purpose, the asset is disposed of, as discussed in the next section. However, the company may be in a cash bind and unable to replace the asset. Or the asset's useful life may have been underestimated at the outset. In any event, companies sometimes continue using fully depreciated assets. The asset account and its related accumulated depreciation account remain in the ledger, even though no additional depreciation is recorded for the asset.

OBJECTIVE 5

Account for disposal of property, plant, and equipment

Disposal of Property, Plant, and Equipment

Eventually, a capital asset ceases to serve a company's needs. The asset may have become worn out, obsolete, or for some other reason, no longer useful to the business. In general, a company disposes of the asset by selling or exchanging it. If the asset cannot be sold or exchanged, then the asset is junked. Whatever the method of disposal, the business should bring depreciation up to date to measure the asset's final book value properly.

To account for disposal, credit the asset account and debit its related accumulated depreciation account. Suppose the final year's depreciation expense has just been recorded for a machine that cost $6,000 and was estimated to have zero residual value. The machine's accumulated depreciation thus totals $6,000. Assuming this asset cannot be sold or exchanged, the entry to record its disposal is

Accumulated Depreciation—Machinery	6,000	
Machinery		6,000
To dispose of a fully depreciated machine.		

If assets are junked prior to being fully depreciated, the company records a loss equal to the asset's book value. Suppose Zellers' store fixtures that cost $4,000 are disposed of in this manner. Accumulated depreciation is $3,000 and book value is therefore $1,000. Disposal of these store fixtures is recorded as follows:

Accumulated Depreciation—Store Fixtures	3,000	
Loss on Disposal of Store Fixtures	1,000	
Store Fixtures		4,000
To dispose of store fixtures.		

Loss accounts such as Loss on Disposal of Store Fixtures decrease net income. Losses are reported on the income statement and are closed to Income Summary along with expenses.

Selling a Capital Asset

Suppose the business sells furniture on September 30, 19X4, for $5,000 cash. The furniture cost $10,000 when purchased on January 1, 19X1, and has been depreciated on a straight-line basis. Managers estimated a 10-year useful life and no residual value. Prior to recording the sale of the furniture, accountants must update depreciation. Since the business uses the calendar year as its accounting period, partial depreciation must be recorded for the asset's expense from January 1, 19X4, to the sale date. The straight-line depreciation entry at September 30, 19X4, is

Sept. 30 Depreciation Expense ($10,000/10 years × $\frac{9}{12}$)	750	
Accumulated Depreciation—Furniture		750
To update depreciation.		

After this entry is posted, the Furniture and the Accumulated Depreciation—Furniture accounts appear as follows. The furniture book value is $6,250 (i.e., $10,000 – $3,750).

Furniture		Accumulated Depreciation—Furniture	
Jan. 1, 19X1 10,000		Dec. 31, 19X1 1,000	
		Dec. 31, 19X2 1,000	
		Dec. 31, 19X3 1,000	
		Sept. 30, 19X4 750	
		Balance 3,750	

The entry to record sale of the furniture for $5,000 cash is

Sept. 30	Cash..	5,000	
	Loss on Sale of Furniture.................................	1,250	
	Accumulated Depreciation—Furniture..........	3,750	
	Furniture...		10,000
	To sell furniture.		

Short Exercise:

Equipment with original cost of $10,000, residual value of $2,000, and 5-year life was sold on 3/31/X3 for $6,400. Accumulated depreciation (SL method) on the asset was $2,500 as of 12/31/X2. Record the sale.

A: First, calculate depreciation from 12/31/X2 to 3/31/X3: ($10,000 – $2,000)/5 × 3/12 = $400. Add this figure to the $2,500 as of 12/31/X2 to bring accumulated depreciation as of 3/31/X3 to $2,900.

Now, make the entry:

Cash................. 6,400
Acc. Depr. 2,900
Loss on Sale ...   700
  Equipment...   10,000

When recording the sale of a capital asset, the business must remove the balances in the asset account (Furniture, in this case) and its related accumulated depreciation account, and also record a gain or a loss if the amount of cash received differs from the asset's book value. In our example, cash of $5,000 is less than the book value of the furniture, $6,250. The result is a loss of $1,250.

If the sale price had been $7,000, the business would have had a gain of $750 (Cash, $7,000 – asset book value, $6,250). The entry to record this transaction would be

Sept. 30	Cash..	7,000	
	Accumulated Depreciation—Furniture..........	3,750	
	Furniture...		10,000
	Gain on Sale of Furniture............................		750
	To sell furniture.		

A gain is recorded when an asset is sold for a price greater than the asset's book value. A loss is recorded when the sale price is less than book value. Gains increase net income. Gains and losses are reported on the income statement and closed to Income Summary along with the revenues.

Exchanging Capital Assets

Businesses often exchange (trade in) their old capital assets for similar assets that are newer and more efficient. For example, a Pizza Pizza restaurant may decide to trade in its 5-year-old delivery car for a new model. To record the exchange, the business must remove from the books the balances for the asset being exchanged and its related accumulated depreciation account.

Assume that Pizza Pizza's old delivery car cost $11,000 and has accumulated depreciation totaling $10,000. The book value, then, is $1,000. The new delivery car, say, a Ford Escort, costs $16,000, and the auto dealer offers a $1,000 trade-in allowance. Pizza Pizza pays cash for the remaining $15,000. The trade-in is recorded with this entry:

Delivery Auto (new)..	16,000	
Accumulated Depreciation—Delivery Auto (old)...........	10,000	
Delivery Auto (old)..		11,000
Cash ($16,000 – $1,000)...		15,000

In this example, the book value and the trade-in allowance are both $1,000, and so no gain or loss occurs on the exchange. Usually, however, an exchange results in a gain or a loss. If the trade-in allowance received is greater than the book value of the asset being given, the business has a gain. If the trade-in allowance received is less than the book value of the asset given, the business has a loss. However, generally accepted accounting principles do not allow losses and gains to be recognized on the exchange of *similar* assets; the cost of the new asset is adjusted to reflect the loss or gain. Gains or losses are allowed on the exchange of *dissimilar* assets. We now turn to the entries for gains and losses on exchanges, continuing our delivery-car example and its data.[3]

Situation 1   Loss on Asset Exchange

Assume that the new Escort has a cash price of $16,000, and the dealer gives a trade-in allowance of $600 on the old vehicle. The pizzeria pays the balance, $15,400 in cash. The loss on the exchange is $400 (book value of old asset given, $1,000, minus trade-in allowance received, $600). The acquisition price of the new automobile is adjusted to reflect the loss, and is $16,400 (i.e., $16,000 + 400). The entry to record this exchange is

Delivery Auto (new)	16,400	
Accumulated Depreciation—Delivery Auto (old)	10,000	
Delivery Auto (old)		11,000
Cash		15,400

Situation 2   Gain on Asset Exchange

Assume that the new Escort's cash price is $16,000, and the dealer gives a $1,300 trade-in allowance. The pizzeria pays the balance in cash. The gain is $300 (trade-in allowance received, $1,300, minus book value of old asset given, $1,000). The acquisition price of the new automobile is $15,700 (i.e., $16,000 − $300). The entry to record this exchange is

Delivery Auto (new)	15,700	
Accumulated Depreciation—Delivery Auto (old)	10,000	
Delivery Auto (old)		11,000
Cash		14,700

STOP & THINK

Suppose Loblaw Companies Limited's comparative income statement for two years included these items:

	19X2	19X1
	($ billions)	
Net sales	$9.4	$9.3
Income from operations	$0.2	$0.5
Gain on sale of store facilities	4	
Income before income taxes	$0.6	$0.5

Which was a better year for Loblaws—19X2 or 19X1?

Answer: From a *sales* standpoint 19X2 was better because sales were higher. But from an *income* standpoint, 19X1 was the better year. In 19X1, merchandising operations—Loblaw's main business—generated $.5 billion of income before interest and taxes. In 19X2, merchandising produced only $0.2 billion of pre-interest and taxes income. Most of the company's income came from selling store facilities. A business cannot hope to continue on this path very long. This example illustrates why investors and creditors are interested in the sources of a company's profits, not just the final amount of net income.

---

[3] GAAP rules for exchanges may differ from income tax rules. In this discussion, we are concerned with the accounting rules.

Internal Control of Capital Assets

Internal control of capital assets includes safeguarding them and having an adequate accounting system. To see the need for controlling capital assets, consider the following real situation. The home office and top managers of Petrol Mfg. Ltd. are in Calgary. The company manufactures gas pumps in Michigan, which are sold in Europe. Top managers and owners of the company rarely see the manufacturing plant and therefore cannot control capital assets by on-the-spot management. What features does their internal control need?

Safeguarding capital assets includes:

1. Assigning responsibility for custody of the assets.
2. Separating custody of assets from accounting for the assets. (This is a cornerstone of internal control in almost every area.)
3. Setting up security measures—for instance, guards and restricted access to capital assets—to prevent theft.
4. Protecting them from the elements (rain, snow, and so on).
5. Having adequate insurance against fire, storm, and other casualty losses.
6. Training operating personnel in the proper use of the asset.
7. Keeping a regular maintenance schedule.

Capital assets are controlled in much the same way that high-priced inventory is controlled—with the help of subsidiary records. For capital assets, companies use a capital asset ledger. Each capital asset is represented by a card describing the asset, and listing its location and the employee responsible for it. These details aid in safeguarding the asset. The ledger card also shows the asset's cost, useful life, and other accounting data. Exhibit 10-11 could be an example for the clothing racks in an Eaton's store.

The ledger card provides the data for computing depreciation on the asset. It serves as a subsidiary record of accumulated depreciation. The asset balance ($19,000) and accumulated depreciation amount ($4,500) agree with the balances in the respective general ledger accounts (Store Fixtures and Accumulated Depreciation—Store Fixtures).

EXHIBIT 10-11 *Capital Asset Ledger Card*

Asset __Clothing racks__   Location __Women's better dresses__

Employee responsible for the asset __Department manager__

Cost __$19,000__   Purchased From __Boone Supply Co. Ltd.__

Depreciation Method __SL__

Useful Life __10 years__   Resale Value __$1,000__

General Ledger Account __Store fixtures__

Date	Explanation	Asset Dr	Asset Cr	Asset Bal	Accumulated Depreciation Dr	Accumulated Depreciation Cr	Accumulated Depreciation Bal
July 3, 19X4	Purchase	19,000		19,000			
Dec. 31, 19X4	Deprec.					900	900
Dec. 31, 19X5	Deprec.					1,800	2,700
Dec. 31, 19X6	Deprec.					1,800	4,500

OBJECTIVE 6

Account for wasting assets and amortization (depletion)

Accounting for Wasting Assets and Depletion

Wasting assets or **natural resources** such as iron ore, coal, oil, gas, and timber are capital assets of a special type. An investment in natural resources could be described as an investment in inventories in the ground (coal) or on top of the ground (timber). As capital assets (such as machines) are expensed or amortized through depreciation, natural resource assets are expensed through depletion. **Depletion expense** is that portion of the cost of natural resources that is used up in a particular period. Depletion expense is computed in the same way as *units-of-production* depreciation.

An oil well may cost $100,000 and contain an estimated 10,000 barrels of oil. The depletion rate would be $10 per barrel ($100,000/10,000 barrels). If 3,000 barrels are extracted during the first year, depletion expense is $30,000 (i.e., 3,000 barrels × $10 per barrel). The depletion entry for the year is

Depletion Expense (3,000 barrels × $10)............................	30,000	
Accumulated Depletion—Oil		30,000

Short Exercise:

Pulp Products purchases for $500,000 land that contains an estimated 500,000 board feet of timber. The land can be sold for $100,000 after the timber has been cut. If Pulp harvests 200,000 board feet in the year of purchase, how much depletion should be recorded?

A: $160,000 ($500,000 − $100,000/ 500,000 = $0.80/board ft. × 200,000)

If 4,500 barrels are removed the second year, that period's depletion is $45,000 (4,500 barrels × $10 per barrel). Accumulated Depletion is a contra account similar to Accumulated Depreciation.

Natural resource assets can be reported as follows:

Capital Assets		
Property, plant, and equipment		
Land		$120,000
Buildings	$800,000	
Equipment..	160,000	
	960,000	
Less: Accumulated depreciation...............................	410,000	
Total property, plant, and equipment		550,000
Oil and Gas Properties		
Oil...	$340,000	
Less: Accumulated depletion*	90,000	
Total Oil and Gas Properties......................................		250,000
Total Capital Assets		$920,000

* Includes the $30,000 recorded above.

Future Removal and Site Restoration Costs There is increasing concern by individuals and governments about the environment. Often, in the past, a company exploiting natural resources, such as a mining company, would simply abandon the site once the ore body was played out. Now, there is legislation in most jurisdictions requiring a natural resource company to remove buildings, equipment, and waste, and to restore the site once a location is to be dismantled and abandoned.

The costs of future removal and site restoration at a property are a charge against all revenues earned from that property; matching suggests that such costs should be accumulated over the economic life of the location. The *CICA Handbook* in Section 3060 requires a natural resource company to accrue future removal and site restoration costs net of expected recoveries by charging income "in a rational and systematic manner." The accrual should be shown as a liability on the balance sheet. When the costs cannot be reasonably determined, a contingent liability should be disclosed in the notes to the financial statements.

OBJECTIVE 7

Account for intangible assets and amortization

Accounting for Intangible Assets and Amortization _____

Intangible assets are a class of long-lived assets that are not physical in nature. Instead, these assets consist of special rights to current and expected future benefits from patents, copyrights, trademarks, franchises, leaseholds, and goodwill.

The acquisition cost of an intangible asset is debited to an asset account. The intangible is expensed through amortization, the systematic reduction of a lump-sum amount. Amortization applies to intangible assets in the same way depreciation applies to property, plant, and equipment, and depletion applies to wasting assets.

Amortization is generally computed on a straight-line basis over the asset's estimated useful life—up to a maximum of 40 years, according to GAAP. But, obsolescence often cuts an intangible asset's useful life shorter than its legal life. Amortization expense for intangibles is written off directly against the intangible asset account rather than held in an accumulated amortization account. The residual value of most intangible assets is zero.

Assume that a business purchases a patent on a special manufacturing process. Legally, the patent may run for 17 years. However, the business realizes that new technologies will limit the patented process's life to 4 years. If the patent cost $80,000, each year's amortization expense is $20,000 ($80,000/4). The balance sheet reports the patent at its acquisition cost less amortization expense to date. After 1 year, the patent has a $60,000 balance ($80,000 – $20,000), after 2 years a $40,000 balance, and so on.

Patents are federal government grants giving a holder the exclusive right for 17 years to produce and sell an invention. Patented products include Bombardier Skidoos and the Spar Aerospace "Canadarm" used on the NASA space shuttle flights which you probably have seen on television. Like any other asset, a patent may be purchased. Suppose a company pays $170,000 to acquire a patent, and the business believes the expected useful life of the patent is only 5 years. Amortization expense is $34,000 per year ($170,000/5 years). The company's acquisition and amortization entries for this patent are

Real-World Example:
Companies protect their exclusive rights to an invention. Polaroid Corporation filed suit against Eastman Kodak Company, charging an infringement of certain Polaroid patents for instant cameras and instant film. Polaroid sought an injunction and damages. An injunction prohibited Kodak from manufacturing and selling such products in the U.S. Eastman Kodak appealed the injunction, but the appeal was denied.

Jan.	1	Patent...	170,000	
		Cash		170,000
		To acquire a patent.		
Dec.	31	Amortization Expense		
		—Patents ($170,000/5).................................	34,000	
		Patent...		34,000
		To amortize the cost of a patent.		

Copyrights are exclusive rights to reproduce and sell a book, musical composition, film, or other work of art. Issued by the federal government, copyrights extend 50 years beyond the author's, composer's, or artist's life. The cost of obtaining a copyright from the government is low, but a company may pay a large sum to purchase an existing copyright from the owner. For example, a publisher may pay the author of a popular novel $1 million or more for the book's copyright. The useful life of a copyright for a popular book may be usually no longer than two or three years, so that each period's amortization amount is a considerable portion of the copyright's cost; on the other hand, some copyrights, especially of musical compositions, such as works by the Beatles, seem to be popular over several decades.

Trademarks and **trade names** (or **brand names**) are distinctive identifications of products or services. For example, The Sports Network has its distinct logo of the yellow letters TSN on a black background shaped like a television screen; Apple Computer has the multi-colored apple with a bite out of it; and the Edmonton Oilers and Toronto Blue Jays have insignia that identify their respective teams. Molson Export, Swiss Chalet chicken, Petro-Canada, and Roots are everyday trade names. Advertising slogans such as Speedy Muffler's "At Speedy you're a somebody," or Shoppers Drug Mart's "Everything you want in a drugstore" are also legally protected.

The cost of a trademark or trade name is amortized over its useful life, not to exceed 40 years. The cost of advertising and promotions that use the trademark or trade name is not a part of the asset's cost but a debit to the advertising expense account.

Franchises and **licenses** are privileges granted by a private business or a government to sell a product or service in accordance with specified conditions. The Calgary Flames hockey organization is a franchise granted to its owners by the National Hockey League. IGA Food Markets and Re/Max Ltd. are well-known franchises. Union Gas holds a franchise to provide gas to residents and businesses in certain parts of the country. The acquisition costs of franchises and licenses are amortized over their useful lives rather than over legal lives, subject to the 40-year maximum.

A **leasehold** is a prepayment that a lessee (renter) makes to secure the use of an asset from a lessor (landlord). For example, most malls lease the space to the mall stores and shops that you visit. Often leases require the lessee to make this prepayment in addition to monthly rental payments. The lessee debits the monthly lease payments to the Rent Expense account. The prepayment, however, is a debit to an intangible asset account entitled Leaseholds. This amount is amortized over the life of the lease by debiting Rent Expense and crediting Leaseholds. Some leases stipulate that the last year's rent must be paid in advance when the lease is signed. This prepayment is debited to Leaseholds and transferred to Rent Expense during the last year of the lease.

Sometimes lessees modify or improve the leased asset. For example, a lessee may construct a fence on leased land. The lessee debits the cost of the fence to a separate intangible asset account, Leasehold Improvements, and amortizes its cost over the term of the lease.

Goodwill in accounting is a more limited term than in everyday use, as in "goodwill among men." In accounting, **goodwill** is defined as the excess of the cost of an acquired company over the sum of the market values of its net assets (assets minus liabilities). Suppose James Richardson & Sons Ltd. acquires Manitoba Express Ltd. at a cost of $10 million. The market value of Manitoba Express's assets is $9 million, and its liabilities total $1 million. In this case, Richardson paid $2 million for goodwill, computed as follows:

Purchase price paid for Manitoba Express Ltd.		$10 million
Sum of the market value of Manitoba Express Ltd.'s assets	$9 million	
Less: Manitoba Express Ltd.'s liabilities....................	1 million	
Market value of Manitoba Express Ltd.'s net assets		8 million
Excess is called *goodwill*		$ 2 million

James Richardson's entry to record the acquisition of Manitoba Express, including its goodwill, would be

Assets (Cash, Receivables, Inventories, Capital Assets, all at market value)	9,000,000	
Goodwill	2,000,000	
Liabilities...		1,000,000
Cash		10,000,000

Goodwill has the following special features:

1. Goodwill is recorded, at its cost, only when it is purchased in the acquisition of another company. Even though a favorable location, a superior product, or an outstanding reputation may create goodwill for a company, it is never recorded by that entity. Instead, goodwill is recorded only by the aquiring company. A purchase transaction provides objective evidence of the value of the goodwill.

2. According to generally accepted accounting principles, goodwill is amortized on a straight-line basis over a period of not less than two years and not to exceed 40 years. In reality, the goodwill of many entities increases in value. Nevertheless, the CICA's Accounting Standards Board specified in Section 1580 that goodwill should be amortized to income on a straight-line basis over the goodwill's expected life. The section prohibits a lump-sum write-off of the cost of goodwill in the year of acquisition either on the income statement or to owners' equity.

International Accounting   Companies in Germany (such as BMW and Volkswagen), in Great Britain (such as British Petroleum and British Airways), and in most other European nations do not have to record goodwill when they purchase another business. Instead they may debit the cost of goodwill directly to owners' equity. These companies never have to amortize the cost of goodwill, so their net income is higher than a Canadian or American company's would be. Canadian and American companies often cry "foul" when bidding against a European firm to acquire another business. Why? Canadians and Americans claim the Europeans can pay higher prices because their income is never reduced for amortization expense.

STOP & THINK

How could companies around the world be placed on the same accounting basis?

Answer: If all companies worldwide followed the same accounting rules, they would be reporting income and other amounts computed similarly. But this is not the case. Companies must follow the accounting rules of their own nation, and there are differences, as the goodwill situation illustrates. This is why international investors keep abreast of accounting methods used in different nations—much the same as a Canadian investor cares whether a company uses FIFO average cost for inventories. An international body, the International Accounting Standards Committee, has a set of accounting standards, but the organization has no enforcement power.

Betterments versus Repairs

When a company makes a capital asset expenditure, it must decide whether to debit an asset account or an expense account. In this context, *expenditure* refers either to a cash or a credit purchase of goods or of services related to the asset. Examples of these expenditures range from replacing the windshield wipers on an automobile to adding a wing to a building.

Expenditures that increase the capacity or efficiency of the asset or extend its useful life are called **betterments**. For example, the cost of a major overhaul that extends a taxi's useful life is a betterment. The amount of the expenditure, said to be *capitalized*, for a betterment is a debit to an asset account. For the cost of a betterment on the taxi, we would debit the asset account Automobile.

Other expenditures do not extend the asset's capacity or efficiency. Expenditures that merely maintain the asset in its existing condition or restore the asset to good working order are called **repairs**; they are expenses and are matched against revenue. Examples include the costs of repainting a taxi, repairing a dented fender, and replacing tires. The work that creates the repair, said to be *expensed*, is a debit to an expense account. For the ordinary repairs on the taxi, we would debit Repair Expense.

Costs associated with intangible assets and natural resources also must be identified as either a betterment or a repair/expense. For example, a license fee paid to the province of Saskatchewan to mine gold is a betterment. This cost should be debited to the Mineral Assets account. The cost of selling the ore—a commission paid to a broker—is like a repair expense and should be debited to an expense account.

The distinction between betterments and repairs is often a matter of opinion. Does the work extend the life of the asset, or does it only maintain the asset in good order? When doubt exists as to whether to debit an asset or an expense, companies tend to debit an expense, for two reasons. First, many expenditures are minor in amount, and most companies have a policy of debiting expense for all expenditures below a specified minimum, such as $1,000. Second, the income tax motive favors debiting all borderline expenditures to expense in order to create an immediate tax deduction. Betterments are not immediate tax deductions.

OBJECTIVE 8
Distinguish betterments from repairs

Short Exercise:
Basiden Ltd. purchased a used truck. Identify the following truck-related expenditures as betterments or repairs:

1. Purchase price of truck, $10,000
2. Painting company logo on truck when purchased, $500
3. Gasoline for truck, $20
4. Hydraulic loader for truck, $1,500
5. 30,000-km inspection, $100

A: Betterment: 1, 2, 4; Repair: 3, 5

EXHIBIT 10-12 *Delivery Truck Expenditures*

Debit an Asset Account for Betterments	Debit Repair and Maintenance Expense for Repairs

Betterment
    Major engine overhaul
    Modification of body for new
      use of truck
    Addition to storage capacity
      of truck
	Repairs
	    Repair of transmission or other
	      mechanism
	    Oil change, lubrication, and
	      so on
	    Replacement tires, windshield,
	      and the like
	    Paint job

Exhibit 10-12 illustrates the distinction between betterments and repairs (expense) for several delivery truck expenditures.

Treating a betterment as a repair, or vice versa, creates errors in the financial statements. Suppose a company incurs the cost of a betterment to enhance the service potential of equipment and erroneously expenses this cost. It is a capital expenditure that should have been debited to an asset account. This accounting error overstates expenses and understates net income on the income statement. On the balance sheet, the equipment account is understated, and so is owner's equity. Capitalizing the cost of an ordinary repair creates the opposite error. Expenses are understated and net income is overstated on the income statement. The balance sheet reports overstated amounts for assets and owners' equity.

Summary Problems for Your Review

Problem 1

The figures that follow appear in requirement 2, Solution to Review Problem, on p. 488.

	Method A Straight-Line			Method B Declining-Balance (Revenue Canada)		
Year	Annual Depreciation Expense	Accumulated Depreciation	Book Value	Annual Depreciation Expense	Accumulated Depreciation	Book Value
Start			$44,000			$44,000
19X5	$4,000	$ 4,000	40,000	$8,800	$ 8,800	35,200
19X6	4,000	8,000	36,000	7,040	15,840	28,160
19X7	4,000	12,000	32,000	5,632	21,472	22,528

Required

Suppose Revenue Canada permitted a choice between these two depreciation methods. Which depreciation method would you select for income tax purposes? Why?

Problem 2

A corporation purchased a building at a cost of $500,000 on January 1, 19X3. Management has depreciated the building by using the straight-line method, a 35-year life, and a residual value of $150,000. On July 1, 19X7, the company sold the building for $575,000 cash. The fiscal year of the corporation ends on December 31.

Required

Record depreciation for 19X7 and record the sale of the building on July 1, 19X7.

SOLUTIONS TO REVIEW PROBLEMS

Problem 1

For tax purposes, most companies select the maximum amount allowed by Revenue Canada, which results in accelerated depreciation of the equipment. Accelerated depreciation minimizes taxable income and income tax payments in the early years of the asset's life, thereby maximizing the business's cash at the earliest possible time. Straight-line spreads depreciation evenly over the life of the asset which would *not* minimize income tax in the same way.

Problem 2

19X7			
July 1	Depreciation Expense—Building		
	[($500,000 – $150,000)/(35 years × ½ year)]	5,000	
	Accumulated Depreciation—Building		5,000
	To update depreciation.		
July 1	Cash..	575,000	
	Accumulated Depreciation—Building		
	[($500,000 – $150,000)/(35 years × 4½ years)] .	45,000	
	Building..		500,000
	Gain on sale of building....................................		120,000
	To record sale of building.		

Summary

1. **Identify the elements of property plant and equipment's cost.** *Capital assets,* of which property, plant, and equipment are a category, are long-lived assets that the business uses in its operation. These assets are not held for sale as inventory.

2. **Explain the concept of amortization (depreciation).** The process of allocating a capital asset's cost to expense over the period the asset is used is called *depreciation.* The cost of all capital assets but land is expensed through *amortization.*

3. **Account for depreciation by three methods.** Businesses may compute the depreciation of property, plant, and equipment by three methods: *straight-line, units-of-production,* and *declining balance.* To measure depreciation, the accountant subtracts the asset's estimated residual value from its cost and divides that amount by the asset's estimated useful life. Most companies use the straight-line method for financial reporting purposes.

4. **Identify the best depreciation method for income tax purposes.** Almost all companies use an accelerated method for income tax purposes. Accelerated depreciation results in greater tax deductions early in the asset's life. These deductions decrease income tax payments and conserve cash that the company can use in its business.

5. *Account for disposal of property, plant, and equipment.* Before disposing of capital assets, of which property, plant, and equipment are a category, the business updates the asset's depreciation. Disposal is recorded by removing the book balances from both the asset account and its related accumulated depreciation account. Disposal often results in recognition of a gain or a loss.

6. *Account for wasting assets and amortization (depletion).* The cost of natural resources, a special category of long-lived assets, is expensed through *depletion*. Depletion of natural resources is computed on a units-of-production basis.

7. *Account for intangible assets and amortization.* Long-lived assets called *intangibles* are rights that have no physical form. The cost of intangibles is expensed through *amortization*. Amortization of intangibles is computed on a straight-line basis over a maximum of 40 years. However, the useful lives of most intangibles are shorter than their legal lives.

8. *Distinguish betterments from repairs.* *Betterments* increase the capacity or the efficiency of an asset or extend its useful life. Accordingly, they are debited to an asset account. *Repairs* merely maintain the asset's usefulness and are debited to an expense account.

Self-Study Questions

Test your understanding of the chapter by marking the correct answer for each of the following questions:

1. Which of the following payments is not included in the cost of land? *(pp. 479–480)*
   a. Removal of old building
   b. Legal fees
   c. Back property taxes paid at acquisition
   d. Cost of fencing and lighting

2. A business paid $120,000 for two machines valued at $90,000 and $60,000. The business will record these machines at *(p. 480)*
   a. $90,000 and $60,000   c. $72,000 and $48,000
   b. $60,000 each   d. $70,000 and $50,000

3. Which of the following definitions fits depreciation? *(p. 483)*
   a. Allocation of the asset's market value to expense over its useful life
   b. Allocation of the asset's cost to expense over its useful life
   c. Decreases in the asset's market value over its useful life
   d. Increases in the fund set aside to replace the asset when it is worn out

4. Which depreciation method's amounts are not computed based on time? *(p. 483)*
   a. Straight-line   c. Declining-balance
   b. Units-of-production

5. Which depreciation method gives the largest amount of expense in the early years of using the asset and therefore is best for income tax purposes? *(p. 484)*
   a. Straight-line   c. Declining-balance
   b. Units-of-production   d. All are equal

6. A company paid $450,000 for a building and was depreciating it by the straight-line method over a 40-year life with estimated residual value of $50,000. After 10 years, it became evident that the building's remaining useful life would be 40 years. Depreciation for the eleventh year is *(pp. 490–491)*
   a. $7,500   c. $10,000
   b. $8,750   d. $12,500

7. Labrador, Inc., scrapped an automobile that cost $14,000 and had book value of $1,100. The entry to record this disposal is *(p. 492)*
   a. Loss on Disposal of Automobile 1,100
         Automobile... 1,100

b. Accumulated Depreciation 14,000

    Automobile.. 14,000

c. Accumulated Depreciation 12,900

    Automobile.. 12,900

d. Accumulated Depreciation 12,900

    Loss of Disposal of Automobile 1,100

    Automobile.. 14,000

8. Depletion is computed in the same manner as which depreciation method? *(p. 496)*

    a. Straight-line   c. Declining balance

    b. Units-of-production

9. Lacy Corporation paid $550,000 to acquire Gentsch, Inc. Gentsch's assets had a market value of $900,000 and its liabilities were $400,000. In recording the acquisition, Lacy will record goodwill of *(p. 498)*

    a. $50,000   c. $550,000

    b. $100,000   d. $0

10. Which of the following items is a repair? *(pp. 499–500)*

    a. New brakes for delivery truck

    b. Paving of a company parking lot

    c. Cost of a new engine for a truck

    d. Building permit paid to construct an addition to an existing building

Answers to the Self-Study Questions follow the Accounting Vocabulary.

Acounting Vocabulary

Accelerated depreciation *(p. 484)*
Amortization *(p. 478)*
Betterment *(p. 499)*
Capital asset *(p. 478)*
Capital cost allowance *(p. 484)*
Copyright *(p. 497)*
Declining-balance (DB) method *(p. 484)*
Depletion expense *(p. 496)*
Depreciable cost *(p. 482)*
Estimated residual value *(p. 482)*
Estimated useful life *(p. 482)*
Franchises and licenses *(p. 498)*
Goodwill *(p. 498)*
Intangible asset *(p. 496)*
Leasehold *(p. 498)*
Patent *(p. 497)*
Repairs *(p. 499)*
Revenue Canada rate *(p. 484)*
Straight-line (SL) method *(p. 483)*
Trademark and trade nameor brand name *(p. 497)*
Units-of-production (UOP) method *(p. 483)*
Wasting asset or natural resource *(p. 496)*

Answers to Self-Study Questions

1. d
2. c [$90,000/($90,000 + $60,000)$120,000 = $72,000;
     $60,000/($90,000 + $60,000)$120,000 = $48,000]
3. b
4. b

5. c
6. a   Depreciable cost = $450,000 − $50,000 = $400,000
       $400,000/40 years = $10,000 per year
       $400,000 − ($10,000 × 10 years) = $300,000/40 years = $7,500 per year
7. d
8. b
9. a $550,000 − ($900,000 − $400,000) = $50,000
10. a

ASSIGNMENT MATERIAL

Questions

1. To what types of long-lived assets do the following expenses apply: depreciation, depletion, and amortization?

2. Describe how to measure the cost of a capital asset. Would an ordinary cost of repairing the asset after it is placed in service be included in the asset's cost?

3. Suppose land is purchased for $100,000. How do you account for the $8,000 cost of removing an unwanted building?

4. When assets are purchased as a group for a single price and no individual asset cost is given, how is each asset's cost determined?

5. Define depreciation. Present the common misconceptions about depreciation.

6. Which depreciation method does each of the following graphs characterize: straight-line, units-of-production, or declining-balance?

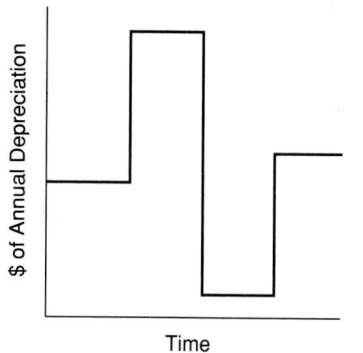
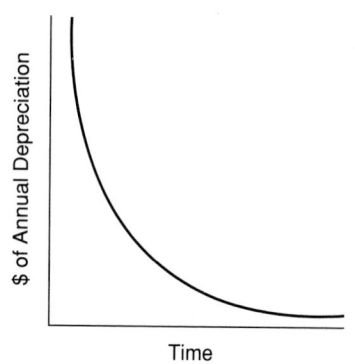
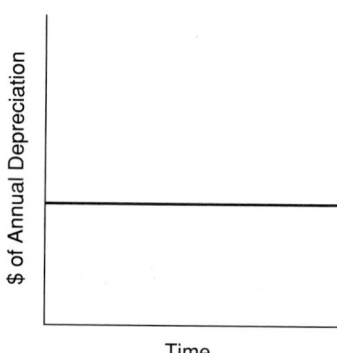

7. Which of the three depreciation methods results in the most depreciation in the first year of the asset's life?

8. Explain the concept of declining-balance depreciation. Which other depreciation method is used in the definition of declining-balance depreciation?

9. The level of business activity fluctuates widely for Harwood Delivery Service, reaching its peak around Christmas each year. At other times, business is slow. What depreciation method is most appropriate for the company's fleet of Chevy Luv trucks?

10. Oswalt Computer Service Center Ltd. uses the most advanced computers available to keep a competitive edge over other service centres. To maintain this advantage, Oswalt usually replaces its computers before they are worn out. Describe the major factors affecting the useful life of a capital asset and indicate which seems more relevant to Oswalt's computers.

11. Which depreciation method does not consider estimated residual value in computing depreciation during the early years of the asset's life?

12. Which depreciation method is best from an income tax standpoint? Why?

13. How does depreciation affect income taxes? How does depreciation affect cash provided by operations?

14. Describe how to compute depreciation for less than a full year, and how to account for depreciation for less than a full month.

15. Ragland Company Ltd. paid $10,000 for office furniture. The company expected it to remain in service for six years and to have a $1,000 residual value. After two years' use, company accountants believe the furniture will last an additional six years. How much depreciation will Ragland record for each of these last six years, assuming straight-line depreciation and no change in the estimated residual value?

16. When a company sells a capital asset before the year's end, what must it record before accounting for the sale?

17. Describe how to determine whether a company experiences a gain or a loss when an old capital asset is exchanged for a new one. Does GAAP favor the recognition of gains or losses? Which accounting concept underlies your answer?

18. Identify seven elements of internal control designed to safeguard capital assets.

19. What expense applies to wasting assets? By which amortization method is this expense computed?

20. How do intangible assets differ from most other assets? Why are they assets at all? What expense applies to intangible assets?

21. Why is the cost of patents and other intangible assets often expensed over a shorter period than the legal life of the asset?

22. Your company has just purchased another company for $400,000. The market value of the other company's net assets is $325,000. What is the $75,000 excess called? What type of asset is it? What is the maximum period over which its cost is amortized under generally accepted accounting principles?

23. Northern Telecom is recognized as a world leader in the manufacture and sale of telephone equipment. The company's success has created vast amounts of business goodwill. Would you expect to see this goodwill reported on Northern Telecom's financial statements? Why, or why not?

24. Distinguish a betterment from a repair. Why are they treated differently for accounting purposes?

Exercises

Exercise 10-1   *Identifying the elements of a capital asset's cost   (Obj. 1)*

J.L. Systems Design Ltd. purchased land, paying $66,000 cash as a down payment and signing a $120,000 note payable for the balance. In addition, the company paid delinquent property tax of $2,000, a legal fee of $500, and a $5,400 charge for leveling the land and removing an unwanted building. The company constructed an office building on the land at a cost of $410,000. It also paid $18,000 for a fence around the boundary of the property, $2,400 for the company sign near the entrance to the property, and $6,000 for special lighting of the grounds. Determine the cost of the company's land, land improvements, and building.

Exercise 10-2   *Allocating cost to assets acquired in a lump-sum purchase   (Obj. 1)*

Dartmouth Research Center Inc. bought three used machines in a $30,000 purchase. An independent appraisal of the machines produced the following figures:

Machine No.	Appraised Value
1	$14,000
2	18,000
3	8,000

Assuming Dartmouth paid cash for the machines, record the purchase in the general journal, identifying each machine's individual cost in a separate Machine account.

Exercise 10-3   *Explaining the concept of amortization*   **(Obj. 2)**

Brian Marling has just slept through the class in which Professor Hanna explained the concept of amortization. Because the next test is scheduled for Wednesday, Brian telephones Michelle White to get her notes from the lecture. Michelle's notes are concise: "Amortization—Sounds like Greek to me." Brian next tries Desirée Mare, who says she thinks amortization is what happens when an asset wears out. Orry Skrypec is confident that amortization is the process of building up a cash fund to replace an asset at the end of its useful life. Explain the concept of amortization for Brian. Evaluate the explanations of Desirée and Orry. Be specific.

Exercise 10-4   *Computing depreciation by four methods*   **(Obj. 3)**

A delivery truck was acquired on January 2, 19X1, for $17,000. The truck was expected to remain in service for 4 years and last 200,000 kilometers. At the end of its useful life, company officials estimated that the truck's residual value would be $1,000. The truck traveled 64,000 kilometers in the first year, 50,000 in the second year, 46,000 in the third year, and 40,000 in the fourth year. Prepare a schedule of depreciation expense per year for the truck using straight-line, units-of-production, and the two declining-balance methods (double-declining-balance and Revenue Canada rates). Assume full depreciation can be charged in the first year under the Revenue Canada method. The Revenue Canada rate is 30 percent. Show your computations.

Exercise 10-5   *Recording partial-year depreciation computed by two methods*   **(Obj. 3)**

Situation 1   Hunt Corporation purchased office furniture on June 3, 19X4, for $2,800 cash. Donna Hunt expects it to remain useful for six years and to have a residual value of $400. Hunt uses the straight-line depreciation method. Record Hunt's depreciation on the furniture for the year ended December 31, 19X4.

Situation 2   Chen Corp. purchased equipment on October 19, 19X2, for $16,500, signing a note payable for that amount. Chen estimated that this equipment will be useful for three years and have a residual value of $1,500. Assuming Chen uses double-declining-balance depreciation, record Chen's depreciation on the machine for the year ended December 31, 19X2.

Exercise 10-6   *Journalizing a change in a capital asset's useful life*   **(Obj. 3)**

A company purchased a building for $980,000 and depreciated it on a straight-line basis over a 30-year period. The estimated residual value was $80,000. After using the building for 15 years, the company realized that wear and tear on the building would force the company to replace it before 30 years. Starting with the 16th year, the company began depreciating the building over a revised total life of 20 years, retaining the $80,000 estimated residual value. Record depreciation expense on the building for years 15 and 16.

Exercise 10-7   *Preparing a property, plant, and equipment ledger record; units-of-production depreciation*   **(Obj. 3)**

Souris Delivery Service Inc. uses a property, plant, and equipment ledger record to account for its delivery vehicles, which are located at the company's service garage. The fleet of vehicles cost $91,000 when purchased from Island Ford Inc. on September 1, 19X2. This cost is the debit balance in the Delivery Vehicles account in the general ledger. Souris uses the units-of-production depreciation method, and estimates a useful life of 640,000 kilometers and a $11,000 residual value for the trucks. The garage supervisor is responsible for the vehicles. The company's fiscal year ends on December 31. Kilometers traveled were 48,000 in 19X2; 168,000 in 19X3; and 150,000 in 19X4. Complete a ledger record for these vehicles through December 31, 19X4.

Exercise 10-8 *Identifying depreciation methods for income tax and financial reporting purposes* **(Obj. 4)**

Using the data in Exercise 10-4, identify the depreciation method that would be most advantageous from an income tax perspective. Which depreciation method do most companies use for reporting to their shareholders and creditors on their financial statements?

Exercise 10-9 *Recording the sale of a capital asset* **(Obj. 5)**

On January 2, 19X1, Oakwood Sales Ltd. purchased store fixtures for $8,700 cash, expecting the fixtures to remain in service for 10 years. Oakwood has depreciated the fixtures by the Revenue Canada rate of 20 percent, assuming that full depreciation can be deducted in the first year. On October 30, 19X8, Oakwood sold the fixtures for $950 cash. Record depreciation expense on the fixtures for the 10 months ended October 30, 19X8, and also record the sale of the fixtures. Oakwood's year end is December 31.

Exercise 10-10 *Exchanging capital assets* **(Obj. 5)**

A machine cost $15,000. At the end of 4 years, its accumulated depreciation was $4,500. For each of the following situations, record the trade-in of this old machine for a new, similar machine.

Situation 1 The new machine had a cash price of $17,400; the dealer allowed a trade-in allowance of $9,000 on the old machine; and you paid the $8,400 balance in cash.

Situation 2 The new machine had a cash price of $18,000; the dealer allowed a trade-in allowance of $10,900 on the old machine; and you signed a note payable for the $7,100 balance.

Exercise 10-11 *Recording wasting assets and depletion* **(Obj. 6)**

Sasquatch Mining Company Ltd. paid $298,500 for the right to extract ore from a 200,000-tonne mineral deposit. In addition to the purchase price, Sasquatch also paid a $500 filing fee and a $1,000 license fee to the province of British Columbia. Because Sasquatch purchased the rights to the minerals only, the company expected the asset to have zero residual value when fully depleted. During the first year of production, Sasquatch removed 35,000 tonnes of ore. Make general journal entries to record (1) purchase of the mineral rights (debit Mineral Asset), (2) payment of fees, and (3) depletion for first-year production.

Exercise 10-12 *Recording intangibles, amortization, and a change in the asset's useful life* **(Obj. 7)**

Part 1 Shah Corporation manufactures high-speed printers and has recently purchased for $4.52 million a patent for the design for a new laser printer. Although it gives legal protection for 17 years, the patent is expected to provide Shah with a competitive advantage for only eight years. Assuming the straight-line method of amortization, use general journal entries to record (1) the purchase of the patent, and (2) amortization for one year.

Part 2 After using the patent for four years, Shah learns at an industry trade show that another company is designing a more efficient printer. Based on this new information, Shah decides, starting with year 5, to amortize the remaining cost of the patent over two additional years, giving the patent a total useful life of six years. Record amortization for year 5.

Exercise 10-13 *Computing and recording goodwill* *(Obj. 7)*

Assume Murphy's Chips Ltd. purchased Chip-O Corp., paying $1 million cash. The market value of Chip-O Corp.'s assets was $1.4 million, and Chip-O Corp. had liabilities of $1.1 million.

1. Compute the cost of the goodwill purchased by Murphy's Chips Ltd.
2. Record the purchase by Murphy's Chips Ltd.
3. Record amortization of goodwill for one year, assuming the straight-line method and a useful life of 10 years.

Exercise 10-14 *Distinguishing betterments from repairs* *(Obj. 8)*

Classify each of the following expenditures as a betterment or a repair (expense) related to machinery: (a) purchase price; (b) sales tax paid on the purchase price; (c) transportation and insurance while machinery is in transport from seller to buyer; (d) installation; (e) training of personnel for initial operation of the machinery; (f) special reinforcement to the machinery platform; (g) income tax paid on income earned from the sale of products manufactured by the machinery; (h) major overhaul to extend useful life by three years; (i) ordinary recurring repairs to keep the machinery in good working order; (j) lubrication of the machinery before it is placed in service; and (k) periodic lubrication after the machinery is placed in service.

Challenge Exercises

Exercise 10-15 *Measuring the effect of an error* *(Obj. 3, 8)*

Le Coque Sportswear is a catalog merchant in France. The company's assets consist mainly of inventory, a warehouse, and automated shipping equipment. Assume that early in year 1 Le Coque purchased equipment at a cost of 3 million francs (F 3 million). Management expects the equipment to remain in service six years. Because the equipment is so specialized, estimated residual value is negligible. Le Coque uses the straight-line depreciation method. Through an accounting error, Le Coque accidentally expensed the entire cost of the equipment at the time of purchase. The company is family-owned and operated as a partnership, so it pays no income tax.

Required

Prepare a schedule to show the overstatement or understatement in the following items at the end of each year over the six-year life of the equipment.

1. Total current assets
2. Equipment, net
3. Net income
4. Owner's equity
5. Debt ratio (Total liabilities/Total assets)

Exercise 10-16 *Reconstructing transactions from the financial statements* *(Obj. 3, 5)*

United Grain Growers Limited comparative balance sheet recently reported these amounts (in thousands of dollars):

	July 31			
	1994		**1993**	
Properties	**Cost**	**Accumulated Depreciation**	**Cost**	**Accumulated Depreciation**
Country elevator properties and equipment, feed plants, seed cleaning plants, warehouses, sheds and research station...................	$194,030	$ 81,078	$174,355	$ 81,627

Terminal elevator properties and equipment	106,887	68,315	109,758	65,415
Miscellaneous equipment	15,312	9,354	7,811	4,316
Properties under capital lease	1,065	319	1,065	107
	$317,294	$159,066	$292,989	$151,465
Net book value		$158,228		$141,524

In the 1994 annual report, United Grain Growers reported depreciation and amortization expense in 1994 of $12,926,000. In addition, the company reported that it had disposed of certain capital assets and acquired others. The company reported that it had lost $976,000 on property disposals.

Required

1. What was the accumulated depreciation of the assets disposed of during 1994?
2. Assume that United Grain Growers acquired assets costing $36,305,000 during 1994. What was the cost price of the assets sold during the year?
3. Write the journal entry to record the disposal of the assets during the year.

Problems   (Group A)

Problem 10-1A   *Identifying the elements of a capital asset's cost* **(Obj. 1)**

Mazzoti Ltd. incurred the following costs in acquiring land and a garage, making land improvements, and constructing and furnishing a home office building.

a. Purchase price of 3½ hectares of land, including an old building that will be used as a garage for company vehicles (land market value is $600,000; building market value is $100,000) $630,000
b. Delinquent real estate taxes on the land to be paid by Mazzoti 3,700
c. Landscaping (additional dirt and earth moving) 3,550
d. Legal fees on the land acquisition 1,000
e. Fence around the boundary of the land 44,100
f. Building permit for the home office building 200
g. Architect fee for the design of the home office building 25,000
h. Company signs near front and rear approaches to the company property 23,550
i. Renovation of the garage 23,800
j. Concrete, wood, steel girders, and other materials used in the construction of the home office building 814,000
k. Masonry, carpentry, roofing, and other labor to construct home office building 734,000
l. Repair of vandalism damage to home office building during construction 4,100
m. Parking lots and concrete walks on the property 17,450
n. Lights for the parking lot, walkways, and company signs 8,900
o. Supervisory salary of construction supervisor (90 percent to home office building, 6 percent to fencing, parking lot and concrete walks, and 4 percent to garage renovation) 55,000
p. Office furniture for the home office building 123,500
q. Transportation of furniture from seller to the home office building 700
r. Landscaping (trees and shrubs) 9,100

Mazzoti depreciates buildings over 40 years, land improvements over 20 years and furniture over 8 years, all on a straight-line basis with zero residual value.

Required

1. Set up columns for Land, Land Improvements, Home Office Building, Garage, and Furniture. Show how to account for each of the foregoing costs by listing the cost under the correct account. Compute the total amount that would be debited to each amount.

2. Assuming that all construction was complete and the assets were placed in service on March 19, record depreciation for the year ended December 31. Round figures to the nearest dollar.

Problem 10-2A *Explaining the concept of depreciation* *(Obj. 2)*

The board of directors of Nanaimo Construction, Inc., is having its regular quarterly meeting. Accounting policies are on the agenda, and depreciation is being discussed. A new board member, a physician, has some strong opinions about two aspects of depreciation policy. Dr. Quan argues that depreciation must be coupled with a fund to replace company assets. Otherwise, he argues, there is no substance to depreciation. He also challenges the 5-year estimated life over which Nanaimo is depreciating company computers. He notes that the computers will last much longer and should be depreciated over at least 10 years.

Required

Write a paragraph or two to explain the concept of depreciation to Dr. Quan and to answer his arguments.

Problem 10-3A *Computing depreciation by three methods and the cash flow advantage of accelerated depreciation for tax purposes* *(Obj. 3, 4)*

On January 2, 19X1, Miske, Inc., purchased three used delivery trucks at a total cost of $63,000. Before placing the trucks in service, the company spent $2,200 painting them, $800 replacing their tires, and $4,000 overhauling their engines and reconditioning their bodies. Miske management estimates that the trucks will remain in service for six years and have a residual value of $16,000. The trucks' combined annual usage is expected to be 28,000 kilometers in each of the first 4 years and 22,000 kilometers in each of the next two years. In trying to decide which depreciation method to use, Julie Miske, the general manager, requests a depreciation schedule for each of the following generally accepted depreciation methods: straight-line, units-of-production, and declining-balance using the Revenue Canada rate of 30 percent. The Revenue Canada method permits only 50 percent of a full year's depreciation in the first year.

Required

1. Assuming Miske depreciates its delivery trucks as a unit, prepare a depreciation schedule for each of the three generally accepted depreciation methods, showing asset cost, depreciation expense, accumulated depreciation and asset book value. Use the formats of Exhibits 10-4 through 10-6.

2. Miske reports to shareholders and creditors in the financial statements using the depreciation method that maximizes reported income in the early years of asset use. For income tax purposes, however, the company uses the depreciation method that minimizes income tax payments in those early years. Consider the first year that Miske uses the delivery trucks. Identify the depreciation methods that meet the general manager's objectives. Assume Miske can deduct full depreciation in the first year for income tax purposes.

3. Assume that cash provided by operations before income tax is $80,000 for the delivery trucks' first year. The income tax rate is 30 percent. For the two depreciation

methods identified in Requirement 2, compare the net income and cash provided by operations (cash flow). Use the format of Exhibit 10-9 for your answer. Show which method gives the net-income advantage, and which method gives the cash-flow advantage. Ignore the earnings rate in the cash-flow analysis.

Problem 10-4A   *Journalizing and posting capital asset transactions; betterments versus repairs*   **(Obj. 1, 3, 5, 8)**

Saskatchewan Power Corporation provides electrical power to Saskatchewan. Assume that the company completed the following transactions:

19X4

Jan.	3	Paid $16,000 cash for a used service truck.
	5	Paid $1,200 to have the truck engine overhauled.
	7	Paid $300 to have the truck modified for business use.
Oct.	3	Paid $814 for transmission repair and oil change.
Dec.	31	Used the double-declining-balance method to record depreciation on the truck. (Assume a four-year life.)
	31	Closed the appropriate accounts.

19X5

Mar.	13	Replaced the truck's broken windshield for $275 cash.
June	26	Traded in the service truck for a new truck costing $23,000. The dealer granted a $4,000 allowance on the old truck, and Saskatchewan Power paid the balance in cash. Recorded 19X5 depreciation for the year to date and then recorded the exchange of trucks.
Dec.	31	Used the double-declining-balance method to record depreciation on the new truck. (Assume a four-year life.)
	31	Closed the appropriate accounts.

Required

1. Open the following accounts in the general ledger: Service Trucks; Accumulated Depreciation—Service Trucks; Truck Repair Expense; and Depreciation Expense—Service Trucks.

2. Record the transactions in the general journal and post to the ledger accounts opened.

Problem 10-5A   *Recording capital asset transactions; exchanges; changes in useful life*   **(Obj. 1, 3, 5, 8)**

A. C. Nielsen Company of Canada Ltd. surveys Canadian viewing trends. Nielsen's balance sheet reports the following assets under Property and Equipment: Land, Buildings, Office Furniture, Communication Equipment, Televideo Equipment, and Leasehold Improvements. The company has a separate accumulated depreciation account for each of these assets except land and leasehold improvements. Amortization on leasehold improvements is credited directly to the Leasehold Improvements account rather than to Accumulated Depreciation—Leasehold Improvements.

Assume that Nielsen completed the following transactions:

Jan.	4	Traded in communication equipment with book value of $31,000 (cost of $96,000) for similar new equipment with a cash cost of $108,000. The seller gave Nielsen a trade-in allowance of $20,000 on the old equipment, and Nielsen paid the remainder in cash.
	19	Purchased office furniture for $45,000 plus six percent sales tax and $300 shipping charge. The company gave a 90-day, 10 percent note in payment.
Apr.	19	Paid the furniture note and related interest.

Aug. 29   Sold a building that had cost $475,000 and had accumulated depreciation of $353,500 through December 31 of the preceding year. Depreciation is computed on a straight-line basis. The building has a 30-year useful life and a residual value of $47,500. Nielsen received $250,000 cash and a $450,000 note receivable.

Sept. 6   Paid cash to renovate leased assets at a cost of $53,000.

Nov. 10   Purchased used communication and televideo equipment from the Decima Research polling organization. Total cost was $90,000 paid in cash. An independent appraisal valued the communication equipment at $75,000 and the televideo equipment at $25,000.

Dec. 31   Recorded depreciation as follows:

Equipment is depreciated by the double-declining-balance method over a five-year life. Record depreciation on the equipment purchased on January 4 and on November 10 separately.

Office furniture has an expected useful life of eight years with an estimated residual value of $5,000. Depreciation is computed using the Revenue Canada rate (20 percent).

Amortization on leasehold improvements is computed on a straight-line basis over the life of the lease, which is six years, with zero residual value.

Depreciation on buildings is computed by the straight-line method. The company had assigned buildings an estimated useful life of 30 years and a residual value that is 10 percent of cost. After using the buildings for 20 years, the company has come to believe that their total useful life will be 35 years. Residual value remains unchanged. The buildings cost $16,000,000.

Required

Record the transactions in the general journal.

Problem 10-6A   *Distinguishing betterments from repairs; preparing a property, plant, and equipment ledger record*   **(Obj. 3, 5, 8)**

Suppose Nova Scotia Boat Repair Co. Ltd. uses property, plant, and equipment ledger records to control its service trucks, purchased from Wallen Motor Corp. The supervisor is responsible for the trucks, which are located at the company's service garage. The following transactions were completed during 19X6 and 19X7:

19X6
Jan. 10   Paid $11,500 cash for a used service truck (truck no. 12).
     11   Paid $1,500 to have the truck engine overhauled.
     12   Paid $250 to have the truck modified for business use.
Aug. 3   Paid $603 for transmission repair and oil change.
Dec. 31   Recorded depreciation on the truck by the double-declining-balance method, based on a 5-year life and a $1,500 residual value.

19X7
Mar. 13   Replaced a damaged bumper on truck no. 12 at a cash cost of $295.
May 12   Traded in service truck no. 12 for a new one (truck no. 14) with a cash cost of $20,500. The dealer granted a $7,000 allowance on the old truck, and Nova Scotia Boat Repair paid the balance in cash. Recorded 19X7 depreciation for year to date and then recorded exchange of the trucks.
Dec. 31   Recorded depreciation on truck no. 14 by the double-declining-balance method, based on a five-year life and a $2,000 residual value.

Required

1. Identify the betterments and the repairs in the transactions. Which expenditures are debited to an asset account? Which expenditures are debited to an expense account?

2. Prepare a separate ledger card for each of the trucks.

Problem 10-7A *Recording intangibles, wasting assets, and the related expenses* **(Obj. 6, 7)**

Part 1 TransCanada PipeLines Ltd. owns gas transmission facilities and other energy-related assets. The company's balance sheet includes the asset Oil Properties.

Suppose TransCanada paid $5 million cash for an oil lease that contained an estimated reserve of 625,000 barrels of oil. Assume that the company paid $350,000 for additional geological tests of the property and $110,000 to prepare the surface for drilling. Prior to production, the company signed a $65,000 note payable to have a building constructed on the property. Because the building provides on-site headquarters for the drilling effort and will be abandoned when the oil is depleted, its cost is debited to the Oil Properties account and included in depletion charges. During the first year of production, TransCanada removed 82,000 barrels of oil, which it sold on credit for $19 per barrel.

Required

Make general journal entries to record all transactions related to the oil and gas property, including depletion and sale of the first-year production.

Part 2 Newfoundland Telephone provides telephone service to most of Newfoundland and Labrador. The company's balance sheet reports the asset Cost of Acquisitions in Excess of the Fair Market Value of the Net Assets of Subsidiaries. Assume that Newfoundland Telephone purchased this asset as part of the acquisition of another company, which carried these figures:

Book value of assets	$640,000
Market value of assets	920,000
Liabilities	405,000

Required

1. What is another title for the asset Cost of Acquisitions in Excess of the Fair Market Value of the Net Assets of Subsidiaries?

2. Make the general journal entry to record Newfoundland Telephone's purchase of the other company for $850,000 cash.

3. Assuming Newfoundland Telephone amortizes Cost of Acquisitions in Excess of the Fair Market Value of the Net Assets of Subsidiaries over 20 years, record the straight-line amortization for one year.

Part 3 Suppose Northern Telecom purchased a patent for $220,000. Before using the patent, Northern Telecom incurred an additional cost of $25,000 for a lawsuit to defend the company's right to purchase it. Even though the patent gives Northern Telecom legal protection for 17 years, company management has decided to amortize its cost over a five-year period because of the industry's fast-changing technologies.

Required

Make general journal entries to record the patent transactions, including straight-line amortization for one year.

Problem 10-8A *Identify the elements of property, plant, and equipment's cost; account for depreciation by two methods; account for disposal of property, plant, and equipment; distinguish betterments from repairs* **(Obj. 1, 3, 5, 8)**

The Dicken's Catering Company has a fiscal year ending September 30th. The company completed the following transactions with regard to property, plant, and equipment:

19X1

Jan.	1	Paid $180,000 plus $5,000 in legal fees (for the lawyers' fees) to purchase the following assets from a competitor who was going out of business:

Asset	Appraised Value	Estimated Useful Life	Estimated Residual Value
Land........................	$100,000	N/A	N/A
Buildings................	60,000	10 years	$4,000
Equipment..............	40,000	5 years	5,000

Dicken's Catering plans to use the straight-line depreciation method for the building and for the equipment.

July	2	Purchased a delivery truck with a list price of $25,000. Dicken's negotiated a $2,000 discount, paid $5,000 down, and promised to pay the balance in 60 days. The truck is expected to be used for 4 years and driven a total of 100,000 kilometers; it is then expected to be sold for $4,000. It will be depreciated using the units-of-production method.
July	3	Paid $1,000 to paint the truck with the company's colors and logo.
Sept.	30	Recorded depreciation on the assets. The truck had been driven 15,000 kilometers since it was purchased.

19X2

Jan.	4	Dicken's paid $2,500 to ABC Equipment Repairs for work done on the equipment. The job consisted of annual maintenance ($500) and the addition of automatic controls ($2,000) which will increase the expected useful life of the equipment to a total of five years and increase its expected residual value by $1,000.
Sept.	30	Recorded depreciation on the assets. The truck had an odometer reading of 54,000 kilometers.
Dec.	1	Traded in one half of the equipment for new equipment. The new equipment had a list price of $25,000 and Dicken's received a trade-in allowance of $10,000.
Dec.	1	Sold the truck for $15,000. The truck had an odometer reading of 65,000 kilometers.

Required

1. Record the transactions of Dicken's Catering Company. Round all amounts to the nearest whole dollar.
2. Show the balance sheet presentation of the assets at the end of December 31, 19X2.

Problem 10-9A *Accounting for depreciation, accounting for wasting assets and amortization, accounting for intangible assets and amortization* **(Obj. 3, 6, 7)**

On July 2, 19X1 the JCR Explorations Ltd. acquired Far North Explorations Ltd. for $5,000,000. At the time of the acquisition, Far North's balance sheet contained the following items which were transferred to JCR Explorations Ltd.:

- Mining Equipment: original cost of $800,000 and a present market value of $780,000. The equipment is expected to last another 10 years and have a residual value of $4,000 at that time.

- Mineral Rights: the rights to mine property by Lesser Slave Lake. The mineral rights originally cost Far North $1,000,000 but now has an appraised market value of $4,000,000. The mine is expected to produce 50,000,000 tons of ore over the next 15 years.

- Leasehold: the rights to rent office space in a nearby town for $4,000 per month for the next 12 years. The leasehold has a market value today of $30,000 because of high rental rates in the area.

- Mortgage Payable: a $410,000 mortgage is outstanding on the mining equipment with interest at current rates.

Required

1. Journalize the purchase of Far North Explorations Ltd. by JCR Explorations Ltd.
2. Journalize the adjusting entries required for the year ending June 30, 19X2, to amortize the cost of the assets—assuming 2,000,000 tons of ore were taken out of the mine. Use the most appropriate methods and time frames from the data given.
3. Show how the assets would appear in the capital assets section of JCR Explorations Ltd.'s balance sheet as of June 30, 19X2.

(Group B)

Problem 10-1B *Identifying the elements of a capital asset's cost* ***(Obj. 1)***

Great-West Life Assurance Co. of Canada incurred the following costs in acquiring land, making land improvements, and constructing and furnishing an office building.

a. Purchase price of four hectares of land, including an old building that will be used for storage (land market value is $280,000; building market value is $20,000)	$216,000
b. Landscaping (additional dirt and earth moving)	8,100
c. Fence around the boundary of the land	17,650
d. Legal fee for title search on the land	600
e. Delinquent real estate taxes on the land to be paid by Great-West Life	5,900
f. Company signs at front of the company property	1,800
g. Building permit for the office building	350
h. Architect fee for the design of the office building	19,800
i. Masonry, carpentry, roofing, and other labor to construct office building	709,000
j. Concrete, wood, steel girders, and other materials used in the construction of the office building	214,000
k. Renovation of the storage building	41,800
l. Repair of storm damage to storage building during construction	2,200
m. Landscaping (trees and shrubs)	6,400
n. Parking lot and concrete walks on the property	29,750
o. Lights for the parking lot, walkways, and company signs	7,300

    p. Supervisory salary of construction supervisor (85 percent to office building, 9 percent to fencing, parking lot, and concrete walks, and 6 percent to storage building renovation)................ 40,000

    q. Office furniture for the office building... 107,100

    r. Transportation and installation of furniture............................... 1,800

Great-West Life depreciates buildings over 40 years, land improvements over 20 years, and furniture over eight years, all on a straight-line basis with zero residual value.

Required

1. Set up columns for Land, Land Improvements, Office Building, Storage Building, and Furniture. Show how to account for each of the foregoing costs by listing the cost under the correct account. Compute the total amount that would be debited to each account.

2. Assuming that all construction was complete and the assets were placed in service on May 4, record depreciation for the year ended December 31. Round off figures to the nearest dollar.

Problem 10-2B   *Explaining the concept of depreciation*   (Obj. 2)

The board of directors of Downtown Parking Lot Limited is reviewing the 19X8 annual report. A new board member, a consulting psychologist with little business experience, questions the company accountant about the depreciation amounts. The psychologist wonders why depreciation expense has decreased from $20,000 in 19X6, to $18,400 in 19X7, and to $17,200 in 19X8. She states that she could understand the decreasing annual amounts if the company had been disposing of properties each year, but that has not occurred. Further, she notes that growth in the city is increasing the values of company properties. Why is the company recording depreciation when the property values are increasing?

Required

Write a paragraph or two to explain the concept of depreciation to the psychologist and to answer her questions.

Problem 10-3B   *Computing depreciation by four methods and the cash flow advantage of declining-balance depreciation for tax purposes*   (Obj. 3, 4)

On January 9, 19X1, Halifax Boat Works, Inc., paid $192,000 for equipment used in manufacturing boats. In addition to the basic purchase price, the company paid $700 transportation charges, $100 insurance for the goods in transit, $4,100 sales tax, and $3,100 for a special platform on which to place the equipment in the plant. Halifax Boat Works management estimates that the equipment will remain in service for five years and have a residual value of $20,000. The equipment will produce 50,000 units in the first year, with annual production decreasing by 5,000 units during each of the next 4 years (that is, 45,000 units in year 2, 40,000 units in year 3, and so on). In trying to decide which depreciation method to use, Jennifer Morse has requested a depreciation schedule for each of the four generally accepted depreciation methods: straight-line, units-of-production, and the two declining-balance methods: double-declining-balance and declining-balance using the Revenue Canada rate of 30 percent.

Required

1. For each of the four generally accepted depreciation methods, prepare a depreciation schedule showing asset cost, depreciation expense, accumulated

depreciation, and asset book value. Use the format of Exhibits 10-4 through 10-7. Assume full depreciation can be deducted in the first year under the Revenue Canada rate method.

2. Halifax Boat Works reports to shareholders and creditors in the financial statements using the depreciation method that maximizes reported income in the early years of asset use. For income tax purposes, however, the company uses the depreciation method that minimizes income tax payments in those early years. Consider the first year Halifax Boat Works uses the equipment. Identify the depreciation methods that meet Halifax Boat Works's objectives. Assume full depreciation can be deducted in the first year under the Revenue Canada rate method.

3. Assume cash provided by operations before income tax is $120,000 for the equipment's first year. The income tax rate is 30 percent. For the two depreciation methods identified in Requirement 2, compare the net income and cash provided by operations (cash flow). Use the format of Exhibit 10-9 for your answer. Show which method gives the net-income advantage, and which method gives the cash-flow advantage. Ignore the earnings rate in the cash-flow analysis.

Problem 10-4B *Journalizing and posting capital asset transactions; betterments versus repairs* *(Obj. 1, 3, 5, 8)*

Assume that a Shoppers Drug Mart store completed the following transactions:

19X2
Jan.   6   Paid $13,000 cash for a used delivery truck.
       7   Paid $800 to have the truck engine overhauled.
       8   Paid $200 to have the truck modified for business use.
Aug. 21   Paid $156 for a minor tuneup.
Dec. 31   Recorded depreciation on the truck by the double-declining-balance method. (Assume a 4-year life.)
       31   Closed the appropriate accounts.

19X3
Feb.   8   Traded in the delivery truck for a new truck costing $16,000. The dealer granted a $4,000 allowance on the old truck, and the store paid the balance in cash. Recorded 19X3 depreciation for the year to date and then recorded the exchange of trucks.
July   8   Repaired the new truck's damaged fender for $625 cash.
Dec. 31   Recorded depreciation on the new truck by the double-declining-balance method. (Assume a four-year life and a residual value of $3,000.)
       31   Closed the appropriate accounts.

Required

1. Open the following accounts in the general ledger: Delivery Trucks; Accumulated Depreciation—Delivery Trucks; Truck Repair Expense; and Depreciation Expense—Delivery Trucks.

2. Record the transactions in the general journal and post to the ledger accounts opened.

Problem 10-5B *Recording capital asset transactions; exchanges; changes in useful life* *(Obj. 1, 3, 5, 8)*

Laidlaw Transportation Ltd. provides nationwide general freight service. The company's balance sheet includes the following assets under property, plant, and equipment: Land, Buildings, Motor Carrier Equipment, and Leasehold Improvements. Assume the company has a separate accumulated depreciation account for each of these assets except land and leasehold improvements. Amortization on leasehold improvements is credited directly to the Leasehold Improvements account rather than to Accumulated Amortization—Leasehold Improvements.

Assume that Laidlaw completed the following transactions at one of its branches:

Jan.   5   Traded in motor-carrier equipment with book value of $37,000 (cost of $130,000) for similar new equipment with a cash cost of $195,000. Laidlaw received a trade-in allowance of $60,000 on the old equipment and paid the remainder in cash.

Feb.   22   Purchased motor-carrier equipment for $136,000 plus 5 percent sales tax and a $200 registration fee. The company gave a 60-day, 12 percent note in payment.

Apr.   23   Paid the equipment note and related interest.

July   9   Sold a building that had cost $550,000 and had accumulated depreciation of $247,500 through December 31 of the preceding year. Depreciation is computed on a straight-line basis. The building has a 30-year useful life and a residual value of $55,000. Laidlaw received $100,000 cash and a $600,000 note receivable.

Aug.   16   Paid cash for leasehold improvements at a cost of $20,500.

Oct.   26   Purchased land and a building for a single price of $300,000. An independent appraisal valued the land at $115,000, and the building at $230,000.

Dec.   31   Recorded depreciation as follows:

Motor-carrier equipment has an expected useful life of five years and an estimated residual value of 5 percent of cost. Depreciation is computed by the Revenue Canada rate method using a rate of 30 percent. Make separate depreciation entries for equipment acquired on January 5 and February 22. (Assets acquired before the 15th of the month are depreciated in that month. Assets acquired after the 15th are not depreciated for that month.)

Amortization on leasehold improvements is computed on a straight-line basis over the life of the lease, which is 10 years, with zero residual value.

Depreciation on buildings is computed by the straight-line method. The company had assigned to its older buildings, which cost $2,000,000, an estimated useful life of 30 years with a residual value equal to 10 percent of the asset cost. However, management has come to believe that the buildings will remain useful for a total of 40 years. Residual value remains unchanged. The company has used all its buildings, except for the one purchased on October 26, for 10 years. The new building carries a 40-year useful life and a residual value equal to 10 percent of its cost. Make separate entries for depreciation on the building acquired on October 26 and the other buildings purchased in earlier years.

Required

Record the transactions in the general journal.

Problem 10-6B   *Distinguishing betterments from repairs; preparing a property, plant, and equipment ledger record*   *(Obj. 3, 5, 8)*

Suppose Pacific Tire Supply Company uses property, plant, and equipment ledger records to control its service trucks, purchased from Paproski Motors Ltd. The supervisor is responsible for the trucks, which are located at the company's service garage. The following transactions were completed during 19X3 and 19X4:

19X3

Jan.   6   Paid $12,420 cash for a used service truck (truck no. 6).
        7   Paid $2,500 to have the truck engine overhauled.
        8   Paid $180 to have the truck modified for business use.
Nov.   5   Paid $107 for replacement of one tire.
Dec.   31   Recorded depreciation on the truck by the double-declining-bal-
            ance method, based on a 4-year useful life and a $1,100 residual
            value.

19X4

Jul.   16   Repaired a damaged fender on truck no. 6 at a cash cost of $877.
Sept.   6   Traded in service truck no. 6 for a new one (truck no. 8) with a cash
            cost of $18,000. The dealer granted a $5,500 allowance on the old
            truck, and Pacific Tire paid the balance in cash. Recorded 19X4 de-
            preciation for year to date and then recorded exchange of the
            trucks.
Dec.   31   Recorded depreciation on truck no. 8 by the double-declining-bal-
            ance method, based on a 4-year life and a $1,500 residual value.

Required

1. Identify the betterments and the repairs in the transactions. Which expenditures
   are debited to an asset account? Which expenditures are debited to an expense
   account?
2. Prepare a separate ledger record for each of the trucks.

Problem 10-7B   *Recording intangibles, wasting assets, and the related expenses*   *(Obj. 6, 7)*

Part 1   Canadian Pacific Ltd. is one of Canada's largest holding companies. The
company's balance sheet includes the assets Natural Gas, Oil, and Coal.

Suppose Canadian Pacific paid $1.8 million cash for a lease giving the firm the
right to work a mine that contained an estimated 125,000 tonnes of coal. Assume
that the company paid $10,000 to remove unwanted buildings from the land and
$45,000 to prepare the surface for mining. Further assume that Canadian Pacific
signed a $20,000 note payable to a landscaping company to return the land surface
to its original condition after the lease ends. During the first year, Canadian Pacific
removed 35,000 tonnes of coal, which it sold on account for $17 per tonne.

Required

Make general journal entries to record all transactions related to the coal, including
depletion and sale of the first-year production.

Part 2   Scott's Hospitality Inc., among its other businesses, operates Kentucky
Fried Chicken franchised restaurants. The company's balance sheet reports the
asset Cost in Excess of Net Assets of Purchased Businesses. Assume that Scott purchased this asset as part of the acquisition of another company, which carried these
figures:

Book value of assets	$2.5 million
Market value of assets	3.1 million
Liabilities	2.3 million

Required

1. What is another title for the asset Cost in Excess of Net Assets of Purchased
   Businesses?
2. Make the general journal entry to record Scott's purchase of the other company
   for $1.3 million cash.
3. Assuming Scott's amortizes Cost in Excess of Net Assets of Purchased Businesses
   over 20 years, record the straight-line amortization for one year.

Part 3   Suppose Scott's Hospitality purchased a Kentucky Fried Chicken franchise license for $260,000. In addition to the basic purchase price, Scott's also paid a lawyer $8,000 for assistance with the negotiations. Management believes the appropriate amortization period for its cost of the franchise license is eight years.

Required

Make general journal entries to record the franchise transactions, including straight-line amortization for one year.

Problem 10-8B   *Identify the elements of property, plant, and equipment's cost; account for depreciation by two methods; account for disposal of property, plant, and equipment; distinguish betterments from repairs* **(Obj. 1, 3, 5, 8)**

The Bishop's Trucking Company has a fiscal year ending September 30th. The company completed the following transactions with regard to property, plant and equipment:

19X1

Jan. 1   Paid $131,000 plus $4,000 in legal fees to purchase the following assets from a competitor who was going out of business:

Asset	Appraised Value	Estimated Useful Life	Estimated Residual Value
Land......................	$80,000	N/A	N/A
Buildings...............	70,000	20 years	$3,000
Equipment.............	50,000	6 years	6,000

Bishop's Trucking plans to use the straight-line depreciation method for the building and for the equipment.

July 2   Purchased a delivery truck with a list price of $30,000. Bishop's negotiated a $3,000 discount, paid $8,000 down and promised to pay the balance in 60 days. The truck is expected to be used for 5 years and driven a total of 120,000 kilometers; it is then expected to be sold for $5,000. It will be depreciated using the units-of-production method.

July 3   Paid $2,000 to paint the truck with the company's colors and logo.

Sept. 30   Recorded depreciation on the assets. The truck had been driven 18,000 kilometers since it was purchased.

19X2

Jan. 4   Bishop's paid $3,800 to ABC Equipment Repairs for work done on the equipment. The job consisted of annual maintenance ($800) and the addition of automatic controls ($3,000) which will increase the expected useful life of the equipment by one year (a total of seven years) and increase its expected residual value by $1,500.

Sept. 30   Recorded depreciation on the assets. The truck had an odometer reading of 56,000 kilometers.

Dec. 1   Traded in one half of the equipment in for new equipment. The new equipment had a list price of $30,000 and Bishop's received a trade-in allowance of $15,000.

Dec. 1   Sold the truck for $18,000. The truck had an odometer reading of 72,000 kilometers.

Required

1. Record the transactions of Bishop's Trucking Company. Round all amounts to the nearest whole dollar.

2. Show the balance sheet presentation of the assets at the end of December 31, 19X2.

Problem 10-9B   *Accounting for depreciation, accounting for wasting assets and amortization, accounting for intangible assets and amortization **(Obj. 3, 6, 7)***

On July 2, 19X1 TTA Explorations Ltd. acquired Off Shore Explorations Ltd. for $3,600,000. At the time of the acquisition, Off Shore's balance sheet contained the following items which were transferred to TTA Explorations Ltd.:

- Mining Equipment: original cost of $700,000 and a present market value of $640,000. The equipment is expected to last another 10 years and have a residual value of $5,000 at that time.

- Mineral Rights: the rights to mine property by Greater Slave Lake. The mineral rights originally cost Off Shore $2,000,000 but now has an appraised market value of $3,000,000. The mine is expected to produce 40,000,000 tons of ore over the next 15 years.

- Leasehold: the rights to rent office space in a nearby town for $3,000 per month for the next 10 years. The leasehold has a market value today of $20,000 because of high rental rates in the area.

- Mortgage Payable: a $510,000 mortgage is outstanding on the mining equipment with interest at current rates.

Required

1. Journalize the purchase of Off Shore Explorations Ltd. by TTA Explorations Ltd.
2. Journalize the adjusting entries required for the year ending June 30, 19X2, to amortize the cost of the assets—assuming 3,000,000 tons of ore were taken out of the mine. Use the most appropriate methods and time frames from the data given.
3. Show how the assets would appear in the capital assets section of TTA Explorations Ltd.'s balance sheet as of June 30, 19X2.

Challenge Problems

Problem 10-1C   *Understanding depreciation and betterments and repairs   **(Obj. 2, 8)***

The president of newly formed McKay Limo Transport Inc., a friend of your family, knows you are taking an accounting course and asks for some advice. He tells you that he is pretty good at running the company but doesn't understand accounting. Specifically, he has two questions:

1. The company has just purchased $1,000,000 worth of regular and stretch limousines. His accountants tell him that he should use accelerated depreciation for his financial statements but he understands that straight-line depreciation will result in lower charges to expense in the early years. He wants to use straight-line depeciation.
2. A friend told him that McKay should capitalize all repairs to the autos and "spread the cost out over the life of the vehicle." He wonders if there is anything wrong with this advice.

Required

Respond to Mr. McKay's questions using your understanding of depreciation and betterments and repairs.

Problem 10-2C *Accounting for wasting assets* **(Obj. 6)**

Challenger Mining Corp. is a new company that has been formed to mine for nickel in Labrador. The ore body is estimated to contain 100,000,000 kilograms of pure nickel for which the world price is $10,829 per tonne. The costs of mine development are estimated to be $80,000,000.

Required

Calculate the costs that would be charged against the nickel production in the form of depletion on a per-1,000-kilogram basis. Estimate any costs you think should be also included. Do not include the costs to mine and refine the ore or shipping and selling costs.

Extending Your Knowledge

Decision Problems

1. Measuring profitability based on different inventory and depreciation methods   (Obj. 3)

Suppose you are considering investing in two businesses, Kanji, Inc. and Fluit Ltd. The two companies are virtually identical, and both began operations at the beginning of the current year. During the year, each company purchased inventory as follows:

Jan.	4	10,000	units at $4	=	$ 40,000
Apr.	6	5,000		5	=	25,000
Aug.	9	7,000		6	=	42,000
Nov.	27	10,000		7	=	70,000
Totals		32,000				$177,000

Over the first year, both companies sold 25,000 units of inventory.

In early January, both companies purchased equipment costing $150,000 that had a 10-year estimated useful life and a $20,000 residual value. Kanji, Inc., uses the first-in, first-out (FIFO) method for its inventory and straight-line depreciation for its equipment. Fluit Ltd. uses last-in, first-out (LIFO) and double-declining-balance depreciation. Both companies' trial balances at December 31 included the following:

Sales revenue...	$300,000
Operating expenses...	80,000

Required

1. Prepare both companies' income statements, disregarding income taxes.

2. Prepare a schedule that shows why one company appears to be more profitable than the other. Explain the schedule and amounts in your own words. What accounts for the different amounts?

3. Is one company more profitable than the other? Give your reason.

2. Plant and equipment and intangible assets   *(Obj. 7, 8)*

The following questions are unrelated except that they apply to fixed assets and intangible assets:

1. The manager of Lakeside Ltd. regularly buys plant and equipment and debits the cost to Repairs and Maintenance Expense. Why would he do that, since he knows this action violates GAAP?

2. The manager of Spruce Beach Limited regularly debits the cost of repairs and maintenance of plant and equipment to Plant and Equipment. Why would she do that, since she knows she is violating GAAP?

3. It has been suggested that, since many intangible assets have no value except to the company that owns them, they should be valued at $1.00 or zero on the balance sheet. Many accountants disagree with this view. Which view do you support? Why?

Ethical Issue

College View Apartments Ltd. purchased land and a building for a lump sum of $2.5 million. To get the maximum tax deduction, College View managers allocated 90 percent of the purchase price to the building and only 10 percent to the land. A more realistic allocation would have been 70 percent to the building and 30 percent to the land.

Required

1. Explain the tax advantage of allocating too much to the building and too little to the land.

2. Was College View's allocation ethical? If so, state why. If not, why not? Identify who was harmed.

Financial Statement Problems

1. Property, plant, and equipment and intangible assets   *(Obj. 4, 5, 8)*

Refer to the Mark's Work Wearhouse Ltd.'s financial statements in Appendix X and answer the following questions.

1. Which depreciation method does Mark's use for the purpose of reporting to shareholders and creditors in the financial statements? What type of depreciation method does the company use for income tax purposes? Why is this method preferable for income tax purposes?

2. What was the amount of depreciation and amortization expense for 1994? Record depreciation expense for 1994.

3. The statement of changes in financial position (Mark's calls it the statement of cash flow) reports purchases of property, plant, and equipment and the proceeds (sale prices) received on disposal of equipment. How much were Mark's additions to property, plant, and equipment during 1994? Journalize Mark's acquisition of these assets. Consider acquisitions only.

4. Mark's Work Wearhouse discloses the cost of fixed assets and their net book value. What was accumulated depreciation at January 30, 1993, and January 29, 1994? Assume that the only entires to the Accumulated Depreciation account in 1994 related to depreciation and amortization expense for 1994 and the accumulated depreciation on the fixed assets disposed of. Calculate the accumulated depreciation on the fixed assets disposed of.

2. *Property, plant, and equipment and intangible assets* (Obj. 3, 5, 7)

Obtain the annual report of a real company of your choosing.

Answer the following questions about the company. Concentrate on the current year in the annual report you select.

1. Which depreciation method or methods does the company use for reporting to shareholders and creditors in the financial statements? Does the company disclose the estimated useful lives of capital assets for depreciation purposes? If so, identify the useful lives.

2. Depreciation and amortization expenses are often combined since they are similar. Many income statements embed depreciation and amortization in other expense amounts. To learn the amounts of these expenses, it often becomes necessary to examine the Statement of Changes in Financial Position. Where does your company report depreciation and amortization? What were these expenses for the current year? (Note: The company you selected may have only depreciation—no amortization.)

3. How much did the company spend to acquire capital assets during the current year? Journalize the acquisitions in a single entry.

4. How much did the company receive on the sale of capital assets? Assume a particular cost and accumulated depreciation of the capital assets sold. Journalize the sale of the capital assets, assuming the sale resulted in a $700,000 loss.

5. What categories of intangible assets does the company report? What is their reported amount?

CHAPTER 11
Current Liabilities and Payroll Accounting

"Airlines with frequent-flier programs must record as a current liability the cost of flying those who will use frequent-flyer miles over the next year," says Joseph D. Wesselkamper, CPA, President of Joseph D. Wesselkamper & Associates, Inc. "When the airline is in partnership with another organization (such as a hotel chain), the problem of determining the current liability becomes more complex."

First there were the frequent-flier programs of the airlines: Fly so many miles on a particular airline, and receive a free ticket to the destination of your choice. Now some hotels—first Westin, then Holiday Inns and CP Hotels—are offering their guests *airline* mileage that makes it easier for people to earn free travel on such airlines as Air Canada and Canadian Airlines as well as on U.S. carriers.

Westin Hotels and Resorts, for example, offer 500 Aeroplan (Air Canada) miles for each stay at a Westin Hotel. Delta Hotels and Resorts are affiliated with Canadian Airlines and give Canadian Plus miles to guests who stay at the hotel. Why would these hotels make such offers? To encourage travelers to stay at Westin or Delta hotels. To the hotel, the cost is a promotion expense. Why would Air Canada or Canadian Airlines allow the hotels to make this offer? To generate revenue: the airlines charge the hotels approximately $0.015 per mile credited to the customer's account (frequent flier rewards always seem to be measured in miles perhaps because the U.S. is the leader in the field).

This real example illustrates the challenge of accounting for liabilities. In this case the airlines have an obligation to provide travel paid for by the hotels.

CHAPTER OBJECTIVES

After studying this chapter, you should be able to

1 Account for current liabilities

2 Account for contingent liabilities

3 Compute payroll amounts

4 Make basic payroll entries

5 Use a payroll system

6 Report current liabilities

A *liability* is an obligation to transfer assets or to provide services in the future. The obligation may arise from a transaction with an outside party. For example, a business incurs a liability when it purchases inventory on account or when it issues a note payable to borrow money.

An obligation may arise in the absence of individual transactions. For example, interest expense accrues with the passage of time. Until this interest is paid it is a liability. Income tax, a liability of corporations, accrues as income is earned. Proper accounting for liabilities is as important as proper accounting for assets. The failure to record an accrued liability causes the balance sheet to understate the related expense and thus overstate owner's or shareholders' equity.

Current liabilities are obligations due within one year or within the company's operating cycle if it is longer than one year. Obligations due beyond that period of time are classified as long-term liabilities.

Let's focus on the airline's transactions in this situation. Suppose that a Westin Hotel grants 100,000 miles of Air Canada Aeroplan frequent-flier credit to its guests. Air Canada's cost is $1,500 (100,000 miles at $0.015 per mile). Assume that Westin pays Aeroplan $1,500. Could you account for these transactions on the books of Air Canada?

Air Canada records a $1,500 liability for unearned service revenue when it receives cash from Westin Motels & Resorts.[1] This is a liability and not a revenue because Air Canada has not yet provided free air travel for the hotel guests. Later, as Westin's hotel guests use their free air travel, Air Canada records the revenue.

We discuss long-term liabilities in Chapter 16. We now turn to accounting for current liabilities, including those arising from payroll expenses. Current liabilities fall into one of two categories: liabilities of a known amount and those whose amount must be estimated. We look first at current liabilities of known amount.

Current Liabilities of Known Amount _____

Accounts Payable

OBJECTIVE 1
Account for current liabilities

Amounts owed to suppliers for products or services that are purchased on open account are accounts payable. We have seen many accounts payable examples in previous chapters. For example, a business may purchase inventories and office supplies on an account payable.

Current liabilities arising from many similar transactions are well suited for computerized accounting. One of the most common transactions of a merchandiser is the credit purchase of inventory. It is efficient to integrate the accounts payable and perpetual inventory systems. When merchandise dips below a predetermined level, the system automatically prepares a purchase request. After the order is placed and the goods are received, inventory and accounts payable data are entered. The

---

[1] See Richard A. Samuelson, "Accounting for Liabilities to Perform Services," *Accounting Horizons*, September 1993, pp. 32–45.

computer then debits Inventory and credits Accounts Payable to account for the purchase. For payments, the computer debits Accounts Payable and credits Cash. The program may also update account balances and print journals, ledger accounts, and the financial statements.

Short-Term Notes Payable

Short-term notes payable, a common form of financing, are notes payable that are due within one year. Companies often issue short-term notes payable to borrow cash or to purchase inventory or capital assets. In addition to recording the note payable and its eventual payment, the business must also accrue interest expense and interest payable at the end of the period. The following entries are typical of this liability:

19X1			
Sept. 30	Purchases...	8,000	
	Note Payable, Short-Term		8,000
	Purchase of inventory by issuing a one-year 10 percent note payable.		
Dec. 31	Interest Expense ($8,000 × .10 × ³⁄₁₂).....................	200	
	Interest Payable...		200
	Adjusting entry to accrue interest expense at year end.		

The balance sheet at December 31, 19X1, will report the Note Payable of $8,000 and the related Interest Payable of $200 as current liabilities. The 19X1 income statement will report interest expense of $200.

The following entry records the note's payment:

19X2			
Sept. 30	Note Payable, Short-Term.................................	8,000	
	Interest Payable...	200	
	Interest Expense ($8,000 × .10 × ⁹⁄₁₂)..................	600	
	Cash [$8,000 + ($8,000 × .10)].......................		8,800
	Payment of a note payable and interest at maturity.		

The cash payment entry must split the total interest on the note between the portion accrued at the end of the previous period ($200) and the period's expense ($600).

The face amount of notes payable and their interest rates and payment dates can be stored for electronic data processing. Computer programs calculate interest, print the interest cheques, journalize the transactions, and update account balances.

Short-Term Notes Payable Issued at a Discount ~ omit

In another common borrowing arrangement, a company may **discount a note payable** at the bank. Discounting means that the bank subtracts the interest amount from the note's face value. The borrower receives the net amount. In effect, the borrower prepays the interest, which is computed on the principal of the note.

Suppose Inco Ltd. discounts a $100,000, 60-day note payable to their bank at 12 percent. The company will receive $98,027, that is, the $100,000 face value less interest of $1,973 ($100,000 × .12 × ⁶⁰⁄₃₆₅). Assume this transaction occurs on November 25, 19X1. Inco's entries to record discounting the note would be:

19X1			
Nov. 25	Cash ($100,000 – $1,973)..	98,027	
	Discount on Note Payable ($100,000 × .12 × ⁶⁰⁄₃₆₅).....	1,973	
	Note Payable, Short-Term.......................................		100,000
	Discounted a $100,000, 60-day, 12-percent note payable to borrow cash.		

Short Exercise:
A $10,000, 11%, 90-day note was issued on Nov. 1. Record the accrual on Dec. 31 and the note payment on Jan 30.
A:

12/31
Interest Expense ($10,000 × 11% × 60/365) 181
  Interest Payable... 181

1/30
Note Payable 10,000
Interest Payable . 181
Interest Expense 90
  Cash 10,271

Short Exercise:
A company borrows $5,000 on a two-month, 9% note on Aug. 31. Record the issuance and payment of the note with interest stated separately. **A:**

8/31
Cash................... 5,000
  Note Payable.... 5,000

10/30
Note Payable 5,000
Interest Expense 75
  Cash................. 5,075

Short Exercise:

For the previous Short
Exercise, record the issuance
and payment of the note with
interest deducted in advance.
A:

8/31
Cash.................. 4,925
Discount on
  Note Payable.... 75
    Note Payable... 5,000

10/30
Int. Expense...... 75
Note Payable..... 5,000
  Cash................ 5,000
  Discount on
    Note Payable... 75

Discount on Note Payable is a contra account to the liability Note Payable, Short-Term. A balance sheet prepared immediately after this transaction would report the note payable at its net amount of $98,027, as follows:

Current liabilities
Note payable, short-term.............................. $100,000
  Less: Discount on note payable .... (1,973)
Note payable, short-term, net .... $ 98,027

The accrued interest at year end must still be recorded, as it would for any note payable. The adjusting entry at December 31 records interest for 36 days as follows:

19X1
Dec. 31 Interest Expense ($100,000 × .12 × $36/365$) 1,184
           Discount on Note Payable...................................... 1,184
         Adjusting entry to accrue interest expense at year
         end.

This entry credits the Discount account instead of Interest Payable. Why? Because the Discount balance represents future interest expense, and the accrual of interest records the current-period portion of the expense. Furthermore, crediting the Discount reduces this contra account's balance and increases the net amount of the Note Payable. After the adjusting entry, only $789 of the Discount remains, and the carrying value of the Note Payable increases to $99,211, as follows:

Current liabilities
Note payable, short-term.. $100,000
  Less: Discount on note payable
    ($1,973 – $1,184).. (789)
Note payable, short-term, net .... $ 99,211

Finally, the business records the note's payment:

19X2
Jan. 24   Interest Expense ($100,000 × .12 × $24/365$) 789
            Discount on Note Payable 789
          To record interest expense.
          Note Payable, Short-Term.. 100,000
            Cash.. 100,000
          To pay note payable at maturity.

After these entries, the balances in the note payable account and the discount account are zero. Each period's income statement reports the appropriate amount of interest expense.

Goods and Services Tax and Sales Tax Payable

There are two basic consumption taxes levied on purchases in Canada that will be visible to the consumer: the goods and services tax (GST) levied by the federal government and provincial sales taxes (PST) levied by all the provinces except Alberta; there are, at present, no sales taxes in the Yukon or the Northwest Territories. There are also excise or luxury taxes, sometimes called "sin taxes," which are a form of sales tax levied by the federal and provincial governments on products such as cigarettes, jewelery, and alcoholic beverages; these taxes are hidden in that they are collected by the manufacturer. The focus of discussion in this section will be on the consumption or visible taxes; the goods and services tax and provincial sales taxes will be discussed in turn below. In order to simplify the discussion, the material concerning calculation and payment of the GST will exclude the PST and the material concerning calculation and payment of the PST will generally exclude the GST.

Goods and Services Tax — omit

In 1991, the federal government passed legislation eliminating existing taxes imposed on manufactured and imported goods. At the same time, it implemented a goods and services tax (GST) that is collected from the ultimate consumer and includes most goods and services consumed in Canada. The tax and its application is covered in an introductory tax course and is beyond the scope of this text; the ensuing discussion deals primarily with basic facts about the tax and how to account for it.

There are three categories of goods and services with respect to the GST:

1. Zero-rated supplies such as basic groceries, prescription drugs, and medical devices;

2. Exempt supplies such as educational services, health care services, and financial services; and

3. Taxable supplies, which basically includes everything that is not zero-rated or exempt.

The GST rate is 7 percent. The tax is collected by the individual or entity (called the *registrant*) supplying the taxable good or service (called *taxable supplies*) to the final consumer and remitted to the Receiver General. Suppliers of taxable goods and services have to pay tax on their purchases, but are able to deduct the amount of GST paid (called an *input tax credit*) from the GST they have collected from their sales of goods and services in calculating the amount due the government. The GST Return and the net tax must be remitted to the Receiver General quarterly for most registrants and monthly for larger registrants.

For example, Mary Janicek purchases a power lawn mower with a view to earning money by cutting grass during the summer.[2] The lawn mower cost $250; the GST would be $17.50. Because Mary is planning to use the mower exclusively to cut grass for a fee, she could recover the $17.50. However, she would have to charge all her customers the 7 percent GST on sales of her lawn-mowing services and remit it to the government. During the three-month first quarter, Mary earned revenue of $2,000.00 and thus collected $2,140.00. She spent $107.00—$100.00 plus GST of $7.00 on gasoline for the mower. Her input tax credit of $24.50 included the $17.50 GST on the lawn mower and $7.00 GST on gasoline for the mower. The entries to record these transactions would be

Equipment	267.50	
Cash		267.50
To record purchase of power mower.		
Supplies Expense	107.00	
Cash		107.00
To record purchase of gasoline for power mower.		
Cash	2,140.00	
Lawn-mowing Revenue		2,000.00
GST Payable		140.00
To record revenue earned from mowing lawns.		

Mary would be required to remit $115.50 ($140.00 – $24.50) as her first quarterly payment. Since Mary would be recovering the GST paid on the purchase of the mower and gasoline, she would credit the recovery to the fixed asset account, Equipment, and the expense account, Supplies Expense. The entry would be as follows:

GST Payable	140.00	
Cash		115.50
Equipment		17.50
Supplies Expense		7.00
To record payment of GST payable net of input tax credits.		

---

[2] In reality, Mary Janicek's business would be below the minimum threshold of $30,000, so Mary is unlikely to be a registrant. The scenario is illustrative.

Because they collect the GST for the federal government, the registrants owe the Receiver General the net tax collected; the account Goods and Services Tax Payable is a current liability. Most companies include GST owing with Accounts Payable and Accrued Liabilities on their balance sheets.

Provincial Sales Tax

Short Exercise:

Record sales of $35,650 and the related 7½% sales tax if (1) the sales tax is recorded separately and (2) the sales tax is included in Sales.

A: (1) Only one entry is required:

Cash............... 38,324
Sales
   Revenue........   35,650
Sales Tax
   Payable   2,674

(2) Two entries are required:

Cash............... 38,324
Sales
   Revenue........   38,324
Sales
   Revenue......... 2,674
Sales Tax
   Payable   2,674

$\left(\$2{,}674 = \$38{,}324 - \dfrac{\$38{,}324}{1.075}\right)$

As was mentioned above, all the provinces, except Alberta (as well as the Yukon and the Northwest Territories), levy a sales tax on sales to the final consumers of products; they are not levied on sales to wholesalers or retailers. The final sellers charge their customers the sales tax in addition to the price of the item sold. At the time of this writing, five provinces charge PST on the sum of the price of the good or service purchased plus the GST; three provinces calculate PST and GST separately; and one province has harmonized the GST and PST. For example, Nova Scotia charges PST on GST; a taxable sale of $100.00 would have GST of $7.00 (.07 × $100.00) and PST of $10.70 [.10 × ($100.00 + $7.00)]. Ontario charges PST and GST separately; a taxable sale of $100.00 would have GST of $7.00 (.07 × $100.00) and PST of $8.00 (.08 × $100.00). Quebec has harmonized the PST and the GST; a taxable sale of $100.00 would have PST and GST of $13.50 [(.065 × $100.00) + (.07 × $100.00)].

Consider Super Stereo Products Inc., an electronics superstore located in Ottawa. Super Stereo does not pay sales tax on its purchase of a TV set from Electrohome but you would have to pay the province of Ontario's 8 percent provincial sales tax to Super Stereo when you buy an Electrohome set from the store. Super Stereo pays the sales tax to the provincial government. Electrohome would not have a sales tax liability at its year end, but Super Stereo probably would. (For purposes of the discussion of sales tax, we will ignore the GST.)

Suppose one Saturday's sales at the Super Stereo store totaled $20,000. The business would have collected an additional 8 percent in sales tax, which would equal $1,600 ($20,000 × .08). The business would record that day's sales as follows:

Cash ($20,000 × 1.08)...	21,600	
Sales Revenue...		20,000
Sales Tax Payable ($20,000 × .08)		1,600
To record cash sales of $20,000 subject to 8 percent sales tax.		

Because the retailers owe the province the sales tax collected, the account Sales Tax Payable is a current liability. Most companies include sales tax payable with Accounts Payable and Accrued charges on their balance sheets.

Companies forward the collected sales tax to the taxing authority at regular intervals, at which time they debit Sales Tax Payable and credit Cash. Observe that Sales Tax Payable does not correspond to any sales tax expense that the business is incurring. Nor does this liability arise from the purchase of any asset. Rather, it is the cash that the business is collecting for the government.

Many companies consider it inefficient to credit Sales Tax Payable when recording sales. They record the sale in an amount that includes the tax. Then prior to paying tax to the province, they make a single entry for the entire period's transactions to bring Sales Revenue and Sales Tax Payable to their correct balances.

Suppose a company located in Vancouver had sales in July of $100,000, subject to the B.C. retail sales tax of 7 percent. Its summary entry to record the month's sales could be

July 31	Cash ($100,000 × 1.07)...	107,000	
	Sales Revenue..		107,000
	To record sales for the month.		

The entry to adjust Sales Revenue and Sales Tax Payable to their correct balances is

July 31	Sales Revenue [$107,000 – ($107,000 ÷ 1.07)]	7,000	
	Sales Tax Payable		7,000
	To record sales tax.		

Companies that follow this procedure need to make an adjusting entry at the end of the period in order to report the correct amounts of revenue and liability on their financial statements.

Current Portion of Long-Term Debt

Some long-term notes payable and long-term bonds payable must be paid in installments. The **current portion of long-term debt**, or *current maturity*, is the amount of the principal that is due within one year. This amount does not include the interest due. Of course, any liability for accrued interest payable must also be reported, but a separate account, Interest Payable, is used for that purpose.

Big Rock Brewery Ltd. owed $169,400 on long-term debt at March 31, 1994, the end of its fiscal year. Slightly more than $80,000 was a current liability because it was due within one year. The remaining $89,000 was a long-term liability. Big Rock's March 31, 1994, balance sheet reported:

Current Liabilities (in part)	
Accounts payable..	$392,663
Current portion of long term debt..............................	80,400

Long-Term Debt	
Long-term debt...	$ 89,000

STOP & THINK

Suppose that Big Rock Brewery reported its full liability as long-term. Identify two ratios that would have been distorted by this accounting error. State whether the ratio values would be overstated or understated and whether they would report an overly positive or negative view of the company.

Answer: Reporting a liability as long-term understates current liabilities and has these effects:

Ratio	Overstated or Understated	View of the Company
Current ratio	Overstated	Overly positive
Acid-test ratio	Overstated	Overly positive

The point of this example is that accounting includes both *recording* transactions and *reporting* the information. Reporting is every bit as important as recording.

Accrued Expenses

As shown in the Big Rock Brewery presentation, accrued expenses, such as interest expense, create current liabilities because the interest is due within the year. Therefore, the interest payable (accrued interest) is reported as a current liability. Other important liabilities for accrued expenses are payroll and the related payroll withholdings, which we discuss in the second part of this chapter.

Unearned Revenues

Unearned revenues are also called *deferred revenues, revenues collected in advance,* and *customer prepayments.* Each account title indicates that the business has received cash from its customers before earning the revenue. The company has an obligation to provide goods or services to the customer.

Short Exercise:

Suppose a contractor collected $300,000 in advance for the installation of special flooring in a building. At year end, one-fourth of the work is completed. What amount of Unearned Revenue should be transferred to Revenue? *A:* $300,000 × 1/4 = $75,000

The Financial Post may be purchased daily or by means of a subscription. When subscribers pay in advance to have *The Financial Post* delivered to their home or business, Financial Post Publications incurs a liability to provide future service. The liability account is called Unearned Subscription Revenue (which could also be titled Unearned Subscription Income or Deferred Subscription Income).

Assume that Financial Post Publications charges $585 for Mary Bish's three-year subscription to *The Financial Post*. Financial Post Publications' entries would be

19X1
Jan. 1   Cash   585
                Unearned Subscription Revenue   585
            To record receipt of cash at start of a three-year
            subscription.

19X1, 19X2, 19X3
Dec. 31   Unearned Subscription Revenue   195
                Subscription Revenue ($585/3)   195
            To record subscription revenue earned at the end of
            each of three years.

Financial Post Publications' financial statements would report this sequence:

| | December 31 | | |
Balance Sheet	Year 1	Year 2	Year 3
Current liabilities*			
Unearned subscription revenue..................................	$390	$195	$-0-

Income Statement	Year 1	Year 2	Year 3
Revenues			
Subscription revenue..	$195	$195	$195

*Technically half the liability should be shown as long-term but most companies simply show the entire liability as current.

Customer Deposits Payable

Some companies require cash deposits from customers as security on borrowed assets. These amounts are called Customer Deposits Payable because the company must refund the cash to the customer under certain conditions.

For example, telephone companies may demand a cash deposit from a customer before installing a telephone. Utility companies and businesses that lend tools and appliances commonly demand a deposit as protection against damage and theft. When the customer ends the service or returns the borrowed asset, the company refunds the cash deposit—if the customer has paid all the bills and has not damaged the company's property. Because the company generally must return the deposit, that cash is a liability. The uncertainty of when the deposits will be refunded and their relatively small amounts cause many companies to classify Customer Deposits Payable as current liabilities. This is consistent with the concept of conservatism.

Certain manufacturers of products sold through individual dealers, such as Avon or Mary Kay, require deposits from the dealers who sell their products; the deposit is usually equal to the cost of the sample kit provided to the merchandiser. Companies, whose products are sold in returnable containers, collect deposits on those containers. The most common example is the deposit on soda pop bottles. In both cases the deposits are shown as current liabilities by the manufacturers. The amounts are relatively small and so are included with accounts payable and accrued charges.

Current Liabilities That Must Be Estimated _____

A business may know that a liability exists but not know the amount. The liability may not simply be ignored. The unknown amount of a liability must be estimated for reporting on the balance sheet.

Estimated current liabilities vary among companies. As an example, let us look at Estimated Warranty Payable, a liability account common among merchandisers.

Estimated Warranty Payable

Many manufacturers and some merchandising companies guarantee their products against defects under *warranty* agreements. The warranty period may extend for any length of time. Ninety-day warranties and one-year warranties are common. Some automobile companies such as General Motors and Chrysler have five-year, 100,000-kilometer warranties on new cars.

Whatever the warranty's lifetime, the matching principle demands that the company record the *warranty expense* in the same period that the business recognizes sales revenue. After all, offering the warranty—and incurring any possible expense through the warranty agreement—is a part of generating revenue through sales. At the time of the sale, however, the company does not know which products are defective. The exact amount of warranty expense cannot be known with certainty, so the business must estimate its warranty expense and open the related liability account—Estimated Warranty Payable (also called Accrued Warranty Costs and Product Warranty Liability). Even though the warranty liability depends on the occurrence of future events, it is accounted for as an actual liability because the obligation for warranty expense has occurred and its amount can be estimated.

Companies may make a reliable estimate of their warranty expense based on their experience. Assume a company made sales of $200,000, subject to product warranties. Company management, noting that in past years between 2 percent and 4 percent of products proved defective, estimates that 3 percent of the products will require repair or replacement during the one-year warranty period. The company records warranty expense of $6,000 ($200,000 × .03) for the period:

Warranty Expense	6,000	
Estimated Warranty Payable.......................................		6,000
To accrue warranty expense.		

Assume that defective merchandise totals $5,800. The company may either repair or replace it. Corresponding entries follow.

Estimated Warranty Payable	5,800	
Cash		5,800
To *repair* defective products sold under warranty.		

Estimated Warranty Payable	5,800	
Inventory..		5,800
To *replace* defective products sold under warranty.		

The expense is $6,000 on the income statement no matter what the cash payment or the cost of the replacement inventory. In future periods, the company may come to debit the liability Estimated Warranty Payable for the remaining $200. However, *when* the company repairs or replaces defective merchandise has no bearing on when the company records warranty expense. The business records warranty expense in the same period as the sale.

Other Estimated Current Liabilities

Estimated Vacation Pay Liability   Most companies grant paid vacations to their employees. The employees receive this benefit during the time they take their

Short Exercise:
A company made sales of $400,000 and estimated warranty repairs at 5% of the sales. Actual warranty outlays were $19,000. Record the sales, the warranty expense, and the warranty outlays.
A:

Accounts Rec.....400,000		
Sales Revenue		400,000

Warranty Expense		
(400,000 × 5%)..20,000		
Est. Warr. Pay		20,000

Est. Warr. Pay..... 19,000		
Cash, Inventory,		
and so on		19,000

vacation, but they earn the compensation by working the other days of the year. The law requires most employers to provide a minimum of two weeks holiday per year, although some employers provide longer holidays to employees who have worked for the company for ten or more years. To match expense with revenue properly, the company accrues the vacation pay expense and liability for each of the 50 workweeks of the year. Then, the company records payment during the two-week vacation period. Employee turnover, terminations, and ineligibility force companies to estimate the vacation pay liability.

Suppose a company's January payroll is $100,000 and vacation pay adds 4 percent (two weeks of annual vacation divided by 50 workweeks each year). Experience indicates that only 80 percent of the vacations owed will be taken, so the January vacation pay estimate is $3,200 ($100,000 × .04 × .80). In Janaury, the company records the vacation pay accrual as follows:

| Jan. 31 | Vacation Pay Expense .... | 3,200 | |
| | Estimated Vacation Pay Liability .... | | 3,200 |

Each month thereafter, the company makes a similar entry for 4 percent of the payroll.

If an employee takes a vacation in August, his or her $2,000 monthly salary is recorded as follows:

Aug. 31	Estimated Vacation Pay Liability	2,000	
	Various Witholding Accounts and		
	Wages Payable[3]		2,000

Short Exercise:

Which of the following items is a current liability at 12/31/94?

1. Note Payable due 3/31/95
2. Customer's accounts receivable with a credit balance
3. Allowance for uncollectible accounts
4. The portion of a note payable due in 1996
5. Accrued interest payable

A: Items 1, 2, and 5 are current liabilities.

Estimated Frequent-Flier Liability of an Airline Company

The chapter-opening story describes how hotel companies are offering guests frequent-flier mileage for free air travel. In that situation the hotels prepay the airlines for the travel. Exhibit 11-1 shows how to account for the airlines' unearned service revenue, based on the chapter-opening story.

The airlines' own frequent-flier plans work differently. Usually there is no hotel operating as an intermediary. Typically, a passenger who travels a certain number of miles can take a free trip or upgrade his or her ticket from coach class to first class. The operating expense of providing this free service creates a liability for the airline. When should the expense and estimated frequent-flier liability be recorded? As the airline earns revenue from its paying customers. Under the matching principle, a company should record expense when it earns the related revenue. Because the ultimate cost of providing the free transportation is uncertain, the airline must estimate this expense and the related liability. Suppose Air Canada records revenue of $1 million in February. Air Canada estimates that this revenue-producing travel will give customers free trips that will cost the company 3 percent of the revenue. Air Canada could record frequent-flier expense and liability as follows:

| Feb. 28 | Aeroplan Expense ($1,000,000 × 0.03) .... | 30,000 | |
| | Estimated Aeroplan liability .... | | 30,000 |

In July, when an Areoplan member takes a free trip costing the airline $150, Air Canada could record the transaction as follows:

| July 8 | Estimated Aeroplan liability .... | 150 | |
| | Various operating expenses .... | | 150 |

The credit side of this entry would depend on the airline's particular situation. The expenses incurred would relate to the cash cost of the services provided to the

---

[3] The various payroll accounts are discussed later in the chapter.

EXHIBIT 11-1   *An Airline's Accounting for Frequent-Flier Mileage Granted by a Hotel Company*

Panel A—Example

In 19X3, Westin Hotels granted 1,000,000 miles of credit to its guests for free travel on Air Canada. Air Canada charges Westin $0.015 per mile, for a total of $15,000 (1,000,000 miles × $0.015). Assume that Air Canada will earn this revenue as follows: $5,000 in 19X4 and $10,000 in 19X5.

Panel B—Accounting Records of Air Canada

Journal Entries	19X3		19X4	19X5
Cash......................................	15,000			
Unearned Service Revenue		15,000		
Unearned Service Revenue..............			5,000	10,000
Service Revenue.............................			5,000	10,000

	December 31,		
Balance Sheet	19X3	19X4	19X5
Current liabilities:			
Unearned service revenue.............	$ 5,000	$10,000	$ –0–
Long-term liabilities:			
Unearned service revenue.............	10,000	–0–	–0–
Income Statement	**19X3**	**19X4**	**19X5**
Service revenue	$ –0–	$5,000	$10,000

Aeroplan passenger such as ticket and baggage handling, and inflight meals and beverages.

Contingent Liabilities

OBJECTIVE 2
Account for contingent liabilities

A *contingent liability* is not an actual liability. Instead, it is a potential liability that depends on a *future* event arising out of a past transaction. For example, a town government may sue the company that installed new street lights, claiming that the electrical wiring is faulty. The past transaction is the street-light installation. The future event is the court case that will decide the suit. The lighting company thus faces a contingent liability, which may or may not become an actual obligation.

It would be unethical for the company to withhold knowledge of the lawsuit from its creditors or from anyone considering investing in the business. A person or business could be misled into thinking the company is stronger financially than it really is. The *disclosure principle* of accounting requires a company to report any information deemed relevant to outsiders of the business. The goal is to arm people with relevant, reliable information for decision-making.

The Accounting Standards Board in Section 3290 requires that *contingent losses* generally be accrued in the financial statements but bars *contingent gains* from being recognized *until* they are realized. This approach follows the principle of conservatism. The Section recognizes that there is always uncertainty underlying contingencies and has identified three levels of uncertainty:

likely: the chance of the occurrence (or non-occurrence) of the future event is high. Warranty expense is an example.

unlikely: the chance of the occurrence (or non-occurrence) of the future event is slight. A golf course promises to pay $25,000 to the first golfer to get a hole-in-one on a particular hole.

not determinable: the chance of the occurrence (or non-occurrence) of the future event cannot be determined. A department store has guaranteed the loans of customers for whom the store installed a new type of roof; the success or failure is unknown and so the cost cannot be estimated.

It is up to management to assess how likely the contingent liability is and thus how, if at all, it should be disclosed.

Sometimes the contingent liability has a definite amount. Recall from chapter 8 that the payee of a discounted note has a contingent liability. If the maker of the note pays at maturity, the contingent liability ceases to exist. However, if the maker defaults, the payee, who sold the note, must pay its maturity value to the purchaser. In this case, the payee knows the note's maturity value, which is the amount of the contingent liability.

Another contingent liability of known amount arises from guaranteeing that a second company will pay a note payable that it owes a third party. This practice, called *cosigning a note*, obligates the guarantor to pay the note and interest if, and only if, the primary debtor fails to pay. Thus the guarantor has a contingent liability until the note becomes due. If the primary debtor pays off, the contingent liability ceases to exist. If the primary debtor fails to pay, the guarantor's liability becomes actual.

Sometimes the amount that will have to be paid, if the contingent liability becomes an actual liability, is not known at the balance sheet date. For example, companies face lawsuits, which may cause possible future obligations of amounts to be determined by the courts. Revenue Canada may have indicated to the entity that a reassessment of its income and taxes has been made or is forthcoming but the company may not know the amount of its liability at the time the financial statements are prepared.

Contingent liabilities are normally disclosed in the notes to the financial statements unless both the confirming future event is likely and the amount of the loss can be reasonably estimated, in which case the amount of the loss should be accrued in the financial statements. When the loss is both likely and estimable, then it is less a contingent loss than a real loss; that is why the loss is accrued or put through the books as of the statement date. For example, suppose Revenue Canada had reassessed a company prior to its year end at December 31, 19X7 disallowing expenses claimed by the company on its 19X5 tax return. If the company decided to accept the reassessment (in which case the confirming future event is likely and the amount known), it should accrue the additional tax payable. If, on the other hand, the company had decided to appeal the reassessment (that is, neither condition is met), the reassessment should be treated as a contingency and shown in the notes.

A few companies draw attention to the footnote describing the contingent liability by making reference to it on the balance sheet. The most common locations for the reference are between liabilities and owners' equity and after owners' equity.

Dreco Energy Services Ltd., an Edmonton-based company that designs, manufactures and sells or rents equipment and supplies related to the oil- and gas-drilling and well-servicing business reports the following in the notes to the financial statements under the heading "Contingencies":

(a) Incidental to the business of the Company, the Company and one or more of its subsidiaries are parties to various lawsuits which allege negligence and liability for product failure or non-performance and claim damages arising therefrom. In management's opinion, to the extent the claims represented by any of these lawsuits are valid, they are either not material or are covered by insurance.

(b) At August 31 (year end), Letters of credit had been issued by the Company in connection with certain contracts and obligations. These letters of credit are released upon performance of the Company's contractual obligations under letters of credit. Should the company default in such performance, the Company will become liable for all or a portion of the outstanding letters of credit.

Mid-Chapter Summary Problem for Your Review

This problem consists of three independent parts:

1. Suppose a Harvey's hamburger restaurant in Nova Scotia made cash sales of $4,000 subject to the 7 percent GST and 11 percent provincial sales tax. Record the sales and the related consumption taxes (Nova Scotia charges PST on GST). Also record payment of the sales tax to the provincial government and the GST to the Receiver General (assume input tax credits amount to $129.00).

2. Suppose at June 30, 19X2, McCain Foods Ltd. reported a 9 percent long-term debt as follows:

Current Liabilities (in part)	millions
Portion of long-term debt due within one year	$ 3.0
Interest payable (20.5 × .09 × ³/₁₂)...	.46

Long-Term Debt and Other Liabilities (in part)	
Long-term debt	$17.5

Assume the company pays interest on its long-term debt on March 31.
Show how McCain would report its liabilities on the year-end balance sheet at June 30, 19X3. Assume the current maturity of its long-term debt is $4 million and the long-term portion is $18 million.

3. What distinguishes a contingent liability from an actual liability?

SOLUTION TO REVIEW PROBLEM

1.

Cash [($4,000 × 1.07) × 1.11]..	4,751	
Sales Revenue		4,000
GST Payable ($4,000 × .07)		280
Sales Tax Payable ($4,280 × .11)...........................		471

To record cash sales and related GST and provincial sales tax.

GST Payable..	280	
Sales Tax Payable	471	
Cash...		622
Various accounts to be credited for the input tax credit		129

To pay GST to the Receiver General, net of the input tax credit, and sales tax to the provincial government.

2. McCain Foods Ltd.'s balance sheet at June 30, 19X3, would be as follows:

Current Liabilities (in part)	millions
Portion of long-term debt due within one year..............	$4.0
Interest payable (22 × .09 × ³/₁₂)...	.50

Long-Term Debt and Other Liabilities (in part)	
Long-term debt...	$18.0

3. A contingent liability is a potential liability, which may or may not become an actual liability. It arises out of a past transaction and depends on a future event to determine if it will become an actual liability.

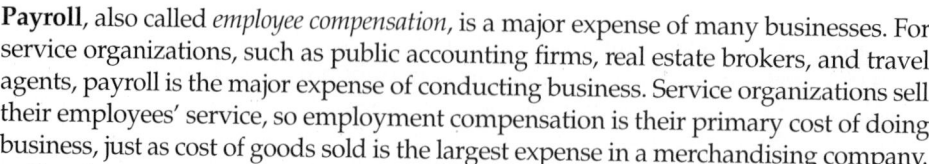

Accounting for Payroll

OBJECTIVE 3
Compute payroll amounts

Payroll, also called *employee compensation*, is a major expense of many businesses. For service organizations, such as public accounting firms, real estate brokers, and travel agents, payroll is the major expense of conducting business. Service organizations sell their employees' service, so employment compensation is their primary cost of doing business, just as cost of goods sold is the largest expense in a merchandising company.

Key Point:
The salaries and wages of a company are usually the single largest expense after cost of goods sold.

Employment compensation takes different forms. Some employees collect a *salary*, which is income stated at a yearly, monthly, or weekly rate. Other employees work for *wages*, which is employee pay stated at an hourly figure. Sales employees often receive a *commission*, which is a percentage of the sales the employee has made. Some companies reward excellent performance with a *bonus*, an amount over and above regular compensation.

Businesses often pay employees at a base rate for a set number of hours—called *straight time*. For working any additional hours—called *overtime*—the employee receives a higher rate.

Assume that Lucy Childres is an accountant for an electronics company. Lucy earns $600 per week straight time. The company workweek runs 40 hours, so Lucy's hourly wage is $15 ($600/40). Her company pays her *time and a half* for overtime. The rate is 150 percent (1.5 times) the straight-time rate. Thus Lucy earns $22.50 for each hour of overtime she works ($15.00 × 1.5 = $22.50). For working 42 hours during a week, she earns $645, computed as follows:

Straight-time pay for 40 hours..................................	$600
Overtime pay for 2 overtime hours (2 × $22.50)......	45
Total pay...	$645

Gross Pay and Net Pay

Many years ago,[4] employees brought home all that they had earned. For example, Lucy Childres would have taken home the full $645 total that she made. Payroll accounting was straightforward. Those days are long past.

The federal government and most provincial governments demand that employers act as collection agents for employee taxes, which are deducted from employee cheques. Insurance companies, labor unions, charitable organizations such as the United Way, and other organizations may also take pieces of employees' pay. Amounts withheld from an employee's cheque are called deductions.

EXHIBIT 11-2   *Gross Pay and Net Pay*

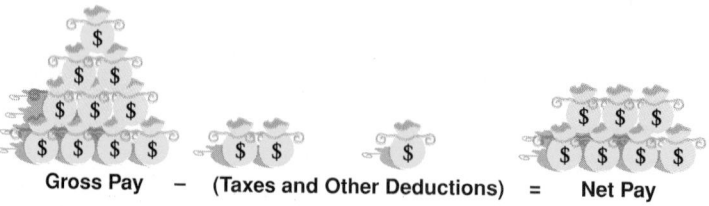

| Gross Pay | − | (Taxes and Other Deductions) | = | Net Pay |

---

[4] Income taxes were first imposed by the federal government in Canada in 1917 as a temporary measure to provide funds for the conduct of Canada's efforts in World War I.

Gross pay is the total amount of salary, wages, commissions, or any other employee compensation before taxes and other deductions are taken out. **Net pay**—the "take-home pay"—equals gross pay minus all deductions. As Exhibit 11-2 shows, net pay is the amount the employee actually takes home.

In addition to employee taxes that employers must withhold from pay, employers themselves must pay some payroll expenses. Many companies also pay employee *fringe benefits*, such as health and life insurance and retirement pay. Payroll accounting has become quite complex. Let us turn now to a discussion of payroll deductions.

Payroll Deductions

Payroll deductions that are *withheld* from employees' pay fall into two categories: (1) *required deductions*, which include employee income tax, unemployment insurance, and Canada Pension or Quebec Pension Plan deductions; and (2) *optional deductions*, which include union dues, insurance premiums, charitable contributions, and other amounts that are withheld at the employee's request. After they are withheld, payroll deductions become the liability of the employer, who assumes responsibility for paying the outside party. For example, the employer pays the government the employee income tax withheld and pays the union the employee union dues withheld.

Required Payroll Deductions

Employee Withheld Income Tax Payable The law requires most employers to withhold income tax from their employees' salaries and wages. The amount of income tax deducted from gross pay is called **withheld income tax**. For many employees, this deduction is the largest. The amount withheld depends on the employee's gross pay and on the number of withholding allowances the employee claims.

Each employee files a Form TD1 with the employer. Exhibit 11-3 is an example of Form TD1. It has been completed by Roberta C. Dean who has a spouse Pierre, who is an author with an estimated income of $3,000, and two children under the age of 18. Roberta claims $6,456 for herself and $2,918 for Pierre, for a total claim of $9,374.[5] Roberta selects a net claim code of 3. Roberta's employer will use the net claim code number to compute the amount of income tax that should be withheld from Roberta's monthly salary.

Revenue Canada provides tax tables each year, which the employer uses with the TD1s to calculate the amount of income tax to be withheld each pay period.

The employer sends its employees' withheld income tax to the government. The amount of the income tax withheld determines how often the employer submits tax payments. Most employers must remit the taxes to the government at least monthly; larger employers must remit two or four times a month, depending on the total amounts withheld. Every business must account for payroll taxes on a calendar-year basis regardless of its fiscal year.

The employer accumulates taxes in the Employees' Withheld Income Tax Payable account. The word *payable* indicates that the account is a liability to the employer, even though the employees are the people taxed.

Employee Withheld Canada (or Quebec) Pension Plan Contributions Payable The **Canada (or Quebec) Pension Plan** (CPP or QPP) provides retirement, disability, and death benefits to employees who are covered by it. Employers are required to deduct premiums from each employee required to make a contribution (basically all employees between 18 and 70 years of age). The maximum pensionable earnings for CPP for 1995 are $34,900 and the basic exemption is $3,400. The premium is 2.7 percent of wages in excess of the basic exemption of $3,400, up to a maximum contribution in a year of $850.50 [($34,900 − $3,400) × .027]. If CPP is being

Real-World Example:
Revenue Canada enforces stiff penalties for underpayment of income taxes by individuals. In 1994, the penalty was 9% of the underpayment amount.

---

[5] Family Allowance was eliminated in 1993. For purposes of discussion, we will use a claim code of 3; an employee may use the code indicated or a lower number.

EXHIBIT 11-3   1995 Personal Tax Credit Return (Form TD1)

 Revenue   Revenu
Canada   Canada

PERSONAL TAX CREDITS RETURN

TD1(E)
Rev. 95

Instructions

You have to complete this return if you have a new employer or payer, and you received one or more of the following types of income:

- salary, wages, commissions, pensions, or any other remuneration; or
- Unemployment Insurance benefits, including training allowances.

Complete a new return no later than seven days after your marital or parental status changes or when you expect a change in your personal credits for the year. It is an offence to file a false return.

If you receive non-employment income, such as a pension or Old Age Security, and you want to have extra tax deducted at source, you can complete Form TD3, *Request for Income Tax Deduction on non-employment income.*

If you have deductions such as registered retirement savings plan contributions, alimony payments, or child care expenses, the amount of tax to be withheld from your income can be reduced. You have to send a written application to your district income tax office. A tax office letter of authority is not needed when a court order states that alimony or maintenance payments have to be deducted at source from an employee's salary.

If you need help, ask your employer or payer, or call the Employer Services Division of your income tax office. The number for this office is listed in the government pages of your telephone book under Revenue Canada.

Confidential calculation on back - Employee's copy

Employer's or payer's copy

Revenue   Revenu
Canada   Canada

PERSONAL TAX CREDITS RETURN

TD1(E)
Rev. 95

After you complete this return, give it to your employer or payer.

Last name (capital letters)	Usual first name and initials	Employee number
DEAN,	Roberta C.	3637

Address	For non-residents only - country of permanent residence	Social insurance number
3817 29th Avenue		7 6 7 6 7 6 7 6 7

	Postal code	Date of birth
Owen Sound, Ontario	N4K 2X9	Year 1 9 3 9 Month 0 2 Day 0 7

1. Basic personal amount
Everyone can claim **$6,456** as the basic personal amount.
- If you choose to claim this amount, enter **$ 6,456**.
- If you choose not to claim this amount (e.g., when you have more than one employer or payer and you have already claimed the basic personal amount), **enter 0** in box **A** on the other side of this return and do not complete sections 2 to 8. You may wish to complete sections 9 to 11.
- If you are a non-resident, and you will be including most of your annual world income (90% or more) when determining your taxable income in Canada, you can claim certain personal amounts. If you are not sure about your non-resident status, or need more information, call the Client Assistance Division of your income tax office.   **Credit claimed $ 6,456**

2. Spousal amount or equivalent-to-spouse amount.

You can claim an amount for supporting your spouse if you are **married or have a common-law spouse.** A common-law spouse is a person of the opposite sex with whom you live in a common-law relationship for any continuous period of at least 12 months, including any period of separation (due to a breakdown in the relationship) of less than 90 days, or with whom you live in a common-law relationship and who is the natural or adoptive parent of your child.

You can claim an equivalent-to-spouse amount if you are **single, divorced, separated, or widowed,** and you support a relative who is:
- residing in Canada (if the relative is your child, the child does not have to reside in Canada);
- living with you in a home you maintain;
- related to you by blood, marriage, or adoption; and
- under 18 years old, except for a relative who has a mental or physical infirmity.

Calculating the amount
If you marry during the year, your spouse's net income includes the income earned before and during the marriage.
If the net income of your spouse or relative for the year will be:
- over $5,918, enter 0;
- $538 or less, enter $5,380; or
- more than $538, complete calculation no. 2 on the back of this return and enter the result as credit claimed.

Any person you claim here cannot be claimed again in section 3.   **Credit claimed $ 2,918**

3. Amount for disabled dependent relatives
With the introduction of the child tax benefit, there is no amount for dependent children who are under the age of 18 at the end of the year. However, you can claim an amount for each disabled dependant who is:
- your or your spouse's child or grandchild, 18 years old or older, and who has a physical or mental infirmity; or
- your or your spouse's parent, grandparent, brother, sister, aunt, uncle, niece, or nephew, who is 18 years old or older, and who has a physical or mental infirmity and is resident in Canada.

Calculating the amount for a disabled dependent relative:
If your dependant's net income for the year will be:
- $2,690 or less, enter $1,583 in section 3 of this return; or
- more than $2,690, complete calculation no. 3 on the back of this return and enter the result as credit claimed.
You can claim an amount for each disabled dependent relative you have.   **Credit claimed $ Nil**

4. Amount for eligible pension
An eligible pension income includes pension payments received from a pension plan or fund as a life annuity, and foreign pension payments. It does not include payments from the Canada or Quebec Pension Plan, Old Age Security, guaranteed supplements, or lump-sum withdrawals from a pension fund.
If you receive an eligible pension income, you can claim your eligible pension income or $1,000, whichever amount is less.   **Credit claimed $ Nil**

5. Age amount.
If your estimated net income from all sources for the year will be:
- $ 25,921 or less, enter $3,482;
- over $25,921, but not over $49,134.33, complete calculation no. 5 on the back of this return and enter the result as credit claimed; or
- over $49,134.33, enter $0.   **Credit claimed $ Nil**

Source: Revenue Canada Taxation. Reproduced with permission of the Minister of Supply and Services Canada.

EXHIBIT 11-3 *(continued)*

Calculation no. 2 • more than $538, calculate:	$ 5,918
Minus: net income of spouse or relative	3,000
Total calculated:	2,918
Report total in section 2 as credit claimed	
Calculation no. 3 • more than $2,690, calculate:	$ 4,273
Minus: dependant's net income	
Total calculated:	
Report total in section 3 as credit claimed	

Calculation no. 5:
• over $25,921, but not over $49,134.33, calculate:
Basic age amount: .... $ 3,482 A.
Reduced by:
1. Annual estimated net income. $ _____
2. Less base amount ....– $ 25,921
3. Line 1 minus line 2 ...... = $ _____
4. Line 3 by 15% .... –   B.
Subtract A from B. If negative, enter 0 $ = _____
Report total in section 5 as credit claimed

Claim Codes	
Total claim amount	Claim codes
No claim amount	0
Minimum $ 6,456	1
$ 6,456.01 - 8,037	2
8,037.01 - 9,619	3
9,619.01 - 11,202	4
11,202.01 - 12,783	5
12,783.01 - 14,364	6
14,364.01 - 15,946	7
15,946.01 - 17,527	8
17,527.01 - 19,109	9
19,109.01 - 20,693	10
$ 20,693.01 - and over Manual calculation required by employer	X
No tax withholding required	E

6. Tuition fees and education amount

Enter your tuition fees, for courses you will take in the year, to attend a university, college, or an institution that the Minister of Human Resources Development has certified. . . . . _____

Add $80 for each month in the year that you will be enrolled full-time in a qualifying educational program at a university, college, or a school offering job retraining courses or correspondence courses, as indicated on Form T2202 or T2202A . . . . _____

Subtract any scholarships, fellowships, or bursaries you will receive in the year (do not report the first $500) . . . . _____

Enter the total amount claimed. If you arrive at a negative amount, **enter 0** . . . . **Credit claimed** $ *Nil*

7. Disability amount

You can claim $4,233 for a person who is severely impaired, mentally or physically, and for whom you will claim the disability amount by using Form T2201, *Disability Tax Credit Certificate.*
Such an impairment has to markedly restrict the person in his or her daily living activities. The impairment has to last, or be expected to last, for a continuous period of at least 12 months.
Enter the total amount claimed: . . . . **Credit claimed** $ *Nil*

8. Amounts transferred from your spouse, relatives, or dependants

You can transfer any of the following amounts that your spouse, relative, or dependants do not need to reduce their federal income tax to zero.

Age amount - If, this year, your spouse will be 65 or older, you can claim any unused balance of the age amount to a maximum of $3,482 . . . . _____

Pension income amount - If your spouse receives eligible pension income, you can claim any unused balance of the eligible pension amount to a maximum of $1,000 . . . . _____

Disability amount - If your spouse, relatives, or dependants are disabled, you can claim their unused balance of the disability amount to a maximum of $4,233 for each person . . . . _____

Tuition fees and education amount - If you are supporting a spouse, relative, or dependants who are attending a university, college, or a certified educational institution, you can claim their unused balance of tuition fees and education amount to a maximum of $4,000 for each person . . . . _____

Enter the total amount calculated . . . . **Credit claimed** $ *Nil*

Total all your personal tax credit amounts from sections 1 to 8 . . . . $ 9,374
Total of credits

At the top of this form, see the claim codes to determine the claim code that applies to you, and enter this code in box **A** . If the total of your tax credits is greater than your employment income for the year, your claim code is "E."   3   **A**

Additional information

9. Additional tax to be deducted

If you receive additional income you may find it convenient to have additional tax deducted from each payment. This will help you avoid having to pay tax when you file your income tax return. If so, state the amount of additional tax you want to have deducted from each payment. If you want to change this extra deduction later, you have to complete a new TD1 return. $ _____

10. Deduction for living in a designated area (e.g., Yukon Territory, or Northwest Territories)

If you live in the Yukon Territory, Northwest Territories, or another designated area for more than six months in a row, beginning or ending this year, you can claim:
• $7.50 for each day that you live in the designated area; or
• $15 for each day that you live in the designated area, if during that time you live in a dwelling that you maintain, and you are the only person living in that dwelling who is claiming this deduction.
For more information, including a list and categories of designated areas, see the income tax guide called *Northern Residents Deduction,* available at any income tax office. $ _____

11. If you reside in **Ontario, Manitoba, Saskatchewan** or **British Columbia**, enter the number of your dependants under 18 years old at the end of the year.

For **Ontario, Manitoba** and **Saskatchewan** residents, only the spouse with the higher net income can indicate an amount. **If you reside in Ontario, Manitoba** or **British Columbia,** the number of children indicated should not include a child claimed for purposes of the equivalent-to-spouse amount.   _____

I certify that, to the best of my knowledge, the information given on this form is correct and complete.

Signature _____   Date _____

calculated for weekly wages, the premium would be calculated as 2.7 percent times wages in excess of the weekly exemption of $65.38 ($3,400/52); similarly, CPP would be calculated for employees paid monthly on wages in excess of the monthly exemption of $283.33. For example, if Martine Violette earned $500.00 in the week ending May 5, 19X2, and if her total CPP withholdings for 19X2 were less than $850.50, her employer would withhold $11.73 [($500.00 – $65.38) × .027] for CPP in calculating her net pay.

Revenue Canada provides tables that the employer uses to calculate how much to deduct from each employee's pay each pay period; the tables take into account the basic exemption of $3,400 of income but also assume that the employee will be working for twelve months. For example, if your total employment income was earned when you worked for two months during the summer and earned $2,500 per month, the withholding would be $63.66 each month ($127.32), the normal deduction for an employee earning $2,500 per month. However, based on your total income of $5,000 (2 × $2,500) and the basic exemption of $3,400, the government will require you to pay $43.20 [($5,000 – $3,400) × .027] and will refund your overpayment of $84.12.

Once the employee reaches the maximum contribution of $850.50, the employer stops deducting for that year. Some employees may have had more than one employer in a year; for example, you may have had a job for the summer and now have a part-time job while you are back at school. Canada requires each employer to deduct Canada Pension Plan contributions; however, you recover the overpayment when you file your income tax return for the year.

The employer must remit the Canada Pension Plan contributions withheld and the employer's share, discussed below, every month to Revenue Canada. Larger employers must remit two or four times a month, depending on the amounts withheld.

Employee Withheld Unemployment Insurance Premiums Payable The **Unemployment Insurance Act** requires employers to deduct unemployment insurance premiums from each employee each time that employee is paid. The purpose of the Unemployment Insurance Fund is to provide assistance to contributors to the fund who cannot work for a variety of reasons. The most common reason is that the employee has been laid off; another reason is maternity leave.

Revenue Canada provides tables for calculating withholdings for a range of pay periods. Employees who work less than 15 hours a week or whose projected annual income will not exceed $8,476 are not required to pay unemployment insurance and thus do not have it deducted from their pay. For example, an employee whose monthly income is $500 would not pay unemployment insurance premiums since the gross pay is less than the minimum of $706.33 ($8,476.00/12). The employee premium is 3.0 percent of earnings to a maximum contribution of $1,271.40 (3.0 percent of maximum insurable earnings of $42,380.00). The premium is calculated by taking the amount earned per pay period and multiplying it by 3.0 percent. For example, an employee earning $2,000 per month would pay a premium of $60.00 ($2,000 × .03).

As with the Canada Pension Plan, Revenue Canada requires every employer to deduct Unemployment Insurance premiums from every eligible employee. Overpayments may be recovered when the employee files his or her income tax return. The tables attempt to spread the withholding over the year for the employee and to ensure that the maximum yearly withholding is not exceeded. As the section at the base of Panel C of Exhibit 11-4 demonstrates, a maximum withholding per pay period is specified; an employee who is paid monthly will have a maximum witholding of $105.95.

The employer must remit the Unemployment Insurance premiums withheld and the employer's share, discussed below, to Revenue Canada every month. Larger employers must remit two or four times a month depending on the amounts withheld.

Optional Payroll Deductions

As a convenience to their employees, many companies make payroll deductions and disburse cash according to employee instructions. Union dues, insurance payments, payroll savings plans, and gifts to charities such as the United Way are examples. The account Employees' Union Dues Payable holds employee deductions for union membership.

EXHIBIT 11-4 *Payroll Withholding Tables*

Panel A Table D-16

Ontario
Semi-Monthly Income Tax Deductions
Basis: 24 Pay Periods Per Year

Semi-Monthly Pay Use appropriate bracket	If the employee's Net Claim Code on Form TD1 Is										
	0	1	2	3	4	5	6	7	8	9	10
From Less than											
1927 – 1953	609.25	535.60	526.60	508.55	490.50	472.50	454.45	436.40	418.40	400.35	382.30
1953 – 1979	620.15	546.50	537.50	519.45	501.40	483.35	465.35	447.30	429.25	411.20	393.15
1979 – 2005	631.00	557.40	548.35	530.35	512.30	494.24	476.20	458.20	440.15	422.10	404.05
2005 – 2031	642.30	568.25	559.25	541.20	523.15	505.15	487.10	469.05	451.05	433.00	414.95
2031 – 2057	654.00	579.15	570.15	552.10	534.05	516.00	498.00	479.95	461.90	443.90	425.80

Panel B Table B-33

Canada Pension Plan Contributions

Semi-Monthly Pay Period

Remuneration From To	C.P.P.	Remuneration From To	C.P.P.	Remuneration From To	C.P.P.	Remuneration From To	C.P.P.
1444.81 – 1445.17	35.19	1914.44 – 1924.43	48.00	2634.44 – 2644.43	67.44	3354.44 – 3364.43	86.88
1445.18 – 1445.54	35.20	1924.44 – 1934.43	48.27	2644.44 – 2654.43	67.71	3364.44 – 3374.43	87.15
1445.55 – 1445.91	35.21	1934.44 – 1944.43	48.54	2654.44 – 2664.43	67.98	3374.44 – 3384.43	87.42
1445.92 – 1446.28	35.22	1944.44 – 1954.43	48.81	2664.44 – 2674.43	68.25	3384.44 – 3394.43	87.69
1446.29 – 1446.65	35.23	1954.44 – 1964.43	49.08	2674.44 – 2684.43	68.52	3394.44 – 3404.43	87.96
1446.66 – 1447.03	35.24	1964.44 – 1974.43	49.35	2684.44 – 2694.43	68.79	3404.44 – 3414.43	88.23
1447.04 – 1447.40	35.25	1974.44 – 1984.43	49.62	2694.44 – 2704.43	69.06	3414.44 – 3424.43	88.50
1447.41 – 1447.77	35.26	1984.44 – 1994.43	49.89	2704.44 – 2714.43	69.33	3424.44 – 3434.43	88.77
1447.78 – 1448.14	35.27	1994.44 – 2004.43	50.16	2714.44 – 2724.43	69.60	3434.44 – 3444.43	89.04

Panel C Table C-21

Unemployment Insurance Premiums

For the maximum premium deduction for various pay periods see bottom of this page.

Remuneration From To	U.I. Premium	Remuneration From To	U.I. Premium	Remuneration From To	U.I. Premium	Remuneration From To	U.I. Premium
1926.17 – 1926.49	57.79	1950.17 – 1950.49	58.51	1974.17 – 1974.49	59.23	1998.17 – 1998.49	59.95
1926.50 – 1926.83	57.80	1950.50 – 1950.83	58.52	1974.50 – 1974.83	59.24	1998.50 – 1998.83	59.96
1926.84 – 1927.16	57.81	1950.84 – 1951.16	58.53	1974.84 – 1975.16	59.25	1998.84 – 1999.16	59.97
1927.17 – 1927.49	57.82	1951.17 – 1951.49	58.54	1975.17 – 1975.49	59.26	1999.17 – 1999.49	59.98
1927.50 – 1927.83	57.83	1951.50 – 1951.83	58.55	1975.50 – 1975.83	59.27	1999.50 – 1999.83	59.99
1927.84 – 1928.16	57.84	1951.84 – 1952.16	58.56	1975.84 – 1976.16	59.28	1999.84 – 2000.16	60.00
1928.17 – 1928.49	57.85	1952.17 – 1952.49	58.57	1976.17 – 1976.49	59.29	2000.17 – 2000.49	60.01
1928.50 – 1928.83	57.86	1952.50 – 1952.83	58.58	1976.50 – 1976.83	59.30	2000.50 – 2000.83	60.02
1928.84 – 1929.16	57.87	1952.84 – 1953.16	58.59	1976.84 – 1977.16	59.31	2000.84 – 2001.16	60.03

Maximum Premium Deduction for a Pay Period of the stated frequency.	Weekly:	24.45	10 pp per year :	127.14
	Bi-Weekly:	48.90	13 pp per year :	97.80
	Semi-Monthly:	52.97	22 pp per year :	57.79
	Monthly:	105.95		

Employer Payroll Costs

Employers bear expenses for at least three payroll costs: (1) Canada Pension Plan contributions, (2) Unemployment Insurance Plan premiums, and (3) Workers' Compensation Plan premiums. In addition, Manitoba and Newfoundland levy a health and post-secondary education tax on employers, while Ontario and Quebec levy a health tax on employers in those provinces. The Northwest Territories has a payroll tax also. As mentioned above, most employers must remit both employee and employer shares monthly. Larger employers must remit twice or four times monthly depending on the size of their payroll. Workers' Compensation payments are remitted quarterly.

Employer Canada Pension Plan Contributions   In addition to being responsible for deducting and remitting the employee contribution to the Canada Pension Plan, the employer must also pay into the program. The employer must match the employee's contribution of 2.7 percent of gross pay in excess of $3,400 to a maximum payment of $850.50. Every employer must do so whether or not the employee also contributes elsewhere. Unlike the employee, the employer may not obtain a refund for overpayment.

Employer Unemployment Insurance Premiums   The employer calculates the employee's premium and remits it together with the employer's share, which is generally 1.4 times the employee's premium, to Revenue Canada. The dollar amount of the employer's contribution would be 1.4 times the maximum employee's contribution of $1,271.40 or $1,779.96. Almost all employers and employees are covered by this program.

Workers' Compensation Premiums   Unlike the previous two programs, which are administered by the federal government, the **Workers' Compensation** plan is provincially administered. The purpose of the program is to provide financial support for workers injured on the job. The cost of the coverage is borne by the employer; the employee does not pay a premium to the fund.

In Manitoba, almost all employees are covered by the program. There are over 70 different categories that the Workers' Compensation Board uses to ascertain the cost of coverage. The category a group of workers is assigned to is based on the risk of injury to workers in that group based on that group's and like groups' experience. The employer pays a premium equal to the rate assessed times the employer's gross payroll. Thus, in February 19X2, the employer estimates gross payroll for 19X2 and sends that information plus any premium owing from 19X1 to the provincial government. Premiums, based on that estimated payroll, are remitted quarterly in most cases. In February 19X3, the employer estimates gross payroll for 19X3, calculates any premium owing for 19X2 based on the excess of actual wages over estimated wages for 19X2, and sends the estimate and premium owing to the provincial government.

Provincial Payroll Taxes   As was mentioned earlier, certain provinces levy taxes on employers to pay for provincial health care while others levy a combined health care and post-secondary education tax to pay for provincial health care and post-secondary education. Quebec and Newfoundland have fixed rates of tax while the other two provinces vary the rate employers are taxed. In Ontario, the rate of tax increases with the annual payroll amount, while it decreases in Manitoba.

Payroll Withholding Tables

We have discussed the tables that employers use in calculating the withholdings that must be made from employees' wages for income taxes, Canada (or Quebec) Pension contributions and Unemployment Insurance premiums. Exhibit 11-4 provides illustrations of all three tables for a resident of Ontario for 1995. Roberta Dean is paid a salary of $2,000 twice a month (semi-monthly). From Panel A, you can

EXHIBIT 11-5   *Typical Disbursement of Payroll Costs by an Employer Company (Ontario)*

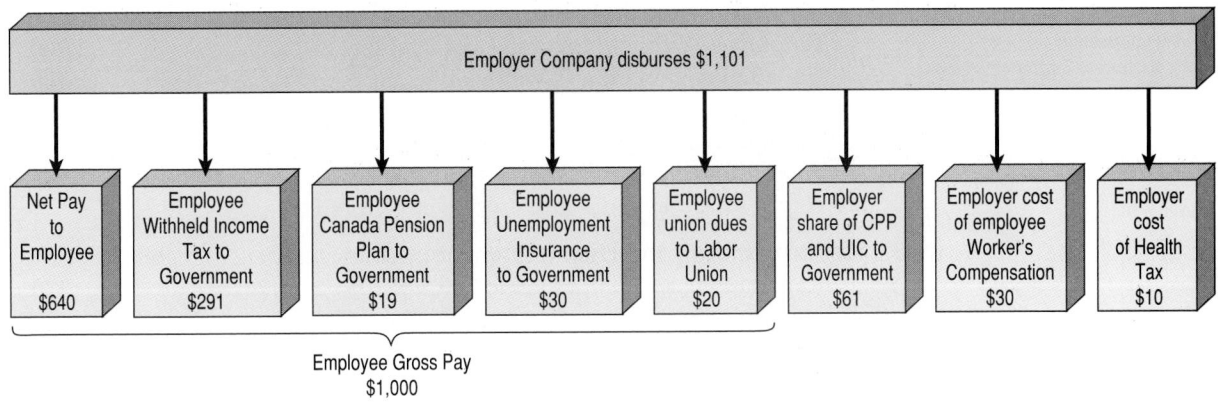

see that, based on her net claim code of 3, she would have income tax of $530.35 withheld. Her Canada Pension deduction, Panel B, would be $50.16 and her Unemployment Insurance premium, Panel C, would be $52.97. The Unemployment Insurance table reads $60.00 but remember the maximum premium is $1,271.40; the box at the bottom of the table states that the maximum deduction for an employee paid twice monthly would be $52.97. The employer's share would be $50.16 for Canada Pension (matches employee's share), while the employer's share for Unemployment Insurance would be $74.16 (1.4 times employee share).

Exhibit 11-5 shows a typical disbursement of payroll costs by an employer company for a single employee who is paid monthly.

Payroll Entries

Exhibit 11-6 summarizes an employer's entries to record a monthly payroll of $10,000 (all amounts are assumed for illustration only).

Entry A in Exhibit 11-6 records the employer's salary expense, which is the gross salary of all employees ($10,000) for a month. From this amount the employer collects for the federal government income tax, Canada Pension (except in Quebec where it is Quebec Pension) and Unemployment Insurance. Union dues are also collected from this amount by the employer on behalf of the union that represents the employees. The remaining amount is the employees' net (take-home) pay of $7,964. In this payroll transaction the employer acts as a collection agent for Revenue Canada (income tax and Canada Pension), the Unemployment Insurance Commission and the union, withholding the employees' contributions from their gross pay.

Entry B represents the employer's share of Canada Pension and Unemployment Insurance. Remember, the employer's share is 1.0 times and 1.4 times the employee's share respectively for these two deductions.

Entry C records employee benefits paid by the employer. This employer is located in Newfoundland and must pay that province's Health and Post-Secondary Tax. In provinces where there is no provincial health insurance tax, some employers pay employee provincial health insurance premiums as a benefit to the employee and other employers do not. Since provincial health insurance premiums must be paid by law, if the employer did not pay them, they would be deducted from the employees' pay in Entry A. This company also has a life insurance plan for its employees for which it pays the premiums.

In the exhibit, the total payroll expense for the month is made up of base salary ($10,000) plus the employer's share of Canada Pension and Unemployment Insurance ($682) plus fringe benefits ($200 + $182) for a total of $11,064. There would also be Workers' Compensation, which, you will recall, is paid completely by the employer.

OBJECTIVE 4

Make basic payroll entries

Short Exercise:

Record the payroll, payroll deductions, and employer payroll costs, given the following information about a Northwest Territories company:

Gross pay............	$190,000
Employee with. inc. tax..............	22,800
Employee with. Can. Pen.	4,900
Employee with. unemp. ins.	5,500
Union dues............	2,945
Employer cost Can. Pen.	1.0
Employer cost unemp. ins.	1.4
Payroll tax.............	1.0%

A:

Payroll entry:

Salary expense......... $190,000	
Emp. With. Inc. Tax Pay	22,800
Can. Pen. Pay..............	4,900
Unemp. Ins. Pay..............	5,500
Union Dues.......	2,945
Salaries Payable	153,855

Employer payroll cost entry:

Can. Pen. and Unemp. Ins. Exp. $12,600	
Can. Pen. Pay..............	4,900
Unemp. Ins. Pay..............	7,700

Fringe benefits:

Territory Payroll Tax Exp.	1,900
Emp. Ben. Pay...............	1,900

EXHIBIT 11-6   *Payroll Accounting by the Employer*

A. Salary Expense (or Wage or Commission Expense)......... 10,000
      Employee Withheld Income Tax Payable..................... 1,200
      Canada Pension Plan Payable............................. 270
      Unemployment Insurance Payable............................ 294
      Employee Union Dues Payable 272
      Salaries Payable to Employees (net pay)..................... 7,964
   To record salary expense and employee withholdings.

B. Canada Pension and Unemployment Insurance Expense   682
      Canada Pension Plan Payable (1.0 × $270)................. 270
      Unemployment Insurance Payable (1.4 × $294) 412
   To record employer's share of Canada Pension and Unemployment Insurance.

C. Provincial Employer's Health and Post-Secondary
      Insurance Tax.. 200
      Employee Life Insurance Expense.................................. 182
      Employee Benefits Payable 382
   To record employee benefits payable by employer.

A company's payments to people who are not employees—outsiders called independent contractors—are *not* company payroll expenses. Consider two CAs, Fermi and Scott. Fermi is the corporation's chief financial officer. Scott is the corporation's outside auditor. Fermi is an employee of the corporation, and his compensation is a debit to Salary Expense. Scott, however, performs auditing service for many clients, and the corporation debits Auditing Expense when it pays her. Any payment for services performed by a person outside the company is a debit to an expense account other than payroll.

The Payroll System

Good business means paying employees accurately and on time. Also, companies face the legal responsibility of remitting amounts withheld from employees and the corporation's matching amounts and employee benefits, as we have seen. These demands require companies to process a great deal of payroll data. Efficient accounting is important. To make payroll accounting accurate and effective, accountants have developed the *payroll system*.

The components of the payroll system are a *payroll register*, a special *payroll bank account*, *payroll cheques*, and an *earnings record* for each employee.

OBJECTIVE 5

Use a payroll system

Payroll Register

Each pay period, the company organizes the payroll data in a special journal called the *payroll register* or *payroll journal*. This register lists each employee and the figures the business needs to record payroll amounts. The payroll register, which resembles the cash disbursement register, or cheque register, also serves as a cheque register by providing a column for recording each payroll cheque number.

A payroll register similar to that in Exhibit 11-7 is used by companies such as Mark's Work Wearhouse. The *Gross Pay* section has columns for straight-time pay, overtime pay, and total gross pay for each employee. Columns under the *Deductions* heading vary from company to company, but every employer must deduct federal income tax, Canada Pension contributions and Unemployment Insurance premiums. Additional column headings depend on which optional deductions the business handles. In Exhibit 11-7, the employer deducts employee withholdings and gifts

EXHIBIT 11-7 *Payroll Register*

Week ended December 27, 19X3

		a	b	c	d	e	f	g	h	i	j	k	l
		Gross Pay			**Deductions**					**Net Pay**		**Account Debited**	
Employee Name	**Hours**	**Straight time**	**Overtime**	**Total**	**Federal Income Tax**	**Canada Pension Plan**	**Unemploy- ment Insurance**	**Winnipeg United Way**	**Total**	**(c–h) Amount**	**Cheque No.**	**Office Salary Expense**	**Sales Salary Expense**
Chen, W.L.*	40	500.00		500.00	83.30	11.73	15.00	2.00	112.03	387.97	1621	500.00	
Drago, C.L.	46	400.00	90.00	490.00	72.95	11.46	14.70	2.00	101.11	388.89	1622		490.00
Ellis, M.	41	560.00	21.00	581.00	118.20	13.92	17.43		149.55	431.45	1623	581.00	
Trimble, E.A**	40	1,360.00		1,360.00	433.25		24.45	15.00	472.70	887.30	1641		1,360.00
Total		12,940.00	714.00	13,654.00	3,167.76	327.70	385.12	155.00	4,035.58	9,618.42		4,464.00	9,190.00

*W.L. Chen earned gross pay of $500. His net pay was $387.97, paid with cheque number 1621. Chen is an office worker, so his salary is debited to Office Salaries Expense.
**E.A. Trimble has exceeded maximum pensionable earnings of $31,500.00 and so has had the maximum, $850.50, deducted.

to the United Way and then sends the amounts to the proper parties. The business may add deduction columns as needed. The *Net Pay* section lists each employee's net (take-home) pay and the number of the cheque issued to him or her. The last two columns indicate the *Account Debited* for the employee's gross pay. (The company has office workers and sales people.)

The payroll register in Exhibit 11-7 gives the employer the information needed to record salary expense for the pay period. Using the total amounts for columns (d) through (l), the employer records total salary expense as follows:

Dec. 27	Office Salaries Expense	4,464.00	
	Sales Salaries Expense	9,190.00	
	Employee Withheld Income Tax Payable.		3,167.76
	Employee Withheld Canada Pension Plan Payable		327.70
	Employee Withheld Unemployment Insurance Payable		385.12
	Employee Gifts to United Way Payable		155.00
	Salaries Payable to Employees		9,618.42

Payroll Bank Account

After the payroll has been recorded, the company books include a credit balance in Salaries Payable to Employees for net pay of $9,618.42. (See column (i) in Exhibit 11-7.) How the business pays this liability depends on its payroll system. Many companies disburse paycheques to employees from a special *payroll bank account*. The employer draws a cheque for net pay ($9,618.42 in our illustration) on its regular bank account and deposits this in the special payroll bank account. Then the company writes paycheques to employees out of the payroll account. When all the paycheques clear the bank, the payroll account has a zero balance, ready for the activity of the next pay period. Disbursing paycheques from a separate bank account isolates net pay for analysis and control, as discussed later in the chapter.

Other payroll disbursements—for withholdings, union dues, and so on—are neither as numerous nor as frequent as weekly or monthly paycheques. The employer pays withholdings, union dues, and charities from its regular bank account.

Payroll Cheques

Many companies pay employees by cheque. A *payroll cheque* is like any other cheque except that its perforated attachment lists the employee's gross pay, payroll deductions, and net pay. These amounts are taken from the payroll register. Exhibit 11-8 shows payroll cheque number 1622, issued to C.L. Drago for net pay of $388.89 earned during the week ended December 27, 19X3. To check your ability to use payroll data, trace all amounts on the cheque attachment to the payroll register in Exhibit 11-7.

Increasingly, companies are paying employees by electronic funds transfer, as the University of Waterloo does. The employee can authorize the company to make all deposits directly to his or her bank. With no cheque to write and deliver to the employee, the company saves time and money. As evidence of the deposit, most companies issue a pay summary slip showing the data for that pay period plus year-to-date data to employees. The employee avoids the trouble of receiving, endorsing, and depositing the paycheque.

Recording Cash Disbursements for Payroll _____

Most employers must make at least three entries to record payroll cash disbursements: net payment to employees, payments of payroll withholdings to the government and payments to third parties for employee fringe benefits.

EXHIBIT 11-8   *Payroll Cheque*

Blumenthal's							1622
Payroll Account							
Winnipeg, Manitoba					12-27 19 X3		

Pay to the Order of _____ C.L. Drago _____ $ | 388.89

Three hundred and eighty-eight & 89/100--------------------- Dollars

Toronto-Dominion Bank
Winnipeg,
Manitoba R2W 3Y1

Anna Figaro
                                                          Treasurer

⑈1119000311⑈ 0787⑈500004654⑈

Pay			Deductions					Net Pay	Cheque No.
Straight-time	Over-time	Gross	Income Tax	C.P.P.	Unemployment Ins.	United Way	Total		
400.00	90.00	490.00	72.95	11.46	14.70	2.00	101.11	388.89	1622

Net Pay to Employees   When the employer pays employees, the company debits Salaries Payable to Employees and credits Cash. Using the data in Exhibit 11-7, the company would make the following entry to record the cash payment (column (i)) for the December 27 weekly payroll:

Dec. 27	Salaries Payable to Employees	9,618.42	
	Cash		9,618.42

Payroll Withholdings to the Government and Other Organizations   The employer must send income taxes withheld from employees' pay and the employee deductions and employer's share of Canada (or Quebec) Pension Plan contributions and Unemployment Insurance premiums to Revenue Canada; the payment for a given month is due on or before the 15th day of the following month. In addition, the employer has to remit any withholdings for union dues, charitable gifts, etc.; the payment would probably be made in the following month. Assume federal income tax of $9,880.00, Canada Pension Plan contributions of $953.90, Unemployment Insurance premiums of $1,109.80, and United Way contributions of $465.00 were deducted in calculating the net pay for the employees of Blumenthal's for the three weeks ended December 6, 13, and 20, 19X3. Based on those amounts and columns (d) through (j) in Exhibit 11-7, the business would record payments to Revenue Canada for $4,553.58 and Winnipeg United Way for $155.00 as follows:

Jan. 7	Employee Withheld Income Tax		
	Payable ($9,880.00 + $3,167.76)	13,047.76	
	Employee Withheld Canada Pension		
	Plan Payable ($953.90 + $327.70)	1,281.60	
	Employee Withheld Unemployment		
	Insurance Payable ($1,109.80 + $385.12)..	1,494.92	
	Canada Pension Plan Expense (1 × $1,281.60)	1,281.60	
	Unemployment Insurance Expense		
	(1.4 × $1,494.92)	2,092.88	
	Cash		19,198.76

Short Exercise:
According to this journal entry, what is the total amount that the business will pay to the government on December 27 for taxes, Canada Pension, and unemployment insurance withheld? **A:** $13,047.76 + $1,281.60 + $1,494.92 = $15,824.28

Jan. 18   Employee Gifts to United Way Payable
                      ($465.00 + $155.00)... 620.00
                            Cash...   620.00

Recall that Manitoba is one of the provinces that levies a tax on payroll to pay for health and post-secondary education in the province. There is no tax on the first $750,000 of payroll, 4.5 percent on the next $750,000, and 2.25 percent on payroll over $1,500,000. Assume that Blumenthal's payroll passed $750,000 with the November 15, 19X3, payroll and that the payroll and benefits totaled $42,000 for the weeks of December 6, 13, and 20, 19X3. Based on those amounts and the total payroll of December 27, 19X3, from Exhibit 11-7, the journal entry to record payment to the Province of Manitoba follows:

Jan. 10   Health and Post-Secondary Education Tax Levy Expense
                      [($42,000.00 + $13,654.00) × .045] 2,504.43
                            Cash 2,504.43

Payments to Third Parties for Fringe Benefits   The employer sometimes pays for employees' dental insurance coverage and for a company pension plan. Assuming the total cash payment for these benefits is $1,927.14, this entry would be

Jan. 10   Employee Benefits Payable.............................. 1,927.14
                            Cash...   1,927.14

Earnings Record

The employer must file Summary of Remuneration Paid returns with Revenue Canada and must provide the employee with a statement of Remuneration Paid, Form T4, at the end of the year. Therefore, employers maintain an earnings record for each employee. Exhibit 11-9 is a five-week excerpt from the earnings record of employee C.L. Drago.

The employee earnings record is not a journal or a ledger, and it is not required by law. It is an accounting tool—like the work sheet—that the employer uses to prepare payroll tax reports. The information provided on the earnings record with respect to year-to-date earnings also indicates when an employee has earned $31,500, the point at which the employer can stop withholding Canada Pension Plan contributions. There is no maximum income tax deduction, and recall from Panel C in Exhibit 11-3 that the Unemployment Insurance premium tables indicate the maximum premium deduction for the various pay periods so that the employer will not deduct more than the maximum.

Exhibit 11-10 is the Statement of Remuneration paid, Form T4 Supplementary, for employee C.L. Drago. The employer prepares this form for each employee and a form called a T4 Summary, which summarizes the information on the T4 Supplementaries issued by the employer for that year. The employer sends the T4 Summary and one copy of each T4 Supplementary to Revenue Canada by February 28 each year. Revenue Canada uses the documents to ensure that the employer has correctly paid to the government all amounts withheld on its behalf from employees together with the employer's share. The employee gets two copies of the T4 Supplementary; one copy must be filed with the employee's income tax return, while the second copy is for the employee's records. Revenue Canada matches the income on the T4 supplementary filed by the employer against the income reported on the employee's income tax return, filed by the employee, to ensure that the employee properly reported his or her income from employment.

EXHIBIT 11-9   Employee Earnings Record for 19X3

Employee Name and Address: Social Insurance No.: 987-010-789

Drago, C.L.
1400 Wellington Crescent
Winnipeg, Manitoba R3P 1E5

Marital Status: Married
Net Claims Code: 4
Pay Rate: $400 per week
Job Title: Salesperson

| Week Ended | Hours | Gross Pay | | | | Deductions | | | | | Net Pay | |
		Straight time	Overtime	Total	To Date	Federal Income Tax	Canada Pension Plan	Unemployment Insurance	Winnipeg United Way	Total	Amount	Cheque No.
Nov. 29	40	400.00		400.00	21,340.00	48.65	9.03	12.00	2.00	71.68	328.32	1525
Dec. 6	40	400.00		400.00	21,740.00	48.65	9.03	12.00	2.00	71.68	328.32	1548
Dec. 13	44	400.00	60.00	460.00	22,200.00	64.65	10.65	13.80	2.00	91.11	368.89	1574
Dec. 20	48	400.00	120.00	520.00	22,720.00	79.10	12.27	15.60	2.00	108.97	411.03	1598
Dec. 27	46	400.00	90.00	490.00	23,210.00	72.95	11.46	14.70	2.00	101.11	388.89	1622
Total		20,800.00	2,410.00	23,210.00		2,809.30	534.87	696.30	104.00	4,144.47	19,065.53	

EXHIBIT 11-10 *Employee Statement of Remuneration Paid (Form T4)*

Revenue Canada | Revenu Canada

T4 – 1994 Supplementary Supplémentaire

STATEMENT OF REMUNERATION PAID
ÉTAT DE LA RÉMUNÉRATION PAYÉE

20-221-127

14 Employment income before deductions / Revenus d'emploi avant retenues	16 Employee's CPP contributions / Cotisations de l'employé au RPC	17 Employee's QPP contributions / Cotisations de l'employé au RRQ	18 Employee's UI premiums / Cotisations de l'employé à l'A-C	20 Registered pension plan contributions / Cotisations à un régime de pension agréé	22 Income tax deducted / Impôt sur le revenu retenu	24 UI insurable earnings / Gains assurables d'A-C	26 Pensionable earnings / Gains donnant droit à pension	28 Exempt / Exemption CPP/QPP UI / RPC/RRQ A-C
23,210 00	534 87		696 30		2,809 30	23,210 00	20,010 00	

Box 14 amount already includes any amount in boxes 30, 32, 34, 36, 38, 40, and 42 / Le montant de la case 14 comprend déjà tous les montants des cases 30, 32, 34, 36, 38, 40 et 42	30 Housing, board, and lodging / Logement, pension et repas	32 Travel in designated area / Voyage dans une région désignée	34 Personal use of employer's auto / Usage personnel de l'auto de l'employeur	36 Interest-free and low-interest loan / Prêts sans intérêt ou à faible intérêt	38 Stock option benefits / Avantages tirés d'une option d'achat d'actions	40 Other taxable allowances and benefits / Autres allocations et avantages imposables	42 Employment commissions / Commissions d'emploi

44 Union dues / Cotisations syndicales	46 Charitable donations / Dons de bienfaisance	50 Pension plan or DPSP registration number / Numéro d'enregistrement d'un RPDB ou d'un régime de pension	52 Pension adjustment / Facteur d'équivalence	10 Province of employment / Province d'emploi	12 Social insurance number / Numéro d'assurance sociale	If your social insurance number is not shown in box 12, see the back of this slip. / Si votre numéro d'assurance sociale ne figure pas dans la case 12, reportez-vous au verso de ce feuillet
	104 00			MANITOBA	978 010 789	

Employee's name and address - Nom et adresse de l'employé

Surname (in capital letters) / Nom de famille (en lettres majuscules) — First name / Prénom — Initials / Initiales

DRAGO, C.L.
1400 WELLINGTON CRESENT
WINNIPEG, MANITOBA
R3P 1E5

Employer's name - Nom de l'employeur: Blumenthal's

56 Employee no. - N° de l'employé:

54 Account number - Numéro de compte: 387-035

Footnotes - Notes:

Return with T4 Summary Return
À retourner avec la déclaration T4 *Sommaire* **1**

Source: Revenue Canada Taxation. Reproduced with permission of the Minister of Supply and Services Canada.

Internal Control over Payrolls _____

The internal controls over cash disbursements discussed in Chapter 7 apply to payroll. In addition, companies adopt special controls in payroll accounting. The large number of transactions and the many different parties involved increase the risk of a control failure. Accounting systems feature two types of special controls over payroll: controls for efficiency and controls for safeguarding cash.

Controls for Efficiency

For companies with many employees, reconciling the bank account can be time consuming owing to the large number of outstanding payroll cheques. For example, a March 30 payroll cheque would probably not have time to clear the bank before a bank statement on March 31. This cheque and others in a March 30 payroll would be outstanding. Identifying a large number of outstanding cheques for the bank reconciliation increases accounting expense. To limit the number of outstanding cheques, many companies use two payroll bank accounts. They make payroll disbursements from one payroll account one month and from the other payroll account the next month. By reconciling each account every other month, a March 30 paycheque has until April 30 to clear the bank before the account is reconciled. Outstanding cheques are essentially eliminated, the time it takes to prepare the bank reconciliation is reduced, and accounting expense is decreased. Also, many companies' cheques become void if not cashed within a certain period of time. This constraint too limits the number of outstanding cheques.

Payroll transactions are ideally suited for computer processing. Employee pay rates and withholding data are stored on computer. Each payroll period, computer operators enter the number of hours worked by each employee. The computer performs the calculations, prints the payroll register and paycheques, and updates the employee earnings records. The program also computes payroll taxes and prepares reports to government agencies. Expense and liability accounts are automatically updated for the payroll transactions. The payroll register is in a computer database form, which allows users to generate a wide variety of reports. At the end of an accounting period, the computerized payroll system automatically computes the amounts for the general ledger system, including any accruals of salary expense incurred but not paid.

Other payroll controls for efficiency include following established policies for hiring and firing employees and complying with government regulations. Hiring and firing policies provide guidelines for keeping a qualified, diligent work force dedicated to achieving the business's goals. Complying with government regulations helps companies avoid paying fines and penalties.

Controls for Safeguarding of Cash

Owners and managers of small businesses can monitor their payroll disbursements by personal contact with their employees. Large corporations cannot do so. These businesses must establish controls to assure that payroll disbursements are made only to legitimate employees and for the correct amounts. A particular danger is that payroll cheques may be written to a fictitious employee and cashed by a dishonest employee. To guard against this crime and other possible breakdowns in internal control, large businesses adopt strict internal control policies.

The duties of hiring and firing employees should be separated from the duties of distributing paycheques. Requiring an identification badge bearing an employee's photograph helps internal control. Issuing paycheques only to employees with badges ensures only actual employees receive pay.

A time-keeping system helps ensure that employees have actually worked the number of hours claimed. Having employees punch time cards at the start and end of the work day proves their attendance—as long as management makes sure that no employee punches in and out for others, too. Some companies have their workers fill in weekly or monthly time sheets.

Again we see that the key to good internal control is separation of duties. The responsibilities of the personnel department, payroll department, accounting department, time-card management, and paycheque distribution should be kept separate.

STOP & THINK

Centurion Homes Ltd. of Calgary, Alberta, builds houses and has four construction crews. The supervisors hire—and fire—workers and keep their hourly records. Each Friday morning the supervisors telephone their workers' hours to the home office, where accountants prepare the weekly paycheques. Around noon the supervisors pick up the paycheques. They return to the construction site and pay the workers at day's end. What is the internal control weakness in this situation? Propose a way to improve the internal controls.

Answer: Construction workers often have limited contact with the home office. When the supervisors control most of the information used in the payroll system, they can forge the payroll records of fictitious employees and pocket their pay. To improve internal control, Centurion could hire and fire all workers through the home office. This practice would establish the identity of all workers listed in the payroll records. Another way to improve the internal controls would be to have a home-office employee distribute paycheques on a surprise basis. Any remaining cheques would arouse suspicion regarding the supervisor. This system would probably prevent supervisors from cheating the company.

OBJECTIVE 6

Report current
liabilities

Reporting Payroll Expense and Liabilities

At the end of its fiscal year, the company reports the amount of *payroll liability* owed to all parties: employees, Revenue Canada, provincial governments, unions, and so forth. Payroll liability is *not* the payroll expense for the year. The liability at year end is the amount that is still unpaid. Payroll expense appears on the income statement, payroll liability on the balance sheet.

Inco Limited reported reported accrued payrolls and benefits of approximately $121 million (Inco reports in U.S. funds in its financial statements) as a current liability on its December 31, 1993, balance sheet (Exhibit 11-11). However, Inco's payroll expense for the year far exceeded $121 million; total operating expenses exceeded $2.3 billion. Exhibit 11-11 also presents the other current liabilities that we have discussed in this chapter.

Exhibit 11-12 summarizes all the current liabilities that we have discussed in this chapter.

EXHIBIT 11-11   *Partial Inco Limited Balance Sheet*

Current Liabilities	(U.S. $ in thousands)
Notes payable	$ 21,133
Long-term debt due within one year	91,701
Accounts payable	125,569
Accrued payrolls and benefits	120,987
Accrued interest	29,265
Other accrued liabilities	97,077
Income and mining taxes payable	6,208
Total current liabilities	$491,940

EXHIBIT 11-12   *Categories of Current Liabilities*

Amount of Liability Known When Recorded	Amount of Liability Estimated When Recorded
Trade accounts payable	Warranty payable
Short-term notes payable	Income tax payable
Sales tax payable	Vacation pay liability
Current portion of long-term debt	
Accrued expenses payable:	
Interest payable	
Payroll liabilities (salaries payable, wages payable, and commissions payable)	
Payroll withholdings payable (employee and employer)	
Unearned revenues (revenues collected in advance of being earned)	
Customer deposits payable	

Summary Problem for Your Review

Beth Denius Ltd., a clothing store, employs one salesperson, Sheila Kingsley. Her straight-time pay is $420 per week. She earns time and a half for hours worked in excess of 35 per week. For Kingsley's wage rate and "net claim code" on her TD1, the income tax withholding rate is approximately 11 percent. Canada Pension is 2.7 percent on income in excess of $65.38 per week, while Unemployment Insurance premiums are 3.0 percent. In addition, Denius pays Kingsley's Blue Cross supplemental health insurance premiums of $31.42 a month and dental insurance premiums of $18.50 a month.

During the week ended February 28, 19X3, Kingsley worked 48 hours.

Required

1. Compute Kingsley's gross pay and net pay for the week.

2. Record the following payroll entries that Denius would make:
   a. Expense for Kingsley's wages including overtime pay
   b. Cost of employer's share of Kingsley's withholdings
   c. Expense for fringe benefits
   d. Payment of cash to Kingsley
   e. Payment Denius must make to Revenue Canada
   f. Payment of fringe benefits for the month

3. How much total payroll expense did Denius incur for the week? How much cash did the business spend on its payroll?

SOLUTION TO REVIEW PROBLEM

Requirement 1

Gross pay:

Straight-time for 35 hours...		$420.00
Overtime pay		
Rate per hour ($420/35 × 1.5)	$18.00	
Hours (48 – 35)	× 13	234.00
Total gross pay..		$654.00

Deductions:

Gross pay		$654.00
Less: Withheld income tax ($654 × .11)...............................	$71.94	
Withheld Canada Pension [($654 – $65.38) × .027].............	15.89	
Withheld Unemployment Insurance ($654 × .03)...............	19.62	107.45
Net pay..		546.55

Requirement 2

a. Sales Salary Expense..	654.00	
Employee Withheld Income Tax Payable		71.94
Employee Canada Pension Payable		15.89
Employee Unemployment Insurance Payable.................		19.62
Wages payable to employee...		546.55
b. Canada Pension Plan Expense ($15.89 × 1)	15.89	
Unemployment Insurance Expense ($19.62 × 1.4)................	27.46	
Employer Canada Pension Plan Payable.........................		15.89
Employer Unemployment Insurance Payable.................		27.46
c. Medical and Dental Expense ($31.42 + $18.50).....................	49.92	
Employee Benefits Payable..		49.92
d. Wages Payable to Employee..	546.55	
Cash..		546.55
e. Employee Withheld Income Tax Payable	71.94	
Employee Canada Pension Payable	15.89	
Employee Unemployment Insurance Payable	19.62	
Employer Canada Pension Plan Payable.............................	15.89	
Employer Unemployment Insurance Payable.....................	27.46	
Cash..		150.80
f. Employee Benefits Payable..	49.92	
Cash..		49.92

Requirement 3

Denius incurred *total payroll expense* of $747.27 (gross salary of $654.00 + employer's cost re Canada Pension of $15.89 + employer's cost re Unemployment Insurance of $27.46 + fringe benefits of $49.92). See entries a to c.

Denius paid cash of $747.27 on payroll (Kingsley's net pay of $546.55 + payment to Revenue Canada of $150.80 + fringe benefits of $49.92). See entries d to f.

Summary

1. Account for current liabilities. *Current liabilities* may be divided into those of *known amount* and those that must be *estimated*. Trade accounts payable, short-term notes payable, and the related liability for accrued expenses are current liabilities of known amount. Current liabilities that must be estimated include warranties payable and corporations' income tax payable.

2. *Account for contingent liabilities*. *Contingent liabilities* are not actual liabilities but potential liabilities that may arise in the future. Contingent liabilities, like current liabilities, may be of known amount or an indefinite amount. A business that faces a lawsuit not yet decided in court has a contingent liability of indefinite amount.

3. *Compute payroll amounts*. *Payroll* accounting handles the expenses and liabilities arising from compensating employees. Employers must withhold income taxes, Canada (or Quebec) Pension Plan contributions, and Unemployment Insurance premiums from employees' pay and send these *withholdings* together with the employer's share of the latter two to the government. In addition, many employers allow their employees to pay for insurance and union dues and to make gifts to charities through payroll deductions. An employee's net pay is the gross pay less all withholdings and optional deductions.

4. *Make basic payroll entries*. An *employer's* payroll expenses include the employer's share of Canada (or Quebec) Pension Plan contributions and Unemployment Insurance premiums; employers also pay provincial health and post-secondary taxes in those provinces which levy them and Workers' Compensation. Also, employers may provide their employees with fringe benefits, such as life insurance coverage and retirement pensions.

5. *Use a payroll system*. A *payroll system* consists of a payroll register, a payroll bank account, payroll cheques, and an earnings record for each employee. Good *internal controls* over payroll disbursements help the business to conduct payroll accounting efficiently and to safeguard the company's cash. The cornerstone of internal control is the separation of duties.

6. *Report current liabilities*. The company reports on the balance sheet all current liabilities that it owes.

Self-Study Questions

Test your understanding of the chapter by marking the correct answer for each of the following questions:

1. A $10,000, 9 percent, one-year note payable was issued on July 31. The balance sheet at December 31 will report interest payable of (*p. 527*)
   a. $0 because the interest is not due yet
   b. $300
   c. $375
   d. $900

2. If the note payable in the preceding question had been discounted, the cash proceeds from issuance would have been (*pp. 527–528*)
   a. $9,100   c. $9,700
   b. $9,625   d. $10,000

3. Which of the following liabilities creates no expense for the company? (*p. 530*)
   a. Interest   c. Unemployment Insurance
   b. Sales tax   d. Warranty

4. Suppose Canadian Tire estimates that warranty costs will equal 1 percent of tire sales. Assume that November sales totaled $900,000, and the company's outlay in tires and cash to satisfy warranty claims was $7,400. How much warranty expense should the November income statement report? (*p. 533*)
   a. $1,600   c. $9,000
   b. $7,400   d. $16,400

5. XYZ Corp. is a defendant in a lawsuit that claims damages of $55,000. On the balance sheet date, it appears unlikely that the court will render a judgment against the company. How should XYZ report this event in its financial statements? (*pp. 535–536*)

a. Omit mention because no judgment has been rendered
b. Disclose the contingent liability in a note
c. Report the loss on the income statement and the liability on the balance sheet
d. Both b and c

6. Emilie Frontenac's weekly pay for 40 hours is $320, plus time and half for overtime. The tax rate, based on her income level and deductions, is 16 percent, the Quebec Pension Plan rate is 2.7 percent on her weekly earnings in excess of $65.38, and the Unemployment Insurance rate is 3.0 percent on her weekly earnings. What is Emilie's take-home pay for a week in which she works 50 hours? *(p. 539)*

a. $346.29   c. $356.40
b. $344.51   d. $359.49

7. Which of the following represents a cost to the employer? *(p. 544)*
   a. Withheld income tax   c. Unemployment Insurance
   b. Canada Pension   d. Both b and c

8. The main reason for using a separate payroll bank account is to *(p. 548)*
   a. Safeguard cash by preventing the writing of payroll cheques to fictitious employees
   b. Safeguard cash by limiting paycheques to amounts based on time cards
   c. Increase efficiency by isolating payroll disbursements for analysis and control
   d. All of the above

9. The key to good internal controls in the payroll area is *(p. 554)*
   a. Using a payroll bank account   c. Using a payroll register
   b. Separating payroll duties   d. Using time cards

10. Which of the following items is reported as current liability on the balance sheet? *(p. 555)*
    a. Short-term notes payable   c. Accrued payroll withholdings
    b. Estimated warranties   d. All of the above

Answers to the Self-Study Questions follow the Accounting Vocabulary.

Accounting Vocabulary

Canada (or Quebec) Pension Plan *(p. 539)*
Current portion of long-term debt *(p. 531)*
Discounting a note payable *(p. 527)*
Gross pay *(p. 539)*
Net Pay *(p. 539*
Payroll *(p. 538)*
Short-term note payable *(p. 527)*
Unemployment Insurance Act *(p. 542)*
Withheld income tax *(p. 539)*
Workers' compensation *(p. 544)*

Answers to Self-Study Questions

1. c $10,000 \times .09 \times \frac{5}{12} = \$375$ 7. d
2. a $\$10,000 - (\$10,000 \times .09) = \$9,100$ 8. c
3. b   9. b
4. c $\$900,000 \times .01 = \$9,000$ 10. d
5. b
6. a Overtime pay: $\$320/40 = \$8 \times 1.5 = \$12$ per hour $\times 10$ hours $= \$120$
      Gross pay $= \$320 + \$120 = \$440$
      Deductions $= (\$440 \times .16) + [(\$440 - \$65.38) \times .027] + [\$440 \times .03]$
      $= \$70.40 + \$10.11 + 13.20 = \$93.71$
      Take-home pay $= \$440.00 - 93.71 = \$346.29$

ASSIGNMENT MATERIAL _____

Questions

1. Give a more descriptive account title for each of the following current liabilities: Accrued Interest, Accrued Salaries, Accrued Income Tax.

2. What distinguishes a current liability from a long-term liability? What distinguishes a contingent liability from an actual liability?

3. A company purchases a machine by signing a $21,000, 10 percent, one-year note payable on July 31. Interest is to be paid at maturity. What two current liabilities related to this purchase does the company report on its December 31 balance sheet? What is the amount of each liability?

4. A company borrowed cash by discounting a $15,000, 8 percent, six-month note payable to the bank, receiving cash of $14,400. (a) Show how the amount of cash was computed. Also, identify (b) the total amount of interest expense to be recognized on this note and (c) the amount of the borrower's cash payment at maturity.

5. Explain how GST that is paid by consumers is a liability of the store that sold the merchandise. To whom is it paid?

6. What is meant by the term *current portion of long-term debt*, and how is this item reported in the financial statements?

7. At the beginning of the school term, what type of account is the tuition that your college or university collects from students? What type of account is the tuition at the end of the school term?

8. Why is a customer deposit a liability? Give an example.

9. Patton Corp. warrants its products against defects for three years from date of sale. During the current year, the company made sales of $300,000. Store management estimated warranty costs on those sales would total $18,000 over the three-year warranty period. Ultimately, the company paid $22,000 cash on warranties. What is the company's warranty expense for the year? What accounting principle governs this answer?

10. Identify two contingent liabilities of a definite amount and two contingent liabilities of an indefinite amount.

11. Describe two ways to report contingent liabilities.

12. Why is payroll expense relatively more important to a service business such as a public accounting firm than it is to a merchandising company such as Zellers?

13. Two persons are studying Allen Ltd.'s manufacturing process. One person is Allen's factory supervisor, and the other person is an outside consultant who is an expert in the industry. Which person's salary is the payroll expense of Allen Ltd.? Identify the expense account that Allen would debit to record the pay of each person.

14. What are two elements of an employee's payroll expense in addition to salaries, wages, commissions, and overtime pay?

15. What determines the amount of income tax that is withheld from employee paycheques?

16. What is the Canada Pension Plan? Who pays it? What are the funds used for?

17. Identify three required deductions and two optional deductions from employee paycheques.

18. Identify three employee benefit expenses an employer pays.

19. Who pays Unemployment Insurance premiums? What are these funds used for?

20. Briefly describe a payroll accounting system's components and their functions.

21. How much Unemployment Insurance has been withheld from the pay of an employee who has earned $52,288 during the current year? What is the employer's Unemployment Insurance expense for this employee?

22. Briefly describe the two principal categories of internal controls over payroll.
23. Why do some companies use two special payroll bank accounts?
24. Identify three internal controls designed to safeguard payroll cash.

Exercises

Exercise 11-1   *Recording sales tax and GST*   **(Obj. 1)**

Make general journal entries to record the following transactions of Ransom Distributors, Inc., for a two-month period. Explanations are not required.

Mar. 31   Recorded cash sales of $83,600 for the month, plus provincial sales tax of 9 percent collected on behalf of the province of Saskatchewan and goods and services tax of 7 percent. Record the two taxes in separate accounts.

Apr. 6   Sent March provincial and goods and services taxes to appropriate authorities. Assume no GST input tax credits.

Exercise 11-2   *Accounting for warranty expense and the related liability*   **(Obj.1)**

The accounting records of Shotwell, Inc., included the following balances at the end of the period:

Estimated Warranty Payable	**Sales Revenue**	**Warranty Expense**
Beg. bal. 4,100	141,000	

In the past, Shotwell's warranty expense has been 7 percent of sales. During the current period, Shotwell paid $10,430 to satisfy the warranty claims of customers.

Required

1. Record Shotwell's warranty expense for the period and the company's cash payments during the period to satisfy warranty claims. Explanations are not required.
2. What ending balance of Estimated Warranty Payable will Shotwell report on its balance sheet?

Exercise 11-3   *Recording note payable transactions*   **(Obj. 1)**

Record the following note payable transactions of Montreal Development, Inc., in the company's general journal. Explanations are not required.

19X2
May 1   Purchased equipment costing $14,000 by issuing a one-year, 8 percent note payable.
Dec. 31   Accrued interest on the note payable.
19X3
May 1   Paid the note payable at maturity.

Exercise 11-4   *Discounting a note payable*   **(Obj. 1)**

On November 1, 19X4, Hui Ltd. discounted a six-month, $12,000 note payable to the bank at 7 percent.

Required

1. Prepare general journal entries to record (a) issuance of the note, (b) accrual of interest at December 31, and (c) payment of the note at maturity in 19X5. Explanations are not required.
2. Show how Hui would report the note on the December 31, 19X4, balance sheet.

Exercise 11-5 *Reporting a contingent liability* (Obj. 2)

Duck Lake Instruments Corp. is a defendant in lawsuits brought against the marketing and distribution of its products. Damages of $230,000 are claimed against Duck Lake but the company denies the charges and is vigorously defending itself. In a recent newspaper interview, the president of the company stated that she could not predict the outcome of the lawsuits. Nevertheless, she said management does not believe that any actual liabilities resulting from the lawsuits will significantly affect the company's financial position.

Required

Describe what, if any, disclosure Duck Lake Instruments should provide of this contingent liability. Total liabilities are $1.6 million. If you believe note disclosure is required, write the note to describe the contingency.

Exercise 11-6 *Accruing a contingency* (Obj. 2)

Refer to the Duck Lake Instruments Corp. situation in the preceding exercise. Suppose that Duck Lake's lawyers advise that preliminary judgment of $50,000 has been rendered against the company.

Required

Describe how to report this situation in the Duck Lake Instrument Corp. financial statements. Journalize any entry required under GAAP. Explanations are not required.

Exercise 11-7 *Reporting current liabilities* (Obj. 6)

The top management of Stattler, Inc., examines the following company accounting records at December 29, immediately before the end of the year:

Total current assets	$ 490,000
Noncurrent assets	1,230,000
	$1,720,000
Total current liabilities	$250,000
Noncurrent liabilities	810,000
Shareholders' equity	660,000
	$1,720,000

Stattler's borrowing agreements with creditors require the company to keep a current ratio of 2.0 or better. How much in current liabilities should Stattler pay off within the next two days in order to comply with its borrowing agreements?

Exercise 11-8 *Computing net pay* (Obj. 3)

Van Pringle is a salesclerk in the electronics department of The Bay in Calgary. He earns a base monthly salary of $800 plus a 9 percent commission on his sales. Through payroll deductions, Van donates $10 per month to a charitable organization and pays dental insurance premiums of $38.25. Compute Van's gross pay and net pay for December, assuming his sales for the month are $82,000. The income tax rate on his earnings is 20 percent, the Canada Pension Plan contribution is 2.7 percent (subject to the basic deduction of $3,400 and the maximum contribution of $850.50), and the Unemployment Insurance Plan premium rate is 3 percent (subject to the maximum premium of $1,271.40). During the first 11 months of the year, Van earned $61,140.

Exercise 11-9 *Computing and recording gross pay and net pay* (Obj. 3, 4)

Vida Berg works for a Quik Trip convenience store for straight-time earnings of $8 per hour, with time and a half for hours in excess of 40 per week. Vida's payroll deductions include income tax of 7 percent, Canada Pension of 2.7 percent on earnings in excess of $65.38 per week, and Unemployment Insurance of 3.0 percent on earnings. In addition, she contributes $5 per week to the United Way. Assuming Vida worked 43 hours during the week, (1) compute her gross pay and net pay for the week, and (2) make a general journal entry to record the store's wage expense for Vida's work, including her payroll deductions. Round all amounts to the nearest cent.

Exercise 11-10   *Recording a payroll*   *(Obj. 3, 4)*

Fortin Department Store Ltd. incurred salary expense of $82,000 for December. The store's payroll expense includes Canada Pension of 2.7 percent (ignore the basic exemption for this question) and Unemployment Insurance of 1.4 times the employee rate of 3.0 percent. Also the store provides the following fringe benefits for employees: dental insurance (cost to the store $2,632.07); life insurance (cost to the store $351.07); and pension benefits through a private plan (cost to the store $707.60). Record Fortin's payroll expenses for Canada Pension and Unemployment Insurance and employee fringe benefits.

Exercise 11-11   *Reporting current and long-term liabilities*   *(Obj. 6)*

Suppose B.C. Kayak Outfitters Ltd. borrowed $500,000 on December 31, 19X0, by issuing 9 percent long-term debt that must be paid in annual installments of $100,000 plus interest each January 2. By inserting appropriate amounts in the following excerpts from the company's partial balance sheet, show how B.C. Kayak Outfitters would report its long-term debt.

| | December 31, | | | | |
	19X1	19X2	19X3	19X4	19X5
Current liabilities					
Current portion of long-term debt.........	$____	$____	$____	$____	$____
Interest payable	$____	$____	$____	$____	$____
Long-term liabilities					
Long-term debt.......................................	$____	$____	$____	$____	$____

Exercise 11-12   *Reporting current and long-term liabilities*   *(Obj. 6)*

Assume Canstar Sports Inc. completed these selected transactions during December 19X6:

1. Sport Spectrum, a chain of sporting goods stores, ordered $60,000 worth of hockey equipment. With its order, Sport Spectrum sent a cheque for $60,000. Canstar will ship the goods on January 3, 19X7.

2. The December payroll of $5,100,000 is subject to employee withheld income tax of 18 percent, Canada Pension Plan expenses of 5.4 percent (employee and employer), Unemployment Insurance deductions of 3.0 percent for the employee and 1.4 times the employee rate of 3.0 percent for the employer. On December 31, Canstar pays employees but accrues all tax amounts.

3. Sales of $200,000,000 are subject to estimated warranty cost of 1.4 percent.

4. On December 2, Canstar signed a $100,000 note payable that requires annual payments of $20,000 plus 9 percent interest on the unpaid balance each December 2.

Required

Report these items on Canstar's balance sheet at December 31, 19X6.

Exercise 11-13   *Accounting for and reporting current liabilities*   **(Obj. 1, 6)**

The balance sheets of PepsiCo, Inc., for four years reported these figures:

| | **Millions** | | | |
	19X4	**19X3**	**19X2**	**19X1**
Total current assets	$ 4,842.3	$ 4,566.1	$ 4,081.4	$ 3,550.8
Noncurrent assets	16,108.9	14,209.0	13,062.0	11.575.9
	$20,951.2	$18,775.1	$17,143.4	$15,126.7
Total current liabilities	$ 4,324.4	$ 3,722.1	$ 4,770.5	$ 3,691.8
Noncurrent liabilities	11,271.1	9.507.6	7,468.7	7,543.8
Stockholders' equity.........................	5,355.7	5,545.4	4,904.2	3,891.1
	$20,951.2	$18,775.1	$17,143.4	$15,126.7

The notes to PepsiCo's 19X4 financial statements report that during 19X3, PepsiCo reclassified $3,450 million of current liabilities as long-term. And during 19X4, PepsiCo reclassified a further $3,500 million as long-term.

Required

1. Compute PepsiCo's current ratio at the end of each year. Describe the trend that you observe.

2. Assume that PepsiCo has not reclassified current liabilities as long-term. Recompute the current ratios for 19X3 and 19X4. Why do you think PepsiCo reclassified the liabilities as long-term? What could the company do to justify the reclassification?

Exercise 11-14   *Analyzing current liability accounts*   **(Obj. 1, 3, 6)**

Inco Limited recently reported notes payable and accrued payrolls and benefits as follows:

| | **December 31,** | |
	1993	**1992**
	(U.S. $ in thousands)	
Current liabilities (partial):		
Notes payable	$ 21,133	$ 1,851
Accrued payrolls and benefits..............................	120,987	144,434

Assume that during 1993, Inco borrowed $35,000,000 on notes payable. Also assume that Inco paid $1,100,000 for employee compensation and benefits during 1993.

Required

1. Compute Inco's payment of notes payable during 1993.
2. Compute Inco's employee compensation during 1993.

Problems   (Group A)

Problem 11-1A   *Journalizing liability-related transactions*   **(Obj. 1)**

The following selected transactions of Econo Auto Service Inc. occurred during 19X4 and 19X5.

Required

Record the transactions in the company's general journal. Explanations are not required.

19X4

Jan. 3 Purchased a machine at a cost of $5,000, signing an 8 percent, six-month note payable for that amount.

     29 Recorded the month's sales of $122,200, three-fourths on credit and one-fourth for cash. Sales amounts are subject to an additional 6 percent provincial sales tax plus 7 percent GST.

Feb. 5 Sent the last month's provincial and GST tax to the appropriate authorities.

     28 Borrowed $300,000 on a 9 percent note payable that calls for annual installment payments of $50,000 principal plus interest.

Apr. 8 Received $1,427 in deposits from distributors of company products. Econo refunds the deposits after six months.

July 9 Paid the six-month, 8 percent note at maturity.

Oct. 8 Refunded security deposits to distributors.

     22 Discounted a $5,000, 7 percent, 90-day note payable to the bank, receiving cash for the net amount after interest was deducted from the note's maturity value.

Nov. 30 Purchased inventory for $3,100, signing a six-month, 10 percent note payable.

Dec. 31 Accrued warranty expense, which is estimated at 3 percent of sales of $1,250,000.

     31 Accrued interest on all outstanding notes payable. Make a separate interest accrual entry for each note payable.

19X5

Jan. 20 Paid off the 7 percent discounted note payable. Made a separate entry for the interest.

Feb. 28 Paid the first installment and interest for one year on the long-term note payable.

May 31 Paid off the 10 percent note plus interest at maturity.

Problem 11-2A   *Identifying contingent liabilities*   **(Obj. 2)**

Covert Buick Company Ltd. is the only Buick dealer in Nanaimo, British Columbia, and one of the largest Buick dealers on Vancouver Island. The dealership sells new and used cars and operates a body shop and a service department. Duke Covert, the general manager, is considering changing insurance companies because of a disagreement with Doug Stillwell, Nanaimo agent for the Dominion of Canada Insurance Company. Dominion is doubling Covert's liability insurance cost for the next year. In discussing insurance coverage with you, a trusted business associate, Stillwell brings up the subject of contingent liabilities.

Required

Write a memorandum to inform Covert Buick Company Ltd. of specific contingent liabilities arising from the business. In your discussion, define a contingent liability.

Problem 11-3A   *Computing and recording payroll amounts*   **(Obj. 3, 4)**

The partial monthly records of The Art Center show the following figures:

Employee Earnings					
(a) Straight-time employee earnings	$16,431		(f) Unemployment Insurance	$	580
			(g) Medical insurance		668
(b) Overtime pay	?		(h) Total deductions		4,141
(c) Total employee earnings	?		(i) Net pay		15,204
Deductions and Net Pay			**Accounts Debited**		
			(j) Salary Expense		?
(d) Withheld income tax	2,403		(k) Wage Expense		4,573
(e) Canada Pension	?		(l) Sales Commission Expense		5,077

Required

1. Determine the missing amounts on lines (b), (c), (e), and (j).

2. Prepare the general journal entry to record The Art Center's payroll for the month. Credit Payrolls Payable for net pay. No explanation is required.

Problem 11-4A   *Computing and recording payroll amounts*   **(Obj. 3, 4)**

Assume that Nancy Jacina is Vice-President of the Bank of Montreal's leasing operations. During 19X6 she worked for the company all year at a $5,625 monthly salary. She also earned a year-end bonus equal to 10 percent of her salary.

Jacina's federal income tax withheld during 19X6 was $1,833 per month. Also, there was a one-time federal withholding tax of $2,416 on her bonus cheque. She paid $144 per month into the Canada Pension Plan until she had paid the maximum. In addition, Jacina paid $106 per month to the Unemployment Insurance Commission through her employer until the maximum had been reached. She had authorized the bank to make the following payroll deductions: life insurance of $19 per month; United Way of Halifax of $35 per month.

The Bank of Montreal incurred Canada Pension expense equal to the amount deducted from Jacina's pay and Unemployment Insurance expense equal to 1.4 times the amount Jacina paid. In addition, the bank paid dental and drug insurance of $32.00 per month and pension benefits of 8 percent of her base salary.

Required

1. Compute Jacina's gross pay, payroll deductions, and net pay for the full year 19X6. Round all amounts to the nearest dollar.

2. Compute Bank of Montreal's total 19X6 payroll cost for Jacina.

3. Prepare the Bank of Montreal's general journal entries to record its expense for
   a. Jacina's total earnings for the year, her payroll deductions, and her net pay. Debit Salary Expense and Executive Bonus Compensation as appropriate. Credit liability accounts for the payroll deductions and Cash for net pay.
   b. Employer payroll expenses on Jacina. Credit liability accounts.
   c. Fringe benefits provided to Jacina. Credit a liability account.

Problem 11-5A   *Journalizing, posting, and reporting liabilities*   **(Obj. 1, 2, 4, 6)**

The general ledger of Concept Systems, Inc., at June 30, 19X3, end of the company's fiscal year, includes the following account balances before adjusting entries. Parentheses indicate a debit balance.

Notes payable, short-term ..	$ 45,000	Employee benefits	
Discount on notes payable..	(600)	payable............................	_____
Accounts payable.................	105,520	Estimated vacation pay	
Current portion of long-		liability.............................	_____
term debt payable............	_____	Sales tax payable	$ 738
Interest payable	_____	Customer deposits	
Salary payable	_____	payable............................	6,950
Employee payroll		Unearned rent revenue	6,000
withholdings payable	_____	Long-term debt payable....	120,000
Employer payroll		Contingent liability............	_____
expenses payable..............	_____		

The additional data needed to develop the adjusting entries at June 30 are as follows:

a. The $45,000 balance in Notes Payable, Short-Term consists of two notes. The first note, with a principal amount of $15,000, was issued on January 31. It matures six months from date of issuance and was discounted at 8 percent. The second note was issued on April 22 for a term of 90 days. It bears interest at 9 percent. It was not discounted. Interest on this note will be paid at maturity.

b. The long-term debt is payable in annual installments of $40,000 with the next installment due on July 31. On that date, Concept Systems will also pay one year's interest at 7 percent. Interest was last paid on July 31 of the preceding year.

c. Gross salaries for the last payroll of the fiscal year were $5,044. Of this amount, employee payroll withholdings payable were $1,088, and salary payable was $3,956.

d. Employer payroll expense payable was $876, and Concept System's liability for employee health insurance was $1,046.

e. Concept Systems estimates that vacation pay expense is 4 percent of gross salaries of $250,000 after adjustment for the last payroll of the fiscal year.

f. On February 1, the company collected one year's rent of $6,000 in advance.

g. At June 30, Concept Systems is the defendant in a $300,000 lawsuit, which the company expects to win. However, the outcome is uncertain.

Required

1. Open the listed accounts, inserting their unadjusted June 30 balances.
2. Journalize and post the June 30 adjusting entries to the accounts opened. Key adjusting entries by letter.
3. Prepare the liability section of the balance sheet at June 30.

Problem 11-6A   *Using payroll register; recording a payroll*   **(Obj. 5)**

Assume that the payroll records of a district sales office of FarWest Lumber Corporation provided the following information for the weekly pay period ended December 21, 19X5:

Employee	Hours Worked	Hourly Earnings Rate	Income Tax	Canada Pension	Unemployment Insurance	United Way	Earnings through Previous Week
Maria Kokoros	42	$18	$183.85	$ 0	$23.22	$10	$39,800
James English	47	8	58.05	9.14	12.12	2	21,100
Louise French	40	11	79.80	10.11	13.20	2	10,300
Robert LaFlair	41	16	129.60	0	19.92	3	37,450

James English and Louise French work in the office, and Maria Kokoros and Robert LaFlair work in sales. All employees are paid time and a half for hours worked in excess of 40 per week. For convenience, round all amounts to the nearest dollar. Show computations.

Required

1. Enter the appropriate information in a payroll register similar to Exhibit 11-7.
2. Record the payroll information in the general journal.
3. Assume that the first payroll cheque is number 319, paid to Maria Kokoros. Record the cheque numbers in the payroll register. Also, prepare the general journal entry to record payment of net pay to the employees.
4. The employer's payroll costs include matching each employee's Canada Pension Plan contribution and paying 1.4 times the employee's Unemployment Insurance premium. Record the employer's payroll costs in the general journal.
5. Why was no Canada Pension deducted for Kokoros and LaFlair?

Problem 11-7A   *Reporting current liabilities*   **(Obj. 6)**

Following are six pertinent facts about events during the current year at Sea Spray Sales Ltd.:

a. On September 30, Sea Spray signed a six-month, 9 percent note payable to purchase inventory costing $50,000. The note requires payment of principal and interest at maturity.

b. On October 31, Sea Spray discounted a $50,000 note payable to the Bank of Nova Scotia. The interest rate on the one-year note is 8 percent.

c. On November 30, Sea Spray received rent of $5,100 in advance for a lease on a building. This rent will be earned evenly over three months.

d. December sales totaled $38,000 and Sea Spray Sales collected provincial sales tax of 11 percent plus Goods and Services tax of 7 percent. This amount will be sent to the appropriate authorities early in January.

e. Sea Spray owes $100,000 on a long-term note payable. At December 31, $20,000 of this principal plus 6 percent accrued interest since July 31 are payable within one year.

f. Sales of $430,000 were covered by Sea Spray's product warranty. At January 1, estimated warranty payable was $8,100. During the year Sea Spray recorded warranty expense of $22,300 and paid warranty claims of $23,600.

Required

For each item, indicate the account and the related amount to be reported as a current liability on Sea Spray's December 31 balance sheet.

Problem 11-8A   *Account for current liabilities; make basic payroll entries; report current liabilities*   **(Obj. 1, 4, 6)**

Discount Auto Supply Ltd. of Red Deer, Alberta, operates an auto parts supply company with the following information available:

- Goods and Services Tax: 7 percent GST is applicable to all purchases and sales.
- Payroll Taxes—the employer's share of Canada Pension and Unemployment Insurance are 1.0 times and 1.4 times respectively. The company pays workers' compensation of 3 percent and estimates vacation pay at 4 percent of all earnings.
- Mortgage Payable: the company has a $200,000 mortgage payable with payments of $2,000 plus interest (@ 12 percent) due on the 20th of each month.

The company prepares quarterly financial statements and had the following transactions for the first three months of 19X1:

Jan. 9 Discounted a $10,000, 8 percent, 60-day note payable to the bank, receiving the net amount in cash.

  20 Made the first payment on the mortgage.

  31 Recorded the month's purchases of $140,000 (not including the GST). All purchases are on credit.

  31 Recorded the month's sales of $250,000 (not including the GST) of which 70 percent were on credit.

  31 Recorded and paid the payroll for the month. Gross earnings were $60,000, with deductions of:
   - Employee income taxes equal to 15 percent,
   - CPP deductions equal to 2 percent
   - UI deductions equal to 3 percent
   - Union dues deduction equal to $1,200.

Feb. 2 Borrowed $50,000 from the bank by signing a 9 percent, 30-day note payable with the principle and interest payable on the due date.

Feb.   7   Paid the GST due from the month of January.

15   Remitted all payroll deductions and contributions to the appropriate bodies.

20   Made the second payment on the mortgage.

28   Recorded the month's purchases of $190,000 (not including the GST). All purchases are on credit.

28   Recorded the month's sales of $310,000 (not including the GST) of which 80 percent were on credit.

28   Recorded and paid the payroll for the month. Gross earnings were $90,000, with deductions of:
- Employee income taxes equal to 15 percent
- CPP deductions equal to 2 percent
- UI deductions equal to 3 percent
- Union dues deduction equal to $1,500.

Mar.   4   Paid the note payable dated February 2nd.

7   Paid the GST due from the month of February.

10   Paid the note payable dated January 9th.

12   Discounted a $15,000, 10 percent, 90-day note payable to the bank, receiving the net amount in cash.

15   Remitted all payroll deductions and contributions to the appropriate bodies.

20   Made the third payment on the mortgage.

30   Recorded the month's purchases of $220,000 (not including the GST). All purchases are on credit.

30   Recorded the month's sales of $390,000 (not including the GST) of which 60 percent were on credit.

30   Recorded and paid the payroll for the month. Gross earnings were $120,000, with deductions of:
- Employee income taxes equal to 15 percent,
- CPP deductions equal to 2 percent
- UI deductions equal to 3 percent
- Union dues deduction equal to $2,400.

Required

1. Journalize all of the transactions and any adjustments that would be required on March 30th (the end of the first quarter). Round all amounts to the nearest whole dollar.

2. Show the current liability section of the balance sheet as of March 30, 19X1.

Problem 11-9A   *Account for current liabilities, account for contingent liabilities, report current liabilities   (Obj. 1, 2, 6)*

Hibernia Farm Equipment Ltd. produces and sells customized farm equipment. The company offers a 60-day, all parts and labor—and an extra 90-day, parts-only—warranty on all of its products. The company had the following transactions in 19X1:

Jan.   31   Sales for the month totaled $60,000, 70 percent of which were on credit. The company collects 7 percent GST on all sales and estimates its warranty costs at 4 percent of sales.

31   Estimated (based on last year's property tax assessment) that the property taxes for the year would be $18,000 (1 percent of the $1,800,000 assessed value). Recorded the estimated property taxes for the month.

Feb.   4   Completed repair work for a customer. The parts ($1,000) and labor ($500) were all covered under the warranty.

Feb.   6   Remitted the appropriate GST for the month of January (they had paid a total of $2,900 in GST on purchases of parts in January).

28   Recorded the estimated property taxes for the month of February.

28   Sales for the month totaled $90,000, 80 percent of which were on credit. The company collects 7 percent GST on all sales and estimates its warranty costs at 4 percent of sales.

Mar.   6   Remitted the appropriate GST for the month of February (they had paid a total of $3,400 in GST on purchases of parts in February).

8   Hibernia received notice that they were being sued by a customer for an accident resulting from the failure of their product. The company's lawyer was reluctant to estimate the likely outcome of the lawsuit, but another customer indicated that a similar case had resulted in a $180,000 settlement.

15   Completed repair work for a customer. The parts ($3,000) and labor ($900) were all covered under the warranty.

20   Completed repair work for a customer. The parts ($1,600) were covered by the warranty, but the labor ($700) was not. Payment is due in 30 days.

31   Sales for the month totaled $70,000, 75 percent of which was on credit. The company collects 7 percent GST on all sales and estimates its warranty costs at 4 percent of sales.

31   Received the property tax assessment for 19X1 which showed the assessed value of their property to be $2,200,000 and a tax rate of 1.2 percent. Made the appropriate adjustment.

Required

1. Journalize the above transactions.
2. Show the appropriate financial statement presentation for all liabilities.

(Group B)

Problem 11-1B   *Journalizing liability-related transactions*   *(Obj. 1)*

The following transactions of Taurus Oil Well Supply Co. Ltd. occurred during 19X2 and 19X3. Record the transactions in the company's general journal. Explanations are not required.

19X2

Feb.   3   Purchased a machine for $6,200, signing a six-month, 8 percent note payable.

28   Recorded the month's sales of $223,000, one third for cash, and two thirds on credit. All sales amounts are subject to the 7 percent Goods and Services tax.

Mar.   7   Sent the last month's Goods and Services tax to the appropriate authority.

Apr. 30   Borrowed $100,000 on a 9 percent note payable that calls for annual installment payments of $25,000 principal plus interest.

May 10   Received $1,125 in security deposits from customers. Taurus refunds most deposits within three months.

Aug.   3   Paid the six-month, 8 percent note at maturity.

10   Refunded security deposits of $1,125 to customers.

Sept. 14   Discounted a $6,000, 7 percent, 60-day note payable to the bank, receiving cash for the net amount after interest was deducted from the note's maturity value.

Nov. 13   Recognized interest on the 7 percent discounted note and paid off the note at maturity.

30   Purchased inventory at a cost of $7,200, signing a 9 percent, three-month note payable for that amount.

Dec. 31   Accrued warranty expense, which is estimated at 1 percent of sales of $2,670,000.

31   Accrued interest on all outstanding notes payable. Make a separate interest accrual entry for each note payable.

19X3

Feb. 28   Paid off the 9 percent inventory note, plus interest, at maturity.

Apr. 30   Paid the first installment and interest for one year on the long-term note payable.

Problem 11-2B   *Identifying contingent liabilities*   (Obj. 2)

Hunting Horn Farm provides riding lessons for children ages 8 through 15. Most students are beginners, and none of them own their own horse. Jan Wiebling, the owner of Hunting Horn, uses horses stabled at her farm and owned by the Erbs. Most of the horses are for sale, but the economy has been bad for several years and horse sales have been slow. The Erbs are happy that Jan uses their horses in exchange for rooming and boarding them. Because of a recent financial setback, Jan cannot afford insurance. She seeks your advice about her business exposure to liabilities.

Required

Write a memorandum to inform Jan of specific contingent liabilities that could arise from the business. It will be necessary to define a contingent liability because she is a professional horse trainer, not a businessperson. Propose a way for Jan to limit her exposure to these possible liabilities.

Problem 11-3B   *Computing and reporting payroll amounts*   (Obj. 3, 4)

The partial monthly records of Souris Metals Ltd. show the following figures:

Employee Earnings

(a) Straight-time earnings......	?
(b) Overtime pay.....................	$ 5,109
(c) Total employee earnings ..	?

Deductions and Net Pay

(d) Withheld income tax.........	11,102
(e) Canada Pension.................	1,852
(f) Unemployment Insurance	2,220

(g) Dental and	
drug insurance.....................	$ 1,373
(h) Total deductions.................	?
(i) Net pay	57,469

Accounts Debited

(j) Salary Expense.....................	31,278
(k) Wage Expense......................	?
(l) Sales Commission Expense	14,807

Required

1. Determine the missing amounts on lines (a), (c), (h), and (k).

2. Prepare the general journal entry to record Souris Metals Ltd's payroll for the month. Credit Payrolls Payable for net pay. No explanation is required.

Problem 11-4B   *Computing and recording payroll amounts*   (Obj. 3, 4)

Assume that Nicole Martel is a commercial lender in National Bank's mortgage department in Sherbrooke. During 19X2, she worked for the bank all year at a $4,800 monthly salary. She also earned a year-end bonus equal to 12 percent of her salary.

Martel's monthly income tax withholding for 19X2 was $1,457. Also, she paid a one-time withholding tax of $2,531 on her bonus cheque. She paid $122.05 per month towards the Quebec Pension Plan until the maximum had been withheld. In addition, Martel's employer deducted $105.95 per month for unemployment insurance until the maximum had been withheld. Martel authorized the following deductions: 1 percent per month of her monthly pay to the National Bank's charitable donation fund and $28.00 per month for life insurance.

National Bank incurred Quebec Pension expense equal to the amount deducted from Martel's pay. Unemployment Insurance cost the bank 1.4 times the amount deducted from Martel's pay. In addition, the bank provided Martel with the following fringe benefits: dental and drug insurance at a cost of $52 per month, and pension benefits to be paid to Martel upon retirement. The pension contribution is based on her income and was $4,114.00 in 19X2.

Required

1. Compute Martel's gross pay, payroll deductions, and net pay for the full year 19X2. Round all amounts to the nearest dollar.

2. Compute National Bank's total 19X2 payroll cost for Martel.

3. Prepare National Bank's summary general journal entries to record its expense for
   a. Martel's total earnings for the year, her payroll deductions and her net pay. Debit Salary Expense and Executive Bonus Compensation as appropriate. Credit liability accounts for the payroll deductions and Cash for net pay.
   b. Employer payroll expenses for Martel. Credit liability accounts.
   c. Fringe benefits provided to Martel. Credit a liability account.
   Explanations are not required.

Problem 11-5B   *Journalizing, posting, and reporting liabilities*   **(Obj. 1, 2, 4, 6)**

Saskatoon Tire Co. Ltd.'s general ledger at September 30, 19X7, the end of the company's fiscal year, includes the following account balances before adjusting entries. Parentheses indicate a debit balance.

Notes payable, short-term....	$49,000	Employee benefits payable	_____
Discount on notes payable...	(1,680)	Estimated vacation pay	
Accounts payable	88,240	liability..............................	_____
Current portion of long-		Sales tax and GST payable	$ 372
term debt payable.............	_____	Property tax payable	1,433
Interest payable......................	_____	unearned rent revenue ...	3,900
Salary payable........................	_____	Long-term debt payable......	220,000
Employee payroll with-		Contingent liabilities	_____
holding taxes payable	_____		
Employer payroll expenses			
payable..............................	_____		

The additional data needed to develop the adjusting entries at September 30 are as follows:

a. The $49,000 balance in Notes Payable, Short-Term consists of two notes. The first note, with a principal amount of $21,000, was issued on August 31, matures one year from date of issuance, and was discounted at 8 percent. The second note was issued on September 2 for a term of 90 days and bears interest at 7 percent. It was not discounted.

b. The long-term debt is payable in annual installments of $55,000, with the next installment due on January 31, 19X8. On that date, Saskatoon Tire will also pay one year's interest at 6.5 percent. Interest was last paid on January 31, 19X7.

c. Gross salaries for the last payroll of the fiscal year were $4,319. Of this amount, employee withholdings were $958, and salary payable was $3,361.

d. Employer payroll costs were $755, and Saskatoon Tire's liability for employee life insurance was $104.

e. Saskatoon Tire estimates that vacation pay is 4 percent of gross salaries of $54,000 after adjustment for the last payroll of the fiscal year.

f. On August 1, the company collected six months' rent of $3,900 in advance.

g. At June 30, Saskatoon Tire is the defendant in a $100,000 lawsuit, which the company expects to win. However, the outcome is uncertain.

Required

1. Open the listed accounts, inserting their unadjusted September 30 balances.
2. Journalize and post the September 30 adjusting entries to the accounts opened. Key adjusting entries by letter.
3. Prepare the liability section of Saskatoon Tire's balance sheet at September 30.

Problem 11-6B   *Using a payroll register; recording a payroll*   **(Obj. 5)**

Assume that payroll records of a branch of Purolator Courier provided the following information for the weekly pay period ended December 18, 19X3:

Employee	Hours Worked	40-Hour Weekly Earnings Rate	Income Tax	Canada Pension	Unemployment Insurance	United Way	Earnings through Previous Week
Tina Fortin	43	$400	$ 80.85	$10.25	$13.35	$3	$17,060
Maria Dixon	46	480	92.30	14.11	17.64	3	29,300
Karol Stastny	41	800	206.95	0	0	8	45,400
David Trent	40	320	48.65	6.87	9.60	2	7,842

Tina Fortin and David Trent work in the office, and Maria Dixon and Karol Stastny are drivers. All employees are paid time and a half for hours worked in excess of 40 per week. For convenience, round all amounts to the nearest dollar. Show computations.

Required

1. Enter the appropriate information in a payroll register similar to Exhibit 11-7.
2. Record the payroll information in the general journal.
3. Assume that the first payroll cheque is number 178, paid to Tina Fortin. Record the cheque numbers in the payroll register. Also, prepare the general journal entry to record payment of net pay to the employees.
4. The employer's payroll costs derive from matching the employee's Canada Pension Plan contribution and paying 1.4 times the employee's Unemployment Insurance premium. Record the employer's payroll costs in the general journal.
5. Why is no Canada Pension or Unemployment Insurance deducted for Stastny?

Problem 11-7B   *Reporting current liabilities*   **(Obj. 6)**

Following are six pertinent facts about events during the year at Misaka Tools (N.B.) Inc.:

a. On August 31, Misaka signed a six-month, 7 percent note payable to purchase a machine costing $31,000. The note requires payment of principal and interest at maturity.

b. On October 31, Misaka received rent of $2,400 in advance for a lease on a building. This rent will be earned evenly over four months.

c. On November 30, Misaka discounted a $10,000 note payable to St. Lawrence Trust. The interest rate on the one-year note is 8 percent.

d. December sales totalled $104,000 and Misaka collected provincial sales tax of 11 percent plus Goods and Services tax of 7 percent. This amount will be sent to the appropriate authorities early in January.

e. Misaka owes $75,000 on a long-term note payable. At December 31, 6 percent interest for the year plus $25,000 of this principal are payable within one year.

f. Sales of $909,000 were covered by Misaka Tool's product warranty. At January 1, estimated warranty payable was $11,300. During the year, Misaka recorded warranty expense of $27,900 and paid warranty claims of $30,100.

Required

For each item, indicate the account and the related amount to be reported as a current liability on Misaka Tool (N.B.) Inc.'s December 31 balance sheet.

Problem 11-8B   *Account for current liabilities; make basic payroll entries; report current liabilities*   *(Obj. 1, 4, 6)*

Lake Front Boat Parts Ltd. of Pigeon Lake, Alberta, operates a marine parts supply company with the following information available:

- Goods and Services Tax: 7 percent GST is applicable to all purchases and sales.
- Payroll Taxes: the employer's share of Canada Pension and Unemployment Insurance is 1.0 times and 1.4 times respectively. The company pays workers' compensation of 3 percent and estimates vacation pay at 4 percent of all earnings.
- Mortgage Payable: the company has a $250,000 mortgage payable with payments of $2,500 plus interest (at 8 percent) due on the 20th of each month.

The company prepares quarterly financial statements and had the following transactions for the first three months of 19X1:

Jan.   9   Discounted a $20,000, 12 percent, 60-day note payable to the bank, receiving the net amount in cash.

      20   Made the first payment on the mortgage.

      31   Recorded the month's purchases of $120,000 (not including the GST). All purchases are on credit.

      31   Recorded the month's sales of $210,000 (not including the GST) of which 80 percent were on credit.

      31   Recorded and paid the payroll for the month. Gross earnings were $70,000, with deductions of:
- Employee income taxes equal to 15 percent
- CPP deductions equal to 2 percent
- UI deductions equal to 3 percent
- Union dues deduction equal to $1,400.

Feb.   2   Borrowed $60,000 from the bank by signing a 10 percent, 30-day note payable with the principal and interest payable on the due date.

      7   Paid the GST due from the month of January.

      15   Remitted all payroll deductions and contributions to the appropriate bodies.

      20   Made the second payment on the mortgage.

      28   Recorded the month's purchases of $180,000 (not including the GST). All purchases are on credit.

      28   Recorded the month's sales of $280,000 (not including the GST) of which 80 percent were on credit.

      28   Recorded and paid the payroll for the month. Gross earnings were $80,000, with deductions of:
- Employee income taxes equal to 15 percent
- CPP deductions equal to 2 percent
- UI deductions equal to 3 percent
- Union dues deduction equal to $1,600.

Mar.   4   Paid the note payable dated February 2nd.

    7   Paid the GST due from the month of February.

    10   Paid the note payable dated January 9th.

    12   Discounted a $25,000, 12 percent, 90-day note payable to the bank, receiving the net amount in cash.

    15   Remitted all payroll deductions and contributions to the appropriate bodies.

    20   Made the third payment on the mortgage.

    30   Recorded the month's purchases of $260,000 (not including the GST). All purchases are on credit.

    30   Recorded the month's sales of $370,000 (not including the GST) of which 60 percent were on credit.

    30   Recorded and paid the payroll for the month. Gross earnings were $110,000, with deductions of:
    - Employee income taxes equal to 15 percent
    - CPP deductions equal to 2 percent
    - UI deductions equal to 3 percent
    - Union dues deduction equal to $2,100.

Required

1. Journalize all of the transactions and any adjustments that would be required on March 30th (the end of the first quarter). Round all amounts to the nearest whole dollar.

2. Show the current liability section of the balance sheet as of March 30, 19X1.

Problem 11-9B   *Account for current liabilities; account for contingent liabilities; report current liabilities   (Obj. 1, 2, 6)*

Custom Equipment Ltd. produces and sells customized farm equipment. The company offers a 60-day, all parts and labor—and an extra 90-day, parts-only—warrantee on all of its products. The company had the following transactions in 19X1:

Jan.   31   Sales for the month totaled $80,000, 75 percent of which were on credit. The company collects 7 percent GST on all sales and estimates its warranty costs at 5 percent of sales.

    31   Estimated (based on last year's property tax assessment) that the property taxes for the year would be $24,000 (1 percent of the $2,400,000 assessed value). Recorded the estimated property taxes for the month.

Feb.   4   Completed repair work for a customer. The parts ($1,500) and labor ($700) were all covered under the warranty.

    6   Remitted the appropriate GST for the month of January (they had paid a total of $3,300 in GST on purchases of parts in January).

    28   Recorded the estimated property taxes for the month of February.

    28   Sales for the month totaled $70,000, 70 percent of which were on credit. The company collects 7 percent GST on all sales and estimates its warranty costs at 4 percent of sales.

Mar.   6   Remitted the appropriate GST for the month of February (they had paid a total of $2,700 in GST on purchases of parts in February).

    8   Custom Equipment received notice that they were being sued by a customer for an accident resulting from the failure of their product. The company's lawyer was reluctant to estimate the likely outcome of the lawsuit, but another customer indicated that a similar case had resulted in a $180,000 settlement.

Mar. 15   Completed repair work for a customer. The parts ($1,900) and labor ($400) were all covered under the warranty.

20   Completed repair work for a customer. The parts ($1,800) were covered by the warranty, but the labor ($500) was not. Payment is due in 30 days.

31   Sales for the month totaled $80,000, 80 percent of which was on credit. The company collects 7 percent GST on all sales and estimates its warrantee costs at 4 percent of sales.

31   Received the property tax assessment for 19X1 which showed the assessed value of their property to be $2,600,000 and a tax rate of 1.2 percent. Made the appropriate adjustment.

Required

1. Journalize the above transactions.
2. Show the appropriate financial statement presentation for all liabilities.

Challenge Problems

Problem 11-1C   *Verifying the completeness of liabilities* **(Obj. 1)**

Public accounting firms acting as auditors of companies are very careful to ensure that all of the company's accounts payable are recorded in the proper period. In other words, they want to ensure that all payables relating to the year under review are recorded as a liability at year end.

Required

Explain why you think auditors are so concerned that all payables owing at year end be properly recorded in the right period.

Problem 11-2C   *Accounting for estimated liabilities* **(Obj. 1)**

There is no consensus on the proper amount for airlines to record with respect to frequent-flier-expense. Two alternative scenarios are presented below:

a. The person claiming a ticket under the frequent flier program would use a seat that otherwise would be empty.

b. The person claiming a ticket under the frequent flier program would use a seat that otherwise would be used by a full-fare-paying passenger.

Required

1. Recommend to the airline how much they should record as a liability under each of the scenarios. Which amount would you suggest the airline record since they don't know which will occur?

2. How would you respond to the person who states that since it is not known if the frequent flier miles will be used, the liability is contingent and need not be expensed until the passenger actually uses the frequent flier miles. This person suggests that because the liability is contingent, not actual, it should be disclosed in the notes.

Extending Your Knowledge

Decision Problems

1. Identifying internal control weaknesses and their solution   *(Obj. 5)*

Hall Custom Homes Ltd. is a large home-building business in Edmonton, Alberta. The owner and manager is Lawrence Hall, who oversees all company operations. He employs 15 work crews, each made up of 6 to 10 members. Construction supervisors, who report directly to Hall, lead the crews. Most supervisors are long-time employees, so Hall trusts them greatly. Hall's office staff consists of an accountant and an office manager.

Because employee turnover is rapid in the construction industry, supervisors hire and terminate their own crew members. Supervisors notify the office of all personnel changes. Also, supervisors forward to the office the employee TD1 forms, which the crew members fill out to claim tax-withholding exemptions. Each Thursday the supervisors submit weekly time sheets for their crews, and the accountant prepares the payroll. At noon on Friday the supervisors come to the office to get paycheques for distribution to the workers at 5 p.m.

Hall's accountant prepares the payroll, including the payroll cheques, which are written on a single payroll bank account. Hall signs all payroll cheques after matching the employee name to the time sheets submitted by the supervisor. Often the construction workers wait several days to cash their paycheques. To verify that each construction worker is a bona fide employee, the accountant matches the employee's endorsement signature on the back of the canceled payroll cheque with the signature on that employee's TD1 form.

Required

1. List one *efficiency* weakness in Hall Custom Homes payroll accounting system. How can the business correct this weakness?
2. Identify one way that a supervisor can defraud Hall Custom Homes under the present system.
3. Discuss a control feature Hall Custom Builders can use to *safeguard* against the fraud you identified in Requirement 2.

2. Questions about liabilities   *(Obj. 1, 2)*

The following questions are not related.

a. A friend comments that he thought that liabilities represented amounts owed by a company. He asks why unearned revenues are shown as a current liability. How will you respond?

b. A warranty is like a contingent liability in that the amount to be paid is not known at year end. Why are warranties payable shown as a current liability, whereas contingent liabilities are reported in the notes to the financial statements?

c. Auditors have procedures for determining whether they have discovered all of a company's contingent liabilities. These procedures differ from the procedures used for determining that accounts payable are correctly stated. How would an auditor identifying a client's contingent liabilities?

Ethical Issue

Microsoft is the defendant in numerous lawsuits claiming unfair trade practices. Microsoft has strong incentives not to disclose these contingent liabilities. However, generally accepted accounting principles require companies to report their contingent liabilities.

Required

1. State why a company would prefer not to disclose its contingent liabilities.

2. Describe how a bank could be harmed if a company seeking a loan did not disclose its contingent liabilities.

3. What is the ethical tightrope that a company must walk in reporting its contingent liabilities?

Financial Statement Problems

1. Current and contingent liabilities (Obj. 1, 2, 6)

Details about a company's current and contingent liabilities appear in a number of places in the annual report. Use the Mark's Work Wearhouse Ltd. financial statements in Appendix A to answer the following questions.

1. Give the breakdown of Mark's current liabilities at January 29, 1994. Give the February, 1994, entry to record the payment of accounts payable and accrued liabilities at January 29, 1994.

2. How much was Mark's long-term debt at January 29, 1994? Of this amount, how much was due in one year? Where did you find information about the make-up of the long-term debt? When is the balance of the long-term debt due?

3. Does Mark's have any commitments coming due in the fiscal year ending in 1995? If so, where did you find information about them? Why are commitments not shown on the balance sheet as a current liability?

4. Does Mark's Work Wearhouse have any contingent liabilities at January 29, 1994? How do you know?

2. Current and contingent liabilities and payroll (Obj. 1, 2, 6)

Obtain the annual report of an actual company of your choosing. Details about the company's current and contingent liabilities and payroll costs may appear in a number of places in the annual report. Use the statements of the company you select to answer the following questions. Concentrate on the current year in the annual report.

1. Give the breakdown of the company's current liabilities at the end of the current year. Journalize the payment in the following year of Accounts Payable reported on the balance sheet.

2. How much of the company's long-term debt at the end of the current year was reported as a current liability? Do the notes to the financial statements identify the specific items of long-term debt coming due within the next year? If so, identify the specific liabilities.

3. Identify the current liability for income taxes at the end of the current year. Give its amount, and record its payment in the next year.

4. Does the company report any unearned revenue? If so, identify the item and give its amount.

5. Where does the company report contingent liabilities—on the face of the balance sheet or in a note? Give important details about the company's contingent liabilities at the end of the current year.

CHAPTER 12
The Foundation for Generally Accepted Accounting Principles

"Communication is a cornerstone for success in all facets of our operations. It is both our responsibility and strong desire to make available to shareholders *all* [emphasis added] relevant information about [the Canadian Imperial Bank of Commerce's] financial position and those of our subsidiaries," says A.L. Flood, Chairman and Chief Executive Officer of the Canadian Imperial Bank of Commerce.[1]

The above quotation indicates that the management of CIBC, Canada's second largest financial institution, is committed to being completely forthcoming to shareholders. Yet creditors and investors (and financial analysts) inevitably want more information. Accountants are caught in the middle. Exhibit 12-1 is illustrative of the political situation accountants face.

As providers of information, accountants design systems to meet the needs of investors and creditors.

This is the objective of financial reporting. But accountants' clients—businesses led by top managers—pay accountants' fees. Top managers are reluctant to disclose every piece of information requested by investors and creditors; too much disclosure will hurt the company's competitive position and, in addition, the gathering and disclosure of information has a cost. The accounting information provided in the annual report and by other means is provided free; it does not generate revenue.

The accounting profession has formulated a theoretical foundation to deal with this conflict between management and creditors and investors and other users. This chapter covers that foundation and illustrates each concept and principle with examples that apply to real situations.

[1] From *Where We Stand*, included with the CIBC 1994 annual report.

CHAPTER OBJECTIVES

After studying this chapter, you should be able to

1 Identify the basic objective of financial reporting

2 Identify and apply the underlying concepts of accounting

3 Identify and apply the principles of accounting

4 Allocate revenue to the appropriate period by four methods

5 Report information that satisfies the disclosure principle

6 Apply the materiality constraint and the conservatism constraint to accounting

EXHIBIT 12-1　*The Politics of Setting Accounting Standards*

| Investors and creditors want more information about companies. | Accountants feel pressure from both groups. | Company managers guard the information they disclose to the public. |

Accounting Standards in Canada

Every technical area seems to have professional associations and regulatory bodies that govern its practice. Accounting is no exception. In Canada, the Canadian Institute of Chartered Accountants (CICA) has had the responsibility for issuing accounting standards that form the basis of generally accepted accounting principles or GAAP. Initially, from 1946, when the first accounting standard was issued by the CICA's Accounting and Auditing Research Committee, until 1972, the CICA assumed for itself the responsibility for issuing accounting standards.[2]

Then in 1972, the Canadian Securities Administrators, a body composed of officials appointed by the provincial governments with securities exchanges to set securities law, issued National Policy Statement 27 (NP 27) designating the *CICA Handbook* as generally accepted accounting principles (GAAP). In 1975, the *Canada Business Corporations Act* did likewise. The *Ontario Securities Act* in 1978 also designated the *CICA Handbook* as GAAP (Exhibit 12-2). In these ways, the CICA became the official promulgator of generally accepted accounting principles. Exhibit 12-2 illustrates how the authority for setting GAAP is delegated to the CICA by the federal and provincial governments and the Securities Administrators.

From the date of the first accounting standard in 1946 until 1968, some 26 "bulletins" were issued by the Accounting and Auditing Research Committee. In 1968, the CICA changed the format of pronouncements; from that date they became *Recommendations* and were the italicized portions of a looseleaf binder entitled the *CICA Handbook*. Sections 1000 to 4999 (Volume I) of the *Handbook* are concerned with accounting, while Sections 5000 to 9200 (Volume II) are concerned with auditing. The Recommendations are standards or regulations that must be followed, except in those rare cases where a particular Recommendation or Recommendations would not lead to fair presentation. In those cases, the accountant should, using professional judgment, select the appropriate accounting principle. An accountant

---

[2] This material is from George J. Murphy, "A Chronology of the Development of Corporate Financial Reporting in Canada: 1850 to 1983." *The Accounting Historians Journal*, Spring, 1986.

EXHIBIT 12-2   *Flow of Authority for Developing GAAP*

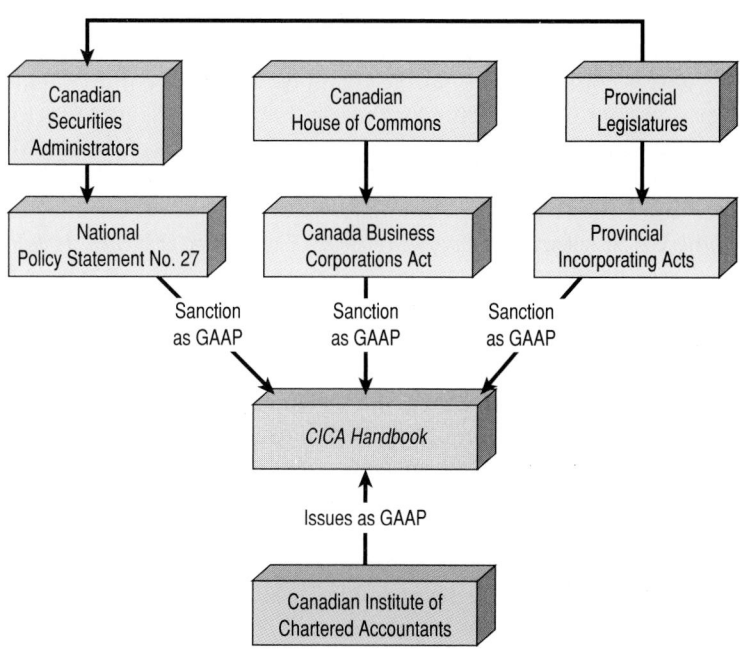

who determines that the *Handbook* is not appropriate and selects some other basis of accounting must be prepared to defend that decision. The *Handbook* also includes *Accounting Guidelines* and *Auditing Guidelines*. They do not have the force of Recommendations and are issued simply to suggest methods for dealing with issues that are not covered by Recommendations. Frequently, they become replaced eventually by Recommendations on the issues.

In 1972, the Accounting and Auditing Research Committee was split into two committees—the Accounting Research Committee (ARC), renamed in 1982, the Accounting Standards Committee (AcSC) and the Auditing Standards Committee (AuSC). In 1992, the two committees were renamed the Accounting Standards Board and the Auditing Standards Board respectively. The former has the responsibility for establishing accounting standards, while the latter has the responsibility for establishing auditing standards. The CICA established another standards committee in 1981, the Public Sector Accounting and Auditing Standards Committee (PSAAC), and a new handbook to contain the standards promulgated by that body. The PSAAC, renamed the Public Sector Accounting and Auditing Standards Board (PSAAB) in 1993, issues standards dealing with accounting by and auditing of public sector entities, such as Transport Canada, provincial liquor commissions, municipalities, hospitals, and school boards. The Recommendations issued by PSAAB have the same force as standards issued by the Accounting Standards Board and the Auditing Standards Board except that they apply only to public sector entities.

Each new accounting Recommendation issued by the Accounting Standards Board becomes part of GAAP, the "accounting law of the land." In the same way that our laws draw authority from their acceptance by the people, GAAP depends on the general acceptance by the business community. Throughout this book, we refer to GAAP as the proper way to do accounting.

Setting accounting standards is a complex process. The *Accounting Standards Board* does research on a particular issue, for example, the proper accounting for a lease. A document called an exposure draft is issued; it is a draft of the proposed new *Handbook* material. The exposure draft is distributed by the Accounting Standards Board to all interested parties who are asked to make comments by a specified date. The Accounting Standards Board considers the responses to the exposure draft and issues a new Recommendation, which becomes part of the *Handbook*. Occasionally, the proposed *Handbook* section is redrafted and re-exposed as a re-exposure draft to get additional comments before it is incorporated into the *Handbook*.

The concern had been expressed for some time that the process described in the preceding paragraph was too long and drawn out; that is, the period between the time when a new accounting issue surfaced and the time a Recommendation setting out the proper accounting procedure for the issue was promulgated was too lengthy. The *Report of the Commission to Study the Public's Expectations of Audits* (Macdonald Commission)[3] suggested that the CICA should set up a procedure for dealing with new or emerging issues more expeditiously.

In 1988, the CICA set up the *Emerging Issues Committee* (EIC) to develop appropriate accounting standards for emerging accounting issues on a timely basis. The abstracts of issues published by the EIC are considered to be an authoritative source of GAAP in the absence of an accounting Recommendation. At the time of this writing, 60 abstracts of issues had been published by the EIC.

Individuals and companies often exert pressure on the Accounting Standards Board in their efforts to shape accounting decisions to their advantage. Occasionally governmental bodies have exerted pressure when they perceived that a proposed standard was not in harmony with government policy. Accountants also try to influence accounting decisions.

We have seen that GAAP guides companies in their financial statement preparation. Independent auditing firms of public accountants hold the responsibility for making sure companies do indeed follow GAAP.

Throughout Chapters 1 to 11, we introduced key concepts and principles as they have applied to the topics under discussion. For example, Chapter 1 introduced the entity concept so that we could account for the transactions of a particular business. In Chapter 3, we discussed the revenue and matching principles as the guidelines for measuring income. Now that you have an overview of the accounting process, we consider the full range of accounting concepts and principles. Collectively, they form the foundation for accounting practice—GAAP.

Sources of Generally Accepted Accounting Principles

While the primary source of GAAP is the Recommendations in the *CICA Handbook*, they cannot possibly cover all the situations that accountants encounter. When situations not covered by the Recommendations in the *CICA Handbook* arise, Section 1000.60 of the *Handbook* suggests that the accountant should use other accounting principles that are

1. Generally accepted by virtue of being general practice (accounting principles that have general acceptance even though they are not codified); or of being industry practice (some industries, such as the Canadian Institute of Public Real Estate Companies, or CIPREC, have developed and enunciated principles for their industry); or

2. In the professional judgment of the accountant, consistent with the Recommendations in the *Handbook*, and developed through consultation with or reference to one or more of the following sources:
   a. Other parts of the *Handbook*
   b. General practice

---

[3] The CICA set up an eight-person commission to study the public's expectations of audits; the commission, named for its chairperson, William A. Macdonald, reported in 1988. For a discussion of the Macdonald Commission's findings, see either the *Report of the Commission to Study the Public's Expectations of Audits* published by the CICA, or the July, 1988 issue of *CAMagazine*.

The commission considered the accounting and auditing standard-setting process as part of its mandate; 6 of the 50 recommendations made by the commission dealt with accounting standards.

c. Accounting Guidelines. The Accounting Standards Board issues Guidelines which are that body's interpretations of Recommendations or opinions on issues that are not yet codified as Recommendations.

d. Abstracts of Issues by the Emerging Issues Committee (discussed earlier)

e. International Accounting Standards. The Canadian Institute of Chartered Accountants, along with the Certified General Accountants Association of Canada and the Society of Management Accountants of Canada, are charter members of the International Federation of Accountants. This body, which includes as members professional accounting organizations in more than 75 countries, is attempting through the International Accounting Standards Committee to harmonize GAAP in those countries by issuing *international accounting standards* (IASs). Other members include the United Kingdom, the United States, the member countries of the European Community, Japan and Australia. Section 1501 of the *Handbook* lists the 31 international accounting standards that have been issued to date. IASs do not override Canadian GAAP as set forth in the *Handbook*, which has precedence as local regulation. The Accounting Standards Board is attempting, where possible, to harmonize the Recommendations in the *CICA Handbook* with the IASs.

f. Authoritative pronouncements from other jurisdictions. The Financial Accounting Standards Board (FASB), the body responsible for setting accounting standards in the United States, has issued a number of accounting standards in areas where there may not be a pronouncement from the CICA.

g. CICA research studies. The CICA has issued a number of research studies, such as *Financial Statements for Pension Plan Participants*, that provide guidance to accountants. In addition, the Certified General Accountants Association of Canada and the Society of Management Accountants of Canada publish research studies dealing with accounting issues.

h. Accounting texts and professional journals such as *CAMagazine* and the *Journal of Accountancy* (published in the U.S. by the AICPA).

If confronted with an accounting issue that is not dealt with by the *CICA Handbook*, you should consider these sources and select the most appropriate treatment, that is, the one that provides the most informative disclosure.

Overview of Generally Accepted Accounting Principles

In December 1988, the then Accounting Standards Committee issued *CICA Handbook* Section 1000, "Financial Statement Concepts." The new section's purpose was to " . . . describe the concepts underlying the development and use of accounting principles in the general purpose financial statements . . . of profit oriented enterprises." The Accouting Standards Committee expected the section to be used by accountants in guiding their professional judgment in the preparation and audit of financial statements.

Accounting principles differ from natural laws like the law of gravity. Accounting principles draw their authority from their acceptance in the business community rather than from their ability to explain physical phenomena. Thus they really are generally accepted by those people and organizations who need guidelines in accounting for their financial undertakings. Exhibit 12-3 diagrams how we move from the objectives of financial reporting to the financial statements.

We now look at the objective of financial reporting. This objective tells what financial accounting is intended to accomplish. Thus it provides the goal for accounting information. Next, we examine particular accounting concepts and principles used to implement the objective. What is the difference between a concept and a principle? The concepts are broader in their application, and the principles are more specific. Last, we discuss the financial statements, the end product of financial accounting, and their elements—assets, liabilities, owner's equity revenues, expenses, and so on.

EXHIBIT 12-3   *Overview of Generally Accepted Accounting Principles*

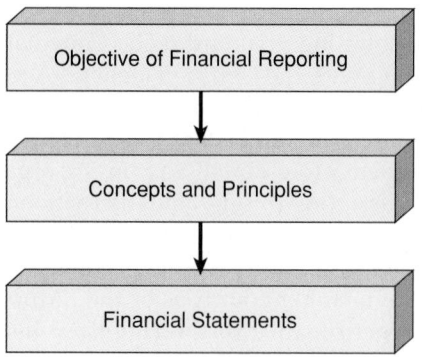

OBJECTIVE 1

Identify the basic
objective of financial
reporting

Objective of Financial Reporting

The basic *objective of financial reporting* is to provide information that is useful in making investment and lending decisions. To be useful in decision-making, the *CICA Handbook*, in Section 1000, states that information in financial statements should be *understandable, relevant, reliable,* and *comparable.*

The information must be *understandable* to users if they are to be able to use it. *Relevant* information is useful for making predictions and for evaluating past performance. *Reliable* information is free from error and the bias of a particular viewpoint; it is in agreement with the underlying events and transactions. *Comparable* information can be compared from period to period to help investors and creditors track the business's progress through time. These characteristics combine to shape the concepts and principles that make up GAAP. Exhibit 12-4 summarizes the qualities that increase the value of accounting information.

EXHIBIT 12-4   *Qualities that Increase the Value of Information for Decision-Making*

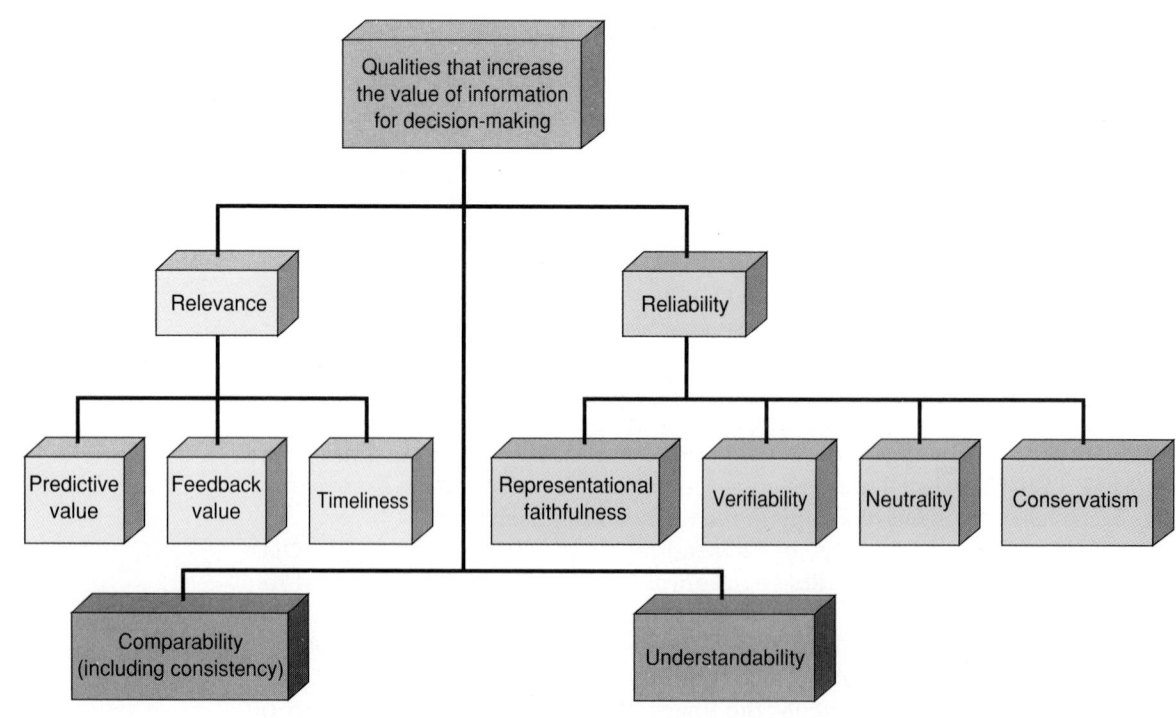

Underlying Concepts

Entity Concept

The **entity concept** is the most basic concept in accounting because it draws a boundary around the organization being accounted for. That is, the transactions of each entity are accounted for separately from transactions of all other organizations and persons, including the owners of the entity. This separation allows us to measure the performance and the financial position of each entity independent of all other entities.

A business entity may be a sole proprietorship (owned and operated by a single individual), a partnership, or a large corporation such as Petro-Canada. The entity concept applies with equal force to all types and sizes of organizations. The proprietor of a travel agency, for example, accounts for his or her personal transactions separately from those of the business. This division allows the proprietor to evaluate the success or failure of the travel agency. If he or she were to mix personal and business accounting records, it would mean losing sight of the information needed to evaluate the business alone.

At the other end of the spectrum, Petro-Canada is a giant company with oil exploration, oil-refining, and retail gasoline sales operations (see Exhibit 12-5). Petro-Canada accounts for each of these divisions separately in order to know which part of the business is earning a profit, which needs to borrow money, and so on. The entity concept also provides the basis for consolidating subentities into a single set of financial statements. Petro-Canada reports a single set of financial statements to the public.

The entity concept also applies to nonprofit organizations such as churches, synagogues, and government agencies. A hospital, for example, may have an emergency room, a pediatrics unit, and a surgery unit. The accounting system of the hospital should account for each separately to allow the managers to evaluate the progress of each unit.

OBJECTIVE 2
Identify and apply the underlying concepts of accounting

Key Point:
The entity concept requires that the transactions of each entity are accounted for separately from the transactions of all other organizations and persons.

Going-Concern Concept

Under the **going-concern** (or **continuity**) **concept**, accountants assume the business will continue operating for the foreseeable future. The logic behind the going-concern concept is best illustrated by considering the alternative assumption: going out of business.

When a business stops, it sells its assets, converting them to cash. This process is called *liquidation*. With the cash, the business pays off its liabilities, and the owners keep any remaining cash. In liquidation, the amount of cash for which the assets are

Key Point:
The going-concern concept assumes that a business will operate long enough for it to recover the cost of its assets.

EXHIBIT 12-5 *The Entity Petro-Canada*

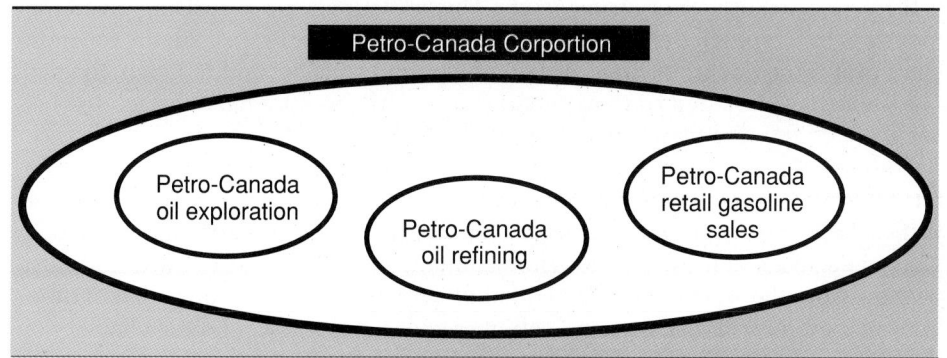

sold measures their current value. Likewise, the liabilities are paid off at their current value. However, if the business does not halt operations—if it remains a going concern—how are its assets and liabilities reported on the balance sheet?

For a going concern, the business reports assets and liabilities based on historical cost. To consider what an asset may be worth on the current market requires making an estimate. This may or may not be objective. Under the going-concern concept, it is assumed the entity will continue long enough for it to recover the costs of its assets.

The going-concern concept allows for the reporting of assets and liabilities as current or long-term, a distinction that investors and creditors find useful in evaluating a company. For example, a creditor wants to know the portion of a company's liabilities that are scheduled to come due within the next year and the portion payable beyond the year. The assumption is that the entity will continue in business and honour its commitments.

Key Point:

For accounting information to be useful, it must be made available at regular intervals. The time-period concept ensures that accounting information is reported at regular intervals.

Time-Period Concept

The **time-period concept** ensures that accounting information is reported at regular intervals. This timely presentation of accounting data aids the comparison of business operations over time—from year to year, quarter to quarter, and so on. Managers, owners, lenders and other people and businesses need regular reports to assess the business's success—or failure. These persons are making decisions daily. Although the ultimate success of a company cannot be known for sure until the business liquidates, decision-makers cannot wait until liquidation to learn whether operations yielded a profit.

Nearly all companies use the year as their basic time period. *Annual* reports are common in business. Companies also prepare quarterly and monthly reports—called *interim reports*—to meet managers', investors', and creditors' need for timely information.

The time-period concept underlies the use of accruals. Suppose the business's accounting year ends at December 31 and the business has accrued—but will not pay until the next accounting period—$900 in salary expense. To tie this expense to the appropriate period, the accountant enters this adjusting entry, as we have seen:

Dec. 31	Salary Expense	900	
	Salary Payable		900

Accrual entries assign revenue and expense amounts to the correct accounting period and thus help produce meaningful financial statements.

Approximately 66 percent of all companies report their financial statements on a calendar-year basis, January through December; the remaining 34 percent's year ends are spread evenly over the other eleven months.

Stable-Monetary-Unit Concept

Accounting information is expressed primarily in monetary terms. The monetary unit is the prime means of measuring assets. This measure is not surprising given that money is the common denominator in business transactions. In Canada, the monetary unit is the dollar; in Great Britain, the pound sterling; and in Japan, the yen. The stable-monetary-unit concept provides an orderly basis for handling account balances to produce the financial statements.

Unlike a liter, a meter, and many other measurements, the value of the monetary unit may change over time. Most of us are familiar with inflation. Groceries that cost $50 three years ago may cost $55 today. The value of the dollar changes. In view of the fact that the dollar does not maintain a constant value, how does a business measure the worth of assets and liabilities acquired over a long span of time? The business records all assets and liabilities at cost. Each asset and each liability on the balance sheet is the sum of all the individual dollar amounts added over time.

For example, if a company bought 40 hectares of land in 1975 for $60,000 and another 40 hectares of land in 1985 for $300,000, the asset Land on the balance sheet carries a $360,000 balance, and the change in the purchasing power of the dollar is ignored. The **stable-monetary-unit concept** is the accountant's basis for ignoring the effect of inflation and making no adjustments for the changing value of the dollar (see Exhibit 12-6). Let us look at the shortcomings of this concept.

Suppose another company paid $600,000 for the same 80 hectares of land in 1995. Its balance sheet would show a much higher amount for the land. How do we compare the two companies' balance sheets? The comparison based on the stable-monetary-unit concept may not be valid because mixing dollar values at different times is like mixing apples and oranges.

Many businesspeople believe that accounting information must be restated for changes in the dollar's purchasing power. In general, however, accounting is based on historical costs.

Accounting Principles

Reliability (Objectivity) Principle

> **OBJECTIVE 3**
> Identify and apply the principles of accounting

The **reliability principle** requires that accounting information be dependable—free from significant error and bias. Users of accounting information may rely on its truthfulness. To be reliable, information must be verifiable by people outside the business. Financial statement users may consider information reliable if independent experts agree that the information is based on objective and honest measurement.

Consider the error from a company's failure to accrue interest revenue at the end of an accounting period. This error results in understated interest revenue and understated net income. Clearly, this company's accounting information is unreliable.

Biased information—data prepared from a particular viewpoint and not based on objective facts—is also unreliable. Suppose a company purchased inventory for $25,000. At the end of the accounting period, the inventory has declined in value and can be replaced for $20,000. Under the lower-of-cost-or-market rule, the company must record a $5,000 loss for the decrease in the inventory's value. Company management may believe that the appropriate value for the inventory is $22,000, but that amount is only an opinion. If management reports the $22,000 figure, total assets and owner equity will be overstated on the balance sheet. Income will be overstated on the income statement.

To establish a *reliable* figure for the inventory's value, management could get a current price list from the inventory supplier or call in an outside professional appraiser to revalue the inventory. Evidence obtained from outside the company usually leads to reliable, verifiable information. The reliability principle applies to all financial accounting information—from assets to owner's equity on the balance sheet and from revenue to net income on the income statement.

EXHIBIT 12-6   *The Stable-Monetary-Unit Concept*

| 1977 | 1996 | 1977 | 1996 |

Due to inflation, a dollar in 1996 is worth less than a dollar was in 1977.   **Under the stable-monetary-unit concept, the effect of inflation is ignored.**

Short Exercise:

Which of the following violates the principle of comparability (consistency)?
1. Firms in the same industry use different accounting methods for a given type of transaction.
2. A company changes from FIFO to LIFO for inventory.
3. A company fails to write down its inventory to the lower of cost or market.
4. A firm fails to adjust its financial statements for changes in the purchasing power of the dollar.

A: 2.

Comparability Principle

The **comparability principle** has two requirements. First, accounting information must be comparable from business to business. Second, each business's financial statements must be comparable (consistent) from one period to the next. The CICA encourages comparability in order to make possible useful analysis from business to business, from period to period.

Standardization of formats for financial statements promote comparability. Using the same terms to describe the statement elements—assets, liabilities, revenues, and so on—aids the comparison process.

Even among companies that adhere to standard formats and standard terms, comparability may be less than perfect. Comparisons of companies that use different inventory methods—LIFO and FIFO, for example—are difficult. When GAAP allows a choice among acceptable accounting methods—in inventory, depreciation and other areas—comparability may be hard to achieve.

Recall that the comparability principle directs each individual company to produce accounting information that is comparable over time. To achieve this quality—which accountants call *consistency*—companies must follow the same accounting practices from period to period. The business that uses FIFO inventory and straight-line for depreciation in one period ought to use those same methods in the next period. Otherwise, a financial statement user could not tell whether changes in income and asset values result from operations or from the way the business accounts for operations.

Companies may change accounting methods, however, in response to a change in business operations. Bombardier may add a new product line that calls for a different inventory method. GAAP allows the company to make a change in accounting method, but the business must include a description of the change and indicate the effect of the change on the financial statements. This disclosure is made in a note to the financial statement.

Cost Principle

The **cost principle** states that assets and services are recorded at their purchase cost and that the accounting record of the asset continues to be based on cost rather than current market value. By specifying that assets be recorded at cost, this principle also governs the recording of liabilities and owner's equity. Suppose that a land developer purchased 20 hectares of land for $50,000 plus a real estate commission of $2,000. Additional costs included fees paid to the municipality ($1,500), utility hookups ($8,000) and landscaping ($20,000), for a total cost of $81,500. The Land account carries this balance because it is the cost of bringing the land to its intended use. Assume that the developer holds the land for one year, then offers it for sale at a price of $200,000. The cost principle requires the accounting value of the land to remain at $81,500.

The developer may wish to lure buyers by showing them a balance sheet that reports the land at $200,000. However, this would be inappropriate under GAAP because $200,000 is merely the developer's opinion of what the land is worth.

The underlying basis for the cost principle is the reliability principle. Cost is a reliable value for assets and services, because cost is supported by completed transactions between parties with opposing interests. Buyers try to pay the lowest price possible and sellers try to sell for the highest price. The actual cost of an asset or service is objective evidence of its value.

Revenue Principle

The **revenue principle** provides guidance on the *timing* of the recording of revenue and the *amount* of revenue to record. The general rule is that revenue should be recorded when it is earned and not before.

Some revenues, such as interest and rent, accrue with the passage of time. Their timing and amount are easy to figure. The accountant records the amount of revenue earned over each period of time.

Other revenues are earned by selling goods or rendering services. Identifying *when* these revenues are earned depends on more factors than the passage of time. Under the revenue principle, three conditions must be met before revenue is recorded: (1) the seller has done everything necessary to expect to collect from the buyer; (2) the amount of revenue can be objectively measured; and (3) collectibility is reasonably assured. In most cases, these conditions are met at the point of sale or when services are performed.

The *amount* of revenue to record is the value of the assets received—usually cash or a receivable. But, situations may arise in which the amount of revenue or the timing of earning the revenue is not easily determined. We turn now to four methods that guide the accountant in applying the revenue principle in different circumstances.

Sales Method   Under the *sales method*, revenue is recorded at the point of sale. Consider a retail sale in a hardware store. At the point of sale, the customer pays the store and takes the merchandise. The store records the sale by debiting Cash and crediting Sales Revenue. In other situations, the point of sale occurs when the seller ships the goods to the buyer. Suppose a mining company sells iron ore to Dofasco. By shipping the ore to Dofasco, the mining company has completed its duty and may expect to collect cash for the revenue earned. If the amount of revenue can be objectively measured and collection is reasonably certain, the mining company can then record revenue. The sale entry is a debit to Accounts Receivable and a credit to Sales Revenue. The sales method is used for most sales of goods and services.

Collection Method   The *collection method* is used only if the receipt of cash is uncertain. Under this method, the seller waits until cash is received to record the sale. This method is a form of cash-basis accounting and, as such, its use is discouraged by Revenue Canada; it is not widely used. Companies that use the collection method do so because they often find it difficult to collect their receivables. They may not reasonably assume that they can collect the revenue, so they wait until the cash is actually received before recording it. The collection method is conservative because revenue is not recorded in advance of its receipt.

Installment Method   The *installment method* is a type of collection method that is used for installment sales. In a typical installment sale, the buyer makes a down payment when the contract is signed and pays the remainder in installments. Department stores (such as Eaton's and Zellers), auto dealers, and appliance stores sell on the installment plan. This method is also used for income tax purposes. Under the installment method, gross profit (sales revenue minus cost of goods sold) is recorded as cash is collected.

Suppose Canadian Tire sells a snowblower for a down payment of $280 plus twelve monthly installments of $25 and 24 monthly installments of $20.00 (a total of $1,060). Canadian Tire's cost of the snowblower is $636, so the gross profit is $424, computed as follows:

Installment sale...	$1,060
Cost of the snowblower sold	636
Gross profit...	$ 424

To determine the gross profit associated with each collection under the installment method, we must compute the gross profit percentage as follows:

$$\text{Gross profit percentage} = \frac{\text{Gross profit}}{\text{Installment sale}} = \frac{\$424}{\$1,060} = 40\%$$

We next apply the gross profit percentage to each year's collections. The result is the amount of gross profit recorded as revenue at the time of cash receipt.

OBJECTIVE 4

Allocate revenue to the appropriate period by four methods

Short Exercise:

A product that cost $500 was in the shipping room when the physical inventory was counted. It was marked "Hold for customer's shipping instructions." The customer's order was dated December 15, 1995, and was filled on December 29, 1995. The goods being held were shipped to the customer on January 5, 1996. Should the sale be recorded in 1995 or 1996?

A: The sale should be recorded in 1995 because the company had done everything needed to complete the sale.

Short Exercise:

A business sells on the installment basis: 19X3 sales are $27,500, down payments are $2,750, and collections on installments total $8,000. Beginning inventory is $4,000, ending inventory is $3,500, and purchases are $16,000. (1) What are cost of goods sold, total gross profit, and the gross profit percentage for the year? (2) What gross profit will the business report if it uses the installment method?

A: (1)
COGS = Beg. Inv. + Pur. – End. Inv. $16,500 = $4,000 + $16,000 – $3,500
GP = Sales – COGS $11,000 = $27,500 – $16,500
GP% = 40% ($11,000/$27,500)
(2)
Down payment .... $ 2,750
Collections.............. 8,000
Total rec'd................ 10,750
                          × 40%
Inst. method GP ...... $ 4,300

Year	Collections	×	Gross Profit Percentage	=	Gross Profit
1	$300	×	40%	=	$120
2	240	×	40	=	96
3	240	×	40	=	96
Total	780	×	40%	=	312

Gross profit of $112 (.40 × $280) would be recorded upon receipt of the down payment.

Accountants would also record gross profit of $120 in year 1, $96 in year 2, and year 3. The total gross profit ($112 + $312 = $424) is the same as under the sales method. However, under the sales method, the full $424 of gross profit would be recorded at the beginning of the contract.

Of course, companies make installment sales year after year. If the company's sales mix changed from year to year, each year's sales may have a different gross profit percentage. In the preceding example, year 1 installment sales earned gross profit of 40 percent. Suppose a company earned a gross profit of 40 percent on installment sales in year 1 and that year 2 sales earn 45 percent, year 3 sales earn 42 percent, and year 4 sales earn 35 percent. The total gross profit for a year is the sum of all the gross profit amounts recorded on cash collections made that year.

Using assumed cash receipts on installment sales made in years 1 to 4, the gross profit computations for the four years appear in Exhibit 12-7.

The installment method is attractive for income tax purposes because it postpones the recording of revenue and thus the payment of taxes. Under generally accepted accounting principles, this method is permissible only when collection of the outstanding balance is not certain. Some companies use the installment method for tax purposes and the sales method for their financial statements.

Percentage-of-Completion Method   Construction of office buildings, bridges, dams, and other large assets often extends over several years. The construction company must decide when to record the revenue. The most conservative approach is to record all the revenue earned on the project in the period when the project is completed. This procedure, called the *completed-contract method,* is acceptable under GAAP in limited circumstances.

EXHIBIT 12-7   *Installment Method for Revenue*

	Gross Profit Percentage	Year 1	Year 2	Year 3	Year 4
		Gross Profit by Year Cash Receipt × Gross Profit Percentage			
Year 1 sales	40%	$80,000 × .40 = $32,000	$120,000 × .40 = $48,000	$140,000 × .40 = $56,000	$160,000 × .40 = $64,000
Year 2 sales	45%		90,000 × .45 = 40,500	100,000 × .45 = 45,000	20,000 × .45 = 9,000
Year 3 sales	42%			75,000 × .42 = 31,500	65,000 × .42 = 27,300
Year 4 sales	35%				30,000 × .35 = 10,500
Total gross profit		$32,000	$88,500	$132,500	$110,800

Ethical Issue: Lincoln Savings and Loan Association of Phoenix, Arizona, went bankrupt during the 1980s. Consider the following actual business transactions:

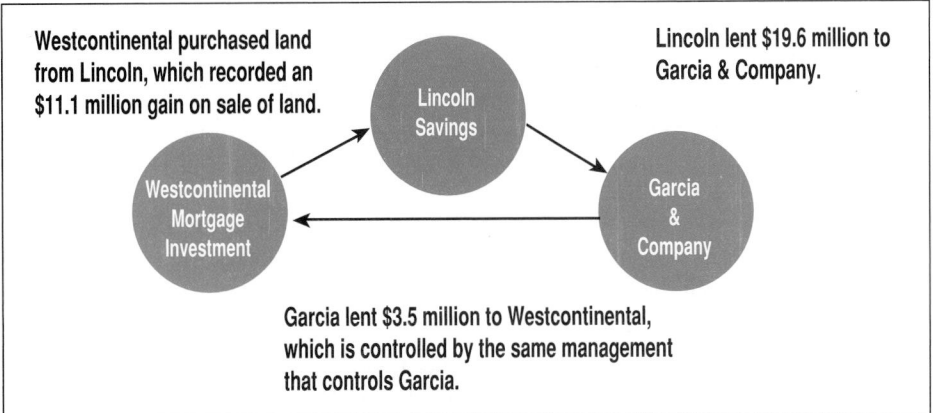

One national accounting firm approved of Lincoln's accounting. The auditors viewed Lincoln's sale of the land as authentic and the gain as real. A second CPA firm, which specializes in accounting for real estate transactions, viewed Lincoln's gain as artificial. That firm's CPAs believed that no sale took place because Westcontinental had received its cash for the purchase from Garcia, which in turn had received its cash from Lincoln. In effect, Westcontinental had none of its own money in the land. Was it ethical for Lincoln Savings to record the gain?

Answer: There is no clear answer. However, when there is a doubt about the ethics of a situation, it is safest to avoid any appearance of unethical conduct. Develop your own ethical guidelines and be prepared to use them in your career. Chances are, your ethical position *will be* challenged.

Under the preferred method, called the *percentage-of-completion method*, the construction company recognizes revenue as work is performed. Each year the company estimates the percentage of project completion as construction progresses. One way to make this estimate is to compare the cost incurred for the year to the total estimated project cost. This percentage is then multiplied by the total project revenue to compute the construction revenue for the year. Construction income for the year is revenue minus cost.

Assume PCL Construction Group Inc. of Edmonton receives a contract to build a power plant for a price of $42 million. PCL estimates total costs of $36 million over the three-year construction period: $6 million in year 1, $18 million in year 2, and $12 million in year 3. Construction revenue and income during the three years are as follows (amounts in millions):

Year	Cost for Year	Total Project Cost	Percentage of Project Completion for Year	Total Project Revenue	Construction Revenue for Year	Construction Income for Year
1	$ 6	$36	$ 6/$36 = $\frac{1}{6}$	$42	$42 × $\frac{1}{6}$ = $ 7	$ 7 – $ 6 = $1
2	18	36	18/ 36 = $\frac{1}{2}$	42	42 × $\frac{1}{2}$ = 21	21 – 18 = 3
3	12	36	12/ 36 = $\frac{1}{3}$	42	42 × $\frac{1}{3}$ = 14	14 – 12 = 2
	$36				$42	$42 $36 $6

The percentage-of-completion method is appropriate when the company can estimate the degree of completion during the construction period, which most construction companies can do. When estimates are not possible, the completed-contract method is required. If PCL had used the completed-contract method, its income statement for year 3 would report total project revenue of $42 million, total project expenses of $36 million, and income of $6 million. The income statements of years 1 and 2 would report nothing concerning this project. Most accountants believe the results under the percentage-of-completion method are more realistic.

Matching Principle

The **matching principle** governs the recording and reporting of expenses. This principle goes hand in hand with the revenue principle to govern income recognition in accounting. Recall that income is revenue minus expense. During any period, the company first measures its revenues by the revenue principle. The company then identifies and measures all the expenses it incurred during the period to earn the revenues. To *match* the expenses against the revenues means to subtract the expenses from the revenues. The result is the income for the period.

Some expenses are easy to match against particular revenues. For example, Loblaw's cost of goods sold relates directly to sales revenue because without the sales, there would be no cost of goods sold. Commissions and fees paid for selling the goods, delivery expense, and sales supplies expense relate to sales revenue for the same reason.

Other expenses are not so easily linked to particular sales because they occur whether or not any revenues arise. Depreciation, salaries, and all types of office expenses of Loblaw's head office in Toronto are in this category. Accountants usually match these expenses against revenue on a time basis. For example, the company's head-office building may be used for general management and marketing. Straight-line depreciation of a 40-year-old building assigns one fortieth of the building's cost to expense each year, whatever the level of revenue. The annual salary expense for a warehouse employee is the person's total salary for the year, regardless of revenue.

Losses, like expenses, are matched against revenue on a time basis. For example, if an asset such as inventory loses value, the loss is recorded when it occurs, without regard for the revenues earned during the period.

Disclosure Principle

OBJECTIVE 5

Report information that satisfies the disclosure principle

The **disclosure principle** holds that a company's financial statements should report enough information for outsiders to make knowledgeable decisions about the company. In short, the company should report sufficient *understandable, relevant, reliable,* and *comparable* information about its economic affairs. This section of the chapter discusses and illustrates types of the more common disclosures; there are others that are covered in later courses.

Summary of Significant Accounting Policies   To evaluate a company, investors and creditors need to know how its financial statements were prepared. This consideration is especially important when the company can choose from several acceptable methods. Companies summarize their accounting policies in the first note to their financial statements. The note may include both monetary amounts and written descriptions. Companies commonly disclose how they have applied accounting principles. For example, the depreciation method, inventory valuation, consolidation basis, fixed assets, and foreign currency translation are five items commonly disclosed.[4]

John Labatt Limited reported the following in its notes to its April 30, 1994 financial statements:

---

[4] *Financial Reporting in Canada*, 1993, Twentieth edition (Toronto: CICA, 1993), p. 26.

Notes to the Consolidated Financial Statements

1. Summary of Significant Accounting Policies [in part]

Basis of presentation
The consolidated financial statements have been prepared in accordance with accounting principles generally accepted in Canada. Significant accounting policies observed in their preparation are summarized below.

Principles of consolidation
The consolidated financial statements include the accounts of all subsidiary companies.

Inventories
Inventories, other than returnable containers, are valued at the lower of cost and net realizable value, with cost being determined on a first-in, first-out basis. Returnable containers are valued at redemption price or at amortized cost not exceeding replacement cost.

Fixed assets
Fixed assets are recorded at cost. Depreciation is provided on a straight-line basis over the estimated useful lives of the assets, generally at annual rates of $2\frac{1}{2}\%$ for buildings and 10% for machinery and equipment.

The Company capitalizes interest costs on major construction projects when the period of construction exceeds one year. Capitalization of interest ceases once operations commence at the facility. Interest capitalized at April 30, 1994 and 1993 was not material.

Other assets
Goodwill is amortized using the straight-line method over the lesser of its estimated life and forty years.

Securities are carried at cost which approximates realizable value.

Investments in and advances to other companies are carried at cost. Income from these investments is recognized when received.

Investments in companies and partnerships over which the Company has significant influence ("partly owned businesses") are accounted for using the equity method.

Contingent Liabilities   Companies are usually eager to disclose good news. The disclosure principle requires them to report bad news as well. For example, a company may be a defendant in a lawsuit with an uncertain outcome. Will the contingency—the possibility of a negative outcome—result in an actual loss to the company? Will it endanger the company's ability to continue as a going concern? Investors, lenders, and other interested parties need the full financial picture. A bank may decide not to loan additional money because of the contingency. A labor union may note the contingency and lower its demand for an increase in employee wages. The disclosure principle requires the company to report whether the lawsuit is likely to result in a liability and, if so, the expected amount.

As discussed in Chapter 11, most companies disclose their contingent liabilities in notes to the financial statements. An example is the following note excerpted from the December 31, 1994, financial statements of Canadian National Railways. CN reported that its contingent liabilities arose from outstanding and possible lawsuits against the company.

c) Contingencies
In the normal course of its operations, the Company becomes involved in various legal actions, including claims relating to injuries, damage to property, and environmental matters. While the final outcome with respect to actions outstanding or pending at December 31, 1994, cannot be predicted with certainty, it is the opinion of management that their resolution will not have a material adverse effect on the System's financial position.

Probable Losses   The disclosure principle directs a business to record and report a probable loss before it occurs if the loss is likely and its amount can be estimated. St. Lawrence Cement Inc. reported in the notes to the financial statements in its 1993 annual report that the company had recorded such a loss in 1992 in connection with a proposed restructuring of its operations. Observe that the restructuring began in 1993 and will be completed in 1994.

> **5. Provision for restructuring costs**
>
> In the fourth quarter of 1992, the Company accrued $12.0 million for the planned restructuring of its Canadian and U.S. operations. . . . The program should be completed in 1994 and the provision taken in 1992 should be sufficient to cover all costs. . . .

Accounting Changes   Consistent use of accounting methods and procedures is important, as we saw in discussing comparability. When a company does change from one accounting method or procedure to another, it must include a description of the change and indicate the effect of the change on net income in the notes to the financial statements. Two common accounting changes are *changes in accounting principles* and *changes in accounting estimates*.

A **change in accounting principle** is a change in accounting method. A switch from the FIFO method to the LIFO method for inventories and a switch from the accelerated depreciation method to the straight-line method are examples of accounting changes. Special rules that apply to changes in accounting principles are discussed in later accounting courses. Whatever the change in principle, the notes to the financial statements must inform the reader that the change has occurred.

IntraWest Corporation disclosed the following accounting change in its September 30, 1994, financial statements, after the company had changed its policy pertaining to recognition of revenue from the sale of properties:

> **Note 2. Change in Accounting Policy**
>
> The Company has changed its accounting policy regarding revenue recognition from the sale of properties. Previously, revenue from the sale of properties was recorded when title was conveyed to the purchaser or, if under construction, on a percentage-of-completion basis, provided certain specified criteria were satisfied. Since the Company's real estate development activities now relate almost exclusively to woodframe buildings which are constructed in less than twelve months, the percentage-of-completion method is no longer considered appropriate.
>
> This change in accounting policy has been applied retroactively. The effect is to reduce non-resort real estate sales revenue by $15,000,000 and non-resort real-estate costs by $13,300,000 in 1993 and to increase non-resort real estate revenue and non-resort real estate costs by the same amounts in 1994. In addition, $6,810,000 of resort real estate sales revenue and $5,874,000 of resort real estate costs which would have been recorded in 1994 will be recognized in 1995.

A **change in accounting estimate** occurs in the course of business as the company alters earlier expectations. A company may record uncollectible accounts expense based on the estimate that bad debts will equal 2 percent of sales. If actual collections exceed this estimate, the company may lower its estimated expense to 1½ percent of sales in the future.

Purolater Courier may originally estimate that a new Ford Econoline delivery van will provide four years' service. After two years of using the truck, Purolator sees that the truck's full useful life will stretch to six years. The company must recompute depreciation based on this new information at the start of the truck's third year of service. Assume that this truck cost $16,000, has an estimated residual value of $2,000 and is depreciated by the straight-line method.

Annual depreciation for each of the first two years of the asset's life is $3,500, computed as follows:

$$\text{Depreciation per year} = \frac{\$16,000 - \$2,000}{4 \text{ years}} = \$3,500$$

Changes in estimate are accounted for by spreading the asset's remaining book value over its remaining life. Annual depreciation after the change in accounting estimate is $1,750, computed in the following manner:

$$\text{Depreciation per year} = \frac{\text{Remaining depreciable book value}}{\text{Remaining life}}$$

$$= \frac{\$16,000 - \$2,000 - (3,500 \times 2)}{6 \text{ total years} - 2 \text{ years used}}$$

$$= \frac{\$7,000}{4 \text{ years}}$$

$$= \$1,750$$

This revised amount of depreciation is recorded in the usual manner.

Hawker Siddeley Canada Inc. disclosed a similar change in accounting estimate in its financial statements for the year ended December 31, 1992:

> **2. Depreciation of property, plant, and equipment**
>
> The Company has revised the rates of depreciation applied to certain property, plant, and equipment other than CGTX Inc.'s railway rolling stock leasing fleet, as of January 1, 1992, in order to more closely reflect the estimated remaining useful lives of such property, plant, and equipment as at that date and the estimated useful lives of property, plant, and equipment acquired after that date.
>
> The effect of the revision of rates has been to reduce depreciation for the year ended December 31, 1992, by $3.0 million. Depreciation for the year ended December 31, 1991, was $19.4 million.

Subsequent Events   A company usually takes several weeks after the end of the year to close its books and to publish its financial statements. Occasionally, events occur during this period that affect the interpretation of the information in those financial statements. Such an occurrence is called a **subsequent event** and should be disclosed in the prior period's statements. The most common examples of subsequent events are issuing shares, borrowing money, paying debts, making investments, selling assets, and becoming a defendant in a lawsuit.

Canadian Imperial Ginseng Products Ltd., a major producer of ginseng products located in British Columbia, reported the following subsequent event in its financial statements for the year ended June 30, 1994.

> **17. Subsequent Events**
>
> The Company issued an Offering Memorandum for a private placement of $3,500,000 of Convertible Bonds dated July 28, 1994. There are three series of bonds as follows: (i) $1,000,000 Series 1 Convertible Bonds at 13%, (ii) $1,000,000 Series 2 Convertible Bonds at 12% and (iii) $1,500,000 Series 3 Convertible Bonds at 11%. The Company may, in its sole discretion, increase the Offering of any or all Series of Bonds by $2,500,000. Bonds are convertible into common shares of the Company at $3.00 per share until July 27, 1995, increasing by $1.00 per annum thereafter until maturity subject to regulatory approval. The bonds mature as to one half on December 31, 1999 and the remaining half on December 31, 2000.

Business Segments   Most large companies operate in more than one area. Each area is called a *business segment*. Lord Kenneth Thomson not only controls Thomson newspapers through a holding company but also The Bay, Zellers, an oil company, and other differing businesses. Canadian Pacific owns hotels, mining companies, steamships, trucking companies, oil companies, and paper companies, as well as real estate interests. Diversification like this is not limited to large international companies. A realtor may also own a restaurant. A farmer may sell farm implements. An automobile dealer may also own a furniture store.

Suppose you are considering investing in a company that is active in the footwear industry but also owns a meat packer and several leisure resorts. Assume the

Canadian footwear industry is in retreat because of intense foreign competition. With income and asset data broken down by business segments, you can determine how much of the company's assets are committed to each segment and which lines of business are most (and least) profitable. Companies disclose segment data in notes to their financial statements.

The following note in the John Labatt Limited April 30, 1994, financial statement meets the GAAP requirement for adequate disclosure of segmented information:

19. Segmented Financial Information

Information by class of business

The classes of business within which the Company operates constitute the Brewing and the Broadcast, Sports and Entertainment segments.

The Brewing segment comprises brewing and marketing activities in Canada, the United States and Italy including export sales, and, in the United Kingdom, the marketing of beer produced and distributed under agreements with U.K. brewers and the ownership of pubs.

The Broadcast, Sports and Entertainment segment comprises broadcast activities, sports franchises, an investment in a sports-related facility, television commercials production, episodic television production and concert promotion businesses, primarily in Canada and the United States.

Corporate and other income and expenses and corporate net assets are allocated between the two business segments. Certain financial information for partly owned businesses is included in the proportion of John Labatt ownership.

	1994	1993
Net sales		
Brewing	$1,769	$1,672
Broadcast, Sports and Entertainment	630	546
	2,399	2,218
Less: Partly owned business	78	83
	$2,321	$2,135
Depreciation and amortization		
Brewing	$83	$74
Broadcast, Sports and Entertainment	16	15
	$99	$89
Earnings before interest, restructuring charges and income taxes		
Brewing	$ 260	$ 218
Broadcast, Sports and Entertainment	32	56
	292	274
Less: Partly owned business	8	9
	$ 284	$ 265
Additions to fixed assets		
Brewing	$ 103	$ 191
Broadcast, Sports and Entertainment	20	12
	$ 123	$ 203
Net assets employed		
Brewing	$ 960	$ 932
Broadcast, Sports and Entertainment	308	238
	1,268	1,170
Cash, short-term investments and securities	562	526
Accounts payable and accrued charges, deferred revenue and taxes payable, netted above	552	532
Total assets of continuing operations	2,382	2,228
Total assets of discontinued operations	154	792
	$2,536	$3,020

Information by geographic area

The Company operates principally in the geographic areas of Canada, the United States and Europe—specifically the United Kingdom and Italy. Geographic segmentation is based on the country in which a business operates.

As no single operation outside Canada constitutes a reportable geographic segment, all such operations are reported together as the International segment.

Corporate and other income and expenses and corporate net assets relating to continuing operations are allocated to the Canada segment. Certain financial information for partly owned businesses is included in the proportion of John Labatt ownership.

	1994	1993
Net sales		
Canada	$1,961	$1,865
International	438	353
	2,399	2,218
Less: Partly owned business	78	83
	$2,321	$2,135
Depreciation and amortization		
Canada	$76	$71
International	23	18
	$ 99	$89
Earnings before interest, restructuring charges and income taxes		
Canada	$ 307	$ 292
International	(15)	(18)
	292	274
Less: Partly owned business	8	9
	$ 284	$ 265
Additions to fixed assets		
Canada	$91	$ 110
International	32	93
	$ 123	$ 203
Net assets employed		
Canada	$ 866	$ 829
International	402	341
	1,268	1,170
Cash, short-term investments and securities	562	526
Accounts payable and accrued charges, deferred revenue and taxes payable, netted above	552	532
Total assets of continuing operations	2,382	2,228
Assets of discontinued operations	154	792
	$2,536	$3,020

To satisfy the disclosure principle, John Labatt discloses net sales, income before taxes, net assets employed, capital asset additions, and depreciation and amortization two ways: by business segments and by geographic area.

Long-term Commitments   Many companies make *long-term commitments* that involve making payments that may be unequal in amount over a series of years. Users of the company's financial statements will have an incomplete picture of the company's future cash flows unless information about the future commitment of payments is disclosed in the notes. An example of such a future commitment of payments is a lease, such as the leases Schneider Corporation enters into in order to conduct its business. Leases are studied in later financial accounting courses. The leases require Schneider to make a series of payments over a number of years. So that a reader of Schneider's financial statements is aware of these future payments and when they are to be made, GAAP requires the year-by-year payments to be disclosed.

Schneider discloses information about its commitments under these leases in the following note from its October 9, 1993, financial statements:

10. Commitments

The following is a schedule of future rental payments required under operating leases at the year end (in thousands of dollars):

1994	$ 3,993
1995	2,033
1996	1,960
1997	956
1998	692
Later years	1,124
	$10,758

Related Party Transactions   A basic assumption underlying the financial statements is that the transactions underlying the numbers in the financial statements were made at arm's length. The usual definition of an arm's-length transaction is a transaction between a buyer and a seller who are independent of each other or unrelated; as such, each can and will work to obtain the most favorable terms for the transaction. Most, and perhaps even all, of a company's transactions will be with unrelated parties. However, some transactions may be between the company and a party related to it. For example, Loblaws stores, owned through Loblaw Companies by George Weston Limited, buy baked goods from Weston Bakeries, owned through Weston Foods by George Weston Limited. Because the two companies have the same parent, they are considered to be related parties.

While most related party or non-arm's-length transactions are conducted at fair prices (the same prices that arm's-length transactions would be), there is a possibility that the buyer or seller obtained a financial advantage that would not have otherwise been possible. For that reason, GAAP requires that related party transactions be disclosed. In its July 31, 1994, financial statements United Grain Growers Limited disclosed information about transactions with various corporations to which United Grain is related:

16. Related Party Transactions

During the normal course of business, the Company shipped grain to the terminal owned by Prince Rupert Grain, insured country properties and inventories with Grain Insurance and Guarantee Company, and sold grain to Leblanc & Lafrance Inc., a wholly-owned subsidiary of 9002-9083 Quebec Inc.

[Note 4. Investments indicates the extent of United Grain's investment in the three companies.]

As an example of a related party transaction, the Statement of Operations shows a line item "Grants from Province of Saskatchewan."

Economic Dependence   Some companies become dependent on other companies as either suppliers or customers. For example, a small manufacturer of furniture may sell all or most of its output to one customer, a department store chain. A small brewer may buy all its bottles from one large glassmaking company. The small manufacturer and the small brewer are said to be economically dependent.

If the department store chain stops buying from the manufacturer, the manufacturer may go out of business before it can develop a new customer base. If the glassmaker stops selling bottles to the brewer, the brewer may get into financial difficulty unless a new supplier can be found quickly. It is important that users of financial statements be aware of economic dependence and so GAAP requires that companies that are economically dependent disclose that fact.

Budd Canada Inc., a Kitchener-Waterloo company that makes automotive parts, provides the following information on its customers in the notes to its September 30, 1992, financial statements. More than 95 percent of its sales are automotive parts.

6. Related Party Information

b) **Other:** The company's automotive parts business is substantially dependent upon products produced for three companies.

Constraints on Accounting

Do financial statements report every detail, no matter how small, to meet the need for understandable, relevant, reliable, and comparable information? The result would be an avalanche of data. To address this problem, accountants use the *materiality concept*. Also, a company's top managers are responsible for its financial statements. To add balance to managers' optimism—which could bias the statements and present too favorable a picture of company operations—accountants follow the *conservatism concept*. We now discuss these constraints on accounting information.

Materiality Concept

The **materiality concept** states that a company must perform strictly proper accounting only for items and transactions that are significant to the business's financial statements. Information is significant—accountants call it *material*—when its omission from or misstatement in the financial statements would influence or change a decision by a statement user. Immaterial (insignificant) items justify less than perfect accounting. The inclusion and proper presentation of *immaterial* items would not affect a statement user's decision. The materiality concept frees accountants from having to compute and report every last item in strict accordance with GAAP. Thus the materiality concept reduces the cost of accounting.

How does a business decide where to draw the line between what is material and what is immaterial? This decision rests to a great degree on how large the business is. Canadian Tire, for example, holds more than $2.4 billion in assets. Management would likely treat as immaterial a $100 purchase of wastebaskets. These wastebaskets may well remain useful for ten years. Strictly speaking, Canadian Tire should capitalize their cost and depreciate the wastebaskets. However, this treatment is not practical. The accounting cost of computing, recording, and properly reporting this asset outweighs the information provided. No statement user—a potential investor or lender, for example—would change a decision based on so insignificant (immaterial) an amount. The cost of accounting in this case outweighs the benefit of the resulting information.

Large companies may draw the materiality line at as high a figure as $10,000 and expense any smaller amount. Smaller firms may choose to expense only those items less than $50. Materiality varies from company to company. An amount that is material to the local service station may not be material to Petro-Canada.

The materiality concept does not free a business from having to account for every item. Canadian Tire, for example, must still account for the wastebaskets. They would credit Cash (or Accounts Payable) to record their purchase, of course, but what account would the company debit? Because the amount is immaterial, management may decide to debit Supplies Expense. No matter what account receives the debit, no statement user's decision would be changed by the information.

Short Exercise:

Which of the following principles or concepts directs a business to record as an expense all items that cost $50 or less, even if the item will be used for more than one accounting period?
1. Disclosure
2. Matching
3. Objectivity
4. Materiality
5. Going-concern
A: 4

Conservatism Concept

Business managers are often optimists. Asked how well the company is doing, its president will likely answer, "Great, we're having our best year ever." Without constraints this optimism could find its way into the company's reported assets and profits. Managers may try to present too favorable a view of the company. For example, they may pressure accountants to capitalize costs associated with fixed assets that should be expensed. This would result in less immediate expense and higher current income on the income statement. The balance sheet would report unduly high fixed asset values and owner's equity. The overall result would be that the managers' performance would appear to be better than it actually was. Traditionally, accountants have been conservative to counter management's optimism.

Conservatism has been interpreted as

Short Exercise:

Choose the accounting principle or concept that is best described by this statement: "Recognize that some accounting measurements take place in a context of significant uncertainty and that possible errors in measurement could occur. Financial statements should understate rather than overstate net assets and income."
1. Materiality
2. Disclosure
3. Entity
4. Reliability
5. Conservatism
A: 5

"Anticipate no profits, but anticipate all losses."

A clear-cut example is the lower-of-cost-or-market (LCM) method for inventories. Under LCM, inventory is reported at the lower of its cost or market value, which results in higher cost of goods sold and lower net income. Thus profits and assets are reported at their lowest reasonable amount. Other conservative accounting practices include the LIFO method for inventories when inventory costs are increasing, accelerated depreciation, and the completed-contract method for construction revenues. These methods result in earlier recording of expenses or later recording of revenues. Both effects postpone the reporting of net income and therefore are conservative.

In recent years, conservatism's effect on accounting has decreased. Conservatism should not mean deliberate understatement of assets, profits, and owner's equity. However, if two different values can be used for an asset or a liability, the concept suggests using the less optimistic value. Conservatism is a secondary consideration in accounting. Understandable, relevant, reliable, and comparable information is the goal, and conservatism is a factor only after these primary goals are met.

You should recognize that conservatism for the company may not be in every users' best interest; conservatism has a down side. If a company follows the cost principle for all its assets, real estate will appear on the balance sheet at cost. If a company located in Vancouver bought land on West Georgia St. 60 years ago, the land would appear on the balance sheet at the cost at that time. Since then, inflation and the strong economic growth that has occurred in Vancouver and British Columbia has increased the value of the land many times. A shareholder of the Vancouver company might sell his or her shares based on the value of the land that is shown on the balance sheet and not on its much higher market value. On the other hand, a new purchaser of the Vancouver company's shares would benefit if the company sold the land and distributed part of the proceeds to existing shareholders. In short, conservatism has much to recommend it—the benefits outweigh the costs—but there are costs.

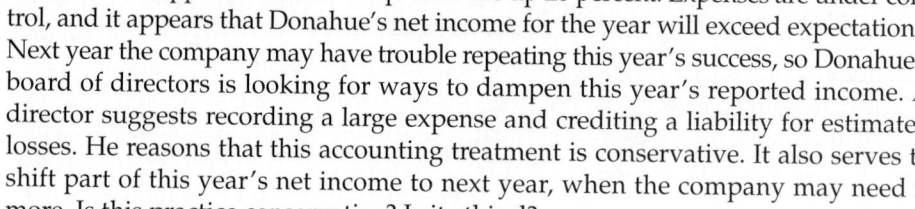

STOP & THINK

Ethical Issue: Suppose Donahue Corp. sales are up 20 percent. Expenses are under control, and it appears that Donahue's net income for the year will exceed expectations. Next year the company may have trouble repeating this year's success, so Donahue's board of directors is looking for ways to dampen this year's reported income. A director suggests recording a large expense and crediting a liability for estimated losses. He reasons that this accounting treatment is conservative. It also serves to shift part of this year's net income to next year, when the company may need it more. Is this practice conservative? Is it ethical?

Answer: This practice is conservative because it would overstate expenses and liabilities and understate net income. The practice is unethical, however, because it would artificially decrease reported income. "Cooking the books" to manage earnings in this manner violates the reliability principle and is therefore unacceptable.

Financial Statements and Their Elements _____

We have examined the concepts and principles that guide businesses in shaping accounting practice. The CICA aims for financial statements that best meet user needs for business information.

This accounting information appears in four statements: the balance sheet, the income statement, the statement of retained earnings, and the statement of changes in financial position (which we cover in Chapter 18). The CICA provides definitions for the elements that make up these statements. Financial information presentation, to be most useful to the greatest number of financial statement users, must be presented in a standard format with well-defined terms, as we learned in our discussion of the comparability concept.

The Canadian Institute of Chartered Accountants in "Financial Statement Concepts," Section 1000 of the *CICA Handbook,* provides authoritative definitions of the elements of financial statements.

Balance Sheet Elements   *Assets* are economic resources controlled by an entity as a result of past transactions or events from which future economic benefits may be obtained. *Liabilities* are obligations of an entity arising from past transactions or events, the settlement of which may result in the transfer or use of assets, provision of services or other yielding of economic benefits in the future. *Equity (Owner's Equity)*, also *net assets*, is the ownership interest in the assets of a profit-oriented entity after deducting its liabilities. Net assets or equity of a non-profit organization is the residual interest after deducting the organization's liabilities.

Income Statement Elements   *Revenues* are increases in economic resources, either by way of inflows or enhancements of assets or reductions of liabilities, resulting from the ordinary activities of an entity, normally from the sale of goods, the rendering of services or the use by others of entity resources yielding rent, interest, royalties or dividends. *Expenses* are decreases in economic resources, either by way of outflows or reductions of assets or incurrences of liabilities, resulting from the ordinary revenue generating or service delivery activities of an entity. *Gains* are increases in equity from peripheral or incidental transactions and events affecting an entity and from all other transactions, events and circumstances affecting the entity except those that result from revenues or equity contributions. *Losses* are decreases in equity from peripheral or incidental transactions and events affecting an entity and from all other transactions, events and circumstances affecting the entity except those that result from expenses or distributions of equity.

Note that *revenues* and *expenses* arise from the business's ongoing central operations, but *gains* and *losses* do not. Sales and interest earned are revenues because most companies make sales and earn interest as part of their central operations. Selling cars and trucks lies at the heart of an automobile dealership. To this business, a gain on the sale of a truck is revenue and a loss on the sale is expense. However, a gain on the sale of a truck is not revenue for a trucking company because that entity buys trucks for use rather than for sale. Selling a truck is not a part of central operations.

Owner's Equity Elements   *Investments by owners* are increases in owner's equity that result from the owner's transferring to the entity something of value. The most common investment is cash, but owners sometimes invest land, buildings, legal services or other assets. In some cases, an owner's investment in the business may consist of paying off its liabilities. *Distributions to owners* are decreases in owner's equity that result from the owner's transferring assets or services from the business to himself or herself, or from the business taking on the owner's liabilities. When the business is a corporation, owner withdrawals are called *dividends*. The most commonly distributed asset is cash, but businesses sometimes distribute other assets, such as stock investments they hold in other companies, to their owners.

PUTTING SKILLS TO WORK

Ratios: Should a Bank Grant a Loan?

We have focused on the principles of accounting that are generally accepted in Canada. Most of the methods of accounting are consistent throughout the world. Double-entry bookkeeping, the accrual accounting system, and the basic financial statements are used worldwide. Differences, however, do exist among countries.

In discussing depreciation—Chapter 10—we emphasized that in Canada the methods used for reporting to tax authorities may differ from the methods used for reporting to shareholders. In contrast, tax reporting and shareholder reporting are identical in many countries. For example, France has "Plan Compatible" that specifies a National Uniform Chart of Accounts used for both tax returns and reporting to shareholders. German financial reporting is also determined primarily by tax laws. In Japan, certain principles are allowed for tax purposes only if they are also used for shareholder reporting.

A company that sells its stock through a foreign stock exchange must follow the accounting principles of the foreign country. For example, Inco Limited, a Canadian company listed on the Toronto Stock exchange, is also listed on the New York Stock Exchange. In fact, Inco reports in U.S. dollars in its annual report. Inco follows Canadian GAAP in its annual report because it is a Canadian company.

Inco complies with U.S. standards by reconciling the disclosures in its annual report with U.S. GAAP by means of a note to the financial statements. Note 17, "Differences Between Canadian and United States Generally Accepted Accounting Principles" explains the differences between the two GAAPs and indicates the effects of those differences on the financial statements.

A significant difference among countries is the extent to which the financial statements account for inflation. In the 1980s the CICA experimented with requiring supplementary disclosure of inflation-adjusted numbers, but there is no requirement for such supplementary disclosure in Canada now. In contrast, some countries have full or partial adjustments for inflation as part of their reporting to both investors and tax authorities. For example, Argentina and Brazil, which have experienced very high inflation rates, require all statements to be adjusted for changes in the general price level.

The globalization of business enterprises and capital markets is creating much interest in establishing common, worldwide accounting standards. There are probably too many cultural, social, and political differences to expect complete worldwide standardization of financial reporting in the near future. However, the number of differences is decreasing. Cooperation among accountants has been fostered by the International Federation of Accountants (IFAC), an organization of accountancy bodies from more than 75 countries. International standards are being formulated and published by the International Accounting Standards Committee (IASC).

International Accounting Differences

Country	Inventories	Goodwill	Research and Development Costs
Canada	LIFO is un-acceptable for tax purposes and is not widely used.	Amortized over useful life, not to exceed 40 years.	Expense research costs. Some development costs may be capitalized.
United States	Specific unit cost, FIFO, LIFO, weighted-average.	Amortized over period not to exceed 40 years.	Expensed as incurred.
Germany	Similar to U.S.	Amortized over useful life or written off immediately.	Expensed as incurred.
Japan	Similar to U.S.	Amortized over 5 years.	May be capitalized and amortized over 5 years.

Note: For inventory, goodwill, and research and development costs, German accounting practices are more similar to those of the United States than to those of other countries. Despite the common heritage of Canada and the United States, Canadian and American accounting practices vary.

Summary Problem for Your Review

This chapter has discussed the following principles and concepts:

Entity concept	Cost principle
Going-concern concept	Revenue principle
Time-period concept	Matching principle
Reliability principle	Disclosure principle
Comparability principle	Materiality concept

Required

Indicate which of these concepts is being violated in each of the following situations:

1. A construction company signs a two-year contract to build a bridge for the province of Nova Scotia. The president of the company immediately records the full contract price as revenue.

2. Competition has taken away much of the business of a small airline. The airline is unwilling to report its plans to sell half its fleet of planes.

3. After starting the business in February 19X2, a gold-mining company keeps no accounting records for 19X2, 19X3, and 19X4. The owner is waiting until the mine is exhausted to determine the success or failure of the business.

4. Assets recorded at cost by a drug-store chain are written up to their fair market value at the end of each year.

5. The accountant for a manufacturing company keeps detailed depreciation records on every asset no matter how small its value.

6. A physician mixes her personal accounting records with those of the medical practice.

7. Expenses are reported whenever the bookkeeper records them rather than when related revenues are earned.

8. The damaged inventory of a discount store is being written down. The store manager bases the write-down entry on his own subjective opinion in order to minimize income taxes.

9. A quick-copy center changes accounting methods every year in order to report the maximum amount of net income possible under generally accepted accounting principles.

10. The owners of a private nursing home base its accounting records on the assumption that the nursing home might have to close at any time. The nursing home has a long record of service to the community.

SOLUTION TO REVIEW PROBLEM

1. Revenue principle
2. Disclosure principle
3. Time-period concept
4. Cost principle
5. Materiality concept
6. Entity concept
7. Matching principle
8. Reliability principle
9. Comparability principle
10. Going-concern concept

Summary

1. Identify the basic objective of financial reporting. The Accounting Standards Board of Canadian Institute of Chartered Accountants (CICA) formulates generally accepted accounting principles (GAAP) to provide understandable, relevant, reliable and comparable accounting information. Information must be *understandable* by users if it is to be used. *Relevant* information allows users to make business predictions and to evaluate past decisions. *Reliable* data are free from error and bias. Accounting information is also intended to be *comparable* from company to company and from period to period.

2. Identify and apply the underlying concepts of accounting. Four concepts underlie accounting. The most basic, the *entity concept*, draws clear boundaries around the accounting entity. The entity, based on the *going-concern concept*, is assumed to remain in business for the foreseeable future. The *time-period concept* is the basis for reporting accounting information for particular time periods such as months, quarters, or years. Under the *stable-monetary-unit concept*, no adjustment is made for the changing value of the dollar.

3. Identify and apply the principles of accounting. Accounting principles provide detailed guidelines for recording transactions and preparing the financial statements. The *reliability* and *comparability principles* require that accounting information be based on objective data and be useful for comparing companies over different time periods. The *cost principle* governs accounting for assets and liabilities, and the *revenue principle* governs accounting for revenues.

4. Allocate revenue to the appropriate period by four methods. Different methods exist to account for revenues, depending on when the revenue has been earned, when it can be measured objectively, and whether collectibility is assured. *Matching* is the basis for recording expenses.

5. Report information that satisfies the disclosure principle. The *disclosure principle* requires companies to report, among other things, their accounting policies, contingent liabilities, probable future losses, accounting changes, subsequent events, business-segment data, long-term commitments and related party transactions.

6. Apply the materiality constraint and the conservatism constraint to accounting. Two constraints on accounting are materiality and conservatism. The *materiality concept* allows companies to avoid excessive cost in accounting for immaterial items. *Conservatism* constrains the optimism of managers by anticipating no profits, but anticipating all losses.

Self-Study Questions

Test your understanding of the chapter by marking the correct answer for each of the following questions:

1. The organization that issues accounting pronouncements that make up GAAP is the *(p. 580)*
   a. Government of Canada
   b. National Securities Administrators
   c. Accounting Standards Board
   d. Ontario Securities Commission

2. Which of the following characteristics of accounting information does the objective of financial reporting omit? *(p. 584)*
   a. Timeliness
   b. Relevance
   c. Reliability
   d. Comparability

3. A new business is starting. The president wishes to wait until significant contracts have been fulfilled before reporting the results of the business's operations. Which underlying concept serves as the basis for preparing financial statements at regular intervals? *(p. 586)*
   a. Entity
   b. Going-concern
   c. Time-period
   d. Stable-monetary-unit

4. Which of these revenue methods is the most conservative? *(pp. 589–591)*
   a. Sales method
   b. Collection method
   c. Percentage-of-completion method
   d. All the above are equally conservative.

5. Suppose a Zellers store sells $10,000 worth of kitchen appliances on the installment plan and collects a down payment of $1,500. Zellers' cost of the appliances is $7,000. How much gross profit will the company report on the down payment under the installment revenue method? *(pp. 589–590)*
   a. $450
   b. $1,500
   c. $3,000
   d. $10,000

6. A construction company spent $180,000 during the current year on a building with a contract price of $900,000. The company estimated total construction cost at $720,000. How much construction *income* will the company report under the percentage-of-completion method? *(pp. 590–592)*
   a. $45,000
   b. $144,000
   c. $180,000
   d. $225,000

7. Which of the following items should be disclosed to satisfy the adequate disclosure principle? *(pp. 592–594)*
   a. Contingent liabilities
   b. Probable losses
   c. Accounting changes
   d. All of the above

8. Important subsequent events should be disclosed because they *(pp. 594)*
   a. Occur immediately after the current period
   b. Describe changes in accounting methods
   c. Reveal losses that have a high probability of occurring in the future
   d. May affect the interpretation of the current-period financial statements

9. Which of the following statements is most in keeping with the materiality concept? *(p. 599)*
   a. Accountants record material losses but are reluctant to record material gains.
   b. Different companies have different materiality limits, depending on their size.
   c. Business-segment data are disclosed to fulfill the materiality concept.
   d. Companies report all the information needed to communicate a material view of the entity.

10. Conservatism would avoid reporting *(pp. 599–600)*
    a. Insignificant data
    b. Too much income
    c. Too little for liabilities
    d. Footnotes

Answers to the Self-Study Questions follow the Accounting Vocabulary.

Accounting Vocabulary

Change in accounting estimate *(p. 594)*
Change in accounting principle *(p. 594)*
Comparability principle *(p. 588)*
Conservatism *(p. 599)*
Cost principle *(p. 588)*
Disclosure principle *(p. 592)*
Entity concept *(p. 585)*
Going-concern or continuity concept *(p. 585)*

Matching principle *(p. 592)*
Materiality concept *(p. 599)*
Reliability principle *(p. 587)*
Revenue principle *(p. 588)*
Stable-monetary-unit concept *(p. 587)*
Subsequent event *(p. 595)*
Time-period concept *(p. 586)*

Answers to Self-Study Questions

1. c	7. d
2. a	8. d
3. c	9. b
4. b	10. b

5. a ($10,000 − $7,000)/$10,000 = .30 × $1,500 = $450
6. a $180,000/$720,000 = .25 × $900,000 = $225,000;
   $225,00 − $180,000 = $45,000

ASSIGNMENT MATERIAL _____

Questions

1. How do accounting principles differ from natural laws?
2. State the basic objective of financial reporting.
3. What three characteristics make accounting information useful for decision-making? Briefly discuss each one.
4. What is the entity concept?
5. How does the going-concern concept affect accounting? What is liquidation?
6. Identify two practical results of the time-period concept.
7. What is the shortcoming of the stable-monetary-unit concept?
8. What are the comparability principle's two requirements?
9. Why is consistency important in accounting?
10. Discuss the relationship between the cost principle and the reliability principle.
11. What three conditions must be met before revenue is recorded? What determines the amount of the revenue?
12. Which revenue recognition method is more conservative, the sales method or the collection method? Give your reason.
13. Suppose Monarch Development Corp. sold land for $200,000 on an installment basis, receiving a down payment of $50,000 to be followed by 12 installments of $12,500 each. If Monarch's cost of the land was $120,000, how much gross profit would Monarch record under the installment method (a) when the down payment is received, and (b) when each installment is received?
14. Briefly discuss two methods of recognizing revenue on long-term construction contracts.
15. Give two examples of expenses that are easy to relate to sales revenue and two examples of expenses that are not so easy to relate to particular sales. On what basis are the latter expenses matched against revenue?
16. ABC Limited agreed on November 22, 19X7 to sell an unprofitable manufacturing plant. ABC estimates on December 31 that the company is likely to incur a $4 million loss on the sale when it is finalized in 19X8. In which year should ABC report the loss? What accounting principle governs this situation?
17. Identify three items commonly disclosed in a company's summary of significant accounting policies.
18. What is a subsequent event? Why should companies disclose important subsequent events in their financial statements?

19. How does information on business segments help an investor?

20. Classify each of the following as a change in accounting principle or a change in accounting estimate:
    a. Change from straight-line to double-declining-balance depreciation.
    b. Change in the uncollectibility of accounts receivable.
    c. Change from LIFO to FIFO for inventory.
    d. Change from the percentage-of-completion method to the completed-contract method for revenue on long-term construction contracts.
    e. Change from an 8-year life to a 10-year life for a machine.
    f. Change in estimated warranty expense rate stated as a percent of sales.

21. Briefly define each of the following terms and explain why information about each is important to users of financial statements:
    a. Related party transactions
    b. Economic dependence

22. Sloan Sales Inc. expenses the cost of capital assets below $500 at the time of purchase. What accounting concept allows this departure from strictly proper accounting? Why would Sloan Sales follow such a policy?

23. Give three examples of conservative accounting methods, stating why the methods are conservative.

24. Identify two balance-sheet elements that are defined independently and give the definition of the third balance sheet element.

25. The four income-statement elements may be divided into two pairs of similar elements. What elements make up these two pairs?

Exercises

Exercise 12-1 *Identifying the objective of financial reporting* *(Obj. 1)*

As a financial analyst with Midland Walwyn, your job is to follow the aerospace industry. Specifically, you compare companies in this industry so that you may recommend to Midland Walwyn clients which companies to invest in. What is the basic objective of financial reporting? Briefly discuss some of the predictions and related evaluations of past performance that an investment analyst would make. Also state why the analyst feels more comfortable using information that has been audited by an independent public accountant.

Exercise 12-2 *Applying accounting concepts* *(Obj. 2)*

The Pacific Tide is a newspaper devoted to cultural affairs in Vancouver and surrounding areas in British Columbia. Its owner, Marla Griffis, is better attuned to cultural affairs than to the business aspects of running a newspaper. Readership is at an all-time high, but the financial position of the business has suffered. For each of the following items indicate the accounting action needed at December 31, the end of the accounting year. Also identify the underlying accounting concept most directly applicable to your answer.

a. On March 31, *The Pacific Tide* had to borrow $200,000 to pay bills. The interest rate of this one-year loan is 7 percent, payable March 31.

b. Griffis intermingles her personal assets with those of the business. In applying for the $200,000 loan, she wanted to include on the company books her Lincoln automobile, which was worth $24,000. Her reasoning was that the business is a proprietorship and that her personal assets are available to the newspaper if needed.

c. Its financial position is so dismal that *The Pacific Tide* is in danger of failure. Assets measured at historical cost total $1.3 million, but their current market value is only $900,000, which barely exceeds liabilities of $850,000. For now it appears that the newspaper will remain in business.

Exercise 12-3   *Reporting assets as a going concern and as a liquidating entity*   **(Obj. 2, 3)**

Robarts Limited has the following assets:

Cash, $9,000.

Accounts Receivable, $25,600; allowance for uncollectible accounts, $4,300.

Office supplies, cost $280; scrap value $70.

Office machinery, cost $72,000; accumulated depreciation $14,000; current sales value, $47,400.

Land, cost $45,000; current sales value $105,000.

Required

1. Assume Robarts continues as a going concern. Compute the amount of its assets for reporting on the balance sheet.

2. Assume Robarts is going out of business by liquidating its assets. Compute the amount of its assets at liquidation value.

Exercise 12-4   *Applying the revenue and matching principles*   **(Obj. 3)**

Burleson, Inc., introduced a new laser disc in December 19X2 and received $100,000 from customers in advance. During 19X3, Burleson shipped the products to customers and received an additional $400,000. In 19X4 Burleson received $300,000 as the final payment for the 19X3 shipments.

Burleson spent $90,000 in 19X2 to advertise the laser discs during 19X3. Cost of goods sold was $160,000. Burleson paid an additional $230,000 during 19X4 for expenses accrued at the end of 19X3.

Required

Show revenues, expenses, and net income for 19X2, 19X3, and 19X4.

Exercise 12-5   *Reporting assets under GAAP*   **(Obj. 3)**

Identify the amount at which each of the following assets should be reported in the financial statements of Maidment Limited. Cite the concept, principle, or constraint that is most applicable to each answer.

a. Maidment purchased a machine for $16,000, less a $1,300 cash discount. To ship the machine to the office, Maidment paid transportation charges of $500 and insurance of $200 while in transit. After using the machine for one month, Maidment purchases lubricating oil costing $150 for use in operating the machine.

b. Inventory has a cost of $42,000, but its current market value is $39,400.

c. Maidment purchased land for $222,000 and paid $2,500 to have the land surveyed, $15,400 to have old buildings removed, and $40,300 for grading land. Maidment is offering the land for sale at $225,000 and has received a $200,000 offer.

Exercise 12-6   *Reporting income under GAAP*   **(Obj. 3)**

San Marcos Electronics Inc. failed to record the following items at December 31, 19X4, the end of its fiscal year:

Accrued salary expense, $1,100.

Prepaid insurance, $700.

Accrued interest expense, $600.

Depreciation expense, $400.

Instead of recording the accrued expenses at December 31, 19X4, San Marcos Electronics recorded the expenses when it paid them in 19X5. The company recorded the insurance as expense when it was prepaid for one year, early in 19X4. Depreciation expense for 19X5 was correctly recorded.

San Marcos Electronics incorrectly reported net income of $10,000 in 19X4 and $7,400 in 19X5 because of the above errors.

Required

Compute San Marcos Electronics' correct net income for 19X4 and 19X5. Compare the corrected trend in net income with the originally reported trend.

Exercise 12-7   *Reporting revenues under GAAP   (Obj. 4)*

For each of the following situations, indicate the amount of revenue to report for the current year ended December 31 and for the following year:

a. Sold gift certificates, collecting $4,000 in advance. At December 31, $1,400 of the gifts have been claimed. The remainder were claimed during the next year.

b. Sold merchandise for $4,400, receiving a down payment of $1,100 and the customer's receivable for the balance. The company accounts for these sales by the sales method.

c. On April 1, loaned $35,000 at 12 percent on a three-year note.

d. Performed $900 of services for a high-risk customer on August 18, accounting for the revenue by the collection method. At December 31, the company had received $200 of the total; $550 was received the following year.

e. On September 1, collected one year's rent of $12,000 in advance on a building leased to another company.

Exercise 12-8   *Computing gross profit under the sales method and the installment method (Obj. 4)*

Levis Appliance Store Ltd. sells on the installment plan. The store's installment sales figures for 19X7 follow:

Sales	$420,000
Down payments received on the sales	80,000
Collections on installments	170,000
Inventory at beginning of 19X7	60,000
Inventory at end of 19X7	42,000
Purchases	216,000

Required

Compute the store's gross profit if it uses (a) the sales method of revenue recognition, and (b) the installment method. Round gross profit percentage to three decimal places.

Exercise 12-9   *Computing construction revenue under the completed-contract method and the percentage-of-completion method   (Obj. 4)*

Red Deer Construction Corp. builds bridges for the province of Alberta. The construction period typically extends for several years. During 19X5, Red Deer completed a bridge with a contract price of $1,000,000. Red Deer's $640,000 cost of the bridge was incurred as follows: $40,000 in 19X3; $360,000 in 19X4; and $240,000 in 19X5. Compute Red Deer's revenue for each year 19X3 through 19X5 if the company uses (a) the completed-contract method, and (b) the percentage-of-completion method. Which method better matches expense with revenue?

Exercise 12-10   *Changing the useful life of a depreciable asset   (Obj. 5)*

Red Deer Construction Corp. uses a crane on its construction projects. The company purchased the crane early in January 19X3 for $600,000. For 19X3 and 19X4 depreciation was taken by the straight-line method based on an eight-year life and an estimated residual value of $80,000. In early 19X5, it became evident that the crane would be useful beyond the original life of eight years. Therefore, beginning in 19X5, McMinn changed the depreciable life of the crane to a total life of ten years. The company retained the straight-line method and did not alter the residual value.

Required

Prepare Red Deer's depreciation entries for 19X4 and 19X5. Identify the accounting principles most important in this situation.

Exercise 12-11   *Identifying subsequent events for the financial statements   (Obj. 5)*

Champlain Inc. experienced the following events after May 31, 19X8, the end of the company's fiscal year, but before publication of its financial statements on July 12:

a. Champlain sales personnel received a contract to supply Favron Systems Inc. with laser equipment.
b. Increased demand for Champlain products suggests that the next fiscal year will be the best in the company's history.
c. On July 6, Champlain is sued for $1 million. Loss of the lawsuit could lead to Champlain's bankruptcy.
d. Champlain collected $210,000 of the $480,000 accounts receivable reported on the May 31 balance sheet. Champlain expects to collect the remainder in the course of business during the next fiscal year.
e. A major customer, who owed Champlain $140,000 at May 31, declared bankruptcy on June 21.

Required

Identify the subsequent events that Champlain should disclose in its May 31, 19X8 financial statements.

Exercise 12-12   *Using accounting concepts and principles   (Obj. 2, 6)*

Identify the accounting concept or principle, if any, that is violated in each of the following situations. You may choose from among *disclosure, conservatism, cost, entity* and *matching*.

a. A manufacturer records depreciation during years when net income is high but fails to record depreciation when net income is low. Revenues are relatively constant.
b. The inventory of a furniture store has a current market value of $163,000. The store reports the inventory at its cost of $181,000.
c. The owner of a placement service used the business bank account to pay her family's household expenses, making no note that the expenses were personal.
d. A manufacturing company changed from the FIFO inventory method to the LIFO method and failed to disclose the accounting change in the financial statements.
e. A paper company that purchased 1,000 hectares of timberland at $800 per hectare in 1982 reports the land at its current market value of $3,000 per hectare.

Exercise 12-13   *Using accounting concepts and principles   (Obj. 2, 6)*

Indicate the accounting concept or principle that applies to the following situations. Choose among *comparability, materiality, reliability, revenue,* and *time period.*

a. Although Ikeda Corp. could increase its reported income by changing depreciation methods, Ikeda management has decided not to make the change.

b. Taco Taco Restaurant was recently sued for $200,000, but the plaintiff has indicated a willingness to settle for less than that amount. Taco Taco hopes to settle for $50,000, but their lawyers believe the settlement will be between $90,000 and $100,000. Taco Taco's auditor reports the settlement as a real liability on the balance sheet. The only remaining issue is whether to report the liability at $50,000 or at $95,000.

c. Econo Leasing Limited is considering publishing quarterly financial statements to provide more current information about its affairs.

d. POA, Inc. is negotiating the sale of $600,000 of inventory. POA has been in financial difficulty and desperately needs to report this sale on its income statement of the current year. At December 31, the end of the company's accounting year, the sale has not been closed.

e. Lancer Distributors Inc. expenses the cost of plant assets that cost less than $400.

Exercise 12-14   *Applying generally accepted accounting principles   (Obj. 2, 3, 6)*

Littlefield Corporation's income statement follows:

Littlefield Company
Income Statement
December 31, 19X9

Revenues:

Sales revenue, including sales taxes of $40,000	$820,000
Discount earned on high-quantity purchases of merchandise inventory (all the goods have been sold)	19,000
Recoveries of accounts receivable previously written off as uncollectible	24,000
Increase in the market value of land	62,000
Interest revenue	9,000
Total revenue	$934,000

Expenses:

Cost of goods sold, including sales taxes of $18,000	$462,000
Salary and related payroll expense	183,000
Depreciation expense	64,000
Reserve for contingent losses	18,000
Household expenses of owner	59,000
Property tax expense	26,000
Utilities expense	17,000
Distributions to owner	61,000
Purchases of property, plant, and equipment	85,000
Loss on sale of investments	12,000
Additional depreciation due to inflation	6,000
Total expenses and losses	$993,000
Net income (loss) for the year	$(59,000)

This income statement has 10 errors. Identify each, and prepare a corrected income statement.

Problems   *(Group A)*

Problem 12-1A   *Identifying the basis for good accounting practices*   **(Obj. 2, 3, 6)**

The following accounting practices are in accord with GAAP. Identify all the accounting concepts and principles that form the basis for each accounting practice. More than one concept or principle may apply.

a. A real estate developer paid $1.3 million for land and held it for three years before selling it for $2 million. There was significant inflation during this period, but the developer reports the $.7 million gain on sale with no adjustment for the change in the value of the dollar.

b. Liabilities are reported in two categories, current and long-term.

c. TGI Friday's, a restaurant, makes such small payments for fire insurance that the company expenses them and makes no year-end adjustment for prepaid insurance.

d. The inventory of a personal computer store declined substantially in value because of changing technology. The store wrote its computer inventory down to the lower of cost or market.

e. A construction company changed from the completed-contract method to the percentage-of-completion method of recording revenue on its long-term construction contracts. The company disclosed this accounting change in the notes to its financial statements.

f. A mining company recorded an intangible asset at the cost of the mineral lease and all other costs necessary to bring the mine to the point of production. After the mine was in operation, the company amortized the asset's cost as expense in proportion to the revenues from sale of the minerals.

g. Because of a downturn in the economy, a jeweler increased his business's allowance for doubtful accounts.

h. The personal residence of the owner of a freight company is not disclosed in the financial statements of the business.

i. A manufacturing company's capital assets are carried on the books at cost under the assumption that the company will remain in operation for the foreseeable future.

j. A clothing store discloses in notes to its financial statements that it uses the FIFO method.

Problem 12-2A   *Identifying the concepts and principles violated by bad accounting practices*   **(Obj. 2, 3, 6)**

The following accounting practices are *not* in accord with generally accepted accounting principles. Identify the single accounting concept or principle that is most clearly violated by each accounting practice.

a. A flood on July 2 caused $150,000 in damage to Yukon Construction Ltd. property. The company did not report the flood as a subsequent event in the June 30 financial statements.

b. Victoria, Inc., overstates depreciation expense in order to report low amounts of net income.

c. The balance sheet of Francine Fortin's design practice includes significant receivables that she will probably never collect. Nevertheless, Fortin's accountant refuses to use the collection method to account for revenue.

d. The current market value of Miska Electronics' inventory is $119,000, but the company reports its inventory at cost of $134,000. The decline in value is permanent.

e. The liabilities of Wash Jet Corporation exceed the company's assets. To get a loan from the bank, Wash Jet's owner, Slade McQueen, includes his personal investments as assets on the balance sheet of the business.

f. Singh Corporation increases the carrying value of its land based on recent sales of adjacent property.

g. Mission Ford Sales Ltd. records expenses on an irregular basis without regard to the pattern of the company's revenues.

h. Waterloo Software Ltd. omits the significant accounting policies note from its financial statements because the company uses the same accounting methods that its competitors use.

i. Royal Iron Works Inc. regularly changes accounting methods in order to report a target amount of net income each year.

j. Alberta Land Inc. reports land at its market value of $820,000, which is greater than the cost of $400,000.

Problem 12-3A   *Using the installment-revenue method*   **(Obj. 4)**

Pine Valley Appliance Store Ltd. makes all sales on the installment basis but uses the sales method to record revenue. The company's income statements for the most recent three years follow:

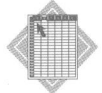

	Year 1	Year 2	Year 3
Sales..	$240,000	$210,000	$290,000
Cost of goods sold.................................	144,000	121,800	179,800
Gross profit...	96,000	88,200	110,200
Operating expenses................................	26,400	28,300	37,300
Net income..	$ 69,600	$ 59,900	$ 72,900
Collections from sales of year 1.............	$100,000	$ 75,000	$ 60,000
2.............		68,000	120,000
3.............			145,000

Required

Compute the amount of net income Pine Valley would have reported if the company had used the installment method for revenue. Ignore the effect of uncollectible accounts and present your answer in the following format:

Installment-method net income	Year 1	Year 2	Year 3
Gross profit..	$?	$?	$?
Operating expenses.................................	26,400	28,300	37,300
Net income (net loss)	$?	$?	$?

Problem 12-4A   *Accounting for construction income*   **(Obj. 4)**

B.C. Shipbuilding Corporation participates in the construction of small ships under long-term contracts. During 19X7, B.C. began three projects that progressed according to the following schedule during 19X7, 19X8, and 19X9:

Project	Contract Price	Total Project Cost	19X7 Cost for Year	19X7 % Completed during Year	19X8 Cost for Year	19X8 % Completed during Year	19X9 Cost for Year	19X9 % Completed during Year
1	$2,100,000	$1,200,000	$ 500,000	42%	$ 700,000	58%	—	—
2	1,200,000	740,000	740,000	100	—	—	—	—
3	7,400,000	6,300,000	1,260,000	20	2,205,000	35	$2,835,000	45%

Required

1. Assume B.C. Shipbuilding uses the completed-contract method for construction revenue. Compute the company's construction revenue and income to be reported in 19X7, 19X8, and 19X9.

2. Compute B.C.'s construction revenue and income to be reported in the three years if the company uses the percentage-of-completion method.

Problem 12-5A   *Accounting for revenues and expenses according to GAAP*   *(Obj. 2, 3, 4)*

Sara Armstrong established Sara's Shoppe in January 19X4 to import woolens from Scotland. During 19X4 and 19X5 Armstrong kept the company's books and prepared the financial statements, although she had no training or experience in accounting. As a result, the accounts contain numerous errors. Armstrong recorded revenue from sales on the collection method, which is not appropriate for the company. Armstrong should have been using the sales method for revenues. She also recorded inventory purchases as the cost of goods sold.

When the value of the company warehouse increased by $50,000 in 19X6, Armstrong recorded an increase in the Building account and credited Revenue. On January 2, 19X4, she borrowed $30,000 on a 9 percent, three-year note. She intended to wait until 19X7, when the note was due, to record the full amount of interest expense for three years. The company's records reveal the following amounts:

	19X4	19X5	19X6
Reported net income (net loss)	$(19,200)	$ 48,600	$ 72,100
Sales	256,700	303,500	366,800
Cash collections from customers	210,400	309,000	317,800
Purchases of inventory	141,000	187,400	202,300
Ending inventory	35,800	59,900	73,400
Accrued expenses not recorded at year end; these expenses were recorded during the next year, when paid	13,500	22,600	30,100
Interest expense recorded	-0-	-0-	-0-
Revenue recorded for increase in the value of the store building			50,000

Required

1. In early 19X7 Armstrong employed you as an accountant. Apply the concepts and principles of GAAP to compute the correct net income of Sara's Shoppe for 19X4, 19X5, and 19X6.

2. How will what you have learned from this problem help you manage a business?

Problem 12-6A   *Identify and apply the underlying concepts and principles of accounting, and their relationship to the basic objective of accounting*   *(Obj. 1, 2, 3)*

Mi-way Corporation is owned and managed by J. Owens, president. You have been hired by Owens as the controller and Owens has given you a number of transactions or events as well as directions on how they should be dealt with.

For each of the following transactions you are required to respond to Owens's directions by:

- describing how you would record the transaction
- identifying which accounting principle(s) or concept(s) is (are) applicable in recording the transaction and why
- identifying how your method helps to fulfill the basic objective of accounting "to provide information that is useful in making investment and lending decisions."

1. Mi-way is approaching the bank to apply for a loan and Owens feels the company's balance sheet should include his personal residence as he would be prepared to sell it to pay off the loan if the company were to default.

2. Mi-way purchased a machine at a bankruptcy sale. The machine had an appraised value of $200,000, but Mi-way was able to purchase it for only $150,000. Owens says the machine presently sells for $240,000 from a supplier and should be recorded at that value and the extra $90,000 credited to revenues due to the work he had to do to find such a bargain.

3. Mi-way has signed a contract to provide $15,000 of services per month for the next six months. The contract calls for payment at the end of the contract and Owens feels that the revenues should all be recorded when received as that is the only time they will have objective evidence of the revenue.

4. Mi-way has purchased a three-year insurance policy which Owens feels should be recorded as an expense immediately as the policy does not allow for any refunds if Mi-way cancels or goes bankrupt.

5. Mi-way has purchased a very specialized machine and Owens feels that its cost should be expensed immediately as it already has no market value due to its special design.

6. Mi-way is being sued by a customer for $500,000. Owens says their lawyer refuses to speculate on their chances in court, but a number of business acquaintances have told them that he can't lose. Owens feels the lawsuit should not be recorded because of the advice he has received and also because he will file for bankruptcy if he does lose, so nothing will be paid anyway.

Problem 12-7A   *Identify and apply the underlying concepts and principles of accounting, and their relationship to the basic objective of accounting; allocate revenue to the appropriate period; apply the materiality constraint and the conservatism constraint to accounting*   **(Obj. 1, 2, 3, 4, 6)**

Give the journal entry required to *properly record* each of the following transactions. Identify any accounting concepts, principles, or constraints that influence how the transaction was recorded and describe why.

1. A company signed a contract for the construction of a building for $500,000. The contract had a penalty clause for late completion. The building was completed late (penalties of $20,000) and the company feels the building should be recorded at $500,000 with the $20,0000 charged to revenues to compensate for those lost due to its lateness.

2. A large company paid $2,000 for the purchase of a number of small tools that are expected to last for 10 years with no residual value expected at that time. The president feels that the straight-line depreciation method would be best.

3. A company has signed a contract to build a shipyard at a total cost of $2,000,000. The company will take three years to complete the job and the contract calls for annual payments of $500,000 at the beginning of each year with the balance due on completion. The company completed 40 percent of the work in the first year and the accountant feels that the sales method should be used, with all revenues recorded when the job is complete and ownership changes hands. However, the board of directors feels that the revenues should be recorded whenever the cash is received as this will make the statements comparable from period to period.

4. A company has completed a $150,000 advertising campaign this year. The president feels that the campaign was much more successful than the ones they have run in previous years and will likely affect sales for the next three years; therefore, the cost should be capitalized and amortized over the three years. The marketing manager feels that the campaign will actually provide benefits for six years and, therefore, that is the appropriate period over which to amortize the costs.

5. A company is being sued for $400,000 by a client for product failure. The company's lawyers estimate that it will take two years to settle and cost the company $250,000. The president does not think the lawsuit should be recorded as the company is not at fault.

6. The owner of a sole proprietorship attended a week-long conference in Europe at a cost of $20,000. The conference would have only cost $4,000, but he took his family and spent an extra week. He feels it should all be expensed to the company as he would not have attended without his family and the extra time.

(Group B)

Problem 12-1B   *Identifying the basis for good accounting practices*   *(Obj. 2, 3, 6)*

The following accounting practices are in accord with generally accepted accounting principles. Identify all the accounting concepts and principles that form the basis for each accounting practice. More than one concept or principle may apply.

a. A fire destroyed the company garage after December 31, 19X7, and before the financial statements were published in early February 19X8. Although the fire loss is insured, reconstruction of the garage will disrupt the company's operations. This subsequent event will be reported in the 19X7 financial statements.

b. A paint company accounts for its operations by dividing the business into four separate units. This division enables the company to evaluate each unit apart from the others.

c. A theater company accrues employee salaries at year end even though the salaries will be paid during the first few days of the new year.

d. Assets are reported at liquidation value on the financial statements of a company that is going out of business.

e. The cost of machinery is being depreciated over a five-year life because independent engineers believe the machinery will become obsolete after that time. (The company had hoped to depreciate the machinery over 10 years to report lower depreciation and higher net income in the early years of the asset's life.)

f. A manufacturing firm built some specialized equipment for its own use. The equipment would have cost $110,000 if purchased from an outside company, but the cost of constructing the equipment was only $89,000. The firm recorded the equipment at cost of $89,000.

g. Depreciation of the head-office building is difficult to relate to particular sales. Therefore, the company records depreciation expense on a time basis.

h. A company wishes to change its method of accounting for revenue. However, the company does not switch because it wants to use the same accounting method that other companies in the industry use.

i. Because it is often difficult to collect installment receivables, a retailer uses the installment method of revenue recognition rather than the sales method.

j. The cost of office equipment such as staplers and wastebaskets is not capitalized and depreciated because of their relative insignificance.

Problem 12-2B   *Identifying the concepts and principles violated by bad accounting practices*   *(Obj. 2, 3, 6)*

The following accounting practices are *not* in accord with generally accepted accounting principles. A few of the practices violate more than one concept or principle. Identify all the accounting concepts and principles not followed in each situation.

a. Tapes Unlimited is continuing in business, but its owner accounts for assets as though the store were liquidating.

b. Major Construction Corporation recognizes all revenue on long-term construction projects at the start of construction.

c. All amounts on the balance sheet and income statement of Business Products Inc. have been adjusted for changes in the value of the dollar during the period.

d. Baxter Grain Ltd. records one half of the depreciation of its grain silos when it purchases them and the other half over their estimated useful lives.

e. Bonnie's Boutique sells high-fashion clothing to customers on credit. Thus far, collection losses on receivables have been very small. Nevertheless, Bonnie Day, the owner, uses the collection method to recognize revenue. The entity's revenue is understated because credit sales are not accounted for properly.

f. Alvarez Importers Ltd. changed from the FIFO method to the LIFO method for inventory but did not report the accounting change in the financial statements.

g. Quebec Ironworks, Inc. applied the lower-of-cost-or-market method to account for its inventory. Quebec Ironworks used an estimate of the inventory value developed by its management. This estimate differed widely from estimates supplied by two independent appraisers. The estimates of the two appraisers were similar.

h. Butler Manufacturing Inc. does not report a lawsuit in which it is the defendant. Alvin Butler, the president, argues that the outcome of the case is uncertain and that to report the lawsuit would introduce subjective data into the financial statements.

i. Todd Sporting Goods Store records cost of goods sold in a predetermined amount each month regardless of the level of sales.

j. Tim Ihnacek is having difficulty evaluating the success of his advertising firm because he fails to separate business assets from personal assets.

Problem 12-3B *Using the installment-revenue method* **(Obj. 4)**

Penticton Construction Ltd. makes all sales on the installment basis but uses the sales method to record revenue. The company's income statements for the most recent three years are as follows:

	Year 1	Year 2	Year 3
Sales	$380,000	$404,000	$370,000
Cost of goods sold	190,000	181,800	199,800
Gross profit	190,000	222,200	170,200
Operating expenses	104,000	121,700	115,100
Net income	$ 86,000	$100,500	$ 55,100
Collections from sales of year 1	$140,000	$151,000	$ 72,000
2		143,000	209,000
3			163,000

Required

Compute the amount of net income Penticton would have reported if the company had used the installment method for revenue. Ignore the effect of uncollectible accounts and present your answer in the following format:

Installment-method net income	Year 1	Year 2	Year 3
Gross profit	$?	$?	$?
Operating expenses	104,000	121,700	115,100
Net income	$?	$?	$?

Problem 12-4B   *Accounting for construction income*   *(Obj. 4)*

Dominion Bridge Inc. constructs bridges under long-term contracts. During 19X5, Dominion began three projects that progressed according to the following schedule during 19X5, 19X6, and 19X7:

Project	Contract Price	Total Project Cost	19X5 Cost for Year	19X5 % Completed during Year	19X6 Cost for Year	19X6 % Completed during Year	19X7 Cost for Year	19X7 % Completed during Year
1	$2,400,000	$1,600,000	$1,600,000	100%	—	—	—	—
2	3,100,000	2,200,000	528,000	24	$1,672,000	76%	—	—
3	1,900,000	1,400,000	280,000	20	840,000	60	$280,000	20%

Required

1. Assume Dominion uses the completed-contract method for construction revenue. Compute the company's construction revenue and income to be reported in 19X5, 19X6, and 19X7.

2. Compute Dominion's construction revenue and income to be reported in the three years if the company uses the percentage-of-completion method.

Problem 12-5B   *Accounting for revenues and expenses according to GAAP*   *(Obj. 2, 3, 4)*

Roberta Tanaka established Tanaka Home Furnishings in January 19X7. During 19X7, 19X8, and most of 19X9, Tanaka kept the company's books and prepared its financial statements, although she had no training or experience in accounting. As a result, the accounts and statements contain numerous errors. For example, Tanaka recorded only cash receipts from customers as revenue. The sales method is appropriate for the business. She recorded inventory purchases as the cost of goods sold. When the current market value of her company's equipment increased by $6,200 in 19X7 and by $1,700 in 19X9, Tanaka debited the Equipment account and credited Revenue. She recorded no depreciation during 19X7, 19X8, and 19X9.

Late in 19X9, Tanaka employed an accountant, who determined that depreciable assets of the firm cost $150,000 on June 30, 19X7, had an expected residual value of $10,000, and a total useful life of eight years. The accountant believes the straight-line depreciation method is appropriate for Tanaka's plant capital. The company's fiscal year ends December 31. At the end of 19X9 the company's records reveal the following amounts in the accompanying table.

	19X7	19X8	19X9
Reported net income (net loss)	$ 39,300	$ (18,200)	$ 51,900
Sales	131,800	164,700	226,100
Cash collections from customers	106,500	151,300	239,600
Purchases of inventory	100,600	136,000	191,700
Ending inventory	20,800	47,400	83,700
Accrued expenses not recorded at year end; these expenses were recorded during the next year, when paid	3,800	2,700	6,800
Depreciation expense recorded	-0-	-0-	-0-
Revenue recorded for increase in the value of equipment	6,200		1,700

Required

1. Apply the concepts and principles of GAAP to compute the correct net income of Tanaka Home Furnishings for 19X7, 19X8, and 19X9.

2. How will what you have learned in this problem help you manage a business?

Problem 12-6B   *Identify and apply the underlying concepts and principles of accounting, and their relationship to the basic objective of accounting   (Obj. 1, 2, 3)*

Yknot Corporation is owned and managed by J. Dewit, president. You have been hired by Dewit as the controller and Dewit has given you a number of transactions or events as well as directions on how they should be dealt with.

For each of the following transactions you are required to respond to Dewit's directions by:

- describing how you would record the transaction
- identifying which accounting principle(s) or concept(s) is (are) applicable in recording the transaction and why
- identifying how your method helps to fulfill the basic objective of accounting "to provide information that is useful in making investment and lending decisions."

1. Yknot has purchased a very specialized machine and Dewit feels that its cost should be expensed immediately as it already has no market value due to its special design.

2. Yknot has signed a contract to provide $12,000 of services per month for the next six months. The contract calls for payment at the end of the contract and Dewit feels that the revenues should all be recorded when received as that is the only time they will have objective evidence of the revenue.

3. Yknot has purchased a four-year insurance policy which Dewit feels should be recorded as an expense immediately as the policy does not allow for any refunds if Yknot cancels or goes bankrupt.

4. Yknot is approaching the bank to apply for a loan and Dewit feels the company's balance sheet should include his personal residence as he would be prepared to sell it to pay off the loan if the company were to default.

5. Yknot is being sued by a customer for $300,000. Dewit says their lawyer refuses to speculate on their chances in court, but a number of business acquaintances have told them that he can't lose. Dewit feels the lawsuit should not be recorded because of the advice he has received and also because he will file for bankruptcy if he does lose, so nothing will be paid anyway.

6. Yknot purchased a machine at a bankruptcy sale. The machine had an appraised value of $280,000, but Yknot was able to purchase it for only $230,000. Dewit says the machine presently sells for $290,000 from a supplier and should be recorded at that value and the extra $60,000 credited to revenues due to the work he had to do to find such a bargain.

Problem 12-7B   *Identify and apply the underlying concepts and principles of accounting, and their relationship to the basic objective of accounting; allocate revenue to the appropriate period; apply the materiality constraint and the conservatism constraint to accounting   (Obj. 1, 2, 3, 4, 6)*

Give the journal entry required to *properly record* each of the following transactions. Identify any accounting concepts, principles, or constraints that influence how the transaction was recorded and describe why.

1. A company signed a contract for the construction of a building for $800,000. The contract had a penalty clause for late completion. The building was completed late (penalties of $50,000) and the company feels the building should be recorded at $800,000 with the $50,0000 charged to revenues to compensate for those lost due to its lateness.

2. A large company paid $1,500 for the purchase of a number of small tools that are expected to last for 8 years with no residual value expected at that time. The president feels that the straight-line depreciation method would be best.

3. A company has signed a contract to build a shipyard at a total cost of $3,000,000. The company will take four years to complete the job and the contract calls for annual payments of $750,000 at the beginning of each year with the balance due on completion. The company completed 30 percent of the work in the first year and the accountant feels that the sales method should be used, with all revenues recorded when the job is complete and ownership changes hands. However, the board of directors feels that the revenues should be recorded whenever the cash is received as this will make the statements comparable from period to period.

4. A company has completed a $200,000 advertising campaign this year. The president feels that the campaign was much more successful than the ones they have run in previous years and will likely affect sales for the next three years; therefore, the cost should be capitalized and amortized over the four years. The marketing manager feels that the campaign will actually provide benefits for seven years and, therefore, that is the appropriate period over which to amortize the costs.

5. A company is being sued for $500,000 by a client for product failure. The company's lawyers estimate that it will take two years to settle and cost the company $350,000. The president does not think the lawsuit should be recorded as the company is not at fault.

6. The owner of a sole proprietorship attended a week-long conference in Europe at a cost of $28,000. The conference would have only cost $6,000, but he took his family and spent an extra week. He feels it should all be expensed to the company as he would not have attended without his family and the extra time.

Challenge Problems

Problem 12-1C   *Understanding reliability and relevance*   (*Obj. 1, 2*)

The objective of financial reporting is to provide useful information for lending and investment decisions. Two characteristics that are mentioned are *relevance* and *reliability*. However, sometimes these two characteristics are in conflict. For example, real estate valued at historical cost in the financial statements is an example where financial information may be reliable but not relevant.

Required

1. What does the above statement mean by the "information may be reliable but not relevant"?
2. Explain how you think accounting theory resolves this apparent conflict.

Problem 12-2C   *Examination of the disclosure principle*   (*Obj. 5*)

Some businesspeople argue that while the disclosure principle is well and good, many of the people benefitting from the disclosure principle are "free riders." That is, they benefit from the information but do not pay for it. The businesspeople go on to argue that there is a high cost to disclosure.

Required

1. Who are the free riders referred to above? Who does bear the cost of the disclosure?
2. Some would argue that society as a whole benefits from fuller disclosure. How would that be true?

Extending Your Knowledge

Decision Problems

1. Measuring income according to GAAP   (Obj. 2, 3, 4)

Gabor Furniture Limited was founded in January 19X5 by Jon and Irene Gabor, who share the management of the business. Irene does the purchasing and manages the sales staff. Jon keeps the books and handles financial matters. The Gabors believe the store has prospered, but they are uncertain about precisely how well it has done. It is now December 31, 19X5, and they are trying to decide whether to borrow a substantial sum in order to expand the business.

They have asked your help because of your accounting knowledge. You learn that the Gabors opened the store with an initial investment of $51,000 cash and a building valued at $100,000. The cash receipts totaled $180,000, which included collections, $15,000 invested by the Gabors, $50,000 borrowed from the bank in the name of the furniture store, and $7,500 of earnings from a family inheritance. The store made credit sales of $105,000 that have not been collected at December 31. The Gabors purchased furniture inventory on credit for $160,000, and inventory at December 31, 19X5, was $75,000. The store paid $90,000 on account.

The 19X5 cash expenses were $92,000. Additional miscellaneous expenses totaled $2,700 at year's end. These expenses included the Gabors' household costs of $10,000 and interest on the business debt. The $5,000 of depreciation on the store building was omitted.

The Gabors have decided to proceed with the expansion plan only if net income for the first year was $40,000 or more. Jon's analysis of the cash account leads him to believe that net income was $49,000, so he is ready to expand. You are less certain than Jon of the wisdom of this decision primarily because the Gabors have mixed personal and business assets.

Required

1. Use a Cash T-account to show how Jon arrived at the $49,000 amount for net income.
2. Prepare the income statement of the furniture store of 19X5.
3. Should the Gabors borrow to expand their business?
4. Which accounting concept or principle is most fundamental to this problem situation?

2. Examining the disclosure principle   (Obj. 3, 5)

Consider the disclosure principle.

1. It has been suggested that the disclosure principle is perhaps one of the most important concepts and principles underlying financial reporting. Why is it so important?
2. "Disclosure of Accounting Policies," Section 1505 of the *CICA Handbook*, was added to the *Handbook* in October, 1974. Discuss the probable impact the addition of Section 1505 had on users of financial statements. Consider users before and after its introduction.
3. Accounting researchers are studying the understandability of financial statements. Why are they doing this? What contribution might their research make?
4. The text suggests that *subsequent events* and *long-term commitments* should be disclosed in the notes to the financial statements. What about these two items makes their disclosure so important to users?

5. *Financial Reporting in Canada*[5] reported that less than one in three of the companies surveyed for its 1993 edition reported the revenue principle or revenue recognition method used in preparing their financial statements. Why do you think these companies reported that information? What might we assume about the other 225 companies in the survey with respect to revenue recognition?

Ethical Issue

Some real estate companies sold land under terms that permitted low down payments by purchasers and stretched payments over many years. In many cases, the land had not yet been subdivided into the individual lots that would be sold. Also, the land often had not been landscaped. Estimating the cost of preparing the land for eventual use was difficult. Under accounting practices widespread in the 1960s and 1970s, real estate companies could record the full amount of the revenue in the year of the sale. These companies were thus able to report unusually high net incomes even though their cash collections were quite low.

Required

1. What three conditions must a company meet in order to record revenue on a sale? Which conditions did the real estate companies meet? Which conditions did they not meet?

2. Which revenue method were companies using during the 1960s and 1970s? In your opinion, was it ethical for these companies to use this method? Give your reason.

3. Which collection method is well suited for this situation? Give your reason.

Financial Statement Problems

1. Disclosure in action   (Obj. 5)

The notes to the financial statements are an integral part of the financial statements. Examine Mark's Work Wearhouse Ltd.'s financial statements in Appendix A, and answer these questions:

1. Note 1, "Significant accounting policies," is perhaps the most important of the notes; it describes the accounting policies followed in preparing the financial statements. Mark's, as a retailer, carries significant quantities of inventory. How is this inventory valued? Why is it important to disclose the basis of valuation of inventory for Mark's?

2. How does Mark's account for store opening expenses? What alternatives are there to the method Mark's uses? How will the different methods affect income? Why is it important that this information be disclosed?

3. Does Mark's have any *extraordinary items, discontinued operations, commitments* or *contingencies*? If so, describe what the notes to the financial statements say about them.

4. Does Mark's report segmented information? What do you think is the reason for this presence or absence?

2. Disclosure in action   (Obj. 5)

Obtain the annual report of an actual company of your choosing. Use the company's financial statements and related notes to answer these questions, illustrating the disclosure principle. Concentrate on the current year in the annual report you select.

---

[5] *Financial Reporting in Canada*, 1993 Twentieth edition (Toronto: CICA, 1993), p. 24.

1. Identify any unusual items, discontinued operations, effects of accounting changes, or extraordinary items reported on the income statements. Examine any notes that give additional details about these special items of income or loss. Identify their individual amounts and state whether each item increased or decreased net income.

2. What are the company's business segments? These may be reported by geographical area, by product line, or in both ways. Identify each segment's revenues and operating income or net income for the current year.

3. Examine the company's multi-year financial summary. Compute the percentage increase or decrease in total revenues over this entire period. Compute the percentage increase or decrease in net income over the same period. Which increased faster, total revenues or net income?

Comprehensive Problems for Part Two

1. Comparing two businesses

At age 25, you created a software package that is now being sold worldwide. You recently sold the business to a large company. Now you are ready to invest in a small resort property. Several locations look promising: Jekyll Island, Nova Scotia; Long Beach, Vancouver Island; and Kingsmere, Quebec. Each place has its appeal, but Jekyll Island wins out. The main allure is that prices there are low, so a dollar will stretch further. Two small resorts are available. The property owners provide the following data:

	Jekyll Island Resort	Bear Creek Hideaway
Cash	$ 34,100	$ 63,800
Accounts receivable	20,500	18,300
Inventory	74,200	68,400
Land	270,600	669,200
Buildings	1,800,000	1,960,000
Accumulated depreciation	(105,000)	(822,600)
Furniture and fixtures	750,000	933,000
Accumulated depreciation	(225,000)	(535,300)
Total assets	$2,619,400	$2,354,800
Total liabilities	$1,124,300	$1,008,500
Owner equity	1,495,100	1,346,300
Total liabilities and owner equity	$2,619,400	$2,354,800

Income statements for the last three years report total net income of $531,000 for Jekyll Island Resort and $283,000 for Bear Creek Hideaway.

Inventories Jekyll Island Resort uses the FIFO inventory method, and Bear Creek uses the LIFO method. If Jekyll Island had used LIFO, its reported inventory would have been $7,000 lower. If Bear Creek had used FIFO, its reported inventory would have been $6,000 higher. Three years ago there was little difference between LIFO and FIFO amounts for either company.

Plant Assets Jekyll Island uses the straight-line depreciation method and an estimated useful life of 30 years for buildings and 10 years for furniture and fixtures. Estimated residual values are $400,000 for buildings, and $0 for furniture and fixtures. Jekyll Island's buildings are 3 years old.

Bear Creek uses the double-declining-balance method and depreciates buildings over 30 years with an estimated residual value of $460,000. The furniture and fixtures, now 3 years old, are being depreciated over 10 years with an estimated residual value of $85,000.

Accounts Receivable   Jekyll Island uses the direct write-off method for uncollectibles. Bear Creek uses the allowance method. The Jekyll Island Resort owner estimates that $2,000 of the company's receivables are doubtful. Prior to the current year, uncollectibles were insignificant. Bear Creek's receivables are already reported at net realizable value.

Required

1. Puzzled at first by how to compare the two resorts, you decide to convert Jekyll Island Resort's balance sheet to the accounting methods and the estimated useful lives used by Bear Creek. Round all depreciation amounts to the nearest $100. The necessary revisions will not affect Jekyll Island Resort's total liabilities.

2. Convert Jekyll Island's total net income for the last three years to reflect the accounting methods used by Bear Creek. Round all depreciation amounts to the nearest $100.

3. Compare the two resorts' finances after you have revised Jekyll Island's figures, with the two resorts' finances beforehand. Which resort looked better at the outset? Which resort looks better when they are placed on equal footing?

2. Group project: refining your business plan for current assets and current liabilities

Review your business plan for an audio/video store (or other business) that you developed at the end of Part 1 (after Chapter 6). Since then, you have learned about internal controls, cash, receivables, inventories, plant assets, and current liabilities (including payrolls). Now revise your business plan to include refinements that apply to cash, receivables, inventories, plant assets, and current liabilities. Include specific internal control procedures that you will undertake to safeguard assets, to encourage employees to follow company policies, and to promote operational efficiency. If required by your instructor, prepare a presentation for class. Direct your report to the employees of your store in order to gain their support for your plan.

VIDEO CASE

CBC ◉

Many Models:
Good for Consumers, Bad for Retailers

When Henry Ford was making his Model T Fords in the early part of this century, he was quoted as saying, "Customers could have a Ford in any color they wanted as long as it was black." His company produced one model and customers bought that model or did without.

Times have changed. In recent years manufacturers have decided to cater to every possible wish that consumers might have and they are producing (and advertising) a wide range of different models of what is basically the same product. The video illustrates the point with a discussion of running/jogging/court/aerobics shoes. The widely varied choice may be wonderful for customers but it is a major headache for retailers.

Individuals might be persuaded to buy an extra pair of shoes, perhaps even two, because such a range is available. But the retailer must stock the full range available in a wide range of sizes or risk losing a sale. And then there are the 1995 models, the new and improved 1996 models, and expectations about what 1997 will bring. The retailer probably has a few 1992, 1993, and 1994 models that have not been sold.

The margin or markup on products such as athletic shoes and in-line skates varies across a range of merchandise. The margin tends to increase as the cost of the item increases. For example, the margin on a pair of plain running shoes (cost—$30.00) might be 40 percent while the margin on a pair of top-of-the-line Air Jordans (cost—$75.00) might be 60 percent.

CASE QUESTIONS

1. What problem does the video and case suggest is facing the retailer at year-end when the financial statements are being prepared?

2. A friend of Percy Williams, owner of The Athletic Sole, a store that specializes in athletic gear of all kinds, suggested Williams use FIFO by type of article (i.e., group all Nike products together) to calculate inventory. Williams has asked you for help. What response would you suggest to the advice given?

3. Would the gross margin method be appropriate for calculating closing inventory for The Athletic Sole? Why or why not?

4. Would a perpetual or periodic inventory system be appropriate? Explain your answer. What information would you include about each product?

CHAPTER 13
Accounting for Partnerships

"For my systems design practice to grow, I had to join forces with at least one other engineer," says Catherine Brown, Partner, Brown & Gaviller, Systems Design Consultants. "Forming a partnership with Russell Gaviller helped me achieve my business goals. But the partnership also raised questions I never faced when I was on my own."

Catherine Brown's systems design practice grew rapidly. After three years, the firm's revenue exceeded $130,000 and net income reached $70,000. After taking the business this far while working alone, Brown faced a tough decision. Should she continue as a sole proprietorship or incorporate the business? She decided that neither option was ideal and chose instead to take on a partner.

Brown's closest friend in engineering at the University of Waterloo, Russell Gaviller, had indicated to Brown that he was thinking of leaving Northern Telecom to go into business for himself or to work for a small consultancy practice. Together, the pair formed the partnership of Brown & Gaviller, Systems Design Consultants. Brown would work on building the business and Gaviller would concentrate on the systems design work.

The partnership form of business introduced some complexities that Brown's proprietorship had avoided. How much cash would Gaviller contribute to the business? He was buying into the client base developed by Brown. How should the partners divide profits and losses? How should a partner who leaves the firm be compensated for his or her share of the business? Brown and Gaviller had to iron out these and many other details.

CHAPTER OBJECTIVES

After studying this chapter, you should be able to

1 Identify the characteristics of a partnership

2 Account for partners' initial investments in a partnership

3 Allocate profits and losses to the partners by different methods

4 Account for the admission of a new partner to the business

5 Account for the withdrawal of a partner from the business

6 Account for the liquidation of a partnership

7 Prepare partnership financial statements

A **partnership** is an association of two or more persons who co-own a business for profit. This definition is common to the various provincial partnership acts which tend to prescribe similar rules with respect to the organization and operation of partnerships in their jurisdiction.

Forming a partnership is easy. It requires no permission from government authorities and involves no legal procedures, with the exception that most provinces require most partnerships to register information such as the name of the partners and the name under which the business will be carried on.[1] When two persons decide to go into business together, a partnership is automatically formed.

A partnership brings together the capital, talents, and experience of the partners. Business opportunities closed to an individual may open up to a partnership. Suppose neither Brown nor Gaviller has enough capital individually to buy a small building for an office. They may be able to afford it together in a partnership. Or they may pool their talents and know-how. Their partnership may offer a fuller range of systems design services than either person could offer alone.

Partnerships come in all sizes. Many partnerships have fewer than ten partners. Some physicians may have ten or more partners while some of the largest law firms in Canada have more than 130 partners.[2] The largest CA firms in Canada have from 270 to more than 650 partners.[3] Exhibit 13-1 lists the 10 largest public accounting firms in Canada.

EXHIBIT 13-1   *The Ten Largest Accounting Partnerships in Canada*

Rank 1993	Firm	1993 Revenue Millions
1	KPMG Peat Marwick Thorne	$475
2	Deloitte & Touche	409
3	Ernst & Young	381
4	Coopers & Lybrand	269
5	Price Waterhouse	240
6	Doane Raymond Grant Thornton	202
7	Arthur Andersen & Co.	193
8	BDO Dunwoody Ward Mallette	186
9	Richter Usher & Vineberg	45
10	Collins Barrow	29

Source: *The Financial Post 500* (Toronto: The Financial Post Company, 1994).

[1] Smyth, J.E., D.A. Soberman, and A.J. Easson, *The Law and Business Administration in Canada*, 6th edition (Scarborough: Prentice Hall Canada Inc., 1991), p. 756.
[2] *The Financial Post 500*, 1994 (Toronto: The Financial Post Company, 1994), p. 152.
[3] *Ibid.*, p. 148.

Characteristics of a Partnership _____

Starting a partnership is voluntary. A person cannot be forced to join a partnership, and partners cannot be forced to accept another person as a partner. Although the partnership agreement may be oral, a written agreement between the partners reduces the chance of a misunderstanding. The following characteristics distinguish partnerships from sole proprietorships and from corporations.

The Written Partnership Agreement

A business partnership is like a marriage. To be successful, the partners must cooperate. However, business partners do not vow to remain together for life. Business partnerships come and go. To make certain that each partner fully understands how a particular partnership operates and to lower the chances that any partner might misunderstand how the business is run, partners may draw up a **partnership agreement**. This agreement is a contract between the partners, so transactions involving the agreement are governed by contract law. The provincial legislatures in Canada have passed their respective versions of a partnership act, the terms of which apply in the absence of a partnership agreement or in the absence of particular matters in the partnership agreement.[4]

The partnership agreement should make the following points clear:

1. Name, location, and nature of the business
2. Name, capital investment, and duties of each partner
3. Method of sharing profits and losses by the partners
4. Withdrawals allowed to the partners
5. Procedures for settling disputes between the partners
6. Procedures for admitting new partners
7. Procedures for settling up with a partner who withdraws from the business
8. Procedures for liquidating the partnership: selling the assets, paying the liabilities, and disbursing any remaining cash to the partners

As partners enter and leave the business, the old partnership is dissolved and a new partnership is formed. Drawing up a new agreement for each new partnership may be expensive and time-consuming.

Limited Life

A partnership has a life limited by the length of time that all partners continue to own the business. When a partner withdraws from the business, that partnership ceases to exist. A new partnership may emerge to continue the same business, but the old partnership has been *dissolved*. **Dissolution** is the ending of a partnership. Likewise, the addition of a new partner dissolves the old partnership and creates a new partnership.

Mutual Agency

Mutual agency in a partnership means that every partner can bind the business to a contract within the scope of the partnership's regular business operations. If Russell Gaviller enters into a contract with a person or another business to provide service, then the firm of Brown & Gaviller—not only Gaviller—is bound to provide

---

[4] Smyth, J.E., D.A. Soberman, and A.J. Easson, *The Law and Business Administration in Canada*, 6th edition. (Scarborough: Prentice Hall Canada Inc., 1991), pp. 744–56.

that service. However, if Gaviller signs a contract to purchase lawn services for his home, however, the partnership would not be bound to pay. Contracting for personal services does not fall within the partnership's regular business operations.

Unlimited Liability

Each partner has an **unlimited personal liability** for the debts of the partnership. When a partnership cannot pay its debts with business assets, the partners must use their personal assets to meet the debt.

Suppose the Brown & Gaviller firm had an unsuccessful year, and the partnership's liabilities exceed its assets by $20,000. Brown and Gaviller must pay this amount with their personal assets. Because each partner has *unlimited liability*, if a partner is unable to pay his or her part of the debt, the other partner (or partners) must make payment. If Gaviller can pay only $5,000 of the liability, Brown must pay $15,000.

Unlimited liability and mutual agency are closely related. A dishonest partner or a partner with poor judgment may commit the partnership to a contract under which the business loses money. In turn, creditors may force *all* the partners to pay the debt from their personal assets. Hence, a business partner should be chosen with great care.

Partners can avoid unlimited personal liability for partnership obligations by forming a *limited partnership*. In this form of business organization, one or more of the general partners assumes the unlimited liability for business debts. In addition, there is another class of owners, limited partners, who can lose only as much as their investment in the business. In this sense, limited partners, have limited liability similar to the limited liability that shareholders in a corporation have.

Co-ownership of Property

Any asset—cash, inventory, machinery, and so on—that a partner invests into the partnership becomes the joint property of all the partners. Also, each partner has a claim to the business's profits.

No Partnership Income Taxes

A partnership pays no income tax on its business income. Instead, the net income of the partnership is divided, and becomes the taxable income of the partners. Suppose Brown & Gaviller earned net income of $150,000, shared equally by partners Brown and Gaviller. Brown & Gaviller would pay no income tax *as a business entity*. However, Brown and Gaviller would pay income tax as individuals on their $75,000 shares of partnership income.

Partner's Owner's Equity Accounts

Accounting for a partnership is much like accounting for a proprietorship. We record buying and selling, collecting, and paying in a partnership just as we do for a business with only one owner. But, because a partnership has more than one owner, the partnership must have more than one owner's equity account. Every partner in the business—whether the firm has two or two hundred partners—has an individual owner's equity account. Often these accounts carry the name of the particular partner and the word *capital*. For example, the owner's equity account for Russell Gaviller would read "Gaviller, Capital." Similarly, each partner has a withdrawal account. If the number of partners is large, the general ledger may contain the single account Partners' Capital or Owners' Equity. A subsidiary ledger can be used for individual partner accounts. Exhibit 13-2 lists the advantages and disadvantages of partnerships (compared to proprietorships and corporations).

EXHIBIT 13-2 *Advantages and Disadvantages of Partnerships*

Concept Highlight

Partnership Advantages	Partnership Disadvantages
Versus Proprietorships:	
1. Can raise more capital.	1. Partnership agreement may be difficult to formulate. Each time a new partner is admitted or a partner withdraws, the business needs a new partnership agreement.
2. Brings together the expertise of more than one person	
3. 1+1>2 in a good partnership. If they work well together, the partners can achieve more than by working alone.	2. Relationships among partners may be fragile.
Versus Corporations:	3. Mutual agency and unlimited personal liability create personal obligations for each partner.
4. Less expensive to organize than a corporation which requires articles of incorporation from a province of the federal government.	
5. No taxation of partnership income which is taxed to the partners as individuals.	

Initial Investments by Partners

OBJECTIVE 2
Account for partners' initial investments in a partnership

Let's see how to account for the multiple owner's equity accounts—and learn how they appear on the balance sheet—by looking at how to account for starting up a partnership.

Partners in a new partnership may invest assets and liabilities in the business. These contributions are entered in the books by recording the assets and liabilities, in the same way as corporations and proprietorships record them, at their agreed-upon values. Subtracting each person's liabilities from his or her assets yields the amount to be credited to the owner's equity account for that person. The partners may hire an independent firm to appraise their assets and liabilities at current market value at the time a partnership is formed. This outside evaluation assures an objective valuation for what each partner brings into the business.

Assume Karen Benz and Chris Hanna form a partnership to manufacture and sell computer software. The partners agree on the following values based on an independent appraisal:

Benz's contributions

- Cash, $10,000; inventory, $70,000; and accounts payable, $85,000
- Accounts receivable, $30,000, less allowance for doubtful accounts of $5,000
- Computer equipment: cost, $600,00; market value, $450,000

Hanna's contributions

- Cash, $5,000
- Computer software: cost, $18,000; market value, $100,000

Benz's investment

June	1	Cash	10,000	
		Accounts Receivable	30,000	
		Inventory	70,000	
		Computer Equipment	450,000	
		Allowance for Doubtful Accounts		5,000
		Accounts Payable		85,000
		Benz, Capital		470,000
		To record Benz's investment in the partnership.		

Key Point:
The major difference in accounting for a proprietorship versus a partnership is the number of capital and drawing accounts. The partnership balance sheet shows a separate capital account for each partner, and there is a separate drawing account for each partner. The asset and liability sections on the balance sheet and the income statement are the same for a proprietorship and a partnership.

Hanna's investment

June	1	Cash	5,000	
		Computer Software	100,000	
		Hanna, Capital...		105,000
		To record Hanna's investment in the partnership.		

The initial partnership balance sheet reports these amounts as shown in Exhibit 13-3.

EXHIBIT 13-3 *Partnership Balance Sheet*

Benz and Hanna
Balance Sheet
June 1, 19X5

Assets			Liabilities	
Cash................................		$ 15,000	Accounts payable....................	$ 85,000
Accounts receivable..... $30,000				
Less: Allowance for				
doubtful accounts....	5,000	25,000	**Capital**	
Inventory		70,000	Benz, capital.............................	470,000
Computer equipment .		450,000	Hanna, capital..........................	105,000
Computer software		100,000	Total capital..............................	575,000
Total assets...................		$660,000	Total liabilities	
			and capital...........................	$660,000

OBJECTIVE 3
Allocate profits and losses to the partners by different methods

Sharing Partnership Profits and Losses

How to allocate profits and losses among partners is one of the most challenging aspects of managing a partnership. If the partners have not drawn up an agreement, or if the agreement does not state how the partners will divide profits and losses, then, by law, the partners must share profits and losses equally. If the agreement specifies a method for sharing profits but not losses, then losses are shared in the same proportion as profits. For example, a partner receiving 75 percent of the profits would likewise absorb 75 percent of any losses.

In some cases, an equal division is not fair. One partner may perform more work for the business than the other partner, or one partner may make a larger capital contribution. In the preceding example, Chris Hanna might agree to work longer hours for the partnership than Karen Benz in order to earn a greater share of profits. Benz could argue that she should receive more of the profits because she contributed more net assets ($470,000) than Hanna did ($105,000). Hanna might contend that his computer software program is the partnership's most important asset, and that his share of the profits should be greater than Benz's share. Arriving at fair sharing of profits and losses in a partnership may be difficult. We now discuss the options available in determining partners' shares.

Sharing Based on a Stated Fraction

Partners may agree to any profit-and-loss-sharing method they desire. Suppose the partnership agreement of Sarah Cagle and Bill Elias allocates two thirds of the business profits and losses to Cagle and one third to Elias. If net income for the year is $90,000, and all revenue and expense accounts have been closed, the Income Summary account has a credit balance of $90,000:

Income Summary

	Bal.	90,000

The entry to close this account and allocate the profit to the partners' capital accounts is

Dec. 31	Income Summary..	90,000	
	Cagle, Capital ($90,000 × ⅔).........................		60,000
	Elias, Capital ($90,000 × ⅓).........................		30,000
	To allocate net income to partners.		

Consider the effect of this entry. Does Cagle get cash of $60,000 and Elias cash of $30,000? No. The increase in the capital accounts of the partners cannot be linked to any particular asset, including cash. Instead, the entry indicates that Cagle's ownership in all the assets of the business increased by $60,000 and Elias's by $30,000.

If the year's operations resulted in a net loss of $66,000, the Income Summary account would have a debit balance of $66,000. In that case, the closing entry to allocate the loss to the partners' capital accounts would be

Dec. 31	Cagle, Capital ($66,000 × ⅔).........................	44,000	
	Elias, Capital ($66,000 × ⅓)	22,000	
	Income Summary....................................		66,000
	To allocate net loss to partners.		

Sharing Based on Capital Contributions

Profits and losses are often allocated in proportion to the partners' capital contributions in the business. Suppose Jim Antoine, Erica Barber, and Tony Culomovic are partners in ABC Company. Their capital accounts have the following balances at the end of the year, before the closing entries:

Antoine, Capital	$ 40,000
Barber, Capital	60,000
Culomovic, Capital	50,000
Total capital balances...	$150,000

Assume that the partnership earned a profit of $120,000 for the year. To allocate this amount based on capital contributions, each partner's percentage share of the partnership's total capital balance must be computed. We simply divide each partner's capital by the total capital amount. These figures, multiplied by the $120,000 profit amount, yield each partner's share of the year's profits:

Antoine:	($40,000/$150,000) × $120,000	=	$ 32,000
Barber:	($60,000/$150,000) × $120,000	=	48,000
Culomovic:	($50,000/$150,000) × $120,000	=	40,000
	Net income allocated to partners	=	$120,000

The closing entry to allocate the profit to the partners' capital accounts is

Dec. 31	Income Summary	120,000	
	Antoine, Capital		32,000
	Barber, Capital		48,000
	Culomovic, Capital................................		40,000
	To allocate net income to partners.		

After this closing entry, the partners' capital balances are

Antoine, Capital ($40,000 + $32,000)	$ 72,000
Barber, Capital ($60,000 + $48,000)	108,000
Culomovic, Capital ($50,000 + $40,000)	90,000
Total capital balances after allocation of net income......................	$270,000

Short Exercise:

Ash, Black, and Cole share profits in a 30:40:30 ratio. Compute each partner's share of net income if the partnership income is $50,000.

A:

Ash:
($50,000 × 30%) = $15,000
Black:
($50,000 × 40%) =   20,000
Cole:
($50,000 × 30%) =   15,000
                     $50,000

Short Exercise:

Ash, Black, and Cole share profits on the basis of capital account balances of $10,000, $20,000, and $70,000, respectively. Compute each partner's share of net income if the partnership net income is $50,000.

A:

Ash:
($10,000/$100,000 ×
        $50,000) = $5,000
Black:
($20,000/$100,000 ×
        $50,000) =   10,000
Cole:
($70,000/$100,000 ×
        $50,000) =   35,000
                     $50,000

Short Exercise:

Ash, Black, and Cole have capital balances of $10,000, $20,000, and $70,000, respectively. The partners share profits and losses as follows: (1) The first $25,000 is allocated on the basis of partners' capital balances. (2) The next $19,000 is allocated on the basis of service, with Ash, Black, and Cole receiving $5,000, $6,000, and $8,000, respectively. (3) The remainder is divided equally.

Compute each partner's share of net income if the partnership earns $50,000.

A:

Ash:
($10,000/$100,000 ×
$25,000) + $5,000
+ $2,000*

= $9,500

Black:
($20,000/$100,000 ×
$25,000) + $6,000
+ $2,000*

= $13,000

Cole:
($70,000/$100,000 ×
$25,000) + $8,000
+ $2,000*

= $27,500

*Remainder shared equally:
($50,000 − $25,000 − $19,000 =
$6,000)

Sharing Based on Capital Contributions and on Service

One partner, regardless of his or her capital contribution, may put more work into the business than the other partners. Even among partners who log equal service time, one person's superior experience and knowledge may command a greater share of income. To reward the harder-working or more valuable person, the profit-and-loss-sharing method may be based on a combination of contributed capital *and* service to the business. Most law firms take service into account in determining partner compensation.

Assume Sheila Randolph and Carolyn Scott formed a partnership in which Randolph invested $60,000 and Scott invested $40,000, a total of $100,000. Scott devotes more time to the partnership and earns the larger salary. Accordingly, the two partners have agreed to share profits as follows:

1. The first $50,000 of partnership profits is to be allocated based on partners' capital contributions to the business.

2. The next $60,000 of profits is to be allocated based on service, with Randolph allocated $24,000 and Scott allocated $36,000.

3. Any remaining amount is allocated equally.

If net income for the first year is $125,000, the partners' shares of this profit are computed as follows:

	Randolph	Scott	Total
Total net income			$125,000
Sharing of first $50,000 of net income, based on capital contributions:			
Randolph ($60,000/$100,000 × $50,000)	$30,000		
Scott ($40,000/$100,000 × $50,000)		$20,000	
Total			50,000
Net income remaining for allocation			75,000
Sharing of next $60,000, based on service:			
Randolph	24,000		
Scott		36,000	
Total			60,000
Net income left for allocation			15,000
Remainder shared equally:			
Randolph ($15,000 × ½)	7,500		
Scott ($15,000 × ½)		7,500	
Total			15,000
Net income left for allocation			$ -0-
Net income allocated to the partners	$61,500	$63,500	$125,000

On the basis of this allocation, the closing entry is

Dec. 31	Income Summary	125,000	
	Randolph, Capital		61,500
	Scott, Capital		63,500
	To allocate net income to partners.		

Sharing Based on Salaries and Interest

Partners may be rewarded for their service and their capital contributions to the business in other ways. In one sharing plan, the partners are allocated salaries plus interest on their capital balances. Assume Edward Massey and Pierre Vanier form an oil-exploration partnership. At the beginning of the year, their capital balances are $80,000 and $100,000 respectively. The partnership agreement allocates annual salary of $43,000 to Massey and $35,000 to Vanier. After salaries are allocated, each partner earns 8 percent interest on his beginning capital balance. Any remaining net income is divided equally. Partnership profit of $96,000 will be allocated as follows:

	Massey	Vanier	Total
Total net income...			$96,000
First, salaries:			
Massey	$43,000		
Vanier		$35,000	
Total..			78,000
Net income remaining for allocation			18,000
Second, interest on beginning capital balances:			
Massey ($80,000 × .08)..	6,400		
Vanier ($100,000 × .08)		8,000	
Total..			14,400
Net income remaining for allocation			3,600
Third, remainder shared equally:			
Massey ($3,600 × ½)	1,800		
Vanier ($3,600 × ½)		1,800	
Total..			3,600
Net income remaining for allocation			$ -0-
Net income allocated to the partners......................	$51,200	$44,800	$96,000

Based on this allocation, the closing entry is

Dec. 31	Income Summary...	96,000	
	Massey, Capital...		51,200
	Vanier, Capital..		44,800
	To allocate net income to partners.		

In the preceding illustration, net income exceeded the sum of salary and interest. If the partnership profit is less than the allocated sum of salary and interest, a negative remainder will occur at some stage in the allocation process. Even so, the partners use the same method for allocation purposes. For example, assume that Massey and Vanier Partnership earned only $82,000:

	Massey	Vanier	Total
Total net income..			$82,000
First, salaries:			
Massey	$43,000		
Vanier		$35,000	
Total...			78,000
Net income remaining for allocation......................			4,000
Second, interest on beginning capital balances:			
Massey ($80,000 × .08)..	6,400		
Vanier ($100,000 × .08)		8,000	
Total...			14,400
Net income remaining for allocation......................			(10,400)
Third, remainder shared equally:			
Massey ($10,400 × ½)	(5,200)		
Vanier ($10,400 × ½)		(5,200)	
Total...			(10,400)
Net income remaining for allocation......................			$ -0-
Net income allocated to the partners......................	$44,200	$37,800	$82,000

Short Exercise:

Ash, Black, and Cole have capital balances of $10,000, $20,000, and $70,000, respectively. The partners share profits and losses as follows: (1) Ash and Cole receive salaries of $6,000 and $7,000, respectively. (2) Interest of 10% is paid on the capital balances. (3) The remainder is divided equally.

Compute each partner's share of net income if the partnership earns $50,000.

A:

Ash:
$6,000 + (10% × $10,000) + $9,000* = $16,000

Black: (10% × $20,000) + $9,000* = $11,000

Cole: $7,000 + (10% × $70,000) + $9,000* = $23,000

*Remainder = [$50,000 – $6,000 – $7,000 – (10% × $100,000)] = $27,000

A net loss would be allocated to Massey and Vanier in the same manner outlined for net income. The sharing procedure would begin with the net loss, and then allocate salary, interest, and any other specified amounts to the partners.

STOP & THINK

Are these salaries and interest amounts business expenses in the usual sense? Explain your answer.

Answer: No, partners do not work for their own business to earn a salary, as an employee does. They do not loan money to their own business to earn interest. Their goal is for the partnership to earn a profit. Therefore, salaries and interest in partnership agreements are simply ways of expressing the allocation of profits and losses to the partners. For example, the salary component of partner income rewards service to the partnership. The interest component rewards a partner's investment of cash or other assets in the business. But the partners' salary and interest amounts are *not* salary expense and interest expense in the partnership's accounting or tax records.

We see that partners may allocate profits and losses based on a stated fraction, contributed capital, service, interest on capital, or any combination of these factors. Each partnership shapes its profit-and-loss-sharing ratio to fit its own needs.

Partner Drawings

Like anyone else, partners need cash for personal living expenses. Partnership agreements usually allow partners to withdraw cash or other assets from the business. Drawings from a partnership are recorded exactly as for a proprietorship. Assume that both Edward Massey and Pierre Vanier are allowed a monthly withdrawal of $3,500. The partnership records the March withdrawal with this entry:

Mar. 31	Massey, Drawing	3,500	
	Vanier, Drawing	3,500	
	Cash		7,000
	Monthly partner withdrawals.		

Real-World Example:
According to the *Income Tax Act*, partners are taxed on their share of partnership income, not on the amount of their withdrawals.

During the year, each partner's drawing account accumulates 12 such amounts, a total of $42,000 ($3,500 × 12). At the end of the period, the general ledger shows the following account balances immediately after net income has been closed to the partners' capital accounts. Assume these beginning balances for Massey and Vanier at the start of the year, and that $82,000 of profit has been allocated on the basis of the preceding illustration.

Massey, Capital			**Vanier, Capital**	
	Jan. 1 Bal. 80,000			Jan. 1 Bal. 100,000
	Dec. 31 Net inc. 44,200			Dec. 31 Net inc. 37,800

Massey, Drawing			**Vanier, Drawing**	
Dec. 31 Bal. 42,000			Dec. 31 Bal. 42,000	

The withdrawal accounts must be closed at the end of the period, as must be done for a proprietorship. The closing entry credits each partner's capital account and debits each capital account.

Admission of a Partner — *Stop here*

OBJECTIVE 4
Account for the admission of a new partner to the business

A partnership lasts only as long as its partners remain in the business. The addition of a new member or the withdrawal of an existing member dissolves the partnership. We turn now to a discussion of how partnerships dissolve—and how new partnerships arise.

Often a new partnership is formed to carry on the former partnership's business. In fact, the new partnership may choose to retain the dissolved partnership's name. Ernst & Young, for example, is an accounting firm from which partners retire, and which admits new partners during the year. Thus the former partnership dissolves and a new partnership begins many times. The business, however, retains the name and continues operations. Other partnerships may dissolve and then re-form under a new name. Let us look now at the ways that a new member may gain admission into an existing partnership.

Admission by Purchasing a Partner's Interest

A person may become a member of a partnership by gaining the approval of the other partner (or partners) for entrance into the firm, *and* by purchasing a present partner's interest in the business. Let us assume that Stephi Fisher and Carlo Levesque have a partnership that carries these figures:

Cash	$ 40,000	Total liabilities	$120,000
Other assets	360,000	Fisher, capital	110,000
		Levesque, capital	170,000
		Total liabilities	
Total assets	$400,000	and capital	$400,000

Business is going so well that Fisher receives an offer from Linda Dynak, an outside party, to buy her $110,000 interest in the business for $150,000. Fisher agrees to sell out to Dynak, and Levesque approves Dynak as a new partner. The firm records the transfer of capital interest in the business with this entry:

Apr. 16	Fisher, Capital		110,000	
	Dynak, Capital			110,000
	To transfer Fisher's equity in the business to Dynak.			

The debit side of the entry closes Fisher's capital account because she is no longer a partner in the firm. The credit side opens Dynak's capital account because Fisher's equity has been transferred to Dynak. The entry amount is Fisher's capital balance ($110,000) and not the $150,000 price that Dynak paid Fisher to buy into the business. The full $150,000 goes to Fisher, including the $40,000 difference between her capital balance and the price received from Dynak. In this example, the partnership receives no cash because the transaction was between Dynak and Fisher, not between Dynak and the partnership. Suppose Dynak pays Fisher less than Fisher's capital balance. That does not affect the entry on the partnership books. Fisher's equity is transferred to Dynak at book value ($110,000).

The old partnership has dissolved. Levesque and Dynak draw up a new partnership agreement, with a new profit-and-loss-sharing ratio, and continue business operations. If Levesque does not accept Dynak as a partner, the Fisher and Levesque partnership would be dissolved, and Dynak would be precluded from buying Fisher's interest.

Short Exercise:

Ted and Fred are partners with capital balances of $16,000 and $24,000, respectively. Profits and losses are shared on the basis of capital balances. Ann offers Fred $60,000 for his interest in the business. What is the entry to record the transfer of capital?

A:

Fred, Capital 24,000
  Ann, Capital 24,000

Admission by Investing in the Partnership

As Russell Gaviller did in our opening story, a person may also be admitted as a partner by investing directly in the partnership rather than by purchasing an existing

Short Exercise:

Ted and Fred are partners with capital balances of $16,000 and $24,000, respectively. Profits and losses are shared on the basis of capital balances. Ted and Fred admit Jill to a 20% interest with a $12,000 investment. What is the entry to record Jill's admission to the partnership:

A:

Cash..................12,000
  Jill, Capital   10,400
  Ted, Capital   640
  Fred, Capital   960
Jill: $10,400 = ($16,000
    + $24,000 + $12,000)
    × 0.2
Ted: $640
    = $16,000/$40,000
    × ($12,000 − $10,400)
Fred: $960
    = $24,000/$40,000
    × ...($12,000
    − $10,400)

partner's interest. The new partner contributes assets—for example, cash, inventory, or equipment—to the business. Assume that the partnership of Robin Ingel and Michael Jay has the following assets, liabilities, and capital:

Cash.....................................	$ 20,000	Total liabilities....................	$100,000
Other assets	240,000	Ingel, capital.......................	70,000
		Jay, capital...........................	90,000
		Total liabilities	
Total assets....................	$260,000	and capital....................	$260,000

Laureen Kahn offers to invest equipment and land (Other assets) with a market value of $80,000 to persuade the existing partners to take her into the business. Ingel and Jay agree to dissolve the existing partnership and to start up a new business, giving Kahn one-third interest—($70,000 + $90,000 + $80,000)/$80,000 = 3—in exchange for the contributed assets. The entry to record Kahn's investment is

July 18	Other Assets	80,000	
	Kahn, Capital................................		80,000
	To admit L. Kahn as a partner with a		
	one-third interest in the business.		

After this entry, the partnership books show:

Cash.....................................	$ 20,000	Total liabilities	$100,000
Other assets		Ingel, capital	70,000
($240,000 + $80,000)......	320,000	Jay, capital	90,000
		Kahn, capital.......................	80,000
		Total liabilities	
Total assets....................	$340,000	and capital	$340,000

Kahn's one-third interest in the partnership does not necessarily entitle her to one third of the profits. The sharing of profits and losses is a separate consideration in the partnership agreement.

Admission by Investing in the Partnership—Bonus to the Old Partners

The more successful a partnership, the higher the payment the partners may demand from a person entering the business. Partners in a business that is doing quite well might require an incoming person to pay them a bonus. The bonus increases the current partners' capital accounts.

Suppose that Hiro Nagasawa and Lisa Schwende's partnership has earned above-average profits for ten years. The two partners share profits and losses equally. The balance sheet carries these figures:

Cash	$ 40,000	Total liabilities...................	$100,000
Other assets.......................	210,000	Nagasawa, capital	70,000
		Schwende, capital.............	80,000
		Total liabilities	
Total assets	$250,000	and capital...................	$250,000

The partners agree to admit Alan Parker to a one-fourth interest with his cash investment of $90,000. Parker's capital balance on the partnership books is $60,000, computed as follows:

Partnership capital before Parker is admitted ($70,000 + $80,000)	$150,000
Parker's investment in the partnership	90,000
Partnership capital after Parker is admitted	$240,000
Parker's capital in the partnership ($240,000 × ¼)	$ 60,000

The entry on the partnership books to record Parker's investment is

Mar. 1	Cash	90,000	
	Parker, Capital		60,000
	Nagasawa, Capital ($30,000 × ½)		15,000
	Schwende, Capital ($30,000 × ½)		15,000
	To admit A. Parker as a partner with a one-fourth interest in the business.		

Parker's capital account is credited for his one-fourth interest in the partnership. The other partners share the $30,000 difference between Parker's investment ($90,000) and his equity in the business ($60,000). This difference is called a *bonus*. It is accounted for as income to the old partners and is, therefore, allocated to them based on their profit-and-loss ratio.

The new partnership's balance sheet reports these amounts:

Cash ($40,000 + $90,000)	$130,000	Total liabilities		$100,000
Other assets	210,000	Nagasawa, capital ($70,000 + $15,000)		85,000
		Schwende, capital ($80,000 + $15,000)		95,000
		Parker, capital		60,000
Total assets	$340,000	Total liabilities and capital		$340,000

Admission by Investing in the Partnership—Bonus to the New Partner

A potential new partner may be so important that the existing partners offer him or her a partnership share that includes a bonus. A law firm may strongly desire a former premier, cabinet minister, or other official as a partner because of the person's reputation. A restaurant owner may want to go into partnership with a famous sports personality like Lanny MacDonald or a singer like k.d. lang.

Suppose Jenny Page and Miko Osuka have a law partnership. The firm's balance sheet appears as follows:

Cash	$140,000	Total liabilities	$120,000
Other assets	360,000	Page, capital	230,000
		Osuka, capital	150,000
Total assets	$500,000	Total liabilities and capital	$500,000

The partners admit Martin Schiller, a former attorney general, as a partner with a one-third interest in exchange for his cash investment of $100,000. At the time of Schiller's admission, the firm's capital is $380,000—Page, $230,000 and Osuka, $150,000. Page and Osuka share profits and losses in the ratio of two thirds to Page and one third to Osuka. The computation of Schiller's equity in the partnership is

Partnership capital before Schiller is admitted ($230,000 + $150,000)	$380,000
Schiller's investment in the partnership	100,000
Partnership capital after Schiller is admitted	$480,000
Schiller's capital in the partnership ($480,000 × ⅓)	$160,000

The capital accounts of Page and Osuka are debited for the $60,000 difference between the new partner's equity ($160,000) and his investment ($100,000). The existing partners share this decrease in capital, which is accounted for as though it were a loss, based on their profit-and-loss ratio. The entry to record Schiller's investment is

Short Exercise:

Ted and Fred are partners with capital balances of $16,000 and $24,000, respectively. They share profits and losses in a 4:6 ratio. Ted and Fred admit Lana to a 20% interest with an $8,000 investment. What is the entry to record Lana's admission as a new partner?

A:

Cash	8,000	
Ted, Capital	640	
Fred, Capital	960	
Lana, Capital		9,600

Ted:
$640 = ($9,600 − $8,000) × 0.4

Fred: $960 = ($9,600 − $8,000) × 0.6

Lana: $9,600 = ($16,000 + $24,000 + $8,000) × 0.2

Aug. 24	Cash	100,000	
	Page, Capital ($60,000 × ⅔)	40,000	
	Osuka, Capital ($60,000 × ⅓)	20,000	
	Schiller, Capital		160,000
	To admit M. Schiller as a partner with a		
	one-third interest in the business.		

The new partnership's balance sheet reports these amounts:

Cash			Total liabilities....................	$120,000
($140,000 + $100,000) ...	$240,000		Page, capital	
Other assets........................	360,000		($230,000 – $40,000)......	190,000
			Osuka, capital	
			($150,000 – $20,000)......	130,000
			Schiller, capital..................	160,000
			Total liabilities	
Total assets	$600,000		and capital......................	$600,000

Withdrawal of a Partner

OBJECTIVE 5

Account for the withdrawal of a partner from the busiess

A partner may withdraw from the business for many reasons, including retirement or a dispute with the other partners. The withdrawal of a partner dissolves the old partnership. The partnership agreement should contain a provision to govern how to settle with a withdrawing partner. In the simplest case, as illustrated on p. 637, a partner may withdraw and sell his or her interest to another partner in a personal transaction. The only entry needed to record this transfer of equity debits the withdrawing partner's capital account and credits the purchaser's capital account. The dollar amount of the entry is the capital balance of the withdrawing partner, regardless of the price paid by the purchaser. The accounting when one current partner buys a second partner's interest is the same as when an outside party buys a current partner's interest.

If the partner withdraws in the middle of the accounting period, the partnership books should be updated to determine the withdrawing partner's capital balance. The business must measure net income or net loss for the fraction of the year up to the withdrawal date, and allocate profit or loss according to the existing ratio. After the books have been closed, the business then accounts for the change in partnership capital.

The withdrawing partner may receive his or her share of the business in partnership assets other than cash. The question then arises of what value to assign the partnership assets: book value or current market value. The settlement procedure may specify that an independent appraisal of the assets to determine their current market value. If market values have changed, the appraisal will result in a revaluing of the partnership assets. Thus the partners share in any market value changes that their efforts caused.

Suppose Ben Isaac is retiring in midyear from the partnership of Green, Maslowski, and Isaac. After the books have been adjusted for partial-period income but before the asset appraisal, revaluation, and closing entries, the balance sheet reports:

Cash...		$ 39,000	Total liabilities.........................	$ 80,000
Inventory....................................		44,000	Green, capital...........................	54,000
Land		55,000	Maslowski, capital	43,000
Building..................	$95,000		Isaac, capital...........................	21,000
Less: Accumulated				
depreciation........	35,000	60,000	Total liabilities	
Total assets..........		$198,000	and capital.........................	$198,000

An independent appraiser revalues the inventory at $38,000 (down from $44,000), and the land at $101,000 (up from $55,000). The partners share the differences between these assets' market values and their prior book values based on their profit-and-loss ratio. The partnership agreement has allocated one fourth of the profits to Green, one half to Maslowski, and one fourth to Isaac. (This ratio may be written 1:2:1 for one part to Green, two parts to Maslowski, and one part to Isaac.) For each share that Green or Isaac has, Maslowski has two. The entries to record the revaluation of the inventory and land are

June 30	Green, Capital ($6,000 × ¼).................................	1,500	
	Maslowski, Capital ($6,000 × ½)	3,000	
	Isaac, Capital ($6,000 × ¼).................................	1,500	
	Inventory ($44,000 – $38,000)		6,000
	To revalue the inventory and allocate the loss in value to the partners.		
30	Land ($101,000 – $55,000)	46,000	
	Green, Capital ($46,000 × ¼)........................		11,500
	Maslowski, Capital ($46,000 × ½)		23,000
	Isaac, Capital ($46,000 × ¼).........................		11,500
	To revalue the land and allocate the gain in value to the partners.		

After the revaluations, the partnership balance sheet reports:

Cash	$ 39,000	Total liabilities.........................	$ 80,000
Inventory...............................	38,000	Green, capital ($54,000 –	
Land	101,000	$1,500 + $11,500)	64,000
Building.................... $95,000		Maslowski, capital ($43,000 –	
Less: Accumulated		$3,000 + $23,000)	63,000
depreciation... 35,000	60,000	Isaac, capital ($21,000 –	
		$1,500 + $11,500)	31,000
		Total liabilities	
Total assets....................	$238,000	and capital	$238,000

The books now carry the assets at current market value, which becomes the new book value; the capital accounts have been adjusted accordingly. Isaac has a claim to $31,000 in partnership assets. How is his withdrawal from the business accounted for?

Withdrawal at Book Value

If Ben Isaac withdraws by taking cash equal to the book value of his owner's equity, the entry would be

June 30	Isaac, Capital..	31,000	
	Cash		31,000
	To record withdrawal of B. Isaac from the partnership.		

This entry records the payment of partnership cash to Isaac and the closing of his capital account upon withdrawal from the business.

Withdrawal at Less Than Book Value

The withdrawing partner may be so eager to leave the business that he or she is willing to take less than his or her equity. This situation has occurred in real estate and oil-drilling partnerships. Assume Ben Isaac withdraws from the business, and agrees to take partnership cash of $10,000 and the new partnership's note for $15,000. This $25,000 settlement is $6,000 less than Isaac's $31,000 equity in the business.

Short Exercise:

Jane, Wayne, and Lane are partners with capital account balances of $20,000, $30,000, and $50,000, respectively. They share profits in a 2:3:5 ratio. Wayne is withdrawing from the business, so the partners have the assets appraised. The building's market value is $4,000 more than its book value. The inventory's market value is $6,000 less than cost. What are the journal entries to revalue these assets?

A:

Building	4,000
Jane, Capital	. . 800
Wayne, Capital............	1,200
Lane, Capital	2,000
Jane, Capital	1,200
Wayne, Capital............	1,800
Lane, Capital	3,000
Inventory	6,000

Short Exercise:

What are the partners' capital account balances after the revaluations in the previous Short Exercise?

A:

Jane: ($20,000 + $800
   – $1,200) = $19,600
Wayne: ($30,000 + $1,200
   – $1,800) = $29,400
Lane: ($50,000 + $2,000
   – $3,000) = $49,000

Short Exercise:

Refer to the Short Exercises on p. 641. Assume that Wayne is willing to accept $20,000 for his partnership interest. What is the journal entry to record his retirement?

A:

Wayne,
  Capital......... 29,400
Cash................... 20,000
Jane, Capital........ 2,686*
Lane, Capital .... 6,714†

*$9,400 × 2/7 = $2,686
†$9,400 × 5/7 = $6,714
Jane and Lane will now share profits in a 2:5 ratio.

The remaining partners share this $6,000 difference—which is a bonus to them—according to their profit-and-loss ratio. However, because Isaac has withdrawn from the partnership, a new agreement—and a new profit-and-loss ratio—must be drawn up. Maslowski and Green, in forming a new partnership, may decide on any ratio that they see fit. Let us assume they agree that Maslowski will earn two thirds of partnership profits and losses, and Green one third. The entry to record Isaac's withdrawal at less than book value is

June	30	Isaac, Capital...	31,000	
		Cash...		10,000
		Note Payable to Ben Isaac......................		15,000
		Green, Capital ($6,000 × ⅓)		2,000
		Maslowski, Capital ($6,000 × ⅔)..............		4,000
		To record withdrawal of B. Isaac from the partnership.		

Isaac's account is closed, and Maslowski and Green may or may not continue the business.

Withdrawal at More Than Book Value

Short Exercise:

Refer to the Short Exercises on p. 641. Assume that Jane and Lane agree to pay Wayne $40,000 for his partnership interest. What is the journal entry to record his retirement?

A:

Jane, Capital 3,029*
Wayne, Capital... 29,400
Lane, Capital ...... 7,571†
Cash................ 40,000

*$10,600 × 2/7 = $3,029
†$10,600 × 5/7 = $7,571

The settlement with a withdrawing partner may allow him or her to take assets of greater value than the book value of that partner's capital. Also, the remaining partners may be so eager for the withdrawing partner to leave the firm that they pay the partner a bonus to withdraw from the business. In either case, the partner's withdrawal causes a decrease in the book equity of the remaining partners. This decrease is allocated to the partners based on their profit-and-loss ratio.

The accounting for this situation follows the pattern illustrated for withdrawal at less than book value—with one exception. The remaining partners' capital accounts are debited because the withdrawing partner receives more than his or her book equity.

Death of a Partner

Death of a partner, like any other form of partnership withdrawal, dissolves a partnership. The partnership accounts are adjusted to measure net income or loss for the fraction of the year up to the date of death, then closed to determine the partners' capital balances on that date. Settlement with the deceased partner's estate is based on the partnership agreement. The estate commonly receives partnership assets equal to the partner's capital balance. The partnership closes the deceased partner's capital account with a debit. This entry credits a payable to the estate.

Alternatively, a remaining partner may purchase the deceased partner's equity. The deceased partner's equity is debited and the purchaser's equity is credited. The amount of this entry is the ending credit balance in the deceased partner's capital account.

Liquidation of a Partnership

OBJECTIVE 6

Account for the liquidation of a partnership

Admission of a new partner or withdrawal or death of an existing partner dissolves the partnership. However, the business may continue operating with no apparent change to outsiders such as customers and creditors. Business **liquidation**, however, is the process of going out of business by selling the entity's assets and paying its liabilities. The final step in liquidation of a business is the *distribution of the remaining cash to the owners*. Before the business is liquidated, the books should be adjusted and closed. After closing, only asset, liability, and partners' capital accounts remain open.

Liquidation of a partnership includes three basic steps:

1. Sell the assets. Allocate the gain or loss to the partners' capital accounts based on the profit-and-loss ratio.
2. Pay the partnership liabilities.
3. Disburse the remaining cash to the partners based on their capital balances.

In actual practice, the liquidation of a business can stretch over weeks or months. Selling every asset and paying every liability of the entity takes time. To avoid excessive detail in our illustrations, we include only two asset categories—Cash and Noncash Assets—and a single liability category—Liabilities. Our examples also assume that the business sells the noncash assets in a single transaction and pays the liabilities in a single transaction.

Assume that Jane Aviron, Elaine Bloch, and Kim Zhang have shared profits and losses in the ratio of 3:1:1. (This ratio is equal to ⅗, ⅕, ⅕, or a 60-percent, 20-percent, 20-percent sharing ratio.) They decide to liquidate their partnership. After the books are adjusted and closed, the general ledger contains the following balances:

Cash	$ 10,000	Liabilities	$ 30,000
Noncash assets	90,000	Aviron, capital	40,000
		Bloch, capital	20,000
		Zhang, capital	10,000
		Total liabilities	
Total assets	$100,000	and capital	$100,000

Sale of Noncash Assets at a Gain

Assume the Aviron, Bloch, and Zhang partnership sells its noncash assets (shown on the balance sheet at $90,000) for cash of $150,000. The partnership realizes a gain of $60,000, which is allocated to the partners based on their profit-and-loss-sharing ratio. The entry to record this sale and allocation of the gain is

Oct.	31	Cash	150,000	
		Noncash Assets		90,000
		Aviron, Capital ($60,000 × .60)		36,000
		Bloch, Capital ($60,000 × .20)		12,000
		Zhang, Capital ($60,000 × .20)		12,000
		To sell noncash assets in liquidation and allocate gain to partners.		

The partnership must next pay off its liabilities:

Oct.	31	Liabilities	30,000	
		Cash		30,000
		To pay liabilities in liquidation.		

In the final liquidation transaction, the remaining cash is disbursed to the partners. *The partners share in the cash according to their capital balances.* (By contrast, *gains* and *losses* on the sale of assets are shared by the partners based on their profit-and-loss-sharing ratio.) The amount of cash left in the partnership is $130,000—the $10,000 beginning balance plus the $150,000 cash sale of assets minus the $30,000 cash payment of liabilities. The remaining cash is put into a 'holding account' to be allocated to the partners once all transactions are complete.

Oct.	31	Aviron, Capital ($40,000 + $36,000)	76,000	
		Bloch, Capital ($20,000 + $12,000)	32,000	
		Zhang, Capital ($10,000 + $12,000)	22,000	
		Cash		130,000
		To disburse cash to partners in liquidation.		

A convenient way to summarize the transactions in a partnership liquidation is given in Exhibit 13-4.

Short Exercise:
Kelly and Keith are partners in a partnership with cash of $10,000 and noncash assets of $50,000. The capital balances of Kelly and Keith are $40,000 and $20,000, respectively. The partners share profits and losses 60:40. The noncash assets are sold for $56,000. All liabilities have been paid. What journal entries record sale of the assets and distribution of cash to the partners?

A:

Cash	56,000	
Noncash Assets		50,000
Kelly, Capital		3,600*
Keith, Capital		2,400†

*$6,000 gain × 60% = $3,600
†$6,000 × 40% = $2,400

Kelly, Capital ($40,000 + $3,600)	43,600	
Keith, Capital ($20,000 + $2,400)	22,400	
Cash		66,000

EXHIBIT 13-4   *Partnership Liquidation—Sale of Assets at a Gain*

	Cash	+ Noncash Assets	= Liabilities+	Capital		
				Aviron (60%) +	Bloch (20%) +	Zhang (20%)
Balances before sale of assets............................	$ 10,000	$ 90,000	$ 30,000	$ 40,000	$ 20,000	$ 10,000
Sale of assets and sharing of gain..............	150,000	(90,000)		36,000	12,000	12,000
Balances	160,000	-0-	30,000	76,000	32,000	22,000
Payment of liabilities	(30,000)		(30,000)			
Balances	130,000	-0-	-0-	76,000	32,000	22,000
Disbursement of cash to partners....................	(130,000)			(76,000)	(32,000)	(22,000)
Balances	$ -0-	$ -0-	$ -0-	$ -0-	$ -0-	$ -0-

After cash is placed in a holding account, the business has no assets, liabilities, or owners' equity. All the balances are zero. By the accounting equation, partnership assets *must* equal partnership liabilities plus partnership capital.

Sale of Noncash Assets at a Loss

Liquidation of a business often includes the sale of noncash assets at a loss. When this occurs, the partners' capital accounts are debited as they share the loss in their profit-and-loss-sharing ratio. Otherwise, the accounting follows the pattern illustrated for the sale of noncash assets at a gain.

STOP & THINK

The liquidation of the Dirk & Cross partnership included the sale of assets at a $150,000 loss. Lorraine Dirk's Capital balance of $45,000 was less than her $60,000 share of the loss. Allocation of losses to the partners created a $15,000 deficit (debit balance) in Dirk's Capital account. Identify ways that the partnership could deal with the negative balance (a capital deficiency) in Dirk's Capital account.

Answer: Two possibilities are:
1. Dirk could contribute assets to the partnership in an amount equal to her capital deficiency.
2. Joseph Cross, Lorraine Dirk's partner, could absorb Dirk's capital deficiency by decreasing his own capital balance.

OBJECTIVE 7

Prepare partnership financial statements

Partnership Financial Statements

Partnership financial statements are much like those of a proprietorship. However, a partnership income statement includes a section showing the division of net income to the partners. For example, the partnership of Leslie Gray and Wayne Hayward might report its income statement for the year ended June 30, 19X6, as shown in

EXHIBIT 13-5 *Financial Statements of a Partnership and a Proprietorship*

Panel A—Partnership

Panel B—Proprietorship

Gray and Hayward Consulting
Income Statement
for the year ended December 31, 19X6

Revenues.....................................		$460
Expenses.....................................		(270)
Net income..................................		$190
Allocation of net income:		
To Gray.................................	$114	
To Hayward...........................	76	$190

Gray Consulting
Income Statement
for the year ended December 31, 19X6

Revenues	$460
Expenses...	(270)
Net income...	$190

Gray and Hayward Consulting
Statement of Owners' Equity
for the year ended December 31, 19X6

	Gray	Howard
Capital, December 31, 19X5.......	$50	$40
Additional investments	10	—
Net income.................................	114	76
Subtotal	174	116
Drawings....................................	(72)	(48)
Capital, December 31, 19X6.......	$102	$68

Gray Consulting
Statement of Owner's Equity
for the year ended December 31, 19X6

Capital, December 31, 19X5..........................	$90
Additional investments.................................	10
Net income...	190
Subtotal...	290
Drawings..	(120)
Capital, December 31, 19X6..........................	$170

Gray and Hayward Consulting
Balance Sheet
for the year ended December 31, 19X6

Assets

Cash and other assets.....................................	$170

Owners' Equity

Gray, capital	$102
Hayward, capital	68
Total capital...	$170

Gray Consulting
Balance Sheet
for the year ended December 31, 19X6

Assets

Cash and other assets.....................................	$170

Owner's Equity

Gray capital...	$170

Panel A of Exhibit 13-5. A proprietorship's financial statements are presented for comparison.

Large partnerships may not find it feasible to report the net income of every partner. Instead, the firm may report the allocation of net income to active and retired partners and average earnings per partner. For example, Exhibit 13-6 shows how the public accounting firm of Main, Price & Anders reported its earnings.

EXHIBIT 13-6   *Reporting Net Income for a Large Partnership*

Main, Price & Anders Combined Statement of Earnings for the year ended August 31, 19X7	
Fees for Professional Services..	$9,144,920
Earnings for the year	$2,978,800
Allocation of earnings	
To partners active during the year—	
Resigned, retired, and deceased partners	$ 199,010
Partners active at year end	2,532,700
To retired and deceased partners—	
Retirement and death benefits	83,100
Not allocated to partners—	
Retained for specific partnership purposes	163,990
	$2,978,800
Average earnings per partner at year end (28 partners)	$ 106,400

Summary Problem for Your Review

The partnership of Taylor and Uvalde is considering admitting Steven Vaughn as a partner on January 1, 19X8. The partnership general ledger includes the following balances on that date:

Cash	$ 9,000	Total liabilities....................	$ 50,000
Other assets........................	110,000	Taylor, capital.....................	45,000
		Uvalde, capital....................	24,000
		Total liabilities	
Total assets.....................	$119,000	and capital.....................	$119,000

Debby Taylor's share of profits and losses is 60 percent and Thomas Uvalde's share is 40 percent.

Required

(Items 1 and 2 are independent.)

1. Suppose Vaughn pays Uvalde $31,000 to acquire Uvalde's interest in the business after Taylor approves Vaughn as a partner.
   a. Record the transfer of owner's equity on the partnership books.
   b. Prepare the partnership balance sheet immediately after Vaughn is admitted as a partner.

2. Suppose that Vaughn becomes a partner by investing $31,000 cash to acquire a one-fourth interest in the business.
   a. Compute Vaughn's capital balance and record his investment in the business.
   b. Prepare the partnership balance sheet immediately after Vaughn is admitted as a partner. Include the heading.

3. Which way of admitting Vaughn to the partnership increases its total assets? Give your reason.

SOLUTION TO REVIEW PROBLEM

Requirement 1

a. Jan.   1   Uvalde, Capital..   24,000
                  Vaughn, Capital.......................................   24,000
                  To transfer Uvalde's equity in the
                  partnership to Vaughn.

b. The balance sheet for the partnership of Taylor and Vaughn is identical to the
   balance sheet given for Taylor and Uvalde in the problem, except Vaughn's name
   replaces Uvalde's name in the title and in the listing of capital accounts.

Requirement 2

a. Computation of Vaughn's capital balance:

Partnership capital before Vaughn is admitted ($45,000 + $24,000)	$ 69,000
Vaughn's investment in the partnership	31,000
Partnership capital after Vaughn is admitted............................	$100,000
Vaughn's capital in the partnership ($100,000 × ¼)	$ 25,000

Jan.   1   Cash   31,000
                  Vaughn, Capital   25,000
                  Taylor, Capital
                     [($31,000 – $25,000) × .60]..................   3,600
                  Uvalde, Capital
                     [($31,000 – $25,000) × .40]..................   2,400
                  To admit Vaughn as a partner with a
                  one-fourth interest in the business.

b.

Taylor, Uvalde, and Vaughn
Balance Sheet
January 1, 19X8

Cash		Total liabilities		$ 50,000
($9,000 + $31,000).................	$ 40,000	Taylor, capital		
Other assets	110,000	($45,000 + $3,600)..............		48,600
		Uvalde, capital		
		($24,000 + $2,400)..............		26,400
		Vaughn, capital		25,000
		Total liabilities		
Total assets..........................	$150,000	and capital		$150,000

Requirement 3

Vaughn's investment in the partnership increases its total assets by the amount of
his contribution. Total assets of the business are $150,000 after his investment, com-
pared to $119,000 before. By contrast, Vaughn's purchase of Uvalde's interest in the
business is a personal transaction between the two individuals. It does not affect the
assets of the partnership regardless of the amount Vaughn pays Uvalde.

Summary

1. *Identify the characteristics, including advantages and disadvantages, of a partnership.* A *partnership* is a business co-owned by two or more persons for profit. The characteristics of this form of business organization are its *ease of formation, limited life, mutual agency, unlimited liability,* and *no partnership income taxes.* In a *limited partnership*, the limited partners have limited personal liability for the obligations of the business.

A written *partnership agreement* establishes procedures for admission of a new partner, withdrawals of a partner, and the sharing of profits and losses among the partners. When a new partner is admitted to the firm or an existing partner withdraws, the old partnership is *dissolved*, or ceases to exist. A new partnership may or may not emerge to continue the business.

2. *Account for partners' initial investments in a partnership.* Accounting for a partnership is similar to accounting for a proprietorship. However, a partnership has more than one owner. Each partner has an individual capital account and a withdrawal account.

3. *Allocate profits and losses to the partners by different methods.* Partners share net income or loss in any manner they choose. Common sharing agreements base the *profit-and-loss ratio* on a stated fraction, partners' capital contributions, and/or their service to the partnership. Some partnerships call the cash drawings of partners *salaries* and *interest*, but these amounts are not expenses of the business. Instead, they are merely ways of allocating partnership net income to the partners.

4. *Account for the admission of a new partner to the business.* An outside person may become a partner by purchasing a current partner's interest or by investing in the partnership. In some cases the new partner must pay the current partners a bonus to join. In other situations the new partner may receive a bonus to join.

5. *Account for the withdrawal of a partner from the business.* When a partner withdraws, partnership assets may be reappraised. Partners share any gain or loss on the asset revaluation on the basis of their profit-and-loss ratio. The withdrawing partner may receive payment equal to, greater than, or less than his or her capital book value, depending on the agreement with the other partners.

6. *Account for the liquidation of a partnership.* In *liquidation* a partnership goes out of business by selling the assets, paying the liabilities, and disbursing any remaining cash to the partners.

7. *Prepare partnership financial statements.* Partnership *financial statements* are similar to those of a proprietorship. However, the partnership income statement commonly reports the allocation of net income to the partners, and the balance sheet has a capital account for each partner.

Self-Study Questions

Test your understanding of the chapter by marking the correct answer for each of the following questions:

1. Which of these characteristics does *not* apply to a partnership? *(p. 629)*
   a. Unlimited life   c. Unlimited liability
   b. Mutual agency   d. No business income tax

2. A partnership records a partner's investment of assets in the business at *(p. 631)*
   a. The partner's book value of the assets invested
   b. The market value of the assets invested
   c. A special value set by the partners
   d. Any of the above, depending upon the partnership agreement

3. The partnership of Lane, Murdock, and Nu divides profits in the ratio of 4:5:3. During 19X6, the business earned $40,000. Nu's share of this income is *(pp. 632–633)*
   a. $10,000   c. $16,000
   b. $13,333   d. $16,667

4. Suppose the partnership of Lane, Murdock, and Nu in the preceding question lost $40,000 during 19X6. Murdock's share of this loss is *(p. 632)*
   a. Not determinable because the ratio applies only to profits
   b. $13,333
   c. $16,000
   d. $16,667

5. The partners of Placido, Quinn, and Rolfe share profits and losses ⅕, ⅙, and ¹⁹⁄₃₀. During 19X3, the first year of their partnership, the business earned $120,000, and each partner withdrew $50,000 for personal use. What is the balance in Rolfe's capital account after all closing entries? *(p. 636)*
   a. Not determinable because Rolfe's beginning capital balance is not given
   b. Minus $10,000
   c. $26,000
   d. $70,000

6. Barb Fuller buys into the partnership of Graff and Harrell by purchasing a one-third interest for $55,000. Prior to Fuller's entry, Ted Graff's capital balance was $46,000, and Louisa Harrell's balance was $52,000; profits and losses were shared equally. The entry to record Fuller's buying into the business is *(p. 638)*

a. Cash	55,000		c. Cash	55,000	
Fuller, Capital ...		55,000	Fuller, Capital		51,000
			Graff, Capital		2,000
			Harrell, Capital......		2,000
b. Graff, Capital	27,500		d. Cash	51,000	
Harrell, Capital.....	27,500		Graff, Capital	2,000	
Fuller, Capital ...		55,000	Harrell, Capital...........	2,000	
			Fuller, Capital		55,000

7. The partners of Thomas, Valik, and Wollenberg share profits and losses equally. Their capital balances are $40,000, $50,000, and $60,000 respectively, when Brenda Wollenberg sells her interest in the partnership to Brent Valik for $90,000. Raymond Thomas and Valik continue the business. Immediately after Wollenberg's retirement, the total assets of the partnership are *(pp. 637–638)*
   a. Increased by $30,000
   b. Increased by $90,000
   c. Decreased by $60,000
   d. The same as before Wollenberg sold her interest to Valik

8. Prior to Bill Hogg's withdrawal from the partnership of Hogg, Hamm, and Bacon, the partners' capital balances were $140,000, $110,000 and $250,000 respectively. The partners share profits and losses ⅓, ¼, and ⁵⁄₁₂. The appraisal indicates that assets should be written down by $36,000. Arthur Hamm's share of the write-down is *(pp. 640–641)*
   a. $7,920   c. $12,000
   b. $9,000   d. $18,000

9. The process of closing the business, selling the assets, paying the liabilities, and disbursing remaining cash to the owners is called *(pp. 642–643)*
   a. Dissolution   c. Withdrawal
   b. Forming a new partnership   d. Liquidation

10. Eric Hirst and Brenda Mallouk have shared profits and losses equally. Immediately prior to the final cash disbursement in a liquidation of their partnership, the books show:

Cash	=	Liabilities	+	Hirst, Capital	+	Mallouk, Capital
$100,000		$-0-		$60,000		$40,000

How much cash should Hirst receive? *(p. 643)*

a. $40,000   c. $60,000

b. $50,000   d. None of the above

Answers to the Self-Study Questions follow the Accounting Vocabulary.

Accounting Vocabulary

Dissolution *(p. 629)*

Liquidation *(p. 642)*

Mutual agency *(p. 629)*

Partnership *(p. 628)*

Partnership agreement *(p. 629)*

Unlimited personal liability *(p. 630)*

Answers to Self-Study Questions

1. a
2. b
3. a   ($40,000 × $\frac{3}{12}$ = $10,000)
4. d   ($40,000 × $\frac{5}{12}$ = $16,667)
5. a
6. c   [($46,000 + $52,000 + $55,000) × $\frac{1}{3}$ = $51,000; $55,000 − $51,000 =
       $4,000; $4,000 ÷ 2 = $2,000 each to Graff and Harrell]
7. d
8. b   ($36,000 × $\frac{1}{4}$ = $9,000)
9. d
10. c

ASSIGNMENT MATERIAL _____

Questions

1. List eight items that the partnership agreement should specify.
2. Ron Montgomery, who is a partner in M&N Associates, commits the firm to a contract for a job within the scope of its regular business operations. What term describes Montgomery's ability to obligate the partnership?
3. If a partnership cannot pay a debt, who must make payment? What term describes this obligation of the partners?
4. How is partnership income taxed?
5. Identify the advantages and disadvantages of the partnership form of business organization.
6. Robin Randall and Sylvia Smith's partnership agreement states that Randall gets 60 percent of profits and Smith gets 40 percent. If the agreement does not discuss the treatment of losses, how are losses shared? How do the partners share profits and losses if the agreement specifies no profit-and-loss-sharing ratio?
7. What determines the amount of the credit to a partner's capital account when the partner contributes assets other than cash to the business?
8. Do partner withdrawals of cash for personal use affect the sharing of profits and losses by the partner? If so, explain how. If not, explain why not.
9. Name two events that can cause the dissolution of a partnership?
10. Briefly describe how to account for the purchase of an existing partner's interest in the business.
11. Jeff Malcolm purchases Sheila Brown's interest in the Brown & Kareem partnership. What right does Malcolm obtain from the purchase? What is required for Malcolm to become Paula Kareem's partner?

12. Sal Assissi and Barb Carter each have capital of $75,000 in their business. They and share profits in the ratio of 55:45. Kathy Denman acquires a one-fifth share in the partnership by investing cash of $50,000. What are the capital balances of the three partners immediately after Denman is admitted?

13. When a partner resigns from the partnership and receives assets greater than his or her capital balance, how is the excess shared by the other partners?

14. Distinguish between dissolution and liquidation of a partnership.

15. Name the three steps in liquidating a partnership.

16. The partnership of Ralls and Sauls is in the process of liquidation. How do the partners share (a) gains and losses on the sale of noncash assets, and (b) the final cash disbursement?

17. Compare and contrast the financial statements of a proprietorship and a partnership.

18. Summarize the situations in which partnership allocations are based on (a) the profit-and-loss ratio, and (b) the partners' capital balances.

Exercises

Exercise 13-1   *Organizing a business as a partnership*   **(Obj. 1)**

Rhonda Hough, a friend from college, approaches you about forming a partnership to export software. Since graduation, Rhonda has worked for the World Bank, developing important contacts among government officials and business leaders in Poland and Hungary. Eager to upgrade their data-processing capabilities, Eastern Europeans are looking for ways to obtain computers. Rhonda believes she is in a unique position to capitalize on this opportunity. With your expertise in finance, you would have responsibility for accounting and finance in the partnership.

Required

Discuss the advantages and disadvantages of organizing the export business as a partnership rather than a proprietorship. Comment on the way partnership income is taxed.

Exercise 13-2   *Recording a partner's investment*   **(Obj. 2)**

Ann Sefcik has operated an apartment-locater service as a proprietorship. She and Kristen Clem have decided to reorganize the business as a partnership. Sefcik's investment in the partnership consists of cash, $2,100; accounts receivable, $10,600 less allowance for uncollectibles, $800; office furniture, $2,700 less accumulated depreciation, $1,100; a small building, $55,000 less accumulated depreciation, $27,500; accounts payable, $3,300; and a note payable to the bank, $10,000.

To determine Sefcik's equity in the partnership, she and Clem hire an independent appraiser. This outside party provides the following market values of the assets and liabilities that Sefcik is contributing to the business: cash, accounts receivable, office furniture, accounts payable, and note payable—the same as Sefcik's book value; allowance for uncollectible accounts, $2,900; building, $71,000; and accrued expenses payable (including interest on the note payable), $1,200.

Required

Make the entry on the partnership books to record Sefcik's investment.

Exercise 13-3   *Computing partners' shares of net income and net loss*   **(Obj. 3)**

Matt Hill and Dave Bristow form a partnership, investing $40,000 and $70,000 respectively. Determine their shares of net income or net loss for each of the following situations:

a. Net loss is $44,000, and the partners have no written partnership agreement.

b. Net income is $66,000 and the partnership agreement states that the partners share profits and losses based on their capital contributions.

c. Net loss is $77,000, and the partnership agreement states that the partners share profits based on their capital contributions.

d. Net income is $125,000. The first $60,000 is shared based on the partner capital contributions. The next $45,000 is based on partner service, with Hill receiving 30 percent and Bristow receiving 70 percent. The remainder is shared equally.

Exercise 13-4   *Computing partners' capital balances*   *(Obj. 3)*

Matt Hill withdrew cash of $62,000 for personal use, and Dave Bristow withdrew cash of $50,000 during the year. Using the data from situation (d) in Exercise 13-3, journalize the entries to close the (a) income summary account, and (b) the partners' drawing accounts. Explanations are not required. Indicate the amount of increase or decrease in each partner's capital balance. What was the overall effect on partnership capital?

Exercise 13-5   *Admitting a new partner*   *(Obj. 4)*

Chris Munroe is admitted to a partnership. Prior to the admission of Munroe, the partnership books show Susan Hecker's capital balance at $100,000 and Louis Vitale's capital balance at $50,000. Compute the amount of each partner's equity on the books of the new partnership under each of the following plans:

a. Munroe pays $60,000 for Vitale's equity. Munroe's payment is not an investment in the partnership but instead goes directly to Vitale.

b. Munroe invests $50,000 to acquire a one-fourth interest in the partnership.

c. Munroe invests $70,000 to acquire a one-fourth interest in the partnership.

Exercise 13-6   *Recording the admission of a new partner*   *(Obj. 4)*

Make the partnership journal entry to record the admission of Munroe under plans a, b, and c in Exercise 13-5. Explanations are not required.

Exercise 13-7   *Withdrawal of a partner*   *(Obj. 5)*

After closing the books, Armstrong & Chan's partnership balance sheet reports owner's equity of $60,000 for Armstrong and $70,000 for Chan. Armstrong is withdrawing from the firm. He and Chan agree to write down partnership assets by $40,000. They have shared profits and losses in the ratio of one third to Armstrong and two thirds to Chan. If the partnership agreement states that a withdrawing partner will receive assets equal to the book value of his owner's equity, how much will Armstrong receive?

Chan will continue to operate the business as a proprietorship. What is Chan's beginning capital on the proprietorship books?

Exercise 13-8   *Liquidation of a partnership*   *(Obj. 6)*

The partnership of Lee, Molnari, and Nix is dissolving. Business assets, liabilities, and partner's capital balances prior to dissolution follow. The partners share profits and losses as follows: Kim Lee, 25 percent; Sandra Molnari, 55 percent; and Ray Nix, 20 percent.

Required

Create a spreadsheet or solve manually—as directed by your instructor—to show the ending balances in all accounts after the noncash assets are sold for $145,000 and for $95,000. Determine the unknown amounts(?):

	A	B	C	D	E	F
1			**Lee, Molnari, and Nix**			
2			**Sale of Noncash Assets**			
3			**(For $145,000)**			
4						
5		**Noncash**		**Lee**	**Molnari**	**Nix**
6	**Cash**	**Assets**	**Liabilities**	**Capital**	**Capital**	**Capital**
7						
8	$ 6,000	$126,000	$77,000	$12,000	$37,000	$6,000
9	145,000	(126,000)		?	?	?
10						
11	$151,000	$ 0	$77,000	$?	$?	$?
12						
13						($A9 – $B8)*.25
14			**(For $95,000)**			
15						
16						
17		**Noncash**		**Lee**	**Molnari**	**Nix**
18	**Cash**	**Assets**	**Liabilities**	**Capital**	**Capital**	**Capital**
19						
20	$ 6,000	$126,000	$77,000	$12,000	$37,000	$6,000
21	95,000	(126,000)		?	?	?
22						
23	$101,000	$ 0	$77,000	$?	$?	$?
24						
						($A21 – $B20)*.25

Identify two ways the partners can deal with the negative ending balance in Nix's capital account.

Challenge Exercise

Exercise 13-9 *Preparing a partnership balance sheet* **(Obj. 7)**

On October 31, 19X9, Crabtree and Evelyn agree to combine their proprietorships as a partnership. Their balance sheets on October 31 are as follows:

	Crabtree's Business		Evelyn's Business	
Assets	**Book Value**	**Current Market Value**	**Book Value**	**Current Market Value**
Cash..	$ 3,700	$ 3,700	$ 8,000	$ 8,000
Accounts receivable (net).......	22,000	20,200	8,000	6,300
Inventory	51,000	46,000	34,000	35,100
Capital assets (net)	121,800	123,500	53,500	57,400
Total assets..............................	$198,500	$193,400	$103,500	$106,800

Liabilities and Capital

Accounts payable	$ 23,600	$ 23,600	$ 9,100	$ 9,100
Accrued expenses payable.....	2,200	2,200	1,400	1,400
Notes payable	75,000	75,000		
Crabtree, capital.......................	97,700	92,600		
Evelyn, capital..........................			93,000	96,300
Total liabilities and capital	$198,500	$193,400	$103,500	$106,800

Required

Prepare the partnership balance sheet at October 31, 19X9.

Problems   (Group A)

Problem 13-1A   *Writing a partnership agreement*   **(Obj. 1)**

Dolores de Souza and Sara Gish are discussing the formation of a partnership to import fabric from Guatemala. Dolores is especially artistic, so she will travel to Central America to buy merchandise. Sara is an excellent salesperson, and has already lined up several large stores to sell the fabric.

Required

Write a partnership agreement to cover all elements essential for the business to operate smoothly. Make up names, amounts, profit-and-loss sharing percentages, and so on as needed.

Problem 13-2A   *Investments by partners*   **(Obj. 2, 7)**

Jon Ringle and Claudette LeBlanc formed a partnership on March 15. The partners agreed to invest equal amounts of capital. Le Blanc invested her proprietorship's assets and liabilities (credit balances in parentheses):

	LeBlanc's Book Value	Current Market Value
Accounts receivable	$ 12,000	$12,000
Allowance for doubtful accounts..	(740)	(1,360)
Inventory...	43,850	31,220
Prepaid expenses...	2,400	2,400
Store equipment	36,700	26,600
Accumulated depreciation..	(9,200)	(-0-)
Accounts payable..	(22,300)	(22,300)

On March 15, Ringle invested cash in an amount equal to the current market value of LeBlanc's partnership capital. The partners decided that LeBlanc would earn 70 percent of partnership profits because she would manage the business. Ringle agreed to accept 30 percent of profits. During the period ended December 31, the partnership earned $80,000. Ringle's drawings were $32,000 and LeBlanc's drawings were $36,000.

Required

1. Journalize the partners' initial investments.
2. Prepare the partnership balance sheet immediately after its formation on March 15.
3. Journalize the December 31 entries to close the Income Summary account and the partner drawing accounts.

Problem 13-3A *Computing partners' shares of net income and net loss* **(Obj. 3, 7)**

Robin Soffer, Kami Karlin, and Joe Schultz have formed a partnership. Soffer invested $20,000, Karlin $40,000, and Schultz $60,000. Soffer will manage the store, Karlin will work in the store three-quarters of the time, and Schultz will not work in the business.

Required

1. Compute the partners' shares of profits and losses under each of the following plans:
   a. Net income is $87,000, and the partnership agreement does not specify how profits and losses are shared.
   b. Net loss is $47,000, and the partnership agreement allocates 45 percent of profits to Soffer, 35 percent to Karlin, and 20 percent to Schultz. The agreement does not discuss the sharing of losses.
   c. Net income is $104,000. The first $50,000 is allocated based on salaries of $34,000 for Soffer and $16,000 for Karlin. The remainder is allocated based on partner capital contributions.
   d. Net income for the year ended September 30, 19X4, is $91,000. The first $30,000 is allocated on the basis of partner capital contributions. The next $30,000 is based on service, with $20,000 going to Soffer and $10,000 going to Karlin. Any remainder is shared equally.

2. Revenues for the year ended September 30, 19X4, were $572,000 and expenses were $481,000. Under plan (d), prepare the partnership income statement for the year.

3. How will what you have learned in this problem help you manage a partnership?

Problem 13-4A *Recording changes in partnership capital* **(Obj. 4, 5)**

Cycle City is a partnership owned by three individuals. The partners share profits and losses in the ratio of 30 percent to Jane Mutchler, 40 percent to Peter Armstrong, and 30 percent to Ivana Marcus. At December 31, 19X6, the firm has the following balance sheet:

Cash.............................		$ 25,000	Total liabilities................	$103,000
Accounts receivable.....	$ 16,000			
Less: Allowance				
for uncollectibles..	1,000	15,000		
Inventory		92,000	Mutchler, capital............	38,000
Equipment....................	130,000		Armstrong, capital.........	49,000
Less: Accumulated			Marcus, capital...............	42,000
depreciation...........	30,000	100,000	Total liabilities	
Total assets....................		$232,000	and capital	$232,000

Mutchler withdraws from the partnership on this date.

Required

Record Mutchler's withdrawal from the partnership under the following plans:

1. Mutchler gives her interest in the business to Lynn Abbelli, her cousin.

2. In personal transactions, Mutchler sells her equity in the partnership to Paul André and Don Craig, who each pay Mutchler $15,000 for one half of her interest. Armstrong and Marcus agree to accept André and Craig as partners.

3. The partnership pays Mutchler cash of $5,000, and gives her a note payable for the remainder of her book equity in settlement of her partnership interest.

4. Mutchler receives cash of $20,000 and a note for $20,000 from the partnership.

5. The partners agree that the equipment is worth $150,000, and that accumulated depreciation should remain at $30,000. After the revaluation, the partnership settles with Mutchler by giving her cash of $10,000 and inventory for the remainder of her book equity.

Problem 13-5A   *Liquidation of a partnership*   *(Obj. 6)*

The partnership of Whitney, Kosse & Itasca has experienced operating losses for three consecutive years. The partners, who have shared profits and losses in the ratio of Fran Whitney 15 percent, Walt Kosse 60 percent, and Emil Itasca 25 percent, are considering the liquidation of the business. They ask you to analyze the effects of liquidation under various assumptions about the sale of the noncash assets. They present the following condensed partnership balance sheet at December 31, end of the current year:

Cash....................................	$ 7,000	Liabilities...........................	$ 63,000
Noncash assets..................	163,000	Whitney, capital................	24,000
		Kosse, capital....................	66,000
		Itasca, capital	17,000
		Total liabilities	
Total assets	$170,000	and capital	$170,000

Required

1. Prepare a summary of liquidation transactions (as illustrated in the chapter) for each of the following situations:
   a. The noncash assets are sold for $175,000.
   b. The noncash assets are sold for $141,000.

2. Make the journal entries to record the liquidation transactions in requirement 1(b).

Problem 13-6A   *Account for partners' investments; allocate profits and losses; account for the admission of a new partner; account for the withdrawal of a partner; prepare partnership balance sheet*   *(Obj. 2, 3, 4, 5, 7)*

19X1

June 10   L. Shannon and S. Lee-Choi have agreed to pool their assets and form a partnership to be called L&S Consulting. They agree to share all profits equally and make the following initial investments:

	Shannon	Lee-Choi
Cash	$ 5,000	$10,000
Accounts receivable (net).........................	11,000	9,000
Office furniture..	12,000	8,000

19X2

May 31   (The fiscal year end) the partnership's reported net income was $45,000.

June   1   Shannon and Lee-Choi agree to accept D. Eurchuk into the partnership with a $60,000 investment for 30% of the business. The partnership agreement is amended to provide for the following sharing of profits and losses:

	Shannon	Lee-Choi	Eurchuk
Annual salary	$30,000	$40,000	$25,000
Interest on capital balance	10%	10%	10%
Balance in ratio of	3 :	2 :	5

19X3

May 31 The partnerships' reported net income was $140,000.

Oct. 10 Shannon withdrew $28,000 from the partnership and Lee-Choi withdrew $19,000 (Eurchuk did not make any withdrawals).

19X4

May 31 The partnership's reported net income was $75,000.

June 2 After a disagreement as to the directions the partnership should be moving in, Eurchuk decided to withdraw from the partnership. The three partners agreed that Eurchuk could take cash of $80,000 in exchange for her equity in the partnership.

Required

1. Journalize all of the transactions for the partnership.
2. Prepare the partners' equity section of the balance sheet as of June 2, 19X4.

Problem 13-7A *Account for partners' investments; allocate profits and losses; account for the admission of a new partner; account for the liquidation of a partnership* **(Obj. 2, 3, 4, 5, 6)**

B. Corbett, J. Yeung and R. Norval started a partnership to operate a management consulting business. The partnership (CY&N Consulting) had the following transactions:

19X1

Jan. 1 Corbett, Yeung, and Norval formed the partnership by signing an agreement that stated that all profits will be shared in a 3:2:5 ratio (Corbett:Yeung:Norval) and by making the following investments:

	Corbett	Yeung	Norval
Cash	$ 4,000	$ 7,000	$23,000
Accounts receivable (net)	14,000	21,000	30,000
Office furniture	0	11,000	0
Computer equipment	26,000	0	9,000

Dec. 31 The partnership reported net income of $25,000 for the year.

19X2

June 7 Corbett and Norval agreed to Yeung's selling his share of the partnership to R. Dawson for $62,000. The new partners agreed to keep the same profit sharing arrangement (3:2:5 for Corbett:Dawson:Norval).

Dec. 31 The partnership reported a net loss of $40,000 for the year.

19X3

Jan. 3 The partners agreed to liquidate the partnership. On this date the balance sheet showed the following items:

Cash	$ 6,000
Accounts receivable	246,000
Allowance for uncollectible accounts	12,000
Office furniture	60,000
Computer equipment	150,000
Accumulated depreciation (total)	46,000
Accounts payable	274,000

The assets were sold for the following amounts:

Accounts receivable	$120,000
Office furniture	65,000
Computer equipment	100,000

Corbett and Dawson both have personal assets but Norval does not.

Required

Journalize all of the transactions for the partnership.

(Group B)

Problem 13-1B   *Writing a partnership agreement*   *(Obj. 1)*

Rudy Aceves and Mary Keim are discussing the formation of a partnership to install payroll accounting systems. Aceves is skilled in systems design, and he is convinced that his designs will draw large sales volumes. Keim is an excellent salesperson, and she has already lined up several clients.

Required

Write a partnership agreement to cover all elements essential for the business to operate smoothly. Make up names, amounts, profit-and-loss sharing percentages, and so on, as needed.

Problem 13-2B   *Investments by partners*   *(Obj. 2, 7)*

On June 30, Joshua Axtell and Zack Riesel formed a partnership. The partners agreed to invest equal amounts of capital. Axtell invested his proprietorship's assets and liabilities (credit balances in parentheses).

On June 30, Riesel invested cash in an amount equal to the current market value of Axtell's partnership capital. The partners decided that Axtell would earn two thirds of partnership profits because he would manage the business. Riesel agreed to accept one third of profits. During the remainder of the year, the partnership earned $60,000. Axtell's drawings were $35,200, and Riesel's drawings were $23,000.

	Axtell's Book Value	Current Market Value
Accounts receivable	$ 7,200	$ 7,200
Allowance for doubtful accounts	(-0-)	(1,050)
Inventory	22,340	24,100
Prepaid expenses	1,700	1,700
Office equipment	45,900	27,600
Accumulated depreciation	(15,300)	(-0-)
Accounts payable	(19,100)	(19,100)

Required

1. Journalize the partners' initial investments.

2. Prepare the partnership balance sheet immediately after its formation on June 30.

3. Journalize the December 31 entries to close the Income Summary account and the partner drawing accounts.

Problem 13-3B   *Computing partners' shares of net income and net loss*   **(Obj. 3, 7)**

Larry Collins, Elinor Davis, and Paul Chiu have formed a partnership. Collins invested $15,000, Davis $18,000, and Chiu $27,000. Collins will manage the store, Davis will work in the store half time, and Chiu will not work in the business.

Required

1. Compute the partners' shares of profits and losses under each of the following plans:
   a. Net loss is $42,900, and the partnership agreement does not specify how profits and losses are shared.
   b. Net loss is $60,000, and the partnership agreement allocates 40 percent of profits to Collins, 25 percent to Davis, and 35 percent to Chiu. The agreement does not discuss the sharing of losses.
   c. Net income is $92,000. The first $40,000 is allocated based on salaries, with Collins receiving $28,000 and Davis receiving $12,000. The remainder is allocated based on partner capital contributions.
   d. Net income for the year ended January 31, 19X8, is $180,000. The first $75,000 is allocated based on partner capital contributions. The next $36,000 is based on service, with Collins receiving $28,000 and Davis receiving $8,000. Any remainder is shared equally.

2. Revenues for the year ended January 31, 19X8, were $870,000 and expenses were $690,000. Under plan (d), prepare the partnership income statement for the year.

3. How will what you learned in this problem help you manage a partnership?

Problem 13-4B   *Recording changes in partnership capital*   **(Obj. 4, 5)**

Personal Finance Services is a partnership owned by three individuals. The partners share profits and losses in the ratio of 28 percent to C. Smythe, 38 percent to Max Lark, and 34 percent to Emily Spahn. At December 31, 19X7, the firm has the following balance sheet:

Cash...............................		$ 12,000	Total liabilities.................	$ 75,000
Accounts receivable	$22,000			
Less: Allowance				
for uncollectibles..	4,000	18,000	Smythe, capital	83,000
Building	$310,000		Lark, capital.....................	50,000
Less: Accumulated			Spahn, capital..................	62,000
depreciation..........	70,000	240,000	Total liabilities	
Total assets................		$270,000	and capital...................	$270,000

Lark withdraws from the partnership on December 31, 19X7, to establish his own consulting practice.

Required

Record Lark's withdrawal from the partnership under the following plans:

1. Lark gives his interest in the business to Terry Boyd, his nephew.

2. In personal transactions, Lark sells his equity in the partnership to Bea Patell and Al Bruckner, who each pay Lark $50,000 for one half of his interest. Smythe and Spahn agree to accept Patell and Bruckner as partners.

3. The partnership pays Lark cash of $15,000, and gives him a note payable for the remainder of his book equity in settlement of his partnership interest.

4. Lark receives cash of $10,000 and a note for $70,000 from the partnership.

5. The partners agree that the building is worth only $280,000, and that its accumulated depreciation should remain at $70,000. After the revaluation, the partnership settles with Lark by giving him cash of $14,100 and a note payable for the remainder of his book equity.

Problem 13-5B   *Liquidation of a partnership*   *(Obj. 6)*

The partnership of Monet, Blair, and Trippi has experienced operating losses for three consecutive years. The partners, who have shared profits and losses in the ratio of Mindy Monet 10 percent, Bert Blair, 30 percent, and Toni Trippi, 60 percent, are considering the liquidation of the business. They ask you to analyze the effects of liquidation under various possibilities about the sale of the noncash assets. They present the following condensed partnership balance sheet at December 31, end of the current year:

Cash..............................	$ 27,000	Liabilities......................................	$131,000
Noncash assets..............	202,000	Monet, capital.............................	21,000
		Blair, capital	39,000
		Trippi, capital	38,000
Total assets	$229,000	Total liabilities and capital....	$229,000

Required

1. Prepare a summary of liquidation transactions (as illustrated in the chapter) for each of the following situations:
   a. The noncash assets are sold for $212,000.
   b. The noncash assets are sold for $182,000.

2. Make the journal entries to record the liquidation transactions in requirement 1(b).

Problem 13-6B   *Account for partners' investments; allocate profits and losses; account for the admission of a new partner; account for the withdrawal of a partner; prepare partnership balance sheet*   *(Obj. 2, 3, 4, 5, 7)*

19X1

June 10   L. DeGracie and S. Langill have agreed to pool their assets and form a partnership to be called D&L Consulting. They agree to share all profits equally and make the following initial investments:

	DeGracie	Langill
Cash	$ 7,000	$12,000
Accounts receivable (net).........................	14,000	7,000
Office furniture...	16,000	9,000

19X2

May 31   (The fiscal year end) the partnership's reported net income was $56,000.

June   1   DeGracie and Langill agree to accept D. Pyefinch into the partnership with a $70,000 investment for 40% of the business. The partnership agreement is amended to provide for the following sharing of profits and losses:

	DeGracie	Langill	Pyefinch
Annual salary........................	$40,000	$30,000	$20,000
Interest on capital balance....	10%	10%	10%
Balance in ratio of.................	2 :	3 :	5

19X3

May 31   The partnership's reported net income is $160,000.

Oct. 10   DeGracie withdrew $30,000 from the partnership and Langill withdrew $20,000 (Pyefinch did not make any withdrawals).

19X4

May 31   The partnership's reported net income is $65,000.

June   2   After a disagreement as to the directions the partnership should be moving in, Pyefinch decided to withdraw from the partnership. The three partners agreed that Pyefinch could take cash of $150,000 in exchange for her equity in the partnership.

Required

1. Journalize all of the transactions for the partnership.
2. Prepare the partners' equity section of the balance sheet as of June 2, 19X4.

Problem 13-7B   *Account for partners' investments; allocate profits and losses; account for the admission of a new partner; account for the liquidation of a partnership (Obj. 2, 3, 4, 5, 6)*

B. Porteo, J. Harvinder, and R. Visser started a partnership to operate a management consulting business. The partnership (PH&V Consulting) had the following transactions:

19X1

Jan.   1   Porteo, Harvinder, and Visser formed the partnership by signing an agreement that stated that all profits will be shared in a 2:3:5 ratio (Porteo:Harvinder:Visser) and by making the following investments:

	Porteo	Harvinder	Visser
Cash..	$ 9,000	$ 6,000	$11,000
Accounts receivable (net).................	15,000	11,000	45,000
Office furniture.................................	0	0	11,000
Computer equipment........................	16,000	29,000	0

Dec. 31   The partnership reported net income of $36,000 for the year.

19X2

June   7   Porteo and Visser agreed to Harvinder's selling his share of the partnership to R. Ewing for $62,000. The new partners agreed to keep the same profit-sharing arrangement (2:3:5 for Porteo:Ewing:Visser).

Dec. 31   The partnership reported a net loss of $50,000 for the year.

19X3

Jan.   3   The partners agreed to liquidate the partnership. On this date the balance sheet showed the following items:

Cash..	$ 9,000
Accounts receivable...	237,000
Allowance for uncollectible accounts	17,000
Office furniture..	56,000
Computer equipment..	180,000
Accumulated depreciation (total)...............................	37,000
Accounts payable...	289,000

The assets were sold for the following amounts:

Accounts receivable	$143,000
Office furniture	62,000
Computer equipment	80,000

Porteo and Ewing both have personal assets but Visser does not.

Required

Journalize all of the transactions for the partnership.

Challenge Problems

Problem 13-1C   *Deciding on a capital structure*   *(Obj. 1, 2)*

Tammy Kahn and T.J. Locke have been in a partnership for five years. The principal business of the partnership is systems design for financial institutions. Gross revenues have increased from $72,000 in 19X1 to $935,000 in 19X6, the year just ended. The number of employees has increased from the two partners in the first year to nine in the most recent year. Kahn and Locke realized that they had to build up the partnership's capital and have withdrawn only part of the annual profits. As a result, their capital accounts have increased from $50,000 (Kahn, $35,000; Locke, $15,000) in 19X1 to $470,000 (Kahn, $260,000; Locke, $210,000) in 19X6.

The two partners realize that they must expand their capital base to expand their operations in order to meet the increasing demand for their systems designs. At the same time they wish to take personal advantage of the partnership's earnings. They have been trying to determine whether they should continue the partnership and borrow the necessary funds, take on one or more partners (several of their employees have expressed interest and have capital to invest), or incorporate and sell a portion of the business to outsiders. With respect to incorporation, a former classmate of Kahn's who works for a stockbroker has indicated he knows of investors who would be interested in buying a share of the business.

Required

Kahn and Locke have come to you to ask for advice. In reponse to your questions, they indicate they will need additional capital of $400,000 to 500,000.

Problem 13-2C   *The effects of accounting decisions on profits*   *(Obj. 3)*

Mary Zalinski, Susan Chiu, and Arnie May have been partners in a nursery/lawn-care business for the past eight years. Zalinski and May work full-time in the business; Chiu has a public accounting business and works about five to ten hours a week on the administrative side of the business. The business has been successful and the partners are considering expansion.

The partnership agreement states that profits will be distributed as follows:

1. Partners will get 15 percent on their average capital balances.
2. Zalinski will get a salary of $35,000; Chiu will get a salary of $5,000; May will get a salary of $35,000.
3. The balance remaining will be distributed on the basis of Zalinski, 40 percent, Chiu, 20 percent; and May, 40 percent.

The agreement also stipulates that the distributions outlined in 1 and 2 will be made even if there are not sufficient profits and that any deficiency will be shared on the basis of 3.

The capital structure was as follows at December 31, 19X3:

Zalinski	$ 60,000
Chiu	590,000
May	120,000
Total	$870,000

There has been some stress in the partnership of late because Zalinski believes that she is contributing a major part of the effort but is earning much less than May; Chiu is upset because she believes that she is earning the least even though her capital is essentially funding the partnership.

Required

Mary Zalinski, Susan Chiu, and Arnie May have come to you to ask for advice as to how they might amicably settle the present dispute. Assume net income in 19X3 was $150,000.

Extending Your Knowledge

Decision Problems

1. Disagreements among partners   (Obj. 3)

Becky Jones invested $20,000 and Tara Schwartz invested $10,000 in a public relations firm that has operated for 10 years. Neither partner has made an additional investment. They have shared profits and losses in the ratio of 2:1, which is the ratio of their investments in the business. Jones manages the office, supervises the 16 employees, and does the accounting. Schwartz, the moderator of a television talk show, is responsible for marketing. Her high profile generates important revenue for the business. During the year ended December 19X4, the partnership earned net income of $87,000, shared in the 2:1 ratio. On December 31, 19X4, Jones's capital balance was $150,000 and Schwartz's capital balance was $100,000.

Required

Respond to each of the following situations:

1. What explains the difference between the ratio of partner capital balances at December 31, 19X4, and the 2:1 ratio of partner investments and profit sharing?
2. Schwartz believes the profit-and-loss-sharing ratio is unfair. She proposes a change, but Jones insists on keeping the 2:1 ratio. What two factors may underlie Swartz's unhappiness?
3. During January 19X5, Jones learned that revenues of $21,000 were omitted from the reported 19X4 income. She brings this to Schwartz's attention, pointing out that her share of this added income is two thirds, or $14,000 and Schwartz's share is one third, or $7,000. Schwartz believes they should share this added income based on their capital balances: 60 percent (or $9,600) to Jones, and 40 percent (or $6,400) to Schwartz. Which partner is correct? Why?
4. Assume that an account payable of $12,000 for an operating expense in 19X4 was omitted from 19X4 reported income. How would the partners share this amount?

2. *Questions about partnerships* *(Obj. 1, 5)*

1. The text suggests that a written partnership agreement may be drawn up between the partners in a partnership. One benefit of an agreement is that it provides a mechanism for resolving disputes between the partners. List five areas of dispute that might be resolved by a partnership agreement.

2. The statement has been made that "If you must take on a partner, make sure the partner is richer than you are." Why is this statement valid?

3. Scare, Brown, and Gunz is a partnership of lawyers. Gunz is planning to move to Australia. What are the options open to her to convert her share of the partnership assets to cash?

Ethical Issue

Gail LaRue and Ben Chui operate the Office Centre, an office supply store in Burnaby, British Columbia. The partners split profits and losses equally, and each takes an annual salary of $50,000. To even out the workload, Chui does the buying and LaRue serves as the accountant. From time to time, they use small amounts of store merchandise for personal use. In preparing for a large private party, LaRue took engraved invitations, napkins, place mats, and other goods that cost $800. She recorded the transaction as follows:

Cost of Goods Sold	800	
Inventory		800

Required

1. How should LaRue have recorded this transaction?
2. Discuss the ethical dimension of LaRue's action.

CHAPTER 14
Corporate Organization, Capital Stock, and the Balance Sheet

"Going public is a good way for a company to raise needed capital," says Malcolm P. Appelbaum, Private Equity Investor of Wand Partners, Inc. "Being publicly traded gets the company more attention in the financial pages and in brokerage-firm research reports. This allows the company, when it's doing well, to raise money more easily and cheaply. These benefits come at the cost of intense scrutiny from shareholders, who expect the company to continue to do well."

Daniel Langlois started his Montreal-based company to develop software that could be used by animators to produce 3-D animation in 1986. It was incorporated as Softimage Inc. In 1987, 35 investors pledged $350,000 to buy a one-third interest in the company. In 1992, Langlois raised US$10 million through an initial public offering. Another US$13.6 million was raised in 1993.

In 1988, Softimage sold its first major software for $120,000. The company continued to develop its software and to grow over the next few years. The funds generated through the stock offerings allowed it to expand to 200 employees and acquire 80 Silicon Graphics workstations. The ability of the software produced by Softimage to make models move in a lifelike manner attracted the attention of movie directors like Steven Speilberg. The special effects in the movies *Jurassic Park* and *The Mask* were produced using Softimage software.

In February, 1994, Bill Gates, chairman of Microsoft Corp., made an offer for Softimage stock, and thus Microsoft acquired Softimage for $130 million of Microsoft stock.

Source: Adapted from Merle MacIsaac, "Wizard of Awe," *Canadian Business*, December, 1994, pp. 29–37.

CHAPTER OBJECTIVES

After studying this chapter, you should be able to

1 Identify the characteristics of a corporation

2 Record the issuance of stock

3 Prepare the shareholders' equity section of a corporation balance sheet

4 Account for the incorporation of a going business

5 Allocate for cash dividends

6 Compute two standard profitability measures: return on assets and return on shareholders' equity

7 Distinguish among market value, redemption value, liquidation value, and book value

8 Account for a corporation's income tax

Key Point:

Corporations are owned by investors who usually are not involved in the daily operation. A corporation's financial statements should provide the information for investors and managers to make sound decisions. Inco reports such information.

OBJECTIVE 1

Identify the characteristics of a corporation

What does it mean to "go public," as Softimage did? A corporation *goes public* when it issues its stock to the general public. Instead, the owners of the corporation—shareholders—can keep the stock *closely held*, that is, owned by a few insiders. A common reason for going public is to raise money for expansion. By offering its stock to the public, a company can hope to raise more money than if the shareholders are a limited group. Softimage probably went public for that reason.

Characteristics of a Corporation

The corporation is the dominant form of business organization in Canada. Although proprietorships and partnerships are more numerous, corporations transact more business and are larger in terms of total assets, sales revenue, and number of employees. Most well-known businesses, such as Bombardier Inc., Cineplex Odeon Corp., and TransCanada PipeLines Ltd. are corporations. Their full names include *Limited, Incorporated*, or *Corporation* (abbreviated *Ltd., Inc.* or *Corp.*) to indicate they are corporations. This chapter and Chapters 15 through 17 discuss corporations.

Why is the corporation form of business so attractive? We now look at the features that distinguish corporations from proprietorships and partnerships.

Separate Legal Entity

A *corporation* is a business entity formed under federal or provincial law. The federal or provincial government grants **articles of incorporation**, which consist of a document that gives the governing body's permission to form a corporation.

A corporation is a distinct entity from a legal perspective. We may consider the corporation as an artificial person that exists apart from its owners, who are called **shareholders**. The corporation has many of the rights that a person has. For example, a corporation may buy, own, and sell property. Assets and liabilities in the business belong to the corporation. The corporation may enter into contracts, sue, and be sued.

The owners' equity of a corporation is divided into shares of **stock**. A person becomes a shareholder by purchasing the stock of the corporation. The articles of incorporation specify how much stock the corporation can issue (sell) and lists the other details of its relationships with the federal or provincial government under whose laws it is incorporated.

Continuous Life and Transferability of Ownership

Most corporations have *continuous lives* regardless of changes in the ownership of their stock. The shareholders of Bombardier or Cineplex Odeon, or TransCanada

PipeLines may transfer stock as they wish. They may sell or trade the stock to another person, give it away, bequeath it in a will, or dispose of it in any other way they desire. The transfer of the stock does not affect the continuity of the corporation. Proprietorships and partnerships, on the other hand, terminate when their ownership changes.

No Mutual Agency

Mutual agency of the owners is not present in a corporation. A shareholder of Loblaws cannot commit the corporation to a contract (unless he or she is also an officer in the business). Mutual agency operates in partnerships but *not* in corporations. For this reason, a shareholder need not exercise the care that partners must in selecting co-owners of the business.

Limited Liability of Shareholders

A shareholder has **limited liability** for corporation debts. He or she has no personal obligation for corporation liabilities. The most that a shareholder can lose on an investment in a corporation's stock is the cost of the investment. Recall that proprietors and partners are personally liable for the debts of their businesses.

The combination of limited liability and no mutual agency means that persons can invest limited amounts in a corporation, without fear of losing all their personal wealth because of a business failure. This feature enables a corporation to raise more capital from a wider group of investors than proprietorships and partnerships.

Because of limited shareholder liability, many banks will lend money to a small corporation only if a third party (usually a corporate officer) guarantees payment of the loan in the event of default by the corporation.

Separation of Ownership and Management

Shareholders own the business, but a *board of directors*—elected by the shareholders—appoints corporate officers to manage the business. Thus shareholders may invest $100 or $1 million in the corporation without having to manage the business or disrupt their personal affairs.

The theory of finance states that the responsibility of management is to maximize the value of the firm for the benefit of the shareholders. However, this separation between owners—shareholders—and management may create problems. Corporate officers may decide to run the business for their own benefit and not to the shareholders' advantage. Shareholders may find it difficult to lodge an effective protest against management policy because of the distance between them and management.

Corporate Taxation

Corporations are separate taxable entities. They pay a variety of taxes not borne by proprietorships or partnerships, such as federal and provincial income taxes. Corporate earnings are subject to **double taxation**. First, corporations pay their own income taxes on corporate income. Then, the shareholders pay personal income tax on the cash dividends (distributions) that they receive from corporations, although the tax rate is usually lower than for regular income. This feature is different from proprietorships and partnerships, which pay no business income tax. Instead, the tax falls solely on the owners who are taxed on their share of the proprietorship or partnership income.

Government Regulation

Strong government regulation is an important disadvantage to the corporation. Because shareholders have only limited liability for corporation debts, outsiders doing business with the corporation can look no further than the corporation itself for any claims that may arise against the business. To protect persons who loan money to a corporation or who invest in its stock, the federal and provincial governments monitor the affairs of corporations. This government regulation consists mainly of ensuring that corporations disclose the business information that investors and creditors need to make informed decisions. For many corporations, adhering to this government regulation is expensive. Exhibit 14-1 lists the advantages and disadvantages of the corporation form of business organization.

EXHIBIT 14-1   *Advantages and Disadvantages of a Corporation*

Corporation Advantages	Corporation Disadvantages
1. Can raise more capital than a proprietorship or partnership can	1. Separation of ownership and management
2. Continuous life	2. Corporate taxation
3. Ease of transferring ownership	3. Government regulation
4. No mutual agency of shareholders	
5. Limited liability of shareholders	

Concept Highlight

Key Point:

Most corporations are authorized to issue many more shares of stock than they intend to issue originally. The corporation can raise additional capital by selling stock in the future without having to request government authorization of more shares.

Organization of a Corporation

Creation of a corporation begins when its organizers, called the **incorporators**, obtain articles of incorporation from the federal or provincial government. The articles of incorporation include the authorization for the corporation to issue a certain number of shares of stock, which are shares of ownership in the corporation. The incorporators pay fees and file the required documents with the incorporating jurisdiction. Then the corporation comes into existence. The incorporators agree to a set of **bylaws**, which act as the constitution for governing the corporation.

The ultimate control of the corporation rests with the shareholders, who receive one vote for each share of voting stock they own. The shareholders elect the members of the **board of directors**, which sets policy for the corporation and appoints the officers. The board elects a **chairperson**, who usually is the most powerful person in the corporation. The board also designates the **president**, who is the chief operating officer in charge of managing day-to-day operations. Most corporations also have vice-presidents in charge of sales, manufacturing, accounting and finance, and other key areas. Often the president and one or more vice-presidents are also elected to the board of directors. Exhibit 14-2 shows the authority structure in a corporation.

The structure of proprietorships, partnerships, and corporations is similar in that all three types of business have owners, managers, and employees. In proprietorships and partnerships, policy decisions are usually made by the owners—the proprietor or the partners. In a corporation, however, the managers who set policy are appointed by the board of directors, and may or may not be owners (shareholders).

All corporations have an annual meeting at which the shareholders elect directors and make other shareholder decisions such as appointing the external auditors. Shareholders unable to attend this annual meeting may vote on corporation matters by use of a *proxy*, which is a legal document that expresses the shareholder's preference and appoints another person to cast the vote.

A corporation keeps a record of its shareholders. The business must notify the shareholders of the annual shareholder meeting, send them financial statements, usually in the form of an annual report, and mail them dividend payments (which

EXHIBIT 14-2   *Authority Structure in a Corporation*

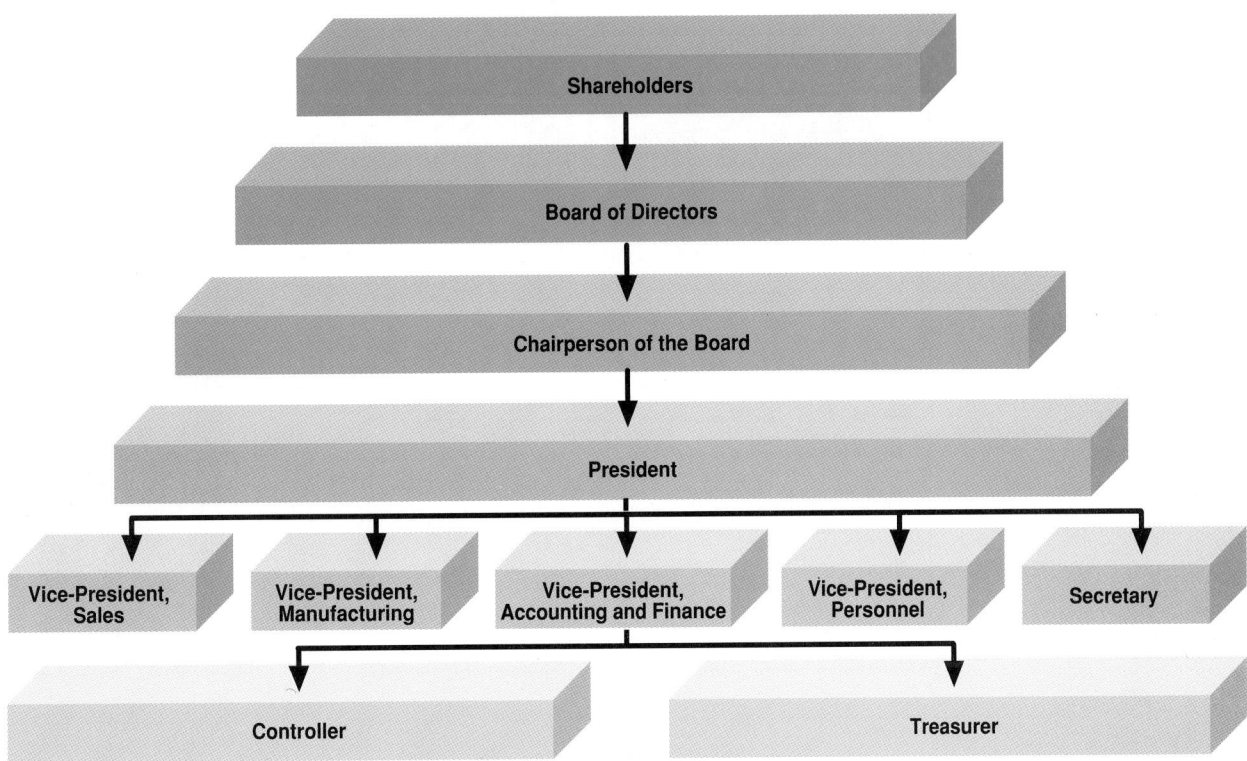

we discuss later in this chapter). Large companies use a registrar to maintain the shareholder list and a transfer agent to issue stock certificates. Banks or trust companies provide these registration and transfer services. The transfer agent handles the change in stock ownership from one shareholder to another.

Capital Stock

A corporation issues *stock certificates* to its owners in exchange for their investments in the business. Because stock represents the corporation's capital, it is often called *capital stock*. The basic unit of capital stock is called a *share*. A corporation may issue a share certificate for any number of shares it wishes—one share, 100 shares, or any other number. Exhibit 14-3 depicts an actual share certificate for 50 shares of National Trustco Inc. stock. The certificate shows the company name, shareholder name, and number of shares.

Stock in the hands of a shareholder is said to be **outstanding**. The total number of shares of stock outstanding at any time represents 100 percent ownership of the corporation.

Shareholders' Equity

The balance sheet of a corporation reports assets and liabilities in the same way as a proprietorship or a partnership. However, owners' equity of a corporation—called **shareholders' equity**—is reported differently. Incorporating acts require corporations to report the sources of their capital. The two most basic sources of capital are investments by the shareholders, called **capital stock** or *share capital*, and the capital earned through the profitable operations of the business, called **retained earnings**.

Key Point:
Note the differences among the following terms:

Authorized stock—the number of shares the corporation can issue. This number is specified in the articles of incorporation but can be increased.

Issued stock—stock that has been sold to a shareholder and for which a stock certificate has been issued.

Outstanding stock—stock that is in the hands of a shareholder.

EXHIBIT 14-3   *Share Certificate*

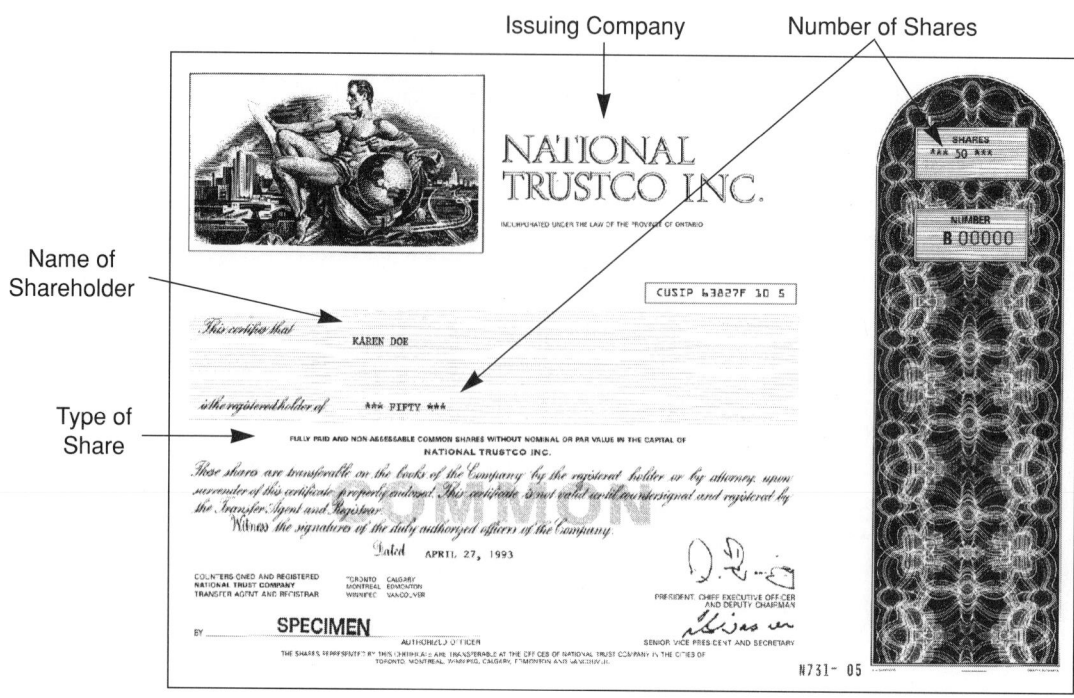

While the *Canada Business Corporations Act* and several of the provincial incorporating acts use the term *stated capital* to describe capital stock, this text will use the more common term, capital stock. Exhibit 14-4 outlines a summarized version of the balance sheet of Canadian Tire Corporation Limited, to show how to report these categories of shareholders' equity.

EXHIBIT 14-4   *Summarized Balance Sheet of Canadian Tire Corporation, Limited (Amounts in millions)*

Assets	$2,669	Liabilities	$1,517
		Shareholders' equity	
		Capital stock	276
		Retained earnings	876
		Total shareholders'	
		equity	**1,152**
		Total liabilities and	
Total assets	$2,669	shareholders' equity	$2,669

Common Stock is one type of capital stock. It is regarded as the permanent capital of the business because it is not subject to withdrawal by the shareholders.

An investment of cash or any other asset in a corporation increases its assets and shareholders' equity. Canadian Tire's entry for receipt of a $20,000 shareholder investment in the business is

Oct.	20	Cash	20,000	
		Common Stock		20,000
		Investment by shareholder.		

Profitable operations produce income, which increases shareholders' equity through an account called Retained Earnings. At the end of the year, the balance of the Income Summary account is closed to Retained Earnings. For example, if Canadian Tire's net income is $80 million, Income Summary will have an $80 million credit balance.

Canadian Tire's closing entry will debit Income Summary to transfer net income to Retained Earnings as follows (in million of dollars):

Dec.	31	Income Summary..	80	
		Retained Earnings..		80
		To close Income Summary by transferring net *income* to Retained Earnings.		

If operations produce a net loss rather than net income, the Income Summary account will have a debit balance. Income Summary must be credited to close it. With a $60,000 loss, the closing entry is

Dec.	31	Retained Earnings..	60,000	
		Income Summary...		60,000
		To close Income Summary by transferring net *loss* to Retained Earnings.		

A large loss may cause a debit balance in the Retained Earnings account. This condition, called a Retained Earnings **deficit** or accumulated deficit, is reported on the balance sheet as a negative amount in shareholders' equity. Dominion Textile Inc. reported the following in 1992:

Shareholders' Equity (in thousands)

Capital stock..	$481,156
Deficit...	(103,068)
Total shareholders' equity..............................	$378,088

If the corporation has been profitable and has sufficient cash, a distribution of cash may be made to the shareholders. Such distributions—called **dividends**—decrease both the assets and the retained earnings of the business. The balance of the Retained Earnings account at any time is the sum of earnings accumulated since incorporation, minus any losses, and minus all dividends distributed to shareholders. Retained Earnings is entirely separate from the capital stock invested in the business by the shareholders.

Some people think of Retained Earnings as a fund of cash. It is not, because Retained Earnings is an element of shareholders' equity, representing a claim against all assets resulting from cumulative earnings minus cumulative dividends since the corporation's beginning. In short, remember that dividends are *paid* out of assets, not out of retained earnings.

Shareholders' Rights

The owner of a share of stock has certain rights that are set out in the corporation's articles of incorporation; these vary from company to company, and even between classes of stock within a company. In addition, the shareholder may have other rights granted by the legislation under which the corporation receives its articles. While those rights outlined in the articles of incorporation are specific to an individual company, those set forth by legislation are shared by shareholders of all companies incorporated under that legislation. The articles of incorporation, for example, may specify that the shareholder of one class of common share is entitled to one vote at shareholders' meetings, while the shareholder of another class common share is not entitled to vote. An example of a shared right is that under the *Canada Business Corporations Act*, shareholders may require the directors of the company to call a meeting of the shareholders.

Some of the rights normally attached to common shares[1] are:

---

[1] The rights enumerated are basic rights common to incorporating legislation generally. For a more complete listing, the interested reader is referred to: *Canada Business Corporations Act with Regulations, 1993*, 9th edition, Don Mills, Ontario: CCH Canadian Limited, 1993; and *Canada Business Corporations Act in The Revised Statutes of Canada*.

1. The right to sell the shares.

2. The right to vote at shareholders' meetings.

3. The right to a proportionate share of any dividends declared by the directors for that class of shares.

4. The right to receive a proportionate share of any assets, on the winding-up of the company, after the creditors and any classes of shares that rank above that class have been paid.

Classes of Stock

Corporations issue different types of stock to appeal to a wide variety of investors. The stock of a corporation may be either common or preferred.

Short Exercise:
For the following list of characteristics of capital stock, indicate whether each characteristic applies to preferred and common stock:

1. Stated dividend
2. Voting rights
3. Priority to receive assets in the event of liquidation
4. Cumulative
5. Callable

A:	Preferred	Common
1.	Yes	No
2.	Maybe	Usually
3.	Yes	No
4.	Yes	No
5.	Maybe	No

Common and Preferred Stock

Every corporation issues *common stock*, the most basic form of capital stock. Unless designated otherwise, the word *stock* is understood to mean "common stock." Companies may issue different classes of common stock. For example, Rogers Communications Inc. has issued Class A common stock, which carries the right to vote, and Class B common stock, which are nonvoting. (Classes of common stock may also be designated Series A, Series B, and so on, with each series having certain unique features such as a fixed dividend or a redemption feature.) The general ledger has a separate account for each class of common stock. In describing a corporation, we would say the common shareholders are the owners of the business.

Investors who buy common stock take the ultimate risk with a corporation. The corporation makes no promises to pay them. If the corporation succeeds, it will pay dividends to its shareholders, but if net income and cash are too low, the shareholders may receive no dividends. The stock of successful corporations increases in value, and investors enjoy the benefit of selling the stock at a gain. But stock prices can decrease, leaving the investors holding worthless stock certificates. Because common shareholders take a risky investment position, they demand increases in stock prices, high dividends, or both. If the corporation does not deliver, the shareholders sell the stock, and its market price falls. Short of bankruptcy, this is one of the worst things that can happen to a corporation because it means that the company cannot raise capital as needed.

Preferred stock gives its owners certain advantages over common shareholders. These benefits include the priority to receive dividends before the common shareholders, and the priority to receive assets before the common shareholders if the corporation liquidates. Often, preferred stock is cumulative which means that if the preferred dividend is not paid in a year, the arrears must be paid to the preferred shareholders before the common shareholders can receive a dividend. Because of the preferred shareholders' priorities, common stock represents the residual ownership in the corporation's assets after the liabilities and the claims of preferred shareholders have been subtracted. Preferred shares usually indicate the annual dividend. Often the right to vote is withheld from preferred shareholders. Lefarge Corporation, the cement and building materials company, has $1.88 convertible preferred shares and $2.44 convertible preferred shares; $1.88 and $2.44 are the annual dividend rates. Companies may issue different classes of preferred stock (Class A and Class B or Series A and Series B, for example). Each class is recorded in a separate account.

Investors who buy preferred stock take less risk than do common shareholders. Why? Because corporations pay a fixed amount of dividends on preferred stock. Investors usually buy preferred stock to earn those dividends. An increase in the market value of preferred stock is less important than an increase in the market value of common stock because preferred stocks' values do not fluctuate much.

Preferred stock operates as a hybrid somewhere between common stock and long-term debt. Like debt, preferred stock pays a fixed dividend. But like stock, the dividend

EXHIBIT 14-5   *Comparison of Common Stock, Preferred Stock, and Long-Term Debt*

	Common Stock	**Preferred Stock**	**Long-Term Debt**
Investment risk	High	Medium	Low
Corporate obligation to repay principal	No	No	Yes
Dividends/Interest	Dividends	Dividends	Tax-deductible interest expense
Corporate obligation to pay dividends/interest	Only after declaration	Only after declaration*	At fixed dates
Fluctuations in market value under normal conditions	High	Medium	Low

*Some preferred stock is cumulative as to dividends.

becomes a liability only after the board of directors has declared the dividend. Also, there is no obligation to pay back true preferred stock in the manner required by debt. Preferred stock that must be redeemed (paid back) by the corporation is a liability masquerading as a stock. Experienced investors treat mandatorily redeemable preferred stock as part of total liabilities, not as part of owners' equity. While preferred shares are a common way for a corporation to raise funds, not all corporations issued preferred shares. All corporations have common shares.

Corporations prefer debt to preferred stock because dividend payments are not tax deductible and interest payments are. Dividends are a distribution of assets created by earnings. On the other hand, individuals might prefer to hold preferred shares because the income tax rate on dividends they receive is lower than the tax rate they pay on interest. It's for that reason that the dividend rate on a company's preferred shares is usually lower than the interest rate on bonds the company issues. Exhibit 14–5 summarizes the similarities and differences among common stock, preferred stock, and long-term debt.

Par Value and No-Par Stock

Par value is an arbitrary amount assigned to a share of stock in the articles of incorporation by the company issuing it. For example, National Trust, through a predecessor company, used to issue common shares with a $2.00 par value. When a common share was sold, $2.00 would be allocated to Common Stock and any consideration received in excess of $2.00 would be recorded as a premium on (that) common stock. Par value shares are gradually being eliminated by the various jurisdictions in Canada and exist today only in a very few of those jurisdictions. The discussion of par value stock is included for completeness, and because it remains a popular class in the United States.

No-par shares are shares of stock that do not have a value assigned to them by the articles of incorporation. The board of directors assigns a value to the shares when they are issued; this value is known as the *stated value*. For example, Dajol Inc. has authorization to issue 100,000 shares of common stock, having no-par value assigned to them by the articles of incorporation. Dajol needs $50,000 at incorporation, and might issue 10,000 shares for $5.00 per share, 2,000 shares at $25.00 per share, or 1,000 shares at $50.00 per share, and so on. The point is that Dajol can assign whatever value to the shares the board of directors wishes. Normally, the stated value would be credited to Common Stock when the stock is issued.

The value of a corporation's capital stock or stated capital is the sum of the shares issued times the stated values of those shares at the time of issue. For example, if YDR Ltd. issued 1,000 common shares at a stated value of $8.00 per share, 2,000 shares at $12.00 per share, and 500 shares at $15.00 per share, its capital stock or stated capital would be $39,500 [(1,000 × $8) + (2,000 × $12) + (500 × $15)].

The *Canada Business Corporations Act* and most provincial incorporating acts now require common and preferred shares to be issued without nominal or par value. The full value of the proceeds from the sale of stock by a company must be allocated to the capital account for that stock. For example, if National Trust were to issue 100 shares of common stock for $2,500 (that is, at a stated value of $25.00 per share), $2,500 would be credited to Common Stock.

Issuing Stock

OBJECTIVE 2

Record the issuance of stock

Large corporations such as NOVA Corporation, McCain Foods Ltd., and John Labatt Ltd. need huge quantities of money to operate. They cannot expect to finance all their operations through borrowing. They need capital that they can raise by issuing stock. The articles of incorporation that the incorporators receive from the federal or provincial government includes an *authorization of stock*—that is, a provision giving the government's permission for the business to issue (to sell) a certain number of shares of stock. Corporations may sell the stock directly to the shareholders, or they may use the service of an *underwriter*, such as the brokerage firms RBC Dominion Securities or Richardson Greenshields. The agreement between a corporation and its underwriter will vary, but typically the underwriter will commit to placing all of the share issue it can with its customers, and to buying any unsold shares for its own account. In another form of contract, the underwriter agrees to do its best to sell all the share issue but makes no guarantees. The underwriter makes its money by selling the shares for a higher price than it pays to the corporation issuing the shares.

Key Point:

Owners invest in a corporation by buying stock. Issuance of stock increases the corporation's assets and shareholders' equity.

Short Exercise:

Answer the following question on the basis of this journal entry for stock issued at $23 per share:

Cash 276,000
  Common
    Stock 276,000

How many shares of stock were issued? **A:**
$276,000/$23
= 12,000 shares

The corporation need not issue all the stock that the articles of incorporation allow—authorized stock can, and often does, exceed issued stock. Management may hold some stock back and issue it later if the need for additional capital arises. The stock that the corporation does issue to shareholders is called *issued stock*. Only by issuing stock—not by receiving authorization—does the corporation increase the asset and owner's equity amounts on its balance sheet.

The price that the shareholder pays to acquire stock from the corporation is called the *issue price*. A combination of market factors—including the company's comparative earnings record, financial position, prospects for success, and general business conditions—determines issue price. Investors will not pay more than market value for the stock. The following sections show how to account for the issuance of stock.

Issuing Common Stock

Short Exercise:

Prepare journal entries for each situation:
A company issues
1. 100,000 shares of no-par common stock for $35 per share. **A:**
Cash 3,500,000
  Common Stock
  (100,000 × $35)
 3,500,000

2. 160,000 shares of no-par common stock in exchange for land valued at $55,000, a building valued at $125,000, and a computer valued at $5,000. **A:**
Equipment.......... 5,000
Building............. 125,000
Land.................. 55,000
  Common
    Stock........... 185,000

Companies often advertise the issuance of their stock to attract investors. *The Financial Post* is the most popular medium for the advertisements, which are also called *tombstones*. Exhibit 14-6 is a reproduction of Acier Leroux Inc.'s tombstone that appeared in *The Financial Post* on April 19, 1995.

Four brokerage firms sold Acier Leroux's stock to their clients. Altogether, Acier Leroux hoped to raise approximately $11 million of capital.

Issuing Common Stock at a Stated Value   Suppose NOVA Corporation issues 80 million shares of its common stock for cash, and the directors determine that the shares will be issued with a stated value of $7.175 per share. The stock issuance entry is

Jan. 8	Cash (80,000,000 × $7.175)................................	574,000,000	
	Common Stock		574,000,000
	To issue common stock at $7.175 per share.		

The amount invested in the corporation, $574 million in this case, is called capital stock. The credit to Common Stock records an increase in the capital stock of the corporation.

EXHIBIT 14-6   *Announcement of Public Offering of Acier Leroux Inc. Stock*

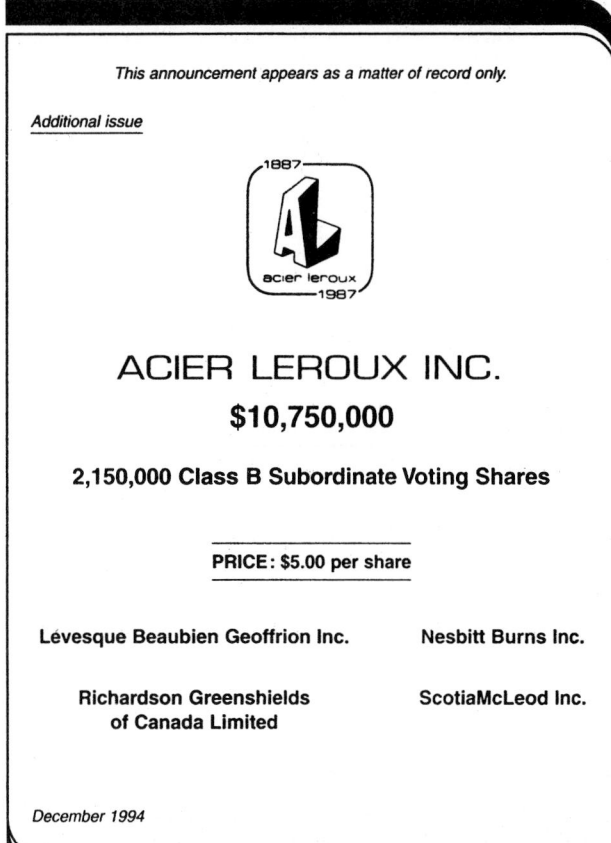

This announcement appears as a matter of record only.

Additional issue

ACIER LEROUX INC.

$10,750,000

2,150,000 Class B Subordinate Voting Shares

PRICE: $5.00 per share

Lévesque Beaubien Geoffrion Inc.   **Nesbitt Burns Inc.**

Richardson Greenshields   **ScotiaMcLeod Inc.**
of Canada Limited

December 1994

The following example illustrates the shareholders' equity section of NOVA Corporation after it had issued the 80 million shares. Assume that the articles of incorporation granted to NOVA authorize it to issue an unlimited number of common shares, that 398,172,048 shares had been issued for a stated value of $5.14 per share prior to January, and that the company had $719 million in retained earnings. The corporation would report shareholders' equity as follows:

Shareholders' Equity (in millions)

Capital stock	
Common stock, unlimited number of shares authorized, 478 million shares issued	$2,621
Retained earnings	719
Total shareholders' equity	$3,340

The authorized common stock reports the maximum number of shares the company may issue under its articles of incorporation.

STOP & THINK

NOVA Corporation actually had total liabilities of $4,916 million on the balance-sheet date just given. What was NOVA's debt ratio?

Answer: The debt ratio is 0.595

$$\frac{\text{Total liabilities}}{\text{Total assets}} = \frac{\$4,916}{\$4,916 + \$3,341} = .595$$

Issuing Common Stock for Assets Other Than Cash   When a corporation issues stock in exchange for assets other than cash, it debits the assets received for their current market value and credits the capital accounts accordingly. The assets' prior book value does not matter because the shareholder will demand stock equal to the market value of the asset given. Kahn Corporation issued 15,000 shares of its common stock for equipment worth $15,000 and a building worth $120,000. The entry is

Nov. 12	Equipment...	15,000	
	Building	120,000	
	Common stock..		135,000
	To issue 15,000 shares of common stock in exchange for equipment and a building.		

Common stock increases by the amount of the assets' current market value, $135,000 in this case; the stated value or value assigned to the shares would be $9.00 ($135,000/15,000) per share.

STOP & THINK

How did this transaction affect Kahn Corporation's capital stock? Retained earnings? Total shareholders' equity?

Answer:

	Capital Stock	Effect on Retained Earnings	Total Shareholders' Equity
	Increase $135,000	None	Increase $135,000

Issuing Par-Value Common Stock at a Premium   A corporation in a province that permits par-value stock usually issues its common stock for a price above par value. The excess amount above par is called a *premium*. Assume Olde Corp. issues 100 shares of $10 par value common stock for a price of $25; the total proceeds would be $2,500 (100 × $25). The $15 per share difference is a premium. This sale of stock increases the corporation's capital stock by $2,500, the total issue price of the stock. Both the par value of the stock and the premium are part of capital stock. A premium on the sale of stock is not gain, income, or profit to the corporation, because the entity is dealing with its own shareholders. This illustrates one of the fundamentals of accounting: a company cannot earn a profit or incur a loss when it sells its stock to or buys its stock from its own shareholders.

The entry to record the issue of one hundred $10 par-value shares at $25 by Olde Corp. would be

Jan. 23	Cash (100 × $25).................................	2,500	
	Common stock (100 × $10)..........................		1,000
	Contributed surplus (100 × $15).................		1,500
	To issue common stock at a premium.		

Since both par-value and premium amounts increase the corporation's capital, they appear in the shareholders' equity section of the balance sheet. At the end of the first year, Olde Corp. would report shareholders' equity on its balance sheet as follows, assuming the articles of incorporation authorize 20,000 shares of $10 par value common stock, 1,000 shares were previously issued at par, and retained earnings is $8,500:

Shareholders' Equity

Capital stock	
Common stock, $10 par, 20,000 shares authorized, 1,100 shares issued	$11,000
Contributed surplus	1,500
Total capital stock	12,500
Retained earnings	8,500
Total shareholders' equity	$21,000

We determine the dollar amount reported for common stock by multiplying the total number of shares issued (1,000 issued previously + 100) by the par value per share.

Issuing Preferred Stock

While not all corporations issue preferred stock, recent editions of *Financial Reporting in Canada* published by the Canadian Institute of Chartered Accountants report that slightly more than two thirds of the 300 companies reporting mentioned preferred shares in the shareholders' equity section of their balance sheets. Accounting for preferred shares follows the pattern illustrated for common stock.

Assume the Lang Corporation articles of incorporation authorize issuance of 5,000 preferred shares with an annual dividend of $11.00 per share. On July 31, the company issues 400 shares at a stated price of $110.00 per share. The issuance entry is

July	31	Cash (400 × $110)	44,000
		Preferred Stock	44,000
		To issue preferred stock.	

Summary Review of Accounting for Stock

Let us review the first half of this chapter by showing the shareholders' equity section of Medina Corporation's balance sheet at May 31 in Exhibit 14-7. (Assume that all figures, which are arbitrary, are correct.) Note the two sections of shareholders' equity: capital stock and retained earnings. Also observe the order of the equity accounts: preferred stock and common stock.

Short Exercise:

From this list, calculate total capital stock and total shareholders' equity:

Common Stock	$16,255
Preferred Stock	6,836
Retained Earnings	18,934

A: Total capital stock = $23,091 ($16,255 + $6,836)
Total shareholders' equity = $42,025 ($23,091 + $18,934)

OBJECTIVE 3

Prepare the shareholders' equity section of a corporation balance sheet

EXHIBIT 14-7 *Part of Medina Corporation's Balance Sheet*

Shareholders' Equity

Capital stock	
Preferred stock, $5.00, 5,000 shares authorized, 400 shares issued	$40,000
Common stock, 5,000 shares authorized, 2,000 shares issued	36,000
Total capital stock	76,000
Retained earnings	3,000
Total shareholders' equity	$79,000

Mid-Chapter Summary Problem for Your Review

1. Test your understanding of the first half of this chapter by answering whether each of the following statements is true or false:

   a. A shareholder may bind the corporation to a contract.

   b. The policy-making body in a corporation is called the board of directors.

   c. The owner of 100 shares of preferred stock has greater voting rights than the owner of 100 shares of common stock.

   d. A company incorporated under the *Canada Business Corporations Act* must assign the proceeds of a stock issue to the capital account for that stock.

   e. All shares of common stock issued and outstanding have voting rights.

   f. Issuance of 1,000 common shares at $12 increases owners' equity by $12,000.

   g. The stated value of a stock is the value assigned to the stock by the company issuing it at the date issued or subscribed.

   h. A corporation issues its preferred stock in exchange for land and a building with a combined market value of $200,000. This transaction increases the corporation's owners' equity by $200,000 regardless of the assets' prior book value.

   i. Preferred stock is a riskier investment than common stock.

2. Tundra Co. Ltd., incorporated under the *Canada Business Corporations Act*, had three transactions during the year involving its common shares. On January 15, 10,000 Class A voting shares were issued with a stated value of $7.80 per share. On February 28, 4,000 Class B non-voting shares with a stated value of $8.50 per share were issued. On August 8, 6,000 Class B shares were issued in exchange for land with a market value of $52,000. Tundra's articles of incorporation state that 50,000 Class A voting and 100,000 Class B non-voting common shares are authorized.

   ### Required

   a. Prepare the journal entry to record the transaction of January 15.

   b. Prepare the journal entry to record the transaction of February 28.

   c. Prepare the journal entry to record the transaction of August 8.

   d. Set up the shareholders' equity section for Tundra Co. Ltd. after the three transactions have taken place.

   e. What is the total capital stock of the company?

   f. How did Tundra withhold the voting privilege from their Class B common shareholders?

SOLUTIONS TO SUMMARY PROBLEM

1. Answers to true-false statements:

a. False	b. True	c. False	d. True	e. False
f. True	g. True	h. True	i. False	

2. a.

Jan. 15	Cash (10,000 × $7.80)	78,000	
	Common Stock—Class A		78,000
	To issue Class A common stock at $7.80 per share.		

   b.

Feb. 28	Cash (4,000 × $8.50)	34,000	
	Common Stock—Class B.......................		34,000
	To issue Class B common stock at $8.50 per share.		

c.   Aug. 8   Land   52,000

               Common Stock—Class B.......................   52,000

               To issue 6,000 shares of common stock in
exchange for land.

d.   Shareholders' Equity

       Capital stock

          Common stock, Class A voting, 50,000
shares authorized, 10,000 shares issued $78,000
Common stock, Class B non-voting,
100,000, shares authorized, 10,000
shares issued......................................   86,000

                                     $164,000

e.   Capital stock is $164,000.

f.   The voting privilege was withheld by specific agreement; the
articles of incorporation specified the Class B common shares
were non-voting.

Donated Capital

Corporations occasionally receive gifts or donations. For example, a city council
may offer a company free land to encourage it to locate in their city. The free land
is called a donation. Also, a shareholder may make a donation to the corporation in
the form of cash, land or other assets, or stock that the corporation can resell.

A donation is a gift that increases the assets of the corporation. However, the donor
(giver) receives no ownership interest in the company in return. A transaction to receive
a donation does not increase the corporation's revenue, and thus it does not affect income.
Instead, the donation creates a special category of shareholders' equity called
donated capital. The corporation records a donation by debiting the asset received at
its current market value, and by crediting Donated Capital, a shareholders' equity account.

Suppose Burlington Ltd. receives 100 hectares of land as a donation from the
city of Lethbridge, Alberta. The current market value of the land is $150,000.
Burlington records receipt of the donation as follows:

Apr. 18   Land...   150,000

               Donated Capital..   150,000

               To receive land as a donation from the city.

Donated capital is reported on the balance sheet after the stock accounts in the
capital stock section of shareholders' equity.

Incorporation of a Going Business

OBJECTIVE 4

Account for the
incorporation of a
going business

You may dream of having your own business someday, or you may currently be a
business proprietor or partner. Businesses that begin as a proprietorship or a partnership often incorporate at a later date. By incorporating a going business, the
proprietor or partners avoid the unlimited liability for business debts. And as we discussed earlier, incorporating makes it easier to raise capital.

To account for the incorporation of a going business, we close the owner equity
accounts of the prior entity and set up the shareholder equity accounts of the corporation. Suppose B.C. Coast Travel Associates is a partnership owned by Joe Suzuki
and Monica Lee. The partnership balance sheet, after all adjustments and
closing entries, reports Joe Suzuki, Capital, of $50,000, and Monica Lee, Capital, of
$70,000. They incorporate the travel agency as B.C. Coast Travel Company, Inc.
with an authorization to issue 200,000 shares of common stock. Joe and Monica

agree to receive common stock equal in stated value to their partnership owners' equity balances. The entry to record the incorporation of the business is

Feb.	1	Joe Suzuki, Capital	50,000	
		Monica Lee, Capital...	70,000	
		Common Stock...		120,000
		To incorporate the business, close the capital accounts of the partnership and issue common stock to the incorporators.		

Organization Cost

The costs of organizing a corporation include legal fees for preparing documents and advising on procedures, fees, and taxes paid to the incorporating jurisdiction, and charges by promoters for selling the company's stock. These costs are grouped in an account titled Organization Cost, which is an asset because these costs contribute to a business's start-up. Suppose Mary's Good Wings and Ribs Ltd. pays legal fees and incorporation fees of $3,500 to organize the corporation under the *Canada Business Corporations Act* in Newfoundland. In addition, an investment dealer charges a fee of $12,000 for selling 20,000 shares of Mary's Good Wings and Ribs Ltd. common stock for $160,000 and receives 2,000 common shares as payment. Mary's Good Wings and Ribs Ltd.'s journal entries to record these organization costs are

Mar.	31	Organization Cost	3,500	
		Cash..		3,500
		Legal fees and incorporation fees to organize the corporation.		
Apr.	3	Cash	160,000	
		Organization Cost...	12,000	
		Common Stock...		172,000
		To record receipt of funds from sale of common stock and issue of shares to investment dealer for selling stock in organization.		

Organization cost is an *intangible asset*, reported on the balance sheet along with patents, trademarks, goodwill, and any other intangibles. We know that an intangible asset should be amortized over its useful life, and organization costs will benefit the corporation for as long as the corporation operates. But how long will that be? We cannot know in advance. Revenue Canada allows corporations to write organization expenses off against taxable income. While the *CICA Handbook* does not require organization costs to be amortized, most companies write organization costs off quickly because of their relatively small size. As is true with other intangibles, amortization expense for the year should be disclosed.

Dividend Dates

A corporation must declare a dividend before paying it. The board of directors alone has the authority to declare a dividend. The corporation has no obligation to pay a dividend until the board declares one, but once declared, the dividend becomes a legal liability of the corporation. Three relevant dates for dividends are

1. **Declaration date** On the declaration date, the board of directors announces the intention to pay the dividend. The declaration creates a liability for the corporation. Declaration is recorded by debiting Retained Earnings and crediting Dividends Payable.

2. **Date of record**   The corporation announces the record date, which follows the declaration date by a few weeks, as part of the declaration. The corporation makes no journal entry on the date of record because no transaction occurs. Nevertheless, much work takes place behind the scenes to identify the shareholders of record on this date properly, because the stock is being traded continuously. Only the people who own the stock on the date of record receive the dividend.

3. **Payment date**   Payment of the dividend usually follows the record date by two to four weeks. Payment is recorded by debiting Dividends Payable and crediting Cash.

Dividends on Preferred and Common Stock

Declaration of a cash dividend is recorded by debiting Retained Earnings and crediting Dividends Payable as follows:

June 19	Retained Earnings	XXX	
	Dividends Payable		XXX
	To declare a cash dividend.		

Payment of the dividend occurs, as was noted above, on the payment date, and is recorded:

July 2	Dividends Payable	XXX	
	Cash..		XXX
	To pay a cash dividend.		

Dividends Payable is a current liability. When a company has issued both preferred and common stock, the preferred shareholders receive their dividends first. The common shareholders receive dividends only if the total declared dividend is large enough to pay the preferred shareholders first.

Pine Industries, Inc., in addition to its common stock, has 9,000 shares of preferred stock outstanding. Preferred dividends are paid at the annual rate of $1.75 per share. Assume that Pine declares an annual dividend of $150,000. The allocation to preferred and common shareholders is

	Total Dividend of $150,000
Preferred dividend (9,000 shares × $1.75 per share).........................	$ 15,750
Common dividend (remainder: $150,000 – $15,750)........................	134,250
Total dividend...	$150,000

If Pine declares only a $20,000 dividend, preferred shareholders receive $15,750 and the common shareholders receive $4,250 ($20,000 – $15,750).

This example illustrates an important relationship between preferred stock and common stock. To an investor, the preferred stock is safer because it receives dividends first (as well as ranking ahead of common shares on dissolution). For example, if Pine Industries earns only enough net income to pay the preferred shareholders' dividends, the owners of common stock receive no dividends at all. However, the earnings potential from an investment in common stock is much greater than from an investment in preferred stock. Preferred dividends are usually limited to the specified amount, but there is no upper limit on the amount of common dividends.

We noted that preferred shareholders enjoy the advantage of priority over common shareholders in receiving dividends. The dividend preference is normally

---

OBJECTIVE 5
Allocate for cash dividends

Short Exercise:
Georgia Strait Corporation was organized on 1/1/X1 with 100,000 shares of stock authorized; 50,000 shares were issued on 1/5/X1. Georgia Strait earned $50,000 during 19X1 and declared a dividend of $0.40 per share on 11/30/X1 payable to shareholders on 1/1/X2. (1) Journalize the declaration and payment of the dividend. (2) Compute the balance of retained earnings on 12/31/X1. *A:*
(1) 11/30/X1 declaration
Retained
  Earnings........... 20,000
    Div. Payable ...   20,000
      (50,000 shares × $0.40)

1/1/X2 payment
Div. Payable 20,000
  Cash.................   20,000
(2) The balance in retained earnings is $30,000 ($50,000 – $20,000). The declaration on 11/30/X1—not the payment on 1/1/X2—reduced retained earnings.

stated as a dollar amount. (In those rare cases where the preferred shares have a par value, the dividend preference may be stated as a percentage of the par value rate.) For example, the preferred stock may be "$3 preferred," meaning that the shareholders receive an annual dividend of $3 per share.

Cumulative and Noncumulative Preferred Stock

The allocation of dividends may be complex if the preferred stock is *cumulative*. Corporations sometimes fail to pay a dividend to their preferred shareholders. The passed dividends are said to be *in arrears*. The owners of **cumulative preferred stock** must receive all dividends in arrears before the corporation pays dividends to the common shareholders. The cumulative feature is not automatic to preferred shares but must be assigned to the preferred shares in the articles of incorporation.

The preferred stock of Pine Industries, Inc. is cumulative. Suppose the company passed the 19X4 preferred dividend of $15,750. Before paying dividends to its common shareholders in 19X5, the company must first pay preferred dividends of $15,750 for both 19X4 and 19X5, a total of $31,500.

Assume that Pine Industries passes its 19X4 preferred dividend. In 19X5, the company declares a $50,000 dividend. The entry to record the declaration is

Sept. 6 Retained Earnings...	50,000	
Dividends Payable, Preferred		
($15,750 × 2)...		31,500
Dividends Payable, Common		
($50,000 − $31,500)...................................		18,500
To declare a cash dividend.		

If the preferred stock is not designated as cumulative, the corporation is not obligated to pay dividends in arrears. Suppose that the Pine Industries preferred stock was not cumulative, and the company passed the 19X4 preferred dividend of $15,750. The preferred shareholders would lose the 19X4 dividend forever. Of course, the common shareholders would not receive a 19X4 dividend either. Before paying any common dividends in 19X5, the company would have to pay the 19X5 preferred dividend of $15,750.

Having dividends in arrears on cumulative preferred stock is not a liability to the corporation. (A liability for dividends arises only after the board of directors declares the dividend.) Nevertheless, a corporation must report cumulative preferred dividends in arrears in the notes to the financial statements. This information alerts common shareholders to how much in cumulative preferred dividends must be paid before any dividends will be paid on the common stock. This gives the common shareholders an idea about the likelihood of receiving dividends and satisfies the disclosure principle.

Note disclosure of cumulative preferred dividends might take the following form. Observe the two references to note 3 in this section of the balance sheet. The "$3.00" after "Preferred stock" is the dividend rate.

Preferred stock, $3.00, 10,000 shares authorized,	
2,000 shares issued (note 3)	$100,000
Retained earnings (note 3)...	414,000

Note 3: Cumulative preferred dividends in arrears. At December 31, 19X2, dividends on the company's $3.00 preferred stock were in arrears for 19X1 and 19X2, in the amount of $12,000 ($3.00 × 2,000 × 2 years).

Participating and Nonparticipating Preferred Stock

The owners of *participating preferred stock* may receive—that is, *participate in*—dividends beyond the stated amount. Assume that the corporation declares a dividend. First, the preferred shareholders receive their dividends. If the corporation has declared a large enough dividend, then the common shareholders receive their dividends. If an additional dividend amount remains to be distributed, common shareholders and participating preferred shareholders share it. For example, the owners of a $4 preferred stock must receive the specified annual dividend of $4 per share before the common shareholders receive any dividends. Then a $4 dividend is paid on each common share. The participation feature takes effect only after the preferred and common shareholders have received the specified $4 rate. Payment of an extra *common* dividend of, say, $1.50 is accompanied by a $1.50 dividend on each participating preferred share.

Participating preferred stock is rare. In fact, preferred stock is nonparticipating unless it is specifically described as participating in the articles of incorporation. Therefore, if the preferred stock in our example is not participating (the usual case), the largest annual dividend that a preferred shareholder will receive in our illustration is $4.

Convertible Preferred Stock

Convertible preferred stock may be exchanged by the preferred shareholders, if they choose, for another specified class of stock in the corporation. For example, the preferred stock of Rainy River Lumber Ltd. is convertible into the company's common stock. A note to Rainy River's balance sheet describes the conversion terms as follows:

> The . . . preferred stock is convertible at the rate of 6.51 shares of common stock for each share of preferred stock outstanding.

If you owned 100 shares of Rainy River's convertible preferred stock, you could convert it into 651 (100 × 6.51) shares of Rainy River Lumber common stock. Under what condition would you exercise the conversion privilege? You would do so if the market value of the common stock that you could receive from conversion exceeded the market value of the preferred stock that you presently held. This way, you as an investor could increase your personal wealth.

Rainy River Lumber convertible preferred stock was issued at $100 per share, and the common stock at $1. The company would record the conversion at the value of the 100 preferred shares on the Rainy River Lumber books, or $10,000 (100 × $100). The conversion of the 100 shares of preferred stock into 651 shares of common stock would be recorded as follows:

Mar. 7	Preferred stock (100 × $100)........................	10,000	
	Common stock (651 shares)....................		10,000
	Conversion of preferred stock into common.		

Summary

Preferred stock, as we see, offers alternative features not available to common stock. Preferred stock may be cumulative or not cumulative, participating or not participating, and convertible or not convertible. In addition, preferred stock is usually preferred when dividends are distributed, and when the assets are distributed to shareholders upon liquidation of the company.

Rate of Return on Total Assets and Rate of Return on Shareholders' Equity

Investors and creditors are constantly evaluating the ability of managers to earn profits. Investors search for companies whose stocks are likely to incease in value. Creditors are interested in profitable companies that can pay their debts. Investment and credit decisions often include a comparison of companies. But a comparison of

---

Short Exercise:

Wheeler Corp. has outstanding 15,000 shares of common stock and 5,000 shares of $1.80 cumulative preferred stock. The company has declared no dividends for the past two years but plans to pay $56,250 this year. Compute the dividends for preferred and common stock if the preferred is nonparticipating. **A:**

Preferred Stock:
Dividends in arrears
($1.80 × 5,000 × 2)
.... $18,000
Current dividend   9,000
Total to Preferred $27,000

Common Stock:
Remainder of dividend
($56,250 − $27,000)
                        29,250
Total dividend........ $56,250

Key Point:

Convertible preferred stock may be exchanged for common stock at the shareholder's option.

Short Exercise:

Record the conversion of 100 shares of $9.00 convertible preferred stock that was originally issued at $150 per share. Each preferred stock is convertible into 4 shares of common stock. **A:**
Preferred Stock
(100 × $150) 15,000
  Common Stock...... 15,000

OBJECTIVE 6

Compute two standard profitability measures: return on assets and return on shareholders' equity

Northern Telecom's net income to the net income of a new company in the electronics industry simply is not meaningful. Northern Telecom's profits run into hundreds of millions of dollars, which likely exceed the new company's total sales. Does that automatically make Northern Telecom a better investment? Not necessarily. To make relevant comparisons between companies different in size, scope of operations, or any other measure, investors, creditors, and managers use some standard profitability measures, including rate of return on total assets and rate of return on shareholders' equity.

The **rate of return on total assets**, or simply **return on assets**, measures a company's success in using its assets to earn income for the persons who are financing the business. Creditors have loaned money to the corporation and earn interest. Shareholders have invested in the corporation's stock and expect the company to earn net income. The sum of interest expense and net income is the return to the two groups that have financed the corporation's activities, and this is the numerator of the return on assets ratio. The denominator is average total assets. Return on assets is computed as follows, using the actual data from the 1993 annual report of Québec-Téléphone (amounts in thousands of dollars):

$$\text{Rate of return on total assets} = \frac{\text{Net income} + \text{Interest expense}}{\text{Average total assets}} = \frac{\$28,971 + \$17,070}{(\$463,060 + \$453,060)/2} = \frac{\$46,041}{\$458,060} = .10$$

Net income and interest expense are taken from the income statement and the notes. Average total assets are computed from the beginning and ending balance sheets. How is this profitability measure used in decision-making? To compare companies. By relating the sum of net income and interest expense to average total assets, we have a standard measure that describes the profitability of of all types of companies. Investment dealers like Levesque Beaubien Geoffrion Inc. and Nesbitt Burns Inc. often single out particular industries as good investments. For example, brokerage analysts may believe that the publishing and printing industry is in a growth phase. These analysts would identify specific publishing and printing companies whose profitabilities are likely to lead the industry and are therefore sound investments. Return on assets is one measure of profitability.

What is a good rate of return on total assets? There is no single answer to this question because rates of return vary widely by industry. For example, consumer products companies earn much higher returns than do utilities or grocery store chains.

Rate of return on common shareholders' equity, often called **return on equity**, shows the relationship between net income and average common shareholders' equity. The numerator is net income minus preferred dividends, information taken from the income statement and statement of retained earnings. The denominator is average common shareholders' equity—total shareholders' equity minus preferred equity. Québec-Téléphone's rate of return on common shareholders' equity for 1993 is computed as follows (amounts in thousands):

$$\text{Rate of return on common shareholders' equity} = \frac{\text{Net income} - \text{Preferred dividends}}{\text{Average common shareholders' equity}} = \frac{\$28,971 - \$553}{(\$211,378 + \$199,882)/2} = \frac{\$28,418}{\$205,630} = .138$$

Observe that the return on equity (14 percent) is higher than the return on assets (10 percent). This difference results from the interest expense component of return on assets. Companies such as Québec-Téléphone borrow at one rate, say, 9 percent, and invest the funds to earn a higher rate, say, 11 percent. The company's creditors are guaranteed a fixed rate of return on their loans. The shareholders, conversely, have no guarantee that the corporation will earn net income, so their investments are riskier. Consequently, shareholders demand a higher rate of return than do creditors, and this explains why return on equity should exceed return on assets. If return on assets is higher than return on equity, the company is in trouble.

Investors and creditors use return on common shareholders' equity in much the same way as they use return on total assets—to compare companies. The higher the rate of return, the more successful the company. A 15 percent return on common shareholders' equity is considered quite good in most industries. Investors also compare a company's return on shareholders' equity to interest rates available in the market. If interest rates are almost as high as return on equity, many investors will lend their money to earn interest rather than invest in common shares. They choose to forego the extra risk of investing in stock when the rate of return on equity is too low.

Different Values of Stock ⌀ stop

The business community refers to several different *stock values*. These values include market value, redemption value, liquidation value, and book value.

Market Value

A stock's **market value**, or *market price,* is the price for which a person could buy or sell a share of the stock. The issuing corporation's net income, financial position, its future prospects, and the general economic conditions determine market value. Daily newspapers report the market price of many stocks. Corporate annual reports generally provide quarterly market price data for the past five or ten years. *In almost all cases, shareholders are more concerned about the market value of a stock than any of the other values discussed below.* Recently, Bank of Montreal common stock was *listed at* (an alternative term is *quoted at*) 29¼ which meant it sold for, or could be bought for, $29.25 per share. The purchase of 100 shares Bank of Montreal common stock would cost $2,925 ($29.25 × 100), plus a commission. If you were selling 100 shares of this stock, you would receive cash of $2,925 less a commission. The commission is the fee an investor pays to a stockbroker for buying or selling the stock.

Redemption Value

Companies may wish to buy back—or redeem—their preferred stock to avoid paying the dividends. Preferred stock that provides for redemption at a set price is called redeemable preferred stock. In some cases, the company has the *option* of redeeming its preferred stock at a set price. In other cases, the company is *obligated* to redeem the preferred stock. The price the corporation agrees to pay for the stock, which is set when the stock is issued, is called *redemption value.*

For example, the redeemable preferred stock of Piney Point Industries, Inc. is "redeemable at the option of the Company at $25 per share." Beginning in 1996, Piney Point is "required to redeem annually 6,765 shares of the preferred stock ($169,125 annually)." Piney Point's annual redemption payment to the preferred shareholders will include this redemption value plus any dividends in arrears.

Liquidation Value

The *liquidation value* of a share of company stock is equal to the net realizable value of the assets less the cash required to pay the liabilities divided by the number of shares outstanding. Liquidation value is rarely equal to either market value or book value.

Short Exercise:
The financial statements of Reeder Corp. reported:

	19X2	19X1
Net income	$40,000	$45,000
Interest expense ..	10,000	12,000
$6.00 Pfd. stock....... (500 shares)	50,000	50,000
Common stock.......	100,000	100,000
Retained earnings..	90,000	80,000
Total assets	420,000	380,000

Dividends of $27,000 were declared and paid to common shareholders in 19X2. Compute (1) the return on assets and (2) the return on common shareholders' equity for 19X2.
A:
(1) 12.5%:

$$\frac{\$40,000 + \$10,000}{(\$420,000 + \$380,000)/2}$$

$$= 0.125$$

(2) 20%:

$$\frac{\$40,000 - (\$6.00 \times 500)}{(\$190,000 + \$180,000)/2}$$

$$= 0.20$$

OBJECTIVE 7
Distinguish among market value, redemption value, liquidation value, and book value

 Real-World Example:
If you buy stock in Inco from another investor, Inco gets no cash. The transaction is a sale between investors. Inco records only the change in shareholder name.

STOP & THINK

Suppose you are a financial analyst who follows Piney Point Industries Inc. as a potential investment. In computing Piney Point's debt ratio, how will you treat the preferred stock in 1995? How will you treat the preferred stock in 1996 and beyond? Give your reason.

Answer: In 1995, you should treat Piney Point's preferred stock as owners' equity because there is no obligation to redeem the stock. In 1996 and beyond, Piney Point preferred stock becomes a liability because the company is *required* to pay the shareholders in order to redeem the stock.

For example, Douglas Ltd. has 10,000 common shares outstanding. The shares are trading on the stock market at $29.50; that is, they have a market value of $29.50 per share. The company's assets have a net realizable value of $336,000, while liabilities amount to $62,000; the liquidation value per share is $27.40 ($336,000 − $62,000) divided by 10,000 shares.

Occasionally, you will read in a business newspaper like *The Financial Post* that a company's break-up value (liquidation value) per share is greater than its market value per share. That means that the total market value of the company's individual assets, minus its liabilities, exceeds the total market value of the company's shares.

Book Value

The **book value** of a stock is the amount of owners' equity on the company's books for each share of its stock. Corporations often report this amount in their annual reports. If the company has only common stock outstanding, its book value is computed by dividing total shareholders' equity by the number of shares outstanding. A company with shareholders' equity of $180,000 and 5,000 shares of common stock outstanding has book value of $36 per share ($180,000/5,000 shares).

If the company has both preferred and common stock outstanding, the preferred shareholders usually have the first claim to owners' equity. Ordinarily, preferred stock has a specified liquidation or redemption value. The book value of preferred stock is its redemption value plus any cumulative dividends in arrears on the stock. Its book value *per share* equals the sum of the redemption value and any cumulative dividends in arrears divided by the number of preferred shares outstanding. After the corporation figures the preferred shares' book value, it computes the common stock book value per share. The corporation divides the common equity (total shareholders' equity minus preferred equity) by the number of common shares outstanding.

Assume that a company balance sheet reports the following amounts:

Shareholders' Equity

Capital stock	
Preferred stock, $6.00, 5,000 shares authorized, 400 shares issued	$ 44,000
Common stock, 20,000 shares authorized, 4,500 shares issued	127,000
Total capital stock	171,000
Retained earnings	85,000
Total shareholders' equity	$256,000

Suppose that four years (including the current year) of cumulative preferred dividends are in arrears and preferred stock has a redemption value of $130 per share.

The book value per share computations for this corporation follow:

Preferred

Redemption value (400 shares × $130)		$ 52,000
Cumulative dividends (400 × $6.00 × 4)		9,600
Shareholders' equity allocated to preferred		$ 61,600
Book value per share ($61,600/400 shares)		$154.00

Common

Total shareholders' equity		$256,000
Less: Shareholders' equity allocated to preferred		61,600
Shareholders' equity available		
for common shareholders		$194,400
Book value per share ($194,400/4,500 shares)		$43.20

Book Value and Decision Making   How is book value per share used in decision-making? Companies negotiating the purchase of a corporation may wish to know the book value of its stock, especially if the stock is not publicly traded. The book value of shareholders' equity may figure into the negotiated purchase price. Corporations—especially those whose shares are not publicly traded—may buy out a retiring executive, agreeing to pay the book value of the person's stock in the company.

Some investors have traditionally compared the book value of a share of a company's stock and with the stock's market value. The idea was that a stock selling below its book value was underpriced and thus was good buy. The relationship between book value and market value is far from clear, however. Book value is a product of the accounting system, which is based on historical costs. Market value, conversely, depends on investors' subjective outlook for dividends and appreciation in the stock's value. Exhibit 14-8 contrasts the book values and ranges of market values for the common stocks of three well-known companies.

Accounting for Income Taxes by Corporations

Corporations pay taxes on their income in the same way that individuals do. Corporate and personal tax rates differ, however. The federal tax rate for manufacturing corporations with income in excess of $200,000 was 21.84 percent while non-manufacturing corporations with income in excess of $200,000 were taxed at a rate of 28.84 percent. Canadian-controlled corporations with income of less than $200,000 and meeting certain other conditions pay taxes at a lower rate. In addition, all the provinces and the Yukon and Northwest Territories levy taxes on corporations at rates ranging from 2.5 percent to 17.0 percent.

For each period, the corporation measures income tax expense and the related income tax payable. Corporate strategy is directed more at minimizing the income tax payable because that is the amount of cash the company must pay the government.

Short Exercise:

Sellers Corp. reported $135,000 of income (income statement) before depreciation. Straight-line (book) depreciation was $16,000, and capital cost allowance was $19,000. Assume a 35% tax rate. (1) Calculate Sellers' income tax expense, income tax payable, and deferred taxes for the year. (2) Is the deferred tax amount a debit or a credit? **A:**
(1) Inc. tax expense:
  ($135,000 − $16,000)
  × 0.35 = $41,650
Inc. tax payable:
  ($135,000 − $19,000)
  × 0.35 = $40,600
Deferred inc. taxes:
  $41,650 − $40,600
  = $1,050
(2) A credit because the expense exceeds the payable.

OBJECTIVE 8

Account for a corporation's income tax

EXHIBIT 14-8   *Book Value and Market Value*

	Year-End Book Value	Fourth-Quarter Market-Value Range
NOVA Corporation	$5.48	$ 9.125 – $10.875
Rogers Communications Inc., Class B	1.85	17.75 – 20.50
Southam Inc.	5.95	16.75 – 21.00

But the main accounting issue centers on the measurement of net income. Therefore accountants strive for a reasonable measure of income tax expense. Total revenues minus total expenses, including income tax expense, produces net income.

Income Tax Expense is based on **pretax accounting income**, or income before income tax, from the income statement. Income Tax Payable is based on **taxable income** from the income tax return filed with Revenue Canada. Taxable income is the basis for computing the amount of tax to *pay* the government. Pretax accounting income and taxable income are rarely the same amount.

$$\begin{array}{ccc} \text{Income} \\ \text{tax} \\ \text{expense} \end{array} = \begin{array}{c} \text{Pretax} \\ \text{accounting} \\ \text{(from income} \\ \text{statement)} \end{array} \times \begin{array}{c} \text{Income} \\ \text{tax} \\ \text{rate} \end{array} \quad \middle\| \quad \begin{array}{c} \text{Income} \\ \text{tax} \\ \text{payable} \end{array} = \begin{array}{c} \text{Taxable} \\ \text{income} \\ \text{(from tax} \\ \text{return)} \end{array} \times \begin{array}{c} \text{Income} \\ \text{tax} \\ \text{rate} \end{array}$$

The authors are indebted to Jean Marie Hudson for this presentation

Some revenues and expenses enter the determination of accounting income in periods different from the periods in which they enter the determination of taxable income. Over a period of several years, total pretax accounting income may equal total taxable income, but for any one year the two income amounts are likely to differ.

The most important difference between pretax accounting income and taxable income occurs when a corporation uses the straight-line method to compute depreciation for the financial statements and the Revenue Canada Rates—introduced in Chapter 10—to calculate depreciation expense (called capital cost allowance) for the tax return and payment of taxes. For any one year, the capital cost allowance claimed on the tax return may differ from accounting depreciation on the income statement.

Suppose Suzy Shier Ltd. had pretax accounting income of $12,000,000 after deducting straight-line depreciation of $1,000,000 in each of two years. Assume the capital cost allowance using Revenue Canada Rates was $2,000,000 in the first year and $0 in the second year. The accounting issue is—What is the correct amount of income tax expense for the two years? By answering this question, we can complete Suzy Shier's income statement. Suzy Shier is located in Quebec so we will use a combined rate of federal and Quebec income tax of 30.7 percent:

Income Statement (partial)

	19X1	19X2
Income before depreciation	$13,000,000	$13,000,000
Depreciation expense....................	1,000,000	1,000,000
Income before income tax	12,000,000	12,000,000
Income tax expense......................	?	?
Net income...................................	$?	$?

Suzy Shier's income tax expense for both years is $3,684,000 ($12,000,000 × .307) regardless of the amount of income tax payable to the government each year. On the tax return, Suzy Shier would report taxable income of $11,000,000 ($13,000,000 – $2,000,000) in 19X1 and $13,000,000 ($13,000,000 – $0) in 19X2. Exhibit 14-9 gives Suzy Shier's entries to record income tax during 19X1 and 19X2.

Total *taxable* income for the two years combined—$24,000,000—is the same as total *pretax accounting* income for the two years. However, each year shows a difference between taxable income and pretax accounting income. With 30.7 percent tax

EXHIBIT 14-9 *Income Tax Entries for a Corporation*

19X1	Income Tax Expense	$3,684,000	
	Income Tax Payable ($11,000,000 × .307)...........		$3,377,000
	Deferred Income Tax		307,000
19X2	Income Tax Expense	3,684,000	
	Deferred Income Tax	307,000	
	Income Tax Payable ($13,000,000 × .307)		3,991,000

rate, income tax payable to the government is $3,377,000 ($11,000,000 × .307) in 19X1 and $3,991,000 ($13,000,000 × .307) in 19X2.

Corporations account for income tax expense and all other expenses on the basis of when the expense occurs, not when it is paid. The process of accruing income taxes during the period that the related income occurs is called *income tax allocation*. The goal of income tax allocation is to match the period's expenses against its revenues. In this case, Suzy Shier Ltd. will record the same amount of income tax expense in both years because pretax accounting income is the same ($12,000,000 each year).

Corporations generally record Income Tax Expense based on the amount of *pretax accounting income* multiplied by the tax rate. Income Tax Payable is credited for an amount equal to *taxable income* multiplied by the tax rate. When these two amounts differ, a new account, Deferred Income Tax, is credited or debited to balance the entry. In Exhibit 14-9, Deferred Income Tax is credited in 19X1 because pretax accounting income ($12,000,000) exceeds taxable income ($11,000,000). The reverse is true in 19X2, and Deferred Income Tax is debited. The 19X2 entry eliminates the preceding credit balance in Deferred Income Tax.

For other corporations, the 19X1 entry may include a debit to Deferred Income Tax. This occurs if taxable income exceeds pretax accounting income. In that case, the credit to Income Tax Payable is greater than the debit to Income Tax Expenses, and the balancing amount is a debit to Deferred Income Tax. Entries in later years will include credits to eliminate the debit balance in Deferred Income Tax. Here is a way to remember whether to debit or credit Deferred Income Tax.

- Debit: Income Tax Expense for the amount equal to *pretax accounting income* multiplied by the income tax rate.
- Credit: Income Tax Payable for the amount equal to *taxable income* multiplied by the income tax rate.
- Debit or Credit: Deferred Income Tax for the amount needed to balance the entry.

Exhibit 14-10 shows Suzy Shier's partial comparative financial statements for 19X1 and 19X2. Income Tax Expense, Income Tax Payable, and Deferred Income Tax come directly from the entries recorded in Exhibit 14-9.

Income Tax Payable and Deferred Income Tax are reported as liabilities on the balance sheet. Income Tax Payable is a current liability because it must be paid within a few months. Deferred income tax is usually a long-term liability, as it is for Suzy Shier Ltd. Why long-term? Because the asset that caused the deferred tax (depreciable property) is classified as long-term.

Study the entries in Exhibit 14-9. Observe that the $307,000 Deferred Income Tax amount for 19X1 was eliminated in 19X2. This is why Deferred Income Tax has a zero balance in Exhibit 14-10.

EXHIBIT 14-10   Income Tax on Corporate Financial Statements

Suzy Shier Ltd.
Partial Income Statement
For the years ended December 31, 19X1 and 19X2

	19X1	19X2
Income before income tax..	$12,000,000	$12,000,000
Income tax expense ($12,000,000 × 0.37 both years)....	3,684,000	3,684,000
Net income..	$ 8,316,000	$ 8,316,000

Suzy Shier Ltd.
Partial Balance Sheet
December 31, 19X1 and 19X2

Liabilities	19X1	19X2
Current:		
Income tax payable..	$3,377,000	$3,991,000
Long-term:		
Deferred income tax..	307,000	–

Summary Problems for Your Review

1. Use the following accounts and related balances to prepare the classified balance sheet of Whitehall, Inc. at September 30, 19X4. Use the account format of the balance sheet.

Common stock,		Inventory..............................	$ 85,000
50,000 shares authorized,		Property, plant, and	
20,000 shares issued........	$156,000	equipment, net..................	225,000
Dividends payable............	4,000	Donated capital	18,000
Cash....................................	9,000	Accounts receivable, net.....	25,000
Accounts payable..............	28,000	Preferred stock, $3.75,	
Retained earnings.............	38,000	10,000 shares authorized,	
Organization cost, net.......	1,000	2,000 shares issued	24,000
Long-term note payable ...	74,000	Accrued liabilities.............	3,000

2. The balance sheet of Trendline Corporation reported the following at March 31, 19X6, end of its fiscal year.

Shareholders' Equity

Preferred stock, $4.00, cumulative 1,000 shares authorized and issued..	$110,000
Common stock, 100,000 shares authorized, 50,000 shares issued	481,500
Donated capital..	55,000
Retained earnings...	330,000
Total shareholders' equity..	$976,500

Required

a. Is the preferred stock cumulative or noncumulative? Is it participating or non-participating? How can you tell?

b. What is the total amount of the annual preferred dividend?

c. Assume the common shares were all issued at the same time. What was the selling price per share?

d. What was the market value of the assets donated to the corporation?

e. Compute the book value per share of the preferred stock and the common stock. The preferred stock has no specified redemption value. No prior year preferred dividends are in arrears, but Trendline has not declared the current-year dividend.

SOLUTIONS TO REVIEW PROBLEMS

1.

Whitehall, Inc.
Balance Sheet
September 30, 19X4

Assets		Liabilities	
Current		**Current**	
Cash	$ 9,000	Accounts payable	$ 28,000
Accounts receivable, net	25,000	Dividends payable	4,000
Inventory	85,000	Accrued liabilities	3,000
Total current assets	119,000	Total current liabilities	35,000
Property, plant, and equipment, net	225,000	Long-term note payable	74,000
Intangible assets		Total liabilities	109,000
Organization cost, net	1,000	**Shareholders' Equity**	
		Capital stock,	
		Preferred stock, $3.75,	
		10,000 shares authorized,	
		2,000 shares issued	$ 24,000
		Common stock,	
		50,000 shares authorized,	
		20,000 shares issued	156,000
		Donated capital	18,000
		Total capital stock	198,000
		Retained earnings	38,000
		Total shareholders' equity	236,000
		Total liabilities and	
Total assets	$345,000	shareholders' equity	$345,000

2. Answers to Trendline Corporation questions:

a. The preferred stock is cumulative as is noted in its description; it is non-participating because it is not specifically labeled otherwise.

b. Total annual preferred dividend: $4,000 (1,000 × $4.00)

c. Price per share: $9.63 ($481,500/50,000 shares issued)

d. Market value of donated assets: $55,000

e. Book values per share of preferred and common stock:

Preferred	
Book value	$110,000
Cumulative dividend for current year (1,000 × $4.00)	4,000
Shareholders' equity allocated to preferred	$114,000
Book value per share ($114,000/1,000 shares)	$ 114.00

Common

Total shareholders' equity...	$976,500
Less: Shareholders' equity allocated to preferred	114,000
Shareholders' equity available	
for common shareholders	$862,500
Book value per share ($862,500/50,000 shares)	$ 17.25

Summary

1. *Identify the characteristics of a corporation.* A corporation is a separate legal and business entity. Continuous life, the ease of raising large amounts of capital and transferring ownership, and limited liability are among the advantages of the corporate form of organization. An important disadvantage is double taxation. Corporations pay income taxes, and shareholders pay tax on dividends. Shareholders are the owners of the corporations. They elect a board of directors, which elects a chairperson and appoints the officers to manage the business.

2. *Record the issuance of stock.* Corporations may issue different classes of stock: common and preferred.

3. *Prepare the shareholders' equity section of a corporation balance sheet.* The balance sheet carries the capital raised through stock issuance under the heading Capital Stock or Contributed Capital in the shareholders' equity section.

4. *Account for the incorporation of a going business.* Close the owner's equity accounts of the prior entry, and open the shareholders' equity accounts of the corporation.

5. *Account for cash dividends.* Only when the board of directors declares a dividend does the corporation incur the liability to pay dividends. Preferred stock has priority over common stock as to dividends, which are stated as a dollar amount per share. In addition, preferred stock has a claim to dividends in arrears if it is cumulative and a claim to further dividends if it is participating. Convertible preferred stock may be exchanged for the corporation's common stock.

6. *Compute two profitability measures: return on assets and return on shareholders' equity.* Return on assets and return on shareholders' equity are two standard measures of profitability. A healthy company's return on equity will exceed its return on assets.

7. *Distinguish among market value, redemption value, liquidation value, and book value.* A stock's market value is the price for which a share may be bought or sold. Redemption value, liquidation value, and book value—the amount of owners' equity per share of company stock—are other values that may apply to stock.

8. *Account for a corporation's income tax.* Corporations pay income tax and must account for the income tax expense and income tax payable. A difference between the expense and the payable creates another account, Deferred Income Tax.

Self-Study Questions

Test your understanding of the chapter by marking the best answer for each of the following questions:

1. Which of the following is a *disadvantage* of the corporate form of business organization? *(pp. 666–668)*
   a. Limited liability of shareholders   c. No mutual agency
   b. Double taxation   d. Transferability of ownership

2. The person with the most power in a corporation is the *(p. 668)*
   a. Incorporator   c. President
   b. Chairperson of the board   d. Vice-president

3. The dollar amount of the shareholder investments in a corporation is called *(p. 669)*
   a. Outstanding stock   c. Capital stock
   b. Total shareholders' equity   d. Retained earnings

4. The arbitrary value assigned to a share of stock by the board of directors is called *(p. 673)*
   a. Market value   c. Book value
   b. Liquidation value   d. Stated value

5. Stock issued by a corporation incorporated under the *Canada Business Corporations Act* normally has *(pp. 672–673)*
   a. No par value
   b. A par value set by management
   c. A par value set by the government
   d. A par value of $10.00

6. Mangum Corporation receives a building for 1,000 shares of common stock. The building's book value is $385,000 and its current market value is $640,000. This transaction increases Mangum's capital stock by *(p. 676)*
   a. $0 because the corporation received no cash
   b. $100,000
   c. $3850,000
   d. $640,000

7. Organization cost is classified as a (an) *(p. 680)*
   a. Operating expense
   b. Current asset
   c. Contra item in shareholders' equity
   d. None of the above

8. Trade Days, Inc. has 10,000 shares of $3.50 cumulative preferred stock, and 100,000 of common stock outstanding. Two years' preferred dividends are in arrears. Trade Days declares a cash dividend large enough to pay the preferred dividends in arrears, the preferred dividend for the current period, and a $1.50 dividend to common. What is the total amount of the dividend? *(p. 681)*
   a. $255,000   b. $220,000   c. $150,000   d. $105,000

9. The preferred stock of Trade Days, Inc. in the preceding question was issued at $55 per share. Each preferred share can be converted into 10 common shares. The entry to record the conversion of this preferred stock into common is *(pp. 683–684)*

a.	Cash	550,000	
	Preferred Stock		500,000
	Common Stock		50,000
b.	Preferred Stock	500,000	
	Capital Stock in Excess of Par—Preferred Stock	50,000	
	Common Stock		550,000
c.	Preferred Stock	550,000	
	Common Stock		550,000
d.	Preferred Stock	550,000	
	Common Stock		400,000
	Capital Stock in Excess of Par —Common Stock		150,000

10. When an investor is buying stock as an investment, the value of most direct concern is *(p. 685)*
    a. Par value   b. Market value   c. Liquidation value   d. Book value

Answers to the Self-Study Questions follow the Accounting Vocabulary.

Accounting Vocabulary

Articles of incorporation *(p. 666)*
Board of directors *(p. 668)*
Book value of stock *(p. 686)*
Bylaws *(p. 668)*
Chairperson (of board) *(p. 668)*
Capital stock *(p. 669)*
Common stock *(p. 670)*
Convertible preferred stock *(p. 683)*
Cumulative preferred stock *(p. 682)*
Deficit *(p. 671)*
Dividends *(p. 671)*
Donated capital *(p. 679)*
Double taxation *(p. 667)*
Incorporators *(p. 669)*
Limited liability *(p. 667)*
Market value of stock *(p. 685)*
No-par *(p. 673)*
Organization cost *(p. 680)*
Outstanding stock *(p. 669)*
Par value *(p. 673)*
Preferred stock *(p. 672)*
President *(p. 668)*
Pretax accounting income *(p. 688)*
Rate of return on common shareholders' equity *(p. 684)*
Rate of return on total assets *(p. 684)*
Retained earnings *(p. 669)*
Return on assets *(p. 684)*
Return on equity *(p. 684)*
Shareholder *(p. 666)*
Shareholders' equity *(p. 669)*
Stock *(p. 666)*
Taxable income *(p. 688)*

Answers to Self-Study Questions

1. b
2. b
3. c
4. d
5. a
6. d
7. d   Intangible asset
8. a   [(10,000 × $3.50 × 3 = $105,000) + (100,000 × $1.50 = $150,000) = $255,000]
9. c
10. b

ASSIGNMENT MATERIAL _____

Questions

1. Why is a corporation called a creature of the government?
2. Identify the characteristics of a corporation.
3. Explain why owners of shares in corporations face a tax disadvantage.
4. Briefly outline the steps in the organization of a corporation.

5. How are the structures of a partnership and a corporation similar and how are they different?

6. Name the four rights of a shareholder. Are preferred shares automatically non-voting? Explain how a right may be withheld from a shareholder.

7. Which event increases the assets of the corporation: authorization of shares or issuance of shares? Explain.

8. Suppose Watgold Ltd. issued 1,000 shares of its $6.65 preferred shares for $120. How much would this transaction increase the company's capital stock? How much would it increase retained earnings? How much would it increase annual cash dividend payments?

9. Woodstock Ltd. issued 100 shares of common stock for $15.00 per share and 200 shares for $16.00 per share. What would be the journal entry to record the combined issue?

10. How does issuance of 1,000 shares of common stock for land and a building, together worth $150,000, affect capital stock?

11. Give an example of a transaction that creates donated capital for a corporation.

12. Journalize the incorporation of the Barnes & Connally partnership.

13. Rank the following accounts in the order they would appear on the balance sheet: Common Stock, Organization Cost, Donated Capital, Preferred Stock, Retained Earnings, Dividends Payable. Also, give each account's balance sheet classification.

14. What type of account is Organization Cost? Briefly describe how to account for organization cost.

15. Briefly discuss the three important dates for a dividend.

16. Mancini Inc. has 3,000 shares of its $2.50 preferred stock outstanding. Dividends for 19X1 and 19X2 are in arrears, and the company has declared no dividends on preferred stock for the current year, 19X3. Assume that Mancini declares total dividends of $35,000 at the end of 19X3. Show how to allocate the dividends to preferred and common (a) if preferred is cumulative, and (b) if preferred is noncumulative.

17. As a preferred shareholder, would you rather own cumulative or noncumulative preferred? If all other factors are the same, would the corporation rather the preferred stock be cumulative or noncumulative? Give your reason.

18. How are cumulative preferred dividends in arrears reported in the financial statements? When do dividends become a liability of the corporation?

19. Distinguish between the market value of stock and the book value of stock. Which is more important to investors?

20. How is book value per share of common stock computed when the company has both preferred stock and common stock outstanding?

21. Why should a healthy company's rate of return on shareholders' equity exceed its rate of return on total assets?

22. Explain the difference between the income tax expense and income tax payable of a corporation.

Exercises

Exercise 14-1   *Organizing a corporation*   *(Obj. 1)*

Carena Datig and Jennifer Scace are opening a limousine service to be named D&S Transportation Limited. They need outside capital, so they plan to organize the business as a corporation. Because your office is in the same building, they come to you for advice. Write a memorandum informing them of the steps in forming a corporation. Identify specific documents used in this process, and name the different parties involved in the ownership and management of a corporation.

Exercise 14-2   *Issuing stock*   **(Obj. 2)**

Rousseau Corp. made the following stock issuance transactions.

Feb. 19   Issued 1,000 shares of common stock for cash of $10.50 per share.
Mar.   3   Sold 300 shares of $4.50 Class A preferred stock for $12,000 cash.
      11   Received inventory valued at $20,000 and equipment with market value of $11,000 for 3,300 shares of common stock.
      15   Issued 1,000 shares of $2.50 Class B preferred stock with stated value of $60 per share.

Required

1. Journalize the transactions. Explanations are not required.
2. How much capital stock did these transactions generate for Rousseau Corp.?

Exercise 14-3   *Recording issuance of stock*   **(Obj. 2)**

The actual balance sheet of Gulf Resources & Chemical Corporation, as adapted, reported the following shareholders' equity. Gulf has two separate classes of preferred stock, labeled as Series A and Series B. All dollar amounts, except for per-share amounts, are given in thousands.

Shareholders' Investment
(same as shareholders' equity)

Preferred stock, authorized 4,000,000 shares (note 7)
  Series A...3... $?
  Series B...20...   ? 18,800
Common stock, authorized 20,000,000, issued and
  outstanding 9,130,000 shares ....8.37..............................   76,455

Note 7: Preferred Stock:	Shares [Issued and] Outstanding
Series A..........................	58,000
Series B..........................	376,000

Required

Assume that the Series A preferred stock was issued for $3 cash per share, the Series B preferred was issued for $20 cash per share, and the common was issued for cash of $8.37 per share. Make the summary journal entries to record issuance of all the Gulf Resources stock. Explanations are not required.

Exercise 14-4   *Recording issuance of no-par stock*   **(Obj. 2)**

Alexanians Inc., located in Burnaby, B.C., is an importer of European furniture and Oriental rugs. The corporation issues 20,000 shares of no-par common stock for $50 per share. Record issuance of the stock.

Exercise 14-5   *Shareholders' equity section of a balance sheet*   **(Obj. 3)**

The articles of incorporation for Dartmouth Corporation authorizes the issuance of 10,000 shares of Class A preferred stock, 5,000 shares of Class B preferred stock, and 10,000 shares of common stock. During a two-month period, Dartmouth completed these stock-issuance transactions:

June 23   Issued 1,000 shares of common stock for cash of $12.50 per share.
July   2   Sold 300 shares of $4.50 Class A preferred stock for $20,000 cash.
July 12   Received inventory valued at $25,000 and equipment with market value of $16,000 for 3,300 shares of common stock.

17   Issued 1,000 shares of $2.50 Class B preferred stock. The issue price was cash of $60 per share.

Prepare the shareholders' equity section of the Dartmouth balance sheet for the transactions given in this exercise. Retained Earnings has a balance of $91,000.

Exercise 14-6   *Capital stock for a corporation*   **(Obj. 2)**

Zhang Corp. has recently organized. The company issued common stock to a lawyer who gave Susan Zhang legal services of $5,000 to help her in organizing the corporation. It issued common stock to another person in exchange for his patent with a market value of $40,000. In addition, Zhang received cash both for 2,000 shares of its preferred stock at $110 per share and for 26,000 shares of its common stock at $15 per share. The city of Red Deer donated 50 hectares of land to the company as a plant site. The market value of the land was $300,000. Without making journal entries, determine the total capital stock created by these transactions.

Exercise 14-7   *Shareholders' equity section of a balance sheet*   **(Obj. 3)**

Pay-n-Sav Corporation has the following selected account balances at June 30, 19X7. Prepare the shareholders' equity section of the company's balance sheet.

Common stock,		Inventory..................................	$112,000
500,000 shares authorized,		Machinery and equipment.....	109,000
120,000 shares issued..................	$120,000	Preferred stock, $1.00,	
Donated capital	81,000	20,000 shares authorized,	
Accumulated depreciation—		11,000 shares issued	308,000
machinery and equipment.........	62,000	Organization cost, net.............	3,000
Retained earnings	119,000		

Exercise 14-8   *Incorporating a partnership*   **(Obj. 4)**

The Kingston Jaybirds are a semiprofessional baseball team that has been operated as a partnership by K. Gruber and B. Conacher. In addition to their management responsibilities, Gruber also plays third base and Conacher sells hot dogs. Journalize the following transactions in the first month of operation as a corporation:

May 14   The incorporators paid legal fees of $840 and other fees of $500 to obtain articles of incorporation.

14   Issued 2,500 shares of common stock to Gruber and 1,000 shares to Conacher. Gruber's capital balance on the partnership books was $20,000, and Conacher's capital balance was $12,000.

18   The city of Kingston donated 20 hectares of land to the corporation for a stadium site. The land's market value was $80,000.

Exercise 14-9   *Computing dividends on preferred and common stock*   **(Obj. 5)**

The following elements of shareholders' equity are adapted from the balance sheet of Transit Freightways Inc. All dollar amounts, except the dividends per share, are given in thousands.

Shareholders' Equity

Preferred stock, cumulative and nonparticipating (note 7)	
Series A, 80,000 shares authorized, 58,000 shares issued	$ 58
Series B, 600,000 shares authorized, 376,000 shares issued	376
Common stock, 1,000,000 shares authorized, 91,300 shares issued.........	913

Note 7: Preferred stock:

Designated Annual
Cash Dividend Per Share

Series A..................	$ .22
Series B	1.20

The Series A preferred has preference over Series B preferred, and the company has paid all dividends through 19X4.

Required

Compute the dividends to both series of preferred and to common for 19X5 and 19X6 if total dividends are $0 in 19X5 and $1,100,000 in 19X6. Round to the nearest dollar.

Exercise 14-10   *Evaluating profitability   (Obj. 7)*

Tempo Services, Inc., reported these figures for 19X7 and 19X6:

	19X7	19X6
Income statement:		
Interest expense	$ 7,400,000	$ 7,100,000
Net income	22,000,000	18,700,000
Balance sheet:		
Total assets	351,000,000	317,000,000
Preferred stock, $1.30, no-par, 100,000		
shares issued and outstanding	2,500,000	2,500,000
Common shareholders' equity	164,000,000	151,000,000
Total shareholders' equity	166,500,000	153,500,000

Compute rate of return on total assets and rate of return on common shareholders' equity for 19X7. Do these rates of return suggest strength or weakness? Give your reason.

Exercise 14-11   *Book value per share of preferred and common stock   (Obj. 7)*

The balance sheet of Delta Systems Ltd. reported the following:

Redeemable preferred stock; redemption value $63,620	$ 48,600
Common shareholders' equity 10,120 shares issued	
and outstanding	216,788
Total shareholders' equity	$265,388

Assume that Delta has paid preferred dividends for the current year and all prior years (no dividends in arrears), and the company has 1,000 shares of preferred stock outstanding. Retained earnings, included in common shareholders' equity, was $135,588. Compute the book value per share of the preferred stock and the common stock.

Exercise 14-12   *Book value per share of preferred and common stock; preferred dividends in arrears   (Obj. 5, 7)*

Refer to Exercise 14-11. Compute the book value per share of the preferred stock and the common stock, assuming that three years' preferred dividends (including dividends for the current year) are in arrears. Assume the preferred stock is cumulative and its dividend rate is $3.00 per share.

Exercise 14-13   *Accounting for income tax by a corporation   (Obj. 8)*

Chrysler Manufacturing Corp. of Manitoba has pretax accounting income of $420,000 in 19X6 and $470,000 in 19X7. Taxable income is $380,000 in 19X6 and $510,000 in 19X7. The combined federal and Manitoba tax rate is 38.8 percent. Record Chrysler's income taxes for both years. What is the balance in the Deferred Income Tax account at the end of each year?

Challenge Exercises

Exercise 14-14   *Accounting for shareholders' equity transactions*   **(Obj. 2, 5)**

Hi Value Stores, Inc., reported these comparative shareholders' equity data:

	January 31, 19X2	January 31, 19X1
Common stock	$ 740,572	$ 529,814
Retained earnings	6,249,138	4,835,710

During 19X2, Hi Value completed these transactions and events:

a. Net income, $1,608,476.

b. Cash dividends, $195,048.

c. Issuance of stock for cash, 914 shares, $21,025.

d. Issuance of stock to purchase other companies (Hi Value debited the Investments account), 5,832 shares, $189,733.

Required

Without making journal entries, show how Hi Value's 19X2 transactions and events accounted for the changes in the shareholders' equity accounts. For each shareholders' equity account, start with the January 31, 19X1, balance and work toward the balance at January 31, 19X2.

Exercise 14-15   *Accounting for income tax by a corporation*   **(Obj. 8)**

Case A—The income statement of Hewitt Corp. reports.

	19X1	19X2
Income before income tax	$25,000	$30,000

The combined federal and provincial income tax rate is 30 percent.

1. How much net income will Hewitt Corp. report each year?
2. Compute the amount of income tax payable from each year's operations.

Case B—Keep all facts as they were in Case A, except that Hewitt uses straight-line depreciation for accounting purposes and Revenue Canada rates for income tax purposes. During 19X1, capital cost allowance exceeds straight-line depreciation by $6,000. In 19X2, capital cost allowance exceeds straight-line by $4,000.

1. How much net income will Hewitt Corp. report each year?
2. Compute the amount of income tax payable from each year's operations.
3. Assume that Hewitt began operations in 19X1. What will be the balance of Deferred Income Tax at the end of 19X1 and at the end of 19X2? Explain the desirable feature of the deferred income taxes.

Problems   (Group A)

Problem 14-1A   *Organizing a corporation*   **(Obj. 1)**

Alan Lauber and Bonnie Krische are opening a restaurant in a growing section of Fredericton, N.B. There are no competing family restaurants in the immediate vicinity. Their most fundamental decision is how to organize the business. Lauber thinks the partnership form is best. Krische favors the corporate form of organization. They seek your advice.

Required

Discuss the advantages and disadvantages of organizing the business as a corporation.

Problem 14-2A   *Journalizing corporation transactions and preparing the shareholders' equity section of the balance sheet*   *(Obj. 2, 3)*

The partnership of Suzuki and Loeb needed additional capital to expand into new markets, so the business incorporated as SL Design Corp. The articles of incorporation from the Government of Canada authorizes SL Design to issue 50,000 shares of $6.00 preferred stock and 100,000 shares of common stock. In its first month, SL Design completed the following transactions:

Dec. 1   Paid incorporation fees of $200 and taxes of $6,100 to the Government of Canada and paid legal fees of $4,000 to organize as a corporation.

2   Issued 300 shares of common stock to the promoter for assistance with issuance of the common stock. The fee was $1,800.

2   Issued 9,000 shares of common stock to Suzuki and 12,000 shares to Loeb in return for the net assets of the partnership. Suzuki's capital balance on the partnership books was $54,000, and Loeb's capital balance was $72,000.

8   Received a small parcel of land valued at $92,000 as a donation from the city of Brandon.

10   Issued 400 shares of preferred stock to acquire a patent with a market value of $50,000.

16   Issued 2,000 shares of common stock for cash of $12,000.

Required

1. Record the transactions in the general journal.
2. Prepare the shareholders' equity section of the SL Design Corp. balance sheet at December 31. The ending balance in Retained Earnings is $42,100.

Problem 14-3A   *Shareholders' equity section of the balance sheet*   *(Obj. 3)*

The following summaries for Millet Corp. and Structural Castings Inc. provide the information needed to prepare the shareholders' equity section of the company balance sheet. The two companies are independent.

Millet Corp.   Millet Corp. is authorized to issue 50,000 shares of common stock. All the stock was issued at $12 per share. The company incurred net losses of $30,000 in 19X1 and $14,000 in 19X2. It earned net incomes of $23,000 in 19X3 and $71,000 in 19X4. The company declared no dividends during the four-year period.

Structural Castings Inc.   Structural Castings' articles of incorporation authorizes the company to issue 5,000 shares of $5.00 cumulative preferred stock and 500,000 shares of common stock. Structural Castings issued 1,000 shares of the preferred stock at $105 per share. It issued 100,000 shares of the common stock for $400,000. The company's retained earnings balance at the beginning of 19X4 was $120,000. Net income for 19X4 was $80,000, and the company declared a $5.00 preferred share dividend for 19X4. Preferred share dividends for 19X3 were in arrears.

Required

For each company, prepare the shareholders' equity section of its balance sheet at December 31, 19X4. Show the computation of all amounts. Entries are not required.

Problem 14-4A   *Analyzing the shareholders' equity of a corporation*   *(Obj. 3, 5)*

Eastern Steel Corporation is a large steel company. Eastern included the following in its shareholders' equity on its balance sheet:

Shareholders' Equity	($ millions)
Preferred Stock	
Authorized 20,000,000 shares in each class; issued:	
$5.00 Cumulative Convertible Preferred Stock, 2,500,000 shares	$ 125
$2.50 Cumulative Convertible Preferred Stock, 4,000,000 shares	100
Common stock	
Authorized 80,000,000 shares; issued 48,308,516 shares	621
Retained earnings..	529
	$1,375

Required

1. Identify the different issues of stock Eastern Steel has outstanding.

2. Is the preferred stock participating or nonparticipating? How can you tell?

3. Suppose Eastern Steel passed its preferred dividends for one year. Would the company have to pay these dividends in arrears before paying dividends to the common shareholders? Give your reason.

4. What amount of preferred dividends must Eastern Steel declare and pay each year to avoid having preferred dividends in arrears?

5. Assume preferred dividends are in arrears for 19X5.
   a. Write note 6 of the December 31, 19X5, financial statements to disclose the dividends in arrears.
   b. Journalize the declaration of a $60 million dividend for 19X6. An explanation is not required.

Problem 14-5A   *Preparing a corporation balance sheet; measuring profitability*   *(Obj. 3, 7)*

The following accounts and related balances of Surgical Products Inc. are arranged in no particular order.

Accounts payable...................	$ 31,000	Accrued liabilities..................	17,000
Retained earnings	?	Long-term note payable........	$104,000
Common stock,		Accounts receivable, net	102,000
100,000 shares		Preferred stock, $.40	
authorized, 42,000		25,000 shares authorized,	
shares issued......................	350,000	3,700 shares issued............	37,000
Dividends payable.................	3,000	Cash	32,000
Total assets, Nov. 30, 19X6	781,000	Inventory.................................	181,000
Net income.............................	36,200	Property, plant, and	
Common shareholders'		equipment, net	378,000
equity, Nov. 30, 19X6	483,000	Organization cost, net	6,000
Interest expense.....................	12,800	Prepaid expenses	13,000
		Patent, net	31,000

Required

1. Prepare the company's classified balance sheet in the account format at November 30, 19X7.

2. Compute rate of return on total assets and rate of return on common shareholders' equity for the year ended November 30, 19X7.

3. Do these rates of return suggest strength or weakness? Give your reason.

4. How will what you have learned in this problem help you evaluate an investment?

Problem 14-6A   *Computing dividends on preferred and common stock*   *(Obj. 5)*

MacLayne Corporation has 5,000 shares of $.50 preferred stock and 100,000 shares of common stock outstanding. During a three-year period, MacLayne declared and paid cash dividends as follows: 19X1, $1,500; 19X2, $12,000; and 19X3, $31,000.

Required

1. Compute the total dividends to preferred stock and common stock for each of the three years if
   a. Preferred is noncumulative and nonparticipating.
   b. Preferred is cumulative and nonparticipating.
2. For requirement 1b, record the declaration of the 19X3 dividends on December 22, 19X3 and the payment of the dividends on January 14, 19X4.

Problem 14-7A   *Analyzing the shareholders' equity of an actual corporation*   *(Obj. 5, 6)*

The balance sheet of Oak Manufacturing, Inc., reported the following:

Shareholders' Investment (same as shareholders' equity)	($ thousands)
Cumulative convertible preferred stock; authorized 20,000 shares..........	$ 45
Common stock, authorized 40,000 shares; issued 16,000 shares	192
Deficit...	(77)
Total shareholders' investment	$160

Notes to the financial statements indicate that 9,000 shares of $.16 preferred stock were issued and outstanding. The preferred stock has a redemption value of $10 per share, and preferred dividends are in arrears for two years, including the current year. On the balance sheet date, the market value of the Oak Manufacturing common stock was $7.50 per share.

Required

1. Is the preferred stock cumulative or noncumulative, participating, or non-participating? How can you tell? •
2. What is the amount of the annual preferred dividend?
3. What class of shareholders controls the company? Give your reason.
4. What is the total capital stock of the company?
5. What is the total market value of the common stock?
6. Compute the book value per share of the preferred stock and the common stock.

Problem 14-8A   *Computing and recording a corporation's income tax*   *(Obj. 8)*

The accounting (not the income tax) records of Valley View Corporation provide the comparative income statement for 19X7 and 19X8:

	19X7	19X8
Total revenue...	$930,000	$990,000
Expenses:		
Cost of goods sold	$430,000	$460,000
Operating expenses...	270,000	280,000
Total expenses before tax...	700,000	740,000
Pretax accounting income	$230,000	$250,000

Total revenue of 19X8 includes revenue of $15,000 that was received late in 19X7. This revenue is included in 19X8 total revenue because it was earned in 19X8. However, revenue that is collected in advance is included in the taxable income of the year when the cash is received. In calculating taxable income on the tax return, this revenue belongs in 19X7.

Also, the operating expenses of each year include depreciation of $50,000 computed on the straight-line method. In calculating taxable income on the tax return, Valley View Corporation uses the Revenue Canada Rates. Capital cost allowance was $80,000 for 19X7 and $20,000 for 19X8.

Required
(Assume a corporate income tax rate of 31 percent.)

1. Compute taxable income for each year.

2. Journalize the corporation's income taxes for each year.

3. Prepare the corporation's single-step income statement for each year.

Problem 14-9A   *Account for the incorporation of an ongoing business; record the issuance of stock; allocate cash dividends; prepare the shareholders' equity section of the balance sheet*   **(Obj. 2, 3, 4, 5)**

Gilbert and Docksteder are partners in a glass recycling business with capital account balances of $50,000 and $80,000 respectively. They are considering incorporating and taking advantage of an offer from the district of Waterloo to establish a new recycling plant. The following transactions then took place:

19X1

Jan.   1   Gilbert and Docksteder incorporated their partnership into URGreen Corporation, with an authorization to issue 50,000 of $1 preferred shares and 100,000 no-par value common shares. Gilbert received 30,000 common shares and Docksteder 50,000 common shares.

         9   The district of Waterloo donated land to the new corporation in exchange for establishing the business in that area. The land had cost the district $30,000 when purchased 10 years ago, but had a market-value today of $90,000.

        15   Paid $3,000 and gave 1,000 common shares to their legal firm for incorporating the business. The total legal fee was $5,000.

Mar.   7   Sold 3,000 preferred shares for $12,000. The preferred shares are convertible on the basis of 4 common shares for each preferred share.

Dec. 31   The company reported net income after taxes of $22,500 for the year, and then closed the income summary account.

19X2

Feb.   14   Declared cash dividends of $15,000, payable on April 8, 19X2, to the shareholders of record on March 1, 19X2. Indicate the amount that would be payable to the preferred and to the common shareholders.

Apr.   8   Paid the cash dividend declared on February 14, 19X2.

July   7   The preferred shareholders converted 1,000 preferred shares into common.

Dec. 31   The company reported net income after taxes of $37,500 for the year, and then closed the income summary account.

19X3

Feb.   16   Declared cash dividends of $20,000, payable on April 10, 19X3, to the shareholders of record on March 13, 19X3. Indicate the amount that would be payable to the preferred and to the common shareholders.

Required

1. Journalize all of the above transactions.

2. Prepare the shareholders' equity section of the balance sheet as of the close of business on March 16, 19X3.

Problem 14-10A   *Record the issuance of stock; allocate cash dividends; account for corporate income taxes, prepare the liability and shareholders' equity sections of the balance sheet*   **(Obj. 2, 3, 5, 8)**

The Northwest Fisheries Company had the following shareholders' equity section of their balance sheet on January, 1, 19X1:

Shareholders' Equity:		
Preferred Stock, $3, cumulative (2 years in arrears), redemption price of $55, 80,000 shares authorized, 10,000 shares issued..	$ 400,000	
Common Stock, class A, $10 par value, 20,000 shares authorized and issued..	200,000	
Common Stock, class B, unlimited number of shares authorized, 60,000 shares issued	960,000	
Contributed Surplus—excess owner par value...............	50,000	
Total	1,610,000	
Retained Earnings...	270,000	
Total Shareholders' Equity		$1,880,000

The company had the following transactions in the following periods:

19X1

Dec. 1   The company declared dividends of $160,000, payable on January 15, 19X2, to the shareholders of record on December 31, 19X1. Indicate the amount that would be payable to the preferred shareholders and to the common shareholders.

       31   The company reported pretax accounting income of $90,000 and taxable income of $85,000 (income taxes = 30%). Record the income taxes and close the income summary account.

19X2

Jan. 7   The company sold 5,000 shares of preferred stock at $40 per share.
      15   Paid the dividend declared on December 1, 19X1.

Feb. 14   The company sold 10,000 shares of common class B stock at $20 per share.

Apr. 17   The company paid the income taxes payable from 19X1.

Dec. 2   The company declared dividends of $70,000, payable on January 15, 19X4, to the shareholders of record on December 31, 19X2. Indicate the amount that would be payable to the preferred shareholders and to the common shareholders.

       31   The company reported pretax accounting income of $100,000 and taxable income of $90,000 (income taxes = 30%). Record the income taxes and close the income summary account.

19X3

Jan. 15   Paid the dividend declared on December 2, 19X2.

Mar. 15   The company decided to redeem 8,000 shares of preferred stock at $55 per share. (Repurchase of stock is covered on page 722 of Chapter 15.)

Required

1. Journalize the above transactions.
2. Prepare the liability and shareholders' equity sections of the balance sheet as of the close of business on March 31, 19X3.
3. Calculate the book value per share of preferred stock.
4. What was the average price that the class A common shares were sold for?

(Group B)

Problem 14-1B   *Organizing a corporation*   *(Obj. 1)*

Ursula Klassen and Stephi Magursky are opening an Office Products Ltd. office supply store in a shopping center in Penticton, B.C. The area is growing, and no competitors are located in the immediate vicinity. Their most fundamental decision is how to organize the business. Klassen thinks the partnership form is best. Magursky favors the corporate form of organization. They seek your advice.

Required

Discuss the advantages and disadvantages of organizing the business as a corporation.

Problem 14-2B   *Journalizing corporation transactions and preparing the shareholders' equity section of the balance sheet*   *(Obj. 2, 3)*

The partnership of Martel and Fortin needed additional capital to expand into new markets. They also wished to avoid the unlimited personal liability of the partnership form of business, so they incorporated the partnership as MF Design, Inc. The articles of incorporation from the federal government authorizes the corporation to issue 10,000 shares of $6.00 preferred stock and 250,000 shares of common stock. In its first month, MF Design Inc. completed the following transactions:

Dec.   1   Paid incorporation taxes of $1,500 and paid legal fees of $2,000 to organize as a corporation.

3   Issued 500 shares of common stock to the promoter for assistance with issuance of the common stock. The promotion fee was $5,000.

3   Issued 5,100 shares of common stock to Martel and 3,800 shares to Fortin in return for the net assets of the partnership. Martel's capital balance on the partnership books was $51,000, and Fortin's capital balance was $38,000.

7   Received a small parcel of land valued at $90,000 as a donation from the city of Moose Jaw.

12   Issued 1,000 shares of preferred stock to acquire a patent with a market value of $110,000.

22   Issued 1,500 shares of common stock for $10 cash per share.

Required

1. Record the transactions in the general journal.
2. Prepare the shareholders' equity section of the ML Design Inc. balance sheet at December 31. The ending Retained Earnings balance is $91,300.

Problem 14-3B   *Shareholders' equity section of the balance sheet*   *(Obj. 3)*

Shareholders' equity information is given for Open Space Ltd. and Alliance Corp. The two companies are independent.

Open Spaces Ltd.   Open Spaces Ltd. is authorized to issue 50,000 shares of common stock. All the stock was issued at $12 per share. The company incurred a net loss of $12,000 in 19X1. It earned net income of $60,000 in 19X2 and $130,000 in 19X3. The company declared no dividends during the three-year period.

Alliance Corp.   Alliance's articles of incorporation authorize the company to issue 10,000 shares of $2.50 preferred stock and 120,000 shares of common stock. Alliance issued 1,000 shares of the preferred stock at $104 per share. It issued 40,000 shares of the common stock for a total of $220,000. The company's retained earnings balance at the beginning of 19X3 was $72,000 and net income for the year was $90,000.

During 19X3, the company declared the specified dividend on preferred and a $.50 per share dividend on common. Preferred dividends for 19X2 were in arrears.

Required

For each company, prepare the shareholders' equity section of its balance sheet at December 31, 19X3. Show the computation of all amounts. Entries are not required.

Problem 14-4B   *Analyzing the shareholders' equity of an actual corporation   (Obj. 3, 5)*

The purpose of this problem is to familiarize you with the financial statement information of a real company, U and I Corp. U and I, which makes food products and livestock feeds, included the following shareholders' equity on its year-end balance sheet at February 28:

Shareholders' Equity	($ thousands)
Voting Preferred Stock, $1.25 cumulative;	
authorized 100,000 shares in each class:	
Class A—issued 75,473 shares	$ 1,736
Class B—issued 92,172 shares	2,120
Common stock: authorized 5,000,000 shares; issued 2,870,950 shares	14,355
Retained earnings	8,336
	$26,547

Required

1. Identify the different issues of stock U and I has outstanding.
2. Is the preferred stock participating or nonparticipating? How can you tell?
3. Give the summary entries to record issuance of all the U and I stock. Assume that all the stock was issued for cash. Explanations are not required.
4. Suppose U and I passed its preferred dividends for one year. Would the company have to pay these dividends in arrears before paying dividends to the common shareholders? Give your reason.
5. What amount of preferred dividends must U and I declare and pay each year to avoid having preferred dividends in arrears?
6. Assume that preferred dividends are in arrears for 19X8.
   a. Write note 5 of the February 28, 19X8, financial statements to disclose the dividends in arrears.
   b. Record the declaration of a $450,000 dividend in the year ended February 28, 19X9. An explanation is not required.

Problem 14-5B   *Preparing a corporation balance sheet   (Obj. 3, 7)*

The following accounts and related balances of Seagram Art & Supply Ltd. are arranged in no particular order.

Trademark, net	$ 9,000	Common shareholders'	
Organization cost, net	14,000	equity, June 30, 19X1.......	322,000
Preferred stock, $.20,		Net income...........................	$ 31,000
10,000 shares		Total assets, June 30,	
authorized and issued......	27,000	19X1	504,000
Cash	13,000	Interest expense...................	6,100
Accounts receivable, net	58,000	Property, plant, and	
Accrued liabilities	26,000	equipment, net	247,000
Long-term note payable........	72,000	Common stock, 500,000	
Inventory.................................	139,000	shares authorized;	

Dividends payable...............	9,000	236,000 shares issued......	258,000
Retained earnings	?	Prepaid expenses	10,000
Accounts payable	31,000		

Required

1. Prepare the company's classified balance sheet in the account format at June 30, 19X2.
2. Compute rate of return on total assets and rate of return on common share-holders' equity for the year ended June 30, 19X2.
3. Do these rates of return suggest strength or weakness? Give your reason.
4. How will what you have learned in this problem help you evaluate an investment?

Problem 14-6B   *Computing dividends on preferred and common stock*   *(Obj. 5)*

Gander Air Corporation has 10,000 shares of $3.50 preferred stock and 50,000 shares of common stock outstanding. Gander Air declared and paid the following dividends during a three-year period: 19X1, $30,000; 19X2, $80,000; and 19X3, $215,000.

Required

1. Compute the total dividends to preferred stock and common stock for each of the three years if
   a. Preferred is noncumulative and nonparticipating.
   b. Preferred is cumulative and nonparticipating.
2. For requirement 1b, record the declaration of the 19X3 dividends on December 28, 19X3, and the payment of the dividends on January 17, 19X4.

Problem 14-7B   *Analyzing the shareholders' equity of a corporation*   *(Obj. 5, 7)*

The balance sheet of Fort Murray Drilling Company Limited reported the following:

Shareholders' Equity

Redeemable non-voting cumulative preferred stock, authorized 10,000 shares (redemption value $358,000)	$320,000
Common stock, authorized 75,000 shares; issued 36,000 shares	285,000
Retained earnings	119,000
Total shareholders' investment..	$724,000

Notes to the financial statements indicate that 8,000 shares of $2.60 preferred stock were issued for $40 per share. Preferred dividends have not been paid for three years, including the current year. On the balance sheet date, the market value of the Fort Murray common stock was $8.50 per share.

Required

1. Is the preferred stock cumulative or noncumulative, participating or nonparticipating? How can you tell?
2. What is the amount of the annual preferred dividend?
3. Which class of shareholders controls the company? Give your reason.
4. What is the total capital stock of the company?
5. What was the total market value of the common stock?
6. Compute the book value per share of the preferred stock and the common stock.

Problem 14-8B   *Computing and recording a corporation's income tax*   **(Obj. 8)**

The accounting (not for income tax) records of Waterhouse Microfilms, Inc., provide the comparative income statement for 19X3 and 19X4:

	19X3	19X4
Total revenue	$680,000	$720,000
Expenses:		
Cost of goods sold	$290,000	$310,000
Operating expenses	180,000	190,000
Total expenses before tax	470,000	500,000
Pretax accounting income	$210,000	$220,000

Total revenue of 19X4 includes rent of $10,000 that was received late in 19X3. This rent is included in 19X4 total revenue because the rent was earned in 19X4. However, rent revenue that is collected in advance is included in taxable income when the cash is received. In calculating taxable income on the tax return, this rent revenue belongs in 19X3.

Also, the operating expenses of each year include depreciation of $40,000 computing under the straight-line method. In calculating taxable income on the tax return, Waterhouse uses the Revenue Canada rates for tax purposes. Capital cost allowance was $60,000 for 19X3 and $20,000 for 19X4.

Required
(Assume a corporate income tax rate of 30 percent.)

1. Compute taxable income for each year.
2. Journalize the corporation's income taxes for each year.
3. Prepare the corporation's single-step income statement for each year.

Problem 14-9B   *Account for the incorporation of an ongoing business; record the issuance of stock; allocate cash dividends; prepare the shareholders' equity section of the balance sheet*   **(Obj. 2, 3, 4, 5)**

Sullivan and Johnson are partners in a glass recycling business with capital account balances of $60,000 and $90,000 respectively. They are considering incorporating and taking advantage of an offer from the district of Waterloo to establish a new recycling plant. The following transactions then took place:

19X1
Jan.   1   Sullivan and Johnson incorporated their partnership into URGreen Corporation, with an authorization to issue 80,000 of $1 preferred shares and 150,000 no-par value common shares. Sullivan received 40,000 common shares and Johnson 60,000 common shares.

9   The district of Waterloo donated land to the new corporation in exchange for establishing the business in that area. The land had cost the district $40,000 when purchased 10 years ago, but had a market value today of $80,000.

15   Paid $2,000 and gave 2,000 common shares to their legal firm for incorporating the business. The total legal fee was $6,000.

Mar.   7   Sold 4,000 preferred shares for $16,000. The preferred shares are convertible on the basis of 4 common shares for each preferred share.

Dec.   31   The company reported net income after taxes of $30,000 for the year, and then closed the income summary account.

19X2
Feb.   14   Declared cash dividends of $20,000, payable on April 8, 19X2, to the

shareholders of record on March 1, 19X2. Indicate the amount that would be payable to the preferred and to the common shareholders.

Apr.   8   Paid the cash dividend declared on February 14, 19X2.

July   7   The preferred shareholders converted 2,000 preferred shares into common.

Dec. 31   The company reported net income after taxes of $45,000 for the year, and then closed the income summary account.

19X3

Feb. 16   Declared cash dividends of $40,000, payable on April 10, 19X3, to the shareholders of record on March 13, 19X3. Indicate the amount that would be payable to the preferred and to the common shareholders.

Required

1. Journalize all of the above transactions.

2. Prepare the shareholders' equity section of the balance sheet as of the close of business on March 16, 19X3.

Problem 14-10B   *Record the issuance of stock; allocate cash dividends; account for corporate income taxes; prepare the liability and shareholders' equity sections of the balance sheet*   **(Obj. 2, 3, 5, 8)**

The Southeast Fisheries Company had the following shareholders' equity section of their balance sheet on January, 1, 19X1:

Shareholders' Equity:

Preferred Stock, $2, cumulative (3 years in arrears), redemption price of $55, 60,000 shares authorized, 15,000 shares issued	$ 600,000	
Common Stock, class A, $10 par value, 10,000 shares authorized and issued	100,000	
Common Stock, class B, unlimited number of shares authorized, 50,000 shares issued	800,000	
Contributed Surplus	50,000	
Total Contributed Capital...	1,550,000	
Retained Earnings	320,000	
Total Shareholders' Equity		$ 1,870,000

The company had the following transactions in the following periods:

19X1

Dec.   1   The company declared dividends of $140,000, payable on January 15, 19X2, to the shareholders of record on December 31, 19X1. Indicate the amount that would be payable to the preferred shareholders and to the common shareholders.

31   The company reported pretax accounting income of $80,000 and taxable income of $75,000 (income taxes = 30 percent). Recorded the income taxes and closed the income summary account.

19X2

Jan.   7   The company sold 5,000 shares of preferred stock at $40 per share.

15   Paid the dividend declared on December 1, 19X1.

Feb. 14   The company sold 20,000 shares of common class B stock at $20 per share.

Apr. 17   The company paid the income taxes payable from 19X1.

Dec.   2   The company declared dividends of $50,000, payable on January 15, 19X4, to the shareholders of record on December 31, 19X2. Indicate the amount that would be payable to the preferred shareholders and to the common shareholders.

31   The company reported pretax accounting income of $90,000 and taxable income of $80,000 (income taxes = 30 percent). Record the income taxes and close the income summary account.

19X3

Jan. 15   Paid the dividend declared on December 2, 19X2.

Mar. 15   The company decided to redeem 5,000 shares of preferred stock at $55 per share.

Required

1. Journalize the above transactions.
2. Prepare the liability and shareholders' equity sections of the balance sheet as of the close of business on March 31, 19X3.
3. Calculate the book value per share of preferred stock.
4. What was the average price that the class A common shares were sold for?

Challenge Problems

Problem 14-1C   *The pros and cons of incorporation*   **(Obj. 1)**

Your friend Mary Lam has come to you for advice. She has a very successful antique store that had sales of more than $400,000 in the year just ended. She would like to expand and will need to borrow $300,000 to finance an enlarged inventory. She has learned that she can buy the store adjoining hers for $200,000 and estimates that $40,000 of renovations would be needed to make the store compatible with her present store. Expansion would mean adding three or four employees to the two employees Mary already has.

Mary's accountant has suggested that she incorporate her business and that Mary hold all the shares. She cited several reasons to Mary including the benefits of limited liability. Mary has talked to her banker about the possibility of incorporating; he pointed out that if she did incorporate, the bank would need personal guarantees for any loans Mary took out.

Required

Consider Mary's situation and discuss the pros and cons of incorporation for Mary. What would you suggest?

Problem 14-2C   *Deciding on an investment in shares*   **(Obj. 6, 7)**

You have just received a bequest from an aunt of $1,000 and you have decided to invest the money in shares of Super Sounds Television (SSTV), a cable televison channel that shows music videos. The company that owns SSTV has common shares, cumulative preferred shares, non-cumulative, convertible preferred shares, and participating, non-cumulative preferred shares. The common shares are trading at $20.00 and currently have been paying a dividend of $1.00 per share. The cumulative preferred shares are selling at $30.00 and have a stated dividend of $1.80. The convertible preferred shares are selling for $86.35 and are convertible at the a rate of 4 common for 1 preferred; the dividend rate is $4.75. The participating preferred shares are trading at $40.00 and have a dividend rate of $2.10.

Required

Evaluate each of the four different shares as an investment opportunity. After performing your analysis, select which shares you will buy and explain your choice.

Extending Your Knowledge

Decision Problems

1. Evaluating alternative ways of raising capital (Obj. 2, 3)

Joe Carter and John Olerud have written a computer program for a video game that they believe will rival Nintendo. They need additional capital to market the product, and they plan to incorporate their partnership. They are considering alternative capital structures for the corporation. Their primary goal is to raise as much capital as possible without giving up control of the business. The partners plan to receive 110,000 shares of the corporation's common stock in return for the net assets of the partnership. After the partnership books are closed and the assets adjusted to current market value, Carter's capital balance is $60,000 and Olerud's balance is $50,000.

The corporation's plans for the articles of incorporation include an authorization to issue 5,000 shares of preferred stock and 500,000 shares of common stock. Carter and Olerud are uncertain about the most desirable features for the preferred stock. Prior to incorporating, the partners have discussed their plans with two investment groups. The corporation can obtain capital from outside investors under either of the following plans:

Plan 1   Group 1 will invest $105,000 to acquire 1,000 shares of $5.00, preferred stock and $70,000 to acquire 70,000 shares of common stock. Each preferred share receives 50 votes on matters that come before the shareholders.

Plan 2   Group 2 will invest $160,000 to acquire 1,400 shares of $6.00 nonvoting, noncumulative, participating preferred stock.

Required

Assume the corporation receives its articles of incorporation.

1. Journalize the issuance of common stock to Carter and Olerud.
2. Journalize the issuance of stock to the outsiders under both plans.
3. Assume net income for the first year is $150,000 and total dividends of $19,100 are properly subtracted from retained earnings. Prepare the shareholders' equity section of the corporation balance sheet under both plans.
4. Recommend one of the plans to Carter and Olerud. Give your reasons.

2. Questions about corporations (Obj. 2, 6)

1. Why do you think capital stock and retained earnings are shown separately in the shareholders' equity section?
2. Mary Reesor, major shareholder of M-R Inc., proposes to sell some land she owns to the company for common shares in M-R. What problem does M-R, Inc., face in recording the transaction?
3. Preferred shares generally are preferred with respect to dividends and on liquidation. Why would investors buy common shares when preferred shares are available?
4. What does it mean if the liquidation value of a company's preferred stock is greater than its market value?
5. If you owned 100 shares of stock in Cara Corporation and someone offered to buy the stock for its book value, would you accept their offer? Why or why not?

Ethical Issue

Note: This case is based on a real situation.

George Campbell paid $50,000 for a franchise that entitled him to market Success Associates software programs in the countries of the European Common Market. Campbell intended to sell individual franchises for the major language groups of western Europe—German, French, English, Spanish, and Italian. Naturally, investors considering buying a franchise from Campbell asked to see the financial statements of his business.

Believing the value of the franchise to be greater than $50,000, Campbell sought to capitalize his own franchise at $500,000. The law firm of McDonald and LaDue helped Campbell form a corporation authorized to issue 500,000 common shares. Lawyers suggested the following chain of transactions:

1. A third party borrows $500,000 and purchases the franchise from Campbell.
2. Campbell pays the corporation $500,000 to acquire all its stock.
3. The corporation buys the franchise from the third party, who repays the loan.

In the final analysis, the third party is debt-free and out of the picture. Campbell owns all the corporation's stock, and the corporation owns the franchise. The corporation balance sheet lists a franchise acquired at a cost of $500,000. This balance sheet is Campbell's most valuable marketing tool.

Required

1. What is unethical about this situation?
2. Who can be harmed? How can they be harmed? What role does accounting play?

Financial Statement Problems

1. Shareholders' equity   (Obj. 2)

The Mark's Work Wearhouse financial statements appear in Appendix A. Answer the following questions about the company's common stock.

1. Where can you find information about Mark's Work Wearhouse capital stock? What classes of capital stock has Mark's issued and are outstanding? How many shares are authorized and how many are issued?
2. Was any stock issued during the year? If yes, at what price were the shares issued?
3. Mark's has a plan whereby the company finances share purchases by employees. What is the name of the plan? How many common shares is the company holding as security for loans made under the plan at January 29, 1994?
4. What is the book value per share at January 29, 1994? The market price of the shares ranged between $1.30 and $1.80 at that time. Why is the market price different from the book price?
5. What did Mark's Work Wearhouse earn per common share in 1994? Where did you find that information?

2. Shareholders' equity   (Obj. 2, 6)

Obtain the annual report of an actual company of your choosing. Answer these questions about the company. Concentrate on the current year in the annual report you select.

1. What classes of stock does the company have outstanding? How many shares are authorized? How many shares were outstanding on the most current balance sheet date?

2. Under what title does the company report additional capital stock?

3. How much is total shareholders' equity? If the total is not labeled, compute total shareholders' equity.

4. Using the company's terminology, journalize the issuance of 100,000 shares of the company's common stock at $55 per share. Recompute all account balances to include the effect of this transaction.

5. Compute the average amount paid in per share of the company's common stock. Then examine the recent market prices of the company's stock in the multiyear summary of financial data. Compare the average amount paid in per share with recent market prices to determine whether the bulk of the company's stock was issued within the recent past. Give the reason for your answer.

CHAPTER 15

Retained Earnings, Dividends, Stock Repurchases, and the Income Statement

"Corporations often restructure their operations and take large one-time losses to enhance future results," says Wilbur L. Ross, Jr., Senior Managing Director of the investment banking firm Rothschild, Inc. "Sophisticated managers simultaneously sell other assets at a gain to offset the impact of the loss. There is usually a small net effect on financial statements but a substantial rise in the price of the stock."

SNC-Lavalin Group Inc., a contracting and engineering firm with operations throughout the world, was puzzled that the stock market was undervaluing its stock. Its earnings were up, management was strong, the balance sheet was healthy, and it had a $2.1 billion order book for engineering projects around the world.

"Given this performance, and despite a concerted investor relations program, [the decline in the stock price] puzzles me," President and CEO Guy Saint-Pierre told shareholders at the company's annual meeting May 10, 1995. He went on to tell the meeting that the company planned to "repurchase 1.4 million [of the company's] shares in an effort to firm up the stock price and boost its liquidity."

The company had strengthened its balance sheet through the sale of subsidiaries that were not part of its engineering-construction core business and had paid off $81 million of its long-term debt. Earnings for the first quarter in 1995 were up more than 1 percent. Pierre Robataille, executive vice-president, reported that the company expected to have revenue in excess of $1 billion. The Board of Directors approved an increase in the quarterly dividend from $.09 to $.10.

The management of SNC-Lavalin believed that the various changes and strong performance would lead to a strengthened stock price. When that did not occur, they decided to repurchase shares as noted above.

Source: Adapted from Kathryn Leger, "SNC-Lavalin feels 'undervalued.'" *The Financial Post*, May 11, 1995, p. 21.

CHAPTER OBJECTIVES

After studying this chapter, you should be able to

1 Account for stock dividends

2 Distinguish stock splits from stock dividends

3 Account for repurchased capital stock

4 Report restrictions of retained earnings

5 Identify the elements of a corporation income statement

6 Account for prior-period adjustments

Businesses like SNC-Lavalin take actions to increase share value. Apparently the company succeeded, because the company's stock price increased by $2.25 per share between the meeting May 10, 1995, and May 24, 1995. If you had owned 1,000 shares of SNC-Lavalin Group stock before the announcement of the planned stock repurchase on May 10, your two-week gain would have been $2,250. An increase in its stock price helps a company raise additional capital if the need arises.

In this case SNC-Lavalin is shrinking—disposing of subsidiaries that are not part of its core business and paying off debt of $81 million. The company has indicated it will repurchase up to 1.4 million shares of stock. This chapter discusses how companies repurchase their own shares. First, however, we continue the discussion of retained earnings and corporate dividends begun in Chapter 14.

Retained Earnings and Dividends

We have seen that the equity section on the corporation balance sheet is called shareholders' equity. The capital stock accounts and retained earnings make up the shareholders' equity section.

Retained Earnings is the corporation account that carries the balance of the business's net income less its net losses from operations and less any declared dividends accumulated over the corporation's lifetime. *Retained* means "held on to." Retained earnings is the shareholders' claim against total assets arising from accumulated income. Successful companies grow by reinvesting the assets they generate by profitable operations. A survey of 300 Canadian corporations in 1992 indicates that the term "Retained Earnings" is used by 78 percent of those reporting; 18 percent used the term "Deficit" while the remaining 4 percent used a variety of terms.[1]

A debit balance in Retained Earnings, which arises when a corporation's accumulated net losses and any declared dividends exceed its accumulated net income, is called a *deficit*. This amount is subtracted from the sum of the credit balances in the other owners' equity accounts on the balance sheet to determine total shareholders' equity. As was noted above, in 1992, 14 percent of 300 companies surveyed had a retained earnings deficit.

At the end of each accounting period, the Income Summary account—which carries the balance of net income for the period—is closed to the Retained Earnings account. Assume the following amounts are drawn from a corporation's temporary accounts:

Income Summary

Dec. 31, 19X1	Expenses	750,000	Dec. 31, 19X1	Revenues	850,000
			Dec. 31, 19X1	Bal.	100,000

---

[1] *Financial Reporting in Canada*, 1993, Twentieth edition (Toronto: CICA, 1993), p. 147.

This final closing entry transfers net income from Income Summary to Retained Earnings:

19X1

Dec. 31	Income Summary	100,000	
	Retained Earnings		100,000
	To close net income to Retained Earnings.		

STOP & THINK

Assume that the beginning balance of Retained Earnings was $720,000. What will Retained Earnings's balance be after this net income?

Answer:

Retained Earnings

Jan. 1, 19X1	Bal.	720,000
Dec. 31, 19X1	Net inc.	100,000
Dec. 31, 19X1	Bal.	820,000

Remember that the account title includes the word *earnings*. *Credits to the Retained Earnings account arise only from net income.* When we examine a corporation's financial statements and want to learn how much net income the corporation has earned and retained in the business, we turn to Retained Earnings.

The Retained Earnings account is not a reservoir of cash waiting for the board of directors to pay dividends to the shareholders. Instead, Retained Earnings is an owners' equity account representing a claim on all assets in general and not on any asset in particular. Its balance is the cumulative, lifetime earnings of the company less its cumulative losses and dividends. In fact, the corporation may have a large balance in Retained Earnings but not have the cash to pay a dividend. Why? One reason could be that the company purchased a building. To *declare* a dividend, the company must have an adequate balance in Retained Earnings. To *pay* the dividend, it must have the cash. Cash and Retained Earnings are two entirely separate accounts sharing no necessary relationship.

Key Point:
Retained Earnings is *not* a bank account. A $500,000 balance in Retained Earnings means that $500,000 of capital has been created by profits reinvested in the business.

Stock Dividends

A **stock dividend** is a proportional distribution by a corporation of its own stock to its shareholders. Stock dividends are fundamentally different from cash dividends because stock dividends do not transfer the assets of the corporation to the shareholders. Cash dividends are distributions of the asset cash, but stock dividends affect *only* the account within shareholders' equity. Stock dividends have *no* effect on total shareholders' equity. Stock dividends increase the capital stock account and decrease Retained Earnings. Both of these accounts are elements of shareholders' equity; total shareholders' equity is unchanged. There is merely a transfer from one shareholders' equity account to another, and no asset or liability is affected by a stock dividend.

The corporation distributes stock dividends to shareholders in proportion to the number of shares they already own. For example, suppose you owned 300 shares of Canadian Pacific Ltd. common stock. If Canadian Pacific distributed a 10 percent common stock dividend, you would receive 30 (300 × .10) additional shares. You would now own 330 shares of the stock. All other Canadian Pacific shareholders would receive additional shares equal to 10 percent of their prior holdings. You would all be in the same relative position after the dividend as you were before.

OBJECTIVE 1
Account for stock dividends

Real-World Example:

In *The Financial Post*, you can read "Dividends" to discover interesting facts about corporations' dividend actions. On May 24, 1995, National Trust reported a $.22 dividend to shareholders of record on June 12, 1995.

Reasons for Stock Dividends

In distributing a stock dividend, the corporation gives up no assets. Why, then, do companies issue stock dividends? A corporation may choose to distribute stock dividends for these reasons:

1. To continue dividends but conserve cash. A company may want to keep cash in the business in order to expand, buy inventory, pay off debts, and so on. Yet the company may wish to continue dividends in some form. To do so, the corporation may distribute a stock dividend. The debit to Retained Earnings indirectly conserves cash by decreasing the Retained Earnings available for the declaration of future cash dividends. Shareholders pay tax on cash dividends but not on stock dividends.

2. To reduce the market price per share of its stock.

Many companies pay low cash dividends and grow by reinvesting their earnings in operations. As they grow, the company's stock price increases. If the price gets high enough, some potential investors may be prevented from purchasing the stock. Distribution of a stock dividend may cause the market price of a share of the company's stock to decrease because of the increased supply of the stock. Suppose the market price of a share of stock is $50. Doubling the number of shares of its stock outstanding by issuing a stock dividend, the market price of the stock is likely to drop by approximately half, to $25 per share. The objective of such a large stock dividend is to make the stock less expensive and thus attractive to a wider range of investors.

Entries for Stock Dividends

The board of directors announces stock dividends on the declaration date. The date of record and the distribution date follow. (This is the same sequence of dates used for a cash dividend.) The declaration of a stock dividend does *not* create a liability because the corporation is not obligated to pay assets. (Recall that a liability is a claim on *assets*.) Instead, the corporation has declared its intention to distribute its stock. Assume General Lumber Corporation has the following shareholders' equity prior to the dividend:

Shareholders' Equity

Capital stock	
Common stock, 50,000 shares authorized, 20,000 shares issued............	$270,000
Total capital stock..	270,000
Retained earnings...	85,000
Total shareholders' equity...	$355,000

Of concern about stock dividends is how to determine the amount to transfer from retained earnings to the capital stock account. The *Canada Business Corporations Act* suggests that the market value of the shares issued is the appropriate amount to transfer, while other incorporating acts allow the directors to set a value on the shares. If market value were to be used, it would be the market value on the date the dividend is declared. If any other value were to be used, it would be determined by the directors at the time of declaration. This issue is not dealt with in the *CICA Handbook*. The market value of the shares issued would seem to be an appropriate valuation in any event and will be used in this text.

Assume General Lumber Corporation declares a 10 percent common stock dividend on November 17. The company will distribute 2,000 (20,000 × .10) shares in the dividend. On November 17 the market value of its common stock is $16 per share. Using the market value approach, Retained Earnings is debited for the market value of the 2,000 dividend shares and Common Stock Dividend Distributable is credited. General Lumber makes the following entry on the declaration date.

Nov. 17 Retained earnings (20,000 × .10 × $16)   32,000

          Common Stock Dividend Distributable ...   32,000

          To declare a 10 percent common stock dividend.

On the distribution (payment) date, the company records issuance of the dividend shares as follows:

Dec. 12 Common Stock Dividend Distributable   32,000

          Common Stock   32,000

          To issue common stock in a stock dividend.

Common Stock Dividend Distributable is a shareholders' equity account. (It is *not* a liability because the corporation has no obligation to pay assets.) If the company prepares financial statements after the declaration of the stock dividend but before issuing it, Common Stock Dividend Distributable is reported in the shareholders' equity section of the balance sheet immediately after Common Stock. However, this account holds the value of the dividend shares only from the declaration date to the date of distribution.

The following tabulation shows the changes in shareholders' equity caused by the stock dividend:

Shareholders' Equity	Before the Dividend	After the Dividend	Change
Capital stock			
Common stock, 50,000 shares			
authorized, 20,000 shares issued	$270,000		
22,000 shares issued		$302,000	**Up by $32,000**
Total capital stock	270,000	302,000	**Up by $32,000**
Retained earnings	85,000	53,000	**Down by $32,000**
Total shareholders' equity	$355,000	$355,000	**Unchanged**

Compare shareholders' equity before and after the stock dividend. Observe the increase in the balance of Common Stock and the decrease in Retained Earnings. Also observe that total shareholders' equity is unchanged from $355,000.

Amount of Retained Earnings Transferred in a Stock Dividend   Stock dividends are said to be *capitalized retained earnings* because they transfer an amount from retained earnings to capital stock. The capital stock accounts are more permanent than retained earnings because they are not subject to dividends. As we saw in the preceding illustration, the amount transferred from Retained Earnings in a stock dividend is the market value of the dividend shares. Therefore, many shareholders view stock dividends as distributions little different from cash dividends.

Stock Splits

A stock dividend may decrease the market price of the stock. A stock *split* also decreases the market price of stock—with the intention of making the stock more attractive. A **stock split** is an increase in the number of outstanding shares of stock coupled with a proportionate reduction in the book value per share of the stock. For example, if the company splits its stock 2 for 1, the number of outstanding shares is doubled and each share's book value is halved. Many large companies in Canada—Dofasco, Toronto-Dominion Bank, St. Lawrence Cement, National Trust, and others—have split their stock.

A second reason for a stock split is that conventional wisdom suggests that the investors in the stock market believe that companies use a stock split to signal an increase in dividends and so will bid up the price of the shares in anticipation of that increase.

Short Exercise:
A corporation issued 1,000 shares of its $15-par common stock as a stock dividend when the stock's market price was $25 per share.
Record the declaration and distribution. Assume that the 1,000 shares issued are 10% of the outstanding shares. ***A:***
(1) *Date of declaration:*
Retained Earnings
   (1,000 × $25) 25,000
    Com. Stock
     Dividend
     Distributable   25,000
Date of distribution:
Com. Stock
   Dividend
   Distributable   25,000
    Com. Stock   15,000

Short Exercise:

Answer these questions to review stock and cash dividends:

1. How is a stock dividend like a cash dividend? **A:** Both are a distribution to shareholders; both reduce Retained Earnings.

2. What happens to total capital stock as a result of cash and stock dividends? **A:** No change with a cash dividend; increase with a stock dividend (by the same amount that Retained Earnings decreases).

3. What happens to total shareholders' equity as a result of cash and stock dividends? **A:** Decrease with cash dividend; no change with stock dividend.

4. Which type of dividend gives taxable income to the shareholder? **A:** Cash dividend.

Assume that the market price of a share of Magna International Inc. common stock is $60 and that the company wishes to decrease the market price to approximately $30. Magna decides to split the common stock 2 for 1 in the expectation that the stock's market price would fall from $60 to $30. A 2-for-1 stock split means that the company would have two times as many shares of stock outstanding after the split as it had before and that each share's book value would be halved. Assume Magna had 10,000,000 shares of common stock issued and outstanding before the split.

Shareholders' Equity (before stock split)	($ millions)
Capital stock	
Common stock, 50,000,000 shares authorized, **10,000,000**	
shares issued..	$ 20
Total capital stock...	20
Retained earnings	200
Total shareholders' equity	$ 220

After the 2-for-1 split, Magna would have 20,000,000 shares (10,000,000 × 2) of common stock outstanding. Total shareholders' equity would be exactly as before the stock split. Indeed, the balance in the Common Stock account does not even change. Only the number of shares issued and the book value per share change. Compare the highlighted figures in the two shareholders' equity presentations.

Shareholders' Equity (after stock split)	($ millions)
Capital stock	
Common stock, 100,000,000 shares authorized, **20,000,000**	
shares issued..	$ 20
Total capital stock...	20
Retained earnings	200
Total shareholders' equity	$ 220

Because the stock split affects no account balances, no formal journal entry is necessary. Instead, the split is recorded in a memorandum entry such as the following:

Aug. 19   Distributed two additional shares of common stock for each old share previously outstanding.

A company may engage in a reverse split to decrease the number of shares of stock outstanding. For example, Magna could split its stock 1 for 4 which would reduce the number of shares issued and outstanding from 10,000,000 to 2,500,000. Reverse splits are rare.

EXHIBIT 15-1   *Effects of Dividends and Stock Splits on Total Shareholders' Equity*

	Effect on Total Shareholders' Equity	
	Declaration	Payment of Cash or Distribution of Stock
Cash dividend...	Decrease	None
Stock dividend...	None	None
Stock split...	None	None

Source: Adapted from Beverly Terry.

Stock Dividends and Stock Splits

OBJECTIVE 2
Distinguish stock splits from stock dividends

A stock dividend and a stock split both increase the number of shares of stock owned per shareholder. Also, neither a stock dividend nor a stock split changes the investor's total cost of the stock owned. For example, assume you paid $3,000 to acquire 150 shares of Potash Corporation of Saskatchewan common stock. If Potash Corporation distributes a 100 percent stock dividend, your 150 shares increase to 300, but your total cost is still $3,000. Likewise, if Potash Corporation distributes a 2-for-1 stock split, your shares increase in number to 300, but your total cost is unchanged. Neither type of stock action is taxable income to the investor.

Both a stock dividend and a stock split increase the corporation's number of shares outstanding. For example, a 100 percent stock dividend and a 2-for-1 stock split both double the outstanding shares and are likely to cut the stock's market price per share in half. They differ in that a stock *dividend* shifts an amount from retained earnings to capital stock, leaving book value per share unchanged. A stock *split* affects no account balances whatsoever but instead changes the book value of the stock.

Exhibit 15-1 summarizes the effects of dividends and stock splits on total shareholders' equity.

Repurchase of Its Stock by a Company ————

OBJECTIVE 3
Account for repurchased capital stock

Corporations may **repurchase stock** from their shareholders for several reasons: (1) the company may have issued all its authorized stock and needs the stock for distributions to officers and employees under bonus plans or stock purchase plans; (2) the purchase may help support the stock's current market price by decreasing the supply of stock available to the public; and (3) management may gather in the stock to avoid a takeover by an outside party.

The *Canada Business Corporations Act* requires a corporation that purchases its own stock to cancel the shares bought; it may do so by treating the purchased shares as authorized but unissued, and issue them in the normal way at a later date or it may cancel them outright. Several of the provincial incorporating acts also require that the shares be treated this way, while other incorporating acts permit the corporation to hold the shares as treasury stock (in effect, the corporation holds the stock in its treasury) and resell them.

Shares that are canceled outright may not be re-issued. The effect of purchasing an outstanding share is to reduce the number of shares issued; the effect of canceling a share outright is to reduce the number of shares authorized.

For practical purposes, treasury stock is like unissued stock: neither category of stock is outstanding in the hands of shareholders. The company does not receive cash dividends on its treasury stock, and treasury stock does not entitle the company to vote or to receive assets in liquidation. The difference between unissued stock and treasury stock is that treasury stock has been issued and bought back.

The repurchase of its own stock by a company decreases the company's assets and its shareholders' equity. The size of the company literally decreases, as shown on the balance sheet. The *Canada Business Corporations Act* and most of the provincial incorporating acts do not permit a corporation to acquire its own shares if such reacquisition would result in the corporation being unable to pay its liabilities as they become due.

For companies incorporated under the *Canada Business Corporations Act* and in jurisdictions where repurchased stock must be canceled or treated as unissued, the Common Stock account is debited. In those jurisdictions where treasury stock is permitted, the entry to record a purchase of treasury stock would include a debit to Treasury Stock and a credit to Cash. The Treasury Stock account has a debit balance, which is the opposite of the other shareholders' equity accounts. Therefore, Treasury Stock is a contra shareholders' equity account; it is deducted from the total of capital stock and Retained Earnings to compute total shareholders' equity.

Repurchase of Capital Stock → Stop

The *CICA Handbook* requires a company that purchases its own shares at a price equal to or greater than the issue price to debt Common Stock (or Preferred Stock as the case may be) for the issue price; any excess should be debited to Retained Earnings. When the shares are purchased at a price less than the issue price, the excess of the issue price over the purchase price should be credited to Contributed Surplus. The balance of Contributed Surplus is not adjusted for shares subsequently reissued. In situations where the shares are issued at different prices, the average issue price should be used. (In jurisdictions where par value stock is permitted, the excess of the price paid over par would be debited to Contributed Surplus.)

Suppose Farwest Drilling Inc. had the following shareholders' equity before purchasing 1,000 of its own shares; its 8,000 shares were issued at the same price, as follows:

Shareholders' Equity

Capital stock

Common stock, 10,000 shares authorized, 8,000 shares issued..............	$20,000
Total capital stock...	20,000
Retained earnings...	14,600
Total shareholders' equity..	$34,600

On November 22, Farwest purchases 1,000 shares of its common stock, paying cash of $7.50 per share; the shares had been issued at $2.50 ($20,000/8,000). The shares are to be canceled, reducing the number of shares authorized. Farwest records the purchase as follows:

Nov. 22	Common Stock..	2,500	
	Retained Earnings	5,000	
	Cash..		7,500
	Purchased 1,000 shares of stock at $7.50 per share.		

The shareholders' equity section of Farwest's balance sheet would appear as follows after the transaction:

Shareholders' Equity

Capital stock

Common stock, 9,000 shares authorized, 7,000 shares issued	$17,500
Total capital stock	17,500
Retained earnings	9,600
Total shareholders' equity	$27,100

Observe that the purchase of the stock decreased the number of shares authorized and decreased the number of shares issued and outstanding. Only outstanding shares have a vote, receive cash dividends, and share in assets if the corporation liquidates. Notice that the dollar amount shown for Capital Stock and Retained Earnings decreased by $2,500 and $5,000 respectively.

Assume the articles of incorporation for Eastern Exploration Ltd., issued under the *Canada Business Corporations Act*, authorized it to issue 100,000 shares of common stock. By February 28 of this year, Eastern had issued 40,000 shares at an average price of $20.00 per share. Common Stock on the balance sheet amounted to $800,000. Retained Earnings was $187,396.

On March 20, Eastern purchases 2,000 shares at $15.00 per share and records the transaction as follows:

March 20	Common Stock (2,000 × $20).......................	40,000	
	Contributed Surplus [2,000 × ($20 – 15)]		10,000
	Cash (2,000 × $15)		30,000
	Purchased 2,000 shares of stock at $15 per share.		

The shareholders' equity section of Eastern Exploration's balance sheet would appear as follows after the transaction:

Short Exercise:

Shareholders' Equity

Capital stock
   Common stock, 98,000 shares authorized, 38,000 shares issued $760,000
   Contributed Surplus (note 6) 10,000
   Total capital stock $770,000
Retained earnings 187,396
   Total shareholders' equity $957,396

Note 6: During the year, the company acquired 2,000 shares of common stock at a price of $15.00 per share; the shares had been issued at $20.00 per share. The shares were canceled.

Sale of Repurchased Capital Stock

A company incorporated under the *Canada Business Corporations Act* may re-issue the shares that it previously had repurchased. The sale would be treated like a normal sale of authorized but unissued stock. As with accounting for the purchase of its own stock, accounting for the re-sale of the stock is different for companies in those jurisdictions that do not require such shares to be canceled as the *Canada Business Corporations Act* does.

STOP & THINK

Stock repurchase transactions have a serious ethical and legal dimension. A company buying its own shares must be extremely careful that its disclosures of information are complete and accurate. Otherwise, a shareholder who sold shares back to the company may claim that he or she was deceived into selling the stock at too low a price. What would happen if a company repurchased its own stock at $17 per share and one day later announced a technological breakthrough that would generate millions of dollars in new business?

Answer: The stock would likely increase in response to the new information. If it could be proved that management withheld the information, a shareholder selling stock back to the company may file a lawsuit to gain the difference per share. The shareholder would claim that the knowledge of the technological advance, he or she would have held the stock until after the price increase. Companies strive to avoid such situations.

No Gain or Loss from Repurchased Capital Stock Transactions

The repurchase and sale of its own stock do not affect net income. Stock repurchase affects *balance sheet accounts*, not income statement accounts. Sale of repurchased stock above cost is an increase in capital stock, not income. Likewise, sale of repurchased stock below cost is a decrease in capital stock, not a loss. Repurchased stock transactions take place between the business and its owners, the shareholders. If the company is able to issue the shares at a price in excess of the price paid for them, the company would earn a "profit" on the transaction. However, the profit is not a real profit; it does not appear on the income statement. Instead, it would be reflected in the Common Stock account, since the proceeds of the sale of shares is credited in total to the Common Stock account. Similarly, if the company issued the shares at a price that was less than the price paid for them, the "loss" would be reflected in the Common Stock account.

Jackson Products, Inc., issued 100,000 shares of common stock at $10. Later, when the market price was $15 per share, Jackson distributed a 10% stock dividend. Then Jackson repurchased 500 shares of stock, at $20 per share. What is the Common Stock balance? *A:* $1,144,773:

100,000 shares × $10
           = $1,000,000
+ 10% × 100,000
  × $15   =   150,000
− 500 shares
  × 10.45 =   5,227
           $1,144,773

Suppose Farwest Drilling sold 500 shares of common stock at $10.00 per share shortly after the purchase of 1,000 shares described above. Farwest records the sale as follows:

Dec.	5	Cash...	5,000	
		Common Stock		5,000
		To sell 500 shares of stock at $10.00 per share.		

If Farwest had sold the 500 shares for $2.00 per share, the sale would be recorded as follows:

Dec.	5	Cash	1,000	
		Common Stock...		1,000
		To sell 500 shares of stock at $2.00 per share.		

Does this mean that a company cannot increase its net assets by repurchasing stock low and selling it high? Not at all. Management may repurchase stock because it believes the market price of its stock is too low. For example, a company may buy 500 shares of its stock at $10 per share. Suppose it holds the stock as the market price rises and resells the stock at $14 per share. The net assets of the company increase by $2,000 [500 shares × ($14 – $10 = $4 difference per share)]. This increase is reported as capital stock and not as income.

Mid-Chapter Summary Problem for Your Review

Pierre Caron, Inc., reported the following shareholders' equity:

Shareholders' Equity

Preferred stock, $1.00	
Authorized: 10,000 shares	
Issued: None...	$ —
Common stock	
Authorized: 30,000 shares	
Issued: 13,733 shares	49,266
Earnings retained in business...	89,320
	$138,586

Required

1. What was the average issue price per share of the common stock?
2. How many shares of Caron's common stock are outstanding?
3. Journalize the issuance of 1,200 shares of common stock at $4 per share. Use Caron's account titles.
4. How many shares of common stock would be outstanding after Caron splits its common stock (computed in requirement 3) 3 for 1?
5. Using Caron account titles, journalize the declaration of a stock dividend when the market price of Caron common stock is $3 per share. Consider each of the following stock dividends independently:
   a. Caron declares a 10 percent common stock dividend on the shares outstanding, after the entry in requirement 3.
   b. Caron declares a 50 percent common stock dividend on the shares outstanding, after the entry in requirement 3.

6. Journalize the following repurchase and sale of its stock transactions by Caron, assuming they occur in the order given:
   a. Caron purchases 500 shares at $8 per share.
   b. Caron purchases 500 shares at $3 per share.
   c. Caron sells 100 shares for $9 per share.

7. How many shares of Caron's common stock would be outstanding after the transactions in requirement 6 take place? Ignore the transactions in requirements 4 and 5.

SOLUTION TO SUMMARY PROBLEM

1. Average issue price of the common stock was $3.59 per share ($49,266/13,733 shares = $3.59).

2. Shares outstanding = 13,733.

3. Cash (1,200 × $4) 4,800
       Common Stock..   4,800
       To issue common stock.

4. Shares outstanding after a 3-for-1 stock split = 44,799, (13,733 + 1200 = 14,933 shares outstanding × 3).

5. a. Earnings Retained in Business
       (14,933 × .10 × $3) 4,480
           Common Stock Dividend Distributable   4,480
       To declare a 10 percent common stock dividend.

   b. Earnings Retained in Business
       (14,933 × .50 × $3) 22,400
           Common Stock Dividend Distributable   22,400
       To declare a 50 percent common stock dividend.

6. a. Common Stock (500 × $3.61)*................................... 1,805
       Retained Earnings [500 × ($8.00 – $3.61)*]................ 2,195
           Cash   4,000
       To purchase 500 shares at $8.00 per share.

   b. Common Stock (500 × $3.61)*................................... 1,805
           Contributed Surplus [500 × ($3.61* – $3.00)].......   305
           Cash   1,500
       To purchase 500 shares at $3.00 per share.

   c. Cash (100 × $9.00) 900
           Common Stock   900
       To sell 100 shares at $9.00 per share.

7. Shares outstanding = 14,033 (13,733 + 1,200 – 500 – 500 + 100)

---

*[($49,266 + $4,800)/(13,733 + 1,200)] = $3.61

Restrictions on Retained Earnings

Dividends and repurchases of capital stock require payments by the corporation to its shareholders. In fact, repurchases of capital stock are returns of capital stock to the shareholders. These outlays decrease the corporation's assets, so fewer assets are available to pay liabilities. Therefore, its creditors may seek to restrict a corporation's dividend payments and capital stock repurchases. For example, a bank may agree to loan $500,000 only if the borrowing corporation limits dividend payments and repurchases of its stock.

To ensure that corporations maintain a minimum level of shareholders' equity for the protection of creditors, as was noted above, incorporating acts restrict the amount

OBJECTIVE 4
Report restrictions of retained earnings

of its own stock that a corporation may repurchase. The maximum amount a corporation can pay its shareholders without decreasing capital stock is its balance of retained earnings. Therefore, restrictions on dividends and stock repurchases focus on the balance of retained earnings.

Companies usually report their retained earnings restrictions in notes to the financial statements. The following disclosure in the 1992 financial statements by TransCanada PipeLines Limited is typical:

Note 17—Restriction on Dividends

Declaration of dividends on both preferred and common shares is restricted under certain preferred share provisions and under several debt instruments. At December 31, 1992, under the most restrictive provisions, approximately $300 million was permitted for the payment of dividends on common shares.

STOP & THINK

Why would a borrower such as TransCanada PipeLines Limited agree to restrict dividends as a condition for receiving a loan?

Answer: To get a lower interest rate. Other things being equal, the greater the borrower's concessions, the more favorable the terms offered by the lender.

Appropriations of Retained Earnings

Appropriations are restrictions of Retained Earnings that are recorded by formal journal entries. A corporation may appropriate (segregate in a separate account) a portion of Retained Earnings for a specific use. For example, the board of directors may appropriate part of Retained Earnings for building a new manufacturing plant, for meeting possible future liabilities or other reasons. A debit to Retained Earnings and a credit to a separate account—Retained Earnings Restricted for Plant Expansion—records the appropriation. The appropriated retained earnings account appears directly above the regular Retained Earnings account on the balance sheet.

Retained earnings appropriations are rare. Corporations generally disclose any retained earnings restrictions in the notes to the financial statements as illustrated in the preceding section. The notes give the corporation more room to describe the nature and amounts of any restrictions. Thus corporations satisfy the requirement for adequate disclosure.

Variations in Reporting Shareholders' Equity _____

Real-world accounting and business practices may use terminology and formats in reporting shareholders' equity that differ from our general examples. We use a more detailed format in this book to help you learn from the components of the shareholders' equity section. Companies assume that readers of their statements already understand the details they omit.

One of the most important skills you will learn in this course is the ability to understand the financial statements of actual companies. Thus we present in Exhibit 15-2 a side-by-side comparison of our general teaching format and the format of the Bank of Montreal taken from a recent annual report. Note the following points with respect to the real-world format illustrated in Exhibit 15-2 and also with regard to actual financial statements:

1. The Bank of Montreal uses the heading Share Capital rather than Capital Stock.

2. Some companies combine all classes of capital stock into a single line item and provide specifics in the notes. The Bank of Montreal has combined the two classes of

EXHIBIT 15-2   *Formats for Reporting Shareholders' Equity**

General Teaching Format		Real-World Format	
Shareholders' Equity **($ amounts in thousands)**		**Shareholders' Equity** **($ amounts in thousands)**	
Capital Stock		Share capital (note 13)	
50,000,000 Class A Preferred shares authorized, 18,703,625 issued	$ 467,591	▶ Preferred shares	$ 717,591
12,500,000 Class B Preferred shares authorized, 10,000,000 issued	250,000	▶ Common shares	2,416,303
Unlimited number of common shares authorized (Proceeds not to exceed $5.5 billion), 119,385,179 issued	2,416,303		
Retained earnings	1,416,215	Retained earnings	1,416,215
Total shareholders' equity	$ 4,550,109	Total shareholders' equity	$4,550,109

Note 13: Share Capital
Authorized

50,000,000	Class A Preferred Shares without par value, issuable in series. The aggregate consideration for all Class A Preferred Shares shall not exceed $1 billion.
12,500,000	Class B Preferred Shares without par value, issuable in series. The aggregate consideration for all Class B Preferred Shares shall not exceed $250 million. These shares may be issued in foreign currencies.
	Unlimited number of Common Shares without par value. The aggregate consideration for all common shares shall not exceed $5.5 billion

* GAAP suggests the presentation of comparative data; in order to simplify the illustration, data are presented for 1991 only.

preferred stock in a single line item but does show preferred and common separately.

3. The preferred and common shares are described fully in the notes with respect to shares authorized and issued; the information in the balance sheet is limited to a description of the class and total amount for which the two classes of shares were issued.

4. Often total shareholders' equity is not specifically labeled.

Corporation Income Statement

A corporation's net income receives more attention than any other item in the financial statements. In fact, net income is probably the most important piece of information about a company. Net income measures the business's ability to earn a profit and answers the question of how successfully the company has managed its operations. To shareholders, the larger the corporation's profit, the greater the likelihood of dividends. To creditors, the larger the corporation's profit, the better able it is to pay its debts. Net income builds up a company's assets and owners' equity. It also helps to attract capital from new investors who hope to receive dividends from future successful operations.

OBJECTIVE 5

Identify the elements of a corporation income statement

Suppose you are considering investing in the stock of two manufacturing companies. In reading their annual reports and examining their past records, you learn that the companies showed the same net income figure for last year and that each company has increased its net income by 15 percent annually over the last five years.

The two companies have generated income in different ways. Company A's income has resulted from the successful management of its central operations (manufacturing). Company B's manufacturing operations have been flat for two years. Its growth in net income has resulted from selling off segments of its business at a profit. Which company would you invest in?

Company A holds the promise of better future earnings. This corporation earns profits from continuing operations. We may reasonably expect the business to match its past earnings in the future. Company B shows no growth from operations. Its net income results from one-time transactions, the selling off of its operating assets. Sooner or later, Company B will have sold off the last of its assets used in operations. When that occurs, the business will have no means of generating income. Based on this reasoning, your decision is to invest in the stock of Company A. Investors would say that Company A's earnings were of *higher quality* than Company B's earnings.

This example points to two important investment considerations: the *trend* of a company's earnings and the *makeup* of its net income. More intelligent investment decisions are likely if the income statement separates the results of central, continuing operations from special, one-time gains and losses. We now discuss the components of the corporation income statement. We will see how the income statement reports the results of operations in a manner that allows statement users to get a good look at the business's operations. Exhibit 15-3 will be used throughout these discussions. The items of primary interest are highlighted for emphasis.

Continuing Operations

Short Exercise:

On 9/1/X9, Active Equipment Corp. sells its division that manufactures mobile homes. The assets are sold at a gain of $850,000. The loss from operations for the year up to the date of sale was $480,000. Tax rate is 30%. How would you present the loss for the year and the sale of the division on the 19X9 income statement? *A:* In the Discontinued Operations section you would list two items:

Operating loss,
  $480,000, less income
  tax savings,
  $144,000.......... $(336,000)
Gain on disposal,
  $850,000, less
  income tax,
  $255,000..........   595,000

We have seen that income from a business's continuing operations helps financial statement users make predictions about the business's future earnings. In the income statement of Exhibit 15-3, the topmost section reports income from continuing operations. This part of the business is expected to continue from period to period. We may use this information to predict that Electronics Corporation will earn income of approximately $54,000 next year.

Note that income tax expense has been deducted in arriving at income from continuing operations. The tax that corporations pay on their income is a significant expense. The combined federal and provincial income tax rates for corporations varies from time to time, for type and size of company, and from province to province; the current rates range from 17 percent to a maximum rate of 46 percent. For computational ease, let us use an income tax rate of 40 percent in our illustrations. This is a reasonable estimate of combined federal and provincial income taxes. The $36,000 income tax expense in Exhibit 15-3 equals the pretax income from continuing operations multiplied by the tax rate ($90,000 × .40 = $36,000).

Discontinued Operations

Most large corporations engage in several lines of business. For example, Canadian Pacific Ltd. is best known for transportation, but it also has subsidiaries in mining, forestry products, real estate, hotels, securities and insurance; several years ago it sold off CP Air. Bombardier Inc., best known for its Skidoos and Seadoos, also owns Short Bros, an airplane-builder in Ireland, manufactures subways cars for a world market, and builds Canadian Airlines jets. We call each significant part of a company a **segment of the business**.

A company may sell a segment of its business. Such a sale is not a regular source of income because a company cannot keep on selling its segments indefinitely. The sale of a business segment is viewed as a one-time transaction. The *CICA Handbook,*

EXHIBIT 15-3   *Corporation Income Statement*

Real-World Example:
Segments represent major lines of business or geographic areas. Rogers Communications Inc. lists its segments as cable television, wireless communication (cellular phones and pagers), and broadcasting. John Labatt Limited reports segmented information both by line of business and geographically, Canada and International.

Electronics Corporation
Income Statement
for the year ended December 31, 19X5

Sales revenue		$500,000
Cost of goods sold		240,000
Gross margin		260,000
Operating expenses (detailed)		181,000
Operating income		79,000
Other gains (losses)		
Gain on sale of machinery		11,000
Income from continuing operations before income tax		90,000
Income tax expense		36,000
Income before discontinued operations		
and extraordinary items		54,000
Discontinued operations		
Operating income, $30,000, less		
income tax of $12,000	$18,000	
Gain on disposal, $5,000, less		
income tax of $2,000	3,000	21,000
Income before extraordinary items		75,000
Extraordinary tornado loss	(10,000)	
Less income tax saving	4,000	(6,000)
Net income		$ 69,000
Earnings per share of common stock		
(30,000 shares outstanding)		
Income before discontinued operations and		
extraordinary items		$ 1.80
Income from discontinued operations		.70
Income before extraordinary items		2.50
Extraordinary loss		(.20)
Net income		$ 2.30

in Section 3475, "Discontinued Operations," requires that the income statement carry information on the segment that has been disposed of under the heading *Discontinued Operations.* This section of the income statement is divided into two components: (1) operating income or (loss) on the segment that is disposed of and (2) gain (or loss) on the disposal. Assume income and gain are taxed at the 40 percent rate. They would be reported as follows:

Discontinued operations	
Operating income, $30,000, less income tax, $12,000	$18,000
Gain on disposal, $5,000, less income tax, $2,000	3,000
	$21,000

Trace this presentation to Exhibit 15-3.

It is necessary to separate discontinued operations into these two components because the company may operate the discontinued segment for part of the year. This is the operating income (or loss) component; it should include the results of operations of the segment from the beginning of the period to the disposal date. There is usually also a gain (or loss) on disposal. The transaction may not have been completed at the company's year end and so the gain (or loss) may have to be estimated. Following the conservatism concept, the estimated loss should be recorded in the accounts at year end while an estimated gain would not be recognized until it was realized.

It is important that the assets, liabilities, and operations of the segment can be clearly identified as separate from those of other operations of the company. The notes to the financial statements should disclose fully the nature of the discontinued operations and other relevant information about the discontinued operations, such as revenue to the date of discontinuance.

Discontinued operations are common in business. Recent examples include the sale, mentioned above, by Canadian Pacific of CP Air to PWA Corp. and the sale by John Labatt Limited of its dairy business including Ault Foods.

Extraordinary Gains and Losses

Extraordinary gains and losses, also called **extraordinary items**, must meet three criteria to be classed as extraordinary. They must have all of these characteristics (*CICA Handbook*, Section 3480):

1. An item is extraordinary only if it is not expected to occur frequently. For example, a company that had property on a flood plain that was covered with water every four or five years could not treat losses from flood waters as extraordinary.

2. An item is extraordinary only if it is not typical of the normal business activities of the company. For example, inventory losses or gains, or losses from the sale of property would not be considered extraordinary, since a company that owned either one might normally expect to suffer a loss as a result of that ownership.

3. A gain or loss is extraordinary only if it does not depend on decisions or determinations made by management. For example, the gain on the sale of property held for expansion would not be an extraordinary gain whereas the gain on the expropriation of land by a municipality would normally be considered extraordinary.

Short Exercise:

How would you report on an income statement: (1) $70,000 extraordinary gain, 30% tax rate, and (2) $120,000 extraordinary loss, 35% tax rate? **A:**

(1) Extraordinary gain..........	$ 70,000
Less income taxes	21,000
Extraordinary gain, net of tax	$ 49,000
(2) Extraordinary loss	$120,000
Less tax savings.....	42,000
Extraordinary loss, net of tax	$ 78,000

In short, to be classed as extraordinary, a transaction must be infrequent, unusual and its result determined externally.

Extraordinary items are reported along with their income tax effect. Assume Electronics Corporation lost $10,000 of inventory in a tornado. This loss, which reduces income, also reduces the company's income tax. The tax effect of the loss is computed by multiplying the amount of the loss by the tax rate. The tax effect decreases the net amount of the loss in the same way that the tax effect on income reduces the amount of net income. An extraordinary loss is reported along with its tax effect as follows:

Extraordinary tornado loss...	$(10,000)	
Less income tax saving	4,000	$(6,000)

Trace this item to the income statement in Exhibit 15-3. An extraordinary gain is reported the same way, net of the income tax on the gain.

Gains and losses from unusual or infrequent transactions, such as gains or losses from fixed asset disposals or losses resulting from employee strikes, would be separately disclosed on the income statement as part of income before discontinued operations and extraordinary items. An example is the gain on the sale of machinery in Exhibit 15-3.

Earnings Per Share (EPS)

The final segment of a corporation income statement presents the company's earnings per share, abbreviated as EPS. In fact, GAAP requires that corporations disclose EPS figures on the income statement or in a note to the financial statements.

Earnings per share is the amount of a company's net income per share of its outstanding common stock. EPS is a key measure of a business's success. Consider Corporation P with net income of $200,000 and 100,000 shares of common stock outstanding. Its EPS is $2 ($200,000/100,000). Corporation Q may also have net income of $200,000 but only 50,000 shares of common stock outstanding. Its EPS is $4 ($200,000/50,000).

$$\text{Earnings per share} = \frac{\text{Net income}}{\text{Shares of common stock outstanding}}$$

$$\text{EPS} = \frac{\$200,000}{100,000} = \$2$$

Corporation P

| Net income: | $200,000 |
| Shares of common stock outstanding: | 100,000 |

$$\text{EPS} = \frac{\$200,000}{50,000} = \$4$$

Corporation Q

| Net income: | $200,000 |
| Shares of common stock outstanding: | 50,000 |

Just as the corporation lists separately its different sources of income from continuing operations, discontinued operations, and so on, it must list separately the EPS figure for income before discontinued operations and extraordinary items and net income for the period. The *CICA Handbook,* in Section 3500.11, suggests that "it may also be desirable to show the per share figure for discontinued operations and extraordinary items to emphasize their significance to the overall results."

Consider the income statement of Electronics Corporation shown in Exhibit 15-3; in 19X5, it had 30,000 common shares outstanding. Income before discontinued operations and extraordinary items was $54,000, income from discontinued operations net of tax was $21,000, and there was an extraordinary loss, net of tax saving, of $6,000. Adhering to the *CICA Handbook,* it presents the following disclosures:

Disclosure required
  Income per share before discontinued operations and
    extraordinary items ($54,000/30,000) $1.80
  Net income per share [($54,000 + $21,000 − $6,000)/30,000].............. 2.30
Disclosure not required, but suggested for clarity
  Income per share from discontinued operations ($21,000/30,000)... .70
  Loss per share from extraordinary items ($6,000/30,000) .... (.20)

Remember that the disclosure required by the *CICA Handbook* is a minimum. It is often in the user's interest to exceed that minimum as was done in Exhibit 15-3. The income statement user can better understand the sources of the business's EPS amounts when presented in this detail.

Weighted Average Number of Shares of Common Stock Outstanding

Computing EPS is straightforward if the number of common shares outstanding does not change over the entire accounting period. For many corporations, however, this figure varies over the course of the year. Consider a corporation that had 100,000 shares outstanding from January through November, then purchased 60,000 of its own shares for cancellation. This company's EPS would be misleadingly high if computed using 40,000 (100,000 − 60,000) shares. To make EPS as meaningful as possible, corporations use the weighted average number of common shares outstanding during the period.

Let us assume the following figures for Diskette Demo Corporation. From January through May, the company had 240,000 shares of common stock outstanding; from June through August, 200,000 shares; and from September through December,

Short Exercise:

The net income of Hart Corp. amounted to $3,750,000. Hart had 200,000 shares of $9.00 preferred stock and 310,000 shares of common stock at the end of the year. At the beginning of the year, Hart had 270,000 shares outstanding and issued 40,000 shares on April 1. Calculate Hart's EPS. **A:**
Weighted average:
$270,000 \times 3/12 =$ 67,500
$310,000 \times 9/12 =$ 232,500
            = 300,000 shares

$$\text{EPS} = \frac{\$3,750,000 - (200,000 \times \$9)}{300,000 \text{ shares}}$$
$$= \frac{\$3,750,000 - \$1,800,000}{300,000}$$
$$= \$6.50$$

210,000 shares. We compute the weighted average by considering the outstanding shares per month as a fraction of the year:

Number of Common Shares Outstanding		Fraction of Year				Weighted Average Number of Common Shares Outstanding
240,000	×	⁵⁄₁₂	(January through May)		=	100,000
200,000	×	³⁄₁₂	(June through August)		=	50,000
210,000	×	⁴⁄₁₂	(September through December)		=	70,000
			Weighted average number of common shares outstanding during the year		=	220,000

The 220,000 weighted average would be divided into net income to compute the corporation's EPS.

Preferred Dividends   Throughout the EPS discussion we have used only the number of shares of common stock outstanding. Holders of preferred stock have no claim to the business's income beyond the stated preferred dividend (unless the preferred stock is participating preferred, but such stock is rare and will be ignored for purposes of this discussion). Even though preferred stock has no claims, preferred dividends do affect the EPS figure. Recall, the EPS is earnings per share of common stock. Also recall that dividends on preferred stock are paid first. Therefore, preferred dividends must be subtracted from income subtotals (income before discontinued operations and extraordinary items and net income) in the computation of EPS.

If Electronics Corporation had 10,000 shares of preferred stock outstanding, each with a $1.50 dividend, the annual preferred dividend would be $15,000 (10,000 × $1.50). The $15,000 would be subtracted from the two income subtotals resulting in the following EPS computations:

Income before discontinued operations and extraordinary items [($54,000 − $15,000)/30,000]	$1.30
Net income [($69,000 − $15,000)/30,000]	1.80

Dilution   Some corporations make their bonds or preferred stock more attractive to investors by offering conversion privileges, which permit the holder to convert the bond or preferred stock into some specified number of shares of common stock. Holders of convertible bonds or convertible preferred stock may exchange their securities for common shares. If in fact the bonds or preferred shares are converted into common stock, then the EPS will be diluted (reduced) because more common shares are divided into net income. Because convertible bonds or convertible preferred shares can be traded in for common stock, the common shareholders want to know the amount of the decrease in EPS that would occur if conversion took place. To provide this information, corporations, with convertible bonds or preferred shares outstanding, present two sets of EPS amounts: EPS based on outstanding common shares (*basic EPS*), and EPS based on outstanding common shares plus the number of additional common shares that would arise from conversion of the convertible bonds and convertible preferred shares into common (*fully diluted EPS*). The topic of dilution can be very complex and is covered more fully in intermediate accounting texts.

EPS is the most widely used accounting figure. Many income statement users place top priority on EPS. Also, a stock's market price is related to a company's EPS. By dividing the market price of a company's stock by its EPS, we compute a statistic called the *price-to-earnings* or *price-earnings ratio. The Financial Post* reports the price-earnings ratios (listed as P/E) daily for hundreds of companies listed on the Toronto, Montreal, and New York Stock Exchanges.

Statement of Retained Earnings

Retained earnings may be a significant portion of a corporation's owners' equity. The year's income increases the retained earnings balance, and dividends decrease it.

EXHIBIT 15-4   *Statement of Retained Earnings*

Electronics Corporation Statement of Retained Earnings for the year ended December 31, 19X5	
Retained earnings balance, December 31, 19X4....................................	$ 130,000
Net income for 19X5..	69,000
	199,000
Dividends for 19X5	(21,000)
Retained earnings balance, December 31, 19X5..................................	$178,000

Retained earnings are so important that corporations prepare a financial statement outlining the major changes in this equity account, much as the statement of owner's equity presents information on changes in the equity of a proprietorship. The statement of retained earnings for Electronics Corporation appears in Exhibit 15-4.

Some companies report income and retained earnings on a single statement. Exhibit 15-5 illustrates how Electronics would combine its income statement and its statement of retained earnings.

Prior-Period Adjustments

What happens when a company makes an error in recording revenues or expenses? Detecting the error in the period in which it occurs allows the company to make a correction before preparing that period's financial statements. But failure to detect the error until a later period means that the business will have reported an incorrect amount of income on its income statement. After closing the revenue and expense accounts, the Retained Earnings account will absorb the effect of the error, and its balance will be wrong until the error is corrected.

> **OBJECTIVE 6**
> Account for prior-period adjustments

EXHIBIT 15-5   *Statement of Income and Retained Earnings*

Electronics Corporation Statement of Income and Retained Earnings for the year ended December 31, 19X5	
Sales revenue...	$500,000
Cost of goods sold	240,000
Net income for 19X5..	69,000
Retained earnings, December 31, 19X4	130,000
	199,000
Dividends for 19X5..	(21,000)
Retained earnings, December 31, 19X5	$178,000
Earnings per share of common stock (30,000 shares outstanding)	
Income before discontinued operations and extraordinary items	$1.80
Income from discontinued operations...	.70
Income before extraordinary items	2.50
Extraordinary loss..	(.20)
Net income...	$2.30

Corrections to the beginning balance of Retained Earnings for errors of an earlier period are called **prior-period adjustments**. The correcting entry includes a debit or credit to Retained Earnings for the error amount and a debit or credit to the asset or liability account that was misstated. The prior-period adjustment appears on the corporation's statement of retained earnings to indicate to readers the amount and the nature of the change in the Retained Earnings balance.

Assume that Paquette Corporation recorded income tax expense for 19X4 as $30,000. The correct amount was $40,000. This error resulted in understating 19X4 expenses by $10,000 and overstating net income by $10,000. A re-assessment from Revenue Canada in 19X5 for the additional $10,000 in taxes alerts the Paquette management to the mistake. The entry to record this prior-period adjustment in 19X5 is

19X5			
June 19	Retained Earnings..	10,000	
	Income Tax Payable		10,000
	Prior-period adjustment to correct error in recording income tax expense of 19X4.		

The debit to Retained Earnings excludes the error correction from the income statement of 19X5. Recall the matching principle. If Income Tax Expense is debited when the prior-period adjustment is recorded in 19X5, then this $10,000 in taxes would appear on the 19X5 income statement. This would not be proper since the expense arose from 19X4 operations.

This prior-period adjustment would appear on the statement of retained earnings, as follows:

Paquette Corporation
Statement of Retained Earnings
for the year ended December 31, 19X5

Retained earnings balance, December 31, 19X4, **as originally reported**	$390,000
Prior-period adjustment—debit to correct error **in recording income tax expense of 19X4**	(10,000)
Retained earnings balance, December 31, 19X4, **as adjusted**..	380,000
Net income for 19X5	114,000
	494,000
Dividends for 19X5..	(41,000)
Retained earnings balance, December 31, 19X5	$453,000

Our example shows a prior-period adjustment for additional expense. To make a prior-period adjustment for additional income, retained earnings is credited and the misstated asset or liability is debited.

Summary Problem for Your Review

The following information was taken from the ledger of Ansong Corporation:

Loss on sale of discontinued		Selling expenses.........................	$ 78,000
operations	$20,000	Common stock,	
Prior-period adjustment		40,000 shares issued	155,000
—credit to Retained		Sales revenue	620,000
Earnings	5,000	Interest expense	30,000
Gain on sale of capital assets.......	21,000	Extraordinary gain	26,000
Cost of goods sold	380,000	Operating income,	
Income tax expense (saving)		discontinued operations.....	30,000
Continuing operations	32,000	Loss due to lawsuit	11,000
Discontinued operations		General expenses......................	62,000
Operating income	12,000	Preferred stock, $8.00,	
Loss on sale..........................	(8,000)	500 shares issued	57,000
Extraordinary gain...................	10,000	Retained earnings,	
Dividends.....................................	16,000	beginning as originally	
		reported	103,000

Required

Prepare a single-step income statement and a statement of retained earnings for Ansong Corporation for the current year ended December 31. Include the earnings per share presentation and show computations. Assume no changes in the stock accounts during the year.

SOLUTION TO SUMMARY PROBLEM

Ansong Corporation
Income Statement
for the year ended December 31, 19XX

Revenue and gains			
Sales revenue..			$620,000
Gain on sale of capital assets.............................			21,000
Total revenues and gains.............................			641,000
Expenses and losses			
Cost of goods sold		$380,000	
Selling expenses...		78,000	
General expenses...		62,000	
Interest expense		30,000	
Loss due to lawsuit..		11,000	
Income tax expense		32,000	
Total expenses and losses			593,000
Income before discontinued operations and			
extraordinary items			48,000
Discontinued operations			
Operating income...	$30,000		
Less income tax...	12,000	18,000	
Loss on sale of discontinued operations	(20,000)		
Less income tax saving	8,000	(12,000)	6,000
Income before extraordinary items.....................			54,000
Extraordinary gain		26,000	
Less income tax		10,000	16,000
Net income			$ 70,000

Earnings per share
Income before discontinued operations and
extraordinary item [($48,000 – $4,000)/40,000 shares]........................ $1.10*
Income from discontinued operations ($6,000/40,000 shares) .... .15
Income before extraordinary items [($54,000 – $4,000)/40,000 shares]....... 1.25
Extraordinary gain ($16,000/40,000 shares) .... .40
Net income [($70,000 – $4,000)/40,000 shares].............................. $1.65*

Computations

$$EPS = \frac{Income - Preferred\ dividends}{Common\ shares\ outstanding}$$

Preferred dividends: 500 × $8.00 = $4,000

---

* These calculations are required; the other EPS calculations are included to make the statements more informative for users.

Ansong Corporation
Statement of Retained Earnings
for the year ended December 31, 19XX

Retained earnings balance, beginning, as originally reported	$103,000
Prior-period adjustment—credit...	5,000
Retained earnings balance, beginning, as adjusted................................	108,000
Net income for current year...	70,000
	178,000
Dividends for current year..	(16,000)
Retained earnings balance, ending	$162,000

Summary

1. **Account for stock dividends.** *Retained Earnings* carries the balance of the business's net income accumulated over its lifetime, less its declared dividends and any net losses. *Cash dividends* are distributions of corporate assets made possible by earnings. *Stock dividends* are distributions of the corporation's own stock to its shareholders.

2. **Distinguish stock splits from stock dividends.** Stock dividends shift amounts from retained earnings to capital stock. *Stock splits* do not change any account balance. Stock splits change the par value of the stock, whereas stock dividends do not. Both increase the number of shares outstanding and lower the market price per share of stock.

3. **Account for repurchased capital.** *Repurchased capital stock* is the corporation's own stock that has been issued and reacquired. The corporation may issue repurchased stock in the normal way but more often cancels the repurchased shares.

4. **Report restrictions on retained earnings.** Retained earnings may be *restricted* by law or contract or by the corporation itself. An *appropriation* is a restriction of retained earnings that is recorded by formal journal entries.

5. **Identify the elements of a corporation income statement.** The corporate *income statement* lists separately the various sources of income—*income before discontinued operations and extraordinary items*, which includes other gains and losses, *discontinued operations*, and *extraordinary gains and losses*. The bottom line of the income statement reports *net income* or *net loss* for the period. *Income tax expense* and *earnings-per-share* figures also appear on the income statement, likewise divided into different categories based on the nature of income. The *statement of retained earnings* reports the causes

for changes in the Retained Earnings account. This statement may be combined with the income statement.

6. Account for prior-period adjustments. The *statement of retained earnings* reports the causes for changes in the Retained Earnings account, including any prior-period adjustments. This statement may be combined with the income statement.

Self-Study Questions

Test your understanding of the chapter by marking the best answer for each of the following questions:

1. A corporation has total shareholders' equity of $100,000, including retained earnings of $19,000. The cash balance is $35,000. The maximum cash dividend the company can declare and pay is *(p. 717)*
   a. $19,000   c. $65,000
   b. $35,000   d. $100,000

2. A stock dividend *(pp. 717–719)*
   a. Decreases shareholders' equity
   b. Decreases assets
   c. Leaves total shareholders' equity unchanged
   d. None of the above

3. Meyer's Thrifty Acres Ltd. has 10,000 shares of common stock outstanding; the stock was issued at $20.00 per share. The stock's market value is $37 per share. Meyer's board of directors declares and distributes a common stock dividend of one share for every ten held. Which of the following entries shows the full effect of declaring and distributing the dividend? *(p. 718)*

   a. Retained Earnings... 37,000
         Common Stock Dividend Distributable   20,000
         Contributed Surplus—Common   17,000

   b. Retained Earnings... 20,000
         Common Stock   20,000

   c. Retained Earnings... 17,000
         Contributed Surplus—Common   17,000

   d. Retained Earnings... 37,000
         Common Stock   37,000

4. Lang Real Estate Investment Corporation declared and distributed a 50 percent stock dividend. Which of the following stock splits would have the same effect on the number of Lang shares outstanding? *(pp. 719–720)*
   a. 2 for 1   c. 4 for 3
   b. 3 for 2   d. 5 for 4

5. A company purchased 10,000 shares of its common stock that had been issued at $1.50 a share paying $6 per share. This transaction *(pp. 721–722)*
   a. Has no effect on company assets
   b. Has no effect on owners' equity
   c. Decreases owners' equity by $15,000
   d. Decreases owners' equity by $60,000

6. A restriction of retained earnings *(p. 725–726)*
   a. Has no effect on total retained earnings
   b. Reduces retained earnings available for the declaration of dividends
   c. Is usually reported by a note
   d. All of the above

7. Which of the following items is not reported on the income statement? *(p. 729)*
   a. Issue price of stock   c. Income tax expense
   b. Extraordinary gains and losses   d. Earnings per share

8. The income statement item that is likely to be most useful for predicting income from year to year is *(pp. 727–730)*
   a. Extraordinary items
   b. Discontinued operations
   c. Income from continuing operations
   d. Net income

9. In computing earnings per share (EPS), dividends on preferred stock are *(p. 732)*
   a. Added because they represent earnings to the preferred shareholders
   b. Subtracted because they represent earnings to the preferred shareholders
   c. Ignored because they do not pertain to the common stock
   d. Reported separately on the income statement

10. A corporation accidentally overlooked an accrual of property tax expense at December 31, 19X4. Accountants for the company detect the error early in 19X5 before the expense is paid. The entry to record this prior-period adjustment is *(pp. 732–733)*

    a. Retained Earnings ...   XXX
          Property tax
              expense   XXX

    b. Property tax
          expense   XXX
       Property tax
          payable..............   XXX

    c. Retained Earnings..   XXX
          Property tax
              payable   XXX

    d. Property tax
          payable   XXX
       Property tax
          expense   XXX

Answers to the Self-Study Questions follow the accounting vocabulary.

Accounting Vocabulary

Appropriation of retained earnings *(p. 726)*
Earnings per share (EPS) *(p. 731)*
Extraordinary item *(p. 730)*
Prior-period adjustment *(p. 734)*
Repurchase of own stock *(p. 721)*
Segment of a business *(p. 728)*
Stock dividend *(p. 717)*
Stock split *(p. 719)*

Answers to Self-Study Questions

1. a
2. c
3. d
4. b
5. d

6. d
7. a
8. c
9. b
10. c

ASSIGNMENT MATERIAL _____

Questions

1. Identify the two main parts of shareholders' equity.

2. Identify the account debited and the account credited from the last closing entry a corporation makes each year. What is the purpose of this entry?

3. Ametek, Inc., reported a cash balance of $73 million and a retained earnings balance of $162.5 million. Explain how Ametek can have so much more retained earnings than cash. In your answer, identify the nature of retained earnings and state how it ties to cash.

4. A friend of yours receives a stock dividend on an investment. He believes stock dividends are the same as cash dividends. Explain why the two are not the same.

5. Give two reasons for a corporation to distribute a stock dividend.

6. A corporation declares a stock dividend on December 21 and reports Stock Dividend Payable as a liability on the December 31 balance sheet. Is this correct? Give your reason.

7. What value is normally assigned to shares issued as a stock dividend?

8. To an investor, a stock split and a stock dividend have essentially the same effect. Explain the similarity and difference to the corporation between a 100 percent stock dividend and a 2-for-1 stock split.

9. Give three reasons why a corporation may repurchase its own shares.

10. What effect does the repurchase of capital stock have on the (a) assets, and (b) issued and outstanding stock of the corporation?

11. What effect does the repurchase and cancellation of common stock have on the (a) assets, (b) authorized stock, and (c) issued and outstanding stock of the corporation?

12. What does the *Canada Business Corporations Act* (CBCA) require a company to do when it repurchases its own stock?

13. Are there any exceptions to the requirement of the CBCA mentioned in question 12? If so, what are they?

14. Incorporating legislation frequently has a prohibition on a corporation purchasing its own stock in certain circumstances. What are those circumstances? Why does the prohibition exist?

15. Why do creditors wish to restrict a corporation's payment of cash dividends and repurchases of the corporation's stock?

16. What are two ways to report a retained earnings restriction? Which way is more common?

17. Identify three items on the income statement that generate income tax expense. What is an income tax saving, and how does it arise?

18. Why is it important for a corporation to report income from continuing operations separately from discontinued operations and extraordinary items?

19. Give two examples of extraordinary gains and losses and four examples of gains and loses that are *not* extraordinary.

20. What is the most widely used of all accounting statistics? What is the price-earnings ratio? Compute the price-earnings ratio for a company with EPS of $2 and a market price of $12 per share of common stock.

21. What is the earnings per share of a company with net income of $5,500 and issued common stock of 12,000 shares?

22. What account do all prior-period adjustments affect? On what financial statement are prior-period adjustments reported?

Exercises

Exercise 15-1   *Journalizing dividends and reporting shareholders' equity*   **(Obj. 1)**

Barr-Knight Systems, Inc., is authorized to issue 100,000 shares of common stock. The company issued 50,000 shares at $4 per share, and all 50,000 shares are outstanding. When the retained earnings balance was $150,000, Barr-Knight declared and distributed a 50 percent stock dividend, using the market value of $1.00 per share. Later, Barr-Knight declared and paid a $.20 per share cash dividend.

Required

1. Journalize the declaration and distribution of the stock dividend.

2. Journalize the declaration and payment of the cash dividend.

3. Prepare the shareholders' equity section of the balance sheet after both dividends.

Exercise 15-2   *Journalizing a stock dividend and reporting shareholders' equity   (Obj. 1)*

The shareholders' equity for Hatashita Jewelry Ltd. on September 30, 19X4 (end of the company's fiscal year), follows:

Shareholders' Equity

Common stock, 100,000 shares authorized,	
50,000 shares issued....................................	$550,000
Retained earnings...	340,000
Total shareholders' equity	$890,000

On November 16, the market price of Hatashita's common stock was $14 per share and the company declared a 10 percent stock dividend. Hatashita issued the dividend shares on November 30.

Required

1. Journalize the declaration and distribution of the stock dividend.
2. Prepare the shareholders' equity section of the balance sheet after the stock dividend.

Exercise 15-3   *Reporting shareholders' equity after a stock split   (Obj. 2)*

Kernohan Distribution Ltd. had the following shareholders' equity at May 31:

Common stock, 200,000 shares authorized, 50,000 shares issued	$280,000
Retained earnings...	210,000
Total shareholders' equity...	$490,000

On June 7, Kernohan split its common stock 4 for 1. Make the memorandum entry to record the stock split, and prepare the shareholders' equity section of the balance sheet immediately after the split.

Exercise 15-4   *Effects of stock issuance, dividends, and stock repurchase transactions (Obj. 1, 2, 3)*

Identify the effects of these transactions on shareholders' equity. Each transaction is independent.

a. Purchase of 1,500 shares of common stock at $4.25 per share.
b. Fifty-percent stock dividend. Before the dividend, 1,000,000 shares of common stock were outstanding; market value was $13.75 at the time of the dividend.
c. Issuance of 50,000 shares of common at $16.50.
d. Ten-percent stock dividend. Before the dividend, 500,000 shares of common stock were outstanding; market value was $7.625 at the time of the dividend.
e. Sale of 600 shares of repurchased stock for $9.00 per share. Cost of the stock was $6.00 per share.
f. Three-for-one stock split. Prior to the split, 60,000 shares of common were outstanding.

Exercise 15-5   *Journalizing repurchase of stock transactions   (Obj. 3)*

Journalize the following transactions of Shoe Renewry, Inc., a national chain of shoe repair shops:

May 19   Issued 10,000 shares of common stock at $15 per share.

Aug. 22 Purchased 900 shares of stock at $14 per share.

Nov. 11 Sold 200 shares of repurchased stock at $16 per share.

Dec. 28 Sold 100 shares of repurchased stock at $13 per share.

Exercise 15-6 *Journalizing repurchase of company stock and reporting shareholders' equity* **(Obj. 3)**

College Book Sales Inc. had the following shareholders' equity on November 30:

Shareholders' Equity

Common stock, 500,000 shares authorized, 50,000 shares issued..	$400,000
Retained earnings..	220,000
Total shareholders' equity	$620,000

On December 19, the company repurchased and retired 2,000 shares of common stock at $7 per share. Journalize this transaction and prepare the shareholders' equity section of the balance sheet at December 31.

Exercise 15-7 *Reporting a retained earnings restriction* **(Obj. 4)**

The agreement under which Yung Corp. issued its long-term debt requires the restriction of $250,000 of the company's retained earnings balance. Total retained earnings is $470,000, and total capital stock is $820,000.

Required

Show how to report shareholders' equity (including retained earnings) on Yung Corp.'s balance sheet, assuming:

a. Yung discloses the restriction in a note. Write the note.

b. Yung appropriates retained earnings in the amount of the restriction and includes no note in its statements.

c. Yung Corp's cash balance is $85,000. What is the maximum amount of dividends Yung can declare?

Exercise 15-8 *Preparing a multiple-step income statement* **(Obj. 5)**

The ledger of Vienna Corporation contains the following information for 19X4 operations:

Cost of goods sold....................	$45,000	Income tax saving—loss on	
Loss on discontinued		discontinued operations...	$ 20,000
operations............................	50,000	Extraordinary gain.................	12,000
Income tax expense—		Sales revenue	130,000
extraordinary gain...............	4,800	Operating expenses	
		(including income tax)......	60,000

Required

Prepare a multiple-step income statement for 19X4. Omit earnings per share. Was 19X4 a good year or a bad year for Vienna Corporation? Explain your answer in terms of the outlook for 19X5.

Exercise 15-9 *Computing earnings per share* **(Obj. 5)**

Benavides Inc. earned net income of $64,000 for the second quarter of 19X6. The ledger reveals the following figures:

Preferred stock, $1.75 per year, 1,600 shares issued and outstanding.......	$ 70,000
Common stock, 42,000 shares issued	420,000

Required

Compute EPS for the quarter, assuming no changes in the stock accounts during the quarter.

Exercise 15-10   *Computing earnings per share*   *(Obj. 5)*

Greenlawn Supply Ltd. had 40,000 shares of common stock and 10,000 shares of $.50 preferred stock outstanding on December 31, 19X8. On April 30, 19X9, the company issued 9,000 additional common shares and ended 19X9 with 49,000 shares of common stock outstanding. Income from continuing operations of 19X9 was $137,200, and loss on discontinued operations (net of income tax) was $8,280. The company had an extraordinary gain (net of tax) of $55,200.

Required

Compute Greenlawn's EPS amounts for 19X9, starting with income before discontinued operations and extraordinary items.

Exercise 15-11   *Preparing a statement of retained earnings with a prior-period adjustment (Obj. 6)*

ReFresh Inc., a soft-drink company, reported a prior-period adjustment in 19X9. An accounting error caused net income of prior years to be overstated by $3.8 million. Retained earnings at January 1, 19X9, as previously reported, stood at $395.3 million. Net income for 19X9 was $92.1 million, and dividends were $39.8 million.

Required

Prepare the company's statement of retained earnings for the year ended December 31, 19X9.

Exercise 15-12   *Preparing a combined statement of income and retained earnings (Obj. 5, 6)*

Dutch Boy Ltd. had retained earnings of $812.6 million at the beginning of 19X7. The company showed these figures at December 31, 19X7:

	($ millions)
Increases in retained earnings	
Net income	$127.1
Decreases in retained earnings	
Cash dividends—preferred...	2.3
common...	85.2
Debit to retained earnings due to purchase of preferred stock	11.3

Required

Beginning with net income, prepare a combined statement of income and retained earnings for Dutch Boy for 19X7. What type of transaction caused the $11.3 million debit to retained earnings?

Challenge Exercise

Exercise 15-13   *Analyzing the effects of a stock dividend and a stock split*   *(Obj. 1, 2)*

Universal Syndicates, Inc., began 19X8 with 3 million shares of common stock issued and outstanding for $9.4 million. Beginning retained earnings was $9.7 million. In

March 19X8 Universal issued 50,000 shares of stock at $50 per share. 19X8 was an exceptional year for Universal. The company's stock price reached an all-time high of $95 late in October. Universal split the stock two for one. Then in December, when the stock's market price was $45 per share, the board of directors declared a 2-percent stock dividend, distributable in January 19X9.

Required

Without making journal entries, show the balance in each shareholders' equity account at December 31, 19X8.

Problems   (Group A)

Problem 15-1A   *Journalizing shareholders' equity transactions*   **(Obj. 1, 3)**

Kapur Corporation completed the following selected transactions during the current year:

Jan.	9	Discovered that income tax expense of the preceding year was overstated by $7,000. Recorded a prior-period adjustment to correct the error.
Feb.	10	Split the company's 100,000 shares of common stock 2 for 1; the old common shares were recalled and new shares were issued.
Mar.	18	Declared a cash dividend on the $5.00 preferred stock (1,000 shares outstanding). Declared at $.20 per share dividend on the common stock outstanding. The date of record was April 2, and the payment date was April 23.
Apr.	23	Paid the cash dividends.
July	30	Declared a 10 percent stock dividend on the common stock to holders of record August 21, with distribution set for September 11. The market value of the common stock was $15 per share.
Sept.	11	Issued the stock dividend shares.
	26	Repurchased 2,500 shares of the company's own common stock at $14 per share. The stock had an average cost of $6 per share.
Nov.	8	Sold 1,000 shares of common stock for $17 per share.
Dec.	13	Sold 500 shares of common stock for $13 per share.

Required

Record the transactions in the general journal.

Problem 15-2A   *Journalizing dividend and repurchase of stock transactions and reporting shareholders' equity*   **(Obj. 1, 2)**

The balance sheet of Souris Sales Ltd. at December 31, 19X5, reported 100,000 shares of common stock authorized, with 30,000 shares issued and a Common Stock balance of $180,000. Souris Sales also had 5,000 shares of $.60 preferred stock authorized and outstanding. The preferred stock was issued in 19X1 at $10.00 per share. Retained Earnings had a credit balance of $104,000. During the two-year period ended December 31, 19X7, the company completed the following selected transactions:

19X6		
Mar.	15	Repurchased 4,000 shares of the company's own common stock at $5 per share.
July	2	Declared the annual $.60 cash dividend on the preferred stock and a $.75-per-share cash dividend on the common stock. The date of record was July 16, and the payment date was July 31.
July	31	Paid the cash dividends.
Nov.	30	Declared a 20 percent stock dividend on the outstanding common stock to holders of record December 21, with distribution set for January 11, 19X7. The market value of Souris Sales common stock was $10 per share.

Dec. 31   Earned net income of $104,000 for the year.

19X7

Jan. 11   Issued the stock dividend shares.
June 30   Declared the annual $.60 cash dividend on the preferred stock. The date of record was July 14, and the payment date was July 29.
July 29   Paid the cash dividends.
Aug. 2   Purchased and retired all the preferred stock at $14 per share.
Oct. 8   Sold 800 shares of common stock for $12 per share.
Dec. 19   Split the common stock 2 for 1 by issuing two new shares for each old share previously issued. Prior to the split, the corporation had issued 32,000 shares.
        31   Earned net income of $117,000 during the year.

Required

1. Record the transactions in the general journal. Explanations are not required.
2. Prepare the shareholders' equity section of the balance sheet at two dates: December 31, 19X6, and December 31, 19X7.

Problem 15-3A   *Increasing dividends to fight off a takeover of the corporation   (Obj. 1)*

Blair Seagram Corporation is positioned ideally in the clothing business. Located in Toronto, Ontario, Seagram is the only company with a highly developed import, design, and distribution network. The company does a brisk business with high-fashion stores. Seagram's success has made the company a prime target for a takeover. Against the wishes of Seagram's board of directors, an investment group from Vancouver is attempting to buy 51 percent of Seagram's outstanding stock. Board members are convinced that the Vancouver investors would sell off the most desirable pieces of the business and leave little of value.

At the most recent board meeting, several suggestions were advanced to fight off the hostile takeover bid. One suggestion is to increase the stock outstanding by distributing a 100 percent stock dividend.

Required

As a significant shareholder of Blair Seagram Corporation, write a short memo to explain to the board whether distributing the stock dividend would make it more difficult for the investor group to take over Blair Seagram. Include in your memo a discussion of the effect that the stock dividend would have on assets, liabilities, and total shareholders' equity, that is, the dividend's effect on the size of the corporation.

Problem 15-4A   *Journalizing prior-period adjustments and dividend and repurchase of stock transactions; reporting retained earnings and shareholders' equity* *(Obj. 1, 3, 6)*

The balance sheet of Prince Albert Development Corp. at December 31, 19X6, reported the following shareholders' equity:

Capital Stock	
Common stock, 100,000 shares authorized, 20,000 shares issued	$500,000
Total capital stock	500,000
Retained earnings	190,000
Total shareholders' equity	$690,000

During 19X7, Prince Albert completed the following selected transactions:

Jan. 11   Discovered that income tax expense of 19X1 was understated by $24,000. Recorded a prior-period adjustment to correct the error.

Apr. 30 Declared a 10 percent stock dividend on the common stock. The market value of Prince Albert Development common stock was $24 per share. The record date was May 21, with distribution set for June 5.

June 5 Issued the stock dividend shares.

July 29 Purchased 2,000 shares of the company's own common stock at $21 per share; average issue price is $25.00.

Nov. 13 Sold 400 shares of common stock for $22 per share.

Nov. 27 Declared a $.30 per share dividend on the common stock outstanding. The date of record was December 17, and the payment date was January 7, 19X8.

Dec. 31 Closed the $62,000 credit balance of Income Summary to Retained Earnings.

Required

1. Record the transactions in the general journal.
2. Prepare a retained earnings statement at December 31, 19X7.
3. Prepare the shareholders' equity section of the balance sheet at December 31, 19X7.

Problem 15-5A *Preparing a single-step income statement and a statement of retained earnings; reporting shareholders' equity on the balance sheet* **(Obj. 5, 6)**

The following information was taken from the ledger and other records of Northumberland Corp. at September 30, 19X6:

Cost of goods sold	$424,000	Preferred stock, $2, 10,000 shares authorized	
Loss on sale of capital assets	8,000	5,000 shares issued	$200,000
Sales returns	9,000	Retained earnings, beginning, as	
Income tax expense (saving):		originally reported	88,000
Continuing operations	72,000	Selling expenses	136,000
Discontinued segment:		Common stock,	
Operating loss	(6,000)	25,000 shares	
Gain on sale	8,000	authorized and issued	200,000
Extraordinary loss	(12,000)	Sales revenue	860,000
Gain on sale of discontinued segment	20,000	Dividends	35,000
Prior-period adjustment—		Interest revenue	4,000
debit to Retained Earnings	6,000	Extraordinary loss	30,000
Sales discounts	18,000	Operating loss,	
Interest expense	11,000	discontinued segment	15,000
General expenses	$113,000	Loss on insurance settlement	12,000

Required

1. Prepare a single-step income statement, including earnings per share, for Northumberland Corp., for the fiscal year ended September 30, 19X6. Evaluate income for the year ended September 30, 19X6, in terms of the outlook for 19X7. Assume 19X6 was a typical year and that Northumberland managers hoped to earn income from continuing operations equal to 10 percent of net sales.
2. Prepare the statement of retained earnings for the year ended September 30, 19X6.
3. Prepare the shareholders' equity section of the balance sheet at that date.
4. How will what you have learned in this problem help you evaluate an investment?

Problem 15-6A   *Preparing a corrected combined statement of income and
retained earnings   (Obj. 5, 6)*

Alexandra Nixon, accountant for Wordsworth Book Stores Ltd., was injured in a
skiing accident. Another employee prepared the accompanying income statement
for the fiscal year ended December 31, 19X3.

The individual amounts listed on the income statement are correct. However,
some accounts are reported incorrectly, and others do not belong on the income
statement at all. Also, income tax (40 percent) has not been applied to all appropriate figures. Wordsworth issued 52,000 shares of common stock in 19X1. The retained earnings balance, as originally reported at December 31, 19X2, was $111,000.

Required

Prepare a corrected combined statement of income and retained earnings for 19X3.
Prepare the income statement in single-step format.

Wordsworth Book Stores Ltd.
Income Statement
19X3

Revenue and gains		
Sales		$362,000
Proceeds from sale of stock		80,000
Gain on retirement of preferred stock		
(issued for $81,000; purchased for $71,000)		10,000
Total revenues and gains		452,000
Expenses and losses		
Cost of goods sold	$105,000	
Selling expenses	56,000	
General expenses	61,000	
Sales returns	11,000	
Dividends	7,000	
Sales discounts	6,000	
Income tax expense	20,000	
Total expenses and losses		266,000
Income from operations		186,000
Other gains and losses		
Gain on sale of discontinued operations	10,000	
Extraordinary flood loss	(20,000)	
Operating loss on discontinued segment	(13,000)	
Prior-period adjustment—understated income		
tax for 19X2	(14,000)	
Total other losses		(37,000)
Net income		$149,000
Earnings per share		$ 2.98

Problem 15-7A   *Computing earnings per share and reporting a retained earnings
restriction   (Obj. 4, 5, 6)*

The capital structure of Vernon Home Builders Inc. at December 31, 19X6, included
20,000 shares of $1.25 preferred stock and 44,000 shares of common stock. The 20,000
preferred shares were issued in 19X3. Common shares outstanding during 19X7
were 44,000 January through May; 50,000 June through August; and 60,500 September
through December. Income from continuing operations during 19X7 was $81,100. The
company discontinued a segment of the business at a gain (net of tax) of $6,630,
and an extraordinary item generated a loss (net of tax) of $33,660. Vernon Home
Builders board of directors restricts $80,000 of retained earnings for contingencies.

Required

1. Compute Vernon Home Builders earnings per share. Start with income from continuing operations. Income of $81,100 is net of income tax.

2. Show two ways of reporting Vernon Home Builders' retained earnings restriction. Retained earnings at December 31, 19X6, was $107,000, and total capital stock at December 31, 19X7, is $314,000. Vernon Home Builders declared no dividends in 19X7.

Problem 15-8A   *Accounting for stock dividends; stock splits; the repurchase of capital stock, and re-issuance of capital stock; calculating earnings per share* **(Obj. 1, 2, 3)**

Tall Trees Company operates a tree-planting service and had the following shareholders' equity on January 1, 19X2.

Shareholders' Equity

Preferred Stock, $1, cumulative (1 year in arrears), redemption price of $12, 40,000 shares authorized, 20,000 shares issued..	$200,000
Common stock, unlimited number of shares authorized, 40,000 shares issued	200,000
Total capital stock	400,000
Retained earnings	360,000
Total shareholders' equity	$760,000

The following transactions took place during 19X2:

Jan.   15   Declared a $90,000 cash dividend, payable on March 1st to the shareholders of record on February 1st. Indicate the amount payable to each class of shareholder.

Feb.   28   Issued 10,000 shares of common stock for $4 per share.

Mar.   1   Paid the cash dividend declared on January 15th.

Apr.   3   Declared a 20 percent stock dividend on the common stock, distributable on May 1st to the shareholders of record on April 15th. The market value of the stock was $4.50 per share.

May   1   Distributed the stock dividend declared on April 3rd.

July   1   Purchased 5,000 shares of the company's own common stock at $3.50 per share.

Sept.   3   Issued 4,000 shares of common stock for $4.80 per share.

Nov.   2   Split the common stock 2 for 1.

Dec.   31   Reported net income of $140,000. Closed the income summary account.

Required

1. Journalize the above transactions.

2. Prepare the shareholders' equity section of the balance sheet as of December 31st.

Problem 15-9A   *Accounting for stock dividends, stock splits, and prior-period adjustments; preparing a combined statement of income and retained earnings; calculating earnings per share*   **(Obj. 1, 2, 5, 6)**

C Growth Company operates a fish farm and had the following shareholders' equity on January 1.

Shareholders' Equity

Preferred Stock, $1, convertible to common on a 2 for 1 basis, 80,000 shares authorized, 40,000 shares issued..	$240,000

Common stock, unlimited number of shares	
authorized, 80,000 shares issued	240,000
Total contributed capital...	480,000
Retained earnings	220,000
Total shareholders' equity	$700,000

The following information is available for the year ending December 31, 19X3:

Feb.   1   Declared a cash dividend of $80,000, payable on March 1st to the share-
holders of record on February 15th. Indicate the amount payable to each
class of shareholder.

Mar.   1   Paid the cash dividend declared on February 1st.

May   2   Declared a 10 percent stock dividend on the common stock, distributable
on July 1st to the shareholders of record on June 15th. The market value of
the stock was $3.50 per share.

July   1   Distributed the common stock dividend declared on May 2nd.

Aug.   8   Received notification from Revenue Canada that C Growth Company had
made a mistake in their filing for 19X1's taxes. The reassessment showed
that they had reported and overpaid $20,000 in taxes. Revenue Canada
has applied the overpayment to taxes presently owing.

Dec.   31   C Growth's records show the following:

Sales for the year	$ 340,000
Cost of goods sold...	160,000
Operating costs...	90,000
Income from discontinued operations...................	10,000
Loss on sale of discontinued operations...............	6,000
Extraordinary loss...	8,000

Close the income summary account assuming the income taxes on discontinued
operations and extraordinary items is 20 percent.

Required

1. Journalize the above transactions.
2. Prepare a combined statement of income and retained earnings for the year
ended December 31, 19X3.

(Group B)

Problem 15-1B   *Journalizing shareholders' equity transactions*   **(Obj. 1, 3)**

Cabot Corporation completed the following selected transactions during 19X6:

Jan.   13   Discovered that income tax expense of 19X5 was understated by $6,000.
Record a prior-period adjustment to correct the error.

      21   Split common stock 3 for 1 by calling in the 10,000 shares of old common
and issuing 30,000 shares of new common.

Feb.   6   Declared a cash dividend on the 10,000 shares of $2.25 preferred stock.
Declared a $.20 per share dividend on the common stock outstanding. The
date of record was February 27, and the payment date was March 20.

Mar.   20   Paid the cash dividends.

Apr.   18   Declared a 50 percent stock dividend on the common stock to holders of
record April 30, with distribution set for May 30. The market value of the
common stock was $15 per share.

May   30   Issued the stock dividend shares.

June   18   Purchased 2,400 shares of the company's own common stock at $12 per
share; average issue price was $8 per share.

Nov.   14   Issued 800 shares of common stock for $10 per share.

Dec.   22   Issued 700 shares of common stock for $16 per share.

Required

Record the transactions in the general journal.

Problem 15-2B *Journalizing dividend and repurchase of stock transactions and reporting shareholders' equity* **(Obj. 1, 2, 3)**

The balance sheet of Video Library Inc. at December 31, 19X7, reported 10,000 shares of $.50 cumulative preferred stock authorized and outstanding. The preferred was issued in 19X1 at $8 per share. Video Library also had 500,000 shares of common stock authorized with 100,000 shares issued at an average price of $4.00 each. Retained Earnings had a balance of $18,000, and the preferred dividend for 19X7 was in arrears. During the two-year period ended December 31, 19X9, the company completed the following selected transactions:

19X8

Feb.	15	Purchased 5,000 shares of the company's own common stock at $4 per share.
Apr.	2	Declared the cash dividend on the preferred stock in arrears for 19X7 and the current cash dividend on preferred. The date of record was April 16, and the payment date was May 1.
May	1	Paid the cash dividends.
	2	Purchased and retired all the preferred stock at $7.50 per share.
Dec.	31	Earned net income of $61,000 for the year.

19X9

Mar.	8	Issued 2,000 shares of common stock for $7 per share.
Sept.	28	Declared a 10 percent stock dividend on the outstanding common stock to holders of record October 15, with distribution set for October 31. The market value of Video Library common stock was $5 per share.
Oct.	31	Issued the stock dividend shares.
Nov.	5	Split the common stock 2 for 1; the old common shares were recalled and new shares were issued.
Dec.	31	Earned net income of $73,000 during the year.

Required

1. Record the transactions in the general journal. Explanations are not required.
2. Prepare the shareholders' equity section of the balance sheet at two dates: December 31, 19X8, and December 31, 19X9.

Problem 15-3B *Repurchasing stock to fight off a takeover of the corporation* **(Obj. 3)**

Inuik Corporation is positioned ideally in its industry. Located in the Northwest Territories, Inuik is the only company with reliable sources for its imported gifts. The company does a brisk business with specialty stores. Inuik's recent success has made the company a prime target for a takeover. An investment group from the Yukon is attempting to buy 51 percent of Inuik's outstanding stock against the wishes of Inuik's board of directors. Board members are convinced that the Yukon investors would sell off the most desirable pieces of the business and leave little of value.

At the most recent board meeting, several suggestions were advanced to fight off the hostile takeover bid. The suggestion with the most promise is to purchase and retire a huge quantity of stock. Inuik has the cash to carry out this plan.

Required

1. As a significant shareholder of Inuik, write a memorandum to explain for the board how the repurchase and retirement of stock would make it more difficult

for the Yukon group to take over Inuik. Include in your memo a discussion of the effect that repurchasing stock would have on stock outstanding and on the size of the corporation.

2. Suppose Inuik management is successful in fighting off the takeover bid and later issues shares at prices greater than the purchase price. Explain what effect these sales will have on assets, shareholders' equity, and net income.

Problem 15-4B   *Journalizing prior-period adjustments and dividend and repurchase of stock transactions; reporting retained earnings and shareholders' equity   (Obj. 1, 3, 6)*

The balance sheet of Belle River Ltd. at December 31, 19X3, presented the following shareholders' equity:

Capital stock

Common stock, 250,000 shares authorized, 50,000 shares issued........	$400,000
Total capital stock...	400,000
Retained earnings...	110,000
Total shareholders' equity...	$510,000

During 19X4, Belle River completed the following selected transactions:

Jan.   7   Discovered that income tax expense of 19X3 was overstated by $12,000. Recorded a prior-period adjustment to correct the error.

Mar. 29   Declared a 50 percent stock dividend on the common stock. The market value of Belle River common stock was $5 per share. The record date was April 19, with distribution set for May 19.

May 19   Issued the stock dividend shares.

July 13   Purchased 2,000 shares of the company's own common stock at $6 per share.

Oct.   4   Sold 1,600 shares of common stock for $8 per share.

Dec. 27   Declared a $.20 per share dividend on the common stock outstanding. The date of record was January 17, 19X5, and the payment date was January 31.

31   Closed the $17,000 credit balance of Income Summary to Retained Earnings.

Required

1. Record the transactions in the general journal.

2. Prepare the retained earnings statement at December 31, 19X4.

3. Prepare the shareholders' equity section of the balance sheet at December 31, 19X4.

Problem 15-5B   *Preparing a single-step income statement and a statement of retained earnings and reporting shareholders' equity on the balance sheet (Obj. 5, 6)*

The following information was taken from the ledger and other records of Banh Sales Corporation at June 30, 19X5:

General expenses	$ 71,000	Sales discounts........................	$ 7,000
Loss on sale of		Extraordinary gain................	27,000
discontinued segment.......	8,000	Operating gain, discontinued	
Prior-period		segment.............................	9,000
adjustment—debit to		Loss on sale of capital	
Retained Earnings	4,000	assets	10,000
Cost of goods sold	319,000	Dividends on preferred	
Income tax expense (saving):		stock	?
Continuing operations......	28,000	Preferred stock, $1.50,	
Discontinued segment:		20,000 shares authorized,	
Operating income	3,600	4,000 shares issued...........	100,000

Loss on sale	$ (3,200)	Dividends on common	
Extraordinary gain	13,800	stock	$ 12,000
Interest expense	23,000	Sales revenue	589,000
Gain on settlement of		Retained earnings	
lawsuit	8,000	beginning, as	
Sales returns	15,000	originally reported	63,000
Contributed surplus from		Selling expenses	87,000
retirement of preferred		Common stock,	
stock	16,000	20,000 shares authorized	
Interest revenue	11,000	and issued	378,000

Required

1. Prepare a single-step income statement, including earnings per share, for Banh Sales Corporation for the fiscal year ended June 30, 19X5. Evaluate income for the year ended June 30, 19X5, in terms of the outlook for 19X6. Assume 19X5 was a typical year and that Banh Sales managers hoped to earn income from continuing operations equal to 8 percent of net sales.

2. Prepare the statement of retained earnings for the year ended June 30, 19X5.

3. Prepare the shareholders' equity section of the balance sheet at that date.

4. How will what you have learned in this problem help you evalute an investment?

Problem 15-6B *Preparing a corrected combined statement of income and retained earnings* **(Obj. 5, 6)**

Roberta Finnie, accountant for The Software Connection Ltd., was injured in a sailing accident. Another employee prepared the following income statement for the fiscal year ended June 30, 19X4:

The Software Connection Ltd. Income Statement June 30, 19X4		
Revenues and gains		
Sales		$833,000
Gain on retirement of preferred stock		
(issued for $70,000; purchased for $59,000)		11,000
Total revenues and gains		844,000
Expenses and losses		
Cost of goods sold	$383,000	
Selling expenses	103,000	
General expenses	74,000	
Sales returns	22,000	
Prior-period adjustment—understated income		
tax for 19X3	4,000	
Dividends	15,000	
Sales discounts	10,000	
Income tax expense	32,000	
Total expenses and losses		643,000
Income from operations		201,000
Other gains and losses		
Extraordinary gain	30,000	
Operating income on discontinued segment	25,000	
Loss on sale of discontinued operations	(40,000)	
Total other gains		15,000
Net income		$216,000
Earnings per share		$ 10.80

The individual amounts listed on the income statement are correct. However, some accounts are reported incorrectly, and others do not belong on the income statement at all. Also, income tax (40 percent) has not been applied to all appropriate figures. The Software Connection issued 24,000 shares of common stock in 19X1. The retained earnings balance, as originally reported at June 30, 19X3, was $209,000.

Required

Prepare a corrected combined statement of income and retained earnings for fiscal year 19X4. Prepare the income statement in single-step format.

Problem 15-7B   *Computing earnings per share and reporting a retained earnings restriction   (Obj. 4, 5, 6)*

Executive Travel Ltd.'s capital structure at December 31, 19X2, included 5,000 shares of $2.50 preferred stock and 130,000 shares of common stock. Common shares outstanding during 19X3 were 130,000 January through February; 119,000 during March; 121,000 April through October; and 128,000 during November and December. Income from continuing operations during 19X3 was $371,885. The company discontinued a segment of the business at a gain of $69,160, and an extraordinary item generated a loss of $49,510. The board of directors of Executive Travel has restricted $280,000 of retained earnings for expansion of the company's office facilities.

Required

1. Compute Executive Travel's earnings per share. Start with income from continuing operations. Income and loss amounts are net of income tax.
2. Show two ways of reporting Executive Travel's retained earnings restriction. Retained earnings at December 31, 19X2 was $127,800, and total capital stock at December 31, 19X3, is $524,610. Executive Travel declared no dividends during 19X3.

Problem 15-8B   *Accounting for stock dividends, stock splits, the repurchase of capital stock, and re-issuance of capital stock; calculating earnings per share (Obj. 1, 2, 3)*

TREESRUS Company operates a tree-planting service and had the following shareholders' equity on January 1.

Shareholders' Equity		
Preferred stock, $1, cumulative (1 year in arrears), redemption price of $24, 40,000 shares authorized, 10,000 shares issued..	$220,000	
Common stock, unlimited number of shares authorized, 30,000 shares issued	150,000	
Total contributed capital...	370,000	
Retained earnings	280,000	
Total shareholders' equity		$650,000

The following transactions took place during 19X1:

Jan.   15   Declared a $60,000 cash dividend, payable on March 1st to the shareholders of record on February 1st. Indicated the amount payable to each class of shareholder.

Feb.   28   Issued 20,000 shares of common stock for $4 per share.

Mar.   1   Paid the cash dividend declared on January 15th.

Apr.   3   Declared a 20 percent stock dividend on the common stock, distributable on May 1st to the shareholders of record on April 15th. The market value of the stock was $5.50 per share.

May	1	Distributed the stock dividend declared on April 3rd.
July	1	Purchased 4,000 shares of the company's own common stock at $4.50 per share.
Sept.	3	Issued 3,000 shares of common stock for $4.80 per share.
Nov.	2	Split the common stock 3 for 1.
Dec.	31	Reported net income of $90,000. Closed the income summary account.

Required

1. Journalize the above transactions.
2. Prepare the shareholders' equity section of the balance sheet as of December 31st.

Problem 15-9B   *Accounting for stock dividends, stock splits, and prior-period adjustments; preparing a combined statement of income and retained earnings; calculating earnings per share   (Obj. 1, 2, 5, 6)*

Fine Fish Company operates a fish farm and had the following shareholders' equity on January 1.

Shareholders' Equity

Preferred stock, $1, convertible to common on a 2 for 1 basis, 60,000 shares authorized, 30,000 shares issued...	$180,000
Common stock, unlimited number of shares authorized, 60,000 shares issued	180,000
Total contributed capital	360,000
Retained earnings	190,000
Total shareholders' equity	$550,000

The following information is available for the year ending December 31, 19X3:

Feb.	1	Declared a cash dividend of $70,000, payable on March 1st to the shareholders of record on February 15th. Indicate the amount payable to each class of shareholder.
Mar.	1	Paid the cash dividend declared on February 1st.
May	2	Declared a 20 percent stock dividend on the common stock, distributable on July 1st to the shareholders of record on June 15th. The market value of the stock was $3.40 per share.
July	1	Distributed the common stock dividend declared on May 2nd.
Aug.	8	Received notification from Revenue Canada that Fine Fish Company had made a mistake in their filing for 19X1's taxes. The reassessment showed that they had reported and overpaid $15,000 in taxes. Revenue Canada has applied the overpayment to taxes presently owing.
Dec.	31	Fine Fish's records show the following:

Sales for the year	$ 430,000
Cost of goods sold..	190,000
Operating costs...	110,000
Income from discontinued operations....................	15,000
Loss on sale of discontinued operations................	8,000
Extraordinary loss..	10,000

Close the income summary account assuming the income taxes on discontinued operations and extraordinary items is 20 percent.

Required

1. Journalize the above transactions.
2. Prepare a combined statement of income and retained earnings for the year ended December 31, 19X3.

Challenge Problems

Problem 15-1C   *Explaining the effects of a stock repurchase*   **(Obj. 3)**

Ritz Corp., a public company listed on the Albert Stock Exchange, had issued 10,000 shares of common stock at incorporation at a price of $8.00. The book value per share was $15.00 at the most recent year end. The company has been paying an annual dividend of $.64 per share.

Recently, when the market price of the stock was $10.00, the company decided to repurchase 1,000 shares at that price.

You and a friend bought 100 shares each when the stock was issued. Your friend wonders whether he should sell his shares back to Ritz since they were offering 25 percent more than he had paid.

Required

Analyze the information provided in order to assist your friend in deciding as to whether or not he should sell his shares back to the company.

Problem 15-2C   *Income from continuing operations, discontinued operations, and extraordinary items*   **(Obj. 5)**

In the late 1980s, the CICA's Accounting Standards Board set out fairly restrictive rules for disclosure of discontinued operations and extraordinary items. The rules limited management's ability to classify a transaction as relating to discontinued operations or as being an extraordinary item.

Required

Explain why management, in the absence of the rules in the *CICA Handbook* described above, might classify a financial event or transaction as extraordinary versus classifying it as part of continuing operations.

Extending Your Knowledge

Decision Problems

1. *Analyzing cash dividends and stock dividends*   (Obj. 1)

Mathieu Fabrics Inc. had the following shareholders' equity on June 30 of the current year, 19X4:

Common stock, 100,000 shares issued	$ 750,000
Retained earnings	830,000
Total shareholders' equity	$1,580,000

In the past, Mathieu has paid an annual cash dividend of $1.50 per share. Despite the large retained earnings balance, the board of directors wished to conserve cash for expansion. In 19X3, the board delayed the payment of cash dividends by one month and in the meantime distributed a 10 percent stock dividend. During the following year, 19X4, the company's cash position improved. The board declared and paid a cash dividend of $1.25 per share.

Suppose you own 4,000 shares of Mathieu Fabrics common stock, acquired three years ago. The market price of the stock was $30 per share before any of the above dividends.

Required

1. How did the stock dividend affect your proportionate ownership in the company? Explain.

2. What amount of cash dividends did you receive in 19X2? What amount of cash dividends will you receive after the above dividend action?

3. Immediately after the stock dividend was distributed, the market value of Mathieu Fabrics stock decreased from $30 per share to $27.27 per share. Does this represent a loss to you? Explain.

4. Suppose Mathieu announces at the time of the stock dividend that the company will continue to pay the annual $1.50 cash dividend per share, even after the stock dividend. Would you expect the market price of the stock to decrease to $27.27 per share as in requirement 3 above? Explain.

2. Earnings and dividends   (Obj. 1, 3, 5)

Answer the following independent questions.

a. An investor noted that the market price of stocks seemed to decline after the date of record. Why do you think that would be the case?

b. The treasurer of Miske Brewing Corp. wanted to disclose a large inventory loss as an extraordinary item because Miske produced too much product just prior to a very cool summer. Why do you think the treasurer wanted to use that particular disclosure? Would such disclosure be acceptable?

c. Corporations sometimes purchase their own stock. When asked why they do so, management often respond that they feel the stock is undervalued. What advantage would the company gain by buying and selling its own stock under these circumstances?

d. Carter Inc. earned a significant profit in the year ended November 30, 19X2, because land it held was expropriated for a new highway. The company proposes to treat the sale of land to the government as other revenue. Why do you think Carter is proposing such treatment? Is this disclosure appropriate?

Ethical Issue

AltaOil Corporation is an independent oil producer in Alberta. In February, company geologists discovered a pool of oil that tripled the company's proven reserves. Prior to disclosing the new oil to the public, top managers of the company quietly bought most of AltaOil stock for themselves personally. After the discovery announcement, AltaOil stock price increased from $13 to $40.

Required

1. Did AltaOil managers behave ethically? Explain your answer.

2. Identify the accounting principle relevant to this situation.

3. Who was helped and who was harmed by management's action?

Financial Statement Problems

1. Retained earnings and earnings per share   (Obj. 3, 5)

Use the Mark's Work Wearhouse Ltd. financial statements in Appendix A to answer the following questions.

1. Mark's Work Wearhouse reports capital stock on the balance sheet and gives details in the notes to the financial statements. At January 29, 1994, how many shares of common stock had Mark's issued during the year ended January 29, 1994? How many shares were outstanding at January 30, 1993?

2. Did the company issue or redeem any shares during 1994? What was the average price per share for stock issued?

3. Prepare a T-account for Retained Earnings to show the beginning and ending balances and all activity during the year ended January 29, 1994.

4. Show how to compute net income *per share* for the year ended January 29, 1994.

2.   *Common stock, retained earnings, and earnings per share (Obj. 3, 5, 6)*

Obtain the annual report of an actual company of your choosing. Answer these questions about the company. Concentrate on the current year in the annual report you select.

1. How many shares of common stock did the company have outstanding at the end of the current year? How many shares had the company issued at the date of the previous balance sheet?

2. Compute average cost per share of common stock.

3. Prepare a T-account for Retained Earnings to show the beginning and ending balances and all activity in the account during the current year.

4. Did the company have any prior-period adjustments during any year reported in the annual report? How can you tell?

5. Show how to compute all earnings (losses) *per share* amounts for the current year.

CHAPTER 16
Long-Term Liabilities

How do investors assess the risk of a bond? Two main rating agencies, Dominion Bond Rating Service Limited and Standard & Poor's, evaluate the risk of—that is, they *rate*—corporate bonds. To make this very subjective judgment, these organizations study the company's management, operations, finances, and outlook for the future. They then assign the bond to a rating category that indicates its risk. The higher the risk, the higher the interest rate on the bond, and vice versa. A central truth of business is that return on investment depends on the risk of the investment. Stated differently, to earn a high rate of return, an investor must take a high degree of risk. An investor who is unwilling to take much risk cannot expect to earn a high rate of return on the investment.

This is equally true whether the investment is a bond, a stock, real estate, a start-up business, an established organization, or any other venture.

The risk-return relationship applies to government bonds as well as corporate bonds. For example, *The Financial Post* reported on April 13, 1995, that Canada's domestic currency debt was downgraded from Aaa to Aa1 by Moody's, a U.S. rating agency. *The Financial Post* reported on April 15 that the interest cost of Canada's debt had gone up slightly in response to the downgrade.

The Economist, on June 3, 1995, reported that credit agencies, such as Standard & Poor's, had given Abbey National, Britain's fourth-largest bank, an AA rating that allowed the bank to borrow at a lower rate. Chrysler's debt was downgraded in 1991 because it was having financial difficulties and its cost of borrowing went up. When Chrysler's financial position improved subsequently as a result of an increase in minivan sales and the introduction of the Neon, its debt was upgraded and its cost of borrowing went down.

LEARNING OBJECTIVES

After studying this chapter, you should be able to

1 Account for basic bonds payable transactions by the straight-line amortization method

2 Amortize bond discount and premium by the effective-interest method

3 Account for retirement of bonds payable

4 Account for conversion of bonds payable

5 Explain the advantages and disadvantages of borrowing

6 Account for lease transactions

A1 Compute the future value of an investment made in a single amount.

A2 Compute the future value of an annuity-type investment.

A3 Compute the present value of a single future amount.

A4 Compute the present value of an annuity.

A5 Determine the cost of an asset acquired through a capital lease.

Large companies such as Bombardier and Air Canada cannot borrow billions from a single lender because no lender will risk that much money on a single company. Banks and other lenders diversify their risk by loaning smaller amounts to numerous customers. That way if a borrower cannot repay, the lender is not devastated. How then do large corporations borrow a huge amount? They issue bonds to the public. **Bonds payable** are groups of notes payable issued to multiple lenders, called bondholders. The idea is that NOVA Corporation can borrow large amounts from thousands of individual investors, each buying a modest amount of NOVA bonds. NOVA receives the amount it needs, and each investor limits his or her risk by diversifying investments—not putting all the "eggs in one basket."

Chapters 14 and 15 covered two ways of financing operations: contributed capital (the stock accounts and additional paid-in capital) and profitable operations (retained earnings). This chapter discusses the third way to finance a company—long-term liabilities, including bonds payable (and notes payable), lease liabilities, and pension liabilities. We treat bonds payable and long-term notes payable together because their accounting is the same. The chapter appendix provides background on the valuation of long-term liabilities.

Key Point:
The following comparison will help you "jump" from equity to debt.

Stocks
1. Stocks represent ownership (equity) of corporation.
2. Shareholder is an owner.
3. Shareholder has the right to receive dividends, if declared.
4. Dividends are optional to corporation.
5. Dividends are not tax-deductible for corporation.
6. Common stock does not have a fixed cost (to corporation) or a fixed return (to shareholder).

(cont)

The Nature of Bonds

To gain access to large amounts of cash, a company may issue bonds. Each bond is, in effect, a long-term note payable that bears interest. Bonds are debts to the company for the amounts borrowed from the investors.

Purchasers of bonds receive a bond certificate, which carries the issuing company's name. The certificate also states the *principal*, which is the amount that the company has borrowed from the bondholder. This figure, typically stated in units of $1,000, is also called the bond's face value, maturity value, or par value. The bond obligates the issuing company to pay the holder the principal amount at a specific future date, called the maturity date, which also appears on the certificate.

Bondholders loan their money to companies for a price: interest on the principal. The bond certificate states the interest rate that the issuer will pay the holder and the

EXHIBIT 16-1   *Bond (Note) Certificate*

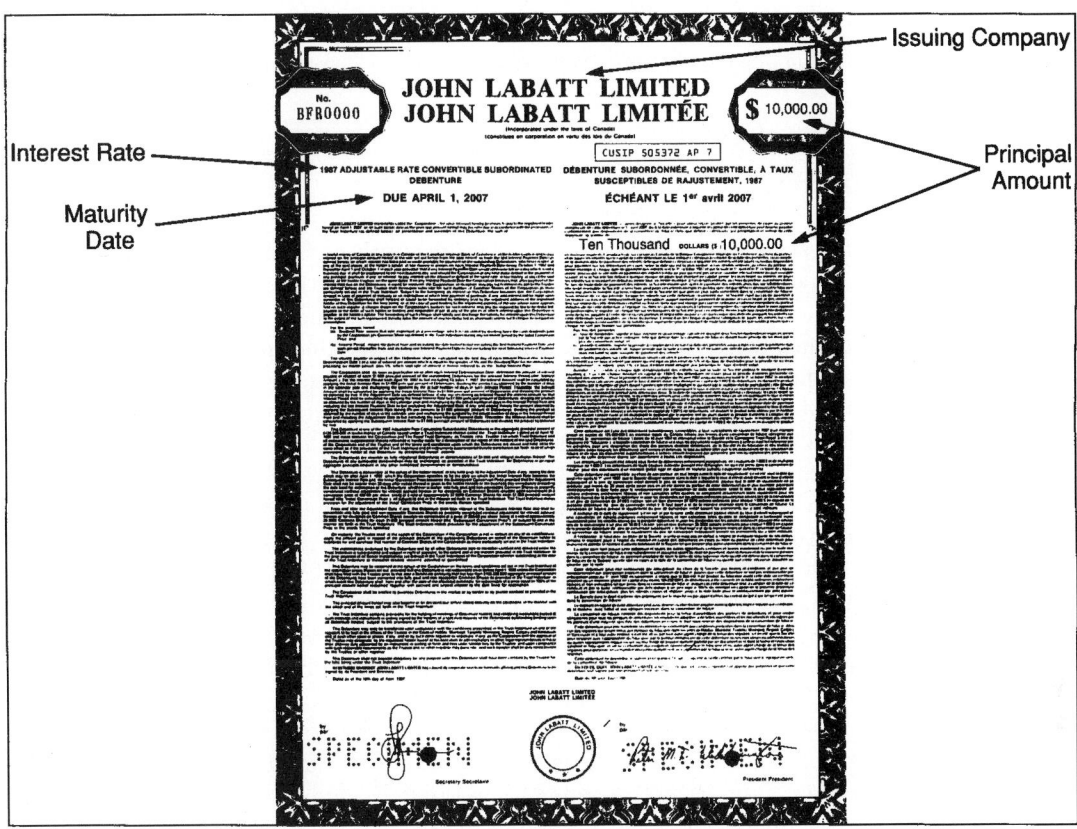

dates that the interest payments are due (generally twice a year). Some bond certificates name the bondholder (the investor). When the company pays back the principal, the holder returns the certificate, which the company retires (or cancels). Exhibit 16-1 shows an actual bond certificate.

The board of directors may authorize a bond issue. In some companies the shareholders—as owners—may also have to vote their approval.

Issuing bonds usually requires the services of a securities firm, like Richardson Greenshields, to act as the *underwriter* of the bond issue. The **underwriter** purchases the bonds from the issuing company and resells them to its clients, or it may sell the bonds for a commission from the issuer, agreeing to buy all unsold bonds.

Types of Bonds

All the bonds in a particular issue may mature at the same time (**term bonds**), or they may mature in installments over a period (**serial bonds**). By issuing serial bonds, the company spreads its principal payments over time and avoids paying the entire principal at one time. Serial bonds are like installment notes payable.

Secured or *mortgage* bonds give the bondholder the right to take specified assets of the issuer if the company *defaults*, that is, fails to pay interest or principal. *Unsecured bonds*, called **debentures**, are backed only by the good faith of the borrower.

7. Corporation is not obligated to repay amount invested by shareholders.

Bonds
1. Bonds represent a debt (liability).
2. Bondholder is a creditor.
3. Bondholder has the right to receive interest.
4. Interest is a contractual obligation of corporation.
5. Interest is a tax-deductible expense of corporation.
6. Bonds have a fixed cost (to corporation) and a fixed return (to bondholder).
7. Corporation must repay bond payable at maturity.

A secured bond is not necessarily more attractive to an investor than is a debenture. The primary motive of a person investing in bonds is to receive the interest amounts and the bonds' maturity value on time. Thus a debenture from a business with an excellent record in meeting obligations may be more attractive to an investor than is a secured bond from a business that has just been started or that has a bad credit record.

Bond Prices

Investors may transfer ownership through bond markets. The bond market in Canada is called the over the counter (OTC) market. It is a network of investment dealers who trade bonds issued by the Government of Canada and Crown corporations, the provinces, municipalities and regions, and corporations. Bond prices are quoted at a percentage of their maturity value using $100 as a base. For example, a $1,000 bond quoted at 100 is bought or sold for $1,000, which is 100 percent of its maturity value. The same bond quoted at 101½ has a market price of $1,015 (101½ percent of its maturity value, or $1,000 × 1.015).

Exhibit 16-2 contains actual price information for bonds of BC Telephone, taken from *The Financial Post*.

On April 13, 1995, BC Telephone's 9.65 percent $1,000 par value bonds, maturing April 18, 2022 (indicated by 22), had a bid price of $104.50, or $1,045.00 which provided a yield of 9.20 percent (the yield rate is based on the market rate and time to maturity). Two months later, *The Financial Post* showed a bid price for the same bonds of $108.50; the yield was 8.82 percent.

One factor that affects the market price of a bond is the length of time left until the bond matures. The earlier the maturity date, the closer the bond will be to its maturity value. Also, the bonds issued by a company with a proven ability to meet all payments commands a higher price than an issue from a company with a poor record. Bond price hinges, too, on the rates of other available investment plans. Is a 9 percent bond the best way to invest $1,000, or does another investment strategy pay a higher rate? Of course, the higher the percentage rate, the higher the market price will be. Buying a 10 percent bond will cost you more than buying an 8 percent bond, given that both issues have the same maturity date and have been issued by equally sound businesses.

A bond issued at a price above its maturity par value is said to be issued at a **premium**, and a bond issued at a price below maturity par value has a **discount**. As a bond nears maturity, its market price moves toward its maturity value. On the maturity date, the market value of a bond equals exactly its maturity value because the company that issued the bond pays that amount to retire the bond.

Present Value[1]

A dollar received today is worth more than a dollar received in the future. You may invest today's dollar and earn income from it. Likewise, deferring any payment gives your money a period to grow. Money earns income over time, a fact called the *time value of money*. Let us examine how the time value of money affects the pricing of bonds.

EXHIBIT 16-2   *Bond Price Information*

Bonds	Int. Rate %	Maturity Date	Bid $	Yield %
BC Telephone	9.65	April 8/22	104.50	9.20

[1] The chapter appendix covers present value in more detail.

Assume a bond with a face value of $1,000 reaches maturity three years from today and carries no interest. Would you pay $1,000 to purchase the bond? No, because the payment of $1,000 today to receive the same amount in the future provides you with no income on the investment. You would not be taking advantage of the time value of money. Just how much would you pay today in order to receive $1,000 at the end of three years? The answer is some amount less than $1,000. Let us suppose that you feel $750 is a good price. By investing $750 now to receive $1,000 later, you earn $250 interest revenue over the three years. The issuing company sees the transaction this way: It pays you $250 interest expense for the use of your $750 for three years.

The amount that a person would invest *at the present time* to receive a greater amount at a future date is called the **present value** of a future amount. In our example, $750 is the present value of the $1,000 amount to be received three years later.

Our $750 bond price is a reasonable estimate. The exact present value of any future amount depends on (1) the amount of the future payment (or receipt), (2) the length of time from the investment to the date when the future amount is to be received (or paid), and (3) the interest rate during the period. Present value is always less than the future amount. We discuss the method of computing present value in the appendix that follows this chapter. We need to be aware of the present-value concept, however, in the discussion of bond prices that follows. Therefore, please study the appendix now.

 Key Point:
Present value is always less than future value. You should be able to invest today's money (present value) so that it will increase (future value). The difference between present value and future value is interest.

Bond Interest Rates

Bonds are sold at market price, which is the amount that investors are willing to pay at any given time. Market price is the bond's present value, which equals the present value of the principal payment plus the present value of the cash interest payments (which are made quarterly, semiannually, or annually over the term of the bond).

Two interest rates work to set the price of a bond. The **contract interest rate**, or **stated interest rate**, is the interest rate that determines the amount of cash interest the borrower pays—and the investor receives—each year. For example, The Toronto-Dominion Bank's 8 percent bonds have a contract interest rate of 8 percent. Thus Toronto Dominion pays $8,000 of interest annually on each $100,000 bond. Each semiannual interest payment is $4,000 ($100,000 × .08 × ½).

The **market interest rate**, or **effective interest rate**, is the rate that investors demand for loaning their money. The market rate varies, sometimes daily. A company may issue bonds with a contract interest rate that differs from the prevailing market interest rate. The Toronto-Dominion Bank may issue its 8 percent bonds when the market rate has risen to 9 percent. Will the Toronto Dominion bonds attract investors in this market? No, because investors can earn 9 percent on other bonds. Therefore, investors will purchase Toronto Dominion bonds only at a price less than the face or maturity value. The difference between the lower price and face value is a *discount* (Exhibit 16-3). Conversely, if the market interest rate

 Key Point:
Because market interest rates fluctuate daily, the contract interest rate will seldom equal the market interest rate on the date the bonds are sold. Bonds sell at a premium if the market rate drops below the bonds' contract rate and at a discount if the market rate rises above the contract rate.

EXHIBIT 16-3 *Price of a Bond*

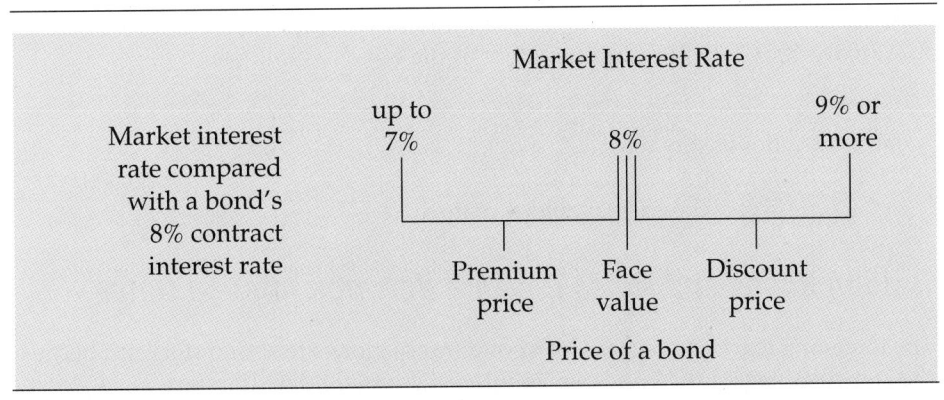

EXHIBIT 16-4   *Factors Affecting Bond Prices*

Factor	Effects on Bond Price
Risk of the issuing corporation	High-risk company ——————▶ Low price
	Low-risk company ——————▶ High price
Length of time to maturity	Long time to maturity ——————▶ Low price
	Short time to maturity ——————▶ High price
Contract interest rate paid by the bond	High contract interest rate ——▶ High price
	Low contract interest rate ——▶ Low price
Market interest rate when the bonds are issued	High market interest rate ——▶ Low price
	Low market interest rate ——▶ High price

is 7 percent, Toronto-Dominion's 8 percent bonds will be so attractive that investors will pay more than face value for them. The difference between the higher price and face value is a *premium*.

Exhibit 16-4 summarizes the effects of the various factors on bond prices.

Issuing Bonds Payable

Suppose the Canadian National Railway System (CN) has $50 million in 8 percent bonds that mature in 10 years. Assume that CN issues these bonds at par on January 1, 1995. The issuance entry is

1995
Jan.   1   Cash   50,000,000
                 Bonds Payable.................................   50,000,000
                 To issue 8%, 10-year bonds at par.

Short Exercise:

The following data will be used to illustrate various points covered in the next several Short Exercises: Assume that Quill Corp. issues, at par, $300,000 of 9%, 10-year bonds on May 31, 1996. The bonds pay interest each May 31 and November 30. What entries record issuance, first semiannual interest payment, and retirement at maturity?

A:

Issuance: 5/31/96
Cash 300,000
   Bonds Payable   300,000
First interest payment:
11/30/96
Interest Expense   13,500
   Cash   13,500
Maturity: 5/31/96
Bonds Payable   300,000
   Cash   300,000

The corporation that is borrowing money makes a one-time entry similar to this to record the receipt of cash and the issuance of bonds. Afterward, investors buy and sell the bonds through the bond markets. The buy-and-sell transactions between investors do not involve the corporation that issued the bonds. It keeps no records of these transactions, except for the names and addresses of the bondholders. This information is needed for mailing the interest and principal payments.

Interest payments for these bonds occur each January 1 and July 1. CN's entry to record the first semiannual interest payment is

1995
July   1   Interest Expense
                 ($50,000,000 × .08 × ½)   2,000,000
                 Cash...   2,000,000
                 To pay semiannual interest on bonds payable.

At maturity, CN will record payment of the bonds as follows:

2005
Jan.   1   Bonds Payable   50,000,000
                 Cash...   50,000,000
                 To pay bonds payable at maturity.

Issuing Bonds and Notes Payable Between Interest Dates

The foregoing entries to record CN's bond transactions are straightforward because the company issued the bonds on an interest payment date (January 1). However, corporations often issue bonds between interest dates.

Suppose Nova Scotia Power issues $75 million of 12 percent debentures due June 15, 2005. These bonds are dated June 15, 1995, and carry the price "100 plus accrued interest from date of original issue." An investor purchasing the bonds after the bond date must pay market value *plus accrued interest*. The issuing company will pay the full semiannual interest amount to the bondholder at the next interest payment date. Companies do not split semiannual interest payments among two or more investors who happen to hold the bonds during a six-month interest period.

Assume that Nova Scotia Power sells $100,000 of its bonds on July 15, 1995, one month after the date of original issue on June 15. Also assume that the market price of the bonds on July 15 is the face value. The company receives one month's accrued interest in addition to the bond's face value. Nova Scotia Power's entry to record issuance of the bonds payable is

1995			
July 15	Cash...	101,000	
	Bonds Payable		100,000
	Interest Payable ($100,000 × .12 × ½)...		1,000
	To issue 12%, 10-year bonds at par, one month after the original issue date.		

Nova Scotia Power's entry to record the first semiannual interest payment is

1995			
Dec. 15	Interest Expense ($100,000 × .12 × ⁵⁄₁₂)........	5,000	
	Interest Payable..	1,000	
	Cash ($100,000 × .12 × ⁶⁄₁₂)......................		6,000
	To pay semiannual interest on bonds payable.		

The debit to Interest Payable eliminates the credit balance in that account from July 15. Nova Scotia Power has now paid off that liability.

Note that Nova Scotia Power pays a full six months' interest on December 15. After subtracting the one month's accrued interest received at the time of issuing the bond, Nova Scotia Power has recorded interest expense for five months ($5,000). This interest expense is the correct amount for the five months that the bonds have been outstanding.

Short Exercise:

Assume that Quill Corp. issues its $300,000, 9%, 10-year bonds at par on September 30, 1996 (four months after the interest date, May 31). What are the entries for the original issuance and the first interest payment? **A:**

Issuance: 9/30/96

Cash................	309,000	
Bonds Payable		300,000
Interest Payable		9,000

($300,000 × 9% × ⁴⁄₁₂
= $9,000)

Interest payment: 11/30/96

Interest Expense	4,500	
Interest Payable	9,000	
Cash		13,500

Six months' interest has been paid in cash, but only two months of interest expense has been incurred by Quill. This is correct because the bonds have been outstanding only two months.

PUTTING SKILLS TO WORK

Sale of Bonds and Notes Between Interest Dates—"Plus Accrued Interest"

Selling bonds and notes between interest dates at market value plus accrued interest simplifies the borrower's accounting. Nova Scotia Power pays the same amount of interest on each note regardless of the length of time the investor has held the note. Nova Scotia Power need not compute each noteholder's interest payment on an individual basis.

When an investor sells bonds or notes to another investor, the price is always "plus accrued interest." Suppose you hold Nova Scotia Power notes as an investment for two months of a semiannual interest period and sell the notes to another investor before you receive your interest. The person who buys the notes will receive your two months of interest on the next specified interest date. Business practice dictates that you must collect your share of the interest from the buyer when you sell your investment. For this reason, all bond or note transactions are "plus accrued interest."

Issuing Bonds Payable at a Discount

Unlike stocks, bonds are often issued at a discount. We know that market conditions may force the issuing corporation to accept a discount price for its bonds. Suppose BCE

Short Exercise:

Assume that Quill Corp. issues its $300,000, 9% bonds on May 31, 1996, when the market rate of interest is just under 10%. The bonds are issued at $97.50. What entry records the issuance? **A:**

5/31/96
Cash 292,500
Discount on
  Bonds Payable   7,500
  Bonds Payable   300,000
($300,000 × 0.975
= $292,500)
The carrying amount on the balance sheet on 5/31/96 is:
Bonds payable $300,000
Less: Discount on
  bonds payable   7,500
Carrying amount $292,500

issues $100,000 of its 8 percent, 10-year bonds when the market interest rate is slightly above 8 percent. The market price of the bonds drops to $98.00, which means 98 percent of face or par value. BCE receives $98,000 ($100,000 × .98) at issuance. The entry is the following:

```
1996
Jan.  1   Cash ($100,000 × .98) ...................................   98,000
          Discount on Bonds Payable .......................    2,000
                Bonds Payable ..........................................           100,000
          To issue 8%, 10-year bonds at a discount.
```

After posting, the bond accounts have the following balances:

Bonds Payable	Discount on Bonds Payable
100,000	2,000

BCE's balance sheet immediately after issuance of the bonds reports:

Long-term liabilities
    Bonds payable, 8%, due 2006 .... $100,000
    Less: Discount on bonds payable 2,000 $98,000

Discount on Bonds Payable is a contra account to Bonds Payable. Subtracting its balance from Bonds Payable yields the book value, or carrying value, of the bonds. The relationship between Bonds Payable and the Discount account is similar to the relationships between Equipment and Accumulated Depreciation and between Accounts Receivable and Allowance for Uncollectible Accounts. Thus BCE's liability is $98,000, which is the amount the company borrowed. If BCE were to pay off the bonds immediately (an unlikely occurrence), BCE's required outlay would be $98,000 because the market price of the bonds is $98,000.

Interest Expense on Bonds Issued at a Discount   We earlier discussed the difference between the contract interest rate and the market interest rate. Suppose the market rate is 8¼ percent when BCE issues its 8 percent bonds. The ¼ percent interest rate difference creates the $2,000 discount on the bonds. BCE borrows $98,000 cash but must pay $100,000 cash when the bonds mature 10 years later. What happens to the $2,000 balance of the discount account over the life of the bond issue? The $2,000 is in reality an additional interest expense to the issuing company. That amount is a cost—beyond the stated interest rate—that the business pays for borrowing the investors' money. The discount has the effect of raising the interest expense on the bonds to the market interest rate of 8¼ percent.

The discount amount is an interest expense not paid until the bond matures. However, the borrower—the bond issuer—benefits from the use of the investors' money each accounting period over the full term of the bond issue. The matching principle directs the business to match expense against its revenues on a period-by-period basis. Each accounting period over the life of the bonds, the discount is allocated to interest expense through amortization.

Straight-line Amortization of Account   We may amortize bond discount by dividing it into equal amounts for each interest period. This method is called *straight-line amortization*. In our example, the beginning discount is $2,000, and there are 20 semiannual interest periods during the bonds' 10-year life. Therefore, ¹⁄₂₀ of the $2,000 ($100) of bond discount is amortized each interest period. BCE's semiannual interest entry on July 1, 1996, is

```
1996
July  1   Interest Expense............................................    4,100
              Cash ($100,000 × .08 × ½)........................            4,000
```

OBJECTIVE 1

Account for basic bonds payable transactions using the straight-line amortization method

Discount on Bonds Payable
($2,000/20)   100

To pay semiannual interest and amortize
discount on bonds payable.

Interest expense of $4,100 is the sum of the contract interest ($4,000, which is paid in cash) plus the amount of discount amortized ($100). Discount on Bonds Payable is credited to amortize (reduce) the account's debit balance. Because Discount on Bonds Payable is a contra account, each reduction in its balance increases the book value of Bonds Payable. Twenty amortization entries will decrease the discount balance to zero, which means that Bonds Payable will have increased by $2,000 up to its face value of $100,000. The entry to pay off the bonds at maturity is

2006
Jan.   1   Bonds Payable   100,000

           Cash...   100,000

           To pay bonds payable at maturity.

Issuing Bonds Payable at a Premium

Why are bonds issued at a premium less common than bonds issued at a discount? Because companies prefer to issue bonds that pay a lower cash interest rate. To illustrate issuing bonds at a premium, let us change the BCE Inc. example. Assume that the market interest rate is 7½ percent when the company issues its 8 percent, 10-year bonds. Because 8 percent bonds are attractive in this market, investors pay a premium price to acquire them. If the bonds are priced at $103.50 (103.5 percent of par value) BCE receives $103,500 cash upon issuance. The entry is

1996
Jan.   1   Cash ($100,000 × 1.035).............................   103,500

           Bonds Payable   100,000

           Premium on Bonds Payable   3,500

           To issue 8%, 10-year bonds at a premium.

After posting, the bond accounts have the following balances:

Bonds Payable	Premium on Bonds Payable
100,000	3,500

BCE's balance sheet immediately after issuance of the bonds reports:

Long-term liabilities
   Bonds payable, 8%, due 2006............................... $100,000
   Premium on bonds payable 3,500 $103,500

Premium on Bonds Payable is added to Bonds Payable to show the book value, or carrying value, of the bonds. BCE's liability is $103,500, which is the amount that the company borrowed. Immediate payment of the bonds would require an outlay of $103,500 because the market price of the bonds at issuance is $103,500. The investors would be unwilling to give up bonds for less than their market value.

Interest Expense on Bonds Issued at a Premium   The ½ percent difference between the 8 percent contract rate on the bonds and the 7½ percent market interest rate creates the $3,500 premium. BCE borrows $103,500 cash but must pay only $100,000 cash at maturity. We treat the premium as a savings of interest expense to BCE. The premium cuts BCE's cost of borrowing the money. We account for the premium much as we handled the discount. We amortize the bond premium as a decrease in interest expense over the life of the bonds.

Short Exercise:

For the $300,000 of 10-year bonds issued by Quill Corp. on May 31, 1996, at 97 ½, what entry on November 30, 1996, records the first semiannual interest payment and amortization of the discount? **A:**

11/30/96

Int. Expense	13,875	
Cash		13,500
Discount on Bonds		
Payable............		375

($300,000 × 0.09 × ⁶/₁₂ = $13,500 interest paid in cash, $7,500 ÷ 20 = $375 amortization)

Discount on Bonds Payable is reduced equally in each of the 20 periods until its balance reaches zero at maturity. The recording of discount amortization *increases* Interest Expense each period. That is, Interest Expense is greater than the cash paid for interest.

Short Exercise:

Assume that Quill Corp.'s $300,000 of 9%, 10-year bonds are issued on May 31, 1996, when the market rate of interest is just over 8%. The bonds are issued at $102.00. (1) What is the entry to record the issuance? (2) What is the entry on November 30, 1996, to record the first semiannual interest payment and amortize the premium? **A:**

(1) 5/31/96

Cash	306,000	
Bonds Payable		300,000
Premiums on		
Bonds Payable		6,000

($300,000 × 1.02 = $306,000)

The carrying amount on the balance sheet on 5/31/96 is

Bonds payable	$300,000
Plus: Premium on	
bonds payable	6,000
Carrying amount	$306,000

(cont.)

(2) 11/30/96

Int. Expense   13,200
Premium on
  Bonds Payable........ 300
    Cash...................... 13,500
($300,000 × 0.09 × ⁶/₁₂ =
$13,500 interest paid in
    cash;
$6,000 ÷ 20 = $300
  amortize.)

Premium on Bonds Payable is
reduced equally in each of the
20 periods until the balance is
fully amortized. The recording
of the premium amortization
decreases Interest Expense
each period. Interest Expense
is less than the cash paid for
interest.

Straight-line Amortization of Premium   In our example, the beginning premium is $3,500, and there are 20 semiannual interest periods during the bonds' 10-year life. Therefore, ¹⁄₂₀ of the $3,500 ($175) of bond premium is amortized each interest period. BCE's semiannual interest entry on July 1, 1996, is

1996					
July	1	Interest Expense...		3,825	
		Premium on Bonds Payable			
		($3,500/20)		175	
		Cash ($100,000 × .08 × %₁₂)			4,000
		To pay semiannual interest and amortize			
		premium on bonds payable.			

Interest expense of $3,825 is the remainder of the contract cash interest ($4,000) less the amount of premium amortized ($175). The debit to Premium on Bonds Payable reduces its credit balance.

STOP & THINK

Consider bonds issued at a discount. Which will be greater, the cash interest paid per period or the amount of interest expense? Answer the same question for bonds issued at a premium.

Answer: For bonds issued at a *discount*, interest expense will be greater than cash interest paid, by the amount of the discount amortized for the period. For bonds issued at a *premium*, cash interest paid will be greater than interest expense, by the amount of the premium amortized for the period.

Reporting Bonds Payable

Bonds payable are reported on the balance sheet at their maturity amount plus any unamortized premium or minus any unamortized discount. For example, at December 31, BCE in the preceding example would have amortized Premium on Bonds Payable for two semiannual periods ($175 × 2 = $350). The BCE balance sheet would show these bonds payable as follows:

Long-term liabilities		
Bonds Payable, 8% due 2006................................	$100,000	
Premium on bonds payable		
[$3,500 – (2 × $175)]..	3,150	$103,150

Over the life of the bonds, twenty amortization entries will decrease the premium balance to zero. The payment at maturity will debit Bonds Payable and credit Cash for $100,000.

Adjusting Entries for Interest Expense _____

Companies issue bonds when they need cash. The interest payments seldom occur on the end of the company's fiscal year. Nevertheless, interest expense must be accrued at the end of the period to measure income accurately. The accrual entry may often be complicated by the need to amortize a discount or a premium for only a partial interest period.

Suppose NOVA Corporation issues $100,000 of its 8 percent, 10-year bonds at a $2,000 discount on October 1, 1996. Assume that interest payments occur on March 31 and September 30 each year. On December 31, NOVA records interest for the three-month period (October, November, and December) as follows:

Short Exercise:
For the previous Short Exercise, (1) what year-end adjusting entry is required on 12/31/96? (2) What entry will follow on 5/31/97? **A:**
(1) 12/31/96
Int. Expense............ 2,200
Premium on
  Bonds Payable...... 50
    Int. Payable......... 2,250
($13,500 × 1/6 = $2,250 and $300 × 1/6 = $50, both for 1 month)
The amounts recorded are 1/6 of the usual semiannual amortization and interest amounts.
(2) 5/31/97
Int. Expense 11,000
Interest Payable 2,250
Premium on
  Bonds Payable 250
    Cash................ 13,500

This entry represents 5 months of interest expense and of amortization and 6 months of interest paid in cash. Interest expense and amortization for the remaining month have been recorded in the 12/31/96 entry.

1996
Dec. 31 Interest Expense.. 2,050
        Interest Payable ($100,000 × .08 × $\frac{3}{12}$)......   2,000
        Discount on Bonds Payable
          ($2,000/10 × $\frac{3}{12}$).....................................   50
        To accrue three months' interest and amortize discount on bonds payable for three months.

Interest Payable is credited for the three months of cash interest that have accrued since September 30. Discount on Bonds Payable is credited for three months of amortization.

The balance sheet at December 31, 1996, reports Interest Payable of $2,000 as a current liability. Bonds Payable appears as a long-term liability, presented as follows:

Long-term liabilities
    Bonds payable, 8%, due 2006 .... $100,000
    Less: Discount on bonds payable ($2,000 − $50).   1,950 $98,050

Observe that the balance of Discount on Bonds Payable decreases by $50. The bonds' carrying value increases by the same amount. The bonds' carrying value continues to increase over its 10-year life, reaching $100,000 at maturity when the discount will be fully amortized.

The next semiannual interest payment occurs on March 31, 1997, as follows:

1997
Mar. 31 Interest Expense 2,050
        Interest Payable 2,000
          Cash ($100,000 × .08 × $\frac{6}{12}$)   4,000
          Discount on Bonds Payable
            ($2,000/10 × $\frac{3}{12}$)   50
        To pay semiannual interest, part of which was accrued, and amortize three months' discount on bonds payable.

Amortization of a premium over a partial interest period is similar except that Premium on Bonds Payable is debited.

Mid-Chapter Summary Problem for Your Review

Assume that Hydro-Québec has outstanding an issue of 9 percent bonds that mature on May 1, 2016. Further, assume that the bonds are dated May 1, 1996, and Hydro-Québec pays interest each April 30 and October 31.

Required

1. Will the bonds be issued at par, at a premium, or at a discount if the market interest rate is 8 percent at date of issuance? What if the market interest rate is 10 percent?

2. Assume Hydro-Québec issued $1,000,000 of the bonds at 104.00 on May 1, 1996.
   a. Record issuance of the bonds.
   b. Record the interest payment and amortization of premium or discount on October 31, 1996.
   c. Accrue interest and amortize premium or discount on December 31, 1996.
   d. Show how the company would report the bonds on the balance sheet at December 31, 1996.
   e. Record the interest payment on April 30, 1997.

SOLUTION TO REVIEW PROBLEM

Requirement 1

If the market interest rate is 8 percent, 9 percent bonds will be issued at a *premium*. If the market rate is 10 percent, the 9 percent bonds will be issued at a *discount*.

Requirement 2

1996				
a. May 1	Cash ($1,000,000 × 1.04)............................	1,040,000	
	Bonds Payable		1,000,000
	Premium on Bonds Payable		40,000
	To issue 9%, 20-year bonds at a premium.		
b. Oct. 31	Interest Expense	44,000	
	Premium on Bonds Payable		
	($40,000/40)	1,000	
	Cash ($1,000,000 × .09 × $\frac{6}{12}$)		45,000
	To pay semiannual interest and amortize premium on bonds payable.		
c. Dec. 31	Interest Expense	14,667	
	Premium on Bonds Payable		
	($40,000/40 × $\frac{2}{6}$).....................................	333	
	Interest Payable		
	($1,000,000 × .09 × $\frac{2}{12}$)		15,000
	To accrue interest and amortize bond premium for two months.		

d. Long-term liabilities

Bonds payable, 9%, due 2016..................	$1,000,000	
Premium on bonds payable		
($40,000 – $1,000 – $333)	38,667	$1,038,667

1997			
e. Apr. 30	Interest Expense	29,333	
	Interest Payable	15,000	
	Premium on Bonds Payable		
	($40,000/40 × $\frac{4}{6}$).....................................	667	
	Cash ($1,000,000 × .09 × $\frac{6}{12}$)		45,000
	To pay semiannual interest, part of which was accrued, and amortize four months' premium on bonds payable.		

SUPPLEMENT TO SUMMARY PROBLEM SOLUTION

Bond problems include many details. You may find it helpful to check your work. We verify the answers to the Summary Problem in this supplement.

On April 30, 1997, the bonds have been outstanding for one year. After the entries have been recorded, the account balances should show the results of one year's cash interest payments and one year's bond premium amortization.

Fact 1	Cash interest payments should be $90,000 ($1,000,000 × .09).
Accuracy check	Two credits to Cash of $45,000 each = $90,000. Cash payments are correct.
Fact 2	Premium amortization should be $2,000 ($40,000/40 semiannual periods × 2 semiannual periods in 1 year).
Accuracy check	Three debits to Premium on Bonds Payable ($1,000 + $333 + $667) = $2,000. Premium amortization is correct.
Fact 3	Also we can check the accuracy of interest expense recorded during the year ended December 31, 1996.
	The bonds in this problem will be outstanding for a total of 20 years, or 240 (that is, 20 × 12) months. During 1996, the bonds are outstanding for 8 months (May through December).
	Interest expense for 8 months *equals* payment of cash interest for 8 months minus premium amortization for 8 months.
	Interest expense should therefore be ($1,000,000 × .09 × $\frac{8}{12}$ = $60,000) minus [($40,000/240) × 8 = $1,333] or ($60,000 − $1,333 = $58,667).
Accuracy check:	Two debits to Interest Expense ($44,000 + $14,667) = $58,667. Interest expense for 1996 is correct.

Effective-Interest Method of Amortization

The straight-line amortization method has a theoretical weakness. Each period's amortization amount for a premium or discount is the same dollar amount over the life of the bonds. However, over that time the bonds' carrying value continues to increase (with a discount) or decrease (with a premium). Thus the fixed dollar amount of amortization changes as a percentage of the bonds' carrying value, making it appear that the bond issuer's interest rate changes over time. This appearance is misleading because in fact the issuer locked in a fixed interest rate when the bonds were issued. The interest rate on the bonds does not change.

We will see how the effective-interest method keeps each interest expense amount at the same percentage of the bonds' carrying value for every interest payment over the bonds' life. The total amount amortized over the life of the bonds is the same under both methods. Canadian GAAP does not specify which method should be used, while U.S. GAAP favors the effective-interest method because it does a better job of matching. However, the straight-line method is popular because of its simplicity.

Effective-Interest Method of Amortizing Discount

Assume that Dofasco Inc. issues $100,000 of its 9 percent bonds at a time when the market rate of interest is 10 percent. Also assume that these bonds mature in five years and pay interest semiannually, so there are 10 semiannual interest payments. The issue price of the bonds is $96,149.[2] The discount on these bonds is $3,851 ($100,000 − $96,149). Exhibit 16-5 illustrates amortization of the discount by the effective-interest method.

Recall that we want to present interest expense amounts over the full life of the bonds at a fixed percentage of the bonds' carrying value. The 5 percent rate—the effective-interest rate—*is* that percentage. We have figured the cost of the money borrowed by the bond issuer—the interest expense—as a constant percentage of the carrying value of the bonds. The dollar *amount* of interest expense varies from period to period but the interest percentage remains the same.

> **OBJECTIVE 2**
> Amortize bond discount and premium by the effective-interest method

> *Key Point:*
> The amount of cash paid each semiannual interest period is calculated with the formula:
> Interest paid = Par value × (Contract rate/2)
> This amount does not change over the term of the bond.

---

[2] We compute this present value using the tables that appear in the appendix to this chapter.

Short Exercise:

Back to Quill Corp. and the $300,000, 9%, 10-year bonds dated 5/31/96. Assume that the bonds are sold on 5/31/96 for $281,337 to yield an effective rate of 10%. Using the effective-interest method, what entry is required on 11/30/96, the first interest payment date? **A:**

11/30/96
Interest Expense 14,067*
Discount on
  Bonds Payable   567†
  Cash   13,500

*$281,337 × 5% = $14,067
†$14,067 − $13,500 = $567

The Discount account has been reduced by $567 and has a new balance of $18,096 ($18,663−$567). The bonds' new carrying value is $281,904 ($300,000 − $18,096).

EXHIBIT 16-5 *Effective-Interest Method of Amortizing Bond Discount*

Panel A: Bond Data

Maturity value—$100,000
Contract interest rate—9%
Interest paid—4½% semiannually—$4,500 ($100,000 × .045)
Market interest rate at time of issue—10% annually, 5% semiannually
Issue price—$96,149

Panel B: Amortization Table

Semiannual Interest Period	A Interest Payment (4½% of Maturity Value)	B Interest Expense (5% of Preceding Bond Carrying Amount)	C Discount Amortization (B − A)	D Discount Account Balance (D − C)	E Bond Carrying Amount ($100,000 − D)
Issue Date				$3,851	$ 96,149
1	$4,500	$4,807	$307	3,544	96,456
2	4,500	4,823	323	3,221	96,779
3	4,500	4,839	339	2,882	97,118
4	4,500	4,856	356	2,526	97,474
5	4,500	4,874	374	2,152	97,848
6	4,500	4,892	392	1,760	98,240
7	4,500	4,912	412	1,348	98,652
8	4,500	4,933	433	915	99,085
9	4,500	4,954	454	461	99,539
10	4,500	4,961*	461	-0-	100,000

*Adjusted for effect of rounding.

Notes

Column A   The semiannual interest payments are constant because they are governed by the contract interest rate and the bonds' maturity value.

Column B   The interest expense each period is computed by multiplying the preceding bond carrying amount by the market interest rate. The effect of this *effective interest rate* determines the interest expense each period. The amount of interest each period increases as the effective-interest rate, a constant, is applied to the increasing bond carrying amount (E).

Column C   The excess of each interest expense amount (B) over each interest payment amount (A) is the discount amortization for the period.

Column D   The discount balance decreases by the amount of amortization for the period (C) from $3,851 at the bonds' issue date to zero at their maturity. Balance of the discount + bonds' carrying amount equal the bonds' maturity value.

Column E   The bonds' carrying amount increases from $96,149 at issuance to $100,000 at maturity.

Key Point:
The amount of semiannual interest expense is calcu-lated with the formula:
Interest expense = Bond carrying value × (Market interest rate/2)
This amount will change each period as carrying value changes over the term of the bond.

The *accounts* debited and credited under the effective-interest amortization method and the straight-line method are the same. Only the amounts differ. We may take the amortization *amounts* directly from the table in Exhibit 16-5. We assume that the first interest payment occurs on July 1 and use the appropriate amounts from Exhibit 16-5, reading across the line for the first interest payment date:

July   1   Interest Expense (column B)   4,807
            Discount on Bonds Payable (column C)..   307
            Cash (column A)   4,500
         To pay semiannual interest and amortize
         discount on bonds payable.

STOP & THINK

Over the life of a bond issued at a *discount,* will the periodic amount of interest expense increase or decrease under the effective-interest amortization method?

Answer: The periodic amount of interest expense *increases* because the carrying amount of the bond *increases* toward maturity value. To see this, refer to columns B and E of Exhibit 16-5.

Effective-Interest Method of Amortizing Premium

Let us modify the Dofasco example to illustrate the effective-interest method of amortizing bond premium. Assume that Dofasco issues $100,000 of five-year, 9 percent bonds that pay interest semiannually. If the bonds are issued when the market interest rate is 8 percent, their issue price is $104,100.[3] The premium on these bonds is $4,100, and Exhibit 16-6 illustrates amortization of the premium by the interest method.

Assuming that the first interest payment occurs on October 31, we read across the line in Exhibit 16-6 for the first interest payment date and pick up the appropriate amounts.

Oct.   31   Interest Expense (column B)   4,164
            Premium on Bonds Payable (column C)......   336
               Cash (column A)...   4,500
         To pay semiannual interest and amortize dis-
         count on bonds payable.

STOP & THINK

How does the method of amortizing bond premium or discount affect the amount of cash interest paid on a bond?

Answer: The amortization method for bond premium or discount has *no effect* on the amount of cash interest paid on a bond. The amount of cash interest paid depends on the contract interest rate stated on the bond. That interest rate, and the amount of cash interest paid, are fixed and therefore remain constant over the life of the bond. To see this, examine column A of Exhibits 16-5 and 16-6.

At year end it is necessary to make an adjusting entry for accrued interest and amortization of the bond premium for a partial period. In our example, the last interest payment occurred on October 31. The adjustment for November and December must cover two months, or one third of a semiannual period. The entry, with amounts drawn from line 2 in Exhibit 16-6 is

[3]Again we compute the present value of the bonds using the tables in this chapter's appendix.

EXHIBIT 16-6   *Effective-Interest Method of Amortizing Bond Premium*

Panel A: Bond Data

Maturity value—$100,000
Contract interest rate—9%
Interest paid—4½% semiannually, $4,500 ($100,000 × .045)
Market interest rate at time of issue—8% annually, 4% semiannually
Issue price—$104,100

Panel B: Amortization Table

	A	B	C	D	E
Semiannual Interest Period	Interest Payment (4½% of Maturity Value)	Interest Expense (4% of Preceding Bond Carrying Amount)	Premium Amortization (A − B)	Premium Account Balance (D − C)	Bond Carrying Amount ($100,000 + D)
Issue Date				$4,100	$104,100
1	$4,500	$4,164	$336	3,764	103,764
2	4,500	4,151	349	3,415	103,415
3	4,500	4,137	363	3,052	103,052
4	4,500	4,122	378	2,674	102,674
5	4,500	4,107	393	2,281	102,281
6	4,500	4,091	409	1,872	101,872
7	4,500	4,075	425	1,447	101,447
8	4,500	4,058	442	1,005	101,005
9	4,500	4,040	460	545	100,545
10	4,500	3,955*	545	-0-	100,000

*Adjusted for effect of rounding.

Notes:

Column A   The semiannual interest payments are a constant amount fixed by the contract interest rate and the bonds' maturity value.

Column B   The interest expense each period is computed by multiplying the preceding bond carrying amount by the effective-interest rate. The amount of interest decreases each period as the bond carrying amount decreases.

Column C   The excess of each interest payment (A) over the period's interest expense (B) is the premium amortization for the period.

Column D   The premium balance decreases by the amount of amortization for the period (C) from $4,100 at issuance to zero at maturity. The bonds' carrying amount – the premium balance = the bonds' maturity value.

Column E   The bonds' carrying value decreases from $104,100 at issuance to $100,000 at maturity.

Dec. 31	Interest Expense ($4,151 × ⅓)...........................	1,384	
	Premium on Bonds Payable ($349 × ⅓).........	116	
	Interest Payable ($4,500 × ⅓).....................		1,500
	To accrue two months' interest and amortize		
	premium on bonds payable for two months.		

The second interest payment occurs on April 30 of the following year. The payment of $4,500 includes interest expense for four months (January through April), the interest payable at December 31, and premium amortization for four months. The payment entry is the following:

Apr. 30   Interest Expense ($4,151 × ⅔)..........................   2,767
    Interest Payable   1,500
    Premium on Bonds Payable ($349 × ⅔).........   233
     Cash..   4,500
    To pay semiannual interest, some of which
    was accrued, and amortize premium on
    bonds payable for four months.

If these bonds had been issued at a discount, procedures for these interest entries would be the same, except that Discount on Bonds Payable would be credited.

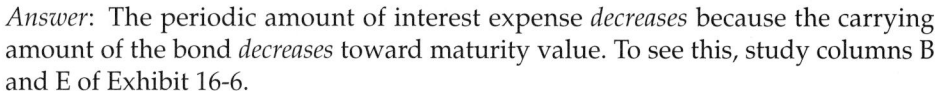

STOP & THINK

For a bond issued at a *premium*, will the periodic amount of interest expense increase or decrease? Assume the effective-interest method.

Answer: The periodic amount of interest expense *decreases* because the carrying amount of the bond *decreases* toward maturity value. To see this, study columns B and E of Exhibit 16-6.

Bond Sinking Fund

Bond indentures, the contracts under which bonds are issued, often require the borrower to make regular periodic payments to a bond sinking fund. A fund is a group of assets that are segregated for a particular purpose. A *bond sinking fund* is used to retire bonds payable at maturity. A trustee manages this fund for the issuer, investing the company's payments in income-earning assets. The company's payments into the fund and the interest revenue—which the trustee reinvests in the fund—accumulate. The target amount of the sinking fund is the face value of the bond issue at maturity. When the bonds come due, the trustee sells the sinking-fund assets and uses the cash proceeds to pay off the bonds. The bond sinking fund provides security of payment to investors in unsecured bonds.

Most companies report sinking funds under the heading Investments, a separate asset category between current assets and capital assets on the balance sheet. A bond sinking fund is not a current asset because it may not be used to pay current liabilities. Accounting for the interest, dividends, and other earnings on the bond sinking fund requires use of the accounts Sinking Fund and Sinking Fund Revenue.

Sobey's Stores Limited has outstanding $9.25 million of 13 percent sinking fund debentures. The company must make annual sinking-fund payments. The entry to deposit $500,000 with the trustee is

Jan. 5 Sinking Fund..   500,000
     Cash..   500,000
    To make annual sinking fund deposit.

If the trustee invests the cash and reports annual sinking fund revenue of $50,000, the fund grows by this amount, and Sobey's makes the following entry at year end:

Apr. 30 Sinking Fund..   50,000
     Sinking Fund Revenue   50,000
    To record sinking fund earnings.

Assume that Sobey's has made the required sinking fund payments over a period of years and that these payments plus the fund earnings have accumulated a cash balance of $9.45 million at maturity. The trustee pays off the bonds and returns the excess cash to Sobey's, which makes the following entry:

Jan.	4	Cash..	200,000	
		Bonds Payable..	9,250,000	
		Sinking Fund.......................................		9,450,000
		To record payment of bonds payable and receipt of excess sinking fund cash at maturity.		

If the fund balance is less than the bonds' maturity value, the entry is similar to the foregoing entry. However, the company pays the extra amount and credits Cash.

Retirement of Bonds Payable

OBJECTIVE 3

Account for retirement of bonds payable

Key Point: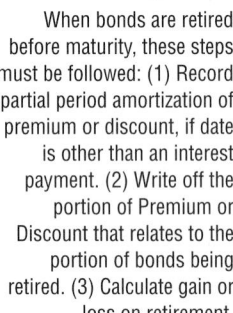

Callable bonds may be paid off at the corporation's option. The bondholder does not have the choice of refusing but must surrender the bond for retirement.

Key Point:

When bonds are retired before maturity, these steps must be followed: (1) Record partial period amortization of premium or discount, if date is other than an interest payment. (2) Write off the portion of Premium or Discount that relates to the portion of bonds being retired. (3) Calculate gain or loss on retirement.

Normally companies wait until maturity to pay off, or retire, their bonds payable. All bond discount or premium has been amortized, and the retirement entry debits Bonds Payable and credits Cash for the bonds' maturity value. But companies sometimes retire their bonds payable prior to maturity. The main reason for retiring bonds early is to relieve the pressure of making interest payments. Interest rates fluctuate. The company may be able to borrow at a lower interest rate and use the proceeds from new bonds to pay off the old bonds, which bear a higher rate.

Some bonds are **callable**, which means that the issuer may *call* or pay off the bonds at a specified price whenever the issuer so chooses. The call price is usually a few percent above the face value or par, perhaps $104.00 or $105.00. Callable bonds give the issuer the benefit of being able to take advantage of low interest rates by paying off the bonds at the most favorable time. An alternative to calling the bonds is to purchase them in the open market at their current market price. Whether the bonds are called or purchased in the open market, the journal entry is the same.

Air Products Canada Ltd. has $7,000,000 of debentures outstanding with unamortized discount of $35,000. Lower interest rates in the market may convince management to pay off these bonds now. Assume that the bonds are callable at $103.00. If the market price of the bonds is $99.25 will Air Products call the bonds or purchase them in the open market? The market price is lower than the call price, so market price is the better choice. Retiring the bonds at $99.25 results in a gain of $175,000.

Face value of bonds being retired............................	$7,000,000
Unamortized discount	35,000
Book value	6,965,000
Market price ($7,000,000 × .9925)............................	6,947,500
Gain on retirement...	$ 17,500

Short Exercise:

Quill Corp. has sold $300,000 of 10-year bonds at a discount. Interest has just been paid, and the remaining carrying value of the bonds is $299,000. Half the bonds are retired when the market price is $96.50. What entry is required? ***A:***
Bonds Payable 150,000*
Discount on
  Bonds Pay. .... 500†
Cash ....144,750‡
(cont.)

The following entry records retirement of the bonds, immediately after an interest date:

June	30	Bonds Payable..	7,000,000	
		Discount on Bonds Payable...............		35,000
		Cash ($7,000,000 × .9925)		6,947,500
		Gain on Retirement of		
		Bonds Payable		17,500
		To retire bonds payable before maturity.		

The entry removes the bonds payable and the related discount from the accounts and records a gain on retirement. Of course, any existing premium would be removed with a debit. If Air Products Canada had retired only half of these bonds, the accountant would remove half of the discount or premium. Likewise, if the price paid to retire the bonds exceeds their carrying value, the retirement entry would record a loss with a debit to the account Loss on Retirement of Bonds. GAAP requires that gains and losses on early retirement of debt, that are both abnormal in size and unusual, be classified as unusual and be reported separately as a line item on the income statement before income tax and discontinued operations and extraordinary items.

Gain on
  Retirement.............. 4,750§

* $300,000 par value × ½
  = $150,000
† $1,000 unamortized discount
  × ½ = $500
‡ $150,000 × 0.965 = $144,750
§ ($150,000 − $500) − $144,750
  = $4,750 gain

Convertible Bonds and Notes

OBJECTIVE 4
Account for conversion of bonds payable

Many corporate bonds and notes payable have the feature of being convertible into the common stock of the issuing company at the option of the investor. These bonds and notes, called **convertible bonds** (or **notes**), combine the safety of assured receipts of principal and interest on the bonds with the opportunity for large gains on the stock. The conversion feature is so attractive that investors usually accept a lower contract, or stated, interest rate than they would on nonconvertible bonds. The lower interest rate benefits the issuer. Convertible bonds are recorded like any other debt at issuance.

If the market price of the issuing company's stock gets high enough, the bondholders will convert the bonds into stock. The corporation records conversion by debiting the bond accounts and crediting the shareholders' equity accounts. The carrying value of the bonds becomes the book value of the newly issued stock. No gain or loss is recorded.

Inco Limited reported in its 1994 annual report

> In July, 1994, the Company issued $172.5 million of 5.75% Convertible U.S. Debentures due 2004 . . . The Debentures . . . are convertible, at the option of holders, into common shares of the Company, at a conversion price of $30 (U.S.) per share.

Assume that $3,000,000 of debentures were converted into 100,000 ($3,000,000/$30) shares of common stock on May 1, 1996. Inco reports its financial statements in U.S. dollars so no conversion to Canadian dollars is necessary. The debentures were issued at par. Inco's entry to record the conversion would be:

```
1996
May  1  Debentures Outstanding......................  3,000,000
            Common Stock..................................                3,000,000
        To record conversion of $3,000,000
        debentures outstanding into 100,000
        common shares.
```

Observe that the carrying value of the debentures ($3,000,000) becomes the amount of increase in shareholders' equity.

Current Portion of Long-Term Debt

Serial bonds and serial notes are payable in serials, or installments. The portion payable within one year is a current liability, and the remaining debt is long-term. At December 31, 1994, Mapco, Inc., had $62 million of 8.7 percent notes payable. The notes are due in $8 million annual installments through 2001 with a final installment of $6 million due in 2002. Therefore, $8 million is a current liability at December 31, 1994, and $54 million is a long-term liability. Mapco reported this installment note payable among its liabilities as follows:

	$ millions
Current liabilities	
Current portion of long-term debt..	$ 8
Long-term debt, excluding amounts payable within one year	54

Mortgage Notes Payable

You have probably heard of mortgage payments. Many notes payable are mortgage notes, which actually contain two agreements. The *note* is the borrower's promise to pay the lender the amount of the debt. The **mortgage**—a security agreement related to the note—is the borrower's promise to transfer the legal title to certain assets to the lender if the debt is not paid on schedule. The borrower is said to pledge these assets as security for the note. Often the asset that is pledged was acquired with the borrowed money. For example, most homeowners sign mortgage notes to purchase their residence, pledging that property as security for the loan. Businesses sign mortgage notes to acquire buildings, equipment, and other long-term assets. Mortgage notes are usually serial notes that require monthly or quarterly payments.

OBJECTIVE 5

Explain the advantages and disadvantages of borrowing

Advantage of Financing Operations with Debt versus Stock

Businesses acquire assets in different ways. Management may decide to purchase or to lease equipment. The money to finance the asset may come from the business's retained earnings, a note payable, a stock issue, or a bond issue. Each financing strategy has its advantages and disadvantages as follows:

Advantages of Financing Operations by

Issuing Stock	Issuing a Note or Bonds
• Creates no liabilities or interest expense, which must be paid even during bad years. Less risky to the issuing corporation.	• Does not dilute stock ownership or control of the corporation. • Results in higher earnings per share because interest expense is tax-deductible and ownership is not diluted.

Exhibit 16-7 illustrates the earnings-per-share (EPS) advantage of borrowing. Suppose a corporation with net income of $300,000 and with 100,000 shares of common stock outstanding needs $500,000 for expansion. Management is considering two financing plans. Plan 1 is to issue $500,000 of 10-percent bonds payable, and Plan 2 is to issue 50,000 shares of common stock for $500,000. Management believes the new cash can be invested in operations to earn income of $200,000 before interest and taxes.

EXHIBIT 16-7   *Earnings-per-Share Advantage of Borrowing*

	Plan 1 Borrow $500,000 at 10%	Plan 2 Issue $500,000 of Common Stock
Net income before interest and income tax ...	$300,000	$300,000
Income before interest and income tax	200,000	$200,000
Less: interest expense ($500,000 × .10)............	50,000	-0-
Income before income tax	150,000	200,000
Less: income tax expense (40%)	60,000	80,000
Project net income	$ 90,000	$120,000
Total company net income	$390,000	$420,000
Earnings per share including expansion		
Plan 1 ($390,000/100,000 shares)	$ 3.90	
Plan 2 ($420,000/150,000 shares)		$ 2.80

The earnings-per-share amount is higher if the company borrows. The business earns more on the investment ($90,000) than the interest it pays on the bonds ($50,000). Earning more income than the borrowed amount increases the earnings for common shareholders, and is called **trading on the equity**. It is widely used in business to increase earnings per share of common stock.

Borrowing has its disadvantages. Interest expense may be high enough to eliminate net income and lead to a cash crisis and even bankruptcy. Also, borrowing creates liabilities that accrue during bad years as well as during good years. In contrast, a company that issues stock can omit its dividends during a bad year.

Recently in Canada we have seen several situations in which a company's interest payments caused financial distress to the organization. The two better-known corporations who have had this problem are Bramalea Ltd. and Trizec Corp. Ltd.

Lease Liabilities

A **lease** is a rental agreement in which the tenant (**lessee**) agrees to make rent payments to the property owner (**lessor**) in exchange for the use of the asset. Leasing allows the lessee to acquire the use of a needed asset without having to make the large initial cash down payment that purchase agreements require. Accountants divide leases into two types when considering the lease from the lessee's perspective: operating and capital. The lessor divides capital leases into three kinds: *operating leases*, *sales-type leases*, in which the lessor is usually a manufacturer or dealer, and *direct financing leases*, in which the lessor is usually not a manufacturer or dealer but provides financing. This text will consider the broader term, *capital lease*, and not the kinds of capital lease.

> ### OBJECTIVE 6
> Account for lease transactions

Operating Leases

Operating leases are usually short-term or cancelable. Many apartment leases and most car-rental agreements extend a year or less. These operating leases give the lessee the right to use the asset, but provide the lessee with no continuing rights to the asset. The lessor retains the usual risks and rewards of owning the leased asset. To account for an operating lease, the lessee debits Rent Expense (or Lease Expense) and credits Cash for the amount of the lease payment. The lessee's books do not report the leased asset or any lease liability (except perhaps a prepaid rent amount or a rent accrual at the end of the period).

Capital Leases

Many businesses use capital leasing to finance the acquisition of some assets. A capital lease is a long-term and noncancelable financing that is a form of debt. How do you distinguish a capital lease from an operating lease? Section 3145 of the *CICA Handbook* defines a **capital lease** as one that transfers substantially all the benefits and risks incident to ownership of property to the lessee. The section goes on to suggest that a lease is a capital lease from the perspective of the lessee if one or more of the following conditions are present at the beginning of the lease:

1. There is reasonable assurance that the lessee will obtain ownership of the leased asset at the end of the lease term.
2. The lease term is of such a length that the lessee will obtain almost all (usually 75 percent or more) of the benefits from the use of the leased asset over its life.
3. The lessor would both recover the original investment and earn a return on that investment from the lease.

A lease which does not meet any of the above conditions is probably an operating lease and should be accounted for as such.

A lease is a capital lease from the perspective of the lessor if any one of the three conditions outlined above is present and *both* the following are present:

1. The credit risk associated with the lease is normal.
2. The amounts of any unreimbursable costs to the lessor are estimable.

Accounting for a Capital Lease   Accounting for a capital lease is much like accounting for a purchase. The lessor removes the asset from his or her books. The lessee enters the asset into his or her accounts and records a lease liability at the beginning of the lease term. Thus the lessee capitalizes the asset on its own financial statements even though the lessee may never take legal title to the property.

A recent survey of 300 companies indicates that while almost 84 percent (251) have long-term debt, one third (96) have capital leases.[4]

Finning Ltd., the heavy equipment company, has its head office in Vancouver. Suppose Finning leases a building, agreeing to pay $10,000 annually for a 20-year period, with the first payment due immediately. This arrangement is similar to purchasing the building on an installment plan. In an installment purchase, Finning would debit Building and credit Cash and Installment Note Payable. The company would then pay interest and principal on the note payable and record depreciation on the building. Accounting for a capital lease follows this pattern.

Finning records the building at cost, which is the sum of the $10,000 initial payment plus the present value of the 19 future lease payments of $10,000 each.[5] The company credits Cash for the initial payment and credits Lease Liability for the present value of the future lease payments. Assume the interest rate on Finning's lease is 10 percent and the present value (PV) of the future lease payments is $83,650.[6] At the beginning of the lease term, Finning makes the following entry:

19X1			
Jan. 2	Leased Building ($10,000 + $83,650)	93,650	
	Cash		10,000
	Lease Liability (PV of future		
	lease payments)		83,650
	To lease a building and make the first annual		
	lease payment on the capital lease.		

Because Finning has capitalized the building, the company records depreciation. Assume the building has an expected life of 25 years. It is depreciated over the lease term of 20 years because the lessee has the use of the building only for that period. No residual value enters into the depreciation computation because the lessee will have no residual asset when the building is returned to the lessor at the expiration of the lease. Therefore, the annual depreciation entry is

19X1			
Dec. 31	Depreciation Expense ($93,650/20)	4,683	
	Accumulated Depreciation		
	—Leased Building		4,683
	To record depreciation on leased building.		

At year end, Finning must also accrue interest on the lease liability. Interest expense is computed by multiplying the lease liability by the interest rate on the lease. The following entry credits Lease Liability (not Interest Payable) for this interest accrual:

---

[4] *Financial Reporting in Canada*, 1993, Twentieth Edition (Toronto: CICA, 1993) pp. 109 and 125.
[5] The chapter appendix explains present value.
[6] The formula for this computation appears in the chapter appendix.

19X1

Dec. 31   Interest Expense ($83,650 × .10)...................... 8,365
                      Lease Liability 8,365
                      To accrue interest on the lease liability.

The balance sheet at December 31, 19X1, reports:

Assets

Capital assets:
    Building under lease... $93,650
    Less: Accumulated depreciation.................................. 4,683 $88,967

Liabilities

Current liabilities:
    Lease liability (next payment due on Jan. 2, 19X2)........................... $10,000

Long-term liabilities:
    Lease liability [beginning balance ($83,650) + interest accrual
        ($8,365) – current portion ($10,000)].. 82,015

In addition, the lessee must report the minimum capital lease payments for the next five years in the notes to the financial statements.

The lease liability is split into current and long-term portions because the next payment ($10,000) is a current liability and the remainder is long-term. The Jan. 2, 19X2, lease payment is recorded as follows:

Jan.   2   Lease Liability 10,000
                      Cash... 10,000
                      To make second annual lease payment on
                      building.

Off-Balance-Sheet Financing

An important part of business is obtaining the funds needed to acquire assets. To finance operations, a company may issue stock, borrow money, or retain earnings in the business. Notice that all three of these financing plans affect the right-hand side of the balance sheet. Issuing stock affects preferred or common stock. Borrowing creates notes or bonds payable. Internal funds come from retained earnings.

Off-balance-sheet financing is the acquisition of assets or services whose resulting debt is not reported on the balance sheet. A prime example is an operating lease. The lessee has the use of the leased asset, but neither the asset nor any lease liability is reported on the balance sheet. In the past, most leases were accounted for by the operating method. However, the *CICA Handbook* in Section 3065 has required businesses to account for an increasing number of leases by the capital lease method. Also, Section 3065 has brought about detailed reporting of operating lease payments in the notes to the financial statements; minimum operating lease payments for the next five years must be reported. The inclusion of more lease information, be they capital or operating leases, makes the accounting information for decision-making more complete. Much useful information is reported only in the notes. Experienced investors study them carefully.

Pension Liabilities

Pensions   Most companies have a pension plan for their employees. A **pension** is employee compensation that is received during retirement. Employees earn the pensions by their service, so the company records pension expense while employees

Key Point:
A pension plan is a contract between a business and its employees. The contract's terms outline the retirement benefits the company will pay to retired employees.

work for the company. While employees may also contribute to a company pension plan, the following discussion relates to employer contributions to a pension plan for employees.

The *CICA Handbook* in Section 3460 gives the rules for measuring pension expense. To record the company's payment into a pension plan, the company debits Pension Expense and credits Cash. Trustees such as trust companies and pension trusts manage pension plans. They receive the employer payments and any employee contributions, then invest these amounts for the future benefit of the employees. The goal is to have the funds available to meet any obligations to retirees.

While employees are perhaps those most interested in the status of their employer's pension plan, others such as creditors are also interested because pension plan assets and obligations can be large in proportion to a company's financial position. A company with a large underfunded pension liability could find itself in financial difficulties that would affect all creditors. For example, the financial statements of Maclean Hunter Limited recently reported that while the company's total assets were $1,753.6 million, the assets in the company's pension plans were $284 million (the accrued liabilities under the plan were estimated at $254 million).

Real-World Example:
There are two types of pension plans: (1) Defined Contribution Plan: The employee, employer, or both must contribute a certain amount each period to the pension fund. The retirement benefits depend on how much is in the fund. (2) Defined Benefit Plan: The amount of the retirement benefit is defined by, say, 80% of salary in the year of retirement. The amount to be contributed to this type of pension fund requires a complex calculation and the services of an actuary.

Section 3460 defines two types of pension plan: a *defined benefit plan*, in which the benefits to be paid to the employee upon retirement are specified and the company must ensure that adequate funds will be available to make the specified payments, and a *defined contribution plan*, in which the contribution is defined and the benefits depend on what is available when the employee retires. Each will be discussed in turn.

A **defined benefit plan** must have an actuarial evaluation at least every three years to ensure that there will be sufficient funds available to make the required payments to each member of the plan on his or her retirement. In conducting the valuation, the plan actuaries will determine the actuarial present value of the plan benefits, compare that to the plan assets and determine whether the plan has a surplus or deficit. Section 3460 requires that the actuarial present value of plan benefits for employee services to the reporting date and the value of pension plan assets be disclosed in the financial statements. A recent annual report issued by National Trustco Inc. includes the following note to the financial statements:

15. PENSION PLAN
The Company maintains a contributory defined benefit plan covering substantially all employees. The plan provides pensions based on length of service and career earnings with periodic upgrades.

Actuarial reports prepared during the year indicate that the present value of the accrued pension benefits and net assets, at market value, available to provide for these benefits as at October 31 are as follows (in thousands):

	1994	1993
Pension fund assets...	$177,730	$166,668
Present value of accrued pension fund benefits	116,805	104,597
	60,925	62,071

The accounting for defined benefits pension plans is complex and is demonstrated in subsequent accounting courses.

A **defined contribution plan** is an accumulation of the employer and employee contributions. The required disclosure is the present value of required future contributions by the company for employee services to the reporting date. For example, the disclosure for Elora Ltd. could be as follows:

NOTES TO THE FINANCIAL STATEMENTS
8. The company has a defined contribution pension plan which covers all the company's employees. The present value of required future contributions in respect of past service by employees of the company was $759,256 at the year end.

Section 3460 of the *CICA Handbook* required companies to disclose pension assets and liabilities for defined benefit plans and unfunded obligations for past service for defined contribution plans, starting in 1990. Before that date, pensions were another example of off-balance-sheet financing. Companies received the benefit of their employees' service but could avoid reporting pension liabilities on the balance sheet.

Summary Problem for Your Review

Québecor Inc. has outstanding an issue of 8 percent convertible bonds that mature in 2012. Suppose the bonds were dated October 1, 1992, and pay interest each April 1 and October 1.

Required

1. Complete the following effective-interest amortization table through October 1, 1994.

   Bond data:

   Maturity value—$100,000
   Contract interest rate—8%
   Interest paid—4% semiannually, $4,000 ($100,000 × .04)

   Market interest rate at time of issue—9% annually, 4½% semiannually
   Issue price—$90.75

   Amortization table:

Semiannual Interest Period	A Interest Payment (4% of Maturity Value)	B Interest Expense (4½% of Preceding Bond Carrying Amount)	C Discount Amortization (B – A)	D Discount Account Balance (D – C)	E Bond Carrying Amount ($100,000 – D)
10-1-92					
4-1-93					
10-1-93					
4-1-94					
10-1-94					

2. Using the amortization table, record the following transactions:
   a. Issuance of the bonds on October 1, 1992.
   b. Accrual of interest and amortization of discount on December 31, 1992.
   c. Payment of interest and amortization of discount on April 1, 1993.
   d. Conversion of one third of the bonds payable into common stock on October 2, 1994.
   e. Retirement of two thirds of the bonds payable on October 2, 1994. Purchase price of the bonds was $102.00.

SOLUTION TO REVIEW PROBLEM

Requirement 1 Amortization Table

Semiannual Interest Period	A Interest Payment (4% of Maturity Value)	B Interest Expense (4 ½% of Preceding Bond Carrying Amount)	C Discount Amortization (B – A)	D Discount Account Balance (D – C)	E Bond Carrying Amount ($100,000 – D)
10-1-92				$9,250	$90,750
4-1-93	$4,000	$4,084	$84	9,166	90,834
10-1-93	4,000	4,088	88	9,070	90,922
4-1-94	4,000	4,091	91	8,987	91,013
10-1-94	4,000	4,096	96	8,891	91,109

Requirement 2

1992

a. Oct. 1 Cash ($100,000 × .9075) 90,750
         Discount on Bonds Payable 9,250
             Bonds Payable 100,000
         To issue 8%, 20-year bonds at a discount.

b. Dec. 31 Interest Expense ($4,084 × 3/6) 2,042
            Discount on Bonds Payable ($84 × 3/6) 42
            Interest Payable ($4,000 × 3/6) 2,000
         To accrue interest and amortize bond discount for three months.

1993

c. Apr. 1 Interest Expense 2,042
         Interest Payable 2,000
            Discount on Bonds Payable ($84 × 3/6) 42
            Cash 4,000
         To pay semiannual interest, part of which was accrued, and amortize three months' discount on bonds payble.

1994

d. Oct. 2 Bonds Payable ($100,000 × 1/3) 33,333
            Discount on Bonds Payable
             ($8,891 × 1/3) 2,964
            Common Stock ($91,109 × 1/3) 30,369
         To record conversion of bonds payable.

e. Oct. 2 Bonds Payable ($100,000 × 2/3) 66,667
         Loss on Retirement of Bonds 7,260
            Discount on Bonds Payable
             ($8,891 × 2/3) 5,927
            Cash ($100,000 × 2/3 × 1.02) 68,000
         To retire bonds payable before maturity.

Summary

1. ***Account for basic bonds payable transactions by the straight-line amortization method.*** A corporation may borrow money by issuing long-term notes and *bonds payable*. A bond contract specifies the maturity value of the bonds, the *contract interest rate*, and the dates for paying interest and principal. Bonds may be secured (*mortgage* bonds) or unsecured (*debenture* bonds).

Bonds are traded through organized markets, such as the over-the-counter market. Bonds are typically divided into $1,000 units. Their prices are quoted at the price per $100.00 bond. *Market interest rates* fluctuate and may differ from the contract rate on a bond. If a bond's contract rate exceeds the market rate, the bond sells at a *premium*. A bond with a contract rate below the market rate sells at a *discount*.

Money earns income over time, a fact that gives rise to the *present-value concept*. An investor will pay a price for a bond equal to the present value of the bond principal plus the present value of the bond interest.

Straight-line amortization allocates an equal amount of premium or discount to each interest period.

2. Amortize bond discount and premium by the effective-interest method. In the *effective-interest method* of amortization, the market rate at the time of issuance is multiplied by the bonds' carrying amount to determine the interest expense each period and to compute the amount of discount or premium amortization.

3. Account for retirement of bonds payable. Companies may retire their bonds payable before maturity. *Callable* bonds give the borrower the right to pay off the bonds at a specified call price, or the company may purchase the bonds in the open market.

4. Account for conversion of bonds payable. *Convertible bonds* and notes give the investor the privilege of trading the bonds in for stock of the issuing corporation. The carrying amount of the bonds becomes the book value of the newly issued stock.

5. Explain the advantages and disadvantages of borrowing. A key advantage of raising money by borrowing versus issuing stock is that interest expense on debt is tax-deductible. Thus borrowing is less costly than issuing stock. Borrowing's disadvantages result from the fact that the company *must* repay the loan and its interest.

6. Account for lease transactions. A *lease* is a rental agreement between the *lessee* and the *lessor*. In an *operating lease* the lessor retains the usual risks and rights of owing the asset. The lessee debits Rent Expense and credits Cash when making lease payments. A *capital lease* is long-term, noncancelable, and similar to an installment purchase of the leased asset. In a capital lease, the lessee capitalizes the leased asset and reports a lease liability.

In the case of *defined benefit pension plans,* companies should report *accrued pension benefits* and *pension assets* in the financial statements; in the case of *defined contribution pension plans*, companies should report *unfunded obligations* for past service.

Self-Study Questions

Test your understanding of the chapter by marking the best answer for each of the following questions:

1. An unsecured bond is called a *(p. 759)*
   a. Serial bond
   b. Registered bond
   c. Debenture bond
   d. Mortgage bond

2. How much will an investor pay for a $100,000 bond priced at $101.875 plus a brokerage commission of $1,100? *(p. 760)*
   a. $100,000
   b. $101,000
   c. $101,875
   d. $102,975

3. A bond with a stated interest rate of 9½ percent is issued when the market interest rate is 9¾ percent. This bond will sell at *(p. 760)*
   a. Par value
   b. A discount
   c. A premium
   d. A price minus accrued interest

4. Ten-year, 11 percent bonds payable of $500,000 were issued for $532,000. Assume the straight-line amortization method is appropriate. The total annual interest expense on these bonds is *(p. 762)*
   a. $51,800
   b. $55,000
   c. $58,200
   d. A different amount each year because the bonds' book value decreases as the premium is amortized

5. Repeat Question 4 but use the effective-interest method of amortization. *(p. 772)*
   a. $51,800
   b. $55,000
   c. $58,200
   d. A decreasing amount each year because the bonds' book value decreases as the premium is amortized

6. Bonds payable with face value of $300,000 and carrying value of $288,000 are retired before their scheduled maturity with a cash outlay of $292,000. Which of the following entries correctly records this bond retirement? *(p. 774)*

   a. Bonds Payable.. 300,000
       Discount on Bonds Payable 12,000
         Cash... 292,000
         Gain on Retirement of Bonds Payable.............. 20,000

   b. Bonds Payable.. 300,000
       Loss on Retirement of Bonds Payable 4,000
         Discount on Bonds Payable 12,000
         Cash... 292,000

   c. Bonds Payable.. 300,000
         Discount on Bonds Payable 6,000
         Cash... 292,000
         Gain on Retirement of Bonds Payable.............. 2,000

   d. Bonds Payable.. 288,000
       Discount on Bonds Payable 12,000
         Gain on Retirement of Bonds Payable.............. 8,000
         Cash... 292,000

7. An advantage of financing operations with debt versus stock is *(pp. 776–777)*
   a. The tax deductibility of interest expense on debt
   b. The legal requirement to pay interest and principal
   c. Lower interest payments compared to dividend payments
   d. All of the above

8. In a capital lease, the lessee records *(pp. 777–779)*
   a. A leased asset and a lease liability   c. Interest on the lease liability
   b. Depreciation on the leased asset   d. All of the above

9. Which of the following is an example of off-balance-sheet financing? *(p. 779)*
   a. Operating lease   c. Debenture bonds
   b. Current portion of long-term debt   d. Convertible bonds

10. A corporation's defined benefit pension plan has accumulated benefit obligations of $830,000 and assets that are worth $790,000. What will this company report for its pension plan? *(p. 780)*
    a. Accumulated benefit obligation of $830,000
    b. Note disclosure of the $40,000 excess of accumulated benefit obligation over plan assets
    c. Long-term pension liability of $40,000
    d. The obligation of $830,000 and the assets of $790,000.

Answers to the Self-Study Questions follow the Accounting Vocabulary.

Accounting Vocabulary

Bonds payable *(p. 758)*
Callable bonds *(p. 774)*
Capital lease *(p. 777)*
Contract interest rate *(p. 761)*
Convertible bonds (or notes) *(p. 775)*
Debentures *(p. 759)*

Defined benefit pension plan *(p. 780)*
Defined contribution pension plan *(p. 780)*
Discount *(p. 760)*
Effective interest rate *(p. 761)*
Lease *(p. 777)*
Lessee *(p. 777)*
Lessor *(p. 777)*
Market interest rate *(p. 761)*
Mortgage *(p. 776)*
Off-balance-sheet financing *(p. 779)*
Operating lease *(p. 777)*
Pension *(p. 779)*
Premium *(p. 760)*
Present value *(p. 761)*
Serial bonds *(p. 759)*
Stated interest rate *(p. 761)*
Term bonds *(p. 759)*
Trading on the equity *(p. 777)*
Underwriter *(p. 759)*

Answers to Self-Study Questions

1. c
2. d   [($100,000 \times 1.01875) + $1,100 = $102,975]
3. b
4. a   [($500,000 \times .11) - ($32,000/10) = $51,800]
5. d
6. b
7. a
8. d
9. a
10. c

ASSIGNMENT MATERIAL _____

Questions

1. Identify three ways to finance the operations of a corporation.
2. How do bonds payable differ from a note payable?
3. How does an underwriter assist with the issuance of bonds?
4. Describe how to report serial bonds payable on the balance sheet.
5. Compute the price to the nearest dollar for the following bonds with a face value of $10,000:
   a. $93.00   b. $88.75   c. $101.375 d. $122.50   e. $100.00
6. In which of the following situations will bonds sell at par? at a premium? at a discount?
   a. 9% bonds sold when the market rate is 9%.
   b. 9% bonds sold when the market rate is 10%.
   c. 9% bonds sold when the market rate is 8%.
7. Identify the accounts to debit and credit for transactions (a) to issue bonds at *par*, (b) to pay interest, (c) to accrue interest at year end, and (d) to pay off bonds at maturity.
8. Identify the accounts to debit and credit for transactions (a) to issue bonds at a *discount*, (b) to pay interest, (c) to accrue interest at year end, and (d) to pay off bonds at maturity.
9. Identify the accounts to debit and credit for transactions (a) to issue bonds at a premium, (b) to pay interest, (c) to accrue interest at year end, and (d) to pay off bonds at maturity.

10. Why are bonds sold for a price "plus accrued interest"? What happens to accrued interest when bonds are sold by an individual?

11. How does the straight-line method of amortizing bond discount (or premium) differ from the effective-interest method?

12. A company retires ten-year bonds payable of $100,000 after five years. The business issued the bonds at $104.00 and called them at $103.00. Compute the amount of gain or loss on retirement. How is this gain or loss reported on the income statement?

13. Bonds payable with a maturity value of $100,000 are callable at $102.50. Their market price is $101.25. If you are the issuer of these bonds, how much will you pay to retire them before maturity?

14. Why are convertible bonds attractive to investors? Why are they popular with borrowers?

15. Why would an investor require the borrower to set up a sinking fund?

16. Contrast the effects on a company of issuing bonds versus issuing stock.

17. Identify the accounts a lessee debits and credits when making operating lease payments.

18. What characteristics distinguish a capital lease from an operating lease?

19. A business signs a capital lease for the use of a building. What accounts are debited and credited (a) to begin the lease term and make the first lease payment, (b) to record depreciation, (c) to accrue interest on the lease liability, and (d) to make the second lease payment?

20. Show how a lessee reports on the balance sheet any leased equipment and the related lease liability under a capital lease.

21. What is off-balance-sheet financing? Give two examples.

22. Distinguish a defined benefit pension plan from a defined contribution pension plan. What must be reported for each in the financial statements?

Exercises

Exercise 16-1   *Issuing bonds payable and paying interest   (Obj. 1)*

Electronix, Inc., issues $300,000 of 8 percent, semiannual, 20-year bonds payable that are dated April 30. Record (a) issuance of bonds at par on May 31, and (b) the next semiannual interest payment on October 31.

Exercise 16-2   *Issuing bonds payable, paying and accruing interest, and amortizing discount by the straight-line method   (Obj. 1)*

On February 1, Logistics Ltd. issues 20-year, 7 percent bonds payable with a face value of $1,000,000. The bonds sell at $98.00 and pay interest on January 31 and July 31. Logistics amortizes bond discount by the straight-line method. Record (a) issuance of the bonds on February 1, (b) the semiannual interest payment on July 31, and (c) the interest accrual on December 31.

Exercise 16-3   *Issuing bonds payable, paying and accruing interest, and amortizing premium by the straight-line method   (Obj. 1)*

Armstrong Corp. issues 20-year, 8 percent bonds payable with a face value of $5,000,000 on March 31. The bonds sell at $101.50 and pay interest on March 31 and September 30. Assume Armstrong amortizes bond premium by the straight-line method. Record (a) issuance of the bonds on March 31, (b) payment of interest on September 30, and (c) accrual of interest on December 31.

Exercise 16-4   *Issuing bonds payable between interest dates   (Obj. 1)*

Refer to the data for Armstrong Corp. in Exercise 16-3. If Armstrong issued the bonds payable on June 30, how much cash would Armstrong receive upon issuance of the bonds?

Exercise 16-5 *Preparing an effective-interest amortization table; recording interest payments and the related discount amortization* **(Obj. 2)**

Chang Sports Supplies Inc. is authorized to issue $500,000 of 7 percent, 10-year bonds payable. On January 2, when the market interest rate is 8 percent, the company issues $400,000 of the bonds and receives cash of $372,660. Chang Sports amortizes bond discount by the effective-interest method.

Required

1. Prepare an amortization table for the first four semiannual interest periods. Follow the format of Panel B in Exhibit 16-5.
2. Record the first semiannual interest payment on June 30 and the second payment on December 31.

Exercise 16-6 *Preparing an effective-interest amortization table; recording interest accrual and payment and the related premium amortization* **(Obj. 2)**

On September 30, 1996, the market interest rate is 7 percent. Kapur Inc. issues $300,000 of 8 percent, 20-year sinking-fund bonds at $110.625. The bonds pay interest on March 31 and September 30. Kapur amortizes bond premium by the effective-interest method.

Required

1. Prepare an amortization table for the first four semiannual interest periods. Follow the format of Panel B in Exhibit 16-6.
2. Record issuance of the bonds on September 30, 1996, the accrual of interest at December 31, 1996, and the semiannual interest payment on March 31, 1997.

Exercise 16-7 *Journalizing sinking-fund transactions* **(Obj. 2)**

Kapur Inc. established a sinking fund for the bond issue in Exercise 16-6. Record payment of $8,000 into the sinking fund on March 31, 1997. Also record sinking-fund revenue of $900 on December 31, 1997, and the payment of the bonds at maturity on September 30, 2016. At maturity date the sinking-fund balance was $296,000.

Exercise 16-8 *Debt payment and discount amortization schedule* **(Obj. 2)**

Home Health Surgical Supply issued $600,000 of 8⅜-percent (0.08375), 5-year bonds payable when the market interest rate was 9½ percent (0.095). Home Health pays interest annually at year end. The issue price of the bonds was $574,082.

Required

Create a spreadsheet model to prepare a schedule to amortize the discount on these bonds. Use the effective-interest method of amortization. Round to the nearest dollar, and format your answer as follows:

	A	B	C	D	E	F
1						
2						Bond
3		Interest	Interest	Discount	Discount	Carrying
4	Date	Payment	Expense	Amortization	Balance	Amount
5	1-1-X1				$☐	$574,082
6	12-31-X1	$☐	$☐	$☐		☐
7	12-31-X2					
8	12-31-X3					
9	12-31-X4					
10	12-31-X5					
		600000*.08375	+F5*.095	+C6-B6	600000-F5	-F5-D6

Exercise 16-9   *Recording retirement of bonds payable   (Obj. 3)*

A.J. Singh Ltd. issued $1,000,000 of 8 percent bonds payable at $97.00 on October 1, 19X0. These bonds mature on October 1, 19X8, and are callable at $101.00. Singh pays interest each April 1 and October 1. On October 1, 19X5, when the bonds' market price is $104.00, Singh retires the bonds in the most economical way available.

Required

Record the payment of interest and amortization of bond discount at October 1, 19X5, and the retirement of the bonds on that date. Singh uses the straight-line amortization method.

Exercise 16-10   *Recording conversion of bonds payable   (Obj. 4)*

Hersch Digital Ltd. issued $400,000 of 8½ percent bonds payable on July 1, 19X4, at a price of $98.50. After 5 years, the bonds may be converted into the company's common stock. Each $1,000 face amount of bonds is convertible into 40 shares of common stock. The bonds' term to maturity is 15 years. On December 31, 19X9, bondholders exercised their right to convert the bonds into common stock.

Required

1. What would cause the bondholders to convert their bonds into common stock?
2. Without making journal entries, compute the carrying amount of the bonds payable at December 31, 19X9. Hersch Digital uses the straight-line method to amortize bond premium and discount.
3. All amortization has been recorded properly. Journalize the conversion transaction at December 31, 19X9.

Exercise 16-11   *Recording early retirement and conversion of bonds payable   (Obj. 3, 4)*

Ruland Holdings Inc. reported the following at September 30:

Long-term liabilities		
Convertible bonds payable, 9%,		
8 years to maturity	$200,000	
Discount on bonds payable	6,000	$194,000

Required

1. Record retirement of one half of the bonds on October 1 at the call price of $101.00.
2. Record conversion of one fourth of the bonds into 4,000 shares of Ruland's common stock on October 1.

Exercise 16-12   *Reporting long-term debt and pension liability on the balance sheet   (Obj. 5)*

Consider the following situations:

a. A note to the financial statements of Mapco, Inc., reported (in thousands):

Note 5: Long-Term Debt	
Total	$537,888
Less: Current portion	22,085
Less: Unamortized discount	1,391
Long-term debt	$514,412

Assume that none of the unamortized discount relates to the current portion of long-term debt. Show how Mapco's balance sheet would report these liabilities.

b. El Campo Incorporated's defined benefit pension plan has assets with a market value of $720,000. The plan's accumulated benefit obligation is $840,000. What should El Campo report in the notes to the financial statements?

Exercise 16-13   *Analyzing alternative plans for raising money*   **(Obj. 5)**

Lindblom Diagnostics Corp. is considering two plans for raising $500,000 to expand operations. Plan A is to borrow at 10 percent, and Plan B is to issue 200,000 shares of common stock. Before any new financing, Lindblom has 200,000 shares of common stock outstanding. Management believes the company can use the new funds to earn income of $420,000 per year before interest and taxes. The income tax rate is 30 percent.

Required

Prepare an analysis like Exhibit 16-7 to determine which plan will result in higher earnings per share.

Exercise 16-14   *Journalizing capital lease and operating lease transactions*   **(Obj. 6)**

A capital lease agreement for equipment requires 10 annual payments of $8,000, with the first payment due on January 2, 19X5, the date of the inception of the lease. The present value of the 9 future lease payments at 10 percent is $51,831.

Required

1. Journalize the following lessee transactions:

    19X5
    Jan.   2   Beginning of lease term and first annual payment.
    Dec.   31   Depreciation of equipment.
            31   Interest expense on lease liability.
    19X6
    Jan.   2   Second annual lease payment.

2. Journalize the January 2, 19X5, lease payment if this is an operating lease.

Challenge Exercises

Exercise 16-15   *Analyzing bond transactions*   **(Obj. 1, 2)**

This (partial) advertisement appeared in *The Financial Post*.

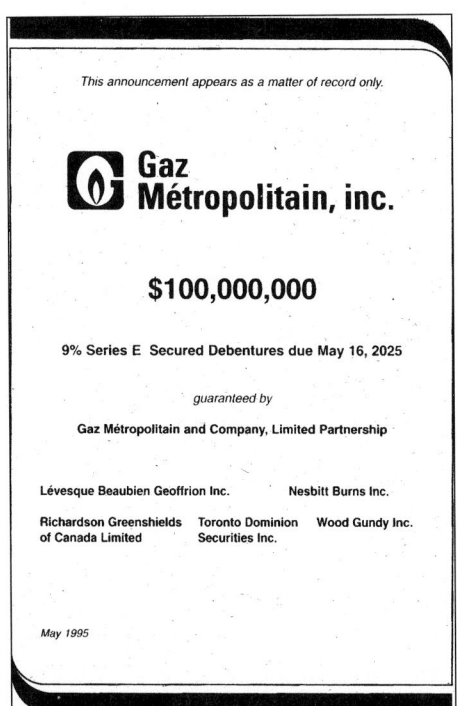

Interest is payable on November 16 and May 16.

Required

Answer these questions:

1. Supposing investors purchased these securities at $98.50 on May 16, 1995. Describe the transaction in detail, indicating who received cash, who paid cash, and how much.

2. Another issue of bonds for $20,000,000 was issued the same day; it bore an interest rate of 12 percent. Why was the rate so much higher for this issue than for Gaz Métropolitan, Inc.?

3. Compute the annual cash interest payment on the bonds.

4. Compute the annual interest expense under the straight-line amortization method.

5. Compute both the first year (from May 16, 1995) and the second year interest expense under the effective-interest amortization method. The market rate at the date of issuance was approximately 9.5 percent.

6. Suppose you purchased $100,000 of these bonds on May 16, 1995. How much cash did you pay? If you had purchased $100,000 of these bonds on May 31, 1995, how much cash would you have paid.

Exercise 16-16   *Accounting for bond transactions*   *(Obj. 1, 2)*

Refer to the real bond situation of Gaz Métropolitan, Inc., in Exercise 16-15. Assume Gaz Métropolitan issued the bonds at a price of $98.50 and that the company uses the effective-interest amortization method. The company's year end is December 31.

Required

Journalize all of Gaz Métropolitan's bond transactions for the period May 16, 1995, through May 16, 1996.

Problems   *(Group A)*

Problem 16-1A   *Journalizing bond transactions (at par) and reporting bonds payable on the balance sheet*   *(Obj. 1)*

The board of directors of Lang Music World Inc. authorizes the issue of $3 million of 7 percent, 10-year bonds payable. The semiannual interest dates are May 31 and November 30. The bonds are issued through an underwriter on June 30, 19X5, at par plus accrued interest.

Required

1. Journalize the following transactions:
   a. Issuance of the bonds on June 30, 19X5.
   b. Payment of interest on November 30, 19X5.
   c. Accrual of interest on December 31, 19X5.
   d. Payment of interest on May 31, 19X6.

2. Check your recorded interest expense for 19X5, using as a model the supplement to the summary problem on pp. 768–769.

3. Report interest payable and bonds payable as they would appear on the Lang Music World Inc. balance sheet at December 31, 19X5.

Problem 16-2A   *Issuing bonds at a discount, amortizing by the straight-line method, and reporting bonds payable on the balance sheet*   *(Obj. 1, 2)*

On March 1, 19X4, K & G Dalgliesh Ltd. issues 8½ percent, 20-year bonds payable with a face value of $500,000. The bonds pay interest on February 28 and August 31. Dalgliesh amortizes premium and discount by the straight-line method.

Required

1. If the market interest rate is 7⅞ percent when Dalgliesh issues its bonds, will the bonds be priced at par, at a premium, or at a discount? Explain.

2. If the market interest rate is 8⅜ percent when Dalgliesh issues its bonds, will the bonds be priced at par, at a premium, or at a discount? Explain.

3. Assume the issue price of the bonds is $96.00. Journalize the following bond transactions:
   a. Issuance of the bonds on March 1, 19X4.
   b. Payment of interest and amortization of discount on August 31, 19X4.
   c. Accrual of interest and amortization of discount on December 31, 19X4, K & G Dalgliesh Ltd.'s year end.
   d. Payment of interest and amortization of discount on February 28, 19X5.

4. Check your recorded interest expense for the year ended February 28, 19X5, using as a model the supplement to the summary problem on pp. 768–769.

5. Report interest payable and bonds payable as they would appear on the Dalgliesh balance sheet at December 31, 19X4.

Problem 16-3A   *Analyzing a company's long-term debt, journalizing its transactions, and reporting the long-term debt on the balance sheet*   **(Obj. 2)**

The notes to Hespler Transport Ltd.'s financial statements recently reported the following data on September 30, year 1 (the end of the fiscal year):

NOTE 4: INDEBTEDNESS
Long-term debt at September 30, year 1 included the following:

6.00% debentures due year 20 with an effective interest rate of 7.66%, net of unamortized discount of $48,152..	$401,848
Other indebtedness with an interest rate of 8.30%, due $12,108 in year 5 and $19,257 in year 6............................	31,365

Assume Hespler amortizes discount by the effective-interest method.

Required

1. Answer the following questions about Hespler's long-term liabilities:
   a. What is the maturity value of the 6 percent debenture bonds?
   b. What are Hespler's annual cash interest payments on the 6 percent debenture bonds?
   c. What is the carrying amount of the 6 percent debenture bonds at September 30, year 1?

2. Prepare an amortization table through September 30, year 4 for the 6 percent debenture bonds. Round all amounts to the nearest dollar, and assume Hespler pays interest annually on September 30.

3. Record the September 30, year 3 and year 4 interest payments on the 6 percent debenture bonds.

4. There is no premium or discount on the other indebtedness. Assuming annual interest is paid on September 30 each year, record Hespler's September 30, year 2 interest payment on the other indebtedness. Round interest to the nearest dollar.

5. Show how Hespler would report the debenture bonds payable and other indebtedness of September 30, year 4.

Problem 16-4A   *Issuing convertible bonds at a premium, amortizing by the effective-interest method, retiring bonds early, converting bonds, and reporting the bonds payable on the balance sheet*   **(Obj. 2, 3, 4)**

On December 31, 19X1, Brandon Disposal Corp. issues 9 percent, 10-year convertible bonds with a maturity value of $300,000. The semiannual interest dates are June 30

and December 31. The market interest rate is 8 percent, and the issue price of the bonds is $106.00 Brandon Disposal amortizes bond premium and discount by the effective-interest method.

Required

1. Prepare an effective-interest method amortization table for the first four semi-annual interest periods.

2. Journalize the following transactions:
   a. Issuance of the bonds on December 31, 19X1. Credit Convertible Bonds Payable.
   b. Payment of interest on June 30, 19X2.
   c. Payment of interest on December 31, 19X2.
   d. Retirement of bonds with face value of $100,000 on July 1, 19X3. Brandon pays the call price of $102.00.
   e. Conversion by the bondholders on July 1, 19X3, of bonds with face value of $150,000 into 10,000 shares of Brandon common stock.

3. Prepare the balance sheet presentation of the bonds payable that are outstanding at December 31, 19X3.

Problem 16-5A *Journalizing bonds payable and capital lease transactions* *(Obj. 1, 6)*

Journalize the following transactions of Jasper Forest Products Ltd.:

19X4
Jan. 1 Issued $500,000 of 8 percent, 10-year bonds payable at $97.00.
1 Signed a 5-year capital lease on equipment. The agreement requires annual lease payments of $20,000, with the first payment due immediately. At 12 percent, the present value of the four future lease payments is $60,750.
July 1 Paid semiannual interest and amortized discount by the straight-line method on our 8 percent bonds payable.
Dec. 31 Accrued semiannual interest expense, and amortized discount by the straight-line method on our 8 percent bonds payable.
31 Recorded depreciation on leased equipment.
31 Accrued interest expense on the lease liability.
31 Recorded bond sinking-fund earnings of $1,000.
19X14
Jan. 1 Paid the 8 percent bonds at maturity from the sinking fund and received excess cash of $7,800.

Problem 16-6A *Financing operations with debt instead of with stock* *(Obj. 5)*

Two businesses must consider how to raise $10 million.

Truro Corporation is in the midst of its most successful period since it began operations in 1952. For each of the past 10 years, net income and earnings per share have increased by 15 percent. The outlook for the future is equally bright, with new markets opening up and competitors unable to manufacture products of Truro's quality. Truro Corporation is planning a large-scale expansion.

Scotia Limited has fallen on hard times. Net income has remained flat for five of the last six years, even falling by 10 percent from last year's level of profits. Top management has experienced unusual turnover, and the company lacks strong leadership. To become competitive again, Scotia Limited desperately needs $10 million for expansion.

Required

1. Propose a plan for each company to raise the needed cash. Which company should borrow? Which company should issue stock? Consider the advantages and

disadvantages of raising money by borrowing and by issuing stock, and discuss them in your answer.

2. How will what you have learned help you manage a business?

Problem 16-7A   *Reporting liabilities on the balance sheet   (Obj. 6)*

The accounting records of Prairie Outfitters Ltd. include the following items:

Bond sinking fund................	$ 80,000	Mortgage note payable,	
Bonds payable, long-term ...	180,000	long-term..........................	$ 67,000
Premium on bonds		Building acquired under	
payable.............................	6,000	capital lease.....................	200,000
Interest payable.....................	9,200	Interest expense...................	47,000
Interest revenue	5,300	Bonds payable,	
Capital lease liability,		current portion	60,000
long-term..........................	73,000	Accumulated depreciation,	
		building	108,000

Required

Show how these items would be reported on the Prairie Outfitters balance sheet, including headings for current liabilities, long-term liabilities, and so on. Note disclosures are not required.

Problem 16-8A   *Amortizing bond discount and premium by the effective-interest method; retirement of bonds; conversion of bonds   (Obj. 2, 3, 4)*

The Quickrite Software Company is authorized to issue $10,000,000, 10-year, 8 percent (4 percent semiannually) convertible bonds payable with interest payable on June 30th and December 31st. The bonds are convertible on the basis of 50 shares of common stock (no par value) for each $1,000 bond. The following transactions took place with regard to the bonds:

19X1

Jan.   1   Sold bonds with $5,000,000 face value. The market rate of interest on this date was 10 percent (5 percent semiannually) and the bonds therefore had a present value of $4,377,400.

June 30   Paid the interest and amortized the discount using the effective interest rate method.

Dec. 31   Paid the interest and amortized the discount using the effective interest rate method.

19X2

April 1   Sold $1,000,000 (face value) of bonds payable at a rate of 102 (including accrued interest). The market rate of interest on this date was 8 percent.

June 30   Paid the interest and amortized the discount using the effective interest rate method.

July   1   Retired $3,000,000 (face value) of the bonds issued on January 1, 19X1, at a rate of 96.

July   1   Bondholders converted $1,000,000 (face value) of bonds issued on January 1, 19X1, for 50,000 shares of common stock.

Required

Round all amounts to the nearest whole dollar.

1. Journalize the transactions.
2. Show the balance sheet presentation of the bonds payable on July 1, 19X2.

Problem 16-9A   *Amortizing bond discount and premium by the effective-interest method; accounting for lease transactions   (Obj. 2, 6)*

The Moonlife Research Company had the following information available on bonds payable outstanding as of December 31, 19X1:

- $5,000,000—Bonds Payable, 12 percent (6 percent semiannually), interest paid on April 1st and October 1st. The bonds had been sold when the market rate of interest was 10 percent.
- $300,000—Premium on Bonds Payable

The following transactions took place after December 31, 19X1:

19X2

Jan.   1   Moonlife signed a lease to rent a building for expansion of their operations. The lease is 5 years, with an option to renew, and calls for annual payments of $20,000 per year payable on January 1st. Moonlife gave a cheque for the first year upon signing the contract. The future payments on the lease have a present value (at 10 percent) of $63,400.

Jan.   1   Moonlife signed a lease for equipment. The lease is for 10 years with payments of $10,000 per year payable on January 1st (first year's payment was made at the signing). At the end of the lease the equipment will become the property of Moonlife; they expect to sell it at that time and estimate the salvage value to be $5,000. The future payments on the lease have a present value (at 10 percent) of $57,590.

April 1   Paid the interest on the bonds payable and amortized the premium using the effective-interest rate method.

Oct.   1   Paid the interest on the bonds payable and amortized the premium using the effective-interest rate method.

Dec. 31   Recorded any adjustments required at the end of the year with regard to the bonds payable and the lease(s).

19X3

Jan.   1   Made the annual payments on the leases.

April 1   Paid the interest on the bonds payable and amortized the premium using the effective-interest rate method.

Oct.   1   Paid the interest on the bonds payable and amortized the premium using the effective-interest rate method.

Dec. 31   Recorded any adjustments required at the end of the year with regard to the bonds payable and the lease(s).

Required

Round all amounts to the nearest whole dollar.

1. Prepare the general journal entries required to record the transactions of 19X2 and 19X3.
2. Show the liability section of the balance sheet on December 31, 19X3.

(Group B)

Problem 16-1B   *Journalizing bond transactions (at par) and reporting bonds payable on the balance sheet   (Obj. 1)*

The board of directors of Shoes by Schultz Ltd. authorizes the issue of $2 million of 8 percent, 20-year bonds payable. The semiannual dates are March 31 and September 30. The bonds are issued through an underwriter on April 30, 19X7, at par plus accrued interest. Shoes by Schultz's year end is December 31.

Required

1. Journalize the following transactions:
   a. Issuance of the bonds on April 30, 19X7.
   b. Payment of interest on September 30, 19X7.
   c. Accrual of interest on December 31, 19X7.
   d. Payment of interest on March 31, 19X8.

2. Check your recorded interest expense for 19X7, using as a model the supplement to the summary problem on pp. 768–769.

3. Report interest payable and bonds payable as they would appear on the Shoes by Schultz Ltd. balance sheet at December 31, 19X7.

Problem 16-2B   *Issuing notes at a premium, amortizing by the straight-line method, and reporting notes payable on the balance sheet*   **(Obj. 1)**

On March 1, 19X6, Hi-Tech Recording Studio Ltd. issues 7¾ percent, 10-year notes payable with a face value of $300,000. The notes pay interest on February 28 and August 31, and Hi-Tech amortizes premium and discount by the straight-line method.

Required

1. If the market interest rate is 8½ percent when Hi-Tech issues its notes, will the notes be priced at par, at a premium, or at a discount? Explain.

2. If the market interest rate is 7 percent when Hi-Tech issues its notes, will the notes be priced at par, at a premium, or at a discount? Explain.

3. Assume the issue price of the notes is $101.00. Journalize the following note payable transactions:
   a. Issuance of the notes on March 1, 19X6.
   b. Payment of interest and amortization of premium on August 31, 19X6.
   c. Accrual of interest and amortization of premium on December 31, 19X6.
   d. Payment of interest and amortization of premium on February 28, 19X7.

4. Check your recorded interest expense for the year ended February 28, 19X7, using as a model the supplement to the summary problem on pp. 768–769.

5. Report interest payable and notes payable as they would appear on the Hi-Tech balance sheet at December 31, 19X6.

Problem 16-3B   *Analyzing a company's long-term debt, journalizing its transactions, and reporting the long-term debt on the balance sheet*   **(Obj. 2)**

Assume that the notes to Regina Transport Ltd.'s financial statements reported the following data on September 30, year 1 (the end of the fiscal year):

NOTE E: LONG-TERM DEBT

5% debentures due year 20, net of unamortized discount of $31,645 (effective-interest rate of 7.5%)	$119,855
Notes payable, interest of 8.67%, due in annual amounts of $22,840 in years 5 through 16...	274,080

Regina Transport amortizes discount by the effective-interest method.

Required

1. Answer the following questions about Regina Transport's long-term liabilities:
   a. What is the maturity value of the 5 percent debenture bonds?
   b. What are Regina Transport's annual cash interest payments on the 5 percent debenture bonds?
   c. What is the carrying amount of the 5 percent debenture bonds at September 30, year 1?

2. Prepare an amortization table through September 30, year 4 for the 5 percent debenture bonds. Round all amounts to the nearest dollar and assume Regina Transport pays interest annually on September 30.

3. Record the September 30, year 3 and year 4 interest payments on the 5 percent debenture bonds.

4. There is no premium or discount on the notes payable. Assuming annual interest is paid on September 30 each year, record Regina Transport's September 30, year 2, interest payment on the notes payable. Round interest to the nearest dollar.

5. Show how Regina Transport would report the debenture bonds payable and notes payable at September 30, year 4.

Problem 16-4B   *Issuing convertible bonds at a discount, amortizing by the effective-interest method, retiring bonds early, converting bonds, and reporting the bonds payable on the balance sheet*   *(Obj. 2, 3, 4)*

On December 31, 19X1, Yang Credit Corp. issues 8 percent, 10-year convertible bonds with a maturity value of $500,000. The semiannual interest dates are June 30 and December 31. The market interest rate is 9 percent, and the issue price of the bonds is $94.00. Yang Credit Corp amortizes bond premium and discount by the effective-interest method.

Required

1. Prepare an effective-interest method amortization table for the first four semi-annual interest periods.

2. Journalize the following transactions:
   a. Issuance of the bonds on December 31, 19X1. Credit Convertible Bonds Payable.
   b. Payment of interest on June 30, 19X2.
   c. Payment of interest on December 31, 19X2.
   d. Retirement of bonds with face value of $100,000 on July 1, 19X3. Yang Credit Corp. purchases the bonds at $96.00 in the open market.
   e. Conversion by the bondholders on July 1, 19X3, of bonds with face value of $200,000 into 50,000 shares of Yang Credit Corp. common stock.

3. Prepare the balance sheet presentation of the bonds payable that are outstanding at December 31, 19X3.

Problem 16-5B   *Journalizing bonds payable and capital lease transactions*   *(Obj. 1, 6)*

Journalize the following transactions of Roger Laminating Inc.:

19X1

Jan.   1   Issued $2,000,000 of 8 percent, 10-year bonds payable at $97.00.

  1   Signed a 5-year capital lease on machinery. The agreement requires annual lease payments of $16,000, with the first payment due immediately. At 12 percent, the present value of the four future lease payments is $48,590.

July   1   Paid semiannual interest and amortized discount by the straight-line method on our 8 percent bonds payable.

Dec. 31   Accrued semiannual interest expense and amortized discount by the straight-line method on our 8 percent bonds payable.

  31   Recorded depreciation on leased machinery.

  31   Accrued interest expense on the lease liability.

19X11

Jan.   1   Paid the 8 percent bonds at maturity.

Problem 16-6B   *Financing operations with debt or with stock*   *(Obj. 5)*

Marketing studies have shown that consumers prefer upscale stores, and recent trends in industry sales have supported the research. To capitalize on this trend, Visual Image Inc. is embarking on a massive expansion. Plans call for opening 10 new stores within the next 18 months. Each store is scheduled to be 30 percent larger than the company's existing stores, furnished more elaborately, and stocked with more expensive merchandise. Management estimates that company operations will provide $2 million of the cash needed for expansion. Visual Image must raise the remaining $1.5 million from outsiders. The board of directors is considering obtaining the $1.5 million either through borrowing or by issuing common stock.

Required

1. Discuss for company management the advantages and disadvantages of borrowing and of issuing common stock to raise the needed cash. Which method of raising the funds would you recommend?
2. How will what you have learned in this problem help you manage a business?

Problem 16-7B   *Reporting liabilities on the balance sheet*   *(Obj. 6)*

The accounting records of Martel Sales Corp. include the following items:

Bonds payable, current portion	$ 75,000		Mortgage note payable, long-term	$ 82,000
Capital lease liability, long-term	54,000		Accumulated depreciation, equipment	46,000
Discount on bonds payable	7,000		Capital lease liability, current	18,000
Interest revenue	5,000		Mortgage note payable, current	23,000
Equipment acquired under capital lease	137,000		Bonds payable, long-term	300,000
Interest payable	13,000			
Interest expense	57,000			

Required

Show how these items would be reported on the Martel Sales balance sheet, including headings for current liabilities, long-term liabilities, and so on. Note disclosures are not required.

Problem 16-8B   *Amortizing bond discount and premium by the effective-interest method; retirement of bonds; conversion of bonds*   *(Obj. 2, 3, 4)*

The Futura Programs Company is authorized to issue $10,000,000, 10-year, 10 percent (5 percent semiannually) convertible bonds payable with interest payable on June 30th and December 31st. The bonds are convertible on the basis of 60 shares of common stock (no par value) for each $1,000 bond. The following transactions took place with regard to the bonds:

19X1

Jan.   1   Sold bonds with $6,000,000 face value. The market rate of interest on this date was 8 percent (4 percent semiannually) and the bonds therefore had a present value of $6,813,000.

June 30   Paid the interest and amortized the premium using the effective interest rate method.

Dec. 31   Paid the interest and amortized the premium using the effective interest rate method.

19X2

April   1   Sold $2,000,000 (face value) of bonds payable at a rate of 102.5 (including accrued interest). The market rate of interest on this date was 10 percent.

June   30   Paid the interest and amortized the premium using the effective interest rate method.

July   1   Retired $3,000,000 (face value) of the bonds issued on January 1, 19X1, at a rate of 101.

July   1   Bondholders converted $2,000,000 (face value) of bonds issued on January 1, 19X1, for 120,000 shares of common stock.

Required

Round all amounts to the nearest whole dollar.

1. Journalize the transactions.
2. Show the balance sheet presentation of the bonds payable on July 1, 19X2.

Problem 16-9B   *Amortizing bond discount and premium by the effective-interest method; accounting for lease transactions   (Obj. 2, 6)*

The Starlife Research Company had the following information available on bonds payable outstanding as of December 31, 19X1:

* $6,000,000—Bonds Payable, 10 percent (5 percent semiannually), interest paid on April 1st and October 1st. The bonds had been sold when the market rate of interest was 12 percent.
* $300,000—Discount on Bonds Payable

The following transactions took place after December 31, 19X1:

19X2

Jan.   1   Starlife signed a lease to rent a building for expansion of their operations. The lease is 6 years, with an option to renew, and calls for annual payments of $15,000 per year payable on January 1st. Starlife gave a cheque for the first year upon signing the lease. The future payments on the lease have a present value (at 10 percent) of $56,865.

Jan.   1   Starlife signed a lease for equipment. The lease is for 10 years with payments of $20,000 per year payable on January 1st (first year's payment was made at the signing). At the end of the lease the equipment will become the property of Starlife; they expect to sell it at that time and estimate the salvage value to be $10,000. The future payments on the lease have a present value (at 10 percent) of $115,180.

April   1   Paid the interest on the bonds payable and amortized the discount using the effective-interest rate method.

Oct.   1   Paid the interest on the bonds payable and amortized the discount using the effective-interest rate method.

Dec.   31   Recorded any adjustments required at the end of the year with regard to the bonds payable and the lease(s).

19X3

Jan.   1   Made the annual payments on the leases.

April   1   Paid the interest on the bonds payable and amortized the discount using the effective-interest rate method.

Oct.   1   Paid the interest on the bonds payable and amortized the discount using the effective-interest rate method.

Dec.   31   Recorded any adjustments required at the end of the year with regard to the bonds payable and the lease(s).

Required

Round all amounts to the nearest whole dollar.

1. Prepare the general journal entries required to record the transactions of 19X2 and 19X3.

2. Show the liability section of the balance sheet on December 31, 19X3.

Challenge Problems

Problem 16-1C   *Understanding present value*   *(Obj. A3, A4)*

A friend tells you that she always buys bonds that are at a discount because "You always get more than you paid when the bond matures."

Required

Discuss your friend's understanding of present value.

Problem 16-2C   *Evaluating alternative methods of financing growth*   *(Obj. 5)*

You have just inherited $1,000 and have decided to buy stock. You have narrowed your choice down to CanLog Logistics Inc. and HiWat Systems Ltd. You carefully read each company's annual report to determine which company's stock you should buy. Your research indicates that the two companies are very similar. CanLog's annual report states "The Company has financed its growth through long- and short-term borrowing," while the HiWat report contains the statement "Your Company has financed its growth out of earnings retained in the business."

CanLog's shares are trading at $25.00 while HiWat's shares are trading at $13.00. You wonder if that is because CanLog has been paying an annual dividend of $2.00 per share while HiWat has been paying a dividend of $1.10.

You recall that the morning newspaper had an article about the economy which predicted that interest rates were expected to rise and stay at a much higher rate than at present for the next two to three years.

Required

Explain which stock you would buy and indicate why you have selected it.

Extending Your Knowledge

Decision Problems

1. *Analyzing alternative ways of raising $5 million (Obj. 6)*

Business is going well for Duck Lake Forest Products, Inc. The board of directors of this family-owned company believes that Duck Lake Forest Products could earn an additional $1,500,000 in income before interest and taxes by expanding into new markets. However, the $5,000,000 that the business needs for growth cannot be raised within the family. The directors, who strongly wish to retain family control of Duck Lake Forest Products, must consider issuing securities to outsiders. They are considering three financing plans.

Plan A is to borrow at 9 percent. Plan B is to issue 100,000 shares of common stock. Plan C is to issue 100,000 shares of nonvoting, $3.75 cumulative preferred stock. The company presently has net income before tax of $6,000,000 and has 500,000 shares of common stock outstanding. The income tax rate is 30 percent.

Required

1. Prepare an analysis similar to Exhibit 16-7 to determine which plan will result in the highest earnings per share of common stock.
2. Recommend one plan to the board of directors. Give your reasons.

2. Questions about long-term debt (Obj. 6 and Appendix)

The following questions are not related.

a. Why do you think corporations prefer operating leases over capital leases? How do you think a shareholder would view an operating lease?
b. Companies like to borrow for longer terms when interest rates are low, and for shorter terms when interest rates are high. Why is this statement true?
c. If you were to win $2,000,000 from Lotto 649, you would receive the $2,000,000, whereas if you were to win $2,000,000 in one of the U.S. lotteries, you would receive 20 annual payments of $100,000. Are the prizes equivalent? If not, why not?

Ethical Issue

Ling-Temco-Vought, Inc. (LTV), manufacturer of aircraft and related electronic devices, borrowed heavily during the 1960s to exploit the advantage of financing operations with debt. At first, LTV was able to earn operating income much higher than its interest expense and was therefore quite profitable. However, when the business cycle turned down, LTV's debt burden pushed the company to the brink of bankruptcy. Operating income was less than interest expense.

Required

Is it unethical for managers to saddle a company with a high level of debt? Or is it just risky? Who could be hurt by a company's taking on too much debt? Discuss.

Financial Statement Problems

1. Long-term debt (Obj. 1, 3)

The Mark's Work Warehouse Ltd. income statement, balance sheet, and statement of changes in financial position in Appendix A provide details about the company's long-term debt. Use the data to answer the following questions.

1. How much cash did Mark's borrow on long-term debt during the year ended January 29, 1994? How much long-term debt did Mark's repay during the year?
2. Journalize in a single entry Mark's interest expense or long-term debt for the year ended January 29, 1994. Assume that Mark's paid 90 percent of the interest expense and accrued the remainder at year end.
3. Mark's balance sheet shows no bank indebtedness yet the income statement shows short-term interest. Why do you think this is the case?
4. Examine the statement of changes in financial position (called the statement of cash flow). Journalize the transactions affecting long-term debt.
5. Does the company have any convertible debt outstanding? If so, how many shares will the company have to issue if the debt is converted?

2. Long-term debt (Obj. 1, 3)

Obtain the annual report of an actual company of your choosing. Answer these questions about the company. Concentrate on the current year in the annual report you select.

1. Examine the statement of changes in financial position. How much long-term debt did the company pay off during the current year? How much new long-term

debt did the company incur during the year? Journalize these transactions using the company's actual account balances.

2. Prepare a T-account for the Long-Term Debt account to show the beginning and ending balances and all activity in the account during the year. If there is a discrepancy, insert this amount in the appropriate place. Do not expect to be able to explain all details in real financial statements!

3. Study the notes to the financial statements. Is any of the company's retained earnings balance restricted as a result of borrowings? If so, indicate the amount of the retained earnings balance that is restricted and the amount that is unrestricted. How will the restriction affect the company's dividend payments in the future?

4. Journalize in a single entry the company's interest expense for the current year. If the company discloses the amount of amortization of premium or discount on long-term debt, use the real figures. If not, assume the amortization of discount totaled $700,000 for the year.

Appendix

Time Value of Money: Future Value and Present Value

The following discussion of future value lays the foundation for present value but is not essential. For the valuation of long-term liabilities, some instructors may wish to begin on page 805.

The term *time value of money* refers to the fact that money earns interest over time. Interest is the cost of using money. To borrowers, interest is the expense of renting money. To lenders, interest is the revenue earned from lending. When funds are used for a period of time, we must recognize the interest. Otherwise we overlook an important part of the transaction. Suppose you invest $4,545 in corporate bonds that pay 10-percent interest each year. After one year, the value of your investment has grown to $5,000. The difference between your original investment ($4,545) and the future value of the investment ($5,000) is the amount of interest revenue you will earn during the year ($455). If you ignored the interest, you would fail to account for the interest revenue you have earned. Interest becomes more important as the time period lengthens because the amount of interest depends on the span of time the money is invested.

Let's consider a second example, but from the borrower's perspective. Suppose you purchase a machine for your business. The cash price of the machine is $8,000, but you cannot pay cash now. To finance the purchase, you sign an $8,000 note payable. The note requires you to pay the $8,000 plus 10-percent interest one year from date of purchase. Is your cost of the machine $8,000, or is it $8,800 [$8,000 plus interest of $800 ($8,0000 × 0.10)]? The cost is $8,000. The additional $800 is interest expense and not part of the cost of the machine. If you ignored the interest, you would overstate the cost of the machine and understate the amount of interest expense.

Future Value _____

OBJECTIVE A1
Compute the future value of an Investment made in a single amount

The main application of future value is the accumulated balance of an investment at a future date. In our first example above, the investment earned 10 percent per year. After one year, $4,545 grew to $5,000, as shown in Exhibit 16A-1. If the money were invested for five years, you would have to perform five such calculations. You would also have to consider the compound interest that your investment is earning. Compound interest is the interest you earn not only on your principal amount but also on the interest you receive on the interest you have already earned. Most business applications include compound interest. The table on the next page shows the interest revenue earned each year at 10 percent:

EXHIBIT 16A-1   *Future Value*

Present Value		Future Value
Time 0	roll forward (accumulate)	1 year
$4,545		$5,000

Present value × (1 + interest rate) = Future value

$4,545   ×   1.10   = $5,000

End of Year	Interest	Future Value
0	—	$4,545
1	$4,545 × 0.10 = $455	5,000
2	5,000 × 0.10 = 500	5,500
3	5,500 × 0.10 = 550	6,050
4	6,050 × 0.10 = 605	6,655
5	6,655 × 0.10 = 666	7,321

Earning 10 percent, a $4,545 investment grows to $5,000 at the end of one year, to $5,500 at the end of two years, and so on. Throughout this discussion we round off to the nearest dollar.

Future Value Tables

The process of computing a future value is called *accumulating* because the future value is *more* than the present value. Mathematical tables ease the computational burden. Exhibit 16A-2, Future Value of $1, gives the future value for a single sum (a present value), $1, invested to earn a particular interest rate for a specific number of periods. Future value depends on three factors: (1) the amount of the investment, (2) the length of time between investment and future accumulation, and (3) the interest rate.

EXHIBIT 16A-2   *Future Value of $1*

Future Value of $1

Periods	4%	5%	6%	7%	8%	9%	10%	12%	14%	16%
1	1.040	1.050	1.060	1.070	1.080	1.090	1.100	1.120	1.140	1.160
2	1.082	1.103	1.124	1.145	1.166	1.188	1.210	1.254	1.300	1.346
3	1.125	1.158	1.191	1.225	1.260	1.295	1.331	1.405	1.482	1.561
4	1.170	1.216	1.262	1.311	1.360	1.412	1.464	1.574	1.689	1.811
5	1.217	1.276	1.338	1.403	1.469	1.539	1.611	1.762	1.925	2.100
6	1.265	1.340	1.419	1.501	1.587	1.677	1.772	1.974	2.195	2.436
7	1.316	1.407	1.504	1.606	1.714	1.828	1.949	2.211	2.502	2.826
8	1.369	1.477	1.594	1.718	1.851	1.993	2.144	2.476	2.853	3.278
9	1.423	1.551	1.689	1.838	1.999	2.172	2.358	2.773	3.252	3.803
10	1.480	1.629	1.791	1.967	2.159	2.367	2.594	3.106	3.707	4.411
11	1.539	1.710	1.898	2.105	2.332	2.580	2.853	3.479	4.226	5.117
12	1.601	1.796	2.012	2.252	2.518	2.813	3.138	3.896	4.818	5.939
13	1.665	1.886	2.133	2.410	2.720	3.066	3.452	4.363	5.492	6.886
14	1.732	1.980	2.261	2.579	2.937	3.342	3.797	4.887	6.261	7.988
15	1.801	2.079	2.397	2.759	3.172	3.642	4.177	5.474	7.138	9.266
16	1.873	2.183	2.540	2.952	3.426	3.970	4.595	6.130	8.137	10.748
17	1.948	2.292	2.693	3.159	3.700	4.328	5.054	6.866	9.276	12.468
18	2.026	2.407	2.854	3.380	3.996	4.717	5.560	7.690	10.575	14.463
19	2.107	2.527	3.026	3.617	4.316	5.142	6.116	8.613	12.056	16.777
20	2.191	2.653	3.207	3.870	4.661	5.604	6.727	9.646	13.743	19.461

The heading in Exhibit 16A-2 states $1. Future value tables and present value tables are based on $1 because unity (the value 1) is so easy to work with. Observe the Periods column and the interest rate columns 4% through 16%. In business applications interest rates are always stated for the annual period of one year unless specified otherwise. In fact, an interest rate can be stated for any period, such as 3 percent per quarter or 5 percent for a six-month period. The length of the period is arbitrary. For example, an investment may promise a return (income) of 3 percent per quarter for six months (two quarters). In that case you would be working with 3-percent interest for two periods. It would be incorrect to use 6 percent for one period because the interest is 3 percent compounded quarterly, and that amount differs somewhat from 6 percent compounded semiannually. Take care in studying future value and present value problems to align the interest rate with the appropriate number of periods.

Let's use Exhibit 16A-2. The future value of $1.00 invested at 8 percent for one year is $1.08 ($1.00 × 1.080, which appears at the junction under the 8% column and across from 1 in the Periods column). The figure 1.080 includes both the principal (1.000) and the compound interest for one period (0.080).

Suppose you deposit $5,000 in a savings account that pays annual interest of 8 percent. The account balance at the end of the year will be $5,400. To compute the future value of $5,000 at 8 percent for one year, multiply $5,000 by 1.080 to get $5,400. Now suppose you invest in a 10-year, 8-percent certificate of deposit (CD). What will be the future value of the CD at maturity? To compute the future value of $5,000 at 8 percent for 10 periods, multiply $5,000 by 2.159 (from Exhibit 16A-2) to get $10,795. This future value of $10,795 indicates that $5,000 earning 8-percent interest compounded annually, grows to $10,795 at the end of 10 years. In this way you can find any present amount's future value at a particular future date. Future value is especially helpful for computing the amount of cash you will have on hand for some purpose in the future.

Future Value of an Annuity

OBJECTIVE A2

Compute the future value of an annuity-type investment

In the preceding example, we made an investment of a single amount. Other investments, called annuities, include multiple investments of an equal periodic amount at fixed intervals over the duration of the investment. Consider a family investing for a child's education. The Dietrichs can invest $4,000 annually to accumulate a college fund for 15-year-old Helen. The investment can earn 7 percent annually until Helen turns 18—a three-year investment. How much will be available for Helen on the date of the last investment? Exhibit 16A-3 shows the accumulation—a total future value of $12,860.

The first $4,000 invested by the Dietrichs grows to $4,580 over the investment period. The second amount grows to $4,280, and the third amount stays at $4,000 because it has no time to earn interest. The sum of the three future values ($4,580 + $4,280 + $4,000) is the future value of the annuity ($12,860), which can be computed as follows:

EXHIBIT 16A-3   *Future Value of an Annuity*

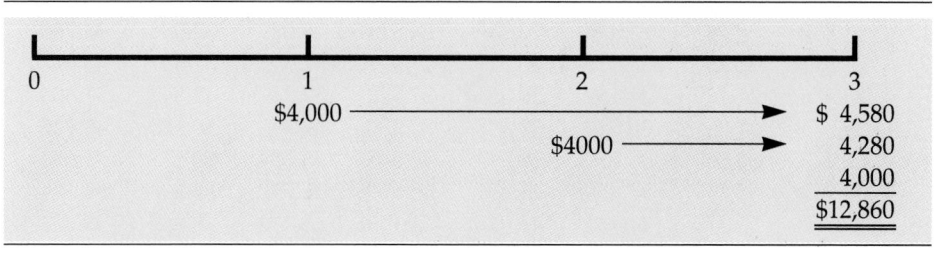

End of Year	Annual Investment	Interest	Increase for the Year	Future Value of Annuity
0	—	—	—	0
1	$4,000	—	$4,000	$4,000
2	4,000 + ($4,000 × 0.07 = $280) =		4,280	8,280
3	4,000 + ($8,280 × 0.07 = $580) =		4,580	12,860

These computations are laborious. As with the Future Value of $1 (a lump sum), mathematical tables ease the strain of calculating annuities. Exhibit 16A-4, Future Value of Annuity of $1, gives the future value of a series of investments, each of equal amount, at regular intervals.

What is the future value of an annuity of three investments of $1 each that earn 7 percent? The answer 3.215 can be found in the 7% column and across from 3 in the Periods column of Exhibit 16A-4. This amount can be used to compute the future value of the investment for Helen's education, as follows:

Amount of each periodic investment	×	Future value of annuity of $1 (Exhibit 16A-4)	=	Future value of investment
$4,000	×	3.215	=	$12,860

This one-step calculation is much easier than computing the future value of each annual investment and then summing the individual future values. In this way you can compute the future value of any investment consisting of equal periodic amounts at regular intervals. Businesses make periodic investments to accumulate funds for equipment replacement and other uses—an application of the future value of an annuity.

EXHIBIT 16A-4   *Future Value of Annuity of $1*

				Future Value of Annuity of $1						
Periods	4%	5%	6%	7%	8%	9%	10%	12%	14%	16%
1	1.000	1.000	1.000	1.000	1.000	1.000	1.000	1.000	1.000	1.000
2	2.040	2.050	2.060	2.070	2.080	2.090	2.100	2.120	2.140	2.160
3	3.122	3.153	3.184	3.215	3.246	3.278	3.310	3.374	3.440	3.506
4	4.246	4.310	4.375	4.440	4.506	4.573	4.641	4.779	4.921	5.066
5	5.416	5.526	5.637	5.751	5.867	5.985	6.105	6.353	6.610	6.877
6	6.633	6.802	6.975	7.153	7.336	7.523	7.716	8.115	8.536	8.977
7	7.898	8.142	8.394	8.654	8.923	9.200	9.487	10.089	10.730	11.414
8	9.214	9.549	9.897	10.260	10.637	11.028	11.436	12.300	13.233	14.240
9	10.583	11.027	11.491	11.978	12.488	13.021	13.579	14.776	16.085	17.519
10	12.006	12.578	13.181	13.816	14.487	15.193	15.937	17.549	19.337	21.321
11	13.486	14.207	14.972	15.784	16.645	17.560	18.531	20.655	23.045	25.733
12	15.026	15.917	16.870	17.888	18.977	20.141	21.384	24.133	27.271	30.850
13	16.627	17.713	18.882	20.141	21.495	22.953	24.523	28.029	32.089	36.786
14	18.292	19.599	21.015	22.550	24.215	26.019	27.975	32.393	37.581	43.672
15	20.024	21.579	23.276	25.129	27.152	29.361	31.772	37.280	43.842	51.660
16	21.825	23.657	25.673	27.888	30.324	33.003	35.950	42.753	50.980	60.925
17	23.698	25.840	28.213	30.840	33.750	36.974	40.545	48.884	59.118	71.673
18	25.645	28.132	30.906	33.999	37.450	41.301	45.599	55.750	68.394	84.141
19	27.671	30.539	33.760	37.379	41.446	46.018	51.159	63.440	78.969	98.603
20	29.778	33.066	36.786	40.995	45.762	51.160	57.275	72.052	91.025	115.380

Present Value

OBJECTIVE A3

Compute the present value of a single future amount

Often a person knows a future amount and needs to know the related present value. Recall Exhibit 16A-1, in which present value and future value are on opposite ends of the same time line.

Suppose an investment promises to pay you $5,000 at the *end* of one year. How much would you pay *now* to acquire this investment? You would be willing to pay the present value of the $5,000, which is a future amount.

Present value also depends on three factors: (1) the amount of payment (or receipt), (2) the length of time between investment and future receipt (or payment), and (3) the interest rate. The process of computing a present value is called *discounting* because the present value is *less* than the future value.

In our investment example, the future receipt is $5,000. The investment period is one year. Assume that you demand an annual interest rate of 10 percent on your investment. With all three factors specified, you can compute the present value of $5,000 at 10 percent for one year. The computation is

$$\frac{\text{Future value}}{(1 + \text{Interest rate})} = \frac{\$5,000}{1.10} = \$4,545$$

By turning the problem around, we verify the present value computation:

Amount invested (present value)	$4,545
Expected earnings ($4,545 × .10)	455
Amount to be received one year from now (future value)	$5,000

This example illustrates that present value and future value are based on the same equation:

$$\text{Present value} \times (1 + \text{Interest rate}) = \text{Future value}$$

$$\frac{\text{Future value}}{(1 + \text{Interest rate})} = \text{Present value}$$

If the $5,000 is to be received two years from now, you will pay only $4,132 for the investment, as shown in Exhibit 16A-5. By turning the data around, we verify that $4,132 accumulates to $5,000 at 10 percent for two years.

Amount invested (present value)	$4,132
Expected earnings for first year ($4,132 × .10)...........................	413
Amount invested after one year..	4,545
Expected earnings for second year ($4,545 × .10)	455
Amount to be received two years from now (future value)	$5,000

EXHIBIT 16A-5   *Two-Year Investment*

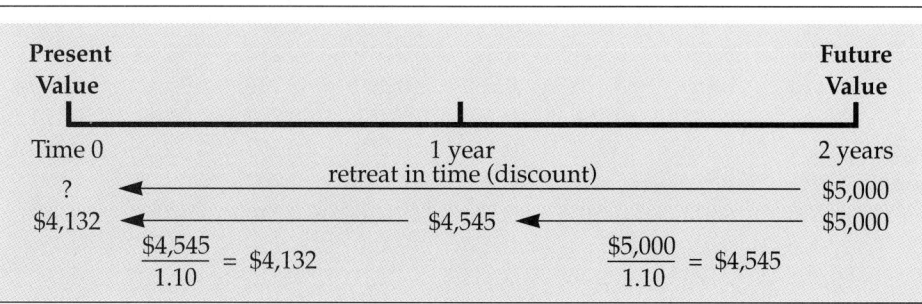

You would pay $4,132—the present value of $5,000—to receive the $5,000 future amount at the end of two years at 10 percent per year. The $868 difference between the amount invested ($4,132) and the amount to be received ($5,000) is the return on the investment, the sum of the two interest receipts: $413 + $455 = $868.

Short Exercise:

Present-Value Tables

What is the present value of $1,000 to be received at the end of 5 years at 10%? **A:** Look in Exhibit 16A-6 at the factor for 5 periods and 10%: 0.621. The present value is: $1,000 × 0.621 = $621. The amount of interest that could be earned over 5 years with an initial investment of $621 is $379 ($1,000 − $621).

We have shown the simple formula for computing present value. However, figuring present value "by hand" for investments spanning many years becomes drawn out. The "number crunching" presents too many opportunities for arithmetical errors. Present-value tables ease our work. Let us re-examine our examples of present value by using Exhibit 16A-6: Present Value of $1.

For the 10 percent investment for one year, we find the junction under 10% and across from 1 in the period column. The table figure of 0.909 is computed as follows: $1/1.10 = 0.909$. This work has been done for us, and only the present values are given in the table. The heading in Exhibit 16A-6 is for $1. To figure present value for $5,000, we multiply 0.909 by $5,000. The result is $4,545, which matches the result we obtained by hand.

For the two-year investment, we read down from 10 percent and across from the period 2 row. We multiply 0.826 (computed as $.90%/1.10 = 0.826$) by $5,000 and get $4,130, which confirms our earlier computation of $4,132 (the difference is due to rounding in the present-value table). Using the table we can compute the present value of any single future amount.

OBJECTIVE A4

Compute the present value of an annuity

Present Value of an Annuity

Return to the investment example beginning on page 805. That investment provided the investor with only a single future receipt ($5,000 at the end of two years). Annuity investments provide multiple receipts of an equal amount at fixed intervals over the investment's duration.

EXHIBIT 16A-6   *Present Value of $1*

Periods	4%	5%	6%	7%	8%	10%	12%	14%	16%
1	0.962	0.952	0.943	0.935	0.926	0.909	0.893	0.877	0.862
2	0.925	0.907	0.890	0.873	0.857	0.826	0.797	0.769	0.743
3	0.889	0.864	0.840	0.816	0.794	0.751	0.712	0.675	0.641
4	0.855	0.823	0.792	0.763	0.735	0.683	0.636	0.592	0.552
5	0.822	0.784	0.747	0.713	0.681	0.621	0.567	0.519	0.476
6	0.790	0.746	0.705	0.666	0.630	0.564	0.507	0.456	0.410
7	0.760	0.711	0.665	0.623	0.583	0.513	0.452	0.400	0.354
8	0.731	0.677	0.627	0.582	0.540	0.467	0.404	0.351	0.305
9	0.703	0.645	0.592	0.544	0.500	0.424	0.361	0.308	0.263
10	0.676	0.614	0.558	0.508	0.463	0.386	0.322	0.270	0.227
11	0.650	0.585	0.527	0.475	0.429	0.350	0.287	0.237	0.195
12	0.625	0.557	0.497	0.444	0.397	0.319	0.257	0.208	0.168
13	0.601	0.530	0.469	0.415	0.368	0.290	0.229	0.182	0.145
14	0.577	0.505	0.442	0.388	0.340	0.263	0.205	0.160	0.125
15	0.555	0.481	0.417	0.362	0.315	0.239	0.183	0.140	0.108
16	0.534	0.458	0.394	0.339	0.292	0.218	0.163	0.123	0.093
17	0.513	0.436	0.371	0.317	0.270	0.198	0.146	0.108	0.080
18	0.494	0.416	0.350	0.296	0.250	0.180	0.130	0.095	0.069
19	0.475	0.396	0.331	0.277	0.232	0.164	0.116	0.083	0.060
20	0.456	0.377	0.312	0.258	0.215	0.149	0.104	0.073	0.051

Consider an investment that promises *annual* cash receipts of $10,000 to be received at the end of each of three years. Assume that you demand a 12 percent return on your investment. What is the investment's present value? What would you pay today to acquire the investment? The investment spans three periods, and you would pay the sum of three present values. The computation is as follows:

Short Exercise:

What is the present value of $1,000 to be received at the end of each of the next five years at 10%? *A:* Look in Exhibit 16A-7 at 5 periods and 10%. The factor is 3.791. The present value of *all five* $1,000 receipts is $1,000 × 3.791 = $3,791.

Year	Annual Cash Receipt	Present Value of $1 at 12% (Exhibit 6A-6)	Present Value of Annual Cash Receipt
1	$10,000	0.893	$ 8,930
2	10,000	0.797	7,970
3	10,000	0.712	7,120
Total present value of investment			$24,020

The present value of this annuity is $24,020. By paying this amount today, you would receive $10,000 at the end of each of three years while earning 12 percent on your investment.

The example illustrates repetitive computations of the three future amounts, a time-consuming process. One way to ease the computational burden is to add the three present values of $1 (0.893 + 0.797 + 0.712) and multiply their sum (2.402) by the annual cash receipt ($10,000) to obtain the present value of the annuity ($10,000 × 2.402 = $24,020).

An easier approach is to use a present value of an annuity table. Exhibit 16A-7 shows the present value of $1 to be received periodically for a given number of periods. The present value of a three-period annuity at 12 percent is 2.402 (the junction of the Period 3 row and the 12 percent column). Thus $10,000 received annually at the end of each of three years, discounted at 12 percent, is $24,020 ($10,000 × 2.402), which is the present value.

EXHIBIT 16A-7   *Present Value of Annuity of $1*

				Present Value of Annuity of $1					
Periods	4%	5%	6%	7%	8%	10%	12%	14%	16%
1	0.962	0.952	0.943	0.935	0.926	0.909	0.893	0.877	0.862
2	1.886	1.859	1.833	1.808	1.783	1.736	1.690	1.647	1.605
3	2.775	2.723	2.673	2.624	2.577	2.487	2.402	2.322	2.246
4	3.630	3.546	3.465	3.387	3.312	3.170	3.037	2.914	2.798
5	4.452	4.329	4.212	4.100	3.993	3.791	3.605	3.433	3.274
6	5.242	5.076	4.917	4.767	4.623	4.355	4.111	3.889	3.685
7	6.002	5.786	5.582	5.389	5.206	4.868	4.564	4.288	4.039
8	6.733	6.463	6.210	5.971	5.747	5.335	4.968	4.639	4.344
9	7.435	7.108	6.802	6.515	6.247	5.759	5.328	4.946	4.607
10	8.111	7.722	7.360	7.024	6.710	6.145	5.650	5.216	4.833
11	8.760	8.306	7.887	7.499	7.139	6.495	5.938	5.453	5.029
12	9.385	8.863	8.384	7.943	7.536	6.814	6.194	5.660	5.197
13	9.986	9.394	8.853	8.358	7.904	7.103	6.424	5.842	5.342
14	10.563	9.899	9.295	8.745	8.244	7.367	6.628	6.002	5.468
15	11.118	10.380	9.712	9.108	8.559	7.606	6.811	6.142	5.575
16	11.652	10.838	10.106	9.447	8.851	7.824	6.974	6.265	5.669
17	12.166	11.274	10.477	9.763	9.122	8.022	7.120	6.373	5.749
18	12.659	11.690	10.828	10.059	9.372	8.201	7.250	6.467	5.818
19	13.134	12.085	11.158	10.336	9.604	8.365	7.366	6.550	5.877
20	13.590	12.462	11.470	10.594	9.818	8.514	7.469	6.623	5.929

Short Exercise:

What is the present value of a $100,000, 12%, 10-year bond priced to yield 14% interest? Interest is paid semiannually.

A:

PV of principal:
$100,000 × 0.258 = $25,800
PV of interest:
$6,000 × 10.594 =   63,564
PV of bond $89,364

The factors are for 20 interest periods, since the 10-year bond pays interest semiannually. The interest rate used to compute the semiannual receipts of cash interest is the bond's stated rate (12%). The interest rate used in the present-value table is the effective rate (14%). How would the issue price of this bond be quoted?

A:

$89,364/$100,000 = 89⅜ approximately.

Present Value of Bonds Payable

The present value of a bond—its market price—is the present value of the future principal amount at maturity plus the present value of the future contract interest payments. The principal is a single amount to be paid at maturity. The interest is an annuity because it occurs periodically.

Let us compute the present value of the 9 percent, five-year bonds of John Labatt. The face value of the bonds is $100,000, and they pay 4½ percent contract (cash) interest semiannually. At issuance the market interest rate is 10 percent, but it is computed at 5 percent semiannually. Therefore, the effective-interest rate for each of the 10 semi-annual periods is 5 percent. We use 5 percent in computing the present value of the maturity and of the interest. The market price of these bonds is $96,149, as follows:

	Effective annual interest rate ÷ 2		Number of semiannual interest payments	
PV of principal				
$100,000 × PV of single amount at 5%		for	10 periods	
($100,000 × .614—Exhibit 16A-6)				$61,400
PV of interest				
($100,000 × .045) × PV of annuity at 5%		for	10 periods	
($4,500 × 7.722—Exhibit 16A-7)				34,749
PV (market price) of bonds................				$96,149

The market price of the John Labatt bonds shows a discount because the contract interest rate on the bonds (9 percent) is less than the market interest rate (10 percent). We discuss these bonds in more detail on p. 769.

Let's consider a premium price for the John Labatt bonds. Assume that the market interest rate is 8 percent at issuance. The effective-interest rate is 4 percent for each of the 10 semiannual periods.

	Effective annual interest rate ÷ 2		Number of semiannual interest payments	
PV of principal				
$100,000 × PV of single amount at 4%		for	10 periods	
($100,000 × .676—Exhibit 16A-6)				$ 67,600
PV of interest				
($100,000 × .045) × PV of annuity at 4%		for	10 periods	
($4,500 × 8.111—Exhibit 16A-7)................				$ 36,500
PV (market price) of bonds................				$104,100

We discuss accounting for these bonds on pp. 769–770.

Capital Leases

OBJECTIVE A5

Determine the cost of an asset acquired through a capital lease

How does a lessee compute the cost of an asset acquired through a capital lease? Consider that the lessee gets the use of the asset but does *not* pay for the leased asset in full at the beginning of the lease. A capital lease is therefore similar to an installment purchase of the leased asset. The lessee must record the leased asset at the present value of the lease liability. The time value of money must be weighed.

The cost of the asset to the lessee is the sum of any payment made at the beginning of the lease period plus the present value of the future lease payments. The lease payments are equal amounts occurring at regular intervals—that is, they are annuity payments.

Consider a 20-year building lease of Finning Ltd., the heavy equipment company. The lease requires 20 annual payments of $10,000 each, with the first payment due immediately. The interest rate in the lease is 10 percent, and the present value of the 19 future payments is $83,650 ($10,000 × PV of annuity at 10 percent for 19 periods, or 8.365 from Exhibit 16A-7). Finning's cost of the building is $93,650 (the sum of the initial payment, $10,000, plus the present value of the future payments, $83,650). The entries for a capital lease are illustrated on pp. 777–778.

Appendix Problems

Problem 16A-1   *Computing the future value of an investment*   **(Obj. A1, A2)**

For each situation, compute the required amount.

a. Langefeld Enterprises Ltd. is budgeting for the acquisition of land over the next several years. Langefeld can invest $300,000 at 9 percent. How much cash will Langefeld have for land acquisitions at the end of five years? At the end of six years?

b. Mercer Associates Inc. is planning to invest $10,000 each year for five years. The company's investment adviser believes that Mercer can earn 6-percent interest without taking on too much risk. What will be the value of Mercer's investment on the date of the last deposit if Mercer can earn 6 percent? If Mercer can earn 8 percent?

Problem 16A-2   *Relating the future and present values of an investment*   **(Obj. A1, A3)**

For each situation, compute the required amount.

a. Bombardier Inc.'s operations are generating excess cash that will be invested in a special fund. During 19X2, Bombardier invests $11,287,000 in the fund for a planned advertising campaign for a new product to be released six years later, in 19X8. If Bombardier investments can earn 10 percent each year, how much cash will the company have for the advertising campaign in 19X8?

b. Bombardier Inc. will need $20 million to advertise a new type of plane in 19X8. How much must Bombardier invest in 19X2 to have the cash available for the advertising campaign? Bombardier investments can earn 10 percent annually.

c. Explain the relationship between your answers (a) and (b).

Problem 16A-3   *Computing the present values of various notes and bonds*   **(Obj. A2, A3)**

Determine the present value of the following notes and bonds:

1. $40,000, five-year note payable with contract interest rate of 11 percent, paid annually. The market interest rate at issuance is 12 percent.

2. Ten-year bonds payable with maturity value of $100,000 and contract interest rate of 12 percent, paid semiannually. The market rate of interest is 10 percent at issuance.

3. Same bonds payable as in number 2, but the market interest rate is 8 percent.

4. Same bonds payable as in number 2, but the market interest rate is 12 percent.

Problem 16A-4   *Computing a bond's present value; recording its issuance at a discount and interest payments*   **(Obj. A3, A4)**

On December 31, 19X1, when the market interest rate is 8 percent, Unitrode Corporation issues $300,000 of 10-year, 7.25 percent bonds payable. The bonds pay interest semiannually.

Required

1. Determine the present value of the bonds at issuance.
2. Assume that the bonds are issued at the price computed in requirement 1. Prepare an effective-interest method amortization table for the first two semiannual interest periods.
3. Using the amortization table prepared in requirement 2, journalize issuance of the bonds and the first two interest payments.

Problem 16A-5   *Deciding between two payment plans   (Obj. A3, A4)*

Yokohama Children's Home needs a fleet of vans to transport the children to singing engagements throughout Japan. Nissan offers the vehicles for a single payment of 6,300,000 yen due at the end of four years. Toyota prices a similar fleet of vans for four annual payments of 1,700,000 yen each. The children's home could borrow the funds at 6 percent, so this is the appropriate interest rate. Which company should get the business, Nissan or Toyota? Base your decision on present value, and give your reason.

Problem 16A-6   *Computing the cost of equipment acquired under a capital lease, and recording the lease transactions   (Obj. A5)*

Montgomery Limited acquired equipment under a capital lease that requires six annual lease payments of $10,000. The first payment is due when the lease begins, on January 1, 19X6. Future payments are due on January 1 of each year of the lease term. The interest rate in the lease is 16 percent.

Required

1. Compute Montgomery's cost of the equipment.
2. Journalize the (a) acquisition of the equipment, (b) depreciation for 19X6, (c) accrued interest at December 31, 19X6, and (d) second lease payment on January 1, 19X7.

CHAPTER 17
Investments and Accounting for International Operations

"[T]he Brooks drug store chain] represents the best purchase I have made in my life," says Jean Coutu, Founder and President of Groupe Jean Coutu (PJC) Inc., a large drug store chain based in Quebec.

Jean Coutu made the comment as his company acquired the 221-store Brooks chain in New England in late 1994. In so doing he increased the number of stores in the group to 470 and increased sales by $425 million to more than $1,300 million. Coutu realized that the only way his company, second only to Shoppers Drug Mart in Canada, could grow was to expand into the United States.

Groupe Jean Coutu found that it could not expand in Canada through acquiring other chains. The company was outperforming the best U.S. drugstores, earning a net margin almost one-third more than than the U.S. stores were earning. The Brooks chain became available and so Jean Coutu paid $147.5 million to acquire it.

Source: Adapted from Kenneth Kidd, "Drugstore Dynamos," *Report on Business Magazine*, May 1995, pp. 57–66.

CHAPTER OBJECTIVES

After studying this chapter, you should be able to

1 Account for stock investments by the cost (LCM) method

2 Use the equity method for stock investments

3 Consolidate parent and subsidiary balance sheets

4 Account for investments in bonds

5 Understand how foreign-currency exchange rates are determined

---

Investments come in all sizes and shapes—from the purchase of an entire company to the purchase of a few shares of a company's stock, to investment in bonds. In earlier chapters we discussed stocks and bonds from the perspective of the company that issued the securities. In this chapter we examine stocks and bonds from the investor's viewpoint.

Why do individuals and corporations invest in stocks and bonds? You would probably make an investment in order to earn dividends and to sell the stock at a higher price than you paid for it. Investment companies such as brokerage firms, mutual funds, insurance companies, and bank trust departments buy stocks and bonds for this same reason.

Most other companies invest in stocks and bonds for a second reason: to influence or to control the other company. Top managers of Jean Coutu Groupe envisioned changes in the drug business, and they hoped to remain competitive in their industry.

In one sense, your purchase of a few shares of stock is similar to Jean Coutu's purchase of Brooks. In both cases, the shareholder—an individual or Jean Coutu— is an owner. But the purchase of an entire company raises questions about how the parent company should account for its investment. We address these questions in this chapter. We also consider the challenging area of accounting for international operations. First, however, let's review how investment transactions take place.

Accounting for Investments

Stock Prices

Investors buy more stocks in transactions among themselves than in purchases directly from the issuing company. Each share of stock is issued only once, but it may be traded among investors many times thereafter. People and businesses buy and sell stocks from each other in markets, such as the Toronto, Montreal, Vancouver, and Alberta Stock Exchanges. Recall that stock ownership is transferable. Investors trade millions of stock shares each day. Brokers like RBC Dominion Securities and Marleau Lemire handle stock transactions for a commission.

A broker may "quote you a stock price," which means state the current market price per share. The financial community quotes stock prices in dollars and one-eighth fractions. A stock selling at 32⅛ costs $32.125 per share. A stock listed at 55¾ sells at $55.75. Financial publications and many newspapers carry daily inform- ation on the stock issues of thousands of corporations. These one-line summaries carry information as of the close of trading the previous day.

Exhibit 17-1 presents information for the common stock of John Labatt, a brewer and food and beverage company, just as it appears in *The Financial Post*.[1]

During the previous 52 weeks, Labatt common stock reached a high of $26.00

---

[1] *The Financial Post*, May 25, 1995, p. 39.

EXHIBIT 17-1   *Stock Price Information*

52 Weeks		Stock	Div Rate	High	Low	Cls or Latest	Net Chge	Vol 100s	Yield %	P/E Ratio
High	Low									
$26	$18\frac{7}{8}$	Labatt, John	0.82	$25\frac{5}{8}$	$25\frac{1}{4}$	$25\frac{1}{4}$	$-\frac{3}{8}$	39,059	3.2	15.1

and a low of $18.875. The annual cash dividend is $.82 per share. *The Financial Post* comes out in the morning so the information relates to the previous day; the high and low prices were $25.625 and $25.25, while the closing price was $25.25 (if there had been no trading on the previous day, the latest, or most recent price, would be given). The closing price on the previous day was down $.375 from the closing price of one trading day earlier. During the previous day, 3,905,900 (39.059 × 100) shares of John Labatt stock were traded. The yield (dividend per share divided by price per share) is 3.2 percent while the P/E ratio (ratio of earnings per share to the share price) is 15.1/1.

What causes a change in a stock's price? The company's net income trend, potential take-overs, the development of new products, court rulings, new legislation, business success, and upward market trends drive a stock's price up, and business failures and bad economic news pull it down. At the time of writing, several groups were attempting to buy control of John Labatt, hence, the large volume of shares being sold. The stock price increased almost $3.00 per share in response to the competing bids for control. The market sets the price at which a stock changes hands.

Investments in Stock

To begin the discussion of investments in stock, we need to define two key terms. The person or company that owns stock in a corporation is the *investor*. The corporation that issued the stock is the *investee*. If you own shares of Labatt common stock, you are an investor and Labatt is the investee.

A business may purchase another corporation's stock simply to put extra cash to work in the hope of earning dividends and gains on the sale of the stock. Alternatively, the business may make the investment to gain a degree of control over the investee's operation. After all, stock is ownership. An investor holding 25 percent of the outstanding stock of the investee owns one fourth of the business. This one-quarter voice in electing the directors of the corporation is likely to give the investor a lot of say in how the investee conducts its business. An investor holding more than 50 percent of the outstanding shares controls the investee.

Let us consider why one corporation might want to gain a say in another corporation's business. The investor may want to exert some control over the level of dividends paid by the investee. Or perhaps the investor regards the investee as a good investment opportunity. The investee might have a line of products closely linked to the investor's own business. This is the case with Brooks and Groupe Jean Coutu. By influencing the investee's business, the investor may be able to exert some control on product distribution, control over critical raw materials or supplies, product-line improvements, pricing strategies, and other important business considerations. A swimming-pool manufacturer might want to purchase stock in a diving-board company, a landscape company, a swimsuit maker, or some other corporation with related business.

Why doesn't the investor simply diversify its own operations? Why didn't Groupe Jean Coutu establish a chain of stores in the U.S.? There already were drug store chains existing in the New England area where Brooks was located and where Groupe Jean Coutu wanted to expand their operations. To start competing with the existing chains would have been too expensive and too risky.

Portfolio Diversification   Investments are not without risk. To offset the ill effects of a sudden downturn in the operations of any one investee, smart investors diversify by holding a portfolio of stocks. The portfolio holds investments in different companies. By diversifying its holdings, the investor gains protection from losing too much if any one investee runs into problems and its stock price plummets.

Classifying Stock Investments

Investments in stock are assets to the investor. The investments may be short-term or long-term. Short-term investments are typically decribed on the balance sheet as **short-term investments**, **marketable securities**, or **temporary investments** and are classified as current assets. To be listed on the balance sheet as current assets, investments must be liquid (readily convertible to cash). Also, the investor's intent is important; the investor must intend either to convert the investments to cash within one year or to use them to pay a current liability. Investments not meeting these two requirements are classified on the balance sheet as **long-term investments**, a category of non-current assets.

Short-term investments include treasury bills, certificates of deposit, and stocks and bonds of other companies. Long-term investments include bond sinking funds, and stocks, bonds, and other assets that the investor expects to hold longer than one year or that are not readily marketable—for instance, real estate not used in the operations of the business. Exhibit 17-2 shows the positions of short-term and long-term investments on the balance sheet.

We report assets in the order of their liquidity. Cash is the most liquid asset, followed by Short-Term Investments, Accounts Receivable, and so on. Long-Term Investments are less liquid than Current Assets but more liquid than Property, Plant, and Equipment.

Accounting for Stock Investments

Accounting for stock investments varies with the nature and extent of the investment. The specific accounting method that GAAP directs us to follow depends first on whether the investment is short-term or long-term and second on the percentage of the investee's voting stock that the investor holds.

Short-term Investments: The Cost Method (with LCM)

OBJECTIVE 1

Account for stock investments by the cost (LCM) method

The **cost method** (with lower of cost or market) is used to account for short-term investments in stock. Cost is used as the initial amount for recording investments

EXHIBIT 17-2   *Reporting Investments on the Balance Sheet*

Current Assets		
Cash..	$X	
Short-term investments..	**X**	
Accounts receivable	X	
Inventories..	X	
Prepaid expenses...	X	
Total current assets..		$X
Long-term investments (or simply **Investments**)		**X**
Property, plant and equipment		X
Intangible assets		X
Other assets		X

and as the basis for measuring gains and losses on their sale. These investments are reported on the balance sheet at the *lower of their cost or market value.* Therefore, we refer to the overall method as cost (with lower of cost or market or LCM).

All investments, including short-term investments, are recorded initially at cost. Cost is the price paid for the stock plus the brokerage commission. Accountants have no separate account for the brokerage commission paid. Suppose that Athabasca Ltd. purchases 1,000 shares of Noranda Inc. common stock at the market price of 36¼ and pays a $500 commission. Athabasca intends to sell this investment within one year or less and, therefore, classifies it as short-term. Athabasca's entry to record the investment is

Aug. 22	Marketable Securities [(1,000 × $36.25) + $500].....	36,750	
	Cash		36,750
	Purchased 1,000 shares of Noranda common stock at $36.25 plus commission of $500.		

Assume Athabasca receives a $.22 per share cash dividend on the Noranda stock. Athabasca's entry to record receipt of the dividends is

Oct. 14	Cash (1,000 × $.22)	220	
	Dividend Revenue		220
	Received $.22 per share cash dividend on Noranda common stock.		

Dividends do not accrue with the passage of time (as interest does). The investee has no liability for dividends until the dividends are declared. An investor makes no accrual entry for dividend revenue at year end in anticipation of a dividend declaration.

However, if a dividend declaration *does* occur before year end, say, on December 28, the investor *may* debit Dividend Receivable and credit Dividend Revenue on that date. The investor would then report this receivable and the revenue in the December 31 financial statements. Receipt of the cash dividend in January would be recorded by a debit to Cash and a credit to Dividend Receivable. The more common practice, however, is to record the dividend as income when it is received.

Receipt of a *stock* dividend is not income to the investor, and no formal journal entry is needed. As we have seen, a stock dividend increases the number of shares held by the investor but does not affect the total cost of the investment. The *cost per share* of the stock investment therefore decreases. The investor usually makes a memorandum entry of the number of dividend shares received and the new cost per share. Assume that Athabasca Ltd. receives a 10 percent stock dividend on its 1,000-share investment in Noranda, which cost $36,750. Athabasca would make a memorandum entry along this line:

Key Point:
Receipt of stock dividends and stock splits is recorded in a memorandum entry.

Nov. 22	Received 100 shares of Noranda common stock in 10 percent stock dividend. New cost per share is $33.41 ($36,750/1,100 shares).

Any gain or loss on the sale of the investment is the difference between the sale proceeds and the cost of the investment. Assume that Athabasca sells 400 shares of Noranda stock for $35 per share, less a $280 commission. The entry to record the sale is

Dec. 18	Cash [(400 × $35) – $280]	13,720	
	Short-Term Investment in Noranda Common Stock (400 × $33.41)		13,364
	Gain on Sale of Investment..................		356
	Sold 400 shares of investment in Noranda common stock.		

Observe that the cost per share of the investment ($33.41) is based on the total number of shares held, including those received as a dividend.

Reporting Short-Term Investments at Lower of Cost or Market (LCM)

Because of accounting conservatism, short-term investments are reported at the lower of their cost or market (LCM or LOCAM) value. Canadian practice, in the absence of standards in the *CICA Handbook*, is to calculate market value on an investment-by-investment basis or on the portfolio as a whole. In either event, the basis of valuation for cost and market values should be disclosed. Assume a company owns three short-term investments with the following costs and market values:

Short Exercise:

The short-term investment portfolio of Nixon Inc. at year end is as follows:

Shares	Cost	Market
Irwin Toy		
1,000	$ 2,000	$ 8,375
National Trust		
5,000	110,000	92,500
Rogers Communications		
700	1,300	10,500
	$113,300	$111,375

Journalize the adjusting entry needed if Nixon values the investments on (1) a portfolio basis; (2) a security-by-security basis.

A: (1) Loss on Marketable
Securities 1,925*
    Marketable
        Securities 1,925
    (2) Loss on Marketable
Securities ....17,500†
    Marketable
        Securities 17,500

* $113,300 – $111,375 = $1,925
†$110,000 – $92,500 = $17,500

Short-term Investment Portfolio

Stock	Cost	Current Market Value
Dofasco Inc.	$155,625	$126,275
Toronto-Dominion Bank	67,000	86,200
George Weston Limited	186,000	174,500
Total	$408,625	$386,975

The investor owning the portfolio has two choices when determining the value of the portfolio for balance sheet purposes. The first considers the portfolio on a security-by-security basis. The investor would write the book value of the two stocks (Dofasco and Weston) whose market price has dropped below the price paid for them, down to their market values of $126,275 and $174,500 respectively. The market price of Toronto-Dominion is greater than cost, so no adjustment would be made to its book value. The journal entry to record the write down would be as follows:

Loss of Marketable Securities	40,850	
Marketable Securities..		40,850

To write down investment in Dofasco ($155,625 – $126,275 = $29,350) and George Weston ($186,000 – $174,500 = $11,500) to market.

The investor's balance sheet would report short-term investments as follows:

Current Assets

Cash	$ XXX
Short-term investments, at lower of cost or market value (note 4)	367,775
Accounts receivable, net of allowance of $XXX	XXX

Note 4. Short-Term Investments
Short-term investments are reported at the lower of their cost or market value. At December 31, 19XX, market value was $386,975.

Under this option, the investor would write down the book value of individual stocks to their market values, where cost was greater than market, irrespective of whether or not the total market value of the portfolio was greater than or less than cost.

The investor's other option would be to apply the LCM rule to the entire portfolio and write it down to market. The journal entry to record the write down would be

Loss on Marketable Securities	21,650	
Marketable Securities...		21,650

To write down investment portfolio to market.

The investor's balance sheet would report short-term investments as follows:

Current Assets

Cash	$ XXX
Short-term investments, at market value (note 4)	386,975
Accounts receivable, net of allowance of $XXX.......................................	XXX

Note 4. Short-term Investments
Short-term investments are reported at the lower of their cost or market value. At December 31, 19XX, cost was $408,625.

Under the second option, if the portfolio cost is lower than market value, the investor reports short-term investments at cost and discloses market value in the note.

Conservatism requires that an investor write the book value of stocks or portfolios down to market when cost exceeds market, but does not permit the investor to write up the book value of those same stocks or portfolios when their market value subsequently rises above the written down book values.

Long-Term Investments

An investor may own numerous investments, some short-term and others long-term. For accounting purposes, the two investment portfolios are not mixed. They are reported separately on the balance sheet, as shown in Exhibit 17-2. *Long-term* is not often used in the account title. An investment is understood to be long-term unless specifically labeled as short-term and included with current assets.

Long-term investments may be of several different types depending on the purpose of the investment and thus the percentage of voting interest acquired. Each of the three types is introduced in the following paragraphs and discussed more fully in turn below.

An investor may make a *portfolio investment* where the purpose is similar to that of short-term investing; the investor will hold the investment to earn dividends or interest but has no long-term interest in the investee. In such a situation, the investor will generally hold less than 20 percent of the voting interest of the investee and would normally play no important role in the investee's operations. Such an investor would normally account for the investment using the *cost method*.

An investor may also make an investment in the investee purchasing between 20percent and 50 percent of the investee's voting stock. The investor will likely be able to exert a *significant influence* over the investee and how the investee operates the business. Such an investor can likely affect the investee's decisions on dividend policy, product lines, sources of supply, and other important matters. An investor holding between 20 and 50 percent would normally account for the investment using the *equity method*.

The investor may make an investment in the investee that exceeds 50 percent of the voting interest and thus is able to control the operations and activities of the investee. Such investees are called subsidiaries; subsidiaries's financial statements are normally *consolidated* with those of the parent.

Long-Term Investments Accounted for by the Cost Method

Accounting for portfolio investments follows the procedures outlined for short-term investments, that is, the cost method. The beginning accounting value is cost, which is debited to an Investments account at the date of purchase. Dividends are treated as income. Gains and losses are recorded on sales. Long-term investments are normally reported on the balance sheet at cost. Section 3050.20 states that if the market price of one of the stocks in the portfolio drops below cost, and the decline is thought to be other than temporary, the stock's book value would be written down to market and carried at that value in the future. The determination of whether or not the decline is temporary is management's.

OBJECTIVE 2
Use the equity method for stock investments

Short Exercise:

Apex Ltd. purchased 40% of Base Ltd.'s stock for $750,000. Base reported $100,000 income and paid $40,000 dividends during the next year. (1) On Apex's books, record the purchase, the net income of Base, and dividends of Base. (2) What is the carrying amount of Apex's investment in Base?

A:

(1) Purchase:
Investment in
   Base 750,000
   Cash 750,000
Net income of Base:
Investment in
   Base 40,000
   Equity-Method
   Invest. Rev. ... 40,000
Dividends of Base:
Cash............... 16,000
   Invest. in
   Base   16,000

(2) $774,000 ($750,000 + $40,000 – $16,000)

Key Point:

A simple T-account illustrates how to account for equity-method investments:

Equity Method

Original cost	Share of losses
Share of income	Share of dividends

Key Point:

An investor who holds 20% of a company's stock can usually elect 20% of the board of directors and gain influence in company decisions. With more than 50% control (majority ownership), the investor can control the affairs of the company.

Long-Term Investments Accounted for by the Equity Method

An investee with a larger stock holding of between 20 percent and 50 percent of the investee's voting stock may significantly influence how the investee operates the business. Since the investor has a voice in shaping business policy and operations, accountants believe that some measure of the business's success and failure should be included in accounting for the investment. We use the equity method to account for investments in which the investor can significantly influence the decision of the investee.

Investments accounted for by the **equity method** are recorded initially at cost. Suppose Nova Corp. pays $400,000 for 30 percent of the common stock of White Rock Corporation. Nova's entry to record the purchase of this investment is

Jan. 6	Investment in White Rock Common Stock .	400,000	
	Cash..		400,000
	To purchase 30% investment in White Rock common stock.		

Under the equity method, Nova, as the investor, applies its percentage of ownership, 30 percent in our example, in recording its share of the investee's net income and dividends. If White Rock reports net income of $125,000 for the year, Nova records 30 percent of this amount as an increase in the investment account and as equity-method investment revenue, as follows:

Dec. 31	Investment in White Rock Common Stock ($125,000 × .30)	37,500	
	Equity-Method Investment Revenue		37,500
	To record 30% of White Rock net income.		

The Investment Revenue account carries the Equity-Method label to identify its source. This labeling is similar to distinguishing Sales Revenue from Service Revenue.

The investor increases the Investment account and records Investment Revenue when the investee reports income because of the close relationship between the two companies. As the investee's owner equity increases, so does the Investment account on the books of the investor.

Nova records its proportionate part of cash dividends received from White Rock. Assuming White Rock declares and pays a cash dividend of $50,000, Nova receives 30 percent of this dividend, recording it as follows:

Jan. 17	Cash ($50,000 × .30)	15,000	
	Investment in White Rock Common Stock		15,000
	To record receipt of 30% of White Rock cash dividend.		

Observe that the Investment account is credited for the receipt of a dividend on an equity-method investment. Why? It is because the dividend decreases the investee's owner's equity and so it also reduces the investor's investment. In effect, the investor received cash for this portion of the investment.

After the above entries are posted, Nova's Investment account reflects its equity in the net assets of White Rock:

Investment in White Rock Common Stock

19X1			19X2		
Jan. 6	Purchase	400,000	Jan.17	Dividends	15,000
Dec. 31	Net income	37,500			
19X2					
Jan. 17	Balance	422,500			

Gain or loss on the sale of an equity-method investment is measured as the difference between the sale proceeds and the carrying value of the investment. For example, sale of one tenth of the White Rock common stock for $41,000 would be recorded as follows:

Feb. 13	Cash	41,000	
	Loss on Sale of Investment...............................	1,250	
	Investment in White Rock Common Stock		
	($422,500 × ⅒)		42,250
	Sold one-tenth of investment in White Rock		
	common stock.		

Companies with investments accounted for by the equity method often refer to the investee as an *affiliated company*. The account title Investments in Affiliated Companies refers to investments that are accounted for by the equity method. Consider John Labatt Ltd. Labatt's investment in the Mexican Brewer, Femsa Cerveza, fell in value when the peso was devalued in early 1995. Labatt announced that it had written its investment in Femsa Cerveza down by $272 million. Labatt would record the transaction as follows (in millions):

Equity-Method Investment Loss.................	272	
Investment in Femsa Cervazo..............		272

Long-Term Investments Accounted for by the Consolidation Method

Most large corporations own controlling interests in other corporations. A **controlling** (or **majority**) **interest** is normally the ownership of more than 50 percent of the investee's voting stock. Such an investment enables the investor to elect a majority of the investee's board of directors and so control the investee. The investor is called the **parent** company, and the investee company, as mentioned earlier, is called the **subsidiary**. For example, Loblaw Companies Limited, the grocery store chain, is 70 percent owned by George Weston Ltd. Galen Weston and the other shareholders of George Weston Ltd. control that company and, because George Weston Ltd. owns Loblaw, they also control Loblaw as diagrammed in Exhibit 17-3.

Why have subsidiaries? Why not have the corporation take the form of a single legal entity? Subsidiaries may limit the parent's liabilities in a risky venture, and may ease expansion into foreign countries. For example, Chieftain International, Inc., the natural gas and oil exploration and production company located in Edmonton, has a U.S. subsidiary, Chieftain International (U.S.) Inc., and two U.K. subsidiaries, Chieftain Exploration (U.K.) Limited and Chieftan International North Sea Limited. Those companies conduct operations for Chieftain in those two countries respectively. Exhibit 17-4 shows selected subsidiaries of three major Canadian companies.

EXHIBIT 17-3 *Ownership Structure of George Weston Ltd.*

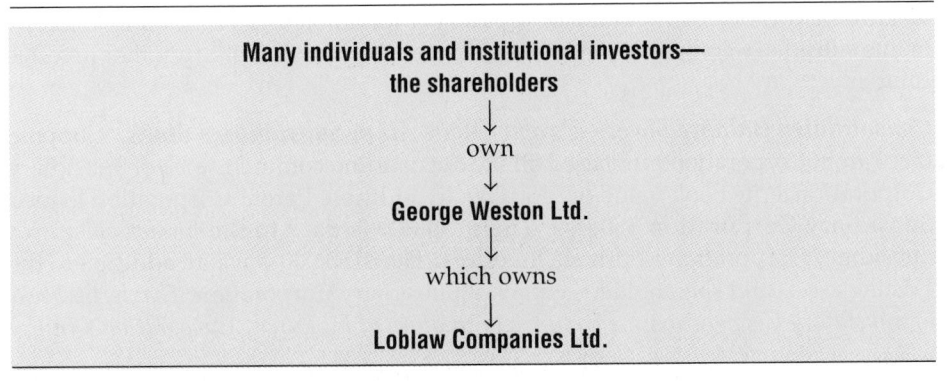

EXHIBIT 17-4   *Selected Subsidiaries of Three Canadian Companies*

Parent Company	Selected Subsidiaries
Bombardier Inc.	de Haviland Inc. (Canada) Learjet Inc. (U.S.) Short Brothers (United Kingdom) Bombardier Eurorail S.A. (Belgium) Bombardier Credit Ltd. (Canada)
Parkland Industries Ltd.	Contact Stores Ltd. Fas Gas Oil Ltd. Fas Gas Transport Ltd. Payless Oil Company Ltd. Service Station Supply Ltd.
Schneider Corporation	Charcuterie Roy Inc. Fleetwood Sausage Ltd. Horizon Poultry Products Inc. Mother Jackson's Open Kitchens Limited J.M. Schneider Inc.

EXHIBIT 17-5
*Accounting Methods
for Stock Investment
by Percentage of
Ownership*

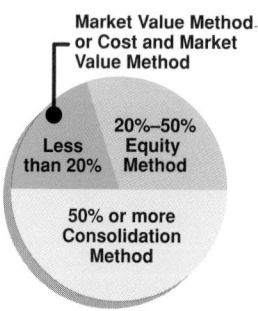

Market Value Method
or Cost and Market
Value Method

Less than 20%

20%–50%
Equity
Method

50% or more
Consolidation
Method

Consolidation accounting is a method of combining the financial statements of two or more companies that are controlled by the same owners. This method implements the entity concept by reporting a single set of financial statements for the consolidated entity, which carries the name of the parent company. Exhibit 17-5 illustrates the accounting method for stock investments according to the percentage of the investor's ownership in the investee company.

Almost all published financial reports include consolidated statements. To understand the statements you are likely to encounter, you need to know the basic concepts underlying consolidation accounting. **Consolidated statements** combine the balance sheets, income statements, and other financial statements of the parent company with those of the subsidiaries into an overall set as if the parents and its subsidiaries were a single entity. The goal is to provide a better perspective on operations than could be obtained by examining the separate reports of each of the individual companies. The assets, liabilities, revenues, and expenses of each subsidiary are added to the parent's accounts. The consolidated financial statements present the combined account balances. For example, the balance in the Cash account of Loblaw Companies is added to the balance in the George Weston Ltd. Cash account, and the sum of the two amounts is presented as a single amount in the consolidated balance sheet of George Weston Ltd. Each account balance of a subsidiary loses its identity in the consolidated statements. George Weston Ltd. financial statements are entitled "George Weston Ltd. and Consolidated Subsidiaries." Loblaw Companies and the names of all other George Weston Ltd. subsidiaries do not appear in the statement titles. But the names of the subsidiary companies are listed in the parent company's annual report. A reader of corporate annual reports cannot hope to understand them without knowing how consolidated statements are prepared. Exhibit 17-6 diagrams a corporate structure whose parent corporation owns controlling interests in five subsidiary companies and an equity-method investment in another investee company.

OBJECTIVE 3

Consolidate parent
and subsidiary
balance sheet

Consolidated Balance Sheet—Parent Owns All of Subsidiary's Stock   Suppose that Parent Corporation purchased all the outstanding common stock of Subsidiary Corporation at its book value of $150,000. In addition, Parent Corporation loaned Subsidiary Corporation $80,000. The $150,000 is paid to the *former owners* of Subsidiary Corporation as private investors. The $150,000 is *not* an addition to the existing assets and shareholders' equity of Subsidiary Corporation. *That is, the books of Subsidiary Corporation are completely unaffected by Parent Corporation's initial*

Exhibit 17-6   *Parent Company with Consolidated Subsidiaries and an Equity Method Investment*

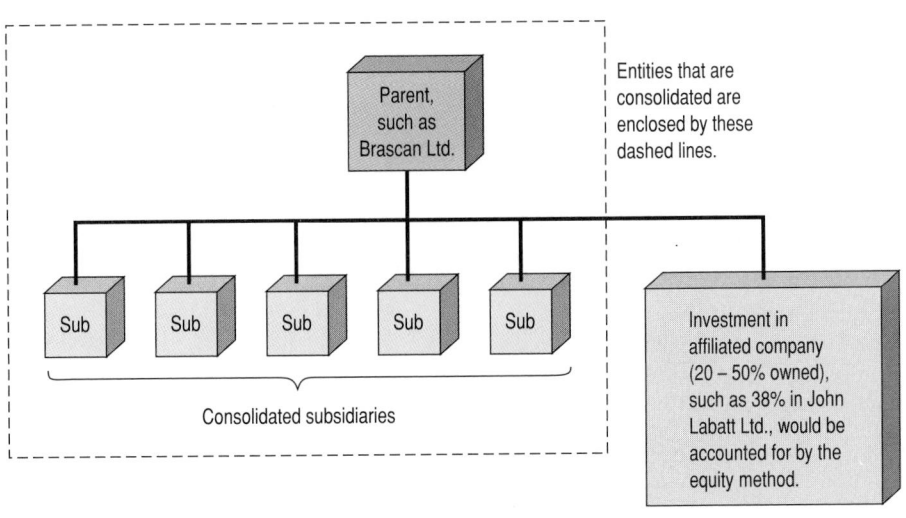

investment and Parent's subsequent acccounting for that investment. Subsidiary Corporation is not dissolved. It lives on as a separate legal entity but with a new owner, Parent Corporation.

Parent Corporation Books[2]			Subsidiary Corporation Books		
Investment in Subsidiary					
Corporation.............	150,000		No entry		
Cash......................		150,000			
Note receivable from			Cash		80,000
Subsidiary................	80,000		Note Payable		
Cash.....................		80,000	to Parent		80,000

Each legal entity has its individual set of books. The consolidated entity does not keep a separate set of books. Instead a work sheet is used to prepare the consolidated statements. A major concern in consolidation accounting is this: Do not double-count—that is, do not include the same item twice.

Companies may prepare a consolidated balance sheet immediately after acquisition. The consolidated balance sheet shows all the assets and liabilities of the parent and the subsidiary. The Investment in Subsidiary account on the parent's books represents all the assets and liabilities of Subsidiary. The consolidated statements cannot show both the investment account *plus* the amounts for the subsidiaries assets and liabilities. Doing so would count the same resources twice. To avoid this double-counting we eliminate (a) the $150,000 Investment in Subsidiary on the parent's books, and the $150,000 shareholder's equity on the subsidiary's books ($100,000 Common Stock and $50,000 Retained Earnings) and (b) the intercompany $80,000 note.

Explanation of Elimination—Entry (a)   Exhibit 17-7 shows the work sheet for consolidating the balance sheet. Consider the elimination entry for the parent-subsidiary ownership accounts, which are intercompany accounts. Entry (a) credits

---

[2] The parent company may use either the cost method or the equity method for work sheet entries to the Investment account. Regardless of the method used, the consolidated statements are the same. Advanced accounting courses deal with this topic.

EXHIBIT 17-7 *Work Sheet for Consolidated Balance Sheet—Parent Corporation Owns All of Subsidiary Corporation's Stock*

Assets	Parent Corporation	Subsidiary Corporation	Eliminations Debit	Eliminations Credit	Consolidated Amounts
Cash..	12,000	18,000			30,000
Notes receivable from Subsidiary....	80,000	—		(b) 80,000	—
Inventory.................................	104,000	91,000			195,000
Investment in Subsidiary...............	150,000	—		(a) 150,000	—
Other assets..............................	218,000	138,000			356,000
Total.......................................	564,000	247,000			581,000
Liabilities and Shareholders' Equity					
Accounts payable.........................	43,000	17,000			60,000
Notes payable.............................	190,000	80,000	(b) 80,000		190,000
Common stock............................	176,000	100,000	(a) 100,000		176,000
Retained earnings........................	155,000	50,000	(a) 50,000		155,000
Total.......................................	564,000	247,000	230,000	230,000	581,000

the parent Investment account to eliminate its debit balance. It also eliminates the subsidiary's shareholders' equity accounts by debiting Common Stock for $100,000 and Retained Earnings for $50,000. The resulting consolidated balance sheet reports no Investment in Subsidiary account, and the Common Stock and Retained Earnings are those of Parent Corporation only. The consolidated amounts are in the final column of the consolidation work sheet.

Explanation of Elimination—Entry (b)   Parent Corporation loaned $80,000 to Subsidiary Corporation, and Subsidiary signed a note payable to Parent. Therefore, Parent's balance sheet includes an $80,000 note receivable and Subsidiary's balance sheet reports a note payable for this amount. This loan was entirely within the consolidated entity and so must be eliminated. Entry (b) accomplishes this. The $80,000 credit in the elimination column of the work sheet offsets Parent's debit balance in Notes Receivable from Subsidiary. After this work sheet entry, the consolidated amount for notes receivable is zero. The $80,000 debit in the elimination column offsets the credit balance of Subsidiary's notes payable, and the resulting consolidated amount for notes payable is the amount owed to those outside the consolidated entity.

STOP & THINK

Examine Exhibit 17-7. Why does the consolidated shareholders' equity ($176,000 + $155,000) exclude the equity of Subsidiary Corporation?

Answer: Because the shareholders' equity of the consolidated entity is that of the parent only, and because the subsidiary's equity and the parent company's investment balance represent the same resources. Therefore, including them both would amount to double-counting.

Parent Company Buys Subsidiary's Stock and Pays for Goodwill   A company may acquire a controlling interest in a subsidiary by paying a price above the book value of the subsidiary's owners' equity, which we assume is equal to the fair value of the subsidiary's net assets (assets minus liabilities). By definition this excess is *goodwill*. What drives a company's market value up? The company may create goodwill through its superior products, service, or location.

The subsidiary does not record goodwill. The goodwill is identified in the process of consolidating the parent and subsidiary financial statements.

Suppose Parent Corporation paid $450,000 to acquire 100 percent of the common stock of Subsidiary Corporation, which had Common Stock of $200,000 and Retained Earnings of $180,000. Parent's payment included $70,000 for goodwill ($450,000 – $200,000 – $180,000 = $70,000).[3] The entry to eliminate Parent's Investment account against Subsidiary's equity accounts is

Common Stock, Subsidiary...	200,000	
Retained Earnings, Subsidiary	180,000	
Goodwill..	70,000	
Investment in Subsidiary		450,000

To eliminate cost of investment in Subsidiary against Subsidiary's equity balances and to recognize Subsidiary's unrecorded goodwill.

In *actual* practice, this entry would be made only on the consolidation work sheet. Here we show it in general journal form for instructional purposes.

The asset goodwill is reported on the consolidated balance sheet among the intangible assets, after capital assets. For example, Bombardier's 1994 financial statement includes goodwill of $6.1 million with "Other Assets." Goodwill is amortized to expense over its useful life, not to exceed 40 years.

Consolidated Balance Sheet—Parent Owns Less Than 100 Percent of Subsidiary's Stock When a parent company owns more than 50 percent (a majority) of the subsidiary's stock but less than 100 percent of it, a new category of owners' equity, called *minority interest,* must appear on the consolidated balance sheet. Suppose Parent buys 75 percent of Subsidiary's common stock. The minority interest is the remaining 25 percent of Subsidiary's equity. Thus **minority interest** is the subsidiary's equity that is held by shareholders other than the parent company. While the *CICA Handbook* is silent on where minority interest should be disclosed on the balance sheet, accepted practice is to list it as a separate item between liabilities and owner's equity.

Assume P Ltd. buys 75 percent of S Ltd.'s common stock. Also, P owes S $50,000 on a note payable to S. Exhibit 17-8 is the consolidation work sheet. Again, focus on the Eliminations columns and the Consolidated Amounts.

EXHIBIT 17-8 *Work Sheet for Consolidated Balance Sheet: Parent (P Ltd.) Owns Less Than 100 Percent of Subsidiary's (S Ltd.) Stock*

Assets	P Ltd.	S Ltd.	Eliminations Debit	Eliminations Credit	Consolidated Amounts
Cash...	33,000	18,000			51,000
Notes receivable from P........................	—	50,000		(b) 50,000	—
Accounts receivable, net.......................	54,000	39,000			93,000
Inventory	92,000	66,000			158,000
Investment in S	120,000	—		(a) 120,000	—
Plant and equipment, net......................	230,000	123,000			353,000
Total..	529,000	296,000			655,000
Liabilities and Shareholders' Equity					
Accounts payable...............................	141,000	94,000			235,000
Notes payable..................................	50,000	42,000	(b) 50,000		42,000
Minority interest	—	—		(a) 40,000	40,000
Common stock	170,000	100,000	(a) 100,000		170,000
Retained earnings	168,000	60,000	(a) 60,000		168,000
Total..	529,000	296,000	210,000	210,000	655,000

---

[3] For simplicity, we are assuming that the fair market value of the subsidiary's net assets (assets minus liabilities) equals the book value of the company's owners' equity. Advanced courses consider other situations.

Key Point:

The elimination entry requires, at most, five steps: (1) Eliminate intercompany receivables and payables. (2) Elim-inate the shareholders' equity accounts of the subsidiary. (3) Eliminate the Investment in Subsidiary account. (4) Record goodwill. (5) Record minority interest.

Entry (a) eliminates P Ltd.'s Investment balance of $120,000 against the $160,000 owner's equity of S Ltd. Observe that all of S's equity is eliminated even though P holds only 75 percent of S's stock. The remaining 25 percent interest in S's equity is credited to Minority Interest ($160,000 × .25 = $40,000). Thus Entry (a) reclassifies 25 percent of S Ltd.'s equity as minority interest. Entry (b) in Exhibit 17-8 eliminates S Ltd.'s $50,000 note receivable against P's note payable of the same amount. The consolidated amount of notes payable ($42,000) is the amount that S Ltd. owes to outsiders.

The consolidated balance sheet of P Ltd., shown in Exhibit 17-9, is based on the work sheet of Exhibit 17-8. The consolidated balance sheet reveals that ownership of P Ltd. and its consolidated subsidiary is divided between P's shareholders (common stock and retained earnings totaling $338,000) and the minority shareholders of S Ltd. ($40,000).

Income of a Consolidated Entity   The income of a consolidated entity is the net income of the parent plus the parent's proportion of the subsidiaries' net income. Suppose Parent Inc. owns all the stock of Subsidiary S-1 Inc. and 60 percent of the stock of Subsidiary S-2 Inc. During the year just ended, Parent earned net income of $330,000, S-1 earned $150,000 and S-2 had a net loss of $100,000. Parent would report net income of $420,000, computed as follows:

Short Exercise:

P Ltd. purchases 80% of S Ltd. for $280,000. Their balance sheets immediately afterward are:

Assets

	P Ltd.	S Ltd.
Cash	$ 200,000	$ 50,000
Accounts rec.	275,000	60,000
Inventory	300,000	80,000
Invest. in S	280,000	
Plant & equip.	500,000	170,000
	$1,555,000	$360,000

Liabilities and Shareholders' Equity

Accounts pay.	$350,000	$ 60,000
Com. stock	500,000	120,000
Ret. earnings	705,000	180,000
	$1,555,000	$360,000

P Ltd. owes S Ltd. $10,000 on account. Prepare the elimination entry in general journal form and the consolidated balance sheet.

A:

Accounts Payable	10,000
Common Stock	120,000
Retained Earnings	180,000
Goodwill	40,000
[$280,000 – ($300,000 × 80%)]	
Investment in S	280,000
Minority Interest	
($300,000 × 20%).	60,000
Accounts Receivable	10,000

Assets

Cash	$ 250,000
Accounts rec.	325,000
Inventory	380,000
Plant & equip.	670,000
Goodwill	40,000
Total	$1,665,000

Liabilities & Shareholders' Equity

Accounts pay	$ 400,000
Minority interest.	60,000
Common stock...	500,000
Ret. earnings	705,000
Total	$1,665,000

	Net Income (Net Loss)	Parent Shareholders' Ownership	Parent Net Income (Net Loss)
Parent Inc.	$330,000	100%	$330,000
Subsidiary S-1	150,000	100	150,000
Subsidiary S-2	(100,000)	60	(60,000)
Consolidated net income ...			$420,000

The parent's net income is the same amount that would be recorded under the equity method. However, the equity method stops short of reporting the investee's assets and liabilities on the parent balance sheet because with an investment in the range of 20–50 percent, the investor owns less than a controlling interest in the investee company.

The procedures for preparation of a consolidated income statement parallel those outlined above for the balance sheet. The consolidated income statement is discussed in an advanced course.

EXHIBIT 17-9   *Consolidated Balance Sheet of P Ltd.*

P Ltd. and Consolidated Subsidiary
Consolidated Balance Sheet
December 31, 19XX

Assets

Cash	$ 51,000
Accounts receivable, net	93,000
Inventory	158,000
Plant and equipment, net	353,000
Total assets	$655,000

Liabilities and Shareholders' Equity

Accounts payable	$235,000
Notes payable	42,000
Minority interest	40,000
Common stock	170,000
Retained earnings	168,000
Total liabilities and shareholders' equity	$655,000

Joint Ventures—Accounted for by the Equity Method

A *joint venture* is a separate entity or project owned and operated by a small group or businesses. Joint ventures are common in risky endeavors such as the petroleum and construction industries. Moreover, they are widely used in regions with developing economies, such as China, eastern Europe, and the Middle East. Many Canadian and U.S. companies that do business abroad enter into joint ventures. Rather than risk a huge investment in uncertain oil exploration, the large oil companies form joint ventures with foreign entities that have known oil sources. For example, Aramco, which stands for Arabian American Oil Company, is a joint venture owned 50 percent by Saudi Arabia. Several multinational oil companies own the remaining 50 percent. Despite the risks of operating in the volatile Middle East, Aramco's partners have enjoyed big profits. The company earned $15 billion during the Persian Gulf War alone. Schneider Corporation has a joint venture with National Meats Inc.; Schneider has a 50 percent interest.

Section 3055 of the *CICA Handbook* requires the use of proportionate consolidation when accounting for a joint venture. Proportionate consolidation means the venturer consolidates its proportionate interest in the assets, liabilities, revenues, and expenses of the joint venture with its own assets, liabilities, revenues, and expenses. For example, assume the venturer, V Ltd., has inventory of $50,000 and a 40 percent interest in the joint venture. The joint venture has inventory of $20,000. V Ltd. would report inventory on its consolidated statements of $58,000 ($50,000 + 40% of $20,000).

Computers and Consolidations

Consider diversified companies such as Intrawest Corporation, the mountain resort industry company with operations at Whistler, Mont Tremblant, Stratton, Vermont, and Keystone, Colorado. The company develops, owns, and runs resorts and resort clubs. The company is also in the property development business but is selling that part of its operations. A company such as Intrawest can prepare its consolidated financial statements automatically with a fully integrated accounting information system. But many wholly-owned subsidiaries retain their own accounting systems. If the subsidiaries have adopted the parent company's standard chart of accounts, a supplementary system can automatically combine the accounts of the parent and subsidiary companies and prepare the consolidated statements. If each subsidiary maintains its own unique chart of accounts, the consolidation must be performed manually. A computer spreadsheet program may still ease the preparation of the consolidated statements. Each subsidiary can enter its statements in a spreadsheet that is electronically linked to a central spreadsheet that automatically updates the consolidated statements. The advantage of the computer spreadsheet becomes clear when you prepare consolidated statements.

Investments in Bonds and Notes

Industrial and commercial companies invest far more in stock than they do in bonds. The major investors in bonds are financial institutions, such as pension plans, trust companies, and insurance companies. For every issuer of bonds payable, at least one investor owns the bonds. The relationship between the issuer and the investor may be diagrammed as follows:

Issuing Corporation		**Investor (Bondholder)**
Bonds payable	⟵⟶	Investment in bonds
Interest expense	⟵⟶	Interest revenue

OBJECTIVE 4

Account for investments in bonds

The dollar amount of a bond transaction is the same for issuer and investor, but the accounts debited and credited differ. However, the accounts are parallel. For example, the issuer's interest expense is the investor's interest revenue.

An investment in bonds is classified either as short-term (a current asset) or as long-term. An investment is a current asset if (1) the investment is liquid (can readily be sold for cash, such as a Government of Canada bond) and (2) the owner intends to convert it to cash within one year or to use it to pay a current liability. An investment that is intended to be held longer than a year is classified as long-term.

Bond investments are recorded at cost, which includes the purchase price and any brokerage fees. Amortization of bond premium or discount is *not* recorded on short-term investments because the investor plans to hold the bonds for so short a period that any amortization would be immaterial. On the other hand, investors hold long-term investments for a significant period and therefore amortize any premium or discount on the bonds.

Let us look at accounting for a *short-term* bond investment. Suppose that an investor purchases $10,000 of bonds on August 1, 19X2, paying $93.00 plus accrued interest and a brokerage commission of $250. The annual contract or stated interest rate is 12 percent, paid semiannually on April 1 and October 1. The cost of the bonds is $9,550 [($10,000 × .93) + $250]. In addition, the investor pays accrued interest for the four months (April through July) since the last interest payment. The investor records the purchase on August 1 as follows:

Aug. 1	Short-Term Investment in Bonds		
	[($10,000 × .93) + $250]............................	9,550	
	Interest Receivable ($10,000 × .12 × $\frac{4}{12}$)	400	
	Cash..		9,950
	To purchase short-term bond investment.		

Accrued interest is *not* included in the cost of the investment but is debited to Interest Receivable.

Short Exercise:

The investor's entry for receipt of the first semiannual interest amount on October 1 is

Oct. 1	Cash ($10,000 × .12 × $\frac{6}{12}$)	600	
	Interest Receivable		400
	Interest Revenue ($10,000 × .12 × $\frac{2}{12}$)		200
	To receive semiannual interest, part of which		
	was accrued.		

At October 1, the investor has held the bonds for two months. The entry correctly credits Interest Revenue for two months' interest. This entry does not include discount amortization on the bonds because the investment is short-term.

At December 31, the investor accrues interest revenue for three months (October, November, and December), debiting Interest Receivable and crediting Interest Revenue for $300 ($10,000 × .12 × $\frac{3}{12}$). The investor's December 31 balance sheet reports the following information (we assume that the market price of the bonds is $96.00):

Current assets	
Short-term investment in bonds (note 4)......................................	$9,550
Interest receivable	300

Note 4: Short-term investments
At December 31, the current market value of short-term investments in bonds was $9,600.

Observe that the investment is reported at cost, with the current market value disclosed in a note. The market value may also be reported parenthetically.

Current assets	
Short-term investment in bonds	
(Current market value, $9,600)...	$9,550
Interest receivable	300

Assume that Quill Corp. is buying bonds as a trading investment. Quill buys $300,000 of 9%, 10-year bonds at $104.00. The bonds pay interest on February 1 and August 1. What are the entries to record (1) the purchase on 8/1/96, (2) the year-end accrual, and (3) the first semiannual receipt of interest?

A:
(1) Purchase on 8/1/96:
Investment
  in Bonds......312,000
Cash ($300,000 ×
  1.04) 312,000
(2) Accrual on 12/31/96:
Interest
  Receivable... 11,250
Interest
  Revenue 11,250
($300,000 × 9% × 5/12)
(3) Interest receipt on 2/1/97:
Cash ($300,000 ×
  0.045) 13,500
Interest
  Receivable... 11,250
Interest Revenue 2,250

The investor measures any gain or loss on sale as the difference between the sale price (less any broker's commission) and the cost of the investment. For example, sale of the bonds for $9,700 will result in a gain of $150. This gain is reported as Other Revenue on a multiple-step income statement or beneath Sales Revenue among the revenues and gains on a single-step statement. A loss would be reported as Other Expense on a multiple-step statement or among the expenses on a single-step statement.

Accounting for *long-term* investments in bonds follows a different pattern because the bonds will be held until their maturity date. At maturity the investor will receive the face value of the bonds. For long-term investments, discount or premium is amortized to account more precisely for interest revenue over the period the bonds will be held. The amortization of discount or premium on a bond investment affects Interest Revenue and the carrying amount of the bonds in the same way as for the company that issued the bonds. Long-term investments in bonds are reported at their *amortized cost*, which determines the carrying amount.

The accountant records amortization on the cash interest dates and at year end, along with the accrual of interest receivable. Accountants rarely use separate discount and premium accounts for investments. Amortization of a discount is recorded by directly *debiting* the Long-Term Investment in Bonds account and *crediting* Interest Revenue. Amortization of a premium is recorded by directly crediting to the Long-Term Investment account. This entry debits Interest Revenue. These entries bring the investment balance to the bonds' face value on the maturity date and record the correct amount of interest revenue each period.

Suppose the $10,000 of 12 percent bonds in the preceding illustration were purchased on April 1, 19X2, as a long-term investment. Interest dates are April 1 and October 1. These bonds mature on April 1, 19X6, so they will be outstanding for 48 months. Assume amortization of the discount by the straight-line method. The following entries for a long-term investment highlight the differences between accounting for a short-term bond investment and for a long-term bond investment:

Apr. 1	Long-Term Investment in Bonds		
	($10,000 × .93)	9,300	
	Cash..		9,300
	To purchase long-term bond investment.		
Oct. 1	Cash ($10,000 × .12 × %₁₂)	600	
	Interest Revenue...		600
	To receive semiannual interest.		
Oct. 1	Long-Term Investment in Bonds		
	[($10,000 – $9,300)/48 × 6]..................................	88	
	Interest Revenue...		88
	To amortize discount on bond investment for six months.		

At December 31, the year-end adjustments are:

Dec. 31	Interest Receivable ($10,000 × .12 × ³⁄₁₂).................	300	
	Interest Revenue...		300
	To accrue interest revenue for three months.		
Dec. 31	Long-term Investment in Bonds		
	[($10,000 – $9,300)/48 × 3]..................................	44	
	Interest Revenue...		44
	To amortize discount on bond investment for three months.		

The financial statements at December 31, 19X2 report the following effects of this long-term investment in bonds (assume the bonds' market price is $102.00):

Balance sheet at December 31, 19X2:

Current assets		
Interest receivable	$ 300	
Total current assets	X,XXX	

Short Exercise:

Refer to the previous Short Exercise but assume that Quill Corp. bought the bonds to hold to maturity. What entries record (1) the purchase on 8/1/96, (2) the year-end accrual, and (3) the first semiannual interest receipt and straight-line amortization of the premium?

A:

(1) Purchase on 8/1/96:
   Invest. in
   Bonds........312,000
   Cash ($300,000 ×
   1.04)........   312,000

(2) Accrual on 12/31/96:
   Interest
   Receivable ... 11,250
   Interest
   Revenue   11,250
   ($300,000 × 9% ×
   5/12)
   Interest
   Revenue   500
   Invest. in
   Bonds......   500
   [($12,000 prem./20
   semiann. int. periods) =
   $600 × 5/6]

(3) Interest receipt on 2/1/97:
   Cash ($300,000 ×
   0.045)........ 13,500
   Interest
   Receivable   11,250
   Interest
   Revenue .. 2,250
   Interest Revenue   100
   Invest. in Bonds 100
   ($600 × 1/6)

EXHIBIT 17-10 *Accounting Methods for Investments*

Type of Investments	Accounting Method
Short-term investment in stock or bonds	
Short-term investment in stock..	Cost (lower of cost or market)
Short-term investment in bonds...	Cost (lower of cost or market)
Long-term investment in stock or bonds	
Long-term investment in stock	
Investor owns less than 20 percent of investee stock	Cost (lower of cost or market if decline in market is not temporary)
Investor owns 20–50 percent of investee stock...............	Equity
Investor owns greater than 50 percent of investee stock	Consolidation
Long-term investment in bonds	Amortized cost

Long-term investments in bonds ($9,300 + $88 + $44)—note 6 9,432

Note 6: Long-term investments.
Long-term bonds are reported at amortized cost. At December 31, 19X1, the current
market value of long-term investments in bonds was $10,200.

Income statement (multiple-step) for the year ended December 31, 19X2:
   Other revenues
      Interest revenue ($600 + $88 + $300 + $44).. $1,032

In particular, note that the long-term bond investments are reported by the *amortized cost* method. Where discount or premium is amortized by the straight-line method, accounting for long-term bond investments follows the pattern illustrated above. Effective-interest amortization amounts for long-term are computed as shown for bonds payable in Chapter 16.

Exhibit 17-10 summarizes the accounting methods for investments.

Mid-Chapter Summary Problem for Your Review

This problem consists of four independent items.

1. Identify the appropriate accounting method for each of the following situations involving investment in common stock:

  a. Purchase of 25 percent and investor plans to hold

  b. Investor intends to sell three months after year end

  c. Purchase of more than 50 percent of investee's stock

2. At what amount should the following long-term investment portfolio be reported on the Decmber 31 balance sheet? All the investments are less than 5 percent of the investee's stock. Journalize any adjusting entry required by these data.

Stock	Investment Cost	Current Market Value
Dreco Energy Services	$10,750	$17,750
Loblaw Companies	5,000	9,125
Four Seasons Hotels	26,250	18,750

3. Investor Ltd. paid $67,900 to acquire a 40 percent equity-method investment in the common stock of Investee Ltd. At the end of the first year, Investee's net income was $80,000, and Investee declared and paid cash dividends of $55,000. Journalize Investor's (a) purchase of the investment, (b) share of Investee's net income, (c) receipt of dividends from Investee, and (d) sale of Investee stock for $80,100.

4. Parent Corp. paid $100,000 for all the common stock of Subsidiary Corp., and Parent owes Subsidiary $20,000 on a note payable. Assume the fair value of Subsidiary's net assets is equal to book value. Complete the following consolidation work sheet:

Assets	Parent Corp.	Subsidiary Corp.	Eliminations Debit	Eliminations Credit	Consolidated Amounts
Cash	7,000	4,000			
Note receivable from Parent	—	20,000			
Investment in Subsidiary	100,000	—			
Goodwill	—	—			
Other assets	108,000	99,000			___
Total	215,000	123,000			___
Liabilities and Shareholders' Equity					
Accounts payable	15,000	8,000			
Notes payable	20,000	30,000			
Common stock	135,000	60,000			
Retained earnings	45,000	25,000	___	___	___
Total	215,000	123,000			

SOLUTION TO SUMMARY PROBLEM

1. a. Equity   b. Cost (LCM)   c. Consolidation
2. There are two possible solutions to this problem:

    a. Report the investments at cost, $45,625, because total cost is less than total market. No journal entry required.

Stock	Investment Cost	Current Market Value
Dreco Energy Services	$10,750	$17,750
Loblaw Companies	5,000	9,125
Four Seasons Hotels	26,250	18,750
Totals	$42,000	$45,625

    b. Report the investments at the lower of cost or market on an investment-by-investment basis because the market value for one or more of the investments (National Trust) is less than cost.

Stock (Note)	Lower of Investment Cost and Current Market Value
Dreco Energy Services	$10,750
Loblaw Companies...	5,000
Four Seasons Hotels	18,750
Total	$34,500

Note: Market value is $45,625.

Adjusting entry:

Unrealized Loss on Long-Term Investments ($26,250 − $18,750)	7,500	
Long-Term Investments...................................		7,500
To write investments down to market value.		

3. a.

Investment in Investee Common Stock...	67,900	
Cash..		67,900
To purchase 40 percent investment in Investee common stock.		

b.

Investment in Investee Common Stock ($80,000 × .40)	32,000	
Equity-Method Investment Revenue..		32,000
To record 40 percent of Investee net income.		

c.

Cash ($55,000 × .40)	22,000	
Investment in Investee Common Stock...		22,000
To record receipt of 40 percent of Investee cash dividend.		

d.

Cash	80,100	
Investment in Investee Common Stock ($67,900 + $32,000 − $22,000)		77,900
Gain on Sale of Investment...		2,200
Sold investment in Investee common stock.		

4. Consolidation work sheet:

Assets	Parent Corp.	Subsidiary Corp.	Eliminations Debit	Eliminations Credit	Consolidated Amounts
Cash...	7,000	4,000			11,000
Note receivable from Parent	—	20,000		(a) 20,000	—
Investment in Subsidiary	100,000	—		(b) 100,000	—
Goodwill..	—	—	(b) 15,000		15,000
Other assets	108,000	99,000			207,000
Total	215,000	123,000			233,000
Liabilities and Shareholders' Equity					
Accounts payable	15,000	8,000			23,000
Notes payable..	20,000	30,000	(a) 20,000		30,000
Common stock	135,000	60,000	(b) 60,000		135,000
Retained earnings.................................	45,000	25,000	(b) 25,000		45,000
Total	215,000	123,000	120,000	120,000	233,000

Accounting for International Operations

OBJECTIVE 5
Understand how foreign-currency exchange rates are determined

Did you know that Inco and Bombardier earn more than seventy-five percent of their revenues outside of Canada? It is common for Canadian companies to do a large part of their business abroad. John Labatt, Molson, Northern Telecom, Alcan Aluminium, and McCain Foods, among others, are very active in other countries.

Accounting for business activities across national boundaries makes up the field of *international accounting*. As communications and transportation improve and trade barriers fall, global integration makes international accounting more important.

Economic Structures and Their Impact on International Accounting

The business environment varies widely across the globe. Toronto, Montreal, and Vancouver reflect the diversity of the market-driven economy of Canada. Japan's economy is similar to ours, although Japanese business activity focuses more on imports and exports. The central government has controlled the economy of China, so private business decisions are only beginning to take root there. In Brazil, extremely high rates of inflation have made historical-cost amounts meaningless. Accountants must continually adjust the price levels because of the rapid change in the value of the cruzeiro, Brazil's monetary unit. International accounting deals with such differences in economic structures.

Foreign Currencies and Foreign-Currency Exchange Rates

Each country uses its own national currency. Assume Spar Aerospace, sells a "space arm" to the U.S. NASA for use on a space shuttle. Will Spar receive Canadian dollars or U.S. dollars? If the transaction takes place in Canadian dollars, NASA must exchange its U.S. dollars for Canadian dollars in order to pay Spar Aerospace in Canadian currency. If the transaction takes place in U.S. dollars, Spar will receive U.S. dollars which it must exchange for Canadian dollars. In either case, a step has been added to the transaction: one company must convert domestic currency into foreign currency, or the other company must convert foreign currency into domestic currency.

The price of one nation's currency may be stated in terms of another country's monetary unit. This measure of one currency against another currency is called the **foreign-currency exchange rate**. In Exhibit 17-11, the dollar value of a French franc is $.27. This means that one French franc could be bought for twenty-seven cents. Other currencies, such as the pound and the yen (also listed in Exhibit 17-11), are similarly bought and sold.

Exhibit 17-11   *Foreign-Currency Exchange Rates*

Country	Monetary Unit	Cost in Canadian Dollars	Country	Monetary Unit	Cost in Canadian Dollars
United States	Dollar	$1.35	Great Britain	Pound	$2.12
European Common Market	European Currency Unit	1.74	Italy	Lira	.0008
France	Franc	.27	Japan	Yen	.0156
Germany	Deutschmark	.93	Mexico	Peso	.228

Source: *The Financial Post*, May 13, 1995, p. 76.

We use the exchange rate to convert the cost of an item given in one currency to its cost in a second currency. We call this conversion a *translation*. Suppose an item costs two hundred French francs. To compute its cost in dollars, we multiply the amount in francs by the conversion rate: 200 French francs × $.27 = $54.

To aid the flow of international business, a market exists for foreign currencies. Traders buy and sell Canadian dollars, U.S. dollars, French francs, and other currencies in the same way that they buy and sell other commodities like beef, cotton, and automobiles. And just as supply and demand cause the prices of these other commodities to shift, so supply and demand for a particular currency cause exchange rates to fluctuate daily. When the demand for a nation's currency exceeds the supply of that currency, its exchange rate rises. When supply exceeds demand, the currency's exchange rate falls.

Two main factors determine the supply and demand for a particular currency: (1) the ratio of a country's imports to its exports, and (2) the rate of return available in the country's capital markets.

The Import/Export Ratio   Japanese exports far surpass Japan's imports. Customers of Japanese companies must buy yen (the Japanese unit of currency) in the international currency market to pay for their purchases. This strong demand drives up the price—the foreign exchange rate—of the yen. France, on the other hand, imports more goods than it exports. French businesses must sell francs in order to buy the foreign currencies needed to acquire the foreign goods. The supply of the French franc increases and so its price decreases.

The Rate of Return   The rate of return available in a country's capital markets affects the amount of investment funds flowing into the country. When rates of return are high in a politically stable country such as Canada, international investors buy stocks, bonds, and real estate in that country. This increases the demand for the nation's currency and drives up its exchange rate.

Currencies are often described in the financial press as "strong" or "weak." What do these terms mean? The exchange rate of a **strong currency,** such as the yen, is rising relative to other nations' currencies. The exchange rate of a **weak currency**, such as the lira, is falling relative to other currencies.

Suppose on May 13 *The Financial Post* listed the exchange rate for the British pound as $2.12. On June 14 the rate has changed to $2.21. We would say that the dollar has fallen against the British pound—the dollar is weaker than the pound—because the pound has become more expensive, and so the dollar now buys fewer pounds. A weaker dollar would make travel to England less attractive to Canadians.

The Financial Post reported a fall in the exchange rate of the Mexican peso from $.228 to $.224. This indicates that the peso is weaker than the dollar. Mexican products are less expensive because each dollar buys more pesos.

In our example situation—in which the pound has risen relative to the dollar and the peso has dropped relative to the dollar—we would describe the pound as the strongest currency, the peso as the weakest currency, and the dollar as somewhere between the other two currencies.

Accounting for International Transactions

When a Canadian company transacts business with a foreign company, the transaction price can be stated either in dollars or in the national currency of the other company. If the price is stated in dollars, the Canadian company has no special accounting difficulties. The transaction is recorded and reported in dollars exactly as though the other company were also Canadian.

Purchases on Account

If the transaction price is stated in units of the foreign currency, the Canadian company encounters two accounting steps. First, the transaction price must be translated into dollars for recording in the accounting records. Second, credit transactions (the most common international transaction) usually cause the Canadian company to experience a **foreign-currency transaction gain** or **loss**. This type of gain or loss occurs when the exchange rate changes between the date of the purchase on account and the date of the subsequent payment of cash.

The credit purchase creates an Account Payable that is recorded at the prevailing exchange rate. Later, when the buyer pays cash, the exchange rate has almost certainly changed. Accounts Payable is debited for the amount recorded earlier, and Cash is credited for the amount paid at the current exchange rate. A debit difference is a loss, and a credit difference is a gain.

Suppose on May 13, 1995, Eaton's Department Store imports Shalimar perfume from a French supplier at a price of 200,000 francs. The exchange rate is $.27 per French franc. Eaton's records this credit purchase as follows:

May 13	Purchases...	54,000	
	Accounts Payable (200,000 × $.27)..............		54,000

Eaton's translates the French franc price of the merchandise (200,000 Fr) into dollars ($54,000) for recording the purchase and the related account payable.

If Eaton's were to pay this account immediately (which is unlikely in international commerce) Eaton's would debit Accounts Payable and credit Cash for $54,000. Suppose, however, that the credit terms specify payment within 60 days. On July 2, when Eaton's pays this debt, the exchange rate has fallen to $.26 per French franc. Eaton's payment entry is

July 2	Accounts Payable..	54,000	
	Cash (200,000 × $.26).....................................		52,000
	Foreign-Currency Transaction Gain...........		2,000

Eaton's has a gain because the company has settled the debt with fewer dollars than the amount of the original account payable. If on the payment date the exchange rate of the French franc had exceeded $.27, Eaton's would have paid more dollars than the original $54,000. The company would have recorded a loss on the transaction as a debit to Foreign-Currency Transaction Loss.

Sales on Account

International sales on account also may be measured in foreign currency. Suppose Bombardier sells some Ski Doos to the German government on December 9. The price of the Ski Doos is 140,000 German marks, and the exchange rate is $.93 per German mark. Bombardier's sale entry is

Dec. 9	Accounts Receivable (140,000 × $.93)	130,200	
	Sales revenue		130,200

Assume Bombardier collects from Germany on December 30, when the exchange rate has fallen to $.92 per German mark. Bombardier receives fewer dollars than the recorded amount of the receivable and so experiences a foreign-currency transaction loss. The collection entry is

Dec. 30	Cash (140,000 × $.92)...	128,800	
	Foreign-Currency Transaction Loss................	1,400	
	Accounts Receivable.....................................		130,200

Foreign-Currency Transaction Gains and Losses are combined for each accounting period. The net amount of gain or loss can be reported as Other Revenue and Expense on the income statement.

Further discussion of foreign currency and international transactions is beyond the scope of this text and will be covered in more advanced courses.

Short Exercise:

(1) On May 13, the exchange rate for German marks was DM = $.93. International Corp. (a Canadian company) purchased inventory from a German company at a cost of 50,000 DM. Record the purchase in dollars. (2) Record the payment on May 31 for a current exchange rate of DM = $.91.

A:

(1) Inventory....... 46,500
   Accounts
    Payable 46,500
(50,000 DM × $.93 = 46,500)
(2) Accounts
   Payable........ 46,500
   Foreign-Currency
   Transaction
    Gain 1,000
   Cash 45,500
(50,000 DM × $.91 = 45,500)

International Accounting Standards _____

For the most part, accounting principles are similar from country to country. However, some important differences exist. For example, some countries, such as Italy, require financial statements to conform closely to income tax laws. In other countries, such as Brazil and Argentina, high inflation rates dictate that companies make price-level adjustments to report amounts in units of common purchasing power. Neither practice is followed as closely in Canada.

Several organizations are working to achieve worldwide harmony of accounting standards. Chief among these is the International Accounting Standards Committee (IASC). Headquartered in London, the IASC operates much as the CICA's Accounting Standards Board in Canada. It has the support of the accounting professions in Canada, the United States, most of the British Commonwealth countries, Japan, France, Germany, the Netherlands, and Mexico. However, the IASC has no authority to require compliance with its accounting standards. It must rely on cooperation by the various national accounting professions. Since its creation in 1973, the IASC has succeeded in narrowing some differences in international accounting standards.

Chapter 12 discussed the membership of three accounting bodies in Canada, the CICA, CGAAC, and SMAC, in the IASC. There was a brief discussion of the relationship between International Accounting Standards (IASs) issued by the IASC and the *CICA Handbook*. The CICA is attempting to harmonize the *Handbook* with the IASs.

Summary Problem for Your Review

Journalize the following transactions of Canada Corp.:

19X5

Nov. 16   Purchased equipment on account for 40,000 Swiss francs when the exchange rate was $1.191 per Swiss franc.

27   Sold merchandise on account to a Belgian company for 700,000 Belgian francs. Each franc is worth $.0479.

Dec. 22   Paid the Swiss company when the franc's exchange rate was $1.185.

31   Adjusted for the change in the exchange rate of the Belgian franc. Its current exchange rate is $.0475.

19X6

Jan.   4   Collected from the Belgian company. The exchange rate is $.0480.

1. Entries for transactions stated in foreign currencies:

19X5			
Nov. 16	Equipment (40,000 × $1.191)	47,640	
	Accounts Payable		47,640
27	Accounts Receivable (700,000 × $.0479)	33,530	
	Sales Revenue...		33,530
Dec. 22	Accounts Payable	47,640	
	Cash (40,000 × $1.185)		47,400
	Foreign-Currency Transaction Gain		240
31	Foreign-Currency Transaction Loss		
	[700,000 × ($.0479 – $.0475)]	280	
	Accounts Receivable		280

19X6

Jan. 4	Cash (700,000 × .0480)......................................	33, 600	
	Accounts Receivable		
	($33,530 – $280)...................................		33,250
	Foreign-Currency Transaction Gain		
	[700,000 × ($.0480 – $.0475)]................		350

Summary

1. *Account for trading investments in stock by the cost (LCM) method.*
Investments are classified as short-term or long-term. *Short-term investments* are liquid, and the investor intends to convert them to cash within one year or less, or to use them to pay a current liability. All other investments are *long-term*.

Different methods are used to account for stock investments, depending on the investor's degree of influence over the investee. All investments are recorded initially at *cost*. Short-term investments are accounted for by the cost method (with lower-of-cost-or-market) and are reported on the balance sheet at the lower of their cost or current market (LCM) value. Dividends received are recorded as income.

2. *Use the equity method for stock investments.* Long-term investments of less than 20 percent of the investee's stock are also accounted for using the cost method. The *equity* method is used to account for investments of between 20 and 50 percent of the investee company's stock. Such an investment enables the investor to significantly influence the investee's activities. Investee income is recorded by the investor by debiting the Investment account and crediting an account entitled Equity-Method Investment Revenue. The investor records receipt of dividends from the investee by crediting the Investment account.

3. *Consolidate parent and subsidiary balance sheets.* Ownership of more than 50 percent of the voting stock creates a *parent-subsidiary* relationship, and the *consolidation* method must be used. Because the parent has control over the subsidiary, the subsidiary's financial statements are included in the consolidated statements of the parent company. Two features of consolidation accounting are (1) addition of the parent and subsidiary accounts to prepare the parent's consolidated statements, and (2) elimination of intercompany items. When a parent owns less than 100 percent of the subsidiary's stock, the portion owned by outside investors is called *minority interest*. Purchase of a controlling interest at a cost greater than the fair value of the subsidiary's net assets creates an intangible asset called *goodwill*. A consolidation work sheet is used to prepare the consolidated financial statements.

4. *Account for investments in bonds.* *Long-term investments* in bonds are accounted for at amortized cost.

5. *Understand how foreign currency exchange rates are determined.* *International accounting* deals with accounting for business activities across national boundaries. A key issue is the translation of foreign-currency accounts into dollars, accomplished through a *foreign-currency exchange rate*. Changes in exchange rates cause companies to experience *foreign-currency transaction gains and losses* on credit transactions.

The International Accounting Standards Committee is working to harmonize accounting principles worldwide.

Self-Study Questions

Test your understanding of the chapter by marking the best answer for each of the following questions:

1. Short-term investments are reported on the balance sheet *(p. 814)*

a. Immediately after cash
b. Immediately after accounts receivable
c. Immediately after inventory
d. Immediately after current assets

2. Byforth, Inc., distributes a 10 percent stock dividend. An investor who owns Byforth stock should *(p. 815)*
   a. Debit Investment and credit Dividend Revenue for the book value of the stock received in the dividend distribution
   b. Debit Investment and credit Dividend Revenue for the market value of the stock received in the dividend distribution
   c. Debit Cash and credit Investment for the market value of the stock received in the dividend distribution
   d. Make a memorandum entry to record the new cost per share of Byforth stock held

3. Short-term investments are reported at the *(p. 816–817)*
   a. Total cost of the portfolio
   b. Total market value of the portfolio
   c. Lower of total cost or total market value of the portfolio or lower of cost or market value on an investment-by-investment basis
   d. Total equity value of the portfolio

4. Putsch Corporation owns 30 percent of the voting stock of Mazelli, Inc. Mazelli reports net income of $100,000 and declares and pays cash dividends of $40,000. Which method should Putsch use to account for this investment? *(p. 817)*
   a. Cost   c. Equity
   b. Market value   d. Consolidation

5. Refer to the facts of the preceding question. What effect do Mazelli's income and dividends have on Putsch's net income? *(pp. 817–819)*
   a. Increase of $12,000   c. Increase of $30,000
   b. Increase of $18,000   d. Increase of $42,000

6. In applying the consolidation method, elimination entries are *(p. 822)*
   a. Necessary
   b. Required only when the parent has a receivable from or a payable to the subsidiary
   c. Required only when there is a minority interest
   d. Required only for the preparation of the consolidated balance sheet

7. Parent Corp. has separate net income of $155,000. Subsidiary A, which Parent owns 90 percent of, reports net income of $60,000, and Subsidiary B, which Parent owns 60 percent of, reports net income of $80,000. What is Parent Corp.'s consolidated net income? *(p. 823)*
   a. $155,000   c. $263,000
   b. $257,000   d. $295,000

8. On May 16, the exchange rate of the German mark was $.93. On May 20, the exchange rate is $.94. Which of the following statements is true? *(p. 831)*
   a. The dollar has risen against the mark.
   b. The dollar has fallen against the mark.
   c. The dollar is weaker than the mark.
   d. The dollar and the mark are equally strong.

9. A strong Canadian dollar encourages *(p. 832)*
   a. Travel to Canada by foreigners
   b. Purchase of Canadian goods by foreigners
   c. Canadians to travel abroad
   d. Canadians to save dollars

10. Ford Motor Company of Canada purchased auto accessories from an English supplier at a price of 500,000 British pounds. On the date of the credit purchase, the exchange rate of the British pound was $2.12. On the payment date, the exchange rate of the pound is $2.15. If payment is in pounds, Ford experiences *(p. 832)*

SOLUTION TO REVIEW PROBLEM

a. A foreign-currency transaction gain of $15,000
b. A foreign-currency transaction loss of $15,000
c. Neither a transaction gain nor loss because the debt is paid in dollars
d. None of the above

Answers to the Self-Study Questions follow the accounting vocabulary.

Accounting Vocabulary

Consolidated statements *(p. 820)*
Controlling (majority) interest *(p. 819)*
Cost method for investments *(p. 814)*
Equity method for investments *(p. 818)*
Foreign-currency exchange rate *(p. 831)*
Long-term investment *(p. 814)*
Marketable security *(p. 814)*
Minority interest *(p. 823)*
Parent company *(p. 819)*
Short-term investment *(p. 814)*
Strong currency *(p. 832)*
Subsidiary company *(p. 819)*
Temporary investment *(p. 814)*
Weak currency *(p. 832)*

Answers to Self-Study Questions

1. a
2. d
3. c
4. c
5. c ($100,000 × .30 = $30,000; dividends have no effect on investor net income under the equity method)
6. a
7. b [$155,000 + ($60,000 × .90) + ($80,000 × .60) = $257,000]
8. a
9. c
10. b [500,000 × ($2.15 – $2.12) = $15,000]

ASSIGNMENT MATERIAL _____

Questions

1. How are stock prices quoted in the securities market? What is the investor's cost of 1,000 shares of BC Telephone $4.50 preferred stock at $63.25 with a brokerage commission of $1,350?

2. What distinguishes a short-term investment from a long-term investment?

3. Show the positions of short-term investments and long-term investments on the balance sheet.

4. Outline the accounting methods for the different types of investment.

5. How does an investor record the receipt of a cash dividend on an investment accounted for by the cost method? How does this investor record receipt of a stock dividend?

6. An investor paid $11,000 for 1,000 shares of stock and later received a 10 percent stock dividend. Compute the gain or loss on sale of 300 shares of the stock for $2,600.

7. At what amount are short-term investments reported on the balance sheet? Are the short-term and long-term investment portfolios mixed, or are they kept separate?

8. When is an investment accounted for by the equity method? Outline how to apply the equity method. Include in your answer how to record the purchase of the investment, the investor's proportion of the investee's net income, and receipt of a cash dividend from the investee. Describe how to measure gain or loss on sale of this investment.

9. Identify three transactions that cause debits or credits to an equity-method investment account.

10. What are two special features of the consolidation method for investments?

11. Why are intercompany items eliminated from consolidated financial statements? Name two intercompany items that are eliminated.

12. Name the account that expresses the excess of cost of an investment over the fair market value of the subsidiary's net assets. What type of account is this, and where in the financial statements is it reported?

13. When a parent company buys less than 100 percent of a subsidiary's stock, a certain type of equity is created. What is it called and how do most companies report it?

14. How would you measure the net income of a parent company with three subsidiaries? Assume that two subsidiaries are wholly (100 percent) owned and that the parent owns 60 percent of the third subsidiary.

15. What is the difference between accounting for a short-term bond investment and a long-term bond investment?

16. Which situation results in a foreign-currency transaction gain for a Canadian business? Which situation results in a loss?
    a. Credit purchase denominated in pesos, followed by weakness in the peso
    b. Credit purchase denominated in pesos, followed by weakness in the dollar
    c. Credit sale denominated in pesos, followed by weakness in the peso
    d. Credit sale denominated in pesos, followed by weakness in the dollar

Exercises

Exercise 17-1   *Journalizing transactions under the cost method*   **(Obj. 1)**

Journalize the following investment transactions of Maral Corp.:

a. Purchased 800 shares (8 percent) of Madison Corporation common stock at $44 per share, with brokerage commission of $300.

b. Received cash dividend of $1 per share on the Madison investment.

c. Sold 200 shares of Madison stock for $49 per share.

Exercise 17-2   *Reporting investments at the lower of cost or market*   **(Obj. 1)**

CP Rail recently reported the following information (not including the question mark) on its balance sheet:

Current Assets	(dollars in millions)
Cash and cash equivalents	$398
Marketable securities [short-term investments], at lower of cost or market	?

Assume that the cost of CP Rail's short-term investments is $130 million and that current market value is $126 million.

Required

Apply the lower-of-cost-or-market method to CP Rail's short-term investments by inserting the appropriate amount in place of the question mark. Write a note to identify the method used to report short-term investments and to disclose cost and market value. Journalize any needed adjustment, assuming the marketable securities were purchased during the current year.

Exercise 17-3   *Journalizing transactions under the equity method*   **(Obj. 2)**

Canadian National Railway System (CN) owns equity-method investments in several companies. Suppose CN paid $2,000,000 to acquire a 30 percent investment in Western Service Corp. Further, assume Western Service reported net income of $640,000 for the first year and declared and paid cash dividends of $420,000. Record the following in CN's general journal: (a) purchase of the investment, (b) CN's proportion of Western Service's net income, and (c) receipt of the cash dividends.

Exercise 17-4   *Recording equity-method transactions directly in the accounts*   **(Obj. 2)**

Without making journal entries, record the transactions of Exercise 17-3 directly in the Investment in Western Service Corp's Common Stock account. Assume that after all the above transactions took place, CN sold its entire investment in Western Service common stock for cash of $2,400,000. Journalize the sale of the investment.

Exercise 17-5   *Comparing the cost and equity methods*   **(Obj. 1, 2)**

Jacina Corporation paid $160,000 for a 40 percent investment in the common stock of Stewart Design, Inc. For the first year, Stewart reported net income of $84,000 and at year end declared and paid cash dividends of $16,000. On the balance sheet date the market value of Jacina's investment in Stewart stock was $153,000.

Required

1. On Jacina's books, journalize the purchase of the investment, recognition of Jacina's portion of Stewart's net income, and receipt of dividends from Stewart under the equity method, which is appropriate for these circumstances.
2. Repeat requirement 1 but follow the cost method for comparison purposes only.
3. Show the amount that Jacina would report for the investment on its year-end balance sheet under the two methods.

Exercise 17-6   *Completing a consolidation work sheet with minority interest*   **(Obj. 3)**

Chin Holdings Ltd., owns an 80 percent interest in Lam Inc. Complete the following to create a consolidation work sheet:

Assets	Chin Holdings Ltd.	Lam Inc.
Cash	49,000	14,000
Accounts receivable, net	82,000	53,000
Note receivable from Chin	—	12,000
Inventory	114,000	77,000
Investment in Lam	90,000	—
Capital assets, net	186,000	129,000
Other assets	22,000	8,000
Total	543,000	293,000

Liabilities and Shareholders' Equity

Accounts payable	44,000	26,000
Notes payable	47,000	36,000
Other liabilities	82,000	131,000
Minority interest	—	—
Common stock	210,000	80,000
Retained earnings	160,000	20,000
Total	543,000	293,000

Exercise 17-7   *Elimination entries under the consolidation method*   **(Obj. 4)**

Assume on December 31 that Doucet Financial Consultants Ltd., a 100 percent owned subsidiary of Schroeder Corp., had the following owner's equity:

Common stock	$200,000
Retained earnings	410,000

Assume further that Schroeder's cost of its investment in Doucet was $610,000 and that Doucet owed Schroeder $32,000 on a note.

Required

Give the work-sheet entry to eliminate (a) the investment of Schroeder and the shareholders' equity of Doucet and (b) the note receivable of Schroeder and note payable of Doucet.

Exercise 17-8   *Recording short-term bond investment transactions*   **(Obj. 4)**

On June 30, Statistical Research, Inc., paid $92.25 for 8 percent bonds of Krebs Limited as a short-term investment. The maturity value of the bonds is $20,000, and they pay interest on March 31 and September 30. Record Statistical Research's purchase of the bond investment, the receipt of semiannual interest on September 30, and the accrual of interest revenue on December 31. At December 31, the bonds' market value is $93.00.

Exercise 17-9   *Recording long-term bond investment transactions*   **(Obj. 4)**

Assume the Krebs Limited bonds in the preceding exercise are purchased as a long-term investment on June 30, 19X3. The bonds mature on September 30, 19X7.

Required

1. Using the straight-line method of amortizing the discount, journalize all transactions on the bonds for 19X3.
2. How much more interest revenue would the investor record in 19X3 for a long-term investment than for a short-term investment in these bonds? What accounts for this difference?
3. Show how the investment would be reported on the balance sheet at December 31.

Exercise 17-10   *Journalizing foreign-currency transactions*   **(Obj. 5)**

Journalize the following foreign-currency transactions:

Nov. 17   Purchased goods on account from a Japanese company. The price was 200,000 yen, and the exchange rate of the yen was $.0156.

Dec. 16   Paid the Japanese supplier when the exchange rate was $.016.

19   Sold merchandise on account to a French company at a price of 60,000 French francs. The exchange rate was $.27.

31 Adjusted for the decrease in the value of the franc, which had an exchange rate of $.26.

Jan. 14 Collected from the French company. The exchange rate was $.28.

Problems   (Group A)

Problem 17-1A *Journalizing transactions under the cost and equity methods* **(Obj. 1, 2)**

Great Western Holdings Limited, the conglomerate, owns numerous investments in the stock of other companies. Assume Great Western Holdings completed the following investment transactions:

19X4

May 1 Purchased 8,000 shares (total issued and outstanding common shares, 38,400) of the common stock of MIC Limited at total cost of $720,000.

July 1 Purchased 1,600 additional shares of MIC Limited common stock at cost of $140,000.

Sept. 15 Received semiannual cash dividend of $1.40 per share on the MIC investment.

Oct. 12 Purchased 1,000 shares of ROX Corporation common stock as a short-term investment, paying $22.50 per share plus brokerage commission of $1,000.

Dec. 14 Received semiannual cash dividend of $.80 per share on the ROX investment.

Dec. 31 Received annual report from MIC Company. Net income for the year was $350,000. Of this amount, Great Western's proportion is 25 percent. The current market for ROX stock is $20,000.

19X5

Feb. 6 Sold 1,920 shares of MIC stock for net cash of $169,700.

Required

Record the transactions in the general journal of Great Western Holdings Limited; the company year end is December 31.

Problem 17-2A *Applying the cost method (with LCM) and the equity method* **(Obj. 1, 2)**

The beginning balance sheet of NOVA Corp. recently included:

Investments in Affiliates $84,057,000

Investments in Affiliates refers to long-term investments accounted for by the equity method. NOVA included its short-term investments among the current assets. Assume the company completed the following investment transactions during the year:

Mar. 3 Purchased 6,000 shares of common stock as a short-term investment, paying $9.25 per share plus brokerage commission of $1,350.

4 Purchased new long-term investment in affiliate at cost of $408,000.

May 14 Received semiannual cash dividend of $.82 per share on the short-term investment purchased March 3.

June 15 Received cash dividend of $27,000 from affiliated company.

Aug. 28 Sold the short-term investment (purchased on March 3) for $10.50 per share, less brokerage commission of $750.

Oct. 24 Purchased other short-term investments for $226,000, plus brokerage commission of $11,400.

Dec. 15 Received cash dividend of $29,000 from affiliated company.

31 Received annual reports from affiliated companies. Their total net income for the year was $620,000. Of this amount, NOVA's proportion is 30 percent.

Required

1. Record the transactions in the general journal of NOVA Corp.

2. Post entries to the Investments in Affiliates T-account, and determine its balance at December 31.

3. Assume the beginning balance of Short-Term Investments was at a cost of $356,400. Post entries to the Short-Term Investments T-account and determine its balance at December 31.

4. Assuming the market value of the short-term investment portfolio is $540,000 at December 31, show how NOVA Corp. would report short-term investments and investments in affiliates on the ending balance sheet. NOVA compares total portfolio cost to total portfolio market value in determining the lower of cost or market. Use the following format:

Cash..	$XXX
Short-term investments, at lower of cost or market ($ _?_ , ___)	
Accounts receivable...	XXX
Total current assets	XXX
Investments in affiliates...	

Problem 17-3A   *Preparing a consolidated balance sheet; no minority interest*   **(Obj. 3)**

Trent Corp. paid $179,000 to acquire all the common stock of Ritz Inc., and Ritz owes Trent Corp. $55,000 on a note payable. Immediately after the purchase on May 31, 19X7, the two companies' balance sheets were as follows:

	Trent Corp.	Ritz Inc.
Assets		
Cash...	$ 18,000	$ 32,000
Accounts receivable, net.........................	64,000	43,000
Note receivable from Stratford..............	55,000	—
Inventory	93,000	153,000
Investment in Ritz	179,000	—
Capital assets, net...................................	205,000	138,000
Total...	$614,000	$366,000
Liabilities and Shareholders' Equity		
Accounts payable	$ 76,000	$ 37,000
Notes payable	118,000	123,000
Other liabilities	44,000	27,000
Common stock...	282,000	79,000
Retained earnings....................................	94,000	100,000
Total..	$614,000	$366,000

Required

1. Prepare a consolidation work sheet.

2. Prepare the consolidated balance sheet on May 31, 19X7. Show total assets, total liabilities, and total shareholders' equity. It is not necessary to classify assets and liabilities as current and long-term.

Problem 17-4A   *Preparing a consolidated balance sheet with goodwill*   **(Obj. 3, 4)**

On August 17, 19X8, Systex Inc. paid $229,000 to purchase all the common stock of Douglas Design Ltd., and Douglas owes Systex $42,000 on a note payable. All historical cost amounts are equal to their fair market value on August 17, 19X8. Immediately after the purchase, the two companies' balance sheets were as follows:

	Systex Inc.	Douglas Design Ltd.
Assets		
Cash	$ 23,000	$ 37,000
Accounts receivable, net	71,000	54,000
Note receivable from Douglas	42,000	—
Inventory	213,000	170,000
Investment in Douglas	229,000	—
Capital assets, net	197,000	175,000
Goodwill	—	—
Total	$775,000	$436,000
Liabilities and Shareholders' Equity		
Accounts payable	$119,000	$ 77,000
Notes payable	190,000	71,000
Other liabilities	33,000	88,000
Common stock	219,000	90,000
Retained earnings	214,000	110,000
Total	$775,000	$436,000

Required

1. Prepare a consolidation work sheet.
2. Prepare the consolidated balance sheet on August 17, 19X8. Show total assets, total liabilities and total shareholders' equity. It is not necessary to classify assets and liabilities as current and long-term.

Problem 17-5A   *Accounting for a long-term bond investment purchased at a discount* **(Obj. 5)**

Financial institutions such as insurance companies and pension plans hold large quantities of bond investments. Suppose Mutual Life Insurance Company purchases $500,000 of 8 percent bonds of Power Corporation for $92.00 on March 31, 19X0. These bonds pay interest on January 31 and July 31 each year. They mature on July 31, 19X8. At December 31, 19X0, the market price of the bonds is $93.00.

Required

1. Journalize Mutual's purchase of the bonds as a long-term investment on March 31, 19X0, receipt of cash interest and amortization of discount on July 31, 19X0, and accrual of interest revenue and amortization of discount at December 31, 19X0. Assume the straight-line method is appropriate for amortizing discount.
2. Show all financial statement effects of this long-term bond investment at December 31, 19X0. Assume a multiple-step income statement.
3. Repeat requirement 2 under the assumption that Mutual purchased these bonds as a short-term investment.

Problem 17-6A   *Computing the cost of a bond investment and journalizing its transactions (Obj. 4)*

On December 31, 19X1, when the market interest rate is 10 percent, an investor purchases $400,000 of Temagemi Corp. 10-year, 9.5 percent bonds at issuance. Determine the cost (present value) of the bond investment. Assume that the investment is long-term. Journalize the purchase on December 31, 19X1, the first semiannual interest receipt on June 30, 19X2, and the year-end interest receipt on December 31, 19X2. The investor uses the effective-interest amortization method. Prepare a schedule for amortizing the premium on the bond investment through December 31, 19X2. If necessary, refer to Chapter 16 and its appendix.

Note: Problem 17-6A is based on the present-value appendix in Chapter 16.

Problem 17-7A   *Journalizing foreign-currency transactions and reporting the transaction gain or loss   (Obj. 6)*

Suppose Xerox of Canada Ltd. completed the following transactions:

Dec.   1   Sold a photocopy machine on account to Pirelli Tire Company for $19,000. The exchange rate of the Italian lira is $.0008, and Pirelli agrees to pay in Canadian dollars.

10   Purchased supplies on account from a U.S. company at a price of U.S. $50,000. The exchange rate of the U.S. dollar is $1.35, and payment will be in U.S. dollars.

17   Sold a photocopy machine on account to an English firm for 100,000 British pounds. Payment will be in pounds, and the exchange rate of the pound is $2.12.

22   Collected from Pirelli. The exchange rate of the lira has not changed since December 1.

31   Adjusted the accounts for changes in foreign-currency exchange rates. Current rates: U.S. dollar, $1.32; British pound, $2.08.

Jan.   18   Paid the U.S. company. The exchange rate of the U.S. dollar is $1.38.

24   Collected from the English firm. The exchange rate of the British pound is $2.11.

Required

1. Record these transactions in Xerox's general journal, and show how to report the transaction gain or loss on the income statement.

2. How will what you have learned in this problem help you structure international transactions?

Problem 17-8A   *Accounting for stock investments using the cost method at LCM and long-term investments in bonds   (Obj. 1, 4)*

Regency Corp. had the following short-term investments in marketable securities (valued at the lower of cost or market on an investment-by-investment basis):

LCM

Air Products Canada Ltd.............................	$128,000
Finning Ltd.	49,000
Regina Transport Ltd.	96,000
Total short-term investments	$273,000

The following transactions took place during 19X1 with regard to Regency's investments:

Jan.   5   Purchased 5,000 shares (2 percent) of Highflyer Ltd. as a short-term investment. The shares were purchased at 23¾ with a commission of $1,200.

31   Highflyer Ltd. reported net income of $2,800,000 and declared a cash dividend of $500,000.

Feb. 15 Received $10,000 from Highflyer Ltd. as a cash dividend.

April 1 Purchased $100,000 (face value) of bonds at 102 as a long-term invest-ment. The bonds pay 10 percent interest (5 percent semiannually) on October 1st and April 1st and mature in 2 years.

Aug. 31 Received a 10 percent percent stock dividend from Highflyer Ltd.

Oct. 1 Received the interest on the bonds.

Nov. 1 Highflyer declared and distributed a 2 for 1 stock split.

Dec. 15 Sold 4,000 shares of Highflyer at 12½ with a commission of $600.

31 Recorded the adjustment for accrued interest on the bonds.

31 The market values of the investments were:

Air Products Canada Ltd.	$134,000
Finning Ltd.	47,000
Highflyer Ltd.	91,000
Regina Transport Ltd.	94,000
Total short-term investments	$366,000

Required

Prepare the general journal entries required to record the transactions of 19X1.

Problem 17-9A   *Accounting for stock investments using the equity method, accounting for investments in bonds, and accounting for transactions stated in a foreign currency* **(Obj. 2, 4, 5)**

KSL Ltd. uses the equity method in accounting for long-term investments and had the following investment transactions:

19X1

Jan. 14 KSL Ltd. purchased 20,000 shares (30 percent) of Goldfinders Ltd. com-mon stock as a long-term investment. The shares were purchased for 14¼ with a commission of $2,200.

Mar. 31 Goldfinders Ltd. reported net income of $100,000 and declared a dividend of $80,000.

April 30 Received $24,000 as a cash dividend from Goldfinders Ltd.

May 1 Purchased $100,000 (U.S. dollar face value) of United America Ltd. bonds at 103 as a short-term investment. The bonds pay interest of 12 percent (6 percent semiannually) each May 1st and November 1st, and mature in 5 years. The exchange rate at the time of the transaction was $1.36 Canadian for each American dollar.

June 20 Received 2,000 shares of Goldfinders Ltd. common stock as a 10 percent stock dividend.

Oct. 1 Goldfinders Ltd. declared and distributed a 3-for-1 common stock split.

Nov. 1 Received the interest on the United America Ltd. bonds when the exchange rate was $1.39 Canadian per American dollar.

Dec. 20 Sold 10,000 shares of Goldfinders Ltd. common stock at 6½ with a com-mission of $800.

31 Adjusted for the accrued interest on the United America Ltd. bonds. The exchange rate was $1.35 Canadian per American dollar.

19X2

May 1 Received the interest on the United America Ltd. bonds when the exchange rate was $1.32 Canadian per American dollar.

Required

1. Prepare the general journal entries required to record these transactions.

2. Show the balance sheet presentation of the investments on May 1, 19X2, assum-ing the United America Ltd. bonds have a market rate of 102 and the exchange rate is $1.34 Canadian per American dollar.

(Group B)

Problem 17-1B   *Journalizing transactions under the cost and equity methods*   *(Obj. 1, 2)*

Segovia Packing Co. Ltd. owns numerous investments in the stock of other companies. Assume Segovia completed the following investment transactions:

19X6

Feb. 12   Purchased 20,000 shares (total issued and outstanding common shares, 90,000) of the common stock of Agribusiness, Inc., at total cost of $715,000.

July   1   Purchased 8,000 additional shares of Agribusiness common stock at cost of $300,000.

Aug.   9   Received annual cash dividend of $.90 per share on the Agribusiness investment.

Oct.   16   Purchased 1,000 shares of Apex Corp. common stock as a short-term investment, paying $43 per share plus brokerage commission of $900.

Nov. 30   Received semiannual cash dividend of $.60 per share on the Apex investment.

Dec. 31   Received annual report from Agribusiness, Inc. Net income for the year was $510,000. Of this amount, ConAgra's proportion is 35 percent.

19X7   The current value of Apex stock is $36,000.

Jan.   14   Sold 4,000 shares of Agribusiness stock for net cash of $141,000.

Required

Record the transactions in the general journal of ConAgra, Inc.

Problem 17-2B   *Applying the cost method (with LCM) and the equity method*   *(Obj. 1, 2)*

The beginning balance sheet of Ranco Limited recently included:

Investments in Affiliates..................... $6,344,000

Investments in Affiliates refers to investments accounted for by the equity method. The company completed the following investment transactions during the year:

Mar.   2   Purchased 2,000 shares of common stock as a short-term investment, paying 12.25 per share plus brokerage commission of $1,000.

        5   Purchased new long-term investment in affiliate at cost of $540,000.

Apr. 21   Received semiannual cash dividend of $.75 per share on the short-term investment purchased March 2.

May 17   Received cash dividend of $47,000 from affiliated company.

July 16   Sold 1,600 shares of the short-term investment (purchased on March 2) for $11 per share less brokerage commission of $920.

Nov.   8   Purchased short-term investments for $136,000, plus brokerage commission of $5,100.

Nov. 17   Received cash dividend of $49,000 from affiliated company.

Dec. 31   Received annual reports from affiliated companies. Their total net income for the year was $550,000. Of this amount, Ranco's proportion is 22 percent.

Required

1. Record the transactions in the general journal of Ranco Limited.

2. Post entries to the Investments in Affiliates T-account and determine its balance at December 31.

3. Assume the beginning balance of Short-Term Investments was cost of $293,600. Post entries to the Short-Term Investments T-account and determine its balance at December 31.

4. Assuming the market value of the short-term investment portfolio is $413,000 at December 31, show how Ranco would report short-term investments and investments in affiliates on the ending balance sheet. Ranco compares total portfolio cost to total portfolio market value in determining the lower of cost or market. Use the following format:

Cash.. $XXX

Short-term investments, at lower of cost or market (_?_ , ___)

Accounts receivable.. XXX

Total current assets.. XXX

Investments in affiliates... ____

Problem 17-3B   *Preparing a consolidated balance sheet; no minority interest* **(Obj. 3, 4)**

Ben Silver Corp. paid $266,000 to acquire all the common stock of Massada Inc., and Massada owes Ben Silver $81,000 on a note payable. Immediately after the purchase on June 30, 19X3, the two companies' balance sheets were as follows:

	Ben Silver Corp.	Massada Inc.
Assets		
Cash.......................................	$ 24,000	$ 20,000
Accounts receivable, net......................	91,000	42,000
Note receivable from Massada...........	81,000	—
Inventory.................................	145,000	214,000
Investment in Massada......................	266,000	—
Capital assets, net.............................	178,000	219,000
Total.......................................	$785,000	$495,000
Liabilities and Shareholders' Equity		
Accounts payable...............................	$ 57,000	$ 49,000
Notes payable.....................................	177,000	149,000
Other liabilities....................................	129,000	31,000
Common stock....................................	274,000	118,000
Retained earnings...............................	148,000	148,000
Total.......................................	$785,000	$495,000

Required

1. Prepare a consolidation work sheet.

2. Prepare the consolidated balance sheet on June 30, 19X3. Show total assets, total liabilities and total shareholders' equity. It is not necessary to classify assets and liabilities as current and long-term.

Problem 17-4B   *Preparing a consolidated balance sheet with minority interest* **(Obj. 3)**

On March 22, 19X4, Viking Travel Corp. paid $280,000 to purchase 80 percent of the common stock of Zurich Sea Travel Inc., and Zurich owes Viking $67,000 on a note payable. Immediately after the purchase, the two companies' balance sheets were as follows:

	Viking Travel Corporation	Zurich Sea Travel
Assets		
Cash	$ 41,000	$ 43,000
Accounts receivable, net	86,000	206,000
Note receivable from Zurich	67,000	—
Inventory	128,000	75,000
Investment in Zurich	280,000	—
Capital assets, net	277,000	168,000
Total	$879,000	$492,000
Liabilities and Shareholders' Equity		
Accounts payable	$ 72,000	$ 65,000
Notes payable	301,000	67,000
Other liabilities	11,000	10,000
Minority interest	—	—
Common stock	141,000	160,000
Retained earnings	354,000	190,000
Total	$879,000	$492,000

Required

1. Prepare a consolidation work sheet.
2. Prepare the consolidated balance sheet on March 22, 19X4. Show total assets, total liabilities, and total shareholders' equity. It is not necessary to classify assets and liabilities as current and long-term.

Problem 17-5B   *Accounting for a long-term bond investment purchased at a premium (Obj. 4)*

Financial institutions such as insurance companies and pension plans hold large quantities of bond investments. Suppose Prairie Mutual Life purchases $600,000 of 9 percent bonds of BC Tel Corporation for $103.00 on July 1, 19X1. These bonds pay interest on March 1 and September 1 each year. They mature on March 1, 19X8.

Required

1. Journalize Prairie Mutual's purchase of the bonds as a long-term investment on July 1, 19X1, receipt of cash interest and amortization of premium on September 1, 19X1, and accrual of interest revenue and amortization of premium at December 31, 19X1. Assume the straight-line method is appropriate for amortizing premium.
2. Show all financial statement effects of this long-term bond investment at December 31, 19X1. Assume a multiple-step income statement.
3. Repeat requirement 2 under the assumption that Prairie Mutual purchased these bonds as a short-term investment. Assume market value was $102.00.

Problem 17-6B   *Computing the cost of a bond investment and journalizing its transactions (Obj. 4)*

On December 31, 19X1, when the market interest rate is 8 percent, an investor purchases $500,000 of Advanced Systems 6-year, 7.4 percent bonds at issuance. Determine the cost (present value) of this long-term bond investment. Journalize the purchase on December 31, 19X1, the first semiannual interest receipt on June 30, 19X2, and the year-end interest receipt on December 31, 19X2. The investor uses the effective-interest amortization method. Prepare a schedule for amortizing the discount on bond investment through December 31, 19X2. If necessary, refer to Chapter 16 and its appendix.

Problem 17-7B *Journalizing foreign-currency transactions and reporting the transaction gain or loss (Obj. 5)*

Suppose Coca-Cola Beverages Ltd. completed the following transactions:

Dec.	4	Sold soft drink syrup on account to a Mexican company for $36,000. The exchange rate of the Mexican peso is $.228, and the customer agrees to pay in Canadian dollars.
	13	Purchased inventory on account from a U.S. company at a price of U.S. $100,000. The exchange rate of the American dollar is $1.35, and payment will be in American dollars.
	20	Sold goods on account to an English firm for 70,000 British pounds. Payment will be in pounds, and the exchange rate of the pound is $2.12.
	27	Collected from the Mexican company. Exchange rate unchanged from December 4.
	31	Adjusted the accounts for changes in foreign-currency exchange rates. Current rates: U.S. dollar, $1.33; British pound, $2.10.
Jan.	21	Paid the American company. The exchange rate of the U.S. dollar is $1.40.
Feb.	17	Collected from the English firm. The exchange rate of the British pound is $2.09.

Required

1. Record these transactions in Coca-Cola's general journal, and show how to report the transaction gain or loss on the income statement.

2. How will what you have learned in this problem help you structure international transactions?

Problem 17-8B *Accounting for stock investments using the cost method at LCM and long-term investments in bonds (Obj. 1, 4)*

Delta Corp. had the following short-term investments in marketable securities (valued at the lower of cost or market on an investment-by-investment basis):

LCM

Air Products Canada Ltd..............................	$ 96,000
Finning Ltd...	127,000
Regina Transport Ltd.	48,000
Total short-term investments	$271,000

The following transactions took place during 19X1 with regard to Delta's investments:

Jan.	5	Purchased 4,000 shares (2 percent) of Lowballer Ltd. as a short-term investment. The shares were purchased at 32¾ with a commission of $1,500.
Jan.	31	Lowballer Ltd. reported net income of $1,900,000 and declared a cash dividend of $400,000.
Feb.	15	Received $8,000 from Lowballer Ltd. as a cash dividend.
April	1	Purchased $100,000 (face value) of bonds at 98 as a long-term investment. The bonds pay 10 percent interest (5 percent semiannually) on October 1st and April 1st and mature in 2 years.
Aug.	31	Received a 10 percent stock dividend from Lowballer Ltd.
Oct.	1	Received the interest on the bonds.
Nov.	1	Lowballer declared and distributed a 2 for 1 stock split.
Dec.	15	Sold 3,000 shares of Lowballer at 16½ with a commission of $700.
	31	Recorded the adjustment for accrued interest on the bonds.
	31	The market values of the investments were:

Air Products Canada Ltd.	$ 93,000
Finning Ltd.	132,000
Lowballer Ltd...	98,000

Regina Transport Ltd.   46,000
Total short-term investments $369,000

Required

Prepare the general journal entries required to record the transactions of 19X1.

Problem 17-9B   *Accounting for stock investments using the equity method, accounting for investments in bonds, and accounting for transactions stated in a foreign currency* *(Obj. 2, 4, 5)*

LZS Ltd. uses the equity method in accounting for long-term investments and had the following investment transactions:

19X1

Jan.   14   LZS Ltd. purchased 30,000 shares (30 percent) of Nickelette Ltd. common stock as a long-term investment. The shares were purchased for 24¼ with a commission of $5,000.

Mar.   31   Nickelette Ltd. reported net income of $200,000 and declared a dividend of $150,000.

April 30   Received $45,000 as a cash dividend from Nickelette Ltd.

May   1   Purchased $200,000 (U.S. dollar face value) of Eagle Crest Ltd. bonds at 97 as a short-term investment. The bonds pay interest of 12 percent (6 percent semiannually) each May 1st and November 1st, and mature in 5 years. The exchange rate at the time of the transaction was $1.38 Canadian for each American dollar.

June 20   Received 3,000 shares of Nickelette Ltd. common stock as a 10 percent stock dividend.

Oct.   1   Nickelette Ltd. declared and distributed a 3-for-1 common stock split.

Nov.   1   Received the interest on the Eagle Crest Ltd. bonds when the exchange rate was $1.36 Canadian per American dollar.

Dec. 20   Sold 30,000 shares of Nickelette Ltd. common stock at 8½ with a commission of $1,000.

      31   Adjusted for the accrued interest on the Eagle Crest Ltd. bonds. The exchange rate was $1.37 Canadian per American dollar.

19X2

May   1   Received the interest on the Eagle Crest Ltd. bonds when the exchange rate was $1.34 Canadian per American dollar.

Required

1. Prepare the general journal entries required to record these transactions.

2. Show the balance sheet presentation of the investments on May 1, 19X2, assuming the Eagle Crest Ltd. bonds have a market rate of 96 and the exchange rate is $1.34 Canadian per American dollar.

Challenge Problems

Problem 17-1C   *Accounting for ownership of shares in another company* *(Obj. 1, 2, 3)*

The text lists general rules for accounting for long-term investments in the voting stock of another corporation. However, the management of the investing company may decide that, in their judgment, the rules do not apply in a particular situation.

Required

1. Identify a situation where an investing company that owns less than 20 percent might believe that the equity method was appropriate.

2. Identify a situation where an investing company that owns between 20 percent and 50 percent might believe that the cost method was appropriate.

3. Identify a situation where an investing company that owns more than 50 percent might believe that the cost method was appropriate.

Problem 17-2C   *Accounting for foreign operations*   **(Obj. 5)**

Canadian exporters are pleased when the Canadian dollar weakens against the U.S. dollar, while the federal and provincial ministers of finance are likely not happy when the dollar weakens.

Required

Explain why a weakening Canadian dollar makes the Canadian exporters happy. Why would a weaker Canadian dollar make the finance ministers unhappy?

Extending Your Knowledge

Decision Problems

1. Understanding the cost and equity methods of accounting for investments   (Obj. 1, 2)

Margaret Joyce is the accountant for Arnprior Inc., whose year end is December 31. The company made two investments during the first week of January, 19X7. Both investments are to be held for at least the next five years as investments. Information about each of the investments follows:

a. Arnprior purchased 30 percent of the common stock of Lonesome Dove Ltd. for its book value of $150,000. During the year ended December 31, 19X7, Lonesome Dove earned $85,000 and paid a total dividend of $40,000.

b. Ten percent of the common stock of Western Music Inc. was purchased for its book value of $50,000. During the year ended December 31, 19X7, Western Music paid Arnprior a dividend of $3,000. Western Music earned a profit of $118,000 for that period. The market value of Arnprior's investment in Western Music was $217,000.

Margaret has come to you as her auditor to ask you how to account for the investments. Arnprior has never had such investments before. You attempt to explain the proper accounting to her by indicating that different accounting methods apply to different situations.

Required

Help Margaret understand by

1. Describing the methods of accounting applicable to these investments.

2. Identifying which method should be used to account for the investments in Lonesome Dove and Western Music.

2. Understanding the consolidation method for investments　(Obj. 3, 4)

Vijay Singh inherited some investments, and he has received the annual reports of the companies in which the funds are invested. The financial statements of the companies are puzzling to Vijay, and he asks you the following questions:

a. The companies label their financial statements as *consolidated* balance sheet, *consolidated* income statement, and so on. What are consolidated financial statements?

b. Notes to the statements indicate that "certain intercompany transactions, loans, and other accounts have been eliminated in preparing the consolidated financial statements." Why does a company eliminate transactions, loans, and accounts? Vijay states that he thought a transaction was a transaction and that a loan obligated a company to pay real money. He wonders if the company is juggling the books to defraud Revenue Canada.

c. The balance sheet lists the asset Goodwill. What is goodwill? Does this mean that the company's stock has increased in value?

d. The shareholders' equity section of one of the companies reports a Translation Adjustment of $87,000. Vijay asks what is being translated and what the amount means.

Required

Respond to each of Vijay's questions.

Ethical Issue

Coast Holdings Limited owns 18 percent of the voting stock of Nashua Corporation. The remainder of the Nashua stock is held by numerous investors with small holdings. Carol Erb, president of Coast Holdings and a member of Nashua's Board of Directors, heavily influences Nashua's policies.

Under the cost method of accounting for investments, Coast Holdings' net income increases as it received dividends from Nashua. Coast Holdings pays President Erb a bonus computed as a percentage of Coast Holdings' net income. Therefore, Erb can control her personal bonus to a certain extent by influencing Nashua's dividends.

A recession occurs in 19X0, and corporate income is low. Erb uses her power to have Nashua Corporation pay a large cash dividend. This action requires Nashua to borrow so heavily that it may lead to financial difficulty.

Required

1. In getting Nashua to pay the large cash dividend, is Erb acting within his authority as a member of the Nashua Board of Directors? Are Erb's actions ethical? Whom can her actions harm?

2. Discuss how using the equity method of accounting for investments would decrease Erb's potential for manipulating her bonus.

Financial Statement Problems

1. Investments in stock　(Obj. 1, 2, 3)

The financial statements for Mark's Work Wearhouse Ltd., are in Appendix A.

Required

The financial statements are labeled "consolidated." What evidence can you find in the financial statements that reveals how Mark's Work Wearhouse accounts for its subsidiaries?

2. Investments in stock   *(Obj. 1, 2, 3)*

Obtain the annual report of an actual company of your choosing. Answer these questions about the company. Concentrate on the current year in the annual report you select.

1. Many companies refer to other companies in which they own equity-method investments as *affiliated companies*. This signifies the close relationship between the two entities even though the investor does not own a controlling interest.

   Does the company have equity-method investments? Cite the evidence. If present, what were the balances in the investment account at the beginning and the end of the current year? If the company had no equity-method investments, skip the next question, and go to question 3.

2. Scan the income statement. If equity-method investments are present, what amount of revenue (or income) did the company earn on the investments during the current year? Scan the statement of changes in financial position. What amount of dividends did the company receive during the current year from companies in which it held equity-method investments? Note: The amount of dividends received may not be disclosed. If not, you can still compute the amount of dividends received—from the following T-account.

Investments, at Equity

Beg. bal. (from balance sheet)	W		
Equity-method revenue (from income statement)	X	**Dividends received (unknown; must compute)**	**Y**
End. bal. (from balance sheet)	Z		

3. The company probably owns some consolidated subsidiaries. You should be able to tell whether the parent company owns 100 percent or less of the subsidiaries. Examine the income statement and the balance sheet to determine whether there are any minority interests. If so, what does that fact indicate?

4. The shareholders' equity section of many balance sheets lists Foreign Currency Translation Adjustment or a similar account title. A positive amount signifies a gain, and a negative amount indicates a loss. The change in this account balance from the beginning of the year to the end of the year signals whether the Canadian dollar was strong or weak during the year in comparison to the foreign currencies. For the company you are analyzing, was the dollar strong or weak during the current year?

Comprehensive Problem for Part Three

1. Accounting for Corporate Transactions

Gateway United Industries Ltd.'s articles of incorporation authorizes the company to issue 500,000 shares of common stock and 200,000 shares of $.50 preferred stock. During the first quarter of operations, Gateway completed the following selected transactions:

Oct. 1 Issued 75,000 shares of common stock for cash of $8 per share.

2 Signed a capital lease for equipment. The lease requires a down payment of $100,000, plus 20 quarterly lease payments of $10,000. Present value of the future least payments is $135,900 at an annual interest rate of 16 percent.

5 Issued 2,000 shares of preferred stock to lawyers who helped organize the corporation. Their bill listed legal services of $22,000.

22 Received land from the province as an incentive for locating in New Brunswick. Fair market value of the land was $120,000.

30 Purchased 5,000 shares (25 percent) of the outstanding common stock of Newbold Corporation as a long-term investment, $75,000.

Nov. 1 Issued $200,000 of 9 percent, 10-year bonds payable at 94.

14 Purchased short-term investments in the common stocks of Bombardier, $22,000, and ATCO Ltd., $31,000.

19 Experienced an extraordinary tornado loss of inventory that cost $21,000. Cash received from the insurance company was $8,000.

20 Repurchased 2,000 shares of the company's common stock at $5.00 per share.

Dec. 1 Received cash dividends of $1,100 on the Bombardier investment.

16 Sold 1,000 shares of the company's stock for cash of $8.25 per share.

29 Received a report from Newbold Corporation indicating the net income for November and December was $70,000.

30 Sold merchandise on account, $716,000. Cost of the goods was $239,000. Operating expenses totaled $174,000, with $166,000 of this amount paid in cash. Gateway uses a perpetual inventory system.

31 Accrued interest and amortized discount (straight-line method) on the bonds payable.

31 Accrued interest on the capital lease liability.

31 Depreciated the equipment acquired by the capital lease. The company uses the double-declining-balance method.

31 Market values of short-term investments: Bombardier stock, $24,000, and the ATCO stock, $30,000.

31 Accrued income tax expense of $110,000.

31 Closed all revenues, expenses, and losses to Retained Earnings in a single closing entry.

31 Declared a quarterly cash dividend of $.125 per share on the preferred stock. Record date is January 11, with payment scheduled for January 19.

Required

1. Record these transactions in the general journal. Explanations are not required.

2. Prepare a single-step income statement for the quarter ended December 31, including earnings per share. Income tax expense of $110,000 should be reported as follows: Income tax expense of $114,000 is used in arriving at income before extraordinary items. The tax effect of the extraordinary loss is an income tax saving of $4,000.

3. Report the liabilities and the shareholder's equity as they would appear on the balance sheet at December 31.

2. Group Project: Refining Your Business Plan to Include Corporate Transactions

Review the business plan for an audio/video store (or other business) that you developed at the end of Part 1 and refined at the end of Part 2. Since that time you have learned about partnerships and more about corporations and international operations.

Revise your business plan to include refinements that apply to shareholders' equity, long-term debt, investments, and international operations. For example, consider the classes of stock you may wish to issue, the amount of long-term debt financing your business may use, and your business's policies on dividends and treasury stock. Will international operations affect your business? Be as specific as possible in refining your plan, and identify all the factors you consider important for success.

VIDEO CASE

CBC ✦

Autoskill International—The Classic Struggle Between Entrepreneurs and Investors

Many businesses in Canada were started by inventors of products or developers of a technology or service who were long on ideas but short on capital. They began as small organizations with a single idea. However, to grow and exploit its idea, the fledgling company needs financial support. One example of a company that began small with a single idea is Bombardier. Bombardier was incorporated in 1902. J. Armand Bombardier's "idea" was a primitive snow machine called a "ski-doo." Now Bombardier is a world-wide company with products ranging from ski-doos and sea-doos through airplanes, subway, and rail equipment. Revenues for the year ended January 31, 1995, totalled $5.8 billion, while assets totaled $5.5 billion. There are still Bombardiers on the Board of Directors.

The lack of capital often forces the entrepreneur to sell part of the company to investors who do have the needed capital. The investors however may have a much different vision for the company than the owners. The investors supply the needed capital but bring potential conflict.

Autoskill is a case in point. Christina Fiedorowicz and Ron Trites, two university neuro-psychologists, formed the company to develop a computer program to teach people to read. The company has expanded using capital provided by outside investors. Sales, mainly to schools, are in the $2 million range.

Wes Nicol, the major investor, controls the Board of Directors. The investors want Autoskill to expand into the home market and increase the value of their investment. They are impatient with Autoskill's slow growth. They want to cut research and put more resources into sales.

Christina and Ron search for other investors who will support their vision but aren't successful. Nicol uses his ownership share to restructure the company; both Christina and Ron lose their roles within the company. Craig Curran brought in by Nicol now runs the company.

CASE QUESTIONS

1. Entrepreneurs needing additional capital have three major sources of funding. Describe the three sources and list the advantages and disadvantages of each.

2. Which of the three sources of funding did Christina and Ron rely on?

3. Could Christina and Ron have incorporated and avoided risking loss of control?

4. What caused Christina and Ron to lose control of the company they founded? Autoskill and the ideas that were incorporated in the software were their ideas after all.

CHAPTER 18
Statement of Changes in Financial Position

"Cash is king," says Don Martin, Manager of Accounting Policy, E.I. du Pont de Nemours (DuPont). "We originally followed returns on investment but didn't really hold businesses [in the DuPont group] responsible for cash flow. If you've got a growing business and you're still plowing more money back into it, you're eating up cash."

Why is cash so important? You can thank heavier debt loads, the uncertainty of asset values, and the high cost of restucturing for a global economy. Cash on hand, even for profit-making enterprises, is not as plentiful as it once was.

Former CEO of Ford Motor Co. of Canada Ltd. Roy Bennett says "There has been a very significant rise in cash-flow awareness in the past five years." Companies like Shell Canada, Northern Telecom, and George Weston are measuring cash flow.

Return on investment (ROI) is important and should also be measured, but cash flow just as important. Cash flow is not affected by the accounting methods used, whereas ROI is so affected. And cash flow can be used to compare operations in different parts of the world.

How can a company generate a large profit and yet have an outflow of cash? The company could be making sales but not collecting its receivables. A merchandiser could be stockpiling inventory that it cannot sell. Or the business could be paying off huge amounts of current liabilities that drain cash. What is the significance of a company's cash-flow problems? The company may run out of cash.

Source: Adapted from John Southerst, "The Smart Money's on Cash," *Canadian Business*, November, 1993, pp. 59–61.

CHAPTER OBJECTIVES

After studying this chapter, you should be able to

1 Identify the purposes of the statement of changes in financial position

2 Distinguish among operating, financing, and investing activities

3 Prepare a statement of changes in financial position by the indirect method

4 Use the financial statements to compute the cash effects of a wide variety of business transactions

5 Prepare a work sheet for the statement of changes in financial position by the indirect method

---

The statement of changes in financial position (SCFP) reports where cash came from and how it was spent. The objective of the three major financial reports—income statement, balance sheet, and statement of changes in financial position—is to enable investors and creditors to make informed decisions about a company. The income statement of a company might present one picture of the company—for example, high income. The statement of changes in financial position, on the other hand, might reveal that the company has a negative cash flow; more cash is flowing out than is flowing in. This example underscores the challenge of financial analysis, that a company's signals may point in different directions. Astute investors and creditors know what to look for; increasingly they are focusing on cash flows.

This chapter discusses the statement of changes in financial position. The *CICA Handbook* in Section 1540, Statement of Changes in Financial Position, "… focuses on the liquid financial resources readily available to the enterprise," which it defines as **cash and cash equivalents**; the enterprise's cash, net of short-term borrowings; and temporary investments. References in this chapter to cash will include cash and cash equivalents. **Cash flows** are cash receipts (increases in cash) and cash payments (disbursements or decreases in cash). The **Statement of Changes in Financial Position** reports cash receipts and cash disbursements classified according to the entity's major activities: operating, financing, and investing. The statement reports a net cash inflow or net cash outflow for each activity and for the overall business. What information does it provide? What decisions does it aid? We address these questions and then show how to prepare the statement. If you understand how to prepare the statement of changes in financial position, you will be in a good position to use the information it provides.

While the most common title of the statement is "Statement of Changes in Financial Position," some Canadian companies use the title "Statement of Cash Flow" or "Statement of Cash Flows." Section 1540 does not specify a particular title.

The CICA, in Section 1540 of the *CICA Handbook*, recognizes the two methods for preparing the statement of changes in financial position: the indirect method, which will be the focus of this chapter, and the direct method, which is mentioned only for completeness. The indirect method is widely used in Canada.

The two methods differ only in the way that net cash flows from operations are calculated; net cash flows from financing activities and net cash flows from investing activities are calculated the same way under either method. The indirect method begins the calculation with net income which is adjusted for items which affect net income and cash flows from operations differently to arrive at net cash flows from operations. The direct method begins with cash receipts from specific operating activities (for example, sales, interest income) from which are deducted cash payments for each major operating activity (for example, cost of goods sold, wages) to arrive at net cash flows from operations.

Basic Concept of the Statement of Changes in Financial Position

The balance sheet reports the cash balance at the end of the period. By examining two consecutive balance sheets, you can tell whether cash increased or decreased during the period. However, the balance sheet does not indicate *why* the cash balance changed. The income statement reports revenues, expenses, and net income—clues about the sources and uses of cash—but it does not tell *why* cash increased or decreased.

The SCFP reports the entity's cash receipts and cash payments during the period—where cash came from and how it was spent. It explains the *causes* for the change in the cash balance. This information cannot be learned solely from the other financial statements.

The income statement and the statement of retained earnings cover the period from beginning to end. The SCFP also covers a span of time and therefore is dated "For the Year Ended XXX" or "For the Month Ended XXX." Exhibit 18-1 illustrates the timing of these statements.

Overview of the Statement of Changes in Financial Position

The statement of changes in financial position is designed to fulfill the following purposes:

1. *To predict future cash flows.* Cash, not reported accounting income, pays the bills. In many cases, a business's sources and uses of cash do not change dramatically from year to year. If so, past cash receipts and disbursements are a reasonably good predictor of future cash receipts and disbursements.

2. *To evaluate management decisions.* If managers make wise investment decisions, their businesses prosper. If they make unwise decisions, the businesses suffer. The statement of changes in financial position reports the company's investment

> **OBJECTIVE 1**
> Identify the purposes of the statement of changes in financial position

EXHIBIT 18-1   *Timing of the Financial Statements*

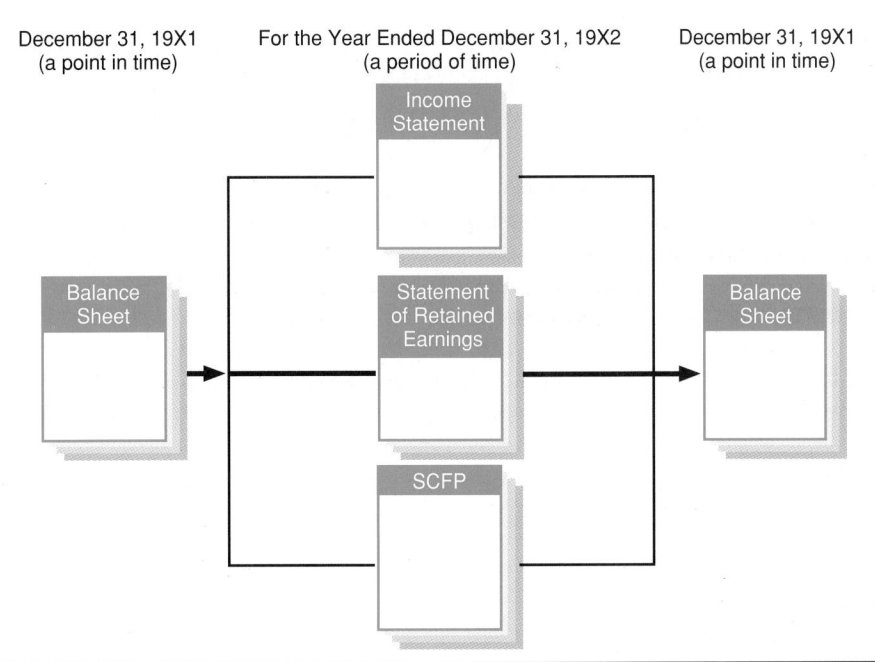

in plant and equipment and thus gives investors and creditors cash-flow information for evaluating managers' decisions.

3. *To determine the ability to pay dividends to shareholders and interest and principal to creditors.* Shareholders are interested in receiving dividends on their investments in the company's stock. Creditors want to receive their interest and principal amounts on time. The statement of changes in financial position helps investors and creditors predict whether the business can make these payments.

4. *To show the relationship of net income to changes in the business's cash.* Usually, cash and net income move together. High levels of income tend to lead to increases in cash, and vice versa. However, a company's cash balance can decrease when net income is high, and cash can increase when income is low. The failures of companies which were earning net income but had insufficient cash have pointed to the need for cash flow information.

Operating, Financing, and Investing Activities

OBJECTIVE 2
Distinguish among operating, financing, and investing activities

A business may be evaluated in terms of three types of business activities. After the business is up and running, operations are the most important activity, followed by financing activities and investing activities. The statement of changes in financial position in Exhibit 18-2 shows how cash receipts and disbursements are divided into operating activities, financing activities, and investing activities for Anchor Ltd., a small manufacturer of glass products. As Exhibit 18-2 illustrates, each set of activities includes both cash inflows—receipts—and cash outflows—payments. Outflows are shown in parentheses to indicate that payments must be subtracted. Each section of the statement reports a net cash inflow or a net cash outflow.

Key Point:
If the revenues and expenses on the income statement are converted to the cash basis, then cash flow from operations is complete. Operating activities include all cash inflows and outflows not associated with financing or investing.

Operating activities create revenues and expenses in the entity's major line of business. Therefore, operating activities affect the income statement, which reports the accrual-basis effects of operating activities. The statement of changes in financial position reports their impact on cash. The largest cash inflow from operating activities is the net income from operations. Items that affect net income and cash flow differently are often subtracted and added as appropriate. For example, depreciation expense is a deduction in calculating net income but does not represent an outflow of cash; therefore, it is added back to net income. The other items will be explored shortly. Exhibit 18-2 shows that Anchor's net cash inflow from operating activities is $68,000. A large positive operating cash flow is a good sign about a company. In the long run, operations must be the main source of a business's cash.

OPERATING ACTIVITIES ARE RELATED TO THE TRANSACTIONS THAT MAKE UP NET INCOME[1]

Financing activities obtain the funds from investors and creditors needed to launch and sustain the business. Financing activities include issuing stock, borrowing money by issuing notes and bonds payable, and making payments to the shareholders—dividends and repurchases of the company's stock. Payments to the creditors include principal payments only. The payment of interest is an operating activity. Financing activities of Anchor Ltd. brought in net cash of $167,000. One thing to watch among financing activities is whether the business is borrowing heavily. Excessive borrowing has been the downfall of many companies.

FINANCING ACTIVITIES ARE RELATED TO THE LONG-TERM LIABILITY ACCOUNTS AND THE OWNERS' EQUITY ACCOUNTS

[1]The authors thank Alfonso Oddo for suggesting this display.

EXHIBIT 18-2   *Statement of Changes in Financial Position*

Anchor Ltd.
Statement of Changes in Financial Position: Indirect Method for Operating Activities
for the year ended December 31, 19X2
(amounts in thousands)

Cash flows from operating activities		
Net income..		$ 41
Add (subtract) items that affect		
net income and cash flow differently:		
Depreciation	$ 18	
Gain on sale of capital assets...	(8)	
Increase in accounts receivable....................................	(13)	
Increase in interest receivable	(2)	
Decrease in inventory..	3	
Increase in prepaid expenses	(1)	
Increase in accounts payable...	34	
Decrease in salary and wage payable..........................	(2)	
Decrease in accrued liabilities.......................................	(2)	27
Net cash inflow from operating activities...............		68
Cash flows from financing activities		
Proceeds from issuance of common stock........................	$ 101	
Proceeds from issuance of long-term debt.......................	94	
Payment of long-term debt...	(11)	
Payment of dividends	(17)	
Net cash inflow from financing activities		167
Cash flows from investing activities		
Acquisition of capital assets..	$(306)	
Loan to another company...	(11)	
Proceeds from sale of capital assets	62	
Net cash outflow from investing activities..................		(255)
Net decrease in cash		$ (20)
Cash balance, December 31, 19X1		42
Cash balance, December 31, 19X2		$ 22

Investing activities increase and decrease the long-term assets available to the business. A purchase or sale of a capital asset like land, a building, or equipment is an investing activity, as is the purchase or sale of an investment in stock or bonds of another company. On the statement of changes in financial position, investing activities include more than the buying and selling of assets that are classified as investments on the balance sheet. Making a loan—an investing activity because the loan creates a receivable for the lender—and collecting on the loan are also reported as investing activities on the statement of changes in financial position. The acquisition of capital assets dominates Anchor's investing activities, which produce a net cash outflow of $255,000.

INVESTING ACTIVITIES ARE RELATED
TO THE LONG-TERM ASSET ACCOUNTS

Investments in capital assets lay the foundation for future operations. A company that invests in plant and equipment appears stronger than one that is selling off its capital assets. Why? The latter company may have to sell income-producing assets in order to pay the bills. Its outlook is bleak.

Overall, Anchor's cash decreased by $20,000 during 19X2. The company began the year with cash of $42,000 and ended with $22,000.

EXHIBIT 18-3   *Cash Receipts and Disbursements Reported on the Statement of Changes in Financial Position*

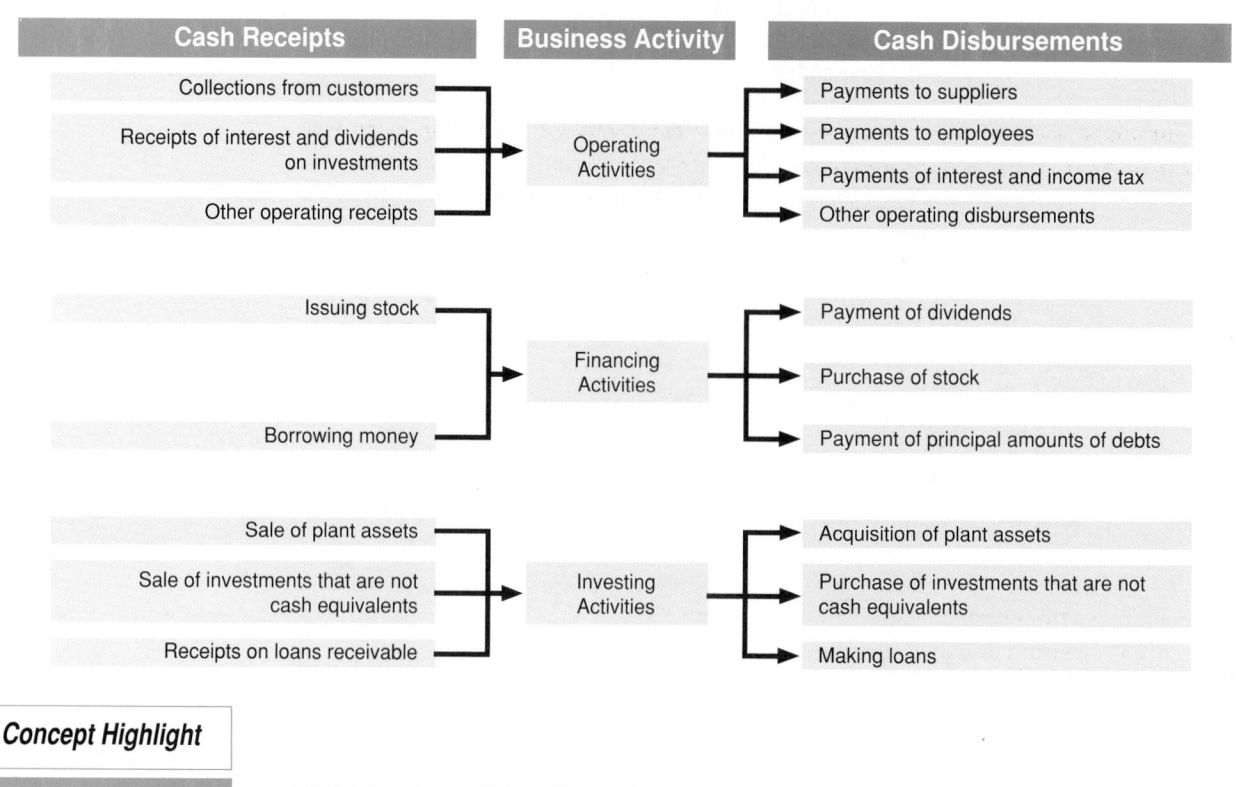

Concept Highlight

Each of these categories of activities includes both cash receipts and cash disbursements, as shown in Exhibit 18-3. The exhibit lists the more common cash receipts and cash disbursements that appear on the statement of changes in financial position.

Discontinued Operations and Extraordinary Items

Just as discontinued operations and extraordinary items are to be shown separately on the income statement, so are they to be shown separately on the statement of changes in financial position. The cash inflow or outflow resulting from discontinued operations or from an extraordinary item should be shown as part of operating, financing or investing activities. For example, recent financial statements of Imasco Limited included a loss from discontinued operations as a reduction of cash from operating activities and as an outflow from investing activities. Intermetco Ltd.'s financial statements show an extraordinary item among operating activities, while those of Provigo Inc. and Selkirk Communications Ltd. include extraordinary items with investing activities.

Interest and Dividends

You may be puzzled by the including of receipts of interest and dividends as operating activities. After all, these cash receipts result from investing activities. Interest comes from investment in loans, and dividends come from investments in stock. Equally puzzling is the including of the payment of interest as part of operations. Interest expense results from borrowing money—a financing activity. Interest and dividends are included as operating activities because they affect the computation of net income. Interest revenue and dividend revenue increase net income, and interest expense decreases income. Therefore, cash receipts of interest and dividends and cash payments of interest are reported as operating activities on the SCFP.

In contrast, note that dividend payments are reported as a financing activity. This is so because they do not enter into the computation of net income but rather are payments to the entity's owners, who finance the business by holding its shares.

Format of the Statement of Changes in Financial Position

Companies' accounting systems are designed for accrual, rather than cash-basis, accounting. This format makes it easier for companies to compute cash flows from operating activities by a short-cut method. The **indirect method** starts with net income and reconciles to cash flows from operating activities. Exhibit 18-4 gives an overview of the process of converting from accrual-basis income to the cash basis for the statement of changes in financial possition.

Section 1540 of the *CICA Handbook* requires that activities generating or requiring cash or cash equivalents be classified as operating, financing, or investing. This text orders the activities, operating, financing, and investing, in the order suggested in Section 1540. However, many Canadian companies follow the order suggested by U.S. standards of operating, investing, and financing activities. While either order is acceptable, it is appropriate to begin the statement with operating activities.

Preparing the Statement of Changes in Financial Position: The Indirect Method

Let's see how to prepare the statement of changes by the indirect method in Exhibit 18-2. Suppose Anchor had assembled the summary of transactions in Exhibit 18-5. These summary transactions give the data for the SCFP, the income statement, and the balance sheet (see Exhibits 18-6 and 18-7). Some transactions affect one statement, and some affect more than one of the three statements. Sales, for example, are reported on the income statement, accounts receivable on the balance sheet, but changes in accounts receivable appear on the SCFP. *The SCFP only reports those transactions with cash effects.*

Preparation of the SCFP follows these steps: (1) identify the activities that increased cash and decreased cash; (2) classify each cash increase and cash decrease as an operating activity, a financing activity, or an investing activity; and (3) identify the cash effect of each transaction. Preparing the statement is discussed next.

Cash Flows from Operating Activities   Operating cash flows are listed first because they are the largest and most important source of cash for most businesses. The failure of a company's operations to generate the bulk of its cash inflows for an extended period may signal trouble. Exhibit 18-2 shows that Anchor is sound; its operating activities generated cash receipts of $68,000.

Short Exercise:

Is net income the amount of cash received from operations?

A: No, net income is computed by the accrual basis. Revenues are recorded when earned, and expenses when incurred. Included in accual-basis net income are some noncash expenses such as depreciation. "Net cash inflow from operations" measures cash-basis net income.

OBJECTIVE 3

Prepare a statement of changes in financial position using the indirect method

Key Point:

After you have listed all the accounts used to convert income statement items to the cash basis, notice that changes in the remaining asset accounts signal an *investing* activity. Changes in the remaining liability and holders' equity accounts signal *financing* activities.

Exhibit 18-4   *Converting from the Accrual Basis to the Cash Basis for the Statement of Changes in Financial Position*

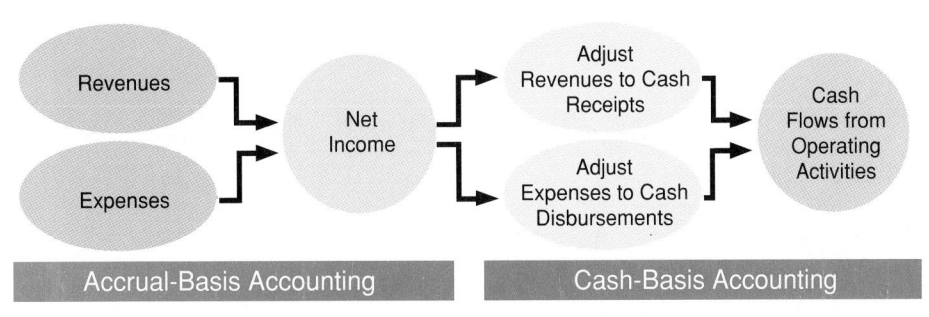

EXHIBIT 18-5   *Summary of Anchor Ltd.'s 19X2 Transactions*

Operating Activities
1. Net income, $41,000.
2. Depreciation expense, $18,000.
3. Increase in accounts receivable, $13,000.
4. Increase in interest receivable, $2,000.
5. Decrease in inventory, $3,000.
6. Increase in prepaid expenses, $1,000.
7. Increase in accounts payable, $34,000.
8. Decrease in salary and wages payable, $2,000.
9. Decrease in accrued liabilities, $2,000.

Financing Activities
10. Proceeds from issuance of common stock, $101,000.
11. Proceeds from issuance of long-term debt, $94,000.
12. Payment of long-term debt, $11,000.
13. Declaration and payment of cash dividends, $17,000.

Investing Activities
14. Cash payments to acquire capital assets, $306,000.
15. Loan to another company, $11,000.
16. Proceeds from sale of capital assets, $62,000 (including $8,000 gain).

Net Income   The calculation of cash flow from operations under the indirect method begins with net income since net income represents an increase in the entity's cash. If the entity had a loss, the loss would be shown as a reduction in cash. The net income figure comes directly from the income statement; Exhibit 18-6 shows Anchor's net income to be $41,000.

Net income includes items that affect net income and cash flow differently. These must be added or subtracted as indicated below and in Exhibit 18-8. The logic behind adding and subtracting the items to arrive at net cash inflow from operating

EXHIBIT 18-6   *Income Statement*

Anchor Ltd. Income Statement for the year ended December 31, 19X2 (amounts in thousands)		
Revenues and gains		
Sales revenue	$284	
Interest revenue	12	
Dividend revenue	9	
Gain on sale of capital assets	8	
Total revenues and gains		$313
Expenses		
Cost of goods sold	$150	
Salary and wage expense	56	
Depreciation expense	18	
Other operating expense	17	
Interest expense	16	
Income tax expense	15	
Total expenses		272
Net income		$ 41

EXHIBIT 18-7   *Comparative Balance Sheet*

Anchor Ltd.
Comparative Balance Sheet
December 31, 19X2 and 19X1
(amounts in thousands)

Assets	19X2	19X1	Increase (Decrease)	
Current				
Cash	$ 22	$ 42	$(20)	
Accounts receivable	93	80	13	Changes in current assets—**Operating**
Interest receivable	3	1	2	
Inventory	135	138	(3)	
Prepaid expenses	8	7	1	
Long-term receivable from another company	11	—	11	Changes in non-current assets—**Investing**
Capital assets, net	453	219	234	
Total	$725	$487	$238	
Liabilities				
Current				
Accounts payable	$ 91	$ 57	$ 34	Changes in current liabilities—**Operating**
Salary and wage payable	4	6	(2)	
Accrued liabilities	1	3	(2)	
Long-term debt	160	77	83	Changes in long-term liabilities and capital stock—**Financing**
Shareholders' Equity				
Common stock	359	258	101	
Retained earnings	110	86	24	Change due to net income—**Operating** and change due to dividends—**Financing**
Total	$725	$487	$238	

activities is discussed below; the mechanics of the transactions is discussed under Objective 4 beginning on page 874.

Depreciation, Depletion, and Amortization Depreciation, depletion, and amortization are deducted from income on the income statement in arriving at net income. These expenses do not involve an outflow of cash so they are added back to net income on the SCFP.

Gains and Losses on the Sale of Assets The cash outflow resulting from a purchase of capital assets and the cash inflow resulting from a sale of capital assets are included as investing activities on the SCFP. The cash inflow from a sale, and thus the net cash flow or flow from investing activities, would be increased by a gain or decreased by a loss on the sale.

Therefore any gain or loss from a sale is double-counted since the gain or loss would also be included as an addition or deduction respectively in determining net income on the income statement. Thus it is necessary to eliminate the gain or loss from the calculation of net cash flows from operations by subtracting the gain (as was done on Exhibit 18-2) or adding back the loss.

Gains and Losses Resulting from Early Extinguishment of Debt Repayment of debt is included as a financing activity on the SCFP. The amount paid out, and thus the net cash flow from financing activities, would be increased by a loss or decreased by a gain that resulted from the repayment of the debt.

EXHIBIT 18-8 *Indirect Method of Determining Cash Flows from Operating Activities*

Add (subtract) items that affect net income and cash flow differently

Net Income
+ **Depreciation**
+ **Depletion**
+ **Amortization**
+ **Loss on disposal or exchange of long-term asset or early extinguishment of debt**
− **Gain on disposal of long-term asset or early extinguishment of debt**
+ **Decrease in current asset other than cash**
− **Increase in current asset other than cash**
+ **Increase in current liability***
− **Decrease in current liability***

Net cash inflow (or outflow) from operating activities

* Short-term notes payable for general borrowing, and current portion of long-term notes payable, are related to financing activities, not to operating activities.

We thank Barbara Gerrity and Jean Marie Hudson for suggesting this exhibit.

To avoid double-counting, it is necessary to eliminate the gain or loss from the calculation of net cash flows from operations by subtracting the gain or adding back the loss.

Changes in the Current Asset and Current Liability Accounts Other Than Cash Most current assets and liabilities result from operating activities; the principal exceptions are short-term notes payable and the current portion of long-term debt which are related to financing activities.

Assume that all of a company's transactions were for cash so that when the company earns revenue cash is increased and when the company incurs an expense, cash is decreased. If such were the case, net income would reflect the total effect of all transactions and would equal cash flows from operations.

However, we know that most companies do not receive cash but rather promises to pay or accounts receivable when they earn revenue. In addition, companies acquire inventories and prepay expenses. Similarly, they disburse cash for their expenses (for example, accounts payable or wages payable) sometime after the expense has been incurred. The combined effect is that net income does not equal cash flows from operations and so net income has to be adjusted to reflect cash from operations.

Two examples will illustrate the point:

1. M Corp. makes a single sale of services to D. Ltd. for $3,000 on December 20 (net income is increased by $3,000). At December 31, 19X1, M's year end, the account is not paid so M has an account receivable on its books; the transaction has zero effect on M's cash flow (cash flow = $0).

   Assume all other transactions made by M Corp. were for cash and that net income was $75,000 plus the $3,000 sale to D or $78,000. The difference between net income and cash flow caused by the credit sale to D is dealt with as follows:

Net income	$78,000
Subtract items that affect net income and cash flow differently:	
Increase in accounts receivable	(3,000)
Cash flow from operations	$75,000

Of course, if the sale had been for cash, cash flow and net income both would have been $78,000.

2. L Ltd. buys data entry services from Q Corp. for $1,000 at December 10, 19X1, but does not pay until after L's year end at December 31 (net income is decreased by $1,000 but there is no effect on cash flow since no payment was made to Q).

Assume all other transactions made by L Ltd. were for cash and that net income was $94,000 minus the $1,000 purchase from Q Corp. or $93,000. The difference between net income and cash flow caused by the credit purchase from Q is dealt with as follows:

Net income	$93,000
Add items that affect net income and cash flow differently:	
Increase in accounts payable	1,000
Cash flow from operations	$94,000

Of course, if the purchase had been for cash, cash flow and net income both would have been $93,000.

Cash Flows from Financing Activities

Cash flows from financing include the following:

Proceeds from Issuance of Stock and Debt Readers of the financial statements want to know how the entity obtains its financing. Issuing stock (preferred and common) and debt are two common ways to finance operations. In Exhibit 18-2, Anchor Ltd. issued common stock of $101,000 and long-term debt of $94,000.

Payment of Debt and Repurchases of the Company's Own Stock The payment of debt decreases Cash, which is the opposite of borrowing money. Anchor Ltd. reports debt payments of $11,000. Other transactions in this category are repurchases of the company's stock.

Payment of Cash Dividends The payment of cash dividends decreases Cash and is therefore reported as a cash payment, as illustrated by Anchor's $17,000 payment in Exhibit 18-2. A dividend in another form—a stock dividend, for example—has no effect on Cash and is *not* reported on the statement of changes in financial position.

Cash Flows from Investing Activities

Many analysts regard investing as a critical activity because a company's investments determine its future course. Large purchases of capital assets signal expansion, which is usually a good sign about the company. Low levels of investing activities over a lengthy period mean the business is not replenishing its capital assets. Knowing these cash flows helps investors and creditors evaluate the direction that managers are charting for the business.

Cash Payments to Acquire Capital Assets and Investments, and Loans to Other Companies These cash payments are similar because they acquire a noncash asset. The first transaction of Anchor Ltd. purchases capital assets, such as land, buildings, and equipment ($306,000) in Exhibit 18-2. In the second transaction, Anchor makes an $11,000 loan and obtains a note receivable. These are investing activities because the company is investing in assets for use in the business rather than for resale. These transactions have no effect on revenues or expenses and thus are not reported

Short Exercise:

Try this example to clarify which amount appears on the SCFP when an asset is sold—the book value, the gain or loss, or the proceeds from the sale: Suppose you sold equipment for $20,000 that originally cost $45,000 and had a book value of $15,000. (1) What entry records the sale? (2) How much cash did you receive? (3) Did you receive an extra $5,000 for the gain? **A:**

(1) Cash	20,000	
Accum. Dep.	30,000	
Equipment..		45,000
Gain		5,000

(2) $20,000 (3) No, so the amount reflected on the cash-flow statement is $20,000.

Short Exercise:

Collins Corp. sold at a $3,000 loss an investment that had cost $25,000. Make the journal entry to help you identify the cash receipt (the number for the SCFP). **A:**

Cash	22,000	
Loss on Sale of Investment	3,000	
Investment		25,000

on the income statement. Another transaction in this category—not shown in Exhibit 18-2—is a purchase of an investment in stocks or bonds of another company.

Proceeds from the Sale of Capital Assets and Investments, and Collections of Loans
These transactions are the opposites of acquisitions of capital assets and investments, and making loans. They are cash receipts from investment transactions.

The sale of the capital assets needs explanation. The statement of changes in financial position reports that Anchor Ltd. received $62,000 cash on the sale of capital assets. The income statement shows an $8,000 gain on this transaction. What is the appropriate amount to show on the statement of changes in financial position? It is $62,000, the cash proceeds from the sale. If we assume Anchor sold equipment that cost $64,000 and had accumulated depreciation of $10,000, the following journal entry would record the sale:

Cash	62,000	
Accumulated Depreciation...	10,000	
Equipment		64,000
Gain on Sale of Capital Assets		
(from income statement)...		8,000

The analysis indicates that the book value of the equipment was $54,000 ($64,000 – $10,000). However, the book value of the asset sold is not reported on the SCFP. Only the cash proceeds of $62,000 are reported on the statement. For the income statement, only the gain is reported. Since a gain occurred, you may wonder why this cash receipt is not reported as part of operations. Operations consist of buying and selling merchandise or rendering services to earn revenue. Investing activities are the acquisition and disposition of assets used in operations. Therefore, the sale of capital assets and the sale of investments should be viewed as cash inflows from investing activities.

STOP & THINK

Suppose Canfor Corp. sold timberland at a $35 million gain. The land cost Canfor $9 million when it was purchased in 1980. What amount will Canfor report as an investing activity on the statement of cash flows?

Answer: Cash receipt of $44 million (cost of $9 million plus the gain of $35 million).

Investors and creditors are often critical of a company that sells large amounts of its capital assets. Such sales may signal an emergency. In other situations, selling off fixed assets may be good news about the company if it is getting rid of an unprofitable division. Whether sales of capital assets are good news or bad news should be evaluated in light of a company's operating and financing characteristics.

Mid-Chapter Summary Problem for Your Review

Acadia Corporation accounting records include the following information for the year ended June 30, 19X8:

a. Salary expense, $104,000.

b. Depreciation expense, $32,000.

c. Proceeds from issuance of common stock, $31,000.

d. Declaration and payment of cash dividends, $22,000.

e. Increase in interest receivable, $5,000.

f. Decrease in salaries payable, $5,000.

g. Increase in accounts receivable, $10,000.

h. Loan to another company, $42,000.

i. Proceeds from sale of capital assets, $18,000, including $1,000 loss.

j. Increase in inventory, $11,000.

k. Income tax expense, $16,000.

l. Credit sales, $358,000.

m. Cash sales, $92,000.

n. Interest revenue, $8,000.

o. Proceeds from issuance of short-term debt, $38,000.

p. Payments of long-term debt, $57,000.

q. Decrease in interest payable, $2,000.

r. Loan collections, $51,000.

s. Proceeds from sale of investments, $22,000, including $13,000 gain.

t. Amortization expense, $5,000.

u. Dividends received in cash, $3,000.

v. Increase in income tax payable, $2,000.

w. Cash payments to acquire capital assets, $83,000.

x. Cost of goods sold, $284,000.

y. Interest expense, $11,000.

z. Cash balance: June 30, 19X7—$83,000
     June 30, 19X8—$54,000

Required

Prepare Acadia Corporation's income statement and statement of changes in financial position for the year ended June 30, 19X8. Follow the SCFP format of Exhibit 18-2 and the single-step format for the income statement as shown in Exhibit 18-6.

SOLUTION TO REVIEW PROBLEM

Acadia Corporation
Income Statement
for the year ended June 30, 19X8
(amounts in thousands)

Revenue and gains		
Sales revenue ($358 + $92)	$450	
Gain on sale of investments	13	
Interest revenue	8	
Dividend revenue	3	
Total revenues and gains		474
Expenses and losses		
Cost of goods sold	$284	
Salary expense	104	
Depreciation expense	32	
Income tax expense	16	
Interest expense	11	
Amortization expense	5	
Loss on sale of capital assets	1	
Total expenses		453
Net income		$ 21

Acadia Corporation
Statement of Changes in Financial Position
for the year ended June 30, 19X8
(amounts in thousands)

Item No. (Reference Only)			
	Cash flows from operating activities		
	Net income		$ 21
	Add (subtract) items that affect net income and cash flow differently		
b.	Depreciation expense	$32	
i.	Loss on sale of capital asset	1	
s.	Gain on sale of investments	(13)	
t.	Amortization expense	5	
e.	Increase in interest receivable	(5)	
f.	Decrease in salaries payable	(5)	
g.	Increase in accounts receivable	(10)	
j.	Increase in inventory	(11)	
q.	Decrease in interest payable	(2)	
v.	Increase in income tax payable	2	(6)
	Net cash inflow from operating activities		15
	Cash flows from financing activities		
o.	Proceeds from issuance of short-term debt	$ 38	
c.	Proceeds from issuance of common stock	31	
p.	Payments of long-term debt	(57)	
d.	Dividends declared and paid	(22)	
	Net cash outflow from financing activities		(10)
	Cash flows from investing activities		
w.	Acquisition of capital assets	$ (83)	
h.	Loan to another company	(42)	
s.	Proceeds from sale of investments	22	
i.	Proceeds from sale of capital assets	18	
r.	Collection of loans	51	
	Net cash outflow from investing activities		(34)
	Net decrease in cash		$(29)
y.	Cash balance, June 30, 19X7		83
y.	Cash balance, June 30, 19X8		$ 54

Computing Individual Amounts for the Statement of Changes in Financial Position

How do accountants compute the amounts for the statement of changes in financial position? Many accountants prepare the SCFP using the income statement amounts and *changes* in the related balance sheet accounts.

Revenue or expense from the income statement	→	Adjustment for the change in the related balance sheet account(s)	→	Amount for the statement of cash flows

OBJECTIVE 4
Use the financial statements to compute the cash effects of a wide variety of business transactions

Accountants label this the T-account approach. Learning to analyze T-accounts in this manner is one of the most useful skills you will acquire from accounting. It will enable you to identify the cash effects of a wide variety of transactions. It will also strengthen your grasp of the accrual basis of accounting.

The following discussions use Anchor Ltd.'s income statement in Exhibit 18-6 and comparative balance sheet in Exhibit 18-7.

The indirect method of computing cash flows from operating activities is also called the *reconciliation method*. It starts with net income and shows the reconciliation from net income to operating cash flows. For example, the consolidated statement of changes in financial position of Fortis Inc. shows "Net income for the year" and adjusts that number by "Items not affecting (generating) cash" and "Change in non-cash working capital" to derive "Cash from operations." The indirect method shows the link between net income and cash flow from operations better than the direct method. That is why Fortis Inc. and many other Canadian companies choose the indirect method over the direct method although both are used. The main drawback of the indirect method is that it does not report the detailed operating cash flows—collections from customers and other cash receipts, payments to suppliers, payments to employees, and payments for interest and taxes.

Exhibit 18-2 is Anchor Ltd.'s statement prepared by the indirect method. One reason companies prefer the indirect method is its ease of preparation from the income statement and the beginning and ending balance sheets.

Computing the Cash Amounts of Operating Activities

The operating section of the statement of changes in financial position begins with net income taken directly from the income statement. Items which affect net income and cash flow differently are added or subtracted to arrive at net cash flow from operations.

Depreciation, Depletion, and Amortization Expenses   It was noted earlier that depreciation, depletion, and amortization expense have no cash effect. Since they are deducted from revenues in the computation of income, they must be added back to reconcile net income to cash flows from operations.

The amounts for depreciation, depletion, and amortization expense are taken directly from the income statement. For example, depreciation expense in Exhibit 18-6 is $18,000.

All expenses with no cash effects are added back to net income on the SCFP. Likewise, revenues that do not provide cash are deducted from net income.

Gains and Losses on the Sale of Capital Assets   Sales of assets are investing activities on the SCFP and, as was pointed out earlier, the cash inflow includes any gain or loss on the sale. Item 16 on Exhibit 18-5 indicates that Anchor received $62,000 from the sale of capital assets and that the $62,000 included a gain of $8,000. Exhibit 18-6 indicates Anchor's net income of $41,000 also includes the $8,000 gain. The double-counting is eliminated by subtracting the amount of the gain from net income in determining cash flows from operations.

The amount of any gain or loss is taken directly from the income statement in preparing the SCFP.

Changes in the Current Asset and Current Liability Accounts Other Than Cash   Exhibit 18-7 provides a comparative balance sheet for Anchor Ltd. and shows the increases or decreases in the asset, liability and shareholders' equity accounts. Recall that changes in the current asset and current liability accounts affect cash flows. The rules are:

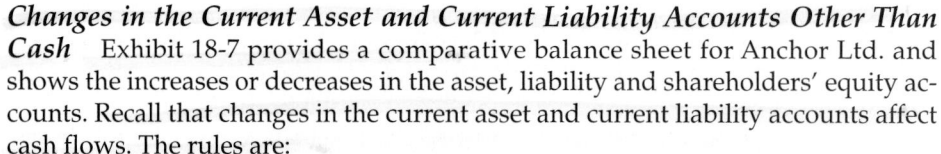

Key Point:

These rules may help with the indirect method: (1) An increase in a current asset is subtracted from net income. (2) A decrease in a current asset is added to net income. (3) An increase in a current liability is added to net income. (4) A decrease in a current liability is subtracted from net income.

1. **An *increase* in a current asset other than cash (or cash equivalents) is subtracted from net income to compute cash flow from operations.** Suppose a company makes a sale. Income is increased by the sale amount. However, collection of less than the full amount leaves Accounts Receivable with an increase. For example, Exhibit 18-7 reports that Anchor Ltd.'s Accounts Receivable increased by $13,000 during 19X2. To compute the impact of revenue on Anchor's cash flow amount, we must subtract the $13,000 increase in Accounts Receivable from net income in Exhibit 18-2. The same logic applies to the other current assets. If they increase during the period, subtract the increase from net income.

2. **A *decrease* in a current asset other than cash is added to net income.** For example, suppose Accounts Receivable's balance decreased by $4,000 during the period. Cash receipts cause the Accounts Receivable balance to decrease, so decreases in Accounts Receivable and the other current assets are added to net income.

3. **A *decrease* in a current liability is subtracted from net income.** The payment of a current liability causes it to decrease, so decreases in current liabilities are subtracted from net income. For example, in Exhibit 18-7, the $2,000 decrease in Accrued Liabilities is subtracted from net income to compute net cash inflow from operating activities.

4. **An *increase* in a current liability is added to net income.** Accounts Payable increased during the year. This increase can occur only if cash is not spent to pay this liability, which means that cash payments are less than the related expense. Thus increases in current liabilities are added to net income.

Exhibit 18-8 summarizes the adjustments needed to convert net income to net cash inflow (or net cash outflow) from operating activities by the indirect method.

Computing the Cash Amounts of Financing Activities

Financing activities affect liability and shareholders' equity accounts, such as Notes Payable, Bonds Payable, Long-Term Debt, Common Stock, and Retained Earnings. The cash amounts of financing activities can be computed by analyzing these accounts.

Computing Issuances and Payments of Long-Term Debt   The beginning and ending balances of Long-Term Debt, Notes Payable, or Bonds Payable are taken from the balance sheet. If either the amount of new issuances or the amount of the payments is known, the other amount can be computed. New debt issuances total $94,000. The computation of debt payments follows from analysis of the Long-Term Debt T-account, using amounts from Anchor Ltd.'s balance sheet, Exhibit 18-7:

Long-term Debt

		Beginning balance	77,000
Payments	**11,000**	Issuance of new debt	94,000
		Ending balance	160,000

Computing Issuances and Repurchases of Stock   The cash effects of these financing activities can be determined by analyzing the various stock accounts. It is convenient to work with a single summary account for stock. Using Exhibit 18-7 data, we have:

Common Stock

		Beginning balance	258,000
Retirements of stock............................	0	**Issuance of new stock**...........	**101,000**
		Ending balance.......................	359,000

Computing Dividend Payments If the amount of the dividends is not given elsewhere (for example, in a statement of retained earnings), it can be computed as follows:

Retained Earnings

		Beginning balance....................	86,000
Dividend declaration	**17,000**	Net income................................	41,000
		Ending balance........................	110,000

Dividends Payable

		Beginning balance....................	XXX
Dividend payments......................	XXX	**Dividend declarations**...........	**XXX** ←
		Ending balance........................	XXX

First, we compute dividend declarations by analyzing the Retained Earnings T-account. Then we solve for dividend payments with the Dividends Payable T-account. Anchor Ltd. has no Dividends Payable account, so dividend payments are the same as declarations.

Computing the Cash Amounts of Investing Activities

Investing activities affect asset accounts, such as Capital Assets, Investments, and Notes Receivable. The cash amounts of investing activities can be identified by analyzing these accounts. Most data for the computations are taken directly from the income statement and beginning and ending balance sheets. Other amounts come from the analysis of accounts in the ledger.

Computing Acquisitions and Sales of Capital Assets Most companies have separate accounts for Land, Buildings, Equipment, and other capital assets. It is helpful to combine these accounts into a single summary for computing the cash flows from acquisitions and sales of these assets. Also, we subtract accumulated depreciation from the assets' cost and work with a net figure for capital assets. This approach allows us to work with a single capital asset account as opposed to a large number of capital asset and related accumulated amortization accounts.

To illustrate, observe that Anchor Ltd.'s balance sheet (Exhibit 18-7) reports beginning capital assets, net of depreciation, of $219,000 and an ending net amount of $453,000. The income statement shows depreciation of $18,000 and an $8,000 gain on sale of capital assets. Further, the acquisitions total is $306,000. How much are the proceeds from the sale of capital assets? First, we must determine their book value, computed as follows:

Key Point:
Proceeds from the sale of an asset need not equal the asset's book value.
Remember:
Book value + Gain = Proceeds
Book value − Loss = Proceeds
The book value information comes from the balance sheet, the gain or loss from the income statement.

Capital Assets (net)

Beginning balance....................	219,000	Depreciation	18,000
Acquisitions	306,000	**Book value of assets sold**	**54,000**
Ending balance.........................	453,000		

Now we can compute the sale proceeds as follows:

Short Exercise:

Greene Corp. reported the following:

Retirement of preferred stock	$45
Sale of bonds issued by Blue Co.	112
Payment of interest on mortgage note	11
Purchase of land	158
Payment of income taxes	38
Sale of common stock	105
Collection of note receivable	63
Payment of dividends	150

What is Greene's net change in cash from investing activities?

A:

($112 − $158 + $63) = $17, a net increase. Categorize the other items. *Operating:* Payment of interest, payment of taxes. *Financing:* Retirement of preferred sock, sale of stock, payment of dividends.

Sale proceeds = Book value sold, + Gain, − Loss,

= $54,000 + $8,000 − $0 = $62,000

Trace the sale proceeds of $62,000 to the statement of changes in financial position in Exhibit 18-2. If the sale resulted in a loss of $3,000, the sale proceeds would be $51,000 ($54,000 − $3,000), and the SCFP would report $51,000 as a cash receipt from this investing activity.

Computing Acquisitions and Sales of Assets Classified as Investments, and Loans and Their Collections   Accountants use a separate category of assets for investments in stocks, bonds, and other types of assets. The cash amounts of transactions involving these assets can be computed in the manner illustrated for capital assets. Investments are easier to analyze, however, because there is no depreciation to account for, as shown by the following T-account:

Investments

Beginning balance	XXX		
Purchases	XXX	Cost of investments sold	XXX
Ending balance	XXX		

New loans cause a debit to a receivable and an outflow of cash. Collections increase cash and cause a credit to the receivable:

Loans and Notes Receivable

Beginning balance	XXX		
New loans made	XXX	Collections	XXX
Ending balance	XXX		

Noncash Financing and Investing Activities _____

Companies make investments that do not require cash. They also obtain financing other than cash. Our example included none of these transactions.

Suppose Anchor Ltd. issued common stock with a stated value of $320,000 to acquire a warehouse. Anchor would journalize this transaction as follows:

Warehouse	320,000	
Common Stock		320,000

Despite the fact that this transaction has no net effect on the statement of changes in financial position, Section 1540.20 of the *CICA Handbook* requires that noncash financing and investing activities be disclosed on the statement and that both sides of the transaction be disclosed separately (that is, it is inappropriate to disclose only the net effect of the transaction). In this case, the proceeds from the issue of the common stock will be included with financing activities, while the purchase of the building will be included with investing activities. The SCFP should indicate that the two transactions are related. The appropriate disclosure is illustrated in the solution to the review problem (Robins Corporation) on p. 882.

As was noted above, the transaction must be shown in its entirety; it is not appropriate to show only the net effect of the transaction. For example, if the purchase had been for common stock of $300,000 and for cash of $20,000, it would not be appropriate to show only the net effect on cash of $20,000. The SCFP would show a financing inflow of $300,000 for the common stock and an investing outflow of $320,000 for the building.

PUTTING SKILLS TO WORK

Nike's Statement of Cash Flows for Operating Activities—Indirect Method

Nike, Inc.
Statement of Changes in Financial Position
(Indirect Method for Operating Activities)
For the Year Ended May 31, 19X7
(in Thousands)

Cash provided (used) by operations:	
Net income	$35,879
Income charges (credits) not affecting cash:	
Depreciation	12,078
Deferred income taxes	8,486
Other	2,494
Changes in certain working capital components:	
Decrease in inventory	59,542
Decrease in accounts receivable	1,174
Decrease in other current assets	4,331
Increase in accounts payable,	
accrued liabilities, and income taxes payable	8,462
Cash provided by operations	132,446
Cash provided (used) by financing activities:	
Additions to long-term debt	30,332
Reductions in long-term debt including current portion	(10,678)
Decrease in notes payable to banks	(18,489)
Proceeds from exercise of options	1,911
Dividends—common and preferred	(15,188)
Cash used by financing activities	(12,112)
Cash provided (used) by investing activities:	
Additions to property, plant, and equipment	(11,874)
Disposals of property, plant, and equipment	1,728
Additions to other assets	(930)
Cash used by investing activities	(11,076)
Effect of exchange-rate changes on cash	(529)
Net increase (decrease) in cash	108,729
Cash and cash equivalents, beginning of year	18,138
Cash and cash equivalents, end of year	$126,867

Nike, Inc., is a well-known maker of athletic shoes and clothing. Nike uses the indirect method to report cash flows from operating activities. Most of the items in Nike's statement of cash flows have been discussed earlier but three need clarification. First, deferred income taxes are added back to net income in the operating section. These taxes do not require current cash payments and are, therefore, similar to accrued liabilities. Second, financing activities include proceeds from exercise of options. This is the amount of cash received from issuance of stock to executives. Third, changes in exchange rates show the cash effect of fluctuations in foreign currencies, a topic that is beyond the scope of this course.

Evaluation of Nike's 19X7 Cash-Flow Results

Nike's cash flows for 19X7 look very strong. Cash increased from $18 million to almost $127 million. Virtually all the cash increase came from operations—a sign of strength. During 19X7, Nike invested in new plant and equipment ($11.9 million) and paid off more than $29 million ($10.7 million + $18.5 million) of debt. The company issued only $30 million of new debt. Nike's board of directors was so confident of the future that the board paid $15 million of dividends, almost half of net income.

STOP & THINK

Examine Anchor Ltd.'s statement of changes in financial position, Exhibit 18-2.
  a. Does Anchor Ltd. appear to be growing or shrinking? How can you tell?
  b. Where did Anchor's cash for expansion come from?
  c. Suppose Accounts Receivable increased by $40,000 (instead of $13,000) during the current year. What would this increase signal about the company?

Answers:

  a. This is an *investing* question. Anchor appears to be growing. The company acquired more capital assets ($306,000) than it sold during the year, and current assets changed very little.
  b. This is a *financing* question. The cash for expansion came from the issuance of common stock ($101,000) and from borrowing ($94,000).
  c. This is an *operating* question. If accounts receivable had increased by $40,000, Anchor Ltd. would have $27,000 less cash ($40,000 minus $13,000). A large increase in accounts receivable may signal difficulty in collecting cash from customers or a sharp increase in sales. A manager, shareholder, or creditor of Anchor Ltd. should compare current-year sales with sales revenue for the preceding year. If sales are up, higher accounts receivable are good news. If sales are down, higher receivables may signal a cash shortage.

OBJECTIVE 5

Prepare a work sheet for the statement of changes in financial position by the indirect method

The Work Sheet Approach to Preparing the Statement of Changes in Financial Position

The main body of the chapter discusses the use of the statement of changes in financial position in decision-making and shows how to prepare the statement using T-accounts. The T-account approach works well as a learning device, especially for simple situations. In practice, however, most companies face complex situations. In these cases, a work sheet can help accountants prepare the SCFP. Here we show how to prepare the SCFP using a specially designed work sheet.

The basic task in preparing the statement of changes in financial position is to account for all the cash effects of transactions that took the business from its beginning financial position to its ending financial position. Like the T-account approach, the work sheet approach helps the accountant identify the cash effects of all transactions of the period. The work sheet starts with the beginning balance sheet and concludes with the ending balance sheet. Two middle columns—one for debit amounts and the other for credit amounts—complete the work sheet. These columns, labeled Transaction Analysis, contain the data for the SCFP. Exhibit 18-9 presents the basic framework of the work sheet. Accountants can prepare the statement directly from the lower part of the work sheet (Panel B in Exhibit 18-9). The advantage of the work sheet approach is that it organizes in one place all relevant data for the statement's preparation. The remaining exhibits are based on the Anchor Ltd. data used earlier in the chapter.

The work sheet can be used with either the indirect method or the direct method for operating activities. As with the T-account approach, cash flows from financing activities and cash flows from investing activities are unaffected by the method used for operating activities.

Transaction Analysis on the Work Sheet

For your convenience, we repeat the Anchor Ltd. transactions from Exhibit 18-5 as Exhibit 18-10.

EXHIBIT 18-9 *The Work Sheet for Preparing the Statement of Changes in Financial Position*

	Balances Dec. 31, 19X1	Transaction Analysis		Balances Dec. 31, 19X2
		Debit	**Credit**	
Anchor Ltd. Work Sheet for Statement of Changes in Financial Position for the year ended December 31, 19X2				
Panel A: Account Titles				
Cash..............................				
Accounts receivable.......				
⟨				
Retained earnings				
Panel B: Statement of Changes in Financial Position				
Cash flows from operating activities......				
Cash flows from financing activities.......				
Cash flows from investing activities.......				
Net increase (decrease) in cash...........................				

EXHIBIT 18-10 *Summary of Anchor Ltd.'s 19X2 Transactions*

Operating Activities
1. Net income, $41,000.
2. Depreciation expense, $18,000.
3. Increase in accounts receivable, $13,000.
4. Increase in interest receivable, $2,000.
5. Decrease in inventory, $3,000.
6. Increase in prepaid expenses, $1,000.
7. Increase in accounts payable, $34,000.
8. Decrease in salary and wages payable, $2,000.
9. Decrease in accrued liabilities, $2,000.

Financing Activities
10. Proceeds from issuance of common stock, $101,000.
11. Proceeds from issuance of long-term debt, $94,000.
12. Payment of long-term debt, $11,000.
13. Declaration and payment of cash dividends, $17,000.

Investing Activities
14. Cash payments to acquire capital assets, $306,000.
15. Loan to another company, $11,000.
16. Proceeds from sale of capital assets, $62,000 (including $8,000 gain).

The transaction analysis on the work sheet appears in the form of journal entries. Only balance sheet accounts appear on the work sheet. There are no income statement accounts. Therefore, Net Income is entered on the work sheet as a credit to Retained Earnings, while Net Loss, if there was one, would be entered as a debit to Retained Earnings.

Net Increase (Decrease) in Cash   The net increase or net decrease in cash for the period is the balancing amount needed to equate the total debits and total credits ($567,000) on the SCFP. In Exhibit 18-11, Anchor Ltd. experienced a $20,000 decrease in cash. This amount is entered as a credit to Cash transaction "17" at the top of the work sheet and a debit to Net Decrease in Cash at the bottom. Totaling the columns completes the work sheet.

Preparing the Statement of Changes in Financial Position from the Work Sheet

To prepare the SCFP, Exhibit 18-2 on page 861 of the text, the accountant has only to rewrite Panel B of the work sheet and add subtotals for the three categories of activities.

Preparing the Work Sheet— Indirect Method for Operating Activities

The indirect method shows the reconciliation from net income to net cash inflow (or net cash outflow) from operating activities. Exhibit 18-11 is the work sheet for preparing the statement of changes in financial position by the indirect method.

The analysis of operating activities, financing activities, and investing activities uses the information presented in Exhibit 18-10. The analysis that follows focuses on cash flows from operating activities. The Anchor Ltd. data come from the income statement (Exhibit 18-6) and the comparative balance sheet (Exhibit 18-7).

Transaction Analysis Under the Indirect Method

Net income transaction (11) is the first operating cash inflow. Net income is entered on the work sheet as a debit to Net Income under cash flows from operating activities and a credit to Retained Earnings. Next come the additions to, and subtractions from, net income, starting with depreciation transaction (2), which is debited to Depreciation on the work sheet and credited to Capital Assets, Net. Transaction (16) is the sale of capital assets. The $8,000 gain on the sale is entered as a credit to Gain on Sale of Capital Assets under operating cash flows—a subtraction from net income. This credit removes the $8,000 amount of the gain from cash flow from operations because the cash proceeds from the sale were not $8,000. The cash proceeds were $62,000, so this amount is entered on the work sheet as a debit under investing activities. Entry (16) is completed by crediting the capital assets' book value of $54,000 ($62,000 − $8,000) to the Capital Assets, Net account.

Entries (3) through (9) reconcile net income to cash flows from operations for increases and decreases in the current assets other than Cash and for increases and decreases in the current liabilities. Entry (3) debits Accounts Receivable for its $13,000 increase during the year. This decrease in cash flows is credited to Increase in Accounts Receivable under operating cash flows. Entries (4) and (6) are similar for Interest Receivable and Prepaid Expenses.

EXHIBIT 18-11 *Work Sheet for Statement of Changes in Financial Position—Indirect Method*

		Transaction Analysis (Amounts in thousands)		
	Balances			**Balances**
Panel A: Account Titles	**Dec. 31, 19X1**	**Debit**	**Credit**	**Dec. 31, 19X2**
Cash	42		(17) 20	22
Accounts receivable	80	(3) 13		93
Interest receivable	1	(4) 2		3
Inventory	138		(5) 3	135
Prepaid expenses	7	(6) 1		8
Long-term receivable from another company	—	(15) 11		11
Capital assets, net	219	(14) 306	(2) 18	
			(16) 54	453
Totals	487			725
Accounts payable	57		(7) 34	91
Salary and wage payable	6	(8) 2		4
Accrued liabilities	3	(9) 2		1
Long-term debt	77	(12) 11	(11) 94	160
Common stock	258		(10) 101	359
Retained earnings	86	(13) 17	(1) 41	110
Totals	487	365	365	725
Panel B: Statement of Changes in Financial Position				
Cash flows from operating activities				
Net income		(1) 41		
Add (subtract) items that affect net income and cash flow differently:				
Depreciation		(2) 18		
Gain on sale of capital assets			(16) 8	
Increase in accounts receivable			(3) 13	
Increase in interest receivable			(4) 2	
Decrease in inventory		(5) 3		
Increase in prepaid expenses			(6) 1	
Increase in accounts payable		(7) 34		
Decrease in salary and wage payable			(8) 2	
Decrease in accrued liabilities			(9) 2	
Cash flows from financing activities				
Proceeds from issuance of common stock		(10) 101		
Proceeds from issuance of long-term debt		(11) 94		
Payment of long-term debt			(12) 11	
Payment of dividends			(13) 17	
Cash flows from investing activities				
Acquisition of capital assets			(14) 306	
Proceeds from sale of capital assets		(16) 62		
Loan to another company			(15) 11	
		353	373	
Net decrease in cash		(17) 20		
Totals		373	373	

The final item in Exhibit 18-11 is the Net Decrease in Cash—transaction (17) on the work sheet—a credit to Cash and a debit to Net Decrease in Cash. To prepare the statement of changes in financial position from the work sheet, the accountant merely rewrites Panel B of the statement, adding subtotals for the three categories of activities.

Noncash Financing and Investing Activities on the Work Sheet   Noncash financing and investing activities can also be analyzed on the work sheet. Because this type of transaction includes both a financing activity and an investing activity, it requires two work sheet entries. For example, suppose Crown Ltd. purchased a building by issuing common stock of $320,000. Exhibit 18-12 illustrates the transaction analysis of this noncash financing and investing activity. Observe that Cash is unaffected.

Work sheet entry (T1) records the purchase of the building, and entry (T2) records the issuance of the stock.

Computers and the Indirect Method of Generating the Statement of Changes in Financial Position _____

The computer can generate the statement of changes in financial position by the indirect method with ease. After the income statement is prepared, the computer picks up net income, depreciation, and the other noncash expenses. Changes in the

EXHIBIT 18-12   *Noncash Financing and Investing Activities on the Work Sheet*

	Balances Dec. 31, 19X1	Transaction Analysis		Balances Dec. 31,19X2
		Debit	**Credit**	
Crown Ltd. Work Sheet for Statement of Changes in Financial Position for the year ended December 31, 19X2				
Panel A: Account Titles				
Cash.............................				
Accounts receivable..................				
Building......................................	650,000	(T1) 320,000		970,000
Common stock...........................	890,000		(T2) 320,000	1,210,000
Retained earnings				
Panel B: Statement of Changes in Financial Position				
Cash flows from operating activities				
Cash flows from financing activities				
Issuance of common stock to purchase building............		(T2) 320,000		
Cash flows from investing activities				
Purchase of building by issue of common stock.			(T1) 320,000	

current assets and the current liabilities and the data for the financing activities and the investing activities are obtained from the specific account balances in the general ledger.

The statement of cash flows created from a computer's general ledger files is not automatically correct from the point of view of generally accepted accounting principles. For example, noncash financing and investing activities of a large organization, such as George Weston, might be incorrectly combined with the company's cash flows. The computerized system must be sophisticated enough to distinguish among various categories of cash activities, analyze the information fed into the computer, and check that its output adheres to generally accepted accounting principles. Management must keep in mind that revisions to a company's computer software are relatively easy and may be made without their knowledge.

Summary Problem for Your Review

Prepare the 19X3 statement of changes in financial position for Robins Corporation, using the indirect method to report cash flows from operating activities.

	December 31,	
	19X3	19X2
Current assets		
Cash and cash equivalents	$19,000	$ 3,000
Accounts receivable	22,000	23,000
Inventories	34,000	31,000
Prepaid expenses	1,000	3,000
Current liabilities		
Notes payable (for inventory purchases)	$11,000	$ 7,000
Accounts payable	24,000	19,000
Accrued liabilities	7,000	9,000
Income and other taxes payable	10,000	10,000

Transaction data for 19X3

Purchase of equipment	$98,000	Depreciation expense	$ 7,000
Payment of cash dividends	18,000	Issuance of long-term note	
Net income	26,000	payable to borrow cash	7,000
Issuance of common stock		Issuance of common stock	
to retire bonds payable	13,000	for cash	19,000
Purchase of long-term		Sale of building	74,000
investment	8,000	Amortization expense	3,000
Issuance of long-term note		Repurchase of own shares	5,000
payable to purchase		Loss on sale of building	2,000
patent	37,000		

SOLUTION TO REVIEW PROBLEM

Robins Corporation
Statement of Changes in Financial Position
for the year ended December 31, 19X3

Cash flows from operating activities		
Net income		$26,000
Add (subtract) items that affect net income and cash flow differently:		
Depreciation	$ 7,000	
Amortization	3,000	
Loss on sale of building	2,000	
Decrease in accounts receivable	1,000	
Increase in inventories	(3,000)	
Decrease in prepaid expenses	2,000	
Increase in notes payable, short-term	4,000	
Increase in accounts payable	5,000	
Decrease in accrued liabilities	(2,000)	19,000
Net cash inflow from operating activities		45,000
Cash flows from financing activities		
Issuance of long-term notes payable*	$ 44,000	
Issuance of common stock**	32,000	
Payment of cash dividends	(18,000)	
Retirement of bonds payable**	(13,000)	
Repurchase of Robins Corporation shares	(5,000)	
Net cash inflow from financing activities		40,000
Cash flows from investing activities		
Purchase of equipment	$(98,000)	
Sale of building	74,000	
Purchase of patent*	(37,000)	
Purchase of long-term investment	(8,000)	
Net cash outflow from investing activities		(69,000)
Net increase in cash and cash equivalents		$16,000

---

* During the year, the company issued a long-term note payable in the amount of $37,000 and used the proceeds to purchase a patent; notes were also issued for $7,000 cash.

** During the year, the company issued common stock in the amount of $13,000 and used the proceeds to retire bonds payable in the same amount; stock was also issued for $19,000 cash.

Summary

1. *Identify the purposes of the statement of changes in financial position.* The *statement of changes in financial position* reports a business's cash receipts, cash disbursements, and net change in cash for the accounting period. It shows *why* cash increased or decreased during the period. A required financial statement, it gives a different view of the business from that given by accrual-basis statements. The SCFP helps financial statement users predict the future cash flows of the entity. Cash includes cash on hand, cash in bank, and *cash equivalents* such as liquid, short-term investments.

2. *Distinguish among operating, financing, and investing activities.* The statement is divided into *operating activities, financing activities,* and *investing activities.* Operating activities create revenues and expenses; financing activities obtain the funds needed to launch and sustain the business; and investing activities affect long-term assets. Each section of the statement includes cash receipts and cash payments and concludes with a net cash increase or decrease. In addition, *non-cash financing activities and investing activities* are also included in the SCFP.

3. Prepare a statement of changes in financial position by the indirect method. The *indirect method* shows the reconciliation from net income to cash flow from operations. Although the *CICA Handbook* permits both the indirect and the direct methods, the indirect method is more widely used in practice.

4. Use the financial statements to compute the cash effects of a wide variety of business transactions. The analysis of the income statement, changes in the balance sheet, and T-accounts aids the computation of the cash effects of business transactions.

5. Prepare a work sheet for the statement of changes in financial position by the indirect method. The work sheet approach is more useful for preparing the statement of changes in financial position in complex situations. The work sheet helps the accountant identify the cash effects of all transactions for the period.

Self-Study Questions

Test your understanding of the chapter by marking the best answer for each of the following questions:

1. The income statement and the balance sheet *(p. 859)*
   a. Report the cash effects of transactions
   b. Fail to report why cash changed during the period
   c. Report the sources and uses of cash during the period
   d. Are divided into operating, financing, and investing activities

2. The purpose of the statement of changes in financial position is to *(pp. 859–860)*
   a. Predict future cash flows
   b. Evaluate management decisions
   c. Determine the ability to pay dividends and interest
   d. All of the above

3. A successful company's major source of cash should be *(p. 860)*
   a. Operating activities   c. Financing activities
   b. Investing activities   d. A combination of the above

4. Dividends paid to shareholders are usually reported on the statement of changes in financial position as a (an) *(p. 860)*
   a. Operating activity   c. Financing activity
   b. Investing activity   d. Combination of the above

5. Which of the following items does not appear on a statement of changes in financial position prepared by the indirect method? *(pp. 863–867)*
   a. Depreciation expense   c. Loss on sale of capital assets
   b. Decrease in accounts receivable   d. Cash payments to suppliers

6. In preparing an SCFP by the indirect method, the accountant will treat an increase in inventory as *(pp. 866–867)*
   a. An increase in investment cash flows   c. A decrease in operating cash flows
   b. A decrease in investment cash flows   d. An increase in operating cash flows

7. Fortier Ltd. sold a long-term investment for $182,000; the selling price included a loss of $4,000. The cash flow from investing activities will show *(pp. 867–868)*
   a. An increase of $182,000   c. A decrease of $182,000
   b. An increase of $186,000   d. None of the above

8. Noncash financing and investing activities *(p. 874)*
   a. Are reported in the main body of the SCFP
   b. Are reported in a separate schedule that accompanies the SCFP
   c. Are reported on the income statement
   d. Are not reported in the financial statements

9. Net income is $17,000, depreciation is $9,000, and amortization is $3,000. In addition, the sale of a capital asset generated a $4,000 gain. Current assets other than cash increased by $6,000, and current liabilities increased by $8,000. What was the amount of cash flow from operations? *(pp. 863–867)*

    a. $23,000   c. $31,000

    b. $27,000   d. $35,000

10. The work sheet approach to the preparation of the SCFP *(p. 880)*

    a. Begins with the change in cash

    b. Ends with the change in cash

    c. Does not as well as the T-account approach for complex situation

    d. Can only be used with the direct method of preparing the SCFP

Answers to the Self-Study Questions follow the Accounting Vocabulary.

Accounting Vocabulary

Cash and cash equivalents *(p. 858)*
Cash flows (disbursements) *(p. 858)*
Financing activity *(p. 860)*
Indirect method *(p. 863)*
Investing activity *(p. 861)*
Operating activity *(p. 860*
Statement of Changes in Financial Position *(p. 858)*

Answers to Self-Study Questions

  1. b

  2. d

  3. a

  4. c

  5. d

  6. c

  7. a

  8. a

  9. b ($17,000 + $9,000 + $3,000 – $4,000 – $6,000 + $8,000 = $27,000)

  10. b

ASSIGNMENT MATERIAL ─────────────────

Questions

1. What information does the SCFP report that is not shown on the balance sheet, the income statement, or the statement of retained earnings?
2. Identify four purposes of the SCFP.
3. Identify and briefly describe the three types of activities that are reported on the SCFP.
4. How is the SCFP dated and why?
5. What is the check figure for the SCFP, where is it obtained, and how is it used?
6. What is the most important source of cash for most successful companies?
7. How can cash decrease during a year when income is high? How can cash increase during a year when income is low? How can investors and creditors learn these facts about the company?

8. DeBerg, Inc., prepares its SCFP using the *indirect* method for operating activities. Identify the section of DeBerg's SCFP where each of the following transactions will appear. If the transaction does not appear on the SCFP, give the reason.

a. Cash	14,000	
Note Payable, Long-Term		14,000
b. Salary Expense	7,300	
Cash		7,300
c. Cash	28,400	
Common Stock		28,400
d. Amortization Expense	6,500	
Goodwill		6,500
e. Accounts Payable	1,400	
Cash		1,400

9. Why and how are depreciation, depletion, and amortization expenses reported on a statement prepared by the indirect method?

10. Summarize the major cash receipts and cash disbursements in the three categories of activities that appear on the SCFP.

11. Marshall Corporation's beginning capital asset balance, net of accumulated depreciation, was $193,000, and the ending amount was $176,000. Marshall recorded depreciation of $37,000 and sold capital assets with a book value of $9,000. How much cash did Marshall pay to purchase capital assets during the period? Where on the SCFP should Marshall report this item?

12. How should issuance of a note payable to purchase land be reported in the statement of changes in financial position? Identify three other transactions that fall in this same category.

13. Which format of the SCFP gives a clearer description of the individual cash flows from operating activities? Which format better shows the relationship between net income and operating cash flow?

14. An investment that cost $65,000 was sold for $80,000, resulting in a $15,000 gain. Show how to report this transaction on a SCFP prepared by the indirect method.

15. Identify the cash effects of increases and decreases in current assets other than cash. What are the cash effects of increases and decreases in current liabilities?

16. Milano Corporation earned net income of $38,000 and had depreciation expense of $22,000. Also, noncash current assets decreased $13,000, and current liabilities decreased $9,000. What was Milano's net cash flow from operating activities?

17. What is the difference between the direct method and the indirect method of reporting financing activities and investing activities?

Exercises

Exercise 18-1   *Identifying the purposes of the statement of changes in financial position*
             (Obj. 1)

Coast Western Builders Ltd., a real estate developer, has experienced an unbroken string of ten years of growth in net income. Nevertheless, the business is facing bankruptcy! Creditors are calling all of Coast Western's outstanding loans for immediate payment, and the cash is simply not available. In trying to explain where Coast Western went wrong, it becomes clear that managers placed undue emphasis on net income and gave too little attention to cash flows.

Required

Write a brief memo, in your own words, to explain for Coast Western managers the purposes of the SCFP.

Exercise 18-2   *Identifying activities for the statement of changes in financial position*   **(Obj. 2)**

Identify each of the following transactions as an operating activity (O), financing activity (F), an investing activity (I), a noncash financing and investing activity (NFI), or a transaction that is not reported on the statement of changes in financial position (N). Assume the indirect method is used to report cash flows from operating activities.

_____ a. Payment of account payable
_____ b. Issuance of preferred stock for cash
_____ c. Payment of cash dividend
_____ d. Sale of long-term investment
_____ e. Amortization of bond discount
_____ f. Collection of account receivable
_____ g. Issuance of long-term note payable to borrow cash
_____ h. Depreciation of equipment
_____ i. Repurchase of common stock
_____ j. Issuance of common stock for cash
_____ k. Purchase of long-term investment
_____ l. Payment of wages to employees
_____ m. Collection of cash interest
_____ n. Cash sale of land
_____ o. Distribution of stock dividend
_____ p. Acquisition of equipment by issuance of note payable
_____ q. Payment of long-term debt
_____ r. Acquisition of building by issuance of common stock
_____ s. Accrual of salary expense

Exercise 18-3   *Classifying transactions for the statement of changes in financial position*
(Obj. 2)

Indicate where, if at all, each of the following transactions would be reported on a SCFP prepared by the indirect method.

a. Salary Expense	4,300	
Cash		4,300
b. Equipment	18,000	
Cash		18,000
c. Cash	7,200	
Long-Term Investment		7,200
d. Bonds Payable	45,000	
Cash		45,000
e. Building	164,000	
Note Payable, Long-Term		164,000
f. Allowance for Doubtful Accounts	1,400	
Accounts Receivable		1,400
g. Dividends Payable	16,500	
Cash		16,500
h. Furniture and Fixtures	22,100	
Note Payable, Short-Term		22,100
i. Accounts Payable	8,300	
Cash		8,300
j. Cash	81,000	
Common Stock		81,000
k. Common Stock	13,000	
Cash		13,000
l. Retained Earning	36,000	
Common Stock		36,000
m. Cash	2,000	
Bonds Payable		2,000
n. Land	87,700	
Cash		87,700

Exercise 18-4   *Preparing the statement of changes in financial position—indirect method*
(Obj. 3)

The income statement and additional data of Yee Trading Corp. follow:

Yee Trading Corp.
Income Statement
year ended September 30, 19X2

Revenues		
Sales revenue..	$229,000	
Dividend revenue..	8,000	$237,000
Expenses		
Cost of goods sold	103,000	
Salary expense...	45,000	
Depreciation expense..	29,000	
Depletion expense	11,000	
Interest expense	2,000	
Income tax expense	9,000	199,000
Net income		$ 38,000

Additional data:

a. Accounts receivable increased by $7,000.

b. Accounts payable increased by $9,000.

c. Payments to employees are $1,000 more than salary expense.

d. Dividends payable increased by $2,000.

e. Acquisition of capital assets is $116,000. Of this amount, $101,000 is paid in cash, $15,000 by signing a note payable.

f. Proceeds from sale of land, $14,000.

g. Proceeds from issuance of common stock, $30,000.

h. Payment of long-term note payable, $15,000.

i. Payment of dividends, $11,000.

j. Increase in cash balance, $?

Prepare Yee Trading's SCFP. Report operating activities by the indirect method.

Exercise 18-5   *Computing amounts for the statement of changes in financial position*
(Obj. 4)

Compute the following items for the SCFP:

a. Beginning and ending Capital Assets, net, are $103,000 and $107,000 respectively. Depreciation for the period is $16,000, and acquisitions of net capital assets are $27,000. Capital assets were sold at a $1,000 gain. What were the cash proceeds of the sale?

b. Beginning and ending Retained Earnings are $45,000 and $73,000 respectively. Net income for the period is $62,000, and stock dividends are $22,000. How much are cash dividend payments?

Exercise 18-6   *Computing cash flows from operating activities—indirect method*   **(Obj. 3)**

The accounting records of Eastern Mills Ltd. reveal the following:

Cash sales.................................	$ 9,000	Increase in current assets	
Gain on sale of land................	5,000	other than cash	$17,000
Acquisition of land	37,000	Payment of dividends............	7,000

Payment of accounts			Collection of accounts		
payable	48,000		receivable		93,000
Net income.............................	21,000		Payment of salaries and		
Payment of income tax...........	13,000		wages		34,000
Collection of dividend			Depreciation............................		12,000
revenue................................	7,000		Decrease in current		
Payment of interest................	16,000		liabilities		23,000

Compute cash flows from operating activities by the indirect method. Use the format of the operating section of Exhibit 18-2.

Exercise 18-7   *Classifying transactions for the statement of changes in financial position (Obj. 3)*

Two transactions of Sports Life Park are recorded as follows:

a. Cash	59,000	
Accumulated Depreciation	83,000	
Equipment		135,000
Gain on Sale of Equipment...................................		7,000
b. Land...	290,000	
Cash		130,000
Note Payable		160,000

Required

Indicate where, how, and in what amount to report these transactions on the SCFP. Sports Life Park reports cash flows from operating activities by the indirect method.

Exercise 18-8   *Preparing the statement of changes in financial position by the indirect method   (Obj. 3)*

Use the income statement of Yee Trading Corp. in Exercise 18-4, plus these additional data:

a. Collections from customers are $7,000 more than sales.

b. Payments to suppliers are $20,000 more than the cost of goods sold.

c. Payments to employees are $1,000 more than salary expense.

d. Dividend revenue, interest expense, and income tax expense equal their cash amounts.

e. Acquisition of capital assets is $116,000. Of this amount, $101,000 is paid in cash, $15,000 by signing a note payable.

f. Proceeds from sale of land, $14,000.

g. Proceeds from issuance of common stock, $30,000.

h. Payment of long-term note payable, $15,000.

i. Payment of dividends, $11,000.

j. Increase in cash balance, $?

k. From the balance sheet:

	September 30,	
	19X2	19X1
Current Assets		
Accounts receivable	$51,000	$58,000
Inventory	83,000	77,000
Prepaid expenses...	9,000	8,000
Current Liabilities		
Notes payable (for inventory purchases).........................	$20,000	$20,000
Accounts payable	35,000	22,000
Accrued liabilities...	23,000	21,000

Prepare Yee Trading's SCFP for the year ended September 30, 19X2, using the indirect method.

Exercise 18-9   *Computing cash flows from operating activities—indirect method*   **(Obj. 3)**

The accounting records of Chen Restaurant Supply Ltd. include these accounts:

Cash				Accounts Receivable			
Mar. 1	5,000			Mar. 1	18,000		
Receipts	47,000	Payments	48,000	Sales	48,000	Collections	47,000
Mar. 31	4,000			Mar. 31	19,000		

Inventory				Equipment			
Mar. 1	19,000			Mar. 1	93,000		
Purchases	37,000	Cost of sales	35,000	Acquisition	6,000		
Mar. 31	21,000			Mar. 31	99,000		

Accumulated Depreciation—Equipment				Accounts Payable			
		Mar. 1	52,000			Mar. 1	14,000
		Depreciation	3,000	Payments	32,000	Purchases	37,000
		Mar. 31	55,000			Mar. 31	19,000

Accrued Liabilities				Retained Earnings			
		Mar. 1	9,000	Quarterly		Mar. 1	64,000
Payments	14,000	Expenses	11,000	dividend	18,000	Net Income	19,000
		Mar. 31	6,000			Mar. 31	65,000

Compute Chen's net cash inflow or outflow from operating activities during March. Does Chen have trouble collecting receivables or selling inventory? How can you tell?

Exercise 18-10   *Interpreting a cash-flow statement—indirect method*   **(Obj. 3)**

Consider three independent cases for the cash-flow data of Prime Motors Inc.:

	Case A	Case B	Case C
Cash flows from operating activities:			
Net income	$ 30,000	$ 30,000	$ 30,000
Depreciation and amortization	11,000	11,000	11,000
Increase in current assets	(19,000)	(7,000)	(1,000)
Decrease in current liabilities	(6,000)	(8,000)	–0–
	$ 16,000	$ 26,000	$ 40,000
Cash flows from financing activities:			
New borrowing	$ 16,000	$ 104,000	$ 50,000
Payment of debt	(21,000)	(29,000)	(9,000)
	$ (5,000)	$ 75,000	$ 41,000
Cash flows from investing activities:			
Acquisition of capital assets	$(91,000)	$(91,000)	$(91,000)
Sales of capital assets	97,000	4,000	8,000
	$ 6,000	$(87,000)	$(83,000)
Net increase (decrease in cash)	$ 17,000	$ 14,000	$(2,000)

For each case, identify from the *cash-flow* statement of changes in financial position how Prime generated the cash to acquire new capital assets.

Challenge Exercise

Exercise 18-11   *Analyzing an actual company's statement of changes in financial position*
(Obj. 3)

Canadian Tire Corporation, Limited's statement of changes in financial position for 1993 and 1994 is reproduced below:

Canadian Tire Corporation, Limited
Consolidated Statements of Operating, Investing, and Financing Activities

For the Years Ended (Dollars in thousands)	December 31, 1994	January 1, 1994
Cash generated from (used for):		
Operating activities		
Net earnings from continuing operations	$114,769	$ 100,384
Items not affecting cash		
Depreciation and amortization of property and equipment	57,424	60,787
Amortization of other assets	2,901	1,279
Loss on disposals of property and equipment	43	4,945
Deferred income taxes	(18,470)	(15,622)
Cash generated from continuing operations	156,667	151,773
Changes in other working capital components	(38,425)	90,867
	118,242	242,640
Investing activities		
Charge account receivables	(168,442)	(55,389)
Additions to property and equipment	(90,567)	(42,362)
Other assets and investments	(9,933)	(892)
Disposals of property and equipment	6,812	4,252
Advances to Associate Dealers	225	1,866
Loans receivable	—	(600)
	(261,905)	(93,125)
Dividends	(35,438)	(36,276)
Financing activities		
Commercial paper	214,793	(44,626)
Class A Non-Voting Share transactions	(21,746)	1,368
Repayment of long-term debt	(21)	(74,783)
Long-term debt issued	—	40,000
Long-term debt issue expense	—	(2,120)
	193,026	(80,161)
Cash generated in the year from continuing operations	13,925	33,078
Discontinued operations		
Cash generated from (used for) operating activities	1,850	(22,001)
Cash used for investing activities	(1,557)	(19,095)
Change in cash position	2,301	46,950
Cash generated in the year from discontinued operations	2,594	5,854
Cash generated in the year	16,519	38,932
Cash position, beginning of year	139,519	100,587
Cash position, end of year	$156,038	$ 139,519

Required

1. Which format does Canadian Tire use for reporting cash flows from operating activities?

2. What was Canadian Tire's largest source of cash during 1994? 1993?

3. The operating activities section of the statement lists (in Thousands) "Changes in other working capital components ($38,425). This amount includes:

> Accounts and loans receivable ....   ($52,791)
> Accounts payable $47,170

Did these accounts' balances increase or decrease in 1994? How can you tell?

4. During 1994, Canadian Tire sold property, plant, and equipment. Assume that the accumulated depreciation on the assets disposed of was $5,000,000. Journalize the sale of the property, plant, and equipment.

5. Does the SCFP of Canadian Tire tell you that The company is growing or shrinking over the two-year period ended December 31, 1994?

6. Why are Canadian Tire's year ends shown as December 31, 1994, and January 1, 1994?

Problems   (Group A)

Problem 18-1A   *Using cash-flow information to evaluate performance*   **(Obj. 1)**

Top managers of STV Broadcasting Corp., are reviewing company performance for 19X4. The income statement reports a 15 percent increase in net income, for the fifth consecutive year with an income increase above 10 percent. The income statement includes a nonrecurring loss without which net income would have increased by 18 percent. The balance sheet shows modest increases in assets, liabilities, and shareholders' equity. The asset posting the largest increase is plant and equipment because the company is halfway through a five-year expansion program. No other assets and no liabilities are increasing dramatically. A summarized version of the SCFP reports the following:

> Net cash inflow from operating activities.............. $310,000
> Net cash inflow from financing activities   70,000
> Net cash outflow from investing activities............   (290,000)
> Increase in cash during 19X4 .... $ 90,000

Required

Write a memo to give top managers of STV your assessment of 19X4 and your outlook for the future. Focus on the information content of the cash flow data.

Problem 18-2A   *Computing amounts for the statement of changes in financial position— indirect method*   **(Obj. 2, 3, 4)**

The 19X3 comparative balance sheet and income statement of Silverado, Inc., follow:

Comparative Balance Sheet

	19X3	19X2	Increase (Decrease)
Current assets			
Cash and cash equivalents..........................	$ 13,700	$ 15,600	$ (1,900)
Accounts receivable	41,500	43,100	(1,600)
Interest receivable	600	900	(300)
Inventories...	94,300	89,900	4,400
Prepaid expenses..	1,700	2,200	(500)
Capital assets			
Land	35,100	10,000	25,100
Equipment, net	100,900	93,700	7,200
Total assets..	$287,800	$255,400	$ 32,400

	19X3	19X2	Increase (Decrease)
Current liabilities			
Accounts payable	$ 16,400	$ 17,900	$ (1,500)
Interest payable	6,300	6,700	(400)
Salary payable	2,100	1,400	700
Other accrued liabilities	18,100	18,700	(600)
Income tax payable	6,300	3,800	2,500
Long-term liabilities			
Notes payable	55,000	65,000	(10,000)
Shareholders' equity			
Common stock	131,100	122,300	8,800
Retained earnings	52,500	19,600	32,900
Total liabilities and shareholders' equity	$287,800	$255,400	$ 32,400

Income Statement for 19X3

Revenues		
Sales revenue		$438,000
Interest revenue		11,700
Total revenues		449,700
Expenses		
Cost of goods sold	$205,200	
Salary expense	76,400	
Depreciation expense	15,300	
Other operating expense	49,700	
Interest expense	24,600	
Income tax expense	16,900	
Total expenses		388,100
Net income		$ 61,600

Silverado had no noncash financing and investing transactions during 19X3. During the year, there were no sales of land or equipment, no issuances of notes payable, and no issue or repurchase of common stock.

Required

1. Prepare the 19X3 SCFP, formatting operating activities by the indirect method.
2. How will what you have learned in this problem help you evaluate an investment?

Problem 18-3A *Preparing the statement of changes in financial position—indirect method* **(Obj. 2, 3)**

Accountants for Maplewood Manufacturing Ltd. have assembled the following data for the year ended December 31, 19X4:

	December 31,	
	19X4	19X3
Current accounts (all result from operations)		
Current assets		
Cash and cash equivalents	$38,600	$34,800 — 3800
Accounts receivable	70,100	73,700 (3600)
Inventories	90,600	96,500 (5900)
Prepaid expenses	3,200	2,100 1100

Current liabilities

Notes payable (for inventory purchases)	$36,300	$36,800 (500)
Accounts payable	72,100	67,500 4600
Income tax payable	5,900	6,800 (900)
Accrued liabilities	28,300	23,200 5,100

Transaction data for 19X4:

Stock dividends	$ 12,600	Payment of cash dividends ...	$48,300	
Collection of loan	10,300	Issuance of long-term debt		
Depreciation expense	19,200	to borrow cash	71,000	
Acquisition of equipment	69,000	Net income	50,500	
Payment of long-term debt by issuing common stock	89,400	Issuance of preferred stock for cash	36,200	
		Sale of long-term investment	12,200	
Acquisition of long-term investment	44,800	Amortization expense	1,100	
Acquisition of building by issuing long-term note payable	118,000	Payment of long-term debt....	47,800	
		Gain on sale of investment	3,500	

Required

Prepare Maplewood's SCFP, using the indirect method to report operating activities.

Problem 18-4A   *Preparing the statement of changes in financial position—indirect method (Obj. 2, 3)*

The comparative balance sheet of Acadia Marine Ltd. at December 31, 19X5, reported the following:

	December 31,	
	19X5	**19X4**
Current assets		
Cash and cash equivalents	$10,600	$12,500 (1900)
Accounts receivable	28,600	29,300 (700)
Inventories	51,600	53,000 (1400)
Prepaid expenses	4,200	3,700 500
Current liabilities		
Notes payable (for inventory purchases)	$ 9,200	$ -0- 9200
Accounts payable	21,900	28,000 (6100)
Accrued liabilities	14,300	16,800 (2500)
Income tax payable	11,000	14,300 (3300)

Acadia Marine's transactions during 19X5 included the following:

Amortization expense	$ 5,000	Cash acquisition of building	$124,000
Payment of cash dividends ...	17,000	Net income	31,600
Cash acquisition of equipment	55,000	Issuance of common stock for cash	105,600
Issuance of long-term note payable to borrow cash	32,000	Stock dividend	13,000
Retirement of bonds payable by issuing common stock	40,000	Sale of long-term investment	6,000
		Depreciation expense	15,000

Required

Prepare Acadia Marine's SCFP for the year ended December 31, 19X5. Use the *indirect* method to report cash flows from operating activities. All current account balances result from operating transactions.

Problem 18-5A   *Preparing the statement of changes in financial position—indirect method*
(Obj. 3)

To prepare the SCFP, accountants for J & K Corporation have summarized 19X8 activity in two accounts as follows:

Cash

Beginning balance.....................	87,100	Payments of operating	
Receipts of dividends.............	1,900	expenses................................	46,100
Collection of loan.....................	18,500	Payment of long-term debt.....	78,900
Sale of investments.................	9,900	Repurchase of common stock.	10,400
Receipts of interest..................	12,200	Payment of income tax	8,000
Collections from customers...	298,100	Payments on accounts	
Sale of common stock.............	60,800	payable.................................	101,600
		Payments of dividends............	1,800
		Payments of salaries	
		and wages..............................	67,500
		Payments of interest................	21,800
		Purchase of equipment............	79,900
Ending balance........................	72,500		

Common Stock

Repurchase of common stock	10,400	Beginning balance...................	103,500
		Issuance for cash	60,800
		Issuance to acquire land.........	62,100
		Issuance to retire long-term	
		debt	21,100
		Ending balance........................	237,100

J & K's 19X8 income statement and selected balance sheet data follow:

J & K Corporation
Income Statement
for the year ended December 31, 19X8

Revenues and gains		
Sales revenue		$281,800
Interest revenue...		12,200
Dividend revenue		1,900
Gain on sale of investments.....................		700
Total revenues and gains		296,600
Expenses		
Cost of goods sold.....................................	$103,600	
Salary and wage expense.........................	66,800	
Depreciation expense	10,900	
Other operating expense..........................	44,700	
Interest expense...	24,100	
Income tax expense...................................	2,600	
Total expenses.......................................		252,700
Net income..		$ 43,900

J & K Corporation
Balance Sheet Data

	Increase (Decrease)
Current assets	
Cash and cash equivalents	$?
Accounts receivable	(16,300)
Inventories	5,700
Prepaid expenses	(1,900)
Loan receivable	(18,500)
Investments	(9,200)
Equipment, net	69,000
Land	62,100
Current liabilities	
Accounts payable	$ 7,700
Interest payable	2,300
Salary payable	(700)
Other accrued liabilities	(3,300)
Income tax payable	(5,400)
Long-term debt	(100,000)
Common stock	133,600
Retained earnings	42,100

Required

Prepare J & K Corporation's SCFP for the year ended December 31, 19X8, using the *indirect* method to report operating activities. All activity in the current accounts results from operations.

Problem 18-6A   *Preparing the statement of changes in financial position—indirect methods*
(Obj. 3, 4)

Seaman-Young Corp.'s comparative balance sheet at September 30, 19X4, included the following balances:

Seaman-Young Corp.
Partial Balance Sheet
September 30, 19X4 and 19X3

	19X4	19X3	Increase (Decrease)
Current assets			
Cash	$ 48,700	$ 17,600	$31,100
Accounts receivable	41,900	44,000	(2,100)
Interest receivable	4,100	2,800	1,300
Inventories	121,700	116,900	4,800
Prepaid expenses	8,600	9,300	(700)
Long-term investments	51,100	13,800	37,300
Equipment, net	131,900	92,100	39,800
Land	47,100	74,300	(27,200)
	$455,100	$370,800	$84,300

Current liabilities

Notes payable, short-term..............................	$ 22,000	$ -0-	$ 22,000
Accounts payable	61,800	70,300	(8,500)
Income tax payable	21,800	24,600	(2,800)
Accrued liabilities..	17,900	29,100	(11,200)
Interest payable	4,500	3,200	1,300
Salary payable..	1,500	1,100	400
Long-term note payable	123,000	$121,400	1,600
Common stock...	113,900	62,000	51,900
Retained earnings...	88,700	59,100	29,600
	$455,100	$370,800	$84,300

Transaction data for the year ended September 30, 19X4:

a. Net income, $93,900.

b. Depreciation expense on equipment, $8,500.

c. Acquired long-term investments, $37,300.

d. Sold land for $38,100, including $10,900 gain.

e. Acquired equipment by issuing long-term note payable, $26,300.

f. Paid long-term note payable, $24,700.

g. Received cash of $51,900 for issuance of common stock.

h. Paid cash dividends, $64,300.

i. Acquired equipment by issuing short-term note payable, $22,000.

Required

Prepare Seaman-Young's SCFP for the year ended September 30, 19X4, using the *indirect* method to report operating activities. All current accounts except short-term notes payable result from operating transactions.

Problem 18-7A   *Distinguish among operating, financing, and investing activities; compute the cash effects of a wide variety of business transactions*   *(Obj. 2, 4)*

Indicate whether or not each of the following items would be shown on a statement of changes in financial position (indirect method).

1. Indicate the effect on "Cash" or "Cash Equivalents" as:
   - source of cash
   - a use of cash
   - no effect on cash

2. If a transaction is either a source or use of cash indicate what type of source or use it is:
   - from operations
   - from financing
   - from investing

3. Give a brief description of why it would or would not affect the statement of changes in financial position.
   a. Depreciation Expense—buildings
   b. A decrease in Merchandise Inventory
   c. An increase in Prepaid Expenses
   d. Amortization of the "premium" on bonds payable
   e. A decrease in Deferred Income Taxes
   f. An increase in marketable securities
   g. Amortization of Goodwill

h. The purchase of equipment in exchange for common shares

i. The payment of interest on long-term debt.

j. The use of an operating line of credit (over-draft allowance)

k. The declaration and distribution of a common stock dividend

l. A decrease in trade accounts payable

m. The sale of office equipment for its book value

n. The borrowing of funds for future expansion through the sale of bonds

o. A gain on the sale of plant assets

Problem 18-8A *Distinguish among operating, financing, and investing activities; use the financial statements to compute the cash effects of a wide variety of business transactions; prepare a statement of changes in financial position by the indirect method* **(Obj. 2, 4)**

Rockpile Industries Inc. had the following financial statements for the year ended December 31st:

Balance Sheet	**19X1**	**19X2**
Assets		
Cash..........	$1,800	$2,600
Marketable securities......	4,000	1,000
Accounts receivable..........	17,500	18,900
Merchandise inventory	61,000	31,800
Prepaid expenses..........	2,300	1,000
Plant and equipment	165,400	177,300
Less accumulated depreciation..........	(12,000)	(16,000)
Land		40,000
Goodwill..........	10,000	9,000
Total assets	$250,000	$265,600
Liabilities		
Accounts payable..........	$ 12,000	$ 14,600
Salaries payable..........	7,000	10,000
Deferred income taxes..........	3,000	1,000
Mortgage payable	40,000	35,000
Total liabilities..........	62,000	60,600
Shareholders' equity		
Preferred shares (10,000 shares)	50,000	50,000
Common shares (50,000 shares in 19X2)..........	50,000	120,000
Retained earnings..........	88,000	35,000
Total shareholders' equity..........	188,000	205,000
Total liabilities & shareholders' equity	$250,000	$265,600

Income Statement
for the year ended December 31, 19X2

Net sales..........	$160,000
Cost of goods sold	90,000
Gross profit margin..........	70,000
Operating expenses	
Selling expenses..........	30,000
Administrative expenses..........	25,000
Interest expense	4,000
Total operating expenses..........	59,000
Operating income..........	11,000
Income taxes (40%)..........	4,400
Net income	$ 6,600

Additional information:

a. The Operating Expenses included:
   - Depreciation Expense on Plant Assets = $18,000
   - Amortization of Goodwill   = $1,000

b. Sold Plant Assets for their book value. The assets cost $43,000 and had been amortized for $14,000.

c. Purchased additional Plant Assets for $54,900.

d. Exchanged Common Shares for land valued at $40,000.

e. Declared and paid cash dividends: Preferred = $23,000, Common = $36,600.

f. Sold 15,000 Common Shares for $2.00 per share.

g. Paid $9,000 (of which $4,000 was interest) on the mortgage.

Required

1. Prepare a statement of changes in financial position for Rockpile Industries Inc. for the year ended December 31, 19X2, using the indirect method.

2. Comment on the results indicated by the statement of changes in financial position.

Problem 18-9A   *Preparing the work sheet for the statement of changes in financial position—indirect method*   **(Obj. A1)**

The 19X3 comparative balance sheet and income statement of Silverado, Inc., follow. Silverado had no noncash financing and investing transactions during 19X3.

Comparative Balance Sheet

	19X3	19X2	Increase (Decrease)
Current asset			
Cash and cash equivalents	$ 13,700	$ 15,600	$ (1,900)
Accounts receivable	41,500	43,100	(1,600)
Interest receivable	600	900	(300)
Inventories	94,300	89,900	4,400
Prepaid expenses	1,700	2,200	(500)
Capital assets			
Land	35,100	10,000	25,100
Equipment, net	100,900	93,700	7,200
Total assets	$287,800	$255,400	$32,400
Current liabilities			
Accounts payable	$ 16,400	$ 17,900	$ (1,500)
Interest payable	6,300	6,700	(400)
Salary payable	2,100	1,400	700
Other accrued liabilities	18,100	18,700	(600)
Income tax payable	6,300	3,800	2,500
Long-term liabilities			
Notes payable	55,000	65,000	(10,000)
Shareholders' equity			
Common stock	131,100	122,300	8,800
Retained earnings	52,500	19,600	32,900
Total liabilities and shareholders' equity	$287,800	$255,400	$32,400

Income Statement for 19X3

Revenues		
Sales revenue		$438,000
Interest revenue		11,700
Total revenues		449,700

Expenses

Cost of goods sold...............................	$205,200	
Salary expense	76,400	
Depreciation expense	15,300	
Other operating expense........................	49,700	
Interest expense...................................	24,600	
Income tax expense..............................	16,900	
Total expenses...........................		388,100
Net income...		$ 61,600

Required

Prepare the work sheet for the 19X3 statement of changes in financial position. Format cash flows from operating activities by the *indirect* method.

(Group B)

Problem 18-1B *Using cash-flow information to evaluate performance* *(Obj. 1)*

Top managers of Charter Flight Service Ltd. are reviewing company performance for 19X7. The income statement reports a 20 percent increase in net income over 19X6. However, most of the increase resulted from an extraordinary gain on insurance proceeds covering fire damage to an airplane. The balance sheet shows large increases in receivables and inventory. The SCFP, in summarized form, reports the following:

Net cash inflow from operating activities..............	$(80,000)
Net cash inflow from financing activities	50,000
Net cash outflow from investing activities............	40,000
Increase in cash during 19X7	$ 10,000

Required

Write a memo to give Charter Flight Service managers your assessment of 19X7 operations and your outlook for the future. Focus on the information content of the cash flow data.

Problem 18-2B *Preparing the statement of changes in financial position—indirect method* *(Obj. 2, 3, 4)*

The 19X5 comparative balance sheet and income statement of Direct Marketing, Inc., follow:

Comparative Balance Sheet

	19X5	19X4	Increase (Decrease)
Current assets			
Cash and cash equivalents..........................	$ 7,200	$ 5,300	$ 1,900
Accounts receivable	28,600	26,900	1,700
Interest receivable	1,900	700	1,200
Inventories..	83,600	87,200	(3,600)
Prepaid expenses..	2,500	1,900	600
Capital assets			
Land	89,000	60,000	29,000
Equipment, net	53,500	49,400	4,100
Total assets..	$266,300	$231,400	$34,900

Current liabilities

Accounts payable	$ 31,400	$ 28,800	$ 2,600
Interest payable	4,400	4,900	(500)
Salary payable	3,100	6,600	(3,500)
Other accrued liabilities	13,700	16,000	(2,300)
Income tax payable	8,900	7,700	1,200
Long-term liabilities			
Notes payable	75,000	100,000	(25,000)
Shareholders' equity			
Common stock	88,300	64,700	23,600
Retained earnings	41,500	2,700	47,000
Total liabilities and shareholders' equity	$266,300	$231,400	$34,900

Income Statement for 19X5

Revenues		
Sales revenue		$213,000
Interest revenue		8,600
Total revenues		221,600
Expenses		
Cost of goods sold	$70,600	
Salary expense	27,800	
Depreciation expense	4,000	
Other operating expense	10,500	
Interest expense	11,600	
Income tax expense	29,100	
Total expenses		153,600
Net income		$ 68,000

Direct Marketing had no noncash financing and investing transactions during 19X5. During the year, there were no sales of land or equipment, no issuances of notes payable, and no issuance or retirement of common stock.

Required

1. Prepare the 19X5 statement of changes in financial position, formatting operating activities by the indirect method.

2. How will what you have learned in this problem help you evaluate an investment?

Problem 18-3B   *Preparing the statement of changes in financial position—indirect method* (**Obj. 2, 3**)

Nav Star Corporation accountants have assembled the following data for the year ended December 31, 19X7:

	December 31,	
	19X7	**19X6**
Current accounts (all result from operations)		
Current assets		
Cash and cash equivalents	$55,700	$22,700
Accounts receivable	69,700	64,200
Inventories	88,600	83,000
Prepaid expenses	5,300	4,100
Current liabilities		
Notes payable (for inventory purchases)	$22,600	$18,300
Accounts payable	52,900	55,800
Income tax payable	18,600	16,700
Accrued liabilities	15,500	27,200

Transaction data for 19X7:

Acquisition of land by issuing long-term note payable	$107,000	Purchase and retirement of common stock	$ 14,300
Stock dividends	31,800	Loss on sale of equipment	11,700
Collection of loan	8,700	Payment of cash dividends	18,300
Depreciation expense	26,800	Issuance of long-term note payable to borrow cash	34,400
Acquisition of building	125,300	Net income	57,100
Retirement of bonds payable by issuing common stock	65,000	Issuance of common stock for cash	41,200
Acquisition of long-term investment	31,600	Sale of equipment	58,000
		Amortization expense	5,300

Required

Prepare Nav Star's SCFP, using the *indirect* method to report operating activities.

Problem 18-4B   *Preparing the statement of changes in financial position—indirect method (Obj. 2, 3)*

The comparative balance sheet of Grassy Narrows Corp. at March 31, 19X7, reported the following:

	March 31,	
	19X7	**19X6**
Current assets		
Cash and cash equivalents	$ 13,600	$ 4,000
Accounts receivable	14,900	21,700
Inventories	63,200	60,600
Prepaid expenses	1,900	1,700
Current liabilities		
Notes payable (for inventory purchases)	$ 4,000	$ 4,000
Accounts payable	30,300	27,600
Accrued liabilities	10,700	11,100
Income tax payable	8,000	4,700

Grassy Narrows' transactions during the year ended March 31, 19X7, included the following:

Acquisition of land by issuing note payable	$ 76,000	Sale of long-term investment	$ 13,700
Amortization expense	2,000	Depreciation expense	9,000
Payment of cash dividend	30,000	Cash acquisition of building	47,000
Cash acquisition of equipment	78,700	Net income	70,000
Issuance of long-term note payable to borrow cash	50,000	Issuance of common stock for cash	11,000
		Stock dividend	18,000

Required

Prepare Grassy Narrows' SCFP for the year ended March 31, 19X7, using the indirect method to report cash flows from operating activities. All current account balances resulted from operating transactions.

Problem 18-5B   *Preparing the statement of changes in financial position—indirect method (Obj. 3)*

To prepare the SCFP, accountants for Pentech Inc. have summarized 19X3 activity in two accounts as follows:

Cash

Beginning balance	53,600	Payments on accounts payable	399,100
Collection of loan	13,000	Payments of dividends	27,200
Sale of investment	8,200	Payments of salaries	
Receipts of interest	12,600	and wages	143,800
Collections from customers	678,700	Payments of interest	26,900
Issuance of common stock	47,300	Purchase of equipment	31,400
Receipts of dividends	4,500	Payments of operating	
		expenses	34,300
		Payment of long-term debt	41,300
		Repurchase of common stock	26,400
		Payment of income tax	18,900
Ending balance	68,600		

Common Stock

		Beginning balance	84,400
		Issuance for cash	47,300
		Issuance to acquire land	80,100
		Issuance to retire long-term	
Repurchase of shares	26,400	debt	19,000
		Ending balance	204,400

Pentech Inc.
Income Statement
for the year ended December 31, 19X3

Revenues		
Sales revenue		$706,300
Interest revenue		12,600
Dividend revenue		4,500
Total revenues		$723,400
Expenses and losses		
Cost of goods sold	$402,600	
Salary and wage expense	150,800	
Depreciation expense	24,300	
Other operating expense	44,100	
Interest expense	28,800	
Income tax expense	16,200	
Loss on sale of investments	1,100	
Total expenses		667,900
Net income		$ 55,500

Pentech Inc. Balance Sheet Data	Increase (Decrease)
Current assets	
Cash and cash equivalents	$?
Accounts receivable	27,600
Inventories	(11,800)
Prepaid expenses	600
Current liabilities	
Accounts payable	$(8,300)
Interest payable	1,900
Salary payable	7,000
Other accrued liabilities	10,400
Income tax payable	(2,700)

Required

Prepare Pentech Corporation's SCFP for the year ended December 31, 19X3, using the indirect method to report operating activities.

Problem 18-6B   *Preparing the statement of changes in financial position—indirect method*
(Obj. 3, 4)

Bosco Bolt Co. Ltd.'s comparative balance sheet at June 30, 19X7, included the following balances:

Bosco Bolt Co. Ltd.
Balance Sheet
June 30, 19X7 and 19X6

	19X7	19X6	Increase (Decrease)
Current assets			
Cash	$ 16,500	$ 8,600	$ 7,900
Accounts receivable	45,900	48,300	(2,400)
Interest receivable	2,900	3,600	(700)
Inventories	68,600	60,200	8,400
Prepaid expenses	3,700	2,800	900
Long-term investment	10,100	5,200	4,900
Equipment, net	82,500	73,600	8,900
Land	42,400	96,000	(53,600)
	$272,600	$298,300	$(25,700)
Current liabilities			
Notes payable, short-term			
(for general borrowing)	$ 13,400	$ 18,100	$ (4,700)
Accounts payable	42,400	40,300	2,100
Income tax payable	13,800	14,500	(700)
Accrued liabilities	8,200	9,700	(1,500)
Interest payable	3,700	2,900	800
Salary payable	900	2,600	(1,700)
Long-term note payable	47,400	94,100	(46,700)
Common stock	59,800	51,200	8,600
Retained earnings	83,000	64,900	18,100
	$272,600	$298,300	$(25,700)

Transaction data for the year ended June 30, 19X7:

a. Net income, $56,200.

b. Depreciation expense on equipment, $5,400.

c. Purchased long-term investment, $4,900.

d. Sold land for $46,900, including $6,700 loss.

e. Acquired equipment by issuing long-term note payable, $14,300.

f. Paid long-term note payable, $61,000.

g. Received cash for issuance of common stock, $3,900.

h. Paid cash dividends, $38,100.

i. Paid short-term note payable by issuing common stock, $4,700.

Required

Prepare Bosco Bolt's SCFP for the year ended June 30, 19X7, using the *indirect* method to report operating activities. All current accounts except short-term notes payable result from operating transactions.

Problem 18-7B   *Distinguish among operating, financing, and investing activities; compute the cash effects of a wide variety of business transactions*   **(Obj. 2, 4)**

Indicate whether or not each of the following items would be shown on a statement of changes in financial position (indirect method).

1. Indicate the effect on "Cash" or "Cash Equivalents" as:
   - source of cash
   - a use of cash
   - no effect on cash

2. If a transaction is either a source of use of cash indicate what type of source or use it is:
   - from operations
   - from financing
   - from investing

3. Give a brief description of why it would or would not affect the statement of changes in financial position.
   a. The receipt of interest on long-term investments
   b. The reduction in the use of an operating line of credit (over-draft allowance)
   c. The declaration and distribution of a common stock dividend
   d. An increase in trade accounts payable
   e. The purchase of office equipment
   f. The borrowing of funds for future expansion through the sale of bonds
   g. A loss on the sale of plant assets
   h. Depreciation Expense—equipment
   i. An increase in Merchandise Inventory
   j. A decrease in Prepaid Expenses
   k. Amortization of the "discount" on bonds payable
   l. An increase in Deferred Income Taxes
   m. A decrease in marketable securities
   n. Amortization of Goodwill
   o. The purchase of equipment in exchange for common shares

Problem 18-8B   *Distinguish among operating, financing, and investing activities; use the financial statements to compute the cash effects of a wide variety of business transactions; prepare a statement of changes in financial position by the indirect method*   **(Obj. 2, 4, 5)**

Mayflower Industries Inc. had the following financial statements for the year ended December 31st:

Balance Sheet	19X1	19X2
Assets		
Cash	$2,400	$1,800
Marketable securities	3,000	1,000
Accounts receivable	22,800	1,800
Merchandise inventory	72,000	30,600
Prepaid expenses	1,900	2,400
Plant and equipment	156,900	190,400
Less accumulated depreciation	(10,000)	(16,000)
Land		50,000
Goodwill	15,000	13,000
Total assets	$264,000	$275,000
Liabilities		
Accounts payable	$ 15,000	$ 14,200
Salaries payable	10,000	18,000
Deferred income taxes	4,000	7,000
Mortgage payable	50,000	40,000
Total liabilities	79,000	79,200

Shareholders' equity

Preferred shares (10,000 shares)	50,000	50,000
Common shares (50,000 shares in 19X2)	50,000	120,000
Retained earnings	85,000	25,800
Total shareholders' equity	185,000	195,800
Total liabilities and shareholders' equity	$264,000	$275,000

Income statement
for the year ended December 31, 19X2

Net sales	$170,000
Cost of goods sold	80,000
Gross profit margin	90,000
Operating expenses	
Selling expenses	50,000
Administrative expenses	28,000
Interest expense	5,000
Total operating expenses	83,000
Operating income	7,000
Income taxes (40%)	2,800
Net income	$ 4,200

Additional information:

a. The Operating Expenses included:
   - Depreciation Expense on Plant Assets = $16,000
   - Amortization of Goodwill   = $2,000

b. Sold Plant Assets for their book value. The assets cost $23,000 and had been amortized for $10,000.

c. Purchased additional Plant Assets for $56,500.

d. Exchanged Common Shares for land valued at $50,000.

e. Declared and paid cash dividends: Preferred = $30,000; Common = $33,400.

f. Sold 20,000 Common Shares for $1.00 per share.

g. Paid $9,000 (of which $5,000 was interested) on the mortgage.

Required

1. Prepare a statement of changes in financial position for Mayflower Industries Inc. for the year ended December 31, 19X2, using the indirect method.

2. Comment on the results indicated by the statement of changes in financial position.

Problem 18-9B   *Preparing the work sheet for the statement of changes in financial position—indirect method*   **(Obj. 5)**

MicroNet Products Ltd.'s comparative balance sheet at September 30, 19X4, follows:

MicroNet Products Ltd.
Comparative Balance Sheet
September 30, 19X4 and 19X3

	19X4	19X3	Increase (Decrease)
Current assets			
Cash	$ 48,700	$ 17,600	$ 31,100
Accounts receivable	41,900	44,000	(2,100)
Interest receivable	4,100	2,800	1,300
Inventories	121,700	116,900	4,800
Prepaid expenses	8,600	9,300	(700)

Long-term investments	55,400	18,100	37,300
Capital assets			
Land	65,800	93,000	(27,200)
Equipment, net	89,500	49,700	39,800
Total assets...	$435,700	$351,400	$ 84,300
Current liabilities			
Notes payable, short-term..............................	$ 22,000	$ -0-	$ 22,000
Accounts payable	61,800	70,300	(8,500)
Income tax payable	21,800	24,600	(2,800)
Accrued liabilities..	17,900	29,100	(11,200)
Interest payable	4,500	3,200	1,300
Salary payable..	1,500	1,100	400
Note payable, long-term	62,900	61,300	1,600
Shareholders' equity			
Common stock..	142,100	90,200	51,900
Retained earnings..	101,200	71,600	29,600
Total liabilities and shareholders' equity............	$435,700	$351,400	$ 84,300

Transaction data for the year ended September 30, 19X4:

a. Net income, $93,900.

b. Depreciation expense on equipment, $8,500.

c. Acquired long-term investments, $37,300.

d. Sold land for $38,100, including $10,900 gain.

e. Acquired equipment by issuing long-term note payable, $26,300.

f. Paid long-term note payable, $24,700.

g. Received cash of $51,900 for issuance of common stock.

h. Paid cash dividends, $64,300.

i. Acquired equipment by issuing short-term note payable, $22,000.

Required

Prepare MicroNet Products' work sheet for the statement of changes in financial position for the year ended September 30, 19X4, using the *indirect* method to report operating activities. Include on the work sheet the noncash financing and investing activities.

Challenge Problems

Problem 18-1C   *Distinguishing between operating, financing, and investing activities*
                     (Obj. 2)

In 1990, the *CICA Handbook* was amended to require, among other things, that the statement of changes in financial position disclose cash flows in and out of the organization from financing and investing activities separate from cash flows from operations.

Required

Explain why you think the CICA's Accounting Standards Board (and the Financial Accounting Standards Board in the U.S.) decided that disclosure of the three different cash flows was to be required.

Problem 18-2C   *Accounting for non-cash financing and investing activities*   *(Obj. 4)*

Initially, the statement of changes in financial position did not require inclusion of noncash financing and investing activities. The statement reported only changes

in working capital and so transactions such as use of long-term debt to purchase capital assets or conversion of debt into equity were excluded.

Required

Discuss the present *CICA Handbook*'s requirements with respect to disclosure of noncash financing and investing decisions and explain why you think the required disclosure does or does not benefit users.

Extending Your Knowledge

Decision Problems

1. Preparing and using the statement of changes in financial position to evaluate operations   (Obj. 4, 5)

The 19X6 comparative income statement and the 19X6 comparative balance sheet of Navasota Inc. have just been distributed at a meeting of the company's board of directors.

In discussing the company's results of operations and year-end financial position, the members of the board of directors raise a fundamental question: Why is the cash balance so low? This question is especially troublesome to the board members because 19X6 showed record profits. As the controller of the company, you must answer the question.

Navasota Inc.
Comparative Income Statement
years ended December 31, 19X6 and 19X5
(amounts in thousands)

	19X6	19X5
Revenues and gains		
Sales revenue	$444	$310
Gain on sale of equipment (sale price, $33)	—	18
Totals	$444	$328
Expenses and losses		
Cost of goods sold	$221	$162
Salary expense	48	28
Depreciation expense	46	22
Interest expense	13	20
Amortization expense on patent	11	11
Loss on sale of land (sale price, $61)	—	35
Totals	339	278
Net income	$105	$ 50

Navasota Inc.
Comparative Balance Sheet
December 31, 19X6 and 19X5
(amounts in thousands)

Assets	19X6	19X5
Cash	$ 33	$ 63
Accounts receivable, net	72	61
Inventories	194	181

Long-term investment	31	-0-
Property, plant, and equipment	361	259
Accumulated depreciation	(244)	(198)
Patents	177	188
Totals	$624	$554

Liabilities and Owner's Equity

Notes payable, short-term (for general borrowing)	$ 32	$101
Accounts payable	63	56
Accrued liabilities	12	17
Notes payable, long-term	147	163
Common stock	149	61
Retained earnings	221	156
Totals	$624	$554

Required

1. Prepare a SCFP for 19X6 in the format that best shows the relationship between net income and operating cash flow. The company sold no capital assets or long-term investments and issued no notes payable during 19X6. The changes in all current accounts except short-term notes payable arose from operations. There were no noncash financing and investing transactions during the year. Show all amounts in thousands.

2. Answer the board members' question: Why is the cash balance so low? In explaining the business's cash flows, identify two significant cash receipts that occurred during 19X5 but not in 19X6. Also point out the two largest cash disbursements during 19X6.

3. Considering net income and the company's cash flows during 19X6, was it a good year or a bad year? Give your reasons.

2. *Using the statement of changes in financial position to evaluate a company's operations   (Obj. 1)*

The statement of changes in financial position, in the not-too-distant past, included information in only two categories: sources of funds and uses of funds. Funds were usually defined as working capital (current assets minus current liabilities). The present-day statement provides information about cash flows from operating activities, financing activities, and investing activities. The earlier statement permitted the information to be about changes in working capital or in cash, while today's SCFP deals specifically with information about flows in cash and cash equivalents.

Required

1. Explain why you think the present day SCFP, with its disclosure of the three different kinds of activities, is or is not an improvement over the earlier model which showed only sources and uses of funds.

2. Is information about cash flows more informative to users than information about working capital flows?

3. Briefly explain why comparative balance sheets and a SCFP are more informative than just comparative balance sheets.

Ethical Issue

Jarvis Travel Agency Ltd. is experiencing a bad year. Net income is only $65,000. Also, two important clients are falling behind in paying the amounts they owe Jarvis, and Jarvis's accounts receivable are ballooning. The company desperately needs a

loan. The Jarvis board of directors is considering ways to put the best face on the company's financial statements. Jarvis's bank emphasizes cash flow from operations. Gwen Morris, the controller, suggests reclassifying as long-term the receivables from the slow-paying clients. She explains to the board that removing the $30,000 rise in accounts receivable will increase net cash inflow from operations. This approach will increase the company's cash balance and may help Jarvis get the loan.

Required

1. Using only the amounts given, compute net cash inflow from operations both without and with the reclassification of the receivables. Which reporting makes Jarvis look better?

2. Where else in Jarvis's SCFP will the reclassification of the receivable be reported? What cash-flow effect will this item report? Evaluate Morris's reasoning.

3. Under what condition would the reclassification of the receivables be ethical? Unethical?

Financial Statement Problems

1. Using the statement of changes in financial position   (Obj. 1, 2, 3, 4, 5)

Mark's Work Wearhouse Ltd.'s statement of changes in financial position appears in Appendix A. Use this statement along with the other material in Appendix A to answer the following questions.

1. By which method of reporting does Mark's report net cash flows from operations? How can you tell?

2. Was Mark's cash flow positive or negative for 1994? Compare cash flow for 1993 and 1994 including the components of the SCFP. Was 1994 a better year or not? Give your reasons.

3. Did the change from 1993 to 1994 in working capital assets other than cash increase or decrease cash? What changes in individual assets and liabilities between 1993 and 1994 had the most significant impact on cash flows in 1994?

2. Computing cash flow amounts and using cash flow data for analysis (Obj. 1, 2, 3, 4, 5)

Obtain the annual report of an actual company of your choosing. Answer the following questions about the company. Concentrate on the current year in the annual report you select:

1. By which method does the company report net cash flows from *operating* activities? How can you tell?

2. Suppose the company reported net cash flows from operating activities by the direct method. Compute these amounts for the current year:
   a. Collections from customers.
   b. Payments to employees. Assume that the sum of Salary Expense, Wage Expense, and other payroll expenses for the current year make up 60 percent of Selling, General, and Administrative Expenses (or expense of similar title).
   c. Payments for income tax.

3. Evaluate the current year in terms of net income (or net loss), cash flows, balance sheet position, and overall results. Be specific.

CHAPTER 19
Using Accounting Information to Make Business Decisions

"For any business to succeed today, there has to be a terrific focus on productivity, growth, and continuous improvement," says J.E. (Ted) Newall, President and CEO of NOVA Corporation of Alberta. "This is by far and away the most competitive decade that anybody in business has seen. It just seems to get tougher every year."

In Newall's first year at NOVA, restructuring costs and losses on the sale of assets resulted in a total loss at the end of 1991 of $923 million. By the end of 1994, the company reported a net income of $575 million.

NOVA Corpation's annual report states "Our objective is to deliver well-above-average returns to our shareholders." The company is improving per-formance as a way of achieving that goal. Many of the measures you will learn about in this chapter can be used to assess how well NOVA is performing.

NOVA also uses many of the measures to assess potential acquisitions and gauge the performance of companies and divisions within the NOVA group. Newall measures all NOVA's business by the same test; if they aren't the best or have no serious chance of reaching that standard, they're not going to last.

Sources: Adapted from Sydney Sharpe, "Ted Newall," and from "Canada's Corporate Elite," *The Financial Post Magazine*, November, 1993, pp. 20 to 26 and page 66; and from "Canada's Corporate Elite," *The Financial Post Magazine*, November, 1994, p. 66.

CHAPTER OBJECTIVES

After studying this chapter, you should be able to

1 Perform a horizontal analysis of comparative financial statements

2 Perform a vertical analysis of financial statements

3 Prepare common-size financial statements

4 Use the statement of changes in financial position in decision-making

5 Compute the standard financial ratios used for decision-making

6 Use ratios in decision-making

As the opening vignette illustrates, business people rely on accounting information to make business decisions. The balance sheet, the income statement, and the statement of changes in financial position provide a large part of the information that is used for making these decisions. In Chapters 1 through 18, we have described the process of accounting and the preparation of the financial statements. We have tried to relate each topic to the real world of business by showing the relevance of the accounting data.

Financial analysis is designed to aid decision making by managers, investors, and creditors. This chapter discusses some of the basic relationships—expressed as trends, percentages, and ratios—in financial statements. Investors, creditors, managers, auditors, and others use these ratios to make decisions—for example, when managers set inventory policies and when banks lend money. The extensive informational value of these ratios is one reason accounting is called the language of business.

Financial Statement Analysis

Financial statement analysis focuses on techniques used by analysts external to the organization, and by managers. Outside analysts rely on publicly available information. A major source of such information is the annual report. As you have learned in previous chapters, the annual report usually includes:

1. The basic financial statements: balance sheet, income statement, statement of retained earnings, and statement of changes in financial position and the notes to the financial statements, including a statement of significant accounting policies;

2. Comparative financial information for at least the prior year;

3. The auditor's report;

4. Management's discussion and analysis (MD&A) of the past financial results and expectations for the future;

5. A management report;

6. Other financial and non-financial information about the company, such as information relating to environmental affairs.

Management's discussion and analysis is a relatively new development in financial reporting. While some companies have been providing a commentary on their past operations and expectations, it is only recently that such disclosure has become required and then only by larger companies registered with the various securities regulators in Canada, such as the Ontario Securities Commission (OSC). The description of MD&A in the OSC's Statement 5.10 is helpful in providing an understanding of the concept:

> MD&A is supplemental analysis and explanation which accompanies but does not form part of the financial statements. MD&A provides management with the opportunity to explain in narrative form its current financial situation and future prospects. MD&A is intended to give the investor the ability to look at

the [company issuing the financial statements] through the eyes of management by providing a historical and prospective analysis of the business of the [issuer]. MD&A requirements ask management to discuss the dynamics of the business and to analyze the financial statements. Coupled with the financial statements this information should allow investors to assess [the issuing company's] performance and future prospects.[1]

An example of MD&A is that provided in the 1994 annual report of Mark's Work Wearhouse Ltd., found in Appendix A. The report begins with a very thorough discussion of the company's operations over the year including detailed information with respect to the company's own stores. The report continues with a discussion of "front-line expenses," or expenses directly related to sales, and "back-line-expenses," or expenses related to support and administration. Next, major changes in the balance sheet over the year are discussed. MD&A continues with a forecast for the income statement and balance sheet; notice the assumptions underlying the forecast are clearly set out. The forecast provides a range from a conservative view to an optimistic view. Notice too that the forecasts are marked unaudited. MD&A concludes with a "Post Mortem" of the year just ended.

Mark's Work Wearhouse is frequently cited by analysts and accounting professionals as providing one of the most informative and "user-friendly" annual reports. The consensus is that management makes a genuine attempt to provide honest information to users no matter how unpleasant, to the company, that information may be.

The MD&A from any company, together with the accounting information in the financial statements of that company helps investors and creditors interpret the financial statements. The balance sheet, income statement, and statement of changes in financial position are based on historical data; they state *what* has happened but rarely provide insights into *why* it has happened. MD&A offers top management's glimpses into the future. Investors and creditors are also interested in where the company is headed.

Objectives of Financial Statement Analysis

Investors who purchase capital stock expect to receive dividends and an increase in the value of the stock. Creditors make loans with the expectation of receiving interest and principal. Both groups risk not receiving their expected returns. They use financial statement analysis to (1) predict the amount of expected returns and (2) assess the risks associated with those returns.

Creditors generally expect to receive specific fixed amounts and have the first claim on the assets, so they are most concerned with assessing short-term liquidity and long-term solvency. **Short-term liquidity** is an organization's ability to meet current payments as they become due. **Long-term solvency** is the ability to generate enough cash to pay long-term debts as they mature.

In contrast, investors are more concerned with profitability, dividends, and future security prices. Why? Because dividend payments depend on profitable operations, and stock price appreciation depends on the market's assessment of the company's prospects. Creditors also assess profitability because profitable operations are the prime source of cash to repay loans.

We divide the tools and techniques that the business community uses in evaluating financial statement information into three broad categories: horizontal analysis, vertical analysis, and ratio analysis.

Horizontal Analysis

Many business decisions hinge on whether the numbers in sales, income, expenses, and so on, are increasing or decreasing over time. Has the sales figure risen from last year? From two years ago? By how much? We may find that the net sales figure

OBJECTIVE 1

Perform a horizontal analysis of comparative financial statements

---

[1]The authors wish to thank Brenda Eprile, CA, Chief Accountant to the Ontario Securities Commission, for her assistance in providing the authors with a copy of OSC Statement 5.10.

has risen by $20,000. This may be interesting, but considered alone it is not very useful for decision-making. An analysis of the *percentage change* in the net sales figure over time improves our ability to use the dollar amounts. It is more useful to know that sales have increased by 20 percent than to know that the increase in sales is $20,000.

The study of percentage changes in comparative statements is called **horizontal analysis**. Computing a percentage change in comparative statements requires two steps: (1) Compute the dollar amount of the change from the earlier (base) period to the later period, and (2) divide the dollar amount of change by the base period amount. Horizontal analysis is illustrated for Schneider Corporation below:

| | **(Dollar amounts in thousands)** | | **Increase (Decrease)** | |
	1994	**1993**	**Amount**	**Percent**
Sales	$767,462	$725,279	$42,183	5.8
Net income	8,019	7,688	331	4.3

The percentage change in Schneider's sales during 1994 is computed as follows:

Step 1,   Compute the dollar amount of change in sales during 1994:

1994	**1993**	**Increase**
$767,462	$725,279	$42,183

Step 2,   Divide the dollar amount of change by the base-period amount to compute the percentage change during the later period:

$$\text{Percentage change} = \frac{\textbf{Dollar amount of change}}{\textbf{Base-year amount}} = \frac{\$42,183}{\$725,279} = 5.8 \text{ percent}$$

During 1994, Schneider's sales increased by 5.8 percent.

Detailed horizontal analyses of a comparative income statement and a comparative balance sheet are shown in the two right-hand columns of Exhibits 19-1 and 19-2 from Schneider Corporation.

EXHIBIT 19-1   *Comparative Income Statement—Horizontal Analysis*

Schneider Corporation
Consolidated Statements of Earnings
years ended October 29, 1994, and October 30, 1993
(Dollar amounts in thousands except per-share amounts)

| | **1994** | **1993** | **Increase (Decrease)** | |
			Amount	**Percent**
Sales	$767,462	$725,279	$42,183	5.8%
Expenses:				
Cost of products sold	677,285	634,107	43,178	6.8
Selling, marketing and administrative	55,372	57,591	(2,219)	(3.9)
Depreciation and amortization	13,237	13,626	(389)	(2.9)
	745,894	705,324	40,570	5.8
Earnings from operations	21,568	19,955	1,613	8.1
Interest expense	7,766	7,138	628	8.8
Earnings before income taxes and minority interest	13,802	12,817	985	7.7
Income taxes	6,152	4,471	1,681	37.6
Earnings before minority interest	7,650	8,346	(696)	(8.3)
Minority interest	369	(658)	1,027	—
Net earnings	$ 8,019	$ 7,688	331	4.3
Earnings per share	$ 1.35	$ 1.31	.04	3.1

EXHIBIT 19-2   *Comparative Balance Sheet—Horizontal Analysis*

Schneider Corporation
Consolidated Balance Sheet
October 29, 1994, and October 30, 1993

	1994	1993	Increase (Decrease) Amount	Percent
Assets				
Current assets:				
Accounts receivable....................	$ 47,121	$ 39,595	$ 7,526	19.0%
Inventories	58,814	48,907	9,907	20.2
Current portion of				
loans receivable	443	443	—	—
Income tax recoverable	274	—	274	—
Other..	2,238	3,073	(835)	(27.1)
Total current assets	108,890	92,018	16,872	18.3
Property, plant, and equipment	110,488	103,382	7,106	6.9
Other assets:				
Loans receivable..........................	2,368	2,496	(128)	(5.1)
Deferred pension.........................	6,133	395	5,738	1,452.7
Production licences and rights...	6,852	7,376	(524)	(7.1)
Intangible assets.........................	9,819	8,419	1,400	16.6
Total other assets........................	25,172	18,686	6,486	34.7
Total assets	$244,550	$214,086	$30,464	14.2
Liabilities and Shareholders' Equity				
Current liabilities:				
Bank advances..............................	$ 21,007	$ 3,369	$17,638	523.5
Outstanding cheques	8,014	7,845	169	2.2
Accounts payable and				
accrued liabilities.....................	47,499	42,714	4,785	11.2
Income taxes payable	—	435	(435)	—
Principal due within one year				
on debentures and loans	8,240	7,484	756	10.1
Total current liabilities................	84,760	61,847	22,913	37.0
Debentures and loans.......................	55,900	59,514	(3,614)	(6.1)
Other liabilities:				
Deferred income taxes................	5,625	3,640	1,985	54.5
Deferred gains	1,372	1,530	(158)	(10.3)
Minority interest	3,978	5,019	(1,041)	(20.7)
Total other liabilities	10,975	10,189	786	7.7
Shareholders' equity:				
Capital stock	20,261	16,052	4,209	26.2
Retained earnings	72,654	66,484	6,170	9.3
Total shareholders' equity	92,915	82,536	10,379	12.6
Total liabilities and				
shareholders' equity	$244,550	$214,086	$30,464	14.2

Trend Percentages

Trend percentages are a form of horizontal analysis. Trends are important indicators of the direction a business is taking. How have sales changed over a five-year period? What trend does gross profit show? These questions can be answered by an analysis of trend percentages over a representative period, such as the most recent five years or the most recent ten years. To gain a realistic view of the company, it is often necessary to examine more than just a two- or three-year period.

Trend percentages are computed by selecting a base year, with each amount during that year set equal to 100 percent. The amounts of each following year are expressed as a percent of the base amount. To compute trend percentages, divide each item for years after the base year by the corresponding amount during the base year. Schneider Corporation showed sales and net earnings for the past seven years as follows:

	(Amounts in millions)						
	1994	**1993**	**1992**	**1991**	**1990**	**1989**	**1988**
Sales	$767	$725	$648	$631	$628	$619	$598
Net earnings (loss)	$8.02	$7.69	$6.28	$5.06	$1.68	$ .02	$2.01

Assume we want trend percentages for a six-year period starting with 1988. We use 1988 as the base year. Trend percentages for net sales are computed by dividing each net sales amount by the 1988 amount of $598 million. Likewise, dividing each year's net earnings amount by the base-year amount ($2.01 million) yields the trend percentages for net earnings. The resulting trend percentages follow (1988, the base year = 100%):

	1994	**1993**	**1992**	**1991**	**1990**	**1989**	**1988**
Net sales	128%	121%	108%	106%	105%	104%	100%
Net earnings	399	383	312	252	84	1	100

Schneider's sales and net earnings have trended upward since a downturn in 1989 and 1990. Net earnings have increased steadily. This information suggests that operations are becoming increasingly more successful.

Vertical Analysis

OBJECTIVE 2

Perform a vertical analysis of financial statements

Horizontal analysis highlights changes in an item over time. However, no single technique provides a complete picture of a business. Another way to analyze a company is called vertical analysis.

Vertical analysis of a financial statement reveals the relationship of each statement item to the total, which is the 100 percent figure. For example, when an income statement is subjected to vertical analysis, net sales is usually the base. Suppose under normal conditions a company's gross profit is 70 percent of net sales. A drop in gross profit to 60 percent may cause the company to report a net loss on the income statement. Management, investors and creditors view a large decline in gross profit with alarm. Exhibit 19-3 shows the vertical analysis of Schneider Corporation's income statement as a percentage of net sales. Exhibit 19-4 shows the vertical analysis of the balance sheet amounts as a percentage of total assets.

The 1994 comparative income statement (Exhibit 19-3) reports that cost of goods sold increased to 88.2 percent of net sales from 87.4 percent in 1993. However, gross profit remained at 97.2 as the other expenses dropped from 1993. The gross profit percentage is one of the most important pieces of information in financial analysis because it shows the relationship between sales and cost of goods sold. All other things equal, a company that can steadily increase its gross profit percentage over a long period is more likely to succeed than a business whose gross profit percentage is steadily declining. The net income percentage remained constant from 1993.

The vertical analysis of Schneider's balance sheet (Exhibit 19-4) yields few surprises. Current assets' percentage of total assets increased slightly in 1994, but so did current liabilities' percentage. Long-term debt decreased from 27.8 percent to 22.9 percent.

Key Point:
To show the relative importance of each item on the income statement, vertical analysis presents everything on that statement as a percentage of net sales:

$$\text{Vertical analysis \%} = \frac{\text{Each income statement item}}{\text{Net sales}}$$

EXHIBIT 19-3   *Comparative Income Statement—Vertical Analysis*

Schneider Corporation
Consolidated Statement of Earnings
years ended Ocotober 29, 1994, and October 30, 1993
(Dollar amounts in thousands)

	1994 Amount	1994 Percent	1993 Amount	1993 Percent
Sales...	$767,462	100.0%	$725,279	100.0%
Expenses:				
Cost of goods sold..................................	677,285	88.3	634,107	87.4
Selling, marketing, and administrative	55,372	7.2	57,591	7.9
Depreciation and amortization	13,237	1.7	13,626	1.9
	745,894	97.2	705,324	97.2
Earnings from operations......................	21,568	2.8	19,955	2.8
Interest expense	7,766	1.0	7,138	1.0
Earnings before income taxes				
and minority interest	13,802	1.8	12,817	1.8
Income taxes...	6,152	.8	4,471	.6
Earnings before minority interest	7,650	1.0	8346	1.2
Minority interest....................................	369	.0	(658)	.1
Net earnings...	$ 8,019	1.0	$ 7,688	1.1
Earnings per share.................................	$ 1.35		$ 1.31	

Common-Size Statements

The percentages in Exhibits 19-3 and 19-4 can be presented as a separate state-ment that reports only percentages (no dollar amounts). Such a statement is called a **common-size statement**.

On a common-size income statement, each item is expressed as a percentage of the net sales amount. Net sales is the "common size" to which we relate the state-ment's other amounts. In the balance sheet, the "common size" is the total on each side of the accounting equation (total assets *or* the sum of total liabilities and share-holders' equity). A common-size statement eases the comparison of different com-panies because their amounts are stated in percentages.

Common-size statements may identify the need for corrective action. Exhibit 19-5 is the common-size analysis of current assets taken from Exhibit 19-4.

Exhibit 19-5 shows cash as a larger percentage of total assets at December 31, 19X4 than at the previous year end. Accounts receivable is a larger percentage of total assets. What could cause an increase in accounts receivable as percentages of total assets? Schneider may have been lax in collecting accounts receivable, which may explain a cash shortage and reveal that the company needs to pursue collection more vigorously. On the other hand, Exhibit 19-1 reveals that sales were up 5.8%. In any event, the company should monitor its cash position and collection of accounts receivable to avoid a cash shortage. Common-size statements provide information useful for this purpose.

Industry Comparisons

We study the records of a company in order to understand past results and predict future performance. Still, the knowledge that we can develop from a single company's records is limited to that one company. We may learn that gross profit has decreased and net income has increased steadily for the last ten years. While this

---

OBJECTIVE 3
Prepare common-size financial statements

Short Exercise:

Calculate the common-size percentages for the following income statement:

Net sales.............	$150,000
COGS..................	60,000
Gross margin......	90,000
Operating exp.	40,000
Operating income	50,000
Income tax exp. 1	15,000
Net income	$ 35,000

A:

Net sales.............	100%
COGS..................	40
Gross margin......	60
Operating exp.	27
Operating income	33
Income tax exp. ...	10
Net income	23%

EXHIBIT 19-4   *Comparative Balance Sheet—Vertical Analysis*

Schneider Corporation
Consolidated Balance Sheet
October 29, 1994 and October 30, 1993
(dollar amounts in thousands)

	1994 Amount	1994 Percent	1993 Amount	1993 Percent
Assets				
Current assets:				
Accounts receivable	$ 47,121	19.3%	$ 39,595	18.5%
Inventories	58,814	24.0	48,907	22.9
Current portion of loans receivable	443	.2	443	.2
Income taxes recoverable	274	.1	—	—
Other	2,238	.9	3,073	1.4
Total current assets	108,890	44.5	92,018	43.0
Property, plant, and equipment	110,488	45.2	103,382	48.3
Other assets:				
Loans receivable	2,368	1.0	2,496	1.2
Deferred pension	6,133	2.5	395	.2
Production licenses and rights	6,852	2.8	7,376	3.4
Intangible assets	9,819	4.0	8,419	3.9
Total other assets	25,712	10.3	18,686	8.7
Total assets	$244,550	100.0%	$214,086	100.0%
Liabilities and Shareholders' Equity				
Current liabilities:				
Bank advances	$21,007	8.6%	$3,369	1.6%
Outstanding cheques	8,014	3.3	7,845	3.7
Accounts payable and accrued liabilities	47,499	19.4	42,714	20.0
Income taxes payable	—		435	.2
Principal due in one year on debentures and loans	8,240	3.3	7,484	3.5
Total current liabilities	84,760	34.6	61,847	28.9
Debentures and loans	55,900	22.9	59,514	27.8
Other liabilities:				
Deferred income taxes	5,625	2.3	3,640	1.7
Deferred gains	1,372	.6	1,530	.7
Minority interest	3,978	1.6	5,019	2.3
Total other liabilities	10,975	4.5	10,189	4.7
Shareholders' equity:				
Capital stock	20,261	8.3	16,052	7.5
Retained earnings	72,654	29.7	66,484	31.1
Total shareholders' equity	92,915	38.0	82,536	38.6
Total liabilities and shareholders' equity	$244,550	100.0%	$214,086	100.0%

information is helpful, it does not consider how businesses in the same industry have fared over this time. Have other companies in the same line of business increased their sales? Is there an industrywide decline in gross profit? Has cost of goods sold risen steeply for other businesses that sell the same products? Managers, investors, creditors and other interested parties need to know how one company compares to other companies in the same line of business.

EXHIBIT 19-5 *Common-Size Analysis of Current Assets*

	Percent of Total Assets	
	1994	**1993**
Schneider Corporation Common-Size Analysis of Current Assets December 31, 1994 and 1993		
Current assets		
Accounts receivable, net..	19.3%	18.5%
Inventories...	24.0	22.9
Other	1.2	1.6
Total current assets...	44.5%	43.0%

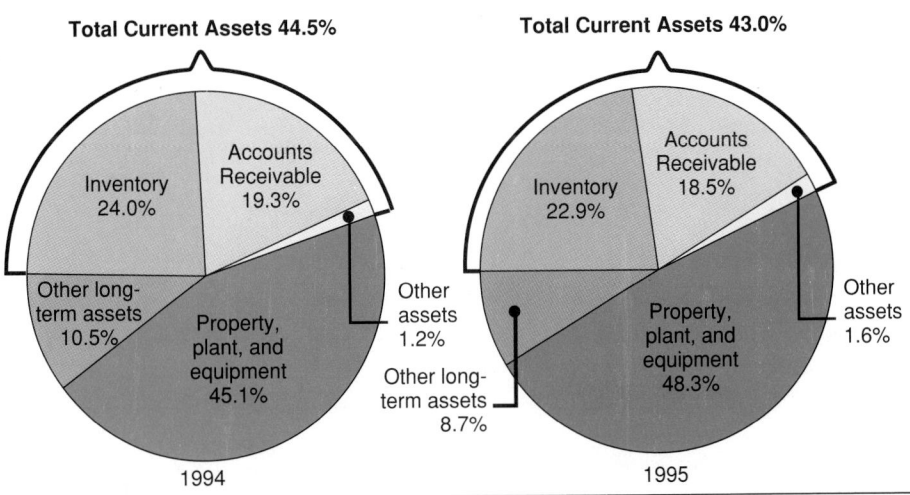

Percent of Total Assets

Total Current Assets 44.5% — 1994
Total Current Assets 43.0% — 1995

Exhibit 19-6 gives the common-size income statement of Bristol-Myers Squibb Company, the pharmaceuticals company, compared with the average for the pharmaceuticals industry. This analysis compares Bristol-Myers Squibb with all other companies in its line of business. The industry averages were adapted from Robert Morris Associates' *Annual Statement Studies*. Analysts specialize in a particular industry and make such comparisons in deciding which companies' stocks to buy or sell. For example, financial-service companies like Richardson Greenshields have paper and forest products industry specialists, merchandising industry specialists, and so on. Boards of directors evaluate top managers based on how well the company compares with other companies in the industry. Exhibit 19-6 shows that Bristol-Myers Squibb compares favorably with competing companies in the pharmaceuticals industry. Its gross profit percentage is much higher than the industry average. The company does a good job of controlling expenses, and as a result, its percentage of income from operations and its net income percentage are significantly higher than the industry average.

Another use of common-size statements is to aid in the comparison of different-sized companies. Suppose you are considering an investment in the stock of a brewer, and you are choosing between John Labatt and the Brick Brewing Co. John Labatt is so much larger than the Brick that a direct comparison of their financial statements in dollar amounts is not meaningful. However, you can convert the two companies' income statements to common size and compare the percentages. You may find that one company has a higher percentage of its assets in inventory and the other company has a higher percentage of its liabilities in long-term debt.

EXHIBIT 19-6   *Common-Size Income Statement Compared with the Industry Average*

Bristol-Myers Squibb Company
Common-Size Income Statement for Comparison with Industry Average
year ended December 31, 1993

	Bristol-Myers Squibb	Industry Average
Net sales	100.0%	100.0%
Cost of products sold	26.5	55.3
Gross profit	73.5	44.7
Operating expenses	50.9	37.7
Earnings from Continuing Operations before Income Taxes	22.6	7.0
Income tax expense	5.4	1.7
Earnings from Continuing Operations	17.2	5.3
Special items (discontinued operations, cumulative effects of accounting changes, and so on)	—	1.1
Net earnings	**17.2%**	**4.2%**

Percent of Net Sales

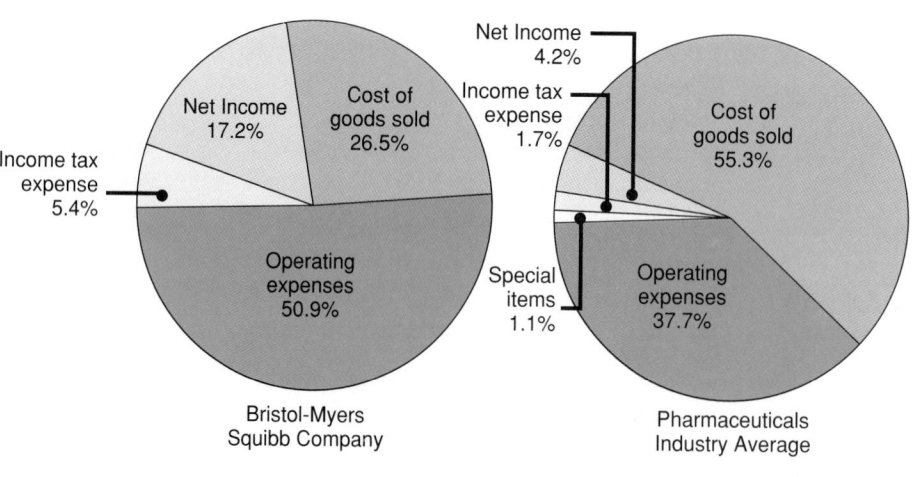

Bristol-Myers Squibb Company

Pharmaceuticals Industry Average

Information Sources

Financial analysts draw their information from various sources. Annual and quarterly reports offer readers a good look at an individual business's operations. Publicly held companies must, in addition, submit annual reports that are more detailed to the provincial securities commission in each province where they are listed on a stock exchange (for example, the Alberta Securities Commission for the Alberta Stock Exchange). Business publications such as the daily and weekend *Financial Post* and the daily *Globe and Mail Report on Business* carry information about individual companies and Canadian industries. The Globe Information Services and The Financial Post Information Service provide data to subscribers on public companies and industries in Canada, too. Credit agencies like Dun and Bradstreet Canada Limited, for example, offer industry averages as part of their financial service.

The Statement of Changes in Financial Position in Decision Making

The chapter so far has centered on the income statement and balance sheet. We may also perform horizontal and vertical analysis on the statement of changes in financial position. In Chapter 18, we discussed how to prepare the statement. To discuss its role in decision making, let us use Exhibit 19-7.

Some analysts use cash flow analysis to identify danger signals about a company's financial situation. For example, the statement in Exhibit 19-7 reveals what may be a weakness in DeMaris Corporation.

First, operations provided a net cash inflow of $52,000, which is much less than the $91,000 generated by the sale of fixed assets. An important question arises: Can the company remain in business by generating the majority of its cash by selling its capital assets? No, because these assets will be needed to manufacture the company's products in the future. Note also that borrowing by issuing bonds payable brought in $72,000. No company can long survive living on borrowed funds. DeMaris must eventually pay off the bonds. Indeed, the company paid $170,000 on older debt. Also, interest expense must be incurred as the price of borrowing. Successful companies like NOVA Corporation, St. Lawrence Cement, and Canadian Pacific generate the greatest percentage of their cash from operations, not from selling their capital assets or from borrowing money. These conditions may be only temporary for DeMaris Corporation, but they are worth investigating.

The most important information that the statement of changes in financial position provides is a summary of the company's use of cash. How a company spends its cash today determines its sources of cash in the future. The company may wisely use its cash to purchase assets that will generate income in the years ahead. However, if a company invests unwisely, cash will eventually run short.

DeMaris's statement of changes in financial position reveals problems. Exhibit 19-7 information indicates that DeMaris invested in no fixed assets to replace those that it sold. The company may in fact be going out of business. Furthermore, DeMaris paid dividends of $33,000, an amount that is very close to its net income. Is the

> **OBJECTIVE 4**
>
> Use the statement of changes in financial position in decision-making

EXHIBIT 19-7 *Statement of Changes in Financial Position*

DeMaris Corporation Statement of Changes in Financial Position for the current year		
Operating activities		
Income from operations..		$ 35,000
Add (subtract) noncash items:		
Depreciation..	$ 14,000	
Net increase in current assets other than cash	(5,000)	
Net increase in current liabilities.....................	8,000	17,000
Net cash inflow from operating activities...........		52,000
Financing activities		
Issuance of bond payable..	$ 72,000	
Payment of long-term debt.......................................	(170,000)	
Repurchase of shares..	(9,000)	
Payment of dividends..	(33,000)	
Net cash outflow from financing activities.........		(140,000)
Investing activities		
Sale of property, plant, and equipment....................	$ 91,000	
Net cash inflow from investing activities...........		91,000
Increase in cash..		$ 3,000

company retaining enough of its income to finance future operations—especially in light of the large amount of long-term debt that DeMaris paid off? Analysts seek answers to questions such as this. They analyze the information from the statement of changes in financial position along with the information from the balance sheet and the income statement to form a well-rounded complete picture of the business.

A popular measure of cash flows is called *free cash flow,* which is net cash inflow from operations minus net cash outflow from investing activities. The Coca-Cola Company discussed its use of free cash flow analysis as follows:

Liquidity and Capital Resources

One of the Company's financial strengths is its ability to generate cash from operations in excess of requirements for capital reinvestment and dividends.

"Free Cash Flow": Free Cash Flow is the cash from operations remaining after the Company has satisfied its business reinvestment opportunities. Management focuses on growing Free Cash Flow to achieve management's primary objective, maximizing shareowner value. The Company uses Free Cash Flow, along with borrowings to make share repurchases and dividend payments. The consolidated statements of cash flows are summarized as follows (in millions):

Year Ended December 31,	**1992**	1991
Cash flows provided by (used in):		
Operations	**$2,232**	$2,084
Investment activities	**(1,359)**	(1,124)
"Free Cash Flow"	**873**	960

Mid-Chapter Summary Problem for Your Review

Perform a horizontal analysis and a vertical analysis of the comparative income statement of TRE Corporation. State whether 19X3 was a good year or a bad year and give your reasons.

TRE Corporation **Comparative Income Statement** **years ended December 31, 19X3 and 19X2**		
	19X3	**19X2**
Total revenues	$275,000	$225,000
Expenses		
Cost of products sold	$194,000	$165,000
Engineering, selling, and administrative expenses	54,000	48,000
Interest expense	5,000	5,000
Income tax expense	9,000	3,000
Other expense (income)	1,000	(1,000)
Total expenses	263,000	220,000
Net earnings	$ 12,000	$ 5,000

SOLUTION TO REVIEW PROBLEM

TRE Corporation
Horizontal Analysis of Comparative Income Statement
years ended December 31, 19X3 and 19X2

	19X3	19X2	Increase (Decrease) Amount	Percent
Total revenues	$275,000	$225,000	$50,000	22.2%
Expenses				
Cost of products sold	$194,000	$165,000	$29,000	17.6
Engineering, selling, and				
administrative expenses	54,000	48,000	6,000	12.5
Interest expense	5,000	5,000	—	—
Income tax expense	9,000	3,000	6,000	200.0
Other expense (income)	1,000	(1,000)	2,000	—
Total expenses	263,000	220,000	43,000	19.5
Net earnings	$ 12,000	$ 5,000	$ 7,000	140.0

TRE Corporation
Vertical Analysis of Comparative Income Statement
years ended December 31, 19X3 and 19X2

	19X3 Amount	Percent	19X2 Amount	Percent
Total revenue.................................	$275,000	100.0%	$225,000	100.0%
Expenses				
Cost of products sold...............	$194,000	70.5	$165,000	73.3
Engineering, selling, and				
administrative expenses.....	54,000	19.6	48,000	21.3
Interest expense.......................	5,000	1.8	5,000	2.2
Income tax expense..................	9,000	3.3	3,000	1.4
Other expense (income)	1,000	0.4	(1,000)	(0.4)
Total expenses...............................	263,000	95.6	220,000	97.8
Net earnings..................................	$ 12,000	4.4%	$ 5,000	2.2%

The horizontal analysis shows that total revenues increased 22.2 percent. This percentage increase was greater than the 19.5 percent increase in total expenses, resulting in a 140 percent increase in net earnings.

The vertical analysis shows decreases in the percentages of net sales consumed by the cost of products sold (from 73.3 percent to 70.5 percent) and the engineering, selling, and administrative expenses (from 21.3 percent to 19.6 percent). These two items are TRE's largest dollar expenses, so their percentage decreases are quite important. The relative reduction in expenses raised 19X3 net earnings to 4.4 percent of sales, compared to 2.2 percent the preceding year. The overall analysis indicates that 19X3 was significantly better than 19X2.

Using Ratios to Make Business Decisions

The heart of financial analysis is the calculation and interpretation of ratios. A ratio expresses the relationship of one number to another number. For example, if the balance sheet shows current assets of $100,000 and current liabilities of $25,000, the ratio of current assets to current liabilities is $100,000 to $25,000. We simplify this numerical expression to the ratio of 4 to 1, which may also be written 4:1 and 4/1.

OBJECTIVE 5
Compute the standard financial ratios used for decision-making

Key Point:

We must learn how to
understand relationships
among the numbers on a
financial statement. Horizontal
and vertical analyses were our
first attempt at studying such
relationships. We now learn
to use ratios, which help even
more in analyzing the
statements. We compare
financial statement amounts
to other items to assess what
the ratio indicates about the
company. How do we assess
a ratio? We must consider
prior years, industry
averages, budgeted ratios,
and so on—only then does a
ratio have meaning.

Other acceptable ways of expressing this ratio include (1) "current assets are 400 percent of current liabilities," (2) "the business has four dollars in current assets for every one dollar in current liabilities," or simply, (3) "the current ratio is 4.0."

We often reduce the ratio fraction by writing the ratio as one figure over the other, for example, 4/1, and then dividing the numerator by the denominator. In this way, the ratio 4/1 may be expressed simply as 4. The 1 that represents the denominator of the fraction is understood, not written. Consider the ratio $175,000 : $165,000. After dividing the first figure by the second, we come to 1.06 : 1, which we state as 1.06. The second part of the ratio, the 1, again is understood. Ratios provide a convenient and useful way of expressing a relationship between numbers. For example, the ratio of current assets to current liabilities gives information about a company's ability to pay its current debts with existing current assets.

A manager, lender, or financial analyst may use any ratio that is relevant to a particular decision. Many companies include ratios in a special section of their annual reports while others use ratios throughout to better explain the company's operations. Québec-Téléphone displays ratio data in the consolidated summary section of its annual report. Exhibit 19-8 shows a sampling of that summary section. Investment services—Moody's, Standard & Poor's Canada, Robert Morris Associates, and others—report these ratios for companies and industries.

Exhibit 19-9 shows some widely used ratios that we discuss here. The ratios may be classified as follows:

1. Ratios that measure the ability to pay current liabilities
2. Ratios that measure the ability to sell inventory and collect receivables
3. Ratios that measure the ability to pay long-term debt
4. Ratios that measure profitability
5. Ratios used to analyze stock as an investment

How much can a computer help in analyzing financial statements for investment purposes? Time yourself as you perform one of the financial-ratio problems in this chapter. Multiply your efforts by, say, 100 companies that you are comparing by means of this ratio. Now consider ranking these 100 companies on the basis of four or five additional ratios.

On-line financial databases, such as Lexis/Nexis and Globe Information Services, offer quarterly financial figures for hundreds of public corporations going back as much as 10 years. Assume that you wanted to compare companies' recent earnings histories. You might have the computer compare hundreds of companies on the basis of price/earnings ratio and rates of return on shareholders' equity and total assets. The computer could then give you the names of the 20 (or however many) companies that appear most favorable in terms of these ratios. Alternatively, you could have the computer download financial statement data to your spreadsheet

EXHIBIT 19-8   *Consolidated Financial Summary of Québec-Téléphone*
(Dollars in thousands except per-share amounts)

Years ended December 31,	1993	1992	1991	1990
Operating Results				
Net earnings	$28,971	$28,849	$26,716	$24,072
Per common share	$1.69	$1.70	$1.59	$1.38
Return on average common share equity	13.9%	14.7%	14.3%	13.6%
Financial Position				
Common share equity	$211,378	$199,882	$188,432	$178,431
Long-term debt	130,000	150,000	157,575	165,142
Debt ratio	42.7%	43.4%	45.3%	46.7%
Interest coverage	3.78	3.58	3.32	3.13

EXHIBIT 19-9   *Ratios Used in Financial Statement Analysis*

Ratio	Computation	Information Provided
Measuring the ability to pay current liabilities		
1. Current ratio	$\dfrac{\text{Current assets}}{\text{Current liabilities}}$	Measures ability to pay liabilities from current assets.
2. Acid-test (quick ratio)	$\dfrac{\text{Cash + short-term investments + net current receivables}}{\text{Current liabilities}}$	Shows ability to pay current liabilities from the most liquid assets.
Measuring the ability to sell inventory and collect receivables		
3. Inventory turnover	$\dfrac{\text{Cost of goods sold}}{\text{Average inventory}}$	Indicates saleability of inventory.
4. Accounts receivable turnover	$\dfrac{\text{Net credit sales}}{\text{Average net accounts receivables}}$	Measures collectibility of receivables.
5. Days' sales in receivables	$\dfrac{\text{Average net accounts receivable}}{\text{One day's sales}}$	Shows how many days it takes to collect average receivables.
Measuring the ability to pay long-term debt		
6. Debt ratio	$\dfrac{\text{Total liabilities}}{\text{Total assets}}$	Indicates percentage of assets financed through borrowing.
7. Times-interest-earned ratio	$\dfrac{\text{Income from operations}}{\text{Interest expense}}$	Measures coverage of interest expense by operating income.
Measuring profitability		
8. Rate of return on net sales	$\dfrac{\text{Net income}}{\text{Net sales}}$	Shows the percentage of each sales dollar earned as net income
9. Rate of return on total assets	$\dfrac{\text{Net income + interest expense}}{\text{Average total assets}}$	Gauges how profitably assets are used.
10. Rate of return on common shareholders' equity	$\dfrac{\text{Net income} - \text{preferred dividends}}{\text{Average common shareholders' equity}}$	Gauges how profitably the assets financed by the common shareholders are used.
11. Earnings per share of common stock	$\dfrac{\text{Net income} - \text{preferred dividends}}{\text{Number of shares of common stock outstanding}}$	Gives the amount of earnings per one share of common stock.
Analyzing stock as an investment		
12. Price/earnings ratio	$\dfrac{\text{Market price per share of common stock}}{\text{Earnings per share}}$	Indicates the market price of one dollar of earnings.
13. Dividend yield	$\dfrac{\text{Dividend per share of common stock}}{\text{Market price per share of common stock}}$	Shows the proportion of the market price of each share of stock returned as dividends to shareholders each period.
14. Book value per share of common stock	$\dfrac{\text{Total shareholders' equity} - \text{preferred equity}}{\text{Number of shares of common stock outstanding}}$	Indicates the recorded accounting value of each share of common stock outstanding.

(that is, place the data in the appropriate cells of your spreadsheet) and compute the ratios yourself.

Accountants use computerized financial analysis a great deal. Public accountants focus on the individual client. They want to know how the client is doing compared with the previous year and compared with other firms in the industry. Auditors want to detect any emerging trends in the company's ratios and compare the results of actual operations with expected results. To do so, an auditor can download monthly financial statistics on a spreadsheet and compute the financial ratios to gain insight into the client's situation.

Measuring the Ability to Pay Current Liabilities _____

Working capital is defined by the following equation:

Working capital = Current assets – Current liabilities

Working capital is widely used to measure a business's ability to meet its short-term obligations with its current assets. In general, the larger the working capital, the better able the business is to pay its debts. Recall that capital or owners' equity is total assets minus total liabilities. Working capital is like a "current" version of total capital. The working capital amount considered alone, however, does not give a complete picture of the entity's working capital position. Consider two companies with equal working capital.

	Company A	Company B
Current assets...........................	$100,000	$200,000
Current liabilities.....................	50,000	150,000
Working capital.......................	$ 50,000	$ 50,000

Both companies have working capital of $50,000, but Company A's working capital is as large as its current liabilities. Company B's working capital, on the other hand, is only one third as large as its current liabilities. Which business has a better working capital position? Company A, because its working capital is a higher percentage of current assets and current liabilities. To use working capital data in decision-making, it is helpful to develop ratios. Two decision tools based on working capital data are the *current ratio* and the *acid-test ratio*.

Current Ratio

The most common ratio using current asset and current liability data is the **current ratio**, which is current assets divided by current liabilities. Recall the makeup of current assets and current liabilities. Inventory is converted to receivables through sales, the receivables are collected in cash, and the cash is used to buy inventory and pay current liabilities. A company's current assets and current liabilities represent the core of its day-to-day operations.

Exhibit 19-10 gives the comparative income statement and balance sheet of Palisades Furniture, Inc. The current ratios of Palisades Furniture, Inc., at December 31, 19X7 and 19X6, follow, along with the average for the retail furniture industry:

	Formula	Current Ratio of Palisades Furniture, Inc.		Retail Furniture Industry Average
		19X7	19X6	
Current ratio $=$	$\dfrac{\text{Current assets}}{\text{Current liabilities}}$	$\dfrac{\$262,000}{\$142,000} = 1.85$	$\dfrac{\$236,000}{\$126,000} = 1.87$	1.80

EXHIBIT 19-10 *Comparative Financial Statements*

Panel A—Comparative Income Statement of Palisades Furniture Inc.

Palisades Furniture, Inc.
Comparative Income Statement
years ended December 31, 19X7 and 19X6

	19X7	19X6
Net sales	$858,000	$803,000
Cost of goods sold	513,000	509,000
Gross profit	345,000	294,000
Operating expenses:		
Selling expenses	126,000	114,000
General expenses	118,000	123,000
Total operating expenses	244,000	237,000
Income from operations	101,000	57,000
Interest revenue	4,000	—
Interest expense	24,000	14,000
Income before income taxes	81,000	43,000
Income tax expense	33,000	17,000
Net income	$ 48,000	$ 26,000

Panel B—Comparative Balance Sheet of Palisades Furniture Inc.

Palisades Furniture, Inc.
Comparative Balance Sheet
December 31, 19X7 and 19X6

Assets	19X7	19X6
Current assets:		
Cash	$ 29,000	$ 32,000
Accounts receivable net	114,000	85,000
Inventories	113,000	111,000
Prepaid expenses	6,000	8,000
Total current assets	262,000	236,000
Long-term investments	18,000	9,000
Property, plant, and equipment, net	507,000	399,000
Total assets	$787,000	$644,000
Liabilities		
Current liabilities:		
Notes payable	$ 42,000	$ 27,000
Accounts payable	73,000	68,000
Accrued liabilities	27,000	31,000
Total current liabilities	142,000	126,000
Long-term debt	289,000	198,000
Total liabilities	431,000	324,000
Shareholders' Equity		
Common stock, no par	186,000	186,000
Retained earnings	170,000	134,000
Total shareholders' equity	356,000	320,000
Total liabilities and shareholders' equity	$787,000	$644,000

Short Exercise:

Use the following income statements and balance sheets for A Co. and B Co.:

	A Co.	B Co.
Cash	$ 31	$ 20
Acc. rec.	45	75
Inventory	21	102
Prepaid expenses	3	3
Plant & equip.		
(net)	200	350
Total assets	$300	$550
Current liabilities	$ 50	$150
Long-term debt	100	240
$.10 Preferred		
stock (10 shares)		10
Common stock	125	100
Retained earnings	25	50
Total liabilities &		
shareholders'		
equity	$300	$550
Net sales	$160	$270
COGS	100	135
Oper. exp.	22	30
Interest exp.	6	30
Income tax exp.	12	25
Net income	$ 20	$ 50

Calculate (1) working capital, (2) the current ratio, and (3) the acid-test ratio. **A:** (1) A Co.: $50 ($31 + $45 + $21 + $3 − $50); B Co.: $50 ($20 + $75 + $102 + $3 − $150); (2) A Co.: 2:1 ($100/$50); B Co.: 1.33:1 ($200/$150); (3) A Co.: 1.52:1 ($76/$50); B Co.: 0.63:1 ($95/$150)

The current ratio decreased slightly during 19X7. Lenders, shareholders, and managers closely monitor changes in a company's current ratio. In general, a higher

Short Exercise:
A Co. and B Co. of the Short Exercise on page 927 have equal amounts of working capital, but their current and acid-test ratios differ. Explain.
A: A Co. has a higher ratio of current assets to current liabilities than B Co., as shown by A's higher current ratio. A Co. should be able to meet current obligations more easily as they come due. A Co. has a higher ratio of quick (liquid) assets to current liabilities than B Co., as indicated by the quick ratio—A is more "liquid" than B. Inventory and prepaid expenses are not "quick" assets. B Co. has more current liabilities than quick assets. B may have trouble paying off current debts because it must convert inventory to receivables or to cash to pay these debts. A Co. appears to have adequate quick assets to meet its debts. A seems to be in a stronger current financial position than B.

current ratio indicates a stronger financial position. A high current ratio suggests that the business has sufficient liquid assets to maintain normal business operations. Compare Palisades Furniture's current ratio of 1.85 with the 1.80 average for the retail furniture industry and with current ratios of some actual companies.

Company	Current Ratio
Southam, Inc. (Communications)	1.02
Canadian Tire Corporation, Limited (Merchandising)	1.59
Guillevin International, Inc. (Wholesale distributor)	1.89
Doman Industries Limited (Forest products)	4.07
United Grain Growers Limited (Agribusiness)	1.29
Budd Canada, Inc. (Manufacturing)	2.96

What is an acceptable current ratio? The answer to this question depends on the nature of the business. The current ratio will generally exceed 1.0, while the norm for most companies is 1.60 to 1.90. Palisades Furniture's current ratio of 1.85 is within the range of those values. In most industries, a current ratio of 2.0 is considered good. The companies listed above are typical of their industries; note that they range from 1.02 to 4.07.

Acid-Test Ratio

The **acid-test** (or *quick*) **ratio** tells us whether the entity could pay all its current liabilities if they came due immediately. That is, could the company pass this *acid test*? The company would convert its most liquid assets to cash. To compute the acid-test ratio, we add cash, short-term investments and net current receivables (accounts and notes receivable, net of allowances) and divide by current liabilities. Inventory and prepaid expenses are the two current assets not included in the acid-test computations because they are the least liquid of the current assets. A business may not be able to convert them to cash immediately to pay current liabilities. The acid-test ratio measures liquidity using a narrower asset base than the current ratio does.

Palisades Furniture's acid-test ratios for 19X7 and 19X6 follow:

Formula		Acid-Test Ratio of Palisades Furniture, Inc.		Retail Furniture Industry Average
		19X7	19X6	
Acid-test ratio =	Cash + short-term investments + net current receivables / Current liabilities	$29,000 + $0 + $114,000 / $142,000 = 1.01	$32,000 + $0 + $ 85,000 / $126,000 = 0.93	0.60

The company's acid-test ratio improved considerably during 19X7 and is significantly better than the industry average. Compare Palisades Furniture's 1.01 acid-test ratio with the acid-test values of some well-known companies:

Company	Acid-Test Ratio
Cara Operations Limited (Food services and office products)	.64
Dofasco Inc. (Steel producer)	1.66
Tembec Inc. (Forest products)	3.46
Renaissance Energy Ltd. (Energy)	.67
SNC-LAVALIN Group Inc. (Engineering Services)	.71

The norm ranges from .20 to 1.00 as reported by Robert Morris Associates. An acid-test ratio of .90 to 1.00 is acceptable in most industries.

Measuring the Ability to Sell Inventory and Collect Receivables _____

The ability to sell inventory and collect receivables is fundamental to business success. Recall the operating cycle of a merchandiser: cash to inventory to receivables and back to cash. This section discusses three ratios that measure the ability to sell inventory and collect receivables.

Inventory Turnover

Companies generally seek to achieve the quickest possible return on their investments. A return on an investment in inventory—usually a substantial amount is no exception. The faster inventory sells, the sooner the business creates accounts receivable, and the sooner it collects cash.

Inventory turnover is a measure of the number of times a company sells its average level of inventory during a year. A high rate of turnover indicates relative ease in selling inventory, whereas a low turnover indicates difficulty in selling. Generally, companies prefer a high inventory turnover. A value of 6 means that the company's average level of inventory has been sold 6 times during the year. In most cases this is better than a turnover of 3 or 4. However, a high value can mean that the business is not keeping enough inventory on hand, and inadequate inventory can result in lost sales if the company cannot fill a customer's order. Therefore, a business strives for the most profitable rate of inventory turnover, not necessarily the highest.

To compute the inventory turnover ratio we divide cost of goods sold by the average inventory for the period. We use the cost of goods sold (not sales) in the computation because both cost of goods sold and inventory are stated *at cost*. Sales is stated at the sales value of inventory and therefore is not comparable to inventory cost.

Palisades Furniture's inventory turnover for 19X7 is

Formula	Inventory Turnover of Palisades Furniture, Inc.	Retail Furniture Industry Average
Inventory turnover = $\dfrac{\text{Cost of goods sold}}{\text{Average inventory}}$	$\dfrac{\$513,000}{\$112,000} = 4.58$	2.70

Cost of goods sold appears in the income statement (Exhibit 19-10). Average inventory is figured by averaging the beginning inventory ($111,000) and ending inventory ($113,000). (See the balance sheet, Exhibit 19-10.) If inventory levels vary greatly from month to month, compute the average by adding the 12 monthly balances and dividing this sum by 12.

Inventory turnover varies widely with the nature of the business. For example, most manufacturers of farm machinery have an inventory turnover close to 3 times a year. By contrast, companies that remove natural gas from the ground hold their inventory for a very short period of time and have an average turnover of 30. Palisades Furniture's turnover of 4.58 times a year is high for its industry, which has an average turnover of 2.70. Palisades Furniture's high inventory turnover results from its policy of keeping little inventory on hand. The company takes customer orders and has its suppliers ship directly to customers.

Inventory turnover rates can vary greatly within a company. At Toys "R" Us, an international retailer of toys and childcare products, diapers and formula turn over more than 12 times a year, whereas seasonal toys turn over less than three times a year. The entire Toys "R" Us inventory turns over an average of three times a year. That inventory is at its lowest point on January 31 and at its highest point around October 31.

To evaluate fully a company's inventory turnover, compare the ratio over time. A sudden sharp decline or a steady decline over a long period suggests the need for corrective action. Analysts also compare a company's inventory turnover to other companies in the same industry and to the industry average.

Short Exercise:

Refer to the Short Exercise on page 927. Take the beginning inventories for A Co. and B Co. to be $19 and $98, respectively. Compute each company's rate of inventory turnover. **A:**

A Co.: $\dfrac{\$100}{(\$21 + \$19)/2} = 5.0$

B Co.: $\dfrac{\$135}{(\$102 + \$98)/2} = 1.35$

Short Exercise:

Evaluate the inventory turnovers of the previous Short Exercise. **A:** A Co. turns its inventory more quickly than B Co., which sells its inventory less than twice a year. The ratio varies widely from industry to industry, but it appears that B is carrying goods that are hard to sell. Or B may be carrying too much inventory for its level of sales.

Short Exercise:

In the Short Exercise on page 927, take the beginning account receivable balances to be $40 and $70, respectively. Compute (1) accounts receivable turnover; (2) days' sales in receivables.

A:

(1) A Co.: $\dfrac{\$160}{(\$45 + \$40)/2} = 3.76$

B Co.: $\dfrac{\$270}{(\$75 + \$70)/2} = 3.72$

(2) A: $160/365 = $0.44; $42.5/$0.44 = 96.6 days

B: $270/365 = $0.74; $72.5/0.74 = 98 days

Accounts Receivable Turnover

Accounts receivable turnover measures a company's ability to collect cash from credit customers. Generally, the higher the ratio, the more successfully the business collects cash, and the better off its operations are. However, too high a receivable turnover may indicate that credit is too tight, causing the loss of sales to good customers. To compute the accounts receivable turnover we divide net credit sales by average net accounts receivable. The resulting ratio indicates how many times during the year the average level of receivables was turned into cash.

Palisades Furniture's accounts receivable turnover ratio for 19X7 is computed as follows:

Formula		Accounts Receivable Turnover of Palisades Furniture, Inc.	Retail Furniture Industry Average
Accounts receivable turnover $=$	$\dfrac{\text{Net credit sales}}{\text{Average net accounts receivable}}$	$\dfrac{\$858,000}{\$99,500} = 8.62$	22.2

The sales figure comes from the income statement. Palisades Furniture makes all sales on credit. If the company makes both cash and credit sales, this ratio is best computed using only net credit sales. Average net accounts receivable is figured using the beginning accounts receivable balance ($85,000) and the ending balance ($114,000). If accounts receivable balances exhibit a seasonal pattern, compute the average using the 12 monthly balances.

Palisades Furniture's receivable turnover of 8.62 is much lower than the industry average. This results because the company is a home-town store that sells to local people who tend to pay their bills over a period of time. Many larger furniture stores sell their receivables to other companies called factors. This practice keeps receivables low and receivable turnover high. But companies that factor (sell) their receivables receive less than face value on their sale. Palisades Furniture follows a different strategy.

Days' Sales in Receivables

Short Exercise:

Evaluate the receivable ratios of the previous Short Exercise. **A:** Both companies' receivables turn over between three and four times a year— it takes about 1/3 to 1/4 of the year to collect the receivables. Compare the 96 and 98 days' sales in receivables with the company's credit terms. If A Co.'s credit terms are 2/10 n/30, then its collection department is doing a poor job of collecting. Or credit is being extended to uncreditworthy customers. A Co. should sell to those customers only on the cash basis.

Businesses must convert accounts receivable to cash. All else equal, the lower the Accounts Receivable balance, the more successful the business has been in converting receivables into cash, and the better off the business.

The **days'-sales-in-receivables** ratio tells us how many days' sales remain in Accounts Receivable. We express the money amount in terms of an average day's sales. This relation becomes clearer as we compute the ratio, a two-step process. First, divide net sales by 365 days to figure the average sales amount for one day. Second, divide this average day's sales amount into the average net accounts receivable.

The data to compute this ratio for Palisades Furniture for 19X7 are taken from the income statement and the balance sheet (Exhibit 19-10).

Formula		Days' Sales in Accounts Receivable of Palisades Furniture, Inc.	Retail Furniture Industry Average
Days' Sales in AVERAGE Accounts Receivable:			
1. One day's sales $=$	$\dfrac{\text{Net sales}}{365 \text{ days}}$	$\dfrac{\$858,000}{365 \text{ days}} = \$2,351$	
2. Days' sales in average accounts receivable $=$	$\dfrac{\text{Average net accounts receivable}}{\text{One day's sales}}$	$\dfrac{\$99,500}{\$2,351} = 42 \text{ days}$	16 days

The computation in two steps is designed to increase your understanding of the meaning of the ratio. We may compute days' sales in average receivables in one step: $99,500/($858,000/365 \text{ days}) = 42$ days.

Palisades Furniture's ratio tell us that 42 average days' sales remain in accounts receivable at the year end and need to be collected. The company will increase its cash inflow if it can decrease this ratio. To detect any changes over time in the firm's ability to collect its receivables, let us compute the days' sales in receivables ratio at the beginning and the end of 19X7.

Days' Sales in ENDING 19X6 Accounts Receivable:

$$\text{One day's sales} = \frac{\$803,000}{365 \text{ days}} = \$2,200$$

$$\text{Days' sales in ending 19X6 accounts receivable} = \frac{\$85,000}{\$2,200} = 39 \text{ days at beginning of 19X7}$$

Days' Sales in ENDING 19X7 Accounts Receivable:

$$\text{One day's sales} = \frac{\$858,000}{365 \text{ days}} = \$2,351$$

$$\text{Days' sales in ending 19X7 accounts receivable} = \frac{\$114,000}{\$2,351} = 48 \text{ days at end of 19X7}$$

This analysis shows a drop in Palisades Furniture's collection of receivables: days' sales in accounts receivable has increased from 39 at the beginning of the year to 48 at year end. The credit and collection department should strengthen its collection efforts. Otherwise, the company may experience a cash shortage in 19X8 and beyond. Palisades Furniture's days' sales in receivables is higher (worse) than the industry average because the company collects its own receivables. Many other furniture stores sell their receivables and carry fewer days' sales in receivables. Palisades Furniture remains competitive because of the personal relationship with customers. Without their good paying habits, the company's cash flow would suffer.

Measuring the Ability to Pay Long-Term Debt _____

The ratios discussed so far give us insight into current assets and current liabilities. They help us measure a business's ability to sell inventory, collect receivables, and to pay current liabilities. Most businesses also have long-term debts. Bondholders and banks that loan money on long-term notes payable and bonds payable take special interest in a business's ability to meet long-term obligations. Two key indicators of a business's ability to pay long-term liabilities are the *debt ratio* and *times-interest-earned ratio*.

Debt Ratio

Suppose you are a loan officer at a bank and you are evaluating loan applications from two companies with equal sales revenue and total assets. Sales and total assets are the two most common measures of firm size. Both companies have asked to borrow $500,000, and each has agreed to repay the loan over a ten-year period. The first customer already owes $600,000 to another bank. The second owes only $250,000. Other things equal, which company is likely to get the loan at the lower interest rate? Company Two is more likely to get the loan. The bank faces less risk by loaning to Company Two. That company owes less to creditors than Company One owes.

This relationship between total liabilities and total assets—called the **debt ratio** — tells us the proportion of the company's assets that it has financed with debt. If the debt ratio is 1, then debt has been used to finance all the assets. A debt ratio of .50 means that the company has used debt to finance half its assets and that the owners of the business have financed the other half. The higher the debt ratio, the higher

Key Point:
The denominator is average total assets. Income is earned throughout the year. For the denominator to be stated for the same time period as the numerator, an average of assets for the year is used.

the strain of paying interest each year and the principal amount at maturity. The lower the ratio, the less the business's future obligations. Creditors view a high debt ratio with caution. If a business seeking financing already has many liabilities, then additional debt payments may be too much for the business to handle. To help protect themselves, creditors generally charge higher interest rates on new borrowing to companies with an already high debt ratio.

Palisades Furniture's debt ratio at the end of 19X7 and 19X6 follow:

		Debt Ratio of Palisades Furniture, Inc.		Retail Furniture Industry Average
Formula		19X7	19X6	
Debt ratio = $\dfrac{\text{Total liabilities}}{\text{Total assets}}$		$\dfrac{\$431{,}000}{\$787{,}000} = .55$	$\dfrac{\$324{,}000}{\$644{,}000} = .50$	.61

Recall from our vertical and horizontal analyses that Palisades Furniture, Inc., expanded operations by financing the purchase of property, plant, and equipment through borrowing, which is common.

Even after the increase in 19X7, the company's debt is not very high. The average debt ratio for most companies ranges around .57 to .67, with relatively little variation from company to company. Palisades Furniture's .55 debt ratio indicates a fairly low-risk debt position in comparison with the retail furniture industry average of .61.

Short Exercise:

Evaluate the ratios of the previous Short Exercise in relation to the ability to repay long-term debt.
A: A Co. has a smaller percentage of total assets tied up in debt; 50% is a low debt ratio. B Co. may have more trouble paying its debts because a larger percentage of its assets are financed by liabilities as compared to equity. B Co. is earning only enough operating income to cover its interest 3.5 times. The lower this ratio, the more difficult it will be for B to pay its interest. A Co. has a much stronger financial position than B Co.

Times-Interest-Earned Ratio

The debt ratio measures the effect of debt on the company's *financial position* (balance sheet) but says nothing about its ability to pay interest expense. Analysts use a second ratio—the **times-interest-earned ratio**—to relate income to interest expense. To compute this ratio, we divide income from operations by interest expense. This ratio measures the number of times that operating income can *cover* interest expense. For this reason, the ratio is also called the *interest-coverage ratio*. A high ratio indicates ease in paying interest expense; a low value suggests difficulty.

Palisades Furniture's times-interest-earned ratios follow:

		Times-Interest-Earned Ratio of Palisades Furniture, Inc.		Retail Furniture Industry Average
Formula		19X7	19X6	
Times-interest-earned ratio =	$\dfrac{\text{Income from operations}}{\text{Interest expense}}$	$\dfrac{\$101{,}000}{\$24{,}000} = 4.21$	$\dfrac{\$57{,}000}{\$14{,}000} = 4.07$	2.00

The company's interest-coverage ratio increased in 19X7. This is a favorable sign about the company, especially since the company's short-term notes payable and long-term debt rose substantially during the year. Palisades Furniture's new capital assets, we conclude, have earned more in operating income than they have cost the business in interest expense. The company's coverage ratio of around 4 is significantly better than the 2.60 average for furniture retailers. The norm for business, as reported by Robert Morris Associates, falls in the range of 2.0 to 3.0 for most companies.

Based on its debt ratio and times-interest-earned ratio, Palisades Furniture appears to have little difficulty paying its liabilities, also called *servicing its debt*.

Measuring Profitability

The fundamental goal of business is to earn a profit. Ratios that measure profitability play a large role in decision-making. These ratios are reported in the business press, by investment services, and in the annual financial reports of companies.

Suppose you are a personal financial planner who helps clients select stock investments. One client has $100,000 to invest in a chemical company. Over the next few years, you expect Methanex Corp. to earn higher rates of return on its investments than analysts are forecasting for the chemicals manufacturer Dupont Canada Inc. Which company's stock will you recommend? Probably Methanex—for reasons you will better understand after studying three rate-of-return measurements.

Short Exercise:
Refer to the Short Exercise on page 927. Compute (1) the debt ratio and (2) the times-interest-earned ratio. **A:**
(1) A Co.: 50% ($150/$300)
    B Co.: 71% ($390/$550)
(2) A Co.: 6.3 times
    ($160 – $100 – $22)/$6
    B Co.: 3.5 times
    ($270 – $135 – $30)/30

Rate of Return on Net Sales

In business, the term *return* is used broadly and loosely as an evaluation of profitability. Consider a percentage called the **rate of return on net sales** or, simply *return on sales*. (The word *net* is usually omitted for convenience, even though the net sales figure is used to compute the ratio.) Palisades Furniture's rate of return on sales ratios follows:

		Rate of Return on Sales of Palisades Furniture, Inc.		Retail Furniture Industry Average
Formula		19X7	19X6	
Rate of return on sales	= $\dfrac{\text{Net income}}{\text{Net sales}}$	$\dfrac{\$48,000}{\$858,000} = .056$	$\dfrac{\$26,000}{\$803,000} = .032$	.008

The increase in Palisades Furniture's return on sales is significant and identifies the company as more successful than the average furniture store. Companies strive for a high rate of return. The higher the rate of return, the more net sales dollars are providing income to the business and the fewer net sales dollars are absorbed by expenses. See how Palisades Furniture's rate of return on sales compares with some other companies:

Company	Rate of Return on Sales
United Dominion Industries Limited (Industrial and building products and engineering)	.031
Loblaw Companies Limited (Retail and wholesale food distribution)	.013
United Grain Growers Limited (Agribusiness)	.006
ATCO Ltd. (Utilities, manufacturing, and oil and gas)	.037

As these rates of return on sales indicate, this ratio varies widely from industry to industry.

One strategy for increasing the rate of return on sales is to develop a product that commands a premium price such as Bombardier's Ski-doo, Laura Secord chocolates, and certain brands of clothing, such as Far West. Another strategy is to control costs. If successful, either strategy converts a higher proportion of sales into net income and increases the rate of return on net sales.

A return measure can be computed on any revenue and sales amount. Return on net sales, as we have seen, is net income divided by net sales. Return on total revenues is net income divided by total revenues. A company can compute a return on other specific portions of revenue as its information needs dictate.

Rate of Return on Total Assets

The **rate of return on total assets** or, simply, *return on assets* measures the success a company has in using its assets to earn a profit. Creditors have loaned money to the company, and the interest they receive is the return on their investment. Shareholders have invested in the company's stock, and net income is their return. The sum of interest expense and net income is the return to the two groups that have financed the company's operations, and this amount is the numerator of the return-on-assets ratio. Average total assets is the denominator.

Palisades Furniture's return-on-assets ratio follows:

Formula		Rate of Return on Total Assets of Palisades Furniture, Inc. 19X7	Retail Furniture Industry Average
Rate of return on assets	=	$\dfrac{\text{Net Income} + \text{interest expense}}{\text{Average total assets}}$	$\dfrac{\$48,000 + \$24,000}{\$715,500} = .101$	.049

Net income and interest expense are taken from the income statement. To compute average total assets, we use beginning and ending total assets from the comparative balance sheet. See how Palisades Furniture's rate of return on assets compares with some other companies:

Company	Rate of Return on Assets
Doman Industries Limited (Forest products)	.035
Dofasco Inc. (Steel producer)	.043
Renaissance Energy Limited (Oil and natural gas)	.047
Methanex Corp. (Chemicals)	.255

Key Point:

Return on shareholders' equity measures how much income is earned for every $1 invested by the common shareholders.

Rate of Return on Common Shareholders' Equity

A popular measure of profitability is **rate of return on common shareholders' equity**, which is often shortened to **return on shareholders' equity**, or simply, *return on equity*. This ratio shows the relationship between net income and common shareholders' investment in the company. To compute this ratio, we first subtract preferred dividends from net income. This calculation leaves only net income available to the common shareholders, which is needed to compute the ratio. We then divide net income available to common shareholders by the average shareholders' equity during the year. Common shareholders' equity is total shareholders' equity minus preferred equity. Palisades Furniture's rate of return on common shareholders' equity follows:

Formula		Rate of Return on Total Assets of Palisades Furniture, Inc. 19X7	Retail Furniture Industry Average
Rate of return on common shareholders' equity	=	$\dfrac{\text{Net income} - \text{preferred dividends}}{\text{Average common shareholders' equity}}$	$\dfrac{\$48,000 - \$0}{\$338,000} = .142$	.093

We compute average equity using the beginning and ending balances [($356,000 + $320,000)/2 = $338,000]. Observe that common shareholders' equity includes Retained Earnings.

Compare Palisades Furniture's rate of return on common shareholder's equity with rates of other companies:

Company	Rate of Return on Common Shareholders' Equity
TransCanada PipeLines Ltd. (Pipeline)	.1286
Hudson's Bay Co. (Retailing)	.1088
Domtar Inc. (Forest Products)	.1141
Thompson Corp. (Publishing)	.1423

Observe that Palisades Furniture's return on equity (14.2 percent) is higher than return on assets (10.1 percent). This difference results from borrowing at one rate—say,

8 percent—and investing the funds to earn a higher rate, such as the firm's 14.2 percent return on shareholders' equity. This practice is called **trading on the equity,** or the use of **leverage**. It is directly related to the debt ratio. The higher the debt ratio, the higher the leverage. Companies that finance operations with debt are said to *lever* their positions. Leverage increases the risk to common shareholders.

For Palisades Furniture and many other companies, leverage increases profitability. That is not always the case, however. Leverage can also have a negative impact on profitability. If revenues drop, debt and interest expense still must be paid. Therefore, leverage is a double-edged sword, increasing profits during good times but compounding losses during bad times.

Earnings per Share of Common Stock

Earnings per share of common stock or, simply, **earnings per share (EPS)** is perhaps the most widely quoted of all financial statistics. EPS is the only ratio that must appear on the face of the income statement. EPS is the amount of net income per share of the company's *common* stock. Earnings per share is computed by dividing net income available to common shareholders by the number of common shares outstanding during the year. Preferred dividends are subtracted from net income because the preferred shareholders have a prior claim to their dividends. Palisades Furniture, Inc., has no preferred stock outstanding and so has no preferred dividends. The firm's EPS for 19X7 and 19X6 follow (the company had 10,000 shares of common stock outstanding throughout 19X6 and 19X7):

Short Exercise:

Refer to the Short Exercise on page 927. Take the companies' beginning total assets to be $280 and $510 and their beginning common shareholders' equity to be $130 and $140, respectively. Compute (1) the rate of return on total assets and (2) the rate of return on common shareholders' equity. **A:**

(1) A Co.: $\dfrac{\$20 + \$6}{(\$280 + \$300)/2} = 9.0\%$

     B Co.: $\dfrac{\$50 + \$30}{(\$510 + \$550)/2} = 15.1\%$

(2) A Co.: $\dfrac{\$20 - \$0}{(\$130 + \$150)/2} = 14.3\%$

     B Co.: $\dfrac{\$50 - \$1}{(\$140 + \$150)/2} = 33.8\%$

		Earnings per Share of Palisades Furniture, Inc.	
Formula		19X7	19X6
Earnings per share of common stock (EPS) $=$	$\dfrac{\text{Net income} - \text{preferred dividends}}{\text{Number of shares of common stock outstanding}}$	$\dfrac{\$48,000 - \$0}{10,000} = \$4.80$	$\dfrac{\$26,000 - \$0}{10,000} = \$2.60$

Palisades Furniture's EPS increased 85 percent. Its shareholders should not expect such a significant boost in EPS every year. Most companies strive to increase EPS by 10 to 15 percent annually, and the more successful companies do so. However, even the most dramatic upward trends include an occasional bad year.

Analyzing Stock as an Investment _____

Investors purchase stock to earn a return on their investment. This return consists of two parts: (1) gains (or losses) from selling the stock at a price that is different from the investors' purchase price, and (2) dividends, the periodic distributions to shareholders. The ratios we examine in this section help analysts evaluate stock in terms of market price or dividend payments.

Price/Earnings Ratio

The **price/earnings ratio** is the ratio of the market price of a share of common stock to the company's earnings per share. This ratio, abbreviated P/E, appears in *The Financial Post* stock listings. P/E plays an important part in evaluating decisions to buy, hold, and sell stocks.

The price/earnings ratios of Palisades Furniture, Inc., follow. The market price of its common stock was $50 at the end of 19X7 and $35 at the end of 19X6. These prices can be obtained from such sources as financial publications, a stockbroker, or an on-line database.

Short Exercise:
In the Short Exercise on page 927, use the following information:

	A Co.	B Co.
Market price per share	$20	30
Shares of common stock outstanding	25	10
Dividend per share	0.75	1.50

Compute the (1) EPS, (2) P/E, and (3) dividend yield. **A:**

(1) A Co.: $\dfrac{\$20 - \$0}{25 \text{ shares}} = \$0.80$

  B Co.: $\dfrac{\$50 - \$1}{10 \text{ shares}} = \$4.90$

(2) A Co.: 25 ($20/$0.80)
  B Co.: 6.1 ($30/$4.90)

(3) A Co.: 3.75% ($0.75/$20)
  B Co.: 5% ($1.50/$30)

Price/Earnings Ratio of Palisades Furniture, Inc.

Formula		19X7	19X6
Price/ earnings ratio	= $\dfrac{\text{Market price per share of common stock}}{\text{Earnings per share}}$	$\dfrac{\$50.00}{\$4.80} = 10.4$	$\dfrac{\$35.00}{\$2.60} = 13.5$

Given Palisades Furniture's 19X7 price/earnings ratio of 10.4, we would say that the company's stock is selling at 10.4 times earnings. The decline from the 19X6 P/E ratio of 13.5 is not a cause for alarm because the numerator (market price of the stock) is not under Palisades Furniture's control. The net income is more controllable, and it increased during 19X7. Like most other ratios, P/E ratios vary from industry to industry. P/E ratios range from 8 to 12 for electric utilities (Nova Scotia Power, for example) to more than 50 for "glamor stocks" such as CIC Canola Industries Canada (61.7), a food products company, and Ranchmen's Resources (55.6), an oil and gas company.

The higher a stock's P/E ratio, the higher its *downside risk*—the risk that the stock's market price will fall. Many investors interpret a sharp increase in a stock's P/E ratio as a signal to sell the stock.

Dividend Yield

Dividend yield is the ratio of dividends per share of stock to the stock's market price per share. This ratio measures the percentage of a stock's market value that is returned annually as dividends, an important concern of shareholders. *Preferred shareholders,* who invest primarily to receive dividends, pay special attention to this ratio.

Palisades Furniture paid annual cash dividends of $1.20 per share in 19X7 and $1.00 in 19X6 and market prices of the company's common stock were $50 in 19X7 and $35.00 in 19X6. Palisades Furniture's dividend yields follow:

Dividend Yield on Common Stock of Palisades Furniture, Inc.

Formula		19X7	19X6
Dividend yield on common stock	= $\dfrac{\text{Dividend per share of common stock}}{\text{Market price per share of common stock}}$	$\dfrac{\$1.20}{\$50.00} = .024$	$\dfrac{\$1.00}{\$35.00} = .029$

An investor who buys Palisades Furniture common stock for $50 can expect to receive almost 2½ percent of their investment annually in the form of cash dividends. Dividend yields vary widely, from 5 to 8 percent for older established firms (like BCE Inc. and Consumers Gas Co. Ltd.) down to a range of 0 to 3 percent for growth-oriented companies (like Rogers Communications and Magna International). Palisades Furniture's dividend yield places the company in the second group.

Book Value per Share of Common Stock

Book value per share of common stock is simply common shareholders' equity divided by the number of shares of common stock outstanding. Common shareholders' equity equals total shareholders' equity less preferred equity. Palisades Furniture has no preferred stock outstanding. Its book value per share of common stock ratios follow. Recall that 10,000 shares of common stock were outstanding at the end of years 19X7 and 19X6.

Formula	Book Value per Share of the Common Stock of Palisades Furniture, Inc.	
	19X7	19X6
Book value per share of common stock $=$ $\dfrac{\text{Total shareholder's equity} - \text{preferred equity}}{\text{Number of shares of common stock outstanding}}$	$\dfrac{\$356{,}000 - \$0}{10{,}000} = \$35.60$	$\dfrac{\$320{,}000 - \$0}{10{,}000} = \$32.00$

Many experts argue that book value is not useful for investment analysis. It bears no relationship to market value and provides little information beyond shareholders' equity reported on the balance sheet. But other investors base their investment decisions on book value. For example, some investors rank stocks on the basis of the ratio of market price to book value. To these investors, the lower the ratio, the more attractive the stock. These investors are called "value" investors, as contrasted with "growth" investors, who focus more on trends in a company's net income.

Limitations of Financial Analysis: The Complexity of Business Decisions

> **OBJECTIVE 6**
> Use ratios in decision-making

Business decisions are made in a world of uncertainty. As useful as ratios may be, they do have limitations. We may liken their use in decision-making to a physician's use of a thermometer. A reading of 39°C indicates that something is wrong with the patient, but the temperature alone does not indicate what the problem is or how to cure it.

In financial analysis, a sudden drop in a company's current ratio signals that *something* is wrong, but this change does not identify the problem or show how to correct it. The business manager must analyze the figures that go into the ratio to determine whether current assets have decreased, current liabilities have increased, or both. If current assets have dropped, is the problem a cash shortage? Are accounts receivable down? Are inventories too low? Only by analyzing the individual items that make up the ratio can the manager determine how to solve the problem. The manager must evaluate data on all ratios in the light of other information about the company and about its particular line of business, such as increased competition or a slowdown in the economy.

Legislation, international affairs, competition, scandals, and many other factors can turn profits into losses, and vice versa. To be most useful, ratios should be analyzed over a period of years to take into account a representative group of these factors. Any one year, or even any two years, may not be representative of the company's performance over the long term.

Efficient Markets, Management Action, and Investor Decisions

Much research about accounting and finance has focused on whether the stock markets are "efficient." An **efficient capital market** is one in which the market prices fully reflect all information available to the public. Stocks are priced in full recognition of all publicly accessible data.

That a market is efficient has implications for management action and for investor decisions. It means that managers cannot fool the market with accounting gimmicks. As long as sufficient information is available, the market as a whole can translate accounting data into a "fair" price for the company's stock.

Suppose you are the president of CompSys Ltd. Reported earnings per share are $4 and the stock price is $40—so the price-earnings ratio is 10. You believe the

corporation's stock is underpriced in comparison with other companies in the same industry. To correct this situation you are considering changing your method of depreciation from accelerated to straight-line. The accounting change will increase earnings per share to $5. Will the stock then rise to $50? Probably not. The company's stock price will likely remain at $40 because the market can understand the accounting change. After all, the company merely changed its method of computing depreciation. There is no effect on the company's cash flows, and its economic position is unchanged.

In an efficient market, the search for "underpriced" stock is fruitless unless the investor has relevant private information. Moreover, it is unlawful to invest based on inside information—information that is available only to corporate management. For outside investors in an efficient market, an appropriate investment strategy seeks to manage risk, to diversify, and to minimize transaction costs. The role of financial statement analysis consists mainly of identifying the risks of various stocks in order to manage the risk of the overall investment portfolio.

Summary Problem for Your Review

The following financial data adapted are from the annual report of The Gap, Inc., which operates The Gap and Banana Republic clothing stores.

The Gap, Inc.
Five-Year Selected Financial Data

Operating Results	19X5	19X4	19X3	19X2	19X1
(Dollar amounts in thousands)					
Net sales	$2,960	$2,519	$1,934	$1,587	$1,252
Cost of goods sold and occupancy expenses, excluding depreciation and amortization	1,856	1,496	1,188	1,007	814
Interest expense (net)	4	4	1	3	3
Income from operations	340	371	237	163	126
Income taxes	129	141	92	65	52
Net earnings	211	230	145	98	74
Cash dividends	44	41	30	23	18
Financial Position					
Merchandise inventory	366	314	247	243	193
Total assets	1,379	1,147	777	579	481
Working capital	355	236	579	129	434
Current ratio	2.06:1	1.71:1	1.39:1	1.69:1	1.70:1
Shareholders' equity	888	678	466	338	276
Average number of shares of common stock outstanding (in thousands)	144	142	142	141	145

Required

Compute the following ratios for 19X5 through 19X2, and evaluate The Gap's operating results. Are operating results strong or weak? Did they improve or deteriorate during the four-year period?

1. Gross profit percentage
2. Net income as percent of sales
3. Earnings per share
4. Inventory turnover
5. Times-interest-earned ratio
6. Rate of return on shareholders' equity

SOLUTION TO REVIEW PROBLEM

	19X5	19X4	19X3	19X2
1. Gross profit percentage	$\dfrac{\$2,960 - \$1,856}{\$2,960}$	$\dfrac{\$2,519 - \$1,496}{\$2,519}$	$\dfrac{\$1,934 - \$1,188}{\$1,934}$	$\dfrac{\$1,587 - \$1,007}{\$1,587}$
	$= 37.3\%$	$= 40.6\%$	$= 38.6\%$	$= 36.5\%$
2. Net income as a percent of sales	$\dfrac{\$211}{\$2,960} = 7.1\%$	$\dfrac{\$230}{\$2,519} = 9.1\%$	$\dfrac{\$145}{\$1,934} = 7.5\%$	$\dfrac{\$98}{\$1,587} = 6.2\%$
3. Earnings per share	$\dfrac{\$211}{144} = \$1.47$	$\dfrac{\$230}{142} = \$1.62$	$\dfrac{\$145}{142} = \$1.02$	$\dfrac{\$98}{141} = \$0.70$
4. Inventory turnover	$\dfrac{\$1,856}{(\$366 + \$314)/2}$	$\dfrac{\$1,496}{(\$314 + \$247)/2}$	$\dfrac{\$1,188}{(\$247 + \$243)/2}$	$\dfrac{\$1,007}{(\$243 + \$193)/2}$
	$= 5.5$ times	$= 5.3$ times	$= 4.8$ times	$= 4.6$ times
5. Times-interest-earned ratio	$\dfrac{\$340}{\$4} = 85$ times	$\dfrac{\$371}{\$4} = 93$ times	$\dfrac{\$237}{\$1} = 237$ times	$\dfrac{\$163}{\$3} = 54$ times
6. Rate of return on shareholders' equity	$\dfrac{\$211}{(\$888 + \$678)/2}$	$\dfrac{\$230}{(\$678 + \$466)/2}$	$\dfrac{\$145}{(\$466 + \$338)/2}$	$\dfrac{\$98}{(\$338 + \$276)/2}$
	$= 26.9\%$	$= 40.2\%$	$= 36.1\%$	$= 31.9\%$

Evaluation: During this four-year period The Gap's operating results were outstanding. Operating results improved, with all ratio values but return on shareholders' equity higher in 19X5 than in 19X2. Moreover, all the performance measures indicate high levels of income and return to investors.

Summary

1. Perform a horizontal analysis of comparative financial statements. Accounting provides information for decision making. Banks loan money, investors buy stocks, and managers run businesses on the basis of the analysis of accounting information. *Horizontal analysis* shows the dollar amount and the percentage change in each financial statement item from one period to the next.

2. Perform a vertical analysis of financial statements. *Vertical analysis* shows the shows the relationship of each item in a financial statement to its total: total assets on the balance sheet and net sales on the income statement.

3. Prepare common-size financial statements. *Common-size statements*—a form of vertical analysis—show the component percentages of the items in a statement. Investment advisory services report common-size statements. Investment advisory services report common-size statements for various industries, and analysts use them to compare a company with its competitors and with the industry averages.

4. Use statement of changes in financial position in decision-making. The *statement of changes in financial position* shows the net cash inflow or outflow caused by a

company's operating, financing, and investing activities. By analyzing the inflows and outflows of cash listed on this statement, an analyst can see where a business's cash comes from and how it is being spent.

   5. *Compute the standard financial ratios used for decision-making.* *Ratios* play an important part in business decision-making because they show relationships between financial statement items.

   6. *Use ratios in decision-making.* Analysis of ratios over a period of time is an important way to track a company's progress.

Self-Study Questions

Test your understanding of the chapter by marking the best answer for each of the following questions:

1. Net income was $240,000 in 19X4, $210,000 in 19X5, and $252,000 in 19X6. The change from 19X5 to 19X6 is a (an) *(p. 914)*
   a. Increase of 5 percent
   b. Increase of 20 percent
   c. Decrease of 10 percent
   d. Decrease of 12.5 percent

2. Vertical analysis of a financial statement shows *(p. 916)*
   a. Trend percentages
   b. The percentage change in an item from period to period
   c. The relationship of an item to the total on the statement
   d. Net income expressed as a percentage of shareholders' equity

3. Common-size statements are useful for comparing *(p. 917)*
   a. Changes in the makeup of assets from period to period
   b. Different companies
   c. A company to its industry
   d. All of the above

4. The statement of changes in financial position is used for decision-making by *(pp. 921–922)*
   a. Reporting where cash came from and how it was spent
   b. Indicating how net income was earned
   c. Giving the ratio relationships between selected items
   d. Showing a horizontal analysis of cash flows

5. Cash is $10,000, net accounts receivable amount to $22,000, inventory is $55,000, prepaid expenses total $3,000, and current liabilities are $40,000. What is the acid-test ratio? *(p. 928)*
   a. .25
   b. .80
   c. 2.18
   d. 2.25

6. Inventory turnover is computed by dividing *(p. 929)*
   a. Sales revenue by average inventory
   b. Cost of goods sold by average inventory
   c. Credit sales by average inventory
   d. Average inventory by cost of goods sold

7. Capp Corporation is experiencing a severe cash shortage due to inability to collect accounts receivable. The decision tool most likely to help identify the appropriate corrective action is the *(pp. 930–931)*
   a. Acid-test ratio
   b. Inventory turnover
   c. Times-interest-earned ratio
   d. Day's sales in receivables

8. Analysis of Mendoza Ltd. financial statements over five years reveals that sales are growing steadily, the debt ratio is higher than the industry average and is increasing, interest coverage is decreasing, return on total assets is declining, and earnings per share of common stock is decreasing. Considered together, these ratios suggest that *(pp. 931–933)*

   a. Mendoza should pursue collections of receivables more vigorously

   b. Competition is taking sales away from Mendoza

   c. Mendoza is in a declining industry

   d. The company's debt burden is hurting profitability

9. Which of the following is most likely to be true? *(pp. 933–934)*

   a. Return on common equity exceeds return on total assets.

   b. Return on total assets exceeds return on common equity.

   c. Return on total assets equals return on common equity.

   d. None of the above

10. How are financial ratios used in decision-making? *(p. 937)*

   a. They remove the uncertainty of the business environment.

   b. They give clear signals about the appropriate action to take.

   c. They can help identify the reasons for success and failure in business, but decision-making requires information beyond the ratios.

   d. They are not useful because decision-making is too complex.

Answers to the Self-Study Questions follow the Accounting Vocabulary.

Accounting Vocabulary

Accounts receivable turnover *(p. 930)*
Acid-test ratio *(p. 928)*
Book value per share of common stock *(p. 936)*
Common-size statement *(p. 917)*
Current ratio *(p. 926)*
Days' sales in receivables *(p. 930)*
Debt ratio *(p. 931)*
Dividend yield *(p. 936)*
Earnings per share (EPS) *(p. 935)*
Efficient capital market *(p. 937)*
Horizontal analysis *(p. 914)*
Inventory turnover *(p. 929)*
Leverage *(p. 935)*
Long-term solvency *(p. 913)*
Price/earnings ratio *(p. 935)*
Rate of return on common shareholders' equity *(p. 934)*
Rate of return on net sales *(p. 933)*
Rate of return on total assets *(p. 933)*
Return on shareholders' equity *(p. 934)*
Short-term liquidity *(p. 913)*
Times-interest-earned ratio *(p. 932)*
Trading on the equity *(p. 935)*
Vertical analysis *(p. 916)*
Working capital *(p. 926)*

Answers to Self-Study Questions

1. b $252,000 − $210,000 = $42,000; $42,000/$210,000 = .20
2. c
3. d
4. a
5. b ($10,000 + $22,000)/$40,000 = .80
6. b
7. d
8. d
9. a
10. c

ASSIGNMENT MATERIAL _____

Questions

1. Identify two groups of users of accounting information and the decisions they base on accounting data.
2. What are three analytical tools that are based on accounting information?
3. Briefly describe horizontal analysis. How do decision-makers use this tool of analysis?
4. What is vertical analysis, and what is its purpose?
5. What use is made of common-size statements?
6. State how an investor might analyze the statement of changes in financial position. How might the investor analyze investing activities data?
7. Why are ratios an important tool of financial analysis? Give an example.
8. Identify two ratios used to measure a company's ability to pay current liabilities. Show how they are computed.
9. Why is the acid-test ratio called by this name?
10. What does the inventory-turnover ratio measure?
11. Suppose the days'-sales-in-receivables ratio of Payette, Inc., increased from 36 at January 1 to 43 at December 31. Is this a good sign or a bad sign about the company? What would Payette management do in response to this change?
12. Company A's debt ratio has increased from .50 to .70. Identify a decision-maker to whom this increase is important, and state how the increase affects this party's decisions about the company.
13. Which ratio measures the *effect of debt* on (a) financial position (the balance sheet) and (b) the company's ability to pay interest expense (the income statement)?
14. Company A is a chain of grocery stores, and Company B is a computer manufacturer. Which company is likely to have the higher (a) current ratio, (b) inventory turnover, and (c) rate of return on sales? Give your reasons.
15. Identify four ratios used to measure a company's profitability. Show how to compute these ratios and state what information each ratio provides.
16. The price/earnings ratio of Inco was 18.8, and the price/earnings ratio of Cominco was 11.5. Which company did the stock market favor? Explain.
17. Irwin Toy paid cash dividends of $.22 (22 cents) per share when the market price of the company's stock was $7.00. What was the dividend yield on Irwin's stock? What does dividend yield measure?
18. Hold all other factors constant and indicate whether each of the following situations generally signals good or bad news about a company:
    a. Increase in current ratio
    b. Decrease in inventory turnover
    c. Increase in debt ratio
    d. Decrease in interest-coverage ratio
    e. Increase in return on sales
    f. Decrease in earnings per share
    g. Increase in price/earnings ratio
    h. Increase in book value per share
19. Explain how an investor might use book value per share of stock in making an investment decision.
20. Describe how decision-makers use ratio data. What are the limitations of ratios?

Exercises

Exercise 19-1   *Computing year-to-year changes in working capital*   **(Obj. 1)**

What was the amount of change, and the percentage change, in Camrose Corporation's working capital during 19X4 and 19X5? Is this trend favorable or unfavorable?

	Year 5	Year 4	Year 3
Total current assets	$312,000	$290,000	$280,000
Total current liabilities	150,000	117,000	140,000

Exercise 19-2   *Horizontal analysis of an income statement*   **(Obj. 1)**

Prepare a horizontal analysis of the following comparative income statement of Syntex Corp. Round percentage changes to the nearest one-tenth percent (three decimal places):

Syntex Corp Comparative Income Statement years ended December 31, 19X9 and 19X8		
	19X9	19X8
Total Revenue	$410,000	$373,000
Expenses		
Cost of goods sold	$202,000	$188,000
Selling and general expenses	98,000	93,000
Interest expense	7,000	4,000
Income tax expense	42,000	37,000
Total expenses	349,000	322,000
Net Income	$ 61,000	$ 51,000

Why did net income increase by a higher percentage than total revenues increased during 19X9?

Exercise 19-3   *Computing trend percentages*   **(Obj. 1)**

Compute trend percentages for net sales and net income for the following five-year period, using year 1 as the base year:

	Year 5	Year 4	Year 3	Year 2	Year 1
		(Amounts in thousands)			
Net sales	$1,410	$1,187	$1,106	$1,009	$1,043
Net income	117	114	83	71	85

Which grew more during the period, net sales or net income?

Exercise 19-4   *Vertical analysis of a balance sheet*   **(Obj. 2)**

Sheila Chan, Inc., has requested that you perform a vertical analysis of its balance sheet to determine the component percentages of its assets, liabilities, and shareholders' equity.

Sheila Chan, Inc.
Balance Sheet
December 31, 19X3

Assets

Total current assets	$ 72,000
Long-term investments	35,000
Property, plant, and equipment, net	217,000
Total assets	$324,000

Liabilities

Total current liabilities	$ 58,000
Long-term debt	118,000
Total liabilities	176,000

Shareholders' Equity

Total shareholders' equity	148,000
Total liabilities and shareholders' equity	$324,000

Exercise 19-5   *Preparing a common-size income statement*   **(Obj. 3)**

Prepare a comparative common-size income statement for Syntex Corp., using the 19X9 and 19X8 data of Exercise 19-2 and rounding percentages to one-tenth percent (three decimal places).

Exercise 19-6   *Analyzing the statement of changes in financial position*   **(Obj. 4)**

Identify any weaknesses revealed by the statement of changes in financial position of Nemmer Electric, Inc.

Nemmer Electric, Inc.
Statement of Changes in Financial Position
for the current year

Operating activities		
Income from operations		$ 52,000
Add (subtract) noncash items		
Depreciation	$ 23,000	
Net increase in current assets other than cash	(15,000)	
Net increase in current liabilities exclusive of short-term debt	11,000	19,000
Net cash inflow from operating activities		71,000
Financing activities		
Issuance of bonds payable	$114,000	
Payment of short-term debt	(171,000)	
Payment of long-term debt	(79,000)	
Payment of dividends	(42,000)	
Net cash outflow from financing activities		(178,000)
Investing activities		
Sale of property, plant, and equipment		101,000
Increase in cash		($ 6,000)

Exercise 19-7   *Computing five ratios*   **(Obj. 5)**

The financial statements of Manixon Ltd. include the following items:

	Current Year	Preceding Year
Balance sheet		
Cash..........	$ 17,000	$ 22,000
Short-term investments.....................	11,000	26,000
Net receivables	64,000	73,000
Inventory.......................................	87,000	71,000
Prepaid expenses.............................	6,000	8,000
Total current assets...........................	185,000	200,000
Total current liabilities......................	121,000	91,000
Income statement		
Net credit sales	$454,000	
Cost of goods sold............................	257,000	

= 68,500
ave = 79

Required

Compute the following ratios for the current year: (a) current ratio, (b) acid-test ratio, (c) inventory turnover, (d) accounts receivable turnover, and (e) days' sales in average receivables.

Exercise 19-8   *Analyzing the ability to pay current liabilities*   **(Obj. 5, 6)**

Red Deer Control Systems, Inc., has requested that you determine whether the company's ability to pay its current liabilities and long-term debts has improved or deteriorated during 19X2. To answer this question, compute the following ratios for 19X2 and 19X1: (a) current ratio, (b) acid-test ratio, (c) debt ratio, and (d) times-interest-earned ratio. Summarize the results of your analysis.

	19X2	19X1
Cash...	$ 21,000	$ 47,000
Short-term investments..........................	28,000	—
Net receivables	102,000	116,000
Inventory.......................................	226,000	263,000
Prepaid expenses.................................	11,000	9,000
Total assets......................................	503,000	489,000
Total current liabilities...........................	205,000	241,000
Total liabilities...................................	261,000	273,000
Income from operations	165,000	158,000
Interest expense...................................	36,000	39,000

Exercise 19-9   *Analyzing profitability*   **(Obj. 5, 6)**

Compute four ratios that measure ability to earn profits for E. Singh Ltd. whose comparative income statement appears below. Additional data follow.

E. Singh Ltd.
Comparative Income Statement
years ended December 31, 19X6 and 19X5

	19X6	19X5
Net sales...	$174,000	$158,000
Cost of goods sold.....................................	93,000	86,000
Gross profit...	81,000	72,000
Selling and general expenses.........................	48,000	41,000
Income from operations	33,000	31,000
Interest expense.......................................	21,000	10,000
Income before income tax	12,000	21,000
Income tax expense....................................	4,000	8,000
Net income...	$ 8,000	$ 13,000

Additional data	19X6	19X5
a. Average total assets...	$204,000	$191,000
b. Average common shareholders' equity	96,000	89,000
c. Preferred dividends	3,000	3,000
d. Shares of common stock outstanding............................	20,000	20,000

Did the company's operating performance improve or deteriorate during 19X6?

Exercise 19-10   *Evaluating a stock as an investment*   **(Obj. 5, 6)**

Evaluate the common stock of Lon Sys Ltd. as an investment. Specifically, use the three stock ratios to determine whether the stock has increased or decreased in attractiveness during the past year.

	Current Year	Preceding Year
Net income	$ 58,000	$ 55,000
Dividends (half on preferred stock)	28,000	28,000
Common shareholders' equity at year end		
(80,000 shares)...	530,000	500,000
Preferred shareholders' equity at year end	200,000	200,000
Market price per share of common stock at year end........	$10.25	$7.75

Challenge Exercises

Exercise 19-11   *Using ratio data to reconstruct a real company's income statement*
              (Obj. 2, 3, 5)

The following data are from the financial statements of McDonald's Corporation, operator of more than 13,000 restaurants in 65 countries.

	Dollars in Millions
Average shareholders' equity	$3,605
Interest expense	$ 413
Preferred stock...	–0–
Operating income as a percent of sales.....	24.04%
Rate of return on sales	11.13%
Rate of return on shareholders' equity......	20.50%
Income tax rate...	37.53%

Required

Complete the following condensed income statement. Report amounts to the nearest million dollars:

Sales	$?
Operating expense....................................	?
Operating income	?
Interest expense..	?
Pretax income...	?
Income tax expense	?
Net income...	$?

Exercise 19-12   *Using ratio data to reconstruct a real company's balance sheet*
              (Obj. 2, 3, 5)

The following data are from the financial statements of Valu Add Stores, Inc.

	Dollars in Thousands
Total liabilities	$11,806
Preferred stock	–0–
Total current assets	$10,196
Accumulated depreciation	$ 448
Debt ratio	57.408%
Current ratio	1.51

Required

Complete the following condensed balance sheet. Report amounts to the nearest thousand dollars:

Current assets		$?
Property, plant, and equipment	$?	
Less Accumulated depreciation	?	?
Total assets		$?
Current liabilities		$?
Long-term liabilities		?
Shareholders' equity		?
Total liabilities and shareholders' equity		$?

Problems   *(Group A)*

Problem 19-1A   *Trend percentages, return on common equity and comparison with the industry   (Obj. 1, 5, 6)*

Net sales, net income, and common shareholders' equity for Bear Utilities Ltd. for a six-year period follow:

	19X7	19X6	19X5	19X4	19X3	19X2
			(Amounts in thousands)			
Net sales	$761	$714	$641	$662	$642	$634
Net income	61	45	32	48	41	40
Ending common shareholders' equity	386	354	330	296	272	252

Required

1. Compute trend percentages for 19X3 through 19X7, using 19X2 as the base year.
2. Compute the rate of return on average common shareholders' equity for 19X3 through 19X7, rounding to three decimal places. In this industry, rates of 13 percent are average, rates above 16 percent are considered good, and rates above 20 percent are viewed as outstanding.
3. How does Bear Utilities' return on common shareholders' equity compare with the industry?

Problem 19-2A   *Common-size statements, analysis of profitability, and comparison with the industry   (Obj. 2, 3, 5, 6)*

Alto Auto Glass Ltd. has asked your help in comparing the company's profit performance and financial position with the average for the auto parts retail industry. The proprietor has given you the company's income statement and balance sheet, and also the following industry average data for retailers of auto parts:

Alto Auto Glass Ltd. Income Statement Compared with Industry Average year ended December 31, 19X6		
	Alto	Industry Average
Net sales	$781,000	100.0%
Cost of goods sold	497,000	65.8
Gross profit	284,000	34.2
Operating expenses	163,000	19.7
Operating income	121,000	14.5
Other expenses	5,000	.4
Net income..........................	$116,000	14.1%

Alto Auto Glass Ltd. Balance Sheet Compared with Industry Average December 31, 19X6		
	Alto	Industry Average
Current assets	$350,000	70.9%
Fixed assets, net...................	74,000	23.6
Intangible assets, net...........	4,000	.8
Other assets	22,000	4.7
Total.......................................	$450,000	100.0%
Current liabilities.................	$207,000	48.1%
Long-term liabilities............	62,000	16.6
Shareholders' equity	181,000	35.3
Total.......................................	$450,000	100.0%

Required

1. Prepare a two-column common-size income statement and a two-column common-size balance sheet for Alto Auto Glass. The first column of each statement should present Alto's common-size statement, and the second column should show the industry averages.

2. For the profitability analysis, compute Alto's (a) ratio of gross profit to net sales, (b) ratio of operating income to net sales, and (c) ratio of net income to net sales. Compare these figures to the industry averages. Is Alto's profit performance better or worse than the industry average?

3. For the analysis of financial position, compute Alto's (a) ratio of current assets to total assets and (b) ratio of shareholders' equity to total assets. Compare these ratios to the industry averages. Is Alto's financial position better or worse than the industry averages?

Problem 19-3A   *Using the statement of changes in financial position for decision-making (Obj. 4)*

You have been asked to evaluate two companies as possible investments. The two companies, similar in size, buy computers, airplanes, and other high-cost assets to lease to other businesses. Assume that all other available information has been analyzed, and the decision on which company's stock to purchase depends on the information given in their statements of changes in financial position shown on the next page.

Required

Discuss the relative strengths and weaknesses of each company. Conclude your discussion by recommending one company's stock as an investment.

Problem 19-4A   *Effects of business transactions on selected ratios (Obj. 4)*

Financial statement data of Menno Industries Ltd. include the following items:

Cash	$ 22,000
Short-term investments	19,000
Accounts receivable, net	83,000
Inventories	141,000
Prepaid expenses	8,000
Total assets	657,000

Allied Leasing Corp.
Statements of Changes in Financial Position
for the years ended September 30, 19X5 and 19X4

	19X5	19X4
Operating activities		
Income from operations	$ 37,000	$ 74,000
Add (subtract) noncash items:		
Total	14,000	(4,000)
Net cash flow from operating activities	51,000	70,000
Financing activities		
Issuance of short-term notes payable	$ 73,000	$ 19,000
Issuance of long-term notes payable	31,000	42,000
Payment of short-term notes payable	(181,000)	(148,000)
Payment of long-term notes payable	(55,000)	(32,000)
Net cash outflow from financing activities	(132,000)	(119,000)
Investing activities		
Purchase of property, plant, and equipment	$ (13,000)	$ (3,000)
Sale of property, plant, and equipment	86,000	79,000
Sale of long-term investments	13,000	—
Net cash outflow from investing activities	86,000	76,000
Increase in cash	$ 5,000	$ 27,000
Cash summary from balance sheet:		
Cash balance at beginning of year	$ 31,000	$ 4,000
Increase (decrease) in cash during the year	5,000	27,000
Cash balance at the end of year	$ 36,000	$ 31,000

Can Lease, Inc.
Statements of Changes in Financial Position
for the years ended September 30, 19X5 and 19X4

	19X5	19X4
Operating activities		
Income from operations	$ 79,000	$ 71,000
Add (subtract) noncash items:		
Total	19,000	—
Net cash inflow from operating activities	98,000	71,000
Financing activities		
Issuance of long-term notes payable	$ 46,000	$ 43,000
Payment of short-term notes payable	(15,000)	(40,000)
Payment of cash dividends	(12,000)	(9,000)
Net cash inflow (outflow) from financing activities	19,000	(6,000)
Investing activities		
Purchase of property, plant, and equipment	$(121,000)	$(91,000)
Sale of long-term investments	13,000	18,000
Net cash outflow from investing activities	(108,000)	(73,000)
Increase (decrease) in cash	$ 9,000	$ (8,000)
Cash summary from balance sheet:		
Cash balance at beginning of year	$ 72,000	$ 80,000
Increase (decrease) in cash during the year	9,000	(8,000)
Cash balance at the end of year	$ 81,000	$ 72,000

Short-term notes payable	49,000
Accounts payable	103,000
Accrued liabilities	38,000
Long-term notes payable	160,000
Other long-term liabilities	31,000
Net income	71,000
Number of common shares outstanding	40,000

Required

1. Compute Menno's current ratio, debt ratio, and earnings per share.
2. Compute each of the three ratios after evaluating the effect of each transaction that follows. Consider each transaction separately.
   a. Purchased merchandise of $26,000 on account, debiting Inventory.
   b. Paid off long-term liabilities, $31,000.
   c. Declared, but did not pay, a $22,000 cash dividend on common stock.
   d. Borrowed $85,000 on a long-term note payable.
   e. Sold short-term investments for $18,000 (cost, $11,000); assume no income tax on the gain.
   f. Issued 5,000 shares of common stock, receiving cash of $120,000.
   g. Received cash on account $19,000.
   h. Paid short-term notes payable, $32,000.

Use the following format for your answer:

Requirement 1		**Current Ratio**	**Debt Ratio**	**Earnings per Share**

Requirement 2	**Transaction (letter)**	**Current Ratio**	**Debt Ratio**	**Earnings per Share**

Problem 19-5A   *Using ratios to evaluate a stock investment*   **(Obj. 5, 6)**

Comparative financial statement data of Wahl Furniture Ltd. appear below:

Wahl Furniture Ltd.
Comparative Income Statement
years ended December 31, 19X4 and 19X3

	19X4	19X3
Net sales...	$462,000	$427,000
Cost of goods sold...	229,000	218,000
Gross profit..	233,000	209,000
Operating expenses...	136,000	134,000
Income from operations	97,000	75,000
Interest expense..	11,000	12,000
Income before income tax	86,000	63,000
Income tax expense...	30,000	27,000
Net income..	$ 56,000	$ 36,000

Wahl Furniture Ltd.
Comparative Balance Sheet
December 31, 19X4 and 19X3
(selected 19X2 amounts given for computation of ratios)

	19X4	19X3	19X2
Current assets			
Cash	$ 96,000	$ 97,000	
Current receivables, net	112,000	116,000	$103,000
Inventories	172,000	162,000	207,000
Prepaid expenses...	16,000	7,000	
Total current assets	396,000	382,000	

Property, plant and equipment, net	189,000	178,000	
Total assets	$585,000	$560,000	598,000
Total current liabilities.....................................	$206,000	$223,000	
Long-term liabilities	119,000	117,000	
Total liabilities	325,000	340,000	
Preferred shareholders' equity, $6.00	100,000	100,000	
Common shareholders' equity.........................	160,000	120,000	90,000
Total liabilities and shareholders' equity........	$585,000	$560,000	

Other information:

a. Market price of Wahl common stock: $49 at December 31, 19X4, and $32.50 at December 31, 19X3.

b. Common shares outstanding: 10,000 during 19X4 and 9,000 during 19X3.

c. Preferred shares outstanding: 1,000 during both years.

d. All sales on credit.

Required

1. Compute the following ratios for 19X4 and 19X3:
   a. Current ratio
   b. Inventory turnover
   c. Accounts receivable turnover
   d. Times-interest-earned ratio
   e. Return on assets
   f. Return on common shareholders' equity
   g. Earnings per share of common stock
   h. Price/earnings ratio
   i. Book value per share of common stock

2. Decide (a) whether Wahl's financial position improved or deteriorated during 19X4, and (b) whether the investment attractiveness of its common stock appears to have increased or decreased.

3. How will what you have learned in this problem help you evaluate an investment?

Problem 19-6A   *Using ratios to decide between two stock investments*   *(Obj. 5, 6)*

Assume you are purchasing an investment and have decided to invest in a company in the air-conditioning and heating business. Suppose you have narrowed the choice to Smajstla, Inc., and DuBois Corp. You have assembled the following selected data:

Selected income statement data for current year

	Smajstla, Inc.	DuBois Corp.
Net sales (all on credit)...	$497,000	$371,000
Cost of goods sold	258,000	209,000
Income from operations..	138,000	79,000
Interest expense...	19,000	—
Net income..	72,000	48,000

Selected balance sheet and market price data at end of current year

	Smajstla, Inc.	DuBois Corp.
Current assets		
Cash	$19,000	$ 22,000
Short-term investments...	18,000	20,000
Current receivables, net	46,000	42,000

Inventories	100,000	87,000
Prepaid expenses	3,000	2,000
Total current assets	186,000	173,000
Total assets	328,000	265,000
Total current liabilities	98,000	108,000
Total liabilities	131,000	108,000
Preferred stock: $5.00 (200 shares)	20,000	
Common stock (10,000 shares)		10,000
(5,000 shares)	12,500	
Total shareholders' equity	197,000	157,000
Market price per share of common stock	$112	$51

Selected balance sheet data at beginning of current year

	Smajstla, Inc.	DuBois Corp.
Current receivables, net	$ 48,000	$ 40,000
Inventories	88,000	93,000
Total assets	270,000	259,000
Preferred shareholders' equity, $5.00 (200 shares)	20,000	—
Common stock (10,000 shares)		10,000
(5,000 shares)	12,500	
Total shareholders' equity	126,000	118,000

Your investment strategy is to purchase the stocks of companies that have low price/earnings ratios but appear to be in good shape financially. Assume you have analyzed all other factors, and your decision depends on the results of the ratio analysis to be performed.

Required

Compute the following ratios for both companies for the current year and decide which company's stock better fits your investment strategy:

1. Current ratio
2. Acid-test ratio
3. Inventory turnover
4. Day's sales in average receivables
5. Debt ratio
6. Times-interest-earned ratio
7. Return on net sales
8. Return on total assets
9. Return on common shareholders' equity
10. Earnings per share of common stock
11. Book value per share of common stock
12. Price/earnings ratio

Problem 19-7A *Prepare a horizontal analysis of a financial statement, compute the standard financial ratios used for decision-making, use ratios in decision-making* **(Obj. 1, 5, 6)**

Standard Boat Batteries Ltd. had the following financial statements available based on a December 31st year end:

Income Statement
for the year ended December 31, 19X2

Net sales	$200,000
Cost of goods sold	110,000
Gross profit margin	90,000
Operating expenses:	
Selling expenses	28,000
Administrative expenses	30,000
Interest expense	6,000
Total operating expenses	64,000

Operating income...		26,000
Income taxes (40%)..		10,400
Net income		$ 15,600

Statement of Retained Earnings
for the year ended December 31, 19X2

Retained earnings—December 31, 19X1		$62,000
Add: net income for 19X2..		15,600
		77,600
Less dividends: preferred...	$10,000	
common	24,600	34,600
Retained earnings—December 31, 19X2		$43,000

Balance Sheet

	19X1	19X2
Assets		
Cash	$ 2,000	$ 3,000
Marketable securities	3,000	5,000
Accounts receivable..	21,000	18,000
Merchandise inventory..	58,000	32,000
Prepaid expenses	3,000	2,000
Plant and equipment...	154,000	178,000
Less accumulated amortization.............................	(12,000)	(35,000)
Goodwill	18,000	16,000
Total assets...	$247,000	$219,000
Liabilities		
Accounts payable	$21,000	$10,000
Notes payable (due in 30 days)	4,000	1,000
Mortgage payable (secured—capital assets)	60,000	35,000
Total liabilities..	85,000	46,000
Shareholders' equity		
Preferred shares (10,000 shares; $1 divid.)		
callable at $6 per share...	50,000	50,000
Common shares		
(19X1 — 5,000 shares, 19X2 — 10,000 shares)........	50,000	80,000
Retained earnings..	62,000	43,000
Total shareholders' equity	162,000	173,000
Total liabilities and shareholders' equity	$247,000	$219,000

Required

1. Perform a horizontal analysis of the comparative balance sheets. For simplicity, you may show only the amount and percentage of change for each item rather than rewriting the balance sheet amounts. Comment on the analysis.

2. Calculate each of the following ratios for the year ended December 31, 19X2. Note the industry standards are provided (in parentheses) for some of the ratios.
   - a. Current ratio (2:1)
   - b. Acid-test ratio
   - c. Inventory turnover
   - d. Days' sales in receivables
   - e. Debt ratio (45%)
   - f. Times-interest-earned ratio
   - g. Rate of return on net sales
   - h. Rate of return on total assets
   - i. Rate of return on common shareholders' equity
   - j. Price/earnings ratio—the market price per share is $10.00 (12.00:1)
   - k. Dividend yield (7%)

3. Comment on the results from part 2 on those ratios for which industry standards were provided (items a, e, j, and k).

Problem 19-8A   *Prepare a vertical analysis of a financial statement, compute the standard financial ratios used for decision-making, use ratios in decision-making*
(Obj. 2, 5, 6)

Byou Hardware Inc. has the following financial statements for the year ending December 31, 19X1, and additional information (all amounts in thousands of dollars):

Balance Sheet December 31, 19X1		Income Statement Year Ended December 31, 19X1	
Assets:		Sales	$ 90,000
Cash	$ 8,000		
Accounts Receivable	22,000	Cost of Goods Sold	50,000
Merchandise Inventory	32,000	Gross Profit	40,000
Prepaid Expenses	10,000		
Plant & Equipment (net)	160,000	Operating Expenses:	
Long-term Investments	90,000	Selling Expense	5,000
Total Assets	$322,000	Administrative Expenses	8,000
Liabilities:		Interest Expense	3,000
Accounts Payable	$ 46,000	Total Operating Expenses	16,000
Salaries Payable	8,000	Operating Income	24,000
Dividends Payable	10,000	Income Taxes	12,000
Bonds Payable	130,000	Net Income	$ 12,000
Total Liabilities	194,000		
Shareholders' Equity:		**Account Balances, January 1, 19X1:**	
Common Stock (5,000 shares)	80,000	Total Assets	$295,000
Retained Earnings	48,000	Accounts Receivable	34,000
Total Shareholders' Equity	128,000	Merchandise Inventory	28,000
Total Equities	$322,000	Retained Earnings	46,000

Required

1. Prepare a vertical analysis of the income statement. The industry standards are Gross Profit of 40 percent and Net Income of 8 percent. Comment on the results.

2. Calculate each of the following for December 31, 19X1 (industry standards are shown in parentheses for some items):
   a. Acid-test ratio (1:1)   f. Rate of return on shareholders' equity
   b. Inventory Turnover (2.0 times)   g. Earnings per share
   c. Days' Sales in Receivables (90 days) h. Price/earnings ratio (market price is
   d. Debt Ratio (40 percent) $16 per share)
   e. Rate of return on total assets   i. Dividend yield
      (6 percent)

3. Comment on the results in part 2 for ratios which had an industry standard provided (items a to e).

4. Byou Hardware Inc. has a policy of increasing purchases (all on credit) in the final month of the year to achieve inventory levels that are 100 percent higher than required. This is done to give the purchasing department a break after a hectic Christmas season. Management is concerned about the effects this policy may have on their acid-test ratio and inventory turnover. Calculate what these ratios would have been without the policy and comment on the results.

(Group B)

Problem 19-1B   *Trend percentages, return on sales, and comparison with the industry*
(Obj. 1, 5, 6)

Net sales, net income, and total assets for Monica Hearn, Inc., for a six-year period follow.

	19X6	19X5	19X4	19X3	19X2	19X1
			(Amounts in thousands)			
Net sales	$347	$313	$266	$281	$245	$241
Net income......................	27	21	11	18	14	13
Total assets	296	254	209	197	181	166

Required

1. Compute trend percentages for 19X2 through 19X6. Use 19X1 as the base year.

2. Compute the rate of return on net sales for 19X2 through 19X6, rounding to three decimal places. In this industry, rates above 5 percent are considered good, and rates above 7 percent are viewed as outstanding.

3. How does Hearn's return on net sales compare to the industry?

Problem 19-2B *Common-size statements, analysis of profitability and comparison with the industry* **(Obj. 2, 3, 5, 6)**

Top managers of Bull's Eye Archery Corp., a sporting goods store, have asked your help in comparing the company's profit performance and financial position with the average for the sporting goods industry. The accountant has given you the company's income statement and balance sheet, and also the following actual data for the sporting goods industry:

Bull's Eye Archery Corp.
Income Statement
Compared with Industry Average
year ended December 31, 19X6

	Bull's Eye	Industry Average
Net sales	$957,000	100.0%
Cost of goods sold	653,000	65.9
Gross profit	304,000	34.1
Operating expenses	257,000	28.1
Operating income	47,000	6.0
Other expenses..................	2,000	0.4
Net income........................	$ 45,000	5.6%

Bull's Eye Archery Corp.
Balance Sheet
Compared with Industry Average
December 31, 19X6

	Bull's Eye	Industry Average
Current assets	$448,000	74.4%
Fixed assets, net..................	127,000	20.0
Intangible assets, net...........	42,000	0.6
Other assets........................	13,000	5.0
Total......................................	$630,000	100.0%
Current liabilities.................	$246,000	35.6%
Long-term liabilities.............	144,000	19.0
Shareholders' equity...........	240,000	45.4
Total......................................	$630,000	100.0%

Required

1. Prepare a two-column common-size income statement and a two-column common-size balance sheet for Bull's Eye Archery. The first column of each statement should present Bull's Eye's common-size statement, and the second column should show the industry averages.

2. For the profitability analysis, compare Bull's Eye's (a) ratio of gross profit to net sales, (b) ratio of operating income (loss) to net sales, and (c) ratio of net income (loss) to net sales. Compare these figures with the industry averages. Is Bull's Eye's profit performance better or worse than average for the industry?

3. For the analysis of financial position, compare Bull's Eye's (a) ratio of current assets to total assets and (b) ratio of shareholders' equity to total assets. Compare these ratios with the industry averages. Is Bull's Eye Archery's financial position better or worse than the average for the industry?

Problem 19-3B   *Using the statement of changes in financial position for decision-making*   **(Obj. 4)**

You are evaluating two companies as possible investments. The two companies, similar in size, are in the commuter airline business. They fly passengers from Toronto to smaller cities in Ontario. Assume that all other available information has been analyzed, and that the decision on which company's stock to purchase depends on the information given in their statements of changes in financial position shown on the next page.

Required

Discuss the relative strengths and weaknesses of Metro Air and Western Ontario Air. Conclude your discussion by recommending one of the company's stocks as an investment.

Problem 19-4B   *Effects of business transactions on selected ratios*   **(Obj. 5, 6)**

Financial statement data of Eye Care Optical Ltd. include the following items:

Cash	$ 47,000
Short-term investments	21,000
Accounts receivable, net	102,000
Inventories	274,000
Prepaid expenses	15,000
Total assets	933,000
Short-term notes payable	72,000
Accounts payable	96,000
Accrued liabilities	50,000
Long-term notes payable	146,000
Other long-term liabilities	78,000
Net income	119,000
Number of common shares outstanding	22,000

Required

1. Compute Eye Care Optical's current ratio, debt ratio, and earnings per share.
2. Compute each of the three ratios after evaluating the effect of each transaction that follows. Consider each transaction separately.
   a. Borrowed $76,000 on a long-term note payable.
   b. Sold short-term investments for $44,000 (cost $66,000); assume no tax effect of the loss.
   c. Issued 14,000 shares of common stock, receiving cash of $168,000.
   d. Received cash on account, $6,000.
   e. Paid short-term notes payable, $51,000.
   f. Purchased merchandise of $48,000 on account, debiting Inventory.
   g. Paid off long-term liabilities, $78,000.
   h. Declared, but did not pay, a $31,000 cash dividend on the common stock.

Use the following format for your answer:

Requirement 1		**Current Ratio**	**Debt Ratio**	**Earnings per Share**

Requirement 2	**Transaction (letter)**	**Current Ratio**	**Debt Ratio**	**Earnings per Share**

Metro Air Ltd.
Statements of Changes in Financial Position
for the years ended November 30, 19X9 and 19X8

	19X9	19X8
Operating activities		
Income from operations	$184,000	$131,000
Add (subtract) noncash items:		
Total	64,000	62,000
Net cash flow from operating activities	248,000	193,000
Financing activities		
Issuance of long-term notes payable	$131,000	$ 83,000
Issuance of short-term notes payable	43,000	35,000
Payment of short-term notes payable	(66,000)	(18,000)
Net cash inflow from financing activities	108,000	100,000
Investing activities		
Purchase of property, plant, and equipment	$(303,000)	$(453,000)
Sale of property, plant, and equipment	46,000	39,000
Sale of long-term investments	—	33,000
Net cash outflow from investing activities	(257,000)	(381,000)
Increase (decrease) in cash	$ 99,000	$ (88,000)
Cash summary from balance sheet:		
Cash balance at beginning of year	$116,000	$204,000
Increase (decrease) in cash during the year	99,000	(88,000)
Cash balance at the end of year	$215,000	$116,000

Western Ontario Air Inc.
Statements of Changes in Financial Position
for the years ended November 30, 19X9 and 19X8

	19X9	19X8
Operating activities		
Income (loss) from operations	$ (67,000)	$154,000
Add (subtract) noncash items:		
Total	84,000	(23,000)
Net cash flow from operating activities	17,000	131,000
Financing activities		
Issuance of long-term notes payable	$ 122,000	$ 143,000
Payment of short-term notes payable	(179,000)	(134,000)
Payment of cash dividends	(45,000)	(64,000)
Net cash outflow from financing activities	(102,000)	(55,000)
Investing activities		
Purchase of property, plant, and equipment	$(120,000)	$ (91,000)
Sale of property, plant, and equipment	118,000	39,000
Sale of long-term investments	52,000	4,000
Net cash inflow (outflow) from investing activites	50,000	(48,000)
Increase (decrease) in cash	$ (35,000)	$ 28,000
Cash summary from balance sheet:		
Cash balance at beginning of year	$131,000	$103,000
Increase (decrease) in cash during the year	(35,000)	28,000
Cash balance at the end of year	$ 96,000	$131,000

Problem 19-5B   *Using ratios to evaluate a stock investment*   *(Obj. 5, 6)*

Comparative financial statement data of Dunn's Brass Foundry, Inc., are as follows:

Dunn's Brass Foundry Inc.
Comparative Income Statement
years ended December 31, 19X6 and 19X5

	19X6	19X5
Net sales	$667,000	$599,000
Cost of goods sold	378,000	283,000
Gross profit	289,000	316,000
Operating expenses	129,000	147,000
Income from operations	160,000	169,000
Interest expense	57,000	41,000
Income before income tax	103,000	128,000
Income tax expense	34,000	53,000
Net income	$ 69,000	$ 75,000

Dunn's Brass Foundry, Inc.
Comparative Balance Sheet
December 31, 19X6 and 19X5
(Selected 19X4 amounts given for computation of ratios)

	19X6	19X5	19X4
Current assets			
Cash	$ 37,000	$ 40,000	
Current receivables, net	208,000	151,000	$138,000
Inventories	352,000	286,000	184,000
Prepaid expenses	5,000	20,000	
Total current assets	602,000	497,000	
Property, plant, and equipment, net	287,000	276,000	
Total assets	$889,000	$773,000	707,000
Total current liabilities	$286,000	$267,000	
Long-term liabilities	245,000	235,000	
Total liabilities	531,000	502,000	
Preferred shareholders' equity, $.80	50,000	50,000	
Common shareholders' equity	308,000	221,000	148,000
Total liabilities and shareholders' equity	$889,000	$773,000	

Other information:

a. Market price of Dunn's Brass Foundry common stock: $30.75 at December 31, 19X6, and $40.25 at December 31, 19X5.
b. Common shares outstanding: 15,000 during 19X6 and 14,000 during 19X5.
c. Preferred shares outstanding: 2,500 during both years.
d. All sales on credit.

Required

1. Compute the following ratios for 19X6 and 19X5:
   a. Current ratio
   b. Inventory turnover
   c. Accounts receivable turnover
   d. Times-interest-earned ratio
   e. Return on assets
   f. Return on common shareholders' equity
   g. Earnings per share of common stock
   h. Price/earnings ratio
   i. Book value per share of common stock

2. Decide (a) whether Dunn's Brass Foundry's financial position improved or deteriorated during 19X6, and (b) whether the investment attractiveness of its common stock appears to have increased or decreased.

3. How will what you have learned in this problem help you evaluate an investment?

Problem 19-6B   *Using ratios to decide between two stock investments*   **(Obj. 5, 6)**

Assume you are purchasing stock in a company in the hospital supply business. Suppose you have narrowed the choice to Scott & White Ltd. and Pediatric Supply Corp. and have assembled the following data:

Selected income statement data for current year

	Scott & White Ltd.	Pediatric Supply Corp.
Net sales (all on credit)	$519,000	$603,000
Cost of goods sold	387,000	454,000
Income from operations	72,000	93,000
Interest expense	8,000	—
Net income	38,000	56,000

Selected balance sheet and market price data at end of current year

	Scott & White Ltd.	Pediatric Supply Corp.
Current assets		
Cash	$ 39,000	$ 25,000
Short-term investments	13,000	6,000
Current receivables, net	164,000	189,000
Inventories	183,000	211,000
Prepaid expenses	15,000	19,000
Total current assets	414,000	450,000
Total assets	938,000	974,000
Total current liabilities	338,000	366,000
Total liabilities	691,000	667,000
Preferred stock $4.00 (250 shares)	25,000	
Common stock (150,000 shares)		150,000
(20,000 shares)	100,000	
Total shareholders' equity	247,000	307,000
Market price per share of common stock	$47.50	$9

Selected balance sheet data at beginning of current year

	Scott & White Ltd.	Pediatric Supply Corp.
Current receivables, net	$193,000	$142,000
Inventories	197,000	209,000
Total assets	909,000	842,000
Preferred shareholders' equity, $4.00 (250 shares)	25,000	
Common stock (150,000 shares)		150,000
(20,000 shares)	100,000	
Total shareholders' equity	215,000	263,000

Your investment strategy is to purchase the stocks of companies that have low price/earnings ratios but appear to be in good shape financially. Assume you have analyzed all other factors, and your decision depends on the results of the ratio analysis to be performed.

Required

Compute the following ratios for both companies for the current year and decide which company's stock better fits your investment strategy:

1. Current ratio
2. Acid-test ratio
3. Inventory turnover
4. Days' sales in average receivables
5. Debt ratio
6. Times-interest-earned ratio
7. Return on net sales
8. Return on total assets
9. Return on common shareholders' equity
10. Earnings per share of common stock
11. Book value per share of common stock
12. Price/earnings ratio

Problem 19-7B   *Prepare a horizontal analysis of a financial statement, compute the standard financial ratios used for decision-making, use ratios in decision-making*   **(Obj. 1, 5, 6)**

Northern Auto Batteries Ltd. had the following financial statements available based on a December 31st year end:

Income Statement
for the year ended December 31, 19X2

Net sales..	$220,000
Cost of goods sold..	120,000
Gross profit margin...	100,000
Operating expenses	
Selling expenses...	35,000
Administrative expenses..	26,000
Interest expense...	6,000
Total operating expenses...	67,000
Operating income..	33,000
Income taxes (40%)..	13,200
Net income...	$ 19,800

Statement of Retained Earnings
for the year ended December 31, 19X2

Retained earnings—December 31, 19X1		$55,000
Add: net income for 19X2..		19,800
		74,800
Less dividends: preferred..	$16,000	
common	23,800	39,800
Retained earnings—December 31, 19X2		$35,000

Balance Sheet

	19X1	19X2
Assets		
Cash	$ 1,000	$ 2,000
Marketable securities	2,000	6,000
Accounts receivable...	24,000	17,000
Merchandise inventory..	57,000	33,000
Prepaid expenses	4,000	1,000
Plant and equipment..	148,000	180,000
Less accumulated amortization.............................	(10,000)	(34,000)
Goodwill	15,000	12,000
Total assets..	$241,000	$217,000
Liabilities		
Accounts payable	$23,000	$12,000
Notes payable (due in 30 days)	5,000	2,000

Mortgage payable (secured—capital assets)	50,000	30,000
Total liabilities	78,000	44,000

Shareholders' equity		
Preferred shares (8,000 shares; $2 divid.)		
callable at $7 per share	48,000	48,000
Common shares		
(19X1 –6,000 shares, 19X2 — 12,000 shares)	60,000	90,000
Retained earnings	55,000	35,000
Total shareholders' equity	163,000	173,000
Total liabilities and shareholders' equity	$241,000	$217,000

Required

1. Perform a horizontal analysis of the comparative balance sheets. For simplicity, you may show only the amount and percentage of change for each item rather than rewriting the balance sheet amounts. Comment on the analysis.

2. Calculate each of the following ratios for the year ended December 31, 19X2. Note the industry standards are provided (in parentheses) for some of the ratios.
   a. Current ratio (2:1)
   b. Acid-test ratio
   c. Inventory turnover
   d. Days' sales in receivables
   e. Debt ratio (45%)
   f. Times-interest-earned ratio
   g. Rate of return on net sales
   h. Rate of return on total assets
   i. Rate of return on common shareholders' equity
   j. Price/earnings ratio—the market price per share is $8.00 (12.00:1)
   k. Dividend yield (7%)

3. Comment on the results from part 2 on those ratios for which industry standards were provided (items a, e, j, and k).

Problem 19-8B *Prepare a vertical analysis of a financial statement, compute the standard financial ratios used for decision-making, use ratios in decision-making* **(Obj. 2, 5, 6)**

Faine's Hardware Inc. has the following financial statements for the year ending December 31, 19X1, and additional information (all amounts in thousands of dollars):

Balance Sheet
December 31, 19X1

Assets:		
Cash	$	6,000
Accounts Receivable		26,000
Merchandise Inventory.....		34,000
Prepaid Expenses...............		12,000
Plant & Equipment (net)...		150,000
Long-term Investments.....		80,000
Total Assets		$308,000
Liabilities:		
Accounts Payable...............	$	39,000
Salaries Payable		7,000
Dividends Payable.............		9,000
Bonds Payable....................		140,000
Total Liabilities...............		195,000
Shareholders' Equity:		
Common Stock (6,000 shares)		70,000
Retained Earnings..............		43,000
Total Shareholders' Equity		113,000
Total Equities..................		$308,000

Income Statement
Year Ended December 31, 19X1

Sales	$ 94,000
Cost of Goods Sold	42,000
Gross Profit........................	52,000
Operating Expenses:	
Selling Expense	7,000
Administrative Expenses	9,000
Interest Expense............	6,000
Total Operating Expenses	22,000
Operating Income..............	30,000
Income Taxes	15,000
Net Income	$ 15,000

Account Balances, January 1, 19X1:

Total Assets	$290,000
Accounts Receivable	36,000
Merchandise Inventory....	26,000
Retained Earnings	37,000

Required

1. Prepare a vertical analysis of the income statement. The industry standards are Gross Profit of 45 percent and Net Income of 12 percent. Comment on the results.

2. Calculate each of the following for December 31, 19X1 (industry standards are shown in parentheses for some items):

   a. Acid-test ratio (1:1)
   b. Inventory Turnover (2.0 times)
   c. Days' Sales in Receivables (90 days)
   d. Debt Ratio (40 percent)
   e. Rate of return on total assets (6 percent)
   f. Rate of return on shareholders' equity
   g. Earnings per share
   h. Price/earnings ratio (market price is $16 per share)
   i. Dividend yield

3. Comment on the results in part 2 for ratios which had an industry standard provided (items a to e).

4. Faine's Hardware Inc. has a policy of increasing purchases (all on credit) in the final month of the year to achieve inventory levels that are 100 percent higher than required. This is done to give the purchasing department a break after a hectic Christmas season. Management is concerned about the effects this policy may have on their acid-test ratio and inventory turnover. Calculate what these ratios would have been without the policy and comment on the results.

Challenge Problems

Problem 19-1C   *Using horizontal analysis to analyze the financial statements of a company (Obj. 1)*

Recently newspapers carried stories about a company that fired three top executives for management fraud. The three had been using improper accounting practices to overstate profits. The improper practices included improperly recording assets on the company's balance sheet, overstating sales, and understating cost of goods sold by inflating inventory numbers. When inventory got out of line, the executives would debit capital assets and credit inventory to further hide their fraud.

   The company had been growing at a very rapid pace, outdistancing its competitors. However, there were warning signals or "red flags" that revealed that all was not well with the company and that suggested that the books might have been "cooked" in order to report the rapid growth. For example, sales grew much faster than did accounts receivable when the company's financial statements were compared with industry data. Inventory turnover was lower than that of competitors while sales were unusually low relative to capital assets.

Required

Which items would be misstated in a horizontal analysis of the company's income statement? Which items would be misstated in a horizontal analysis of the company's balance sheet? Indicate the direction of the misstatement.

Problem 19-2C   *Understanding the impact of improper accounting practices on the financial statements of a company   (Obj. 5)*

Refer to the information given in Problem 19-1C.

Required

1. Sales grew faster than receivables. Would this situation create an unusually high or unusually low turnover?

2. Why was the fact that sales grew faster than receivables relative to other companies in the industry a "red flag"?

3. Explain why inventory turnover was too low.

4. Why was the fact that inventory turnover was low relative to other companies a "red flag"?

5. Compare the company's receivable turnover with inventory turnover. Does the comparison suggest a "red flag"? If so, what is it?

Extending Your Knowledge

Decision Problems

1. *Identifying action to cut losses and establish profitability*   (Obj. 2, 5, 6)

Suppose you manage Wheel Sports, Inc., a sporting goods and bicycle shop, which lost money during the past year. Before you can set the business on a successful course, you must first analyze the company and industry data for the current year in an effort to learn what is wrong. The data appear below.

Wheel Sports, Inc., Balance Sheet Data

	Wheel Sports, Inc.	Industry Average
Cash and short-term investments	3.0%	6.8%
Trade receivables, net	15.2	11.0
Inventory	64.2	60.5
Prepaid expenses	1.0	0.0
Total current assets	83.4	78.3
Capital assets, net	12.6	15.2
Other assets	4.0	6.5
Total assets	100.0%	100.0%
Notes payable, short-term, 12%	17.1%	14.0%
Accounts payable	21.1	25.1
Accrued liabilities	7.8	7.9
Total current liabilities	46.0	47.0
Long-term debt, 11%	19.7	16.4
Total liabilities	65.7	63.4
Common shareholders' equity	34.3	36.6
Total liabilities and shareholders' equity	100.0%	100.0%

Wheel Sports, Inc., Income Statement Data

	Wheel Sports, Inc.	Industry Average
Net sales	100.0%	100.0%
Cost of sales	(68.2)	(64.8)
Gross profit	31.8	35.2
Operating expense	(37.1)	(32.3)
Operating income (loss)	(5.3)	2.9
Interest expense	(5.8)	(1.3)
Other revenue	1.1	.3
Income (loss) before income tax	(10.0)	1.9
Income tax (expense) saving	4.4	(.8)
Net income (loss)	5.6%	1.1%

Required

On the basis of your analysis of these figures, suggest four courses of action Wheel Sports should take to reduce its losses and establish profitable operations. Give your reasons for each suggestion.

2.   *Understanding the components of accounting ratios*   (Obj. 5, 6)

a.   Krista Chen has asked you about the stock of a particular company. She finds it attractive because it has a high dividend yield relative to another stock she is also considering. Explain to her the meaning of the ratio and the danger of making a decision based on it alone.

b.   Limeridge Ltd.'s owners are concerned because the number of days' sales in receivables has increased over the previous two years. Explain why the ratio might have increased.

c.   Mark Lott is the controller of Hunan Industries Inc., whose year end is December 31. He prepares cheques for suppliers in December and posts them to the appropriate accounts in that month. However, he holds on to the cheques and actually mails them to the suppliers in January. What financial ratio(s) are most affected by the action? What is Lott's purpose in undertaking this activity?

Ethical Issue

Kross Corp.'s long-term debt agreements make certain demands on the business. Kross may not repurchase company stock in excess of the balance of Retained Earnings. Also, Long-term Debt may not exceed Shareholders' Equity, and the current ratio may not fall below 1.50. If Kross fails to meet these requirements, the company's lenders have the authority to take over management of the corporation.

Changes in consumer demand have made it hard for Kross to sell its products. Current liabilities have mounted faster than current assets, causing the current ratio to fall to 1.47. Prior to releasing financial statements, Kross management is scrambling to improve the current ratio. The controller points out that an investment can be classified as either long-term or short-term, depending on management's intention. By deciding to convert an investment to cash within one year, Kross can classify the investment as short-term (a current asset). On the controller's recommendation, Kross's board of directors votes to reclassify long-term investments as short-term.

Required

1.   What effect will reclassifying the investment have on the current ratio? Is Kross Corp.'s financial position stronger as a result of reclassifying the investment?

2.   Shortly after releasing the financial statements, sales improve and so, then, does the current ratio. As a result, Kross management decides not to sell the investments it had reclassified as short-term. Accordingly, the company reclassifies the investments as long-term. Has management behaved unethically? Give your reason.

Financial Statement Problems

1.   *Measuring profitability and analyzing stock as an investment* (Obj. 5, 6)

Use the financial information in the Mark's Work Wearhouse Ltd. financial statements in Appendix A to chart the company's progress through the fiscal years 1994, 1993, and 1992 to answer the following requirements.

Required

1.   Compute the following ratios that measure profitability and that are used to analyze stock as an investment:

a. Percentage of net income to sales
b. Rate of return on total assets
c. Rate of return on common shareholders' equity
d. Net income per share

2. Compute these ratios at the end of each of the two most recent years.
    a. Current ratio
    b. Debt ratio

3. Compute inventory turnover for each of the two most recent years.

4. Do your answers to Questions 1 to 3 support management's analysis in the management discussion and analysis in Appendix A.

2. *Measuring profitability and analyzing stock as an investment* *(Obj. 5, 6)*

Obtain the annual report of an actual company of your choosing.

Required

1. Use the financial statements and the multi-year summary data to chart the company's progress during the three most recent years including the current year. Compute the following ratios that measure profitability and which are used to analyze stock as an investment.

    Profitability Measures
    a. Return on net sales
    b. Return on common shareholders' equity
    c. Return on total assets

    Stock Analysis Measure
    d. Price/earnings ratio (If given, use the average of the "high" and "low" stock prices for each year.)

2. Is the trend in the profitability measures consistent with the trend in the stock analysis measure? Evaluate the company's overall outlook for the future.

Comprehensive Problems for Part Four

1. Analyzing a company for its investment potential

The information provided below is taken from the Land's End 1994 annual report.

Land's End, Inc.
Five-Year Consolidated Financial Summary
(Dollar amounts in thousands except per-share data)

	1994	1993	1992	1991	1990
Income statement data					
Net sales	$869,975	$733,623	$683,427	$601,991	$544,850
Pretax income	69,870	54,033	47,492	24,943	47,270
Percent to net sales	8.0%	7.4%	7.0%	4.1%	8.7%
Net income before accounting change	42,429	33,500	28,732	14,743	29,071
Cumulative effect of accounting change	1,300	—	—	—	—
Net income	43,729	33,500	28,732	14,743	29,071
Net income (pro forma for 1986 and 1987)	43,729	33,500	28,732	14,743	29,071

Per share of common stock

Net income per share before accounting change	$ 2.36	$ 1.85	$ 1.53	$ .75	$ 1.45
Cumulative effect of accounting change	.07	—	—	—	—
Net income per share	$ 2.43	$ 1.85	$ 1.53	$ .75	$ 1.45
Cash dividends per share	$ .20	$ .20	$ .20	$ .20	$ .20
Common shares outstanding	17,956	18,028	18,472	19,218	19,881

Balance sheet data

Current assets	$192,276	$137,531	$131,273	$107,813	$ 99,714
Current liabilities	91,049	67,315	74,548	60,774	43,915
Property, plant, equipment, and intangibles, net	81,554	74,272	74,527	77,576	67,218
Total assets	273,830	211,803	205,800	185,400	166,932
Noncurrent liabilities	5,496	5,100	4,620	7,800	8,413
Shareholders' investment	177,285	139,388	126,632	116,826	114,604

Other data

Net working capital	$101,227	$ 70,216	$ 56,725	$ 47,050	$ 55,799
Capital expenditures	16,958	9,965	5,347	17,682	25,160
Depreciation and amortization expense	8,286	7,900	7,428	7,041	5,251
Return on average shareholders' investment	28%	25%	23%	13%	28%
Return on average assets	18%	16%	15%	8%	18%
Debt/equity ratio	—	—	1%	3%	4%

Analyze the data for the fiscal years ended 1990 through 1994 to decide whether or not to invest invest in the common stock of Land's End. Include the following sections in your analysis, and fully explain your final decision.

- Trend analysis
- Profitability analysis
- Measuring ability to sell inventory
- Cash flow analysis (net cash inflow or outflow from operating activities)
- Measuring ability to pay debts

To compute some of the items not given in the Five-Year Summary, you will need the following data:

	(Dollar amounts in millions)					
	1994	**1993**	**1992**	**1991**	**1990**	**1989**
Cost of sales......................	$512	$427	$395	$359	$316	—
Cash....................................	$21.6	$22.7	$1.4	$27.3	$8.3	$32.1
Inventory...........................	$150	$106	$113	$74	$86	—

2. Group Project: Refining your business plan to analyze accounting information
In Part 4 of this book (Chapters 18 and 19) you learned how to analyze the cash effects of transactions and to report those effects on the statement of changes in financial position. You also learned a number of ratios that managers, investors, and creditors use for decision making. How will you use what you have learned to (a) manage a business and (b) evaluate investments?

VIDEO CASE

Foreign Currency and the Canadian Dollar

The exchange rate, or price of the Canadian dollar in terms of other currencies, is established by foreign currency traders in Canada and in other markets around the world—London, New York and Tokyo are among the leading financial markets. When the demand in international markets for the Canadian dollar exceeds the supply of dollars being offered (more buyers than sellers), the price of the Canadian dollar relative to other currencies such as the U.S. dollar increases. We say the Canadian dollar is strengthening. When the supply in international markets for the Canadian dollar exceeds the demand for dollars (more sellers than buyers), the price of the Canadian dollar relative to other currencies such as the U.S. dollar decreases. We say the Canadian dollar is weakening.

The two major factors that affect the exchange rate are the ratio of a country's imports to its exports and the rate of return available in the country's capital markets. There are other factors at play. One factor cited is the perceptions of currency traders about issues such as the financial stability of a country and the traders' expectations about a country's economic prospects.

Two considerations that impact on traders' perceptions that are cited are Canada's deficit and the North American Free Trade Agreement (NAFTA). As the video "Dollar Dive" points out, a fall in the value of one currency, in this case the Mexican peso, makes traders nervous and can lead to declines in the value of other currencies such as the Canadian dollar. Canada's deficit and need to borrow on world markets is one factor cited in the video that leads to a decline

in the value of the Canadian dollar. "...Canada ...has now become an honorary member of the third world..." is a quote from the *Wall Sreet Journal*. The contention that a country's debt may be a factor is supported by the fact that a decline in value was not experienced by the German mark; Germany does not have as significant debt problems as Canada does.

Some experts have blamed NAFTA for Canada's foreign currency woes. However, the Mexican foreign minister José Angel Gurria suggests that NAFTA is not the cause. Robert Hormats, Vice-Chairman of Goldman Sachs, a large U.S. investment dealer with Canadian interests, agrees that NAFTA was not a factor. The U.S. dollar was not significantly affected by the peso's fall.

CASE QUESTIONS

1. How would a Canadian exporter view the fall in the value of the Canaian dollar?

2. How would a provincial government that had borowed outside Canada view the fall in the value of the Canadian dollar.

3. What would the effect of the fall in the value of the peso have on an investment in Mexico by a Canadian company such as John Labatt Ltd.? Assume the peso decines in value by 50 percent while the decline in the value of the Canadian dollar is 10 percent.

4. What is the effect of the fall of the peso on debt of a Canadian company that must be repaid in British pounds.

Published Financial Statements

MANAGEMENT'S DISCUSSION AND ANALYSIS

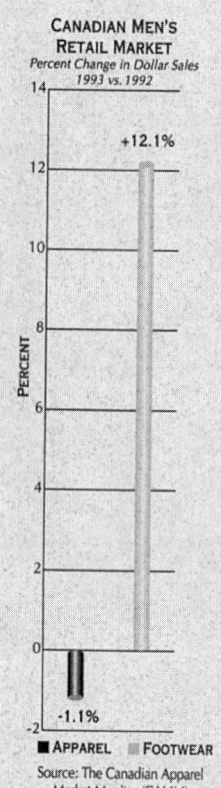

CANADIAN MEN'S RETAIL MARKET
Percent Change in Dollar Sales 1993 vs. 1992

+12.1%

-1.1%

■ APPAREL ▨ FOOTWEAR

Source: The Canadian Apparel Market Monitor (CAMM)

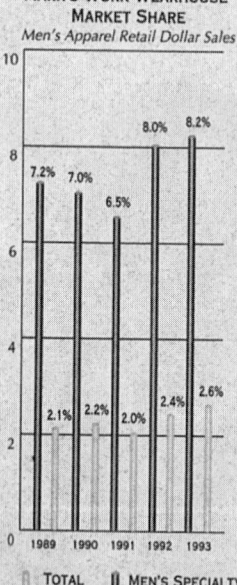

MARK'S WORK WEARHOUSE MARKET SHARE
Men's Apparel Retail Dollar Sales

7.2% 7.0% 6.5% 8.0% 8.2%

2.1% 2.2% 2.0% 2.4% 2.6%

1989 1990 1991 1992 1993

▨ TOTAL MARKET ▊ MEN'S SPECIALTY STORE MARKET

Source: The Canadian Apparel Market Monitor (CAMM)

MD&A SUMMARY

Having completed the second full year of operations since the late '91 restructuring, the Company is "back into the black" and is ready to move from its "survival phase" to its "post turnaround phase".

OPERATIONS

During a year in which total retail sales in Canada were up only a modest 4% and Canadian men's apparel sales were actually down 1%, the Company's corporate stores posted a $24.6 million or 18.4% sales increase. These large gains resulted in the Company increasing its market share from 2.4% to 2.6% in the men's apparel retail market and from 8% to 8.2% in the men's specialty store market.

This increase breaks down geographically as follows:

Western Canada	$10.2 million
Ontario	$10.7 million
Quebec/Atlantic	$3.7 million

On a same store basis, sales were up $17.5 million or 14.6%. The Company's franchise stores also performed well with a $9.2 million or 17.5% same store sales increase. This year's sales increases occurred over a 52-week retail year, whereas the retail year previous was 53 weeks.

Corporate store sales increased or decreased by category as shown in the chart, "Corporate Store Sales by Category".

From a dollar perspective, increases in private label bottoms, accessories and both footwear categories accounted for $17 million of the $24.6 million increase. The significant increase

CORPORATE STORE SALES BY CATEGORY	INCREASE	DECREASE
Work apparel	11.3%	-
Men's casual wear	17.1%	-
Western wear	246.5%	-
Brand name bottoms	-	4.8%
Industrial footwear	17.2%	-
Accessories	28.2%	-
Casual outerwear	13.6%	-
Industrial outerwear	20.0%	-
Private label bottoms	49.8%	-
Casual footwear	66.7%	-
Ladies wear	-	36.4%

in the Company's private label bottoms business can be attributed to the implementation of a key component in the Company's 1991 Strategic Plan. In that Plan, the Company set out to "grow" its private label bottoms business, while maintaining its brand label bottoms business at the volume levels in existence for margin performance reasons. The gains realized on the Company's footwear categories have increased its market share from 2.6% to 4.5% of the men's Canadian footwear market, and from 15.4% to 23.3% of the men's over $90 price point items in the men's Canadian work footwear market.

The Company's increase of 17.1% in men's casual wear was also significant, considering last year's 16.1% increase. Growth in western wear was confined to Western Canada and represents only 2.5% of the Company's sales. The Company's market ranking and individual product ranking after this past year's gains is illustrated in the chart attached.

Richard Faust, Senior Buyer, Bottoms was instrumental in achieving a 49.8% increase in private label bottoms.

Notably, the Company's large sales gains were achieved without sacrificing margins. The Company actually recorded a modest four-tenths of a point margin gain from 36.3% at January 30, 1993 to 36.7% at January 29, 1994. Purchase mark up (after merchandise and freight costs) was a full point above the previous year, achieved by changing business blend and purchasing the same quality commodities at better prices, not by significant retail price increases. Although higher than the prior year, mark downs were managed to a slightly lower percentage of sales rate. Higher customer adjustments and the elimination of volume rebates by one of the Company's key suppliers offset some of the purchase mark up and mark down gains to result in the moderate four-tenths of a point improvement. While shrinkage was managed to a similar percentage of sales as in the prior year, the Company is not pleased with its $2.5 million cost in this area.

In conclusion, the Company delivered an extra $9.7 million in gross margin dollars, of which $9.0 million was sales growth and $700,000 a slight improvement in margin rate. The purchase mark up in the Company's opening

inventories continues to improve, reaching 43.4% at January 29, 1994 from 41.2% at January 30, 1993, 40.2% at January 25, 1992, and 39.1% at January 26, 1991.

It should be noted that front line expenses declined as a percentage of sales from 29.8% at January 30, 1993 to 28.7% at January 29, 1994. On a same store basis, the increase in front line expenses was $2.5 million or 7.1%. Of the large front line staff cost increase, $891,000 was in bonuses paid to store staff with the balance split between higher staff costs (to generate the sales gains) and higher store labor costs (attributable to the implementation of the Company's new computer system in fiscal 1994). Advertising costs were $1,754,000 greater than a year ago and 5.5% of sales compared to 5.3% of sales in the previous year. It should be noted that $14 million of the Company's $24.6 million sales increase came during the Company's National Event advertising campaigns.

During the year, the franchise contribution improved by $1.1 million for two reasons: franchise royalties were higher due to their sales

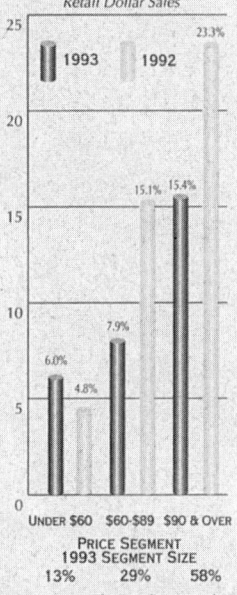

MARK'S WORK WEARHOUSE
MARKET SHARE
*Men's Work Shoes/Boots
Retail Dollar Sales*

Source: The Canadian Apparel
Market Monitor (CAMM)

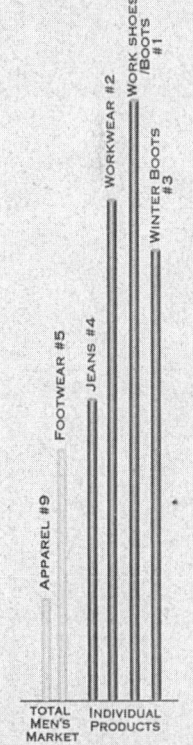

MARK'S WORK WEARHOUSE
MARKET SHARE RANKING
Men's Apparel/Footwear 1993

Source: The Canadian Apparel
Market Monitor (CAMM)

Front line expenses increased by $5,567,000 or 14% as follows:

Front Line Expenses	January 1993	January 1994	Increase (Decrease)
		(thousands of dollars)	
Staff	11,115	14,220	3,105
Advertising	7,018	8,772	1,754
Other	3,906	4,595	689
Occupancy	14,886	15,579	693
Depreciation	1,736	1,686	(50)
Interest (short-term)	1,152	528	(624)
	39,813	45,380	5,567

gains, and bad debt write-offs were some $600,000 less than the previous year when 12 franchise stores were closed and/or repossessed.

The Company was able to "hold the line" on back line staff and administration; however, software development costs, depreciation and interest on long-term debt climbed as the result of costs involved with installing the Company's new computer system. As outlined in the fixed asset and long-term debt notes of the Company's financial statements, all computer services including equipment were outsourced at year end. In future years, interest on long-term debt

and depreciation of computer hardware costs will appear as lease costs for computer services, along with any software development and support costs.

The combination of the $9.7 million increase in gross margin dollars, the $5.5 million increase in front line expenses, the $1.1 million improvement in franchise contribution, and the $1.2 million increase in back line costs produced just over a $4 million improvement in the Company's bottomline helping it get "back into the black" for the first time since January 27, 1990.

> The Company was able to "hold the line" on back line staff and administration costs.

Back line costs increased by $1,194,000 or 8.7% as follows:

Back Line Expenses	January 1993	January 1994	Increase (Decrease)
		(thousands of dollars)	
Staff	6,631	6,311	(320)
Administration and other	2,665	2,252	(413)
Occupancy	888	984	96
Depreciation	1,294	1,874	580
Software development costs	1,342	1,913	571
Interest (long-term)	978	1,658	680
	13,798	14,992	1,194

Clothes That Work.
Mountain Gear 3-in-1 jacket.

BALANCE SHEET

During the course of the past two years, the Company concluded the following major financing transactions:

Financing Transactions	January 1993 Inflows (Outflows)	January 1994 Inflows (Outflows)
	(thousands of dollars)	
Issue of subordinated debentures Series A (excludes accrued interest)	3,850	
Repayment of subordinated debentures Series A (excludes accrued interest)		(3,850)
Issue of subordinated debentures Series B	500	
Issue of 8,000,000 common shares (net of issue costs)	7,200	
Issue of 4,572,364 common shares (net of issue costs)		3,500
Issue of common shares to employees under employee share purchase, stock options plans and by private placement	450	270
Issue of convertible subordinated debentures		3,000
Outsourcing of all computer services including equipment previously under capital lease		(7,400)

The major refinancings noted above, coupled with significantly improving operations, resulted in the Company's year end cash position advancing from a negative $2,778,000 at January 25, 1992 to a positive $3,761,000 at January 29, 1994. The Company's working capital improved by a further $4,380,000 this past year after having posted a $10,474,000 improvement in the previous year. The Company is satisfied with its 1.62/1 current ratio at January 29, 1994, compared to 1.64/1 at January 30, 1993 and 1.11/1 at January 25, 1992. The Company has also improved its debt-to-equity ratio to 1.72/1 at January 29, 1994 from 2.04/1 at January 30, 1993 and 4.07/1 at January 25, 1992. The Company is not satisfied, however, with the level of inventory and supplier payables at January 29, 1994 and will focus on improving turnover in the coming year to reduce these balances.

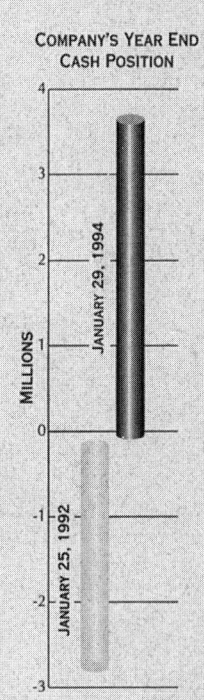

COMPANY'S YEAR END CASH POSITION

FORECAST

Earnings per common share for the 52 weeks ending January 28, 1995 are forecast to be in the range of 17 cents to 28 cents per share.

This forecast represents, in management's judgement, the most likely set of conditions and the Company's most likely course of action. The reader is cautioned that some assumptions used while preparing our forecast, although considered reasonable at the time of preparation, may prove to be incorrect. The actual results achieved during the forecast period will inevitably vary from the forecast results, and variations may be material.

The Company completed these forecasts on March 30, 1994. The financial reports issued by the Company to its shareholders during the forecast year will contain either a statement that there are no significant changes to be made to the forecast range or an updated earnings per share forecast accompanied by explanations of significant changes.

> Earnings per common share for the 52 weeks ending January 28, 1995 are forecast to be in the range of 17 cents to 28 cents per share.

	Actual 52 Weeks Ended January 29, 1994	Forecast (unaudited) 52 Weeks Ended January 28, 1995	
KEY ASSUMPTIONS (dollars in thousands)		Conservative	Optimistic
Same store sales increase - corporate	14.6%	4.1%	8.2%
Same store sales increase - franchise	17.5%	0.0%	11.2%
Gross margin rate	36.7%	37.0%	37.0%
Inventory turnover	2.4	2.4	2.5
Number of corporate store openings	5	3	3
Number of store closings	6	2	2
Sales increases from part-year fiscal 1994 corporate stores becoming full-year stores in fiscal 1995	-	$ 6,710	$ 6,710
Sales from new store openings	-	$ 2,585	$ 2,585
Number of franchise stores	43	42	42
Operating line – interest rates	7.6%	8.4%	8.4%
Capital expenditures			
Real estate and other	$ 2,957	$ 3,500	$ 3,500
Systems	$ 1,782	$ —	$ —
New equity financing (net)	$ 3,542	$ —	$ —
Long-term debt financing			
Convertible subordinated debt	$ 3,000	$ —	$ —
Capital leases	$ 1,927	$ —	$ —
Long-term debt repayments			
Subordinated debt	$ 4,406	$ —	$ —
Capital leases	$ 7,443	$ —	$ —

INCOME STATEMENT

(In thousands)

	Actual	Forecast (unaudited)	
	52 Weeks Ended January 29, 1994	52 Weeks Ended January 28, 1995	
		Conservative	Optimistic
Sales	$158,066	$169,120	$175,215
Cost of sales	99,999	106,527	110,361
Gross margin	58,067	62,593	64,854
Front line expenses	45,380	47,277	47,530
Front line contribution	12,687	15,316	17,324
Franchise contribution	3,571	3,392	3,822
Net front line contribution	16,258	18,708	21,146
Back line expenses	14,992	14,695	14,646
Income from operations	1,266	4,013	6,500
Income taxes	—	—	—
Net income	$ 1,266	$ 4,013	$ 6,500

BALANCE SHEET

(In thousands)

	Actual	Forecast (unaudited)	
	52 Weeks Ended January 29, 1994	52 Weeks Ended January 28, 1995	
		Conservative	Optimistic
Assets			
Current assets			
Inventories	$ 32,333	$ 27,296	$ 26,144
Other	17,840	13,972	16,766
	50,173	41,268	42,910
Other assets	632	632	632
Fixed assets	5,590	6,807	6,807
	$ 56,395	$ 48,707	$ 50,349
Liabilities			
Current liabilities	$ 30,923	$ 19,567	$ 18,722
Deferred gain	1,727	1,382	1,382
Long-term debt	3,000	3,000	3,000
	35,650	23,949	23,104
Shareholders' equity			
Capital stock	25,793	25,793	25,793
(Deficit)	(5,048)	(1,035)	1,452
	20,745	24,758	27,245
	$ 56,395	$ 48,707	$ 50,349
Net cash generated (deployed)	$ 2,821	$ (6,287)	$ (2,119)

"POST MORTEM" ON THE PRIOR YEAR'S FORECAST

Sales of $158,066,000 exceeded the operating budget by $10,540,000 or 7.1% and exceeded the conservative forecast by $14,776,000 or 10.3%. This occurred because of very strong sales gains beyond forecasts in Alberta, Metro Toronto, Southern Ontario and Eastern Ontario throughout the year, the result of aggressive inventory positions and marketing campaigns.

Margin rates were lower than forecasted due to heavier mark downs, customer adjustments, shrinkage, and freight costs, but thanks to the significant sales overrun to plan, $1,167,000 or 2.1% more gross margin dollars than the operating budget and $2,800,000 or 5.1% more gross margin dollars than the conservative forecast, were generated.

Front line expenses came in some $515,000 or 1.1% over the operating budget and some $814,000 or 1.8% over the conservative forecast. Most front line expenses came in under the operating budget and conservative forecast except for staff costs which were $1,200,000 over the operating budget and $1,700,000 over the conservative forecast. This was a result of sales bonuses, extra staff costs to generate sales gains, and extra staff costs to implement the Company's new computer system.

The franchise contribution surpassed the operating budget and conservative forecast by $423,000 due to higher royalties as franchise store sales significantly exceeded plans.

Back line expenses came in some $1,343,000 or 9.8% over the operating budget and some $1,648,000 or 12.4% over the conservative forecast. Back line expense overruns to both plans occurred in the areas of system software development, long-term debt interest on system equipment acquired under capital lease, and telecommunication cost overruns related to the new system. Back line staff costs were under plan amounts and co-op advertising recoveries from suppliers fell short of expectations. The net result is a net income $268,000 short of the operating budget, but $761,000 above the conservative forecast to produce a result near the top of the Company's forecast range.

From a balance sheet perspective, the Company concluded the year with higher inventory, franchise receivables and supplier payables than planned, resulting in a poorer debt-to-equity ratio than forecast, but producing a current ratio better than the conservative forecast.

> Very strong sales gains beyond forecasts in Alberta, Metro Toronto, Southern Ontario and Eastern Ontario throughout the year were the result of aggressive inventory positions and marketing campaigns.

Clothes That Work for recreation.
LEVI's® denim shirts and RED TAB® jeans.

FINANCIAL STATEMENTS AND NOTES

MANAGEMENT'S RESPONSIBILITY FOR FINANCIAL STATEMENTS

The accompanying consolidated financial statements of the Company were prepared by management in accordance with accounting principles generally accepted in Canada applied on a consistent basis and conforming on a historical cost basis in all material respects with International Accounting Standards. The significant accounting policies, which management believes are appropriate for the Company, are described in Note 1 of the financial statements. The financial information contained elsewhere in this Annual Report is consistent with that in the financial statements.

Management is responsible for the integrity and objectivity of the financial statements. Estimates are necessary in the preparation of these statements and, based on careful judgements, have been properly reflected. Management has established systems of internal control which are designed to provide reasonable assurance that assets are safeguarded from loss or unauthorized use, and to produce reliable accounting records for the preparation of financial information.

The Board of Directors is responsible for ensuring that management fulfills its responsibilities for financial reporting and internal control. The Audit Committee of the Board is responsible for reviewing the annual consolidated financial statements and reporting to the Board, making recommendations with respect to the appointment and remuneration of the Company's auditor and reviewing the scope of the audit.

Management recognizes its responsibility for conducting the Company's affairs in compliance with established financial standards and applicable laws and maintains proper standards of conduct for its activities.

John A. Murphy, Senior Vice-President, Control

AUDITORS' REPORT

TO THE SHAREHOLDERS OF MARK'S WORK WEARHOUSE LTD.

We have audited the consolidated balance sheet of Mark's Work Wearhouse Ltd. as at January 29, 1994, January 30, 1993 and January 25, 1992 and the consolidated statements of operations, retained earnings (deficit) and cash flow for each of the years then ended. These financial statements are the responsibility of the Company's management. Our responsibility is to express an opinion on these financial statements based on our audits.

We conducted our audits in accordance with generally accepted auditing standards. These standards require that we plan and perform an audit to obtain reasonable assurance whether the financial statements are free of material misstatement. An audit includes examining, on a test basis, evidence supporting the amounts and disclosures in the financial statements. An audit also includes assessing the accounting principles used and significant estimates made by management, as well as evaluating the overall financial statement presentation.

In our opinion, these consolidated financial statements present fairly, in all material respects, the financial position of the Company as at January 29, 1994, January 30, 1993 and January 25, 1992 and the results of its operations and the changes in its financial position for each of the years then ended in accordance with generally accepted accounting principles.

Price Waterhouse Chartered Accountants, Calgary, Alberta
April 22, 1994

CONSOLIDATED BALANCE SHEET

	January 25, 1992	January 30, 1993	January 29, 1994
		(thousands)	
Assets			
Current assets			
Cash	$ —	$ 940	$ 3,761
Accounts receivable (Note 2)	10,625	7,807	12,931
Income taxes recoverable	1,794	348	100
Inventories	30,606	27,994	32,333
Prepaid expenses and deposits	1,362	1,106	1,048
	44,387	38,195	50,173
Other assets (Notes 3 and 11)	1,186	531	632
Fixed assets (Notes 4 and 7)	8,955	8,909	5,590
	$ 54,528	$ 47,635	$ 56,395
Liabilities			
Current liabilities			
Bank indebtedness (Note 5)	$ 2,778	$ —	$ —
Accounts payable and accrued liabilities	36,361	21,394	30,743
Current portion of long-term debt (Note 6)	852	1,931	180
	39,991	23,325	30,923
Deferred gain (Note 4)	504	477	1,727
Long-term debt (Note 6)	3,280	8,166	3,000
Shareholders' Equity			
Capital stock (Note 8)	14,321	21,981	25,793
Retained earnings (deficit)	(3,568)	(6,314)	(5,048)
	10,753	15,667	20,745
	$ 54,528	$ 47,635	$ 56,395

Commitments (Note 7)

Approved by the Board

Director

Director

CONSOLIDATED STATEMENT OF OPERATIONS

	52 weeks ended January 25, 1992	53 weeks ended January 30, 1993 (thousands)	52 weeks ended January 29, 1994
Front line operations (Note 1a)			
Sales	$ 132,742	$ 133,453	$ 158,066
Cost of sales	85,959	85,063	99,999
Gross margin	46,783	48,390	58,067
Front line expenses			
Personnel, advertising and other	21,037	22,039	27,587
Occupancy	14,556	14,886	15,579
Depreciation and amortization	2,238	1,736	1,686
Interest – short-term	1,258	1,152	528
	39,089	39,813	45,380
Front line contribution	7,694	8,577	12,687
Franchise contribution (Notes 12 and 1b)	3,000	2,475	3,571
Net front line contribution before back line expenses	10,694	11,052	16,258
Back line operations (Note 1a)			
Back line expenses			
Personnel, administration and other	11,184	9,296	8,563
Occupancy	985	888	984
Depreciation and amortization	1,566	1,294	1,874
Software development costs	660	1,342	1,913
Interest – long-term	1,096	978	1,658
Other items (Note 9)	1,959	—	—
	17,450	13,798	14,992
Earnings (loss) from operations before income taxes	(6,756)	(2,746)	1,266
Income taxes (Note 10)			
Current (recovery)	(1,794)	—	—
Deferred	1,351	—	—
	(443)	—	—
Net earnings (loss) from continuing operations	(6,313)	(2,746)	1,266
Discontinued operations (Note 11)			
Loss from operations	(196)	—	—
Loss on disposal, net of current tax recovery of $150,000 in 1992	(2,250)	—	—
Net earnings (loss)	$ (8,759)	$ (2,746)	$ 1,266
Earnings (loss) per common share			
From continuing operations	(64)¢	(17)¢	6¢
Net	(89)¢	(17)¢	6¢

CONSOLIDATED STATEMENT OF RETAINED EARNINGS (DEFICIT)

	52 weeks ended January 25, 1992	53 weeks ended January 30, 1993 (thousands)	52 weeks ended January 29, 1994
Retained earnings (deficit) at beginning of year	$ 5,191	$ (3,568)	$ (6,314)
Net earnings (loss)	(8,759)	(2,746)	1,266
Retained earnings (deficit) at end of year	$ (3,568)	$ (6,314)	$ (5,048)

CONSOLIDATED STATEMENT OF CASH FLOW

	52 weeks ended January 25, 1992	53 weeks ended January 30, 1993 (thousands)	52 weeks ended January 29, 1994
Cash generated (deployed)			
Operations			
Cash receipts	$ 129,712	$ 136,000	$ 152,942
Payments for inventories and operating expenses	(146,651)	(143,990)	(144,862)
Interest on long-term debt	(1,096)	(978)	(1,658)
Income taxes	2,069	1,446	248
	(15,966)	(7,522)	6,670
Financing			
Proceeds of long-term debt	477	6,756	4,927
Retirement of long-term debt	(7,092)	(942)	(12,246)
Issuance of share capital	—	7,660	3,812
	(6,615)	13,474	(3,507)
Investing			
Purchase of fixed assets	(1,648)	(3,160)	(4,739)
Change in net assets of discontinued automotive operation	2,610	499	—
Other assets	346	427	(101)
Disposition of fixed assets	1,501	—	4,498
Settlement with senior executives	(874)	—	—
	1,935	(2,234)	(342)
Net cash generated (deployed)	(20,646)	3,718	2,821
Cash (bank indebtedness) at beginning of year	17,868	(2,778)	940
Cash (bank indebtedness) at end of year	$ (2,778)	$ 940	$ 3,761

NOTES TO CONSOLIDATED FINANCIAL STATEMENTS

January 29, 1994

(dollar amounts in tables in thousands except earnings per share)

1. SIGNIFICANT ACCOUNTING POLICIES

The Company operates in the retail clothing industry in Canada. These financial statements are prepared by management in accordance with accounting principles generally accepted in Canada and conform, on a historical cost basis, in all material respects with International Accounting Standards.

(a) Basis of presentation and reclassification – The consolidated financial statements include the accounts of the Company and its subsidiaries, all of which are wholly owned.

During the year ended January 30, 1993, the Company reclassified elements of its statement of operations to distinguish between front line, franchise and back line activities to be more representative of the Company's business organization. Front line operations represent those activities where the Company's people and facilities come face-to-face with the customers, and back line operations represent those activities which support the effective performance of front line activities.

During the year ended January 25, 1992, the Company disposed of substantially all of the assets of its wholly owned subsidiary, Pro-Formance Automotive Ltd. ('Proformance'), and these financial statements reflect the Proformance operations on a discontinued basis using accounts of Proformance on a one-month delay basis for its fiscal year ended December 31. Reference is made in Notes 3 and 11.

(b) Franchise contribution – Initial franchise fees are recorded as income when the cash has been received, the store has been opened and any other material conditions relating to the sale have been substantially performed. Royalties, which are based on sales by the franchise, are recorded as income as they are earned. Costs are expensed as incurred as part of either front line or back line expenses as the majority of costs are not specifically identifiable as franchise costs, with the exception of bad debt write offs, which reduce the franchise contribution.

(c) Inventories – Inventories are accounted for by the retail method and are carried at the lower of estimated cost and anticipated selling price, less an expected average gross margin.

(d) Fixed assets – Depreciation is designed to amortize fixed assets on a straight line basis over their estimated useful lives at the following annual rates:

Leasehold improvements	Term of the lease
Furniture, fixtures and equipment	20%

(e) Computer services – The Company's outsourcing agreement with Information Systems Management (Alberta) Corporation requires declining payments over the next five years (Note 7). Since the services presently contemplated are to be the same for each of those years, the related costs are to be recognized in amounts equal to one-fifth of the total payments, reduced by the amortization of the gain (Note 4).

(f) Store opening expenses – Costs incurred in connection with the opening of a new store are charged against earnings in the year in which the store commences operations.

(g) Software development costs – Costs incurred to develop or acquire software for the Company's management information systems are expensed as incurred.

(h) Earnings per share – Basic earnings per share are calculated using the weighted average number of Common Shares outstanding during the year. Fully diluted earnings per share were calculated as though the Common Shares related to the conversion of the Company's 8% Convertible Subordinated Debentures had been issued on January 28, 1994. This calcuation was not dilutive. Exercise of outstanding options would not be dilutive.

2. ACCOUNTS RECEIVABLE

	1992	1993	1994
Receivable from franchise stores	$ 8,477	$ 7,524	$ 12,047
Other accounts receivable	3,465	2,652	3,739
	11,942	10,176	15,786
Allowance for doubtful accounts	(1,317)	(2,369)	(2,855)
	$ 10,625	$ 7,807	$ 12,931

3. OTHER ASSETS

	1992	1993	1994
Net assets of discontinued automotive operation (Notes 1a and 11)	$ 499	$ —	$ —
Employee relocation loans, secured	387	231	150
Notes receivable	300	300	300
Other	—	—	182
	$ 1,186	$ 531	$ 632

4. FIXED ASSETS

	1992		1993		1994	
	Cost	Net book value	Cost	Net book value	Cost	Net book value
Leasehold improvements	$ 6,945	$ 1,374	$ 7,038	$ 1,306	$ 3,003	$ 1,802
Furniture, fixtures and equipment	13,817	3,824	14,047	3,328	7,741	3,788
Equipment under capital lease (Note 7)	5,431	3,757	6,806	4,275	—	—
	$ 26,193	$ 8,955	$ 27,891	$ 8,909	$ 10,744	$ 5,590

Pursuant to an agreement dated December 31, 1993, effective February 1, 1994, the Company disposed of all its computer equipment under capital lease to Information Systems Management (Alberta) Corporation and entered into a five-year agreement by which it outsourced its computer operations, including computer equipment, to Information Systems Management (Alberta) Corporation. The gain realized on the disposition has been deferred and is being amortized as a reduction of outsourcing costs over the 60-month term of the agreement.

Effective August 1, 1991, the Company sold and leased back its corporate office and warehouse facility. The gain realized on the sale has been deferred and is being amortized as a reduction of occupancy expense over the 128-month term of the lease.

5. BANK INDEBTEDNESS

The Company has revolving credit facilities for demand loans as follows:

	Amount	Interest Rate
Operating	$11,500	prime + 1%
Operating – Bulge	$ 5,500	prime + 1.25%
Letter of Credit Facility	$ 1,500	1.25%

The operating line of credit could be limited to $9,500,000 in the February 1 to May 1 period if certain projected sales targets are not met. The operating line of credit and the letter of credit facility are limited to the lesser of $13,000,000 and the aggregate of 60% of inventories and 50% of accounts receivable, as defined. The operating bulge facility increases the operating line of credit and the letter of credit facility to a total of $18,500,000 for the period May 1, 1994 to December 31, 1994 subject to the same limits based on inventories and accounts receivable.

Security provided includes a first fixed and floating charge debenture on the assets of the Company together with a registered general assignment of book debts and assignment of inventories.

6. LONG-TERM DEBT

	1992	1993	1994	
	Amount Outstanding	Amount Outstanding	Amount Outstanding	Due within one Year
8% Convertible Subordinated Debentures	$ —	$ —	$ 3,000	$ —
Subordinated debentures				
– Series A, 11.4%	—	4,004	—	—
– Series B, prime + 2%	—	532	180	180
Capital lease obligations –				
1993 16.1%; 1992 16.4% average				
interest rate, repayable over five years	4,086	5,515	—	—
Other	46	46	—	—
Total	4,132	10,097	3,180	$ 180
Less: Amount due within one year	852	1,931	180	
	$ 3,280	$ 8,166	$ 3,000	

On January 28, 1994, the Company issued, by way of private placement to institutional investors, $3,000,000 8% Convertible Subordinated Debentures. The Debentures mature on February 3, 1997 and are convertible into Common Shares of the Company at a price of $1.85 per share. The net proceeds of the offering, together with working capital, were used to repay the 11.4% Subordinated Debentures Series A. The Series B Subordinate Debentures were repaid in full in February of 1994.

The aggregate repayments of principal required to meet long-term debt obligations are as follows:

1995	$ 180
1996	—
1997	3,000
1998	—
1999	—
	$ 3,180

7. COMMITMENTS

The Company has entered into operating lease agreements terminating at various dates to 2008. The minimum annual rentals, excluding tenant operating costs, under these agreements are as follows:

1995	$ 8,250
1996	7,303
1997	6,355
1998	5,166
1999	3,621
Thereafter	10,794
	$ 41,489

In addition to minimum annual rentals, contingent rentals may be payable under certain store leases on the basis of sales in excess of stipulated amounts.

On December 31, 1993, the Company entered into a five-year agreement effective February 1, 1994 through February 1, 1999 with Information Systems Management (Alberta) Corporation by which it outsourced its computer operations and disposed of its computer equipment previously held under capital lease. The minimum annual cash costs for services under this agreement are as follows:

1995	$ 2,946
1996	3,044
1997	2,207
1998	1,789
1999	1,064
Thereafter	180
	$ 11,230

Minimum annual costs for services could escalate if the Company were to require increased services beyond current requirements.

8. CAPITAL STOCK

The authorized capital stock of the Company is divided into 100,000,000 First Preferred Shares of no par value and an unlimited number of Common Shares of no par value.

The Articles of the Corporation were amended on May 12, 1992 to redesignate the previously existing Restricted Voting Shares as Common Shares, after the previously existing Class A Shares had been converted into Restricted Voting Shares. A further amendment to the Articles was made on August 13, 1992 to remove the previously existing Class A Shares from the capital structure of the Company and increase the number of Common Shares that the Company is authorized to issue to an unlimited number.

The issued capital stock of the Company is as follows:

	1992	1993	1994
Class A Shares			
(1992 – 877,000)	$ 2	$ —	$ —
Restricted Voting Shares			
(1992 – 8,964,832)	14,319	—	—
23,139,817 Common Shares			
(1993 – 18,289,453)	—	21,981	25,793
	$ 14,321	$ 21,981	$ 25,793

During the year ended January 29, 1994, 4,572,364 Common Shares were issued for a total consideration of $3,795,062 less costs of issue of $252,553, pursuant to a rights offering. Further, pursuant to an employment contract, 150,000 shares were issued during the year ended January 29, 1994 by private placement to an executive officer for $138, 000. In addition, pursuant to the exercise of employee stock options, 128,000 Common Shares were issued during the year ended January 29, 1994 for a total consideration of $131,500.

During the year ended January 30, 1993, 8,000,000 Restricted Voting Shares, redesignated as Common Shares, were issued for a total consideration of $8,000,000 less costs of issue of $795,688, pursuant to a Special Warrants issue. Also during the year ended January 30, 1993, 450,621 Common Shares were issued to employees under the Company's Employee Share Purchase Plan for a total consideration of $455,487. Under the Plan, the Company is permitted, but not obligated, to provide financial assistance by way of loans to employees to permit them to acquire Common Shares against the security of the Common Shares being purchased. As at January 29, 1994, 125,362 Common Shares were presently held as security for $126,756 of financing provided by the Company under the Plan.

No Class A Shares or Restricted Voting Shares were issued or cancelled during the year ended January 25, 1992.

Options to purchase Common Shares granted to directors, employees, an employee who will be joining the Company, and one former employee pursuant to a settlement arrangement, and outstanding as at January 29, 1994 are as follows:

Number of Common Shares	Exercise Price	Expiry Date
135,000	$0.85	January 31, 1996
15,000	$0.94	January 31, 1996
810,000	$1.00	January 17, 1997
180,000	$1.20	March 25, 1997
75,000	$1.00	January 15, 1998
235,000	$0.85	January 20, 1998
655,000	$1.45	January 19, 1999

Pursuant to a settlement with Morley A. Blumes, the Company granted him an option to acquire up to 75,000 Common Shares of the Company at $1.00 per share. The option expires on January 15, 1998 and the Company may require that it be exercised if the trading price of the Common Shares of the Company exceeds $4.50 for 20 consecutive trading days. (Note 9).

9. OTHER ITEMS

	1992	1993	1994
Loan settlement with a senior executive	$ (429)	$ —	$ —
Settlement with a senior executive	(1,530)	—	—
	$ (1,959)	$ —	$ —

In connection with the issuance of Special Warrants during the period January 29, 1992 through February 7, 1992 and the agreement by Marcus W. Blumes to convert all issued Class A Shares into Restricted Voting Shares, the Company agreed to a settlement of the loans due from Mr. M.W. Blumes. In connection with the termination of employment of Morley A. Blumes and the settlement of all other outstanding disputes between the Company and Morley A. Blumes, including set off against amounts owing by Morley A. Blumes to the Company, the Company agreed to a settlement with Morley A. Blumes. (Note 8).

10. INCOME TAXES

The provision for income taxes varies from the amount computed by applying the combined federal and provincial income tax rates as follows:

	1992		1993		1994	
Federal and provincial income taxes	(43.3)%	$ (2,925)	(44.3)%	$(1,216)	44.2%	$ 560
Increase (decrease) resulting from:						
Realization of net capital						
loss carryforward	(2.0)%	(137)	—	—	—	—
Deferred income tax writedown	20.0%	1,351	—	—	—	—
Capital taxes	.7%	49	3.1%	85	5.4%	68
Benefit of unrecognized (recognized) amounts	17.0%	1,152	44.4%	1,219	(49.3)%	(624)
Other	1.0%	67	(3.2)%	(88)	(.3)%	(4)
Provision for income taxes (recovery)	(6.6)%	$ (443)	—	$ —	—	$ —

The Company has an August tax year end. For the tax year ended August 28, 1993, the Company had net capital losses carried forward in the aggregate amount of $769,000 which will be available to offset future taxable capital gains, if any. The possible benefit of these net capital losses has not been recognized. The Company also has an excess of undepreciated capital cost of its depreciable fixed assets over the net book value of those fixed assets and other amounts not yet taken as deductions for income tax purposes totalling $2,437,000 which are available to reduce future years' earnings for income tax purposes, the benefits of which are not recognized in the accounts. The Company also had non-capital losses, carried forward for tax purposes, of $9,947,000 as at August 28, 1993, the benefits of which have not been recognized in the accounts. These losses are available for carryforward and begin to expire in 1995.

11. DISCONTINUED OPERATIONS

Effective June 1991, the Company undertook a formal plan to dispose of its three automotive dealerships. The sales of substantially all of the operating assets of those dealerships were completed in the fourth quarter of fiscal 1992. Net cash proceeds from the sales of $2,727,000, after deducting selling expenses and the assumption or payments of debts of the automobile dealerships, were used in December, 1991 to repay bank term loans of the Company. Results of those operations were as follows:

	1992	1993	1994
Revenue	$ 23,263	$ —	$ —
Net earnings (loss)			
Before income taxes	$ (164)	$ —	$ —
Income taxes	32	—	—
	$ (196)	$ —	$ —

The book value of the net assets of the automotive operation at June 30, 1991 and at the balance sheet dates was as follows:

	June 30, 1991	January 25, 1992	January 30, 1993	January 29, 1994
Working capital	$ 1,226	$ 241	$ —	$ —
Fixed assets, net	9,974	258	—	—
Long-term debt	(6,610)	—	—	—
Other	387	—	—	—
	$ 4,977	$ 499	$ —	$ —

12. FRANCHISE OPERATIONS

	1992	1993	1994
Franchise royalties and			
initial franchise fees	$ 3,630	$ 3,573	$ 4,071
Bad debt provisions on			
franchise receivables	(630)	(1,098)	(500)
Franchise contribution (Note 1b)	$ 3,000	$ 2,475	$ 3,571
Number of franchise stores			
Open at beginning of year	53	57	45
New openings	4	—	—
Franchising of corporate stores	3	—	—
Closed	(2)	(7)	(1)
Converted to corporate stores	(1)	(5)	(1)
Open at end of year	57	45	43
Number of corporate stores			
Open at year end	86	91	91

13. RETIREMENT PLAN

A defined contribution retirement plan was implemented in September, 1989 for the benefit of the Company's permanent employees. In conjunction with that plan, a past service pension plan was adopted and fully funded in August, 1989. The cost of that plan was deferred and is being charged to earnings over five years at $64,000 per year.

14. SELECTED QUARTERLY FINANCIAL INFORMATION (UNAUDITED)

52 weeks ended January 29, 1994

	First	Second	Third	Fourth
Sales	$24,869	$28,833	$39,791	$64,573
Gross margin percentage	37.6%	34.3%	37.1%	37.3%
Earnings (loss) before income taxes	$(2,971)	$(3,728)	$(489)	$8,454
Net earnings (loss) per share	(14)¢	(16)¢	(02)¢	37¢
Corporate stores at end of quarter	88	90	93	91

53 weeks ended January 30, 1993

	First	Second	Third	Fourth
Sales	$20,340	$23,195	$31,342	$58,576
Gross margin percentage	37.2%	34.8%	36.8%	36.2%
Earnings (loss) before income taxes	$ (3,429)	$ (3,766)	$ (1,350)	$ 5,799
Net earnings (loss) per share	(35)¢	(23)¢	(7)¢	32¢
Corporate stores at end of quarter	84	83	89	91

52 weeks ended January 25, 1992

	First	Second	Third	Fourth
Sales	$21,834	$23,808	$33,110	$53,990
Gross margin percentage	36.9%	34.4%	36.9%	33.9%
Earnings (loss) before income taxes	$ (3,718)	$ (3,981)	$ (2,815)	$ 3,758
Net earnings (loss) per share	(23)¢	(46)¢	(26)¢	06¢
Corporate stores at end of quarter	91	91	91	86

Appendix B

Present-Value Tables and Future-Value Tables

This appendix provides present-value tables (more complete than those appearing in Chapter 16 and Chapter 26) and future-value tables.

Table B-1 *Present Value of $1*

Periods	1%	2%	3%	4%	5%	6%	7%	8%	9%	10%	12%
1	0.990	0.980	0.971	0.962	0.952	0.943	0.935	0.926	0.917	0.909	0.893
2	0.980	0.961	0.943	0.925	0.907	0.890	0.873	0.857	0.842	0.826	0.797
3	0.971	0.942	0.915	0.889	0.864	0.840	0.816	0.794	0.772	0.751	0.712
4	0.961	0.924	0.888	0.855	0.823	0.792	0.763	0.735	0.708	0.683	0.636
5	0.951	0.906	0.883	0.822	0.784	0.747	0.713	0.681	0.650	0.621	0.567
6	0.942	0.888	0.837	0.790	0.746	0.705	0.666	0.630	0.596	0.564	0.507
7	0.933	0.871	0.813	0.760	0.711	0.665	0.623	0.583	0.547	0.513	0.452
8	0.923	0.853	0.789	0.731	0.677	0.627	0.582	0.540	0.502	0.467	0.404
9	0.914	0.837	0.766	0.703	0.645	0.592	0.544	0.500	0.460	0.424	0.361
10	0.905	0.820	0.744	0.676	0.614	0.558	0.508	0.463	0.422	0.386	0.322
11	0.896	0.804	0.722	0.650	0.585	0.527	0.475	0.429	0.388	0.350	0.287
12	0.887	0.788	0.701	0.625	0.557	0.497	0.444	0.397	0.356	0.319	0.257
13	0.879	0.773	0.681	0.601	0.530	0.469	0.415	0.368	0.326	0.290	0.229
14	0.870	0.758	0.661	0.577	0.505	0.442	0.388	0.340	0.299	0.263	0.205
15	0.861	0.743	0.642	0.555	0.481	0.417	0.362	0.315	0.275	0.239	0.183
16	0.853	0.728	0.623	0.534	0.458	0.394	0.339	0.292	0.252	0.218	0.163
17	0.844	0.714	0.605	0.513	0.436	0.371	0.317	0.270	0.231	0.198	0.146
18	0.836	0.700	0.587	0.494	0.416	0.350	0.296	0.250	0.212	0.180	0.130
19	0.828	0.686	0.570	0.475	0.396	0.331	0.277	0.232	0.194	0.164	0.116
20	0.820	0.673	0.554	0.456	0.377	0.312	0.258	0.215	0.178	0.149	0.104
21	0.811	0.660	0.538	0.439	0.359	0.294	0.242	0.199	0.164	0.135	0.093
22	0.803	0.647	0.522	0.422	0.342	0.278	0.226	0.184	0.150	0.123	0.083
23	0.795	0.634	0.507	0.406	0.326	0.262	0.211	0.170	0.138	0.112	0.074
24	0.788	0.622	0.492	0.390	0.310	0.247	0.197	0.158	0.126	0.102	0.066
25	0.780	0.610	0.478	0.375	0.295	0.233	0.184	0.146	0.116	0.092	0.059
26	0.772	0.598	0.464	0.361	0.281	0.220	0.172	0.135	0.106	0.084	0.053
27	0.764	0.586	0.450	0.347	0.268	0.207	0.161	0.125	0.098	0.076	0.047
28	0.757	0.574	0.437	0.333	0.255	0.196	0.150	0.116	0.090	0.069	0.042
29	0.749	0.563	0.424	0.321	0.243	0.185	0.141	0.107	0.082	0.063	0.037
30	0.742	0.552	0.412	0.308	0.231	0.174	0.131	0.099	0.075	0.057	0.033
40	0.672	0.453	0.307	0.208	0.142	0.097	0.067	0.046	0.032	0.022	0.011
50	0.608	0.372	0.228	0.141	0.087	0.054	0.034	0.021	0.013	0.009	0.003

Table B-1   *(cont'd)*

14%	15%	16%	18%	20%	25%	30%	35%	40%	45%	50%	Periods
					Present Value						
0.877	0.870	0.862	0.847	0.833	0.800	0.769	0.741	0.714	0.690	0.667	1
0.769	0.756	0.743	0.718	0.694	0.640	0.592	0.549	0.510	0.476	0.444	2
0.675	0.658	0.641	0.609	0.579	0.512	0.455	0.406	0.364	0.328	0.296	3
0.592	0.572	0.552	0.516	0.482	0.410	0.350	0.301	0.260	0.226	0.198	4
0.519	0.497	0.476	0.437	0.402	0.328	0.269	0.223	0.186	0.156	0.132	5
0.456	0.432	0.410	0.370	0.335	0.262	0.207	0.165	0.133	0.108	0.088	6
0.400	0.376	0.354	0.314	0.279	0.210	0.159	0.122	0.095	0.074	0.059	7
0.351	0.327	0.305	0.266	0.233	0.168	0.123	0.091	0.068	0.051	0.039	8
0.308	0.284	0.263	0.225	0.194	0.134	0.094	0.067	0.048	0.035	0.026	9
0.270	0.247	0.227	0.191	0.162	0.107	0.073	0.050	0.035	0.024	0.017	10
0.237	0.215	0.195	0.162	0.135	0.086	0.056	0.037	0.025	0.017	0.012	11
0.208	0.187	0.168	0.137	0.112	0.069	0.043	0.027	0.018	0.012	0.008	12
0.182	0.163	0.145	0.116	0.093	0.055	0.033	0.020	0.013	0.008	0.005	13
0.160	0.141	0.125	0.099	0.078	0.044	0.025	0.015	0.009	0.006	0.003	14
0.140	0.123	0.108	0.084	0.065	0.035	0.020	0.011	0.006	0.004	0.002	15
0.123	0.107	0.093	0.071	0.054	0.028	0.015	0.008	0.005	0.003	0.002	16
0.108	0.093	0.080	0.060	0.045	0.023	0.012	0.006	0.003	0.002	0.001	17
0.095	0.081	0.069	0.051	0.038	0.018	0.009	0.005	0.002	0.001	0.001	18
0.083	0.070	0.060	0.043	0.031	0.014	0.007	0.003	0.002	0.001		19
0.073	0.061	0.051	0.037	0.026	0.012	0.005	0.002	0.001	0.001		20
0.064	0.053	0.044	0.031	0.022	0.009	0.004	0.002	0.001			21
0.056	0.046	0.038	0.026	0.018	0.007	0.003	0.001	0.001			22
0.049	0.040	0.033	0.022	0.015	0.006	0.002	0.001				23
0.043	0.035	0.028	0.019	0.013	0.005	0.002	0.001				24
0.038	0.030	0.024	0.016	0.010	0.004	0.001	0.001				25
0.033	0.026	0.021	0.014	0.009	0.003	0.001					26
0.029	0.023	0.018	0.011	0.007	0.002	0.001					27
0.026	0.020	0.016	0.010	0.006	0.002	0.001					28
0.022	0.017	0.014	0.008	0.005	0.002						29
0.020	0.015	0.012	0.007	0.004	0.001						30
0.005	0.004	0.003	0.001	0.001							40
0.001	0.001	0.001									50

Table B-2   *Present Value of Annuity $1*

Periods	1%	2%	3%	4%	5%	6%	7%	8%	9%	10%	12%
					Present Value						
1	0.990	0.980	0.971	0.962	0.952	0.943	0.935	0.926	0.917	0.909	0.893
2	1.970	1.942	1.913	1.886	1.859	1.833	1.808	1.783	1.759	1.736	1.690
3	2.941	2.884	2.829	2.775	2.723	2.673	2.624	2.577	2.531	2.487	2.402
4	3.902	3.808	3.717	3.630	3.546	3.465	3.387	3.312	3.240	3.170	3.037
5	4.853	4.713	4.580	4.452	4.329	4.212	4.100	3.993	3.890	3.791	3.605
6	5.795	5.601	5.417	5.242	5.076	4.917	4.767	4.623	4.486	4.355	4.111
7	6.728	6.472	6.230	6.002	5.786	5.582	5.389	5.206	5.033	4.868	4.564
8	7.652	7.325	7.020	6.733	6.463	6.210	5.971	5.747	5.535	5.335	4.968
9	8.566	8.162	7.786	7.435	7.108	6.802	6.515	6.247	5.995	5.759	5.328
10	9.471	8.983	8.530	8.111	7.722	7.360	7.024	6.710	6.418	6.145	5.650
11	10.368	9.787	9.253	8.760	8.306	7.887	7.499	7.139	6.805	6.495	5.938
12	11.255	10.575	9.954	9.385	8.863	8.384	7.943	7.536	7.161	6.814	6.194
13	12.134	11.348	10.635	9.986	9.394	8.853	8.358	7.904	7.487	7.103	6.424
14	13.004	12.106	11.296	10.563	9.899	9.295	8.745	8.244	7.786	7.367	6.628
15	13.865	12.849	11.938	11.118	10.380	9.712	9.108	8.559	8.061	7.606	6.811
16	14.718	13.578	12.561	11.652	10.838	10.106	9.447	8.851	8.313	7.824	6.974
17	15.562	14.292	13.166	12.166	11.274	10.477	9.763	9.122	8.544	8.022	7.120
18	16.398	14.992	13.754	12.659	11.690	10.828	10.059	9.372	8.756	8.201	7.250
19	17.226	15.678	14.324	13.134	12.085	11.158	10.336	9.604	8.950	8.365	7.366
20	18.046	16.351	14.878	13.590	12.462	11.470	10.594	9.818	9.129	8.514	7.469
21	18.857	17.011	15.415	14.029	12.821	11.764	10.836	10.017	9.292	8.649	7.562
22	19.660	17.658	15.937	14.451	13.163	12.042	11.061	10.201	9.442	8.772	7.645
23	20.456	18.292	16.444	14.857	13.489	12.303	11.272	10.371	9.580	8.883	7.718
24	21.243	18.914	16.936	15.247	13.799	12.550	11.469	10.529	9.707	8.985	7.784
25	22.023	19.523	17.413	15.622	14.094	12.783	11.654	10.675	9.823	9.077	7.843
26	22.795	20.121	17.877	15.983	14.375	13.003	11.826	10.810	9.929	9.161	7.896
27	23.560	20.707	18.327	16.330	14.643	13.211	11.987	10.935	10.027	9.237	7.943
28	24.316	21.281	18.764	16.663	14.898	13.406	12.137	11.051	10.116	9.307	7.984
29	25.066	21.844	19.189	16.984	15.141	13.591	12.278	11.158	10.198	9.370	8.022
30	25.808	22.396	19.600	17.292	15.373	13.765	12.409	11.258	10.274	9.427	8.055
40	32.835	27.355	23.115	19.793	17.159	15.046	13.332	11.925	10.757	9.779	8.244
50	39.196	31.424	25.730	21.482	18.256	15.762	13.801	12.234	10.962	9.915	8.305

Table B-2 *(cont'd)*

14%	15%	16%	18%	20%	25%	30%	35%	40%	45%	50%	Periods
0.877	0.870	0.862	0.847	0.833	0.800	0.769	0.741	0.714	0.690	0.667	1
1.647	1.626	1.605	1.566	1.528	1.440	1.361	1.289	1.224	1.165	1.111	2
2.322	2.283	2.246	2.174	2.106	1.952	1.816	1.696	1.589	1.493	1.407	3
2.914	2.855	2.798	2.690	2.589	2.362	2.166	1.997	1.849	1.720	1.605	4
3.433	3.352	3.274	3.127	2.991	2.689	2.436	2.220	2.035	1.876	1.737	5
3.889	3.784	3.685	3.498	3.326	2.951	2.643	2.385	2.168	1.983	1.824	6
4.288	4.160	4.039	3.812	3.605	3.161	2.802	2.508	2.263	2.057	1.883	7
4.639	4.487	4.344	4.078	3.837	3.329	2.925	2.598	2.331	2.109	1.922	8
4.946	4.772	4.607	4.303	4.031	3.463	3.019	2.665	2.379	2.144	1.948	9
5.216	5.019	4.833	4.494	4.192	3.571	3.092	2.715	2.414	2.168	1.965	10
5.453	5.234	5.029	4.656	4.327	3.656	3.147	2.752	2.438	2.185	1.977	11
5.660	5.421	5.197	4.793	4.439	3.725	3.190	2.779	2.456	2.197	1.985	12
5.842	5.583	5.342	4.910	4.533	3.780	3.223	2.799	2.469	2.204	1.990	13
6.002	5.724	5.468	5.008	4.611	3.824	3.249	2.814	2.478	2.210	1.993	14
6.142	5.847	5.575	5.092	4.675	3.859	3.268	2.825	2.484	2.214	1.995	15
6.265	5.954	5.669	5.162	4.730	3.887	3.283	2.834	2.489	2.216	1.997	16
6.373	6.047	5.749	5.222	4.775	3.910	3.295	2.840	2.492	2.218	1.998	17
6.467	6.128	5.818	5.273	4.812	3.928	3.304	2.844	2.494	2.219	1.999	18
6.550	6.198	5.877	5.316	4.844	3.942	3.311	2.848	2.496	2.220	1.999	19
6.623	6.259	5.929	5.353	4.870	3.954	3.316	2.850	2.497	2.221	1.999	20
6.687	6.312	5.973	5.384	4.891	3.963	3.320	2.852	2.498	2.221	2.000	21
6.743	6.359	6.011	5.410	4.909	3.970	3.323	2.853	2.498	2.222	2.000	22
6.792	6.399	6.044	5.432	4.925	3.976	3.325	2.854	2.499	2.222	2.000	23
6.835	6.434	6.073	5.451	4.937	3.981	3.327	2.855	2.499	2.222	2.000	24
6.873	6.464	6.097	5.467	4.948	3.985	3.329	2.856	2.499	2.222	2.000	25
6.906	6.491	6.118	5.480	4.956	3.988	3.330	2.856	2.500	2.222	2.000	26
6.935	6.514	6.136	5.492	4.964	3.990	3.331	2.856	2.500	2.222	2.000	27
6.961	6.534	6.152	5.502	4.970	3.992	3.331	2.857	2.500	2.222	2.000	28
6.983	6.551	6.166	5.510	4.975	3.994	3.332	2.857	2.500	2.222	2.000	29
7.003	6.566	6.177	5.517	4.979	3.995	3.332	2.857	2.500	2.222	2.000	30
7.105	6.642	6.234	5.548	4.997	3.999	3.333	2.857	2.500	2.222	2.000	40
7.133	6.661	6.246	5.554	4.999	4.000	3.333	2.857	2.500	2.222	2.000	50

Present Value

Table B-3 *Future Value of $1*

Periods	1%	2%	3%	4%	5%	6%	7%	8%	9%	10%	12%	14%	15%
						Future Value							
1	1.010	1.020	1.030	1.040	1.050	1.060	1.070	1.080	1.090	1.100	1.120	1.140	1.150
2	1.020	1.040	1.061	1.082	1.103	1.124	1.145	1.166	1.188	1.210	1.254	1.300	1.323
3	1.030	1.061	1.093	1.125	1.158	1.191	1.225	1.260	1.295	1.331	1.405	1.482	1.521
4	1.041	1.082	1.126	1.170	1.216	1.262	1.311	1.360	1.412	1.464	1.574	1.689	1.749
5	1.051	1.104	1.159	1.217	1.276	1.338	1.403	1.469	1.539	1.611	1.762	1.925	2.011
6	1.062	1.126	1.194	1.265	1.340	1.419	1.501	1.587	1.677	1.772	1.974	2.195	2.313
7	1.072	1.149	1.230	1.316	1.407	1.504	1.606	1.714	1.828	1.949	2.211	2.502	2.660
8	1.083	1.172	1.267	1.369	1.477	1.594	1.718	1.851	1.993	2.144	2.476	2.853	3.059
9	1.094	1.195	1.305	1.423	1.551	1.689	1.838	1.999	2.172	2.358	2.773	3.252	3.518
10	1.105	1.219	1.344	1.480	1.629	1.791	1.967	2.159	2.367	2.594	3.106	3.707	4.046
11	1.116	1.243	1.384	1.539	1.710	1.898	2.105	2.332	2.580	2.853	3.479	4.226	4.652
12	1.127	1.268	1.426	1.601	1.796	2.012	2.252	2.518	2.813	3.138	3.896	4.818	5.350
13	1.138	1.294	1.469	1.665	1.886	2.133	2.410	2.720	3.066	3.452	4.363	5.492	6.153
14	1.149	1.319	1.513	1.732	1.980	2.261	2.579	2.937	3.342	3.798	4.887	6.261	7.076
15	1.161	1.346	1.558	1.801	2.079	2.397	2.759	3.172	3.642	4.177	5.474	7.138	8.137
16	1.173	1.373	1.605	1.873	2.183	2.540	2.952	3.426	3.970	4.595	6.130	8.137	9.358
17	1.184	1.400	1.653	1.948	2.292	2.693	3.159	3.700	4.328	5.054	6.866	9.276	10.76
18	1.196	1.428	1.702	2.026	2.407	2.854	3.380	3.996	4.717	5.560	7.690	10.58	12.38
19	1.208	1.457	1.754	2.107	2.527	3.026	3.617	4.316	5.142	6.116	8.613	12.06	14.23
20	1.220	1.486	1.806	2.191	2.653	3.207	3.870	4.661	5.604	6.728	9.646	13.74	16.37
21	1.232	1.516	1.860	2.279	2.786	3.400	4.141	5.034	6.109	7.400	10.80	15.67	18.82
22	1.245	1.546	1.916	2.370	2.925	3.604	4.430	5.437	6.659	8.140	12.10	17.86	21.64
23	1.257	1.577	1.974	2.465	3.072	3.820	4.741	5.871	7.258	8.954	13.55	20.36	24.89
24	1.270	1.608	2.033	2.563	3.225	4.049	5.072	6.341	7.911	9.850	15.18	23.21	28.63
25	1.282	1.641	2.094	2.666	3.386	4.292	5.427	6.848	8.623	10.83	17.00	26.46	32.92
26	1.295	1.673	2.157	2.772	3.556	4.549	5.807	7.396	9.399	11.92	19.04	30.17	37.86
27	1.308	1.707	2.221	2.883	3.733	4.822	6.214	7.988	10.25	13.11	21.32	34.39	43.54
28	1.321	1.741	2.288	2.999	3.920	5.112	6.649	8.627	11.17	14.42	23.88	39.20	50.07
29	1.335	1.776	2.357	3.119	4.116	5.418	7.114	9.317	12.17	15.86	26.75	44.69	57.58
30	1.348	1.811	2.427	3.243	4.322	5.743	7.612	10.06	13.27	17.45	29.96	50.95	66.21
40	1.489	2.208	3.262	4.801	7.040	10.29	14.97	21.72	31.41	45.26	93.05	188.9	267.9
50	1.645	2.692	4.384	7.107	11.47	18.42	29.46	46.90	74.36	117.4	289.0	700.2	1,084

Table B-4   *Future Value of Annuity of $1*

Periods	1%	2%	3%	4%	5%	6%	7%	8%	9%	10%	12%	14%	15%
1	1.000	1.000	1.000	1.000	1.000	1.000	1.000	1.000	1.000	1.000	1.000	1.000	1.000
2	2.010	2.020	2.030	2.040	2.050	2.060	2.070	2.080	2.090	2.100	2.120	2.140	2.150
3	3.030	3.060	3.091	3.122	3.153	3.184	3.215	3.246	3.278	3.310	3.374	3.440	3.473
4	4.060	4.122	4.184	4.246	4.310	4.375	4.440	4.506	4.573	4.641	4.779	4.921	4.993
5	5.101	5.204	5.309	5.416	5.526	5.637	5.751	5.867	5.985	6.105	6.353	6.610	6.742
6	6.152	6.308	6.468	6.633	6.802	6.975	7.153	7.336	7.523	7.716	8.115	8.536	8.754
7	7.214	7.434	7.662	7.898	8.142	8.394	8.654	8.923	9.200	9.487	10.09	10.73	11.07
8	8.286	8.583	8.892	9.214	9.549	9.897	10.26	10.64	11.03	11.44	12.30	13.23	13.73
9	9.369	9.755	10.16	10.58	11.03	11.49	11.98	12.49	13.02	13.58	14.78	16.09	16.79
10	10.46	10.95	11.46	12.01	12.58	13.18	13.82	14.49	15.19	15.94	17.55	19.34	20.30
11	11.57	12.17	12.81	13.49	14.21	14.97	15.78	16.65	17.56	18.53	20.65	23.04	24.35
12	12.68	13.41	14.19	15.03	15.92	16.87	17.89	18.98	20.14	21.38	24.13	27.27	29.00
13	13.81	14.68	15.62	16.63	17.71	18.88	20.14	21.50	22.95	24.52	28.03	32.09	34.35
14	14.95	15.97	17.09	18.29	19.60	21.02	22.55	24.21	26.02	27.98	32.39	37.58	40.50
15	16.10	17.29	18.60	20.02	21.58	23.28	25.13	27.15	29.36	31.77	37.28	43.84	47.58
16	17.26	18.64	20.16	21.82	23.66	25.67	27.89	30.32	33.00	35.95	42.75	50.98	55.72
17	18.43	20.01	21.76	23.70	25.84	28.21	30.84	33.75	36.97	40.54	48.88	59.12	65.08
18	19.61	21.41	23.41	25.65	28.13	30.91	34.00	37.45	41.30	45.60	55.75	68.39	75.84
19	20.81	22.84	25.12	27.67	30.54	33.76	37.38	41.45	46.02	51.16	63.44	78.97	88.21
20	22.02	24.30	26.87	29.78	33.07	36.79	41.00	45.76	51.16	57.28	72.05	91.02	102.4
21	23.24	25.78	28.68	31.97	35.72	39.99	44.87	50.42	56.76	64.00	81.70	104.8	118.8
22	24.47	27.30	30.54	34.25	38.51	43.39	49.01	55.46	62.87	71.40	92.50	120.4	137.6
23	25.72	28.85	32.45	36.62	41.43	47.00	53.44	60.89	69.53	79.54	104.6	138.3	159.3
24	26.97	30.42	34.43	39.08	44.50	50.82	58.18	66.76	76.79	88.50	118.2	158.7	184.2
25	28.24	32.03	36.46	41.65	47.73	54.86	63.25	73.11	84.70	98.35	133.3	181.9	212.8
26	29.53	33.67	38.55	44.31	51.11	59.16	68.68	79.95	93.32	109.2	150.3	208.3	245.7
27	30.82	35.34	40.71	47.08	54.67	63.71	74.48	87.35	102.7	121.1	169.4	238.5	283.6
28	32.13	37.05	42.93	49.97	58.40	68.53	80.70	95.34	113.0	134.2	190.7	272.9	327.1
29	33.45	38.79	45.22	52.97	62.32	73.64	87.35	104.0	124.1	148.6	214.6	312.1	377.2
30	34.78	40.57	47.58	56.08	66.44	79.06	94.46	113.3	136.3	164.5	241.3	356.8	434.7
40	48.89	60.40	75.40	95.03	120.8	154.8	199.6	259.1	337.9	442.6	767.1	1,342	1,779
50	64.46	84.58	112.8	152.7	209.3	290.3	406.5	573.8	815.1	1,164	2,400	4,995	7,218

Glossary

Accelerated depreciation method See declining-balance method *(p. 484)*.

Account The detailed record of the changes that have occurred in a particular asset, liability, or shareholders' equity during a period *(p. 54)*.

Account payable A liability that is backed by the general reputation and credit standing of the debtor *(p. 10)*.

Account receivable An asset, a promise to receive cash from customers to whom the business has sold goods or services *(p. 10)*.

Accounting The system that measures business activities, processes that information into reports and financial statements, and communicates the findings to decision-makers *(p. 2)*.

Accounting cycle Process by which accountants produce an entity's financial statements for a specific period *(p. 162)*.

Accounting equation The most basic tool of accounting: Assets = Liabilities + Owner's Equity *(p. 10)*.

Accounting information system The combination of personnel, records, and procedures that a business uses to meet its need for financial data *(p. 280)*.

Accounts receivable turnover Ratio of net credit sales to average net accounts receivable. Measures ability to collect cash from credit customers *(p. 930)*.

Accrual-basis accounting Accounting that recognizes (records) the impact of a business event as it occurs, regardless of whether the transaction affected cash *(p. 111)*.

Accrued expense An expense that has been incurred but not yet paid in cash *(p. 121)*.

Accrued revenue A revenue that has been earned but not yet received in cash *(p. 122)*.

Accumulated depreciation The cumulative sum of all depreciation expense from the date of acquiring a capital asset *(p. 119)*.

Acid-test ratio Ratio of the sum of cash plus short-term investments plus net current receivables to current liabilities. Tells whether the entity could pay all its current liabilities if they came due immediately. Also called the quick ratio *(pp. 409, 928)*.

Adjusted trial balance A list of all the ledger accounts with their adjusted balances *(p. 125)*.

Adjusting entry Entry made at the end of the period to assign revenues to the period in which they are earned and expenses to the period in which they are incurred. Adjusting entries help measure the period's income and bring the related asset and liability accounts to correct balances for the financial statements *(p. 116)*.

Aging of accounts receivable A way to estimate bad debts by analyzing individual accounts receivable according to the length of time they have been due *(p. 395)*.

Allowance for Doubtful Accounts A contra account, related to accounts receivable, that holds the estimated amount of collection losses. Also called allowance for Uncollectible Accounts *(p. 392)*.

Allowance for Uncollectible Accounts Another name for allowance for Doubtful Accounts *(p. 392)*.

Allowance method A method of recording collection losses based on estimates made prior to determining that the business will not collect from specific customers *(p. 392)*.

Amortization The term the CICA Handbook uses to describe the systematic changing of the cost of a capital asset; it is often called depreciation when applied to property, plant and equipment, and depletion when applied to wasting assets. The term is also used to describe the writing off to expense of intangible assets *(pp. 118, 478)*.

Appropriations Restriction of retained earnings that is recorded by a formal journal entry *(p. 726)*.

Articles of incorporation The document issued by the federal or provincial government giving the incorporators permission to form a corporation *(p. 666)*.

Asset An economic resource a business owns that is expected to be of benefit in the future *(p. 10)*.

Auditing The examination of financial statements by outside accountants, the most significant service that public accountants perform. The conclusion of an audit is the accountant's professional opinion about the financial statements *(p. 50)*.

Bad-debt expense Another name for uncollectible account expense *(p. 392)*.

Balance sheet List of an entity's assets, liabilities and owner equity as of a specific date. Also called the statement of financial position *(p. 18)*.

Bank collection Collection of money by the bank on behalf of a depositor *(p. 344)*.

Bank reconciliation Process of explaining the reasons for the difference between a depositor's records and the bank's records about the depositor's bank account *(p. 344)*.

Bank statement Document for a particular bank account showing its beginning and ending balances and listing the month's transactions that affected the account *(p. 342)*.

Batch processing Computerized accounting for similar transactions in a group or batch *(p. 285)*.

Betterment Expenditure that increases the capacity or efficiency of an asset or extends its useful life. Capital expenditures are debited to an asset account *(p. 499)*.

Board of directors Group elected by the shareholders to set policy for a corporation and to appoint its officers *(pp. 7, 668)*.

Bonds payable Groups of notes payable (bonds) issued to multiple lenders called bondholders *(p. 758)*.

Book value of a capital asset The asset's cost less accumulated amortization (or depreciation) *(p. 119)*.

Book value of stock Amount of owners' equity on the company's books for each share of its stock *(p. 686)*.

Book value per share of common stock Common shareholders' equity divided by the number of shares of common stock outstanding *(p. 936)*.

Bylaws Constitution for governing a corporation *(p. 668)*.

Callable bonds Bonds that the issuer may call or pay off at a specified price whenever the issuer wants *(p. 774)*.

Canada (or Quebec) Pension Plan All employees and self-employed persons in Canada (except in Quebec where the pension plan is the Quebec Pension Plan) between 18 and 70 years of age are required to contribute to the Canada Pension Plan administered by the Government of Canada *(p. 539)*.

Capital Another name for the owner's equity of a business *(p. 10)*.

Capital assets Long-lived assets, like property, plant and equipment, wasting assets, and intangible assets used in the operation of a business. Their value is in use *(pp. 118, 478)*.

Capital cost allowance Depreciation allowed for income tax purposes by Revenue Canada; the rates allowed are called capital cost allowance rates *(p. 484)*.

Capital lease Lease agreement that transfers substantially all of the benefits and risks of ownership from the lessor to the lessee *(p. 777)*.

Capital stock A corporation's capital from investments by the shareholders. Also called share capital *(p. 669)*.

Cash-basis accounting Accounting that records only transactions in which cash is received or paid *(p. 111)*.

Cash disbursements journal Special journal used to record cash payments by cheque *(p. 297)*.

Cash equivalents Highly liquid short-term investments that can be converted into cash with little delay *(p. 858)*.

Cash flows Cash receipts and cash payments (disbursements) *(p. 858)*.

Cash receipts journal Special journal used to record cash receipts *(p. 293)*.

Chairperson (of board) Elected person on a corporation's board of directors; usually the most powerful person in the corporation *(p. 668)*.

Change in accounting estimate A change that occurs in the normal course of business as a company alters earlier expectations *(p. 594)*.

Change in accounting principle A change in accounting method, such as from the FIFO method to the LIFO method for inventories and a switch from declining-balance depreciation to straight-line *(p. 594)*.

Chart of accounts List of all the accounts and their account numbers in the ledger *(p. 71)*.

Cheque Document that instructs the bank to pay the designated person or business the specified amount of money *(p. 341)*.

Closing entries Entries that transfer the revenue, expense, and owner withdrawal balances from these respective accounts to the capital account *(p. 171)*.

Closing the accounts Step in the accounting cycle at the end of the period that prepares the accounts for recording the transactions of the next period. Closing the accounts consists of journalizing and posting the closing entries to set the balances of the revenue, expense, and dividend accounts to zero *(p. 170)*.

Common-size statement A financial statement that reports only percentages (no dollar amounts); a type of vertical analysis *(p. 917)*.

Common stock The most basic form of capital stock. In describing a corporation, the common shareholders are the owners of the business *(pp. 11, 670)*.

Comparability principle Specifies that accounting information must be comparable from business to business and that a single business's financial statements must be comparable from one period to the next *(p. 588)*.

Conservatism Concept by which the least favorable figures are presented in the financial statements *(pp. 449, 599)*.

Consignment Transfer of goods by the owner (consignor) to another business (consignee) who, for a fee, sells the inventory on the owner's behalf. The consignee does not take title to the consigned goods *(p. 440)*.

Consistency principle A business must use the same accounting methods and procedures from period to period or disclose a change in method *(p. 448)*.

Consolidated statements Financial statements of the parent company plus those of majority-owned subsidiaries as if the combination were a single legal entity *(p. 820)*.

Contingent liability A potential liability that will become an actual liability only if a future event does occur *(p. 406)*.

Contract interest rate Interest rate that determines the amount of cash interest the borrower pays and the investor receives each year. Also called the stated interest rate *(p. 761)*.

Control account An account whose balance equals the sum of the balances in a group of related accounts in a subsidiary ledger *(p. 292)*.

Controlling (majority) interest Ownership of more than 50 percent of an investee company's voting stock *(p. 819)*.

Convertible bonds (or notes) Bonds (or notes) that may be converted into the common stock of the issuing company at the option of the investor *(p. 775)*.

Convertible preferred stock Preferred stock that may be exchanged by the preferred shareholders, if they choose, for another class of stock in the corporation *(p. 683)*.

Copyright Exclusive right to reproduce and sell a book, musical composition, film, or other work of art. Issued by the federal government, copyrights extend 50 years beyond the author's life *(p. 497)*.

Corporation A business owned by shareholders that begins when the federal government or provincial government approves its articles of incorporation. A corporation is a legal entity, an "artificial person," in the eyes of the law *(p. 6)*.

Cost method for investments The method used to account for short-term investments in stock and for long-term investments when the investor holds less than 20 percent of the investee's voting stock. Short-term investments should be written down to market if the market declines below cost; long-term investments carried under the cost method should be written down to market if the decline is thought to be other than temporary *(p. 814)*.

Cost of goods sold The cost of the inventory that the business has sold to customers, the largest single expense of most merchandising businesses. Also called cost of sales *(p. 222)*.

Cost of sales Another name for cost of goods sold *(p. 222)*.

Cost principle States that assets and services are recorded at their purchase cost and that the accounting record of the asset continues to be based on cost rather than current market value *(p. 588)*.

Credit The right side of an account *(p. 57)*.

Creditor The party to a credit transaction who sells a service or merchandise and obtains a receivable *(p. 390)*.

Cumulative preferred stock Preferred stock whose owners must receive all dividends in arrears before the corporation pays dividends to the common shareholders *(p. 682)*.

Current asset An asset that is expected to be converted to cash, sold, or consumed during the next 12 months, or within the business's normal operating cycle if longer than a year *(p. 175)*.

Current liability A debt due to be paid within one year or one of the entity's operating cycles if the cycle is longer than a year *(p. 175)*.

Current portion of long-term debt Amount of the principal that is payable within one year *(p. 531)*.

Current ratio Current assets divided by current liabilities. Measures the ability to pay current liabilities from current assets *(pp. 177, 926)*.

Database program Computer program that organizes information so that it can be systematically assessed in a variety of report forms *(p. 288)*.

Days' sales in receivables Ratio of average net accounts receivable to one day's sales. Tells how many days' sales remain in Accounts Receivable awaiting collection *(pp. 410, 930)*.

Debentures Unsecured bonds, backed only by the good faith of the borrower *(p. 759)*.

Debit The left side of an account *(p. 57)*.

Debt ratio Ratio of total liabilities to total assets. Tells the proportion of a company's assets that it has financed with debt *(pp. 178, 931)*.

Debtor The party to a credit transaction who makes a purchase and creates a payable *(p. 390)*.

Declining-balance method (DB) A type of depreciation method that writes off a relatively larger amount of an asset's cost nearer the start of its useful life than does the straight-line method *(p. 484)*.

Default on a note Failure of the maker of a note to pay at maturity. Also called dishonor of a note *(p. 407)*.

Deficit Debit balance in the retained earnings account *(p. 671)*.

Defined benefits pension plan Benefits to be paid to the employee upon retirement are specified *(p. 780)*.

Defined contribution pension plan The contribution to the plan is defined and the benefits to be paid to the employee depend on funds available at retirement *(p. 780)*.

Depletion expense That portion of a wasting asset's natural resource cost that is used up in a particular period. Depletion expense is computed in the same way as units of production depreciation *(p. 496)*.

Deposit in transit A deposit recorded by the company but not yet by its bank *(p. 344)*.

Depreciable cost The asset's cost minus its estimated residual value *(p. 482)*.

Depreciation Another name for amortization *(p. 118)*.

Direct write-off method A method of accounting for bad debts by which the company waits until the credit department decides that a customer's account receivable is uncollectible and then debits Uncollectible-Account Expense and credits the customer's Account Receivable *(p. 397)*.

Disclosure principle A business's financial statements must report enough information for outsiders to make knowledgeable decisions about the business *(pp. 448, 592)*.

Discount Amount of bond's issue price under its maturity (par) value *(p. 760)*.

Discounting a note payable A borrowing arrangement in which the bank subtracts the interest amount from the note's face value. The borrower receives the net amount *(p. 527)*.

Discounting a note receivable Selling a note receivable before its maturity *(p. 405)*.

Dishonor of a note Failure of the maker of a note to pay a note receivable at maturity. Also called default on a note *(p. 402)*.

Dissolution Ending of a partnership *(p. 629)*.

Dividend yield Ratio of dividends per share of stock to the stock's market price per share. Tells the percentage of a stock's market value that the company pays to shareholders as dividends *(p. 936)*.

Dividends Distributions by a corporation to its shareholders *(p. 671)*.

Donated capital Special category of shareholders' equity created when a corporation receives a donation (gift) from a donor who receives no ownership interest in the company *(p. 679)*.

Double taxation Corporations pay their own income taxes on corporate income. Then, the shareholders pay personal income tax on the cash dividends that they receive from corporations *(p. 667)*.

Earnings per share (EPS) Amount of a company's net income per share of its outstanding common stock *(pp. 731, 935)*.

Effective interest rate Another name for market interest rate *(p. 761)*.

Efficient capital market One in which the market prices fully reflect all information available to the public *(p. 937)*.

Electronic fund transfer (EFT) System that transfers cash by digital communication rather than paper documents *(p. 342)*.

Entity An organization or a section of an organization that, for accounting purposes, stands apart from other organizations and individuals as a separate economic unit. This is the most basic concept in accounting *(p. 8)*.

Entity concept States that the transactions of each entity are accounted for separately from the transactions of all other organizations and persons *(p. 585)*.

Equity method for investments The method used to account for investments in which the investor has 20 to 50 percent of the investor's voting stock and can significantly influence the decisions of the investee. The investment account is debited for ownership in the investee's net income and credited for ownership in the investee's dividends *(p. 818)*.

Estimated residual value Expected cash value of an asset at the end of its useful life. Also called Residual value, Scrap value and Salvage value *(p. 482)*.

Estimated useful life Length of the service that a business expects to get from an asset; may be expressed in years, units of output, miles or other measures *(p. 482)*.

Expense Decrease in owner's equity that occurs in the course of delivering goods or services to customers or clients *(p. 11)*.

Extraordinary item A gain or loss that is not typical of the business and does not depend on a management decision *(p. 730)*.

Financial accounting The branch of accounting that provides information to people outside the business *(p. 4)*.

Financial statements Business documents that report financial information about an entity to persons and organizations outside the business *(p. 2)*.

Financing activity Activity that obtains the funds from investors and creditors needed to launch and sustain the business; a section of the statement of changes in financial position *(p. 860)*.

First-in, first-out (FIFO) method Inventory costing method by which the first costs into inventory are the first costs out to cost of goods sold. Ending inventory is based on the costs of the most recent purchases *(p. 442)*.

FOB destination Terms of a transaction that govern when the title to the inventory passes from the seller to the purchaser—when the goods arrive at the purchaser's location *(p. 440)*.

FOB shipping point Terms of a transaction that govern when the title to the inventory passes from the seller to the purchaser—when the goods leave the seller's place of business *(p. 440)*.

Foreign-currency exchange rate The measure of one currency against another currency *(p. 831)*.

Franchises and licenses Privileges granted by a private business or a government to sell a product or service in accordance with specified conditions *(p. 498)*.

General journal Journal used to record all transactions that do not fit one of the special journals *(p. 289)*.

General ledger Ledger of accounts that are reported in the financial statements *(p. 290)*.

Generally accepted accounting principles (GAAP) Accounting guidelines, formulated by the CICA's Accounting Standards Committee, that govern how businesses report their financial statements to the public *(p. 8)*.

Going-concern or continuity concept Accountants' assumption that the business will continue operating in the foreseeable future *(p. 585)*.

Goodwill Excess of the cost of an acquired company over the sum of the market values of its net assets (assets minus liabilities) *(p. 498)*.

Gross margin Excess of sales revenue over cost of goods sold. Also called gross profit *(p. 214)*.

Gross margin method A way to estimate inventory based on a rearrangement of the cost of goods sold model: Beginning inventory + Net purchases = Cost of goods available for sale. Cost of goods available for sale – Cost of goods sold = Ending inventory. Also called the Gross profit method *(p. 453)*.

Gross margin percentage Gross margin divided by net sales revenue. A measure of profitability *(p. 234)*.

Gross pay Total amount of salary, wages, commissions, or any other employee compensation before taxes and other deductions are taken out *(p. 539)*.

Gross profit Another name for gross margin *(p. 214)*.

Hardware Electronic equipment that includes computers, disk drives, monitors, printers, and the network that connects them *(p. 281)*.

Horizontal analysis Study of percentage changes in comparative financial statements *(p. 914)*.

Imprest system A way to account for petty cash by maintaining a constant balance in the petty cash account, supported by the fund (cash plus disbursement tickets) totaling the same amount *(p. 355)*.

Income from operations Another name for operating income *(p. 231)*.

Income statement List of an entity's revenues, expenses, and net income or net loss for a specific period. Also called the statement of operations *(p. 18)*.

Income summary A temporary "holding tank" account into which the revenues and expenses are transferred prior to their final transfer to the Retained Earnings account *(p. 171)*.

Incorporators Persons who organize a corporation *(p. 669)*.

Indirect method Format of the operating activities section of the statement of changes in financial position that starts with net income and shows the reconciliation from net income to operating cash flows. Also called the reconciliation method *(p. 863)*.

Intangible asset An asset with no physical form, a special right to current and expected future benefits *(p. 496)*.

Interest The revenue to the payee for loaning out the principal, and the expense to the maker for borrowing the principal *(p. 401)*.

Interest period The period of time during which interest is to be computed, extending from the original date of the note to the maturity date *(p. 401)*.

Interest rate The percentage rate that is multiplied by the principal amount to compute the amount of interest on a note *(p. 401)*.

Internal control Organizational plan and all the related measures adopted by an entity to meet management's objectives of discharging statutory responsibilities, profitability, prevention and detection of fraud and error, safeguarding of assets, reliability of accounting records, and timely preparation of reliable financial information *(p. 334)*.

Inventory profit Difference between gross margin figured on the FIFO basis and gross margin figured on the LIFO basis *(p. 444)*.

Inventory turnover Ratio of cost of goods sold to average inventory. Measures the number of times a company sells its average level of inventory during a year *(pp. 235, 929)*.

Investing activity Activity that increases and decreases the long-term assets available to the business; a section of the statement of changes in financial position *(p. 861)*.

Journal The chronological accounting record of an entity's transactions *(p. 60)*.

Last-in, first-out (LIFO) method Inventory costing method by which the last costs into inventory are the first costs out to cost of goods sold. This method leaves the oldest costs—those of beginning inventory and the earliest purchases of the period—in ending inventory *(p. 443)*.

Lease Rental agreement in which the tenant (lessee) agrees to make rent payments to the property owner (lessor) in exchange for the use of the asset *(p. 777)*.

Leasehold Prepayment that a lessee (renter) makes to secure the use of an asset from a lessor (landlord) *(p. 498)*.

Ledger The book of accounts *(p. 54)*.

Lessee Tenant in a lease agreement *(p. 777)*.

Lessor Property owner in a lease agreement *(p. 777)*.

Leverage Another name for trading on the equity *(p. 935)*.

Liability An economic obligation (a debt) payable to an individual or an organization outside the business *(p. 10)*.

Limited liability No personal obligation of a shareholder for corporation debts. The most that a shareholder can lose on an investment in a corporation's stock is the cost of the investment *(p. 667)*.

Liquidation The process of going out of business by selling the entity's assets and paying its liabilities. The final step in liquidation of a business is the distribution of any remaining cash to the owners *(p. 642)*.

Liquidity Measure of how quickly an item may be converted to cash *(p. 175)*.

Long-term asset An asset other than a current asset *(p. 175)*.

Long-term investment Separate asset category reported on the balance sheet between current assets and capital assets *(p. 814)*.

Long-term liability A liability other than a current liability *(p. 175)*.

Long-term solvency The ability to generate enough cash to pay long-term debts as they mature *(p. 913)*.

Lower-of-cost-or-market (LCM) rule Requires that an asset be reported in the financial statements at the lower of its historical cost or its market value (current replacement cost for inventory) *(p. 450)*.

Maker of a note The person or business that signs the note and promises to pay the amount required by the note agreement. The maker is the debtor *(p. 401)*.

Management accounting The branch of accounting that generates confidential information for internal decision-makers of a business, such as top executives *(p. 4)*.

Market interest rate Interest rate that investors demand in order to loan their money. Also called the Effective interest rate *(p. 761)*.

Market value of stock Price for which a person could buy or sell a share of stock *(p. 685)*.

Marketable security Another name for short-term investment *(p. 814)*.

Matching principle The basis for recording expenses. Directs accountants to identify all expenses incurred during the period, measure the expenses, and match them against the revenues earned during that same span of time *(pp. 113, 592)*.

Materiality concept A company must perform strictly proper accounting only for items and transactions that are significant to the business's financial statements *(pp. 449, 599)*.

Maturity date The date on which the final payment of a note is due. Also called the due date *(p. 401)*.

Maturity value The sum of the principal and interest due at the maturity date of a note *(p. 401)*.

Menu A list of options for choosing computer functions *(p. 284)*.

Minority interest A subsidiary company's equity that is held by shareholders other than the parent company *(p. 823)*.

Modules Separate compatible units of an accounting package that are integrated to function together *(p. 286)*.

Mortgage Borrower's promise to transfer the legal title to certain assets to the lender if the debt is not paid on schedule *(p. 776)*.

Multiple-step income statement Format that contains subtotals to highlight significant relationships. In addition to net income, it also presents gross margin and income from operations *(p. 233)*.

Mutual agency Every partner can bind the business to a contract within the scope of the partnership's regular business operations *(p. 629)*.

Net earnings Another name for net income or net profit *(p. 11)*.

Net income Excess of total revenues over total expenses. Also called net earnings or net profit *(p. 11)*.

Net loss Excess of total expenses over total revenues *(p. 11)*.

Net pay Gross pay minus all deductions; the amount of employee compensation that the employee actually takes home *(p. 539)*.

Net profit Another name for net income or net earnings *(p. 11)*.

Net purchases Purchases less purchase discounts and purchase returns and allowances *(p. 263)*.

Net sales Sales revenue less sales discounts and sales returns and allowances *(p. 224)*.

Network The system of electronic linkages that allow different computers to share the same information *(p. 281)*.

Nominal account Another name for a temporary account *(p. 171)*.

Nonsufficient funds (NSF) cheque A "hot" cheque, one for which the maker's bank account has insufficient money to pay the cheque *(p. 344)*.

No-par stock Shares of stock that do not have a value assigned to them by the articles of incorporation *(p. 673)*.

Note payable A liability evidenced by a written promise to make a future payment *(p. 10)*.

Note receivable An asset evidenced by another party's written promise that entitles you to receive cash in the future *(p. 10)*.

Off-balance-sheet financing Acquisition of assets or services with debt that is not reported on the balance sheet *(p. 779)*.

On-line processing Computerized processing of related functions, such as the recording and posting of transactions on a continuous basis *(p. 285)*.

Operating activity Activity that creates revenue or expense in the entity's major line of business. A section of the statement of changes in financial position. Operating activities affect the income statement *(p. 860)*.

Operating cycle The time span during which cash is paid for goods and services that are sold to customers who then pay the business in cash *(p. 175)*.

Operating expenses Expenses, other than cost of goods sold, that are incurred in the entity's major line of business: rent, depreciation, salaries, wages, utilities, property tax and supplies expense *(p. 231)*.

Operating income Gross margin minus operating expenses plus any other operating revenues. Also called income from operations *(p. 231)*.

Operating lease Usually a short-term or cancelable rental agreement *(p. 777)*.

Organization cost The costs of organizing a corporation, including legal fees, taxes, and charges by promoters for selling the stock. Organization cost is an intangible asset *(p. 680).*

Other expense Expense that is outside the main operations of a business, such as a loss on the sale of capital assets *(p. 231).*

Other revenue Revenue that is outside the main operations of a business, such as a gain on the sale of capital assets *(p. 231).*

Outstanding cheque A cheque issued by the company and recorded on its books but not yet paid by its bank *(p. 344).*

Outstanding stock Stock in the hands of a shareholder *(p. 669).*

Owner's equity The claim of an owner of a business to the assets of the business. Also called capital *(p. 10).*

Par value Arbitrary amount assigned to a share of stock *(p. 673).*

Parent company An investor company that owns more than 50 percent of the voting stock of a subsidiary company *(p. 819).*

Partnership An unincorporated business with two or more owners *(pp. 6, 628).*

Partnership agreement Agreement that is the contract between partners specifying such items as the name, location, and nature of the business; the name, capital investment, and duties of each partner; and the method of sharing profits and losses by the partners *(p. 629).*

Patent A federal government grant giving the holder the exclusive right for 17 years to produce and sell an invention *(p. 497).*

Payee of a note The person or business to whom the maker of a note promises future payment. The payee is the creditor *(p. 401).*

Payroll Employee compensation, a major expense of many businesses *(p. 538).*

Pension Employee compensation that will be received during retirement *(p. 779).*

Percentage of sales approach A method of estimating uncollectible receivables as a percentage of the net credit sales (or net sales) *(p. 395).*

Periodic inventory system Type of inventory accounting system in which the business does not keep a continuous record of the inventory on hand. Instead, at the end of the period the business makes a physical count of the on-hand inventory and applies the appropriate unit costs to determine the cost of the ending inventory *(pp. 215, 438).*

Permanent account Another name for a real account—asset, liability, or shareholders' equity—that is not closed at the end of the period *(p. 171).*

Perpetual inventory system Type of accounting inventory system in which the business keeps a continuous record for each inventory item to show the inventory on hand at all times *(pp. 216, 437).*

Petty cash Fund containing a small amount of cash that is used to pay minor expenditures *(p. 354).*

Postclosing trial balance List of the ledger accounts and their balances at the end of the period after the journalizing and posting of the closing entries. The last step of the accounting cycle, the postclosing trial balance ensures that the ledger is in balance for the start of the next accounting period *(p. 173).*

Posting Transferring of amounts from the journal to the ledger *(p. 61).*

Preferred stock Stock that gives its owners certain advantages over common shareholders, such as the priority to receive dividends before the common shareholders and the priority to receive assets before the common shareholders if the corporation liquidates *(p. 672).*

Premium Excess of bond's issue price over its maturity (par) value *(p. 760)*

Prepaid expense A category of miscellaneous assets that typically expire or get used up in the near future. Examples include prepaid rent, prepaid insurance, and supplies *(p. 116).*

Present value Amount a person would invest now to receive a greater amount at a future date *(p. 761).*

President Chief operating officer in charge of managing the day-to-day operations of a corporation *(p. 668).*

Pretax accounting income Income before income tax from the income statement *(p. 688)*.

Price/earnings ratio Ratio of the market price of a share of common stock to the company's earnings per share. Measures the value that the stock market places on $1 of a company's earnings *(p. 935)*.

Principal amount The amount loaned out by the payee and borrowed by the maker of a note *(p. 401)*.

Prior-period adjustment A correction to retained earnings for an error of an earlier period *(p. 734)*.

Promissory note A written promise to pay a specified amount of money at a particular future date *(p. 401)*.

Proprietorship An unincorporated business with a single owner *(p. 6)*.

Purchases journal Special journal used to record all purchases of inventory, supplies and other assets on account *(p. 295)*.

Quick ratio Another name for the Acid-test ratio *(p. 409)*.

Rate of return on common share-holders' equity Net income minus preferred dividends, divided by average common shareholders' equity. A measure of profitability. Also called return on common shareholders' equity *(pp. 684, 934)*.

Rate of return on net sales Ratio of net income to net sales. A measure of profitability. Also called return on sales *(p. 933)*.

Rate of return on total assets The sum of net income plus interest expense divided by average total assets. This ratio measures the success a company has in using its assets to earn income for the persons who finance the business. Also called return on assets *(pp. 684, 933)*.

Real account Another name for a permanent account *(p. 171)*.

Receivable A monetary claim against a business or an individual, acquired mainly by selling goods and services and by lending money *(p. 390)*.

Reliability principle Requires that accounting information be dependable (free from error and bias). Also called the Objectivity principle *(p. 587)*.

Repair Expenditure that merely maintains an asset in its existing condition or restores the asset to good working order. Repairs are expensed (matched against revenue) *(p. 499)*.

Repurchase of own stock A corporation may repurchase its own stock that it has issued previously *(p. 721)*.

Retained earnings A corporation's capital that is earned through profitable operation of the business *(pp. 11, 669)*.

Return on assets Another name for rate of return on total assets *(p. 684)*.

Return on equity Another name for rate of return on common shareholders' equity *(p. 684)*.

Return on shareholders' equity Another name for rate of return on common shareholders' equity *(pp. 684, 934)*.

Revenue Increase in owner's equity that is earned by delivering goods or services to customers or clients *(p. 11)*.

Revenue Canada rate The maximum depreciation rate (also called the Capital cost allowance rate) that Revenue Canada allows a taxpayer to use in calculating depreciation expense (also called capital cost allowance) in determining taxable income *(p. 484)*.

Revenue principle The basis for recording revenues; tells accountants when to record revenue and the amount of revenue to record *(pp. 113, 588)*.

Reversing entry An entry that switches the debit and the credit of a previous adjusting entry. The reversing entry is dated the first day of the period following the adjusting entry *(p. 209)*.

Sales Another name for sales revenue *(p. 214)*.

Sales discount Reduction in the amount receivable from a customer, offered by the seller as an incentive for the customer to pay promptly. A contra account to sales revenue *(p. 223)*.

Sales journal Special journal used to record credit sales *(p. 290)*.

Sales returns and allowances Decrease in the seller's receivable from a customer's return of merchandise or from granting the customer an allowance from the amount the customer owes the seller. A contra account to sales revenue *(p. 223)*.

Sales revenue Amount that a merchandiser earns from selling inventory before subtracting expenses Also called sales *(p. 214)*.

Segment of a business One of various separate divisions of a company *(p. 728)*.

Serial bonds Bonds that mature in installments over a period of time *(p. 759)*.

Server The main computer in a network, where the program and data are stored *(p. 281)*.

Shareholder A person who owns stock in a corporation *(pp. 6, 666)*.

Shareholders' equity Owners' equity of a corporation *(p. 669)*.

Short-term investment Investment that is readily convertible to cash and that the investor intends either to convert to cash in one year or to use to pay a current liability; also called a marketable security, a current asset *(p. 814)*.

Short-term liquidity Ability to meet current payments as they come due *(p. 913)*.

Short-term note payable Note payable due within one year, a common form of financing *(p. 527)*.

Single-step income statement Format that groups all revenues together and then lists and deducts all expenses together without drawing any subtotals *(p. 234)*.

Software Set of programs or instructions that cause the computer to perform the work desired *(p. 281)*.

Special journal An accounting journal designed to record one specific type of transaction *(p. 289)*.

Specific unit cost method Inventory cost method based on the specific cost of particular units of inventory *(p. 441)*.

Spreadsheet A computer program that links data by means of formulas and functions; an electronic worksheet *(p. 287)*.

Stable-monetary-unit concept Accountants' basis for ignoring the effect of inflation and making no adjustments for the changing value of the dollar *(p. 587)*.

Stated interest rate Another name for the contract interest rate *(p. 761)*.

Statement of Changes in Financial Position Reports cash receipts and cash disbursements classified according to the entity's major activities: operating, financing, and investing *(pp. 18, 858)*.

Statement of earnings Another name for income statement *(p. 18)*.

Statement of financial position Another name for the balance sheet *(p. 18)*.

Statement of operations Another name for the income statement. Also called statement of earnings *(p. 18)*.

Statement of retained earnings Summary of the changes in the retained earnings of a corporation during a specific period *(p. 18)*.

Stock Shares into which the owners' equity of a corporation is divided *(p. 666)*.

Stock dividend A proportional distribution by a corporation of its own stock to its shareholders *(p. 717)*.

Stock split An increase in the number of outstanding shares of stock coupled with a proportionate reduction in the book value of the stock *(p. 719)*.

Straight-line (SL) method Depreciation method in which an equal amount of depreciation expense is assigned to each year (or period) of asset use *(p. 483)*.

Strong currency A currency that is rising relative to other nations' currencies *(p. 832)*.

Subsequent event An event that occurs after the end of a company's accounting period but before publication of its financial statements and which may affect the interpretation of the information in those statements *(p. 595)*.

Subsidiary company An investee company in which a parent company owns more than 50 percent of the voting stock *(p. 819)*.

Subsidiary ledger Book of accounts that provides supporting details on individual balances, the total of which appears in a general ledger account *(p. 292)*.

Taxable income Income from the income tax return filed with Revenue Canada;

the basis for computing the amount of tax to pay the government *(p. 688).*

Temporary account Another name for a nominal account. The revenue and expense accounts which relate to a particular accounting period and are closed at the end of the period are temporary accounts. For a corporation, the Dividends account is also temporary *(p. 171).*

Temporary investments Another name for Short-term investments *(p. 814).*

Term bonds Bonds that all mature at the same time for a particular issue *(p. 659).*

Time-period concept Ensures that accounting information is reported at regular intervals *(pp. 114, 586).*

Times-interest-earned ratio Ratio of income from operations to interest expense. Measures the number of times that operating income can cover interest expense. Also called the Interest-coverage ratio *(p. 932).*

Trademarks and trade names or brand names Distinctive identifications of a product or service *(p. 497).*

Trading on the equity Earning more income on borrowed money than the related expense, thereby increasing the earnings for the owners of the business *(pp. 777, 935).*

Transaction An event that affects the financial position of a particular entity and may be reliably recorded *(p. 12).*

Trial balance A list of all the ledger accounts with their balances *(p. 65).*

Underwriter Organization that purchases the bonds from an issuing company and resells them to its clients, or sells the bonds for a commission, agreeing to buy all unsold bonds *(p. 759).*

Unearned revenue A liability created when a business collects cash from customers in advance of doing work for the customer. The obligation is to provide a product or a service in the future. Also called deferred revenue *(p. 122).*

Unemployment Insurance Act All employees and employers in Canada must contribute to the Unemployment Insurance Fund which provides assistance to unemployed workers *(p. 542).*

Units-of-production (UOP) method Depreciation method by which a fixed amount of depreciation is assigned to each unit of output produced by the capital asset *(p. 483).*

Unlimited personal liability When a partnership (or a proprietorship) cannot pay its debts with business assets, the partners (or the proprietor) must use personal assets to meet the debt *(p. 630).*

Vertical analysis Analysis of a financial statement that reveals the relationship of each statement item to the total, which is 100 percent *(p. 916).*

Voucher Document authorizing a cash disbursement *(p. 353).*

Wasting assets or natural resources Capital assets that are natural resources *(p. 496).*

Weak currency A currency that is falling relative to other nations' currencies *(p. 832).*

Weighted-average cost method Inventory costing method based on the weighted-average cost of inventory during the period. Weighted average cost is determined by dividing the cost of goods available for sale by the number of units available. Also called the average cost method *(p. 441).*

Withheld income tax Income tax deducted from employees' gross pay *(p. 539).*

Work sheet A columnar document designed to help move data from the trial balance to the financial statements *(p. 162).*

Workers' compensation A provincially administered plan which is funded by contributions by employers and which provides financial support for workers injured on the job *(p. 544).*

Working capital Current assets minus current liabilities; measures a business's ability to meet its short-term obligations with its current assets *(p. 926).*

Index

Check Figures for Problems

P1-1A No check figure
P1-2A Shareholders' equity $120,600
P1-3A Total assets $61,000
P1-4A Total assets $190,000
P1-5A June 11 Investment of cash by owner $5,000
P1-6A Net income $88,000; Total assets $273,000
P1-7A Shareholders' equity $28,050
P1-8A Total assets $26,600
P1-9A Total assets $84,500
P1-1B No check figure
P1-2B Shareholders' equity $137,600
P1-3B Total assets $68,000
P1-4B Total assets $107,000
P1-5B Aug. 9 Collected cash on account
P1-6B Net income $59,000; Total assets $82,000
P1-7B Shareholders' equity $38,200
P1-8B Total assets $35,150
P1-9B Total assets $86,350
P1-1C No check figure
P1-2C No check figure
Decision Problems (DP) No check figures
Financial Statement Problems (FSP) No check figures

P2-1A Net loss $10,000
P2-2A No check figure
P2-3A Trial balance $29,100
P2-4A Trial balance $37,300
P2-5A Trial balance $47,000
P2-6A Trial balance $101,800
P2-7A No check figure
P2-8A Cash $3,700
P2-1B Net income $45,000
P2-2B No check figure
P2-3B Trial balance $35,500
P2-4B Trial balance $52,700
P2-5B Trial balance $61,700
P2-6B Trial balance $93,700
P2-7B No check figure
P2-8B Cash $3,300
P2-1C No check figure
P2-2C No check figure
DP 1 Net income $4,850
DP 2 No check figure
FSP 1 No check figure
FSP 2 No check figure

P3-1A Cash net loss, $1,500; accrual net income, $1,150
P3-2A No check figure
P3-3A No check figure
P3-4A No check figure
P3-5A Adjusted trial balance, $62,500
P3-6A Total assets, $105,030
P3-7A Total assets, $41,250
P3-8A Net income overstated by $24,300
P3-9A Operating income, $25,600
P3-1B Cash net loss, $2,400; accrual net income, $1,400
P3-2B No check figure
P3-3B No check figure
P3-4B No check figure
P3-5B Adjusted trial balance, $49,810
P3-6B Total assets, $42,810
P3-7B Total assets, $43,150
P3-8B Net income overstated by $15,550
P3-9B Operating income, $21,700
P3-1C No check figure
P3-2C No check figure
DP 1 Ending adjusted shareholders' equity, April 30, $155,400
DP 2 No check figure
FSP 1 End bals. (thousands): Prepaid expenses and deposits $1,106
FSP 2 No check figure
P3A-1 End bals.: Unearned Service Rev. $2,400; Service Rev. $800

P4-1A Net income, $10,670
P4-2A Ending shareholders' equity, $77,720; current ratio 19X1, 1.17
P4-3A Ending shareholders' equity, $31,000
P4-4A Postclosing trial balance, $143,000
P4-5A Net income, $5,750
P4-6A Ending shareholders' equity, $61,800; current ratio 19X6, 1.20
P4-7A d. Overall effect—net income understated, $460
P4-8A Net income, $200
P4-9A Net income, $600
P4-1B Net income, $9,820
P4-2B Ending shareholders' equity, $26,440; current ratio 19X2, 1.18
P4-3B Ending shareholders' equity, $47,000
P4-4B Postclosing trial balance, $112,000

P4-5B Net income $4,990

P4-6B Ending shareholders' equity, $56,900; current ratio, 19X3, 1.31

P4-7B d. Overall effect—net income overstated, $980

P4-8B Net income, $5,000

P4-9B Net income, $900

P4-1C No check figure

P4-2C No check figure

DP 1 Net income $33,540

DP 2 No check figure

FSP 1 Debt ratio 1994: 0.63

FSP 2 No check figure

P4A-1 Salary Expense bal., Sept. 5, $120

P5-1A No check figure

P5-2A Feb. 27 payment/receipt, $2,900

P5-3A Cost of goods sold, $132,300

P5-4A Net income, $85,130

P5-5A Net income, $50,710; inventory turnover 19X4, 1.42

P5-6A Net income, $50,390

P5-7A Ending Retained Earnings, $54,760

P5-8A Gross margin, $7,430

P5-9A Retained earnings, $5,600

P5-1B No check figure

P5-2B June 26 payment/receipt $2,500

P5-3B Cost of goods sold, $101,000

P5-4B Net loss, $23,210

P5-5B Net income, $39,460; gross margin percentage 19X5, 49%

P5-6B Net income, $36,240

P5-7B Ending Retained Earnings $53,060

P5-8B Gross margin $6,812

P5-9B Retained earnings, $10,480

P5-1C No check figure

P5-2C No check figure

DP 1 Corrected shareholders' equity $53,380

DP 2 No check figure

FSP 1 Gross profit percentage 1994, 0.37; Inventory turnover 1994, 3.32

FSP 2 No check figure

P5S-1 Feb. 27 payment/receipt $1,700

P5S-2 Net income $88,050

P6-1A No check figure

P6-2A Total cash, $35,933

P6-3A Total cash, $4,289

P6-4A Total cash, $17,130

P6-5A Total cash, $48,320

P6-6A Total cash, $25,979

P6-1B No check figure

P6-2B Total cash, $58,160

P6-3B Total cash, $10,190

P6-4B Total cash, $15,473

P6-5B Total cash, $54,340

P6-6B Total cash, $43,159

P6-1C No check figure

P6-2C No check figure

DP 1 Total cash receipts on account, $5,774

DP 2 No check figure

CP 1 Net income $19,400; current ratio 2.88; gross margin percentage 38%

CP 2 Net income $1,027; total assets $116,727

CP 3 No check figure

CP 4 No check figure

P7-1A No check figure

P7-2A No check figure

P7-3A No check figure

P7-4A Adj. book bal. $4,368.77

P7-5A Adj. book bal. $13,670

P7-6A Cash short and over $12 Dr.

P7-7A No check figure

P7-8A Cash short and over, $190 Dr.

P7-9A Adjusted book balance, $2,445

P7-1B No check figure

P7-2B No check figure

P7-3B No check figure

P7-4B Adj. book bal. $6,503.33

P7-5B Adj. book bal. $8,657

P7-6B Cash short and over $18.35 Cr.

P7-7B No check figure

P7-8B Cash sort and over, $180 Dr.

P7-9B Adjusted book balance, $1,765

P7-1C No check figure

P7-2C No check figure

DP 1 Adj. bank bal., $19,358; Adj. book bal. $19,858

DP 2 No check figure

FSP 1 No check figure

FSP 2 No check figure

P7A-1 Vouchers Payable, Jan. 31, $18,424

P7A-2 Vouchers Payable, July 31, $20,965

P8-1A Uncollect.-acct. expense, direct method, $3,500; allow. method $8,860

P8-2A No check figure

P8-3A Allow. for uncollect. Accts. $3,293

P8-4A Allow. for Doubtful Accts. $9,663

P8-5A No check figure

P8-6A Accrued interest revenue $190

P8-7A 19X4 Inventory turnover 3.4 times

P8-8A Uncollectible account expense, May 31, allowance method, $3,477

P8-9A Uncollectible account expense, $25,060

P8-1B Uncollect.-acct. expense, direct method, $8,900; allow. method $12,800

P8-2B No check figure

P8-3B Allow. for Uncollect. Accts. $5,099

P8-4B Allow. for Doubtful Accts. $3,809

P8-5B No check figure

P8-6B Accrued interest revenue $394

P8-7B 19X6 Inventory turnover 7.5 times

P8-8B Uncollectible amount expense, May 31, allowances method, $4,562

P8-9B Uncollectible amount expense, $38,080

P8-1C No check figure

P8-2C No check figure

DP 1 Net income, 19X3, $61,800

DP 2 No check figure

FSP 1 Day's sales in receivables 23.94

FSP 2 No check figure

P9-1A Cost of goods sold, $1,590

P9-2A LIFO end. inventory $18,269

P9-3A FIFO inventory profit $500

P9-4A Gross margin: Weighted-average $2,435; FIFO $2,587; LIFO $2,289

P9-5A FIFO gross margin $4,978

P9-6A FIFO ed. inventory $360

P9-7A Net income: 19X1 $27 million; 19X2 $9 million; $19X3 $11 million

P9-8A Est. cost of end. inventory $340,000

P9-9A Estimated ending inventory, $41,610

P9-10A FIFO inventory, $39,600

P9-1B Cost of goods sold $3,906

P9-2B Wtd.-avg. COGS $11,482

P9-3B FIFO inventory profit $263

P9-4B Gross margin: Weighted-average $61,686; FIFO $62,195; LIFO $61,255

P9-5B FIFO gross margin $111.2 million

P9-6B FIFO end. inventory $540

P9-7B Net income: 19X4 $11 million; 19X5 $63 million; 19X6 $65 million

P9-8B Est. cost of end. inventory $175,000

P9-9B Estimated ending inventory, $94,350

P9-10B FIFO inventory, $35,000

P9-1C No check figure

P9-2C No check figure

DP-1 Net income before tax without purchase: FIFO $415,000; LIFO $355,000 Net income before tax with purchase: FIFO $415,000; LIFO $200,000

DP-2 No check figure

FSP 1 Net purchases $104,338

FSP 2 No check figure

P10-1A Depr.-Land improv. $3,900; Home office bldg. $30,503; Garage $2,175; Furniture $11,644

P10-2A No check figure

P10-3A Depr. 19X6 - SL $9,000; UOP $7,636; Revenue Canada, 0

P10-4A Depr. Exp. 19X5, before closing $7,938

P10-5A No check figure

P10-6A Cost of truck no. 14 $20,390

P10-7A Part 1: Depletion $724,880

P10-8A No check figure

P10-9A Capital assets $5,129,900

P10-1B Depr.-Land improve. $2,217; Office bldg. $16,286; Storage bldg. $1,013; Furniture $9,075

P10-2B No check figure

P10-3B Depr. 19X5: SL $36,000; UOP $27,000; DDB $5,920; Revenue Canada $28,020

P10-4B Depr. Exp. 19X3, before closing, $8,867

P10-5B No check figure

P10-6B Cost of truck no. 8, $17,533

P10-7B Part 1: Depletion $525,000

P10-8B No check figure

P10-9B Capital assets, $3,789,500

P10-1C No check figure

P10-2C No check figure

DP 1 Net income: Kanji $79,000; Fluit $41,000

DP 2 No check figure

FSP 1 2. Depreciation and amortization expense, $3,560,000

FPS 2 No check figure

P11-1A No check figure

P11-2A No check figure

P11-3A Total employee earnings $19,345

P11-4A Total annual cost of employee $87,082

P11-5A Total liab. $306,784

P11-6A Net pay $1,726

P11-7A No check figure

P11-8A Current liabilities, 687,344

P11-9A Current liabilities, $13,300

P11-1B No check figure

P11-2B No check figure

P11-3B Wage exp. $27,931

P11-4B Total annual cost of employee $71,881

P11-5B Total liab. $377,126

P11-6B Net pay $1,667

P11-7B No check figure

P11-8B Current liabilities, $665,928

P11-9B Current liabilities, $17,100

P11-1C No check figure

P11-2C No check figure

DP 1 No check figure

DP 2 No check figure

FSP 1 No check figure

FSP 2 No check figure

P12-1A No check figure

P12-2A No check figure

P12-3A Net income year 2, $30,260

P12-4A Income, percentage-completion method, 19X8, $903,000

P12-5A Correct net inc. 19X4, $46,700

P12-6A No check figure

P12-7A No check figure

P12-1B No check figure

P12-2B No check figure

P12-3B Net inc. year 2, $32,450

P12-4B Income, percentage-completion method 19X5, $1,116,000

P12-5B Correct net inc. 19X7, $66,650

P12-6B No check figure
P12-7B No check figure
P12-1C No check figure
P12-2C No check figure
FSP 1 No check figure
FSP 2 No check figure
DP 1 Net income $37,800
DP 2 No check figure
CP 1 Jekyll Island total assets, revised $2,237,900; Jekyll Island net income, revised $184,500
CP 2 No check figure

P13-1A No check figure
P13-2A 2. Ringle, Capital $48,560; LaBlanc, Capital $48,560
P13-3A 2. Net income: Soffer, $35,333; Karlin, $30,333; Schultz, $25,334
P13-4A 4. Debit: Mutchler, Capital $38,000; Armstrong, Capital $1,143; Marcus, Capital $857
P13-5A 1. b. Cash to: Whitney $20,700; Kosse $52,800; Itasca $11,500
P13-6A Shannon, capital, $110,873
P13-7A Less on realization, Jan. 3, 19X3, $113,000
P13-1B No check figure
P13-2B 2. Axtell, Capital $40,450; 2. Riesel, Capital $40,450
P13-3B 2. Net income: Collins $69,750; Davis $53,500; Chiu $56,750
P13-4B 4. Debit: Lark, Capital $50,000; Smythe, Capital $13,548; Spahn, Capital $16,452
P13-5B 1. b. Cash to: Monet, $19,000; Blair, $33,000; Trippi, $26,000
P13-6B DeGracie capital $109,912
P13-7B Loss on realization, Jan. 3, 19X3 $134,000
P13-1C No check figure
P13-2C Distribution to Zalinski, $4,600
DP 1 No check figure
DP 2 No check figure

P14-1A No check figure
P14-2A Total shareholders' equity $323,900
P14-3A Total shareholders' equity: Millet, $650,000; Structural, $695,000
P14-4A 6. b. Com. div. $15,000,000
P14-5A Total assets $743,000; Return on common equity 0.067
P14-6A 2. 19X3 Div. pay.: Pfd. $2,500; Com. $28,500
P14-7A BV per share: Pfd. $10.32; Com. $4.195
P14-8A 1. Taxable income: 19X7, $215,000; 19X8, $265,000
3. Net income: 19X7, $158,700; 19X8, $162,500
P14-9A Shareholders' equity, $259,000
P14-10A Shareholders' equity, $1,774,500
P14-1B No check figure
P14-2B Total shareholders' equity $400,300
P14-3B Total shareholders' equity: Open Spaces $778,000; Alliance Corp. $461,000

P14-4B 6. b. Com. div. $30,888
P14-5B Total assets $490,000; Return on common equity 0.090
P14-6B 2. 19X3 Div. Pay.: Pfd. $35,000; Com. $180,000
P14-7B BV per share: Pfd. $52.55; Com. $8.43
P14-8B 1. Taxable income: 19X3, $200,000; 19X4, $230,000 3. Net income: 19X3, $147,000; 19X4, $154,000
P14-9B Shareholders' equity, $265,000
P14-10B Shareholders' equity, $2,352,500
P14-1C No check figure
P14-2C No check figure
DP 1 Total shareholders' equity: Plan 1, $415,900; Plan 2, $400,900
DP 2 No check figure
FSP 1 No check figure
FSP 2 No check figure

P15-1A No check figure
P15-2A Total shareholders' equity: Dec. 31, 19X6, $395,500; Dec. 31, 19X7, $449,100
P15-3A No check figure
P15-4A Total shareholders' equity $688,680
P15-5A Total shareholders' equity $493,000
P15-6A RE, Dec. 31, 19X3, $179,200; EPS = $1.72
P15-7A EPS = $.57; Total shareholders' equity $475,070
P15-8A Shareholders' equity, $851,700
P15-9A Retained earnings, $208,800
P15-1B No check figure
P15-2B Total shareholders' equity: Dec. 31, 19X8, $454,000; Dec. 31, 19X9, $541,000
P15-3B No check figure
P15-4B Total shareholders' equity $524,880
P15-5B Total shareholders' equity $596,800
P15-6B RE, June 30, 19X4, $308,000; EPS = $4.91
P15-7B EPS = $3.07; Total shareholders' equity $1,043,945
P15-8B Shareholders' equity, $746,400
P15-9B Retained earnings, $221,800
P15-1C No check figure
P15-2C No check figure
DP 1 No check figure
DP 2 No check figure
FSP 1 2. Average price $.84 per share
FSP 2 No check figure

P16-1A 2. 19X5 Interest exp. $105,000
P16-2A 4. Interest exp. $43,500
P16-3A 9/30/Yr. 4 Bond carrying amount $414,084
P16-4A 12/31/X3 Bond carrying amount $314,688
P16-5A 12/31/X4 Interest exp. (bonds) $20,750
P16-6A No check figure
P16-7A Total long-term liab. $326,000
P16-8A Long-term liabilities, $1,187,367
P16-9A Long-term liabilities, $5,172,126

P16-1B 2. 19X7 Interest exp. $106,667
P16-2B 4. Interest exp. $22,950
P16-3B 9/30/Yr. 4 Bond carrying amount $124,423
P16-4B 12/31/X3 Bond carrying amount $474,920
P16-5B 12/31/X1 Interest exp. (bonds) $83,000
P16-6B No check figure
P16-7B Total long-term liab. $429,000
P16-8B Long-term liabilities, $3,101,131
P16-9B Long-term liabilities, $5,908,746
P16-1C No check figure
P16-2C No check figure
DP 1 EPS Plan A $7.77
DP 2 No check figure
FSP 1 No check figure
FSP 2 No check figure
P16A-1 a. $461,700 (5 yrs.)
P16A-2 a. $20,000,564
P16A-3 2. $112,472; 3. $127,140
P16A-4 12/31/X2 Bond carrying amount $285,629
P16A-5 PV Nissan 4,989,600¥, PV Toyota 5,890,500¥
P16A-6 Depr. exp. $7,123 Interest exp. $5,238

P17-1A Loss on sale, Feb. 6, 19X5, $17,112
P17-2A 2. Investment in affiliates, Dec. 31, $84,595,000
P17-3A Consol. total assets $746,000
P17-4A Consol. total assets $969,000
P17-5A 2. Long-term investment $463,600
P17-6A Cost of bond $387,578
P17-7A A. Foreign currency transaction loss $10,500
P17-8A Short-term investments (LCM), $345,332
P17-9A Short-term investments in bonds, $136,680
P17-1B Loss on sale Jan. 14, 19X7, $25,900
P17-2B 2. Investment in affiliates, Dec. 31, $6,909,000
P17-3B Consol. total assets $933,000
P17-4B Consol. total assets $1,024,000
P17-5B 2. Long-term investments $616,650
P17-6B Cost of bond $486,123
P17-7B A. Foreign currency transaction loss $7,100
P17-8B Short-term investments (LCM), $353,330
P17-9B Short-term investments in bonds, $257,280
P17-1C No check figure
P17-2C No check figure
DP 1 No check figure
DP 2 No check figure
FSP 1 No check figure
FSP 2 No check figure
CP 1 3. Total liab.: Current $161,250; Long-term $289,536; Total shareholders' equity: $906,274
CP 2 No check figure

P18-1A No check figure
P18-2A Net cash inflow from operations $75,600

P18-3A Net cash inflow from operations $84,000
P18-4A Net cash inflow from operations $50,500
P18-5A Net cash inflow from operations $67,200
P18-6A Net cash inflow from operations $67,400
P18-7A No check figure
P18-8A Net cash flow from operating activities $58,300
P18-9A Transacation analysis debits, $93,200
P18-1B No check figure
P18-2B Net cash inflow from operations $69,600
P18-3B Net cash inflow from operations $80,200
P18-4B Net cash inflow from operations $90,600
P18-5B Net cash inflow from operations $72,800
P18-6B Net cash inflow from operations $61,100
P18-7B No check figure
P18-8B Net cash flow from operating activities $94,300
P18-9B Transaction analysis debits, $234,300
P18-1C No check figure
P18-2C No check figure
DP 1 Net cash inflow from operations $140,000
DP 2 No check figure
FSP 1 Net cash from operations 1994 $6,670,000
FSP 2 No check figure

P19-1A 19X7: 1. Net sales 120%; 2. .165
P19-2A Net income 14.9%; SE 40.2%
P19-3A Invest in Can Lease
P19-4A 2. a. Current ratio 1.38; Debt ratio .60; EPS no effect
P19-5A 19X4: Inven. turnover 1.37; Return on assets .117; EPS $5.00
P19-6A Buy Smajstria; Price/earnings 7.9
P19-7A Current ratio 5.5:1
P19-8A Acid test ratio .47:1
P19-1B 19X6: 1. Net sales 144%; 2. .078
P19-2B Net income 4.7%; SE 38.1%
P19-3B Invest in Metro Air
P19-4B 2. b. Current ratio 2.00; Debt ratio .49; EPS $4.41
P19-5B 19X6: Inven. turnover 1.18; Return on assets .152; EPS $4.47
P19-6B Buy Pediatric Supply; Price/earnings 24.3
P19-7B Current ratio 4.2:1
P19-8B Acid test ratio .59:1
P19-1C No check figure
P19-2C No check figure
DP 1 No check figure
DP 2 No check figure
FSP 1 3. Inventory turnover 1994, 3.267
FSP 2 No check figure
CP 1 Inventory turnover 1994, 4.0; net cash inflow 1994, $21.1 million; debt ratio 1994, 35%
CP 2 No check figure

Photo Credits

1 Courtesy of Mark's Work Wearhouse; **53** Liaison/Pono Presse; **109** Courtesy Air Canada; **161** Courtesy Motorola Inc.; **213** Courtesy Bombardier Inc./Canadair; **279** Courtesy Mobile Computing Corp.; **333** Prentice Hall Library; **389** Prentice Hall Library; **435** Yale; **477** Henry Georgi/Mont Tremblant Resort; **525** Courtesy Westin Hotels & Resorts; **579** Chiasson/Canapress; **627** Dick Hemingway; **665** Edward Gajdel; **715** Courtesy SNC-LAVALIN Group Inc.; **757** Courtesy Standard & Poor's; **811** Courtesy Le Groupe Jean Coutu (PJC) Inc.; **857** Bob Carroll; **911** Courtesy Nova Corporation.